D0348027

Hawaii

Jeff Campbell

**Glenda Bendure, Ned Friary, Molly Green,
China Williams, Luci Yamamoto**

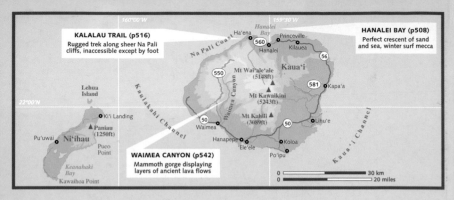

KALALAU TRAIL (p516)
Rugged trek along sheer Na Pali cliffs, inaccessible except by foot

HANALEI BAY (p508)
Perfect crescent of sand and sea, winter surf mecca

WAIMEA CANYON (p542)
Mammoth gorge displaying layers of ancient lava flows

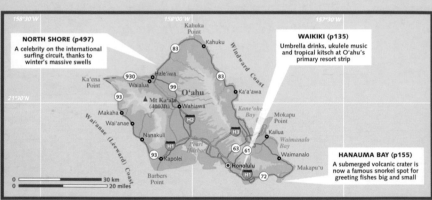

NORTH SHORE (p497)
A celebrity on the international surfing circuit, thanks to winter's massive swells

WAIKIKI (p135)
Umbrella drinks, ukulele music and tropical kitsch at O'ahu's primary resort strip

HANAUMA BAY (p155)
A submerged volcanic crater is now a famous snorkel spot for greeting fishes big and small

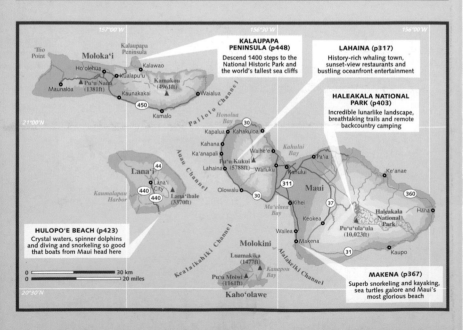

KALAUPAPA PENINSULA (p448)
Descend 1400 steps to the National Historic Park and the world's tallest sea cliffs

LAHAINA (p317)
History-rich whaling town, sunset-view restaurants and bustling oceanfront entertainment

HALEAKALA NATIONAL PARK (p403)
Incredible lunarlike landscape, breathtaking trails and remote backcountry camping

HULOPO'E BEACH (p423)
Crystal waters, spinner dolphins and diving and snorkeling so good that boats from Maui head here

MAKENA (p367)
Superb snorkeling and kayaking, sea turtles galore and Maui's most glorious beach

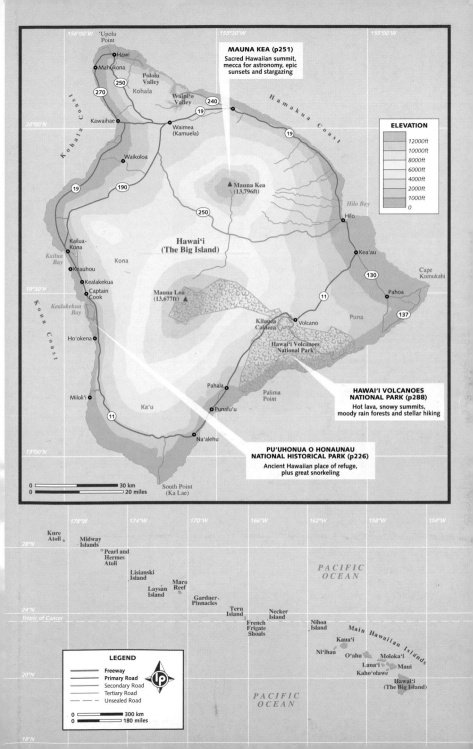

MAUNA KEA (p251)

Sacred Hawaiian summit, mecca for astronomy, epic sunsets and stargazing

HAWAI'I VOLCANOES NATIONAL PARK (p288)

Hot lava, snowy summits, moody rain forests and stellar hiking

PU'UHONUA O HONAUNAU NATIONAL HISTORICAL PARK (p226)

Ancient Hawaiian place of refuge, plus great snorkeling

ELEVATION

12000ft
10000ft
8000ft
6000ft
4000ft
2000ft
1000ft
0

'Upolu Point
Hawi
Mahukona
Kohala
Pololu Valley
Waipi'o Valley
Kawaihae
Waimea (Kamuela)
Hamakua Coast
Kohala Coast
Waikoloa
Hilo Bay
Hilo
Kailua-Kona
Hawai'i (The Big Island)
Kona
Mauna Kea (13,796ft)
Kea'au
Cape Kumukahi
Kailua Bay
Keauhou
Kealakekua
Captain Cook
Mauna Loa (13,677ft)
Pahoa
Puna
Kealakekua Bay
Kona Coast
Ho'okena
Kilauea Caldera
Volcano
Hawai'i Volcanoes National Park
Miloli'i
Pahala
Palima Point
Ka'u
Punalu'u
Na'alehu
South Point (Ka Lae)

0 — 30 km
0 — 20 miles

Kure Atoll
Midway Islands
Pearl and Hermes Atoll
Lisianski Island
Laysan Island
Maro Reef
Gardner Pinnacles
Tern Island
Necker Island
French Frigate Shoals
Nihoa Island
PACIFIC OCEAN
Kaua'i
Ni'ihau
O'ahu
Main Hawaiian Islands
Moloka'i
Lana'i
Maui
Kaho'olawe
Hawai'i (The Big Island)
Tropic of Cancer
PACIFIC OCEAN

LEGEND

Freeway
Primary Road
Secondary Road
Tertiary Road
Unsealed Road

0 — 300 km
0 — 180 miles

On the Road

JEFF CAMPBELL
Coordinating Author
Where do you find winter in Hawaii? On Mauna Loa! Hiking above 11,000ft took my breath away… with every step. Somehow I kept plodding, till I stood at the rim of the summit caldera. Only from the top can you appreciate what an elemental giant Mauna Loa is. I'm still overwhelmed.

CHINA WILLIAMS This is me and my candlelit dinner of marlin jerky and bottled water during the blackout that followed the October 2006 Hawaiian earthquake. The tremor lasted long enough for me to realize that I had no obvious 'safe' place to go so I stood in a corner and hoped that it would stop. The kind B&B owner kept me fed, watered and lighted.

LUCI YAMAMOTO Only in Hawaii do I crave shave ice. It tastes different here. Maybe it's the hot weather, or the colorful syrup bottles. Maybe I just like watching the old-timers turning blocks of ice into powdery snow…and the way folks of all ages gather outside, on rickety benches, eating and talking story.

MOLLY GREEN I've spent many an hour peddling organic produce at farmers markets throughout the Bay Area, and appreciate a good farm stand. I freaked out when we hit the South Kona Fruit Stand (p226). That pineapple I'm holding became breakfast the next morning.

NED FRIARY What a one-of-a-kind place Haleakala National Park is. There are things like this silversword that exist no place else on the planet. And it's amazing how you can go from a dry cindery landscape into a rainforest with rare birds in just a couple of miles.

GLENDA BENDURE Heaven smells like lavender, I'm sure of it. And wandering around a whole farm of lavender, backed by an ethereal cloud forest, is close to bliss. Maui's Upcountry fills the senses: the greens are greener, the blossoms brighter, the earthy scents earthier. Sounds like an exaggeration, but it's true.

THE SPIRIT OF ALOHA

Encouraging travel to Hawaii may be the easiest job in the world. Its well-known iconography has long evoked 'paradise': the emerald cliffs and white-sand beaches, the waxed surfboards and grimacing tiki, the aloha shirts, ukuleles and swaying hula girls. This string of islands in the Pacific Ocean – this precious lei of volcanic flowers – is so celebrated it hardly seems necessary to introduce it.

Beyond umbrella-shaded cocktails and kitschy souvenirs, another Hawaii awaits. Hawaii's blend of diverse peoples commune over a rowdy potluck, sprinkled with a gentle Hawaiian greeting that embodies hospitality, respect, love and welcome: aloha. Bring the spirit of aloha, and you may indeed find paradise.

④

O'ahu

In Hawaiian, O'ahu means 'the gathering place,' and no island provides a more vivid experience of Hawaii's complex society. O'ahu holds more than three-quarters of the state's residents, who annually trouble the neat categories of census takers. East and West, traditional and modern, farmer and executive, tourist and soldier: all meet, clash, fuse, merge and spark on O'ahu.

⑥

① Honolulu

This teeming multiethnic metropolis is a cultural and culinary feast. Learn about Hawaii's monarchy at 'Iolani Palace (p104), about Polynesian culture at the Bishop Museum (p115), about Hawaii's fine arts at the Hawai'i State Art Museum (p105). Then, get eating (p124).

② Waikiki

The cliché of 'Hawaii as paradise' was first concocted on the idyllic beaches of Waikiki (p139), where bartenders still pour this heady cocktail and entertainment includes both luau extravaganzas (p151) and authentic local music (p150).

③ Pearl Harbor

Hawaii's many active US military bases, particularly located on O'ahu, signal its continued strategic importance. For the most dramatic reminder of why, visit the USS *Arizona* Memorial (p133), commemorating WWII history.

④ North Shore

While Native Hawaiians invented the sport of surfing, the North Shore (p171) is the birthplace of modern-day, big-wave riding where, during winter, legends carve a thunderous sea.

⑤ Hanauma Bay

Any visit to Hawaii worth bragging about includes going eyeball to eyeball with tropical fishes in their coral-reef high-rises. Hanauma Bay (p155) is O'ahu's most famous fishbowl for snorkeling and diving.

⑥ Byodo-In Temple

The Japanese have been a prominent thread in Hawaii's cultural tapestry for over 140 years. The most striking commemoration of this influence is the timeless Byodo-In Temple (p165), where visitors can ring its enormous brass bell for good luck.

Hawai'i (the Big Island)

Among the Neighbor Islands – the five populated islands not named O'ahu – the Big Island stands out, both in size and diversity. In fact, it is unique as the only island still growing: Kilauea is the world's most active volcano. History, outdoor adventure, resorts, rural towns, city life: it's all right here.

⑤ Mauna Kea
Standing on the sacred summit of Mauna Kea (p251) – the earth's largest volcanic mountain – is a preeminent collection of astronomical observatories. Bring along a jacket, and enjoy perhaps the clearest night sky on the planet.

⑥ Hamakua Coast
Hawaii's moody verdant beauty, overgrown and pulsing with mana (spiritual power), is captured along the Hamakua Coast (p259) at Waipi'o Valley (p262), Laupahoehoe (p266), and forgotten stretches of the Old Mamalahoa Hwy (p266).

① Hawai'i Volcanoes National Park
If you're lucky, walk right up to hot lava (p297) in this tremendous national park (p288), which has some of the best, most varied hiking in Hawaii – or, well, probably anywhere.

② Hilo
Poor Hilo (p267). 'The Rainiest City in the USA,' they call it. Hardly anyone comes to admire its weathered charm, thriving farmers market (p273), lively gallery scene and great museums (p271). But they should.

③ Kona Coast
The sunny Kona Coast, lined with beaches and anchored by Kailua-Kona (p201), contains one of Hawai'i's most important ancient Hawaiian sites, Pu'uhonua o Honaunau National Historical Park (p226). The coffee's pretty good too (p219), we hear.

④ Waimea (Kamuela)
Cowboys and cattle ranches are not the first things that spring to mind when you mention 'Hawaii,' but without them there'd be no slack-key guitar. Waimea (p246), the heart of cowboy country, offers horse rides and gourmet fixins.

Maui

Maui, Maui, Maui. Class valedictorian, most popular, hopelessly attractive, drives the best car. A little smug, sometimes, but still so funny and easy-going, everyone wants to be her friend. Many couples come to Maui hoping to cradle their love in a gentle tropical paradise, slipping into a dreamy timeless forever. And dang if it doesn't work.

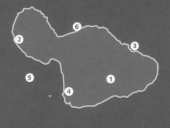

1 Haleakala National Park

Normally, we leave getting up before dawn to the sporty types, but for sunrise at Haleakala Crater (p403), a jaw-dropping 7.5 miles wide, we make an exception. Still, we don't hit the trails until after breakfast.

2 Lahaina

In the historic whaling town of Lahaina (p317), you can watch the sunset reflected in your lover's eyes, then enjoy one of the best luau (p328) in Hawaii. Romantics should consider the Ka'anapali resorts (p336) as well.

3 Road to Hana

One of the pleasures of touring Hawaii is that the journey is usually as heart-stoppingly dramatic as the destination. Take, for instance, the cliff-hugging Road to Hana (p373): 54 bridges, 600 curves, waterfalls galore and two sweaty palms gripping the wheel.

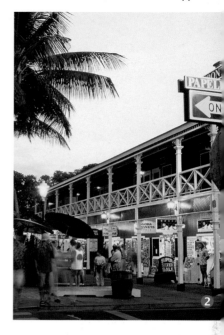

4 Makena

For idyllic Hawaiian beaches free of condos and resorts, amble to Makena (p367), whose several strands are popular with snorkelers, sea turtles, wedding parties and all manner of sunbathers (with and without bathing suits).

5 Whale-watching

Apparently humpback whales find Maui romantic too. Every winter, thousands frolic off Maui's western coast (p83), courting, mating, calving and breaching in what can only be pure joy.

6 Ho'okipa Beach

Ho'okipa Beach (p370) is to windsurfing what O'ahu's North Shore is to big-wave surfing. Watching the experts do their stuff is a great show. Plus, nearby Pa'ia (p369) has a low-key funky vibe and excellent eats.

Kaua'i

Active volcanoes, as on the Big Island, slope smoothly – their unlined profiles indicating their youth. Extinct volcanoes, as on Kaua'i, show the caresses of age. Here, nature's fingers have dug deep creases and fluted sharp edges, sculpting an intricate, emerald-bright jewel in the sea. Bring your boots, for this art gallery is all outdoors.

① Na Pali Coast

The most dramatic face of this wrinkled green island is to be discovered along the Na Pali Coast (p516). Hike the cliffs along the Kalalau Trail (p516) or admire them from below in a kayak (p510), but don't miss them.

② Waimea Canyon

Known as the 'Grand Canyon of the Pacific,' spectacular Waimea Canyon (p542) is not quite *that* big, but campers and hikers will still run out of days before they run out of trails.

③ Po'ipu Beach

The sunny southern coast has family-friendly condos aplenty, particularly around Po'ipu Beach (p521). Make sand castles with the kids, or take a scuba diving trip to Ni'ihau (p524).

④ Hanalei Bay

Kaua'i's North Shore provides a cornucopia of activities: surfing, kayaking, snorkeling, diving. Gorgeous Hanalei Bay (p508) is the center of the action, along with the easy-going, surf-bum town Hanalei (p507).

⑤ Wailua River

Age has also endowed Kaua'i with navigable rivers. Wailua River (p481) is so popular with kayakers and tours it's now regulated, but other nice waterways include Hule'ia River (p471) and Hanalei River (p509).

⑥ Hanapepe

Hanapepe (p534) is a low-key Old West town that's now a de facto artists colony. Browse the galleries anytime, but definitely plan to be here for the lively Friday 'Art Nights' (p535).

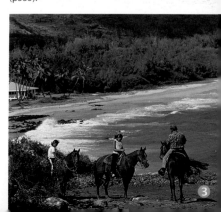

Moloka'i & Lana'i

Hawaii's two smallest inhabited islands couldn't be more different: Moloka'i is mysterious, very Hawaiian and only modestly developed for tourism. Lana'i, once awash in pineapple fields, has been reinvented as an upscale retreat and golf resort. Both are unhurried to the max. So which nickname appeals to you: the Friendly Isle or the Private Island?

❶ Kalaupapa Peninsula

The mule ride down the steep cliffs to Kalaupapa Peninsula (p448), a historic leprosy settlement and now national park, is Moloka'i's signature experience: moving, tragic, beautiful and adventurous all at once.

❷ Kamakou Preserve

Nature radiates with so much power in Hawaii, it's easy to believe but a thin veil separates gods and goddesses from our world. The difficult-to-reach, raw forests of Moloka'i's Kamakou Preserve (p444) are the stuff such dreams are made of.

❸ Halawa Valley

One of Hawaii's most scenic coastal drives is from Moloka'i's Kaunakakai (p435) to the stunning Halawa Valley (p442), passing sacred heiau (ancient temples), historic fishponds, quiet beaches and local communities.

❹ Golf Resorts

You can enjoy Lana'i without setting foot in its two resorts, Resort Lana'i at Manele Bay (p424) and the Lodge at Koele (p421), but you'd miss the indulgent spas, pro golf courses, gourmet restaurants, elegant bars…

❺ Hulopo'e Beach

Most places in the world don't have any sparkling white-sand beaches from which you might snorkel with dolphins and scuba dive in underwater grottoes. So the fact that Lana'i has just one, at Hulopo'e Beach (p423), isn't bad.

❻ Lana'i City

Lana'i's only town, Lana'i City (p418) is one of Hawaii's most evocative historic plantation towns. It still feels like 50 years ago, with tin-roofed houses, simple wooden facades and no stoplights.

Contents

Regional Map Contents

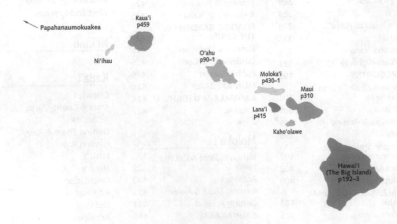

Papahanaumokuakea

Ni'ihau

Kaua'i
p459

O'ahu
p90–1

Moloka'i
p430–1

Lana'i
p415

Maui
p310

Kaho'olawe

Hawai'i
(The Big Island)
p192–3

Getting Started

A successful Hawaii trip begins with reasonable expectations and a realistic budget. The equation is relatively simple: the more time you have, the more islands you can visit. If time is short, don't waste it jumping from island to island – instead, see one island well.

A good rule of thumb is to allow a week or two for each of the four main islands, particularly if you want to experience the entire island. O'ahu, Maui, Kaua'i and Hawai'i have a lot to offer; a week on each may even feel rushed. While it's possible to fit in two main islands in a week, it's only satisfying if your desires are specific: if you're seeking only certain activities or a few particular sights. If you have two weeks, we would suggest visiting either one main island, two main islands or, at most, two main islands and a quick trip to Moloka'i or Lana'i. (This last trip will be more comfortable if you allow three weeks.)

Avoid the temptation to see three or all four main islands in one trip – unless you've got three to four weeks and a wad of cash. Traveling between the islands is relatively easy, and easy to do on a whim, but it still costs more and takes more time than checking out the other side of the island you're on. For instance, the islands may be small, but you'll need a car. How many cars do you want to rent in two weeks? And no, unfortunately you can't cut costs by relying on Hawaii's meager public transit. It'll drive you *lolo*. The only exception is Honolulu, which has a good bus system (p132).

Also, as always, plan ahead and make reservations for the things you don't want to miss. Does that hotel or tour sound nice? Book it now, particularly if you're visiting in high season. You don't need advance reservations for most activities, but why get your heart set on a luau, B&B or guided hike and arrive to find it full? If you have kids, don't worry; it's easy for families to travel in Hawaii.

For itinerary suggestions, see the Itineraries chapter.

WHEN TO GO

There is no bad time to be in Hawaii. The busiest seasons are mid-December through March and June through August – but this has more to do with weather and vacation schedules *elsewhere*. Weather in Hawaii varies only a little year-round – a bit rainier in winter, a bit hotter in summer.

See climate charts (p556) for more information.

For certain activities, however, the seasons are a consideration: in winter, the biggest waves hit the islands, which makes it prime time for surfers. Windsurfers will find their optimal conditions in summer. Whale-watching happens mainly January to March. For more on activities, see p73.

DON'T LEAVE HOME WITHOUT...

- A swimsuit, hat and sunglasses for afternoons at the beach (p75)
- Light jacket, fleece layers and rain gear for evenings and inland adventures (p84)
- Hotel (p552) and tour (p563) reservations and your passport
- Binoculars for whale-watching (p83) and birding, and flashlights for exploring lava tubes
- Rubbah slippahs and hiking boots (p85), because beach-wear and trail-wear don't mix
- Snorkel gear if you're planning lots of time in the water (p75)
- A spirit of aloha and a hang-loose attitude (p43)

READ THIS BOOK, NOW FORGET IT

We love travel guides (we really do!), but we also know they are no replacement for a spirit of discovery. The very best travel experiences, not just in Hawaii but anywhere, are the ones you create yourself. They are the unexpected people you meet, the wonderful restaurant you found while escaping the rain, the trails you followed that no one mentioned.

Even in a heavily visited and small place like Hawaii there are tons of 'undiscovered' places. Indeed, we've sprinkled this book with 'Detours' to help inspire your own independent explorations.

In other words, read this book. Then forget it. Put it down. It's your trip.

Bargain-hunters should travel from April to May through September to mid-November, when you have the best chance of netting off-season rates in lodgings, plus everything is a little more relaxed and tours are not as full.

Prices can spike around the big holidays – Thanksgiving, Christmas, New Year and Easter – and during special events. Perhaps you are dying to see O'ahu's Hula or Pro Bowls, or you long to catch Hilo's Merrie Monarch Festival (p276), if not, avoid these places at these times. For Hawaii-wide festivals and events, see p559. For a list of the best events worth including in a trip, see opposite.

COSTS & MONEY

HOW MUCH?

Aloha shirt $20-70

Mai tai $5-7

Pound of Kona coffee $20-30

Pound of *poke* $5-10

Weekly snorkel rental $15-20

Hawaii can be an expensive destination, but it doesn't have to be. Once you've covered the cost of your airline flight and a rental car, you can travel as cheaply here as anywhere in the US. Of course, you can also spend a mint. It all depends on your needs and style of travel.

Flights from the mainland USA (p567) run from around $400 to $700. Interisland flights (p568) have recently gotten much cheaper, starting from $30 to $40 one way. For more on airfares, see p566.

On average, Hawaii travelers spend $175 per day per person on everything else: rental car, hotel, food, gas, tours and so on. Budget for this much, and you can enjoy a comfortable midrange trip. It's very easy to spend lots more than this (particularly in Honolulu and at resorts), and it's also easy to spend less – bring a tent.

Rental cars (p571) cost from $185 to $240 per week; as above, the only place to even think of doing without one is within Honolulu.

As for sleeping, each island has the full range of options (see p552). All have state and county campgrounds costing from $3 to $10 a night, and Maui and the Big Island have excellent national parks with free camping. Hostel dorm beds run around $20. In hostels, rural B&Bs and spartan hotels, you can find private rooms for $50 to $70. For standard middle-class hotels, expect to pay from $100 to $150 nightly. At deluxe beachfront hotels, rates reach $200 a night (and tack on another $30 to $50 in Waikiki). Celebrating a romantic occasion? Hawaii has some of the world's finest hostelries, and they are yours for $300 a night and up. Some places offer weekly discounts (always ask), and weekly or monthly condo rentals offer good value.

How and where you eat will have a big impact on your budget. If you prefer to cook, rent places with kitchens (standard in condos), though be prepared for the highest grocery prices in the US (most of Hawaii's food is imported). Farmers markets are common, and are the best places for inexpensive fresh produce (see the island chapters). If you stick to plate lunches and local *grinds* (food), meals will rarely top $10 per person, and many a fine dinner can be had for $20 to $30. Gourmet cuisine comes with gourmet prices, of course (but you knew that). For more, see p54.

TOP 10

HAWAII — *Kaho'olawe*

FAVE FESTIVALS & EVENTS

Here are some of our favorite Hawaii celebrations. See also the Festivals & Events sections in the island chapters. For more food festivals, see p58. For more Hawaii-wide events, see p559. For even more perusing, go to www.calendar.gohawaii.com.

1 Merrie Monarch Festival – Easter; Big Island (p276)

2 May Day (aka Lei Day) – May; all main islands (p559)

3 International Festival of Canoes – mid-May; Maui (p324)

4 Taste of Honolulu – June; O'ahu (p122)

5 Prince Lot Hula Festival – July; O'ahu (p122)

6 Aloha Festivals – late August through early October; all main islands (p559)

7 Hawaii International Film Festival – October; all main islands, p122)

8 Ironman Triathlon World Championship – late October; Big Island (p207)

9 Kona Coffee Cultural Festival – early November; Big Island (p207)

10 Triple Crown of Surfing – November; O'ahu (p79)

HAWAII NOVELS & MEMOIRS

To get inside the heart of Hawaiian sensibilities and local life, crack open one or two of these poetic, beautiful and sometimes pidgin-laced volumes.

1 *Hawaii* by James Michener

2 *Da Word* by Lee Tonouchi

3 *Wild Meat and the Bully Burgers* by Lois-Ann Yamanaka

4 *Comfort Woman* by Nora Okja Keller

5 *All I Asking for Is My Body* by Milton Murayama

6 *Talking to the Dead* by Sylvia Watanabe

7 *Hotel Honolulu* by Paul Theroux

8 *Volcano* by Garrett Hongo

9 *Growing Up Local: An Anthology of Poetry and Prose from Hawaii* edited by Eric Chock et al

10 *The Seven Orchids* by Ian MacMillan

BEST PLACES TO HONOR THE SUN

In Hawaii, the sun rises up out of the ocean and sets there too. Observing these luminous moments are, shall we say, a little bit popular. Try it from any one of these perches and you'll see why.

1 Diamond Head – sunrise; O'ahu (p155)

2 Yokohama Bay – sunset; O'ahu (p188)

3 Mauna Kea summit – sunset; Big Island (p251)

4 Hawai'i Volcanoes National Park, near flowing lava – sunset; Big Island (p297)

5 Haleakala Crater – sunrise; Maui (p405)

6 Big Beach – sunset; Maui (p368)

7 Lahaina – sunset; Maui (p317)

8 Lagoons' Kiele Course – sunrise; Kaua'i (p471)

9 Hanalei Bay pier – sunset; Kaua'i (p508)

10 Princeville Resort lawn – sunset; Kaua'i (p503)

TRAVEL LITERATURE

Here, we provide recommendations for some illuminating, moving non-fiction accounts of Hawaiian history, culture and the natural world.

To listen to a Hawaiian king 'talk story,' read *Legends and Myths of Hawaii* by David Kalakaua (aka, the Merrie Monarch). Of ancient Hawaii, he writes, 'but a thin veil then divided the living from the dead, the natural from the supernatural,' and he captures this shimmering quality in his evocative tales – which seamlessly mix real history (of Kamehameha I, Captain Cook, the burning of the temples) with living mythology.

For some suggestions of Hawaii fiction, see p23 and p51.

Gavan Daws is the pre-eminent Hawaii historian. For the modern era, from the arrival of Captain Cook in 1778 to statehood in 1959, read his beautiful *Shoal of Time*.

For a glimpse of Native Hawaiian culture today, pick up *Voices of Wisdom: Hawaiian Elders Speak* by MJ Harden. In it 24 *kupuna* (elders – including well-known folk like Herb Kawainui Kane) discuss nature, activism, hula, spirituality, music and more.

Big Island resident Peter Adler fills his *Beyond Paradise* with wry, self-deprecating meditations on life in modern-day Hawaii. He ruminates on growing avocados, climbing Mauna Loa, bugs, Kaho'olawe and on how Hawaii chose its 'unofficial' state fish (the *humuhumunukunukuapua'a*).

For a sharp and pointed argument in favor of Hawaiian sovereignty, check out *From a Native Daughter* by Haunani-Kay Trask.

So much can be said, and has been written, about Hawaii's natural world. A good place to begin is *A World Between Waves*, edited by Frank Stewart. This varied essay collection covers everything from volcanoes to whales, and includes a fantastic WS Merwin account of Captain Cook's first voyage from the perspective of the naturalists on board.

Finally, don't leave the islands without reading *Pidgin to Da Max* by Douglas Simonson (aka Peppo), which is so funny it inspired a second volume (*Hana Hou*), *Pupus to Da Max* and a collector's edition. It's shaka, brah! Garans. (But please, follow the 'nonlocal caution.')

INTERNET RESOURCES

Hawaii Visitors & Convention Bureau (www.gohawaii.com) The state's official tourism site.

Hawaii Ecotourism Association (www.hawaiiecotourism.org) This nonprofit certifies and lists outfitters, tours and hotels committed to ecotourism.

Honolulu Advertiser (www.honoluluadvertiser.com) The state's main daily newspaper.

Lonely Planet (www.lonelyplanet.com) Hawaii travel news and links to other useful web resources.

Office of Hawaiian Affairs (www.oha.org) Learn about current Native Hawaiian issues, news and life.

Ulukau: The Hawaiian Electronic Library (www.ulukau.org) Online Hawaiian-to-English (and vice versa) dictionaries and key Hawaiian texts.

Itineraries

On the four main islands, one to two weeks allows a full experience of each island. For shorter visits, see the 'in…days' boxed texts for some itinerary suggestions: O'ahu (p98); The Big Island (p194); Maui (p317); and Kaua'i (p460).

CLASSIC ROUTES

O'AHU   **One to Two Weeks**
To begin, immerse yourself in **Honolulu** (p101) and **Waikiki** (p135) for four days. In between sessions at **Waikiki's beaches** (p139); **eat your heart out** in the city; tour **Chinatown** (p121); visit the **Bishop Museum** (p115), **'Iolani Palace** (p104) and the **Honolulu Academy of Art** (p111); see **Pearl Harbor** (p132); hear some live **Hawaiian music** (p150); and, of course, hike **Diamond Head** (p153). Now relax. Leave the city heading east: spend a leisurely day snorkeling (or diving) at **Hanauma Bay** (p155). The next day, surf, kayak or windsurf at the beaches along **Waimanalo Bay** (p158) or **Kailua Bay** (p161). Consider lingering along the rural **Windward Coast** (p159), otherwise make tracks for the **North Shore** (p171) and the famous beaches around **Waimea** (p173). In winter, watch some big-wave surfing; in summer, snorkel with sea turtles. If the clock's run out, drive scenic Kamehameha Hwy through **central O'ahu** (p182) and hit the airport; otherwise, veer right on H1 and explore the **Wai'anae Coast** (p184), perhaps hiking to **Ka'ena Point** (p188). Now go ahead, end with a **luau** (p151) – it's fun!

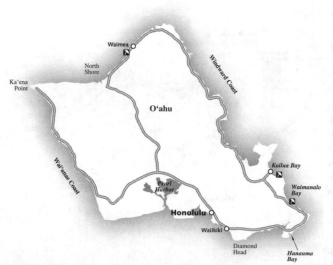

For big city, big waves and big fun, a week or two on O'ahu gives unrepentant urbanites a chance to experience world-class snorkeling, windsurfing, diving and, of course, surfing – without sacrificing fine grinds, high *culchah* or tiki-bar cocktails. You'll drive 125 miles or so.

MAUI
One to Two Weeks

You're on your honeymoon, right? Well, we're not waiting around for laggards. Just keep up. Start off in the old whaling town of **Lahaina** and explore its treasure trove of **historic sites** (p322), perhaps celebrating your arrival with the superb **Old Lahaina Luau** (p328). Head north into **West Maui** (p330). In winter, spot whales breaching offshore, particularly at **Papawai Point Scenic Viewpoint** (p332) and take a **whale-watching tour** (p324). It's a special occasion, so indulge in a resort at **Ka'anapali** (p333) and enjoy its excellent beaches; spend two days if you must (three if you're really in love), but then let's go! Drive around the peninsula, stopping at gorgeous **Kapalua Beach** (p340), and okay, yes, snorkel with spinner dolphins at **Slaughterhouse Beach** (p341), but eventually get around on the scenic **Kahekili Hwy** (p343) and down to **South Maui** (p356): book a snorkel cruise to **Molokini Crater** (p311), check out more whales from **Kihei** (p356), and kayak and snorkel around **Makena** (p367). Look at the time – only a day left!? Well get thee to **Haleakala National Park** (p403) before you go. Those staying longer should spend two days **hiking** (p408) this awesome crater and catching the sunrise from the **summit** (p405). Then drive the cliff-hugging **Road to Hana** (p373), stopping frequently to gape in wonder. Those smart enough to stay the full two weeks can take their time, overnight in **Hana** (p373), and still fit in a windsurf at **Kanaha Beach** (p348) before departure time. And by the way, congratulations!

For an adventure-packed holiday that doesn't skimp on the pampering, Maui combines comfy resorts with splendid beaches, whale-watching, unbelievable snorkeling, the world's largest volcanic crater and the harrowing Hana Hwy, just for good measure. Activity hounds: 300+ miles of driving. Honeymooners: 2.

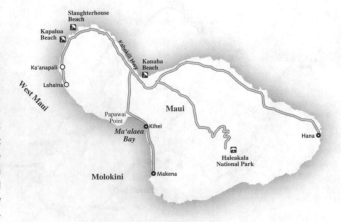

THE BIG ISLAND   One to Two Weeks

Variety is the name of the game on the Big Island. Start from **Kailua-Kona** (p201) in the west, and go counter-clockwise around the island. First, spend a day shaking off your jet lag on the white-sand strands within **Kekaha Kai State Park** (p231). The next day kayak and snorkel at **Kealakekua Bay** (p218), and imbibe the ancient mana of **Pu'uhonua o Honaunau National Historical Park** (p226). Spend your third day driving through **Ka'u** (p301) – stopping at **Ka Lae** (p305), **Green Sands Beach** (p306) and **Punalu'u Beach** (p303) to admire the sea turtles – on the way to **Hawai'i Volcanoes National Park** (p288). If you can, spend two days (or more) exploring the park: take the **Kilauea Iki Trail** (p296), trek to **hot lava** (p297) and take a full day to hike **Mauna Loa** (p258) or the **Napau Crater Trail** (p297). If you have only two more days, spend one in **Hilo** (p267), exploring its downtown, the farmers market and the excellent museums. Return on your last day along the **Hamakua Coast** (p259), making sure to see **Waipi'o Valley** (p262). With more time, base yourself in Hilo for three nights: make sure to get lost in **Puna** (p283), and catch the sunset and stargazing from **Mauna Kea** (p251). Returning along the Hamakua Coast, now hike into Waipi'o Valley and pull into the cowboy town of **Waimea** (p246) for gourmet fixins and maybe a horse ride. With a final day or two, explore **North Kohala** (p240): trek to the **Pololu Valley** (p246), visit **Mo'okini Heiau** (p243) and explore **Hawi** (p243) for more great eats. When it's time to leave, say goodbye from ever-lovely **Hapuna Beach** (p237).

The Big Island offers the diversity of a continent within the space of a small island. In 320 miles, go from rain forests to lava deserts, pastureland to snowy mountains, white-sand beaches to flowing magma, a cowboy town to a working-class city, and tourist resorts to rural B&Bs.

KAUA'I
One to Two Weeks

If you've chosen Kaua'i, you're looking for adventure, but we're going to start you off easy: **Po'ipu** (p521). Enjoy a day or two in a condo at the sunny beaches here and limber up on the **Maha'ulepu Heritage Trail** (p524). However, scuba divers should jump right in: book a trip to the waters around **Ni'ihau** (p524). Now, tighten your hiking boots and spend the next two days in **Waimea Canyon State Park** (p542) and **Koke'e State Park** (p545): trek the bogs of the **Alaka'i Swamp** (p547), traverse knife-edged 2000ft cliffs on the **Awa'awapuhi Trail** (p547) and wear yourself out on the **Kukui Trail** (p544). Next, drive to road's end at **Polihale State Park** (p542) for moody atmosphere and, if it's Friday, chill out among **Hanapepe's art galleries** (p535). Well-rested, head east: hit **Wailua** (p478) and kayak the **Wailua River** (p481) or the less-crowded **Hule'ia River** (p471). If time is tight, skip Wailua and just get yourself to the **North Shore** (p497), which deserves three or four days. Get in some snorkeling and windsurfing at **'Anini Beach** (p501), check out the surf-bum town of **Hanalei** (p507), while surfing and kayaking in **Hanalei Bay** (p508), and then hit road's end at **Ha'ena State Park** (p515), for more snorkeling and diving at **Ke'e Beach** (p515). Okay, feeling warmed up? **Na Pali Coast State Park** (p516) is all that's left: if it's May to September, **kayak** 17 miles along the coast (p510); otherwise, hike the **Kalalau Trail** (p516). Are you here for 14 days? Do both. Whichever, you've saved the best for last and can go home tired and satisfied.

When Hollywood needs 'tropical paradise,' it comes to Kaua'i, and so should you. The eldest main island is a faceted emerald of canyons and cliffs, waterfalls and rivers, bays and beaches. Don't tell the others, but Kaua'i is the prettiest child. You'll drive 175 miles.

ISLAND HOPPING

O'AHU, MAUI & LANA'I   Two Weeks

This trip is for lovers, honeymooners and those aging boomers who like to mix activities and culture, who like staying in one place, and who prefer to end strenuous beach days with a glass of wine and real entertainment. Start on O'ahu, basing yourself in **Waikiki** (p135) for a week. Set your own pace, but mix explorations of **Honolulu's** major cultural **sights** (p104) with hikes in the **Tantalus and Makiki Valley** (p119), a jaunt up **Diamond Head** (p153), snorkeling in **Hanauma Bay** (p155) and windsurfing at **Kailua Beach Park** (p161). Fit in **Pearl Harbor** (p132), a look at the **North Shore** (p171) and end each day with some fine **Honolulu dining** (p124) and lots of good **Hawaiian music** (p150).

Now go to Maui for four or five days. Again, make it easy: get a nice room for the duration at **Lahaina** (p317) or **Ka'anapali** (p333). There are enough beaches, whale-watching cruises and activities in **West Maui** (p330) to fill your days, but also visit **Haleakala National Park** (p403) and take a snorkel trip to **Molokini** (p311).

Finally, stay in one of **Lana'i's world-class resorts** (p421 or p424) for three or four nights. If things have been a little hectic up to now, slow down. Play a round or two of **golf** (p420), snorkel at **Hulopo'e Beach** (p423) or take in the vistas from the **Munro Trail** (p426), but mainly, relax. Enjoy the **Spa at Manele** (p424) and the company of your traveling companion.

See the Transportation chapter for details on island-hopping by air (p568) and/or boat (p570).

You've got time, you've got money and you want to see a lot for a minimum of effort. Combine O'ahu, Maui and Lana'i – you'll go from the busiest city to the quietest island and, in between, choose from a banquet of top-shelf activities. You'll drive 400 miles, or much less.

THE BIG ISLAND, MOLOKA'I & KAUA'I   Two Weeks

This trip is for those who consider a six-hour hike a half-day's work and who prefer their 'view lanai' to be a patch of grass outside their tent flap. We won't camp the whole way; we'll mix in enough hotels to keep this a vacation. Start on the Big Island at **Kailua-Kona** (p201): the first day, book a **hotel** (p207), snorkel at **Kahalu'u Beach** (p213) and visit **Pu'uhonua o Honaunau National Historical Park** (p226). Then spend three nights and four days camping and hiking in **Hawai'i Volcanoes National Park** (p288). Spend a night or two in **Hilo** (p267), shop the **farmers market** (p273) and catch the sunset from **Mauna Kea** (p251). Next, camp at **Laupahoehoe Point** (p266) while exploring short hikes on the **Hamakua Coast** (p259). Then, visit **Waipi'o Valley** (p262), either camping at **Kalopa State Park** (p265) or backpacking to **Waimanu Valley** (p264).

Next, spend three days on Moloka'i. Good camping is scarce, so stick to a **Kaunakakai hotel** (p436). Day one: explore **East Moloka'i** (p439), checking out **Halawa Valley** (p442) and perhaps **Moa'ula Falls** (p442). Day two: penetrate the raw forests of the **Kamakou Preserve** (p444). Day three: trek to the **Kalaupapa Peninsula** (p448).

With five or six days in Kaua'i, spend two camping and hiking at **Koke'e State Park** (p545) and **Waimea Canyon State Park** (p542), then boogie up to the **North Shore** (p497), mixing some camping at **'Anini Beach** (p501) or **Ha'ena Beach** (p508) with lodgings in **Hanalei** (p510). Spend time swimming, snorkeling and surfing, but don't leave without hiking or backpacking the **Na Pali Coast's** *amazing* **Kalalau Trail** (p516). All in all, it's a hiker's dream.

If you want to live in the scenery (not just admire it), consider combining the Big Island, Moloka'i and Kaua'i, which offer the hiking and backcountry adventures of a lifetime, plus lots of ancient and modern-day Hawaiian culture. It's 550 miles (driving, not hiking).

Snapshot

Hawaii may be promoted as 'paradise,' but it struggles with the same problems facing any society today – a widening gap between rich and poor, an escalating cost of living, social tensions, limited resources and environmental stresses. In 2006, with a booming economy and high approval ratings, Republican Governor Linda Lingle was re-elected to her second term. In her inauguration speech, she surprised many by boldly announcing it was time for Hawaii's economy to be fundamentally restructured: away from land development and toward human development and technological innovation.

If history is a guide, accomplishing such a shift won't be easy – land has always been the source of wealth and power in Hawaii. However, as the governor and many others recognize, the quality and pace of modern development in Hawaii isn't sustainable. That word – 'sustainability' – is likely to become the Hawaiian mantra for decades.

On the face of it, Hawaii is doing great: in 2005, the state economy ranked ninth in the nation with record growth in tourism, the state's largest industry, and a surging real-estate market (from 2001 to 2006, the median house price on O'ahu doubled to $630,000). For more on the economy, see p46.

However, this economic growth is bypassing most state residents. Rampant land development and the annual arrival of over 7 million visitors is hurting both the environment (p70) and island and Native Hawaiian culture. In other words, Hawaii's economy is threatening to destroy what feeds it.

The real-estate market has largely been fueled by wealthy second-home buyers and off-island speculators, who build new subdivisions and resorts, sometimes with little regard for environmental and community impacts. Middle- and lower-income residents are actually worse off, since their gains in personal income can't keep pace with escalating fuel, medical and housing costs. Rents in Hawaii are the highest in the nation (the median in 2005 was $995 per month), and the gap between rich and poor widens daily.

For years, residents have quipped that Hawaii's high cost of living was simply their 'paradise tax,' but as more working families are driven into homelessness (see p185), there is less humor about the situation.

As for how residents feel about tourism, surveys show they are conflicted. They understand how important the industry is to Hawaii, and with their deeply held beliefs in the aloha spirit, they feel a true sense of welcome toward visitors. But they look at the traffic jams, exclusive resorts, unlicensed 'vacation rentals' in residential areas, shifts to low-wage service jobs, the commutes, escalating rents and home prices – and they feel their quality of life vanishing. On any given day, one out of nine people on O'ahu is a tourist. On Maui and Kaua'i, it's one out of three. Many residents complain that the state mostly caters to short-term visitors over the health and welfare of its citizens.

Native Hawaiians feel particularly trampled. Many see their culture trivialized as a promotional tool and then commodified for tourists. Then, in the name of economic development, their ancestral places and sacred landscapes are disturbed and built over (p65). Today, there are growing calls among Native Hawaiians for not just federal recognition, such as offered by the Akaka Bill, sitting before congress (p42), but for nothing less than the reinstatement of national sovereignty (www.reinstated.org).

Overall, this can't last. So, as the state develops a 'Sustainability Plan' (p69) for its tourism industry, the governor offers a new vision: one where a highly educated citizenry jumps onto the 21st-century's high-tech wave and surfs into a healthier, more sustainable future.

FAST FACTS

Population: 1,275,194

Gross state product: $54 billion

Average wage: $36,355

Miles of coastline: 750

State flower: hibiscus *(Pua aloalo)*

Number of tourists in Hawaii each day, on average: 180,000

Energy produced from oil: 89%; from alternative sources: 5%

Size: 6450 sq miles; the USA's fourth smallest state

Percentage of marriages that are interethnic: nearly 60%

State motto: *Ua Mau Ke Ea O Ka Aina I Ka Pono* (The Life of the Land Is Perpetuated in Righteousness)

History

Perilous Pacific voyages, western colonization, kingdom politics and intrigue, and the Hawaiian Renaissance are just a few of the things that make Hawaii's history so compelling and so evocative.

ANCIENT HAWAI'I
Voyage & Discovery

Contrary to many history books, British Captain James Cook did not 'discover' the Hawaiian Islands when he sighted the island of O'ahu in 1778 on his third voyage of exploration to the Pacific.

The truth of the matter is that the world's most isolated land mass had been discovered almost 2000 years earlier by intrepid explorers from the East. Archaeologists and anthropologists often disagree exactly where these explorers came from; some believe they sailed from Southeast Asia, others, from China. Either way, there is consensus that their eastward migratory path took them to the southern Polynesian islands of Tonga, Samoa and the Marquesas Islands. From there, they ventured blindly into the unknown Pacific Ocean where they stumbled upon (and subsequently settled) a group of uninhabited and beautiful islands.

It is estimated that the journey from the Marquesas to Hawai'i in large double-hulled voyaging canoes took them at least four months, without any landings along the way to stock up on fresh food and water. In canoes

---

HOKULE'A: STAR OF GLADNESS

Imagine sailing on a 62ft double-hulled canoe across the Pacific Ocean, trying to find a miniscule island hundreds, if not thousands, of miles away. Then toss the modern navigational tools – radar, satellite positioning systems, radios – overboard. A daunting scenario to say the least!

But that is exactly what some intrepid modern-day sailors have done seven times in the last 30 years. In 1976, to re-create the incredible journey of the early settlers in Hawai'i, the Polynesian Voyaging Society (www.pvs.hawaii.org) built and launched a modern-day reproduction of an ancient Hawaiian long-distance sailing canoe named *Hokule'a* (*Star of Gladness*). After months of intense training, a remarkable 4800-mile voyage was made to Tahiti and back – navigational tools left on land – making the vessel and its crew instant symbols of Hawaiian pride.

This historic achievement was followed by voyages to Tahiti again in 1980; Aotearoa (New Zealand), Tonga, Samoa, the Society Islands and the Cook Islands in 1985; Rarotonga in 1992; the Marquesas Islands in 1995; and Rapa Nui (Easter Island) in 1999.

In the last seven years the *Hokule'a* and its crews have stayed closer to home, exploring the Northwestern Hawaiian Islands (p550). These journeys have been linked with school programs that teach students about navigation, exploration, ocean and land resource conservation and cultural preservation. Among many other things, the Navigating Change Educational Partnership (www.cooperativeconservationamerica.org/viewproject.asp?pid=38) has connected over 1800 students via special ship-to-classroom telecommunications systems so that crew members and students can communicate directly with each other during the course of the voyage. Teachers incorporate into their curriculums science, history, ecology and conservation lessons that are directly associated with the activities of the crew.

TIMELINE

1779	1810
Captain James Cook is killed at Kealakekua Bay on the island of Hawai'i	King Kamehameha the Great unites the Islands under one kingdom

only 60ft long and 14ft wide, with very limited storage capacity for food and supplies, this was an astounding achievement. They had no modern maps or navigational tools such as satellites, compasses and sextons; their only guides were the wind, stars and wave patterns – incredible!

Early Society

Hawaiian society developed much along the lines of other Polynesian island groups, which were ruled by chiefs. In Hawai'i the social hierarchy was made up of four major classes of people.

The highest rank in the social order was the *ali'i* (chiefly) class. One's rank as an *ali'i* was determined by the mother's family lineage, making Hawai'i a matriarchal society.

The second class contained *ali'i ai moku* (high chiefs) who ruled individual islands, and *ali'i 'ai ahupua'a* (lesser chiefs) who ruled subdistricts on each island called *ahupua'a*. Also ranked second were the kahuna (masters) – individuals trained in specific skills such as canoe building, religious practices, healing arts, martial arts, navigation and other specialties. Kahuna were considered to be experts in their field and were highly regarded.

The third, and largest, class of people in the social hierarchy were the *maka'ainana* (commoners). The *maka'ainana* were not owned by the *ali'i*, and were free to live wherever they pleased. However they were obligated to support the *ali'i* through taxes paid in the form of food, goods and labor in building large temples or other important structures.

Lastly there was the *kauwa* (outcast) class, which was looked down upon and generally did not mix with the other classes, except as slaves.

Some describe traditionally Hawaiian society as being like feudal European society, with lords owning the land as well as the people. But this is inaccurate. The *ali'i* were considered to be caretakers, not owners, of the land and people they ruled, with the sacred duty to care for the land, its resources and its residents on behalf of the gods.

ANCIENT RELIGION

Religion was the cornerstone of early Hawaiian society, consisting of a pantheon of gods and deities. All individual, family and community activities were governed by strict religious laws and regulations, known as the *kapu* (taboo) system. This system governed what people ate, whom they married, when they fished or harvested crops, and just about every other aspect of daily life.

The four major gods were Ku, the god of war; Kane, the god of fresh water, sunlight, procreation and fertility; Kanaloa, the god of the ocean; and Lono, the god of peace and agriculture.

Among the lesser gods were Pele, the goddess of volcanoes (p34); Laka, the goddess of hula; and Hina, the moon goddess. Most land features, such as valleys, beaches, mountains and rivers, also had their own protector gods.

The ancient Hawaiians believed that when they died, their spirits lived on in the form of *'aumakua* (guardian spirits). These spirits often assumed earthly forms of animals such as sharks, owls, birds, fish, chickens and pigs. *'Aumakua* provided guidance and protection to the living, and in return the living family protected the animal form of their ancestors.

An Ocean in Mind, by Will Kyselka (1987), is a compelling first-hand account about Kyselka's many journeys in the Pacific rediscovering traditional Polynesian voyaging.

1820	1825
First missionaries arrive in the Islands	First successful commercial sugar plantation is established

PELE'S FIERY POWER

Pele, the goddess of fire and volcanoes, is legendary in Hawaii. The goddess, who lives in Halema'uma'u Crater in the Big Island's Kilauea volcano (p292), is responsible for the fiery eruptions and lava flows that both destroy and create land throughout the Islands.

In one of the most famous of the many Pele stories, Pele fell in love with a man named Lohi'au while on a dream journey to the island of Kaua'i. Upon awakening, Pele asked her favorite sister, Hi'iaka (the hula goddess) to go and fetch Lohi'au so she could take him as her lover. While on Kaua'i, Hi'iaka and Lohi'au fell in love. Pele saw this in her dreams and, in a fit of revenge, sent lava flows to kill Lohi'au and to destroy Hi'iaka's beloved ohia forest grove.

Today many Hawaiians still believe that Pele takes on the mortal form of an old woman dressed in white, and have recounted stories about seeing her wandering at night in dark and isolated areas. In these sightings Pele has often asked for assistance of some kind, and if it was not given she has inflicted harm or bad luck.

FROM 'DISCOVERY' TO MONARCHY TO ANNEXATION
Arrival of Captain Cook

One fateful day, an event occurred in the Islands that would change the traditional world of Hawaiians in ways inconceivable at the time. On January 18, 1778, British naval explorer Captain James Cook, on his third 'Voyage of Discovery' to the Pacific Ocean, sighted the island of O'ahu while en route to the Pacific Northwest, where he was to search for a possible 'northwest passage' from the Pacific Ocean to the Atlantic Ocean via Hudson Bay.

Voyages of Discovery: Captain Cook and the Exploration of the Pacific, by Lynne Withey (1989) tells the story of Cook's three great voyages to the Pacific and his death in the Islands.

Cook's appearance marked the end of Hawai'i's more than 500 years of complete isolation from the rest of the world, and the beginning of the decline of one of the most sophisticated civilizations in the Pacific.

The most immediate impact of Cook's visit to the 'Sandwich Isles,' as Cook named them, was the introduction of venereal diseases, which quickly spread throughout the Islands, killing hundreds of Hawaiians. Then in February 1779, while on his second visit to the islands, Cook anchored in the idyllic Kealakekua Bay to repair his two ships, the *HMS Discovery* and the *HMS Resolution,* and to refresh food supplies. On February 14 Hawaiians attacked Cook and some of his men after Cook tried to take a chief hostage in retaliation for the theft of one of his shore boats. A short battle ensued and Cook, four of his men, and 17 Hawaiians were killed.

Kamehameha the Great

Up until the 1790s, each of the islands in Hawaii were independently ruled by *ali'i 'ai moku.* These high chiefs sometimes fought against one another in attempts enlarge their domains. In 1790 the ruling chief of the island of Hawai'i, Kamehameha, began a monumental campaign to conquer all of the other islands. After 20 years of warfare and diplomatic efforts, he achieved his goal and became the first *ali'i* to rule over all of the islands.

King Kamehameha I is credited with bringing long-term peace and stability to a society that was often in flux because of power struggles among the *ali'i.* While he was a heroic warrior and supreme ruler with absolute powers under the *kapu* system, he was also a just and diplomatic monarch who was greatly admired by his people. Kamehameha ruled for 24 years until his death in 1819. His demise threw Hawaiian society into great turmoil. By this time

1840	1855
First whaling ship enters Honolulu from Nantucket	First sugar plantation contract laborers arrive from China

westerners had then been in the islands for 41 years and had planted the seeds of religious discontent against the ancient *kapu* system, which was upheld by Kamehameha I.

Upon his death, the title of *Mo'i* (supreme ruler) went to Kamehameha's 23-year-old son Liholiho (Kamehameha II) and a new position, Kuhina Nui (regent) was given to Queen Ka'ahumanu, who became co-ruler with Liholiho. Both Liholiho and Ka'ahumanu had been greatly influenced by westerners and were eager to renounce the *kapu* system. Upon their orders, many of the ancient religious heiau (temples) and *ki'i* (idols) were destroyed, and they openly ate together, which was strictly forbidden under the old system which forbade men and women from eating together. These royal actions signaled the beginning of the end of more than 2000 years of tradition, greatly unsettling the entire Hawaiian population and opening a doorway to the American missionaries who would arrive in the Islands only 11 months later.

Whalers, Traders & Hawaiian Pit Stop

After Cook's ships returned to England, news of his discovery quickly spread throughout Europe and America, opening the floodgates to a foreign invasion of other explorers, traders, adventures, missionaries and fortune hunters.

By the 1820s Hawai'i had a foreign resident population of about 500 and was a crucial site in the development of the trade and whaling industries in the Pacific, becoming the critical link in the growing trade route from China to the Pacific Northwest. British, American, French and Russian traders all used Hawai'i as a mid-Pacific station to reprovision their ships and to buy sandalwood from the chiefs, which was a highly lucrative commodity in China.

Similarly, whalers found Hawai'i to be the perfect place to reprovision and to transfer their catch to ships heading for America. This allowed them to stay in the Pacific for much longer periods of time, thereby boosting their annual catch and their profits. By the 1840s, Hawai'i had become the whaling capital of the Pacific, with hundreds of ships and thousands of whalers stopping in Hawaiian ports each year.

Kamehameha: The Boy Who Became a Warrior King, by Ellie Crowe (2003), is a children's book that provides a glimpse into the life of the famous chief who united Hawai'i's many chiefdoms into one kingdom.

THE MYSTERIES OF CAPTAIN COOK'S DEATH

While many people have some knowledge of Captain James Cook, his legacy in the Pacific, and his death in Hawai'i, most do not know that two artifacts related to his death have been the source of ongoing debate over the years.

The so-called 'Cook Dagger,' owned by the Royal British Columbia Museum in Victoria, Canada, is reputed to be the dagger that a Hawaiian used to kill Cook at Kealakekua Bay in 1779. This dagger may have been owned by Cook or one of his men and given to the Hawaiians in a trade deal prior to the battle in which Cook was killed. If true, the irony of this is inescapable.

The second artifact in question is the 'Cook Arrow,' now the property of the Australian Museum in Sydney. Until recently it was at the center of intrigue because part of it was believed to have been made from one of Captain Cook's leg bones. For years Cook historians have wanted DNA testing done on the arrow to verify its origins, but the Australian Museum had always declined, insisting that the testing would partially destroy the arrow.

In 2004 the museum finally relented and had the arrow tested. The result? The bone is definitely not from Cook's appendage. In fact, the material is not human bone at all but bone from an unidentified type of animal.

1866	1893
First leprosy victims are sent into exile at Kalaupapa, Moloka'i	Hawaiian monarchy is overthrown and Queen Lili'uokalani is deposed

Saving 'Heathen' Souls

On April 19, 1820, the brig *Thaddeus* landed in Kona on the Big Island, delivering the first group of missionaries to the Islands. By a twist of fate, these American Congregationalists from New England arrived at a fortuitous time, when Hawaiian society was in great upheaval after the death of King Kamehameha the Great.

It made the missionaries' efforts to save the souls of the 'heathen' Hawaiians much easier, especially among the *ali'i* who immediately engaged in the reading and writing lessons offered by the missionaries in the Hawaiian language. By the middle of the 1850s, Hawai'i had a higher literacy rate than the United States. Between the 1830s and 1900, more than 100 Hawaiian-language newspapers were published in the Islands.

But the missionaries also helped to destroy traditional Hawaiian culture. They prohibited the dancing of the hula because of its 'lewd and suggestive movements,' they denounced the traditional Hawaiian chants and songs that paid homage to the Hawaiian gods, and in the late 1800s they managed to proscribe the speaking of the Hawaiian language in schools, as another means of turning Hawaiians away from their 'hedonistic' cultural roots – a major turnaround from the early missionary days when all students were taught in Hawaiian.

The Rise of Sugar

Foreigners were quick to see that Hawai'i was a perfect place to grow sugarcane. Beginning in the 1830s, planters began establishing small plantations, using mostly Hawaiian labor. However, industry growth was stymied by insufficient numbers of Hawaiian laborers – introduced diseases, such as typhoid, influenza, smallpox and syphilis, had, over 50 years, caused a severe decline in the Native Hawaiian population.

This shortage led to the importation of workers from overseas, starting in the 1860s, first from Japan, then from China, and then from the Portuguese islands of Madeira and the Azores. Most of these laborers signed two- to three-year contracts for wages as low as $1 per month, plus housing and medical expenses. Many of these immigrants intended to return to their homelands after their contracts expired, but most ended up staying in the Islands.

The influx of imported foreign labor and the rise of the sugar industry had a major impact on the Islands' social structure. Caucasian plantation owners and sugar agents rose to become the elite upper economic and political class, while the Hawaiians and foreign laborers became the lower class, without much of a middle class in between.

SWEET KINGS: FROM SUGAR TO PINEAPPLE TO FLOWERS

In 1960 the sugar industry was the largest industry in the Islands, with 26 sugar plantations and 228,000 acres of land under cultivation. In the 1980s and 1990s, plantations began to shrivel up and disappear at an alarming rate because of the high cost of labor compared to foreign sites like Mexico and the Philippines. Today there are just two working plantations cultivating only 22,000 acres of sugarcane. Sugar is now the state's third largest individual crop. Hawaii's next agricultural king, pineapple, remains number one, but seed crops are poised to take its crown. However, in terms of income, each of these crops now trails flowers (and nurseries), which generated $100 million in sales in 2005. For more on Hawaii's economy, see p46.

1900	1912
Hawaii becomes a US territory	Duke Kahanamoku wins Olympic gold and silver at Stockholm

The Great Mahele

Two of the most significant government actions of the monarchy period were promulgation of Hawaii's first constitution in 1840, and enactment of the Great Mahele in 1848, both of which occurred during the reign of King Kamehameha III (Kauikeaouli). Having been born and raised in Hawaii after Western contact had occurred, this king struggled to retain traditional Hawaiian social and political systems amidst increasing demands by foreigners for greater representation in government affairs and the right to own land, both of which were denied to all people under the absolute monarchy.

Bowing to this pressure, King Kamehameha III promulgated a constitution which established a constitutional monarchy with limited citizen representation. Largely because of this new power foreigners pressed hard for more changes, and in 1848 they were able to enact the Mahele, a sweeping land reform act which took all the lands in the kingdom and redistributed them into three parts: as crown lands (kings and heirs), chief lands, and government lands (for the benefit of the general public). This was followed in 1850 by the Kuleana Act, which awarded 30,000 acres of government lands to Hawaiian commoners, and gave foreigners the right to purchase some lands.

These actions effectively abolished the traditional concept of land stewardship under the chiefs and opened the way for land to be owned in fee. Despite the Kuleana Act, most of the lands designated for the exclusive rights of Hawaiians found their way into foreign hands. Hawaiians became increasingly disenfranchised from the land and the self-sufficiency it provided, while foreigners grew more and more land- and money-rich.

Hawaii School Reports – Hawaii History (www .hawaiischoolreports .com/history) is an excellent place to search for historical information about the Islands, from ancient times to the present.

Civil War Makes Sugar King

The sugar industry was stable in the 1850s, but the outbreak of the Civil War in 1861 led to a boom. The northern states relied heavily on the southern states for sugar, so they had to turn elsewhere – and that place was Hawai'i. Sugar sales soared throughout the war, but slowed down when the war came to an end in 1865. The industry languished until 1874, when King Kalakaua was elected to the throne, following the death of King Lunalilo. Kalakaua immediately lobbied the United States for a reciprocity treaty, which would end foreign import taxes and increase profits. The United States agreed to such a treaty in 1875 and sugar production instantly skyrocketed, rising from 21 million pounds in 1874 to 58 million pounds in 1878 and 114 million pounds in 1883.

Five sugar-related companies, known as the Big Five, quickly rose to dominate the industry. Castle & Cooke, Alexander and Baldwin, C Brewer & Co, American Factors and Theo H Davies & Co – all controlled by white businessmen – not only dominated the sugar industry, but also the economic and political spheres of the Islands. The leaders of these corporations, while bitter business rivals, saw that it was in their best interests to work together as an alliance to keep the balance of power in their favor. This business alliance would also turn into a secret antimonarchy organization known as the Hawaiian League, which would bring an end to the monarchy and the independent Kingdom of Hawaii.

Overthrow of the Monarchy

In 1887 the members of the Hawaiian League wrote a new constitution and through threat of violence by the newly formed Honolulu Rifles (whose rifles were fixed with bayonets), forced King Kalakaua to sign it. This constitution,

1925	1941
The first air flight between the mainland and Hawaii is made	Pearl Harbor attacked by Japanese forces; US enters WWII

which became known as the 'Bayonet Constitution,' essentially stripped the office of the monarch of most of its powers, effectively making King Kalakaua a figurehead. It also gave voting rights only to those who could meet highly restrictive income and property ownership criteria, effectively limiting voter eligibility to wealthy businessmen and landowners, most of whom were Caucasian.

When King Kalakaua died in 1891, his sister and heir, Princess Lili'uokalani, ascended the throne. The queen was a staunch supporter of her brother's efforts to retain powers of the monarch, and she too fought against foreign intervention and control.

In 1892 Queen Lili'uokalani began drafting a new constitution that would restore many of the powers of the crown lost in the Bayonet Constitution. But before she could proclaim this constitution, the leaders of the Hawaiian League, called the Committee of Thirteen, hatched a plan to take over the monarchy by force of arms. To augment the 150-strong Honolulu Rifles, the Committee requested support from US Minister John L Stevens. Stevens ordered 150 sailors and marines from a visiting US ship, the USS *Boston,* docked in Honolulu Harbor, to come ashore. Knowing that he could not officially order these men to participate in the coup d'état without authorization from Washington, Stevens justified his actions by saying that the ship's men were brought out 'only to protect American citizens in case of resistance.' Historians disagree as to the motives of Minister Stevens, with some saying he stood to gain personal land grants for his support, while others say he was only acting in the best interests of all of the Americans residing in Honolulu at the time.

Because the Kingdom of Hawai'i had no standing army, only palace guards, the queen stepped down under protest and appealed to her people to resist confrontation so that there would be no bloodshed. After the coup a provisional government was declared by the Committee of Thirteen, who immediately sought and received recognition as the new government from Minister Stevens and all other foreign-embassy representatives in Hawaii, thus ending 83 years of the Hawaiian monarchy. Eighteen months later, the Republic of Hawaii was declared.

Although the queen acquiesced to the Committee of Thirteen's demands, she saw them as having committed an act of treason against the sovereign Hawaiian government, and made every effort to bring the situation to the attention of the United States, with the belief that when Congress found out about the overthrow and Minister Steven's unauthorized role in it, they would take swift action to restore the crown and sovereignty of the kingdom. The queen had good reason to believe that restoration would be possible – in 1843 British Pacific Fleet Commander, Admiral Richard Thomas, restored the crown after British subject Lord George Paulet illegally took over the Islands by threat of force for seven weeks. (Each year on July 31, the date when the monarchy was restored, many people celebrate Restoration Day at Thomas Square in Honolulu.)

In 1895, while annexation was being debated in Washington, a group of Hawaiian royalists led by Robert Wilcox attempted a counter-revolution, which was quickly put down. The deposed queen was accused of being a co-conspirator, and after being found guilty of 'misprision' by a tribunal court, she was sentenced to five years of hard labor in prison. This sentence was later reduced to nine months' house arrest at 'Iolani Palace and a $5000 fine.

After serving her sentence, Lili'uokalani continued to lobby Congress for restoration, but to no avail. She died in 1917, 14 years after the overthrow,

---

Of Hawaii's eight ruling monarchs, only King Kamehameha I begot children who inherited the throne.

Tom Coffman provides an intriguing account of the overthrow of the Hawaiian monarchy, annexation and the drive for statehood in *Nation Within: The Story of America's Annexation of the Nation of Hawaii* (2003).

---

a tragic but heroic figure to the Hawaiian people and others who supported the monarchy.

Annexation

After the overthrow of the monarchy, the new government leaders, most of whom were members of the Hawaiian League, pushed hard for annexation, believing that it would bring greater economic and political stability to the Islands, and more profits to Caucasian run businesses. Whereas United States law required that any entity petitioning for annexation must have the backing of the majority of its citizens through a public vote, the leaders of the Republic did not offer such a vote to the people. In 1887 in protest, more than half of the Islands' population, most of whom were Hawaiian, signed an anti-annexation petition, which was sent to Congress to demonstrate that the majority of the people were opposed to the idea.

Despite overwhelming support for home rule, as demonstrated by the Anti-Annexation Petition, Congress supported annexation. On July 7, 1898, President William McKinley signed a joint congressional resolution approving annexation for the five-year-old Republic of Hawaii. Many historians feel that Hawaii would not have been annexed if it had not been for the outbreak of the Spanish-American War in April 1898, which sent thousands of US troops to the Philippines, making Hawaii a crucial Pacific staging point for the war.

From 1900, when Hawaii became a US territory, until 1941, when the US entered WWII, Hawaii's sugar-based economy developed rapidly, bolstered by a burgeoning pineapple industry. A marginal tourism market began to expand as more passenger ships began arriving and new hotels were built. Hawaii was no longer a sleepy haven for the rich and famous; the Islands were on the move economically, socially and politically.

HAWAIIAN HOMESTEAD LANDS

After Hawaii became a territory in 1900, Hawaiians began to lobby Congress to return certain lands that had been illegally taken when the monarchy was overthrown in 1893. This movement was led by Prince Jonah Kuhio, former leader of the Home Rule Party, which represented Hawaiians and continued to fight for Hawaiian independence. When Kuhio was elected to Congress in 1903, he lobbied hard for land reparations.

It was not until 1920 that the US Congress passed the Hawaiian Homes Commission Act. This set aside almost 200,000 acres of government land to be leased, for free, to Native Hawaiians, who had lost most of their ancestral lands and cultural heritage because of Western colonization and political control.

Although this program was well intended, it has long been plagued with problems. Much of the lands designated for homesteading are located in isolated areas with no infrastructure such as roads and access to water and electricity. Government bureaucracy has caused applicants to be placed on a waiting list – not just for weeks or months, but for years. Many individuals have gone to their graves waiting for land.

Currently, even though there are designated homestead lands still available, there are more than 8000 individuals and families on the waiting list, which has caused many applicants to vent their frustrations through numerous public appeals and protests. With no clear remedy in site, this situation is likely to continue for years to come.

1960	1965
Hilo, on Hawai'i, is devastated by a tsunami generated off the coast of South America	Hawaii's Patsy Mink becomes first woman of Asian ancestry to be elected to Congress

WAR, STATEHOOD & BEYOND
Day of Infamy

On December 7, 1941, when bomb-laden Japanese airplanes appeared above the Pearl Harbor area, most residents thought they were mock aircrafts being used in US Army and Navy practice maneuvers (which were frequent due to the threat of possible conflict with Japan). Even the loud anti-aircraft gunfire didn't raise much concern.

But when sirens began to wail and huge clouds of smoke appeared from the ships anchored in the harbor, everyone turned on their radios and were shocked to hear the announcement: 'This is not a test, this is the real McCoy!'

Within the next hour the Japanese invasion force, consisting of 47 ships and submarines and 441 aircraft, assaulted other military installations around O'ahu resulting in the damaging or destruction of hundreds of ships, airplanes and support facilities, and the deaths or injury of more than 3000 military and civilians. Pearl Harbor, the USA's most important naval base in the Pacific, and the main target of the Japanese, suffered the most damage, with 9 battleships, destroyers and other ships sunk; and 7 battleships, cruisers and destroyers damaged. The greatest loss was that of the battleship USS Arizona, which exploded in a spectacular hail of fire, oil, metal and smoke, killing 1,177 crew members. This devastating attack instantly propelled the USA into WWII.

The impact of the war on Hawaii was dramatic. The Army took control of the islands, martial law was declared, civil rights were suspended, rationing of gasoline and nightly blackouts were imposed, and all citizens were issued gas masks.

> It took Hawaii 59 years – longer than any other territory in the Union – to become a state after becoming a territory in 1900.

While thousands of Japanese Americans on the mainland were rounded up and sent to internment camps across the United States, most of the Japanese in Hawaii were spared because they made up most of the labor force in the sugar fields; to send them away would mean certain collapse of the industry and the sugar-dependent economy of the Islands.

However this did not mean that the Japanese in the Islands were not treated with suspicion. Their loyalty to the United States was still questioned and they were not allowed to join the armed forces. In 1943, because of political pressure, the US government reversed its decision and approved the formation of an all-Japanese combat unit, the 100th Infantry Battalion. While only 3000 men were needed for this unit, more than 10,000 men answered the recruitment call.

In 1943 the all-Japanese 442nd Regimental Combat Team, formed with 3800 men from Hawaii and the mainland, was sent to fight overseas. And fight bravely they did. By the end of the war the 442nd had received more commendations and medal awards than any other army unit in the war. The 100th Infantry Battalion also received special recognition when they helped to rescue – with great loss to their own unit – the so-called 'Lost Battalion,' comprised of several units of the 77th Division from New York, which was stranded behind enemy lines in the Vosges Mountains in France.

Final Push for Statehood

Between 1900, when Hawaii became a territory of the United States, and 1959 when it became a state, numerous statehood bills were introduced in Congress, only to be shot down. One of the primary reasons for this lack of support was racial prejudice against Hawaii's multiethnic population. Southern congressmen were very vocal in their belief that making Hawaii a state would open the

---

MILITARY OCCUPATION

The military's presence in Hawaii has been an increasing source of controversy in the Islands in recent decades. During WWII the military took over large segments of public lands throughout the state, most of which were never returned. One significant exception is Kaho'olawe (p412).

While everyone recognizes that military spending (including wages for civilian workers) is significant and important to the overall economy of Hawaii, many want to reclaim lands taken during the war. They also criticize the military for its poor environmental record and for the negative environmental of impact military training (p70). The most heated debate today centers on the development of a Stryker Brigade unit (to be stationed on O'ahu and the Big Island), which is part of the federal government's plan to fight terrorism.

---

doors to Asian immigration and the so-called 'Yellow Peril' threat that was so rampant at the time. Many also believed that Hawaii's labor unions were hotbeds of communism, and that Hawaiian government leaders, most of whom were of Hawaiian and Asian descent, lacked the intelligence and moral character necessary to facilitate Hawaii's arduous transition from territory to state.

The notoriety of the 442nd Regimental Combat Team and 100th Infantry Battalion in WWII went a long way toward reducing anti-Japanese sentiments on the mainland and increasing support for statehood. After the war, with Pearl Harbor's strategic location in the Pacific still fresh in the minds of Congress, Hawaii jockeyed hard against Alaska to become the 49th state admitted to the Union.

In 1959 Hawaii's Daniel K Inouye was the first person of Asian ancestry to become a member of Congress when he was elected to the House of Representatives.

Hawaii was greatly disappointed in June 1958 when Congress voted to admit Alaska as number 49. However, disappointment soon turned into a renewed sense of urgency and eight months later, in March 1959, Congress voted again, this time admitting Hawaii into the Union. On August 21, President Eisenhower signed the admission bill that officially deemed Hawaii the 50th state.

The Tourism Boom

Statehood had an immediate economic impact on the Islands, most notably in the boosting of the tourism industry. Coupled by the advent of jet airplanes, which could transport thousands of people per week to the Islands, tourism exploded, creating a hotel-building boom previously unmatched in the United States. Tourism quickly became the second-largest industry in the Islands, behind sugar production.

Over the next 30 years, the ever-growing tourism industry impacted almost every area of life in the Islands. By the 1990s many people believed that the industry had grown out of control, and efforts were made to limit tourism growth, but without much success.

In 1991 with the onset of the first war in Iraq, the tourism industry suffered a major setback, as did almost all tourist destinations around the world, resulting in a trickle-down effect that impacted negatively on hundreds of businesses and thousands of workers, from hotel employees to food vendors, taxi drivers, restaurant staff and even *lei* sellers. Adding to this effect was 1992's Hurricane 'Iniki (p496), which caused millions of dollars in damage, mostly to the island of Kaua'i, where the tourism industry was crippled overnight.

It took Hawaii nearly 10 years to recover from these two catastrophic events. Today the industry is thriving once again and doing better than ever.

1982	1992
Hurricane 'Iniki kills four people and causes US$250 million in damages	The world's largest optical telescope is installed at Mauna Kea on Hawai'i

STATEHOOD CELEBRATION PARTY!

When Hawaii delegate to Congress John A Burns called Hawaii from Washington, DC, on the morning of March 12, 1959, to announce that the House of Representatives had passed Hawaii's statehood bill by a vote of 323 to 89, pandemonium erupted. Church bells rang, ship horns bellowed, cars cruised the streets with people hanging out the windows blowing horns, firecrackers thundered, many schools and businesses shut for the day, and thousands of people paraded down confetti-strewn streets hugging and shouting. It had taken Hawai'i 58 years of continuous lobbying to attain statehood and the people would not be denied their long-awaited chance to celebrate.

Over the next three days, celebration activities would also include official ceremonies at 'Iolani Palace, a huge street party in Waikiki, parades, bonfires, fireworks displays and a massive entertainment program at the Honolulu Stadium that included hundreds of hula dancers, singers and bands.

After things settled down, government leaders began the arduous task of preparing a new state government. Elections were held, dozens of new state offices and staff positions were created and filled, and for the first time citizens were able to vote for their own governor, instead of having one appointed to them. It was a monumental endeavor.

Hawaiian Renaissance

In the 1960s, while tourism brought much needed cash into the new state, it also brought further erosion of traditional Hawaiian culture, which was replaced more and more with American culture. Traditionally Hawaiian luau became westernized and commercialized, Hawaiian music in Waikiki was replaced by rock-and-roll, and the Hawaiian language could rarely be heard in public. Traditional grass and *ti*-leaf hula skirts were replaced with glitzy colored cellophane skirts, and fresh flower lei were replaced with fake plastic ones.

Native Books Na Mea Hawai'i (http://native bookshawaii.com) is the best place to find books about Hawaii and a wide assortment of handmade items produced by local artists and craft makers.

But in the 1970s, much of this began to change thanks to two historical events. In 1974 a small group of people committed themselves to building and sailing a replica of a long-distance voyaging canoe. When the Polynesian Voyaging Society completed the *Hokule'a* (p32) and sailed it to and from Tahiti in 1976, a new interest in traditional Hawaiian knowledge and activities was born.

The same year, a small grassroots group of Hawaiians from Moloka'i, called the Protect Kaho'olawe 'Ohana (PKO), began to protest the bombing of the island of Kaho'olawe, which had been taken by the US government during WWII and used as a practice bombing site (p412).

Polynesian Voyaging Society (www.pvs.hawaii .org) includes information about the famous canoe *Hokule'a*, canoe building, and Polynesian navigation and migration, as well as interesting personal stories.

The political actions of the PKO, which included the illegal occupation of the island, awakened a new interest in reclaiming not only Kaho'olawe and other military lands, but in reclaiming many Hawaiian cultural practices, which had nearly been obliterated by American culture. Men and women began enrolling in hula schools in large numbers, many new Hawaiian-music groups were formed and Hawaiian-language classes emerged in the schools.

This renaissance also spawned an interest in Hawaiian sovereignty. Some groups want Hawaii to secede from the United States and reestablish a monarchy, others want a nation-within-a-nation model. Some are seeking federal recognition and funding to address Native Hawaiian health and social disparities, and the alienation of Hawaiians, resulting from 100 years of American domination and control. Currently before the US Congress is the Akaka Bill, submitted by Hawaii Senator Daniel Akaka, which calls for such recognition and funding.

1996	2001
Hawaii astronaut Ellison Onizuka dies in Challenger disaster	After being hit by a US submarine, Japanese ship sinks in Hawaiian waters and nine die

The Culture

Hawaii's 'hang loose' vibe emanates primarily from its overwhelming natural setting. No one can ignore the pull of the land and sea. But beyond a love of nature, Hawaii's residents are diverse, making cultural generalities impossible. Can a lawyer in downtown Honolulu have much in common with a line cook in Hanalei? Surprisingly, yes. (Both might be surfers who catch waves at dawn.) Even as newcomers flock to the islands, bringing mainland manners and money, a distinct local culture staunchly persists: Hawaiian residents remain bound by local food, pidgin, sports and island-casual style. Most obviously, you'll notice that they are all wholeheartedly proud of their state. Hawaii *no ka 'oi* (Hawaii is the best)!

REGIONAL IDENTITY

Located 2500 miles from the nearest continent, Hawaii is practically another country. Here, streets all have Hawaiian names, mixed-race people are the norm, school kids can play the ukulele and define an *ahupua'a* (see p33), and poi is an everyday food. Here, you'll find no daylight saving time, no major change of seasons and no snakes or skunks.

The geographical distance puts local, rather than national, news on the front page. Indeed, Washington seems far away, as does Hollywood, New England and especially the Midwest and the South. Of course, when a Hawaii connection exists, locals go wild. Senator Barack Obama, the Illinois Democrat who catapulted to rock-star fame during his run for President, grew up in Honolulu and graduated from the exclusive Punahou School in 1979, and locals are embracing him as a long-lost native son. At the time of press (2007), he was seeking the Democratic nomination for the 2008 Presidential race.

Personality-wise, most locals are easygoing and low-key. If in-your-face New York assertiveness and buttoned-up New England preppiness dissipate as one goes west, Hawaii is the epitome of laid-back cool. To locals (especially seniors and Asians), it is best to avoid embarrassing confrontations and to 'save face' by keeping quiet. If you attend community meetings or activist

---

WHO'S WHO

Haole White person (except local Portuguese). Often further defined as 'mainland haole' or 'local haole.'

Hapa Person of mixed ancestry, most commonly referring to *hapa haole* who are part white and part Asian.

Hawaiian Person of Native Hawaiian ancestry. It's a faux pas to call any Hawaii resident 'Hawaiian' (as you would a Californian or Texan), thus ignoring the existence of an indigenous people.

Kama'aina Person who is native to a particular place. A Hilo native is a *kama'aina* (literally defined as 'child of the land') of Hilo and not of Kona. It assumes a deep knowledge of and connection to the place. In the retail context, '*kama'aina* discounts' apply to any resident of Hawaii (ie anyone with a Hawaii driver's license).

Local Person who grew up in Hawaii. Locals who move away retain their local 'cred,' at least in part. But longtime transplants (see below) never become local. To call a transplant 'almost local' is a welcome compliment, despite its emphasis on the insider-outsider mentality.

Neighbor Islander Person who lives on any Hawaiian Island other than O'ahu.

Transplant Person who moves to the islands as an adult.

Note: In this book, Hawai'i (with the *'okina* punctuation mark) refers to the island of Hawai'i (Big Island), while Hawaii (without the *'okina*) refers to the state. We use this distinction to avoid confusion between the island and the state, but the *'okina* spelling is officially used for both.

rallies, chances are, the most vocal, liberal and passionate will be mainland transplants. Of course, as more and more mainlanders settle in Hawaii, the traditional stereotypes are fading.

Underlying a statewide identity are quirks particular to each island and each town. As the only big city, Honolulu constitutes its own category – it's the sole option for designer boutiques, innovative restaurants, rock concerts, pro or NCAA football games and any semblance of nightlife. On O'ahu, locals tend to categorize one another by high school. ('Where you wen' grad?' is the standard opening line upon meeting for the first time.)

Neighbor Islands are considered 'country' or even *da boonies* (the boondocks). In general, Neighbor Islanders tend to dress more casually, talk more pidgin, wear less makeup, differentiate more between local and nonlocal, and fend off yuppie trends (at least for a while). In small towns, luxury cars, designer shoes and Ivy League degrees have limited clout. Instead, the status vehicle is a monster truck for off-roading. And no Prada suit can rival a suntanned, ripped surfer's finesse on the waves.

That said, tourist-hotspot Maui is more bustling and sophisticated than tropical Kaua'i, where no town population tops 10,000. And, on the Big Island, Hilo (sensible, leisurely, rainy and predominantly Japanese) is nothing like Kailua-Kona (fun-loving, touristy, sunny and 'haole-fied').

Modern Hawaii culture is a catchy mix of pop culture, and the islands are a fantasy destination both for travelers and for settlers. But behind the polished image lies longstanding Native Hawaiian issues. In fall 2006, the US Court of Appeals ruled that Kamehameha Schools (an influential private school founded by the great-granddaughter and last royal descendant of Kamehameha the Great) can legally limit enrollment to students of Hawaiian ancestry – a decision heralded by the majority of locals, Hawaiian or not. But still stalled in the US Congress is the Native Hawaiian Government Reorganization Act introduced by Senator Daniel Akaka to formally ac-

IN THE NEWS

■ **Fixed mass-transit: is it the answer?** To combat Honolulu's traffic nightmare, Mayor Mufi Hannemann approved legislation for a controversial fixed mass-transit system (either rail or bus). Building the 28-mile route, which will run from Kapolei to UH Manoa, is estimated to cost almost $5 billion (probably an underestimate). Everyone agrees mass-transit is needed but opponents argue that Honolulu lacks the density to warrant a *fixed* system.

■ **You're not too old for a booster seat, buddy!** As of January 2007, all children under age eight must use a booster seat when riding in automobiles in Hawaii. Drivers who violate the law are fined between $100 and $500 and are required to attend a four-hour safety class.

■ **Light up waaaaay over there** Smoking is prohibited in all public places in Hawaii, including restaurants, bars, offices, airports and shops. Enacted in late 2006, the law requires that smokers be at least 20ft away from the entrance to any business.

■ **Who will grace Hawaii's commemorative quarter?** Hawaii's state commemorative quarter will feature either Kamehameha the Great, a surfer or a hula dancer – each chosen to epitomize Hawaii. Look for it in 2008.

■ **No more endless summers** Hawaii public schools adopted a uniform 'year-round' academic calendar in 2006. Before, the calendar had long been traditional (three-month summer vacation) or, since the late 1980s, determined independently by individual schools. Now, students break for one week in October, three weeks for Christmas, two weeks in spring break and seven weeks for summer.

knowledge Native Hawaiians' indigenous status and to permit them a future governing body.

Interested parties probably already know that *pakalolo* (marijuana) remains Hawaii's top crop ($1 billion annually) and that medical marijuana was legalized in 2000. The troublesome drug problem is the use of 'ice' (crystal methamphetamine), which has been rampant in Hawaii since the 1990s, especially in rural communities.

LIFESTYLE

Tourists view Hawaii as a tropical-vacation fantasyland, but daily life for most locals is simple and family-oriented. Socializing revolves around children and extended family. At popular parks and beaches on weekends, you'll see high-spirited potluck gatherings that can last all day. School sports events are packed with eager parents, plus the gamut of aunties and uncles (whether real relatives or not).

Especially on Neighbor Islands, it's impossible to be anonymous. One cannot avoid crossing paths with familiar faces. It's not unusual to bump into old schoolmates at the supermarket or at PTA meetings. If locals meet someone new, they compare notes on family background and connections – not to one-up each other, but to find common bonds.

Read *Honolulu Advertiser* columnists' blogs at http://blogs.honolulu advertiser.com to get the gist of the local psyche.

The workday starts and ends early, and while workaholism is not unknown, most people in Hawaii live more balanced and relaxed lives than do their mainland counterparts. The balmy climate encourages outdoor activity, especially early-bird golf or surfing.

The aloha shirt remains appropriate for business and social functions, but only if cotton or silk and, ideally, a Reyn Spooner design. The muumuu as street attire has been outmoded since the 1980s, but it's certainly appropriate for hula dancers or Hawaiian *tutu* (grandmothers).

Honolulu dwellers are generally more fashion conscious, technologically savvy and cosmopolitan than Neighbor Islanders, but such personal differences depend mostly on exposure to the outside world. Most locals strive for the conventional 'American dream': kids, home ownership, stable work and ample free time. Generally, those with less-standard lifestyles (eg B&B owners, artists, unmarrieds and world travelers) are mainland transplants.

Actually, much of the so-called local lifestyle stems from plantation-era, working-class customs. The highly educated and upper-income classes can fall outside the stereotypical definition of 'local' because they tend to speak no pidgin and aspire to the same Ivy League dreams as their mainland counterparts.

One might assume that locals routinely circumnavigate their home islands (even the Big Island is compact by mainland standards), but residents tend to stick to their regions. On Kaua'i, a rural Waimea resident might drive to Lihu'e but once a quarter to stock up at Wal-Mart and Costco.

Politically, most residents are middle-of-the-road Democrats and tend to vote along party, racial, ethnic, seniority and local/nonlocal lines. The re-election of Senator Daniel Akaka in 2006 was held by many as an example of loyalty to a to a Native Hawaiian elder statesman – despite questions about his efficacy as a politician. His opponent in the primary election was about 30 years younger, haole and viewed as less local, despite having grown up on the Big Island.

In the 2004 Presidential election, residents gave John Kerry 54% and George W Bush 45% of the popular vote. Interestingly, the Kerry/Bush ratio was a close 51% to 48% on O'ahu.

Among Hawaii's lifestyle cons are rampant traffic, high energy costs, limited affordable housing and comparatively low wages. Yet most agree that nothing compares to living in Hawaii and leave only if absolutely necessary.

ECONOMY

Hawaii's economic base has varied over the years from sandalwood to whaling, sugarcane, pineapple, military and tourism. Since statehood, tourism has been Hawaii's leading employer, revenue producer, and growth sector. In 2005, 7.5 million people visited the islands and spent $11.9 billion, and tourism now employs over twice as many residents (22%) as does the state's second-largest employer, the military (8% to 10%).

Since the sugar industry died in Hawaii (except on Kaua'i and on Maui), diversified agriculture has been the focus. Indeed, coffee, macadamia nuts, guava, orchids, papaya and aquaculture have proven successful, but of course no single crop will ever replace sugar (see p36). In 2005, total agricultural sales were $576 million, of which $79 million was from pineapple and $59 million from sugarcane. (Granted, the billion-dollar underground marijuana industry makes such figures seem paltry.)

Other industries include film and TV production and manufacturing (which is disadvantaged due to Hawaii's costly shipping distance from the US mainland). Hawaii also benefits from the influx of big-box retailers. Soon, Target and Walgreens will join the other big boys, including Costco, Wal-Mart, Kmart and Home Depot. (Note: most locals are big-time shoppers with no qualms about patronizing chains that gobble mom-and-pop shops.)

Hawaii's unemployment rate, which has been averaging below 3%, consistently ranks among the lowest nationwide. The minimum wage is $7.25, much higher than the federal minimum of $5.15. And yet, in 2005, the average annual wage was $36,355 – compared with $40,675 nationwide – while inflation and cost of living remain sky-high, making it hard for residents to 'get ahead.' For more on Hawaii's current economy, see the Snapshot, p31.

POPULATION

Over 70% of Hawaii's 1.3 million residents live on O'ahu. Thus Honolulu remains Hawaii's only real city. On O'ahu, population density is 1500 people per sq mile – low compared to mainland cities. But across the Hawaiian Islands, average density is less than 190 people per sq mile (and is especially low on the vast Big Island).

THE NINTH HAWAIIAN ISLAND

Want to strike a conversation with a random bunch of locals? Ask them about their last trip to…Vegas!

Considered the 'Ninth Hawaiian Island,' Las Vegas is a repeat travel destination for locals of all ages, but especially seniors. They gladly tolerate 105°F summers, freezing winters and casinos thick with cigarette smoke for a week of slot machines, Cirque du Soleil and all-you-can-eat buffets. Most take advantage of the well-oiled Honolulu–Vegas circuit, which offers irresistibly cheap packages at Sam Boyd's string of downtown hotels.

Why Vegas? First, locals are unfazed by tropical splendor and prefer vacationing in the glitzy spectacle of theme-park hotels and buzzing casinos. Second, gambling (and the chance to win big) is compelling, especially because Hawaii is one of only two states that ban gambling (the other is Utah). Third, locals enjoy hanging out with other locals – and in Vegas, they're guaranteed to bump into folk from home.

A sizable community of Hawaii expatriates lives in Vegas, largely due to the low cost of living. But most locals shake their heads in disbelief. Vegas is fun, but there's no place like Hawaii.

Ethnically, Hawaii is unique. First, it is among only four states in which whites do not form a majority. Second, it has the largest percentage of Asian Americans (58%, predominantly Japanese and Filipino) among all states. Third, Hawaii has the highest mixed-race percentage (24%) among all states. Fourth, Hawaii was the first majority-minority state in the USA since the early 20th century – and its current minority (nonwhite) population constitutes a whopping 77%.

The number of Native Hawaiians has dropped steadily ever since Captain Cook's arrival, and today roughly 80,000 (5%) of Hawaii's people identify themselves as Native Hawaiian. This figure is misleading, however, and experts estimate the number of pure Native Hawaiians to be under 5000, less than half of 1% of the population.

Despite Hawaii's majority-minority, haole (whites) nevertheless comprise the largest single ethnic group, averaging 22% of the population in the islands, with especially high numbers on Neighbor Islands, where they average 30% of the population (compared to only 20% on Oʻahu). The Japanese are the second-largest ethnic group in the state with 16%, closely followed by the Filipinos at 14%. The Chinese comprise only 3% of the population overall, and most live on Oʻahu.

Hawaii's reputation as an ethnic melting pot is not quite accurate. Towns greatly vary in ethnic composition. On the Big Island, Hilo comprises 16% whites and 27% Japanese, while Kailua-Kona is just the opposite, with 36% whites and 6% Japanese. The two towns have comparable numbers of mixed-race and Hawaiian persons. Still, while schoolchildren might stick together by race, especially Japanese and haole kids, half of all marriages in Hawaii are mixed-race.

MULTICULTURALISM

Hawaii's diversity is both eclectic and narrow at once. That's because Hawaii's unique blend of races, ethnicities and cultures is quite isolated from the rest of the world. On one hand, Hawaii is far removed from any middle-American, white-bread city. On the other, it also lacks major exposure to certain races and ethnicities, particularly blacks and Mexican Hispanics, that are prevalent in the mainland USA population

Any discussion regarding multiculturalism must address whether we are talking about locals (insiders) or nonlocals (outsiders).

Among locals, social interaction has hinged on old plantation stereotypes and hierarchies since statehood. During plantation days, whites were the wealthy plantation owners, and for years afterward, minorities would joke about their being the 'bosses' or about their privileges due to race. As the Japanese rose to power both economically and politically, they tended to capitalize on their 'minority' status, emphasizing their insider status as former plantation laborers. But the traditional distinctions and alliances are fading now as the plantation generation dies away.

Of course, any tensions among local groups are quite benign compared with racial strife on the mainland USA. Locals seem slightly perplexed at the emphasis on 'political correctness'. Among themselves, locals good-naturedly joke about island stereotypes, eg talkative Portuguese, stingy Chinese, goody-goody Japanese and know-it-all haole. Hawaii's much-loved comedians of the 1970s and 1980s – Andy Bumatai, Frank DeLima and Rap Reiplinger – used such stereotypes to hilarious comic effect.

When nonlocals enter the picture, the balance shifts. Generally, locals feel bonded with other locals. While tourists and transplants are welcomed with open arms, they must earn the trust and respect of the locals. It is unacceptable for an outsider to assume an air of superiority and to try to

Among the US population, Hawaii residents have the longest life expectancy: 79.8 years for those born in the year 2000.

WATCH THE HANDS

Ancient Hawaiians had no written language. Thus hula and chanting were their means of communication and creative expression. Hula was not solely entertainment. Rather, dancers used hand gestures, facial expression and rhythmic movement to illustrate historical events and legendary tales and to venerate the gods. Back then they wore *kapa* (bark cloth), never the now-stereotypical grass skirts.

When the Christian missionaries arrived, they viewed hula dancing as too licentious and suppressed it. The hula might have been lost forever if King Kalakaua, the 'Merrie Monarch,' had not revived it in the late 1800s.

Today's commercial hula shows, which emphasize swaying hips and nonstop smiling, might be compelling but they're not 'real' hula. Serious students join a *hula halau* (school), where they undergo rigorous training and adopt hula as a life practice. Dancers learn to control every part of the body, as subtle differences in gestures can change the meaning entirely.

In hula competitions, dancers vie in *kahiko* (ancient) and *'auana* (modern) categories. *Kahiko* performances are raw and primordial, accompanied only by chanting, and they use a bent-knee stance to allow dancers to absorb earth's energy. *Kahiko* dancers' costumes show primary colors and often lots of skin. (In the mid 1980s, one male group surprised the audience when the men wore little more than a G-string!) Accompanied by harmonious singing and string instruments, *'auana* seems more like mainstream hula, with western-influenced dresses and pants, sinuous arm movements and smiling faces.

The best event at which to watch authentic hula is the Merrie Monarch Festival (p276), held at Easter time. Free shows are held four times a year at Hawai'i Volcanoes National Park (p299). Other hula festivals include the Prince Lot Hula Festival held in July on O'ahu (p123), the Kaua'i Mokihana Festival Hula Competition (p526) held in October and the Moloka'i Ka Hula Piko in May (p436).

'fix' local ways. If white, such people will inevitably fall into the category of 'loudmouth haole.'

That said, prejudice against haole is minimal. If called a haole, don't worry. It is generally not an insult or threat (and if it is, you'll know). Essentially, locals are warm and gracious to those who appreciate island ways.

RELIGION

Hawaiian Legends of the Guardian Spirits by Caren Loebel-Fried tells *aumakua* (guardian spirit) legends, illustrated with beautiful, striking woodblock prints.

Ancient Hawaiian religion fell to the wayside when the *kapu* system collapsed and Christian missionaries arrived (see History, p36). But Hawaiians took the traditions underground; today, one sees glimpses of the old religion in local ceremonies. Christian sermons often include both Hawaiian and English words and public ceremonies, such as ground breaking, feature a kahuna to bless the land. Hawaiians' activism against development is rooted in *aloha 'aina* (love of the sacred land).

Today, while most locals do not claim adherence to a particular faith, religion remains quite significant as a social force. Undoubtedly the largest group in Hawaii is Roman Catholic, with roughly 240,000 adherents, a large percentage of whom are Filipino immigrants. The next largest group is the Church of Jesus Christ of Latter-Day Saints, with around 43,000 adherents, including many converts from the South Pacific.

As for Protestant Christianity, the mainstream, less conservative groups – including the United Church of Christ, which arrived with the early missionaries – are struggling with declining membership. Conversely, nondenominational and often-fundamentalist evangelical churches are burgeoning.

Buddhists number an estimated 100,000 in Hawaii, the highest statewide percentage of Buddhists in the USA, but the number of younger adherents is dwindling. Most Japanese Buddhists in Hawaii are nonmeditating

Shin Buddhists, but the **Honolulu Diamond Sangha** (☎ 735-1347; www.diamondsangha .org) is an established Zen organization founded in 1959 by master teacher Robert Aitken.

ARTS
Music

Tune your radio to a local station and hear the gamut of island sounds, from traditional hula *mele* (songs) to '70s Hawaiian folk rock, to reggae-inspired Jawaiian. Three instruments typify the Hawaiian sound:

The Hawaiian steel guitar *(kika kila)* today rarely steals the spotlight, but it ranks among Hawaii's greatest musical contributions. It is perhaps the only modern instrument invented in the US and it inspired the creation of resonator guitars, such as the Dobro, that are integral to bluegrass, blues and other genres.

Mexican cowboys first introduced the guitar to Hawaiians in the 1830s. Fifty years later, young Joseph Kekuku (born 1874) began playing a guitar flat on his lap, sliding a knife or comb across the strings. He continued the technique at Kamehameha School for Boys, where a shop teacher helped him create a steel bar and a converter nut to lift the strings off the fretboard.

Kekuku and other Hawaiians burst on the international scene, introducing the steel guitar and hapa-haole (Hawaiian music with English lyrics) sounds during the early 1900s. Other influential steel guitarists include Sol Hoʻopiʻi, Jerry Byrd and Barney Isaacs, all now deceased, plus living stars Alan Akaka, Bobby Ingano and Gregory Sardinha.

Universally beloved is the ukulele, derived from the *braguinha*, a Portuguese instrument introduced to Hawaii in the late 19th century. Ukulele means 'jumping flea' in Hawaiian, referring to the way players' deft fingers would swiftly 'jump' around the strings. Hawaii's ukulele masters include Eddie Kamae, Herb Ohta and Jake Shimabukuro.

Today, the most famous and commercially successful Hawaiian genre is slack-key guitar *(ki hoʻalu,* which means 'loosen the key'), a fingerstyle method in which the strings are slacked from their standard tuning. Generally the

For a humorous and heartwarming rendition of the Bible, see Da Jesus Book: Hawaii Pidgin New Testament.

ISLAND SOUNDS

Familiarize yourself with the dynamic panoply of Hawaiian music by starting with the following icons:

Genoa Keawe (www.genoakeawe.com) No one epitomizes Hawaii like 'Aunty Genoa,' whose extraordinary signature falsetto sets the standard. Now in her late 80s, she still performs at the Waikiki Beach Marriott Resort (p146) every Thursday.

Gregory 'Rocky' Sardinha Versatile, talented Sardinha studied with the late great Jerry Byrd and today performs regularly throughout the islands. Catch him on Thursday and alternating Saturday evenings at House Without a Key (p149) at the Halekulani Hotel.

Israel Kamakawiwoʻole No discussion of Hawaiian music is complete without honoring 'Braddah Iz,' whose *Facing Future* is Hawaii's all-time bestselling album. Locals felt kinship to his genuine Hawaiian soul. When he died in 1997 at age 38 of morbid obesity, his body lay in state at the Capitol in Honolulu (an honor bestowed only to two others before him, Governor John A Burns and US Senator Spark Matsunaga).

Jake Shimabukuro (www.jakeshimabukuro.com) An ukulele virtuoso and exhilarating performer, Shimabukuro is known for lightning-fast fingers and a talent for playing any musical genre on the ukulele. Check his tour schedule online.

Kealiʻi Reichel (www.kealiireichel.com) Charismatic vocalist Reichel is also a *kumu hula* (hula teacher) and the founder of a Hawaiian-language immersion school on Maui. Since recording his award-winning first CD in 1994, he has earned a permanent place in Hawaii's musical pantheon. Check his website for concert details.

To learn more about slack-key guitar, start at George Winston's Dancing Cat label, www .dancingcat.com. An online community for guitar and ukulele players is available at www .taropatch.net.

thumb plays the bass and rhythm chords, while the fingers play the melody and improvisations in a picked style. Traditionally, slack-key tunings were closely guarded family secrets.

Among the most influential steel and slack-key guitarists is Gabby Pahinui (1921–80), who played with the legendary Sons of Hawaii and later formed the Gabby Pahinui Hawaiian Band with four of his sons. Today's top slack-key masters include Dennis Kamakahi, Keola Beamer and Ledward Ka'apana, among others.

In 2005, a Grammy Award for Best Hawaiian Music Album was established. Both the first and second winners were slack-key compilations: *Slack Key Guitar, Volume 2* (www.palmrecords.com/cd_slack_key_2.html) and *Masters of Hawaiian Slack Key Guitar, Volume 1* (www.slackkey.com/CD2004.htm). The focus on slack-key has dismayed some, who think Hawaiian lyrics and vocals deserve the spotlight.

Hawaiian Arts & Crafts

Woodworking is an ancient skill that remains popular and commercially viable. In old Hawai'i, the best artisans used giant logs to build canoes. Today, the usual creations are hand-turned wooden bowls and furniture, impossibly smooth and polished, made from a variety of hardwood. Traditionally koa was the wood of choice but, for variety, other gorgeous island woods are also used. Don't be fooled by cheap monkeypod bowls made in the Philippines.

Lei making is a popular craft that touches daily life. Locals continue to wear lei for special events, such as weddings and public ceremonies. Traditionally, lei were subtler in their beauty, made of *mokihana* (small, green berries native only to Kaua'i), *maile* (fragrant, dark-green, oblong leaves) and other

---

TIKI THROUGH THE AGES

Ancient Hawaiians carved wooden tiki (called *ki'i* in Hawaiian) to embody the gods. Fierce, intimidating tiki guarded heiau (places of worship) and loomed over ceremonies of human sacrifice. Only the best artists, chosen in youth, were trained to carve the stylized figures.

But in 1819, the *kapu* system fell and Christianity took its place. Native Hawaiians themselves destroyed the tiki that symbolized the repressive old system. Today less than 200 ancient tiki from the late 1700s remain.

Modern, commercial, all-American tiki culture began in Hollywood in 1934, when 'Donn Beach' founded Don the Beachcomber, a South Seas bar that featured Cantonese cuisine, exotic rum punches, fire torches and flower lei. Around the same time, in Oakland, Victor Bergeron established a tiki-themed restaurant called Trader Vic's. Both became national chains (Trader Vic's went international), offering the mainlander's view of island life.

After WWII, servicemen returned from far-flung Pacific locales, inspiring James Michener to write *Tales of the South Pacific*, which won the 1948 Pulitzer Prize. By the 1950s, tiki culture reached full frenzy, with the emergence of Hollywood-style surfer movies, Martin Denny's album *Exotica*, aloha shirts, Waikiki and its International Marketplace (invented by Donn Beach), and Hawaii's admission as the 50th state in 1959.

By the 1970s, America's fascination with the tiki aesthetic was passé, trumped by new influences, whether the Beatles, Jimi Hendrix, Vietnam or hippie culture. Tiki bars closed and kitschy paraphernalia were tossed or packed away.

Instead, the Hawaiian Renaissance (p42) emerged, with renewed interest in native arts, including hula, music, voyaging and ancient tiki. Today, see genuine tiki relics at museums and parks, such as Pu'uhonua O Honaunau (p226) and Bishop Museum (p115).

And what about those tacky tiki mugs in your attic? Today they're back in demand for their camp value.

HAWAIIAN QUILTING *Lisa Dunford*

With vibrant colors and graphic patterns, the striking beauty of Hawaiian appliqué quilts is easy to see. But look more closely and discover the story behind the beauty. Each part has meaning, and each design is thought to contain the very spirit of the crafter (early quilts were buried with their makers, so their souls couldn't go wandering).

Missionaries introduced quilting to the Islands in the 1800s, but Hawaiian women already sewed *kapa* (bark cloth) to make bedding, imprinting the top with natural motifs. Most scholars believe appliqué quilting took hold because of its 19th-century popularity in the US and easy adaptation to *kapa*-like designs. (Local lore has it that patchwork quilting was rejected because island women didn't have fabric scrap bags – who are we to argue?)

Still today, traditional quilts usually have one bright fabric, say magenta, which is cut into a repeating pattern after being folded it in fourths or eighths (remember making paper snowflakes in grade school?). The bright fabric is then appliquéd, usually by hand, onto a white or natural foundation cloth, and the design is quilted around in an echo pattern.

At the center of the quilt is the *piko* (navel); an open center is seen as a gateway linking the spiritual world and the physical one, a solid core symbolizes the strength of the family. A border, or lei, symbolizes the continuity of life. Fruits and plants have meaning, too (don't look for human figures though, they could come alive at night):

- breadfruit – abundance
- pineapple – hospitality
- mango – wishes granted
- taro – strength

If you want to buy one of these treasures, expect to pay thousands. (If prices are low, the quilts were likely made in the Philippines.) Better still, create your own. Some top-end hotels and fabric shops offer quilting classes. Two of the most highly regarded traditional Hawaiian quilters, **Poakalani Serreo** (www.nvo.com/poakalani) and **Nalani Goard** (www.hawaiianquilting.net), conduct day classes and give demonstrations at various O'ahu sites.

greenery. Today's popular tourist lei feature flashy or fragrant flowers, such as plumeria or dendrobium orchids, or polished *kukui* nuts (candlenuts). Beware, most *kukui*-nut lei are cheap imports from the Philippines.

Intricate collectors' lei are sewn with shells and seeds. The prized Ni'ihau shell lei is required by state law to include genuine shells from Ni'ihau for at least 80% of the lei. Made with tiny, rare, lustrous shells, these lei can cost between $125 for the simplest choker and $25,000 for the finest, matching strands.

Lauhala weaving is another traditional craft now mass-produced abroad and sold to unwitting tourists. Weaving the *lau* (leaves) of the *hala* (pandanus) tree is the fun part, while preparing the leaves, which have razor-sharp spines, is difficult, messy work. Traditionally *lauhala* served as mats and floor coverings, but today smaller items such as hats, placemats and baskets are most common. Kimura Lauhala Shop (p216) and other such specialty shops sell the real deal.

Literature

Until the late 1970s, nonlocal writers, whose stories focused on Hawaii from the Western viewpoint, dominated Hawaii literature. Popular titles include *Hawaii*, James Michener's ambitious saga of Hawaii's history, and *Hotel Honolulu*, Paul Theroux's novel about a washed-up writer who becomes the manager of a rundown Waikiki hotel. Also widely read is Isabella Bird, the 19th-century British adventurer, whose writing captures the islands' exoticism to outsiders.

In *Lei Aloha* by Marsha Heckman, the artistry of Hawaiian lei making comes alive with gorgeous photos and compelling interviews with lei makers.

Vintage muumuu and aloha shirts are reborn at www.denisetjarks.com (handbags) and www .muumuuheaven.com (skirts).

Since the late '70s, and especially from the '90s, locally born writers have redefined the meaning of Hawaii literature. The new Hawaii literature doesn't treat the islands as an exotic setting but instead focuses on the lives of local characters. **Bamboo Ridge Press** (www.bambooridge.com), which publishes contemporary local fiction and poetry in a biannual journal, *Bamboo Ridge*, has launched many local writers' careers. Some have hit the national scene, such as Nora Okja Keller, whose first novel, *Comfort Woman*, won the 1998 American Book Award, and Lois-Ann Yamanaka, who introduced pidgin to literary circles with *Saturday Night at the Pahala Theatre* (1993 Pushcart Prize winner) and several critically acclaimed novels such as *Behold the Many*.

Much locally written literature features pidgin English, especially in dialogue. If you're new to pidgin, *Growing Up Local: An Anthology of Poetry and Prose from Hawaii* (Bamboo Ridge Press) is a good introduction. While four-letter words pepper many local works, this collection contains none and is widely used in high school and college ethnic-literature classes nationwide.

Highly amusing are the pidgin writings by Lee Tonouchi, a lecturer in the English Department at Kapiolani Community College on O'ahu, who was hired after submitting an application written entirely in pidgin. A prolific writer and playwright, he makes an intriguing, subversive argument for legitimizing pidgin. His books include *Da Word* (short stories), *Living Pidgin: Contemplations on Pidgin Culture* (essays) and, most recently, *Da Kine Dictionary* (pictorial dictionary).

Cinema & TV

Hollywood's love affair with Hawaii began in 1913 and bloomed in the 1930s, when the islands captured the public's imagination as a sultry, carefree paradise. In film classics such as *Waikiki Wedding* (featuring Bing Crosby's Oscar-winning song, 'Sweet Leilani'), *Blue Hawaii* (an Elvis favorite) and a spate of WWII dramas, including the 1953 classic *From Here to Eternity*, viewers saw Hawaii through foreigners' eyes.

Hundreds of feature films have been shot in Hawaii, including box-office hits such as *Raiders of the Lost Ark*, *Godzilla*, *Waterworld*, *Pearl Harbor* and *Jurassic Park* and its two sequels. Hawaii benefits financially from its film industry, but unless homegrown films are produced, expect to see the same themes and stereotypes (and fake pidgin accents) in Hollywood movies. Essentially, Hawaii is often just a colorful backdrop for mainland characters.

Viewers might not even realize they're seeing Hawaii onscreen, as the islands often serve as stand-ins for Costa Rica, Africa, Vietnam and other such settings. Kaua'i, the most prolific island 'set,' has appeared in over 70 films. Diehard fans can visit their favorite Kaua'i sites through Hawaii Movie Tours (p488).

Hawaii has hosted 23 major TV series since 1968, including *Hawaii Five-O*, which to many symbolized edgy Honolulu urban life, and the 1980s' *Magnum PI*, which put Tom Selleck and his red Ferrari on the map. O'ahu is currently enjoying the spotlight as the location for ABC's hit series *Lost*, about a group of island castaways stranded after a plane crash. The show, which debuted in 2004 and won an Emmy Award for Outstanding Drama Series in 2005, attracts avid fans who journey to O'ahu to find key filming locations (see www.gohawaii.about.com/od/oahuactivities/ss/lost_locations.htm).

Hawaii is also an attractive place for on-location specials. In 2006, the PBS series *Antiques Roadshow* was filmed on O'ahu, and two MTV reality series (*Island Fever*, about a group of young folk, and *Living Lahaina*, about the adventures of surf instructors) were shot on Maui.

In *Tiki of Hawaii: A History of Gods and Dreams,* Sophia V Schweitzer traces tiki culture from its ancient Hawaiian spiritual roots to the post-WWII tiki-bar craze.

For more information about the industry, contact the **Hawaii Film Office** (www.hawaiifilmoffice.com).

SPORTS

Alas, Hawaii is too remote and unpopulated to attract a major professional sports team. If any team did come here, it would enjoy tremendous fan support because locals love team sports. As it stands, they rally behind the University of Hawai'i (UH) Warriors football team. While women's and men's volleyball have long boasted powerhouse teams, UH football, the only National Collegiate Athletic Association (NCAA) Division I program, is definitely the main draw, regularly attracting thousands of fans to the 50,000-seat Aloha Stadium on O'ahu.

In 2006 UH beat Arizona State University 41-24 in the **Sheraton Hawaii Bowl** (www.sheratonhawaiibowl.com), a post-season NCAA Division I-A game held on Christmas Eve or Day. Quarterback Colt Brennan completed 33 of 42 passes for 559 yards and five touchdowns, setting the NCAA single-season record for touchdown passes. The Warriors also broke the NCAA record for most points in a season, scoring a total of 657.

The Aloha Bowl also hosts the **AFC-NFC Pro Bowl** (www.nfl.com/probowl), the NFL's all-star game, which draws sell-out crowds the first week in February.

The two hottest sports are surfing and golf, which both attract dedicated participants and spectators. For awesome surfing, head to O'ahu's North Shore (p171) to see the Triple Crown of Surfing Championship and the Quiksilver In Memory of Eddie Aikau Invitational in November and December. For more on surfing, see p79.

Golf is wildly popular among all ages, and locals avidly follow their favorite pros. Michelle Wie, a 2007 Punahou graduate who turned pro at age 16, is Hawaii's golden child. (Locals also adore Tiger Woods.) In January, two major PGA tournaments draw spectators here: the Sony Open in Hawaii at Wai'alae Country Club on O'ahu and the Mercedes-Benz Championship at Kapalua Plantation Course (p342) on Maui. Unfortunately, the elite PGA Grand Slam ended its 13-year run on Kaua'i by moving to Bermuda in 2007. Other major sporting events include the Ironman Triathlon World Championship (p207) and the **EA Sports Maui Invitational** (www.mauiinvitational.com), the nation's premier preseason college basketball tournament.

In 2004, at age 14, Michelle Wie became the youngest person (and the fourth female) to play in a PGA tour event (Sony Open).

Too old to surf? In *Surfing For Life* (www.surfingforlife.com), documentary filmmaker David L Brown profiles 10 lifelong surfers, champions in their youth and still catching waves in their 70s, 80s and 90s.

Food & Drink

In Hawaii, eating goes beyond habit – it verges on *hobby*. People talk about food, they constantly snack, they grow their own vegetables, they trade recipes, they never skip meals, they fish and hunt, they celebrate with huge potluck feasts, and they eat with gusto.

Once you experience Hawaii's delicious gustatory variety, you'll understand why. The sensational flavors showcase the plantation-era ethnic cuisines, from Japanese teriyaki to Chinese dumplings to Hawaiian *kalua* pork (smoky-flavored, traditionally roasted underground). But the Hawaii versions of the classics are noticeably different. Over time the cuisines influenced one another and became…local.

Bear in mind, when the first Polynesians landed here, the only indigenous edibles were ferns, *ohelo* berries and other barely sustaining plants. The Polynesians brought *kalo* (taro), *'ulu* (breadfruit), *'uala* (sweet potato), *mai'a* (banana), *ko* (sugarcane), *niu* (coconut) and mountain apple, plus chickens, pigs and dogs for meat – and they discovered an abundance of seafood.

In Hawaii, you'll notice two levels of fare. On one hand, you can splurge at celebrated restaurants featuring revolutionary Hawaii Regional Cuisine or elegant Japanese delicacies. On the other hand, you can go local and eat everyday *grinds* (food), such as takeout *poke* (cubed, marinated raw fish), *saimin* noodle soup and Spam *musubi* (rice ball). Often eaten with disposable chopsticks on disposable plates, local street food is tasty and filling. Alas, it can also be fried, salty, gravy-laden and meaty.

If you look closely you will realize that the highbrow creations are just finer versions of down-home *grinds* (food). The underlying flavors – including *shoyu* (soy sauce), ginger, seaweed, rice, fresh fish and tropical fruit – are analogous.

STAPLES & SPECIALTIES

Whether you're eating highbrow or lowbrow cuisine, a handful of commonalities are found in Hawaii dining. First, Hawaii is a rice-eating society. While you might find couscous or smashed potatoes at fancy restaurants, everyday meals (especially at home) are incomplete without sticky, medium-grain, white rice. Not flaky rice. Not wild rice, nor flavored rice. Definitely not Uncle Ben's. Locals can devour mounds of the sticky stuff and, lucky for them, Asian restaurants often include unlimited rice with a meal.

Second, the top condiment is soy sauce (ubiquitously called by its Japanese name, *shoyu*), trailed by ketchup. Salsa, the number-one US condiment, is found mainly at Mexican restaurants.

Third, meat, chicken or fish is often integral to a dish. Locals are generally meat-and-rice folks. A favorite breakfast combo includes rice, fried egg and spicy Portuguese sausage (or bacon, ham, Spam etc). At upscale restaurants, fresh fish is often the highlight.

Fourth, the local pantry is relatively simple to stock, assuming access to a normal supermarket and a diverse farmers market. If one is seeking premium imported olives, no worries. O'ahu, Hawai'i, Maui and Kaua'i have yuppie gourmet shops or supermarkets with fine-foods aisles. Especially in Honolulu, the wine-and-cheese contingent is growing, creating a viable market for such imports. (But the beer-and-*pupu* crowd still rules most of Hawaii.)

Hawaii is the only US state that grows coffee and chocolate.

Honolulu Star-Bulletin food columnist Betty Shimabukuro compiled the best of her readers' requested recipes in By Request: The Search for Hawaii's Greatest Recipes.

HAWAII'S SOUL FOOD

Don't miss a taste of *poke* (pronounced 'PO-keh'), a savory raw-fish dish you'll see everywhere. In Hawaiian, *poke* means to slice into pieces. Thus, the dish is typically bite-sized cubes of marinated raw fish (often *'ahi*) mixed with *ogo* (seaweed) and *inamona*, a flavoring made of roasted and ground *kukui* (candlenut). The standard marinade includes *shoyu*, sesame oil, salt, green onion and chili pepper. Today, varieties feature all types of seafood, herbs, spices, nuts, fruits, vegetables and even tofu.

Poke is usually an appetizer or side dish, but it can make a healthful meal. Fine restaurants often raise *poke* to gourmet status in their preparations. On the mainland, that once-daring, now-clichéd tuna tartare on the menu is just a copycat of this everyday Hawaiian classic.

Find outstanding *poke* at Suisan Fish Market (p278), Eskimo Candy Seafood (p362), Tanioka's Fish Market (p135) and Fish Express (p474). *Poke* fans, don't miss the Aloha Festival's **Poke Contest** (www.pokecontest.com), originated in 1992 by celebrity chef Sam Choy.

Local Food

Unless you plan to dine only at resort restaurants, you'll eat mainly local food, a broad term that encompasses take-out plate lunches, grocery snacks, hole-in-the-wall diners, and fast food. Due to the diverse ethnic influences (plus a dose of all-American classics such as the hamburger), virtually all palates will be pleased.

The usual rule of thumb applies here: when choosing an eatery or a dish, follow the locals, not other tourists.

Bento Sold at deli counters, corner stores and *okazu-ya* (see below), this prepackaged Japanese-style box lunch includes rice and your choice of meat or fish, along with pickles, cooked vegetables and other Japanese garnishes.

Crack seed One taste and you'll be hooked. Crack seed is Chinese-style preserved fruit (often plum, cherry, mango or lemon) with a powerful flavor that blends sweet, sour and salty. Find dozens of varieties – dry or wet, seed or seedless – prepackaged at grocers or sold by the pound at candy shops. The most popular is *li hing mui*, which is used today to spice up everything from cookies to margaritas!

For a mouth-watering array of crack seed, see www.crackseedcenter .com, the website of Crack Seed Center (above), a longtime favorite at Ala Moana Shopping Center.

Loco moco An only-in-Hawaii combination of rice, two eggs (any style but typically fried) and hamburger patty, topped with gravy and a dash of *shoyu*. Originated at Café 100 (p277) in Hilo, this meal-in-a-bowl is surprisingly appetizing. Meatless versions are available.

Manapua The local version of Chinese *char siu bao* features lots of bright-red *char siu* (Chinese barbecued pork) filling and either a steamed or baked bun. One *manapua* is large enough for a meal.

Okazu-ya Often hole-in-the-wall establishments, *okazu-ya* are Japanese delicatessens where you can cobble together a tasty take-out meal. Locals first choose a starch, such as *musubi* (rice ball), *maki* (hand-rolled) sushi, or fried noodles. Then they pick from dozens of side dishes, eg tofu patties, shrimp and vegetable tempura, *nishime* (stew of root vegetables and seaweed), Japanese-style fried chicken, teriyaki beef or broiled mackerel. Go early, as most open at dawn and sell out by the early afternoon.

Plate lunch Eaten mainly for lunch, this fixed-plate meal includes 'two scoop rice,' a scoop of macaroni salad (mayonnaise-laden and often including potato and grated carrot) and your choice of a hot protein entrée, such as *tonkatsu* (breaded pork cutlets), fried mahimahi or teriyaki chicken. Nonlocals might find typical plate lunches unbelievably calorie-laden and unhealthy. But you can occasionally request tossed greens and brown rice. Traditionally, plate lunches were served on paper plates but now Styrofoam clamshell containers are common.

Pupu Defined as snacks or appetizers, *pupu* are 'grazing' foods. In Hawaii, a *pupu* party is more than just cheese and crackers – it might include *poke*, fried shrimp, *edamame* (boiled fresh soy-beans in the pod), sushi and other finger foods. If available, try boiled peanuts in the shell, which are appealingly salty and crunchy.

Saimin A soup of chewy Chinese egg noodles and Japanese broth, garnished with your choice of toppings, such as green onion, dried nori, *kamaboko* (steamed fish cake), egg roll or *char siu*.

Shave ice On a hot day, nothing can beat a mound of ice, shaved as fine as powdery snow, packed into a cup and drenched with sweet syrups in eye-popping hues. Purists stick with only ice but, for added decadence, try sweet azuki bean paste or ice cream underneath.

Native Hawaiian

Among Hawaii's diverse cuisines, Native Hawaiian preparations will probably be the most unfamiliar to tourists. You can find the most-popular dishes at restaurants, lunch counters and grocers – or you can try them all at a luau (see Celebrations, p58).

The centerpiece of a Hawaiian feast is *kalua* pig, roasted underground in an *imu* (pit of red-hot stones). In the pit, layers of crushed banana trunks and *ti* leaves cover the stones, creating a bed for the pig, which is stuffed with more hot stones. Everything is buried under *ti* leaves, a layer of mats and then dirt, sealing in the hot steam. To *kalua* means to cook using this method. Cooking time is four to eight hours, depending on the quantity of food. The result is smoky, salty, succulent pork. Traditional *kalua* cooking is hard to find nowadays, as few resorts (or folks at home) still cook pork underground. Instead, locals oven-roast pork seasoned with salt and liquid smoke.

The Hawaiians' primary starch was the sacred wetland taro, which was steamed and mashed into poi. The slightly sticky and pasty consistency of poi can be adjusted by adding water. You might hear locals describe poi texture by the number of fingers needed to scoop it into the mouth: one-, two- and three-finger poi. Poi is highly nutritious, low in calories, easily digestible and relatively bland, but for most nonlocals, it is an acquired taste. Poi serves as a counterpoint to the strong flavors and textures of other dishes so, if tasted on its own, it might seem too plain and gooey.

Other commonly eaten Hawaiian foods are *laulau* (bundle of pork or chicken and salted butterfish, wrapped in taro leaf, which cooks to a soft texture similar to spinach, and steamed in a covering of *ti* leaf); *lomilomi* salmon (a dish of minced, salted salmon, diced tomato and green onion); baked *'ulu*; raw *'opihi* (limpets picked off the reef at low tide); *pipikaula* (beef jerky); *haupia* (a stiff pudding made of coconut cream and arrowroot); and raw *'a'ama* (black crab).

Hawaii Regional Cuisine

Two decades ago, foodies sniffed at Hawaii cuisine. Sure, you could slum it on local *grinds* at the beach, and the multitude of midrange Asian eateries was satisfactory. But fine dining typically meant heavy, European fare that ignored locally grown ingredients and the unique mélange of ethnic flavors.

SPAM CAPITAL OF THE USA

If you're too embarrassed to eat Spam on the mainland, welcome to Hawaii – the only place you can eat Hormel's iconic canned ham with pride! Here in the Spam capital of the USA, locals consume almost seven million cans per year.

Of course, Spam looks and tastes different in Hawaii. It is always eaten cooked (typically sautéed to a light crispiness in sweetened *shoyu*), not straight from the can, and served as a tasty meat dish – Spam and eggs, Spam and rice, Spam and vegetables.

The affinity for Spam is probably a legacy of plantation cookery, when fresh meat wasn't always available. Even today, whenever the islands are threatened by a hurricane or dock-workers' strike, locals stock up on water, batteries, toilet paper, 20lb bags of rice and…Spam. For variety, folks also stock their cupboards with Vienna sausage, Libby's corned beef, and canned sardines and tuna.

The most-common preparation is Spam *musubi:* a block of rice with a slice of fried Spam on top (or in the middle), wrapped with a strip of black sushi nori. Created in the 1960s or '70s, it has become a classic, and thousands of *musubi* are sold daily at grocers, lunch counters and convenience stores.

Check out the annual **Waikiki Spam Jam** (www.spamjamhawaii.com), a happening block party honoring Hawaii's favorite canned meat.

HOLD THE PINEAPPLE SALSA

Once Hawaii Regional Cuisine hit the gourmet radar, many island restaurants tried to join the party. Hence, you see the same catchword preparations on menus: macadamia-crusted fish, sugarcane-skewered shrimp, pineapple-topped *anything*.

But it takes more than tropical catchwords to create genuine Hawaii Regional Cuisine. Or, rather, it takes *less*. The best chefs are actually simplifying their preparations to showcase the premium, island-grown ingredients themselves.

Wanna-bes tend to try too hard, with too many sauces and too many flavors, creating dishes like spicy coconut crab cakes with wasabi aioli, or seafood spring rolls drizzled with teriyaki glaze, alongside pineapple-chili salsa. Yikes.

The key to Hawaii Regional Cuisine is the use of local and seasonal ingredients: Kamuela tomatoes, Nalo greens, Kilauea goat cheese and honey, Kula onions, Hanalei taro, and Hamakua mushrooms, ginger and vanilla. For example, Town (p128) restaurant uses steak from North Shore Cattle Company in Hale'iwa and all-organic produce from a Waianae farm.

The current interest in locally grown produce is a boon to small-scale farmers, who now have an eager commercial market. Chefs are always on the lookout for novel ingredients, after all. The *real* catchwords are fresh, handpicked, organic and locally grown.

By the early 1990s, French- and American-trained island chefs finally decided to create their own cuisine. They partnered with local farmers, ranchers and fishers to feature island-grown produce and transformed their favorite childhood dishes into grown-up, gourmet masterpieces. The movement was dubbed 'Hawaii Regional Cuisine' and the pioneering chefs became celebrities. Best known worldwide is Roy Yamaguchi, who opened his original Roy's (p155) in 1988, but whose empire of 34 restaurants across the US, Japan and Guam can seem a tad ubiquitous.

Critics uniformly praise Alan Wong's namesake restaurant (p128), founded in 1995, for elevating down-home favorites to the gourmet level. For example, it substitutes lobster mousse for rice in hot California rolls, and dresses tomatoes with *li hing mui* vinaigrette. Another oft-lauded culinary master is Chef Mavro's (p127) George Mavrothalissitis, who goes right to the source for the finest local ingredients. He is known for pairing each imaginative main with an appropriate wine (chosen by a blind taste-test panel). Another star is Japanese-trained chef Hiroshi Fukui, of Hiroshi Eurasian Tapas (p125), who takes traditional, precise Japanese cuisine to another level by adding unexpected island touches.

Food Lover's Guide to Honolulu by Joan Namkoong is more than a restaurant guide – it's an indispensable resource on all local edibles, from plate lunches to dim sum to Hawaii Regional Cuisine.

DRINKS
Non-Alcoholic

World-renowned Kona coffee typically costs $20 to $40 per pound, depending on the grade. Aficionados rave about its mellow flavor that has no bitter aftertaste. The upland slopes of Mauna Loa and Hualalai on the Big Island's Kona district offer the ideal climate – sunny mornings and rainy afternoons – for coffee cultivation. Coffee is also grown on O'ahu, Maui, Moloka'i and especially Kaua'i. But only 100% Kona has gourmet cachet.

Old-fashioned soda pop made a comeback in 2004 with **Waialua Soda Works** (☎ 371-7556; www.waialuasodaworks.com), a husband-and-wife operation that creates the real 'real thing' in glass bottles. Flavors feature local ingredients and currently include pineapple, mango, root beer and vanilla cream.

Fruit juices are available, but supermarket cartons and cans are typically sugary blends. Two fruit-juice tonics you might see at farmers markets, health-food shops and hippie cafés are *'awa* (kava), a mild sedative, and *noni* (Indian mulberry), which some consider a cure-all. Both fruits are

Kaua'i Coffee Company produces 3.5 million pounds or 60% of the state's coffee.

pungent, if not repulsive, in smell and taste, so they are typically mixed with other juices.

Alcoholic

In Hawaii, beer is the everyman of drinks. It's cheap, unpretentious and widely available. In general, men drink more than women, especially among Asians.

National brands such as Coors are popular but the microbrew trend is thriving. Most of the established companies have lively brewpubs, such as Kona Brewing Company (p210) on the Big Island, Maui Brewing Company (p339), Sam Choy's Big Aloha Brewery (p135) on O'ahu and Waimea Brewing Company (p540) on Kaua'i.

Some of the best beers come from companies that are strictly breweries (no pub), eg Mehana Brewing Company on the Big Island, which produces a mild ale called 'Roy's Special Reserve' for Roy Yamaguchi's restaurants statewide, and Keoki Brewing Company on Kaua'i, which supplies Waikiki's 'Pink Palace,' the Royal Hawaiian Hotel (p147), with a pink lager.

Among mainland transplants and the upper-income, professional crowd, wine is growing in popularity. Wine-tasting parties and clubs are not uncommon, and wine sales have skyrocketed. In 2003 Lyle Fujioka opened a wine bar called Formaggio (p129), where you can pick from over 40 selections by the glass. Especially in Honolulu, top-tier restaurants take their wines seriously, offering impressive lists, often selected by Chuck Furuya (who was Hawaii's only master sommelier for over 15 years, until Roberto Viernes became the second master in 2005 at age 31).

On Maui and the Big Island, you can sample tropical wines, such as the popular pineapple wine of Tedeschi Vineyards (p403) or the imaginative guava or macadamia-honey concoctions of Volcano Winery (p300).

Craving an 'umbrella' drink? For tourists only, rum and vodka are transformed into the mai tai, piña colada and Blue Hawaii.

CELEBRATIONS

When locals get together for informal gatherings at beaches, parks and homes, the centerpiece is the potluck buffet, a massive spread of homemade dishes. On standard American holidays, mainstream foods appear

---

EAT, DRINK AND HULA

Ancient Hawaiians celebrated auspicious occasions – a child's birth, war victory or successful harvest – with a feast to honor the gods and share their bounty. Originally called aha 'aina (gathering for a meal), the modern term, luau, which refers to the taro leaves always served at such feasts, has become a household word.

The best luau are private, family affairs, thrown for a Hawaiian wedding or a baby's first birthday, without fire-eaters and Tahitian dancers and the rousing 'Aloooooooooooha!' greeting. Guests feast on raw shellfish delicacies never served at commercial luau, and the entertainment is a lively local band, which might spur the tutu (grandmothers) to get up and dance hula with their grandchildren.

But unless you have connections, your only option is a commercial luau show. Most are large, well-choreographed affairs that include an all-you-can-eat buffet and flashy Polynesian performances. The food tends to be mediocre, featuring the Hawaiian standards like poi and kalua pig – plus roast beef, teriyaki beef, fried rice and motley options designed to please all.

Recommended luau include the following: Kona Village Resort luau (Big Island, p232), Old Lahaina Luau (Maui, p328), Feast at Lele (Maui, p328), Smith's Tropical Paradise (Kaua'i, p486) and Royal Hawaiian Hotel Luau (O'ahu, p151).

(eg Easter eggs, Super Bowl beer and Thanksgiving turkey) along with nontraditional local fare such as rice (instead of mashed potatoes), sweet-potato tempura (instead of yams) and hibachi-grilled teriyaki beef (instead of roast beef).

Food festivals often showcase island crops, such as the Kona Coffee Cultural Festival (p207), East Maui Taro Festival (p380) and Maui Onion Festival (p335). Beer drinkers should mark their calendars for the Kona Brewers Festival (p207). Only in Hawaii will you find the Aloha Festivals Poke Contest (p55) and the Waikiki Spam Jam (p56).

Gourmet culinary events are all the rage across the islands; they vary in price and formality. Maui boasts a spate of such events, including A Taste of Lahaina (p325) and the Kapalua Wine & Food Festival (p342). Kaua'i's Taste of Hawaii (p484) is the ultimate Sunday brunch, while the Big Island's **A Taste of the Hawaiian Range** (☎ 322-4892; www.ctahr.hawaii.edu/taste) is an affordable treat for the carnivorous. Search for others at www.calendar .gohawaii.com.

In *Japanese Cooking Hawai'i Style*, Muriel Miura, who hosted popular 1970s local cooking shows, demonstrates everyday favorites with a practical, no-fuss approach.

WHERE TO EAT & DRINK

Informal dining is Hawaii's forte. For takeout, head to '70s-style drive-ins, *okazu-ya* lunch shops and, primarily on O'ahu, *kaukau* wagons (lunch trucks). For sit-down meals, diner-style restaurants abound. Often with Formica tables and vinyl chairs, no view and no decor, they provide quick service and decent food at decent prices. If you've got an appetite or want variety, all-you-can-eat seafood and prime-rib buffets at hotels are your ticket. The better buffets serve sushi and sashimi.

For gourmet cuisine, stick to Honolulu, which is not only Hawaii's state capital, but also its food capital. The major cutting-edge trends start here.

Get a food-obsessed insider's take on local restaurants (primarily on O'ahu) at http://ono kinegrindz.typepad.com.

HAWAII'S TOP EATS

Plate Lunch

- Fort St Bar & Grill (O'ahu; p124)
- Café 100 (Big Island; p277)
- Aloha Mixed Plate (Maui; p326)
- Mark's Place (Kaua'i; p530)
- Rainbow Drive-In (O'ahu; p147)

Shave Ice

- Itsu's Fishing Supplies (Big Island; p279)
- Hawaiian Blizzard (Kaua'i; p493)
- Local Boys Shave Ice (Maui, p361)
- Waiola Bakery & Shave Ice (O'ahu; p147)
- Matsumoto's (O'ahu; p180)

Only in Hawaii

- Hamura Saimin (Kaua'i; p474)
- Manago Hotel Restaurant (Big Island; p225)
- Up in Smoke (Maui; p376)
- Teshima Restaurant (Big Island; p217)
- Nico's at Pier 38 (O'ahu; p135)

Hawaii Regional Cuisine (Honolulu)

- Hiroshi Eurasian Tapas (p125)
- 3660 on the Rise (p128)
- Alan Wong's (p128)
- Chef Mavro (p127)
- Roy's (p155)

Hawaii Regional Cuisine (Neighbor Islands)

- I'O (Maui; p327)
- Merriman's (Big Island; p235)
- Pineapple Grill (Maui; p343)
- Ke'ei Café (Big Island; p220)
- Bar Acuda (Kaua'i; p512)

At the time of research, stylish Japanese tapas-style eateries were all the rage. In 2007 Waikiki, trying to upgrade from its slew of middle-America chains, welcomed Nobu Waikiki (p149) at the Waikiki Parc Hotel (p145) and Roy's at the Waikiki Beach Walk. Discerning Chinese-cuisine eaters should also focus on Honolulu. Its lively Chinatown offers the state's only outstanding Chinese cuisine – from steaming *manapua* to fresh *char siu* to dim sum banquets.

On Neighbor Islands, restaurants typically open and close (by 10pm) early. For late-night dining, you'll have to seek out bars or 24-hour eateries like O'ahu favorite **Zippy's** (www.zippys.com). In general, locals tip slightly less than mainlanders do, but still up to 20% for good service and at least 15% for the basics.

For groceries, head to farmers markets and locally owned supermarkets. Granted, most locals and tourists alike cannot resist the deals at Costco. Note that in Hawaii, 75% of groceries are imported from the mainland, including milk and eggs (unless labeled 'Island Fresh'), chicken, pork, produce and most beef. Thus, if absolute freshness matters to you, choose locally caught fish and locally grown produce.

VEGETARIANS & VEGANS

Locals might think vegetarians and vegans are missing out, but noncarnivores can feast in Hawaii, too. The multitude of Asian eateries ensures vegetable and tofu options, even in rural towns, while healthy versions of traditional local fare are now available, especially at establishments run by mainlanders influenced by 'California cuisine.' Popular offerings include tofu (or fresh *'ahi* for pesci-vegetarians) wraps, meal-sized salads and grilled-vegetable sandwiches or plates (often with wholewheat bread or brown rice).

That said, high-end restaurants do tend to highlight seafood. Vegans, especially, must seek out the few eateries that use no animal products, such as Blossoming Lotus (p494) on Kaua'i. Your best bet is to forage for yourself at farmers markets or at health food stores, which unfortunately can be pricey.

Meatless diets are growing increasingly common, but mainly among mainland transplants and young women. Most locals eat everything in moderation and might view vegetarianism as extreme or a haole (Caucasian)/hippie thing. If you start admonishing others about the evils of meat eating, you won't make any friends.

When ordering at restaurants, be sure to ask whether a dish is indeed meatless; soups and sauces often contain meat, chicken or fish broth.

'If you really want to act local, buy a *goza*...pack a picnic and head to the nearest park.'

EATING WITH CHILDREN

Excluding a few formal restaurants, kids are welcome almost everywhere. Hawaii is a family-oriented, extremely casual place. Sit-down restaurants are quick to accommodate children with high chairs and booster seats.

During the day, eat outdoors! The balmy weather allows for impromptu plate lunches at the beach or fresh fruit at roadside stands. If you really want to act local, buy a *goza* (inexpensive roll-up straw mat sold at ABC and Longs Drug stores), pack a picnic and head to the nearest park.

Locals share a big sweet tooth, so finding treats is easy (perhaps too easy). Premium ice cream, shave ice, home-style cookies, Portuguese sweet bread and chocolate-covered macadamias are omnipresent temptations. As for main dishes, the local palate tends toward the sweet and straightforward – without too much garlic, bitter greens, pungent cheeses and strong spices – which typically agrees with kid tastes.

You might assume that all fancy restaurants frown on parties that include kids; but many actually cater to them with special menus. Although the trend toward loud dining rooms (Roy's, for example, is notorious for having a sky-high decibel level) is unfortunate, at least kid chatter will blend into the overall din. At hotel luau, kids receive a discount (and sometimes free admission when accompanied by a paying adult). Commercial luau might seem like cheesy Vegas shows to adults, but kids will probably enjoy the flashy dances and fire tricks.

HABITS & CUSTOMS

Locals eat meals early and on the dot: typically 6am breakfast, noon lunch and 6pm dinner. Restaurants are jammed around the habitual mealtimes, but they clear out an hour or two later, as locals are not lingerers. If you dine at 8:30pm you might not have to wait at all! But bear in mind that restaurants also close early and night owls must hunt for places to eat.

Locals tend to consider food quantity as important as quality – and the portion sizes are telling (more so at budget and midrange restaurants than at ritzy ones). If you're a light eater, feel free to split a meal or to take home the leftovers.

Home entertainment for local folks always revolves around food, which is usually served 'potluck style' with all the guests adding to the anything-goes smorgasbord. Locals rarely serve dinner in one-at-a-time courses. Rather, meals are served 'family style,' where diners help themselves. Throwaway paper plates and wooden chopsticks make for an easy cleanup, and the rule is 'all you can eat' (and they definitely mean it!).

If you're invited to someone's home, show up on time and bring a dish, preferably homemade (but a bakery cake or pie is always appreciated). Remove your shoes at the door. And don't be surprised if you're forced to take home a plate or two of leftovers.

Learn how to choose and cook good produce with *The Hawai'i Farmers Market Cookbook,* edited by Joan Namkoong and Haley Matson-Mathes, which includes interviews with farmers.

SNACK ATTACK

When traveling, locals' suitcases are filled with more than clothing. They take *omiyage* (gifts or souvenirs) from their hometown to the people they visit. And they bring back more *omiyage* for the folk at home.

The typical *omiyage* gift is a sweet treat that is made in limited quantities only on one island. Some of these delicacies are too fragile to survive a journey to the mainland, so try them while on vacation.

- Big Island – Big Island Candies macadamia and chocolate treats (p280); 100% Kona coffee; Tex Drive-In *malasada* (p261); Two Ladies Kitchen *mochi* (p279)

- Kaua'i – Aunty Lilikoi condiments (p540); *liliko'i* chiffon pie or fresh saimin noodles from Hamura Saimin (p474); Taro Ko chips (p536); Kilauea honey

- Maui – Tasaka Guri-Guri sherbet (p348); Sam Sato's *manju* (p352); Komoda Store & Bakery cream puffs (p397); Kitch'n Cook'd potato chips

- Moloka'i – Kanemitsu Bakery sweet bread (p437)

- O'ahu – Coco Puffs from Liliha Bakery (p125); Royal Kitchen *manapua* (p125); Ted's Bakery pies (p176)

On all islands, head to farmers markets for locally grown, locally made gifts, eg fruit preserves, honey, vanilla beans and extracts, coffee and much more. Hawaii-grown papayas are outstanding and worth carrying home, but they must be certified to leave the island; it's best to buy pre-certified boxes of fruit.

COOKING COURSES

In Honolulu, gourmet cooking classes are offered by **Gourmet Cooking Hawaii** (☎ 735-7788; www.gourmetcookinghawaii.com) twice a month, taught by Chef Mavro and other celebrity chefs; and by **Kapi'olani Community College** (☎ 734-9211; www .kcc.hawaii.edu), which offers a professional culinary program plus noncredit classes on weekends and evenings. Top-end hotels such as the Halekulani Hotel (p146) offer occasional classes.

EAT YOUR WORDS

In the comfort of your own kitchen, experiment with local recipes found at www.hawaii .edu/recipes.

Deciphering a menu is relatively easy, but among familiar English words is enough Hawaiian, Japanese and pidgin lingo to stump you. If someone offered you an 'ono piece of *mochi*, would you try it? Don't miss out. Learn the following common food terms; for pidgin and Hawaiian pronunciation tips, see p578.

Food Glossary

adobo – Filipino chicken or pork cooked in vinegar, *shoyu*, garlic and spices

arare – *shoyu*-flavored rice crackers; also called *kaki mochi*

'awa – kava, a native plant used to make an intoxicating drink

bento – Japanese-style box lunch

broke da mout – delicious; literally 'broke the mouth'

char siu – Chinese barbecued pork

crack seed – Chinese-style preserved fruit; a salty, sweet and/or sour snack

donburi – meal-sized bowl of rice and main dish

furikake – Japanese condiment typically containing dried seaweed, sesame seeds and bonito flakes

grind – to eat

grinds – food; *ono kine grinds* is good food

guava – fruit with green or yellow rind, moist pink flesh and lots of edible seeds

gyoza – grilled dumpling usually containing minced pork or shrimp

haupia – coconut-cream dessert

hulihuli chicken – rotisserie-cooked chicken

imu – underground earthen oven used to cook *kalua* pig and other luau food

inamona – roasted and ground *kukui* (candlenut), used to flavor *poke*

kalo – Hawaiian word for taro

kalua – Hawaiian method of cooking pork and other luau food in an *imu*

kaukau – food

kamaboko – cake of pureed, steamed fish; used to garnish Japanese dishes

katsu – deep-fried fillets, usually chicken; see *tonkatsu*

laulau – bundle of pork or chicken and salted butterfish, wrapped in taro and *ti* leaves and steamed

li hing mui – sweet-salty preserved plum; type of crack seed; also refers to the flavor powder

liliko'i – passion fruit

loco moco – dish of rice, fried egg and hamburger patty topped with gravy or other condiments

lomilomi salmon – minced, salted salmon, diced tomato and green onion

luau – Hawaiian feast

mai tai – 'tiki bar' drink typically containing rum, grenadine, and lemon and pineapple juices

malasada – Portuguese fried doughnut, sugar-coated, no hole

manapua – Chinese steamed or baked bun filled with *char siu*

manju – Japanese bun filled with sweet bean paste

mochi – Japanese sticky-rice dumpling

nishime – Japanese stew of root vegetables and seaweed

noni – type of mulberry with smelly yellow fruit, used medicinally

nori – Japanese seaweed, usually dried

ogo – crunchy seaweed, often added to *poke*; *limu* in Hawaiian

ohelo – shrub with edible red berries similar in tartness and size to cranberries
'ono – delicious
'ono kine grinds – good food
pho – Vietnamese soup, typically beef broth, noodles and fresh herbs
pipikaula – Hawaiian beef jerky
poi – staple Hawaiian starch made of steamed, mashed taro
poke – cubed, marinated raw fish
ponzu – Japanese citrus sauce
pupu – snacks or appetizers
saimin – local-style noodle soup
shave ice – cup of finely shaved ice sweetened with colorful syrups
shoyu – soy sauce
soba – buckwheat noodles
star fruit – translucent green-yellow fruit with five ribs like the points of a star and sweet, juicy pulp
taro – plant with edible corm used to make poi and with edible leaves eaten in *laulau; kalo* in Hawaiian
teishoku – fixed, multicourse Japanese meal
teppanyaki – Japanese style of cooking with an iron grill
tonkatsu – breaded and fried pork cutlets, also prepared as chicken *katsu*
tsukemono – Japanese pickled vegetables
ume – Japanese pickled plum

NAME THAT FISH

In Hawaii, most fish go by Hawaiian and/or Japanese names. For more information, see the Hawai'i Seafood Buyers' Guide at www.hawaii.gov /dbedt/seafood.

'ahi – yellowfin or bigeye tuna, red flesh, excellent raw or rare
aku – skipjack tuna, red flesh, strong flavor; *katsuo* in Japanese
kajiki – Pacific blue marlin; *a'u* in Hawaiian
mahimahi – dolphin fish or dorado, pink flesh, popular cooked
nairage – striped marlin; *a'u* in Hawaiian
onaga – red snapper, soft and moist
ono – wahoo, white-fleshed and flaky
opah – moonfish, firm and rich
'opakapaka – pink snapper, delicate flavor, premium quality
'opelu – mackerel scad, pan-sized, delicious fried
shutome – swordfish, succulent and meaty
tako – octopus, chewy texture

Environment

Any discussion of the Hawaiian Islands begins and ends with two things: volcanoes and isolation. That the islands exist at all is due to a 'hot spot' beneath the earth's mantle, which has been spewing molten rock and creating a string of massive shield volcanoes for more than 70 million years. These volcanoes bubble out of the sea in the most geographically isolated spot on the planet, over 2000 miles from any continent. Because to this profound, ancient isolation, Hawaii's environment constitutes a rare living textbook in Darwinian evolution – one so fragile that it is vanishing before our eyes. Hawaii accounts for approximately 75% of all documented plant and animal extinctions in the USA, and it is the 'endangered species capital of the world' (with 329 and counting). Today, the species that bears most of the responsibility for that status – humans – is working harder than ever to change that status.

THE LAND

The entire Hawaiian archipelago is made up of over 50 volcanoes that extend 2200 miles and is called the Hawaiian Island–Emperor Seamount chain. They are created by a rising column of molten rock – a 'hot spot' – under the Pacific Plate; as the plate moves westward (at a rate of about 3.2in a year), the magma pierces through the crust like a sewing needle, creating volcanoes.

Hawaii: The Islands of Life (1989) has strikingly beautiful photos of the flora, fauna and landscapes being protected by the Nature Conservancy of Hawaii, with text by Gavan Daws.

As each volcanic island moves off the hot spot, it stops erupting and starts eroding. At the far northwestern end of the chain, the islands have receded back below the ocean surface to become seamounts. Moving eastward, the islands get progressively taller and younger until you reach Hawai'i, the Big Island, the still-growing, million-year-old child of the group. Straddling the hot spot, Hawai'i's Kilauea (p288) is the world's most active volcano. Since 1983 it has been erupting almost nonstop; in the last decade, it's added over 500 acres of new land to the Big Island.

Under the sea about 20 miles east of Hawai'i, however, a new volcano is erupting – Lo'ihi. In 30,000 years or so, it will emerge from the water to become the newest island in the Hawaiian chain.

Within the state of Hawaii, there are eight main islands, only six of which are populated. West of Kaua'i, the minuscule islands and atolls of the Northwestern Hawaiian Islands (p550) stretch for a thousand miles. In all, Hawaii constitutes only 6423 sq miles. This accounts for about 1% of the total US landmass, an area slightly larger than the state of Connecticut. On the Big Island, Ka Lae is the southernmost point in the US, a latitude equivalent to Hong Kong, Bombay and Mexico City.

WILDLIFE

Born barren, the Hawaiian islands were originally populated only by those plants and animals that could traverse 2000 miles of ocean – flying themselves, floating on the wind, or riding the waves. Seeds came in bird wings, insects on driftwood. Scientists estimate that successful species arrived once every 70,000 years – and they included no amphibians, no browsing animals, no pines, no mosquitoes and only two mammals: a bat and a seal.

Hawaii's coral reefs constitute 84% of all US reefs, and they are home to about 550 species of fish (nearly 30% are endemic).

However, the flora and fauna that made it occupied an unusually rich, diverse land, containing nearly every ecological or life zone. In a prime example of 'adaptive radiation,' the 250 flowering plants that arrived evolved into 1800 native species; 350 kinds of insects became 10,000. Lacking predators

---

STONES & BONES

When land is developed in Hawaii, more than earth and plants can be disturbed. Construction workers frequently dig up the *iwi* (bones) and *moepu* (funeral objects) of ancient Hawaiian burial sites. Locals tell 'chicken-skin' stories of machinery breaking down and refusing to operate until the bones are removed and prayers are said. Today, it's common practice for a Hawaiian priest to bless sites before construction begins.

Some estimate that the foundations of all of Waikiki's resorts contain *iwi*, because the sand used to make the concrete contained it. Native Hawaiians didn't begin to protest this long-standing problem until 1988, when the construction of the Ritz Carlton Kapalua on Maui unearthed 1100 skeletal remains. As a result of protests the hotel moved inland, and a plaque now marks the sacred burial ground.

Also as a consequence, in 1990 Congress enacted the **Native American Graves Protection and Repatriation Act** (www.hawaii.gov/dlnr/hpd/hpburials.htm), and Hawaii established burial councils on each island to oversee the repatriation of remains. Since then about 3000 sets of remains have been reinterred, and about 250 cases are reviewed annually. But the program has been the source of even more complaints, from chronic underfunding and a lack of standards to the preponderance of industry representation on the councils.

Hui Malama (www.huimalamainakupuna.org), which is a nonprofit group created to care for the *iwi* and *moepu*, has stirred up the most controversy. In 2000 the Bishop Museum 'loaned' Hui Malama 83 sacred funeral objects, and the group promptly returned them back to the caves from whence they'd originally been looted by European explorers in 1905. This guerrilla action of repatriation met with furious protests, not just from the museum but from some other Native Hawaiian groups.

In 2006 the items were 'recovered' from the caves, and a judge ordered Hui Malama and the Bishop Museum to split the $330,000 cost. Hui Malama can't pay, so it's now an open question of how they'll continue.

Meanwhile, construction digs up new bones nearly every other day…

---

or much competition, new species dropped defensive protections: thorns, poisons and strong odors disappeared. This process accounts for why such high percentages of native Hawaiian species are also endemic, or unique to the islands (90% of native plants, 98% of native insects), and why they fare so poorly against modern invaders.

When Polynesians arrived, they brought new animals and plants. These species are termed 'Polynesian introductions'; they include pigs, chickens, rats, coconuts, bananas, taro and about two dozen other species, not to mention people. Most of these species mixed comfortably with preexisting native species, though these new Hawaiians, with their agriculture, caused major changes to the landscape and led the first wave of species extinctions.

So-called alien or nonnative species refer to those that arrived after late-18th-century Western contact. They include relatively benign crops and ornamental plants, as well as notoriously invasive and devastating pests – such as cattle, fountaingrass, miconia and ivy gourd. Delicately balanced ecosystems have been decimated by even a single invader (for instance, rabbits on Laysan Island, see p550). Today, over half of the original 140 (known) native animal species and about 10% of endemic plant species are extinct.

Progress reports make depressing reading (comparing the current situation to a 'holocaust'), but success stories do occur, proving that with sufficient effort and the right conditions, nature can rehabilitate itself. In many ways, the Hawaiian islands are a unique laboratory in the global effort to discover 'sustainable' methods of conservation – preserving diversity, and by extension our own skins.

With 329 endangered species, Hawaii keeps the US Fish & Wildlife Service (FWS; www.fws.gov/pacificislands) on its toes: its website has official numbers and updates.

Animals

Prior to the arrival of humans, the islands were home primarily to birds, snails, insects and spiders.

BIRDS

Native Hawaiian birdlife is so varied, it deserves a book of its own.

The Hawaii Audubon Society (www.hawaii audubon.com) publishes the best bird guide and their website has bird-viewing suggestions for each island and a good image gallery.

Many of Hawaii's birds are spectacular examples of adaptive radiation. For instance, all 57 species of endemic Hawaiian honeycreepers most likely evolved from a single finch ancestor. Today, over half of those bright-colored species – along with two-thirds of all native Hawaiian birds – are extinct, the victims of more aggressive, nonnative birds, predatory feral animals (like mongooses) and infectious avian diseases against which they have no immunity (see opposite). Over 30 bird species remain endangered.

The endangered nene, Hawaii's state bird, is a long-lost cousin of the Canada goose. Nene usually nest in sparse vegetation on rugged lava flows, to which their feet adapted by losing most of their webbing. While eight other species of Hawaiian geese (now extinct) became flightless, nene remain strong flyers. Nene once numbered as many as 25,000 on all the islands, but by the 1950s there were only 50 left. Intensive breeding programs have raised their numbers to over a thousand on three islands: Maui, Kaua'i and Hawai'i.

Other notable endangered birds include the 'alala (Hawaiian crow), of which only two are known to exist in the wild, in South Kona on the Big Island. Similarly, only two po'ouli, a species of honeycreeper, are known to exist, on Maui, but since they have not been seen since 2003, the species is now presumed extinct.

The only hawk native to Hawaii, the 'io was a symbol of royalty. They breed only on the Big Island, nesting mainly in native forests (a pair lives in Kalopa State Park, p265). The population seems to be holding steady at over 1400.

LAND MAMMALS

Domestic and wild introductions (which have got loose and become feral) include rabbits, goats, sheep, pigs and horses. Some, like Maui axis deer and Big Island cattle, were sent as 'gifts' to Hawaiian kings. The now-ubiquitous mongoose was originally introduced to control sugarcane rats. Today, feral animals are the most destructive force in Hawaii, and getting rid of them is central to reestablishing native landscapes and saving certain endangered species (see opposite).

The endangered 'ope'ape'a (Hawaiian hoary bat), one of Hawaii's two endemic mammals, has reddish-gray, white-tinged fur, making it appear

---

HONU

Native Hawaiians revere the green sea turtle, which they call honu. Often considered a personal 'aumakua (family deity), honu's image frequently appears in petroglyphs (and today in tattoos). For ancient Hawaiians, sea turtles were a delicious and prized source of food, but their capture and consumption were typically governed by strict religious and traditional codes.

As with all seven types of sea turtles (four of which can be found in Hawaii), the green sea turtle is now endangered and protected by federal law. Adults can grow over 3ft long and weigh more than 300lb. Young turtles are omnivorous, but adults (unique among sea turtles) become strict vegetarians. This turns their fat green – hence their name.

Green sea turtles can be found throughout the Hawaiian Islands; they are often seen feeding in shallow lagoons, bays and estuaries. However, their main nesting sight is the French Frigate Shoals in the Northwestern Hawaiian Islands (p550). Here, up to 700 females (90% of the population) come to lay their eggs every year.

OF PIGS, MOSQUITOES & HONEYCREEPERS

Nothing illustrates the fragile interdependence of Hawaiian ecosystems better than the story of how pigs are driving Hawaiian birds to extinction.

Not directly, of course, but the chain of cause-and-effect is undeniable.

Most likely the descendents of domestic pigs brought by early European explorers, feral pigs in fact cause such complete and widespread devastation to native wet forests that Mardy Lane, a ranger at Hawai'i Volcanoes National Park, says, 'Pigs are public enemy number one.' Despite the park's ongoing eradication program, thousands still live within its boundaries. Asked if feral pigs will ever be eliminated, Lane shrugs in frustration: 'I don't know.'

Outside of federal lands, eradication efforts are few, and one estimate is that there may be one feral pig for every 20 state residents.

Pigs trample and kill native fauna, destroy the forest understory and spread far and wide the seeds of invasive plants. They love native tree-fern stems, knocking them over and eating the tender insides – and the bowl-like cavities left behind catch rainwater and create ideal breeding pools for mosquitoes.

These common mosquitoes – presumed to have arrived in water casks in 1826 – pick up avian malaria and avian pox (also introduced from the European continent) and spread it to native birds, particularly honeycreepers, who lost their natural immunity to these diseases as they evolved.

Even in wet forests, water typically drains into the porous volcanic soil, and mosquitoes have trouble breeding. It's a simple equation: no feral pigs, far fewer mosquitoes, far less avian malaria and far more honeycreepers.

Lane is not alone in her feelings. As the eminent historian Gavan Daws wrote: 'To the Hawaiian forest, the pig is death.'

'hoary' (grayed by age). With a foot-wide wingspan, these tree-dwellers exist predominantly around forests on the leeward sides of the Big Island, Maui and Kaua'i.

MARINE MAMMALS

Up to 10,000 migrating North Pacific humpback whales come to Hawaiian waters for calving each winter (January through March), and whale watching (p83) is a major highlight. The fifth largest of the great whales, the endangered humpback can reach lengths of 45ft and weigh up to 45 tons. Other whales migrate through (such as rarely seen blue and fin whales), and Hawaii is home to a number of dolphins. The most notable is the intelligent spinner dolphin, so named for its acrobatic leaps from the water.

Hawaii's other endemic mammal, the Hawaiian monk seal, breeds primarily in the remote Northwestern Hawaiian Islands, but it occasionally appears on Big Island beaches. The current population is around 1400.

Angel fish change sex as they mature: they begin female and become male.

Plants

Mile for mile, Hawaii has the highest concentration of climate or ecological zones on earth. And whether you're in tropical rain forests or dry forests, high-altitude alpine deserts or coastal dunes, marshes or grassy plains – extravagantly diverse flora occupies every niche.

Of course, what we see today is not what the first Polynesians saw. Most 'Hawaiian' agricultural products are imports – papayas, pineapples, mangoes, bananas, macadamia nuts, coffee. Also, over half of Hawaii's native forest is now gone – due to logging, conversion to agriculture, invasive species and so on – and only 10% of Hawaii's dry forest remains. As a rule, low-lying areas have been more heavily altered by human development and invasive species than higher-altitude terrains. Of Hawaii's 1300 endemic native plant species, over 100 are extinct and 273 are endangered.

FLOWERS

What's wrong with a place where it's common for women to wear flowers in their hair? The classic hibiscus is native to Hawaii, but many varieties have also been introduced, so that now more than 5000 varieties grow on the islands. However, it's perhaps fitting that the state flower, the yellow *Hibiscus brackenridgei*, was added to the endangered species list in 1994. The *koki'o ke'oke'o*, a native white hibiscus tree that grows up to 40ft high, is the only Hawaiian hibiscus with a fragrance. Other common native plants include the royal *ilima*, used for making lei, and the seed-filled *liliko'i* (passion fruit).

Hawaii is also abloom with scores of introduced ornamental and exotic tropical flowers, including blood-red anthuriums with heart-shaped leaves, brilliantly orange-and-blue bird-of-paradise and a myriad of drooping heliconia. There are hundreds of varieties of both cultivated and native wild orchids and ornamental ginger varieties.

Competition is stiff, but one of the better all-in-one pocket field guides to native flora is Flowers and Plants of Hawaii *by Paul Wood.*

FORESTS

The most bewitching of native Hawaiian forest trees is the koa, nowadays found only at higher elevations. Growing up to 100ft high, this rich hardwood is traditionally used to make canoes, surfboards and even ukuleles.

Hawaii was once rich in fragrant *'iliahi* (sandalwood) forests, but these were sold off to foreign traders by the mid-19th century. Rare nowadays, these tall trees are found in Hawai'i Volcanoes National Park.

The widespread and versatile ohia is one of the first plants to colonize lava flows. Its distinctive tufted flowers consist of petalless groups of red, orange, yellow and (rarely) white stamens. Native forests of ohia and *hapu'u* (tree ferns) are vital, endangered habitats.

Brought by early Polynesian settlers, the *kukui* (candlenut tree) has light silver-tinged foliage that stands out brightly in the forest. The oily nuts from Hawaii's state tree are used for making lei, dyes and candles.

Other notable trees include ironwood, a nonnative conifer with drooping needles, which act as natural windbreaks and prevent erosion from beaches; majestic banyan trees, which have a canopy of hanging aerial roots with trunks large enough to swallow small children; and towering monkeypods, a common shade tree, which has dark glossy green leaves, puffy pink flowers and longish seed pods.

Ancient Hawaiians didn't have metals and never developed pottery, so plants fulfilled most of their needs. Ethnobotanist Beatrice Krauss describes this fascinating history in Plants in Hawaiian Culture.

NATIONAL, STATE & COUNTY PARKS

Hawaii has two national parks, Haleakala National Park on Maui and Hawai'i Volcanoes National Park on the Big Island. They contain some of the best hiking in Hawaii, and indeed, the world. Both have volcanoes as centerpieces, contain an astonishing range of environments and preserve important stands of native forest. In 1916, both areas were combined within Hawai'i National Park, then in the 1960s, Haleakala National Park and Hawai'i Volcanoes National Park were reestablished as independent entities. Hawai'i Volcanoes was named a Unesco World Heritage site in 1987.

In addition, the islands have five national historical parks, sites and memorials, all but one preserving ancient Hawaiian culture: three are on the Big Island, notably Pu'uhonua O Honaunau (Place of Refuge); one is on Moloka'i, Kalaupapa Peninsula; and in Honolulu is the famed *USS Arizona Memorial*, dedicated to WWII's Pearl Harbor attack. For information on all of Hawaii's national parks, visit www.nps.gov/state/hi.

Hawaii has 10 **national wildlife refuges** (NWR; www.fws.gov/pacificislands) on four islands: O'ahu, Maui, Kaua'i and Hawai'i. Most are open to the public; since their primary focus is preserving endangered plants and waterbirds, they are a delight for bird-watchers.

Hawaii has 52 state parks and recreational areas on five islands (excluding Lanaʻi). These diverse parks include some absolutely stunning places (like Waimea Canyon on Kauaʻi); a few also have campsites and cabins. They are managed by the **Division of State Parks** (☎ 587-0300; www.hawaii.gov/dlnr/dsp), which has local offices on each island that issue camping permits. Finally, each island also has county beach-parks and other areas, many of which allow camping; see each island chapter for contact information. For general questions about state-managed areas, the website for the **Department of Land & Natural Resources** (DLNR; ☎ 587-0320; www.state.hi.us/dlnr/; Kalanimoku Bldg, 1151 Punchbowl St, Honolulu) has some useful, downloadable publications on hiking and aquatic safety, beach access and conservation. DLNR's **Division of Forestry and Wildlife** (www.dofaw.net) manages Hawaii's 109,000-acre Natural Area Reserves System; the system's 19 reserves are open to hiking, but other activities are restricted.

For a list of Hawaii's top 20 natural areas, see p70.

IS 'SUSTAINABLE TOURISM' AN OXYMORON?

Hawaii has a problem: tourism is booming.

Of course, Hawaii wants tourists – the economy needs them (p46) – but many are openly wondering: is Hawaii's dependence on tourism a devil's bargain? Is it possible to accommodate over seven million visitors every year and sustain Hawaii's fragile environment and its unique culture? Can Hawaii meet the needs and desires of visitors and still maintain an infrastructure and quality of life that nurtures residents?

To answer these vital questions, Hawaii has embarked on a pioneering effort to define and quantify 'sustainable tourism,' then to manage their tourism industry so as to achieve it. This ambitious program is called **Hawaii 2050** (www.hawaii2050.org), since the hopeful goal is to realize Hawaii's model of sustainability by the year 2050.

It began with the 2002 Sustainable Tourism Project, in which a diverse group of experts and stakeholders was charged with, in effect, creating the initial blueprint. They were to devise the measuring tools for tracking tourism's many impacts and effects in Hawaii; they then were to define 'sustainability' and outline the necessary pragmatic steps.

In 2006, they published their report. While not exactly beach reading, it's a fascinating snapshot of Hawaii as it struggles to define its essential self and how it might best thrive. (The report can be found on the Hawaii 2050 website, on the 'Research' page.)

Interestingly, the task force couldn't agree on a definition of what sustainable tourism is. But they were able to agree on what sustainability should look like. They developed six central goals, leaving the road to achieving them sketchily outlined for now.

Paraphrased, they believe tourism has become 'sustainable' when the following has occurred:

■ Reflects Hawaii's deepest values, particularly *malama ʻaina* (nourishing the land) and aloha (welcome).

■ Provides economic benefit to all sectors of society.

■ Works in harmony with Hawaii's ecosystems, enhancing and preserving them.

■ Helps perpetuate Hawaii's ethnic cultures, particularly Native Hawaiian culture.

■ Reinforces Hawaii's heritage of tolerance and respect among ethnicities and between residents and visitors.

■ Protects communities' sense of place for current and future generations.

These sound like reasonable, even laudable goals for any industry. So, as the 'product' of this particular industry, we visitors can try to ensure that our time on the islands achieves no less (see p72).

Through 2007, Hawaii's counties will be holding monthly community meetings on all the islands to get input from Hawaii's citizens about what they think. Out of this dialogue, a 'Sustainability Plan' will be created and submitted to the state legislature for formal adoption in 2008.

HAWAII'S TOP 20 NATURAL AREAS

Natural area	Features	Activities	Visit	Page
O'ahu				
Hanauma Bay Nature Preserve	enormous coral reef in volcanic ring	snorkeling, swimming	year-round	p155
Malaekahana State Recreation Area	sandy beach, Moku'auia (Goat Island) bird sanctuary	swimming, snorkeling, camping, bird-watching	May-Oct	p170
Big Island				
Hawai'i Volcanoes National Park	lava fields, mile-wide craters, fern forests	hiking, camping	year-round	p288
Kealakekua Bay	pristine waters, coral reefs, underwater caves	snorkeling, diving, kayaking	year-round	p222
Laupahoehoe Point	ragged coast, steep cliffs, restless sea	camping	year-round	p266
Mauna Kea	Hawaii's highest peak	hiking, star gazing, ancient Hawaiian sites	year-round	p251
Pu'uhonua O Honaunau National Historical Park	ancient 'place of refuge',	hiking, snorkeling, exploring tide pools	year-round	p226
Waipi'o Valley	remote, fertile valley, black-sand beach	waterfalls, hiking	year-round	p262
Moloka'i				
Kalaupapa National Historic Park	historic & remote leprosy colony, mule riding	hiking, touring	year-round	p448
Kamakou Preserve	pristine rain forest, gorgeous valley vistas, waterfalls, montane bog	hiking, bird-watching	May-Oct	p444

ENVIRONMENTAL ISSUES

Environmental concerns are entangled in just about every issue facing Hawaii. However, more people and organizations than ever before are raising environmental alarms, educating the public and working toward solutions.

There is widespread agreement that the two most dire problems facing native landscapes are feral animals (from goats to mongooses) and the introduction and uncontrolled proliferation of invasive, habitat-modifying plants. Even in Hawaii's most protected areas – national parks and state reserves – inadequate budgets hamper eradication and rehabilitation efforts. The **Nature Conservancy** (www.nature.org), a nonprofit organization that purchases land to protect rare ecosystems, is very involved in Hawaii, and it has developed its own ecoregional plan (www.hawaiiecoregionplan.info).

In contrast to the land, Hawaii's coral reefs are comparatively healthy – and they are likely to get healthier with the 2006 establishment of the Papahanaumokuakea Marine National Monument (p550). That said, overfishing continues to be a major concern. In 2007 state legislation restricted the use of lay gill nets – mesh netting sometimes strung for a thousand feet that indiscriminately traps all sea creatures. **Fair Catch** (www .faircatchhawaii.org) is leading the effort to ban lay gill nets entirely.

In recent years, rising populations and real estate profits have spurred a building boom, some of it by off-island speculators with little concern for

Natural area	Features	Activities	Visit	Page
Maui				
Haleakala National Park (Kipahulu Section)	towering waterfalls, cascading pools, ancient sites	hiking, swimming,	year-round	p381
Haleakala National Park (Summit Section)	large dormant volcano	hiking, camping	year-round	p403
Makena State Park	glorious, unspoiled, expansive beaches (one is clothing-optional),	swimming, sunset watching	year-round	p368
Hana Hwy	38 miles of rugged steep cliffs, green valleys, waterfalls	hiking, camping	year-round	p373
Lana'i				
Hulopo'e Beach	dolphins frolicking in a pristine bay	swimming, snorkeling	year-round	p423
Kaua'i				
Koke'e State Park	waterfalls, trails for overnighters & daytrippers	hiking	year-round	p545
Na Pali Coast	beaches, waterfalls, classic 11-mile backpack trek, hiking	camping, swimming, snorkeling	May-Oct	p516
Polihale State Park	remote miles-long white-sand beach	sunset-watching, partying, camping	year-round	p542
Waimea Canyon State Park	unbeatable views of 'Grand Canyon of the Pacific'	hiking, mountain biking, camping	Apr-Nov	p542
Northwestern Hawaiian Islands				
Midway Island	Laysan albatross colony, epic coral reef, WWII history	bird-watching, snorkeling, hiking	Nov-Jul	p551

environmental impacts. New sprawling subdivisions and resorts have put even more pressure on a limited watershed and nearly full landfills. Plus, new construction is increasingly uncovering and disturbing archaeological and cultural sites like burial mounds (see the boxed text, p65).

The long-standing friction over Hawaii's military presence continues. The military is notoriously noncompliant with environmental regulations, and its training maneuvers frequently have a substantial impact on cultural sights and local communities. For instance, in 2006, after years of denial, the army admitted to using depleted uranium at O'ahu's Schofield Barracks, and in 2005 it was discovered that the army dumped 8000 tons of chemical weapons off western O'ahu during WWII, which it now claims are nonhazardous (and so does not need to clean up!). One of the biggest current conflicts, though, is over the military's plan to expand its holdings and conduct maneuvers with Stryker combat vehicles on O'ahu and the Big Island.

Future development of Mauna Kea's summit (on the Big Island, p251) is another hot-button topic. Environmental groups and Hawaiians adamantly oppose any new astronomical observatories. In 2006 they scored a victory when a proposal for six new 'outrigger' telescopes around the Keck observatories was abandoned after a judge ruled that scientists couldn't build any more structures without first developing a comprehensive summit management plan and environmental impact statement.

The Pacific Basin Information Node (http://pbin .nbii.gov/) sounds like a conspiracy, but it's a fantastic network of sources for information on all aspects of Hawaii's environment.

HAVE A GREEN TRIP

Call it ecotourism, sustainable tourism, responsible travel: by whatever name, going green is an attitude and an approach, not merely a set of guidelines or a list of approved tour operators. It's about traveling with awareness, respect and care. It's about having a light footprint. It's something you can practice while lying on the beach or backpacking in the rain forest.

In Hawaii it's as simple as traveling in whatever way that for you embodies the two essential Hawaiian values of *malama 'aina* (nourishing the land) and aloha: care for the land and loving welcome. Hawaii is itself struggling with how to realize these ideals in its tourism industry (p69).

But there *are* things you can do: before coming, clean your shoes and shake out your tent so that you don't inadvertently bring seeds or insects, introducing yet another invasive species. When hiking, stay on the trail; when snorkeling, stay off the coral. Don't take plant cuttings, black sand or lava rocks. Don't disturb cultural sites.

Don't approach marine mammals (most are protected, making it illegal to do so); let dolphins, whales, seals and sea turtles swim in peace. If you see a wild animal in distress, report it to the State of Hawaii's **Division of Conservation & Resource Enforcement** (Docare; ☎ 587-0077).

Respect 'Kapu – No Trespassing' signs (unless a trustworthy local says it's okay): you see so many because residents feel their privacy and quality of life are constantly being encroached upon. Patronize local businesses, such as those listed at www.kauaimade.org.

Learn about Hawaiian culture from those who actually practice it; a great start is through Maui's **Kauahea** (www.kauahea.org), created by the director of the Maui Arts & Cultural Center (p348)

Speaking of tour operators, the **Hawaii Ecotourism Association** (www.hawaiiecotourism.org) is a nonprofit organization that recommends and certifies outfitters, tours and hotels committed to ecotourism and sustainable travel. Check them out before making reservations.

Less strictly focused (with some paid advertisements) is the ecotourism website **Alternative Hawaii** (www.alternative-hawaii.com).

Those who want to take the next step and volunteer will find a wealth of opportunities, from whale counts to trail maintenance and much more. See p564 for a list of recommendations, and contact **Malama Hawaii** (www.malamahawaii.org), a partnership network of community groups and other nonprofit organizations.

Hawaiian Natural History, Ecology, and Evolution (2002) by Alan Ziegler is a great comprehensive study of the complex interaction of Hawaiian ecosystems, over time and with human society.

Similarly controversial is the development of Hawaii's Superferry, a high-speed ferry set to begin interisland travel in 2007. Many complain that it's been rushed into operation without studying its potential impacts on the environment and on local communities near the docks.

The **Sierra Club** (www.hi.sierraclub.org) is perhaps Hawaii's most active environmental organization, with groups on O'ahu, Maui, Kaua'i and Hawai'i. In addition to political lobbying and legal actions, it publishes an informative newsletter and sponsors activities and outings. The **Hawaii Audubon Society** (www.hawaiiaudubon.com) is also very active and provides good opportunities for visitors to get involved.

Kahea (www.kahea.org) is a leading community-based activist group that tackles environment, development and Hawaiian cultural rights issues.

Two more good sources of information are **Environment Hawai'i** (www.environment-hawaii.org), a watchdog group that publishes a wide-ranging monthly newsletter, and **Hawaii Ecosystems at Risk** (www.hear.org), whose diverse website focuses on invasive species and eradication efforts.

Outdoors

Underwater discovery in the waters of Hawaii (p76)

The two phrases that come closest to defining Hawaii and a Hawaiian sensibility are *aloha 'aina* and *malama 'aina*. These translate as 'love of the land' and 'care for the land.'

In Native Hawaiian culture, the land always comes first. Gods embody themselves in the landscape, and islanders are keenly aware that they live on precious, limited islands in a boundless sea. You aren't likely to find another place in the world showered with more affection, respect and pure joy by its inhabitants.

Besides, just look at the place.

The name 'Hawaii' is synonymous with nature at its most luscious, sensuous and divine. Experiencing this, luxuriating in the unbelievable richness of nature's full glory, is central to any visit. It's also big, big fun, and ancient Hawaiians were not immune to that either. Island history pulses to the rhythm of games, sport and competition – making it no different in kind to life today. When surf's up on O'ahu's North Shore, business stops, and that tells you everything you need to know about island priorities.

Are you coming to revel in nature and the thrill of the outdoors? Of course you are. The only question is, which island(s) should you visit and what activities should you try. Let's start figuring that out.

First, each island chapter opens with a map showing the best locations for each activity, and chapters begin with an 'Activities' section that overviews the range of what each island offers and gives details on island-wide gear rentals, lessons, outfitters and tour operators.

Rolling surf at Kekaha Beach (p541), with Ni'ihau (p456) in the distance

ANN CE

top five

PLACES TO GET OUTDOORS

Hawai'i Volcanoes National Park, Big Island (p295)
Hike to hot lava

Molokini, Maui (p311)
Snorkel a submerged volcanic crater

North Shore, O'ahu (p171)
Surf legendary big waves

Na Pali Coast, Kaua'i (p510)
Kayak 17 miles of stunning coastline

Haleakala Crater, Maui (p410)
Cycle 38 miles from mountain to ocean

Surfing, Honolua Bay (p341), Maui.
KARL LEHMANN

At Sea

The Pacific Ocean. You probably noticed it on the flight over. Here are all the ways you can play in it.

SWIMMING

Would you care for sand that is white, black, green, orange, tan or some combination? Perhaps you'd like a sea-glass beach? Or one pebbled, rocky or cratered with lava rock tide pools? Every island is ringed with a phenomenal variety of beaches, and each possesses idyllic photo-op strands, perfect for swimming. Water temperatures range from 72°F to 80°F year-round.

The islands have four distinct coastal areas – north shore, south shore, leeward (west) coast and windward (east) coast – each of which has its own peculiar water conditions. As a general rule, the best places to swim in the winter are along the south shores, and in the summer, the north shores. When it's rough on one side, it's usually calm on another, so you can generally find a suitable place.

O'ahu has fabulous beaches, including Waikiki Beach (p135) – don't automatically snub it just because it's famous. Maui is frequently credited with having the 'best beaches,' and it certainly has a lion's share of great ones. However, in this chapter, we're going to try to avoid bestowing titles like 'best.' After all, the Big Island's Hapuna Beach (p237) has been rated one of the top beaches in the world, and Kaua'i has silken strands that could send beach-lovers into a coma. There's nothing second-rate about those places.

The only island where swimming isn't great is Moloka'i, which has nice beaches, but generally too much wind, making waters rough.

Tide pool, Puako (p237), Big Island
CASEY MAHANEY

Manta ray, Molokini (p311)
CASEY MAHANEY

Green sea turtle (p66)
SIMON FOALE

SNORKELING

In Hawaii, the most beautiful scenery and spectacular creatures are often found underwater. Hawaii has extensive coral reefs that are home to some 550 species of fish, and its waters are frequented by, among others, green sea turtles (p66) manta rays, spinner dolphins and humpback whales, which you can sometimes hear singing underwater!

The best part is that this unforgettable aquarium is just offshore. Simply don a mask and snorkel and swim with your face down. It doesn't take athletic prowess or training, and it's cheap. A weekly rental – including snorkel, mask, fins and usually a bag to carry them in – averages out at $2 to $4 a day, depending on the quality of the gear.

Each island has some fantastic and easy-access snorkeling spots, in addition to snorkeling cruises that get you to places you can't reach from shore. On O'ahu, Hanauma Bay (p155) is phenomenal (and regulated to keep it from being loved to death). On Maui, you can't miss Malu'aka Beach (p367), which is also known as 'Turtle Beach' for self-evident reasons. From Maui, cruises also get you to the partly submerged volcanic crater of Molokini (p311).

The Big Island has both coral reefs, as at Kealakekua Bay (p222), and lava rock tide pools, as at Kapoho (p286). A top spot on Kaua'i is Ke'e Beach (p515). Lana'i and Moloka'i also have world-class snorkeling, at Hulopo'e Beach (p423) and Dixie Maru Beach (p455).

The only thing to keep in mind is that, when snorkeling, it's easy to forget yourself – and suddenly find you've drifted out too far or that conditions have changed. Never snorkel alone; make sure others are in the water or on the beach. See also p78

SCUBA DIVING

Snorkeling not getting you deep enough? Scuba dive and you can explore even more extensive coral reefs, shipwrecks and lava tubes, and admire the ocean's pelagic creatures on their own terms.

Hawaii is a mecca for divers, and it's a great place to learn. Most dive companies offer both single-day 'intro' dives for beginners and reasonably priced open-water certification courses. Experienced divers needn't bring anything other than a swimsuit and certification card. Diving is more expensive than snorkeling (two-tank dives run $90 to $150, courses $350 to $500), but you'll like the return on your investment.

Every island has highly recommended dive spots for all abilities – how to choose? Oʻahu's Hanauma Bay (p155) and the Big Island's Kona Coast (p194) are particularly good places for novice divers. Oʻahu is also notable for wreck diving off the south coast, while the Big Island offers lava tubes and nighttime sojourns with manta rays (p206).

Off Maui, the granddaddy of fishbowls is crescent-shaped Molokini (p311), and nearby Lanaʻi offers the grottoes, caves and arches of Cathedrals, off Hulopoʻe Beach (p423). Kauaʻi also has excellent diving; the most reliable is off the south coast.

Experienced divers who want the dive of a lifetime should consider booking a trip to recently reopened Midway Island (p551) in the Northwestern Hawaiian Islands.

The **Professional Association of Diving Instructors** (PADI; ☎ 800-729-7234; www.padi.com) and the **National Association of Underwater Instructors** (NAUI; www.naui.org) certify scuba divers.

For more information on dive spots in Hawaii, pick up Lonely Planet's *Diving & Snorkeling Hawaii*.

RESPONSIBLE DIVING

The popularity of diving is placing immense pressure on many sites. Please consider the following tips when diving, to help preserve the ecology and beauty of reefs.

- Avoid touching living marine organisms with your body or dragging equipment across the reef. Polyps can be damaged by even the gentlest contact. Never stand on coral. If you must hold on to the reef, only touch exposed rock or dead coral.

- Be conscious of your fins. Even without contact, the surge from heavy fin strokes near the reef can damage delicate organisms. When treading water in shallow reef areas, take care not to kick up clouds of sand. Settling sand can easily smother the delicate organisms of the reef.

- Do not use reef anchors, and take care not to ground boats on coral.

- Don't collect (or buy) coral or shells. Aside from the ecological damage, taking home marine souvenirs depletes the beauty of a site and spoils the enjoyment of others.

- Don't leave any rubbish, and remove any litter you find. Plastics in particular are a serious threat to marine life. Turtles can mistake plastic for jellyfish and eat it.

- Minimize your disturbance of marine animals. It is illegal to approach endangered marine species too closely; these include most whales, dolphins, sea turtles and the Hawaiian monk seal. In particular, do not ride on the backs of turtles, as this causes them great anxiety.

- Practice and maintain proper buoyancy control. Major damage can be done by divers descending too fast and colliding with the reef. Make sure you are correctly weighted and that your weight belt is positioned so that you stay horizontal. Be aware that buoyancy can change over the period of an extended trip: initially you may breathe harder and need more weight; a few days later you may breathe more easily and need less weight.

- Resist the temptation to feed fish. You may disturb their normal eating habits, encourage aggressive behavior or feed them food that is detrimental to their health.

- Spend as little time in underwater caves as possible, as your air bubbles may be caught within the roof and leave previously submerged organisms high and dry.

Divers Alert Network (DAN; ☎ 919-684-8111, 800-446-2671; www.diversalertnetwork.org) gives advice on diving emergencies, insurance, decompression services, illness and injury.

Boards ready for action, Waikiki (p135) ANN CECIL

SURFING

Native Hawaiians invented surfing, which has evolved in Darwinian fashion into every board sport practiced today. In Hawaii, surfing is both its own intense subculture as well as a casual part of everyday life. Many island kids learn to surf the same way Canadians learn to ski – from the moment they can stand.

For an introduction to the sport and its place in Hawaiian history, see *Surfer* magazine editor Jake Howard's special section (opposite). Each chapter also contains a boxed text by Jake describing that island's particular surf scene, as well as its most notable surfing spots.

Hawaii's biggest waves roll into the north shores of the islands from November through February. Summer swells, which break along the south shores, aren't as frequent or as large as their winter counterparts.

When it comes to surfing, O'ahu stands head and shoulders above the Neighbor Islands. With its excellent and wide variety of surf spots, O'ahu is where all the major competitions happen; its epic North Shore (p171) is home to surfing's 'Triple Crown.' All of which makes for a sometimes very crowded, high-octane scene. While all the other islands have good, even great, surfing, they tend to be much more laid-back.

Of course, surfing lessons and board rentals are available at just about every tourist locale with rideable waves; a two-hour group lesson typically costs $55 to $75. The **Surf News Network** (www.surfnewsnetwork.com) provides a comprehensive weather-and-wave report.

OCEAN SAFETY

Never turn your back on the ocean. You'll hear this a lot in Hawaii. It means, whether on the shore or in the water – no matter how much fun you're having – always pay attention. Familiarity with Hawaiian waters breeds a healthy mistrust of what the ocean will do. Water conditions can change abruptly, and it's best to never swim alone. Drowning is the leading cause of accidental death for visitors.

- **Rip Currents** Rips, or rip currents, are fast-flowing ocean currents that can drag swimmers out into deeper water. Anyone caught in one should either go with the flow until it loses power or swim parallel to shore to slip out of it.
- **Rogue Waves** All waves are not made the same. They often come in sets, some bigger, some smaller, and sometimes, one really big 'rogue wave' sweeps in and literally drags napping sunbathers into the ocean.
- **Shorebreaks** Waves breaking close to shore are called shorebreaks. When only a couple of feet high, they're generally fine for novice bodysurfers. Large shorebreaks, though, can slam down with enough force to knock you out.
- **Undertows** Particularly along steeply sloped beaches, undertows occur where large waves wash back directly into incoming surf. If you get caught in one and pulled under the water, don't panic. Go with the current until you get beyond the wave.

For information about tsunami, see p558.

WELCOME TO HAWAII, WHERE THE SURF'S ALWAYS UP *Jake Howard, Surfer magazine*

Whether you are waxing up for your first surf adventure or seasoned enough to test your mettle on the world's most monstrous waves, nowhere is there a better, more idyllic place to be a surfer than the islands of Hawaii. With a plethora of schools and rental outfitters popping up across the archipelago, it's the perfect locale to get your feet – and your board – wet for the first time. Once you paddle out into that luxurious 75°F water, you'll understand why it's impossible to conceive of a Hawaii without surfing, and surfing without Hawaii.

Island-specific surfing information can be found in each island's chapter.

Early Riders

Imagine a world governed by the sea – specifically, the merits of your surfing talent. If you surf well, you rise through the feudal ranks – maybe someday even sliding all the way from the outer reefs to the inner sanctum of royalty. Surf poorly and, well, find yourself relegated to the life of a peasant.

While ancient Hawaiians lacked a written language, making the exact date of surfing's inception unknowable, researchers have traced petroglyphs and specific oral chants to approximately AD 1500, which leads them to believe that surfing existed in Polynesian culture long before that. One thing that they are sure of is that wave riding was an integral part of the old Hawaiian *kapu* (taboo) system of governing.

In ancient Hawaii, kings didn't have castles, they had surfboards. The *ali'i* (ruling class) sought the finest craftsmen to scour the jungles for just the right *wiliwili* tree. The tree would then go through an intricate prayer ritual before it was felled and whittled down to a 14ft to 16ft *olo* (a primitive long-board that weighed in excess of 100lb). Once ground smooth by *pohaku puna* (granulated coral) and *oahi* (rough stone), the new boards were adorned with a dark stain derived from *ti* root and polished with *kukui* oil until gleaming with a glossy finish. Another ceremony was then held, and the board was 'christened' before finally being ridden.

As with the rest of the western hemisphere, life in Hawaii remained relatively unchanged for hundreds of years. Then in 1778 Captain James Cook 'discovered' the island chain (p34), becoming the first European to behold the wonder of surfing. Despite Cook's unfortunate demise in 1779, word of the island paradise quickly got out and, by 1820 missionaries from New England began arriving. They promptly started stamping out the 'hedonistic' act of surfing and, save a few holdouts, by 1890 surfing was all but extinct.

It was during the early 1900s that modern surfing's first icon, Duke Kahanamoku, stepped off the beach into history. Kahanamoku grew up on the sands of Waikiki where, along with a handful of others, he swam, fished, dove and rode the reefs on traditional *olo*-style boards. In 1911 Duke and the Waikiki beachboys caught the attention of author Jack London, whose detailed accounts in *Cruise of the Snark* almost immediately captured the imagination of the Western world. Throughout the course of the 20th century Kahanamoku spread the gospel of surfing, traveling the world demonstrating the Hawaiian 'Sport of Kings.'

Modern Masters

Understandably, Hawaii is home to some of the best surfers in the world. Since the 1960s, when the Islands became the premier destination for traveling surfers, local Hawaiians have remained at the forefront of their sport. With surfing enjoying overwhelming popularity, thanks in large part to early surf films – most notably, Bruce Brown's influential *The Endless Summer* (1964) – as well as the emergence of *Surfer* magazine in 1960, the very roots of professional surfing began to take hold on O'ahu. Stars of the day, such as Gerry Lopez and Rory Russell, were the first to bring home legitimate paychecks for simply going surfing. Due to his casual grace and effortless style in the hollow waves of the Banzai Pipeline (p173), Lopez established himself as Mr Pipeline.

Pipeline would continue to be the surf scene's focal point, led by local riders like

Dane Kealoha, Johnny Boy Gomes, and brothers Michael and Derek Ho. In 1993 Derek would go on to be Hawaii's first, but not last, world champion. Heading into the 1980s, Sunny Garcia, a strong-willed youngster from the west side of O'ahu, ascended the world ranks, finally claiming the title in 2000. Shortly thereafter, Kaua'i-born brothers Bruce and Andy Irons began to rise in prominence. While Bruce quickly developed into one of the best free surfers in history, Andy went on a competitive tear, winning three world titles in a row from 2002 through 2004.

To claim the **Triple Crown of Surfing** (www.triplecrownofsurfing.com) is one of the most distinguishing accomplishments a professional surfer can achieve. The three contests, which take place every winter on O'ahu's North Shore at Hale'iwa, Sunset Beach and Pipeline, showcase the world's top surfers on the world's top waves. Notable Triple Crown champions include eight-time world champion Kelly Slater, Andy Irons and Sunny Garcia.

Girls in Curls

In 2002 *Blue Crush*, a big-budget film portraying the trials and tribulations of three young surfer girls trying to make it on O'ahu's North Shore, introduced women around the country to the sport and lifestyle that for so long has been dominated by men. Surf-industry insiders would come to know it as the '*Blue Crush* boom.' But women in Hawaii didn't need a cheesy Hollywood movie to show them what riding waves was all about; they've been doing it since the beginning. In the 1890s, as surfing was on the brink of extinction, Princess Ka'iulani (who would later come to be celebrated in a Robert Louis Stevenson poem), riding her *olo*, almost single-handedly saved the sport, influencing Duke and his contemporaries.

Then 70 years later another woman emerged as a beacon of the aloha spirit. Makaha's Rell Sunn, or 'Auntie Rell,' as she was known, started an unknowable number of young surfers on their paths to enlightenment. Sunn made it a point to give the gift of surfing to as many underprivileged island children as she could, most notably through her annual *menehune* contest (named for the legendary little people credited with building many of Hawaii's heiau), which she ran from 1976 until she succumbed to cancer in 1998. Even today Sunn's influence remains strong, as her surf contest is still a can't-miss event for the kids of O'ahu's Makaha.

Following in Sunn's footsteps, China Uemura's Wahine Classic runs in Waikiki every year and continues to foster youth and women's surfing. The torch has also been passed to talents such as Carissa Moore and Coco Ho (daughter of Pipe Master Michael Ho). Still in their teens, these two girls may be the ones to redefine women's pro surfing and to eliminate the gender barrier altogether.

Nuts & Bolts

When it comes to a 'surfari' in paradise, few places in the world are easier to jump right into than Hawaii. You can forget everything from surf wax to your toothbrush, and you'll survive; you just may have to pay a little bit more out of pocket to get what you need. Because almost everything in Hawaii has to be imported, it's one of the more expensive places to visit, but in almost all towns and cities there's access to everything the traveling surfer may need.

It may be cheaper to bring your own boards but before you fly, check for any hidden airline baggage fees. (Check inter-island carrier policies too; some do have board restrictions.) Most of the airlines charge from $50 to $100 per board; plus they're notoriously bad about handling board bags, more often than not resulting in damage.

If you don't want the hassle of flying with boards, some of the best surfboards in the world are hand-shaped in Hawaii. On O'ahu's North Shore, traveling professional surfers will often put their boards up for sale in local surf shops after their stay, and it's quite easy to find some quality used boards if you know what you're looking for. On average a brand-new surfboard runs about $400, while used boards vary from $150 to $350 depending on their condition.

Local shops are not only the best places to find great boards, but they're great centers of information. Whether you're curious about conditions, looking for sunscreen or needing lessons, surf shops are the nerve centers for the wave-bound community.

To find out about surf and weather conditions, www.surfline.com offers top-of-the-line webcams and forecasts, but it is a for-fee service. Free but less in-depth reports and forecasts are on offer at www.wavewatch.com, along with quality webcams. **North Shore lifeguards** (www.northshorelifeguards.com) are another great source of information. Also the **Honolulu Advertiser** (http://the.honoluluadvertiser.com/current/sp/surf) posts daily surf reports online.

It's All about Respect

As a tourist in Hawaii, there are some places you go, and there are some places you don't go. For many local families the beach parks are meeting places where generations gather to celebrate life under the sun. They're tied to these places by a sense of community and culture, and they aren't eager for outsiders to push them out. As a conscious traveler it's important to understand this. Most folks who live in Hawaii are happy to share the spots that have become gentrified over the past 100 years, and usually will greet you with open arms – but they do reserve the right to protect some of their sacred surf grounds.

In the water, basic surf etiquette is vital. The person 'deepest,' or furthest outside, has the right of way. When somebody is already up and riding, don't take off on the wave in front of them. Also, remember you're a visitor out in the lineup, so don't expect to get every wave that comes your way. There's a definite pecking order and, frankly, as a tourist you're at the bottom. That being said, usually if you give a wave, you'll get a wave in return. In general, be generous in the water, understand your place and surf with a smile, and you should be fine.

Bodysurfing & Bodyboarding

Why stand up when you can ride the waves lying down? Bodysurfing and bodyboarding are wave activities for anybody – and they are suitable at some swimming and many surfing beaches. Places to search out include Brennecke's Beach (p522) on Kaua'i; White Sands Beach (p204) on the Big Island; Sandy Beach Park (p157) and Makapu'u Beach Park (p157) on O'ahu; and Kihei (p356) on Maui.

WINDSURFING

Boasting a variety of both steady and seasonal winds, Hawaii ranks as one of the world's premier places for windsurfing. In general, the best winds blow from June through September, but trade winds keep windsurfers happy all year.

Maui's Ho'okipa Beach (p370) is windsurfing's equivalent of O'ahu's North Shore. It's huge, dangerous and fast, and windsurfing's top international competitions are held here. And, also like O'ahu, Maui stands out among the islands for its abundance of good windsurfing spots. Kanaha Beach Park (p348) and Ma'alaea Bay (p355) are two places mere mortals might try.

Experienced windsurfers should also include Moloka'i in their itinerary: wind whips through the ocean channels at either end of the island, creating top-notch conditions.

If you're looking to learn, O'ahu's Kailua Bay (p161) is super-fantastic. It is consistently good year-round and, when the winds pick up, suitably challenging. One of the best windsurfing schools is here, **Naish Hawaii** (www.naish.com), founded by world champion Robby Naish; lessons run $45 to $75.

Kaua'i and the Big Island are not prime islands for windsurfing, but they each have at least one beach perfect for learning the sport: on Kaua'i, head for 'Anini Beach (p501), and on the Big Island, aim for 'Anaeho'omalu Bay (p234).

Kitesurfing, Pa'ia (p369), Maui
KARL LEHMANN

KITESURFING

A recent entry into the pantheon of wave sports, kitesurfing is, if you'll pardon the expression, really taking off. It's becoming even more popular than windsurfing, even though it takes a good deal of strength, coordination and practice to learn. Kitesurfing, also called kiteboarding, is a little like strapping on a snowboard, grabbing a parachute and gliding/flying over the water. It's a very impressive feat to watch, and if you already know how to windsurf, surf or wakeboard, there's a good chance you'll master it quickly.

Any place that's good for windsurfing is good for kitesurfing. Which means that Maui should dominate the attention of kitesurfers, aspiring or otherwise. In fact, 'Kite Beach' is the nickname for the southwestern end of Kanaha Beach Park (p348), where you can find instruction and rentals. O'ahu's Kailua Bay (p161) is also a great place to learn. Lessons vary (from $125 to $240, depending on duration) and cost a little more than windsurfing.

KAYAKING

When they aren't made of beaches, Hawaii's coastlines are sculpted epiphanies of ragged sea cliffs and precipitous green valleys towering over desolate pocket strands. You cannot drive or walk to many of these places, but you can reach them in a kayak.

Every island has some bit of coast that rewards kayakers with their own portion of heaven. Kaua'i is famous for its 17-mile, summer-only paddle along the unseemly beautiful Na Pali Coast (p510). Kaua'i is also the only island to offer river kayaking. The famous Wailua River (p481) has become so popular it is now almost entirely restricted to guided tours, but Kaua'i has other choices, like the North Shore's Hanalei River (p325).

From O'ahu's Kailua Bay (p161), kayakers can reach two deserted islands that are now seabird sanctuaries. On the Big Island, only boats and kayakers can get to the best snorkeling spots in Kealakekua Bay (p222).

On Maui, kayakers can sport with sea turtles, spinner dolphins and humpback whales (in winter; see opposite) at Makena (p367) and La Perouse Bay (p369). If you have some experience, Moloka'i also offers splendid kayaking from Halawa Beach (p442) and past the magnificent sea cliffs at Kalaupapa (p450).

For outrigger canoeing, see opposite.

WHALE WATCHING

Each winter, mainly from January to March, about two-thirds of the entire North Pacific humpback whale population – roughly 10,000 whales – comes to the shallow coastal waters off the Hawaiian islands for breeding, calving and nursing. Five main areas are protected as the **Hawaiian Islands Humpback Whale National Marine Sanctuary** (http://hawaii humpbackwhale.noaa.gov). Visiting the sanctuary waters during this time is a hot-ticket item.

The western coastline of Maui and the eastern shore of Lana'i are the chief birthing and nursing grounds, but the west coast of the Big Island also sees lots of activity, including the acrobatic 'breaching' displays, for which humpbacks are famous. However, all islands offer whale-watching tours and have areas where you can spot whales from shore.

Sanctuary headquarters are in Kihei (p356) in Maui; those really keen should volunteer for the annual Sanctuary Ocean Count (p564).

FISHING

The sea has always been Hawaii's breadbasket. Today, approximately 30% of Hawaii households fish recreationally, and 10% still practice some subsistence fishing. You will see locals everywhere casting from shore (shorefishing), and no fishing license is required to join them (only freshwater fishing requires a license). However, regulation upon regulation governs what you can catch and when; see the website of the state **Department of Aquatic Resources** (www.hawaii.gov/dlnr/dar).

Most visiting anglers, though, are more interested in deep-sea sportfishing charters for such legendary quarry as 'ahi (yellowfin tuna), swordfish, spearfish, mahimahi (dolphinfish) and, most famous of all, Pacific blue marlin, which can reach 1000lb. Hawaii has some of the world's best sportfishing, chiefly off the Big Island's Kona Coast (p206), Moloka'i (p430) and Kaua'i (p462).

OUTRIGGER CANOEING: THE ORIGINAL SUPERFERRY

Hawaii was settled by Polynesians paddling outrigger canoes across 2000 miles of open ocean, so you could say canoeing was Hawaii's original sport. Europeans, who marveled at so much when they first arrived, were awestruck at the skill Native Hawaiians displayed in their canoes near shore. They could time launches and landings perfectly, and they paddled for play among the waves like dolphins.

Today, over 40 canoe clubs keep outrigger canoeing alive and well, mainly through racing in single, double and six-person canoes. The main season is from January to May, and the **Hawaii Island Paddlesports Association** (HIPA; www.hawaii paddling.org) is the major organization.

The most impressive long-distance events, though, happen in the fall. In the **Queen Lili'uokalani** (www.kaiopua.org) on the Big Island in early September, teams go 18 miles from Kailua Bay to Honaunau Bay. But this is just a warm-up. In late September and early October, men and women compete separately in a 41-mile race across the channel from Moloka'i to O'ahu (p436).

Many races are open to nonresidents; get canoe club info, schedules and advice through www.y2kanu.com. If you just want to dip a paddle, outrigger canoe trips are offered on the Wailua River on Kaua'i (p480) and at Kihei on Maui (p359). And certainly, don't miss Maui's mid-May International Festival of Canoes (p325) in Lahaina, where master carvers create the boats, then launch them.

On Land

Of course, if you spend all *your time in the water and on the beach, you'll miss one of the richest and most varied ecosystems on the planet. Now get off your towel and hit the trail!*

HIKING

It's really not fair. Not to your vacation plans nor to all the other truly lovely places in the world. But pound for pound, these tiny islands can't be topped for heart-stopping vistas, soulful beauty and constant variety. The hiker is overwhelmed at every turn – finally collapsing in despair upon realizing that only by living here is there any hope of seeing everything. (Say...)

Short of relocating, you'll have to make choices. We wish we could make one or two of the islands sound skippable, but none is. Thankfully, this means wherever and whenever you visit – and whether you prefer raw jungly backpacks or short paved nature trails – you'll come home with treasured experiences.

For pure variety, the Big Island wins by a nose. Hawai'i Volcanoes National Park (p288) contains an erupting volcano, for goodness sake, plus steaming craters, lava deserts and native rainforests. Then, there are two nearly 14,000ft mountains to scale – Mauna Loa (p258) and Mauna Kea (p251) – and the haunting Waipi'o Valley (p262).

Kaua'i's legendary Kalalau Trail (p516) on the Na Pali Coast edges spectacularly fluted sea cliffs, while an abundance of trails crisscross Koke'e State Park (p545) and Waimea Canyon State Park (p542), aka the 'Grand Canyon of the Pacific.'

Hiking Manoa Falls Trail (p118), O'ahu
KARL LEHMANN

Maui's volcano may be dormant, but Haleakala National Park (p403) provides awe-inspiring descents across the caldera's enormous moonscape. The death-defying Hana Hwy (p373) offers many short excursions; for more vistas, hit the Waihe'e Ridge Trail (p343).

On O'ahu, you will of course pilgrimage to the top of Diamond Head (p153), but above the city are lush trails in Tantalus and Makiki Valley (p119). On the windward coast, Ahupua'a 'O Kahana State Park (p167) is rewarding.

Moloka'i's Kalaupapa Trail descends into Kalaupapa National Historical Park (p448), which preserves a leprosy settlement, and Pepe'opae Trail in the Kamakou Preserve (p444) is 'verdant' defined.

'Ioa Needle (p353), 'Iao Valley, Maui ADINA TOVY AMSEL

'TRAILS TO GO ON'

Established in 1988, **Na Ala Hele** ('Trails to Go On'; www.hawaiitrails.org) is affiliated with Hawaii's Division of Forestry & Wildlife, and it coordinates public access to hiking trails statewide, while also maintaining and preserving historical trails. Currently there are 97 trails and 85 access roads (totaling 675 miles) within the system. Na Ala Hele's website provides trail descriptions, while on the ground, trailheads are marked with its logo signpost – a brown sign featuring a yellow hiking petroglyph figure.

Many more trails remain to be completed (such as the Big Island's Ala Kahakai National Trail; p197), and Na Ala Hele can't keep up. Unbelievably, funding for Hawaii's **Division of Forestry & Wildlife** (Dofaw; Map pp106-7; ☎ 587-0062; www.dofaw.net; Suite 132, 567 S King St, Honolulu) ranks 47th in the US. So, if Hawaii's trails really inspire you, consider contacting Dofaw and volunteering to help Na Ala Hele keep going.

And what of Lana'i? Okay, it has only one first-rate hike, but take the Munro Trail (p426) on a clear day and you'll survey all the main islands but distant Kaua'i.

For more on hiking, check out Lonely Planet's *Hiking in Hawaii*.

Hiking Preparations & Safety

All the islands have paved nature trails and botanical gardens that require no 'preparations' to speak of. Anyone looking to spend hours (or days) on dirt trails should bring sturdy hiking boots, rain gear and a fleece sweater – weather is changeable, and trails can be rocky, uneven and muddy. If you'll be tackling a mountain, bring a winter coat (even in summer). A flashlight is also important: it gets dark fast after the sun sets. And, of course, a hat, sunscreen and lots of water are mandatory.

As for safety, see the hike descriptions for specific advice, as the range of potential hazards varies tremendously: from volcanic fumes to flash floods to crumbling cliffs. Keep in mind, however, that true wilderness abuts civilization throughout Hawaii. Prepare for a short hike outside Honolulu the same as you would for a long hike in the middle of nowhere.

Biking, Haleakala National Park (p403) LEE FOSTER

CYCLING & MOUNTAIN BIKING

Cycling and mountain biking in Hawaii is more about quality than quantity. Generally speaking, local biking communities are well organized, host group rides and promote responsible cycling. In addition to established trails and routes, there are miles of 4WD roads that can be converted to a cyclist's pleasure.

The Big Island may have the most opportunities. As the home of the Ironman Triathlon (p207), it is well prepared for both cyclists and mountain bikers. Both can find happiness at Hawai'i Volcanoes National Park (p288), while mountain bikers also get the 45-mile Mana Rd (p251) circling Mauna Kea and the 6.5-mile beach trail to Pine Trees (p230) on the Kona Coast.

One of the coolest (but crowded) cycles is the 38-mile sunrise descent from the top of Haleakala (p410) on Maui. On Kaua'i, you can pedal the Waimea Canyon Trail (p545) and Powerline Trail (p484), a picturesque ridge-top route from Wailua to Princeville.

Dedicated cyclists and mountain bikers shouldn't miss Moloka'i, which has 40 miles of trails; the best are in the Moloka'i Forest Reserve (p444).

GOLF

Pssst, hey, did you know that golf is Hawaii's best-kept secret – what? It was on TV?

Oh, well, so everybody knows. If you've ever spoiled a good walk chasing golf balls, you owe yourself a treat. Do it in Hawaii. Maybe you don't want to shell out $150 to $200 for a round at one of the elite resort courses (or maybe you do), but Hawaii also has lots of cheaper ($35 to $50 per round), well-loved municipal courses with egregious scenery you can't get back home. Kaua'i's **Kukuiolono Golf Course** (p530) costs only $8!

ARE YOU AN IRONMAN OR A TINMAN?

Sure, sure, you could enter the famous Ironman Triathlon World Championship (www .ironmanlive.com) and swim 2.4 miles, bike 112 miles and run 26.2 miles nonstop, but why show off? Do you have what it takes to be an aluminum man or a tinman?

Since the Ironman race began in 1978 (and still occurs each October on the Big Island; p207), several lesser metals have inspired their own triathlons. O'ahu's **Tinman Triathlon** (http://tinmanhawaii.com) has been going strong for over 25 years. It's a comparative dash: contestants do an 800m (about half a mile) swim, 40km (about 25-mile) bike and 10km (about 6-mile) run. Tinman winners finish in under two hours; the Ironman world record is a skooch over eight hours. Now really, which would you rather do?

In fact, Hawaii is chockful of races of all kinds that mix competition with gorgeous scenery. Why not sign up for Maui's Xterra World Championship (p368), which ends with a bike ride up the slopes of Haleakala? How about the Big Island's Kilauea Volcano Wilderness Run (p299) around Kilauea Caldera?

If you've got that competitive fire, check out the **Big Island Race and Training Schedule** (www.bigislandraceschedule.com) and click on the Hawaii Race Links. Here you'll find swims, runs, paddles, bikes and multisport races for a rainbow of alloys.

EXTREME SPORTS

Never let it be said that ancient Hawaiians didn't know how to play. Every ruler and god eventually had to prove their prowess in sports. Stories of Lono say he outshone all the islands' best athletes: leaping further, canoeing faster, wrestling better, killing sharks with stones, bringing snowballs from atop Mauna Kea and catching 20 hurled spears with his bare hands.

Lono also had no rival with the *holua* – an ancient sled that was 6in to 8in wide and 6ft to 12ft long. That's right, it was about as wide as this book's height and raced down a mountain at speeds up to 50mph. Losing your balance could mean death – but greatness isn't proved without risk, right? Of course, some are hoping to revive this ancient Hawaiian extreme sport (www.hawaiibc.com).

Hopefully they won't make the same mistake as one careless Hawaiian youth long ago. He refused the challenge of a frail old woman asking to borrow his *holua,* and she turned into a very angry Pele – who with thunder under her feet and lightning in her hair, surfed a crested wave of lava down the mountain, killing all who'd laughed at her.

Now that's extreme.

Lana'i, dominated by two world-class golf resorts (p420), is the prime destination for the unrepentant, well-heeled duffer who wants to do nothing but. Otherwise, O'ahu, Kaua'i, Maui and the Big Island all offer very challenging, professionally designed, drop-dead gorgeous resort courses and a host of other choices. Playing in the afternoon is usually discounted.

HORSEBACK RIDING

All of the main islands offer memorable horseback riding. But since ranches, rodeos, cattle and cowboys are a big part of the Big Island and Maui, save your serious riding for these spots. Maui's most unique offering is guided horse trips down crunchy cinder-rock trails into Haleakala (p400). On the Big Island, *paniolo* (Hawaiian cowboy) headquarters are in Waimea (p246) at Parker Ranch. Horse rides into Waipi'o Valley (p262) are also a highlight.

YOGA & RETREATS

For others, the Zen of the mind is preferred to the Zen of the back swing. Hawaii offers both active yoga studios for folks who want to keep up with their practice while on holiday, as well as full-on retreats for those who feel that meditation is a vacation.

Maui has much to entice the alternatively inclined (p317). Kaua'i has a relative abundance of yoga studios; one recommended retreat is Mana Yoga in Princeville (p502). The Big Island is sprinkled with yoga studios along the Kona Coast and in Hilo, but Puna (p283) is the place for retreats.

Horseback riding is a quiet activity at pastoral Parker Ranch (p247), Waimea, Big Island

ANN CECIL

Majestic Waimea Canyon, Waimea Canyon State Park (p542), Kaua'i.

O'ahu

There are a lot of beach resorts in the world where you can escape into a manufactured fantasy, where everything is staged for the scrapbook photograph. And then there's O'ahu, known in Hawaiian as 'the gathering place.'

The most developed of the Hawaiian islands, O'ahu is the state's center of government and culture – a role it usurped from Maui. It is one of the world's best combinations of urban living, natural beauty and rural community. You can indulge your vacation dreams of umbrella drinks and suntans as well as eat at ethnic hole-in-the-walls and pick-up local pidgin. It is a perfect counterpoint for people who get bored with resorts and the ease of being a tourist.

On the mainland, you'd have to drive halfway across a state to find the diversity that O'ahu has within an hour's drive. Honolulu is a traffic-jammed city more akin to Asia than Europe. There's no ethnic majority; everyone who can claim a fairly homogenous racial identity is in a minority. The intermingling of O'ahu's ethnic groups is best captured with a food anecdote: Honolulu's American-style diners serve a noodle dish known as saimin that claims parentage from Japan, China, Korea and the Philippines. A mixed-up family tree found only in Hawaii.

The island was one of the first to implant itself in the world's collective longing for a tropical vacation, thanks to the success of Waikiki. Many come for the Waikiki vacation package, and all are pleasantly surprised by what lies beyond the hotel. A short distance away are dramatic mountain ranges, aqua-blue coral bays and wide sandy beaches. There's snorkeling in the old volcanic crater of Hanauma Bay, monster waves at the surfing haven of the North Shore, genuine Hawaiian ukulele bands, hiking through tropical forests and a general aloha spirit.

HIGHLIGHTS

- Watch the wave riders at **Sunset Beach** (p173)
- Swim with sea turtles at **Kailua Beach Park** (p161)
- Listen to Hawaiian songs at the beach bars of **Waikiki** (p149)
- Climb **Diamond Head Crater** (p153) in time for dawn
- Munch on shrimp scampi from the lunch trucks at **Kahuku** (p170)
- Hike in the **Makiki Valley** (p119)
- Glider ride over the **North Shore** (p181)
- See spinner dolphins up close on the **Wai'anae** (p188)

| ■ POPULATION: 905,266 | ■ AREA: 608 SQ MILES | ■ OFFICIAL FLOWER: ILIMA (A TYPE OF HIBISCUS) |

O'AHU

O'AHU

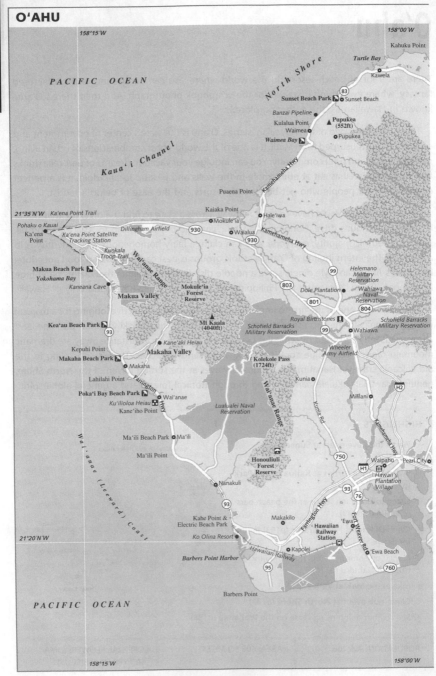

PACIFIC OCEAN

Kaua'i Channel

158°15'W

158°00'W

Kahuku Point

North Shore

Turtle Bay

Kawela

Sunset Beach Park

Sunset Beach

Banzai Pipeline

Kulalua Point

▲ Pupukea (552ft)

Waimea

Waimea Bay

Pupukea

Kamehameha Hwy

Puaena Point

Kaiaka Point

Hale'iwa

21°35'N'W   Ka'ena Point Trail

Mokule'ia

Pohaku o Kauai

Ka'ena Point Satellite Tracking Station

Dillingham Airfield

930

Waialua

Kamehameha Hwy

Ka'ena Point

930

Kuaokala Troop Trail

99

Helemano Military Reservation

Makua Beach Park

803

Dole Plantation

Wahiawa Naval Reservation

Yokohama Bay

Kaneana Cave

Makua Valley

Mokule'ia Forest Reserve

801

804

Schofield Barracks Military Reservation

Kea'au Beach Park

93

▲ Mt Kaala (4040ft)

Kane'aki Heiau

Royal Birthstones

Schofield Barracks Military Reservation

99

Wahiawa

Kepuhi Point

Makaha Valley

Kolekole Pass (1724ft)

Wheeler Army Airfield

Makaha Beach Park

Makaha

H2

Lahilahi Point

Farrington Hwy

Kunia

Mililani

Poka'i Bay Beach Park

Wai'anae

Lualualei Naval Reservation

Wai'anae Range

Kunia Rd

Ku'ilioloa Heiau

Kane'iho Point

Ma'ili Beach Park

Ma'ili

Honouliuli Forest Reserve

750

Waipahu

Pearl City

Ma'ili Point

H1

Hawaii's Plantation Village

Wai'anae (Leeward) Coast

Nanakuli

93

93

76

'Ewa

Kahe Point & Electric Beach Park

Makakilo

Fort Weaver Rd

'Ewa Beach

Hawaiian Railway Station

Ko Olina Resort

Kapolei

Farrington Hwy

760

21°20'N'W

95

Barbers Point Harbor

Hawaiian Railway

PACIFIC OCEAN

Barbers Point

158°15'W

158°00'W

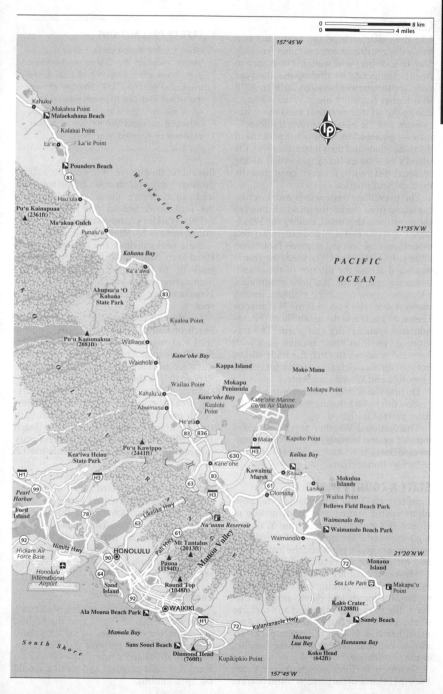

0 —————— 8 km
0 —————— 4 miles

157°45'W

Kahuku
Makahoa Point
Malaekahana Beach
Kalanai Point
La'ie
La'ie Point
Pounders Beach
83
Hau'ula
Pu'u Kainapuaa
(2361ft)
Ma'akua Gulch
Punalu'u

Windward Coast

PACIFIC
OCEAN

21°35'N W

Kahana Bay
Ka'a'awa
Ahupua'a 'O
Kahana
State Park
83
Kualoa Point

Pu'u Kaaumakua
(2681ft) Waikane
Waiahole

Kane'ohe Bay
Kappa Island
Moko Manu

Wailau Point
Mokapu
Peninsula
Kane'ohe Bay Kealohi
Kahalu'u Point
Ahuimanu

Mokapu Point

He'eia
83 836
Malae
Kapoho Point
Kane'ohe Marine
Corps Air Station

Kea'iwa Heiau
State Park
Pu'u Kawippo
(2441ft)
630
H3
H1
99
Kane'ohe Kawainui
63 83 Marsh
Pearl
Harbor H3
Ford
Island 78
61
Olomana
Lanikai

Kailua Bay
Kailua
Mokulua
Islands
Wailea Point
Bellows Field Beach Park

92
Hickam Air
Force Base
Nimitz Hwy
90
HONOLULU
64
Sand
Island
92
WAIKIKI
Ala Moana Beach Park

Likelike Hwy
63

Pali Hwy
61 Mt Tantalus
(2013ft)
Pauoa
(1194ft)
Round Top
(1048ft)

Nu'uannu Reservoir

Manoa Valley

Waimanolo

Waimanalo Bay
Waimanalo Beach Park

21°20'N W

72
Manana
Island

Sea Life Park
Makapu'u
Point

Koko Crater
(1208ft)
Sandy Beach

Honolulu
International
Airport

South Shore

Mamala Bay
Sans Souci Beach
Diamond Head
(760ft)
Kupikipkio Point

H1
72 Kalanianaole Hwy

Moana
Lua Bay
Koko Head
(642ft)
Hanauma Bay

157°45'W

CLIMATE

Like the entire archipelago, O'ahu has two barely discernable seasons: summer (roughly May to October) and winter (November to April). Temperatures throughout the year vary approximately between 70°F to 80°F with higher humidity likely in the summer; during the winter months it rains more frequently. But the island has several microclimates – governed by the weather patterns of the trade winds and their interaction with the island's two mountain ranges – that define seasonal differences for each coast and the mountainous interior.

The prevailing trade winds move across the island from the northeast, where most of the moisture is deposited, making the Windward Coast (the east side) and eastern Ko'olau mountain range lush and relatively cooler than other parts of the island. The winds then move westward across the interior of the island, bumping against the Wai'anae mountains, which exacts any remaining moisture, leaving the west side (also known as the Wai'anae or Leeward Coast) and the South Shore (Honolulu and Waikiki) dry and warm. The traditional Hawaiian home is often built with louvered windows to catch the trade winds, but air-con is a welcome invention for coastal Honolulu and Waikiki residents.

During the winter months, Kona winds reverse this trend bringing intense rain to the drier parts of the island.

The National Weather Service provides **recorded weather forecasts** (☎ 973-4381) and **marine conditions** (☎ 973-4382) for all of O'ahu. See p556 for climate charts.

STATE & COUNTY PARKS

Even though O'ahu is the state's most populous island, nature sits right outside of Honolulu's glass skyscrapers and Waikiki's high-rise hotels. The entire coastline is dotted with county beach parks and the lush mountain interior is crisscrossed by hiking trails.

Most of the county beach parks are well-maintained with parking and bathroom facilities, lifeguards and picnic areas so that the entire island can enjoy surf and turf free of charge (in most cases). In addition to the usual beach activities, the beach parks are also communal backyards where families come to celebrate.

Smack dab in Honolulu is Ala Moana Beach Park (p111), one of the prettiest urban beaches

---

SAFETY PRECAUTIONS

When visiting beach parks, hiking trails or 'secret' spots off the side of the highway, don't leave any valuables in the car or the trunk. Car break-ins are common all over the island and can happen within a matter of minutes. Some locals leave their cars unlocked to avoid the hassles of broken windows or jimmied door locks.

---

this side of the equator. A few minute's climb through ginger plants and canopy trees will lead you to views of the urban skyline along the Tantalus & Makiki Valley hiking trails (p119). Waikiki's famous strip of sand is portioned out as a handful of public parks.

State parks include the iconic Diamond Head State Monument (p153), with hiking trails up to the top of Waikiki's skyline-dominating mountain. Further east is scenic Hanauma Bay (p155), a famous snorkeling spot.

On the east coast are the tame swimming beach of Kailua Beach Park (p161) and the wild and rugged coastline of Malaekahana State Recreation Area (p170). Slicing into the moist mountains is Ahupua'a 'O Kahana State Park (p167) in the Kahana Valley.

Some of the most famous North Shore surfing breaks occur just offshore from modest beach parks, including 'Ehukai Beach Park (p173), home to Pipeline. Pupukea Beach Park (p173) is a conservation success story protecting tidal pools and the turtle habitat of Shark's Cove.

Occupying the sacred northwestern tip of the island is Ka'ena Point State Park (p188), the nesting home to several Pacific seabirds, and a spectacular sight of lava cliffs and furious crashing waves. The Wai'anae Coast doesn't register on many tourist itineraries, but its beach parks are blessedly free of crowds, save for a few locals and sunbathing sea turtles.

Camping

You can pitch a tent at many county and state parks on the island. You'll find the highest concentration of facilities on the Windward Coast, beneath the majestic Ko'olau range. At all of the island's parks, rip-offs and car break-ins are a problem and visitors should take precautions.

There are four state parks on the island with camping areas: interior Kea'iwa Heiau State Park (p120) in the Ko'olau Range, Sand Island State Recreation Area in the greater Honolulu area; Malaekahana State Recreation Area (p170) and Ahupua'a 'O Kahana State Park (p167), both on the Windward Coast. These are managed by the Division of State Parks, **Department of Land and Natural Resources** (Map pp106-7; ☎ 887-0300; www.hawaii.gov/dlnr/dsp; State Office Bldg, 1151 Punchbowl St, Honolulu, HI 96813; ⏰ 8am-3:30pm Mon-Fri), which maintains an O'ahu district office. This office handles permit requests and payment of camping fees, both of which must be arranged before arrival. O'ahu state campgrounds are open Friday to Wednesday, except Sand Island State Recreation Area, which is open Friday to Monday. Camping permits cost $5. At Malaekahana, a private nonprofit group operates a concession campground.

There are 15 county beach parks that allow camping from Friday to Wednesday morning (no camping on Wednesday and Thursday nights), but free permits most be arranged in person at the **Department of Parks & Recreation** (Map pp106-7; ☎ 523-4525; Honolulu Municipal Bldg, 650 S King St, cnr Alapai St; ⏰ 8am-4pm Mon-Fri) in downtown Honolulu or at one of the satellite city halls, including an office at the **Ala Moana Center** (Map p112; Ground fl, 1450 Ala Moana Blvd; ⏰ 9am-5pm Mon-Fri, 8am-4pm Sat). For locations and hours of other satellite city halls, call the **City Hotline** (☎ 973-2600).

The most popular county campgrounds are Kualoa Regional Park, Waimanalo Bay, and Bellows Field Beach Parks. Other county beach parks are used as permanent shelters by the island's homeless, who flout camping regulations (see also the boxed text, p185). Periodically the county will kick out illegal campers from one coast, sending them over to the other coast. Because the homeless population migrates to different beach parks, we recommend visiting the county campground before arranging accommodation so that you can measure personal feelings of safety and comfort.

Camping is allowed along certain trails and one backcountry site (Peacock Flats) managed by the **Division of Forestry & Wildlife** (Map pp106-7; ☎ 587-0166; Room 325, State Office Bldg, 1151 Punchbowl St, Honolulu, HI 96813; ⏰ 7:45am-4:30pm Mon-Fri). Visit the website (www.hawaiitrails.org) for a list of trails, topographic maps and camping avail-

ability. Camping permits must be arranged in person either at the division's main office or at the Makiki Heights office (Map p115; ☎ 973-9778; 2135 Makiki Heights Dr, Honolulu, HI 96822; ⏰ 7:45am-4:30pm).

ACTIVITIES
Water Activities
SWIMMING
O'ahu is ringed by more than 50 gorgeous white-sand beaches and the island's four distinct coastal areas provide year-round swimming. When it's rough on one side, it's generally calm on another.

Recommended South Shore beaches include Waikiki (p139) and Ala Moana (p111). On the Windward Coast, Kailua Beach Park (p161), Kualoa Regional Park (p166), Malaekahana (p170) and Waimanalo Bay (p158) are good choices.

North Shore beaches, while too rough for swimming much of the winter, can be calm during summer.

The Wai'anae Coast extends from Ka'ena Point to Barbers Point, where the best year-round swimming is at Poka'i Bay Beach Park (p186).

SNORKELING, DIVING & OCEAN TRIPS
Hanauma Bay Nature Preserve (p155) on the South Shore offers excellent snorkeling year-round. In summer, follow the locals (both divers and snorkelers) to the North Shore's Pupukea Beach Park (p173). On the Wai'anae Coast, head to Electric Beach (p184) and Makaha Beach Park. In the winter, most divers head to the South Shore wrecks off the coast

---

TOP 10 BEACHES

- **Kailua Beach Park** (p161)
- **Sunset Beach Park** (p173)
- **Yokohama Beach** (p188)
- **Malaekahana State Recreation Area** (p170)
- **Makaha Beach Park** (p186)
- **Ala Moana Beach Park** (p111)
- **Sans Souci Beach** (p141)
- **Waimanalo Beach Park** (p158)
- **Waimea Bay Beach Park** (p175)
- **Sandy Beach** (p157)

of Waikiki and spots between Koko Head and Kupikipiki'o Point (Black Point). The following operators offer diving tours and rent gear:

Breeze Hawaii Diving Adventure (Map pp136-7; ☎ 735-1857; www.breezehawaii.com; 3014 Kaimuki Ave, Honolulu)

Aaron's Dive Shop (Map p162; ☎ 262-2333; www .hawaii-scuba.com; 307 Hahani St, Kailua)

Aloha Dive Shop (Map p154; ☎ 395-5922; www .alohadiveshop.com; No1 Marina Bldg, 377 Keahole St, Hawai'i Kai)

Deep Ecology (Map p177; ☎ 637-7946, 800-578-3992; www.deepecologyhawaii.com; 66-456 Kamehameha Hwy, Hale'iwa)

Between Christmas and April, humpback whales often with babies in tow visit the harbors of northern and western O'ahu. Hawaiian spinner dolphins are year-round residents on the Wai'anae Coast and are known for their graceful acrobatics. Deep Ecology (p179) and Wild Side Specialty Tours (p186) offer whale- and dolphin-watching tours; both companies are well-regarded for their conservation efforts.

Boom Boom Sportfishing (☎ 306-4162; www.boom boomsportfishing.com; Ko Olina Marina & Wai'anae Harbor,

Wai'anae Coast) offers charter and shared fishing excursions.

SURFING & OTHER WATER SPORTS

O'ahu is on the international surfing circuit, attracting itinerant wave riders to the North Shore's massive winter breaks and hosting several high-profile competitions. It was also here that surfers figured out how to adapt their boards to ride swells that had never before been conquered. North Shore might be the surf celebrity, but breaks all around the island have their own personalities and status among the surfing hierarchy. See the boxed text, below for a rundown of the surf scene.

Kailua Bay (p161) is the number-one spot for windsurfing, with year-round trade winds and good flat-water and wave conditions. Other prime windsurfing spots include Diamond Head Beach (p155), and Sunset Beach Park (p173). In Waikiki, Fort DeRussy Beach (p139) is the main windsurfing spot. Rentals and local information is available from the mentioned beach parks.

The most popular places for kayaking overlap with the windsurfing destinations (except

---

O'AHU SURF BEACHES & BREAKS   *Jake Howard*

Hawaiian for 'the gathering place,' O'ahu has become a hub for the islands' surf economy. Because O'ahu has some of the most diverse surf breaks in the islands, boarders of all skill levels can find what they're looking for here.

In Waikiki, slow and mellow combers (long curling waves) provide the perfect training ground for beginners. Board rentals abound at spots like Central Waikiki Beach (p140) and local beachboys are always on hand for lessons at spots like mellow **Queen's**, mushy left- and right-handed **Canoes**, gentle but often crowded **Popular's** and ever-popular **Publics**. In Honolulu proper, **Ala Moana** (p111) offers a heavy tubing wave. Waves in this area are best during summer, when south swells arrive from New Zealand and Tahiti.

Reckon yourself a serious surfer? A pilgrimage to the famed North Shore is mandatory. In winter, when the waves can reach heights of more than 30ft, spots like **Waimea Bay** (p175), **Pipeline** (p173) and **Sunset Beach** (p173) beckon to the planet's best professional surfers.

While home to some great waves, O'ahu's Wai'anae Coast has turf issues; the locals who live and surf here cherish this area and are trying to hold onto its last vestiges of Hawaiian culture and community. In the winter, large west swells can make for big surf at places like **Makaha Beach Park** (p186), but tread lightly: the locals know each other here, so there will be no question that you're from out of town.

If you're looking for a multipurpose wave, **Diamond Head Beach** (p155) is friendly to short-boarders, long-boarders, windsurfers and kitesurfers. And for a good day of bodysurfing, **Sandy's** and **Makapu'u** on the island's southeast shore are ideal. If you go out here, do so with caution: the pounding waves and shallow bottom have caused some serious neck and back injuries.

For surf reports, call **Surf News Network** (☎ 596-7873), a recorded surf-condition telephone line that reports winds, wave heights and tide information, or check out **Hawaii Surfing News** (www.holoholo.org/surfnews) online.

O'AHU FLORA & FAUNA

Most of the islets off O'ahu's Windward Coast are sanctuaries for seabirds, including terns, noddies, shearwaters, Laysan albatrosses, tropic birds, boobies and frigate birds. Moku Manu (Bird Island) off Mokapu Peninsula has the greatest number of species.

The 'elepaio, a brownish bird with a white rump, and the 'amakihi, a small yellow-green bird, are the most common endemic forest birds on O'ahu. The 'apapane, a vibrant red honeycreeper, and the 'I'iwi, a bright vermilion bird, are less common.

The only other endemic forest bird, the O'ahu creeper, may already be extinct. This small yellowish bird looks somewhat like the 'amakihi, which makes positive identification difficult. The last sighting of the O'ahu creeper was in 1985 on the Poamoho Trail. The James Campbell National Wildlife Refuge (p171) provides limited viewing of several endangered seabirds.

O'ahu has wild pigs and goats in its mountain valleys. Brush-tailed rock wallabies, accidentally released in 1916, reside in the Kalihi Valley. Although rarely seen, the wallabies are of interest to zoologists because they may be the last members of a subspecies thought to be extinct in their native Australia.

There are several excellent botanical gardens on the island, each in a different ecological setting. The largest and most diverse, Foster Botanical Garden (p110) features orchids and palms, many bordering on the science-fiction variety. Among the stars of this garden is a Bo tree, a descendant of the tree under which the Buddha sat. At the Ho'omaluhia Botanical Garden (p164) in Kane'ohe, you can enjoy a stroll or drive through a lush rain-forest garden.

---

for Sunset Beach). **Go Bananas** (Map pp136-7; ☎ 737-9514; www.gobananaskayaks.com; 799 Kapahulu Ave, Honolulu) rents top-notch gear and can steer people to less crowded spots.

Land Activities

HIKING

Despite being the most populated island, O'ahu has some wonderfully remote and appealing hiking trails, many of which sit smack dab in Honolulu. Everyone hikes up prominent Diamond Head Crater (p153), in Waikiki, as much for the view as for a touristy version of a pilgrimage. The trails in Tantalus & Makiki Valley (p119) are lush, diverse and are pleasantly devoid of crowds. You can also go waterfall spotting at Manoa Falls Trail (p118).

On the rainier Windward Coast, you'll find a wet and verdant scramble through Ahupua'a 'O Kahana State Park (p167). A wild and ocean-whipped landscape unfolds along the Ka'ena Point Trail (p189) on the Wai'anae Coast.

This book sketches the most popular and accessible hikes. For more detailed information, check out O'ahu Trails by Kathy Morey or The Hikers Guide to O'ahu by Stuart Ball. Trail maps can be obtained online (www.haw aiitrails.org) or at the Division of Forestry & Wildlife offices (see Camping p92).

Hiking clubs generally organize guided trips open to the public; check the Friday editions of daily newspapers or the Honolulu Weekly for announcements. The following clubs offer guided hikes, educational opportunities or additional hiking information.

Hawaii Trail & Mountain Club (http://htmclub.org) A volunteer organization dating from 1910.

Hawaii Nature Center (Map p115; ☎ 955-0100; www.hawaiinaturecenter.org) Sponsors hikes and volunteer opportunities.

Hawaii Audubon Society (☎ 528-1432; www .hawaiiaudubon.com) Leads bird-watching hikes.

Sierra Club (☎ 538-6616; www.hi.sierraclub.org) Leads weekend hikes and other outings around O'ahu.

RUNNING, CYCLING & MOUNTAIN BIKING

Kapi'olani Park (p141) and Ala Moana Beach Park (p111) are two favorite jogging spots, as is the 4.6-mile run around Diamond Head crater (p153). O'ahu has about 75 foot races each year, including the Honolulu Marathon (www.honolulumarathon.org).

The **Hawaii Bicycling League** (☎ 735-5756; www .hbl.org) holds rides around O'ahu nearly every weekend, ranging from 10-mile jaunts to 60-mile treks. For information on cycling as a means of transport around O'ahu, see p99.

Some of O'ahu's hiking trails are multi-use for mountain-bikes. Popular coastal rides include Ka'ena Point (p188) and nearby Kealia and Kuakola Trails (p182). Interior mountain-trail rides include the Maunawili network (p158).

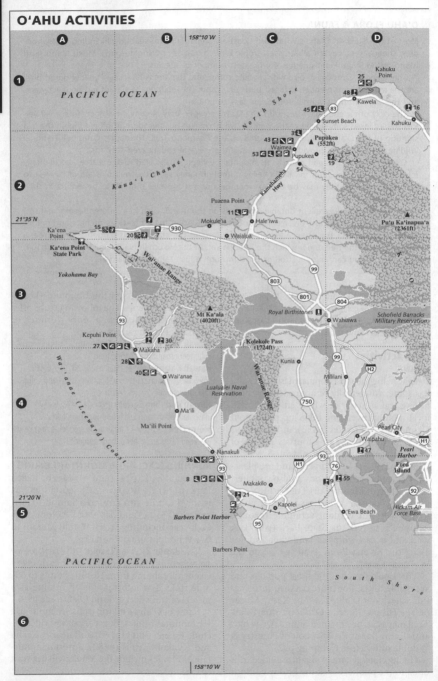

O'AHU ACTIVITIES

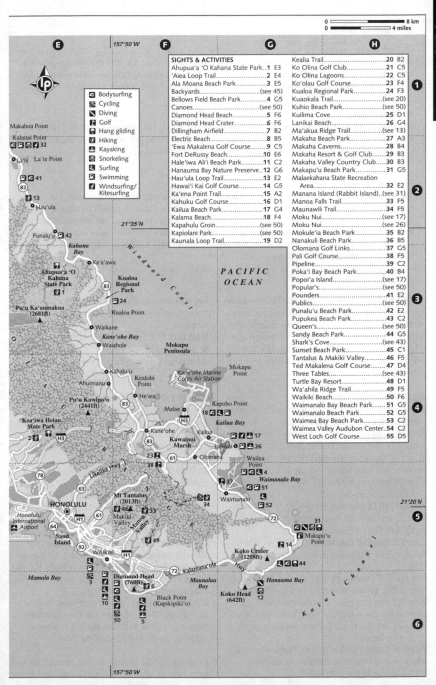

0 ———— 8 km
0 ———— 4 miles

SIGHTS & ACTIVITIES

Ahupua'a 'O Kahana State Park...1	E3
'Aiea Loop Trail...........................2	E4
Ala Moana Beach Park................3	E5
Backyards.............................(see 45)
Bellows Field Beach Park............4	G5
Canoes..............................(see 50)
Diamond Head Beach.................5	F6
Diamond Head Crater.................6	F6
Dillingham Airfield......................7	B2
Electric Beach............................8	B5
'Ewa Makalena Golf Course........9	C5
Fort DeRussy Beach..................10	E6
Hale'iwa Ali'i Beach Park..........11	C2
Hanauma Bay Nature Preserve..12	G6
Hau'ula Loop Trail....................13	E2
Hawai'i Kai Golf Course............14	G5
Ka'ena Point Trail.....................15	A2
Kahuku Golf Course.................16	D1
Kailua Beach Park....................17	G4
Kalama Beach..........................18	F4
Kapahulu Groin...................(see 50)
Kapiolani Park.....................(see 50)
Kaunala Loop Trail..................19	D2

Kealia Trail............................20	B2
Ko Olina Golf Club..................21	C5
Ko Olina Lagoons...................22	C5
Ko'olau Golf Course................23	F4
Kualoa Regional Park...............24	F3
Kuaokala Trail.....................(see 20)
Kuhio Beach Park.................(see 50)
Kuilima Cove..........................25	D1
Lanikai Beach..........................26	G4
Ma'akua Ridge Trail..............(see 13)
Makaha Beach Park.................27	A3
Makaha Caverns......................28	B4
Makaha Resort & Golf Club......29	B3
Makaha Valley Country Club.....30	B3
Makapu'u Beach Park...............31	G5
Malaekahana State Recreation
Area.....................................32	E2
Manana Island (Rabbit Island)..(see 31)
Manoa Falls Trail......................33	F5
Maunawili Trail.......................34	F5
Moku Nui...........................(see 17)
Moku Nui...........................(see 26)
Mokule'ia Beach Park...............35	B2
Nanakuli Beach Park.................36	B5
Olomana Golf Links..................37	F5
Pali Golf Course......................38	F5
Pipeline.................................39	C2
Poka'i Bay Beach Park..............40	B4
Popoi'a Island.....................(see 17)
Popular's...........................(see 50)
Pounders.................................41	E2
Publics...............................(see 50)
Punalu'u Beach Park.................42	E2
Pupukea Beach Park.................43	C2
Queen's............................(see 50)
Sandy Beach Park....................44	G5
Shark's Cove.......................(see 43)
Sunset Beach Park....................45	C1
Tantalus & Makiki Valley............46	F5
Ted Makalena Golf Course.........47	D4
Three Tables.......................(see 43)
Turtle Bay Resort.....................48	D1
Wa'ahila Ridge Trail.................49	F5
Waikiki Beach..........................50	F6
Waimanalo Bay Beach Park........51	G5
Waimanalo Beach Park..............52	G5
Waimea Bay Beach Park............53	C2
Waimea Valley Audubon Center..54	C2
West Loch Golf Course..............55	D5

O'AHU

EXPLORING O'AHU...

In Two Days

Got only a weekend in the sun? Then it's all about you and Waikiki. Explore the various beaches, enjoy the evening music at Kuhio Beach Park (p151) and eat dinner at Ono Hawaiian Food (p148). The next day hike up Diamond Head (p153) and splash out for dinner at Chef Mavro's (p127).

In Four Days

With two extra days, you can go snorkeling at Hanauma Bay (p156) and rent a car to explore the Windward Coast (p159) and the North Shore (p171). Stop off at whatever little beach catches your fancy and be sure to dine at one of the seafood lunch trucks.

For the Foodie

The other islands might excel in the castaway and outdoor-activities department, but O'ahu dominates in food. The all-American diner, such as Rainbow Drive-In (p147), is alive and well here with that special Hawaiian culinary twist. You can down sushi and sake at Imanas Tei (p128), dim sum at Legend Seafood Restaurant (p125), a salmon plate lunch at Diamond Head Market & Grill (p147) and chase it with a coco-puff dessert from Liliha Bakery (p125). If the bikini gets tight, you've conquered the island.

Bike Hawaii (☎ 734-4214, 877-682-7433; www.bike hawaii.com) organizes mountain biking tours of the island; the company founder, John Alford, is the author of several mountain-biking guides to the islands. Barnfield's Raging Isle Surf & Cycle (p179) rents bikes and can provide trail information.

GOLF & TENNIS

O'ahu has several 18-hole municipal golf courses; for general information, visit the City & County website (www.honolulu.gov /des/golf/golf.htm). Green fees for 18 holes at any of these municipal courses are $42 per person. The reservation system is the same for all municipal courses: call ☎ 296-2000.

Municipal courses:

Ala Wai Golf Course (Map pp136-7; ☎ 733-7387; 404 Kapahulu Ave, Honolulu) Popular course on the edge of Waikiki with views of Diamond Head.

'Ewa Villages Golf Course (☎ 681-0220; 91-1760 Park Row, 'Ewa) Challenging course 32 miles west of Honolulu.

Kahuku Golf Course (☎ 293-5842; 56-501 Kamehameha Hwy, Kahuku, Windward Coast) Stunning coastal views that more than make up for the somewhat rough greens at this nine-hole public course. There's no shop or restaurant, but you can rent pull carts and golf clubs. Did we mention the wind?

Pali Golf Course (☎ 266-7612; 45-050 Kamehameha Hwy, Kane'ohe) Picturesque setting on the Windward Coast; a 30-minute drive from Waikiki.

Ted Makalena Golf Course (☎ 671-880; 93-059 Waipio Point Access Rd, Waipahu) Flat course near Pearl Harbor.

West Loch Golf Course (☎ 675-6076; 91-1126 Okupe St, 'Ewa Beach) An 18-hole, par-71 course with ocean views, water features and a challenging layout highlight.

Private courses:

Hawai'i Kai Golf Course (Map p154; ☎ 395-2358; www.hawaiikaigolf.com; 8902 Kalaniana'ole Hwy, Hawai'i Kai; green fees $37-100) Two 18-hole courses: the 2323yd Robert Trent Jones Sr–designed executive course, and a 6614yd championship course. It is 13 miles east of Waikiki.

Ko Olina Golf Club (☎ 676-5300; www.koolinagolf .com; 92-1220 Ali'inui Dr; 18 holes $160) Golf Digest's pick as one of the top 75 resort courses in the USA and former host of the LPGA Tour and senior PGA Tour.

Ko'olau Golf Course (☎ 236-4653; www.koolaugolf club.com; 45-550 Kionaole Rd, Kane'ohe; green fees $80-125) A top-100 US golf course on the Windward Coast.

Makaha Valley Country Club (☎ 695-9578; www .makahavalleycc.com; 84-627 Makaha Valley Rd, Wai'anae; green fees $80) The views to the ocean are worth the fees alone; located on the Wai'anae Coast.

Olomana Golf Links (☎ 259-7926; www.olomana golflinks.com; 41-1801 Kalaniana'ole Hwy, Waimanalo; green fees $80) Two distinctive, challenging nine-hole courses on the Windward Coast of the island.

O'ahu has 182 public tennis courts, as well as courts at several Waikiki hotel and resort facilities. If you're staying in Waikiki, the most convenient locations are **Ala Moana Beach Park** (☎ 592-7031), **Kapi'olani Park Tennis Courts** (☎ 971-2525), and the **Diamond Head Tennis Center** (☎ 971-7150; 3908 Paki Ave) at the Diamond Head end of Kapi'olani Park.

HANG GLIDING & SKYDIVING

Skydiving and glider rides are offered at Dillingham Airfield on the North Shore; for details, see p181.

GETTING THERE & AWAY
Air

The vast majority of flights into Hawaii land at the **Honolulu International Airport** (Map p102; HNL; ☎ 836-6413; 300 Rodgers Blvd, Honolulu; www.honoluluairport .com), which is 6 miles west of downtown Honolulu and 9 miles west of Waikiki. It is the only commercial airport on O'ahu and serves as the hub for the main interisland air carriers with frequent services to all of the Neighbor Islands. For details on interisland and mainland travel, see the Transportation chapter (p568).

At the airport, you'll find **visitor information booths** (☎ 836-6413) near the baggage claim, the international-arrivals area, interisland terminal, and at both ends of the main lobby. There are also car-hire counters for some rental agencies (Alamo, for example, is located offsite). A free shuttle connects several terminals of the airport. It can be picked up in front of the main lobby (on the upper level) and in front of the interisland gates.

Foreign-currency exchange counters are located in strategic sections of the airport; in the international arrivals hall, most operate between 6am to midnight. You can also find ATMs throughout the airport.

For more detailed airport information, visit www.hawaii.gov/dot/airports and navigate to the O'ahu page.

Sea

The new interisland **Hawaii Superferry** (www .hawaiisuperferry.com; fares $50-60) operates daily services between O'ahu and Maui and O'ahu and Kaua'i. For more information on the superferry, see p570. By 2009 additional routes to other Neighbor Islands will be added.

GETTING AROUND

O'ahu is an easy island to get around, whether you travel by public bus, private car, moped or taxi.

To/From the Airport

From the airport you can get to Honolulu and Waikiki by local bus, airport shuttle services, taxi or hire car. For other points on the island, it will be more convenient to rent a car.

You can travel to downtown Honolulu, Ala Moana Center and Waikiki via public bus 19 or 20 from the airport. The fare is $2 and buses run every 30 to 40 minutes from 5am to 11:15pm Monday to Friday, to 11:15pm on weekends. Do note that there are luggage restrictions.

There are also several door-to-door airport shuttles. **Roberts Hawaii** (☎ 954-8652; www .robertshawaii.com) operates a shuttle between any Waikiki hotel and the cruise-ship port. For airport arrivals, proceed to the ground transport median outside baggage claim; buses pick up passengers every 20 minutes. Other shuttle services include **Hawaii Super Transit** (☎ 841-2928) and **Reliable Shuttle** (☎ 924-9292; www.reliableshuttle.com), which can accommodate other drop-off points in Honolulu. Use the courtesy phone in the baggage-claim area to contact the Reliable Shuttle agent for airport pick-up. Fares for airport shuttles cost $10/20 one way/roundtrip; and there are sometimes surcharges for surfboards, baby gear and other baggage.

The ride from the airport to Waikiki averages between 20 and 45 minutes, depending on your destination and traffic. For trips to the airport, you'll need to make advance reservations.

Cab fares to Honolulu or Waikiki from the airport will cost about $30.

If you're driving yourself, the easiest way to Waikiki is via the Nimitz Hwy (92), which turns into Ala Moana Blvd. Although this route hits more local traffic, it's hard to get lost on it; follow the signs 'To Waikiki.' If you're into life in the fast lane, connect instead with the H1 Fwy heading east. On the return trip to the airport from Waikiki, beware of the poorly marked interchange where H1 and Hwy 78 split; if you're not in the right-hand lane at that point, you could easily end up on Hwy 78. It takes about 25 minutes to get from Waikiki to the airport via H1 *if* you don't hit traffic.

Bicycle

It's certainly possible to cycle your way around O'ahu, but cyclists should consider taking the bus to get beyond the greater Honolulu traffic. Most buses are equipped with bicycle racks, which can carry two bicycles, at no extra charge.

The state's **Highways Division** (www.state.hi.us /dot/highways/bike/oahu) publishes a *Bike O'ahu* map with biking trails, including clear road-safety categories.

Bus

O'ahu's public bus system, which is called **TheBus** (www.thebus.org), is extensive and easy to use. The many routes link metropolitan Honolulu with Waikiki, beach parks in Kailua, the surf scene on the North Shore or the snorkeling spot of Hanauma Bay – just to name a few.

Ala Moana Center is Honolulu's central transfer point. Each bus route can have a few different destinations, and buses generally keep the same number whether inbound or outbound. If you're in doubt, ask the bus driver. They're used to disoriented and jet-lagged visitors.

All buses are wheelchair accessible, and all can accommodate two bicycles at no extra charge. Be prepared for the frigid air-conditioning. A bus in Honolulu is probably the coldest place on O'ahu, regardless of the season.

REASONS TO LOVE THEBUS *suzlinda*

■ **How To Explore O'ahu** O'ahu is easy to explore with an impressive network of buses (unimaginatively named 'TheBus') taking you to the doorstep of every big-name attraction or right off the beaten path. The cost is $2 per ride, no change provided, so come prepared.

■ **What You Get for $2** Even if the driver does not offer, when you pay for your ride be sure to ask for a transfer, which can be used for a return trip or another leg on another bus for anywhere from two hours (by company policy) to six-plus, depending upon the generosity of the driver.

■ **What You Get for $20** For anyone who plans to ride TheBus extensively for just a few days there is an Explorer Pass that provides unlimited rides for the four consecutive days of your choosing and is available for $20 at any of the prolific ABC stores in Waikiki.

■ **What You Get for $40** The best bargain is on the month-long pass which, for the cost of one day's car rental, provides unlimited rides in a calendar month. They can be purchased throughout the month for $40 and are obviously a much better deal earlier in the month.

■ **Why You Should Just Pay for a Pass** Having a pass is the best way to truly explore the island (by bus) as it offers the freedom to jump off at unplanned stops without continually paying another $2 to get back on. This being said, it is important to note a few features of TheBus.

■ **Your Personal Driver** Hands-down the best resource for exactly which stop is closest to where you want to go, what restaurant is best, and what the locals are doing, TheBus drivers are almost always friendly and always helpful.

■ **Island Time – Try Wait** It's not a myth, and if you can relax and go with the flow, TheBus is for you. While they publish schedules, when riding TheBus it's good to not be in a hurry. In fact, it's best if you have a destination in mind, but no particular time frame.

■ **If You Do Have A Time Frame...** Be at the bus stop about 10 minutes before the bus is scheduled to arrive, and be willing to wait 20 minutes past the time it's scheduled to arrive. Oahu traffic is notoriously dodgy – be glad you aren't having to deal with it.

■ **Locals Love to 'Talk Story'** It's usually not too difficult to get a local to strike up a conversation on TheBus, but be ready to spend some time listening as most are eager to share knowledge of their beautiful home with you. Just remember to sit back and enjoy the journey.

(blu,list) v. to recommend a travel experience. www.lonelyplanet.com/bluelist

BLUELIST.

FARES
The one-way fare for all rides is $2 for adults, $1 for children aged six to 18 and for seniors 65 years and older; children under the age of six ride free. You can use either coins or $1 bills; bus drivers don't give change. One free transfer per paid ride is available.

Visitor passes ($20) are valid for unlimited rides within a consecutive four-day period and can be purchased at any of the ubiquitous ABC stores in Waikiki and Ala Moana Center. Monthly bus passes ($40), valid for unlimited rides in a calendar month, can be purchased at **TheBus Pass Office** (Map p102; ☎ 848-4444; 811 Middle St, Honolulu; ☿ 7:30am-4pm Mon-Fri), satellite city halls, Foodland, Star and Times supermarkets.

SCHEDULES & INFORMATION
Bus schedules vary depending on the route; many operate from about 5:30am to 8pm daily, though some main routes, such as Waikiki, continue until around midnight. Buses run reasonably close to scheduled times, although waiting for the bus that isn't full anywhere between Ala Moana and Waikiki on a Saturday night can be a particularly memorable experience.

TheBus has a great **route information service** (☎ 848-5555; ☿ 5:30am-10pm). As long as you know where you are and where you want to go, the staff will tell you not only which bus to catch, but also when the next one will arrive. This same service also has a TDD service for the hearing impaired.

Routes and timetables are available on the website or you can get printed timetables for individual routes free from any satellite city hall, including the one at the Ala Moana Center.

Car
Directions on O'ahu are given using the Hawaii-wide terms *mauka* (toward the mountains) and *makai* (toward the ocean).

The following car-hire agencies have service desks or shuttle pick-up from the airport baggage claim area. For toll-free reservations numbers and websites, see p571.
Alamo (☎ 833-4585)
Avis (☎ 834-5536)
Budget (☎ 537-3600)
Enterprise (☎ 836-2213)
Dollar (☎ 834-5536)
Hertz (☎ 831-3500)
National (☎ 826-6890)

DRIVING DISTANCES & TIMES

Although actual times may vary depending upon traffic conditions, the average driving times and distances from Waikiki to points of interest around O'ahu are as follows:

Destination	Miles	Time
Hale'iwa	29	50min
Hanauma Bay	11	25min
Honolulu Airport	9	20min
Ka'ena Point State Park	43	1¼hr
Kailua	14	25min
La'ie	34	1hr
Makaha Beach	36	1hr
Mililani	15	30min
Nu'uanu Pali Lookout	11	20min
Sea Life Park	16	35min
Sunset Beach	37	65min
USS *Arizona* Memorial	12	30min
Waimea	34	1hr

HONOLULU

pop 362,000
In the pecking order of US cities, Honolulu gets no respect, being relegated to a piece of TV trivia from the days of polyester. But Hawaii's biggest city is an undercover gem. Step off the plane into the jumble of utilitarian towers and you're meeting Asia with an American passport. If the mainland erased the ethnic differences of Europeans into one collective mass of Caucasians, Honolulu has done the same with its Asian immigrants creating its own hybrid family tree, shorthand language, deferential culture and a heaping dose of Hawaiian hospitality.

The fringes of Honolulu – from rainbow-striped mountains to sparkling seas – make for better scenery than the overlapping urban grid, but cruise into the congested arteries to meet a foodie capital where every resident knows a little shop that dishes up the best of a handful of local inventions and foreign imports. This is a home-cooking city that puts the moms and pops to work in little storefront restaurants where the menu is written on a whiteboard and the tables are wiped down with a rag. It has also imported the Asian tradition of food courts, a modern adaptation of the old-fashioned market,

O'AHU

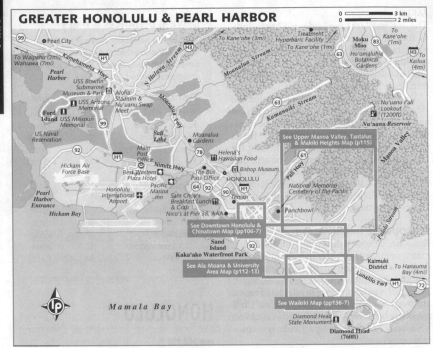

GREATER HONOLULU & PEARL HARBOR

where dining options are paramount to a good time.

Leagues ahead of its potential rivals, Honolulu doesn't have to compete for the fickle prize of hippest, fastest-paced or up-and-coming city. It easily mixes urban living with country manners, where a lane change elicits a friendly *shaka* (hand greeting) as thanks, and where comfortable aloha shirts are acceptable business attire.

Honolulu offers a range of attractions and activities. It boasts a lovely city beach, some excellent museums, elegant public gardens and an abundance of good restaurants.

HISTORY

The fall of O'ahu to Kamehameha the Great in 1795 signaled the beginning of a united Hawaiian kingdom. The new king moved to Honolulu in 1809 to control the vigorous international trade taking place in the harbor.

In the 1820s Honolulu's first bars and brothels opened up to crews of whaling ships; Christian missionaries began arriving about the same time, presumably for different purposes. Sugar plantations, established in the 1830s, soon became Hawaii's major industry.

Contract workers from Asia, North America and Europe were brought in to fill the labor shortage, marking a surge in immigration exemplified by today's ethnic diversity.

Honolulu replaced Maui as capital of the Kingdom of Hawai'i in 1845. Increasingly, Western expatriates dominated Hawaiian affairs. In 1893 a small group of these new Hawaiian citizens seized control of Hawai'i from Queen Lili'uokalani and declared it their own 'republic;' in 1898 Hawaii was formally annexed by the USA as its newest territory (see p39).

Honolulu continued to grow as a commercial center. In 1901 electric streetcars were introduced. The next decades saw a revival of Hawaiian culture as the sounds of falsetto voices and steel guitars filled the airwaves of territorial radio.

Following the Japanese attack on Pearl Harbor in 1941 Honolulu became the site of a harsh cultural, political and economic clampdown on the resident Japanese American population by military leaders. The 1950s closed with a plebiscite on statehood in which 90% of islanders voted 'yes.'

O'AHU

Modern air travel and increased prosperity on the mainland provided Honolulu with a thriving tourism industry that replaced the declining shipping industry. Today Honolulu is a modern metropolis that dominates the government and cultural life of the state.

ORIENTATION

Honolulu sprawls along the South Shore of the island without bothering to delineate clear boundaries. Still, the city proper is generally considered to extend west to the airport and east to Kaimuki.

Two major thoroughfares run the length of the city: Ala Moana Blvd (Hwy 92) skirts the coast from the airport to Waikiki, and the H1 runs between Ala Moana Blvd and the mountains. H1 connects to all other freeways on the island. Interestingly enough, it's a US interstate freeway – no small achievement for an island in the middle of the Pacific. In between are several grids bisected by one-way streets overlapping at irregular angles, making navigation within central Honolulu difficult.

King and Beretania Sts are the primary conduits into downtown Honolulu, which contains O'ahu's state and federal government buildings, including the state capitol and 'Iolani Palace.

Chinatown is immediately north of downtown Honolulu, roughly bounded by Honolulu Harbor, Bethel St, Vineyard Blvd and River St. The Aloha Tower and cruise-ship terminals sit on the oceanside *(makai)* of Chinatown.

Kapi'olani Blvd and University Ave are the main thoroughfares connecting the Ala Moana area and the University of Hawai'i, situated in beautiful Manoa Valley beneath the southern Ko'olau range.

Southeast of downtown Honolulu, Waikiki is the tourist epicenter. Just southeast of Waikiki, is Diamond Head, the city's most striking geological landmark. All of Waikiki is within the boundaries of greater Honolulu, but is covered in a separate section later in this chapter.

INFORMATION
Bookstores
Bestsellers (Map pp106-7; ☎ 528-2378; 1001 Bishop St; ☷ 10am-5:30pm Mon-Fri, 9am-3pm Sat) Good selection of travel guides, novels and maps.
Borders Books & Music (Map p112; ☎ 591-8995; 1200 Ala Moana Blvd, Ward Center; ☷ 9am-10pm) Extensive news and travel sections.

Native Books/Na Mea Hawaii (Map p112; ☎ 596-8885; www.nativebookshawaii.com; Ward Warehouse, cnr Ala Moana Blvd & Ward Ave; ☷ 10am-9pm Mon-Sat, 10am-5pm Sun) Specializes in Hawaiiana titles and gifts. Also holds cultural performances and classes.
Rainbow Books & Records (Map p112; ☎ 955-7994; www.rainbowbookshawaii.com; 1010 University Ave; ☷ 10am-10pm Sun-Thu, 10am-11pm Fri & Sat) Carries new and used books, CDs and records.
UH Manoa Campus Bookstore (Map p112; ☎ 956-8022; Campus Center, 2465 Campus Rd; ☷ 8:15am-4:45pm Mon-Fri, 8:15am-11:45am Sat) Carries Hawaiian studies titles and school paraphernalia.

Emergency
Police (☎ 529-3111) For nonemergencies.
Police, Fire & Ambulance (☎ 911) For all emergencies.
Suicide & Crisis Line (☎ 832-3100) Operates 24 hours.

Internet Access
Coffee Talk (☎ 737-7444; 3601 Wai'alae Ave, Kaimuki; per hr $5; ☷ 5am-11pm Sun-Thu, 5am-midnight Fri & Sat) Free wi-fi and computer terminals.
Net Stop Coffee (Map p112; ☎ 955-1020; 2615 S King St; per hr $5; ☷ 9am-midnight) A casual cybercafé near the university with wi-fi and terminals.
Qi Café (Map p112; ☎ 699-5624; 1750 Kalakaua Ave; ☷ 7am-7pm) Café with free wi-fi across from the convention center.

Libraries
Hawaii State Library (Map pp106-7; ☎ 586-3500; 478 S King St, cnr Punchbowl; ☷ 10am-5pm Mon & Wed, 9am-5pm Tue, Thu, Fri & Sat) The main branch of the state system; there are 23 neighborhood and district library branches.

Media
NEWSPAPERS & MAGAZINES
There are a half dozen free magazines listing events, visitor information and business coupons available in Waikiki. The following are geared toward the local community.
Honolulu Advertiser (www.honoluluadvertiser.com) One of Honolulu's two main daily newspapers.
Honolulu Star-Bulletin (www.starbulletin.com) The other main daily.
Honolulu Weekly (www.honoluluweekly.com) Free weekly papers covering progressive politics and in-the-know entertainment.

RADIO & TV
The following radio and TV stations broadcast local news, music and programs.
KHPR (88.1FM) Hawaii Public Radio.
KHET (Channel 11) Hawaii Public TV.

O'AHU

KIPO (89.3FM) Hawaii Public Radio.

KTUH (90.3FM) Broadcasting from the University of Hawai'i.

KIKU (Channel 20) Multicultural TV programming.

KINE (105.1FM) Classic and contemporary Hawaiian music.

Medical Services

Hyperbaric Treatment Center (Map p102; ☎ 587-3425; 347 N Kuakini St) Divers with the bends are taken here.

Queen's Medical Center (Map pp106-7; ☎ 538-9011; 1301 Punchbowl St) One of O'ahu's several hospitals with 24-hour emergency services.

Straub Clinic & Hospital (Map p112; ☎ 522-4000; 888 S King St, cnr Ward Ave) Offers 24hr emergency services as well as neighborhood clinics across the island.

Money

The following banks have branches and ATMs conveniently located throughout the island.

Bank of Hawaii (☎ 888-643-3888; https://www.boh .com)

First Hawaiian Bank (☎ 844-4444; www.fhb.com)

Post

The telephone number for all post offices is ☎ 800-275-8777.

Ala Moana post office (Map p112; Ala Moana Center, 1450 Ala Moana Blvd) On the inland side on the ground floor.

Downtown post office (Map pp106-7; 335 Merchant St, cnr Richards St) In the old Federal Building.

Main post office (Map p102; Honolulu International Airport, 3600 Aolele St, Honolulu, HI 96820; ☉ 7:30am-3pm Mon-Fri) If you're expecting to receive mail by general delivery (poste restante), it is only accepted at this location and then held for 30 days.

Mo'ili'ili post office (Map p112; 2700 S King St) A block east of University Ave.

Uptown post office (Map pp106-7; 1170 Nu'uanu Ave) Near Chinatown.

Tourist Information

Hawaii Visitors and Convention Bureau (☎ 800-464-2924; www.gohawaii.com/oahu) There is a physical office located in Waikiki (Map p136–7).

O'ahu Visitors Bureau (☎ 523-3802, 877-525-6248; www.visit-oahu.com) An excellent website.

SIGHTS

So you've only come for the beaches, but you'll find that Honolulu is an easy city to explore with sections of neoclassical architecture, an intriguing history and a mix of ethnic communities. The largest concentration of historical and cultural sights are clustered in downtown and adjacent Chinatown, both of which are well-suited for getting around on foot. Because most people stay in Waikiki, directions are given for transport from there.

Downtown

'IOLANI PALACE

No other place evokes a more poignant sense of Hawaiian history than the **'Iolani Palace** (Map pp106-7; ☎ 522-0822; docent-led tours adult/child 5-12 $20/5, audio tours $12/5; ☉ hours vary depending on the tour), a historic house museum where royalty feasted and plots and counterplots simmered.

'Iolani was the residence of King Kalakaua and Queen Kapi'olani from 1882 to 1891, and of Queen Lili'uokalani for two years after that. At this time, much of the Hawaiian monarchy observed the diplomatic protocols of the Victorian world. The king traveled abroad meeting with leaders around the globe and received many foreign emissaries in 'Iolani Palace. Although the palace was modern and opulent for its time, it did little to assert Hawaii's sovereignty over more powerful US business interests, who used force to overthrow the Hawaiian kingdom in 1893.

Two years after the coup, the once Queen Lili'uokalani was convicted of treason and spent nine months as a prisoner in her former home. The palace also served as the capitol of the republic, then the territory and later the state of Hawaii. In 1969 the government moved into the current state capitol, leaving 'Iolani Palace a shambles. a lengthy multimillion dollar reconstruction project restored the palace to its former glory and it reopened as a museum in 1978, although many of the original royal artifacts had been lost or stolen over time.

On the 1st floor are re-creations of the palace's reception rooms, including a grand hallway, dining room and throne hall. The red-and-gold **throne room** features the original thrones of the king and queen and was the site of celebrations that were full of pomp and pageantry. On the 2nd floor are the residential quarters, including the room in which the queen was imprisoned and the confessional quilt that she made during this period.

The interior of the palace can only be seen on a guided tour (9am to 11:15am, every

20 minutes) or on a self-guided audio tour (11:45am to 3pm, every 10 minutes). Children under five years are welcome to explore the basement-level galleries, but not the 1st and 2nd floors of the palace. Sometimes you can join a tour on the spot, but it's advisable to call ahead for reservations; to protect the floors visitors must wear hospital-style booties.

The palace grounds, which are free and open to the public during daylight hours, predate the palace. A simpler house on these grounds was used by King Kamehameha III, who ruled from 1825 to 1854, and in ancient times a Hawaiian temple stood here. The former Royal Household Guards **barracks** is now the palace ticket window. The domed **pavilion**, originally built for the coronation of King Kalakaua in 1883, is still used for the inauguration of governors, and every Friday afternoon concerts are performed here by the Royal Hawaiian Band.

King Kamehameha II and Queen Kamamalu lay buried in the grassy mound surrounded by a wrought-iron fence until 1865, when their remains were moved to the Royal Mausoleum in Nu'uanu. The huge **banyan tree** between the palace and the state capitol is thought to have been planted by Queen Kapi'olani.

QUEEN LILI'UOKALANI STATUE

Symbolically positioned between the palace and the state capitol is the bronze **statue** (Map pp106–7) of Hawaii's last queen. Lili'uokalani holds the Hawaii constitution, which she wrote in 1893 (fear of which caused US businessmen to depose her); *Aloha Oe*, a popular hymn she composed; and *Kumulipo*, the Hawaiian chant of creation.

STATE CAPITOL

Built in the 1960s, Hawaii's **state capitol** (Map pp106-7; ☎ 586-6400; 415 S Beretania St) is not your standard gold dome. It's a poster-child of conceptual post-modernism: the two cone-shaped legislative chambers represent volcanoes; the supporting columns symbolize palm trees. Trade winds blow gently through an open rotunda, and a large pool representing the ocean surrounding Hawaii encircles the entire structure. Visitors are free to walk through the rotunda and past the legislative chambers.

In front of the capitol stands a statue of **Father Damien**, the Belgian priest who in 1873 volunteered to work among leprosy victims on Moloka'i (see p449). The stylized sculpture was created by Venezuelan artist Marisol Escobar. Directly opposite on S Beretania St, an **eternal torch** memorializes soldiers who died in WWII.

WASHINGTON PLACE

The former governor's official residence, **Washington Place** (Map pp106-7; ☎ 586-0248; admission by donation; 🕑 by appointment Mon-Fri) is now a historic house museum intended to open up cultural legacies to the Hawaiian people. The large colonial-style building, surrounded by stately trees, was erected in 1846 by US sea captain John Dominis. The captain's son, also named John, became the governor of O'ahu and married the Hawaiian princess who later became Queen Lili'uokalani. After the queen was dethroned and released from house arrest, she lived at Washington Place until her death in 1917. A plaque near the sidewalk on the left side of Washington Place is inscribed with the words to *Aloha Oe*.

HAWAI'I STATE ART MUSEUM

A long-overdue addition to Honolulu's museum scene, **Hawai'i State Art Museum** (Map pp106-7; ☎ 586-0900; www.hawaii.gov/sfca; 2nd fl, Capitol District Bldg, 250 S Hotel St; admission free; 🕑 10am-4pm Tue-Sat) showcases the best of traditional and contemporary art from Hawaii's diverse ethnic artistic community. A variety of artistic styles are on display, from fine art and sculpture to contemporary photography and mixed-media. Revolving exhibits reveal how a blending of Western, Asian and traditional Pacific folk-art forms have shaped a unique island aesthetic.

The downtown museum is easy to spot: it's a Spanish Mission–style gem that dates from 1928 when it was home to the Army & Navy YMCA.

ST ANDREW'S CATHEDRAL

The French Gothic **St Andrew's Cathedral** (Map pp106-7; ☎ 524-2822; cnr Alakea & S Beretania Sts; 🕑 tours 11am Sun) was King Kamehameha IV's personal homage to the architecture and faith of the Church of England. Following the tradition of the church's English founder, the Hawaiian king and his consort, Queen Emma, founded the Anglican Church of Hawaii in 1858. King Kamehameha V had the cornerstone laid in 1867 four years after the death of Kamehameha IV on St Andrew's Day – hence the name.

O'AHU

DOWNTOWN HONOLULU & CHINATOWN

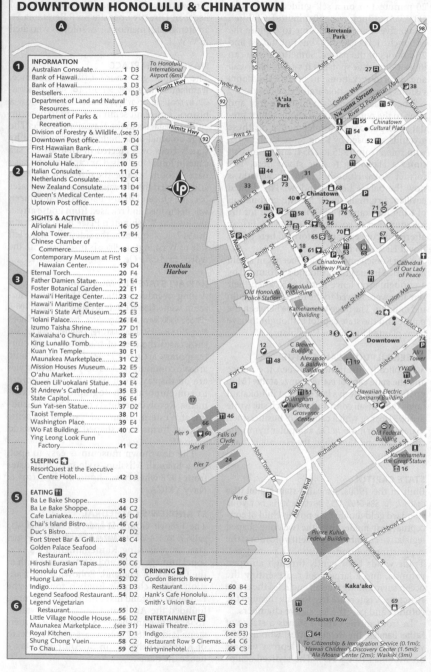

❶ INFORMATION
Australian Consulate................1 D3
Bank of Hawaii.........................2 C2
Bank of Hawaii.........................3 D3
Bestsellers...............................4 D3
Department of Land and Natural
  Resources...............................5 F5
Department of Parks &
  Recreation..............................6 F5
Division of Forestry & Wildlife..(see 5)
Downtown Post office............7 D4
First Hawaiian Bank................8 C3
Hawaii State Library................9 E5
Honolulu Hale.......................10 E5
❷ Italian Consulate...................11 C4
Netherlands Consulate...........12 C4
New Zealand Consulate..........13 D4
Queen's Medical Center........14 F4
Uptown Post office.................15 D2

SIGHTS & ACTIVITIES
Ali'iolani Hale.......................16 D5
Aloha Tower..........................17 B4
Chinese Chamber of
  Commerce.............................18 C3
Contemporary Museum at First
  Hawaiian Center...................19 D4
❸ Eternal Torch........................20 F4
Father Damien Statue.............21 E4
Foster Botanical Garden.........22 E1
Hawai'i Heritage Center..........23 C2
Hawai'i Maritime Center.........24 C5
Hawai'i State Art Museum.......25 E3
'Iolani Palace........................26 E4
Izumo Taisha Shrine...............27 D1
Kawaiaha'o Church.................28 E5
King Lunalilo Tomb.................29 E5
Kuan Yin Temple....................30 E1
Maunakea Marketplace...........31 C2
Mission Houses Museum.........32 E5
O'ahu Market.........................33 C2
Queen Lili'uokalani Statue......34 E4
St Andrew's Cathedral............35 E3
State Capitol..........................36 E4
Sun Yat-sen Statue.................37 D2
Taoist Temple........................38 D1
Washington Place...................39 E4
Wo Fat Building......................40 C2
Ying Leong Look Funn
  Factory..................................41 C2

SLEEPING ❑
ResortQuest at the Executive
  Centre Hotel.........................42 D3

❺ EATING ❑
Ba Le Bake Shoppe...............43 D3
Ba Le Bake Shoppe...............44 C2
Cafe Laniakea........................45 C2
Chai's Island Bistro................46 C4
Duc's Bistro...........................47 D2
Fort Street Bar & Grill............48 C4
Golden Palace Seafood
  Restaurant.............................49 C2
Hiroshi Eurasian Tapas...........50 C6
Honolulu Café........................51 C4
Huong Lan..............................52 D2
Indigo....................................53 D3
Legend Seafood Restaurant....54 D2
Legend Vegetarian
  Restaurant.............................55 D2
❻ Little Village Noodle House....56 D2
Maunakea Marketplace.......(see 31)
Royal Kitchen........................57 D1
Shung Chong Yuein...............58 C2
To Chau.................................59 C2

DRINKING ❑
Gordon Biersch Brewery
  Restaurant.............................60 B4
Hank's Cafe Honolulu...........61 C3
Smith's Union Bar..................62 C2

ENTERTAINMENT ❑
Hawaii Theatre......................63 D3
Indigo...............................(see 53)
Restaurant Row 9 Cinemas....64 C6
thirtyninehotel.......................65 C3

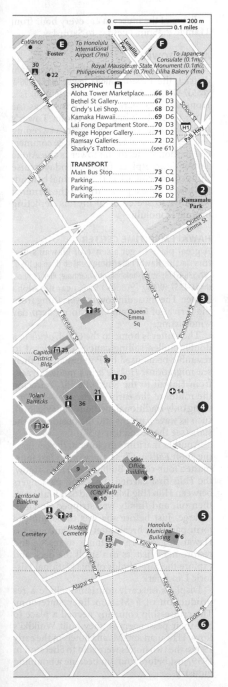

The construction of stone and glass was shipped from England. The impressive window of hand-blown stained glass forms the western facade reaching from the floor to the eaves. In the right-hand section of the stained glass the Reverend Thomas Staley, the first bishop sent to Hawaii by Queen Victoria, stands with Kamehameha IV and Queen Emma.

Historic tours are typically scheduled after the 10am service, but call ahead to confirm.

ALI'IOLANI HALE

The first major government building constructed by the Hawaiian monarchy in 1874, **Ali'iolani Hale** (Map pp106–7; House of Heavenly Kings) now houses the Hawaii Supreme Court and the state legislature. It was originally designed by Australian architect Thomas Rowe to be a royal palace, although it was never used as such. It was on the steps of Ali'iolani Hale, in January 1893, that Sanford Dole proclaimed the provisional government and the overthrow of the Hawaiian monarchy.

A **statue** of Kamehameha the Great, cast in Florence in the 1880s, stands in front of Ali'iolani Hale. Each year on June 11, the state holiday honoring the king, the statue is ceremoniously draped with colorful layers of 12ft lei.

KAWAIAHA'O CHURCH

O'ahu's oldest church, **Kawaiaha'o Church** (Map pp106-7; ☎ 522-1333; cnr Punchbowl & S King Sts; admission free; ☷ 8am-4pm Mon-Fri) was built on the site where the first missionaries built a grass-thatch church shortly after their arrival in 1820. The original structure seated 300 people on *lauhala* mats, woven from *hala* (pandanus) leaves.

This New England Gothic–style Congregational church, completed in 1842, is constructed of 14,000 coral slabs, each weighing about 1000lb, which Hawaiian divers chiseled out of Honolulu's underwater reef – a task that took four years. The clock tower was donated by Kamehameha III, and the old clock, installed in 1850, still keeps accurate time. The rear seats of the church, marked by *kahili* (feather staffs) and velvet padding were for royalty and are still reserved for their descendants.

The **tomb of King Lunalilo**, the successor to Kamehameha V, is at the main entrance.

Lunalilo ruled for only one year before his death in 1874 at the age of 39. The **cemetery** at the rear of the church is a bit like a who's who of colonial history. Early missionaries are buried alongside other notables of the day, including the infamous Sanford Dole, who became the first territorial governor of Hawaii after the overthrow of Queen Lili'uokalani.

HONOLULU HALE

City Hall, also known as **Honolulu Hale** (Map pp106-7; ☎ 523-2489; 530 S King St), was designed and built in 1927 as a Spanish mission by CW Dickey, Honolulu's then famous architect. Now on the National Register of Historic Places, it has a tiled roof, decorative balconies, arches and pillars, some ornate frescoes, and an open-air courtyard sometimes used for concerts and art exhibits. On the front lawn, an **eternal-flame memorial** honors the victims of the September 11 terrorist attacks on the US mainland.

MISSION HOUSES MUSEUM

Containing three of the original buildings of the Sandwich Islands Mission headquarters, the **Mission Houses Museum** (Map pp106-7; ☎ 531-0481; 553 S King St; 1hr guided tours adult/child 6-18 $10/6; ⊙ 10am-4pm Tue-Sat) is authentically furnished with handmade quilts on the beds, settees in the parlor and iron cooking pots in the stone fireplaces.

The first missionaries packed more than their bags when they left Boston; they actually brought a prefabricated wooden house, now called the **Frame House**, around the Horn with them! Designed to withstand cold New England winter winds, the small windows instead block out Honolulu's cooling trade winds, keeping the two-story house hot and stuffy. Erected in 1821, it's the oldest wooden structure in Hawaii.

The coral-block **Chamberlain House** was the early mission storeroom, a necessity as Honolulu had few shops in those days. Upstairs are hoop barrels, wooden crates packed with dishes, and the desk and quill pen of Levi Chamberlain. He was appointed by the mission to buy, store and dole out supplies to the missionary families, who survived on a meager allowance – as the account books on his desk testify.

The **Printing Office** housed a lead-type press used to print the Bible in Hawaiian.

Tours of the museum are every hour from 11am to 2:45pm Tuesday to Saturday.

ALOHA TOWER

Built in 1926 at the edge of the downtown district, the 10-story **Aloha Tower** (Map pp106-7; ☎ 537-9260; Pier 9; admission free; ⊙ 9am-5pm) is a Honolulu landmark that for years was the city's tallest building. The Aloha Tower's top-floor observation deck offers a sweeping 360-degree view of Honolulu's large commercial harbor. Beneath the tower is the Aloha Tower Marketplace (p131). Today cruise ships still disembark at the terminal beneath the tower. Take a peek through the terminal windows to see colorful murals depicting bygone Honolulu.

HAWAI'I MARITIME CENTER

A great place to get a sense of Hawaii's history is the **Hawai'i Maritime Center** (Map pp106-7; ☎ 536-6373; http://holoholo.org/maritime; Pier 7; adult/child 6-17 $7.50/4.50; ⊙ 8:30am-5pm), near the Aloha Tower. The museum covers everything from the arrival of Captain Cook to modern-day windsurfing.

The center is home to the 60ft *Hokule'a*, a double-hulled sailing canoe constructed to resemble boats used by Polynesians in their sea migrations. *Hokule'a* has made voyages from Hawaii to the South Pacific, retracing the routes of the early Polynesian seafarers, using only traditional methods of navigation, such as wave patterns and the position of the stars (see the boxed text, p32).

Another maritime explorer at the center is the 266ft *Falls of Clyde*, the world's last four-masted four-rigger. Built in 1878 in Glasgow, the *Falls* first carried sugar and passengers between Hilo (Big Island) and San Francisco, then oil, and finally was stripped down to a barge. Just before she was to be sunk to form part of a breakwater off Vancouver, a Hawaiian group raised funds to rescue and restore her. Visitors can stroll the deck and explore the cargo holds of this National Historic Landmark.

Displays on early tourism include a reproduction of a Matson liner stateroom. The cruise-ship company needed a place to bed their passengers so they built Waikiki's Royal Hawaiian and Moana hotels in the early 1900s; the two hotels were sold to Sheraton in 1959, just before tourism became a booming industry.

O'AHU

CONTEMPORARY MUSEUM AT FIRST HAWAIIAN CENTER

The downtown gallery of the **Contemporary Museum** (Map pp106-7; ☎ 526-1322; www.tcmhi.org; 999 Bishop St; admission free; ☺ 8:30am-4pm Mon-Thu, 8:30am-6pm Fri) fills the briefcase district with modern art. Changing exhibits feature renowned international and local artists. The building includes a four-story-high glass wall with 185 prisms designed by famed New York glass artist Jamie Carpenter. The headquarters of the museum is in a charming residential house in Makiki Valley; see p114.

HAWAII CHILDREN'S DISCOVERY CENTER

If the beach somehow fails to stimulate your children, get them some hands-on-learning at the **Hawaii Children's Discovery Center** (☎ 524-5437; www.discoverycenterhawaii.org; 111 Ohe St; adult/child 2-17 $8/6.75; ☺ 9am-1pm Tue-Fri, 10am-3pm Sat & Sun). Occupying a 37,000-sq-ft waterfront site, once the city's old incinerator, its origins are evidenced by the surviving smokestack reaching skyward from the building's center.

Although older kids may find some exhibits interesting, the museum is principally geared toward elementary school–aged children. The museum has five main sections extending over three stories. The **Tot Spot** includes toys and games for toddlers. **Fantastic You!** explores the human body, allowing kids to walk through a mock stomach. More traditional displays are found in the **Your Town** section, where kids can drive an interactive fire engine, be bank tellers or TV interviewers. The other two sections, **Hawaiian Rainbows** and **Your Rainbow World**, relate specifically to Hawaii, and allow children to navigate a ship and swim with dolphins.

You can get here from Waikiki via bus 19 or 20; it's a five-minute walk from the nearest bus stop on Ala Moana Blvd to the museum, and just opposite Kaka'ako Waterfront Park.

KAKA'AKO WATERFRONT PARK

South of downtown Honolulu and just off Ala Moana Blvd at the end of Cooke St, little Kaka'ako Waterfront Park (Map p102) is protected from much of the city noise by a small grassy rise. Roller bladers cruise along the rock-fringed promenade, which offers clear views of Diamond Head, Waikiki and Honolulu Harbor. The 28-acre park attracts experienced surfers in the morning and picnickers in the afternoon. It's not a safe swimming beach, but the tricky surf break is near

the shore, making Kaka'ako a great place to watch surfers and boogie boarders up close. Facilities include a modern pavilion, picnic tables, showers, rest rooms and free parking.

ROYAL MAUSOLEUM STATE MONUMENT

Housing the remains of Kings Kamehameha II, III, IV and V, as well as King David Kalakaua and Queen Lili'uokalani (Hawaii's last reigning monarchs), is the **Royal Mausoleum** (☎ 587-0300; 2261 Nu'uanu Ave; admission free; ☺ 8am-4:30pm Mon-Fri). Conspicuously absent are the remains of Kamehameha the Great, the last king to be buried in secret in accordance with Hawaii's old religion. Built in 1864, the original mausoleum is now a chapel; the caskets are in nearby crypts. Other gravestones honor Kamehameha I's British confidant John Young and American Charles Reed Bishop, husband of Princess Bernice Pauahi Bishop.

The Royal Mausoleum is on Nu'uanu Ave, just before it meets the Pali Hwy. You can get there by taking Nu'uanu Dowsett bus 4 from Waikiki. Guided tours are available by reservation.

Chinatown

The location of this long-running mercantile district is no accident. Between the port and what was once the countryside, enterprising Chinese planted utilitarian businesses selling farm products, nuts and bolts and daily services to the city folks, as well as visiting ship crews. Many of the early businesses were established in the 1860s by Chinese laborers who had completed their sugarcane plantation contracts or by the descendents of the initial wave of immigrants.

In December 1899 bubonic plague broke out in the area. The 7000 Chinese, Hawaiians

---

FLOWER POWER

Chinatown herbalists are both physicians and pharmacists, with walls small wooden drawers, each filled with a different herb. They'll size you up, feel your pulse and listen to you describe your ailments before deciding which drawers to open, mixing herbs and flowers and wrapping them for you to take home and boil together. The object is to balance yin and yang forces. You can find herbalists at the Chinatown Cultural Plaza, and along N King and Maunakea Sts.

and Japanese who made the crowded neighborhood their home were cordoned off and forbidden to leave. When more plague cases arose, the all-powerful Board of Health ordered the Honolulu Fire Department to burn the wooden buildings on the *mauka* side of Beretania St, between Nu'uanu Ave and Smith St, on January 20, 1900. But the wind suddenly picked up and the fire spread out of control, racing toward the waterfront. Nearly 40 acres of Chinatown burned to the ground, leaving 4000 residents homeless. Despite the adverse setting, the Chinese held their own and rebuilt a new Chinatown.

Success, not fire, would ultimately drive the original Chinese families out of the neighborhood. Some of the most influential Chinese families on the island date back five generations and now own prime real estate and influential business empires. They've also moved out of the low-rent district of Chinatown to wealthier suburbs, leaving behind the petri dish for the next wave of immigrants: Vietnamese, Laotians and Filipinos.

A visit to Chinatown is basically an eating tour, but there are several sights worth exploring after your meal. See the Walking Tour (p121) for a suggested route through the district.

KEKAULIKE ST
The commercial heart of Chinatown revolves around the markets and food shops on Kekaulike St. Noodle factories, pastry shops and produce stalls line the street crowded with hobbling grandmothers and errand-running families. The **O'ahu Market** (Map pp106-7; cnr Kekaulike & N King Sts; ☺ 7am-5pm) sells everything a Chinese cook needs: ginger root, fresh octopus, quail eggs, slabs of tuna, jasmine rice, long beans and salted jellyfish. The market has been an institution since 1904. In 1984 the tenants organized and purchased the market themselves to save it from falling into the hands of developers. You owe yourself a bubble tea if you spot a pig's head in the market.

Just up the street is **Ying Leong Look Funn Factory** (Map pp106-7; ☎ 537-4304; 1028 Kekaulike St; ☺ 9am-5pm), one of half-a-dozen family-run noodle factories in the neighborhood. Catch this shop in the early morning and a dusting of flour will cover every surface.

At the foot of the pedestrian lane is **Maunakea Marketplace** (Map pp106-7; 1120 Maunakea St; ☺ 7am-5pm), which is a precursor to today's megastores (see also p125). Food supplies, prepared meals and even some Chinatown souvenirs get sold all under one roof.

HAWAI'I HERITAGE CENTER
Local volunteers with family ties to the community run this friendly **gallery** (Map pp106-7; ☎ 521-2749; 1117 Smith St; ☺ 9am-2pm, Mon-Sat) that covers changing exhibitions of O'ahu's Chinese and other ethnic communities. The center also hosts a historic walking tour of Chinatown (see p122).

FOSTER BOTANICAL GARDEN
O'ahu's natural heritage is exotic and beautiful. Plants you've only ever read about can be spotted in all their lush greenery at the **Foster Botanical Garden** (Map pp106-7; ☎ 522-7066; 180 N Vineyard Blvd; adult/child 6-12 $5/1; ☺ 9am-4pm), O'ahu's main botanical garden. In 1850 German botanist William Hillebrand purchased 5 acres of land from Queen Kalama and planted the trees now towering in its center. In 1867 Captain Thomas Foster bought the property, continuing to plant the grounds. In the 1930s the garden became the property of Honolulu.

An impressive 14-acre collection of tropical flora, the garden is laid out according to plant groups: palms, plumeria and poisonous plants. The **economic garden** has nutmeg, allspice and cinnamon, as well as a black pepper vine that climbs 50ft up a gold tree, a vanilla vine, and other herbs and spices that have commercial value. The **herb garden** was the site of the first Japanese-language school in O'ahu and where many Japanese immigrants sent their children to learn Japanese, hoping to maintain their cultural identity and the possibility of some day returning to Japan. During the bombing of Pearl Harbor a stray artillery shell exploded in a room full of students. A memorial marks the site. At the other end of the park, the **wild orchid garden** makes a good place for close-up photography.

Among the garden's many extraordinary plants is a tree so rare it has no common name – the East African *Gigasiphon macrosiphon*. It is thought to be extinct in the wild. The native Hawaiian *loulu* palm, taken long ago from O'ahu's upper Nu'uanu Valley, may also be extinct in the wild. The garden's chicle, New Zealand kauri tree and Egyptian doum palm are all reputed to be the largest of their kind in the USA. Oddities include the cannonball tree, the sausage tree and the double coconut palm capable of producing a 50lb nut.

All of the trees are labeled, and a free self-guided tour booklet is available at the entrance. Included in the admission price is an hour-long tour, starting at 1pm Monday through Saturday.

KUAN YIN TEMPLE
Near the entrance of Foster Botanical Garden, the **Kuan Yin Temple** (Map pp106-7; ☎ 533-6361; 170 N Vineyard Blvd; ☺ daylight hours) is a bright-red Buddhist temple with a green ceramic-tile roof. The ornate interior is richly carved and filled with the sweet, pervasive smell of burning incense.

The temple is dedicated to Kuan Yin Bodhisattva, Goddess of Mercy, whose statue is the largest in the prayer hall. Devotees burn paper 'money' for prosperity and good luck. Offerings of fresh flowers and fruit are placed at the altar. The large citrus fruit that is stacked pyramid-style is the pomelo, considered a symbol of fertility because of its many seeds.

Honolulu's multiethnic Buddhist community worships at the temple, and respectful visitors are welcome.

TAOIST TEMPLE
Founded in 1889, the Lum Sai Ho Tong Society was one of more than 100 societies started by Chinese immigrants in Hawaii to help preserve their cultural identity. This one was for the Lum clan, which hails from an area west of the Yellow River. At one time the society had more than 4000 members, and even now there are nearly a thousand Lums in the Honolulu phone book.

The society's **Taoist temple** (Map pp106-7; cnr River & Kukui Sts) honors the goddess Tin Hau, a Lum child who rescued her father from drowning and was later deified. Many Chinese claim to see her apparition when they travel by boat. The temple is not usually open to the general public, but you can admire the building from the outside.

IZUMO TAISHA SHRINE
Across the river from the Taoist temple, this Shinto **shrine** (Map pp106-7; ☎ 538-7778, 522-7060; 215 N Kukui St; ☺ 9am-4pm) was built by Japanese immigrants in 1923. During WWII the property was confiscated by the city of Honolulu and wasn't returned to its congregation until 1962. Incidentally, the 100lb sacks of rice that sit near the altar symbolize good health, while ringing the bell at the shrine entrance is considered an act of purification for those who come to pray. School children from Japan journey to this shrine each year as a gesture of peace.

Ala Moana & University Area
Ala Moana means 'Path to the Sea.' It is also the name of the area west of Waikiki, which includes Honolulu's largest beach park and the state's largest shopping center.

ALA MOANA BEACH PARK
One of the most photogenic parks in the country, Ala Moana Beach Park (Map p112) stretches out alongside the ocean claiming nearly a mile-long golden beach buffered by statuesque shade trees with downtown Honolulu's skyscrapers forming a mini-mountain range in the distance. Honolulu residents go jogging here, play volleyball and enjoy weekend picnics. It has full beach facilities, several softball fields, tennis courts and free parking.

Ala Moana is safe for swimming and a good spot for distance laps. However, at low tide the deep channel running the length of the beach can be a hazard to poor swimmers who don't realize it's there. A former boat channel, it drops off suddenly to over head depth. If you measure laps, it's 500m between the lifeguard tower at the Waikiki end and the white post in the water midway between the third and fourth lifeguard towers.

The 43-acre peninsula jutting from the east side of the park, the Aina Moana State Recreation Area, more commonly known as **Magic Island**, is where high-school outrigger-canoe teams often practice in the late afternoon during the school year. In summer this is also a hot surf spot. There's a nice walk around the perimeter of Magic Island, and picturesque sunsets, with sailboats pulling in and out of the adjoining Ala Wai Yacht Harbor.

If you're taking the bus from Waikiki, buses 8, 19 and 20 stop on Ala Moana Blvd opposite the beach park.

HONOLULU ACADEMY OF ARTS
An exceptional, and exceptionally broad, **museum** (Map p112; ☎ 532-8700; www.honoluluacademy.org; 900 S Beretania St; adult/child 12-18 $7/4; ☺ 10am-4:30pm Tue-Sat, 1-5pm Sun) covers the artistic traditions of almost every continent, with a leading role in the area of Pacific Rim art.

O'AHU

ALA MOANA & UNIVERSITY AREA

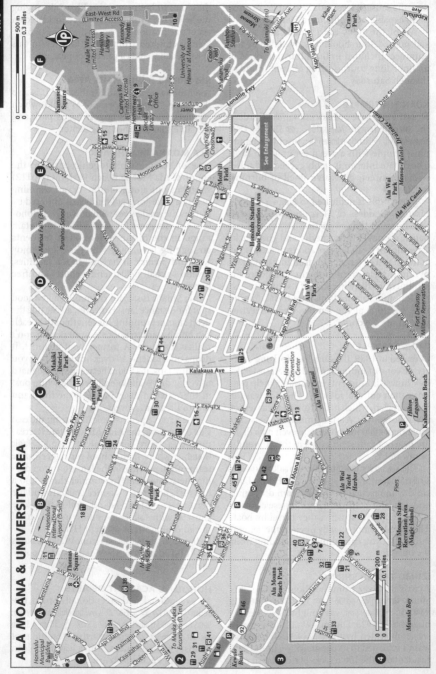

The splendid Asian gallery is considered one of the finest Asian art collections in the USA, and it gives almost equal weight to both Japanese and Chinese works, ranging from scenes of Kyoto, painted by the renowned Japanese artist Kano Motohide, to the extensive Ming dynasty collection. The latter includes pivotal works by Shen Zhou, credited with establishing a composition technique that significantly influenced Ming painting styles. The museum's collection has been bolstered by the acquisition of the Richard Lane Collection, a leading Japanese art scholar with a focus on woodblock printed books.

The Henry R Luce Pavilion, a 10,000-sq-ft contemporary section, contains Hawaiian artifacts and paintings on the upper level.

A gallery of European art of the 19th and 20th centuries exhibits paintings by Henri Matisse, Paul Cezanne, Claude Monet, Paul Gauguin, Vincent van Gogh and Camille Pissarro. The museum also contains works of 16th- to 18th-century European artists Pieter de Hotch, Sir Thomas Lawrence and Carlo Bonavia, and a number of Madonna-and-child oils from 14th-century Italy.

Pacific art collections include ceremonial carvings, war clubs and masks from Papua New Guinea, and body ornaments and navigational stick charts from Micronesia. The museum owns some fine eclectic pieces,

sculptures and miniature figurines from India, and fertility figures and ceremonial carvings from Africa.

The museum also conducts **tours** (☎ 532-3853; ⏲ 8:30am, 11am, 1:30pm Wed-Sat) to Shangri La, Doris Duke's estate near Diamond Head. The tobacco heiress was an avid Islamic-art collector and her secluded home incorporates elements of Islamic design as well as religiously significant works. Tours ($25) depart from the museum and are not recommended for children under 12; reservations are advised.

Bus 2 from Waikiki stops out front. In addition to metered parking, there is a museum parking lot between S Beretania and S King Sts.

UNIVERSITY OF HAWAI'I AT MANOA

Born too late to take advantage of the tweedy academic architecture of the mainland, **University of Hawai'i at Manoa** (UH; Map p112; ☎ 956-8111; cnr University Ave & Dole St), the central campus of the statewide university system, is a modern complex filled with shade trees and well-bronzed students.

UH has strong programs in astronomy, second-language studies, geophysics, marine sciences, and Hawaiian and Pacific studies. The campus attracts students from islands throughout the Pacific. Staff at the **Ticket Information & ID Center** (Map p112; ☎ 956-7236; Room 212,

Campus Center) provide campus maps and can answer general questions about the university. Free one-hour **walking tours** of the campus, emphasizing history and architecture, leave from the Campus Center at 2pm on Monday, Wednesday and Friday; to join a tour, simply arrive 10 minutes early. A self-guided *Campus Art* brochure, available at the information center, provides a walking tour of outdoor sculptures and other works by distinguished Hawaiian artists.

At the east side of campus is the **East-West Center** (Map p112; ☎ 944-7111; Burns Hall, East-West Rd), an internationally recognized education and research organization established by the US Congress in 1960 to promote mutual understanding among the peoples of Asia, the Pacific and the USA. Professional and student researchers work and study at the center, examining development policy, the environment and other Pacific issues. Changing exhibitions of Asian art and culture are displayed in the East-West Center's **gallery** (☎ 944-7177; admission free; ⏰ 8am-5pm Mon-Fri, noon-4pm Sun). The center often has other multicultural programs open to the public, including seminars, concert and dance performances.

Ka Leo O Hawaii, the free student newspaper, lists lectures, music performances and other campus happenings. Pick it up at university libraries and other places around campus.

Bus 4 runs between the university and Waikiki; bus 6 travels between the university and Ala Moana.

Upper Manoa Valley, Tantalus & Makiki Heights

Just 2 miles from downtown Honolulu, a narrow switchback road cuts its way up the lush green forest reserve land of Tantalus and Makiki Valley (Map p115). The road climbs up almost to the top of 2013ft Mt Tantalus, with swank mountainside homes tucked in along the way. The 8.5-mile circuit is Honolulu's finest scenic drive, offering splendid views of the city below.

Among the profusion of dense tropical growth, bamboo, ginger, elephant-ear taro and fragrant eucalyptus trees are easily identified. Vines climb to the top of telephone poles and twist their way across the wires. Branching off of the main road are trails that wind through the verdant forest. For hiking information, see p118.

The Makiki Heights area below the forest reserve is one of the most exclusive residential areas in Honolulu. There's a bus service as far as Makiki Heights, but none around the Tantalus-Round Top loop road.

CONTEMPORARY MUSEUM

Occupying an estate with 3.5 acres of tropical and meditative gardens, the **Contemporary Museum** (Map p115; ☎ 526-0232; www.tcmhi.org; 2411 Makiki Heights Dr; adult/child over 12 $5/3; ⏰ 10am-4pm Tue-Sat, noon-4pm Sun) is an engaging modern-art museum, with views of Honolulu below. Admission is free every third Thursday of the month.

The estate house was constructed in 1925 for Mrs Charles Montague Cooke, whose other former home is the present site of the Honolulu Academy of Arts (p111). A patron of the arts, she played a founding role in both museums.

The main galleries feature changing exhibits of paintings, sculpture and other contemporary artwork by local, national and international artists. A newer building on the lawn holds the museum's most prized piece, a vibrant environmental installation by David Hockney based on sets for *L'Enfant et les Sortilèges*, Ravel's 1925 opera.

Docent-led tours, conducted at 1:30pm, are included in the admission price. An excellent courtyard café serves lunch.

The museum, near the intersection of Mott-Smith and Makiki Heights Drs, can be reached by bus 15 from downtown Honolulu.

PU'U 'UALAKA'A STATE PARK

For a marvelous panoramic view over Honolulu, visit **Pu'u 'Ualaka'a State Park** (Map p115; ⏰ 7am-6:45pm). The park entrance is 2.5 miles up Round Top Dr from Makiki St. It's half a mile in to the lookout; bear to the left when the road forks.

The sweeping view extends from Kahala and Diamond Head on the far left, across Waikiki and downtown Honolulu, to the Wai'anae Range on the right. To the southeast is the University of Hawai'i at Manoa, easily recognized by its sports stadium; to the southwest you can see clearly into the green mound of Punchbowl crater; the airport is visible on the coast, with Pearl Harbor beyond that.

If you're taking photos, the best time is during the day; however, this is also a fine place to watch the evening settle over the city.

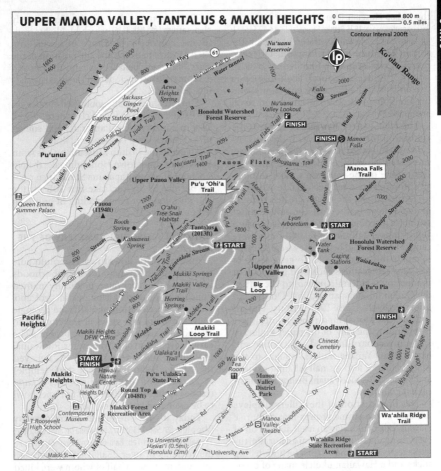

UPPER MANOA VALLEY, TANTALUS & MAKIKI HEIGHTS

Arrive half an hour before dusk to see the hills before they're in shadow.

LYON ARBORETUM

Nature trails wind through this highly regarded **arboretum** (Map p115; ☎ 988-0456; wwwdev .hawaii.edu/lyonarboretum; 3860 Manoa Rd; admission by donation; ☼ 9am-4pm Mon-Fri), founded in 1918 and managed by the University of Hawai'i.

Dr Harold Lyon is credited with introducing 10,000 exotic trees and plants to Hawaii. Approximately half of these are represented in this 193-acre arboretum. This is not a landscaped tropical flower garden, but a mature and largely wooded arboretum where related species are clustered in a seminatural state.

Among the plants in the Hawaiian ethno-botanical garden are mountain apple, bread-fruit and taro; *ko*, the sugarcane brought by early Polynesian settlers; *kukui*, which was used to produce lantern oil; and *ti*, which was used for medicinal purposes during ancient times and for making moonshine after Westerners arrived.

To reach the arboretum by car take Manoa Rd to its end. Catch bus 5 to Manoa Valley and get off at the last stop; it is then a 0.6 mile walk.

Greater Honolulu
BISHOP MUSEUM
Considered the finest Polynesian cultural- and natural-history museum in the world,

the **Bishop Museum** (Map p102; ☎ 847-3511; www
.bishopmuseum.org; 1525 Bernice St; adult/child 4-12 $15/12;
☺ 9am-5pm) is Hawaii's version of the Smith-
sonian Institute in Washington, DC. The
museum was originally founded in 1889 in
honor of Princess Bernice Pauahi Bishop, a
descendant of the Kamehameha family, and
originally housed only Hawaiian and royal
artifacts.

The main gallery, **Hawaiian Hall**, covers the
cultural history of Hawaii with displays including a full-sized *pili*-grass thatched house,
carved temple images and shark-toothed war
clubs. One of the museum's most impressive holdings is a feather cloak once worn
by Kamehameha the Great, created entirely
of the yellow feathers of the now-extinct
mamo, a predominately black bird with a
yellow upper tail. Some 80,000 birds were
caught and plucked before they were released
to create this single cloak. To get a sense of
just how few feathers each bird had, look at
the nearby taxidermic *mamo*, to the left of
the Queen Lili'uokalani exhibit. On the 2nd
floor, artifacts from 19th-century Hawaii
include traditional *tapa* robes (cloth made
by pounding the bark of the paper mulberry
tree), missionary-inspired quilt work and
barter items Yankee traders brought to the
islands; there's also a small whaling exhibit,
and Princess Bernice Pauahi Bishop's whimsical hat collection.

The final section of the gallery displays
artifacts of the ethnic groups that comprise
Hawaii today. Like Hawaii itself, it has a bit of
everything, including samurai armor, Portuguese festival costumes, Taoist fortune-telling
sticks and a Hawaiian ukulele made of coconut shells. An impressive 55ft sperm whale
skeleton hangs from the ceiling, opposite a
koa-tree royal racing canoe. The Hawaiian
Hall will reopen in the spring of 2008 after
an extensive renovation.

The **Kahili Room**, a small gallery off the main
hall, features portraits of Hawaiian royalty and
a display of *kahili*, the feathered staffs used at
coronations and royal funerals. A **Polynesian
Hall** covers the cousin cultures of Polynesia,
Micronesia and Melanesia.

The new **Science Adventure Center** uses interactive exhibits to explain Hawaii's unique
natural environment from volcanoes, ocean
behavior and biodiversity.

The museum's modern wing, the **Castle
Building**, has changing traveling exhibitions.

The museum is also home to O'ahu's only
planetarium (☎ 848-4136), which highlights traditional Polynesian methods of navigation,
such as wave patterns and the position of the
stars. Shows are held at 11:30am, 1:30pm and
3:30pm, and are included in the museum admission price.

The gift shop off the lobby sells books on
the Pacific not easily found elsewhere, as well
as some quality Hawaiian crafts and souvenirs. A snack shop is open until 4pm.

To get to the Bishop Museum by bus from
Waikiki or downtown Honolulu, take the No
2 School St bus to Kapalama St and turn right
on Bernice St. By car, take exit 20B off the
H1, go inland on Houghtailing St and turn
left on Bernice St.

NATIONAL MEMORIAL CEMETERY OF THE PACIFIC

A mile north of downtown Honolulu surrounded by freeways and neighborhoods
is a bowl-shaped crater poetically named
Punchbowl, formed by a long-extinct volcano.
Sitting at an elevation of 500ft, the geologic
souvenir offers fine views of the city, out to
Diamond Head and the Pacific beyond. The
early Hawaiians called the crater Puowaina,
the 'hill of human sacrifices.' It's believed
there was a heiau (an ancient stone temple)
at the crater and that the slain bodies of *kapu*
(taboo) breakers were brought to Punchbowl
to be cremated upon the altar.

Today it's the site of a 114-acre **cemetery**
(Map p102; ☎ 566-1430; 2177 Puowaina Dr; admission free;
☺ 8am-5:30pm Oct-Feb, 8am-6:30pm Mar-Sep), where
the remains of over 25,000 US soldiers are
interred, more than half of whom were killed
in the Pacific during WWII.

The remains of Ernie Pyle, the distinguished
war correspondent who covered both world
wars and was hit by machine gun fire on Ie
Shima during the final days of WWII, lie in
section D, grave 109. Five stones to the left, at
grave D-1, is the marker for astronaut Ellison
Onizuka, the Big Island native who perished
in the 1986 *Challenger* space-shuttle disaster.
Their resting places are marked with the same
style of flat granite stone that marks each of
the cemetery's graves.

A huge marble court **memorial** at the rear of
the cemetery is inscribed with the names of
the 26,289 Americans missing in action from
WWII and the Korean War. An adjacent court
displays the names of another 2489 soldiers

missing from the Vietnam War. For a good view of the city, walk to the **lookout**, 10 minutes' south of the memorial.

If you're driving to Punchbowl, take the H1 to the Pali Hwy. There's a marked exit as you start up the Pali Hwy; watch closely, because it comes up quickly! From there, follow signs through a series of narrow streets up to the cemetery.

Alternatively take bus 2 from Waikiki to downtown Honolulu and get off at Beretania and Alapai Sts, where you transfer to bus 15. Ask the driver where to get off; from there it's about a 15-minute walk to Punchbowl.

QUEEN EMMA SUMMER PALACE

The **summer palace** (Map p115; ☎ 595-6291; www .daughtersofhawaii.com; 2913 Pali Hwy; adult/child $6/1; ☼ 9am-4pm) of Queen Emma, consort of Kamehameha IV, is open to the public as an historic house museum.

Emma was three-quarters royal Hawaiian and a quarter English. She was a granddaughter of the captured British sailor John Young, who became a friend and adviser to Kamehameha I. The house is also known as Hanaiakamalama, the name of John Young's home in Kawaihae on the Big Island, where he served as governor.

The Youngs left the luxurious home to Queen Emma, who often slipped away from her more formal downtown home to spend time at this retreat – a bit like an old Southern plantation house – columned porch, high ceilings and louvered windows catching the cool breeze.

Forgotten following Emma's death in 1885, the home was to be razed in 1915, because the estate was being turned into a public park. The Daughters of Hawaii, whose members are descendants of early missionaries, rescued it and now operate it as a museum.

The interior looks much as it did in Queen Emma's day – decorated with period furniture collected from five of her homes, including a koa cabinet displaying a set of china from Queen Victoria; Emma's tiger-claw necklace, a gift from a maharaja of India; and feather cloaks and capes once worn by Hawaiian royalty.

To get here, take bus 4 (Nu'uanu Dowsett Ave) from Waikiki, or bus 55, 56 or 57 from the Ala Moana Center. Be sure to let the bus driver know where you're going, so you don't miss the stop. If driving, the palace is at the 2-mile marker of the Pali Hwy (Hwy 61).

Pali Highway (Hwy 61): Honolulu to Kailua

Slicing into the lush core of O'ahu, this scenic highway is the perfect vantage point to adore the emerald glow of Ko'olau Range. If it has been raining heavily every fold and crevice in the mountains will have a lacy waterfall streaming down its face, like open wounds of liquid silver. Past the 4-mile marker, look up and to the right to see two notches cut about 15ft deep into the crest of the *pali* (cliff). These notches are thought to have been dug as cannon emplacements by Kamehameha I.

The highway's official purpose is to link Honolulu and Kailua (p160), on the Windward Coast. The original route was via an ancient footpath that wound its way perilously over these cliffs. In 1845 the path was widened into a horse trail and, later again, into a cobblestone road that would allow carriage traffic to pass. The **Old Pali Hwy** was built along the same route in 1898. It was abandoned in the 1950s after tunnels were blasted through the Ko'olau Range for the present multilane highway.

You can still drive a loop of the Old Pali Hwy, which is now called **Nu'uanu Pali Dr** and begins half a mile past the Queen Emma Summer Palace. The drive is through a cathedral of trees all draped with hanging vines and philodendrons. The lush vegetation along Nu'uanu Pali Dr includes banyan trees with hanging aerial roots, tropical almond trees, bamboo groves, impatiens, angel trumpets and golden cup – a tall climbing vine with large golden flowers.

This detour returns you to the Pali Hwy just in time to exit to the **Nu'uanu Pali Lookout** (Map p102) with its broad view of the Windward Coast from a height of 1200ft. From the windy lookout you can see Kane'ohe straight ahead, Kailua to the right, and Mokoli'i Island (Chinaman's Hat) and the coastal fishpond ('Apu'u Fishpond) at Kualoa Regional Park beyond Kane'ohe.

Another section of the abandoned Old Pali Hwy winds down from the right of the lookout, ending abruptly at a barrier near the current highway about a mile away. Few people realize the road is here, let alone venture down it. It makes a nice walk and takes about 20 minutes one way. There are good views looking back up at the jagged Ko'olau Range and out across the valley.

As you get back on the highway, it's easy to miss the sign leading you out of the parking

O'AHU

THE BATTLE OF NU'UANU

O'ahu was the final island conquered by Kamehameha the Great in his campaign to unite Hawaii under his rule. On the quiet beaches of Waikiki he landed his fleet of canoes to battle Kalanikupule, the new king of O'ahu.

Heavy fighting started around the Punchbowl, and continued up Nu'uanu Valley. But O'ahu's spear-and-stone warriors were no match for Kamehameha's troops, including a handful of Western sharpshooters. The defenders made their last stand at the narrow ledge along the current-day Nu'uanu Pali Lookout. Hundreds were driven over the top to their deaths. A hundred years later, during the construction of the Old Pali Hwy, more than 500 skulls were found at the base of the cliffs.

Some O'ahu warriors, including their king, escaped into the upland forests. But when Kalanikupule surfaced a few months later, he was sacrificed by Kamehameha to the war god, Ku. Kamehameha's taking of O'ahu marked the last battle ever fought between Hawaiian troops.

---

lot, and instinct could send you in the wrong direction. As you drive out of the parking lot, go to the left if you're heading toward Kailua, to the right if heading toward Honolulu.

ACTIVITIES

Many first-time visitors to Honolulu are surprised by the city's boundaries; there don't seem to be any! But head inland, and within a few miles you wind up in lush green valleys, accompanied by passing showers and rainbows. Excellent hiking trails cover the area.

Hiking

You can spend days enjoying the solitude of the hills surrounding the city. The **Hawaii Nature Center** (Map p115; ☎ 955-0100; www.hawaiinaturecenter .org) conducts family programs and hikes on most weekends; see their website for a schedule of events. Further up the road, the state **Division of Forestry & Wildlife** (Map p115; ☎ 973-9778; www .hawaiitrails.org; 2135 Makiki Heights Dr; ☒ 7:45am-4:30pm Mon-Fri) distributes free trail maps, including the Honolulu Mauka Trail System maps covering the Tantalus-Makiki. There's also a drinking fountain, next to a soda vending machine, good for filling empty water bottles.

UPPER MANOA VALLEY

Crowning the university area is the Upper Manoa Valley (Map p115), where a forest reserve protects the emerald hills. Manoa Rd runs into the valley through the well-to-do residential neighborhood of Woodlawn before reaching the trailhead to Manoa Falls and the Lyon Arboretum (p114).

Manoa Falls Trail is a beautiful and easy hike climaxing at a silver-threaded waterfall. The trail runs above a rocky streambed and through lush vegetation, moss-covered stones and tree trunks, seemingly miles from any of Honolulu's concrete. The only sounds come from chirping birds and the rushing stream and waterfall. All sorts of trees line the path, including tall *Eucalyptus robusta*, with their soft, spongy, reddish bark; flowering orange African tulip trees; and other lofty varieties that creak like wooden doors in old houses. Many of them were planted by the Lyon Arboretum, which at one time held a lease on the property.

Wild purple orchids and red ginger grow near the falls, adding a colorful element to the tranquil scene. The falls are steep, dropping about 100ft into a small shallow pool. Occasional falling rocks make swimming inadvisable and the local health department warns against swimming in the water for fear of leptospirosis (see p574).

The hike runs three-quarters of a mile and takes about 30 minutes one way with a 400ft gain in elevation. The trail can be a bit muddy and slippery.

Just before reaching Manoa Falls, **'Aihualama Trail** branches off, providing a broad view of the Manoa Valley, just a short way up the path. After about a five-minute walk, you'll enter a bamboo forest with some massive old banyan trees. When the wind blows, the forest releases eerie crackling sounds. It's an engaging forest – enchanted or spooky, depending on your mood. You can hike the muddy trail as a 15- to 20-minute side spur from the Manoa Falls trail or orchestrate a much longer hike by connecting with **Pauoa Flats**, which leads to **Pu'u 'Ohi'a Trail** and **Nu'uanu Valley Lookout** (see below).

To reach the trailhead by car from Waikiki, take McCully St heading into Honolulu to

Wilder Ave and turn right on Punahou St. Take the left fork (Manoa Rd) when the road splits in two. Follow this road to the parking lot ($5). By bus, take No 5 to Manoa; the bus stop is an easy walk to the trailhead.

TANTALUS & MAKIKI VALLEY
This green belt (Map p115) cinching central Honolulu transports hikers deep into a sylvan embrace. Within view of the urban core, bird song fills the air, and lilikoi fruit are produced in such abundance that many litter the forest floor. A network of hiking trails runs throughout the forest reserve and are rarely crowded, despite their accessibility. Perhaps because the drive itself is so nice, the only walking most people do is between their car and the scenic lookouts.

Makiki Forest
One of the most popular routes through this reserve is the **Makiki Loop Trail**, a popular 2.5-mile hike that starts at the Maunalaha Trail linking the Makiki Valley Trail and Kanealole Trail. The loop cuts through a lush and varied tropical forest, mainly of nonnative species introduced to reforest an area denuded by the sandalwood trade in the 19th century.

The Maunalaha Trail crosses a bridge, passes taro patches and climbs up the eastern ridge of Makiki Valley, passing Norfolk pine, bamboo and fragrant allspice and eucalyptus trees, with some clear views along the way. After three-quarters of a mile, you'll come to a four-way junction, where you'll take the left fork and continue on the **Makiki Valley Trail**. The trail goes through small gulches and across gentle streams bordered by patches of ginger. Near the Moleka Stream crossing,

there are mountain apple trees (related to allspice and guava) that flower in the spring and bear fruit in the summer. Edible yellow guava and strawberry guava also grow along the trail, which offers great glimpses of the city below. The **Kanealole Trail** begins as you cross Kanealole Stream and then follows the stream back to the baseyard, three-quarters of a mile away. The trail leads down through a field of Job's tears; the beadlike bracts of the female flowers of this tall grass are often used for lei. Kanealole Trail is usually muddy, so wear shoes with good traction and pick up a walking stick.

From the same trailhead, you can do a 6-mile trek that leads to sweeping views of the valley and the ocean beyond. Known as the **Big Loop** (approximately 7 miles), start on Maunalaha Trail, then take Moleka to Manoa Cliff, Kalawahine and Nahuina Trails. Reconnect with Kanealole Trail to return you to the starting point.

The starting point for these hikes is at the Makiki Forest baseyard, which is about half a mile up Makiki Heights Dr if approaching from Makiki St. The turn-off is a little lane at a sharp bend in the main road. There's a parking lot nearby and offices for the Hawaii Nature Center and a branch of the Division of Forestry & Wildlife (see opposite).

You can also reach the baseyard by taking bus 15, which runs between downtown and Pacific Heights. Get off near the intersection of Mott-Smith and Makiki Heights Drs and walk one mile along Makiki Heights Dr to the baseyard.

Pu'u 'Ohi'a (Mt Tantalus) Trail
The Pu'u 'Ohi'a Trail, in conjunction with the Pauoa Flats Trail, leads up to a lookout with a view of the Nu'uanu reservoir and valley. It's less than 2 miles one way, but makes a hardy hike. The trailhead is at the very top of Tantalus Dr, 3.6 miles up from its intersection with Makiki Heights Dr. There's a large turnoff opposite the trailhead where you can park.

Pu'u 'Ohi'a Trail begins with reinforced log steps, and leads past ginger, lush bamboo groves and lots of eucalyptus, a fast-growing tree planted to protect the watershed. About a half-mile up, the trail reaches the top of 2013ft **Mt Tantalus** (Pu'u 'Ohi'a).

From below Mt Tantalus, the trail leads to a service road and a telephone relay station. To the right of the building, the trail continues

---

JEWELS OF THE FOREST

O'ahu has an endemic genus of tree snail, the *Achatinella*. The forests were once loaded with these colorful snails, which clung like gems to the leaves of trees. They were too attractive for their own good, however, and hikers collected them by the handfuls around the turn of the 20th century. Even more devastating has been the deforestation of habitat and the introduction of a cannibal snail and predatory rodents. Of 41 *Achatinella* species, only 19 remain today and all are endangered.

until it reaches the **Manoa Cliff Trail** where you'll go left. Walk on for a short distance until you come to another intersection, where you'll turn right onto the **Pauoa Flats Trail**. This trail leads down into Pauoa Flats and on to the lookout, where you'll see the Pali Hwy below and the green Ko'olau mountain range. The flats area can be muddy; be careful not to trip on exposed tree roots. Retrace your steps to return to the trailhead parking lot, approximately 2.75 miles away.

You can extend this hike to link with **Manoa Falls** (p118), but you'll need a shuttle car at the falls parking lot as public transport doesn't serve the Pu'u 'Ohi'a trailhead. You'll pass two trailheads before reaching the lookout. The first is Nu'uanu Trail, on the left, which runs three-quarters of a mile along the western side of Upper Pauoa Valley, and offers views of Honolulu and the Wai'anae Range. The second is **'Aihualama Trail**, a bit further along on the right, which takes you 1.3 miles through tranquil bamboo groves and past huge old banyan trees to Manoa Falls.

WA'AHILA RIDGE TRAIL

Sitting above Diamond Head and the Kahala area, the **Wa'ahila Ridge Trail** (Map p115) offers a cool retreat amid Norfolk pines, native plants, and ridge views to Waikiki, Manoa Valley and adjacent Palolo Valley. The 4.8-mile trail covers a variety of terrain in a short time, making for an enjoyable afternoon stroll. The trail begins at the back of St Louis Heights subdivision, east of Manoa Valley.

Take bus 14 to Peter Pl, and walk about 15 minutes to the trailhead.

WAIMANO TRAIL

The trailhead for another popular hike begins above Pearl City (Map p102) and ends at a spectacular *pali* lookout atop the Ko'olau Range. The challenging Waimano Trail covers 7 miles in each direction, and it's a stretch to do it in one day. A better approach is to set up at the campground about 2 miles in, hike to the *pali* lookout the next morning, and back to the trailhead in the afternoon. You'll go boulder-hopping, ridge-scaling and stream-crossing through a relatively untouched native Hawaiian forest, all in pursuit of the *pali* views at the summit.

You'll want to pick up a trail map from the Division of Forestry & Wildlife (p118). To reach the trailhead, take the H1 freeway to Moanalua Rd (exit 10), then to Waimano Home Rd. Park at the end of the road on a dirt pull-out.

KEA'IWA HEIAU STATE PARK

This 334-acre **park** (Map pp90-1; ☎ 483-2511; Aiea Heights Dr; admission free; ☼ 7am-dusk) is known for a sacred heiau and moderate hiking trail. Camping is also available.

At the park entrance is **Kea'iwa Heiau**, a 100ft-by-160ft, single-terraced, stone temple built in the 1600s and used by *kahuna lapaau* (herbalist healers). The kahuna used hundreds of medicinal plants and grew many on the grounds surrounding the heiau. Among those still found here are *noni* (Indian mulberry), whose pungent yellow fruits were used to treat heart disease; *kukui*, the nuts of which were an effective laxative; breadfruit, the sap of which soothed chapped skin; and *ti* leaves, which were wrapped around a sick person to break a fever.

Not only did the herbs have medicinal value, but the temple itself was considered to possess life-giving energy. The kahuna was able to draw from the powers of both. Today, people wishing to be healed visit the heiau, leaving offerings that reflect the multiplicity of Hawaii's cultures: rosary beads, New Age crystals and sake cups sit beside flower lei and rocks wrapped in *ti* leaves.

The 4.5-mile **'Aiea Loop Trail** begins at the top of the park's paved loop road next to the rest rooms and comes back out at the campground, about a third of a mile below the start of the trail. This easy-to-moderate trail starts off in a forest of eucalyptus trees and runs along the ridge, passing Norfolk Island pines, ironwood, edible guava and native *ohia lehua*, which has feathery red flowers.

There are sweeping urban vistas of Pearl Harbor, Diamond Head and the Ko'olau Range. About two-thirds of the way in, the wreckage of a C-47 cargo plane that crashed in 1943 can be spotted through the foliage on the east ridge.

The park **campsites** are well maintained but because many are open, there's not a lot of privacy. If you're camping in winter, make sure your gear is waterproof, as it rains frequently at this 880ft elevation. The park has rest rooms, showers and drinking water. There's a resident caretaker by the front gate, and the gate is locked at night for security. Camping is not permitted on Wednesday and Thursday, and permits (p92) must be obtained in advance.

The park is 3 miles northeast of Pearl Harbor. Head west on Moanalua Hwy (78) and take the Stadium/Aiea turnoff onto Moanalua Rd. Turn right onto Aiea Heights Dr at the second traffic light. The road winds up through a residential area 2.5 miles to the park.

WALKING TOUR

Honolulu's most walkable and engaging neighborhood is Chinatown, a district filled with markets, restaurants and home-grown shops only found in Hawaii.

A good place to start is **Chinatown Gateway Plaza (1)**, where stone lions mark the official entrance. Turn left onto Nu'uanu Ave, where the granite-block sidewalks were built with

---

WALK FACTS

Start Chinatown Gateway Plaza
Finish Chinatown Gateway Plaza
Distance 1.2 miles
Duration two hours

---

the discarded ballasts of trade ships that brought tea from China in the 19th century in exchange for sandalwood, to the corner of N King St, and peek into the **First Hawaiian Bank (2)**, where the retro architecture includes wooden teller cages with bars.

Turn right on N King St, then after a block turn right on Smith St. Poke your head into the **Hawai'i Heritage Center (3**; p110). Continue along Smith to N Hotel St, which is being revitalized from a red-light district to a hot club scene. Turn left on N Hotel St, and go one block to Maunakea St, forming a photogenic corner shot of Chinese-style architecture. The **Wo Fat (4)** building on the corner is Chinatown's signature building and was twice rebuilt after the fires of 1886 and 1900. Walk down Maunakea St, stopping at **Shung Chong Yuein cake shop (5**; p125) on your left. Here you can buy *jung*, a mixture of sticky rice and shredded pork wrapped in bamboo leaves, or a sweet treat of candied ginger.

Turn right again onto N King St, past the red dragon columns guarding the **Bank of Hawaii (6)**. If you're hungry, sample the $1.50 dim sum at the **Golden Palace Seafood Restaurant (7**; p125)

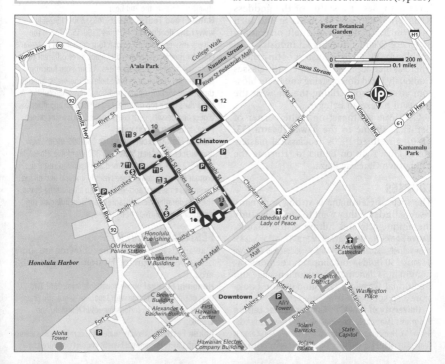

before proceeding to the corner of Kekau-like St and the bustling **O'ahu Market (8**; p110), where boxes of iced fish and fresh produce await morning shoppers. Do a quick detour to **Ba Le Bake Shoppe (9**; p124), a local Vietnamese sandwich shop and success story for the newest generation of Honolulu's immigrants. What was a small-scale business started by a Vietnamese refugee is now a local franchise, supplying baguettes Waikiki hotels.

Backtrack to the short Kekaulike St pedestrian mall and turn left toward the bustling **Maunakea Marketplace (10**; p125), where the fish is so fresh it's still jumping. Stroll right on through the marketplace's dozen ethnic lunch counters, turning left as you emerge onto Pauahi St. Take a right at River St and pass the **Dr Sun Yat-sen statue (11)**, honoring the Chinese revolutionary. The utilitarian building beside the bronze statue is the **Chinatown Cultural Plaza (12)**, a modern block lacking in old-fashioned atmosphere but filled with quintessential Chinatown businesses: weekend dim sum restaurants, tailors, acupuncturists and calligraphers. In a small courtyard, people light incense and leave mangoes at a statue of the goddess Kuan Yin. Follow N Beretania St and turn right on Maunakea St and left on Pauahi St, where O'ahu's thriving lei industry is in full bloom. You'll pass clusters of tiny shops where skilled lei makers, some with glasses studiously tilted down, string and braid blossom after blossom, filling the air with the scents of pikake and ginger.

Continue southeast until the corner of Bethel St, home to the **Hawaii Theatre (13**; p130), a restored 1920s neoclassical masterpiece. Turn right on Bethel to return to the Chinatown Gateway Plaza.

COURSES

The spell of Hawaiiana is strong and many visitors find that they want to seriously study the unique arts and culture of the islands. **Native Books/Na Mea Hawaii** (Map p112; ☎ 596-8885; www.nativebookshawaii.com; Ward Warehouse; cnr Ward Ave & Kamakee St) holds workshops and demonstrations in hula dancing, Hawaiian language and traditional weaving. On Sundays the bookstore also sponsors 1pm concerts.

University of Hawai'i's Campus Center Leisure Programs (Map p112; ☎ 956-6468; www.hawaii.edu/cclp; Room 101, Hemenway Hall, University of Hawai'i, 2445 Campus Center Rd) offers a variety of short-term courses

open to the general public. Some courses, like the body-boarding class, are completed in a day, though most others, including hula, yoga and slack-key guitar classes, meet a couple of times a week during a month-long session.

Temari (Map p102; ☎ 536-4566; www.temaricenter.com; 1754 Lusitana St), a nonprofit center, helps educate the public about traditional Asian-Pacific arts through courses in origami, lei making and esoteric art forms like gyotaku, which uses fish rubbings to create an image.

TOURS

There is no shortage of tours on the island, especially if you're eyeing a trip to Hilo Hattie or a yawn-inducing bus ride to the Dole Plantation. But if you'd like to know more about Honolulu's history, consider one of these low-key options.

Hawai'i Heritage Center (Map pp106-7; ☎ 521-2749; 1117 Smith St; ⏾ 9:30-11.30am Wed & Fri; tours $10) Leads walking tours of Chinatown, beginning at the gallery on Smith St.

Chinese Chamber of Commerce (Map pp106-7; ☎ 533-3181; 42 N King St; ⏾ 9:30-11:30am Mon; tours $10) Runs walking tours of Chinatown beginning at the chamber office on the 2nd floor.

Hawaii Food Tours (☎ 926-3663, 800-715-2468; www.hawaiifoodtours.com; tours $100-150) This is the eater's answer to sightseeing. A former chef and restaurant critic for the *Honolulu Advertiser* leads three different tours to appeal to all kinds of appetites. A four-hour lunchtime tour samples Honolulu's ethnic hole-in-the-walls; another three-hour tour focuses on traditional Hawaiian cuisine. A third visits three top gourmet restaurants for appetizers, dinner and dessert, each course paired with a fine wine. Prices include transportation.

Mauka Makai Excursions (☎ 866-896-0596; www.hawaiianecotours.net; Suite 106, 350 Ward Ave, Honolulu; tours $52-85)A Hawaiian owned and operated cultural ecotour company doing three types of cultural and hiking excursions to several ancient Hawaiian sites on the island. The hike durations and distances vary depending on the excursion; rates include hotel pick-ups.

FESTIVALS & EVENTS

Hawaiians love a party; the following are some of the best held in the Honolulu and Waikiki area.

Honolulu Festival (www.honolulufestival.com) Two days of cultural exchange with Japanese dance and drama performers in March; various venues in Honolulu and Waikiki.

Kokua Festival (www.kokuafestival.com) Hawaii's salute to Earth Day is this annual benefit concert organized by local musician Jack Johnson during April in the Waikiki Shell. All proceeds go to the Kokua Hawaii Foundation, a nonprofit supporter of environmental education.

Spam Jam (www.spamjamhawaii.com) April sees a Waikiki street festival devoted to Hawaii's favorite potted meat product: spam.

Taste of Honolulu (info@tasteofhonolulu.com) A three-day food and music affair sampling the city's best cooking is held in June in the Honolulu Civic Center. There's a bit of everything, from top-of-the-food-chain to humble mom-and-pop eateries. More than 30 musical groups keep the place jumping, but island grinds (food) are what bring thousands of locals to this one-of-a-kind event.

Prince Lot Hula Festival (www.mgf-hawaii.org) The state's oldest and largest non-competitive hula event is held in July at the Moanalua Gardens (Map p102).

Ukulele Festival (www.roysakuma.net) Held annually in July at the Kapi'olani Park Bandstand, Waikiki, this festival of the 'jumping flea' instrument spotlights legendary Hawaiian musicians and a ukulele orchestra.

Aloha Festival (http://alohafestivals.com) The month long, statewide festival of Hawaiian culture keeps the whole of O'ahu busy during September with block parties, parades and music festivals.

Hawaii International Film Festival (www.hiff.org) This celebration of celluloid packs the city's movie theatres with imported and homegrown films in October.

Hawaii International Jazz Festival (www.hawaiijazz .com) Jazz thrives on O'ahu in November at this annual festival held in City Hall and showcasing local and international talent.

SLEEPING

Honolulu proper doesn't have much in the way of accommodations since Waikiki functions as the nearest bedroom community for tourists. Unless you love cities or are visiting relatives, you're better off following the package-tour bus to Waikiki as well.

Budget

Hosteling International Honolulu (Map p112; ☎ 946-0591; http://hostelsaloha.com; 2323A Seaview Ave; member/nonmember dm $16/19, r $42/48; ☑ check-in 8am–noon & 4pm–midnight) This small, well-run hostel is in a quiet residential neighborhood near the university. Dorms are sunny and breezy with sex-segregated rooms. Private rooms are for couples only. HI membership is sold on-site; the cost is $28 for Americans, $18 for foreign visitors. Many students use this hostel as a landing pad before finding an apartment, so they are often full at the beginning of the semester. The hostel has a TV lounge, guest kitchen, laundry room, lockers and bulletin boards.

Central Branch YMCA (Map p112; ☎ 941-3344; www .ymcahonolulu.org; 401 Atkinson Dr; s with shared bathroom $35, s/d $43/55; ☒ ℗ $8) On the east side of the Ala Moana Center, just outside Waikiki, this YMCA was described by the desk clerk as being an old building with plumbing problems. The rooms with shared bathroom are available to men only and are small and simple, resembling those in a student dorm. Rooms with bathrooms are open to both men and women. Guests receive YMCA privileges, including free use of the sauna, pool and gym. There's a coin laundry, TV lounge and snack bar.

Midrange

Pagoda Hotel (Map p112; ☎ 941-6611, 800-367-6060; www.pagodahotel.com; 1525 Rycroft St; r $100-112, ste $170; ☒ ☒ ℗ $6) North of the Ala Moana Center, the Pagoda Hotel is a mid-20th-century survivor with outdated but charming decor and a local sense of place. The hotel is divided into two sections: a 12-story tower of hotel rooms and suites and a motel-style complex of studios with kitchenettes. The hotel is especially popular with families from the Neighbor Islands, mainly as an alternative to jumping into the bustling Waikiki scene.

Manoa Valley Inn (Map p112; ☎ 947-6019; www .manoavalleyinn.com; 2001 Vancouver Dr; r with shared bathroom $100-120, r $140-190, incl continental breakfast; ☒ ℗ free) On a quiet side street near the university, this restored Victorian inn is on the National Register of Historic Places and has a stunning view of Honolulu. The inn's common areas and guest rooms are furnished with antiques and is the closest that Honolulu has to a mainland-style B&B, but it receives mixed reviews about service and upkeep.

Pacific Marina Inn (Map p102; ☎ 836-1131, 800-548-8040; www.castleresorts.com; 2628 Waiwai Loop; r from $110; ☒ ☒ ℗) A mile east of the airport, this three-decker motel is just that – a roadside motel with small, bare-bones rooms. There are often internet discounts; and a shuttle will pick you up from the airport.

Best Western Plaza Hotel (Map p102; ☎ 836-3636, 800-800-4683; www.bestwesternhonolulu.com; 3253 N Nimitz Hwy; r $145-185; ☒ ☒ ℗ $15) If you've got an overnight layover in Honolulu before puddle-jumping to neighboring islands, this airport hotel is an adequate bedmate. Ask for a rear room away from traffic noise. There is a complimentary shuttle to and from the airport and high-speed internet in the lobby.

Ala Moana Hotel (Map p112; ☎ 955-4811, 800-367-6025; www.alamoanahotel.com; 410 Atkinson Dr; r $150-190, ste from $300; 🅇 🅇 🅿 $15) Looming above the Ala Moana Center, near the Hawaiian Convention Center, this multistory condotel has standard executive-strength rooms with smart but conservative trimmings. Prices rise as you climb higher up in the tower to gain either a city or ocean view. You'll share the check-in line with airline crews and conventioneers.

Top End

ResortQuest at the Executive Centre Hotel (Map pp106-7; ☎ 539-3000, 877-997-6667; www.resortquesthawaii .com; 1088 Bishop St; ste $220-320 incl continental breakfast; 🅇 🅇 🅿 $15) Honolulu's only downtown hotel is geared entirely for businesspeople. All accommodations are suites outfitted with the gadgets to run mobile empires, including free high-speed internet. The hotel is on the upper floors of a high-rise, so most of the rooms have fine city views. Pricier rooms have ocean views and kitchen facilities. There's a fitness center, a heated lap pool, and a business center with secretarial services and laptop rentals.

EATING

You might sleep and play in Waikiki, but you should eat in Honolulu, which has an incredible variety of restaurants that mirror the city's multiethnic composition. If the islands weren't so far away from the mainland, you'd hear more buzz about this slumbering chowhound capital.

Downtown

If you're feeling peckish after a day of historical sightseeing, there is a cluster of inexpensive restaurants within easy walking distance of 'Iolani Palace. For dining after dark, Aloha Tower Marketplace and Restaurant Row both sport a few well-regarded, Honolulu-born options.

BUDGET

Ba Le Bake Shoppe (Map pp106-7; ☎ 521-4117; 1154 Fort St Mall; mains $5; 🕑 7am-6pm Mon-Fri, 7am-3pm Sat) A corruption of the word 'Paris,' this Vietnamese bakery-café is one of an islandwide chain established by a recent Vietnamese immigrant. The simple shop is best known for its chewy baguette sandwiches, but you can also scratch that spring-roll itch. For a caffeine jolt, there's an equally chewy cup coffee served with loads of sugar and milk, either hot or iced. There is another outlet on N King St.

Honolulu Café (Map pp106-7; ☎ 533-1555; Pacific Guardian Center, 741 Bishop St; mains $5-7; 🕑 6am-5pm Mon-Fri) This breezy café is set in the old Dillingham Transportation Building, one of the hubs of the US robber barons who ruled Hawaii's economy. The light fare features mainly sandwiches and salads and the café is an easy walk away from the franchise options at Aloha Tower Marketplace.

Cafe Laniakea (Map pp106-7; ☎ 524-8789; 1040 Richards St; mains $5-12; 🕑 11am-2pm Mon-Fri) Chic and health-conscious, this café runs with an entirely different crowd than your average mess hall. Set in the courtyard at the historic Julia Morgan-designed YWCA, the café has a changing menu committed to local and organic (when possible) ingredients. And because Honolulu has never heard of pretension, the upscale meals are close to down-home prices.

Fort Street Bar & Grill (Map pp106-7; ☎ 523-1500; Topa Financial Center, 745 Fort St; mains $8-15; 🕑 11am-2pm & 5-9pm Mon-Fri) Local foodies' favorite for dressed-down Hawaiian contemporary food, this unpretentious spot is Colin Nishida's latest addition to the Side Street Inn (see p129) family. The office workers roll in after work for light plates and karaoke.

MIDRANGE

Chai's Island Bistro (Map pp106-7; ☎ 585-0011; Aloha Tower Marketplace; lunch $12-20, dinner $25-40; 🕑 11am-4pm Tue-Fri, 4-10pm daily) Mixing Hawaiian ingredients and music together, Chai's is a smarter in-town version to the overpriced meals in Waikiki. You'll find award-winning Pacific Rim cuisine, harvesting much of its menu from the sea. Some of Hawaii's top musicians perform at dinner.

TOP 10 HONOLULU & WAIKIKI EATS

- **Indigo** (p126)
- **Hiroshi Eurasion Tapas** (opposite)
- **Kaka'ako Kitchen** (p126)
- **Fort Street Bar & Grill** (right)
- **Imanas Tei** (p127)
- **Duc's Bistro** (p126)
- **Little Village Noodle House** (opposite)
- **Legend Seafood Restaurant** (opposite)
- **Town** (p128)
- **Ono Hawaiian Food** (p148)

Hiroshi Eurasian Tapas (Map pp106-7; ☎ 533-4476; Restaurant Row, 500 Ala Moana Blvd; mains $18-22; ☑ 5:30-9:30pm) A longtime player on the Honolulu culinary scene, Hiroshi Fukui, the former chef of L'Uraku, has emerged with his own restaurant and a subtle twist on the reigning fusion styles. Regarded as East–West fusion, most dishes begin with a Japanese home-cooking base and are matched with unlikely playmates: such as Kona kampachi (yellowtail) carpaccio, harvested on the Big Island, served with local tomatoes and a *ponzu* (citrus) vinaigrette.

Chinatown

Chinatown is packed with little hole-in-the-walls and an emerging presence of tiny boutique eateries. Weekend dim sum, Vietnamese noodles and spicy Thai are just a few of the neighborhood's specialties.

BUDGET

Shung Chong Yuein (Map pp106-7; ☎ 531-1983; 1027 Maunakea St; items around $1.50) Come early for Chinese baked goods like almond cookies and other pastries at bargain prices. This is also the place to buy dried and sugared foods – everything from candied ginger and pineapple to candied squash and lotus root.

Royal Kitchen (Map pp106-7; ☎ 524-4461; Chinatown Cultural Plaza, River St; mains per piece $1; ☑ 6:30am-5pm) A simple takeaway shop, Royal Kitchen is famous for its baked *manapua* (Chinese-style buns) with a selection of fillings: *char-siu* (barbecued pork), chicken curry, vegetarian, sweet potato, *kalua* (cooked in a pit) pig and more.

To Chau (Map pp106-7; ☎ 533-4549; 1007 River St; mains $4-7; ☑ 8am-2:30pm) Always packed, this Vietnamese restaurant holds fast to its reputation as Honolulu's serving best *pho* (Vietnamese noodle soup). Beef, broth and vegetables – the dish is a complete meal in itself, but the menu includes other Vietnamese standards should your glasses need defogging.

Huong Lan (Map pp106-7; ☎ 538-6707; Chinatown Cultural Plaza, Maunakea St; mains $5-9; ☑ 8am-5pm Thu-Tue) One of Honolulu's many beloved *pho* shops, Vietnamese families fill the booths with adept noodle wrangling and spirited conversations.

Maunakea Marketplace (Map pp106-7; N Hotel St; mains from $5; ☑ 7am-3:30pm) For local grinds at its most brawny, head to the food court in this marketplace, where you'll find about 20 mom-and-pop vendors dishing out home-style Chinese, Filipino, Thai, Vietnamese, Korean and Japanese food. You can chow down at tiny wooden tables crowded into the central walkway.

Liliha Bakery (☎ 531-1651; 515 N Kuakini, cnr Liliha St; mains $6-8; ☑ 24hr Tue-Sun) Sugary cereals aren't just for breakfast anymore. This bakery and diner causes a traffic jam for its coco-puff pastries. Too nutritious you say? Then take a seat and order hamburger steak or other lumberjack faves at this spot northeast of Downtown.

Little Village Noodle House (Map pp106-7; ☎ 545-3008; 1113 Smith St; mains $7-15; ☑ 10:30am-10:30pm Sun-Thu, 10:30am-midnight Fri & Sat; ℗) A quiet and air-conditioned restaurant in Chinatown? That's only the beginning at this little village kitchen covering almost every region of China, with special attention to the northern provinces. Forget chop suey and sticky sweet and sour, the dishes here are garlicky, fiery or just the right dose of saltiness. Any fish in black-bean sauce here is the gold standard for Honolulu. Noodles, including O'ahu style duck noodles, are another forte. Little Village is clean, friendly and full of surprises, not the least of which is free parking just behind the restaurant.

MIDRANGE & TOP END

Legend Vegetarian Restaurant (Map pp106-7; ☎ 532-8218; Chinatown Cultural Plaza, River St; mains $8-13; ☑ 10:30am-2pm Thu-Tue) This Buddhist vegetarian, lunch-only spot is known for several fish and pork analogs that even meat eaters acknowledge as tasty. Favorites include the vegetarian butter fish and sweet-and-sour vegetarian pork, along with a huge selection of dim sum offerings.

Golden Palace Seafood Restaurant (Map pp106-7; ☎ 521-8268; 111 N King St; mains $8-15; ☑ 7am-10pm) It says seafood on the sign outside, but it is really the $1.50 dim sum that brings in Chinatown's midmorning regulars. All the dim sum components are here: impatient wait staff, mystery meatballs, pink tablecloths and Asian kitschy art. You get only a quick peek inside the bamboo steamers and no accompanying explanation. Tasty requests include *char siu bao* (steamed pork buns), shrimp or chive dumplings and *look funn* (steamed rice noodles).

Legend Seafood Restaurant (Map pp106-7; ☎ 532-1868; Chinatown Cultural Plaza, 100 N Beretania St; mains $8-20; ☑ 10:30am-2pm Mon-Fri, 8am-2pm Sat & Sun,

5:30-9:30pm daily) Bright and busy, this impersonal banquet restaurant peddles seafood, but is best known for dim sum. Spinach and scallop dumplings get wheeled around on the steam cart, followed by the fry cart, and the dessert cart. The bite-size morsels are more extensive here than at other dim sum restaurants, but you've got more competition from the savvy patrons.

Duc's Bistro (Map pp106-7; ☎ 521-2900; 1188 Maunakea St; lunch $10-19, dinner $15-32; ☒ 11:30am-2pm & 5-10pm Mon-Fri, 5-10pm Sat) Honolulu's power brokers hang out at his swank French-Vietnamese bistro with a tiny Manhattan-like bar. Fusion highlights include noodles in lime sauce, seafood paella, vermicelli with spring rolls, and avocado and green papaya salad. A small jazz combo performs on most evenings.

Indigo (Map pp106-7; ☎ 521-2900; 1121 Nu'uanu Ave; mains $16-26; ☒ 11:30am-2pm Tue-Fri, 6-9:30pm Tue-Sat) A favorite for the theater crowd, Indigo has a relaxed, open-air courtyard and menu decorated with contemporary Eurasian cuisine. Creative dim sum appetizers include 'ahi (yellowfin tuna) tempura rolls and goat cheese wontons. Dinner features such dishes as tangerine-glazed ribs, ginger-miso salmon and mahogany duck. An award-winning wine list matches the inspired menu. See p130 for a review of its bars.

Ala Moana

The bulk of Honolulu's local restaurants – including Korean, Japanese, and various local fusions – can be found in and around Ala Moana area. The Ala Moana Center is also a hub for affordable but stylish dining.

BUDGET

My Favorite Place (Map p112; ☎ 949-2727; 1694 Fern St; mains $5-8; ☒ 6-9pm Mon-Fri, 9am-9pm Sat) This homey café has bargain-basement prices and a full spread of local eats leaning more toward Korean dishes, accompanied by pictures if you haven't yet sorted out the difference between saimin and loco moco.

Maiki Market Food Court (Map p112; 1st fl, Ala Moana Center; mains $5-12; ☒ 10am-8pm) On the mainland no self-respecting eater would be caught hanging out in a shopping center food court after the age of 17. But cross the Pacific in the other direction and you'll understand how Asia has brought the old-style market into air-conditioned comfort. This particular nucleus for communal grazing includes small

outposts of favorite Honolulu restaurants, like Yummy Express, which serves Korean-style lunch plates with your choice of a fork or chopsticks.

Tsukiji Fish Market (Map p112; Ho'okipa Tce, Ala Moana Center; mains $5-20; ☒ 10am-10pm) Christened by the famous Tokyo fish market of the same name, this newcomer to Ala Moana's dining scene is an all-in-one Japanese food feast with a full-service fish market surrounded by sushi and yakitori bars, noodle stalls and other street-food options.

Kaka'ako Kitchen (Map p112; ☎ 596-7488; Ward Center, 1200 Ala Moana Blvd; mains $7-12; ☒ 7am-10pm Mon-Sat, to 5pm Sun) A downscale sister of upscale 3660 On the Rise (see p128), Kaka'ako uses the same fresh ingredients and creative flair in a plate-lunch presentation: Styrofoam container, outdoor seating and plastic utensils. Local favorites include shoyu chicken, wild salmon or ginger-sake 'ahi steak with your choice of brown or white rice and an organic salad.

Stanley's BBQ Chicken (Map p112; Auahi St, mains $8-12; ☒ 8am-5pm Sat) Parked in the lot out in front of Marukai 99 Superstore, this smoke-belching lunch wagon cranks out island tunes and lots of barbecued chicken worth getting messy for.

Mekong I (Map p112; ☎ 591-8841; 1295 S Beretania St; mains $8-12; ☒ 11am-2pm Mon-Fri, 5-9:30pm daily) One of the oldest Thai restaurants in Honolulu, it's a small unpretentious place with a reputation for flavorful and fiery dishes.

Jimbo Restaurant (Map p112; ☎ 947-2211; 1936 S King St; mains $9-10; ☒ 11am-2:50pm & 5-9:50pm) This family friendly restaurant is known throughout the island for its handmade soba and udon noodles. Order them in broth or fried and slurp your way to happiness along with the old married couples who no longer bother talking to each other and young daters who giggle at everything.

MIDRANGE & TOP END

Auntie Pasto's (Map p112; ☎ 523-8855; 1099 S Beretania St; mains $8-13; ☒ 11am-10:30pm Mon-Fri, 4-11pm Sat & Sun) A local chain, this silly-named Italian-American restaurant is set in an atmospheric shophouse of windows and tiles. It doesn't seem very 'Hawaii' but locals come to look pretty and eat sensibly.

Pavilion Cafe (Map p112; ☎ 532-8734; 900 S Beretania St; mains $10-15; ☒ 11:30am-1:30pm Tue-Sat) In the Honolulu Academy of Arts, this upscale café has a lovely courtyard setting overlooking the museum's water fountains. The kitchen specializes in gourmet salads and sandwiches, but also makes an innovative pasta of the day. It's a good place to relax and a wonderfully indulgent way to support the arts. Reservations are suggested, particularly if there's a special exhibition at the museum.

Shokudo Japanese (Map p112; ☎ 941-3701; Ala Moana Pacific Center, 1585 Kapi'olani Blvd; mains $10-15; 11:30am-1am Sun-Thu, to 2am Fri & Sat) This sake-tini and Japanese restaurant is a fashionable venue for hip Honolulu residents sporting tats, piercings and club wear. It's a date place for yuppies but still full of enough aloha for the extended families. Dressed-up versions of Japanese dishes are the main event with silky homemade tofu as the show stealer.

Yanagi Sushi (Map p112; ☎ 537-1525; 762 Kapi'olani Blvd; mains $10-20; 11am-2pm daily, 5:30pm-2am Mon-Sat, 5:30pm-10pm Sun) Yanagi is one of Honolulu's most popular late-night places for sushi, along with other Japanese dishes prepared to perfection. Ask about the 'late birds' meal specials available after 10:30pm.

Sorabol (Map p112; ☎ 947-3113; 805 Ke'eaumoku St; lunch $10-12, dinner $15-20; 24hr) Sorabol feeds the lunching ladies by day and the bleary-headed clubbers before dawn. Detractors often sniff that its reputation is undeserved but the rest of the city has undying loyalty for this Korean auntie. *Kal-bi* (Korean barbeque) and steamed butterfish are specialties.

Sushi Sasabune (Map p112; ☎ 947-3800; 1419 S King St; mains $10-15; 6-10pm) From freshness to carving to presentation, The art of sushi is all here in *omakase* style (chef's choice), meaning you are the student and the man behind the sushi bar is the teacher. This bravado annoys some but endears others. The choices might wander from familiar to challenging – all served on warm rice, intended to better melt the flavors – and the construction is often unrecognizable compared to the fish pellets you get at sushi buffets.

Willows (Map p112; ☎ 952-9200; 901 Hausten St; lunch/dinner buffet $20/30, weekend buffet $22-30; 11am-2pm & 5:30-9pm) Once high-fashion for the choice-starved Depression era, buffet restaurants are now as dated as jello moulds. But Hawaii is so charmingly anachronistic, who could resist joining the multigenerational families at this Honolulu landmark complete with a garden setting. Few restaurants have a more loyal following than this one, where a chef carves

prime rib and suckling pig to accompany *'ahi poke* (cubed raw fish mixed with soya, sesame oil, salt, chili pepper and other condiments), crab legs and more. Discounts for children apply.

Chef Mavro (Map p112; ☎ 944-4714; 1969 S King St; 3-/4-course dinner $98/115) The most avant-garde of Honolulu's haute restaurants, Chef Mavro creates conceptual dishes using green tea–dusted zucchini-blossom tempura appetizer with a glass of German Moselle wine. Textures and fragrances are just as important as flavor and great care is used to pair food and wine.

University Area

Near the University of Hawai'i is a cluster of student-oriented health and antihealth restaurants.

BUDGET

Bubbies (Map p112; ☎ 949-8984; 1010 University Ave, cnr Coyne St; ice cream $3-5; noon-midnight, to 1am Fri & Sat, to 11:30pm Sun) In a college strip skilled at pouring draughts, this neighborhood ice-cream shop is the sweet-tooth's alternative to beer. Homemade ice cream comes in luscious tropical flavors or decadent chocolate-on-chocolate creations.

Imanas Tei (Map p112; ☎ 941-2626; 2626 S King St; mains $5-15; 5-11:30pm Mon-Sat) They call it an *izakaya* (a Japanese pub serving food), and sake fans come here first for the liquid version of rice and then graze their way through the menu of sushi and crowd-pleasing *nabemono* (do-it-yourself meat and vegetable soups). The restaurant is tucked behind Puck's Alley.

Well Bento (Map p112; ☎ 941-5261; 2nd fl, 2570 S Beretania St; mains $6-10; 10:30am-9pm) This inconspicuous hole-in-the-wall is the macrobiotic alternative to the plate lunch, serving 'Zen' veggies and grilled tofu, as well as seared chicken or fish. This is only a take-out place but it is an easy walk to Old Stadium park for a midday picnic. Cash only.

Down to Earth Natural Foods (Map p112; ☎ 947-7678; 2525 S King St; mains from $7; 7:30am-9pm) Honolulu's largest natural-foods supermarket has a small sandwich and salad café with lots of vegetarian options. The grocery section has a decent selection of local and organic produce including Hawaii's tasty papaya and apple bananas.

Spices (Map p112; ☎ 949-2679; 2671-D S King St; mains $7-10; 5:30-10pm Tue-Sun) This pan–Southeast Asian restaurant has spiced up the university

O'AHU

dining scene with Thai curries, Lao soups and Burmese noodles. The restaurants sets a modern but neighborhood-friendly table free of suffocating ethnic kitsch.

MIDRANGE & TOP END
Waioli Tea Room (Map p115; ☎ 988-5800; 2950 Manoa Rd; à la carte dishes $10-15; ✆ 10:30am-2pm Mon-Fri, 8am-2pm Sat & Sun) What a gorgeous setting wrapped up in shade trees and long, flowing vines in a green nook of Manoa Valley. The stone house is a vintage specimen from the·days when it was the kitchen for the Salvation Army Young Ladies' Orphanage, whose bakery truck was so successful that it threatened to put local shops out of business. The main event here is the afternoon high tea ($18.75) from 2pm to 4pm. But others filter in for breakfast chats with friends or to shower moms with appreciation. The food isn't as good as the scenery, but sometimes pretending is good enough.

Contemporary Cafe (Map p115; ☎ 523-3362; Contemporary Museum, 2411 Makiki Heights Dr; mains $9-12; ✆ 11am-2:30pm Tue-Sat, noon-2:30pm Sun) This is a genteel treat, with a pleasant lawn setting at the Contemporary Museum in Makiki Valley. There are healthy nibbles from salads to sandwiches, and you can just pop in for lunch without paying the museum admission.

Alan Wong's (☎ 949-2526; 1857 S King St; appetizers $11-16, mains $27-38; ✆ 5-10pm) One of Hawaii's top restaurants, this high-energy place specializes in upmarket Hawaiian regional cuisine. Chef Wong is one of Hawaii's most celebrated chefs and offers a creative menu with an emphasis on fresh local ingredients. Appetizers include tempura 'ahi, while mains feature fresh seafood – such as Wong's signature dish, ginger-crusted onaga (red snapper). Each night there's also a five-course 'tasting menu' ($65). Reservations are recommended. There are other branches in the Ala Moana Shopping Centre and Waikiki.

Kaimuki
Wai'alae Ave, the commercial strip of this low-key neighborhood east of Waikiki, is Honolulu's home-grown 'restaurant row' with cozy bistros, cafés and old-school bakeries.

BUDGET
Sconee's Bakery (☎ 734-4024; 1117 12th Ave; mains $1.50-2; ✆ 7:30am-2pm) Children literally skip with excitement to this neighborhood bake

shop known for guava bars, cupcakes and buttery scones.

Coffee Talk (☎ 737-7444; 3601 Wai'alae Ave; ✆ 6:30am-8pm) For a coffee-producing state, Hawaii hasn't been jolted by the 'café' culture phenomenon, making this Kaimuki hangout all the more unique. Start the day with a slow wind-up of java, people-watching and crossword-puzzling. And then chase it with a peanut-butter cookie or scone.

Days of Aloha (☎ 735-5166; 11th Ave Atrium Marketplace, 1137 11th Ave; mains $4-7; ✆ 11am-9pm Tue-Fri, 9am-9pm Sat, 9am-6pm Sun) Tucked behind the commercial strip Wai'alae Ave, this vintage Hawaiian-style café serves tasty salads and sandwiches, Italian sodas and coffee drinks. On Saturday night, there's live Hawaiian music, and you can bring your own beer.

Hale Vietnam (☎ 735-7581; 1140 12th Ave; mains $7-12; ✆ 11am-10pm) This top-notch favorite has delicious Vietnamese food at moderate prices. A delightful starter is the temple rolls, a slight twist on the familiar spring roll with the addition of steamed yam. The yellow curries are also excellent, and come in vegetarian, beef and chicken variations.

MIDRANGE & TOP END
Town (☎ 735-5900; 3435 Wai'alae Ave at 9th Ave; mains $9-17; ✆ 6:30-2:30pm & 5-10pm) This modern bistro introduces the urban concept of partially naked eating – not the patrons, but the food. The ingredients are quality specimens – like steaks from North Shore Cattle Company or organic produce from local farms – and the interference from the kitchen is minimal so that individual flavors can be appreciated. The pasta and gnocchi dishes also receive praise.

Maguro-ya (☎ 732-3775; 3665 Wai'alae Ave; mains $12-15; ✆ 11am-1pm Tue-Sat, 5-9:30pm Tue-Sun) This handsome Japanese eatery is among the town's best for sushi and traditional teishoku (combination) dinners of fresh fish, tempura and sashimi.

3660 On the Rise (☎ 737-1177; 3660 Wai'alae Ave; appetizers $7-10, mains $22-28; ✆ 5:30-9pm Tue-Sun) One of the top-end Hawaii regional restaurants, 3660 will woo diners skeptical of white tablecloths. The dishes are sensible without being flamboyant and include familiar surf-and-turf ingredients that either seared or pan-cooked. But the result is far from country-club fare thanks to the thoughtful additions of Hawaiian flavors. The restaurant is between 12th and 13th Aves.

DRINKING

Any self-respecting bar or club in Honolulu has a *pupu* (snack) menu to complement the liquid sustenance and some bars are justly famous for their appetizers as well as their good-times atmosphere. One key Hawaiian drinking term to know is *pau-hana*, meaning 'happy hour.' For more options in nearby Waikiki, see p149.

Smith's Union Bar (Map pp106-7; ☎ 538-9145; 19 N Hotel St; ⊙ 6pm-1am Mon-Tue, 6pm-2am Wed-Sat) You have to be a dive-bar aficionado to appreciate Smith's Union, which first opened in 1935 when this section of Chinatown was a red-light district and playground for merchant seamen. For the wage-slave hipsters, it is a front-loading hangout before hitting the district's most recent incarnation: a trendy club zone.

Hank's Cafe Honolulu (Map pp106-7; ☎ 526-1410; 1038 Nu'uanu St; ⊙ 1:30pm-midnight) You can't get more low-key than at this neighborhood bar on the edge of Chinatown. Owner Hank Taufaasau is a jack-of-all-trades when it comes to the barfly business: the walls are decorated with Polynesian-themed art, live music rolls in nightly and regulars have made it home.

Gordon Biersch Brewery Restaurant (Map pp106-7; ☎ 599-1405; 1st fl, Aloha Tower Marketplace; ⊙ 11am-midnight Sun-Thu, 11:30am-1am Fri & Sat) It isn't the most original choice, but the San Francisco–based brewpub has a relaxed waterfront perch near enough to Honolulu sightseeing areas that you can reward culture-spotting with hops-chasings. Live rhythm and blues and contemporary Hawaiian rock get a weekend billing.

TOP 10 HONOLULU & WAIKIKI ENTERTAINMENT SPOTS

- **Indigo** (p130)
- **Side Street Inn** (right)
- **Tiki's Grill & Bar** (p149)
- **Kuhio Beach Torch Lighting & Hula Show** (p151)
- **Hank's Cafe Honolulu** (above)
- **Aku Bone Lounge** (p130), Waikiki
- **Lewers Lounge** (p150)
- **Duke's Canoe Club** (p149)
- **Anna Bannana's** (p130)
- **Brew Moon** (right)

Brew Moon (Map p112; ☎ 593-0088; Ward Center, 1200 Ala Moana Blvd ⊙ 11am-11pm Sun-Thu, to 2am Fri & Sat) This high-energy place might feel a little contrived in the midst of tidy Ward Center, but the homemade beers are a requisite pick for the microbrew crowd. The pub menu also gets a nod from the city's roaming stomachs. Watch for wallet-friendly happy hour specials. There's a second location in Waikiki: above the Local Motion shop (1958 Kalakaua Ave).

Mai Tai Bar (Map p112; ☎ 947-2900; 3rd fl, Ala Moana Center; ⊙ 11am-1am) A happening bar in the middle of a shopping center? We don't make the trends, we just report them, and during Friday happy hours this suburban-style bar is packed with a see-and-flirt crowd. It has consistently won people's choice awards in various bar surveys, thanks to easy parking and access to retail therapy.

Side Street Inn (Map p112; ☎ 591-0253; 1225 Hopaka St; ⊙ 10am-1:30pm Mon-Fri, 4pm-1am daily) High hopes might be dashed upon arrival at this back-alley bar and restaurant, but the industrial location is part of the charm. Basically a sports bar for a local crowd, Side Street has muscled its way on to night-hoppers agenda with its pan-fried pork chops, mellow atmosphere and late-night following.

Formaggio (☎ 739-7719; Market City Shopping Center, 2919 Kapi'olani Blvd; ⊙ 5pm-midnight Mon-Thu, Fri & Sat 5pm-2am) The neighborhood of Kaimuki leads Honolulu in early adaptation of international trends and this wine-and-cheese bar pairs a sip of Italian sophistication along with a tumbler of mellow Hawaii. With a soundtrack of smooth jazz, the local crowd savors conversation and spirits, not just a race to oblivion.

ENTERTAINMENT

For a listing of live music, new clubs or cultural events, check out the free *Honolulu Weekly*, which comes out on Wednesday, and *Honolulu Advertiser's* TGIF section, which comes out conveniently enough on Friday.

Nightclubs

Honolulu's club scene centers around newly revitalized N Hotel St and Nu'uanu Ave in Chinatown. This was once the city's notorious red-light district and the historic beat of police detective Chang Apana, who served as the model for the Charlie Chan character. Ala Moana Center has developed its 3rd floor into a club zone suited for suburbanites. Some of the eateries in Restaurant Row also make space for a DJ and a dance floor after the dinner period.

Indigo (Map pp106-7; ☎ 521-2900; 1121 Nu'uanu Ave; admission free; ☺ 11:30am-2pm Tue-Fri, 6pm-midnight Tue-Sun) This popular nouveau restaurant and its affiliated nightclub put the 'life' back into Honolulu's nights. Divided into different theme lounges, Indigo mixes cocktails in the Opium Den & Champagne Bar and spins tunes in the Green Room. Jazz and live music are featured during the week, and electronica is slotted for the weekend.

thirtyninehotel (Map pp106-7; ☎ 599-2552; 39 N Hotel St; ☺ 4pm-2am Tue-Sat) More arty than clubby, this multimedia space is a gallery by day and low-key dance scene at night. Guest DJs from the mainland don their aloha wear for special weekend appearances, while jazz tests the acoustics on Tuesday.

Pearl (Map p112; ☎ 955-9517; 3rd fl, Ala Moana Center; ☺ 4pm-2am Mon-Thu, 10pm-4am Fri-Sun) Part of the nightlife complex of Ala Moana Center, this New York–style club is dressed up with an onyx bar, lounge areas, chandelier-lit terraces and an urban groove for those cocktail-savvy 30-somethings.

Live Music

Honolulu has had a long love affair with jazz, and speakeasy-style bars still seat the horns next to the patrons. Hawaiian music is another beloved genre and most clubs will feature a showcase night; Waikiki is the most reliable hub for traditional and contemporary Hawaiian music.

Anna Bannanas (Map p112; ☎ 946-5190; 2440 S Beretania St; 9pm-2am Thu-Sun) A reliable college bar, part roadhouse and arthouse, Anna Bananas

goes beyond its retro atmosphere to feature alt-rock, punk and metal bands.

Jazz Minds Art & Cafe (Map p112; ☎ 945-0800; 1661 Kapi'olani Blvd; ☺ 4pm-2am Mon-Sat) Intimate and subdued, this jazz lounge pulls in the city's best talent from NewJass Quartet, Groove Improv Artists to Honolulu Jazz.

Wards Rafters (☎ 735-8012, 3810 Mauna Loa Ave, Kaimuki; ☺ 3-6pm Sun) You might not get invited to a family luau, but you can make your way to another type of family affair. Usually once a week, Jackie Ward opens up her converted attic space to various musicians from O'ahu's tight-knit jazz community. It's a word-of-mouth place that informs regulars of gigs via an email mailing list. You can call with questions and consider bringing a gift of flowers for the host. BYOB.

Aku Bone Lounge (Map p112; ☎ 589-2020; 1201 Kona St; ☺ 5pm-2am) This is down-home Hawaii – a low-key bar with a tasty *pupu* menu, cold Bud Light and a rubber-slippers crowd. Most nights are for karaoke, which are sung by patrons from the comfort of their own tables, but live Hawaiian music takes over for the other nights .

Theater, Dance & Concerts

Honolulu boasts a symphony orchestra, an opera company, ballet troupes, chamber orchestras and community theater groups.

Hawaii Theatre (Map pp106-7; ☎ 528-0506; 1130 Bethel St) In a beautifully restored historic building on the edge of Chinatown, this is a major venue for dance, music and theater. Performances range from top contemporary Hawaiian musicians, to modern dance and film festivals. It also hosts the Ka Himeni Ana competition

---

CRUISING FOR ART

Smartly dressed professionals now flock to once seedy Nu'uanu Ave in Chinatown, not for the treats of skid row but for art, socializing, music and clubbing. The city's **Gallery Walk** (first Friday of the month, 5pm to 9pm) is prime time for Chinatown's art galleries, which set out free *pupu* (snacks) and entertainment to lure browsers. You can pick up a gallery walking map from any of the featured galleries. A good place to start is at **Pegge Hopper Gallery** (Map pp106-7; ☎ 524-1160; 1164 Nu'uanu Ave), which represents the distinctive paintings of the gallery's namesake artist. If you collect tats instead of mats, check out **Sharky's Tattoo** (Map pp106-7; ☎ 585-0076; 1038 Nu'uanu Ave), which incorporates Hawaiian traditional tattoos in modern designs. **Bethel St Gallery** (Map pp106-7; ☎ 524-3552; 1140 Bethel St) is an artist-owned cooperative displaying works of sculpture, painting and glassware. Shake off all that culture with a visit to **Hank's Cafe Honolulu** (p129), which serves the thirsty locals shots of art, spirits and live music. Or grab dinner at a nearby eatery before hitting the splashy club scene that cranks up later in the evening.

in which famous Hawaii musicians play in the falsetto style.

Blaisdell Center (Map p112; ☎ 591-2211; 777 Ward Ave) The center presents concerts, Broadway shows and family events, such as the Honolulu Symphony and the American Ballet Theatre, and occasional big-name rock musicians, such as Sting.

The **Doris Duke Theatre** (Map p112; ☎ 532-8768; 900 S Beretania St), at the Honolulu Academy of Arts, and the **East-West Center** (Map p112; ☎ 944-7111), adjacent to the university, both present multicultural theater performances and concerts.

Cinemas

Varsity (Map p112; ☎ 296-1818; 1006 University Ave) The two-screen theater near the university usually shows foreign, arthouse and other alternative films.

Doris Duke Theatre (Map p112; ☎ 532-8768; Honolulu Academy of Arts, 900 S Beretania St) This theater showcases American independent cinema, foreign films and avant-garde shorts.

Movie Museum (☎ 735-8771; 3566 Harding Ave, Kaimuki) This Kaimuki gem is a fun place to watch classic oldies, such as *Citizen Kane* and *Casablanca*, in a theater with just 20 comfy chairs. Movies are shown Thursday to Monday evenings and weekend afternoons. Reservations are recommended.

Honolulu also has several megaplexes showing first-run feature films:
Restaurant Row 9 Cinemas (Map pp106-7; ☎ 526-4171; Restaurant Row, 500 Ala Moana Blvd)
Ward Stadium 16 (Map p112; ☎ 593-3000; 1044 Auahi St).

SHOPPING
Downtown & Chinatown
Aloha Tower Marketplace (Map pp106-7; ☎ 566-2337; 1 Aloha Tower Dr; www.aloha-tower.com; ⏱ 9am-9pm Mon-Sat, 9am-7pm Sun) This handsome harborfront shopping center is anchored by the 184ft Aloha Tower. The open-air marketplace is a kid-friendly shopping venue with several restaurants and bars hosting live Hawaiian music. Daily hula shows and once-weekly ukulele lessons are also held here.

Lai Fong Department Store (Map pp106-7; ☎ 781-8140; 1118 Nu'uanu Ave; ⏱ hours vary) For antiques, junk and kitsch, this is a great place to browse. It sells a variety of antiques and knickknacks, including Chinese silk clothing, Oriental porcelain and old postcards of Hawaii dating back to the first half of the 20th century.

> ### TOP 10 HONOLULU & WAIKIKI SHOPPING SPOTS
> - **Ala Moana Center** (below)
> - **Native Books/Na Mea Hawaii** (p132)
> - **Manuheali'i** (p132)
> - **Cindy's Lei Shop** (below)
> - **Nu'uanu Swap Meet at Aloha Stadium** (p134)
> - **Royal Hawaiian Shopping Center** (p152)
> - **Island Treasures Antiques** (p152)
> - **Bailey's Antique & Aloha Shop** (p152)
> - **Diamond Head Farmer's Market** (p148)
> - **Hula Supply Center** (p132)

Cindy's Lei Shop (Map pp106-7; ☎ 536-6538; 1034 Maunakea St; ⏱ 6am-8pm Mon-Sat, 6am-6pm Sun) A friendly, inviting place with lei made of *maile* (a native twining plant), lantern *ilima* (a native ground cover) and Micronesian ginger, as well as more common orchids and plumeria.

Ramsay Galleries (Map pp106-7; ☎ 537-2787; 1128 Smith St) Features finely detailed pen-and-ink drawings by the artist Ramsay and changing exhibits of high-quality works by other local artists.

Kamaka Hawaii (Map pp106-7; ☎ 531-3165; 550 South St) If you've been hankering to make your own music, this shop specializes in handcrafted ukuleles made on O'ahu, with prices starting at around $500.

Ala Moana & University Area
Ala Moana Center (Map p112; ☎ 955-9517, 1450 Ala Moana Blvd; ⏱ 9:30am-9pm Mon-Sat, 10am-7pm Sun) Holy fashion, this attractive open-air shopping mall could compete on an international runway with some of Asia's most famous malls. And the shoppers are top-shelf fashionistas, stocking up on couture. The usual mall anchors are here, (Sears and Macy's) as are the designer name brands (you name it) and the trendy teen brands (Abercrombie & Fitch). A favorite for local color is the Crack Seed Center, where you can just scoop from jars full of pickled mangoes, candied ginger, dried cuttlefish and banzai (rice crackers, nuts and dried fish) mix. The ground floor or the shopping center is also the hub for TheBus service.

O'AHU

Ward Warehouse (Map p112; ☎ 591-8411; cnr Ward Ave & Kamakee St; ☼ 10am-9pm Mon-Sat, 10am-6pm Sun) Just across the street from Ala Moana Beach Park, this two-story shopping centre has several tasteful Hawaiiana shops, from fashion to gifts. Within the center is Native Books/Na Mea Hawaii (☎ 596-8885), which sells beautiful silk-screened fabrics, koa wood bowls, Hawaiian quilts and much more.

Manuheali'i (Map p112; ☎ 942-9868; 930 Punahou St; ☼ 9:30am-6pm Mon-Fri, 9am-4pm Sat, 9am-1pm Sun) When Hawaii gals need a party dress, many look to this homegrown shop for original and modern designs. The flowing rayon dresses take inspiration from the traditional muumuu, but are transformed into contemporary looks that range from daring to sassy.

T&L Muumuu Factory (Map p112; ☎ 941-4183; 1423 Kapi'olani Blvd; ☼ 9am-6pm Mon-Sat, 10am-4pm Sun) So much flammable aloha wear in one space – it is worth a visit just for the oddity factor. This is an auntie's shop, where polyester still represents progress. Bold-print muumuus run in sizes from skeletal to queen, and *pu'u* skirts are just funky enough to wedge into an urban outfit.

Hula Supply Center (Map p112; 941-5379; 2346 S King St; ☼ 9am-5:30pm Mon-Fri, 9am-5pm Sat) For 60 years, Hawaiian musicians and dancers have come here to get their feather lei, calabash drum gourds, hula skirts, nose flutes and the like.

Montsuki (☎ 734-3457; 1148 Koko Head Ave, Kaimuki; ☼ 10m-5pm) Designers Janet and Patty Yamasaki refashion classic kimono and obi designs into modern dresses. Hybrid wedding dresses, formal attire or sleek day wear can all be custom-crafted even for short-term visitors.

GETTING THERE & AROUND
To/From the Airport
Honolulu International Airport is a 9-mile, 25-minute drive northwest of downtown via Ala Moana Blvd/Nimitz Hwy (92) or the H1. If you are heading there during rush hour, give yourself extra time. For more information on transport and driving directions to/from Honolulu International Airport, see p99.

Bus
The Ala Moana Center, on Ala Moana Blvd just northwest of Waikiki, is the central bus terminal for TheBus, the island's public-bus network. From Ala Moana, you can connect to points within Honolulu as well as other parts of the island. See the individual listings

for bus-access details. For general information about the service, see p100.

Car
Often, directions in Honolulu are given based on landmarks: for example, if someone tells you to go 'Ewa,' it means to go west of Honolulu towards the area of the same name. Alternatively 'Diamond Head' is often used as a general term for sights east of Honolulu.

Parking is available at several municipal parking lots in the downtown Honolulu area. Chinatown is full of one-way streets, traffic is thick and parking can be tight, so consider taking the bus even if you have a car. However, there are public parking garages at the Chinatown Gateway Plaza on Bethel St and the Ali'i Center on Alakea St. Note that N Hotel St is open to bus traffic only.

Rush hour in Honolulu starts around 7am to 9am and 3pm to 6pm weekdays. You can also expect heavy traffic when heading toward Honolulu in the morning and away in the late afternoon on the Pali and Likelike Hwys. The H1, the main South Shore freeway, is the key to getting around the island. It connects with the Kalaniana'ole Hwy (72), which runs along the southeast coast; with the Pali (61) and Likelike (63) Hwys, which lead to the Windward Coast; with the Farrington Hwy (93), which leads up the Wai'anae (Leeward) Coast; with H2 and the Kamehameha Hwy (99, 83) on the way to the North Shore; and with H3, which runs from Pearl Harbor through the Ko'olau Range, ending on the Windward Coast.

Taxi
Taxis are readily available at the airport and larger hotels, but are otherwise generally hard to find. Phone **TheCab** (☎ 422-2222), **Charley's** (☎ 531-1333) or **City Taxi** (☎ 524-2121) to book a taxi. They have meters and charge a flag-down fee of $2.25 to start. From there, fares increase in 30¢ increments at a rate of $2.40 per mile. There's an extra charge of 40¢ for each suitcase or backpack.

PEARL HARBOR

The sparkling bay of Pearl Harbor (Map p102), west of Honolulu, lives in the US history books not for its original stock of pearl oysters or its scenic setting, but instead for the Japanese air attacks of December 7, 1941

O'AHU

SURPRISE ATTACK

The so-called 'Day of Infamy' began at 7:55am on December 7, 1941 with a wave of more than 350 Japanese planes swooping over the Ko'olau Range headed toward the unsuspecting US Pacific Fleet in Pearl Harbor.

The battleship USS *Arizona* took a direct hit and sank in less than nine minutes, trapping its crew beneath the surface. About 80% of its crew (1177 men) died. It wasn't until 15 minutes after the bombing started that American anti-aircraft guns began to shoot back at the Japanese warplanes. Twenty-one other US military vessels were sunk or seriously damaged and 347 airplanes were destroyed. Some 2335 US soldiers were killed during the two-hour attack.

In hindsight, there were two significant warnings prior to the attack that were disastrously dismissed or misinterpreted. Roughly an hour before the Japanese planes arrived, USS *Ward* spotted a submarine conning tower approaching the entrance of Pearl Harbor. The Ward immediately attacked with depth charges and sank what turned out to be one of five midget Japanese submarines launched to penetrate the harbor. At 7:02am a radar station on the north shore of O'ahu reported planes approaching. Even though they were coming from the west rather than the east, they were assumed to be American planes from the US mainland.

---

on the US Pacific fleet headquartered here. It was one of the few foreign attacks on US soil in modern history and hurtled the country into military action during WWII.

Today the harbor is still the home to an active naval and air-force base. To memorialize the attack on Pearl Harbor, the National Park Service maintains a museum and shrine at the sunken USS *Arizona*. Nearby are two other historical military attractions: the USS *Bowfin* Submarine Museum and Park and the Battleship *Missouri*, where General Douglas MacArthur accepted the Japanese surrender marking the end of WWII. Together, for the US, these three sites represent the beginning, middle and end of the war. To visit all three sites, dedicate at least a half-day, preferably in the morning when they are less crowded and traffic is less serious. Weekday afternoon rush hour typically runs from around 2pm or 3pm until 7pm.

USS ARIZONA MEMORIAL

One of the most significant WWII attractions in the USA, this **site** (☎ 422-2771, 24hr recorded information 422-0561; www.nps.gov/usar; admission free; ✆ 7:30am-5pm, closed Thanksgiving, Christmas & New Year's Day) presents the history of the Pearl Harbor attack and commemorates the fallen service members. Run by the National Park Service, the memorial comprises two sections: the mainland visitor center and offshore shrine. Within the visitor center is a museum that presents WWII memorabilia and a model of the battleship and shrine, as well as a documentary film for historical background. The

offshore shrine was built over the midsection of the sunken USS *Arizona* with deliberate geometry to represent initial defeat, ultimate victory and eternal serenity. One of three chambers inside the shrine acts as the final resting place for the service people killed during the attack; their names are engraved into the marble wall. In the central room are cutaway well sections through which visitors can see the skeleton of the ship. All facilities have disabled access.

Boat trips to the shrine depart from the visitor center every 15 minutes between 7:45am and 3pm on a first-come, first-served basis (weather permitting). At the visitors center, you'll be given a ticket stating the minute of the hour that the tour will begin.

The memorial is one of Hawaii's busiest attractions and can receive an average of 5000-plus people during the summer months. Generally, the shortest waits are in the morning, and as the day goes on, waits of a couple of hours are not uncommon.

CHECK YOUR BAGS

There are strict security measures at the USS *Arizona* and the USS *Missouri* memorials. You are not allowed to bring in any items that allow concealment, including purses, camera bags, fanny packs, backpacks, diaper bags, shopping bags and the like. Also, cameras or video cameras larger than 12in can not be brought into the sites at all. You may, of course, bring normal-sized cameras.

USS BOWFIN SUBMARINE MUSEUM & PARK

If you have to wait an hour or two for your USS *Arizona* Memorial tour to begin, you might want to stroll over to the adjacent **USS Bowfin Submarine Museum & Park** (☎ 423-1341; www.bowfin.org; submarine & museum adult/child $10/4, museum only $4/2, combination ticket with USS Missouri $21/11; 8am-5pm). Run by a private nonprofit organization, this park contains the moored WWII-era USS *Bowfin* submarine as well as the Pacific Submarine Museum.

Launched in 1942, the *Bowfin* completed nine war patrols and sank 44 ships in the Pacific before the end of WWII. Visitors take a self-guided audio tour of the submarine that explores the life of the crew. The affiliated museum traces the development of submarines from their early origins to the nuclear age.

Surrounding the submarine and museum is a small park (admission is free) from where you can view the missiles and torpedoes spread around the grounds. Look through the periscopes or inspect the Japanese *kaiten,* a suicide torpedo that was developed as a last-ditch effort to ward off invasion. It was the marine equivalent of the kamikaze pilot and his plane. A volunteer was placed in the torpedo before it was fired. He then piloted it to its target. At least one US ship, the USS *Mississinewa,* was sunk by a *kaiten*. It went down off Ulithi Atoll in November 1944.

BATTLESHIP MISSOURI MEMORIAL

The decommissioned battleship **USS Missouri** (☎ 423-2263; www.ussmissouri.org; adult/child $15/8, audio tour $22/14, combination ticket with USS Bowfin $21/11; 9am-5pm), nicknamed 'Mighty Mo,' provides a unique historical 'bookend' to the US campaign in the Pacific during WWII. If you're a history buff the USS *Missouri* is a worthwhile sight, but if your time or money is limited a visit to the USS *Arizona* Memorial will suffice.

The 887ft-long USS *Missouri* launched near the end of WWII and served as a flagship during the battles of Iwo Jima and Okinawa. On September 2, 1945, the formal Japanese surrender that ended WWII took place on the battleship's deck.

The USS *Missouri* is now docked on Ford Island, just a few hundred yards from the sunken remains of the USS *Arizona* and is managed by the nonprofit USS *Missouri* Memorial Association. A general admission tour of the ship takes approximately two hours. You can poke about the officers' quarters, visit the wardroom that now houses exhibits on the ship's history and walk the deck where General Douglas MacArthur accepted the Japanese surrender. There are more expensive tours that include a docent-led tour of the 'combat engagement center' where you can watch a simulated naval battle.

It's not possible to drive directly to Ford Island, because it's an active military facility. Instead, a shuttle bus picks up visitors from the USS *Bowfin* Park every 10 minutes from 9am to 5pm.

EATING

Because traffic can be tricky on this side of the island, you might want to schedule in a meal to wait out rush hour.

BARGAIN HUNTING

OK, so where's the best place to hunt for pineapple-shaped ukuleles, cheap Hawaiian CDs and '50s kitsch ceramics? Hands-down the honors go to the **Nu'uanu Swap Meet** (Map p102; ☎ 486-6704; Aloha Stadium, 99-500 Salt Lake Blvd; admission $0.50; 6am-3pm Wed, Sat & Sun) in the Pearl Harbor area. The Aloha Stadium, best known as the host to nationally televised football games and top-name music concerts, transforms itself three days a week into Hawaii's biggest and best swap meet. For local flavor, this flea market is hard to beat, with some 1500 vendors selling an amazing variety of items, from beach gear and bananas to T-shirts and old Hawaii license plates.

This is such a big event that there are private shuttle bus services from Waikiki that operate on swap meet days; for information, call **VIP Trans** (☎ 836-0317), which runs every 30 minutes from 7am to 3:15pm from Waikiki hotels only (one way $6), or **Reliable Shuttle** (☎ 924-9292), operating every hour 6:30am to 1:30pm (roundtrip $15).

To reach Aloha Stadium by bus, take the No 20 from Waikiki, or the No 42 from Ala Moana Shopping Center. By car, take the H1 Fwy west, get off at Stadium/Halawa exit, and follow the 'Stadium' signs.

AN ACQUIRED TASTE?

Admit it, you don't like poi, or so you say.

Of the many Hawaiian foods to try, from briny *lomilomi* salmon and *kalua* pig, to raw sashimi and crunchy seaweed, one Hawaiian staple still remains off-limits to most island visitors – the pasty, slightly sour, pounded taro root known as poi. It has been relegated to a culinary outpost for things bland and purplish.

But poi is mainly used as a tangy dipping sauce for nearly everything on the table, never as a dish on its own. And the best poi is slightly aged, not the fresh (bland) stuff of the tourist luau.

So it may be time for another try. Really, all we are saying is: give poi a chance.

Helena's Hawaiian Food (☎ 845-8044; 1240 N School St; per person $5-10; ☷ 10am-7:30pm Tue-Fri) Wedged between a radiator shop and the highway, this humble Honolulu institution dates back to 1946. In 2000 this modest storefront restaurant joined Honolulu's bigwigs when it was honored with a James Beard award. Owner Helena Chock still runs the kitchen, handles the cash register and chats with customers. The menu is mostly à la carte dishes, some smoky and salty, others sweet or spicy. You start with poi (fermented taro) or rice, then add a couple of small plates of *lomilomi* (minced and salted, with tomato and green onion) salmon, briny shortribs or *kalua* pig, and you've got a mini-luau for under $10.

Tanioka's Fish Market (☎ 671-3779; www.taniokas .com; 94-903 Farrington Hwy, Waipahu; ☷ 9am-5pm Mon-Fri, 9am-3pm Sun) Once a small family venture, this Waipahu market, west of Pearl Harbor, has evolved into an enterprise selling over 40 varieties of poke, including a gut-busting 300 pounds of limu poke and 200 pounds of shoyu poke a day.

Nico's at Pier 38 (☎ 540-1377; 1133 N Nimitz Hwy; mains $7-8; ☷ 6:30am-6pm Mon-Fri, 6:30am-2:30pm Sat) French chef Nico was inspired by the dressed-down island food scene to merge his classical training with the reliable plate lunch. French standards such as steak frite appear alongside fresh fish sandwiches and local belly fillers including chicken katsu.

Sam Choy's Breakfast, Lunch & Crab (☎ 545-7979; 580 N Nimitz Hwy; mains $8-18; ☷ 7am-3pm & 5-9pm) Hawaii knows how to do over-the-top meals as well as the mainland with huge portions of seafood specials, local food and crab dinners. Lots of tourists find their way here for the surf-and-turf combos that are as accessible but higher quality than hotel fare. Don't forget to sample some of the onsite microbrews made by Big Aloha Brewery.

GETTING THERE & AWAY

The USS *Arizona* Memorial and USS *Bowfin* Park are off Kamehameha Hwy (99) on the US Naval Reservation just south of the Aloha Stadium.

If you're coming from Honolulu, take H1 west to exit 15A (Stadium/USS *Arizona* Memorial). Make sure you follow the highway signs for the USS *Arizona* Memorial and not the signs for Pearl Harbor. There's plenty of free parking at the visitor center.

It's also easy to get there by public bus. Buses 20, 42 and City Express-A are the most direct from Waikiki to the visitor center, taking about an hour. Bus 20 makes a stop at the airport, adding about 15 minutes to the travel time.

VIP Trans (☎ 839-0911) picks up passengers from Waikiki hotels several times a day, charging $10 roundtrip. The ride takes around 40 minutes and runs from 9:30am to 5:15pm.

Beware of private boat cruises to Pearl Harbor that leave from Kewalo Basin; they don't stop at the visitor center and passengers are not allowed to board the USS *Arizona* Memorial.

WAIKIKI

Like an aging Hollywood diva, Waikiki has experienced a decided arc to its career as a fashionable tropical resort. Before air travel, only the wealthy and the nobility had access to Waikiki's languorous beach and temperate climate. Then it burst into the popular imagination as the quintessential exotic vacation complete with flower lei, aloha shirts and romance, all within a few hours' airplane ride. Celebrities sang about it, beach boys strummed ukuleles, and fresh-faced kids walked on water thanks to long wooden surfboards. For an older generation, Waikiki still holds this golden-era title, but little of the historic glamour remains.

O'AHU

WAIKIKI

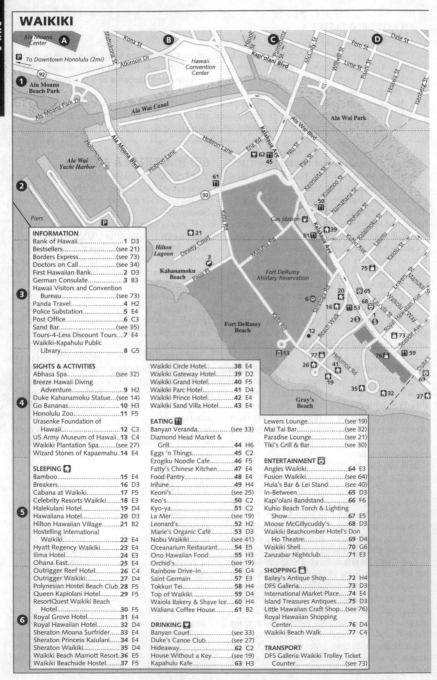

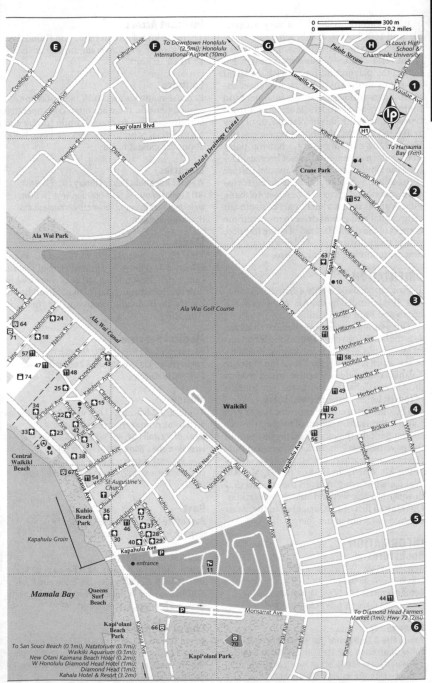

O'AHU

What endures instead is a very accessible and tourist-oriented beach resort now crowded with high-rise towers and suburban chain restaurants – Vegas with a beach. No longer the playground for the rich, Waikiki sits firmly in the lap of the middle class, including conventioneers, family reunioners and round-the-world travelers. More adventurous types bristle at the idea of Waikiki, until they arrive and find that the tourist veneer doesn't blot out the natural beauty – bowing palm trees, golden sunsets and velvet breezes. Despite the familiar, traditional Hawaiian culture is proudly on display at beachside performance spaces and generic-looking hotel bars. Plus Waikiki is just a small part of a vibrant state capital and a short drive to more remote corners of the island. Instead of being trapped, you've really just arrived. And as a reward you deserve an umbrella drink or two.

ORIENTATION

Technically Waikiki is only a district of Honolulu. It is bounded by the Ala Wai Canal, the ocean and Kapi'olani Park.

Three parallel roads cross Waikiki: Kalakaua Ave, the beach road named after King David Kalakaua; Kuhio Ave, the main drag for Waikiki's buses, which is named after Prince Jonah Kuhio Kalaniana'ole; and Ala Wai Blvd, which borders the Ala Wai Canal. This forms the tight nucleus of tourist hotels, restaurants and bars.

The outskirts are a tad more local. Ala Wai Canal is the nearby residential neighborhood's closest park. In the mornings, joggers pound the pavement and in the late afternoon outrigger canoe teams dice up the water en route to the Ala Wai Yacht Harbor. In 1922 the Ala Wai Canal was dug to divert the streams that flowed into the wetland marsh of Waikiki. Old Hawaii lost out, as farmers had the water drained out from under them.

INFORMATION
Bookstores
Bestsellers (☎ 953-2378; Hilton Hawaiian Village, 2005 Kalia Rd; ☷ 10am-9pm)
Borders Express (☎ 922-4154; Waikiki Shopping Plaza, 2250 Kalakaua Ave; ☷ 9:30am-9:30pm)

Emergency
Police, Fire & Ambulance (☎ 911) For all emergencies.
Police Substation (☎ 529-3801; 2405 Kalakaua Ave; ☷ 24hr) If you need help, or just friendly directions, there's a small police station at Kuhio Beach.

Internet Access
There are lots of internet shops on Kuhio Ave, but few offer wi-fi. Average surfing costs are $5 to $6 an hour.

Laundry
Because many visitors to Waikiki stay for extended periods, there are often coin-operated laundry facilities in hotels, condo towers and commercial storefronts. Ask at your hotel about the closest facility.

Libraries
Waikiki-Kapahulu Public Library (☎ 733-8488; 400 Kapahulu Ave; ☷ 10am-5pm Tue, Wed, Fri & Sat, noon-7pm Thu) This small library carries mainland and Honolulu newspapers.

Media
Free tourist magazines, such as *This Week O'ahu*, *101 Things to Do* and *Best of O'ahu*, can readily be found on street corners and in hotel lobbies throughout Waikiki. In addition, there's the *Honolulu Weekly* and the *Honolulu Advertiser*.

Medical Services
Doctors on Call (☎ 971-6000; Sheraton Princess Kaiulani Hotel, 120 Ka'iulani Ave) A 24-hour clinic with X-ray and lab facilities.

Money
There are 24-hour ATMs at these banks, as well as at numerous other locations.
Bank of Hawaii (☎ 543-6900; 2228 Kalakaua Ave)
First Hawaiian Bank (☎ 943-4670; 2181 Kalakaua Ave) Displays some interesting Hawaiian murals by internationally renowned French artist Jean Charlot.

Post
Post office (☎ 973-7515; 330 Saratoga Rd) In the center of Waikiki, with free parking.

Tourist Information
Hawaii Visitors and Convention Bureau (☎ 923-1811, 800-464-2924; Suite 801, Waikiki Shopping Plaza, 2270 Kalakaua Ave) Its visitor information office has tourist brochures, free maps and helpful staff.

Travel Agencies
Panda Travel (☎ 738-3898, 800-303-6702; www .pandaonline.com; 1017 Kapahulu Ave; ☷ 8am-5:30pm Mon-Fri, 9am-1pm Sat) Makes arrangements for hotels, car rentals, package deals, cruises, etc.

O'AHU

Tours-4-Less Discount Tours (☎ 923-2211; 159 Ka'iulani Ave) Student and discount travel information.

DANGERS & ANNOYANCES

You can't walk down Kalakaua Ave without encountering one or two hustlers pushing time-shares or discounts to clubs, luau or sunset cruises. At night you can expect to see a few provocatively dressed prostitutes cruising for well-dressed Japanese businessmen. All in all, however, Waikiki is fairly tame, and you're unlikely to encounter any real problems.

SIGHTS & ACTIVITIES
Beaches

The 2-mile stretch of white sand commonly referred to as Waikiki Beach runs from Hilton Hawaiian Village in the west to Kapi'olani Park in the east. Along the way, the beach changes names and personalities.

In the early morning, the surprisingly quiet beach belongs to walkers and joggers. Strolling down the beach toward Diamond Head at dawn can actually be a meditative experience. By midmorning it looks like a normal resort beach – body-board, surfboard and catamaran concessionaires and lots of beached bodies. By noon it's challenging to walk along the packed beach without stepping on anyone.

As the beachfront developed, landowners haphazardly constructed seawalls and offshore barriers (called groins) to protect their properties, blocking the natural forces of sand accretion, making erosion a serious problem at Waikiki. Most of Waikiki's legendary white sands have been barged in from Papohaku Beach on Moloka'i.

Offshore, Waikiki is good for swimming, body-boarding, surfing, sailing and other beach activities most of the year, and there are lifeguards and showers interspersed along the beach. Between May and September, summer swells make the water a little rough for swimming, but great for surfing. The best snorkeling is in the area toward Diamond Head at Sans Souci Beach.

The following beaches run from west to east.

KAHANAMOKU BEACH

Fronting the Hilton Hawaiian Village, Kahanamoku Beach is protected by a breakwater at one end and a pier at the other, with a coral reef running between the two. It's a calm swimming area with a gently sloping sandy bottom.

It was named for Duke Kahanamoku, a surfer and swimmer who won an Olympic gold medal in the 100m freestyle in 1912, and went on to become a Hawaiian celebrity and legend.

FORT DERUSSY BEACH

Connected by a footpath to Kahanamoku Beach, Fort DeRussy Beach is one of the least-crowded of the Waikiki beaches and borders 1800ft of the Fort DeRussy Military Reservation.

The water is usually calm and good for swimming. When conditions are right, the beach is used by windsurfers, boogie boarders and board surfers. There are two beach huts, open daily, which rent windsurfing equipment, boogie boards, kayaks and snorkel sets. Public fee parking is available in front of the US Army Museum of Hawai'i.

In addition to lifeguards and showers, you'll find an inviting grassy lawn with palm trees offering some sparse shade, providing an alternative to frying on the sand.

BE YOUR OWN TOUR GUIDE

It's possible to make a cheap day excursion circling the island by bus, beginning at the Ala Moana Center in Waikiki. The Wahiawa–Circle Island bus 52 goes clockwise up Hwy 99 to Hale'iwa and along the North Shore. At the Turtle Bay Resort, on the northern tip of O'ahu, it switches signs to No 55 and comes down the scenic Windward Coast to Kane'ohe and back over the Pali Hwy to Ala Moana. The Kane'ohe–Circle Island bus 55 does the same route in reverse. These buses operate every 30 minutes from 5am to around 11pm daily. If you take the circle-island route nonstop, it takes about four hours.

For a shorter excursion from Waikiki, you can make a loop around southeast O'ahu by taking bus 58 to Sea Life Park and then bus 57 up to Kailua and back into Honolulu. Because you'll need to change buses, ask the driver for a transfer when you first board.

O'AHU

GRAY'S BEACH

Located near the Halekulani Hotel, Gray's Beach has suffered some of the strip's worst erosion. Because the seawall in front of the Halekulani was built so close to the waterline, the part of the beach facing the hotel is often totally submerged, though the waters off the beach are shallow and calm. What little remains preserves the memory of a boarding house called Gray's-by-the-Sea that stood on the site in the 1920s. In the 1930s it was home to the original Halekulani Hotel, the predecessor to today's swank high-rise.

CENTRAL WAIKIKI BEACH

Between the Royal Hawaiian Hotel and the Sheraton Moana Surfrider, Waikiki's busiest section of sand and surf is great for sunbathing, swimming and people watching.

Most of the beach has a shallow bottom with a gradual slope. The only drawback for swimmers is the beach's popularity with beginner surfers and the occasional catamaran, so be careful. **Queen's** and **Canoes**, Waikiki's best-known surf breaks, are offshore.

On the Diamond Head side of the police station, there are four boulders, known as the **Wizard Stones of Kapaemahu**, which are said to contain the secrets and healing powers of four sorcerers: Kapaemahu, Kinohi, Kapuni and Kahaloa, who visited from Tahiti in ancient times, and before returning transferred their powers to these stones.

Just east of the stones is a bronze **statue** of Duke Kahanamoku (1890–1968), Hawaii's most decorated athlete, standing with one of his long-boards. Considered the 'father of modern surfing,' Duke, who lived in Waikiki, gave surfing demonstrations around the world, from Sydney, Australia, to Rockaway Beach, New York. Many local surfers took issue with the placement of the statue, Duke standing with his back to the sea, a position they say he never would have assumed in real life. So, the city moved the statue as close to the sidewalk as possible, thus moving it further from the water.

KUHIO BEACH PARK

Paralleling the beach is a low breakwater seawall (called the Kapahulu Groin) running about 1300ft out from a covered storm drain, commonly referred to as the Wall. The seawall was built to control sand erosion, forming two nearly enclosed swimming pools. Local kids walk out on the breakwater, but it can be dangerous to the uninitiated due to a slippery surface and breaking surf.

The pool closest to the Wall is best for swimming, with the water near the breakwater reaching depths of 5ft and greater. However, because circulation is limited, the water gets murky, acquiring a noticeable film of suntan oil. The 'Watch Out Deep Holes' sign refers to holes in the pool's sandy bottom created by swirling currents. Be cautious in the deeper areas of the pool, as the holes can take waders by surprise.

This park is marked on its east end by the **Wall**, a walled storm drain with a walkway on top that juts out into the ocean. This is Waikiki's hottest boogie-boarding spot, where kids will ride straight for the wall and then veer away at the last moment, drawing 'oohs' and 'ahs' from the tourists who gather to watch them on the little pier above.

The park, incidentally, is named after Prince Kuhio, who maintained his residence here. His house was torn down in 1936, 14 years after his death, in order to expand the beach. The old-timers gathering each afternoon playing chess and cribbage on sidewalk pavilions and the kids boogie boarding give this section of the beach a real sense of Hawaiian life.

The city spent millions of dollars removing one lane of Kalakaua Ave fronting the park to extend the beach and adding water fountains, landscaping and a grassy hula mound that hosts weekly cultural displays.

KAPI'OLANI BEACH PARK

Starting at the Wall and extending down to the Natatorium, beyond Waikiki Aquarium, is Kapi'olani Beach Park.

However, **Queen's Surf** is the common name given to the wide midsection of Kapi'olani Beach. The stretch in front of the pavilion is popular with the gay community, and its sandy bottom offers decent swimming. The beach between Queen's Surf and The Wall is shallow and has broken coral.

Kapi'olani Beach Park is a relaxed place with far less of the frenzied activity by Waikiki's beachfront hotels. It's a popular weekend picnicking spot for local families who unload the kids to splash in the water as they line up the BBQ grills.

There are rest rooms and showers at the Queen's Surf pavilion. The surfing area off-

SUNSET ON THE BEACH

Cast off your self-imposed TV solitude and join the crowds for weekend movie screenings on Waikiki's Queen's Surf Beach, across from Kapi'olani Park. More than just popcorn and celluloid, the evening becomes a festive scene that attracts an equal measure of locals and visitors. Dubbed 'Sunset on the Beach,' the city-sponsored event is as much fun as a luau.

Food and music help the sun set and when darkness falls a huge screen is unscrolled above the stage and a feature movie is shown. Sometimes they opt for a movie with island connections, such as *Blue Hawaii* – the 1961 classic starring Elvis Presley – while other nights it's a popular first-run Hollywood flick. See www.sunsetonthebeach.net for movie schedule.

shore is called **Publics** and sees some good surf waves in winter.

SANS SOUCI BEACH

Also known as **Kaimana Beach** because of its proximity to the New Otani Kaimana Beach Hotel, Sans Souci attracts sunbathers and swimmers keen to avoid the main tourist scene. Despite being by itself, it also has a lifeguard station and outdoor showers.

Many residents come to Sans Souci to swim their daily laps out to a wind sock marker and back. A shallow coral reef close to the shore makes for calm, protected waters and provides reasonably good snorkeling. More coral can be found by following the Kapua Channel as it cuts through the reef, although if you swim here beware of currents that can pick up. Check conditions with the lifeguard before venturing out.

Historic Hotels

From the cityscape pictures that decorate the set of *Wheel of Fortune,* you'd never know that Waikiki has architecture older than game show host Pat Sajak. But indeed, there are two historic hotels, the Royal Hawaiian and the

TEA CEREMONIES

Ensconced in a mellow Japanese teahouse, is the **Urasenke Foundation of Hawaii** (☎ 433-6553; http://urasenke.org; 245 Saratoga Rd), which presents a traditional tea ceremony once or twice a month, depending on the season, bringing a rare bit of serenity to busy Saratoga Rd. Students dressed in kimonos perform the ceremony on tatami mats in a formal tearoom; for those participating, it can be a meditative experience. Guests are asked to wear socks, as they must leave their shoes at the door.

Sheraton Moana Surfrider, that both retain their period character. These beachside hotels are on the National Register of Historic Places and within walking distance of each other on Kalakaua Ave.

Sheraton Moana Surfrider (☎ 922-3111, 800-325-3535; www.sheraton.com/hawaii; 2365 Kalakaua Ave; free tours 11am & 5pm Mon, Wed & Fri) was originally christened the Moana Hotel in 1901. Built in the style of an old plantation inn, the Moana joined what was then an exclusive neighborhood for Hawaiian royalty and business tycoons. The patrons in the early years included aristocrats and princes. If you don't join the tour, visit the mezzanine museum, which displays period photographs and hotel memorabilia, including scripts from the *Hawaii Calls* radio show.

Royal Hawaiian Hotel (☎ 923-7311, 800-325-3535; www.sheraton-hawaii.com; 2259 Kalakaua Ave; free tours 2-3pm Mon, Wed & Fri) is a pink Art Deco palace with Moorish-style turrets and archways. During the days of luxury liners, the sea voyage to Hawaii took approximately five days and the aristocratic and celebrity passengers who docked in Honolulu needed a fitting setting for their transplanted society, thus the hotel became an extension of the ocean-liner business run by Matson Navigation. Today, historic tours explore the architecture and lore of this grand dame.

Kapi'olani Park

At the Diamond Head end of Waikiki is Hawaii's first public park, the nearly 200-acre Kapi'olani Park, a gift from King Kalakaua to the people of Honolulu in 1877. The king dedicated the park to his wife, Queen Kapi'olani.

The park is the city's communal backyard, hosting sports games and family picnics under shady banyan trees. The park's tourist attractions include the Kapi'olani Beach Park

O'AHU

O'AHU FOR NA KEIKI

O'ahu spills over with activities for kids. To check out the wild side, head to the petting area of the **Honolulu Zoo** (below). Across the street, the **Waikiki Aquarium** (below) has a touch tank geared especially for *na keiki* (children). At **Hanauma Bay** (p155), kids can glimpse schools of parrotfish and other colorful reef inhabitants.

For an enlightening bit of history, visit the **Bishop Museum** (p115), where shark-toothed war clubs await inspection. The museum's planetarium is the only one in the Pacific that chronicles the navigational systems of the first Polynesians to reach the islands. At the **Hawai'i Maritime Center** (p108) kids can check out the *Hokule'a*, the sailing canoe that was built to retrace the routes of early clever seafarers.

There are numerous safe beaches for families with small children. Waikiki has several 'kiddie pool' beaches. On the Windward Coast, **Kailua Beach Park** (p161) is equally safe and appealing.

(p140), Waikiki Aquarium and the Honolulu Zoo. Outdoor musical events are also held at the park (see p151).

WAIKIKI AQUARIUM

Located next to a living reef on the Waikiki shoreline, this modern university-managed **aquarium** (☎ 923-9741; www.waquarium.org; 2777 Kalakaua Ave; adult/child 4-13/child over 13 $9/2/4; ☸ 9am-5pm) dates from 1904, and includes an impressive shark gallery where visitors can watch circling reef and zebra sharks through a 14ft-wide window.

The aquarium is a great place to identify colorful coral and fish you've seen while snorkeling or diving. Tanks re-create various Hawaiian reef habitats, including those found in a surge zone, a sheltered reef, a deep reef and an ancient reef. There are rare Hawaiian fish with names like the bearded armorhead and the sling-jawed wrasse, along with moray eels, giant groupers and flash-back cuttlefish wavering with pulses of light.

In addition to Hawaiian marine life, you'll find exhibits on other Pacific ecosystems. Noteworthy are the giant Palauan clams that were raised from dime-sized hatchlings in 1982 and now measure more than 2ft, the largest in the USA. The aquarium's outdoor tank is home to rare Hawaiian monk seals.

HONOLULU ZOO

This reputable **zoo** (☎ 971-7171; adult/child 6-12 $8/1; ☸ 9am-4pm), at the northern end of Kapi'olani Park, features some 300 species spread across 42 acres of tropical greenery. A highlight is the naturalized African Savanna section, which has lions, cheetahs, white rhinos, giraffes, zebras, hippos and monkeys.

The zoo also has an interesting reptile section, a good selection of tropical birds (including native Hawaiian birds) and a small petting zoo for children.

NATATORIUM

This padlocked building once housed a 100m-long saltwater swimming pool built, in 1927 to honor Hawaii's WWI veterans. Two Olympic gold medalists – Johnny Weissmuller and Duke Kahanamoku – both trained in this tide-fed pool and there were once hopes of hosting the Olympics on O'ahu, with this pool as the focal point. The Natatorium is on the National Register of Historic Places but restoration projects have been stalled in political bureaucracy.

US Army Museum of Hawai'i

This **museum** (☎ 955-9552; www.hiarmymuseum soc.org; Fort DeRussy Military Reservation; admission free; ☸ 10am-4:15pm Tue-Sun) traces the military history of consolidation of power under King Kamehameha in the 1700s to the US army's ongoing role on the island. Located at Fort DeRussy Military Reservation, the museum occupies Battery Randolph, a reinforced concrete building erected in 1911 as a coastal artillery battery. The battery once held two formidable 14-inch disappearing guns with an 11-mile range, designed to recoil into the concrete walls for reloading after firing, which shook the whole neighborhood. A 55-ton lead counterweight then returned the carriage to position. Also on display is a Cobra helicopter and various military tanks and machinery.

On the 2nd floor of the complex is the Pacific Regional Visitor Center, which documents the flood-control and water-management projects of the US Army Corps of Engineers in Hawaii.

The surrounding area is part of Fort DeRussy, a US army post used mainly as a recreation center for the armed forces. This large chunk of Waikiki real estate was acquired by the US army a few years after Hawaii was annexed by the USA. Prior to that it was swampy marshland and a favorite duck-hunting spot for Hawaiian royalty. The Hale Koa Hotel on the property is open only to military personnel, but there's public access to the beach and the adjacent military museum. The section of Fort DeRussy between Kalia Rd and Kalakaua Ave has public footpaths that provide a shortcut between the two roads.

Spas

What's a beach vacation without the proper pampering? And this tropical destination has an indigenous tradition of body massage coupled with a gentle aloha spirit.

Abhasa Spa (☎ 922-8200; www.abhasa.com; Royal Hawaiian Hotel; 2259 Kalakaua Ave; massage from $110) emits a soothing island glow with cabana massage rooms surrounded by a tidy tropical garden. Local treatments include the Hawaiian-style of massage called *lomi lomi* (loving hands) and *pohaku* (heated lava rocks that relax tense muscles).

Waikiki Plantation Spa (☎ 926-2880; www.waikiki plantationspa.com; Penthouse Level, Outrigger Waikiki, 2335 Kalakaua Ave; massage from $100) specializes in holistic Hawaiian therapies, including *lomi lomi* and *pohaku*; some therapists incorporate a spiritual aspect to the massage with a concluding chant or prayer. The relaxation deck overlooking the water adds another spiritual dimension.

FESTIVALS & EVENTS

Many of the celebrations and festivals held in Waikiki are part of city- or island-wide events. See p122 for some listings.

SLEEPING

Waikiki's main beachfront strip, Kalakaua Ave, is lined with high-rise hotels that all look the same. What you're shopping for is an ocean view for the best price as the rooms are generic in their decor and layout. Do be aware that 'ocean view' and its cousins 'ocean front' and 'partial ocean view' are all liberally

used and often require a periscope to spot the waves. When making reservations, check the hotel's online room map or call a reservation agent at the hotel for guidance.

The primary chains that dominate the strip include ResortQuest, Sheraton, Outrigger and Aqua. The Outrigger group (which also owns Ohana) is a locally owned company and has won many state tourism awards for its promotion of Hawaii cultural events. Aqua is a newcomer to Waikiki and is renovating many of the older hotels off the beachfront into condotels with stylish lobbies. Like Vegas, Waikiki would like to upgrade its image but the small waves toward chic and fabulous have not yet reached shore.

The hotels listed here in no way tackle all the options, but we do cover either stand-out chain options or small, sometimes family-owned, spots that don't have a high-profile. Moving a few blocks inland to Kuhio Ave and near the Ala Wai Canal significantly reduces the costs of the room.

Since price should be the guiding principle for finding a hotel room in Waikiki, we suggest the online booking services that offer airfare-and-accommodation packages. If you're looking for a condo rental, contact **Pacific Islands Reservations** (☎ 808-262-8133; www .waikiki-condo-rentals.com). When we use the term 'studio,' this refers to a standard hotel room with a kitchenette (burner, sink, refrigerator and microwave). With so many competing for the available accommodations, prices in

---

TOP 10 WAIKIKI SLEEPS

Spanning every budget, there's a little nook in Waikiki just for you. Here are some suggestions:

- **Royal Grove Hotel** (p144)
- **Hawaiiana Hotel** (p144)
- **Waikiki Circle Hotel** (p145)
- **Waikiki Grand Hotel** (p144)
- **New Otani Kaimana Beach Hotel** (p145)
- **Royal Hawaiian Hotel** (p147)
- **Kahala Hotel & Resort** (p155)
- **Sheraton Princess Kaiulani** (p145)
- **Sheraton Moana Surfrider** (p146)
- **Halekulani Hotel** (p146)

O'AHU

Waikiki tend to be higher than in the rest of the state for comparable lodgings. For this section only we have defined budget options as costing under $100, midrange $100 to $300 and top end as $301.

Budget

HOSTELS

In the shadows of the beach-facing high-rises, little Lemon Rd is filled with backpacker-style hostels catering to around-the-worlders and the under-25 set. Accommodations include standard dorms; semiprivate rooms, in which one section of the dorm has its own private bedroom but shared facilities; and private rooms. Configurations vary but each hostel will have a shared kitchen and common area as well as travelers information. There are no curfews or other restrictions, except the usual requirement for travelers to show a passport or an onward ticket.

Hostelling International Waikiki (☎ 926-8313; 2417 Prince Edward St; dm/d $20/48; ☒ check-in 8am-noon & 4pm-midnight; ▣ ℗ $5) On a backstreet a few blocks from Waikiki Beach, this HI hostel has seven-bed dorms that are sex-segregated in an older, low-rise apartment complex. Along with the dorms, there are also private rooms. The accommodations are adequate but won't have you jumping for joy. There's a $3 surcharge if you're not an HI member; HI membership can be purchased onsite for $28 for US citizens, $18 for foreign visitors. Unlike most other HI hostels, there's no dormitory lockout or curfew.

Polynesian Hostel Beach Club (☎ 922-1340; www .hostelhawaii.com; 2584 Lemon Rd; dm $20-23, semiprivate s/d $45/54, private r $67-75; ▣ ℗ $5) More of a travelers scene, this cheery hostel features co-ed dorms (10-, six- and four-bed), cable TV and shared kitchen.

Waikiki Beachside Hostel (☎ 923-9566, 866-478-3888; www.waikikibeachsidehostel.com; Suite B101, 2556 Lemon Rd; dm $25-35, semiprivate r $75-82; ▣ ℗ $5) The rooms at this hostel are more expensive than its neighbors because each dorm comes equipped with kitchenettes and cable TV. There are four-bed and eight-bed dorm rooms – co-ed and female only – as well as semiprivate rooms.

HOTELS

Waikiki Prince Hotel (☎ 922-1544; 2431 Prince Edward St; r $45-65; ☒ ℗ $8) If you don't need a lot of bells and whistles, this no-frills option is basic,

clean and affordable. More expensive rooms have kitchenettes. It's a couple of minutes' walk to the beach.

Royal Grove Hotel (☎ 923-7691; www.royalgrove hotel.com; 151 Uluniu Ave; studios in old/new wing $47/64; ☒ ▣ ℗ $8) If you've outgrown dorms but not your youthful thriftiness, then this classic low-rise hotel is a dream come true. Simple and affordable, it is a favorite of retirees returning each winter to their home-away-from-home complete with a pet bird and a piano in the lobby. Rooms are centered around a small pool courtyard. Economy rooms in the oldest wing have no air-con and are exposed to traffic noise. Rooms in the main wing have air-con and a small lanai (porch). Both types of room have a kitchenette.

Midrange

Waikiki Gateway Hotel (☎ 955-3741, 800-247-1903; www.waikiki-gateway-hotel.com; 2077 Kalakaua Ave; r $100-133, studios $160; ☒ ▣ ℗ $11) Within walking distance to quiet Fort DeRussy beach, this hotel is first and foremost a bargain considering its location, but don't arrive expecting top-shelf amenities. The few perks include free internet and continental breakfast.

Hawaiiana Hotel (☎ 923-3811, 800-367-5122; www .hawaiianahotelatwaikiki.com; 260 Beach Walk; r $105-235; ☒ ▣ ℗ $15) Cottage-style rooms shaded by a lush garden create an escape into an old-fashioned era. The setting is low-key charm and comfort with rooms accented in lavender, rattan furnishings and ceiling fans.

Waikiki Grand Hotel (☎ 923-1814, 800-321-2558; www.queenssurf.com; 134 Kapahulu Ave; r $105-250; ☒ ▣ ℗ $12) Opposite the zoo, this hotel has individually owned units with unique decorations. A spot check into one revealed a clean plantation style, a nice break from the factory-issued hotel comforter. The hotel is also known for Hula's, a popular gay bar.

Breakers (☎ 923-3181, 800-426-0494; www.breakers -hawaii.com; 250 Beach Walk; studios from $120; ☒ ▣ free) This older, Polynesian-style hotel is a throwback to earlier times, with a landscaped garden and floor-to-ceiling louvered windows. First-floor garden rooms can sleep up to five. All rooms are large and have kitchenettes.

Celebrity Resorts Waikiki (☎ 923-7336; www.celeb rityresorts.com; 431 Nohonani St; studios from $130, ste from $144; ☒ ℗ $10) Despite the easy-to-overlook name, this low-key, three-story hotel merits paparazzi attention. It's clean and friendly, in a quieter part of Waikiki, with about half of its rooms overlooking a landscaped garden. Studios can sleep up to four people (with a sleeper couch) and one-bedrooms can cram in six. Look for the small sign and green awning.

Waikiki Sand Villa Hotel (☎ 922-4744, 800-247-1903; www.waikikisandvillahotel.com; 2375 Ala Wai Blvd; r from $140-185; 🔀 🖳 🔊 🅿 $10) Popular with Japanese and Chinese visitors, this unassuming high-rise opposite the Ala Wai Canal has a friendly laid-back atmosphere. The rooms are compact, but most can sleep four people. For the best views, ask for a corner unit or snag a premium room with a view of the mountains. There's also a nice pool and Jacuzzi area and internet bar for surf and suds.

Queen Kapiolani Hotel (☎ 922-4671, 800-367-2317; www.queenkapiolani.com; 150 Kapahulu Ave; r $140-220; 🔀 🅿 $8) Sort of like your great aunt's sitting room, this older hotel has a distinct sense of place and time with a breezy open-air lobby, faux chandeliers, weather-worn carpets and faded paintings of Hawaiian royalty. It is at the quieter end of Waikiki closer to the local beaches. Rooms vary greatly from acceptable to cramped. Most ocean-view rooms have lanai with unobstructed views of Diamond Head.

New Otani Kaimana Beach Hotel (☎ 923-1555, 800-356-8264; www.kaimana.com; 2863 Kalakaua Ave; r $150-250, studios $180-250, ste $250-330; 🔀 🅿 $15) Just half a mile from the throbbing hub of Waikiki, the New Otani Kaimana Beach Hotel sits oceanside in front of little Sans Souci Beach Park. For the seclusion and beach access, this may be one of the best values in Waikiki. The rooms are small, but the view is big, and all have roomy lanai.

Bamboo (☎ 922-7777, 866-406-2782; www.aquabamboo.com; 2425 Kuhio Ave; r $157-163, ste $180-200; 🔀 🔊 🅿 $15) An intimate boutique, this hotel has small, Eurasian style rooms. There is a complimentary continental breakfast and wi-fi in the lobby. The pool is saltwater should you tire of the ocean.

Ilima Hotel (☎ 923-1877, 800-801-9366; www.ilima.com; 445 Nohonani St; studios $167-200, ste $240-280; 🔀 🔊 🅿) A tad on the frumpy side, the Ilima is in a less hurried section of Waikiki, between the Ala Wai Canal and the International Marketplace. Units are roomy and bright, with large lanai, two double beds and fully equipped kitchens; the deluxe studios have free DSL connection. Free local phone calls.

Waikiki Circle Hotel (☎ 800-922-7866, 923-1571; www.aston-hotels.com; 2464 Kalakaua Ave; r $175-205; 🔀)

This tubular building must have been *très chic* back in the playful era of post-modernism, but today this survivor is all about value not fashion. About half of the rooms, complete with lanai, get a full view of the ocean for the price that other hotels charge for a parking lot view. The drawback is that the rooms aren't big enough to practice your hula routine.

Sheraton Princess Kaiulani (☎ 922-5811, 800-500-8313; www.sheraton-hawaii.com; 120 Ka'iulani Ave; r from $185; 🔀 🔊 🅿 $15) Known as the 'PK,' this Sheraton property was built in the 1950s by Matson Navigation to help turn Waikiki into a middle-class destination. The location puts you in the busy heart of Waikiki without the inflated prices of many other central hotels.

Cabana at Waikiki (☎ 926-5555, 877-902-2121; www.cabana-waikiki.com; 2551 Cartwright Rd; r $200-225; 🔀 🔊 🅿 $12) The well-appointed Cabana caters to the gay community and is only minutes from Waikiki's gay bar Hula's and Queen's Surf Beach. Each of the 15 units can sleep four people, and comes with a queen bed and sofa bed, kitchenette and lanai. Furnishings are on the tropical side. Rates include continental breakfast and access to a hot tub and gym.

Waikiki Parc Hotel (☎ 921-7272, 800-422-0450; www.waikikiparc.com; 2233 Helumoa Rd; r from $205; 🔀 🔊 🅿 $15) Across the street from its more upmarket sister operation, the Halekulani, the Parc has a pleasantly understated elegance. The rooms are average in size, but have nice touches, such as ceramic-tiled floors, shuttered lanai doors and bathtubs. Check out their online packages that include lodging and car rental or additional rooms for families traveling together.

Hilton Hawaiian Village (☎ 949-4321, 800-445-8667; www.hawaiianvillage.hilton.com; 2005 Kalia Rd; r from $210; 🔀 🔊 🅿 $12) On the Fort DeRussy side of Waikiki, the Hilton is Waikiki's largest hotel – practically a self-sufficient city of towers, restaurants, bars and shops. This is obviously a huge lodging factory but the beach is serene and wide.

Ohana East (☎ 922-5353, 800-462-6262; www.ohanahotels.com; 150 Ka'iulani Ave; d $219, ste $319; 🔀 🔊 🅿 $15) One of the Ohana's more upscale hotels, the East is centrally located, has all the amenities of a large-scale hotel and is utterly forgettable, which is a plus, we promise.

ResortQuest Waikiki Beach Hotel (☎ 922-2511, 800-922-7866; www.ResortQuestHawaii.com; 2570 Kalakaua Ave; r from $260; 🔀 🔊 🅿 $15) Renovated into a bright and bustling hotel, this ocean-view

O'AHU

number is all the rage on internet-booking sites and is frequently sold out. The location is central, the decor is exuberant and if you get a discount then you too will be a devotee.

Hyatt Regency Waikiki (☎ 923-1234, 800-926-3415; www.hyattwaikiki.com; 2424 Kalakaua Ave; r from $280; ⌗ ⌸ Ⓟ $12) From the outside, it's hard to miss the Hyatt's twin towers with its mega-capacity and oceanfront views in the Regency club rooms. Inside, the lobby-level garden atrium and cascading waterfalls soothes the cacophony of screaming kids and bickering families. The illusion of intimacy carries through into accommodations where rooms are limited to 18 per floor.

Top End

Although Waikiki stands firmly in the lap of middle-class standards, there are a few beachfront hotels that can compete with the top-shelf. And then of course a beachfront location accounts for a high-end price tag.

Outrigger Reef Hotel (☎ 923-3111, 800-688-7444; www.outriggerreef.com; 2169 Kalia Rd; r from $300; ⌗ ⌸ Ⓟ $18) The Outrigger Reef lacks the historic charm of its other beachfront neighbors but it has managed to nudge its way into a beachfront location. Rooms are modern and functional and the average guest dresses a little more suburban than urban.

Sheraton Waikiki (☎ 922-4422, 800-325-3535; www.sheraton-hawaii.com; 2255 Kalakaua Ave; r from $320; ⌗ ⌸ Ⓟ $15) This megahotel looms over the historic Royal Hawaiian Hotel with modern utility; a bustling lobby, shops and enough room to accommodate tour groups, family reunions and conferences.

Halekulani Hotel (☎ 923-2311, 800-367-2343; www.halekulani.com; 2199 Kalia Rd; r from $325; ⌗ ⌸ Ⓟ $18) Subdued and elegant, this is the hotel where you're more likely to need an evening gown than a fanny pack. Its modern sophistication ranks it as a favorite with the *Condé Nast Traveler* and *Travel & Leisure* set. Service is regarded as effortless with in-room check-ins and other humane treatments. Rooms come with all the modern gadgets, including complimentary wi-fi and deep-soak tubs.

W Honolulu Diamond Head (☎ 922-1700, 888-528-9465; www.whotels.com; 2885 Kalakaua Ave; r from $335; ⌗ ⌸ Ⓟ $18) The W brand has dug into a quiet spot on Sans Souci Beach, delivering its tech- and fashion-friendly identity to the Blackberry-carrying vacationers.

Sheraton Moana Surfrider (☎ 922-3111, 800-325-3535; www.starwoodhotels.com; 2365 Kalakaua Ave; r from $350; ⌗ ⌸ Ⓟ $12) Built in 1901, the Moana was Hawaii's first beachfront hotel. Several restorations and a couple of modern wings later, it manages to maintain its original colonial character. The lobby is graceful and historic with high plantation-style ceilings and Hawaiian artwork. The rooms in the original building have been restored to an early-20th-century look, with understated wooden trim-

---

WAIKIKI GIMMICKS

There's no denying it, Waikiki is tourist central with all the attendant drawbacks: overpriced hotel meals, weak alcoholic fruity drinks and a unique culture reduced to a coconut bra. Don't fight it, just embrace it for all of its commodified cheesiness. Of the many entertainment gimmicks that line the strip, here are a few standouts.

Oceanarium Restaurant (☎ 921-6111; Pacific Beach Hotel, 2490 Kalakaua Ave; weekend brunch buffet $21-26, dinner buffet $34; ☺ 6am-10pm) Dine with the fishes at this hotel restaurant and aquarium. The dining room wraps around a three-story aquarium brimming with colorful tropical fish and more pensive sharks and rays. The occupants of the tank are only for decoration, not for consumption. Divers feed the tropical fish at noon, 1pm, 6:30pm and 8pm.

Top of Waikiki (☎ 923-3877; www.topofwaikiki.com; 21st fl, Waikiki Business Plaza, 2270 Kalakaua Ave; sunset dinner $14; ☺ 5-9:30pm) Once a hallmark of progress, the revolving restaurant was first introduced at a world's fair in the 1960s but it has since become a relic of simpler times. Rotating at about one revolution per hour, this tower-top restaurant absorbs a 360-degree view from mountain to sea and back again. There's food involved too, but the novelty is the slow-motion sit-and-spin.

International Market Place (☎ 971-2080; 2330 Kalakaua Ave; ☺ 10am-10pm) For the ultimate in tourist trinket shopping, try this busy and rambling open-air collection of clothing and jewelry stalls, palm trees and snack shops, all in the heart of Waikiki. You'll find everything from seashell necklaces and refrigerator magnets to T-shirts and Hawaiian music CDs.

mings of koa and cherry. But you get more room in the newer wing and 'partial ocean view' is more generous than it sounds.

Outrigger Waikiki (☎ 923-0711, 800-688-7444; www .outrigger.com; 2335 Kalakaua Ave; r $350; 🍴 🛍 P $18) This beachfront hotel was the first of the Outrigger chain and remains its flagship property. Set on a prime stretch of sand, there's a vacation 'party' atmosphere to the place with beachside events and the good-times restaurant-bar Duke's Canoe Club (p149). Complimentary wi-fi in the lobby and direct dial calls to the US mainland.

Waikiki Beach Marriott Resort (☎ 922-6611, 800-367-5121; www.marriottwaikiki.com; 2552 Kalakaua Ave; r from $375; 🍴 🛍 P $19) A huge complex of towers and connected hallways, the Marriott requires a GPS to navigate. Rooms are dolled up in a canary yellow and the K-Tower soaks up views of stoic Diamond Head. This isn't for the exclusive crowd, as the comfort seekers here are many and fairly anonymous. It also features weekly poolside performances by the grand lady of Hawaiian falsetto, Auntie Genoa Keawe.

Royal Hawaiian Hotel (☎ 923-7311, 800-325-3535; www.starwood.com/hawaii; 2259 Kalakaua Ave; r from $430; 🍴 🛍 P $15) Now a Sheraton property, the Royal Hawaiian was Waikiki's first true luxury hotel, and today it still softens the rough edges of Waikiki's less aristocratic side. This pink, Moorish-style building is all ambiance with cool and airy walkways and soaring ceilings. Rooms in the historic section maintain a classic appeal, some with their own quiet garden view.

EATING

The heart of Waikiki is filled with food but much of it delivers caloric quantity over flavor quality – early-bird specials are still a Waikiki signature and suburban chains, like the Cheesecake Factory, are wooing away the crowds who eat with brand-name fidelity. Kuhio Ave is filled with cheap grazing choices, from breakfast spots to ethnic noodle houses that can fuel you through a day of surf-riding and beach-strolling.

The surfside hotels have restaurants that catch the sea breezes with various dining options, from dawn to dusk. Surf-and-turf are the usual suspects and worth a gander. But for night-time meals, you're better off getting out of the Waikiki stew and into Honolulu. On the periphery of Waikiki, you'll find some great neighborhood restaurants along Kapahulu Ave heading towards the university.

Budget

Leonard's (☎ 737-5591; 933 Kapahulu Ave; pastries 65¢-$1; 🕙 6am-9pm) This Portuguese bakery is known throughout Honolulu for its *malasadas*, a type of sweet, fried dough rolled in sugar, like a doughnut without the hole. Try the *haupia malasada*, with a coconut cream filling, and you'll be hooked.

Waiola Bakery & Shave Ice (☎ 735-8886; 525 Kapahulu Ave) Developing a shave ice palate is a point of pride for locals and this modest storefront delivers some crucial requirements: superfine shave ice and a large assortment of unique flavors. Go beyond the obvious tropical syrups into lychee or sprinkle a little azuki bean on top.

Fatty's Chinese Kitchen (☎ 922-9600; 2345 Kuhio Ave; dishes $3-8; 🕙 10:30am-10:30pm) Have a seat at this hole-in-the-wall next to the Miramar hotel for some of the cheapest and saltiest grub in Waikiki. The atmosphere is purely local, with a dozen seats lining a long bar just a grease splatter away from the cook.

Tokkuri Tei (☎ 739-2800; 611 Kapahulu Ave; dishes $3-15; 🕙 11am-1:45pm Mon-Fri, 5:30pm-midnight Sat) Bring your sense of adventure to this cozy *izakaya* (Japanese bar serving small plates) with upbeat versions of sushi standards. The decor is Japanese lanterns and bookcases store customers' favorite bottles of drink. Try the house poke (made with fish roe), grilled *shiso maki* (shiso leaf and pork) or soft-shell crab drizzled with a sweet chili vinaigrette.

Saint Germain (☎ 924-4305; 2301 Kuhio Ave; snacks $5; 🕙 7am-9pm) The setting is an ordinary storefront through which even the mourning doves saunter with bravado. Starting with delicious croissants, this little French bakery presents a tasty variety of soups, salads and hearty baguette sandwiches, all made fresh to order with a dozen vegetarian and meat fillings to select from.

Rainbow Drive-In (☎ 737-0177; cnr Kapahulu & Kanaina Aves; dishes $5; 🕙 7:30am-9pm) There aren't many drive-ins left in the world, and this old-fashioned survivor is an only-in-Hawaii subset. From the takeaway counter, construction workers and gangly teens order all the local favorites: chili served over rice, teriyaki burgers and saimin (local-style noodle soup).

Diamond Head Market & Grill (☎ 732-0077; 3158 Monsarrat Ave; dishes $6-10; 🕙 grill 10:30am-9pm, market

7:30am-9pm) Fast-food for an upscale neighborhood, this takeaway counter and deli market feeds families who don't want to heat up the kitchen as well as career bachelors with healthy versions of plate lunches. The salmon plate gets an approving nod from others in line and there are picnic tables beside the parking lot for immediate consumption. In the market, you can stock up on salads and picnic supplies.

Marie's Organic Café (☎ 926-3900; 2155 Kalakaua Ave; dishes $6-10; ☽ 11am-8pm Mon-Sat) In the same complex as Planet Hollywood, this health-food store has a small café for organic veggie sandwiches, salads and wraps. The green barley mousse with a dab of azuki paste is both a dessert and an oddity.

Eggs 'n Things (☎ 949-0820; 1911 Kalakaua Ave; dishes $7-10; ☽ 11pm-2pm) Never empty, this bustling diner specializes in hearty breakfast fare, from thick pancakes done up with whip cream to steak and eggs. The odd hours reflect its clientele, early morning tourists, graveyard shift workers and post-clubbers.

Waliana Coffee House (☎ 955-1764; 1860 Ala Moana Blvd; dishes $7-14; ☽ 24hr) Opposite the Hilton Hawaiian Village, this all-night coffee shop serves heaping portions along with tropical fruity drinks with plenty of aloha. Sit at the bar and swap tales with an O'ahu newbie.

Ezogiku Noodle Cafe (☎ 923-2013; cnr Lemon Rd & Paoakalani Ave; dishes $8; ☽ 11am-11pm) This is where many Waikiki hotel employees go during their lunch and dinner breaks for steaming bowls of Japanese ramen, curries and fried rice. It's cheap, fast and the closest you'll get to a subway noodle shop this side of Tokyo.

Stock up your kitchenette at **Food Pantry** (☎ 923-9831; 2370 Kuhio Ave; ☽ 6am-1am), a local grocery store. Its prices are higher than those of the chain supermarkets, outside Waikiki, but you don't have to fire up the car to get here.

Midrange

Ono Hawaiian Food (☎ 737-2275; 726 Kapahulu Ave; meals $8-11; ☽ 11am-8pm Mon-Sat) It ain't your touristy version of a luau, but this little local diner cuts out the showmanship and concentrates on homegrown Hawaiian fare. Along with crowded aging tables and sports paraphernalia, locals and tourists shoehorn themselves in for *kalua* pig plate, *lomilomi* salmon, or *lau lau* (meat wrapped in ti or taro leaves and steamed) served either with rice or poi. Arrive by 6pm to avoid a long wait; cash only.

Irifune (☎ 737-1141; 563 Kapahulu Ave; mains $10-15; ☽ 11:30am-1:30pm & 5:30-9:30pm Tue-Sat) Follow the locals to this cramped eatery, decorated with Japanese country kitsch, and serving up creative appetizers like *gyoza* (fried dumplings) stuffed with tofu and cream cheese. A top dinner choice is the garlic 'ahi, seared ever so gingerly, and a variety of combination plates. Alcohol is not served, but you can bring your own beer.

Keoni's (☎ 922-9888; Ohana East, 2375 Kuhio Ave; dishes $10-25; ☽ 7am-11pm) One of the spin-offs from the nearby place offers a mix of Thai and American dishes. There are breakfasts and lunch specials.

Keo's (☎ 951-9355; Kuhio Ave; mains $12-18; ☽ 5-11pm) The owner Keo Sananikone, claiming Laotian heritage, teethed unfamiliar palates on the flavors and spices of Thai curries and stir fries. Whereas Chinese food is usually relegated to a greasy-spoon setting, Keo's is a dressed-up night out.

FARMERS MARKETS

While the rest of the US mainland has to hibernate in the winter, Hawaii's temperate climate means a year-round harvest celebrated at local farmers markets.

Diamond Head Farmers Market (Map p154; Kapi'olani Community College parking lot, 4303 Diamond Head Rd; ☽ 7:30am-11:30am Sat) is O'ahu's premier gathering of farmers and their fans. Everything sold at the market is local and has a loyal following, such as Don Akiyama's jams that are made with berries from the Big Island, and North Shore's Big Wave Tomatoes. Different restaurants are invited each week to prepare meals should you come only to 'window' shop.

Ward Farmers Market (Map p112; Auahi St; ☽ 3-5pm Mon-Sat, 7am-1pm Sun), across the street from Ward Center, is this almost daily fresh market and grocery. For the average tourist, a visit here is more like sightseeing for food and is a good introduction to Hawaiian and Asian dishes and ingredients, from local produce to prepared meals. The market covers the budget range from blue collar to gourmet imports.

TINY BUBBLES

Don Ho, a survivor of Waikiki's 1960s lounge set, sang his hit tune *Tiny Bubbles* for the last time in the spring of 2007 during his weekly gig at the Waikiki Beachcomber Hotel. A local boy, Ho started playing Waikiki's music clubs in the early '60s after leaving the air force. Part Chinese, Hawaiian and European, Ho peddled his breezy and saucy style on the mainland, massaging the audience into enthusiastic sing-alongs. An engaging performer, he managed to survive the demise of lounge and ride the wave of kitsch, delivering a quintessential dose of Hawaii to old timers, young ones and even a few visiting celebrities.

Top End

Nobu Waikiki (☎ 921-7272; Waikiki Parc Hotel; 2233 Helumoa Rd; mains $20-40; ☐ 5:30-10:30pm) Chef Matsuhisa's Japanese fusion restaurant has won a trip to Waikiki, a fitting home for his hybrid dishes.

Kyo-ya (☎ 947-3911; 2057 Kalakaua Ave; lunch $22, dinner $26-34; ☐ 11am-1:30pm Mon-Sat, 5:30-9:15pm daily) Kyo-ya is the full deal, a formal Japanese restaurant with kimono-clad waitresses specializing in *kaiseki* (multi-course meals). The lengthy menu includes several sashimi and tempura pairings, along with butterfish misoyaki and a traditional Kyoto-style grill served with several small courses. Both the setting and food presentation are elegant, and it's a favorite spot among islanders for a special night out.

Banyan Veranda (☎ 921-4600; Sheraton Moana Surfrider, 2365 Kalakaua Ave; mains $28-$42, set menu $57; ☐ 5:30-9pm) For a romantic dinner, visit the hotel's historic courtyard veranda. The menu, which changes nightly, features French and Pacific Rim–influenced dishes, accompanied by Hawaiian music. Another Veranda highlight is afternoon tea ($30; 1pm to 4pm Monday to Saturday, 3pm to 4pm Sunday), with finger sandwiches, scones and traditional sweets.

Orchid's (☎ 923-2311; Halekulani Hotel, 2199 Kalia Rd; breakfast buffet $45; ☐ 7:30-11am & 11:30am-2pm Mon-Sat, 9am-2:30pm Sun, 6-10pm daily) The Sunday brunch buffet at Orchid's is a grand spread that includes sashimi, sushi, prime rib, smoked salmon, roast suckling pig, an array of salads and fruits, and a rich dessert bar. It's a pampering treat, complete with a fine ocean view, orchid sprays on the tables, and a soothing flute and harp duo. Reservations recommended.

La Mer (☎ 923-2311; Halekulani Hotel, 2199 Kalia Rd; mains $40-55; ☐ 6-10pm) Regarded as the island's ultimate fining dining room, this French-inspired restaurant absorbs a stunning ocean view. A neoclassical French menu places the emphasis on Provençal cuisine with a bow to local ingredients. The dining here is formal, though men are no longer required to wear jackets as once was the case; long-sleeved shirts will do.

DRINKING

Waikiki's bars have two unifying trends: umbrella drinks and Hawaiian music, together at last. The beachfront hotels have oceanside bars but most have all the ambiance of a garage; we've listed some of the standouts here. If you want Hawaiian music without the booze, see the options listed under Entertainment. Bars are typically open from 4:30pm to midnight.

Tiki's Grill & Bar (☎ 923-8454; ResortQuest Waikiki Beach Hotel, 2570 Kalakaua Ave) The quintessential Waikiki bar, Tiki's delivers all the stereotypes expected for its location and name: frozen fruity drinks, a view of the ocean and lots of Polynesian kitsch. Live music completes the mood.

Duke's Canoe Club (☎ 922-2268; Outrigger Waikiki, 2335 Kalakaua Ave) This beachside courtyard is Waikiki's most popular venue for contemporary Hawaiian music. There's entertainment featuring the biggest names – including Kapena and Henry Kapono. It's a great scene with lots of drunken souvenir photo-taking and vacationland camaraderie. The food ain't bad either.

Paradise Lounge (☎ 949-4321; Hilton Hawaiian Village, 2005 Kalia Rd; ☐ music 8-10:30pm) On Friday or Saturday nights, head to the Hilton Hawaiian Village to catch Jerry Santos and Olomana, one of the classic Hawaiian groups performing today.

Mai Tai Bar (☎ 923-7311; Royal Hawaiian Hotel, 2259 Kalakaua Ave; ☐ music 4:30-10:30pm) At the Royal Hawaiian's low-key bar you can catch some great local groups and a view of the breaking surf.

O'AHU

HAWAIIAN MUSIC

You might be surprised to learn that some of Hawaii's leading local musicians play regular gigs at the Waikiki hotels and bars. In fact, on an average stage the star power, albeit limited to the islands, rivals that of any Hollywood outing. Here are some regular names to watch for at local gigs.

- **Ledward Ka'apana** – Slack key guitarist with a falsetto singing voice, Ka'apana typically plays at the Royal Hawaiian's Mai Tai Bar.

- **Kapena** – Having formed 15 years ago as a high-school band, Kapena didn't win the Kaimuki high-school battle of the bands but went on to be an influential force in modern island music. Founding member Kelly Boy De Lima is often credited with renewing interest in ukulele music. The band plays at Dukes and at the Royal Hawaiian's Mai Tai Bar.

- **Sam Kapu III** – Part of a musical dynasty, Sam Kapu mainly performs traditional ukulele music as well as three-part harmonies with his regular trio. He typically plays at the Sheraton hotels and the Royal Hawaiian.

- **Kapono** – A local singer-songwriter, Henry Kapono Ka'aihue is O'ahu's renaissance man having produced albums since the 1970s, along with his sometimes collaborator Cecilio Rodriguez. Now that his live-music venue Kapono's has closed, he can be found gigging at Duke's when he's in town.

- **Makana** – A leading proponent of the slack key rock, Makana plays Indigo and Chai's Island Bistro.

- **3 Scoops of Aloha** – A popular Jawaiian-style band whose name means 'more than enough aloha,' it typically plays at the Royal Hawaiian's Mai Tai Bar and Sheraton's Sand Bar.

- **Opihi Pickers** – Led by ukulele player Imua Garza along with various family members, this band blends traditional and contemporary features. It plays at Duke's.

- **Pilihoa** – Acoustic band that sings in tight falsetto style, this trio plays weekly at Aku Bone.

- **Jerry Santos and Olomana** – Classic ukulele and falsetto performers who play at Chai's Island Bistro and Hilton Hawaiian Village's Paradise Lounge.

- **Jake Shimabukuro** – The 'Jimi Hendrix of the uke' has been lured away from the islands by the record companies, but his brother Bruce plays weekly gigs at the Sheraton Waikiki.

- **Royal Hawaiian Band** – Hawaii's 'official' band appears monthly at Kapi'olani Bandstand and on the 'Iolani Palace lawn. It's a quintessential Hawaiian scene that caps off with the audience joining hands and singing Queen Lili'uokalani's *Aloha Oe* in Hawaiian. Call ☎ 922-5331 for performance schedules.

House Without a Key (☎ 923-2311; Halekulani Hotel, 2199 Kalia Rd; ☽ music 5-8:30pm) One of the classier beachside bars, House Without a Key lazes underneath an old Kiawe tree, complete with sunset cocktails, and Hawaiian music and hula entertainment.

Banyan Court (☎ 922-4600; Sheraton Moana Surfrider, 2365 Kalakaua Ave; ☽ music 5:30-10pm) You can listen to music beneath the same old banyan tree where 'Hawaii Calls' broadcast its nationwide radio show for four decades beginning in 1935.

Sand Bar (☎ 922-4422; Sheraton Waikiki, 2255 Kalakaua Ave; ☽ music 6pm-8:30pm) This cabana-like bar has views of Diamond Head and live Hawaiian music nightly, including 'keiki hula,' when a children's hula group displays its stuff.

Lewers Lounge (☎ 923-2311; Halekulani Hotel, 2199 Kalia Rd; ☽ music 8:30-midnight) Waikiki as an aristocratic playground is still alive in this sophisticated lounge. Cocktails are made from scratch using fresh (not canned) juices, including exotic tropical flavors like lychee and ginger. And the famed jazz bassist Bruce Hamada and his trio provide a smooth jazz serenade most nights.

Hideaway (☎ 682-2731; 1913 Dudoit Ln; ☽ 3-10pm Mon-Thu, 3pm-2am Fri & Sat, 6:30am-6:30pm Sun) This gritty watering hole is incongruously located close to Waikiki, but only shows up in a few drunken vacation snapshots. The crowd is mainly a steady supply of regulars who feel at home with the cheap beer and an eclectic jukebox.

Kapahulu Kafe (☎ 732-7486; 766 Kapahulu Ave) Why rot your guts with the fermented juices when you can chill-out with Hawaii's homegrown stimulant, kava? Between the University and Waikiki, this kava bar is a mellow introduction to the herbal drink, plus an arty venue for a weekly calendar of local acoustic acts.

ENTERTAINMENT
Hawaiian Music, Hula & Luau
Waikiki is the undeniable center of traditional Hawaiian music and dance performances – from falsetto trios to community hula troupes. Starting at about sunset, most nights, outdoor performances occupy the beachfront bars, shopping centers and Kuhio Beach Park. Many of the oceanfront hotels also sponsor various craft and culture events; check with the concierge about schedules.

Kuhio Beach Torch Lighting & Hula Show (☎ 843-8002; admission free; Hula Mound, Kuhio Beach; ☻ 6:30-7:30pm) Some of O'ahu's best hula troupes perform at the sacred hula mound near the Duke Kahanamoku Statue on the Waikiki strip. Other performances include traditional torch lighting and conch shell ceremony, and Hawaiian music. The shows are sponsored by the Mayor's Office of Culture & Arts (www .honolulu.gov/moca).

International Market Place (2330 Kalakaua Ave; admission free; ☻ shows 7pm Fri-Sun) Hula and contemporary Hawaiian bands fill the food court with culture at this souvenir shopping bazaar.

Royal Hawaiian Shopping Center (☎ 922-0588; 2201 Kalakaua Ave; ☻ shows 6:30pm Tue-Sun) On the 2nd floor of this shopping center are various musical and hula performances. In addition, the shopping center sponsors cultural classes in hula dance, lei-making and playing the ukulele.

Royal Hawaiian Hotel Luau (☎ 931-8383; 2259 Kalakaua Ave; adult/child 5-12 $97/53; ☻ shows 6pm Mon) So you've got your heart set on a 'genuine' luau? Make it easy on yourself: expect touristy, stay close to home and pick the prettiest setting. *Voilà*, the Royal Hawaiian Hotel holds the only oceanfront luau in Waikiki amidst its elegant grounds. There are no long bus rides, the food is quite decent and the dancers' per-

formances professional – and the price tag is no joke.

Concerts
Waikiki Shell (☎ 527-5400; www.blaisdellcenter.com; Kapi'olani Park) This beautiful outdoor amphitheater hosts classical and contemporary twilight musical concerts – with Diamond Head in the background. Symphony, jazz, rock and Hawaiian music concerts occur throughout the year. Ticketing is handled through the Blaisdell Center box office.

Free musical events – including the Royal Hawaiian Band and the symphony – are staged at **Kapi'olani Park Bandstand** at various times throughout the year.

Nightclubs
The nightclub scene has migrated to Honolulu but if you don't feel like making the trek, the following have dance floors for getting your ya-yas out.

Moose McGillycuddy's (☎ 923-0751; 310 Lewers St; admission $3-5; ☻ 9pm-1am Mon-Sat) A restaurant by day, this place turns into a raucous college nightspot, with live Top-40 bands, bikini contests and ladies' nights.

Zanzabar Nightclub (☎ 924-3939; Waikiki Trade Center, 2255 Kuhio Ave; admission from $10; ☻ 9pm-4am) The kind of club that advertises on the radio, Zanzabar is flashy and slightly cheesy but a strobe-lit good time nonetheless. Theme nights and karaoke fill the weekly schedule. Weekdays are 18 plus, weekends 21 plus.

Gay & Lesbian Venues
What the Waikiki scene may lack in venues, it makes up for in aloha. Two local monthly magazines, *DaKine* and *Odyssey*, keep up with gay and lesbian events. The *Honolulu Weekly* also carries listings.

Hula's Bar & Lei Stand (☎ 923-0669; 2nd fl, Waikiki Grand Hotel, 134 Kapahulu Ave; ☻ 10am-2am) This friendly open-air bar is Waikiki's main gay venue. It also has a great ocean view of Diamond Head.

Also recommended:

Angles Waikiki (☎ 926-9766; 2256 Kuhio Ave; ☻ 10am-2am) A bar by day, a nightclub by night, with dancing, a pool table and video games.

Fusion Waikiki (☎ 924-2422; 2260 Kuhio Ave; ☻ 10pm-4am Sun-Thu, 8pm-4am Fri & Sat) This place has karaoke and drag shows.

In-Between (☎ 926-7060; 2155 Lauula St; ☻ 4pm-2am Mon-Sat, 2pm-2am Sun) A gay karaoke bar.

ALOHA MY WARDROBE

It is a shame when a perfectly good piece of cloth becomes permanently associated with vacationing pensioners. This is the mainland reputation of what is otherwise a common wardrobe feature in the islands: the aloha shirt. These brightly colored, well-ventilated shirts are perfect for the weather and the spirit of the islands. Beyond the bold and not-so-beautiful specimens found in granddad's closet, some designs are subdued and patterned after native flora, while others reflect the shirt's Japanese heritage with traditional kimono patterns. The evolution of the aloha shirt began in the 1920s when Honolulu-based tailors started to recycle leftover kimono fabric into a button-down, short-sleeved, untucked shirt that suited the tourists' tastes. During WWII, aloha wear (and island production of the shirts) hit its peak, even sneaking into business attire with its signature vibrant tropical patterns. First rayon and then polyester replaced the original silk fabric. By the turn of the new millennium, Hawaii had lost most of its shirt factories to China. But the local labels that survive have resuscitated the retro look of the 1920s and 1930s.

SHOPPING

Waikiki does not suffer a shortage of shopping malls, souvenir stalls, swimsuit and T-shirt shops, quick-stop convenience marts or fancy boutiques.

Bailey's Antique & Aloha Shop (☎ 734-7628; 517 Kapahulu Ave) A great shop for the eclectic collector, Bailey's covers the evolution of the aloha shirt from vintage 1920s when kimono silk was used to the 1970s polyester specials. Of the new generation of shirts, Bailey's only carries Hawaii-made labels, including Kona Bay and Pineapple Juice.

Island Treasures Antiques (☎ 922-8223; 2nd fl, Waikiki Town Center, 2301 Kuhio Ave; ⊗ 2-8pm Tue-Sat, 2-6pm Sun) Looking for Hawaii kitsch? Then this mid-20th-century antique shop is for you. It carries everything you need to decorate your basement Tiki bar.

Royal Hawaiian Shopping Center (☎ 922-0588; 2201 Kalakaua Ave) One of Waikiki's biggest shopping centers, the Royal Hawaiian has dozens of shops selling jewelry and designer clothing. It is also home to Little Hawaiian Craft Shop, which carries a range of local crafts, from *kukui*-nut key chains and Hawaiian-style quilting kits to high-quality koa bowls.

Waikiki Beach Walk (Lewers St) Part of the Outrigger Enterprises' much-anticipated makeover of Waikiki, this new shopping center includes a Trump Tower hotel, Hawaii-based shops and restaurants.

Waikiki Shopping Plaza (☎ 923-1191; 2250 Kalakaua Ave) Just opposite the Royal Hawaiian Shopping Center, this three-story plaza features close to 75 shops and eateries, most with an Asian theme, along with drop-in weekend classes in the art of making lei and shell necklaces.

GETTING AROUND
To/From the Airport

See p99 for transport options to/from Honolulu International Airport.

Bus

O'ahu's public bus system, **TheBus** (☎ 848-5555; www.thebus.org), runs frequent routes to/from Waikiki. Most of the Waikiki bus stops are along Kuhio Ave. Here are a few useful lines:

Route No	Destination
2 & 13	Downtown Honolulu, including 'Iolani Palace and Chinatown
8 & 58	Ala Moana Center, the bus system's main hub and transfer point to other lines
19 & 20	Ala Moana Center, Aloha Tower Marketplace and Honolulu International Airport

Car & Moped

Parking cheaply in Waikiki can be a challenge. Many hotels charge $8 to $15 a day for guest parking. The cheapest metered lot is at Honolulu Zoo. There's a large public parking lot at Ala Wai Yacht Harbor at the west end of Waikiki, with a 24-hour limit. At the east end of Waikiki, there's a parking lot along Monsarrat Ave at Kapi'olani Park with no time limit.

There are several Waikiki-based car-rental offices affiliated with the national agencies, but lines tend to be long on weekends. For general rental information and toll-free numbers, see p571.

Mopeds can be another great way of getting around Waikiki, but they're really best suited to people who already have experience riding in city traffic. Motorcycles rent for about $100 for four hours and mopeds for $25 to $65 for four hours.

Trolley

There are trolley-style buses that offer services between Waikiki and Honolulu's main tourist sights. This service doesn't offer much in the way of value compared to public transportation, but it is tailored to the tourist and often seems more convenient.

Waikiki Trolley (☎ 593-2822; www.waikikitrolley.com) runs three color-coded lines (red, pink and blue). An all-day pass (adult/child $25/12) allows you to jump on and off the trolley as often as you like. You can purchase tickets at the **DFS Galleria Waikiki ticket counter** (330 Royal Hawaiian Ave). Below is a brief outline of the routes:

Red Line (Honolulu City Shuttle) Starts at Hilton Hawaiian Village running along Kalakaua Ave, loops around Kuhio Ave into Honolulu via S Beretania St with stops at Honolulu Academy of Arts, 'Iolani Palace, Aloha Tower Marketplace, Foster Botanical Garden and the Bishop Museum. Trolleys run hourly 9:10am to 5:30pm and the entire route takes about 2½ hours.

Pink Line (Ala Moana Shopping Shuttle) Starts at DFS Galleria Waikiki running along Kalakaua Ave, loops around Kuhio Ave to Ala Moan Blvd into Honolulu to Ala Moana Center. Trolleys run every 10 minutes from 9:30am to 9pm, and the entire route takes one hour. You can also buy one-way tickets for $2.

Blue Line (Ocean Coast Line) Starts at DFS Galleria Waikiki running along Kalakaua Ave to Honolulu Zoo, Waikiki Aquarium, Diamond Head, Hanauma Bay and Sea Life Park. Trolleys run every 45 minutes from 9am to 4:30pm and the entire route takes three hours. There's also an express line that run twice a day.

Hilo Hattie Trolley (☎ 537-6500) is a free shopping shuttle designed to get you from your Waikiki hotel to the retailer's superstore on Nimitz Hwy, with stops at Ala Moana Center and Aloha Tower Marketplace. It runs every 20 minutes from 8:20am to 4:50pm between 10 Waikiki hotels and the shopping centers, though you can end up waiting longer for one that's not full.

SOUTHEAST COAST

Past the strip malls and residential upscale neighborhoods of Kahala and Hawai'i Kai begins a coastal drive that will take your breath away. The Kalaniana'ole Hwy (72) swells and dips like the raging sea as it rounds Koko Head,

southeast O'ahu's prominent headland formed by volcanic activity some 10,000 years ago. The road twists through narrow passageways in lava cliffs and overlooks sweeps of sand and crashing waves. This is usually the point at which visitors really fall in love with O'ahu – they've rented a car for a circle-island tour or are en route to snorkel in famous Hanauma Bay. Scenic overlooks allow mere mortals to embrace this landscape of intricately carved bays and beaches. Most of this portion of southeastern O'ahu is protected by the Koko Head Regional Park.

DIAMOND HEAD STATE MONUMENT

The massive backdrop to Waikiki, Diamond Head rises 763ft to its fish-shaped summit. The bare and scalloped land mass is a tuff cone and crater formed by a violent steam explosion deep beneath the earth's surface long after most of O'ahu's volcanic activity had stopped. Today Diamond Head is a **state monument** (☎ 733-4512; admission walk-in $1, car $5; ☾ hiking 6am-4pm), popular for its hiking trail to the crater rim with panoramic views.

The Hawaiians called it Le'ahi and built a *luakini* (temple for human sacrifices) on the top. But ever since 1825, when British sailors found calcite crystals sparkling in the sun and mistook them for diamonds, it's been called Diamond Head.

In 1909 the US army established Fort Ruger at the edge of the crater, building a network of tunnels, topping the rim with cannon emplacements, bunkers and observation posts. Reinforced during WWII, the fort has been a silent sentinel whose guns have never fired.

The trail to the summit was built in 1910 to service the military observation stations along the crater rim. Although a fairly steep hike, with an elevation gain of 560ft, it's only three-quarters of a mile to the top and plenty of people of all ages hike up. The return trip takes about an hour, and you should definitely pack your own water.

The crater is dry and scrubby with kiawe (a relative of the mesquite tree), grasses, koa trees and wildflowers. The small yellow-orange flowers along the way are native *ilima*, O'ahu's official flower.

Starting up the trail, the summit lies ahead a bit to the left, at roughly 11 o'clock. About 20 minutes up the trail, hikers enter a long, dark tunnel. The roof is high enough to walk without bumping your head (there is a handrail),

O'AHU

SOUTHEAST COAST

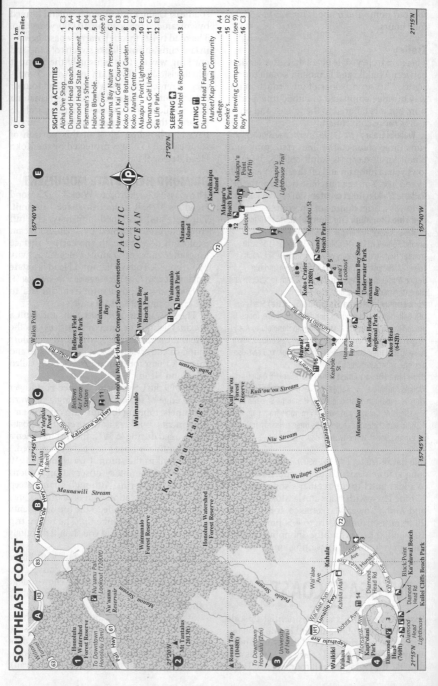

SIGHTS & ACTIVITIES	
Aloha Dive Shop	1 C3
Diamond Head Beach	2 A4
Diamond Head State Monument	3 A4
Fisherman's Shrine	4 D4
Halona Blowhole	5 D4
Halona Cove	(see 5)
Hanauma Bay Nature Preserve	6 D4
Hawai'i Kai Golf Course	7 D3
Koko Crater Botanical Garden	8 D3
Koko Marina Center	9 C4
Makapu'u Point Lighthouse	10 E3
Olomana Golf Links	11 C1
Sea Life Park	12 E3

SLEEPING 🏨	
Kahala Hotel & Resort	13 B4

EATING 🍴	
Diamond Head Farmers Market/Kapi'olani Community College	14 A4
Keneke's	15 D2
Kona Brewing Company	(see 9)
Roy's	16 C3

and your eyes should adjust enough to make out shadows in the darkness. The tunnel curves, and no light is visible until close to the end making it a little spooky; the park advises hikers to use a flashlight.

The tunnel should be the climax of this long climb, but coming out into the light hikers face a steep 99-step staircase, followed by a shorter tunnel, a narrow spiral staircase inside an unlit bunker and the last of the trail's 271 steps. And when you reach the top, be careful – there are steep drops.

From the summit there's a fantastic 360-degree view – the southeast coast to Koko Head and Koko Crater, and the Wai'anae (Leeward) Coast to Barbers Point and the Wai'anae Range, with Kapi'olani Park and the Waikiki Shell below. The lighthouse, coral reefs, sailboats and sometimes even surfers waiting for a wave at Diamond Head Beach are also visible. The summit can be quite windy, as evidenced by the several caps and hats you'll see scattered just below the lookout. So hold on!

To reach Diamond Head from Waikiki, take bus 22 or 58, both of which run about twice an hour. It's a 20-minute walk from the bus stop to the trailhead at the parking lot. By car from Waikiki, take Monsarrat Ave to Diamond Head Rd and then take the right turn after Kapi'olani Community College into the crater.

DIAMOND HEAD BEACH

Diamond Head Beach draws both surfers and windsurfers, plus a few picnickers. Conditions are suitable for intermediate to advanced windsurfers, and when the swells are up it's a great place for wave riding. This little beach has showers, but no other facilities.

As there's not much to see here unless the wind and surf are up, most people coming this way are touring by car. To get there from Waikiki, follow Kalakaua Ave to Diamond Head Rd. There's a parking lot just beyond the lighthouse. Walk east past the end of the lot and you'll find a paved trail down to the beach. If you don't have your own transport, bus 14 runs from Waikiki about once an hour.

Sleeping & Eating

There are food options (and a fancy hotel) between Diamond Head and Waikiki in the upscale developments of Hawai'i Kai and Kahala.

Kahala Hotel & Resort (☎ 739-8888, 800-367-2525; www.kahalaresort.com; 5000 Kahala Ave; r from $400; ✗ ⟡ Ⓟ $18) One of the state's most exclusive luxury hotels. This is where the rich and famous go when they want to avoid the Waikiki scene, a 15-minute drive away. The hotel is classic without being trendy and can accommodate children thanks to its quiet stretch of beach and dolphin lagoon.

Kona Brewing Company (☎ 394-5662; Koko Marina Center, 7192 Kalaniana'ole Hwy/Hwy 72, Hawai'i Kai; mains $11-22; ☉ 11am-11pm) This hip eatery is known first for its microbrews, like Longboard Lager and Castaway IPA, and then for its local-style *pupu* (small plates), such as *'ahi* appetizers and wood-fired pizzas. Hawai'i Kai is an eastern suburb of Waikiki.

Roy's (☎ 396-7697; 6600 Kalaniana'ole Hwy/Hwy 72, Hawai'i Kai; mains $20-40; ☉ 5:30-9:30pm Sun-Thu, 5-10pm Fri & Sat) Chef Roy Yamaguchi's namesake restaurants are sometimes referred to as the Spago of the islands. The O'ahu-born enterprise was an early innovator of Hawaiian Regional Cuisine (p56), which emphasizes fresh local ingredients and blends European, Asian and Polynesian flavors. Today, Roy's restaurants have populated the islands and mainland, but this Hawai'i Kai location, east of Waikiki, is one of the originals. A more centrally located restaurant is slotted for the new Waikiki Beach Walk (corner of Kalia Rd and Lewers St).

HANAUMA BAY NATURE PRESERVE

A stunning ensemble of sapphire and turquoise hues mix together in modern-art abstractions in this bowl-shaped bay, the remnants of an eroded crater. Just below the sparkling surface are coral reefs, some of which are 7000 years old. These craggy and ancient underwater formations are a city for fish, providing food, shelter and an interspecies 'pick-up' scene. Schools of glittering silver fish, bright blue flashes of parrotfish and perhaps a sea turtle are just a few of the regulars who are so used to snorkelers that many will go eyeball to face mask with you.

Before Hanauma (Curved Bay) was designated a marine life conservation district in 1967, it was a popular fishing spot in danger of being stripped of its primary inhabitants. Despite its protected status today, the beloved bay is still a threatened ecosystem – it is constantly in danger of being loved to death by the huge number of annual visitors. Some of the park's seemingly bureaucratic rules are actually intended to manage the number of people who access the park at one time and, in turn, protect the attraction.

Information

Hanauma is both a county nature preserve and a state underwater **park** (☎ 396-4229; www .hanaumabayhawaii.org; adult/child under 13 $5/free; ☾ 6am-6pm Nov-Mar, 6am-7pm Apr-Oct, closed Tue; Ⓟ $1). Past the ticket booth at the entrance is an information center with educational displays about the geology and ecology of the bay. All visitors are expected to watch a video, intended to stagger the crowds and inform people of environmental precautions. At beach level, there are rental-gear concessions, lockers, lifeguards and bathrooms.

The bay gets very busy, especially in summer, and parking is limited. To beat the crowds come early (around 6am) when all the locals show up, and avoid Mondays and Wednesdays.

Sights & Activities

The bay is well-protected from the vast ocean by various reefs and the inlet's natural curve, making conditions favorable for snorkeling year-round. The fringing reef closest to shore has a large, sandy opening known as the **Keyhole Lagoon**, which is the best place for novice snorkelers. The deepest water is 10ft, though it's very shallow over the coral. The Keyhole is well protected and usually very calm. Because most visitors are beginners, this is also the most crowded part of the bay later in the day

---

WATER SAFETY: SNORKELING 101

Which is safer – snorkeling in a peaceful bay on the surface, or diving with air tanks to depths of 40ft or more? Believe it or not, far more snorkelers drown in Hawaiian waters than do scuba divers. A scuba diver in distress is usually apparent, and help is at hand, generally the dive group leader. Snorkelers, however, are a solitary lot. When floating in a face-down position, even the smallest wave can flood the breathing tube of a snorkeling mask. Fins can make it difficult to get upright quickly, especially if the snorkeler has started to panic. What to do? Snorkel with a partner and check on each other frequently.

---

and visibility can be poor from swimming. Be careful not to step on the coral or to accidentally knock it with your fins. Feeding the fish is also prohibited

For confident snorkelers and strong swimmers, it's better on the outside of the reef, where there are large coral heads, bigger fish and fewer people; to get there follow the directions on the signboard or ask the lifeguard at the southwest end of the beach. There are two channels on either side of the bay that experience very strong currents. Don't attempt to swim outside the reef when the water is rough or choppy.

Areas that are off limits to visitors include **Toilet Bowl** and **Witches Brew**, once-popular natural wonders along the outer edges of the bay that proved too hazardous for casual visitors. Toilet Bowl is a small natural pool in the lava rock connected to the sea by an underwater channel, which enables water to surge into the bowl and then flush out from beneath. The cove at the southern side of the point is Witches Brew, so named for its swirling, turbulent waters, where rogue waves have caught a number of unsuspecting hikers.

Getting There & Away

Hanauma Bay is about 10 miles from Waikiki along Kalaniana'ole Hwy (72). The parking lot sometimes fills up by midmorning, so the earlier you get there the better. If the lot is full, you could park at Koko Marina Center and walk uphill to the entrance.

Buses 22 and 58 both go to Hanauma Bay (58 goes on to Sea Life Park). However, 22 is slightly preferable, as it stops at the entrance to Hanauma Bay; 58 lets you off about a quarter of a mile below the entrance. Buses travel to Hanauma Bay from Kuhio Ave in Waikiki from 8:15am to 4:25pm. The last bus returning from Hanauma Bay departs at 5:40pm weekdays bound for Waikiki, and at 5:55pm on Saturday and Sunday.

HALONA BLOWHOLE AREA

Heading east from Hanauma Bay, the road skirts past several lookouts and the geographical oddity of the **Halona Blowhole**. Here the water surges through a submerged tunnel in the rock and spouts up through a hole in the ledge. It's preceded by a gushing sound, created by the air that's being forced out by the rushing water. The action depends on water conditions – sometimes it's barely discernible, while at other times it's a showstopper. Down to the right of the parking lot is **Halona Cove**, the little beach where the classic risqué love scene with Burt Lancaster and Deborah Kerr in *From Here to Eternity* was filmed in the 1950s. A small **stone monument** atop Halona Point was erected by Japanese fisherfolk to honor those lost at sea.

The blowhole is 1.75 miles past Hanauma Bay.

SANDY BEACH

On this sandy spit of land, the ocean heaves and thrashes like a furious beast. It is understandably one of the island's most dangerous beaches with a punishing shorebreak, powerful backwash and strong rip currents. And the experienced body-boarders spend hours trying to mount the skull-crushing waves. When the swells are big, board surfers hit the left side of the beach. As a spectator, Sandy Beach provides excellent theater for the showdown between man versus nature, as well as a buxom and sandy observation point.

This is no place to frolic in the waves and red flags flown on the beach indicate hazardous water conditions. Even if you don't notice the flags, always check with the lifeguards before entering the water.

Not all the action is in the water. The grassy strip on the inland side of the parking lot is used by people looking skyward for their thrills – it's both a hang-glider landing site and a popular locale for flying kites.

The park has rest rooms and showers. Bus 22 from Waikiki stops in front of the beach. On weekends, you can usually find a food wagon in the parking lot, selling plate lunches and drinks.

KOKO CRATER

One of the tallest and best-preserved tuff cones, Koko Crater now supports a small county **botanical garden** (☎ 522-7060; admission free; ☼ 9am-4pm), planted with plumeria, oleander and cacti and other dryland species. The garden itself is not that interesting but the Hawaiian myth associated with the crater makes it unusually arousing. According to Hawaiian legend, Koko Crater is the imprint left by the vagina of Pele's sister Kapo, which was sent here from the Big Island to lure the pig-god Kamapua'a away from Pele (the volcano goddess).

To get there, take Kealahou St off Kalaniana'ole Hwy (Hwy 72) opposite the northern end of Sandy Beach. Just over half a mile in, turn onto Kokonai Rd and then left onto the one-lane road to Koko Crater Stables and continue 0.3 miles to the garden.

MAKAPU'U POINT & BEACH PARK

This point of land has a precipitous view of the ocean from its 647ft pedestal. The coastal **lighthouse** at its tip marks the easternmost point of O'ahu. The gate to the mile-long service road is locked to keep out private vehicles, but hikers can park off the highway just beyond and walk in. Although not difficult, it's an uphill walk, and conditions can be hot and windy. The path and the lighthouse lookout give fine coastal views and, during winter, whales are sometimes visible offshore.

About a third of a mile further along the highway, a scenic **roadside lookout** spies across the coastline at aqua-blue waters outlined by white sand and black lava beds – an even more spectacular sight when hang-gliders take off from the cliffs, O'ahu's top hang-gliding spot. Offshore is **Manana Island**, also known as Rabbit Island. This aging volcanic crater is populated by feral rabbits and wedge-tailed shearwaters, coexisting so closely that birds and rabbits sometimes share the same burrows. The island looks vaguely like the head of a rabbit, ears folded back. You could also try to imagine it as a whale. In front of it is the smaller, flat **Kaohikaipu Island**. There's a coral reef between the two islands that divers sometimes explore, but to do so requires a boat.

Below the lookout is **Makapu'u Beach Park**, one of the island's top winter bodysurfing spots, with waves reaching 12ft and higher. It also has the island's best shorebreak. As with Sandy Beach, Makapu'u is strictly the domain of experienced bodysurfers who can handle rough water and dangerous currents. Surfboards are prohibited. In summer the waters can be calm and good for swimming. Two native Hawaiian plants are plentiful – *naupaka* by the beach and yellow-orange *ilima* by the parking lot.

Makapu'u Point is about 1.3 miles north of Sandy Beach.

SEA LIFE PARK

Hawaii's only **marine park** (☎ 259-7933; www.sealifeparkhawaii.com; 41-202 Kalaniana'ole Hwy; adult/child 4-12 $32/25; ☼ 9:30am-5pm) combines all the celebrities of the sea into a variety of zoo- and circus-like exhibits. The highlight of the park is a huge

300,000-gallon aquarium filled with sea turtles, eels, eagle rays, hammerhead sharks and an array of colorful reef fish. There is also a penguin habitat, a turtle lagoon with green sea turtles, and a seabird sanctuary with red-footed boobies, albatrosses and great frigate birds.

There are also several interactive displays that include performances and 'swim' time with dolphins, stingrays and sea lions. These programs have additional admission fees and various combo packages are available.

You can visit the park's cafeteria and gift shop without paying admission, and from there you can also get a free glimpse of the seal and sea lion pools. Though a parking fee ($3) is charged in the main lot, if you continue past the ticket booth to the area marked 'additional parking,' there's no fee.

Buses 22 (Beach Bus), 57 (Kailua/Sea Life Park) and 58 (Hawai'i Kai/Sea Life Park) all stop at the park.

WAIMANALO BAY

A wide, inviting stretch of beach unfolds for 5.5 miles from Makapu'u Point to Wailea Point. What could be just the usual palm-fringed beach and sparkling sea is punctuated by offshore islands and a coral reef a mile offshore that keeps the breaks at a reasonable distance.

Waimanalo has three beach parks. Camping is possible at each of the beach parks; see p92 for obtaining permits. As elsewhere, don't leave valuables in your car as break-ins are common. Bus 57 stops on the main road in front of the Waimanalo parks.

Sights
WAIMANALO BEACH PARK
Waimanalo Beach Park has a long strip of soft white sand and little puppy waves excellent for swimming. The park has a shady patch of ironwood trees and views of the lower Ko'olau Range rise up on the inland side of the park. Manana Island and Makapu'u Point are visible to the south.

This is an in-town county park with a grassy picnic area, lifeguards, rest rooms and showers. Camping is allowed in an open area near the road.

WAIMANALO BAY BEACH PARK
A spacious park with lots of sun and shade, Waimanalo Bay's biggest waves break onshore here drawing dedicated board surfers and bodysurfers. Through a wide forest of

ironwoods, you'll find a thick mane of blond sand for long walks and ocean ogling.

This county park is about a mile north of Waimanalo Beach Park and has shady beachside campsites. There's a lifeguard station, picnic area, showers and rest rooms.

BELLOWS FIELD BEACH PARK
The **beach** (☷ noon Fri-8am Mon) fronting Bellows Air Force Base is a long beach with fine sand and a natural setting backed by ironwood trees. The small shorebreak waves are good for beginner bodysurfers and board surfers.

There's a lifeguard, showers and rest rooms; the 50 campsites are set out among the trees. The entrance is 1.5 miles from Hwy 72. Although it's military property, camping permits are issued through the county.

Activities
HIKING
The safe, usually dry and relatively easy **Kuli'ou'ou Ridge Trail** offers 360-degree views of Honolulu and the Windward Coast. Along this 5.4-mile roundtrip trail, you can ramble along forest switchbacks before making a short but steep climb to the windy summit of the Ko'olau Range for great ocean views. To reach the trail, take bus 1 (Hawai'i Kai) to Kuli'ou'ou Rd, from where it's a 1-mile walk inland to Kala'au Pl. The trailhead is at the end of the cul-de-sac.

Maunawili Falls Trail (Map p159) is considered one of the best pooling waterfall hikes on the island. It is a very popular segment of a 10-mile trail system (known broadly as Maunawili Trail), which gently contours around a series of *pali* lookouts through the Ko'olau Range from the west near Pali Hwy to the east near Waimanalo town.

To reach the falls trailhead (2.5 miles roundtrip) head toward the Maunawili subdivision, just outside of Kailua. From the Pali Hwy heading toward the coast, turn right onto Auloa Rd and at the first fork take Maunawili Rd. The road eventually intersects with Kelewina St and a gated access road that marks the trail head.

Maunawili Connector Trail links the falls trail with the longer **Maunawili Trail**. From the Waimanalo side, by car or bus 57, go to Waimanalo town center along the Kalaniana'ole Hwy (72). Turn inland onto Kumuhau St, then right onto Waikupanaha Rd. About a quarter mile along this road, look for a break in the fence at a gravel pull-out and the familiar Na Ala Hele (see p85) trailhead sign.

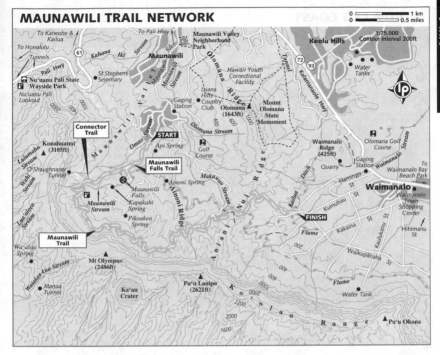

MAUNAWILI TRAIL NETWORK

To reach the trail from the Pali Hwy (61) side by car, look for a hairpin turn just after the tunnels, and a parking area marked 'scenic lookout,' where the trailhead begins. Via the 57 bus, get off at Maunawili Rd, near Castle Medical Center. From there, follow Maunawili Rd about 1.8 miles to the trailhead.

Sleeping & Eating

All three of Waimanalo's beach parks have camping, see the individual listings above. Nearby Kailua has more to offer sleepy travelers. **Keneke's** (Kalaniana'ole Hwy/Hwy72; lunch $7-8) is a local eatery just north of Waimanalo Beach Park, near the post office.

WINDWARD COAST

The island's eastern side is characterized by the dramatic Ko'olau Range, which runs head-long toward the shore as if riding an unseen wave. These verdant vertical monuments are separated by deep scalloped valleys and catch the moist trade winds for their own bathing rituals.

In the southern corner of the coast are the affluent bedroom communities of Kane'ohe and Kailua, which are only 10 miles from Honolulu. North of Kane'ohe, the Windward Coast becomes surprisingly rural with humble roadside shacks and small Hawaiian-owned papaya, banana and vegetable farms. The Kamehameha Hwy starting around Waiahole and Waikane is really just a modest two-lane road that runs the length of the entire coast, doubling as Main St for each of the small towns along the way. Stop at any beach park and the pecking chickens will outnumber visitors. Rusting cars decorate lawns and the only rush is midday when the cross-island tourists hit the roads.

Because the Windward Coast is exposed to the northeast trade winds, it's a popular area for anything that requires a sail – from windsurfing to yachting. There are attractive swimming beaches in Kailua, Kualoa and Malaekahana – although many other sections of the coast are too silted to be much more than a snapshot. Swimmers should keep a careful eye out for the stinging Portuguese man-of-wars that are sometimes washed in during storms.

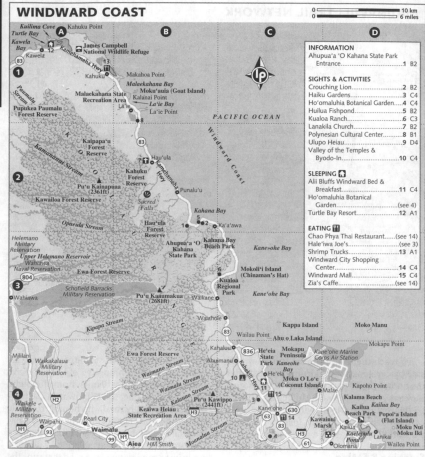

WINDWARD COAST

Three highways cut through the Ko'olau Range from central Honolulu to the Windward Coast. The Pali Hwy (61) goes straight into Kailua center. The Likelike Hwy (63) runs directly into Kane'ohe, and, although it doesn't have the scenic stops the Pali Hwy has, it is in some ways more dramatic. The H3 freeway begins near Pearl Harbor and cuts a scenic path through the mountains to Kailua. For this book, the Windward Coast runs from Kailua in the south to Kahuku town in the north.

KAILUA

pop 38,000

Little more than a beachfront village, Kailua is windward O'ahu's largest town, which is a fairly easy title to win. The long graceful bay

protected by a coral reef is Kailua's claim to fame and many seasoned O'ahu visitors leapfrog over touristy Waikiki for Kailua's residential beachcombing ambiance. The weather and wave conditions are also ideal for swimming, kayaking, windsurfing and kitesurfing. Along the shore, mid-20th-century cottages, most cooled by the trade winds not the modern convenience of air conditioning, crowd into little neighborly lanes. The town has a fine variety of restaurants, supported in part by a steady stream of Honolulu residents.

History

In ancient times Kailua (meaning 'two seas') was a place of legends and home to several Hawaiian chiefs and, allegedly, the island's first *menehune* (the 'little people' who built many of Hawaii's fishponds, heiau and other stonework, according to legend). Kailua once served as a political and economic center for the region. Rich in stream-fed agricultural land, fertile fishing grounds and protected canoe landings, the area supported at least three temples, one of which, Ulupo Heiau (p162), you can still visit today.

Information

Bank of Hawaii (☎ 266-4600; 636 Kailua Rd) On the town's main road.

Bookends (☎ 261-1996; 600 Kailua Rd; ☽ 9am-8pm Mon-Sat, 9am-5pm Sun) Next to the Times Supermarket, selling books, maps and a few mainland newspapers.

Hakuyosha Hawaii Laundromat (☎ 261-4566; 345 Hahani St)

Kailua Information Center & Chamber of Commerce (☎ 261-2727; www.kailuachamber.com; Suite 103, 600 Kailua Rd; ☽ 10am-4pm Mon-Fri) In the Kailua Shopping Center, the office has maps, brochures and information on accommodations and outdoor activities around Kailua.

Kailua Public Library (☎ 266-1996; 239 Kuulei Rd; ☽ 10am-5pm Mon, Wed & Fri, 1-8pm Tue & Thu) A good place to find kids' books.

Morning Brew (☎ 262-7770; 572 Kailua Rd; ☽ 7am-8pm) Offers internet access and wireless connections for laptops.

Post office (☎ 266-3996; 335 Hahani St) In the town center.

Sights & Activities

KAILUA BAY

A wide arc of sand drapes around the jewel-colored waters of Kailua Bay with formidable volcanic headlands pinning either side. Above the tender waves, sea turtles poke their heads and, along the beach, residents swap chit-chat during early morning dog walks. Tucked back behind the dunes are long yards and modest one-story homes, belying their present-day multimillion dollar price tags.

The beach is divided into three sections from north to south: Kalama Beach Park, Kailua Beach Park and Lanikai Beach. The beach all along the bay has a gently sloping sandy bottom with generally calm waters. Swimming is usually good year-round. Onshore trade winds transform the bay into a windsurfing and kiteboarding rink, while offshore islands make good kayaking trips.

Kailua Beach Park is the primary access point for visitors and has public facilities off the southeastern end of S Kalaheo Ave. The park has an interior patch of ironwood trees and the usual public facilities.

Windsurfing, kitesurfing and kayaking companies have concession stands near the parking lot of this beach park. Some also have in-town shops.

Hawaiian Watersports (☎ 262-5483; 354 Hahani St; rentals $55-65; ☽ 9am-5pm) Rents gear and leads guided tours.

Kailua Sailboards & Kayaks (☎ 262-2555; www.kailuasailboards.com; Kailua Beach Center, 130 Kailua Rd; rentals $40-60; ☽ 9am-5pm) Rents equipment, gives lessons and operates kayaking tours.

Naish Hawaii (☎ 262-6068, 800-767-6068; www.naish.com; 155 Hamakua Dr; rentals from $25-35; ☽ 9am-5:30pm) Run by a windsurfing champion and offers wind and kitesurfing equipment rentals and introductory lessons.

To get to Kailua Beach Park, take bus 56 or 57 from Ala Moana Center in Honolulu and transfer to bus 70 in Kailua. If you're driving, simply stay on Kailua Rd, which begins at the end of the Pali Hwy (61) and continues as the main road through town, ending at the beach park.

Kalama Beach, on the northern side of the bay, has the roughest shorebreak and is popular with experienced body-boarders. Surfers usually head for the northernmost end of Kailua Bay at Kapoho Point or further still to Zombies Break.

If you follow the coastal road as it continues southeast of Kailua Beach Park, you'll shortly come to Lanikai, an exclusive residential neighborhood, fronted by **Lanikai Beach**, which was once one of the prettiest stretches of powdery white sand in Hawaii. Today, the ocean has characteristically withdrawn its onshore deposits leaving mainly man-made erosion barriers. The area has become a more popular option for kayakers heading to the twin Mokulua Islands, Moku Nui and Moku Iki, which sit directly offshore from Lanikai.

From Kailua Beach Park, the road turns into the one-way Aalapapa Dr, which comes back around as Mokulua Dr to make a 2.5-mile loop. There are 11 narrow beach access walkways off Mokulua Dr. For the best stretches of beach, start at the walkway opposite Kualima Dr. There is no public parking in Lanikai and street parking is scarce, so consider parking at Kailua Beach Park.

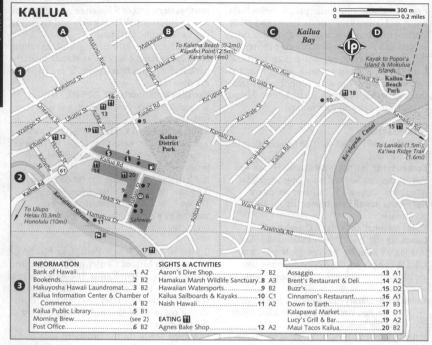

Three islands off Kailua and Lanikai are seabird sanctuaries and only accessible by kayak. Landings are allowed on **Popoi'a Island** (Flat Island), directly off the south end of Kailua Beach Park. The twin **Mokulua Islands**, Moku Nui and Moku Iki, sit directly off Lanikai. It's possible to kayak from Kailua Beach Park to Moku Nui, but landings are prohibited on Moku Iki, the smaller of the two islands. Landings are allowed on Moku Nui, which has a beautiful beach for sunbathing and snorkeling.

ULUPO HEIAU

The building of Ulupo Heiau (Map p160), a sizable, open-platform temple of stones piled 30ft high and 140ft long, is attributed to *menehune*, the little people who legends say created much of Hawaii's stonework, finishing each project in one night. Fittingly, Ulupo means 'night inspiration.' In front of the temple, thought to have been a *luakini* (place for human sacrifice), is an artist's rendition of the site as it probably looked in the 18th century. From the path across the top of the heiau, hikers get a view of Kawainui Marsh.

Ulupo Heiau is a mile south of Kailua Rd, behind the YMCA. Coming up the Pali Hwy from Honolulu, take Uluoa St, the first left after passing the Hwy 72 junction. Turn right on Manu Aloha St and right again onto Manu O'o St.

KAWAINUI & HAMAKUA MARSHES

Kawainui Marsh (Map p160) is one of Hawaii's largest freshwater marshes and provides flood protection for the town of Kailua. The inland water catchment is also one of the largest remaining fishponds used by ancient Hawaiians. Legend says the edible mud of the ancient fishpond was home to a *mo'o* (lizard spirit).

Downstream from Kawainui is the smaller Hamakua Marsh, which provides habitat for rare Hawaiian birds in their natural habitat, including the *'alae 'ula* (Hawaii moorhen), *ae'o* (Hawaiian stilt) and *'alae ke'oke'o* (Hawaiian coot). Bird-watchers flock to this 22-acre sanctuary at the south side of the town center. Simply park behind the Down to Earth natural health-food store on Hamakua Dr.

Sleeping

Kailua has no hotels but there are numerous European-style B&Bs and vacation-home rentals either on the beach or within walking distance.

Mainlanders familiar with B&Bs in showcase homes with gourmet meals will be surprised by Kailua's version of hospitality. Most are simply rooms in private suburban homes run by area residents. Some offer 'studios,' which have a separate entrance, private bathroom and sometimes a kitchenette. B&Bs in Kailua are also governed by antiquated local regulations that result in a 'word-of-mouth' lodging network. Most cannot display signs and none is permitted to offer a hot breakfast; fresh bakery muffins and local fruit are the usual substitute. Most places also provide beach gear, barbeque facilities and the like.

Kailua's B&Bs also follow their own peculiar booking system: most require a deposit (usually by money order or travelers check), a minimum stay of three nights, and request advance reservations. Some B&B owners have mentioned that Lonely Planet readers are (in)famous for calling last minute from the airport.

The accommodations listed below can be booked directly with the host or through the **Bed & Breakfast Association of O'ahu** (☎ 262-8286; www.stayoahu.com). This association also handles customer complaints, monitors standards and helps match visitors with the right kind of accommodations. For vacation rentals, in which you rent an entire home, check out the options at **Pacific Islands Reservations** (☎ 262-2342; www.oahu-hawaii-vacation.com) or **Vacation Rentals By Owner** (www.vrbo.com).

There are no budget accommodations in Kailua; the following are listed from least expensive to most expensive. Readers should call for directions.

Paradise Palms Bed & Breakfast (☎ 254-4234; www.paradisepalmshawaii.com; r $85-95) Done up in homey guest-room decor, you'll feel like you're visiting new-found relatives at this suburban home. The beds claim most of the floor space and are the stars of the show with 800-thread count sheets. Because the rooms are small, this is not an ideal option for families with kids. It is on a main road but two blocks from the beach.

Tree Top (☎ 261-9712; d $90-95; 🖳) Spacious and simply decorated, Tree Tops has converted space above the family home that is ideal for hosting out-of-town families (including pets) needing no-fuss quarters. This is a 10-minute drive to the beach from a residential neighborhood.

Hawaiian Beach Vacations (☎ 261-5455; www .hawaiianbeachvacation.com; d $90-150) Just a leisurely stroll to the beach, this large modern house has several different lodging configurations that can sleep and feed big families or condensed couples. The owner is an artist and oil paintings of her family decorate the walls.

Kailua Tradewinds (☎ 262-1008; d $95; 🖳) Next door to Papaya Paradise is a more kid-friendly option in a modern plantation-style house. Breakfast isn't provided, but a kitchenette is available.

Papaya Paradise B&B (☎ 261-0316; www.kailua oahuhawaii.com; d $100; 🖳) A suburban home run by a retired couple has a big outdoor sitting area and quiet lodging options best suited for more mature audiences. The backyard has a handsome view of Olomana Mountain. Papaya is half a mile from the beach.

Amanda's Vacation Rentals (☎ 262-8981; www .amandasvacationrentals.com; d $100-110; 🖳) A low-key option for couples and families, Amanda's has apartment-style accommodations and is a five-minute walk to the beach.

Beach Lane B&B (☎ 262-8286; www.beachlane.com; d $105-145) Just a minute's walk to the beach, this classic cottage B&B has breezy rooms (some with peeping views of the ocean) best suited for couples or small families. The owner speaks Danish, German, Norwegian, Swedish and English.

Kailua Beach Accommodations (☎ 262 5409; www .hawaiibestrentals.com; d $115-195) Smack dab on the beach, this oceanfront home has several spacious options for couples and families as well as a wide yard fronting the beach.

Lanikai Plantations (☎ 561-1851; d $150-175) This large modern home in upscale Lanikai is high energy with a front-yard trampoline, kayaks and plans for a pool and other outdoor toys. There is direct beach access behind the house, but this end of the bay has suffered considerable erosion.

Tee's at Kailua (☎ 261-0771; www.teesinn.com; d $165-195; 🖳) This suburban home is activity oriented: you can kayak directly to the beach from the canal beside the house or load up on other sweating-in-the-sun information. Guests have access to the yard containing a vegetable and herb garden used in the complimentary

O'AHU

breakfasts and snacks. Tee's is a five-minute drive from the beach.

Hale Ihilani (☎ 261-6220; d $250; ▣) This suburban home is outfitted in contemporary tropical decor creating a private and romantic honeymoon nook complete with a small garden lit by tiki torches. The beach is two blocks away.

Eating

Agnes Bake Shop (☎ 262-5367; 46 Ho'olai St; snacks $2-3; ⊙ 6am-6pm Tue-Sat, 6am-2pm Sun) This bakery makes whole-grain breads, inexpensive pastries and tempting Portuguese *malasadas*, which are served fresh. Match them with a cup of coffee and the newspaper and let the vacation begin.

Kalapawai Market & Deli (☎ 262-4359; 305 S Kalaheo Ave; snacks $2-6; ⊙ 6am-9pm) En route to the public beach access, this local landmark is the place to pick up coffee or made-to-order sandwiches. Early morning customers often toast their own bagels while helping themselves to fresh coffee. There's also a broad selection of wine and beer.

Buzz's (☎ 261-4661; 413 Kawailoa Rd; lunch $9-15, dinner $20-32; ⊙ 11am-3pm & 5-11pm) Opposite Kailua Beach Park, this local hangout has an open patio, a straightforward lunch menu of fish and burgers, and surprisingly upscale dinner options for such a casual audience. Credit cards are not accepted.

Cinammon's Restaurant (☎ 261-8724; 315 Uluniu St; breakfast $5-10, lunch $8-12; ⊙ 7am-2pm Sun-Wed, 7am-8:30pm Thu-Sat) Breakfast with a local touch is the attraction at this busy Kailua eatery, with eggs Benedict mahimahi and banana pancakes among the standouts.

Maui Tacos Kailua (☎ 261-4155; Suite 102, 539 Kailua Rd; dishes $3-6; ⊙ 9am-9pm) This island-wide chain serves fresh fish tacos (soft or crispy, $3.75) and hearty burritos ($6), along with a help-yourself assortment of semi-spicy salsas.

Assaggio (☎ 261-2772; 354 Uluniu St; lunch $10-15, dinner $15-22; ⊙ 5-10pm Tue-Sat) This restaurant serves very good Italian dishes in a somewhat upmarket setting. The menu is extensive, with more than 50 pasta, seafood, steak and chicken dishes, including chicken Assaggio, a tasty dish brimming with garlic.

Brent's Restaurant & Deli (☎ 262-8588; 629A Kailua Rd; dishes $7-12; ⊙ 7am-2pm) From lox and eggs to sandwiches like the Banker and Gone to Brooklyn, this New York–style deli is the closest you'll get to Manhattan, plus the weather's better.

Lucy's Grill & Bar (☎ 230-8188; 33 Aulike St; appetizers $7-12, dinner $16-26; ⊙ 5-10pm) Nestled in windward Kailua at the end of the Pali Hwy, this contemporary bistro is one of the best dining and drinking options outside of Honolulu. The menu is a fusion of Hawaiian-Euro-Asian, ranging from salt-crusted rib-eye steak to a spinach and caramelized onion pizza with *liliko'i* (passion fruit) puree. Along with a breezy outdoor patio, there's a full bar that overlooks the dining area and open kitchen. And if you like exotic bar drinks, check out local concoctions like the pineapple martini or Li Hing Mui margarita made from a famous sweet and sour 'crack-seed' candy.

Down To Earth (☎ 262-3838; 201 Hamakua Dr; ⊙ 8am-10pm) is a large natural food store with everything from organic produce to power bars, plus a hot veggie and vegan deli.

KANE'OHE
pop 36,500

Although Kane'ohe is blessed with a large and reef-sheltered bay, the military has claimed the setting for industrial purposes rather than recreation. The near-constant trade winds that sweep across the bay are ideal for sailing. The work-a-day town doesn't receive as many visitors as cute Kailua, but it does have several inland attractions to make it worth a stop on a round-the-island tour or even a cross-island excursion from the Pearl Harbor area.

Orientation

Two highways run north to south through Kane'ohe. Kamehameha Hwy (836) is closer to the coast and goes by He'eia State Park. The Kahekili Hwy, which is more inland, intersects the Likelike Hwy and continues on north past the Byodo-In temple. The highways merge into a single route, Kamehameha Hwy (83), a few miles north of Kane'ohe.

Kane'ohe Marine Corps Air Station occupies the whole of Mokapu Peninsula. The H3 Fwy terminates at its gate.

Sights & Activities
HO'OMALUHIA BOTANICAL GARDEN

A lush and lovely vantage point for admiring the land and sea of the Windward Coast, this county **botanical garden** (Map p160; ☎ 233-7323; 45-680 Luluku Rd; admission free; ⊙ 9am-4pm) occupies a 400-acre corner at the foot of the Ko'oalu Range. It is planted with trees and shrubs from the world's tropical regions and was originally designed by the US Army Corps of Engineers as flood protection for the valley.

This peaceful natural preserve is networked by trails winding through the green park up to a 32-acre lake (no swimming). A small **visitor center** features displays on the park's history, flora and fauna, and Hawaiian ethnobotany. Guided two-hour nature hikes are offered at 10am Saturday and 1pm Sunday.

The park is at the end of Luluku Rd, 2.25 miles north of the Pali Hwy via the Kamehameha Hwy. Buses 55 and 56 stop at the Windward City Shopping Center, opposite the start of Luluku Rd, from where the visitor center is a 1.5-mile walk uphill. There is also camping (see right).

VALLEY OF THE TEMPLES & BYODO-IN

The **Valley of the Temples** (Map p160; ☎ 239-8811; adult/child $2/1; ⏰ 9am-5pm) is an interdenominational cemetery in a stunning setting just off the Kahekili Hwy. For most visitors the main attraction is Byodo-In, the 'Temple of Equality.' Dedicated in 1968 to commemorate the 100th anniversary of Japanese immigration to Hawaii, Byodo-In is a replica of the 950-year-old temple in Kyoto, Japan. The temple's symmetry is a classic example of Japanese Heian architecture and garden design symbolizing the Pure Land of Mahayana Buddhism. The seated 9ft-tall tall Buddha in the main hall is positioned to catch the first rays of morning sunlight.

The reds of the elegant temple against the deep green of the Ko'olau Range is strikingly picturesque, especially when mist settles over the *pali*. A three-ton brass bell beside the large pond is said to bring tranquility and good fortune to those who ring it. It's all very Japanese, right down to the gift shop selling imported sake cups, *daruma* (good luck) dolls and happy Buddhas. For a panoramic view of the valley, head up to the hilltop mausoleum with the cross.

A calendar of cultural events are hosted at Byodo-In; call ☎ 239-9844 for upcoming events.

There are no buses directly to Byodo-In, but bus 55 can drop passengers off near the cemetery entrance on Kahekili Hwy, 1.5 miles north of Haiku Rd. From there, it's 0.75 miles to the temple.

HAIKU GARDENS

A more meditative place is hard to imagine than **Haiku Gardens** (Map p160; 46-336 Haiku Rd; admis-sion free; ⏰ dawn-dusk), a little valley containing a lily pond, an abundance of fragrant tropical flowers and lots of birdsong. The gardens, cradled by the Ko'olau Range, are picture perfect. The path starts at the side of Hale'iwa Joe's restaurant and takes only about 15 minutes down and back. To get there from Kamehameha Hwy, turn west on Haiku Rd just past the Windward Mall; after crossing Kahekili Hwy, continue on Haiku Rd for a quarter of a mile. Haiku Gardens is on the right.

HE'EIA STATE PARK

He'eia State Park (Map p160) on Kealohi Point, just off Kamehameha Hwy, has a good view of He'eia Fishpond on the right and He'eia-Kea Harbor on the left. The **fishpond**, an impressive survivor from the days when stone walled ponds of fish raised for royalty were common on Hawaiian shores, remains largely intact despite the invasive mangroves.

Moku O Lo'e (Coconut Island), just offshore to the southeast, was once a royal playground, named for the coconut trees planted there by Princess Bernice Pauahi Bishop. In the 1930s it was the estate of Christian Holmes, heir to the Fleischmann fortune, who dredged the island, doubling its size to 25 acres. During WWII it was also used as an R&R facility. In the 1960s the island was used in the filming of the popular *Gilligan's Island* TV series. Today the Hawaii Institute of Marine Biology of the University of Hawai'i occupies part of the island.

Sleeping

Ho'omaluhia Botanical Garden (Map p160; ☎ 233-7323; 45-680 Luluku Rd) You're allowed to camp here between 9am on Friday and 4pm on Monday. With a resident caretaker and gates that close at night to noncampers, the park is one of the safest places to camp on O'ahu. Like other county campgrounds, there's no fee. You can get a permit in advance at any satellite city hall, or simply go to the park between 9am and 4pm daily to get one; be sure to call first to confirm that space is available. For more information on obtaining camping permits, see p92.

Alii Bluffs Windward Bed & Breakfast (Map p160; ☎ 235-1124, 800-235-1151; www.hawaiiscene.com/alii bluffs; 46-251 Ikiiki St; r $70-80; 🖳) Hospitality is the attraction at this cozy suburban home filled with the owners' affable personalities, original artwork and comfortable furnishings. Scottish

O'AHU

host Don Munro and his partner De, a retired New York fashion designer, give guests the run of the house and the small backyard. Each of the two available rooms has a bathroom. There's a view of Kane'ohe Bay, although it's a drive to the beach.

Eating

Chao Phya Thai Restaurant (Map p160; ☎ 235-3555; Windward City Shopping Center, cnr Kamehameha Hwy & Kaneohe Bay Dr; dishes $7-12; ⏰ 11am-2pm Mon-Sat, 5-9pm daily) This family-run eatery serves very decent northeastern Thai food, including green papaya salad and sticky rice, along with Thai standard favorites like *pad thai* (stir-fried rice noodles) and curries. No liquor, but you can BYO.

Zia's Caffe (Map p160; ☎ 235-9427; 45-620 Kamehameha Hwy; dishes $8-16; ⏰ 11am-10pm Mon-Fri, 4-10pm Sat & Sun) Opposite Windward City Shopping Mall, Zia's is popular with local families looking for good value and decent portions of Italian standards, like spaghetti and meatballs and shrimp scampi, along with mussels marinara, vegetable lasagna and Caesar salad. The place has an open feel and a kids' menu.

Hale'iwa Joe's (Map p160; ☎ 247-6671; 46-336 Haiku Rd; mains $15-30; ⏰ 11:30am-10pm) The Haiku Gardens location is half the attraction here – a romantic, open-air setting overlooking a large lily pond tucked beneath the Ko'olau Range, and dating from the mid-1800s. The restaurant features excellent Pacific Rim fare, including ceviche and coconut shrimp tempura, along with hearty meat dishes and prime rib. You can also drop by the gardens during the day, or just before sunset when it closes for a happy-hour (4:30pm to 6:30pm Monday to Friday) drink and a predinner stroll. To get there from Kamehameha Hwy, turn west on Haiku Rd just past Windward Mall; after crossing Kahekili Hwy, continue on Haiku Rd a quarter of a mile.

If you're looking for something convenient, the city's two main shopping centers – **Windward City Shopping Center** (Map p160; 45-480 Kane'ohe Bay Dr) and **Windward Mall** (Map p160; 46-056 Kamehameha Hwy) – have lots of inexpensive food options.

NORTH OF KANE'OHE TO KAHANA VALLEY

Traveling along Kamehameha Hwy (83) north across the bridge beside the landmark Hygienic Store is a physical and cultural depart-

ure from the gravitational pull of Honolulu. You've officially crossed into rural O'ahu, where the highway becomes a two-laner and the ocean shares the shoulder. You'll cruise through dappled sunlight, various collections of valleys inhabited by small towns without noticeable landmarks and small family farms.

Just inland from the town of Waikane in the Waikane Valley, large tracts of land were taken over for military training and target practice during WWII, that continued until the 1960s. The government now claims the land has so much live ordnance that it can't be returned to the families it was leased from. This is a source of ongoing contention with local residents, who are upset that much of the inner valley remains off-limits. Not surprisingly, this is where you are more likely to encounter Hawaiian sovereignty sentiments.

Kualoa Regional Park

This 153-acre county park on Kualoa Point provides an expansive vista of offshore islands and inland mountains. In ancient times Kualoa was once one of the most sacred places on O'ahu. When a chief stood on Kualoa Point, passing canoes lowered their sails in respect. The children of chiefs were brought here to be raised, and it may have been a place of refuge where *kapu* (taboo) breakers and fallen warriors could seek reprieve from the law. Because of its rich significance to Hawaiians, Kualoa Regional Park is listed in the National Register of Historic Places.

The park is largely open lawn with a few palm trees shading a long, thin strip of beach with safe swimming. Pali-ku (Vertical Cliffs) – the mountains looming precipitously across the road – look like a scene from a classic Chinese watercolor when the mist settles.

According to Hawaiian legend, the main offshore island, **Mokoli'i**, is the tail of a nasty lizard slain by a god and thrown into the ocean. Following the immigration of Chinese laborers to Hawaii, this conical-shaped island also came to be called Papale Pake (China-man's Hat).

Apua Pond, a 3-acre brackish salt marsh located on the point, is a nesting area for the endangered *aeo* bird (Hawaiian stilt). Beyond the park, you'll see a bit of **Moli'i Fishpond**, visible through the trees as a distinct green line in the bay where the rock walls are covered with mangrove, *milo* (a native shade tree) and pickleweed. There are picnic tables, rest rooms, showers and a lifeguard. Camping is allowed from Friday through Sunday (for permits to visit, see p92).

Kualoa Ranch

Rarely is such a touristy attraction located in such a stunning location, making a stop at this Hawaiian-style dude ranch almost irresistible. **Kualoa Ranch** (Map p160; ☎ 237-7321; www.kualoa.com; 49-560 Kamehameha Hwy, Kualoa; tours from $20-140) has a range of activities, from horseback riding to narrated nature tours, on its scenic property. Tour groups, especially Japanese, make up the bulk of visitors.

Part of the prehistoric-looking landscape was used as a backdrop for the TV show *Lost*, and movies such as *Jurassic Park, Godzilla, Windtalkers* and *George of the Jungle*. Daily tours take visitors deep into the Ka'a'awa Valley where these scenes were shot.

Back in 1850 Kamehameha III leased about 625 acres of this land for $1300 to Dr Judd, a missionary doctor who became one of the king's advisers. Judd planted the land with sugarcane, built flumes to transport it and imported Chinese laborers to work the fields. You can still see the remains of the mill's stone stack, and a bit of the crumbling walls, half a mile north of the beach park alongside the road.

Ka'a'awa

In the Ka'a'awa area, the road hugs the coast and the *pali* moves right on in, with barely enough space to squeeze a few houses between the base of the cliffs and the road. **Swanzy Beach Park**, a narrow neighborhood beach used mainly by fisherfolk, is fronted by a shore wall. Across the road from the park is a convenience store, a gas station and a hole-in-the-wall post office – pretty much the center of town, such as it is.

Crouching Lion

The Crouching Lion (Map p160) is a rock formation at the back of a roadside restaurant just north of the 27-mile marker.

The legend goes like so: the rock is a demigod from Tahiti who was cemented to the mountain during a jealous struggle between the volcano goddess Pele and her sister Hiiaka. When he tried to free himself by crouching, he was turned to stone. To find him, stand at the restaurant sign with your back to the ocean and look straight up to the left of the coconut tree and the cliff above.

Michael's Restaurant & Sports Lounge (☎ 237-8511; 51-666 Kamehameha Hwy; lunch $10-20, dinner $10-40; ⏱ 11am-10pm) is the recently renamed Crouching Lion restaurant that shares real estate with the famous landmark. During the day, lots of day-trippers stop in for a light lunch and view of the ocean, while evenings see more locals grabbing a beer and a round of pool.

KAHANA VALLEY

This lush valley is both fertile with plant life and Hawaiian artifacts. During ancient times the islands were divided into *ahupua'a* – pie-shaped land divisions reaching from the mountains to the sea – providing everything the Hawaiians needed for subsistence. Modern subdivisions and town boundaries have erased this traditional organization everywhere except here, the only publicly owned *ahupua'a* in Hawaii.

Before Westerners arrived, Kahana Valley was planted with wetland taro which thrived in the rainy valley. Archaeologists have identified the remnants of more than 130 agricultural terraces and irrigation canals, as well as the remains of a heiau, fishing shrines and numerous house sites.

In the early 20th century the area was planted with sugarcane, which was hauled north to the Kahuku Mill via a small railroad. During WWII the upper part of Kahana Valley was taken over by the military and used for training soldiers in jungle warfare. In 1965 the state bought Kahana Valley from the Robinson family of Kaua'i (owners of the island of Ni'ihau) in order to preserve it from development, and today it is home to about 30 Hawaiian families in the lower valley. The upper valley remains undeveloped and is mostly used by locals who hunt feral pigs on weekends.

Sights & Activities

AHUPUA'A 'O KAHANA STATE PARK

One mile beyond the Crouching Lion, Ahupua'a 'O Kahana State Park (formerly Kahana Valley State Park) is in an incredibly rainy and unspoiled valley.

The park's most important site is **Huilua Fishpond** (Map p160), on Kahana Bay, a survivor of the traditional ponds used by the Hawaiians to cultivate fish. Early fishpond technology typically used fresh and saltwater sources and strategic placement to protect it from large swells. Management of the pond was a communal effort governed by local beliefs in the magical powers of stones and protective lizards.

You can walk through the valley on either of two hiking trails. The **orientation center** provides a trail map, but it isn't always open to visitors; trails tend to be poorly maintained and conditions slippery.

The most accessible of the park trails is the 1.25-mile **Kapa'ele'ele Ko'a & Keaniani Lookout Trail**, which commences at the orientation center, and continues along the old railroad route past the Kapa'ele'ele Ko'a fishing shrine to Keaniani Kilo, a lookout that was used in ancient times for spotting schools of fish. The longer **Nakoa Trail**, named for the koa trees that are found along the 2.5-mile loop through a tropical rain forest, crosses over the Kahana Stream twice, passing by a swimming hole.

Sleeping

There are 10 beachside campsites at the park, but they're primarily used by island families. Camping is allowed with a permit from the state.

PUNALU'U

This inconspicuous seaside community is just another string of houses along the highway that most visitors drive by en route to the North Shore. But it is close enough to the surfer scene that the accommodations become more affordable options.

Punalu'u Beach Park has a long, narrow beach with an offshore reef that protects the shallow inshore waters in all but stormy weather. Be cautious near the mouth of the Waiono Stream and in the channel leading out from it, as currents are strong when the stream is flowing quickly or when the surf is high.

Sleeping & Eating

Punalu'u Guesthouse (☎ 946-0591; 53-504 Kamehameha Hwy; 2-bed dm per person $25) Cheap without being a flophouse, this three bedroom house has been converted into an informal hostel, managed by the owners of Hostelling International Honolulu. You need to make all arrangements in Honolulu as walk-ins are not accepted. There's a communal kitchen, an on-site house 'parent' and guests often get together at dinnertime. All rooms share a bathroom.

Pat's at Punalu'u (53-567 Kamehameha Hwy) This oceanfront condominium is a bit neglected on the outside, but the privately owned units are often well maintained. There's no front desk; instead, rental arrangements are handled either by the owners or by agents. Try **Paul Comeau Condo Rentals** (☎ 293-2624, 800-467-6215; www.patsinpunaluu.com; PO Box 589, Ka'a'awa, HI 96730; studios $100, 1-bedroom/2-bedroom units $125/235), which handles several units at Pat's at Punalu'u with a three-day minimum stay. Papaya Paradise B&B also rents a unit at Pat's.

Ching's Punalu'u Store (Kamehameha Hwy; ◷ 10am-5pm) This market and deli dates back to 1935 when it was founded by a local jack-of-all trades. A small shrine to the original owner resides beside the deli counter. In addition to the normal corner-store goods, you can pick up pre-made poi, butter *mochi* (Japanese sticky rice cake) and plantation iced tea (pineapple and mint) as well as bait (but not sushi).

Shrimp Shack (☎ 256-5589; Kamehameha Hwy; mains $10; ◷ 11am-6pm) A sunny yellow truck parked next door to Ching's is one of many roadside food attractions along this strip of highway. Deep-fried coconut shrimp and other plate lunches are devoured at shaded picnic tables overlooking the road and the ocean beyond.

HAU'ULA

Aside from a couple of gas pumps and a 7-Eleven store, the main landmark in town is the stone ruins of **Lanakila Church** (c 1853; Map p160), perched on a hill next to the newer Hau'ula Congregational Church. Across the road is rundown **Hau'ula Beach Park**. Camping is allowed, though it's mostly the domain of folks living out of their cars. Better beach parks include nearby **Kokololio** and **Kakele**, but currents can be strong.

Behind the soggy commercial strip is a scenic backdrop of hills and Norfolk pines where the Division of Forestry & Wildlife maintains two trails: **Hau'ula Loop** and **Ma'akua Ridge**. Both trails share the same access point and head into beautiful hills in the lower Ko'olau Range. The Hau'ula Loop, which clambers through Waipilopilo Gulch and onto a ridge over Kaipapa'u Valley, is not only better maintained but more rewarding, both for its views and the native flora along the way, including sweet-smelling guava, and ohia trees with feathery red blossoms, as well as thick groves of shaggy ironwood trees and towering Norfolk pines. The 2.5-mile hike is a popular path with locals and families, and usually takes between one and two hours. The signposted trailhead for both hikes is at a bend in Hau'ula Homestead Rd, about a quarter of a mile from Kamehameha Hwy. Hau'ula Homestead Rd is in town north of Hau'ula Beach Park.

LA'IE

La'ie will seem like a big city compared to its rural neighbors. It is presently the center of the Mormon community in Hawaii with a large population of Mormon Samoans. In ancient times, this is thought to have been the site of a *pu'uhonua* (place of refuge) – a place where *kapu* breakers and fallen warriors could seek refuge.

The first Mormon missionaries to Hawaii arrived in 1850. After an attempt to establish a Hawaiian 'City of Joseph' on the island of Lana'i failed amid a land scandal, the Mormons moved to La'ie. In 1865 they purchased 6000 acres of land in the area and slowly expanded their influence.

Information

Bank of Hawaii (☎ 293-9238; La'ie Shopping Center, 55-510 Kamehameha Hwy) Has a 24-hour ATM.

Post office (☎ 293-0337; La'ie Shopping Center, 55-510 Kamehameha Hwy; ☺ 9am-3:30pm Mon-Fri, 9:30-11:30am Sat)

Sights & Activities

LA'IE HAWAII TEMPLE

In 1919 the Mormons constructed this miniversion of the great Salt Lake **temple** (☎ 293-9297; 55-600 Naniloa Loop; ☺ 10am-5pm), at the end of a wide promenade. It is formal and stately, like nothing else on this end of the Windward Coast. There is a visitor center where enthusiastic guides will show you pictures of the interior of the temple (off-limits to non-Mormons) and talk to you extensively about the wonders of their faith. Nearby is the Hawaii branch of Brigham Young University, with scholarship programs attracting students from islands throughout the Pacific.

POLYNESIAN CULTURAL CENTER

A nonprofit theme park showcasing the cultures of Polynesia, the **Polynesian Cultural Center** (PCC; Map p160; ☎ 293-3333, 800-367-7060; www.polynesia.com; 55-370 Kamehameha Hwy; adult/child 3-11 $36/25, with evening show $50/35; ☺ noon-9pm Mon-Sat) is owned by the Mormon Church and is one of O'ahu's

biggest attractions, second only to the USS *Arizona* Memorial.

The park has seven theme villages representing Samoa, New Zealand, Fiji, Tahiti, Tonga, the Marquesas and Hawaii. The 'villages' contain authentic-looking huts and ceremonial houses, many elaborately built with twisted ropes and hand-carved posts. The huts hold weavings, tapa, feather work and other handicrafts. People of Polynesian descent dressed in native garb demonstrate poi pounding, coconut-frond weaving, dances and games. There's a replica of an old mission house and missionary chapel representative of those found throughout Polynesia in the mid-19th century.

Many of the people working here are Pacific Island students from nearby Brigham Young University. The interpreters are amiable and you could easily spend a few hours wandering around chatting or trying to become familiar with a craft or two.

The basic admission also includes winding boat rides through the park and a sort of floating talent show; a tram tour of the Mormon temple grounds and BYU campus; and ocean-theme movies at the IMAX theater. Crowds of tourists are the norm here, and most visits usually fill the day and evening. If you want to stay for the Ali'i Luau (buffet), your best option is the all-inclusive package for $80/56.

BEACHES

The beaches of La'ie are a lot more attractive than those to the immediate south. Better yet, though, is Malaekahana State Recreation Area (p170), just outside of town.

Pounders, half a mile south of the main entrance to PCC, is an excellent bodysurfing beach, but the shorebreak, as the name of the beach implies, can be brutal. Summer swimming is generally good, but watch out for a strong winter current. The area around the old landing is usually the calmest.

Hukilau Surf Shop (☎ 293-9229; 55-730 Kamehameha Hwy; rentals $5-25; ☺ 10am-6pm Mon-Sat) rents all sorts of watersports gear and can give you the lowdown on all the best places for action that day.

From **La'ie Point** there's a good view of the mountains to the south and of tiny offshore islands believed to be the surviving pieces of a *mo'o* (giant lizard) slain by a legendary warrior. The islet to the left with the hole in it is **Kukuiho'olua**, otherwise known as Puka Rock. To get to La'ie Point, head seaward on Anemoku St, opposite the La'ie Shopping Center, then turn right on Naupaka St and go straight to the end.

Sleeping & Eating

Laie Inn (☎ 293-9282, 800-526-4562; www.laieinn.com; 55-109 Laniloa St; d $95-100; ❊ ❋) This unassuming two-story motel next to the Polynesian Cultural Center is nothing special from the outside, but all rooms surround an attractive courtyard swimming pool with a lanai.

Hukilau Cafe (☎ 293-8616; 55-662 Wahinepe'e St; dishes $6-8; ❧ 7am-2pm Tue-Fri, 7-11:30am Sat) Just north of the elementary school, this friendly hole-in-the-wall serves Hawaiian-sized breakfast and lunch, like sweet bread French toast, or roast pork, salad and rice.

Foodland supermarket (☎ 293-4443; La'ie Shopping Center, Kamehameha Hwy) If you're looking to eavesdrop on community gossip, then hit this grocery store during prime time: right after school. It does not sell alcohol (thanks to the Mormons), but all the other staples are here.

MALAEKAHANA STATE RECREATION AREA

You'll feel all sorts of intrepid pride when you discover this wild and rugged beach, just north of town. A long, narrow strip of sand stretches between Makahoa Point to the north and Kalanai Point to the south with a thick inland barrier of ironwoods.

Swimming is generally good year-round, although there are occasionally strong currents in winter. This popular family beach is also good for many other water activities, including bodysurfing, board surfing and windsurfing. Kalanai Point, the main section of the park, is less than a mile north of La'ie and has picnic tables, BBQ grills, camping, rest rooms and showers.

Moku'auia (Goat Island), a state bird sanctuary just offshore, has a small sandy cove with good swimming and snorkeling. It's possible to wade over to the island – best when the tide is low and the water's calm. Be careful of the shallow coral (sharp) and sea urchins (sharper). When the water is deeper, you can also swim across to the island, but beware of a rip that's sometimes present off the windward end of the island. Be sure to ask the lifeguard about water conditions and whether it's advisable to cross.

Sleeping

Malaekahana has the best campgrounds on the Windward Coast, with two locations to choose from. You can pitch a tent for free in the park's main Kalanai Point section if you have a state park permit.

You can rent a rustic cabin or camp without needing a permit in the Kahuku section (Makahoa Point) of the park, which has a separate entrance off Kamehameha Hwy, half a mile north of the main park entrance. **Friends of Malaekahana** (☎ 293-1736; tent site per person $8.34, 4–6-person yurts $130) maintains this end of the park. Best of all, this is the only place on O'ahu that allows Wednesday and Thursday overnight camping. Reservations strongly recommended.

KAHUKU

Kahuku is a former sugar town with rows of identically modest cabins lining the main road. The mill that once stood in the center of town belonged to the Kahuku Plantation, which produced sugar from 1890 until it closed in 1971. The operation was a relatively small concern, unable to keep up with the increasingly mechanized competition. When the mill shut down, Kahuku's economy skidded into a slump that continues to linger today.

Today the town's claim to fame is food (both fresh and fried) and football. Shrimp ponds at the north side of Kahuku supply O'ahu's restaurants and nearby shrimp trucks (Map p160). Just south of the Kahuku Sugar Mill, **Giovanni's Shrimp Truck** (☎ 293-1839; dishes $9-12; ❧ 11am-6pm) was one of the original truck-wagons to park along the highway and dish up the locally grown shrimp to sightseers. Giovanni's is best known for a tasty half-pound of shrimp scampi smothered in garlic and butter.

If the first doesn't always mean the best to you, then go further down the road to **Kahuku Famous Shrimp** (☎ 455-1803; dishes $8-12; ❧ 10am-6pm), which offers a few more choices, like spicy squid, and a tasty shrimp and veggie stir-fry. This truck occupies the parking lot of a low-slung shopping center on the site of the old mill, where only the smokestack remains.

Roadside stands outside of town sell the famous Kahuku corn, a sweet variety that often gets name-brand billing on Honolulu menus.

As for football, Kahuku High's Red Raiders (www.kahukufootball.org) consistently ranks as one of the best teams in all Hawaii.

Four miles outside of town heading toward Turtle Bay Resort, **James Campbell National Wildlife Refuge** (☎ 637-6330) encompasses a rare freshwater wetland that provides habitat for Hawaii's four species of endangered waterbirds – the Hawaiian coot, the Hawaiian stilt, the Hawaiian duck and the Hawaiian moor hen. During stilt nesting season, normally from mid-February to October, the refuge is off-limits to all visitors. The rest of the year, it can only be visited as part of a guided tour provided by refuge staff (at 4pm every Thursday, 9am on the first two Saturdays of the month and 3:30pm on the remaining Saturdays of the month from October 1 to February 15). Tours are free, but reservations are required and can be made by calling the refuge itself.

NORTH SHORE

More famous off the island than on, the North Shore is a pilgrimage stop for the ever-expanding troupe of migrating surfers, who chase around the globe for seasonal waves. In the winter when the conditions are right, the ocean swells several stories high, changing color from blue to green to frothy white as it beats upon the shoreline. The power is unimaginable, even more so when sunburned bodies skip in and out of the swells with speed and grace.

Before Bruce Brown's 1964 classic, *Endless Summer* captured and inspired the surfing generation, the North Shore had more in common with the northern part of the Windward Coast than with the beach scene of Southern California. Fishing villages dotted the shoreline, later yielding to sugar plantations and small-scale farming. By the early 1900s the O'ahu Railroad & Land Company had linked the North Shore with Honolulu, bringing in the first beachgoers from the city. Hotels and private beach houses sprang up for a time, but largely disappeared by the 1940s when the railroad pulled out. By the 1950s Waikiki surfers started taking on North Shore waves and big-time surfing competitions followed a few years later.

Today North Shore surfing breaks such as Pipeline (or more formally Banzai Pipeline),

Waimea and Sunset Beach attract top surfers from around the globe and grace the covers of every surf magazine ever published. Kids from the heartland of Iowa can recount scenes from surf movies filmed at these mythic places. The two-lane Kamehameha Hwy that skirts the coast is often bumper-to-bumper with traffic, not because of commuters, but because of spectators coming to worship the niche sport.

Meanwhile the beatnik towns of the North Shore, long known for their pebble-floored roadside diners and sun-drenched mellowness, are making the transition to the global trends of a resort town. Oceanfront shacks are now multimillion-dollar vacation homes for wealthy mainlanders, provoking a local backlash united under the bumper sticker slogan: 'Keep North Shore Country.'

TURTLE BAY

Sitting upon the crown of northeastern O'ahu, the coves and lava beds that define the area in and around Turtle Bay (Kawela Bay) is a stunning marker between the Windward Coast and the North Shore. The Turtle Bay Resort claims a portion of this landscape with a view-perfect hotel, golf course, condo village and public access to the nearby beaches. A controversial plan that was recently approved by the city of Honolulu will add five more hotels to this pristine area, stretching from Kahuku Point to Kawela Bay. North Shore residents fiercely oppose the project, while struggling Kahuku residents see an opportunity for jobs and economic development. If the project progresses, this quiet corner will take on more activity, for better or for worse.

Beaches

Shallow **Kuilima Cove**, which is fronted by the Turtle Bay Resort, is protected by a shallow reef, creating one of the area's best swimming spots. The nearby coral is perfect for snorkeling. Public parking is available inside the resort.

Just a mile east of Kuilima Cove is **Kaihalulu Beach**, a beautiful, curved, white-sand beach backed by ironwoods. The rocky bottom makes for poor swimming, but the shoreline attracts morning beachcombers. Go another mile east to reach scenic **Kahuku Point**, where local fishers cast throw-nets and pole fish from the rocks.

O'AHU

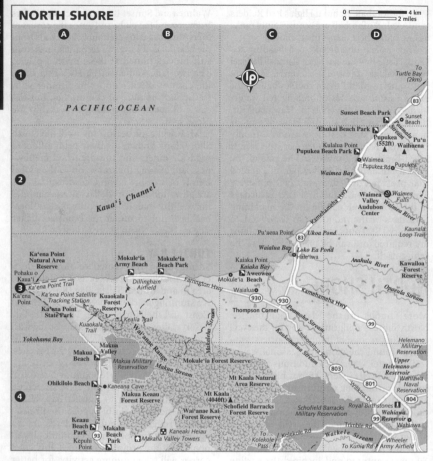

NORTH SHORE

Turtle Bay Resort

Out-of-sync with the North Shore's beatnik reputation, the **Turtle Bay Resort** (Map p160; ☎ 293-6000; www.turtlebayresort.com; 57-091 Kamehameha Hwy, Kahuku) has brought all the modern conveniences of resort life to an unlikely corner of the island. The resort has two top-rated 18-hole courses (one designed by George Fazio and the other by Arnold Palmer); 10 tennis courts, highly rated by *Tennis Magazine*; and horseback riding on slow-paced trails and sunset rides.

SLEEPING & EATING
The sleeping options at the resort include the multistory **hotel** (☎ 293-6000; r from $430) and the adjacent **condominiums** (studios from $100; 1-bedroom

units $105-165; 2-bedroom units $180-275). Each of the hotel rooms has a lanai with a breathtaking ocean view. Booking arrangements for the condos are handled by **Turtle Bay Condos** (☎ 293-2800, 888-266-3690; www.turtlebaycondos.com) or **Estates at Turtle Bay** (☎ 293-0600, 888-200-4202; www.turtlebay-rentals.com). Team Real Estate at Hale'iwa (p179) also deals with Turtle Bay condo bookings.

Lei Lei's Bar & Grill (☎ 293-8811; Turtle Bay Resort, 57-091 Kamehameha Hwy; meals $8-22; ☺ 7am-10pm) Of the resort's several eateries facing the golf course, this is a destination all on its own for locals in the know. The eclectic menu includes oyster shooters, sandwiches, baby back ribs and several Japanese-accented dishes, such as seafood scampi with udon noodles.

WAIMEA & AROUND
pop 2450

The community of Waimea and its surf-related shops nap along the two-lane ocean-front road waiting for the swells. The beaches and their related surf breaks are celebrities, known across the globe by no-name kids, proven pros and itinerant surfers. In the peak of the season, there's an almost holy aura to the famous sites: surfers and spectators have reached the fabled land. For the full-time residents, the sand and sea are virtual community centers, with friends meeting up, hanging out or just hitting the water on good days – or for that matter, on bad days. The surfer ethos of being laid-back is in full effect until things get crowded and then a dash of big-city aggression kicks in.

The Waimea Valley was once heavily settled, the lowlands terraced in taro, the valley walls dotted with houses and the ridges topped with heiau sites. Waimea River, now blocked at the beach, originally opened into the bay and was a passage for canoes traveling to villages upstream. Surfing has been associated with Waimea since the 15th century, when Hawaiians took to *he'e nalu* (wave-sliding).

Sights & Activities
SUNSET BEACH PARK

Consider this beach park to be the bikini queen of all North Shore beaches. Leggy white sands, perfect proportions of sea and sky and a nearly golden halo of sunlight. In winter, the beauty becomes a beast with monster waves and challenging breaks that make it a classic winter surfing destination. The tremendous surf activity causes the slope of the beach to become increasingly steep as the season goes on. **Backyards** is a complete reef break off Sunset Point at the northern end and draws a lot of tow surfers as well as top windsurfers. There are strong currents and a shallow reef, but Backyards often has the island's biggest waves for sailing.

Winter swells create a powerful rip, but come summer, the shoreline begins to smooth out and the waves mellow. The beach has rest rooms, showers and a lifeguard tower.

'EHUKAI BEACH PARK

From the road this looks like just another inconspicuous beach park, but offshore is one of surfing's most revered breaks: **Pipeline**. More formally christened 'Banzai Pipeline,' this break is considered one of the deadliest because of the shallow reef that transforms the waves into towering but collapsible tubes. This is where the first big-wave surfers proved it could be done, where pro surfers compete and where emerging riders come to get noticed by photographers and corporate sponsors. The annual world surfing qualifiers is usually held here at the end of January, while the Pipeline Masters competition (part of the Triple Crown of Surfing) typically occurs in the beginning of December.

The park is opposite the Sunset Beach Elementary School. Facing the ocean, walk 300ft to the left to find the world-famous break. Conditions mellow out in summer, when it's good for swimming. The beach has a lifeguard, rest rooms and showers.

PUPUKEA BEACH PARK

Best known for its jagged rock formations and tide pools, this park is divided into two sections – Three Tables and Shark's Cove – and is a popular snorkeling and dive site. When the swells are high, it is better viewed from land for its aquatic acrobatics: the waves crash into the elevated rocks spraying white foam with orchestral timing.

Gear can be rented from Planet Surf, across the street from the Foodland supermarket. Parking is available across from the auto repair shop and across from the grocery store. Bus 52 stops out front.

Shark's Cove

This cove is beautiful both above and below the water's surface. The origin of the cove's name is uncertain, but sharks are no more common here than anywhere else on the island. Shark's Cove is part of the Pupukea Marine Life Conservation District, dedicated to conserving the unusual coral reef here, noteworthy because it is resistant to the impact of big winter waves.

From May to October, when the seas are generally calm, Shark's Cove offers excellent snorkeling and diving. Turtles are commonly sighted and often crawl up onto the ledges so that the waves and smaller fishes can clean their shells of algae. A fair number of beginning divers take lessons here, while the underwater caves and caverns will thrill advanced divers. The caves can be found around the cove's northeast point. There have been a number of drownings in these caves,

O'AHU

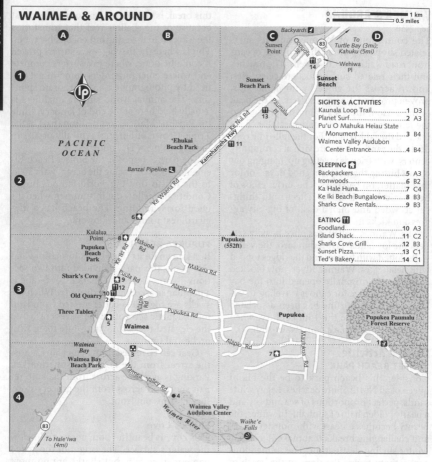

WAIMEA & AROUND

and divers in particular should only explore them with a local expert. Most caves have little natural light, and if sediment is stirred up from swells, the result can be zero visibility and disorientation.

The large boulders out on the end of the point to the far right of the cove are said to be followers of Pele, the volcano goddess. As an honor, she gave them immortality by turning them to stone.

Three Tables

Three Tables gets its name from the flat ledges that rise just above the water. In summer when the ocean is calm, the curious formations are fun to explore on a snorkeling or diving trip. In the deeper water, you'll find more fish,

coral caves, lava tubes and arches. In winter, dangerous rips flow between the beach and the tables, making the area inaccessible. Beware of sharp rocks and coral.

WAIMEA VALLEY AUDUBON CENTER

Across from Waimea Bay Beach Park, this elegant **botanical garden** (☎ 638-9199; http://waimea .audubon.org; 59-864 Kamehameha Hwy; adult/child under 4/child 4-12 $8/free/5; ⏰ 9:30am-5pm) has more than 5000 species. There are sections of ginger, hibiscus, heliconia, native food plants and medicinal species, including many that are endangered. A waterfall sits at the end of the main path through the garden, 0.8 miles from the entrance. The park has several ancient stone platforms and terraces dating back hundreds of years, as well as replicas of thatched buildings similar to those used by early Hawaiians.

Bus 52 stops on the highway in front on the center, from where it's nearly a half-mile walk inland to the entrance. (From Hale'iwa town, you can catch the bus to the Audubon Center from the bus stop opposite Bank of Hawaii on Kamehameha Hwy.) There is no transportation inside the center.

WAIMEA BAY BEACH PARK

Beautiful, deeply set with turquoise waters and a wide white-sand beach almost 1500ft long, Waimea Bay was sacred to the ancient Hawaiians and still retains sacred status with modern-day surfers. Savage high surf and mean rips transform the picturesque bay in winter into a pin-up model for the daring wave riders. On big days, say when waves reach over 30ft, crowds of spectators throng the safety of the beach to watch surfers perform their near-suicidal feats. This is where the classic big wave surf competition in honor of Eddie Aikau is held.

On winter's calmer days the body-boarders are out in force, but even then sets come in hard and people get pounded. Winter water activities here are not for novices. The water is usually calm enough for swimming and snorkeling from June to September. There are showers, rest rooms and picnic tables, and a lifeguard is on duty daily.

PU'U O MAHUKA HEIAU STATE MONUMENT

Attributed to the legendary *menehune*, Pu'u o Mahuka Heiau, a long, low-walled platform temple perched on a bluff above Waimea, is the largest heiau on O'ahu. The terraced stone walls are a couple of feet high, although most of the heiau is now overgrown. It's an excellent site for a temple, with a commanding view of both Waimea Valley and Waimea Bay. West, the view extends along the coast to Ka'ena Point.

To get to the heiau, turn up Pupukea Rd at Foodland supermarket. The marked turnoff is about half a mile up the road; from there it's three-quarters of a mile in. There's a good view of Pupukea Beach Park on the drive up.

KAUNALA LOOP TRAIL

The little-known **Kaunala Loop** trail sits quietly above Waimea Valley, a good place to mix an easy valley walk with a moderate ridge climb for sweeping views of Waimea Bay. Ancient Hawaiians believed the waters of Waimea were sacred, and after seeing the bay from viewpoints high atop this trail, it would be hard not to agree.

To get to the trailhead, turn up Pupukea Rd at the Foodland supermarket and continue for 2.5 miles. This 4.5-mile hike averages about two hours. This trail is officially open to the public only on weekends and state holidays. Hunting is allowed, so hikers should wear bright colors and don't go wandering off the trail. Also bring water. No permit is required.

Sleeping

The bulletin board at Pupukea's Foodland supermarket has notices of roommates wanted and the occasional vacation rental listing,

---

MEASURING WAVES, HAWAIIAN STYLE

Say you're in the water, when you turn around to notice – a bit late perhaps – a very large wave coming your way. Didn't you hear on the radio that the surf was going to be about 3ft to 4ft today? OK, so where did this massive seven-footer come from that is about to change your life? If it's any consolation, your question is the subject of a long-brewing debate that centers around two competing methods for measuring the height of an approaching wave.

Hawaiian surfers measure the height of the wave from the back; the rest of the world, including California to Australia, measures its height from the front, or face (officially, the distance from the trough in front of a wave to its peak). On average, the face height is nearly double the back height.

The difference is dramatic enough to have convinced the Honolulu office of the National Weather Service to lobby for adopting the international standard in reporting local wave conditions; it cites 60 ocean drownings during high-surf periods since 1980. Many surfers are bummed by the new standard, but lifeguards and rescue squads are relieved. They want people to have a realistic idea of what to expect when they hit the beach – so the next time you get creamed by a six-footer, you won't be able to say you weren't warned.

O'AHU

so check it out if you're thinking of staying a while. There are also a number of private home owners who rely on word-of-mouth advertising, as well as vacation rental agencies (p179).

BUDGET

Backpackers (☎ 638-7838; www.backpackers-hawaii .com; 59-788 Kamehameha Hwy; dm $25, r $65-75, cabin $170-280, studios $125-150) Opposite Three Tables, this one-time surfers' hangout has expanded into *the* round-the-world traveler spot. Rarely do you find such a budget backpacker joint in the USA and some of the accommodations will seem airlifted from the Southeast Asian pancake trail. The apartment-style model is used here: you rent a room or a dorm bed in a self-contained unit with shared bathroom, kitchen and common space. The best of the mix are in Plantation Village, more accurately a collection of grubby shacks with a communal atmosphere. You won't pay very much and you won't get very much – a win-win. More of a mixed bag are the studios and main house; because rooms vary in quality (and air ventilation) ask to check out a few options before committing. A two-night minimum is required, and there's a free shuttle that picks up guests from Waikiki.

Shark's Cove Rentals (☎ 638-7980, 888-883-0001; www.sharkscoverentals.com; 59-672 Kamehameha Hwy; r $75-185) This well-managed property consists of four adjacent houses that are directly across from Pupukea Beach Park. The houses are divided into apartment-style dorms: each of the self-contained apartment has three private bedrooms with bunk beds, shared bathroom and shared kitchen. In the main house, overlooking the water, the units have a private bathroom but shared kitchen and common space. The owners are enthusiastic about their guests and their enjoyment of the North Shore.

MIDRANGE & TOP END

Ironwoods (☎ 293-2554; richard27@hawaii.rr.com; 57-531 Kamehameha Hwy; studios per day $75) Two miles south of Sunset Beach, this private home owned by a lovely couple claiming two decades on the North Shore rents out an oceanfront studio with a loft bedroom. The quarters are a bit cramped and you'll need to climb a steep ladder to bed down for the night but the beach is just footsteps from the house. There's a five-night minimum stay.

Ka Hale Huna (☎ 638-7924; www.vrbo.com/59784; off Pupukea Rd; studios $100) Perched on the mountain that overlooks the sea, this private home rents out a very private studio with a lanai facing a wooded canyon filled with bird activity. The unit has a kitchenette, a sun-filled room, outdoor BBQ grill and access to the shade and fruit trees of the garden. The beach is a 15-minute drive away.

Ke Iki Beach Bungalows (☎ 638-8229, 866-638-8229; www.keikibeach.com; 59-579 Ke Iki Rd; 1-bedroom units $135-195, 2-bedroom units $175-210) Snuggled between two legendary surfing spots, Waimea Bay and Sunset Beach, this quaint collection of cottages and studios faces its own stretch of blonde beach. In summer the sea is gentle and inviting, but in winter the waves snarl and curl, frothing an ice blue as they pound the shore. Ke Iki's 12 units are not lavish, but are smartly decorated and comfortable. Every apartment has a full kitchen. Tropical touches include overhead ceiling fans and outdoor hammocks and showers.

Eating

Ted's Bakery (☎ 638-8207; 59-024 Kamehameha Hwy; snacks $1-3; ◷ 7am-6pm) Beloved by all, this sweet-tooth mecca peddles piles and piles of cinnamon rolls and butter buns to surfers, daytrippers and construction workers. If you miss out on those, then settle for a slice of chocolate *haupia* (coconut) pie or moist carrot cake. It is opposite Sunset Beach.

Shark's Cove Grill (☎ 638-8300; snacks $7-10; ◷ 8:30am-7pm) This little white trailer parks along the highway 100yd north of Foodland and has good burgers, fish sandwiches and chicken teriyaki plates. There are a few sunny tables, and a view of the beach.

Sunset Pizza (☎ 638-7660; 59-174 Kamehameha Hwy; pizza $10-18; ◷ 7am-9pm) Opposite Sunset Beach Park, this place has great pizza and slow service, plus meatball subs and slices.

Island Shack (☎ 638-9500; 59-254 Kamehameha Hwy; mains $9-14; ◷ 8:30am-9:30pm) Look for the giant wooden *ki'i* (Tiki) figure across from Rocky Point north of Waimea. It's open-air picnic style, complete with gravel floor and wobbly plastic tables. Fresh fish plates and veggie sandwiches dominate a menu with a Brazilian touch. 'Ahi tuna with rice and beans. Cash only.

The **Foodland** (☎ 638-8081; 59-720 Kamehameha Hwy; ◷ 6am-10pm) supermarket opposite Pupukea Beach Park has the best grocery prices and selection on the North Shore. It also has a good deli selling fresh *'ahi poke* and inexpensive fried chicken, perfect for a beachside picnic.

HALE'IWA

pop 2500

Hale'iwa still retains a sleepy outpost ambiance despite being the commercial center of the North Shore scene. Nearly every service person and business owner in this town watches the waves more closely than the clock. And there's a communal bond between the disparate characters who unpack their lives here. The accomplished business owners of today were once the young kids hustling waiter jobs just to earn enough to underwrite the surfing life. And when the waves are up, Hale'iwa turns into a ghost town.

Orientation

Most of Hale'iwa's shops are along Kamehameha Hwy, the main street. Hale'iwa has a picturesque boat harbor bounded on both sides by beach parks, including Hale'iwa Ali'i Beach Park, known for the North Shore's safest year-round swimming conditions.

The Anahulu River, flowing out along the boat harbor, is spanned by the Rainbow Bridge. In 1832 John and Ursula Emerson, the first missionaries to come to the North Shore, built Hale'iwa, meaning house *(hale)* of the great frigate bird *(iwa)*, a grass house and missionary school on the riverbank, which gave its name to the village.

Information

Coffee Gallery (☎ 637-5355; North Shore Marketplace, 66-250 Kamehameha Ave; per hr $4; free wi-fi; ☼ 6am-8pm) Internet access also available at this café.

First Hawaiian Bank (☎ 637-6235; 66-135 Kamehameha Hwy) On the northern side of Hale'iwa Shopping Plaza.

Hale'iwa Pharmacy (☎ 637-9393; 66-149 Kamehameha Hwy) In Hale'iwa Shopping Plaza.

Post office (☎ 637-1711; 66-437 Kamehameha Ave) At the south side of town.

Dangers & Annoyances

Because there is a transient population on the North Shore, car and vacation rental break-ins are common. Don't leave any valuables in your car when parked at beach parks and

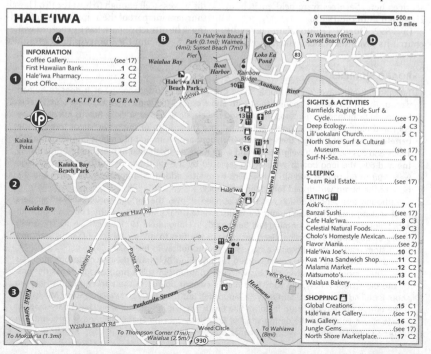

HALE'IWA

0 — 500 m
0 — 0.3 miles

INFORMATION	
Coffee Gallery..........................(see 17)	
First Hawaiian Bank.........................1	C2
Hale'iwa Pharmacy..........................2	C2
Post Office................................3	C2

SIGHTS & ACTIVITIES	
Barnfields Raging Isle Surf & Cycle..................................(see 17)	
Deep Ecology.................................4	C3
Lili'uokalani Church..........................5	C1
North Shore Surf & Cultural Museum...........................(see 17)	
Surf-N-Sea.....................................6	C1

SLEEPING	
Team Real Estate.........................(see 17)	

EATING	
Aoki's...7	C1
Banzai Sushi.............................(see 17)	
Cafe Hale'iwa................................8	C3
Celestial Natural Foods.....................9	C3
Cholo's Homestyle Mexican.....(see 17)	
Flavor Mania............................(see 2)	
Hale'iwa Joe's..............................10	C1
Kua 'Aina Sandwich Shop..............11	C2
Malama Market...........................12	C2
Matsumoto's..............................13	C1
Waialua Bakery.............................14	C2

SHOPPING	
Global Creations...........................15	C1
Hale'iwa Art Gallery......................(see 17)	
Iwa Gallery..................................16	C2
Jungle Gems.............................(see 17)	
North Shore Marketplace..........17	C2

To Hale'iwa Beach Park (0.1mi); Waimea (4mi); Sunset Beach (7mi)

To Waimea (4mi); Sunset Beach (7mi)

Waialua Bay

Loko Ea Pond

Boat Harbor

Rainbow Bridge

Hale'iwa Ali'i Beach Park

Hale'iwa Rd

Anahulu River

PACIFIC OCEAN

Emerson Rd

Kaiaka Point

Kaiaka Bay Beach Park

Kaiaka Bay

Cane Haul Rd

Hale'iwa

Pa'ala'a Rd

Haleiwa Rd

Kiiki'i Stream

Paukauila Stream

Waialua Beach Rd

To Mokule'ia (1.3mi)

To Thompson Corner (1mi); Waialua (2.5mi)

Weed Circle

Twin Bridge Rd

Helemano Stream

To Wahiawa (8mi)

follow all the safety regulations required by the rental agencies.

Sights
NORTH SHORE SURF & CULTURAL MUSEUM

You can get a sense of how integral surfing is to the town's character by visiting this funky **museum** (☎ 637-8888; North Shore Marketplace, 66-250 Kamehameha Ave; admission by donation; ☯ most afternoons), where the tone is marked by a key North Shore word, 'usually' – it's staffed by volunteers, so the hours are flexible. The volunteers are into surfing, of course, so when the surf's up expect the place to be closed up! There's a good collection of vintage surfboards, period photos and classic surf posters, along with reasonably priced lost beach jewelry.

LILI'UOKALANI CHURCH

Although the current building was constructed in 1961, the **Lili'uokalani Church** (☎ 637-9364; 66-090 Kamehameha Ave; ☯ most mornings) congregation dates from 1832. It is a Protestant church named for Queen Lili'uokalani, who spent summers on Anahulu River and attended services here. Services were held entirely in Hawaiian until the 1940s.

In 1892 Queen Lili'uokalani gave the church its seven-dial clock, which shows the hour, day, month and year, as well as the phases of the moon. The queen's 12-letter name replaces the numerals on the clock face. The church is open whenever the minister is in, usually mornings.

BEACHES

The in-town beach parks provide a nice patch of green to host family luau and community soccer scrimmages. Although these beach parks are close to the harbor, the wave action does attract annual surf competitions and lots of local attention.

After seeing so many stunning beaches along the North Shore, it is perfectly acceptable to shrug at a few and **Hale'iwa Beach Park** is a good candidate. This park is on the north side of Waialua Bay, where the beach is protected by shallow shoals and a breakwater. The waters are usually calm, though north swells occasionally ripple the bay. This 13-acre park has full beach facilities and a good view of Ka'ena Point.

The smaller waves at **Hale'iwa Ali'i Beach Park** are a popular surf break for local kids who are just learning their backyard sport. In winter the waves swell enough to host the Pro Hawaii tournament, part of the Triple Crown of Surfing. The attractive park has a generous white-sand beach and the knotty-pine community

---

BOARD SHAPERS

Tackling the big waves on the North Shore owes as much to technology as it does to human daring. The big waves that pound the North Shore during the winter months were unnavigable to the old-fashioned long-boards that cruised the classic waves of Waikiki. Boards needed to be light and nimble so that a surfer could crawl into the bosom of the wave, shoot through the barrel and kick out through the white top. Polyurethane foam and fiberglass, introduced in the 1950s and 60s, solved the weight issue and were more easily shaped into ergonomic designs. By the mid-60s, the long-boards were being replaced by the short-boards: surfboards on average were 10ft to 6ft shorter and 8lb lighter. Fins were later added for stability in the water and the nose of the board was tipped for added buoyancy.

Although this general design was being applied all over the surfing world, backyard shapers were making their own adaptations for their favorite breaks. In O'ahu, Gerry Lopez, along with Jack Shipley, established Lightning Bolt Surfboards in Honolulu in 1971, specifically for the North Shore break known as Pipeline. Gerry was one of the first to master this now famous spot and his custom-made boards became a necessary tool to follow in his wake.

Today, board shapers who once worked for Lightning Bolt have their own custom shops, as does a new crop of tech-savvy shapers who use computer-imaging programs to tweak designs. Of the old-school variety, Bill Barnsfield makes custom boards in the backend of his Hale'iwa shop, Barnfield's Raging Isle Surf & Cycle (opposite). But the revitalized Waialua Sugar Mill (p181) is the official nucleus for board factories filled with glassers, air brushers, and legendary shapers. This is where you'll find the design shop of Eric Arakawa, who shapes for Andy Irons; and Dan Moore's Outereef, which makes tow boards.

building served as the lifeguard headquarters in the TV series *Baywatch Hawaii*, which used this beach park as its main setting during filming in Hawaii from 1999 to 2001.

The 53-acre **Kaiaka Bay Beach Park** is on Kaiaka Bay, about a mile west of town. This is a good place for a picnic, as there are shady ironwood trees, but the in-town beaches are better for swimming. Two streams empty out into Kaiaka Bay, muddying up the beach after heavy rainstorms. Kaiaka has rest rooms, picnic tables, showers and campsites.

Activities
DIVING & SNORKELLING
During the winter, North Shore dive operators take trips to Shark's Cove (p173) in the summer months and to South Shore wrecks in the winter. Between Christmas and April, humpback whales visit the harbors of northern and western O'ahu.

Deep Ecology (☎ 637-7946, 800-578-3992; www .deepecologyhawaii.com; 66-456 Kamehameha Hwy; dives $95-129) is a small North Shore family operation well regarded by local divers. It rents out gear and runs dive, snorkeling and whale-watching trips. One of the owners was instrumental in convincing the state to designate Shark's Cove as the Pupukea Marine Life Conservation District. When out on dives, the company also helps untangle turtles caught in fishing line. Whale-watching trips head out in small Zodiac boats for a more intimate experience.

CYCLING & MOUNTAIN BIKING
Bike riding on the North Shore ranges from paved bike paths next to the Kamehameha Hwy to challenging tracks above Waimea Bay and wider trails around Ka'ena Point (p189). For bike hire, head to **Barnfield's Raging Isle Surf & Cycle** (☎ 637-7707; www.ragingisle.com; North Shore Marketplace, 66-250 Kamehameha Hwy; bike rental per day $40-60; ☺ 10am-6:30pm). Check the website for trail information.

SURFING
If you're a beginner, the North Shore does have a few tame breaks, including Chun's Reef, Pu'uena Point and Hale'iwa Ali'i Beach Park. Even if you've ridden a few waves in Waikiki, it is advisable to do a lesson with one of the many freelancing surfers so that you get an introduction to the underwater hazards. Everyone offers lessons on the side,

so ask around for recommendations or keep an eye out for homemade brochures.

Sleeping
Except for Turtle Bay Resort, there are no official hotels on the North Shore. Vacation rentals are the most common lodging options. There are a few European-style B&Bs as well as budget-style hostels. People occasionally rent out rooms in their homes; check the bulletin boards at Malama Market in Hale'iwa or Foodland supermarket in Pupukea. Hale'iwa's only camping option is at Kaiaka Bay Beach Park (left). See Waimea for more sleeping options.

VACATION RENTALS
Vacation rentals can range from one-bedroom condos to five-bedroom houses. There is usually a seven-night minimum stay and often a cleaning fee. Most houses have modern decor and kitchen amenities, outdoor grill and beach gear. The following companies get reliably good feedback:

Sand Sea Beachfront Vacation Homes (☎ 637-2568, 800-442-6901; www.sandsea.com; PO Box 239, Hale'iwa, Hi 96712; 2-/8-bedroom houses from $200/750) In business since 1979, this agency specializes in renting privately owned beachfront homes along the North Shore. There are usually about 40 to choose from; see their website for details.

Team Real Estate (☎ 637-3507, 800-982-8602; www .teamrealestate.com; Suite D-103, North Shore Marketplace, 66-250 Kamehameha Hwy; 1-bedroom condo $110, beachfront homes from $300) This company represents Turtle Bay Resort condos and beachfront homes along the North Shore.

Eating
BUDGET
Flavor Mania (☎ 637-9363; Hale'iwa Shopping Center, 66-145 Kamehameha Hwy; ☺ 11am-6pm) This is an old-fashioned ice-cream parlor serving homemade flavors. To complete the retro feel, there are also a few old-school video games.

Coffee Gallery (☎ 637-5571; North Shore Marketplace, 66-250 Kamehameha Hwy; snacks $2-6; ☺ 6am-8pm) Follow your nose to this mellow café serving fresh-roasted coffees (including local Hawaii beans), pastries and hearty sandwiches. Internet access is also available.

Kua 'Aina Sandwich Shop (☎ 636-6067; 66-214 Kamehameha Hwy; snacks $4-7; ☺ 11am-8pm) Many locals swear that this cool eatery grills up the island's best burgers along with big salads

---

SWEET TREAT

For many people, the circle-island drive isn't complete without lining up for shave ice at **Matsumoto's** (☎ 637-4827; 66-087 Kamehameha Hwy; snacks $2-5) tin-roofed general store. Often Honolulu families drive to the North Shore with one purpose: to stand in line here and walk out with a dripping, delicious shave ice cone, drenched with island flavors, such as *liliko'i* (passion fruit), banana, mango and pineapple.

Hawaiian shave ice is drenched with industrial-strength sweet syrup like the snow cones found on the US mainland, but it's much better because the ice is more finely shaved. A medium-sized cone with a combination of flavors usually costs about $2, a bit more if you add a local favorite, red azuki bean. The entire concoction begins dripping into a sticky mess the second you get it, so don't dawdle.

Although most tourists flock to Matsumoto's, many locals prefer **Aoki's** (66-117 Kamehameha Hwy; snacks $1.50-3).

---

and fresh fish sandwiches. It's a North Shore favorite and, with luck, you'll find a table on the shady lanai.

Waialua Bakery (☎ 637-9079; 66-200 Kamehameha Hwy; snacks $4-7; 🕑 8am-4pm Mon-Sat) Your average hippy outpost for smoothies and sandwiches that sprouts effortlessly in bohemian corners like Hale'iwa.

Cafe Hale'iwa (☎ 637-5516; 66-460 Kamehameha Hwy; breakfast $5-7, lunch $8-10; 🕑 7am-12:30pm Mon-Sat) An unpretentious joint with Formica tables and walls plastered with surf memorabilia, Cafe Hale'iwa is a popular haunt for both local surfers and day-trippers. It offers good food at cheap prices. A popular breakfast choice is the egg sandwich or mahi and eggs. Lunch is mostly sandwiches and Mexican fare.

Malama Market (☎ 637-4520; 66-190 Kamehameha Hwy; 🕑 7am-9pm), next to Kua 'Aina Sandwich Shop, is the place for general grocery items, while **Celestial Natural Foods** (☎ 637-6729; 66-443 Kamehameha Ave; 🕑 9am-6pm Mon-Sat, 10am-6pm Sun) carries a small assortment of fresh produce and health foods.

MIDRANGE & TOP END

Cholo's Homestyle Mexican (☎ 637-3059; North Shore Marketplace, 66-250 Kamehameha Hwy; meals $8-14; 🕑 8am-9pm) Cholo's has decent Mexican food with a North Shore touch, meaning that the margaritas flush more faces red than a day of surfing.

Banzai Sushi (☎ 637-4404; North Shore Marketplace, 66-250 Kamehameha Hwy; dinner $10-15; 🕑 5-9:30pm) Owned by a Brazilian, this sushi restaurant does a lot more than just maki rolls. South American–style ceviche, surf videos and lounging on pillows helps to capture the post-surfing glow.

Hale'iwa Joe's (☎ 637-8005; 66-001 Kamehameha Hwy; appetizers $7-10, lunch $8-15, dinner $18-26; 🕑 11:30am-9:30pm) A hometown setting for hearty seafood-inspired meals, this North Shore institution is a weekly date for almost every resident and even more tourists. Favorites include Emma's Poke (marinated raw *'ahi*) and crunchy coconut shrimp, nibbled on the lanai overlooking the harbor.

Shopping

Hale'iwa shopping ranges from the trendy to the quirky, and most of the shops and galleries are either in or nearby the North Shore Marketplace (66-250 Kamehameha Hwy).

Jungle Gems (☎ 637-6609; North Shore Marketplace, 66-250 Kamehameha Hwy) For unusual handmade jewelry and elaborate beadwork.

Global Creations (☎ 637-1505; 66-079 Kamehameha Hwy) For mainstream furnishings, clothing, Hawaiian trinkets and that last-minute gift shopping.

Aloha Island Art (North Shore Marketplace, 66-250 Kamehameha Hwy) In front of Jungle Gems, this outdoor stand sells unique gyotaku prints, based on a Japanese art form of handpainted fish prints. Artist Michael Hemperly uses handmade papers and sells his original works when the winds are too calm to go windsurfing.

Hale'iwa Art Gallery (☎ 637-3368; North Shore Marketplace, 66-250 Kamehameha Hwy) This modern art space carries North Shore and Polynesian artists, including Alfred Furtado, who is known for painting vivid pictures of hula dancers, many of whom are relatives by marriage.

Iwa Gallery (☎ 637-4865; 66-119 Kamehameha Hwy; 🕑 10:30am-6:30pm) This smaller gallery carries primarily the wax candle works of owner Scott

Bechtol; his most popular pieces are the crying Tiki candles, designed so that the wax drips out of the candle like tears.

WAIALUA

A former sugar plantation town, Waialua is a welcome return to the 'country' that North Shore residents are so fond of sloganizing. The center of town is a ghost town with a boarded up bank and a weedy promenade. The other landmark is the old sugar mill, which closed down in 1996 bringing an end to the last commercial sugar operation on O'ahu.

The **Waialua Sugar Mill** (www.sugarmill hawaii.com) has been redeveloped into a model center for locally owned shops and businesses. **North Shore Soap Factory** (☎ 637-8400; www.hawaiianbathbody.com) makes soaps and bath products from island-grown ingredients, such as plumeria, papaya, and guava under the brand Hawaiian Bath & Body. **Island-X Hawaii** (☎ 637-2624; www.islandxhawaii.com) sells fresh Waialua-grown coffee straight from the processing center out the back door, as well as Waialua-made soda. On Saturdays from 8am to noon the **Waialua Farmers Market** sets up in the parking lot of the sugar mill to show off the wares of local farmers. Many of the former plantation workers now farm small plots of land leased from the Dole pineapple corporation, an agreement reached to help workers retrenched as a result of the sugar mill's closure. There are also small-scale surfboard makers and other light-industry operations keeping the old mill decidedly brawny.

If you miss the farmers market, stop in at **Brown Bottle** (☎ 637-6728; 67-292 Goodale Ave; ⏱ 7am-10:30pm), a liquor store that sells fresh produce grown by a local farmer.

The Waialua area remains economically depressed, with many of the surrounding fields overgrown with feral sugarcane. Other sections are newly planted with coffee trees – a labor-intensive crop that holds out promise for new jobs. You can see the coffee trees, planted in neat rows, as you come down the slopes into Waialua.

Sleeping

Camp Mokule'ia (☎ 637-6241; www.campmokuleia .com; 68-729 Farrington Hwy, Waialua; campsite per person $7) Halfway between Hale'iwa and Dillingham Airfield, the church-owned retreat is open to the public with reservations. The camp is spread out through a partially shaded ironwood grove facing the ocean. Facilities are clean and basic, including showers, toilets and cooking areas.

Tree of Life Retreat (☎ 637-9363; 68-007 Aweoweo St; r $80-145) In a cozy beachside neighborhood of Waialua, this private residence is a meditation B&B, offering three bedrooms (two with shared bathroom) to fellow devotees of daily meditation, yoga and the spiritual arts. Guests have access to the kitchen and outdoor grill area. The house is across the street from lowkey Aweoweo Beach, a shallow bay good for swimming and turtle spotting.

MOKULE'IA & AROUND

Here's to the end of the road, the last few stretches of human habitation before the island terminates into the deep and fearsome ocean. The Farrington Hwy (930) is your honorable guide; it runs west from Thompson Corner to Dillingham Airfield and Mokule'ia Beach. Both this road and the road along the Wai'anae Coast are called Farrington Hwy, but they don't connect, as each side reaches a dead end about 2½ miles short of Ka'ena Point.

Mokule'ia Beach Park

Mokule'ia Beach is a 6-mile stretch of sand running from Kaiaka Bay toward Ka'ena Point. It is windswept and deserted, seeing a few GIs and local fishers and maybe some teenagers at night. There's a consistent lava rock shelf that runs along much of its shoreline. The fairly consistent winds here make it a very popular spot with windsurfers, particularly in spring and autumn. In the winter there are dangerous currents. The only beach facilities are at the beach park, opposite Dillingham Airfield. Camping is allowed with a county camping permit.

Dillingham Airfield

The trade winds that visit O'ahu create perfect conditions for sail planes to glide over the scenic North Shore. All sailplane operations on the island are headquartered at Dillingham Airfield at the west end of the Farrington Hwy, just past Mokule'ia Beach Park.

Mr Bill's Original Glider Rides (☎ 677-3404; Dillingham Airfield; 30min glide $100) and **Soar Hawaii Sailplanes** (☎ 637-3147; Dillingham Airfield) offer introductory rides lasting from 10 minutes to one hour for one to two people. Rates range

O'AHU

O'AHU

from $40 to $158 per person. They also offer training and acrobatic rides.

Skydive Hawaii (☎ 637-9700; Dillingham Airfield; www.hawaiiskydiving.com; per person $225) offers tandem jumps with an instructor, usually a friendly stranger with whom you jump out of a perfectly good airplane, free fall for a minute and float down for another 10 minutes. The whole process, including basic instruction, takes about 1½ hours. Participants must be at least 18 years of age and weigh less than 200lb. Planes take off daily, weather permitting.

Mokule'ia Army Beach to Ka'ena Point

Mokule'ia Army Beach, opposite the western end of Dillingham Airfield, has the widest stretch of sand on the Mokule'ia shore. Once reserved exclusively for military personnel, the beach is now open to the public, although it is no longer maintained and there are no facilities. The beach is unprotected and has very strong rip currents, especially during high surf in winter.

From Army Beach you can proceed another 1.5 miles down the road, passing still more white-sand beaches with aqua-blue waters. You'll usually find someone shore-casting and a few folks living out of their junker cars. The terrain is scrub land reaching up to the base of the Wai'anae Range, while the shoreline is wild and windswept. The area is not only desolate, but can also be a bit trashed.

The Farrington Hwy ends at the beginning of the dirt path leading to rocky Ka'ena Point (p188), which connects to the Wai'anae Coast. You can hike or mountain bike around the point but you can't drive. To get to the other side by car, you'll have to backtrack to the highways that buzz through Central O'ahu.

Hiking Trails

The five-mile **Kealia Trail** ascends from Dillingham Airfield above Ka'ena Point for more than a mile of cliff-face switchbacks. But this segment isn't very interesting as it follows a dusty 4WD road used by local hunters. The Kealia Trail later joins forces with **Kuaokala Trail** to bring hikers to a justly celebrated viewpoint over Makua Valley and the high Wai'anae Range. This trail is best for those wishing to avoid the hassle of securing a permit and driving around the Wai'anae Coast just to hike the Kuaokala Trail, accessible from the Ka'ena Point Satellite Tracking Station (p188).

CENTRAL O'AHU

Central O'ahu forms a saddle between the Wai'anae Range on the west and the Ko'olau Range on the east. Aside from a few historical areas and scenic vistas, most people just zoom up through central O'ahu on their way to the North Shore.

Three routes lead north from Honolulu to Wahiawa, the region's central town. The freeway, H2, is the fastest route, whereas Kunia Rd (750), the furthest west, is the most scenic. The least interesting of the options, Farrington Hwy (99), catches local traffic as it runs through Mililani, a nondescript residential community. From Wahiawa two routes, Kaukonahua Rd (803) and Kamehameha Hwy (99), lead through scenic pineapple country to the North Shore.

HAWAII'S PLANTATION VILLAGE

The lives of the people who came to Hawaii to work on the sugarcane plantations are showcased at **Hawaii's Plantation Village** (Map pp90-1; ☎ 677-0110; 94-695 Waipahu St, Waipahu; adult/child 4-11 $13/5; ⏰ guided tours on the hour from 10am-2pm Mon-Sat). The setting is particularly evocative, as Waipahu was one of O'ahu's last plantation towns, and its rusty sugar mill, which operated until 1995, still looms on a knoll directly above this site.

The site encompasses homes and buildings typical of plantation villages of the early 20th century. Period furnishings illustrate the lifestyles of the different ethnic groups – Hawaiian, Japanese, Chinese, Korean, Portuguese, Puerto Rican and Filipino. The Chinese cookhouse (c 1909) was originally on this site, and the Japanese shrine (1914) was moved here; the other structures are 'authentic' replicas. You need to join a tour to visit the site.

To get there by car, take the H1 Fwy to exit 7, turn left onto Paiwa St, then right onto Waipahu St, continue past the sugar mill. The village is on the left. Bus No 42 runs between Waikiki and Waipahu every 30 minutes and takes about 1½ hours. The village is 5 miles northwest of Pearl Harbor.

HONOULIULI FOREST RESERVE

Honouliuli Forest Reserve is home to nearly 70 rare and endangered plant and animal species. The land once belonged to Hawaiian royalty and was named Honouliuli – meaning dark harbor – for the dark, fertile lands that stretch from the waters of Pearl Harbor to the summit of the Wai'anae Range.

The **Nature Conservancy** (☎ 587-6220; www.nature .org\hawaii) leads monthly hikes to two trails in the Honouliuli Forest Reserve on the slopes of the Wai'anae Range north of Kapolei. Palikea Ridge Trail is the easier of the two hikes, while the Kalua'a Loop Trail is considered intermediate.

KUNIA ROAD (HIGHWAY 750)

Kunia Rd is a worthwhile detour, and only adds a few miles to the drive through central O'ahu. The first mile, after turning from H1, winds through creeping suburbia, soon followed by vast plantation lands. The route runs along the foothills of the Wai'anae Range and the countryside remains solidly agricultural all the way to Schofield Barracks Military Reservation, along the way passing pineapple fields. There is little development – just red earth carpeted with long green strips of pineapples stretching to the edge of the mountains.

Within the military reservation, **Kolekole Pass** (elevation 1724ft) occupies the gap in the Wai'anae Range that Japanese fighter planes once flew through on December 7, 1941 just minutes before attacking Pearl Harbor. This flight scene was recreated here in 1970 for the shooting of the popular war film *Tora! Tora! Tora!*

Kolekole Pass sits above Schofield Barracks Military Reservation. The pass can be visited providing the base isn't on military alert. Access to the pass is through Lyman Gate at Schofield Barracks Military Reservation. Follow the signs to a small parking area on the side of the mountain where a five-minute walk to the top ends at a clearing with a view straight down to the Wai'anae Coast.

In Hawaiian mythology, the large, ribbed stone that sits atop the ridge here is said to be the embodiment of a woman named Kolekole who took the form of this stone in order to become the perpetual guardian of the pass.

WAHIAWA

Wahiawa, whose name means 'place of noise' in Hawaiian, is just that: shockingly crowded with used car lots, tattoo parlors and general GI businesses associated with five nearby military bases and reservations.

Sights & Activities
ROYAL BIRTHSTONES

Just north of Wahiawa is the area known as **Kukaniloko**, which marks a group of royal birthstones (Map pp90–1) where Hawaiian queens gave birth to generations of royalty. The stones date from the 12th century. Legend held that if a woman lay properly against the stones while giving birth, her child would be blessed by the gods, and indeed, many of O'ahu's great chiefs were born at this site.

These stones are one of only two documented birthstone sites in Hawaii (the other is on Kaua'i; p482). Many of the petroglyphs on the stones are of recent origin, but the eroded circular patterns are original.

To get to the site from town, head three-quarters of a mile north on Kamehameha Hwy from its intersection with California Ave. Turn left onto the red dirt road directly opposite Whitmore Ave. The stones, marked with a state monument sign, are a quarter of a mile down the road, through a pineapple field, among a stand of eucalyptus and coconut trees. You'll need to park your car shortly after the turnoff; don't leave valuables unattended.

DOLE PLANTATION

About halfway between Wahiawa and Hale'iwa on the North Shore, the food empire behind this **attraction** (Map pp90-1; ☎ 621-8408; 64-1550 Kamehameha Hwy; ☙ 9am-5:30pm) is almost synonymous with Hawaii. What started out as a fruit stand in the heart of O'ahu's pineapple country is now a bustling gift shop with various kid-friendly activities. Miles of pineapple fields surround the complex and Dole's processing plant sits across the street.

The pineapple industry in O'ahu was established in 1901 by James D Dole, a cousin of Sanford B Dole, then president of the Republic of Hawaii after the overthrow of the queen. Not only was Dole successful at growing pineapples in the temperamental soil but he introduced industrialization into the time-consuming process of canning the fruit so that it could reach the mainland market faster and cheaper.

The **plantation garden tour** (adult/child $3.75/3) is a walking tour through a garden of commercial species grown in O'ahu. You can explore on your own or on a guided tour (9:30am to 4:30pm). The **Pineapple Express Train** (adult/child $7.50/5.50; ☙ every 15min 9am-5pm) explores the whole complex, including the production portion of the plantation, aboard a steam train with narration. If you feel like doing it all, go for the train/garden combo ticket, which costs $9.50/7.50 per adult/child.

Kids are the biggest fans of the 'world's largest maze' (adult/child $5/3), especially on overcast days when the sun isn't a problem. The maze covers nearly 2 acres and contains 1.7 miles of pathways with a station-based game associated with certain points to chase away the monotony. Most people take 30 to 45 minutes to get through, or give up in boredom. The posted record is six minutes.

WAI'ANAE COAST

A little bit of Appalachia by the sea, the Wai'anae Coast still stands separate from the rest of the island. To outsiders it is a wasteland where the modern world can stow its unmentionables – the electric plant, the garbage dump and the slums – without sullying its own backyard. The majority of residents are Hawaiians and their visible lives reflect very little monetary success in the O'ahu experiment of multiethnic commerce.

Despite being cash poor, this is the soul of the island where the tender voice of Makaha native son Braddah Iz captured the Eden reality, a beautiful landscape in which the dwellers had eaten the fruit of knowing and suffering. The houses might be shacks, the climate might be dry, but the stretch of sand and sea that defines this coast is not only beautiful but physically and emotionally nourishing to the residents. And to the interior are wedge-shaped mountains and deep valleys crowned with daily rainbows.

Few tourists find their way out here and the area has a reputation for being initially unreceptive to outsiders. One of the coast's biggest towns, Nanakuli earned its name, which means 'to turn away,' when the villagers would avoid interacting with visitors because they could not afford to offer drinking water, an expected gesture of hospitality, due to the scarcity of the resource. Today's residents might guard themselves from the outside for other reasons – gentrification is on its way, signaled by the arrival of Starbucks and a new resort – but for the gentle traveler who seeks experiences over snapshots, this insular coast is Hawaii without

the name brand, a real place of beauty, legend and living.

Farrington Hwy (93) runs the length of the coast scooting past squatty towns and liquor stores on one side and white-sand beaches on the other. Further up the coast habitation yields to the velvet-tufted mountains and rocky coastal ledges leading all the way to the sacred tip of the island at Ka'ena Point.

KO OLINA RESORT

O'ahu's newest resort development, Ko Olina (Map pp90–1) signals upscale things to come for this corner of the coast. Thanks to resort magic, this somewhat marginal piece of real estate now boasts a manicured complex with a hotel, residential villas and condos, private club, marina and several man-made beach lagoons. The Ko Olina Lagoons were constructed by the developers to fix the little problem of no natural beach on the property. The four sculpted lagoons are open to the public and all have inviting white-sand beaches and kid-friendly water conditions. The lagoons are constructed with small islets at their mouths, a design that creates channels for water circulation. Swimmers should be aware of the seaward currents going out through the middle channels; signs posted at each lagoon detail water-safety issues.

A shoreline path connects the four lagoons, making an enjoyable stroll. Each lagoon has rest rooms, showers and parking spaces for about 20 cars.

Sleeping

JW Marriott Ihilani Resort & Spa (☎ 679-0079, 800-626-4446; www.ihilani.com; Ko Olina Resort, 92-1001 Olani St; r from $300; ✷ ☐ ☲) With a gorgeous beachside setting, this resort hotel has luxurious rooms and offers an upscale respite from the Waikiki scene. Packages that include spa treatments and golf are available.

KAHE POINT

Across from the power plant on Farrington Hwy (93) is **Kahe Point Beach Park**, which does not have a beach, just the rocky cliffs of Kahe Point that are favored by fishers. What it does offer is a fine view of the sandy beaches that lie to the north, as well as running water, picnic tables and rest rooms.

To the north is **Electric Beach** or Tracks. It is a calm place to swim in summer and frequented by surfers in winter. The offshore cooling pipe

O'AHU'S HOMELESS POPULATION

Every big city in the USA has a homeless population, due in part to an inadequate mental health-care system, drug and alcohol abuse and a certain cultural legacy of wanderers and drifters. But in O'ahu, where many of the city-managed beach parks have become permanent homeless encampments, the profile of the average homeless person is quite different than those on the mainland. Many of this group are low-income families who have been pushed out of the island's housing boom.

The state doesn't have an accurate figure of how many people are living at the parks, but estimates in 2006 put the number at about 1000 people living on the beach of the Wai'anae Coast. Other sources quote between 12,000 to 15,000 island-wide and include extended families living together in cramped quarters. With the state's strong economy and increasing national housing prices, many rental properties, especially in the now gentrifying Wai'anae Coast, have sold to owner-occupants, in turn diminishing the available rental units and driving up rents. A studio apartment that cost $400 per month in Makaha now costs about $800.

Many low-income families – some with service-industry or construction jobs, others receiving some form of government assistance – can't afford the increase and can't find alternatives within the state's public-housing system or the federally funded Section 8 housing-assistance program. Because rents have increased, the number of people who receive Section 8 subsidies has decreased. Another aggravating factor is that the state's diminishing stock of public housing, with no new construction in the past decade. In 2006 the governor announced plans for the construction of seven subsidized housing projects and two emergency shelters have recently been completed.

While many see the state's proposals as a step in the right direction, few are hopeful that the homeless situation can be fully solved by construction projects. As once-marginalized communities, such as those on the Wai'anae Coast, become more upscale, the working poor who do not own their own homes will be displaced if housing prices continue to surge. In 2001 the average cost for a single family home on the Wai'anae Coast, the least desirable part of the island, was $125,000. Today it is $340,000. These leaps in real-estate prices are out of sync with median annual incomes, which average about $45,000 for a household on the island. If the market doesn't undergo a correction, then families higher up on the economic ladder may soon face the same problems that the currently displaced encounter today.

---

from the power plant has created an artificial reef that acts like an ocean cafeteria for colorful fish. Snorkeling and diving tours often make a stop here. Watch out for the current created at the end of the pipe.

To get to the beach, take the first turnoff after the power plant and drive over the abandoned railroad tracks.

NANAKULI

Nanakuli, the biggest town on the Wai'anae Coast, is the site of a Hawaiian Homesteads settlement, having one of the largest native Hawaiian populations on O'ahu. It also has supermarkets, a courthouse, a bank and fast-food joints.

The **Nanakuli Beach Park** is lined by a broad sandy beach that attracts swimmers, snorkelers and divers during the calmer summer season. In winter, high surf creates rip currents and dangerous shorebreaks. To get to this park, with a playground, sports fields and

full facilities, turn left at the traffic lights on Nanakuli Ave. Although camping is available, Nanakuli is one of many Wai'anae beaches that have become semipermanent homeless encampments.

MA'ILI BEACH PARK

Ma'ili has a long, grassy roadside park with a seemingly endless stretch of white beach. Like other places on this coast, the water conditions are often treacherous in winter, which pleases the local surfers, but calm enough for swimming in summer. There's a lifeguard station and rundown facilities; coconut palms provide shade.

WAI'ANAE

Wai'anae is the second-largest town on the Wai'anae Coast and has the greatest concentration of everyday services: from grocery stores to the commercial boat harbor and a well-used beach park.

Protected by Kane'ilio Point and a long breakwater, **Poka'i Bay Beach Park** features the calmest year-round swimming on the Wai'anae Coast. Waves seldom break inside the bay, and the sandy sea floor slopes gently, making the beach a popular spot for families. Snorkeling is fair near the breakwater, where fish gather around the rocks. You can watch local canoe clubs rowing in the late afternoon and lots of family luau on weekends. There are showers, rest rooms and picnic tables, and a lifeguard on duty daily.

Wild Side Specialty Tours (☎ 306-7273; www.sail hawaii.com; Wai'anae Harbor; tours $75-95) This family-owned business takes small groups out into the wonderful marine world off the Wai'anae Coast. Tours with staff marine biologists typically include dolphin spotting and whale watching (in season). If the conditions are right and everyone observes 'wet-etiquette' (the marine version of polite behavior), guests can snorkel alongside wild dolphins. The business donates a portion of its profits to Wild Dolphin Foundation (www.wilddolphin.org), a non-profit conservation organization.

Kane'ilio Point, along the south side of the bay, is the site of **Ku'ilioloa Heiau**. Partly destroyed by the army during WWII, this stone temple has been reconstructed by local conservationists. To get there, turn onto Lualualei Homestead Rd, heading seaward, at the traffic light immediately north of the Wai'anae post office.

Eating

Wai'anae Ice House (☎ 696-6685; Wai'anae Harbor; lunch from $7; ☼ 4am-6pm Mon-Sun) Fish fresh off the boat land in this nondescript bunker run by affable Victor Rapoza. His daughters whip up the catch of the day into affordable plate lunches.

Hannara Restaurant (☎ 696-6137; 86-078 Farrington Hwy; mains $3-7; ☼ 6am-8pm Mon-Sat, to 3pm Sun) Rub shoulders with the Wai'anae crowd at this bustling local grinds place featuring macadamia-nut pancakes and *kalua* pig.

Southern Swell (☎ 306-6593; 87-070 Farrington Hwy; mains $7-15; ☼ 6am-7pm Tue-Sun) A family barbeque recipe smuggled to the islands from Florida introduces the true grit cuisine of the mainland South to a worthy tropical companion. Cash only.

MAKAHA

Makaha means 'ferocious,' and in days past the valley was notorious for the bandits who waited along the cliffs to ambush passing travelers. Today Makaha is best known for its world-class surfing, fine beach and O'ahu's best-restored heiau. If you're looking for accommodation, this area offers the coast's best options.

Sights

MAKAHA BEACH PARK

Big heaps of sand and the usual collection of hard bodies checking out the waves define this crescent-shaped beach. Some of O'ahu's most daunting winter surf pounds this shoreline and attracts experienced local surfers. Although the corporate-sponsored events have shifted to the North Shore, Makaha Beach hosts the Buffalo Big Board Classic, with competitors using old-style 'tankers' reaching 15ft. The competition has diversified to include other board shapes and riders and is a de facto Hawaiian cultural event.

When the surf isn't up, Makaha is a popular swimming beach. In summer the slope of the beach is relatively flat, while in winter the wave action results in a steeper drop. As much as half the beach washes away during winter, but even then Makaha is still impressive. Snorkeling is good offshore during the calmer summer months. The Makaha Caverns feature underwater arches and tunnels at depths of 30ft to 50ft. Makaha Beach has showers and rest rooms, and lifeguards are on duty.

KANE'AKI HEIAU

Set within the Makaha Valley the **Kane'aki Heiau** (☎ 695-8174; admission free; ☼ 10am-2pm Tue-Sun) is one of the best restored sacred sites on the island. According to legend the rain goddess was impressed with the fishing prowess of a local chief. His generous offering to her was reciprocated with generous rainfall to the parched valley and in turn a heiau was built in her honor. The site was later used as a *luakini*, a type of temple dedicated to the war god Ku and a place for human sacrifices. Kamehameha worshipped here, and it remained in use until the time of his death in 1812.

Restoration, undertaken by the Bishop Museum and completed in 1970, added two prayer towers, a taboo house, drum house, altar and god images. The heiau was reconstructed using traditional ohia tree logs and *pili* (a bunchgrass, commonly used for thatching houses) from the Big Island. The immediate setting surrounding the heiau remains undisturbed, though it's in the midst of a residential estate.

To get there, take Kili Dr to the Makaha Valley Towers condominiums, and turn right onto Huipu Dr. Half a mile down on the left is Mauna Olu St, leading into Mauna Olu Estates. The guard at the Mauna Olu Estates gatehouse grants entry to nonresidents who are visiting the heiau, a short drive past the gatehouse. Following rain, access is difficult, so call in advance.

Sleeping

Makaha accommodations options include several beachside condos that are rented out by realty agents as well as an inland resort hotel. While most condo rates are quoted for monthly stays, you may be able to negotiate shorter periods.

Makaha Beach Cabanas (☎ 372-0855; www.beach lovershawaii.com; units from $1700-2000/month) This company handles rentals at two condominium complexes: Makaha Cabanas and Makaha Surfrider. The Cabanas occupy a quiet stretch of beach known only to the locals and cozy one-bedroom units open out directly to the bleach-blond sand. Although the building is far from fancy, Surfrider has comfortable one- to two-bedroom units that can accommodate larger groups and families; there's also a swimming pool.

Hawaii Hatfield Realty (☎ 696-7121, 696-4499; www .hawaiiwest.com; Suite 201, 85-833 Farrington Hwy, Wai'anae; units from $500/week) Hawaii Hatfield arranges long-term rentals for Makaha Shores, a condo complex at the northern end of Makaha Beach.

Makaha Resort & Golf Club (☎ 695-9544; www .makaharesort.net; 84-626 Makaha Valley Rd; r from $205, 1-bedroom units $325; ⚅ ⚄) With a panoramic view clear down to the ocean, this small hillside resort makes for an unbeatable golfing getaway. The hotel itself is mellow without a lot of design fuss.

MAKUA VALLEY

Enough rain from the North Shore sneaks around the tip of the island to keep this valley covered in a fresh fuzz of green. It's an impressive collection of coastal scenery, devoid of commercial or residential development, that is widely embraced by Hawaiians in myth, song, sustenance and recreation. According to Hawaiian legend, this valley was the creation site of the first man ('Makua' in Hawaiian means 'parent') and the departure point for souls after

they cast off their human form. Traditional Hawaiian sea burials are held along the sandy beaches and handmade memorials to the recently departed dot the rocky ledges.

More than 4000 acres of the valley belong to the US military, which first occupied the area after the Japanese attack on Pearl Harbor. The military's continued use of the land for firing and training exercises, as well as controlled burns, has incurred public outrage and lawsuits that contend the military's activity threatens environmentally sensitive habitats for in excess of 40 endangered plant and animal species, as well as cultural and archaeological sites. Despite the controversy, few concessions have been made.

Kea'au Beach Park

Kea'au Beach Park is a long, open, grassy strip, bordering a rocky shore. A sandy beach begins at the very northern end of the park, with a rough reef, sharp drop and high seasonal surf. North along the coast, you'll see lava sea cliffs, white-sand beaches and patches of kiawe, while, on the inland side, you'll glimpse a run of little valleys.

Facilities include campsites, showers, picnic tables and rest rooms.

Makua Beach

It difficult to award such a presumptuous title as most beautiful beach, but few would be faulted if they preferred this undeveloped stretch of coast where scenery and cultural significance intermingle. The postcard proportions are here: a perfect arc of white sand is backed by the pyramid-shaped mountains of the Wai'anae Range. This is the site of many traditional Hawaiian burials at sea, including that of beloved musician Israel Kamakawiwo'ole, better known as Braddah Iz.

Locals crawl out of their nine-to-five lives on holiday weekends to absorb the sun and spirit of the beach. The powerful shorebreaks are popular with body-boarders and high surf waves appear in winter and spring. Spinner dolphins are frequent visitors and snorkeling is good at the northern end.

There are two parking lots on either side of the beach, but no facilities.

Kaneana Cave

Massive Kaneana Cave was once completely underwater but the initial earthquake that created the fissure was eventually whittled into a subterranean womb by continued wave action as the ocean slowly receded. The geologic formation also plays an important part in a Hawaiian creation myth. The cave is named for the god of creation Kane and from this earthly womb came man who populated the coast.

Hawaiian *kahuna* (priests) once performed their rituals inside the cave's inner chamber. Older Hawaiians consider it a sacred place and some won't enter for fear it's haunted. The cave is on the right-hand side of the road about two miles north of Kea'au Beach Park.

Ka'ena Point Satellite Tracking Station

The US Air Force operates a satellite tracking station high on the ridge of O'ahu's northwesternmost tip. It was originally built for use in the country's first reconnaissance satellite program (known as Corona), but now supports weather, early warning and communications systems. The station is not open to the public but the surrounding acreage is managed by the **Division of Forestry & Wildlife** (☎ 587-0166), which can issue hiking permits to the trail system that connects the Wai'anae Coast to the North Shore. Part of the land is also open to hunting and is popularly used by locals.

The dusty 2.5-mile **Kuaokala Trail** (Map p172) follows a high ridge to Mokule'ia Forest Reserve. At the trail's highest point (1960ft) is an overlook with great views. On a clear day hikers can see Mt Ka'ala, the highest peak on O'ahu, and part of the Wai'anae Range. The trail connects to the Kealia Trail (p182), whose trailhead starts near the Dillingham Airfield in the North Shore.

KA'ENA POINT STATE PARK

Ka'ena Point State Park is an undeveloped 853-acre coastal strip that runs along both sides of Ka'ena Point, the westernmost point of O'ahu. Until the mid-1940s the O'ahu Railroad ran up here from Honolulu and continued around the point, carrying passengers on to Hale'iwa on the North Shore.

In addition to being a state park, Ka'ena Point has been designated a natural area reserve because of its unique ecosystem. The extensive dry, windswept coastal dunes that rise above the point are the habitat of many rare native plants, including the endangered *Kaena akoko* – found nowhere else.

More common plants are the beach *naupaka,* with white flowers that look like they've been torn in half; *pau-o-Hiiaka,* a vine

with blue flowers; and beach morning glory, sometimes found wrapped in the parasite *kaunaoa.*

Seabirds seen at Ka'ena Point include shearwaters, boobies and the common noddy – a dark-brown bird with a grayish crown. You can often see schools of spinner dolphins off the beach and, in winter, humpback whales. The reserve is a nesting site for the rare Laysan albatross, and Hawaii's endangered monk seals occasionally bask in the sun here.

Sights & Activities
YOKOHAMA BAY

Locals say this is the best sunset spot on the island. It certainly has the right orientation and an attractive mile-long sandy beach. Being the last sandy beach also helps the symbolic appreciation of the setting sun. The bay is so named for the large numbers of Japanese fishers who came here during the railroad days.

Winter brings huge pounding waves, making Yokohama a popular seasonal surfing and bodysurfing spot best left to the experts because of the submerged rocks, strong rips and dangerous shorebreak.

Swimming is limited to the summer, and then only when calm. When the water's flat, it's possible to snorkel; the best spot with the easiest access is at the south side of the park. Rest rooms, showers and a lifeguard station are at the south end of the park.

KA'ENA POINT

You don't have to be versed in Hawaiian legends to know that something mystical occurs at this dramatic convergence of land and sea at the far northwestern tip of the island. Powerful ocean currents altered by the O'ahu landmass have been battling against each other for millennia. The watery blows crash on to the long lava bed fingers sending frothy explosions skyward. All along this untamed coastal section, nature is at its most furious and beautiful – an incongruous harmony.

Early Hawaiians believed that when people went into a deep sleep or lost consciousness, their souls would wander. Souls that wandered too far were drawn west to Ka'ena Point. If they were lucky, they were met here by their *'aumakua* (ancestral spirit helper), who led their souls back to their bodies. If unattended, their souls would be forced to leap from Ka'ena Point into the endless night, never to return.

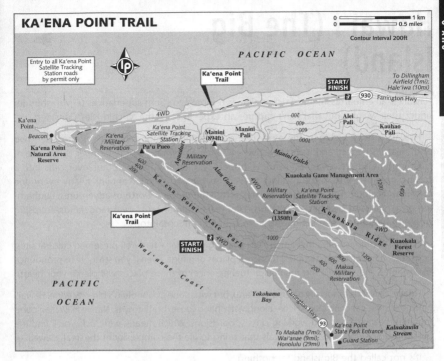

The 2.5-mile (one-way) coastal **Ka'ena Point Trail** runs from the end of the paved road at Yokohama Bay to Ka'ena Point, following the old railroad bed. You'll see tide pools, sea arches, fine coastal views and the lofty sea cliffs of the Wai'anae Range. The hike is unshaded, so take plenty of water, even if you plan on a short hike; there are no facilities in this hot and dry corner of the island.

On clear days, Kaua'i is visible from the point. According to legend, it was at Ka'ena Point that the demigod Maui attempted to cast a huge hook into Kaua'i and pull it next to O'ahu to join the islands. But the line broke and Kaua'i slipped away, with just a small piece remaining near O'ahu. Today this splintered rock, off the end of Ka'ena Point, is known as Pohaku o Kaua'i.

Don't leave anything valuable in your car unless you're prepared to lose it. You can also access the trail from the North Shore, west of Dillingham Airfield (see p181).

Hawai'i (The Big Island)

Hawai'i is an embarrassment of riches. One is tempted to spout superlatives till you shudder under their weight, but that can't capture an experience of the 'Orchid Isle.' Consider:

Hawai'i is twice as big as the other islands combined. Among its five volcanoes are two of the earth's largest, and its most active – Kilauea. But what you'll remember is the awe of standing in a surreal lava wasteland as, hopefully, glowing magma pours over cliffs into a boiling ocean – earth in the making. Hawai'i, so big and so tall, contains nearly every one of earth's ecological zones. This translates into a full quiver's worth of adventures: sunbathing on white-sand beaches, snorkeling coral reefs, riding horses over rangelands, traipsing through rain forests, and stargazing from subarctic mountaintops.

Hawai'i, birthplace of Kamehameha – Hawaii's great ruler – has well-preserved cultural sites, from ancient stone heiau (temples) to sacred places of refuge. Even if you struggle to pronounce their names, the shimmering mana (spiritual essence) of these places will pierce your heart.

Finally, Hawai'i is as socially diverse as O'ahu, but with none of Honolulu's big-city edge. Hawai'i holds the state's second city – Hilo – along with 'hang-loose, brah' towns, Native Hawaiian communities, beach resorts and working-class subdivisions. Which means, with luck, you'll find the best souvenir – encounters with locals that bring to life the complexity of the 'real' Hawaii.

It's not called the Big Island for nothing.

HIGHLIGHTS

- Hike the smoking craters and lava terrain of **Hawai'i Volcanoes National Park** (p288)
- Almost brush bellies while diving with **Pacific manta rays** (p205)
- Lounge with wild horses on the black-sand beach in **Waipi'o Valley** (p262)
- Watch the sun set and the stars blaze from **Mauna Kea** (p251)
- Discover historic downtown **Hilo** (p267) – its museums, historic buildings and ice shave
- Explore an ancient place of refuge, **Pu'uhonua o Honaunau National Historical Park** (p226)
- Indulge yourself in **Hawi's restaurants** (p243)
- Visit a small-time **Kona coffee farm** (p219)
- Admire the awesome Moku'aweoweo Caldera atop **Mauna Loa's summit** (p258)
- **Kayak in a sea cave** (p205) off the Kona Coast

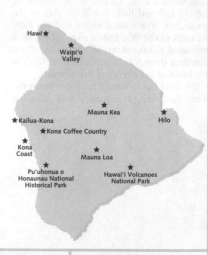

Hawi ★
Waipi'o Valley ★
★ Mauna Kea
★ Kailua-Kona ★ Hilo
★ Kona Coffee Country
Kona Coast
★ Mauna Loa
★ Pu'uhonua o Honaunau National Historical Park
★ Hawai'i Volcanoes National Park

■ POPULATION: 167,293	■ AREA: 4028 SQ MILES	■ OFFICIAL FLOWER: RED LEHUA 'OHI'A

HAWAI'I (THE BIG ISLAND)

CLIMATE

Big Island climates are fairly stable year-round. As a rule, it's cooler as you move inland and up, and it's wetter on the windward north and east coasts. The western Kona Coast is perennially sunny and usually hot, though go a few miles upland into coffee country and the air is considerably cooler.

On the eastern coast, Hilo is notoriously rainy, with an annual rainfall of over 100in. But temperatures remain balmy and, except for rainstorms, the typical drizzle is innocuous and short-lived. Good luck finding someone to predict the Windward Coast weather; even newspapers simply print endless variations on 'sunny, with a chance of rain.'

At 4000ft, Hawai'i Volcanoes National Park (and the nearby town of Volcano) is cooler than Hilo, with chilly nights and occasional rainstorms. But the coolest town on the island is Waimea, where afternoon fog rolls across the grassy plains daily.

On the windward side of Mauna Kea, along the northeastern Hamakua Coast, around 300in of rain falls annually – but this water usually gets squeezed out on the mountain's flanks, and at around 2500ft, the coast and summit are much clearer. In fact, only about 15in of precipitation falls on the summits of Mauna Kea and Mauna Loa, mostly as winter snow that caps these peaks with white.

In January the average daily high temperature is 65°F at Hawai'i Volcanoes National Park, 79°F in Hilo and a toasty 81°F in Kailua-Kona. August temperatures rise only 5°F or so. Nighttime lows are about 15°F less. For more on climate, see p21.

The National Weather Service Hilo provides recorded forecasts for the Big Island (☎ 961-5582) and for island water conditions (☎ 935-9883). **Hawai'i Volcanoes National Park** (☎ 985-6000) has recorded information on eruption activity and viewing points.

NATIONAL, STATE & COUNTY PARKS

Hawai'i Volcanoes National Park (p288) is one of the Big Island's main attractions and one of the USA's most interesting and varied national parks, hosting about 1.3 million visitors annually. Day-trippers can drive around Kilauea Caldera easily, but you could fill several days or even a week with hikes and explorations without exhausting this lava wonderland.

Several national and state historical parks preserve ancient Hawaiian sights. The best

may be Pu'uhonua o Honaunau (p226), an ancient place of refuge in South Kona, and remote Mo'okini Heiau (p243), a haunting place of worship in North Kohala. However, Kealakekua Bay (p218), where Captain Cook met his demise, Kaloko-Honokohau (p230) and Pu'ukohola Heiau (p239) are also interesting.

Many of the island's finest beaches lie on parkland, such as the world-renowned Hapuna Beach (p237). The row of beaches within Kekaha Kai State Park (p231) are also idyllic, though only Manini'owali is accessible by paved road (and thus more crowded).

Other parks worth seeking out on the Windward Coast are Kalopa (p265), preserving a native forest; Laupahoehoe (p266), moody site of a tsunami disaster; and Akaka Falls (p267), the prettiest 'drive-up' waterfalls in Hawai'i. Though it's not a park per se, don't miss Waipi'o Valley (p262) either.

Camping

Good campgrounds are not overabundant on Hawai'i, but there are enough so that you can circumnavigate the island in a tent, and a few are memorably wonderful. Some parks also offer simple cabins.

NATIONAL PARKS

Hawai'i Volcanoes National Park has two good, free, drive-up campgrounds, some A-frame cabins for rent and great backcountry camping opportunities. See p288 for more information.

STATE PARKS

Camping is allowed at Kalopa State Park (p265), which has great facilities and a caretaker, and at MacKenzie State Recreation Area (p287), which is rather desolate and currently not recommended. Permits are required; the fee is $5 per family campsite.

Three state parks have cabins, all of them recommended. Hapuna Beach State Recreation Area (p237) has six A-frame cabins sleeping up to four people ($20 per night). Kalopa State Park (p265) has two group cabins sleeping up to eight people ($55 per night). Mauna Kea State Park (p251) maintains five cabins sleeping up to six people ($35 per night, Friday to Sunday only).

To make a reservation and obtain a permit, contact the **Division of State Parks** (Map p268; ☎ 974-6200; www.hawaii.gov/dlnr/dsp; Suite 204, 75 Aupuni St, PO Box 936, Hilo, HI 96721; ⌚ 8am-3:30pm

HAWAI'I (THE BIG ISLAND)

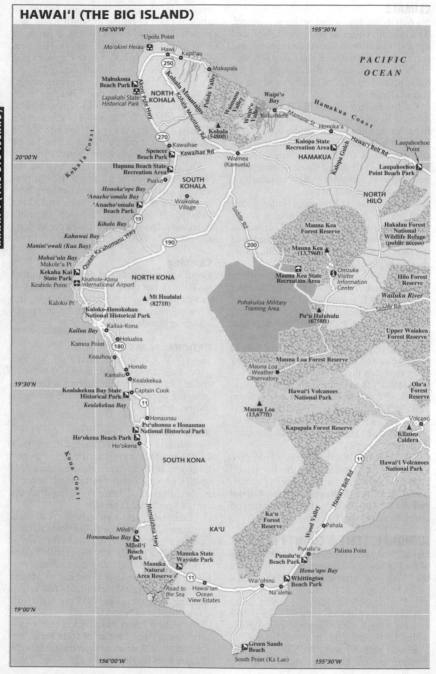

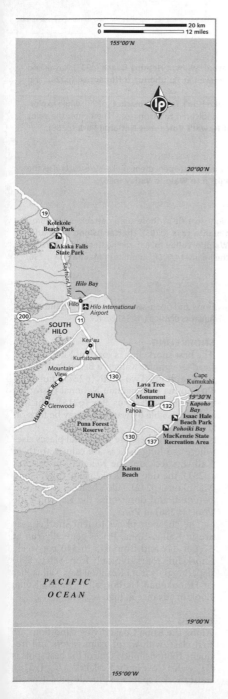

Mon-Fri), which accepts reservations in order of priority: first walk-ins, then mail requests, then phone requests. Note that the phone is rarely answered and long-distance calls aren't returned. The website has an application form you can print and mail in, and the office has a binder with photos of every campsite and cabin. The maximum length of stay per permit is five consecutive nights. You can obtain another permit for the same park only after 30 days have passed.

Cabins are popular with island families and require booking well in advance. Cancellations do occur, however; if you're flexible with dates, you might be able to one get without advance reservations.

COUNTY PARKS
The county allows camping at 10 of its beach parks. Proceeding clockwise around the island, these are: Spencer (p238), Mahukona (p242) and Kapa'a (p242) in South Kohala; Laupahoehoe (p266) and Kolekole (p266) on the Hamakua Coast; Isaac Hale (p286) in Puna; Punalu'u (p303) and Whittington (p304) in Ka'u; and Miloli'i (p228) and Ho'okena (p227) in South Kona.

Particularly on weekends, county parks can be noisy places, as they're popular with late-night revelers. Spencer can get quite crowded, which is why it's patrolled by a security guard, who sort of keeps a lid on things. Parks to expressly avoid are Isaac Hale (until it's renovated), Whittington, and Miloli'i, as they are very isolated. Laupahoehoe is one of the prettiest campgrounds, but it's windy.

Camping permits are required, and can be obtained (up to a year in advance) by mail, online or in person from the **Department of Parks & Recreation** (Map p268; ☎ 961-8311; www .co.hawaii.hi.us/parks/parks.htm; Suite 6, 101 Pauahi St, Hilo, HI 96720; ☺ 7:45am-4pm Mon-Fri). The website lists facilities and availability at each county park. You can also make reservations through the Hilo office and pick up the permit at the department's branch offices around the island. The Hilo office has binders with photos of each campsite, and staff offer helpful advice about noise and safety issues.

Daily camping fees are $5 for adults, $2 for teens and $1 for children 12 and under; internet booking costs $1 more. Camping is allowed for up to two weeks, except between June and August, when the limit is one week.

THE BIG ISLAND...

In Two Days
If you arrive in **Kona** (p201), spend your days leeward: swim at **Hapuna Beach** (p237), kayak and snorkel at **Kealakekua Bay** (p218), visit ancient Hawaii at **Pu'uhonua o Honaunau** (p226), and tour a **coffee plantation** (p219).

If you arrive in **Hilo** (p267), stay windward. Browse Hilo's **farmers market** (p273); while exploring Hilo's historic downtown, visit '**Imiloa** (p272), dedicated to Mauna Kea. Then enter the wilds of **Puna** (p283) and pay your respects to Pele at **Hawai'i Volcanoes National Park** (p288).

In Four Days
Combine the leeward and windward itineraries, and between them make sure to cruise the verdant **Hamakua Coast** (p259) and include a hike into **Waipi'o Valley** (p262).

On a Surf-and-Turf Adventure
Did you come to play hard? In a week, you might just fit in these unforgettable adventures: **kayaking Kealakekua Bay** (p218), **diving with manta rays** (p205), **charter fishing for marlin** (p206), **riding horses in Kohala** (p241), **hiking Waipi'o Valley** (p263), seeing hot lava at **Hawai'i Volcanoes National Park** (p297), and reaching the nearly 14,000ft summits of **Mauna Kea** (p256) or **Mauna Loa** (p258).

ACTIVITIES
The Big Island is heaven for hikers and those wanting a diverse range of activities. When it comes to the water, Hawai'i's western shore has top-quality choices for everything – even if other islands may boast even longer white-sand beaches, even bigger waves or even larger coral reefs. When it comes to hiking, though, the Big Island suffers no comparison: where else can you walk from live lava at the coast to the snowcapped summits of the world's largest volcanoes?

Water Activities
SWIMMING
The Big Island has over 300 miles of shoreline, but only the Kona Coast has the kind of dreamy white-sand beaches that grace tourist brochures. The best swimming spots are in South Kohala and North Kona: Hapuna Beach (p237) is frequently cited as 'the best,' but Manini'owali (p231) and Kauna'oa Bay (p238), by the Mauna Kea Beach Hotel, are pretty sweet, too.

Elsewhere, the coast can be rocky and the seas rough, but protected coves can be found. Time it right, and Hilo's beaches (p274) can be great, and nearby Puna has a hot pond (p286) and lava tide pools (p286).

There are recommended public swimming pools in Hilo (p275), Kailua-Kona (p204), Kapa'au (p244), and Pahoa (p283). For direc-

tions and open-swim schedules, call the county **Aquatics Division** (☎ 961-8694).

SNORKELING
The best snorkeling is south of Kailua-Kona: head straight for Kahalu'u Beach Park (p213) in Keauhou; Two-Step (p227), north of Pu'uhonua o Honaunau National Historical Park; and Kealakekua Bay (p218), which is only accessible by water and may be tops on the island.

That said, there are wonderful places elsewhere (so long as seas are calm): north of Kailua, check out the Kekaha Kai beaches (p231), the tide pools of Puako, (p237), and Mahukona (p242). Hilo's beaches (p274) can be good, and don't miss the Kapoho Tide Pools (p286) in Puna.

The cheapest places to rent snorkel gear are in Kailua-Kona. Prices generally run at $7 per day and from $15 to $40 per week. Snorkeling tours (typically from $80 to $90) depart mainly from Keauhou Bay, Kailua Pier or Honokohau Harbor, all in Kailua-Kona. Book in advance in high season.

DIVING
Along the Kona Coast diving conditions are first class, with warm, calm waters and frequent 100ft visibility. One of the best spots is Ka'awaloa Cove in the Kealakekua Bay (p218); most snorkel spots also provide good dives. In

Kailua-Kona you can also arrange a thrilling night dive to see manta rays (p206). The best conditions are in spring and summer, but diving is decent year-round. On the Hilo side, the diving conditions tend to be mediocre, but good dives are possible (such as at Leleiwi Beach, p275).

Most dive outfits are located in Kailua-Kona (see p206) and charge from $95 to $140 for a two-tank dive; Hilo also has a dive shop (p275).

KAYAKING

Kayaking in lovely Kealakekua Bay (p218) is a must. The most popular launching spot is Napo'opo'o Beach, where you paddle across the bay toward the Captain Cook Monument for snorkeling and explorations.

Racers, or those interested in watching outrigger canoe racers, should contact the **Hawai'i Island Paddlesports Association** (www.hawaiipaddling .com) for its January to May race schedule. And don't miss the **Queen Lili'uokalani outrigger race** (www.kaiopua.org) on Labor Day weekend.

SURFING

Big Island surf spots often have rugged lava-rock shorelines that require nimble maneuvering. Another hindrance is *wana* (sea urchins that resemble pincushions), which abound at some beaches. For an overview of the main spots, see the boxed text, below.

You can rent a surfboard from local surf shops ($15 to $25 per day) or stands near beaches ($30 per day; about $20 for two hours).

WINDSURFING

Beginner windsurfers will find an ideal spot to learn at 'Anaeho'omalu Beach Park (p234) in Waikoloa, where you can rent equipment and take lessons. Things get more exciting when the spring trade winds kick up, but if windsurfing's your only interest, seek out Maui.

FISHING

Deep-sea fishing is an obsession on the Kona Coast, which is the world's number-one spot for catching Pacific blue marlin, a spectacular fighting fish with a long swordlike bill. The waters are also rich with *'ahi* (yellowfin tuna) and *aku* (bonito or skipjack tuna), swordfish, spearfish and mahimahi (white-fleshed fish also called 'dolphin'). June to August typically sees the biggest hauls for blue marlin, while January to June is the best time for striped marlin. Most of the world records for catches of such fish belong to Kona fishers. For information on charter tours, see p206.

BIG ISLAND SURF BEACHES & BREAKS Jake Howard

Because Hawai'i is the youngest island in the chain and the coastline is still quite rugged, it's often assumed there isn't much in the way of surfable waves. As a result places like O'ahu and Kaua'i have stolen the surf spotlight in recent years, but archaeologists and researchers believe that Kealakekua Bay (p218) is probably where ancient Polynesians started riding waves. Today a fun little left-hander called Ke'ei breaks near the bay.

Unlike its neighboring islands, whose north and south shores are the primary center of swell activity, the east and west shores are the Big Island's focal points. Because swells are shadowed by the other islands, as a general rule the surf doesn't get as big here. The Kona Coast offers the best opportunities, with north and south swell exposures as well as the offshore trade winds. Kawaihae Harbor (p239) is surrounded by several fun, introductory reefs near the breakwall, while further south, around the newly opened Kekaha Kai State Park (p231) is a considerably more advanced break that challenges even the most seasoned surfers. If you have a 4WD vehicle or don't mind an hour-long hike, be sure to check out heavy reef breaks like Mahai'ula (p231) and Makalawena (p231). They break best on northwest swells, making the later winter months the prime season.

On east Hawai'i, just outside of Hilo (p274), are several good intermediate waves. Richardson Ocean Park is a slow-moving reef break that's great for learning, and just west of town is Honoli'i, a fast left and right peak breaking into a river mouth. Further up the Hamakua Coast is Waipi'o Bay (p262), and while access to myriad beaches requires a long walk or a 4WD vehicle, the waves and scenery are worth the effort.

Top bodyboarding and bodysurfing spots include Hapuna Beach (p237), White Sands Beach (p204), and the beaches at Kekaha Kai State Park (p231).

THE BIG ISLAND ACTIVITIES

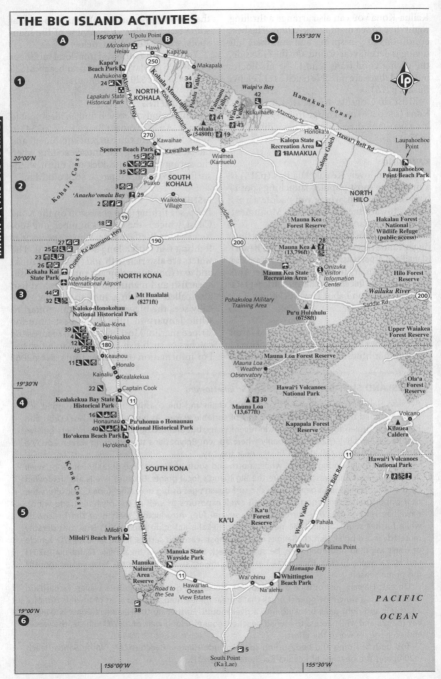

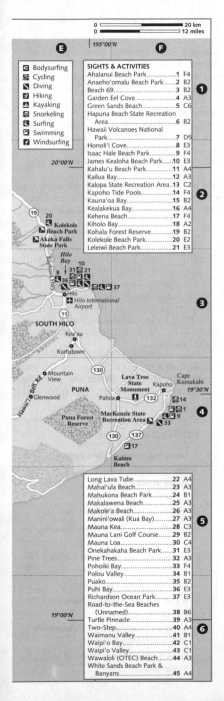

For Kona fishing reports, the well-published **Jim Rizzutto** (www.fishinghawaiioffshore.com) will let you know who's catching what. For schedules of tournaments, check in with the **Hawaii Big Game Fishing Club** (www.hbgfc.org).

Land Activities

HIKING

The Big Island has fantastic hiking. The widest variety of trails and terrain is at Hawai'i Volcanoes National Park (p288): hot lava, coastal cliffs, grassy plains, rain forests, lava deserts, steaming craters, mountain summits. It's all here.

Hawai'i has not one but two nearly 14,000ft summits that can be day hiked, Mauna Loa (p258) and Mauna Kea (p256). Want verdant valleys? Try the relatively short hike to Pololu Valley (p246) in North Kohala, or, from the Hamakua Coast, drop into wondrous Waipi'o Valley (p262), which can be extended into a two-night backpack to Waimanu Valley (p264).

More good trails await at Kalopa State Recreation Area (p265) and Kohala Forest Reserve (p251). **Na Ala Hele** (☎ 331-8505; www .hawaiitrails.org) is a state-sponsored group that maintains a number of trails, and its website lists more. It is also working to restore the 175-mile **Ala Kahakai National Trail** (www.nps .gov/state/hi), which when finished will edge the island from Hawai'i Volcanoes National Park, around South Point and up the Kona Coast to 'Upolu Point; for now, only a couple dozen miles are accessible along the Kona Coast.

For tours (including hikes to hot lava), **Hawaiian Walkways** (☎ 775-0372, 800-457-7759; www .hawaiianwalkways.com) and **Hawaii Forest & Trail** (☎ 331-8505, 800-464-1993; www.hawaii-forest.com) are the Big Island's best outfits; both are winners of Hawaii Ecotourism Board awards and offer guided hikes to places you might not see otherwise. The Sierra Club's **Big Island Moku Loa Group** (☎ 965-5460; www.hi.sierraclub.org/Hawaii/outings .html; suggested nonmember donation $3) also offers a range of recommended, low-cost hiking tours. For all, reserve in advance.

CYCLING & MOUNTAIN BIKING

With wide-open spaces, the Big Island is ideal for both road and mountain biking. Outside Kailua-Kona, Hwy 19 has bicycle lanes, and cyclists can enjoy Crater Rim Dr in Hawai'i Volcanoes National Park (p291). Avid mountain bikers can tackle the 45-mile

---

ALL SHOOK UP

On October 15, 2006, a 30-second, 6.7-magnitude earthquake occurred off the northwest coast of the Big Island. No one was killed, but the quake did an estimated $200 million in damage – cracking over a thousand homes, breaking irrigation ditches, causing landslides, forcing the closure of a South Kohala resort (Mauna Kea Beach Hotel), and injuring two famous heiau (ancient temples): Mo'okini and Pu'ukohola.

The earthquake – and its approximately 160 aftershocks – also stirred up residents and sent a small shudder through the tourism industry, whose numbers dipped the next month.

But earthquakes are simply part of life when your islands are made of volcanoes. As a state, Hawaii ranks third in the US in earthquake activity, and the Big Island is responsible for most of them – averaging 200 or so tiny tremors weekly. It's rare for a big quake to hit, but as October 15 reminded everyone, they will happen.

So, as one of this guide's authors found out (see p4), you never know when Hawaii will do one of its Elvis impersonations; but hopefully, the Big Island sights mentioned above and others that were closed at the time of research (as noted throughout this chapter) will have reopened by your arrival.

Mana Rd loop (p251) circling Mauna Kea and the 6.5-mile beach trail to Pine Trees (p230) on the Kona Coast, plus plenty more miles of 4WD roads and rocky trails. To find out more information about Big Island mountain biking, contact **People's Advocacy for Trails Hawaii** (☎ 326-9495) in Kona or **Big Island Mountain Bike Association** (☎ 961-4452; www.interpac.net/~mtbike) in Hilo.

For cycling tours, contact **Orchid Isle Bicycling** (☎ 327-0087, 800-219-2324; www.cyclekona.com; day tour $125). It offers multiday trips in addition to day tours, and you can custom-design your own. For women only, **Woman Tours** (☎ 800-247-1444; www.womantours.com; tours from $2100) organizes two one-week Big Island cycle tours.

Feeling competitive, but not quite up to the standard for the Ironman Triathlon (p207)? The **Big Island Race and Training Schedule** (www.bigislandraceschedule.com) lists bicycle, foot and swimming races, plus it has more bike-trail suggestions.

For bicycle rentals, head to the main towns, Hilo (p281) and Kailua-Kona (p212).

HORSEBACK RIDING

The Big Island is *paniolo* (Hawaiian cowboy) country, and the pastureland of Waimea and North Kohala are perfect for horseback riding. An efficient outfit is the family-run Dahana Ranch Roughriders (see p248).

GOLF

The Big Island boasts more than 20 golf courses, including the world-class courses at the South Kohala resorts. Most experts regard the Mauna Kea & Hapuna Golf Courses (p238) as the island's best, closely followed by the Mauna Lani golf course (p235) and Waikoloa Beach & Kings' Courses (p234). The Four Seasons Hualalai Course (p232), designed by Jack Nicklaus, is also highly regarded but open only to club members and hotel guests.

For a sweet deal, head to the Hilo Municipal Golf Course (p275), where the locals play, rain or shine. Or try the very scenic Volcano Golf & Country Club (p300), near the national park.

TOP FESTIVALS & EVENTS

- **Great Waikoloa Ukulele Festival** (p234) March.
- **Merry Monarch Festival** (p276) March or April.
- **Hamakua Music Festival** (p260) May.
- **Fourth of July Parker Ranch Rodeo** (p249) July 4.
- **Aloha Festivals Ka Ho'ola'a o Na Ali'i** (p299) August or September.
- **Poke Contest** (p238) September.
- **A Taste of the Hawaiian Range** (p234) September to October.
- **Ironman Triathlon World Championship** (p207) Late October.
- **Kona Coffee Cultural Festival** (p207) November.

TENNIS

Many county parks on the Big Island have municipal tennis courts that are well maintained. Call the **Department of Parks & Recreation** (☎ 961-8311) in Hilo for a list of public tennis courts. The large hotels sometimes allow non-guests to rent court time.

GETTING THERE & AWAY
Air

An increasing number of flights go directly to Kona and Hilo airports, though many flights also route through Honolulu first. Kona is the busier of the two airports, with the bulk of mainland and international flights.

Hilo International Airport (ITO; ☎ 935-5707) Off Hwy 11, just under a mile south of the intersection of Hwys 11 and 19.

Kona International Airport at Keahole (KOA; ☎ 329-3423) On Hwy 19, 7 miles north of Kailua-Kona. For directions to/from the airport, see right.

See p566 for airline contact details, and more information on flights to the Big Island, from both the mainland and abroad.

The two major interisland carriers are **Hawaiian Airlines** (☎ 800-367-5320; www.hawaiianair.com) and **Aloha Airlines** (☎ 800-367-5250; www.alohaair lines.com), plus newcomer **Go!** (☎ 888-435-9462; www.iflygo.com). For all three, interisland flights require a stopover in Honolulu (except one Hawaiian Airlines flight from Kailua-Kona to Maui). Service through Honolulu is regular; each airline has about 10 flights daily from both Hilo and Kailua-Kona. Current fare wars have prices down to $30 to $40 one way.

Another option is **Island Air** (☎ 800-652-6541; www.islandair.com), which offers three to five flights daily from Hilo to Honolulu; specials run at $30, but typically are more like $50 to $65. Island Air is the only carrier that flies between Kailua-Kona and Hilo ($20 one way); a single round-trip daily serves commuters. Most Big Island visitors opt to drive.

See p568 for more on interisland flights.

GETTING AROUND

The Big Island is divided into six districts: Kona, Kohala, Waimea, Hilo, Puna and Ka'u. The Hawai'i Belt Rd circles the island, covering the main towns and sights. It's possible but not efficient or convenient to get around by bus. Really, if you want to explore, you need a car.

The best foldout map is the Hawaii Street Guide *Big Island Manini Map*. This is a slimmer version of the *Ready Mapbook* series' encyclopedic, but bulky, books covering east and west Hawai'i (but worth it for a long stay on the Big Island). Another good foldout map is Nelles' *Hawai'i: The Big Island*. The colorful Franko's map of *Hawai'i, the Big Island* features water sports and is sold at dive shops.

To/From the Airports

Most Big Island visitors rent cars, and car-hire booths for the major agencies (see p200) line the road outside the arrivals area at both airports.

HILO INTERNATIONAL AIRPORT

Taxis can be found curbside; the approximate fare from Hilo airport to downtown Hilo is $17.

KONA INTERNATIONAL AIRPORT AT KEAHOLE

Taxis can also be found curbside; the approximate fare from the airport to Kailua-Kona is $25, and to Waikoloa it's $45.

Shuttle-bus services typically cost as much as taxis. **Speedi Shuttle** (☎ 329-5433, 877-242-5777; www.speedishuttle.com) will get you to destinations up and down the Kona Coast, plus Waimea, Honoka'a and Hawai'i Volcanoes National Park (though that'll cost $150-plus). Call 48 hours in advance. If you make a round-trip booking, the return fare is discounted 10%.

Bicycle

The best way to cycle around the Big Island is with the support of a tour. Though do-able on one's own, it's a challenge, particularly if the weather doesn't cooperate. However, because Kona is the hub for the Ironman Triathlon, you'll find top-notch bike shops that sell and can repair high-caliber equipment.

Bus

Unless you don't plan to stay long or go far, don't base your trip on using the county-run **Hele-On Bus** (☎ 961-8744; www.co.hawaii.hi.us/mass _transit/heleonbus.html; ◷ 7:45am-4:30pm Mon-Fri). Even though all buses are free (for now; the county votes again in October 2007), and even though routes cover the island, service is minimal, and most routes only run Monday to Friday;

none run on Sunday. Schedules are available at the Big Island Visitors Bureau (p271) and the information kiosk at Hilo's Mo'oheau bus terminal (p281). All buses originate from Mo'oheau terminal, unless otherwise noted. You need permission from the driver to board with a surfboard or boogie board; these items, in addition to luggage, backpacks and bicycles, are charged a $1 fee.

Car & Motorcycle

From Kona to Hilo, the northern half of the belt road is 92 miles, and the nonstop journey takes over two hours. The southern Kona-Hilo route is 125 miles and takes approximately three hours nonstop.

Before renting a car, consider whether you want to drive Saddle Rd, the only route to Mauna Kea and Mauna Loa. Though the condition and reputation of this road is improving (see p258), most rental companies still prohibit driving their cars on it. Currently, Harper, National and Alamo are the only companies that allow driving on Saddle Rd, and only Harper rents 4WDs that can be driven past Mauna Kea's visitor center to the summit.

There are car-hire booths at Kona and Hilo airports:

Alamo Hilo (☎ 961-3343); Kona (☎ 329-8896)
Avis Hilo (☎ 935-1290); Kona (☎ 327-3000)
Budget Hilo (☎ 935-6878); Kona (☎ 329-8511)
Dollar (☎ Hawaii reservations 800-367-7006)
Hertz Hilo (☎ 935-2896); Kona (☎ 329-3566)
National Hilo (☎ 935-0891); Kona (☎ 329-1674)
Thrifty (☎ 877-283-0898)

For more information on the national chains, including toll-free numbers and websites, see p571.

Harper Car & Truck Rentals (Map p268; ☎ 969-1478, 800-852-9993; www.harpershawaii.com; 456 Kalaniana'ole Ave, Hilo) is the local car-hire agency. It is the only company that rents 4WDs that can be driven to Mauna Kea's summit, but they are expensive and the insurance coverage (which is supplemental, not primary) has a high deductable. Rates fluctuate greatly by season and demand, but for a 4WD anticipate spending at least $130 per day, and always ask for rate quotes including taxes.

Taxi

On the Big Island, cab drivers are typically locals who are familiar with the island, and they often act as tour guides. It's easy to find

ROAD DISTANCES & TIMES

From Hilo

Destination	Miles	Time
Hawi	86	2¼hr
Honoka'a	40	1hr
Kailua-Kona	92	2½hr
Na'alehu	64	1¾hr
Pahoa	16	½hr
Hawai'i Volcanoes NP	28	½hr
Waikoloa	80	2¼hr
Waimea	54	1½hr
Waipi'o Lookout	50	1¼hr

From Kailua-Kona

Destination	Miles	Time
Hawi	51	1¼hr
Hilo	92	2½hr
Honoka'a	61	1½hr
Na'alehu	60	1½hr
Pahoa	108	3hr
Hawai'i Volcanoes NP	98	2½hr
Waikoloa	18	¾hr
Waimea	43	1hr
Waipi'o Lookout	70	1¾hr

a cab at either airport, but most companies are small, with no advertisements or *Yellow Pages* listings. Cabs don't run all night or cruise for passengers, so in town you'll need to call ahead. The standard flag-down fee is $2, plus $2 per mile thereafter.

Tours

BUS & VAN

Several longtime tour operators offer around-the-island tours, which are essentially a mad dash through Kailua-Kona, Hawai'i Volcanoes National Park, Punalu'u black-sand beach, Hilo's Rainbow Falls, the Hamakua Coast and Waimea. Trust us, you'll get only a quick glimpse of the island.

Roberts Hawaii (☎ 954-8652, 866-898-2519; www.robertshawaii.com), **Jack's Tours** (☎ 969-9507, 800-442-5557; www.jackshawaii.com) and **Polynesian Adventure Tours** (☎ 329-8008, 800-622-3011; www.polyad.com) offer daylong circle-island bus tours (with variations) that cost from $65 to $80. All three companies pick up passengers at hotels in Waikoloa, Kailua-Kona and Keauhou; the exact time varies, but expect to leave at around sunrise and get back around sunset.

For something more unusual, contact **Hawaii AgVentures** (☎ 324-6011, 800-660-6011; www .hawaiiagventures.com) and ask about creating a personalized tour of local farms – perhaps Kona chocolate, local cheese or fruit orchards. Rates depend on group size and tour.

HELICOPTER

For a thrilling bird's-eye view of the island, try a helicopter tour. Lava tours (all leaving from Hilo) are far and away the most popular – most fly over Kilauea Caldera, the active Pu'u 'O'o vent and then hover over live lava flows. Before booking, confirm exactly what you'll see, and make sure all seats are window seats. Noise-canceling headsets are nice – and some promise 'doors off' tours. Other helicopter tours (some leaving from Kona) take in the valleys of the Kohala and Hamakua Coasts. Expect to pay $175 and up for a 45- to 55-minute lava tour, while two-hour valley trips run to $350 and more.

Helicopter tours are canceled during inclement weather but may fly when it's overcast; wait for a sparkling clear day if you can. Free tourist magazines have discount coupons, but the best deals are found by booking ahead through the internet.

Blue Hawaiian Helicopters (☎ 961-5600, 800-745-2583; www.bluehawaiian.com) Reliable, dependable and high volume.

Island Hoppers (☎ 329-0018, 800-538-7590; www .fly-hawaii.com/above) Has cheaper 50-minute 'flightseeing tours' by small prop plane.

Paradise Helicopters (☎ 329-6601; www.paradise copters.com) A good reputation for more personal tours.

Sunshine Helicopters (☎ 871-0722, 800-469-3000; www.sunshinehelicopters.com)

Tropical Helicopters (☎ 866-961-6810; www .tropicalhelicopters.com)

KAILUA-KONA

pop 10,000

Kailua-Kona (aka Kailua or Kona) sits on a sparkling blue bay with white-sand beaches and is beamed with tropical sunshine almost every day of the year. Dormant Mt Hualalai watches over this attractive town, a favorite with retirees. The central part of the city is dominated by tourism, its main drag filled with ABC stores selling cheap tourist souvenirs, and a surplus of hotels and condominiums. Sunburned vacationers in matching aloha attire fill downtown

streets, living their Hawaiian vacation dream. But it is possible to get onto an alternative track here and enjoy Kailua's mellow scene, excellent restaurants and plenty of ocean activities.

HISTORY

Kamehameha the Great lived his last years in Kailua-Kona, worshipping at Ahu'ena Heiau, his own temple. But soon after his death in 1819, his son Liholiho broke the *kapu* (taboo) by dining with women. When no godly wrath ensued, the traditional belief in Hawaiian gods collapsed. When the first missionaries sailed into Kailua Bay in 1820, the Hawaiian Islands transformed into a Christian society.

In the 19th century the city was a leisure retreat for Hawaiian royalty. Still standing on Ali'i Dr, Hulihe'e Palace (p203) a favorite getaway for King David Kalakaua (1836–91), aka the Merry Monarch, the last king of Hawai'i and the catalyst for a Hawaiian cultural resurgence.

While Hilo is the governmental seat of the island, Kailua's economic clout has skyrocketed since the 1970s, mainly through tourism and the world-renowned Kona coffee.

ORIENTATION

The highways and major roads in the Kona district parallel the coastline, making navigation easy. Kailua-Kona is south of the airport on Hwy 19 (Queen Ka'ahumanu Hwy), which becomes Hwy 11 (Mamalahoa Hwy) at Palani Rd. Kaiwi St, Palani Rd and Henry St are the primary and most direct links between the highway and Kailua town. Ali'i Dr is Kailua's main street, and runs from the center of town 5 miles along the coast. The stretch of Ali'i from the intersection with Palani Rd to where Kahakai Rd comes in is the most touristic area, filled with shopping gallerias and bustling pedestrian traffic. From there, condo complexes, private homes and a few hotels dominate the coastline all the way to Keauhou. Kuakini Hwy parallels northern Ali'i Dr and flows into Hwy 11, and it can be a quicker way to get around, though it has few connections to Ali'i, with Lunapule Rd being the southernmost.

INFORMATION
Bookstores

Borders Books Music & Café (☎ 331-1668; cnr Henry St & Hwy 11; ☼ 9am-9pm Sun-Thu, to 10pm Fri & Sat) Largest bookseller in Kailua-Kona, with many US and foreign newspapers.

HAWAI'I (THE BIG ISLAND)

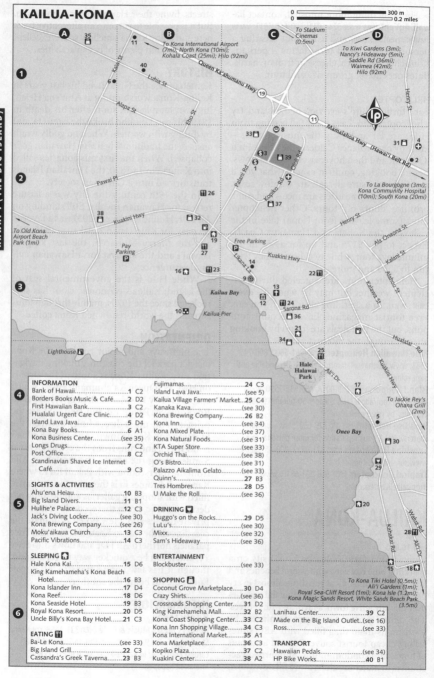

KAILUA-KONA

Kona Bay Books (☎ 326-7790; 74-5487 Kaiwi St; ◎ 10am-6pm) Kailua-Kona's last used-book store, with a limited selection of used CDs and new and used books.

Emergency

Police (☎ 935-3311) For nonemergencies.
Police, Fire & Ambulance (☎ 911) For emergencies.
Sexual Assault Hotline (☎ 935-0677)

Internet Access

Island Lava Java (☎ 327-2161; Ali'i Sunset Plaza, 75-5799 Ali'i Dr; per hr $10; ◎ 6am-10pm) Free wireless access with purchase; three computers are provided for paid access.
Kona Business Center (☎ 329-0006; Suite B-1A, Kona International Market, 74-5533 Luhia St; per hr $8; ◎ 8:30am-5:30pm Mon-Fri) All-purpose copy center for faxing and internet access.
Scandinavian Shaved Ice Internet Café (☎ 331-1626; 75-5699 Ali'i Dr; per hr $8; ◎ 10am-9:30pm Mon-Sat, noon-9:30pm Sun) Two computers are right in the café, and four are in a room behind it with a separate entrance.

Media

NEWSPAPERS

Hawai'i Island Journal (www.hawaiiislandjournal.com) Free bimonthly alternative paper with arts and entertainment listings.
Hawaii Tribune-Herald (www.hawaiitribune-herald .com) The Big Island's main daily newspaper.
West Hawaii Today (www.westhawaiitoday.com) Kona Coast's daily newspaper.

RADIO

A station guide is available at www.hawaii radiotv.com/BigIsleRadio.html
KANO 90.7 FM Hawaii Public Radio broadcasts music, talk and news.

Medical Services

Hualalai Urgent Care Clinic (☎ 327-4357; 75-1028 Henry St; ◎ 8am-5pm Mon-Fri, 9am-5pm Sat) For nonemergency medical care. Appointments are recommended.
Kona Community Hospital (☎ 322-9311; www .kch.hhsc.org; 79-1019 Haukapila St, Kealakekua) Located about 10 miles south of Kailua-Kona.
Longs Drugs (☎ 329-1380; Lanihau Center, 75-5595 Palani Rd; ◎ 8am-9pm Mon-Sat, to 6pm Sun) A centrally located drugstore with a pharmacy.

Money

Bank of Hawaii (☎ 326-3903; Lanihau Center, 75-5595 Palani Rd) Has a 24-hour ATM.

First Hawaiian Bank (☎ 329-2461; 74-5593 Palani Rd) Also with a 24-hour ATM.

Post

Post office (☎ 331-8307; 74-5577 Palani Rd; ◎ 8:30am-4:30pm Mon-Fri, 9:30am-1:30pm Sat) Access is via the Lanihau Center.

Tourist Information

In the absence of any official tourist-information post, the best sources include hotel staff, B&B proprietors and the internet.

DANGERS & ANNOYANCES

'Tourist information' or 'discount activities' storefronts along Ali'i Dr are most often fronts for aggressive salespeople looking to push condominium time-shares. Stay away or get sucked in!

SIGHTS

Being more a town of action, Kailua has few sights. But what few there are hold great historical significance and have withstood the test of time. Other than the beaches, Kailua's sights are concentrated at the northern end of picturesque Ali'i Dr in the center. To get the most out of your visit, take the Historical Society's excellent walking tour (see p207).

Hulihe'e Palace

Hawai'i's second governor, 'John Adams' Kuakini, commissioned this simple, elegant two-story house in 1838 as his private residence. Used as a vacation getaway for Hawaiian monarchs, the house, built with lava rock in 1885, was plastered over inside and out by King Kalakaua, who preferred a more polished style after his travels abroad.

Prince Kuhio, who inherited the palace from his uncle Kalakaua, found himself short of cash and auctioned off the furnishings and artifacts. Luckily, his wife and other female royalty meticulously numbered each piece and recorded the name of the bidder. Eventually the Daughters of Hawai'i, a group founded in 1903 by daughters of missionaries, tracked down the owners and persuaded many to donate the pieces for display in the **museum** (☎ 329-1877; www.huliheepalace.org; 75-5718 Ali'i Dr) they established at the palace. The palace suffered structural damage in the 2006 earthquake, and the Kona Historical Society closed the museum pending restoration. Check with the museum for an update.

After reopening, the museum will again display Western antiques, collected on royal jaunts to Europe, and Hawaiian artifacts, such as a table inlaid with 25 kinds of native Hawaiian wood, and several of Kamehameha the Great's war spears.

The pleasant, oceanfront grounds of the palace remain open. A **fishpond** behind the palace is no longer stocked but holds a few colorful tropical fish. Curiously, it also once served as a queen's bath and a canoe landing.

Ahu'ena Heiau

After Kamehameha the Great established his kingdom's royal court in Lahaina on Maui, he returned to his Kamakahonu residence on Kailua Bay, where he died in May 1819. His personal **temple** is at the tip of an outcrop on the northern end of Kailua Bay, and surrounded by water on three sides. It has been reconstructed with palm-leaf shacks and carved wooden *ki'i* (statues). Do not climb on this sacred site.

Here, **Kamakahonu beach** is a miniature cove fronting King Kamehameha's Kona Beach Hotel. The waters are calm and safe for children, and the hotel's beach hut rents beach gear.

Moku'aikaua Church

On April 4, 1820, the first Christian missionaries to the Hawaiian Islands sailed into Kailua Bay. When they landed, they were unaware that Hawai'i's old religion had been abolished on that very spot just a few months before. King Liholiho gave them this site, just a few minutes' walk from Kamehameha's Ahu'ena Heiau, to establish Hawai'i's first Christian church.

Completed in 1836, the **church** (☎ 329-1589; 75-5713 Ali'i Dr) is a handsome building with walls of lava rock held together by sand and coral lime mortar. The posts and beams, hewn with stone adzes, and smoothed down with chunks of coral, are made from resilient ohia, and the pews and pulpit are made of koa, the most prized native hardwood. The steeple tops out at 112ft, making the church the tallest structure in Kailua. The building was angled to invite the trade winds to sweep through its simple and serene interior.

Kailua Pier

The town's pier, built in 1915, was once a major cattle-shipping area. Cattle driven down from hillside ranches were stampeded into the water and forced to swim out to waiting steamers, where they were hoisted aboard by sling and shipped to Honolulu slaughterhouses.

As sportfishing charters now use Honokohau Harbor north of town, Kailua Pier is mainly used by dive boats and cruise ships, though its hoist and scales are still used for weigh-ins during billfish tournaments.

Beaches

WHITE SANDS BEACH PARK

This attractive beach is a mini-paradise with crystal turquoise waters and shady palms. Its ability to lose its sand literally overnight during high winter surf has earned it nicknames such as Magic Sands and Disappearing Sands. When its rocks and coral are exposed, the beach becomes too treacherous for most swimmers. Gradually the sand magically returns, transforming the shore back into its former beachy self. White Sands is always packed and is an ideal bodyboarding and bodysurfing spot. Facilities include rest rooms, showers, picnic tables and a volleyball court; a lifeguard is on duty. The park is about 4 miles south of the center.

OLD KONA AIRPORT STATE PARK

Despite being only a mile from downtown and worth visiting, this 217-acre park is often overlooked by visitors. Its lengthy shore offers solitude and the relaxing sound of waves crashing, and it's a good place to picnic or stroll.

The old airport runway skirts a long sandy beach laced with thick strips of black lava rock. Though there are a couple of breaks allowing entry into the water, fishing, not swimming, is the major activity here. At low tide, the rocks reveal countless aquariumlike **tide pools** holding tiny sea urchins, crabs and bits of coral. One at the southern end of the park is large enough to be a *keiki* (child) pool.

The waters offshore of the park and adjacent private properties are a marine life-conservation district. **Garden Eel Cove**, reached by a short walk from the north end of the beach, is a good area for scuba divers and confident snorkelers. The reef fish are large and plentiful, and a steep coral wall in deeper waters harbors moray eels and a wide variety of sea creatures. When the surf's up, local surfers flock to an offshore break at 'Shark Rocks.'

Facilities include rest rooms, showers and covered picnic tables on a lawn dotted with

---

THE BIG ISLAND FOR NA KEIKI

- Get underwater with **Atlantis Submarines** (p207).

- Say 'hi' to Max at **Pana'ewa Rainforest Zoo** (p274).

- Learn to **surf** (p207).

- Go tide-pooling at **Kapoho Tide Pools** (p286) and **Old Kona Airport State Park** (opposite).

- Join local kids playing and swimming at **Hilo's beaches** (p274).

- Picnic and net fish at **Lili'uokalani Park** (p273).

- Catch a $1 movie at Hilo's **Kress Cinema** (p280).

- Learn about space and astronauts at **Onizuka Space Center** (p231).

- Go snorkeling in **Kealakekua Bay** (p222).

- Tired of sand in your suit? The whole family can swim at **Pahoa Community Aquatic Center** (p284).

---

beach heliotrope and short coconut palms. The former runway disposes of any parking worries. Next to it is a mile-long loop that locals use as a track. To the south, the county's **Kailua Park Complex** (☎ 327-3553) has a gym, a pool, soccer and softball fields, four night-lit tennis courts, a horseshoe-toss pit, and play structures.

To get here, follow Kuakini Hwy to its end.

ACTIVITIES

Most of Kailua's activities involve getting wet. For information on renting a bicycle, see p212.

Note that the area's snorkeling, diving and kayaking tours have been gathered here, so you can see the range of options. Descriptions note whether tours leave from Kailua Pier, Honokohau Harbor to the north or Keauhou Harbor to the south.

Snorkeling

Snorkeling cruises (aka 'Dolphin Cruises') are plentiful around Kailua, with good reason. A half-day (four hours) spent snorkeling promises wonderful views, good times and lessons in Hawaiian history and ocean life. There are

usually morning or afternoon departures – opt for the morning as that's the time when water conditions are best.

The most common (and crowded) snorkeling destination is **Kealakekua Bay** (p222) to the south. The coast south of Kailua has beautiful lava cliffs and caves, while the northern coast is a flat lava shelf with great snorkeling aplenty. Ultimately, the captain decides the best destination for the day's conditions.

Do not miss the opportunity to do a **night snorkel or dive with Pacific manta rays**. With 'wing' spans of 8ft to 12ft, these gentle creatures will amaze you with their sheer size. Light attracts plankton, which draws the manta rays to feed.

Cruise prices usually include snorkeling gear, beverages and snacks. There are often discounts if you book online. Recommended operators:

Captain Zodiac (☎ 329-3199, 800-422-7824; www .captainzodiac.com; half-day cruise adult/child 4-12 $87/72) Captain Zodiac makes daily trips to Kealakekua Bay in 24ft rigid-hull inflatable Zodiacs with up to 16 passengers and a fun pirate theme. Departs from Honokohau Harbor, with pickups possible at the Kailua-Kona and Keauhou piers.

Fairwind (☎ 322-2788, 800-677-9461; www.fair-wind .com; Fairwind II adult/child $69/43, incl meal adult $99-105, child under 4 free-$29, child 4-12 $59-65, Hula Kai per person incl meal $119-139) The *Fairwind II* – a scrappy 100-passenger catamaran with a 15ft slide kids adore – sails daily to Kealakekua Bay. Cruises on the luxury Hydrofoil catamaran *Hula Kai* are longer and go to the day's best and most crowd-free spots. Divers are accommodated. Book in advance, as Fairwind does the highest volume in the area. Departs from Keauhou Bay.

Kamanu Charters (☎ 329-2021, 800-348-3091; www .kamanu.com; adult/child $75/45) Snorkel without crowds at Pawai Bay, just north of the protected waters of the Old Kona Airport State Park. The 36ft catamaran, which motors down and sails back, takes a maximum of 24 people. Departs from Honokohau Harbor.

Sea Hawaii Rafting (☎ 325-7444, 937-7809; www .seahawaiirafting.com; half-day $95, charters per hr $300) With over 13 years of experience in Kona's waters, excellent guide Kris Henry can tailor trips to your preferences. His rigid-hull, inflatable Zodiac can accommodate up to 20 passengers, with a trip minimum of four. Kris is extremely knowledgeable about the area, great with kids and an all-around great guy. His interest in sharing Hawaii's mana stems from his part-Hawaiian heritage. Departs from Honokohau Harbor.

Sea Paradise (☎ 322-2500, 800-322-5662; www .seaparadise.com; snorkel cruise incl 2 meals adult/child

$95/59, 2-tank dive $125, sunset cruise $95, manta snorkel adult/child $79/59, manta dive $110) Highly recommended Sea Paradise offers morning snorkel cruises to Kealakekua Bay, dive trips and a sunset dinner sail on a classy 46ft catamaran with a fun and professional crew. The manta night cruises include James Wing, a manta-ray expert and professional videographer, and are the area's best. Departs from Keauhou Bay.

Sea Quest (☎ 329-7238; www.seaquesthawaii.com; morning cruise adult/child $85/72, afternoon cruise $64/54) Sea Quest takes between two and six passengers (up to 12 on request) out on 22ft and 26ft rigid-hull inflatable rafts. The recommended morning cruise includes both Honaunau and Kealakekua Bays, while the afternoon cruise concentrates on Kealakekua Bay. Departs from Keauhou Bay.

Diving

Near the shore, divers can see steep drop-offs with lava tubes, caves and diverse marine life. In deeper waters there are 40 popular boat-dive areas, including an airplane wreck off Keahole Point.

One well-known dive spot is **Red Hill**, an underwater cinder cone about 10 miles south of Kona. It has beautiful lava formations – including ledges and lots of honeycombed lava tubes nicely lit by streaks of sunlight – as well as coral pinnacles and brightly colored nudibranchs (mollusks).

Two-tank dives range from $95 to $140. One-tank night dives and manta-ray dives cost between $65 and $120. The larger five-star PADI operations offer certification courses for around $500.

See the snorkel outfits on p205, as some accommodate divers. Kailua-Kona's dive operations are numerous and largely have great reputations:

Aloha Dive Company (☎ 325-5560, 800-708-5662; www.alohadive.com) A personable small company run by locals Mike and Buffy Nakachi and Earl Kam. Groups are limited to six on the 28ft boat.

Big Island Divers (☎ 329-6068; 800-488-6068; www.bigislanddivers.com; 74-5467 Kaiwi St) Personable staff with expansive shop (number-one Aqua-Lung dealer on the island). Offers night and manta-ray dives.

Dive Makai (☎ 329-2025; www.divemakai.com) A small, friendly operation run by a husband-and-wife team with a 31ft boat. In business for nearly three decades, they provide thorough predive briefings, have a diver-to-guide maximum ratio of 6:1 and keep dives unstructured. Offers night and manta-ray dives.

Jack's Diving Locker (☎ 329-7585, 800-345-4807; www.jacksdivinglocker.com; Coconut Grove Marketplace, 75-5819 Ali'i Dr) One of the best outfits for introductory dives, as well as night manta-ray dives. Housed at a 5000ft facility, with a store, classrooms, a tank room and a 12ft-deep dive pool. Its two 38ft boats and one 23ft craft handle up to 12 divers each. Jack's has a reputation for preservation and setting up moorings.

Kayak Tours

There's no better or more ecologically sound way to explore the Kona Coast than by kayak. Tours are generally led by certified lifeguards and they're appropriate for novices. Prices include snacks and all required gear.

These recommended operators also rent kayaks (all are located south of Kailua):

Adventures in Paradise (☎ 323-3005, 866-824-2337; www.bigislandkayak.com; 81-6367 Hwy 11, Kealakekua; tour $80) This outfit, on Hwy 11 at Keopula Rd, is friendly, professional and very good with beginners. Its snorkeling tours have a two-person minimum and a three- to four-kayak maximum.

Aloha Kayak Company (☎ 322-2868; www.alohakayak.com; Hwy 11, Honalo; morning adult/child $65/32, afternoon $50/25) This Hawaiian-owned outfit's tours include snorkeling, sea caves, cliff jumping and historical orientation. The morning tour is longer and includes lunch. Glass-bottomed kayaks are available.

Kona Boys (☎ 328-1234; www.konaboys.com; 79-7539 Hwy 11, Kealakekua; sunset $125, camping incl meals $250-350) Kona Boys is professional with a laid-back surfer's vibe. It does sunset paddles, which include night snorkeling, and overnight camping paddles.

Ocean Safaris (☎ 326-4699; www.oceansafariskayaks.com; Keauhou Harbor; dolphin tour $35, cave tour $64) Ocean Safaris does the same snorkeling, sea cave and cliff-jumping tour, as well as an early dolphin-sighting tour.

Whale Watching

The season for humpback whales usually starts around January and runs to March or April. Most snorkeling, diving or fishing operations offer whale-watching tours during humpback season. Marine-mammal biologist Dan McSweeney of **Whale Watch** (☎ 322-0028, 888-942-5376; www.ilovewhales.com; 3hr cruise adult/child $69/59; ☼ Jul-Apr) leads excursions to see the sperm, false killer, dolphin and melon-headed whales, plus five dolphin species, that can be seen in Kona waters year-round. Hydrophones allow passengers to hear whale songs.

Fishing

Kona has more than 100 charter fishing boats; many are listed in the *Fishing* freebie, which is available at airports and around town. The standard cost for joining an existing party starts at $80 per person for a four-hour (half-day) trip. Otherwise, a charter for up to six people runs between $300 and $600 for a half-day, and $500 and $900 for a full day, depending on the boat. Prices include equipment.

Recommended boat booking centers:

Charter Desk (☎ 329-5735, 888-566-2487; www .charterdesk.com)

Charter Services Hawaii (☎ 334-1881, 800-567-2650; www.konazone.com)

Kona Charter Skippers Association (☎ 936-4970, 800-762-7546; www.konabiggamefishing.com)

Surfing

What little surf there is on the Leeward Coast is not in Kailua-Kona. **Banyans**, near the banyan tree north of White Sands Beach (p204), has some waves. Otherwise head for nearby Kahalu'u Beach (p213) or Pine Trees (p230). For tips or board rental, head to friendly and family-run **Pacific Vibrations** (☎ 329-4140; pacvibe@hawaii.rr.com; 75-5702 Likana Lane; board per day $10-20; ⏰ 10am-5:30pm Mon-Fri, to 3:30pm Sat). For lessons, contact **Surfer Bear** (☎ 936-3654; www .surferbearhawaii).

Yoga

Located in a private home, **Yoga Hale** (☎ 938-9980; www.yogahale.com; 77-6530 Naniloa Dr; drop-in class $15; ⏰ 7:30am & 6pm Mon-Fri, 9:30am Sat & Sun) offers excellent classes in yin, prenatal, hot and Vinyasa yoga. The latter is quite a work out.

TOURS

Atlantis Submarines (☎ 329-6626, 800-548-6262; www.atlantisadventures.com; adult/child $80/40; ⏰ 10am, 11:30am & 1pm) Submarine rides last 35 minutes and descend 100ft in a coral crevice in front of the Royal Kona Resort. The sub has 26 portholes and carries 48 passengers.

Kailua Bay Charter Company (☎ 324-1749; www .konaglassbottomboat.com; 50min tour adult/child $30/12; ⏰ Mon-Sat) See Kailua's coastline, underwater reef, fish, and perhaps dolphins or whales, from a 36ft glass-bottom boat with a pleasant crew and onboard naturalist. Easy boarding for elderly or mobility-impaired passengers.

Kona Brewing Company (☎ 334-2739; North Kona Shopping Center, 75-5629 Kuakini Hwy; www.kona brewingco.com; admission & tour free; ⏰ 10:30am & 3pm Mon-Fri) Founded in 1994, the Big Island's first micro-brewery now ships its handcrafted brews to outer islands and beyond. Tours of this family-run Kona icon include sampling.

Kona Historical Society (☎ 323-3222, 326-9092; www.konahistorical.org; 90min tour $15; ⏰ 9am &

10:30pm Wed-Fri, occasionally Tue & Sat) This worthwhile and informational walking tour covers historical sites in downtown Kailua-Kona, and includes a book. There's a four-person minimum and a cruise-ship maximum.

FESTIVALS & EVENTS

Hawaiian International Billfish Tournament (☎ 329-6155; www.konabillfish.com) August. This grand-daddy of Kona fishing tournaments is accompanied by a week of festive entertainment.

Ironman Triathlon World Championship (www .ironmanlive.com) Third Saturday in October. The legendary event combines a 2.4-mile ocean swim, 112-mile bike race and 26.2-mile marathon in the ultimate race. About 1700 men and women from around the world qualify to compete each year, finishing with times from eight to 17 hours.

Kona Brewers Festival (☎ 331-3033, 334-1884; www.konabrewersfestival.com; admission $40) Second Saturday in March. This 'just folks' festival features samples from 30 craft breweries and gourmet eats from scores of local restaurants. Proceeds benefit local environmental and cultural organizations. Buy tickets in advance.

Kona Coffee Cultural Festival (☎ 326-7820; www .konacoffeefest.com; button $3) November. For 10 days during harvest season the community celebrates Kona coffee pioneers and their gourmet brew. Events include a cupping competition (akin to wine tasting), art exhibits, farm tours, parades and a coffee-picking race (a recent winner picked over 23lb in three minutes!).

SLEEPING

The center of Kailua-Kona has few hotels and is dominated by condominium complexes strung along Ali'i Dr. A few B&Bs are located in the hills above town, a bit of a drive from the center. Reservations for all are recommended in the high season.

Condos tend to be cheaper than hotels for longer stays, and they offer more comfort. Condo vacation rentals are handled by owners or on behalf of owners by property management agencies. Commonly used management agencies:

ATR Properties (☎ 329-6020, 888-311-6020; www .konacondo.com)

Kona Hawaii Vacation Rentals (☎ 329-3333, 800-244-4752; www.konahawaii.com)

Knutson & Associates (☎ 329-6311, 800-800-6202; www.konahawaiirentals.com)

SunQuest Vacations & Property Management Hawaii (☎ 329-6438, from US 800-367-5168, from Canada 800-800-5662; www.sunquest-hawaii.com)

Budget

Kona Tiki Hotel (☎ 329-1425; www.konatiki.com; 75-5968 Ali'i Dr; r incl breakfast $65, with kitchenette $88; P ⚊) This is a sweet deal for a no-frills room (sans TV or phone) in a vintage three-story complex on the ocean. Most rooms have a queen-size and a twin bed, and all have a refrigerator and breezy oceanfront lanai (balcony). No credit cards.

CONDOMINIUMS

Kona Islander Inn (☎ 329-9393, 800-622-5348; www .konahawaii.com; 75-5776 Kuakini Hwy; kitchenette studios $70-90; P ⊠ ⚊) The low prices and proximity to downtown cause this complex to be a bit overrun. Go for units on upper floors and those furthest from Ali'i Dr. There's a major lack of parking.

Kona Isle (☎ 329-6311; 75-6100 Ali'i Dr; 1-bedroom units $60-115; P ⊠ ⚊) Buildings in this complex, arranged around a central green bordered by flowering plants, enjoy a quiet reputation. An oceanfront area has a sand 'beach,' palms and a saltwater pool.

Midrange

Kiwi Gardens (☎ 326-1559; www.kiwigardens.com; incl breakfast r with shared bathroom $105, r $125; P) The rural upland neighborhood setting is beautiful and quiet, with distant ocean views and lush greenery. The B&B, located in a characterless modern stucco home, is nonetheless more just a place to lay your head. Rooms have screened-in lanai and unremarkable but homey furnishings. Kids will get a kick out of a common area with '50s decor, a vintage soda fountain and a jukebox.

Nancy's Hideaway (☎ 325-3132, 866-325-3132; www .nancyshideaway.com; 73-1530 Uanani Pl; studios/cottages incl breakfast $125/145; P) Tree ferns and pretty landscaping surround the pink one-bedroom cottage and stand-alone studio at Nancy's, located in a quiet, rural neighborhood. The modern, immaculate accommodations are bright and free of frilly kitsch and much character. Private lanai have distant ocean views, and cats and peacocks roam the property. If you seek remote tranquility, Nancy's is worth the 6-mile drive up the mountain from Kailua. Children under 13 are not encouraged.

King Kamehameha's Kona Beach Hotel (☎ 329-2911, reservations 800-367-6060; www.konabeachhotel.com; 75-5660 Palani Rd; r $170-250; P ⊠ ⚊) It must be the oceanfront location in the heart of downtown that keeps this classic Kailua hotel in business, because it is certainly not the hotel itself. The

TOP SLEEPS: LEEWARD SIDE

■ **Holualoa Inn** (p216)
■ **Hale o Luna** (p302)
■ **Horizon Guest House** (p226)
■ **Banana Patch** (p220)
■ **Luana Inn** (p224)
■ **Kona Magic Sands Resort** (below)

lobby has modest displays of traditional Hawaiian artifacts, but an elevator ride leads to dreary hallways and outdated rooms with worn carpet and furnishings. Go for ocean-view rooms, as those with a partial view mostly overlook an unsightly rooftop. Parking is $9.50 per day.

Ask for the most recently renovated rooms in these conveniently located standbys:

Kona Seaside Hotel (☎ 329-2455, 800-560-5558; www.konaseasidehotel.com; 75-5646 Palani Rd; r $118-165, with kitchenette $170; P ⊠ ⚊) Attracts business travelers and an older clientele.

Uncle Billy's Kona Bay Hotel (☎ 329-1393, 800-367-5102; www.unclebilly.com; 75-5744 Ali'i Dr; r $119; P ⊠ ⚊) Popular with tour groups and fairly noisy.

CONDOMINIUMS

Kona Magic Sands Resort (☎ 329-3333; 77-6452 Ali'i Dr; studio units $95-125; P ⊠ ⚊) The compact studios in this three-story building are kept cool and quiet by cinderblock construction, and each has a full kitchen, rattan furnishings and an oceanfront lanai. A good pool area and White Sands Beach next door make this complex great value.

Hale Kona Kai (☎ 329-2155, 800-421-3696; http://hkk.kona@verizon.net; 75-5870 Kahakai Rd; 1-bedroom units $140-165; P ⊠ ⚊) An unremarkable three-story block of often upgraded units all face the ocean at the Hale Kona Kai. Each is comfortable and has a lanai; corner units' lanai wrap around.

Top End

Royal Kona Resort (☎ 329-3111, reservations 800-447-6925; www.royalkona.com; 75-5852 Ali'i Dr; r $210-385; P ⊠ ⚊) There's no more prominent piece of architecture in Kailua than the Royal Kona Resort's three oceanfront towers. The place is popular with package tours, and the lobby relentlessly reminds guests that this is Hawaii with loud piped music, lava rock everywhere and gaudy ocean-themed bathrooms. Huge

Easter Island heads overlook the restaurant, which is straight out of the '70s. Guests can enjoy excellent, spacious rooms and a saltwater lagoon. Kids stay and eat for free.

CONDOMINIUMS

Royal Sea-Cliff Resort (☎ 329-8021, 800-688-7444; www.outrigger.com; 75-6040 Ali'i Dr; studios $159, 1-bedroom units $189-245, 2-bedroom units $239-305; P ✗ ☎) Condo complex or upscale hotel? It's hard to tell at the seven-floor Royal, by the ubiquitous Outrigger chain. A verdant atrium and artificial stream run the length of the impressive open-air interior, leading down to two oceanfront pools and a sauna. The modern units have stylish furnishings, full kitchen, washing machine and dryer. The covered parking is a true blessing.

Kona Reef (☎ 329-2959, 800-367-5004; www.castleresorts.com; 75-5888 Ali'i Dr; 1-bedroom units $240-295, 2-bedroom units $400-450; P ✗ ☎) The Reef has more spacious condos than other complexes, and it faces the ocean. The four-floor complex is very well kept, though it has an '80s stucco look with little greenery. Castle Resorts manages almost half of the units and has a helpful office onsite.

EATING

You can find every type of bad food in Kailua-Kona…unless you know where to go. Don't succumb to the touristy charm of Ali'i Dr. If you're after quality food with flavor, it's more likely in a shopping center outside of downtown than overlooking the ocean. While worthwhile midrange restaurants are few, Kailua-Kona abounds with excellent lowcost eateries. Last, don't be afraid to use your rental car: Keauhou and South Kona have some great eats.

Budget

Palazzo Aikalima Gelato (☎ 327-3388; Kona Coast Shopping Center, 74-5588 Palani Rd; ⏰ 10am-9:30pm Sun-Thu, to 10pm Fri & Sat) If you're serious about your frozen desserts, this all-natural, artisanal gelato and sorbet should impress.

U Make the Roll (☎ 326-1322; Kona Marketplace, 75-5725 Ali'i Dr; sushi rolls $3.95-4.50; ⏰ 11am-7pm Mon-Fri, to 4pm Sat) Hidden on the back side of the center, you'll never find this sushi stand unless you're searching. The rolls can be loose, but the price is right.

Island Lava Java (☎ 327-2161; Ali'i Sunset Plaza, 75-5799 Ali'i Dr; meals $7-14; ⏰ 6am-10pm) It's inevitable that you'll end up at this popular café at least

MUST-TRY FOODS IN HAWAI'I
waialugirl

- **Malasadas** Compliments of the Portuguese, a *malasada* is a sugar-dusted fried dough puff, occasionally stuffed with various flavors of custard. Who needs Krispy Kreme?

- **Spam musubi** A brick of rice with a proud slice of Spam on top, wrapped with a strip of seaweed. It's such a fulfilling snack, it's available at every 7-Eleven.

- **Mochi ice cream** Perhaps out of a fortuitous experiment, balls of ice cream are wrapped in sweet *mochi* (Japanese sticky rice cake) to create the most delicious treats in the local grocer's freezer. Don't miss the ones at Bubbies ice cream parlors.

- **Popcorn and mochi crunch** At the movies local-style: pour your buttered popcorn into the cardboard box, add *mochi crunch* (Japanese rice crackers), mix and enjoy! Mochi crunch is available at all concession stands.

- **Shave ice** Call it 'shaved' ice, and everyone will know you're from out of town. The fine-cut Hawaiian version of the snow cone is far tastier. A good one feels like silk to the tongue. It's the most refreshing snack to top off a day of fun in the sun.

(blu,list) v. to recommend a travel experience. www.lonelyplanet.com/bluelist **BLUELIST.**

once. If you don't come for a satisfying egg or pancake breakfast, then you'll hit the excellent grill for a sandwich or bistro salad, since it serves later than most. Or maybe you'll need that afternoon Kona coffee and a sweet treat. Whichever it is, you can enjoy it with a view of the bay and a lounge in the sun.

Ba-Le Kona (☎ 327-1212; Kona Coast Shopping Center, 74-5588 Palani Rd; sandwiches $5, soups & plates $8; ⏰ 10am-9pm Mon-Sat, 11am-7pm Sun) Everyone gushes about Ba-Le's flavorful Vietnamese fare, like its green-papaya salad topped with shrimp, rice-paper summer rolls and traditional *pho* noodle soups. Satisfying sandwiches made with freshly baked French bread or croissants, cold rice-noodle salads and rice plates come with your choice of lemongrass chicken, tofu, beef or pork. The dining room is chilly and stark, with the usual florescent-tube lighting, but the food is worth it.

Kona Mixed Plate (☎ 329-8104; Kopiko Plaza, Kopiko Rd; plates $8.50; 🕙 10am-8pm Mon-Sat) Visitors never find this place, tucked in a shopping center behind Burger King. Burgers and saimin (local-style noodle soup) are on the lit-up menu, but the real deal here is plate lunches. Choose between a long list of meat and fish options, veggie stir-fry or tempura.

Orchid Thai (☎ 327-9437; Kuakini Center, Kaiwi St; lunch specials $9; 🕙 11am-2:45pm & 5-8:45pm Mon-Sat) The place is simple (folding chairs!), but Orchid is without a doubt the Leeward Coast's best Thai. A lunch special includes rice, a veggie summer roll and a dish of your choice. Bring your own alcohol.

Big Island Grill (☎ 326-1153; 75-5702 Kuakini Hwy; plate lunches $9, mains $13; 🕙 6-10am & 11am-9pm) Big food with no frills sums up the Big Island Grill. There's been little effort to dress up the former fast-food building that houses this local favorite. Judging by the perpetually packed dining room, no one minds. Framed pictures of sports teams line the entry, and young staff members hurry around in aloha shirts serving plates heaped with rice or mashed potatoes, veggies and teriyaki beef or battered fish to local families. The extensive menu should please all.

Kanaka Kava (☎ 327-1660; Coconut Grove Marketplace, 75-5803 Ali'i Dr; salads $12-14; 🕙 10am-10pm Sun-Wed, to 11pm Thu-Sat) Drop by this tiny locals' spot to sample Zachary's kava ($4; the mildly relaxing juice of the *'awa* plant) or his organic salads topped with a choice of fish, shellfish, chicken, tofu or *poke* (cubed raw fish marinated in soy sauce, oil and chili pepper). The Hawaiian à la carte items, including squid luau (feast) and taro steamed with coconut milk, rival the fare at any upscale place.

Midrange

Kona Brewing Company (☎ 329-2739; 75-5629 Kuakini Hwy; sandwiches & salads $7-12, small/large pizzas $15/22; 🕙 11am-9pm Sun-Thu, to 10pm Fri & Sat) Locals and tourists alike crowd around the bright, noisy bar for handcrafted brews at the Big Island's first microbrewery. Specialty ales include Big Wave Golden, which blends traditional pale and honey malts, and *liliko'i* (passion fruit) wheat. Try the four-beer sampler ($7). Diners enjoy salads and thin-crust pizzas from a stone oven, on a torch-lit patio surrounded by

leafy plants. This place packs, so reserve ahead and anticipate limited parking.

Cassandra's Greek Taverna (☎ 334-1066; 75-5669 Ali'i Dr; mains lunch $11, dinner $18; 🕙 11am-10pm) If you must give in to Ali'i Dr's touristy, open-air, upper-floor restaurants, Cassandra's is the place to do it. The Greek fare is tasty, if a bit overpriced, and a couple of appetizers with a cold beer and a clear view of canoe paddlers in the bay is a great finish to an afternoon. The bar has pool tables and gets rowdy in the later hours.

Fujimamas (☎ 327-2125; 75-5719 Ali'i Dr; mains lunch $11, dinner $16-23; 🕙 11:30am-2:30pm & 5-11pm) Fujimamas blends hip, eclectic ambience, something Kailua's restaurant scene sorely lacks, with chic presentation, making it a very exciting new addition. The heavily Japanese-influenced menu includes sushi, wok dishes and 'things that make you go ummm.' The handmade Chinese noodles with mushrooms and truffle oil ($16) get wide acclaim, as does the grilled pork chop on tempura sweet potato bread with apple chutney and miso sesame sauce ($23). Oh, and leave room for the insane desserts, such as banana tempura on tropical French toast.

Jackie Rey's Ohana Grill (☎ 327-0209; Sunset Shopping Plaza, 75-5995 Kuakini Hwy; mains lunch $11, dinner $23; 🕙 lunch 11am-2pm & pupu 2-5pm Mon-Fri, dinner 5-9pm daily) Jackie Rey's dining room is bright and casual, attracting those looking for good value and a conventional dining experience. The menu presents typical meat and seafood dishes with influences from all over the globe, from macadamia-nut pesto to ginger coconut sauce, tabbouleh salad to spicy pineapple salsa. For lunch, try the seared *'ahi poke* wrap with stir-fried vegetables ($13). For dinner, try the pork loin with coconut shrimp stuffing and honey Jack Daniel's glaze ($22). Also serves *pupu* (snacks).

Kona Inn (☎ 329-4455; 75-5744 Ali'i Dr; mains lunch $9-16, dinner $17-28; 🕙 11:30am-9:30pm) If you're after

---

TOP EATS: LEEWARD SIDE

- **Ke'ei Café** (p220)
- **Fujimamas** (above)
- **Bamboo** (p244)
- **Hualalai Grille by Alan Wong** (p232)
- **O's Bistro** (opposite)

a straightforward salad and sandwich lunch or steak and seafood dinner served in a handsome environment, the Kona Inn is your place. The inn opened in 1929 as the Big Island's first hotel, and maintains a historical air. The dining room has koa furnishings and gleaming hardwood floors, and overlooks a lawn and the crashing waves beyond.

Also recommended:

Quinn's (☎ 329-3822; 75-5864 Palani Rd; sandwiches $10, meals $19-24; ⏰ 11am-11pm) This divey-looking seafood restaurant has many devoted fans and is your best bet for a late meal.

Tres Hombres (☎ 329-2173; 75-5864 Walua Rd; mains $13-20; ⏰ 11:30am-9pm) The dining area is uninteresting and the service inconsistent, but if you crave Mexican, this is Kailua's best.

Top End

O's Bistro (☎ 327-6565; Crossroads Shopping Center, 75-1027 Henry St; dinner mains $15-32; ⏰ 10am-9pm) As a dining experience, the jury is out on this upscale bistro, with an unlikely location in the Safeway shopping center. Some ooh and ah over its eclectic menu, which jumps from Thai fried chicken and rice-noodle salad to kalamata linguine, from fish tacos to Peking duck. Others say the urban-chic interior gets too crowded and so noisy that it becomes difficult to hold a conversation. Vegetarians will delight in the 'food without faces' menu.

La Bourgogne (☎ 329-6711; Kuakini Plaza, 77-6400 Nalani St, at Hwy 11; mains $24-32; ⏰ 6-10pm Tue-Sat) For many Kona residents, this intimate French restaurant is the hands-down choice for special occasions. The windowless dining room is a little musty, but the food is impeccable and it's the finest dining available in Kona. Venison chop with sherry and pomegranate glaze ($35) and roasted rabbit in white wine, aromatic vegetables and lavender ($28) are possibilities. Waitstaff expertly navigate the extensive wine list. Reservations are a must.

Groceries

For groceries, **KTA Super Store** (☎ 329-1677; Kona Coast Shopping Center, 74-5594 Palani Rd; ⏰ 5am-midnight) and **Kona Natural Foods** (☎ 329-2296; Crossroads Shopping Center, 75-1027 Henry St; ⏰ 8:30am-9pm Mon-Sat, to 7pm Sun, deli to 4pm daily) should have everything you need. Each has a deli, and at KTA you'll find sushi and local specialties. For local produce, the **Kailua Village farmers market** (Ali'i Dr; ⏰ 9am-5pm Thu-Sun) is good, but the Keauhou farmers market (see p215) is better.

> ### BEST PLACES FOR A SUNSET DRINK: LEEWARD SIDE
>
> ■ **Huggo's on the Rocks** (below)
> ■ **Verandah Lounge** (p215)
> ■ **Beach Tree Bar** (p232)
> ■ **Ocean Bar** (p237)

DRINKING

There are a fair number of bars in Kailua-Kona, most of them generic sports-bar types. If you're not into drinking at Kona Brewing Company (opposite) or Cassandra's (opposite), then one of these spots should suit you.

Sam's Hideaway (☎ 326-7267; Kona Marketplace, 75-5725 Ali'i Dr; ⏰ 10-1:30am) Sam's has cheap drinks and a grumpy bartender, and is dim and untouristy, making it the perfect dive bar.

LuLu's (☎ 331-2633; Coconut Grove Marketplace, 75-5819 Ali'i Dr; ⏰ 11am-10pm) On an upper floor, open-air LuLu's is large, loud and full of gimmicks. Dollar bills cover the walls and 30 TVs fire away. For a night of scamming and debauchery on the dance floor, head for LuLu's.

Mixx (☎ 329-7334; King Kamehameha Mall, 75-5626 Kuakini Hwy; pupu $6-15; ⏰ noon-late) Mixx attracts an older crowd in the late afternoon and evening for wine by the glass and tapas-style *pupu* plates. As the evening goes on, the crowd becomes younger, especially if there's a DJ spinning or it's salsa night.

Huggo's on the Rocks (☎ 329-1493; 75-5828 Kahakai Rd; ⏰ 11:30am-11pm Sun-Thu, to midnight Fri & Sat) Take in a view of the bay from beneath the bar's thatched roof or at a table with your feet in the sand. The open-air setting is ideal for sunset, and the mai tais and *pupu* are renowned. There's live music nightly.

ENTERTAINMENT
Luau

It's hard to differentiate between Kailua-Kona's two colorful, albeit hokey, luau: both include a ceremony, a buffet dinner with Hawaiian specialties, an open bar and a Polynesian dinner show featuring a cast of flamboyant dancers, musicians and fire performers. Ask to watch staff bury the pig in the *imu* (underground oven) the morning of the luau.

Journeys of the South Pacific (☎ 329-3111; www .konaluau.com; Royal Kona Resort; adult/child 6-11 $72/27; ⏰ 6pm Mon, Wed & Fri)

King Kamehameha's Kona Beach Hotel (☎ 329-4969; www.islandbreezeluau.com; adult/child 5-12 $65/29; ⏱ 5pm Tue-Fri & Sun)

Cinemas

Either catch a Hollywood flick on one of the 10 screens at **Stadium Cinema** (☎ 327-0444; Makalapua Shopping Center; 74-5475 Kamaka'eha Ave) or rent one from **Blockbuster** (☎ 326-7694; Kona Coast Shopping Center, 74-5588 Palani Rd; ⏱ 10am-10pm, to midnight Fri & Sat), which requires ID and a credit card to set up an account.

SHOPPING

Downtown Kailua is jammed with small, mostly tourist-tacky, shops selling souvenirs, aloha shirts, surf gear, island crafts and beach accessories. Quality is hard to find.

Kona International Market (☎ 329-6262; 74-5533 Luhia St; ⏱ 9am-5pm Tue-Sun) This awesome new complex is made up of five large warehouse buildings filled with individual stalls selling everything imaginable, including gifts, beach gear, boutique-quality clothing, produce and flowers. There's a food court as well as ample parking.

Ali'i Gardens (☎ 334-1381; 75-6129 Ali'i Dr; ⏱ 9am-5pm Wed-Sun) This pretty outdoor gift and souvenir market has a mix of imports and locally made crafts.

Made on the Big Island Outlet (☎ 326-4949; King Kamehameha's Kona Beach Hotel; ⏱ 10am-6pm) This store stocks a wide selection of top-notch island crafts, edibles, clothing and oddities, including take-home potted bonsai.

Crazy Shirts (☎ 329-2176; Kona Marketplace, 75-5719 Ali'i Dr; ⏱ 9am-9pm) The iconic T-shirt company, founded in 1964, offers unique island designs on heavyweight cotton. A Kilauea motif is dyed using volcanic ash, and the Kona Brewing Company line is dyed using…beer!

TOP PLACES FOR TRADITIONAL CRAFTS

- Holualoa (p216)
- Hilo Farmers Market (p273)
- Hawi (p244)
- Kona International Market (above)
- Kainaliu (p218)
- Honokaa Marketplace (p261)
- Dan De Luz's Woods (p282)

Ross (☎ 329-8772; Kona Coast Shopping Center, 74-5588 Palani Rd; ⏱ 10am-6pm Mon-Thu, 9:30am-9:30pm Fri & Sat, 9:30am-6pm Sun) If you find your rental lacking bedding or kitchen utensils, or you forgot your bathing suit, head for this discount store.

GETTING THERE & AWAY
Air

The island's primary airport is **Kona International Airport at Keahole** (KOA; ☎ 329-3423; www.hawaii.gov/dot/airports/hawaii/koa; Hwy 19), located 7 miles north of Kailua-Kona. When booking flights keep in mind that late-afternoon weekday traffic is brutal on southbound Hwy 19.

Bus

The free Hele-On Bus (see p199) runs from Kailua-Kona to Captain Cook (four daily on weekdays, one hour 20 minutes) from 9:15am to 4:15pm. It runs to Pahala (two hours) and South Kohala (one hour 25 minutes) once daily. It runs to Hilo (3½ hours) once daily from Monday to Saturday, and to Oceanview Estates (one hour) once daily on Tuesday and Saturday. It runs to Kapa'au (2½ to four hours) once daily on Tuesday, Thursday and Saturday.

Car

The trip from Hilo to Kailua-Kona is 92 miles and takes 2½ hours; for other driving times and distances, see p200.

GETTING AROUND
To/From the Airport

If you're not picking up a rental car, taxis can be found curbside; the fare averages $25 to Kailua-Kona and $45 to Waikoloa. **Speedi Shuttle** (☎ 329-5433, 877-242-5777; www.speedishuttle.com) charges about the same, and only charges a couple of dollars for each additional person. Book in advance.

Bicycle

Bicycle is an ideal way to get around Kailua. **Hawaiian Pedals** (☎ 329-2294; www.hawaiianpedals.com; Kona Inn Shopping Village, 75-5744 Ali'i Dr; per day $20; ⏱ 9am-9pm) rents mountain and hybrid bikes. Affiliated **HP Bike Works** (☎ 326-2453; www.hpbikeworks.com; 74-5599 Luhia St; per day $35-50; ⏱ 9am-6pm Mon-Sat) rents higher-end bikes. Rentals include helmet, lock, pump and patch kit.

Car

Ali'i Dr in downtown Kailua-Kona gets very congested in the late afternoon and evening. Free public parking is available in a lot between

Likana Lane and Kuakini Hwy. Shopping centers along Ali'i Dr usually provide free parking for patrons behind their center.

The highways running past Kailua experience horrific commuter gridlock. Avoid southbound Hwy 19 and Hwy 190 between 4pm and 6pm, and northbound Hwy 11 between 6am and 8am. Radar speed traps are common on Hwy 19 between Kailua and the airport.

Bus

The free Hele-On Bus (see opposite) and the Keauhou Resort's shuttle (see p215) both make stops within Kailua-Kona.

Taxi

Call ahead for pickup.
Aloha Taxi (☎ 329-7779; ☽ 5am-10pm)
D&E Taxi (☎ 329-4279; ☽ 6am-9pm)

AROUND KAILUA-KONA

At its southern end Kailua-Kona flows right into Keauhou, without a discernible divide. In the cool mountains above sits the artist community of Holualoa.

Keauhou Resort Area

Keauhou is an upscale resort area with a well-groomed feel and a beautiful coastline. Once the site of a major Hawaiian settlement, the area is now home to a large shopping center, 36 holes of golf, two large hotels and a handful of condo complexes. You'll likely make it this way to snorkel or for a departure from Keauhou Harbor, though Keauhou's restaurants do deserve a visit.

INFORMATION

The following are in the **Keauhou Shopping Center** (Map p217; ☎ 322-3000; www.keauhou-resort .com/shopping.asp; cnr Ali'i Dr & Kamehameha III Rd):
Bank of Hawaii (☎ 322-3380; ☽ 9am-6pm Mon-Fri, 9am-2pm Sat & Sun) Has a 24-hour ATM.
Keoki's Surfin' Ass Café (☎ 322-9792; per hr $8; ☽ 6:30am-8pm Mon-Fri, 6:30am-6:30pm Sat & Sun) Offers internet access and sends and receives faxes.
Longs Drugs (☎ 322-5122; ☽ 8am-9pm Mon-Sat, to 6pm Sun) A drugstore with a pharmacy.
Post office (☎ 329-8307; ☽ 9am-4pm Mon-Fri, 10am-3pm Sat)

SIGHTS & ACTIVITIES
St Peter's Church

The 'Little Blue Church' is one of Hawai'i's most-photographed, and a favorite choice for weddings. Made of clapboard with a corrugated-tin roof, it sits almost in Kahalu'u Bay.

Built in the 1880s, St Peter's was moved from White Sands Beach to this site in 1912. It now sits on an ancient Hawaiian religious site, Ku'emanu Heiau. Hawaiian royalty, who surfed Kahalu'u Bay, paid their respects at this temple before hitting the waves.

Kahalu'u Beach Park

The island's best easy-access snorkeling spot, **Kahalu'u Bay** is a giant natural aquarium loaded with colorful marine life. Rainbow parrotfish, silver needlefish, brilliant yellow tangs, Moorish idol and butterfly fish are among the numerous tropical fish often seen here. Don't touch the coral while snorkeling. At high tide, green sea turtles often swim into the bay to feed or rest on the beach. Give these endangered animals their space.

An ancient breakwater, which according to legend was built by the *menehune* (Hawai'i's mythical race of little people), is on the reef and protects the bay. This **surf spot** is popular with locals and usually packed. It's normally a long-board wave, but when the surf is high Kahalu'u can harbor strong rip currents that pull northward into the rocks. If you're a novice, talk to a lifeguard about the day's conditions before paddling out.

The beach park is hardly a peaceful spot, with traffic zooming by, a packed parking lot and throngs of tourists. Visit in the first or last hours of daylight to beat the crowds. The tiny beach, whose salt-and-pepper sands are composed of black lava and white coral, has a huge banyan tree kids love. Facilities include showers, rest rooms, picnic tables and grills. A lifeguard is on duty.

Historical Sites & Tide Pools

Tie in a visit to Kahalu'u Bay with a visit to the historical sites and tide pools on the grounds of the Outrigger Keauhou Beach Resort (see p214). The sites are along easy paths – ask at the front desk for a site map.

At the north end are the ruins of **Kapuanoni**, a fishing heiau, and the reconstructed **summer beach house of King Kalakaua** next to a spring-fed pond that served as a royal bath. To the south are other heiau sites, including the remains of the **Ke'eku Heiau**, a probable *luakini* (temple of human sacrifice).

A *pahoehoe* (smooth lava) rock shelf in front of the Outrigger contains scads of **tide**

pools. Here you'll see sea urchins, small tropical fish and, at high tide, green sea turtles.

Just south of the Outrigger is the now-defunct Kona Lagoon Hotel. At very low tide **petroglyphs** are revealed on a flat lava tongue in front of the northern side of the closed hotel, with most of them about 25ft from the shore.

Original Hawaiian Chocolate Factory

A tiny **chocolate factory** (☎ 322-2626; www.original hawaiianchocolatefactory.com; 78-6772 Makenawai St; ☽ by appointment) on the slopes of Mt Hualalai, Bob and Pam Cooper's mom-and-pop company is unique in that they grow, harvest, process and package only Big Island cocoa. On a free tour of their operation you'll see cocoa fruit in lovely shades of yellow, gold and fuchsia, and learn about how they process their estate chocolate.

Keauhou Bay

This bay, which has a launch ramp and a small boat harbor, is one of the most protected on the west coast. On it, a small grassy area has a couple palm-shaded picnic tables, showers and rest rooms. Two sand volleyball courts stand between the headquarters of the local outrigger canoe club and the lapping bay.

Against the hillside, just south of the dive shacks, a plaque marks the site where Kamehameha III was born in 1814. The young prince was said to have been stillborn and brought back to life by a visiting kahuna (priest).

To get to the bay, turn *makai* (seaward) off Ali'i Dr onto Kamehameha III Rd. See p205 for information about excursions out of this harbor.

Hula Rehearsals & Classes

The Halau Kala'akeakauikawekiu hula group holds public rehearsals on the grounds of the **Sheraton Keauhou Bay Resort** (78-128 Ehukai St; ☽ 2:30-5pm & 5:30-6:30pm Wed, 8am-1pm Sat). Technically only guests are invited to watch, but perhaps you were 'just on your way to the restaurant.'

On Monday at 5pm on the grounds of the Outrigger Keauhou Beach Resort, magical local instructor Kumu Keala Ching teaches super-traditional hula and chanting classes. Watch respectfully or join in.

Aloha Fridays

On Friday the Keauhou Shopping Center offers ukulele lessons (advanced at 10am, beginner at 11am), a lei-making class (at noon) and a Polynesian dance show (at 6pm). All are free, though ukulele are not provided.

FESTIVALS & EVENTS

The **Kona Chocolate Festival** (☎ 937-7596; www.kona chocolatefestival.com; Outrigger Keauhou Beach Resort; gala $35; ☽ 4th Sat in Mar) is a weekend-long event including workshops, lectures, farm tours (ranging from free to $30 per person), culminating in a gala evening featuring the chocolate creations of local chefs, and candy and ice-cream makers. Proceeds benefit the local Waldorf School.

SLEEPING

Outrigger Keauhou Beach Resort (☎ 322-3441, reservations 800-688-7444; www.outrigger.com; 78-6740 Ali'i Dr; r $239-279; P ☒ ☒) Resort seems a big word for this low-key, oceanfront hotel, though it does have a pool and six tennis courts and it couldn't be closer to Kahalu'u Beach. As it's built perpendicular to the shoreline, ocean views vary from full to partial; north-facing rooms have a good view regardless. Rooms have lanai and are in fine shape; their decor is hotel standard. The ground floor of the hotel is on the plain side and delightfully free of outside walls, allowing the ocean breeze to flow right through. Grounds are leafy and include tide pools and historical sites. Parking is $5 per day.

Condominiums

For property-management agencies, see p207.

Keauhou Resort Condominiums (☎ 800-367-5286; 78-7039 Kamehameha III Rd; 1-bedroom units $85-125; ☒ ☒) This well-maintained complex surrounds the Kona Country Club golf course and is extremely convenient to the shopping center and highway. A two-bedroom unit for up to four people is only an additional $25 per day.

Outrigger Kanaloa at Kona (☎ 322-9625, reservations 800-959-5662; www.outrigger.com; 78-261 Manukai St; 1-bedroom units $279-349, 2-bedroom units $299-479; ☐ ☒ ☒) These tropical townhouse-style condominiums have exposed-beam ceilings and sit on an oceanfront lava ledge. A daily maid service is included.

EATING

Habaneros (☎ 324-4688; Keauhou Shopping Center; à la carte $3-7, plates $7.50-9; ☽ 9am-9pm Mon-Sat) Habaneros unites a diverse crowd, its only commonality the search for a decent taqueria. Retirees, the after-beach crowd and Latin American coffee pickers (the latter being the true indicator that this place is 'numbah one') savor burritos, tacos and plates of fajitas elbow-to-elbow at two long counters. Cash only.

Peaberry & Galette (☎ 322-6020; Keaubou Shopping Center; crepes $7.50-12.50; ☺ 9:30am-8pm Mon-Thu, to 10pm Fri & Sat, to 6pm Sun) Let the modern ambient tunes and the espresso machine dose you up on uberhipness at this too-cool-for-school creperie. The salade niçoise and quiche do not disappoint, though the disposable cups and utensils do. The sweet or savory crepes are beautifully presented if a little under-filled. Italian, not local, coffee is served.

Kama'aina Terrace (☎ 322-3441; Outrigger Keauhou Beach Resort; buffet adult/child 6-12 $35/17.50; ☺ 6:30-10:30am & 5:30-9pm) Oceanfront and breezy, the Outrigger holds several inviting dining events in addition to its regular menu. A seafood and prime-rib buffet including traditional Hawaiian dishes and sushi is held every Friday from 5:30 to 9pm. On Sunday there's a lavish brunch buffet ($28.95) from 9:30am to 12:30pm. The Sunset Specials include salad, a main course, sorbet and coffee or tea ($24.95, available from 5:30pm to 6:30pm Sunday to Thursday).

Kenichi (☎ 322-6400; Keauhou Shopping Center; sushi $7-15, mains $20-30; ☺ 11:30am-1:30pm Tue-Fri & 5pm-last client daily) Many attempt Pacific fusion; Kenichi does it right. The likes of cranberry miso sauce, balsamic reduction and curry with mint-scented yogurt sauce fill a menu of fresh, quality seafood and meat. The portions are small yet memorable. Sushi and *pupu* could be combined for a less spendy meal. It's a shame the environment doesn't match the standard of the food, with an extremely plain dining room and an unadulterated outdoor area the only options.

For groceries and deli takeout, head for **KTA Super Store** (☎ 322-2311; Keauhou Shopping Center; ☺ 7am-10pm) or **Kona Natural Foods** (☎ 322-1800; Keauhou Shopping Center; ☺ 9am-7pm Mon-Sat, 10am-5pm Sun, deli 9am-4:30pm Mon-Sat). Keauhou's **farmers market** (Keauhou Shopping Center; ☺ 8am-noon Sat) is the Leeward Coast's best.

DRINKING & ENTERTAINMENT

Verandah Lounge (☎ 322-3441; Outrigger Keauhou Beach Resort; ☺ 4-10:30pm) The waves crashing against a lava ledge in front of this wraparound bar make for an awesome drinking experience.

Live Hawaiian music sets the tone from 6pm to 9pm daily.

Kamaha'o (☎ 930-4828; www.kaikehawaii.com; Sheraton Keauhou Bay Resort, 78-128 Ehukai St; adult/child 6-15 $79/40; ☺ Mon, Wed & Fri) Focusing on Hawaiian myths and legends, the Sheraton's luau also includes contemporary performing arts, dinner and an open bar.

Keauhou Cinema (☎ 324-0172; Keauhou Shopping Center) Hollywood flicks fill seven screens at this theater with stadium seating.

GETTING AROUND

A free **shuttle** (☎ 322-0088) runs a route between the Sheraton Keauhou Bay Resort and the Outrigger Keauhou Beach Resort, between 8am and 8pm. It makes four daily trips into downtown Kailua-Kona. Anyone can ride; for a schedule see the front desk of any Keauhou hotel or www.konagolf.com/konagolf/shuttle.cfm.

Holualoa
pop 6100

Holualoa has an enviable location on the cool, lush slopes of Mt Hualalai, some 1400ft above Kailua-Kona. But fine views of Kailua Bay's sparkling turquoise waters are not the primary reason to come to this tiny, historical coffee village. Local artists are the focus here, and their works range from indigenous Hawaiian crafts to sophisticated fine art. So take a stroll along the highway, duck in and out of shops and galleries, and talk story with locals and prominent creators. Most businesses close on Sunday and Monday.

SIGHTS & ACTIVITIES
Donkey Mill Art Center

Rustic and unpretentious, the Holualoa Foundation for Arts & Culture's **art center** (☎ 322-3362; www.donkeymillartcenter.org; 78-6670 Hwy 180; admission free; ☺ 10am-4pm Tue-Sat) displays impressive collections and offers workshops taught by recognized artists in a variety of mediums. The center's building, built in 1953, was once a coffee mill with a donkey painted on its roof, hence the name. It's 3 miles south of the village center.

Coffee Farm Tours

Several of Holualoa's coffee farms offer free tours where you'll learn about the meticulous handpicking, sun-drying and careful roasting of their renowned Kona coffee. Tours end with steaming samples of their product.

Kona Blue Sky Coffee (☎ 877-322-1700; www.kona blueskycoffee.com; 76-973A Hualalai Rd; ☺ 9am-3:30pm Mon-Sat) is grown on the 400-acre Twigg-Smith Estate. Tours include a short video. The Kona Le'a Plantation is home to **Holualoa Kona Coffee Company** (☎ 877-322-9937, 800-334-0348; www.kona lea.com; 77-6261 Hwy 180; ☺ 8am-4pm Mon-Fri) coffee without the use of pesticides or herbicides on its beautiful farm.

Malama I'ka Ola Holistic Health Center

This **health center** (☎ 324-6644; 76-5914 Hwy 180) offers yoga classes and massage, in addition to alternative skin and healthcare treatments.

SLEEPING & EATING

Kona Hotel (☎ 324-1155; Hwy 180; s/d with shared bathroom $30/35-40) To stay at this historic wooden boarding house constructed in 1926 is to step into the developing world. Rooms are basically fine and can have amazing views, but the fairly clean communal bathrooms have been neglected for decades. Rooms cannot be locked (but do latch from the inside), likely the reason the Inaba family likes to get a look at you before confirming availability. Don't bother calling.

Holualoa Inn (☎ 324-1121, 800-392-1812; www.holua loainn.com; 76-5932 Hwy 180; incl breakfast r $260-290, ste $285-310; ☒) This classy, six-room inn on 30 acres in the heart of Holualoa is easily the nicest place to stay in the greater Kailua-Kona area. The ability to pop out and pick something up from the corner store is not compromised by isolation and spectacular views of Kailua Bay. Warm wood paneling, imported Asian furniture and tasteful original artwork are found throughout the attractive, western red cedar building. Enjoy a glass of wine and the sunset in the living room with its fireplace and red eucalyptus floors, or take a refreshing dip in the beautiful pool with a shell mosaic. The luxuriously soft sheets and fluffy down comforters promise a good night's sleep in the thematically decorated rooms. Children under 13 are not encouraged. One-night stays are an additional $45.

Holualoa Café (☎ 322-2233; Hwy 180; ☺ 6:30am-3pm Mon-Sat) Holualoa's only eatery has a limited selection of drinks, sandwiches and salads, but it does have espresso!

SHOPPING

Ipu Hale Gallery (☎ 322-9096; Hwy 180; ☺ 10am-4pm Tue-Sat) Next to the Holualoa Café, this gallery sells *ipu* (gourds) decoratively carved with gorgeous Hawaiian imagery in an ancient method unique to the Hawaiian island of Ni'ihau. Lost after the introduction of Western crockery, the art form was revived by a Big Island scholar just 15 years ago.

Holualoa Ukulele Gallery (☎ 324-4100; Hwy 180; ☺ 10:30am-4:30pm Tue-Sat) In the historic Holualoa post-office building, Sam Rosen sells ukulele handcrafted by himself as well as other craftsmen at prices only serious buyers would consider. Signed portraits of local ukulele legends Jake Shimabukuro and 'Ohta-san' give the gallery a professional seal of approval.

Kimura Lauhala Shop (☎ 324-0053; cnr Hualalai Rd & Hwy 180; ☺ 9am-5pm Mon-Fri, to 4pm Sat) Three generations of Kimuras weave quality *lauhala* (pandana plant) products here, as they have since the 1930s. Originally, they purchased *lauhala* products from Hawaiian weavers and sold them at the family's general store. When demand increased they took on the production themselves, assisted by local farming wives, who do piecework at home outside of coffee season. Don't fall prey to cheap imports – the *lauhala* hats, placemats, baskets, bags and floor mats sold here are the real deal.

GETTING THERE & AWAY

From Kailua-Kona, turn *mauka* (inland) on Hualalai Rd off Hwy 11, and wind 3 miles (including hairpin turns) up to Hwy 180; turn left for most sights. If coming from North Kona, Hina Lani St and Palani St are straighter shots to Hwy 180 than Hualalai Rd, though a little indirect. From South Kona, head up Hwy 180 immediately north of Honalo.

SOUTH KONA COAST

Lush and balmy, with stunning ocean views, South Kona is the Hawai'i of people's fantasies, and perhaps the most beautiful section of the Leeward Coast. After leaving Kailua-Kona, Hwy 11 climbs swiftly, passing through a series of tiny upland towns with elevations hovering around 1500ft. Each town sits on a steep mountainside covered with thick, verdant foliage peppered with wild plumeria, banana, lychee and papaya trees, and towering palms.

This is the acclaimed Kona Coffee Belt (see the boxed text, p219), consisting of 22 miles filled with coffee farms and plenty of coffee-tasting rooms. Frequent afternoon showers

SOUTH KONA COAST

0 — 4 km
0 — 2 miles

SIGHTS & ACTIVITIES
Adventures in Paradise.........4 B3
Aloha Kayak Company...........5 B2
Amy BH Greenwell
  Ethnobotanical Garden........6 B3
Big Island Yoga Center.........7 B2
Captain Cook Monument........8 B3
Daifukuji Soto Mission..........9 B2
Greenwell Farms................10 B2
Greenwell General Store
  Museum.......................11 B2
Higashihara Park...............12 B1
Hiki'au Heiau..................13 B3
Ka'awaloa Cove................14 B3
Kings' Trail Rides.............15 B3
Kona Boys.....................16 B2
Kona Coast Macadamia Nut &
  Candy Factory...............17 C4
Kona Coffee Living History
  Farm........................18 B3
Long Lava Tube...............19 A2
St Benedict's Painted Church..20 C4
Two-Step......................21 B4

SLEEPING
Aloha Guest House.............22 C4
Luana Inn....................23 B3
Manago Hotel.................24 B3
Pineapple Park...............25 B3

EATING
Adriana's....................26 B3
Aloha Angel Café.............27 B2
Bong Brothers................28 C4
Choicemart..................(see 26)
Coffee Shack.................29 C3
Coffees 'n' Epicurea.........30 C3
Evie's Natural Foods.........31 B2
Ke'ei Café...................32 B2
Kona Seafood.................33 C3
Manago Hotel................(see 24)
Nasturtium Café & Bakery....34 B2
South Kona Fruit Stand......35 C4
Super J's....................36 C4
Teshima Restaurant..........37 B2

ENTERTAINMENT
Aloha Theatre................(see 27)

SHOPPING
Art Farm....................38 B3
Discovery Antiques...........39 B2
Island Books.................40 B2
Kealakekua Ranch Center.....(see 26)
Keauhou Shopping Center.....41 A1
Oshima Store.................42 B2

INFORMATION
Bank of Hawaii...............(see 41)
Keoki's Surfin' Ass Café.....(see 41)
Kona Community Hospital......1 B2
Longs Drugs.................(see 41)
Orchid Isle Café.............2 B2
Post Office...................3 B2
Post Office..................(see 41)

Kahalu'u Bay
Kahalu'u Beach Park
He'eia Bay
Keauhou Bay
To Holualoa (2mi)
To Kailua-Kona (4mi)
Keauhou
Honalo
Kainaliu
Halekii St
Kealakekua
Onouli St
Captain Cook
Captain Cook Monument Trail
Kealakekua Bay State Historical Park
Manini Beach
Kealakekua Bay
Ke'ei Bay
PACIFIC OCEAN
Napo'opo'o Rd
Pu'uhonua Rd
Middle Ke'ei Rd
St Benedict's Painted Church Rd
Mamalahoa Hwy
Honaunau
Keone'ele Cove
Pu'uhonua O Honaunau National Historical Park (Place of Refuge)
Keokea
To Ho'okena (5mi); Miloli'i (20mi); Ka Lae (50mi)

lower temperatures, and keep coffee and macadamia-nut crops happy.

Here the pace is slow and the vibe laid-back, with pockets of old Hawaii that seem frozen in time. Though its beaches are few, South Kona boasts some of the island's best snorkeling, diving and kayaking spots. Few public roads connect Hwy 11 to the coast, so ocean access is limited to one road each in Captain Cook, Honaunau, Ho'okena and Miloli'i.

HONALO
pop 2000
At a bend in the road, and the intersection of Hwys 11 and 180, sits little Honalo. The Buddhist temple **Daifukuji Soto Mission** is the most interesting structure in the tiny stretch.

The exterior is nothing special, but kick off your shoes and duck inside to check out its two ornate altars. Keep an ear out for the *taiko* (Japanese drum) group while perusing old photos of the congregation. North of town is **Higashihara Park** (7am-8pm). Its mac-daddy wooden play structure, cement whale, and playing field should keep kiddies entertained for hours. It's on the *makai* side, just south of the 114-mile marker.

It's hard to miss **Teshima Restaurant** (322-9140; Hwy 11; mains $9-12; 6:30am-1:45pm & 5-9pm) – the most prominent building in town – and you shouldn't. Teshima has been serving up delicious Japanese food since the 1940s and is an institution on the Kona coast. Four generations of Teshimas still work in this low-key, family restaurant; you're likely to see 'Grandma' (in her 90s) clearing tables. A good sampler is the *teishoku* (set meal) of miso soup, sashimi, fried fish, sukiyaki, *tsukemono* (pickled vegetables) and rice. No credit cards accepted.

KAINALIU

Finally, a stretch of Hwy 11 invites you to park your car and walk around. Shops and eateries sit in a tightly packed little row, and Kainaliu has successfully overcome the regional disregard for sidewalks. The focal point of town, and it could be argued South Kona, is the **Aloha Theatre** (☎ 322-2323; www.alohatheatre.com). Community theater, dance performances and touring musical acts all take the stage here. Check the bulletin board for current happenings, which could include indie film screenings and festivals.

Funky imports shops, a few fine galleries of authentic local art and dusty, timeless, old-style stores will catch the shopper's eye. Locals joke that there is nothing you can't find at **Oshima** (☎ 322-3844; Hwy 11; ⏰ 7:30am-7:45pm Mon-Sat, 7:30am-6:45pm Sun), making it a good family-run alternative to the big box stores in Kailua-Kona. It stocks everything from groceries and pharmaceuticals to snorkel gear and surf wear. **Island Books** (☎ 322-2006; Hwy 11) is the best used bookstore for miles, with a good Hawaiiana section and an extremely knowledgeable owner. Move fast or get caught in his enjoyable chatter.

Evie's Natural Foods (☎ 322-0739; Mango Center, Hwy 11; snacks $3-13; ⏰ 9am-9pm Mon-Fri, to 5pm Sat & Sun) stocks health-food staples and some organic produce. Its café (open 9am to 6:45pm) doesn't get rave reviews (especially for service), but health-conscious types will likely enjoy the basic breakfasts, smoothies, sandwiches, salads and hot dishes.

Adjoining the theater, **Aloha Angel Café** (☎ 322-3383; Hwy 11; breakfast & lunch $6-13, dinner $15-23; ⏰ 7:30am-8pm, to 2:30pm Tue & Wed) offers a more traditional restaurant experience. Sit in the bright dining room among potted plants and whirling ceiling fans or enjoy a distant ocean view from the narrow back terrace. The extensive menu may wow you more than the food itself, but the array of tasty burgers, wraps, curries, and veggie and meat plates should satisfy all.

KEALAKEKUA
pop 1700

A few stoplights and a chain fast-food restaurant will alert you that Kealakekua is the commercial center of Kona's upland towns. What you can see strung over a long stretch of Hwy 11 isn't anything special, but on each side lies a tropical jungle growing wild. Kealakekua makes a convenient base to both explore South Kona and enjoy Kailua-Kona's activities. Its name means 'Path of the Gods,' to recognize a chain of 40 heiau that once ran from Kealakekua Bay all the way to Kailua-Kona.

Information

A **post office** (☎ 322-1656; cnr Hwy 11 & Haleki'i Rd), four banks with ATMs, and the primary hospital serving the leeward side, **Kona Community Hospital** (☎ 322-9311; www.kch.hhsc.org; 79-1019 Haukapila St) are in close proximity. The **Orchid Isle Café** (☎ 323-2700; 81-6637 Hwy 11; per hr $8; ⏰ 6am-4pm Mon-Fri, 7am-2pm Sat & Sun) offers internet access.

Sights
KONA COFFEE LIVING HISTORY FARM

To get a seriously accurate feel for rural Japanese-immigrant life in the early 20th century, visit the Kona Historical Society's 7-acre, working **coffee farm** (☎ 323-2006; www.konahistorical.org; adult/child $15/7.50; ⏰ tours on the hour 9am-2pm Mon-Fri). A former resident of the farm is also a society member, and she's stocked the docents up with all sorts of juicy details about farm life. You'll get a look at the Uchida family's former orchards, house, processing mill, drying roofs and traditional Japanese bathhouse. Don't sweat the ticket price – it's worth it. Cruise ship and school groups often dominate certain time slots, so call ahead.

GREENWELL GENERAL STORE MUSEUM

The **Kona Historical Society** (☎ 323-3222; www.konahistorical.org) has turned the old stone-and-mortar Greenwell General Store into a **museum** (admission $4; ⏰ 9am-3:30pm Mon-Sat) version of what it was in 1890. They've meticulously filled it with authentic period goods such as farm equipment and cans. It's between the 110- and 111-mile markers, immediately south of Greenwell Farms. The society's headquarters are behind it.

GREENWELL FARMS

This, one of Kona's longest-standing coffee farms, is run by the fourth generation of the Greenwell family. Established in 1850, their beautiful 35-acre **farm** (☎ 888-592-5662; www.greenwellfarms.com; Hwy 11; ⏰ 8am-5pm Mon-Sat, tours until 4pm) quickly became known worldwide as a large-scale producer of quality Kona coffee. Henry

KONA COFFEE

On the slopes of Hualalai and Mauna Loa sit roughly 650 coffee farms on a strip of land just 2 miles wide and 22 miles long. Most farms are modest 3-acre independent farms. From this stunningly gorgeous yet unassuming region comes the world-renowned Kona coffee.

Missionaries introduced the coffee tree to Hawaii in 1828. By the turn of the century, coffee was an important cash crop throughout the state. However the instability of coffee prices eventually drove island farmers out of business – except on the Big Island, where Kona coffee was extraordinary enough to sell at a profit during gluts in world markets.

Why is Kona coffee so special? First, *Coffea arabica* flourishes in a climate with sunny mornings and rainy afternoons, which is typical in Kona at elevations between 500ft and 2800ft. Second, coffee thrives in rich volcanic soil and mild, frost-free temperatures. Third, only a select variety of *arabica* called 'Kona Typica' (and never the inferior *robusta*) qualifies to produce the superior beans. Finally, Kona farmers use meticulous methods to cultivate their crops, with all planting and picking done by hand.

The fruit of the coffee plant starts as green berries, turning yellow, orange and then deep red (called 'cherry') when ripe. The cherries don't ripen all at once, so they must be picked several times from August to late January. It takes 8lb of cherry (about 4000 beans) to produce 1lb of roasted coffee.

Don't be fooled by cheap coffee labeled 'Kona Coffee' in giant lettering, followed by the miniscule word 'blend' – which means it is probably only 10% Kona coffee. Quality depends not only on the label but also on factors such as roasting, grade of the beans, and whether the beans are 'estate' (all from one farm) or a blend of Kona beans from different farms. You might also care about whether beans are organically grown or not. Genuine Kona coffee can be found in several ways:

- Look for the **Kona Coffee Council** (www.kona-coffee-council.com) seal of approval on the bag.
- Check for a 'purge valve' on the bag (another sign it's the real deal), which allows air and heat to escape from freshly roasted beans. The bag should be well inflated.
- The price should be around $20 per pound.

There are over 100 private labels for 100% Kona coffee. From Holualoa to Honaunau, tiny 'backyard' growers abound, and just about every business sells beans on the side. The pioneering coffee farmers of the early 1900s were mostly entrepreneurial Japanese families who wanted to escape the yoke of sugarcane-plantation life by leasing the coffee lands then being abandoned. They kept the industry alive, but as subsequent generations left farming, those original family farms have mostly died out.

In recent years there has been an explosion of 'gentleman farms' run by mainland transplants. Coffee estates, it seems, have developed a cachet similar to that of Napa Valley vineyards. This might be good news for the Big Island: while Kona coffee production had dropped to a low point by 1980, the gourmet-coffee craze during the past two decades has spurred sales of the highly aromatic Kona beans.

Most small coffee farms would be happy to show you around and talk to you about their process, with the hope that you'll become a dedicated client. For contact information, go to www.konacoffeefarms.org. For a list of farms that accept guest workers to live onsite for as little as one week, see www.hofa.org.

Greenwell achieved this fame by trading dry goods from his general store for other farmers' coffee cherry, which he blended with his own. If you come late in the afternoon during harvest season, a long line of farm trucks will tell you that that practice continues today. Take a free tour, sample around 10 types of coffee or enjoy the freebie fruit at a shady picnic table. The farm is between the 110- and 111-mile markers.

AMY BH GREENWELL ETHNOBOTANICAL GARDEN

For a look at the Hawaiian landscape before it came under Western influence, take the time to wander through this small **ethnobotanical garden** (☎ 323-3318; www.bishopmuseum.org/green well/; suggested donation adult/child $4/free; ☯ 8:30am-5pm Mon-Fri, free guided tours 1pm Wed & Fri, 10am 2nd Sat of month). Wide, grassy stretches separate beds with three categories of plants: endemic (native and exclusive), indigenous (native but found elsewhere) and Polynesian (introduced by the islands' original settlers). Informative plaques explain which plants were used for dye, surfboards and so on, but take a tour to get the most out of your visit. The garden puts on workshops a few times monthly. Bring insect repellant. The garden is just south of the 110-mile marker.

Activities
MAMALAHOA HOT TUBS & MASSAGE
Soak away your worries in one of two jarrah wood tubs at **Mamalahoa Hot Tubs & Massage** (☎ 323-2288; www.mamalahoa-hottubs.com; ☯ by appointment noon-8pm Wed-Sat), set in a lush garden. The tubs, sheltered by thatched roofs that allow for stargazing, are simultaneously open yet private. Hawaiian hot stone and Lomi Lomi are among the massage styles offered. A half-hour tub and one-hour massage package costs $85.

BIG ISLAND YOGA CENTER
For Iyengar yoga, **Big Island Yoga Center** (☎ 329-9642; www.bigislandyoga.com; 81-6623 Hwy 11; drop-in class adult/senior $14/10) is the place. The studio occupies the 2nd floor of a beautiful old house, and is bright and stocked with mats and props.

Sleeping
Heading south from Kailua-Kona, Kealakekua is where South Kona's B&B plethora begins.

Pineapple Park (☎ 323-2224, 877-800-3800; www.pineapple-park.com; 81-6363 Hwy 11; dm $25, r with/without bathroom $85/65; ☯ office 7am-8pm; ▣) The only hostel on this side of the island, Pineapple Park is naturally a magnet for budget backpacker types. Private rooms are overly decorated but comfortable, and all guests have use of a lanai, a kitchen, laundry facilities and free wi-fi. Clean up before you show up or the grumpy owner might well turn you away. It's located between the 110- and 111-mile markers, with a line of colorful kayaks ($35/55 for singles/doubles) out front.

Banana Patch (☎ 322-8888, 800-988-2246; www.bananabanana.com; studios $99, 1-/2-bedroom cottages d $125/150) These secluded cottages sit in a garden so lush that you'd never think you were a few quick turns off the highway. Each is attractively decorated (well, maybe a bedspread or the fake flowers could go) with stained-glass lamps, plush carpets and updated fixtures. Cook your heart out in the fully-equipped kitchen, or lounge on a deck or stone lanai. The full privacy of each cottage allows for nudie tubbing and sunbathing if you're so inclined. Though they are well-ventilated, expect a little dampness due to the leafy setting. Rates are based on a one-week stay.

Areca Palms Estate B&B (☎ 800-545-4390, 323-2276; www.konabedandbreakfast.com; Hwy 11; r incl breakfast $110-145; ☯ office 9am-6pm; ▣) Enter the gate and you'll immediately perceive that this B&B has substance. A wide, neatly trimmed lawn surrounds the house shaded by – you guessed it – giant areca palms. The owners, from Oregon, prove you need not be local-born to epitomize the aloha spirit. Their immaculate house resembles an airy cedar lodge, with loads of natural wood, country-style furnishings and exposed-beam ceilings. Extras like a large common living room, an outdoor Jacuzzi and thick robes stashed in the closet add to your comfort. Their breakfasts get rave reviews, and the location is very convenient to the highway.

Eating
Kealakekua is low on casual eats but has two of the best restaurants in South Kona.

Nasturtium Café & Bakery (☎ 322-5083; Hwy 11; mains $11-16; ☯ 11am-4pm Tue-Fri, 10:30am-2:30pm Sat) Nasturtium takes nourishing its clients so seriously that a mission statement is posted at the entrance. Only hormone-free animal proteins and organic produce are used to create soups, salads, sandwiches and wraps with a gourmet touch. The fresh island fish quesadilla with chevre and pineapple salsa ($13.75) is divine, as is the organic gingered macadamia-nut tart ($6.50). Enjoy live flamenco or slack-key guitar (Wednesday through Saturday) on the outdoor patio or in the bright dining area in a converted barn building. It's between the 112- and 113-mile markers.

Ke'ei Café (☎ 322-9992; mains $11-19; ☯ 10:30am-2pm & 5-8:30pm Mon-Fri, 5-8:30pm Sat) Widely renowned as one of the best restaurants on the island, Ke'ei is the spot for quality and flavor in an unpretentious environment. Off the main tourist track, this family-friendly restaurant eclectically blends Asian flavors, island fruits and the occasional Brazilian approach. Seafood is the focus here, though veggie dishes and other meats round out the constantly changing menu. Wood floors, colorful artwork and gleaming wooden tables create warmth, while high ceilings and French doors, open to limited outdoor seating, allow air to circulate. Reservations are recommended for dinner. It's just south of the 113-mile marker.

THE FINAL DAYS OF CAPTAIN COOK

After first landing in what he called the 'Sandwich Islands' (see p34) Captain Cook's expedition continued its journey into the North Pacific. Failing to find the fabled passage through the Arctic, Cook sailed back to Hawaii, landing at Kealakekua Bay on January 17, 1779, one year after his first sighting of O'ahu, and once again at the time of the annual *makahiki* festival.

Cook's initial arrival at Waimea Bay (p536) on Kaua'i had coincided with the *makahiki*, a period when all heavy work and warfare was suspended in order to pay homage to Lono (the god of agriculture and peace) and to participate in games and festivities. To the Hawaiians, Cook appeared to be the *kinolau* (earthly form) of the great god and was thus revered. Dozens of canoes had ventured out to greet the tall ship, and when he was ushered to shore every effort was made to accommodate this god on earth.

Since the previous year, word of Captain Cook's arrival had spread to the other islands. His welcome at Kealakekua Bay was even more spectacular, with more than 1000 canoes in the water surrounding his ships and 9000 people on shore to greet him. Cook later wrote in his journal, 'I had nowhere in the course of my voyages seen so numerous a body of people assembled in one place,' quite unaware that he was seen as the second coming of Lono.

Once landed, Cook and his men were greeted by Chief Kalaniopu'u and feted in grand Hawaiian style, with a big luau accompanied by hula dancing, boxing demonstrations and an abundance of the local brew, *'awa*.

After two weeks of R and R, including sexual indulgences, Cook restocked his ships and departed Kealakekua Bay on February 4 and headed north once again. En route the ships ran into a storm off the northwest coast of the Big Island, where the *Resolution* broke a foremast. Uncertain of finding a safe harbor in the area, Cook returned to Kealakekua Bay on February 11.

Although Cook was welcomed back to the island, Kalaniopu'u was concerned about Cook's reappearance because it meant that he would again need to provide food, which had become nearly depleted from Cook's first stay. This time mutual respect and admiration turned to animosity as both parties strayed beyond the bounds of diplomacy and goodwill. Each side engaged in thievery and issued insults, and tensions escalated.

After a cutter (rowboat) was stolen, Cook ordered a blockade of Kealakekua Bay and went to shore to take Kalaniopu'u as a hostage until the boat was returned, a tactic that had worked well for him with other island groups. As a ruse, Cook invited Kalaniopu'u onto the *Resolution* to talk about the recent disputes. This plan sat well with the chief, whose culture dictated that disputes be settled by *ho'oponopono*, where everyone airs their grievances and does not leave until a mutual resolution is found.

En route to the shore with Cook, Kalaniopu'u received word that the Englishmen on the big ships had shot and killed a lower chief, who had been attempting to exit the bay in his canoe. Eyewitness accounts on the British and Hawaiian sides differ as to exactly what happened next, but reports generally agree that, after word of the chief's death at the hands of the sailors reached the Hawaiians, a brutal battle ensued along the shore, resulting in the deaths of five Englishmen, including Captain Cook, and 17 Hawaiians.

The death of Cook stunned both sides and ended the battle. The sailors wanted to leave, but the Hawaiians took Cook's body away and the British wanted to retrieve it. Over the next two weeks both sides negotiated the release of Cook's body, which had been dismembered in the fashion accorded high chiefs. Several ensuing skirmishes resulted in the death of about 50 Hawaiians. Some, but not all, of Cook's remains were returned to his ship, after which they were buried at sea according to naval tradition.

HAWAI'I (THE BIG ISLAND)

Shopping

Discovery Antiques (☎ 323-2239; Hwy 11; ☺ 10am-5pm Mon-Sat, 11am-4pm Sun) Packed with cases of Hawaiian antiques and curiosities, this shop is great for a unique find. Keep the kids distracted with locally made ice cream sold right in the store.

CAPTAIN COOK

pop 3200

Captain Cook has quite a bit to offer the traveler: a score of B&Bs, some tasty down-home food and the island's best bay for snorkeling and kayaking. Modest government offices mark the center of this unpretentious town, along with an abandoned theater building and the historical Manago Hotel. As Hwy 11 winds south, gaps between buildings grow large, and lush greenery lit by bright flowers dominates the landscape. The area offers commanding ocean views.

Sights

KEALAKEKUA BAY STATE HISTORICAL PARK

Kealakekua Bay is a wide, calm bay shouldered by a low lava point to the north, tall reddish *pali* (cliffs) in the center and miles of green mountain slopes to the south. The bay, which is both a state park and a marine-life conservation district, has a wide variety of life in its pristine waters, including spinner dolphins.

Napo'opo'o Rd, off Hwy 11, winds 4.5 miles down to the bay, past a coffee factory and tiny, honor-system **farm stands** selling fresh fruit and lei. The thick, lush foliage becomes drier and thinner as you descend from the rainier uplands. The bay often stays sunny even when it's raining up on the highway. The road ends at the parking lot for **Napo'opo'o Beach and Wharf**. The beach is merely a patch of sand, and is a poor swimming or snorkeling spot. Veer right at the base of Napo'opo'o Rd for **Hiki'au Heiau**, a large platform temple. Veer left for Manini Beach and Ke'ei Bay.

The northern end of the bay is called **Ka'awaloa Cove**, a decent diving and excellent snorkeling spot accessible only by sea. On it is the white obelisk of the **Captain Cook Monument**, which sits near the spot where Captain Cook was killed during a 1779 skirmish (see p221). In 1877, as an act of diplomacy, the Kingdom of Hawai'i gifted the 16 sq ft of land the monument stands on to Britain. The following year, Cook's countrymen erected the 27ft monument to honor his death. The ruins

of the ancient village of Ka'awaloa sit on the land behind the monument.

Pali Kapu o Keoua, the 'sacred cliffs of Keoua,' were named for a chief and rival of Kamehameha I. Numerous caves in the cliffs were the burial places of Hawaiian royalty, and it's speculated that some of Captain Cook's bones were placed here as well. The caves that are difficult to access probably still contain bones. Do not disturb these sacred sites.

The southern shoreline of Kealakekua Bay is rocky and exposed to regular northwest swells, so swimming and snorkeling conditions are poor. Surrounded by homes, **Manini Beach** is a small patch of sand with a few picnic tables. A break in the rough lava allows water access, but the swells can be daunting. Surfers head to the point just south of Manini Beach. The best entry is on the right.

Further south is **Ke'ei Bay**, good for surfing and paddling, not for swimming. To get there, take the rough dirt road past the turnoff for Manini Beach (if you reach Ke'ei Transfer Station, you've gone too far). At the bay, there's a beach, a small canoe launch and a few shacks, but no facilities – and residents who prefer not to be disturbed.

A narrow road continues another couple of miles south through scrub brush to Pu'uhonua o Honaunau National Historical Park (p226). Roadside grasses conceal trenches.

Activities

SNORKELING

Ka'awaloa Cove in Kealakekua Bay is among the island's (and Hawaii's!) premier snorkeling spots. The water is protected from ocean swells and is exceptionally clear. Sea stars and eels weave through coral gardens, and schools of colorful fish feed and hide. If you're lucky, sea turtles and spinner dolphins might cruise by – remember to keep your distance (see opposite).

Snorkeling is limited to a narrow section running the length of the shore. Immediately behind it an underwater cliff drops off 70ft to 100ft. The water confident can seek out an underwater lava arch toward the point. Don't touch bottom while snorkeling, as stepping on coral effectively kills it.

To get to Ka'awaloa Cove, either rent a kayak (see opposite) or take a snorkeling cruise (see p205). Morning is the best time to go, when the winds are calm and sunlight the most guaranteed.

THE DOLPHIN CONTROVERSY

Hand-painted signs posted at the top of Napo'opo'o Rd urge passersby to 'leave the dolphins in peace.' As it's the most frequented snorkeling spot on the island, the controversy surrounding perceived harassment of dolphins comes to a head at Kealakekua Bay. Dolphins are nocturnally active, and they enter bays like Kealakekua during the day to rest and procreate. In their desire to see them, snorkelers and New Age folks seeking 'dolphin healings' have been known to chase dolphins, which infuriates local animal-rights activists. Laws require that people remain a minimum of 50yd from large marine animals such as dolphins and turtles. These laws are obviously very difficult to enforce, but, since these species are protected, animal-rights activists pressure local, state and federal officials to live up to the letter of the law. Their preferred solution: restrict visitor access to the bay. Groups have been known to monitor snorkelers by binocular and report distance violations. For the animals' well-being, and the future of visitor access to this beautiful bay, maintain a healthy distance should you be lucky enough to see dolphins or turtles.

KAYAKING

The calm waters of Kealakekua Bay make for a great paddle, even for novices. Outfitters along Hwy 11 rent kayaks and snorkeling kits, as do a few free agents around the parking lot. A good outfitter will include in your rental paddles, life jackets, backrests, a dry bag, a soft cooler and a scratch-free way to strap the kayak to your car. It's forbidden to launch kayaks around the Hiki'au Heiau – the Napo'opo'o Wharf provides a comfortable launching point for independent kayakers.

The paddle to the cove takes 30 to 45 minutes. The cove can become a zoo when the snorkeling cruises arrive, so avoid mid-morning and mid-afternoon. The earlier you paddle out, the more likely you'll have calm winds and the bay to yourself. Following the 2006 earthquake the coastguard prohibited kayaks from being beached at Ka'awaloa Cove, meaning you'll likely have to pull it along with you while snorkeling.

It is illegal for guided kayak tours (but not individuals) to launch from the Napo'opo'o Wharf, but one outfitter listed below launches from private land and leads guided paddles on Kealakekua Bay. Kayak tours through other waters launch from the Kailua-Kona area (see p206).

Recommended outfitters:

Adventures in Paradise (☎ 323-3005, 866-824-2337; www.bigislandkayak.com; 81-6367 Hwy 11, Kealakekua; kayaks s/d $35/60; ⊗ 8am-sunset) Friendly, professional and remarkably thorough, this outfitter goes the extra mile in sharing firsthand familiarity with Big Island waters. Renters are shown a short video on technique and safety, which practically guarantees a successful voyage. At the intersection of Hwy 11 and Keopuka Rd.

Aloha Kayak Company (☎ 322-2868; www.aloha kayak.com; Hwy 11, Honalo; kayaks s/d/tr $35/60/70, half-day $25/45/55; ⊗ 8am-5pm) This popular, Hawaiian-owned outfit is the only one to offer half-day (from noon to dark) rates and glass-bottomed kayaks. Rentals include a leash to tether the kayak to you.

Kona Boys (☎ 328-1234; www.konaboys.com; 79-7539 Hwy 11, Kealakekua; kayaks s/d $47/67, tour incl lunch $159; ⊗ 7:30am-5pm) A laid-back yet professional outfit with a cool surfing vibe. Its guided paddle in Kealakekua Bay has a four-person minimum.

DIVING

Between the Napo'opo'o landing and the southern tip of Manini Beach, marine life abounds amid coral, caves, crevices and ledges in waters up to 30ft deep. But the bay's best diving spot is Ka'awaloa Cove, where depths range from about 5ft to 120ft – the diversity of coral and fish is exceptional.

The aptly named Long Lava Tube, just north of Kealakekua Bay, is an intermediate dive site. Lava 'skylights' allow light to penetrate through the ceiling, yet nocturnal species are often active during the day, and you may see crustaceans, morays and even Spanish dancers. Outside are countless lava formations sheltering critters such as conger eels, triton's trumpet shells and schooling squirrelfish.

HIKING

For a hardy hike, take the **Captain Cook Monument Trail** to the coast. The trail is not particularly steep or uneven, but it's not well maintained unless recently cleared by horseback riders. Following the 2006 earthquake the final section of the trail allowing access to the monument, Kealakekua Bay, Queen's Bath (a brackish spring-fed pool) and the cliffs was closed. Ask around to see if it's been reopened. If it hasn't, you could attempt to explore the coast north of the bay.

To get to the trailhead, turn *makai* off Hwy 11 onto Napo'opo'o Rd and drive past two telephone poles. Park at the third pole, where you'll see an orange arrow pointing at the trailhead. Start walking downhill on the dirt road (not the chained asphalt road). After 200yd stay to the left at the fork in the road. The route is fairly simple, but when in doubt stay to the left. After the lava ledge the trail intersects a 4WD road that continues straight north along the coast for miles.

The hike takes about an hour down, and it's hot and largely unshaded. There are no facilities at the bottom of the trail, so bring lots of water.

HORSEBACK RIDING

Kings' Trail Rides (☎ 323-2388, 345-0616; www.kona cowboy.com; 81-6420 Mamalahoa Hwy; rides Mon-Fri/Sat & Sun $135/150; ☺ 9am-4pm Mon-Fri, occasionally Sat & Sun) With the closure of the final stretch of the Captain Cook Monument Trail, Kings' is leading horseback trips to the coastline just north of Kealakekua Bay. Trips include lunch and possibly snorkeling if waters are very calm. It's near the 111-mile marker, with a 'www.konacowboy.com' sign.

Sleeping

Captain Cook is awash with B&Bs and has the only proper hotel in South Kona.

Manago Hotel (☎ 323-2642; www.managohotel .com; Hwy 11; s/d with shared bathroom $30/33, with private bathroom s $51-56, d $54-59, Japanese s/d $70/73) A stay at the Manago is like stepping into a time machine and makes for an absolutely classic Hawaiian experience. The Manago began in 1917 as a restaurant catering to salesmen on the then-lengthy journey between Hilo and Kona. Then came a boarding house, with the same rooms with shared bathroom (and substantial highway noise) that are still available today. A modern block of no-frills motel-style rooms sits behind the historical building, each with an institutional-feeling bathroom and a sliding glass door to a small lanai overlooking an orchard of sorts. There's little noise to wake you save for a rooster or two. It's between the 109- and 110-mile markers.

Edge of the World (☎ 328-7424, 800-660-8491; www .konaedge.com; incl breakfast s $65-114, d $70-119; ☐)

Run by a professor-turned-farmer and his wife, this low-key B&B is on 5 acres including coffee and macadamia nut groves. The couple speaks a variety of languages and rents three rooms in their hodgepodge redwood home. Guests have access to a hot tub on a breezy lanai with a wonderful view and will be provided with a plethora of local info. The hot breakfast includes organic ingredients. Trade may be considered. The B&B is located down a complex series of roads near the Manago Hotel.

Cedar House (☎ 328-8829; 866-328-8829; www .cedarhouse-hawaii.com; incl breakfast r $110-115, cottages $135, with kitchenette $145; ☐) This attractive B&B, located on a coffee farm, offers a range of accommodations including a stand-alone cottage and a two-floor apartment. The handsome main house is indeed built of cedar and redwood, with lots of windows and a deck to take in panoramic coastline and farm views. All rooms have private entrances, wi-fi and good views. The decor can be a little on the bright side but is generally updated and tasteful. Cedar House is located a winding 1-mile drive above the Kealakekua Ranch Center.

Luana Inn (☎ 328-2612; www.luanainn.com; 82-5856 Napo'opo'o Rd; r incl breakfast $150-180, ste with kitchen $200; ☐ ☒) Rather unlike its counterparts, everything about this new B&B is spacious, uncluttered and tastefully understated. Furnishings are modern and colors muted throughout guest rooms, which all have private entrances. The hosts, a young couple who take their mission very seriously, can be counted on to be attentive and provide meticulous info about the area, should you need them. If not, you'll be left to your solitude and the sunny pool overlooking Kealakekua Bay. The buffet-style breakfast includes local organic ingredients and homemade baked goods and yogurt. Internet access is available in a guest office. The grounds are a little barren – Luana's only downfall – so focus your attention on the amazing bay view!

Also recommended:

Rainbow Plantation B&B (☎ 323-2393, 800-494-2829; www.rainbowplantation.com; r incl breakfast $79-99; ☐) An overgrown tropical farm with several accommodations, including a retired boat! Located at the northern end of town.

Belle Vue (☎ 800-772-5044; www.kona-bed-breakfast .com; r incl breakfast $95-165) A French-owned B&B with flowery decor and a wide verandah with an amazing view. Within walking distance of central Captain Cook.

Eating

Captain Cook has a few little culinary gems, all of which are listed below.

Adriana's (☎ 217-7405; Kealakekua Ranch Center, Hwy 11; à la carte items $2-9; ✆ 10am-7pm Mon-Fri) Adriana and her family make the best Mexican food in South Kona, with a twist from their native El Salvador. Take your pick of nachos, quesadillas, tacos, burritos or tamales (order ahead for *pupusa*). Take it to go or eat at cement tables outside.

Super J's (☎ 328-9566; 83-5409 Hwy 11; plate lunches $3.50-9; ✆ 10am-6:30pm Mon-Sat) *Laulau* and *kalua* pig (cooked traditionally in an underground oven) with cabbage plate lunches are your only options at this old-school Hawaiian take-out food stand. It's south of the 107-mile marker.

Manago Hotel (☎ 323-2642; Hwy 11; mains $7.50-13.50; ✆ 7-9am, 11am-2pm & 5-7:30pm Tue-Sun) The Manago's history as a old-time roadhouse comes through loud and clear in its no-frills dining room and super-fast food prep. The menu is little more than a board on the wall, listing burgers and meat dishes such as the famous pork chops and a variety of well-prepared fish. Staff cheerfully bustle about greeting neighbors and delivering self-serve sides such as pickled *ogo* (seaweed), mac-potato salad, pumpkin, baked beans and white rice. Breakfast is a set menu ($5) with optional plate-sized pancakes an inch thick. You must eat here at least once.

Coffee Shack (☎ 328-9555; 83-5799 Hwy 11; meals $8-12; ✆ 7:30am-3pm) The Shack has an amazing view from its intimate, open-air deck surrounded by tropical foliage. The place is perched precariously on the *makai* side of the highway and has very limited parking. The breakfasts, hearty salads, sandwiches and pizzas are consistently OK, while, ironically, the coffee gets bad reviews. Consider sliding in for a beer right before closing. It's between the 108- and 109-mile markers.

Surprisingly, **Choicemart** (☎ 323-3994; Kealakekua Ranch Center, Hwy 11; ✆ 6am-9pm Mon-Sat, to 8:30pm Sun), South Kona's largest grocery store, stocks some organic produce and a good selection of wine and health foods.

Shopping

Art Farm (☎ 323-3495; Hwy 11; ✆ 10am-5pm Mon-Sat, to 4pm Sun) This unique gift store located immediately north of the Manago Hotel carries work by local artists.

HONAUNAU

pop 2400

Tiny Honaunau is little more than a place to roll through on your way to Pu'uhonua o Honaunau National Historical Park, but it does boast a few sights. Many residents in the Honaunau and Napo'opo'o area are small coffee and macadamia-nut growers. The area is lush and beautiful, with dramatic sea views.

Sights

ST BENEDICT'S PAINTED CHURCH

John Berchmans Velghe was a Catholic priest who came to Hawai'i from Belgium in 1899. Upon taking responsibility for St Benedict's **church** (☎ 328-2227; Painted Church Rd; admission free), he moved it 2 miles up from its original location on the coast near the *pu'uhonua* (place of refuge). It's not clear whether he did this as protection from tsunami or as an attempt to rise above – both literally and symbolically – a significant Hawaiian cultural site and what Christianity considered to be pagan ways.

Father John then painted the walls with a series of biblical scenes to aid in teaching the Bible. He designed the wall behind the altar to resemble the Gothic cathedral in Burgos, Spain. The painted palm leaves climbing the slender support columns add a more Hawaiian touch.

KONA COAST MACADAMIA NUT & CANDY FACTORY

At the Kamigaki family's **factory** (☎ 328-8141, 800-242-6887; www.konaoftheworld.com; Middle Ke'ei Rd; admission free; ✆ 8am-4:30pm Mon-Fri, to 4pm Sat, 11am-3pm Sun), you can gather some basic information

---

TOP LOCAL GRINDS

▪ **Teshima Restaurant** (p217)

▪ **Manago Hotel** (above)

▪ **Hawaiian Style Cafe** (p249)

▪ **Big Island Grill** (p210)

▪ **Kona Mixed Plate** (p210)

▪ **Café 100** (p277)

▪ **Kuhio Grille** (p278)

▪ **Tex Drive-In** (p261)

▪ **Hana Hou** (p304)

▪ **Triple K Grindz** (p283)

about (surprise!) mac nuts and try out a husking machine. The dusty barn 'showroom' overlooks the real operation out back, where nuts are husked and sorted. The real attraction is the store, which sells all sorts of mac-nut products and delectable chocolates. Be forewarned that opening hours are flexible.

Sleeping

Aloha Guest House (☎ 328-8955, 800-897-3188; www.alohaguesthouse.com; 84-4780 Mamalahoa Hwy; r incl breakfast $140-250; 🖳) The only word for the commanding views of the coast from this upscale B&B: unforgettable. Each of the five units is classily appointed and includes a custom-designed glass shower, a refrigerator and access to an outdoor Jacuzzi and a microwave. There's free use of computer, printer, photocopier and fax. Youthful, personable hosts speak German and serve full breakfasts. It's located 1 mile up an access road at the southern extreme of Captain Cook.

Horizon Guest House (☎ 328-2540; www.horizonguesthouse.com; r $250; 🖳 🐾) For a little piece of high-class heaven, check yourself into Horizon. Whether taking in the insane view from the infinity pool, enjoying breakfast (and the same view) on your private lanai or snuggling under the handmade Hawaiian quilt, you're sure to feel pampered here. With only four rooms, there'll never be a crowd in the classily decorated living or dining room available for guest use. Take note that the closest place to have more than a casual meal is about 12 miles of winding highway north.

Eating

South Kona Fruit Stand (☎ 328-8547; 84-4770 Hwy 11; 🕙 9am-6pm Mon-Sat) This cute fruit stand is more like a fruit boutique – don't miss it. It sells both its own and other farms' organic produce, and has a bar blending all sorts of heavenly tropical smoothies. It's on the *mauka* side between the 103- and 104-mile markers.

Coffees 'n' Epicurea (☎ 328-0322; 83-5315 Hwy 11; 🕙 6:30am-6pm) A coffee-tasting room is an unlikely place for this patisserie with flaky pastries, delicate éclairs and gorgeous pies. (The baker defected from the Kohala Coast resorts.) A back patio has greenery and some seating, and its gift shop is surprisingly sophisticated, obviously catering to a crowd beyond the tour-bus norm. It's on the *makai* side at the 106-mile marker.

Bong Brothers (☎ 328-9289; www.bongbrothers.com; Hwy 11; deli items $3-5; 🕙 9am-6pm Mon-Fri, 10am-5:30pm Sun) Your best bet for food in Honaunau is vegetarian deli takeout from Bong Brothers, a small health food and gift store located in an historic 1929 building. The green papaya salad ($3) is delicious, as are the smoothies, soups, curries and burritos. Organic produce fills baskets on the front porch, and a rocking chair there is perfect for watching the characters come and go.

Kona Seafood (☎ 328-9777; Hwy 11; 🕙 10am-6:30pm Mon-Thu, to 7pm Fri, to 5pm Sat & Sun) For fresh seafood, *poke* and other local specialties by weight, stop at Kona Seafood. It's at the 106-mile marker.

PU'UHONUA O HONAUNAU NATIONAL HISTORICAL PARK

Visiting this impressive **national park** (☎ 328-2288, 328-2326; www.nps.gov/puho; 1-week pass adult/car $3/5; 🕙 7am-8pm, visitor center 8am-5:30pm) fronting Honaunau Bay is a memorable experience. The park's tongue twister of a name simply means 'place of refuge at Honaunau.'

History

In ancient Hawai'i, the *kapu* system regulated daily life. A common person could not look at the *ali'i* (chief) or walk in his footsteps. Women could not prepare food for men or eat with them. One could not fish, hunt or gather timber except during certain seasons.

If one broke the *kapu* the penalty was always death. The belief was that the violation angered the gods, who might retaliate with volcanic eruptions, tidal waves, famine or earthquakes. Thus, to appease the gods, the violator was hunted down and killed.

However there was one escape. Commoners who broke a *kapu* could get a second chance, if they reached the sacred ground of a *pu'uhonua* (place of refuge). Similarly, a *pu'uhonua* also gave sanctuary to defeated warriors and men who were too old or young, or who were unable to fight during times of war.

To reach the *pu'uhonua* was a challenge. Since the grounds immediately surrounding the refuge were royal and therefore couldn't be crossed, *kapu* breakers had to swim through open ocean, braving sharks and currents, to reach safety. Once inside the sanctuary, priests performed ceremonies of absolution to placate the gods. *Kapu* breakers could then return home for a fresh start. The *pu'uhonua* at Honaunau was used for several centuries before being abandoned around 1819.

Sights

A half-mile **walking tour** passes the park's major sites, which are marked by numbered plaques – the visitor center gives out a brochure map with cultural information. Avoid visiting at midday as the park is relatively uncovered. While most of the sandy trail is accessible by wheelchair, the sites near the water require you to traverse rough lava rock.

The first section of the park is the royal grounds, where Kona *ali'i* and their warriors lived. **Hale o Keawe Heiau**, the temple on the point of the cove, was built around 1650 and contains the bones of 23 chiefs. It was believed that the mana of the chiefs remained in their bones and bestowed sanctity on those who entered the grounds. A fishpond, lava tree molds, a hand-carved koa canoe, and a few thatched huts and shelters can also be seen in this section. Look for sea turtles at **Keone'ele Cove**, which was once the royal canoe landing.

Carved wooden *ki'i* standing up to 15ft high front an authentic-looking heiau reconstruction. Leading up to the heiau is the **Great Wall** separating the royal grounds from the *pu'uhonua*. Built around 1550, this stone wall is more than 1000ft long and 10ft high. Inside the wall are two older heiau and legendary stones.

An oceanfront **picnic area** with tables and BBQs in a palm tree grove lies just south of the park center. It's a pretty sweet spot. Here **tide pools** in *pahoehoe* lava rock contain tiny black *pipipi* (tiny black mollusks), coral, black-shelled crabs, small fish, sea hares and sea urchins.

Activities

Breeze through the park's easy hiking trail, then hit the water at an epic snorkeling spot. Ultra-traditional **hula and chanting classes** taught by magical Kumu Keala Ching take place in the park at 5pm on Friday. There's usually a beginner in every class, but respectful observing is also permitted.

SWIMMING & SNORKELING

Immediately north of the park is Two-Step, one of the coast's best snorkeling spots, also popular with kayakers and canoe paddlers. Leave your car in the park's lot, and hang a left outside the entrance.

There's no beach – snorkelers step off a lava ledge beside the boat ramp into about 10ft of water, which quickly drops to about 25ft. Some naturally formed steps (hence the spot's name) make it fairly easy to get in and out of the water.

Visibility is excellent, especially with the noon sun overhead, with good-sized reef fish and a fine variety of corals close to shore. When the tide is rising, the water is deeper and it brings in more fish. The predatory 'crown of thorns' starfish can be seen here feasting on live coral polyps. Cool, freshwater springs seep out of the ground, creating blurry patches in the water. Divers can investigate a ledge a little way out that drops off about 100ft.

HIKING

A pretty 2-mile-return-trip hike leads to the site of the abandoned village of Ki'ilae. The visitor center lends a booklet describing the marked archaeological sites along the unshaded **1871 Trail**, which begins off the road to the picnic area.

You'll pass a collapsed lava tube and a *holua* (sled course) *ali'i* raced wooden sleds down before reaching the steep **Alahaka Ramp**, which once allowed riders on horseback to travel between villages. Halfway up the ramp is **Waiu-O-Hina lava tube**, which opens to the sea. At the time of research it was closed pending geological assessment.

At the top of the ramp, incredible vistas over ocean coves spread out below. Continue to the spot where Ki'ilae Village once stood, heading back where a gate marks the park boundary.

Festivals

On the weekend closest to July 1, the park puts on a **cultural festival** with traditional displays and food, *hukilau* (net fishing) and a 'royal court.'

HO'OKENA

Most tourists breeze on by Ho'okena, missing one of South Kona's few sandy beaches on a beautiful bay. Ho'okena itself is little more than a tiny fishing community with a county **beach park** and no businesses to speak of. The locals are friendlier than their neighbors in Miloli'i, but they still can view outsiders with wariness.

Ho'okena was once a bustling village. King Kalakaua dispatched his friend Robert

Louis Stevenson here in 1889 to show him a typical Hawaiian village. Stevenson stayed a week with the town's judge and wrote about Ho'okena in *Travels in Hawaii*. In the 1890s, Chinese immigrants moved into Ho'okena, setting up shops and restaurants. A tavern and a hotel opened, and the town got rougher and rowdier. In those days, Big Island cattle were shipped from the Ho'okena landing to market in Honolulu. When the circle-island road was built, the steamers stopped coming and people moved away. By the 1920s, the town was all but deserted.

Ho'okena's beach is medium-sized with soft dark sands backed by a steep green hillside. The bay's waters are often calm and great for swimming and kayaking. The snorkeling is decent, with a fair amount of coral, some fish, and often dolphins and sea turtles, though it drops off pretty quickly. Be aware of strong currents further out. When the winter surf is up, local kids hit the waves with bodyboards.

The beach park has a picnic pavilion, bathrooms, showers and a hang-loose vibe, but no drinking water. Camping here is pretty choice, so much so that some folks live out of the campground for short periods. Sites are right on the sand, and the shady ones fill up quickly. A county permit (p553) is required. A farm stand on the *makai* side of Hwy 11 around the 99-mile marker sells some organics.

The turnoff is between the 101- and 102-mile markers. A narrow road winds 2 miles down to the beach. Veer left at the bottom.

MILOLI'I

Miloli'i residents feel their fishing village is one of the most traditional left in Hawai'i – and they'd like to keep it that way. Though fishermen zipping around in motorized boats and makeshift homes where the old fishing shacks once stood may not look 'traditional' (nor is the village's current problem with crystal methamphetamine, or 'ice'), but the total lack of tourism certainly is. Villagers generally prefer their isolation and are not enthusiastic about tourists rolling through town. It may be most respectful to honor their desire for solitude.

Miloli'i means 'fine twist.' Historically, the village was known for its skilled sennit twisters, who used bark from the *olona* (a native shrub) to make fine cord and highly valued fishnets. Many villagers continue to make a living from the sea.

The village sits at the edge of an expansive 1926 lava flow that covered the nearby fishing village of Ho'opuloa. Homes dot the hillside or are spread throughout a desolate lava field. At the end of the road is a tiny, ratty beach park with bathrooms and an expanse of tide pools. A county permit is required (see p553) to camp on the rocky shore. The turnoff is just south of the 89-mile marker. It's 5 miles down a steep and winding single-lane road to the village.

NORTH KONA COAST

The volcanoes step back and give the shore some breathing room here on the North Kona Coast. But they've left their mark on this slim, gently sloping shelf, a dark landscape dominated by crisscrossing layers of chunky *'a'a* (rough lava) and frozen tongues of *pahoehoe*. The heat comes in brutal waves here, the leeward lack of wind compounded by the jet-black earth.

This harsh environment is unwelcoming toward life and has appropriately remained unpopulated. But, strangely, growing in numbers along the coast where fishing villages once stood are world-renowned resorts with buildings so colorful and golf courses so green they appear to be mirages. Developers recognized the unique beauty found in the sharp contrast of turquoise water, white sand and black land. Only time will tell if their lavish projects will meet the same fate as the fishing villages, wiped out by a tsunami in 1946.

Escape the heat and make your way to the beaches, North Kona's original mirages. Their white sands won't disappoint and the difficulty required to reach a few of them will make your success all the sweeter.

HONOKOHAU HARBOR

To alleviate traffic off Kailua Pier this harbor was built in 1970. It is Kona's largest small-boat harbor, and, located just 2 miles north of the city, it is the convenient launching point for many an ocean activity. To reach the harbor, turn *makai* on Kealakehe Parkway just north of the 98-mile marker.

Sights & Activities

To catch a glimpse of the weigh-ins from charter fishing boats, park near the harbor's gas station and walk to the dock behind the

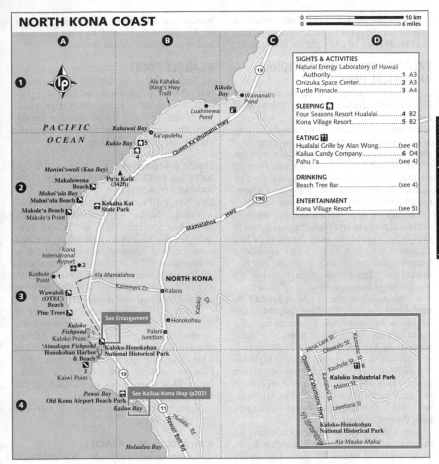

NORTH KONA COAST

0 ————————— 10 km
0 ————————— 6 miles

SIGHTS & ACTIVITIES
Natural Energy Laboratory of Hawaii
  Authority.....................................**1** A3
Onizuka Space Center....................**2** A3
Turtle Pinnacle.............................**3** A4

SLEEPING
Four Seasons Resort Hualalai..........**4** B2
Kona Village Resort.......................**5** B2

EATING
Hualalai Grille by Alan Wong..........(see 4)
Kailua Candy Company...................**6** D4
Pahu i'a......................................(see 4)

DRINKING
Beach Tree Bar.............................(see 4)

ENTERTAINMENT
Kona Village Resort.......................(see 5)

HAWAI'I (THE BIG ISLAND)

adjacent building. The best times are around 11am and 3pm. Boats flying white flags scored 'ahi, blue flags mean marlin, and inverted flags signify a catch-and-release excursion.

See p205 for information about snorkeling and diving tours departing from this harbor.

SNORKELING & DIVING

The area south of Honokohau Harbor all the way to Kailua Bay is a marine-life conservation district (accessible by boat) promising good snorkeling and diving.

Straight out from Honokohau Harbor, **Turtle Pinnacle** is a premier dive site for spotting and photographing turtles, which congregate here to let small fish feed off the algae and

parasites on their shells. Frogfish, octopi and pipefish are also frequently sighted.

Off **Kaiwi Pt**, south of Honokohau Harbor, sea turtles, large fish and huge eagle rays swim around some respectable drop-offs. Nearby is **Suck 'Em Up**, a couple of lava tubes. The swell pulls divers through like an amusement-park ride.

Eating

Kailua Candy Company (☎ 329-2522, 800-622-2462; www.kailua-candy.com; cnr Kamanu & Kauhola Sts, Kaloko Light Industrial Area; ☒ 8am-6pm Mon-Sat, to 4pm Sun) Founded in 1977, this stark chocolate shop once ranked in *Bon Appetit* magazine as among America's top 10. Try its celebrated macadamia-nut *honu* ('turtles;' nuts and caramel covered with chocolate) and truffles in flavors like passion fruit, Kona coffee and guava-rum. To get here, turn *mauka* on Hina Lani St off Hwy 19 and right on Kamanu St.

KALOKO-HONOKOHAU NATIONAL HISTORICAL PARK

Covering 1160 acres of oceanfront between Kaloko and Honokohau Harbor, this **national park** (☎ 329-6881; www.nps.gov/kaho; ☺ visitor center 8:30am-4pm, park 24hr) includes fishponds, ancient heiau and house sites, burial caves, petroglyphs, *holua*, and a restored 1-mile segment of the ancient King's Trail footpath. Despite all this, the park is virtually unknown, even by locals. It is speculated that the bones of Kamehameha were buried in secret near Kaloko.

Though it may appear a desolate, seemingly endless expanse of lava rock, the park is worth exploring. Visit in the early morning or late afternoon (or when it's overcast), as midday temperatures can be unbearable on the unshaded trails. Trails cross rough chunks of '*a'a* (rough, jagged lava), so wear good shoes.

At the park's northern end is **Kaloko Fishpond**. Further south, '**Aimakapa Fishpond**, is the largest on the Kona Coast. Separated from the ocean by a stone wall, fish were raised in these ponds until distributed by the *ali'i*. Mangrove, an introduced species, was painstakingly removed from these fishponds by park workers in order to re-attract native birds. *Aeo* (Hawaiian black-neck stilt) and '*alae ke'oke'o* (Hawaiian coot), both endangered native waterbirds, have thrived here since.

Green sea turtles are often seen resting on the salt-and-pepper sands of **Honokohau Beach**, at the southern end of the park. The turtles are endangered and protected by law; do not disturb them. The water here is decent for swimming and snorkeling, although the bottom is a bit rocky. At the southern end of the beach is '**Ai'opio Fishtrap** and a heiau. In ancient times, fish swam into an opening in the rock wall at high tide and were trapped inside when the tide fell.

Inland from the northern end of Honokohau Beach, **Kahinihiniula** (Queen's Bath) is a brackish spring-fed pool. Although in the middle of a lava flow, the pool is linked to the ocean and rises at high tide. It is marked by stone cairns and Christmas berries, always a good sign that freshwater is nearby.

The main entrance to the park is between the 96- and 97-mile markers. A gate on the highway marks a northern entrance. For southern access, enter Honokohau Harbor on Kealakehe Parkway, take your first right and continue to a signed entrance.

KEAHOLE POINT

At Keahole Point the seafloor drops steeply just offshore, providing a continuous supply of both cold water from 2000ft depths and warm surface water. These are ideal conditions for – you'll never guess – ocean thermal-energy conversion (OTEC).

Sights & Activities

NATURAL ENERGY LABORATORY OF HAWAII AUTHORITY

The Natural Energy Laboratory of Hawaii Authority (Nelha) was created by the state in 1974 to research OTEC and related technologies. Nelha has successfully generated electricity and continues to research methods to transform OTEC into an economically viable energy resource. **Public lectures** (☎ 329-7341; www.nelha.org; per person $5; ☺ 10-11:30am Wed & Thu) are held (reservations required).

Today Nelha also sponsors a variety of commercial ventures, including aquaculture production of *ogo*, algae, abalone, lobster and black pearls. One of Nelha's tenants is a Japanese company that desalinates pristine Hawaiian seawater and sells it as a tonic in Japan. Their huge ponds are visible from the entire slopes above the highway.

The turnoff to Nelha is between the 94- and 95-mile markers.

WAWALOLI (OTEC) BEACH

The Nelha access road leads to **Wawaloli Beach**, a great spot for exploring tide pools covering the rocky lava coastline. Swimming conditions are poor, but the beach has bathrooms and is quiet. Enjoy a sunset picnic at the picnic tables while the kids play in a *keiki* pool (shallow tide pool) and waves crash against the rocks. The airport's proximity can be a little annoying.

PINE TREES

Pine Trees, one of west Hawai'i's best **surfing breaks**, is just south of Nelha. Why Pine Trees? Early surfers spied mangrove trees near the break, which they thought were pines. No mangroves (or pines) are visible today, but the name stuck.

The break is along a long, pretty beach that is rocky enough to make swimming difficult.

There is surf at a number of points along this stretch depending on the tide and swell. The final bay gets the most consistent yet more forgiving waves. An incoming midtide is favorable in general, but as the swell picks up in the winter these breaks often close out. This place attracts a crowd, so if you plan to paddle out, you'll have to 'talk story with da locals to find da powah surf, brah!'

When the access road to Nelha veers to the right, look left for a well-worn 4WD road leading about 2 miles further south to Pine Trees. You could walk, but the heat can be intense. Gates are closed between 8pm and 6am.

ONIZUKA SPACE CENTER

Astronaut Ellison S Onizuka Space Center (☎ 329-3441; Kona Airport; adult/child $3/1; ❋ 8:30am-4:30pm) pays tribute to the Big Island native who perished in the 1986 *Challenger* space-shuttle disaster. The little museum sits between the departure and arrival buildings and features exhibits and educational films about space and astronauts. Items on display include a moon rock, a NASA space suit and scale models of spacecraft.

KEKAHA KAI STATE PARK

For remote, pristine, white-sand beaches head for **Kekaha Kai** (❋ 9am-7pm Thu-Tue). Formerly known as Kona Coast State Park, most of this 1600-acre park is completely undeveloped fields of chunky 'a'a lava devoid of plant life. But its beautiful beaches, only one of which has paved access, are the reason to come here. If you plan to hike in either set out early or prepare for punishing heat both from the exposed trails and the dark ground. Wear good shoes and bring lots of water.

Sights & Activities
MAHAI'ULA BEACH
The park's largest, this **beach** has salt-and-pepper sand, along with coral rubble. The inshore waters are shallow, and the bottom is gently sloping. Snorkeling and swimming are usually good, but, during periods of high surf, which are not infrequent in winter, surfing is the sport of choice on the bay's north side. There are picnic tables and portable toilets.

The unpaved (barely passable in a 2WD), 1.5-mile road to Mahai'ula Beach is between the 90- and 91-mile markers. From the first parking area, take a five-minute walk north.

MANINI'OWALI (KUA BAY)
Manini'owali, also called Kua Bay, is idyllic, with crescent-shaped white sands and turquoise waters. Due to its easy access, Manini'owali packs on weekends. Most of the year, the conditions are suited to swimmers, and in winter, the waves kick up for bodyboarders and bodysurfers. Winter storms can generate currents that temporarily strip the beach of its sand.

The beach has bathrooms and showers, but very little vegetation or shade, and unshaded picnic tables. On the way down to the beach you'll see **Pu'u Ku'ili**, a 342ft grassy cinder cone. Access is via a paved road just south of the 88-mile marker.

MAKALAWENA & MAKOLE'A BEACHES
These **beaches** require either a 4WD or a hike and have no facilities. On weekdays they see few visitors. Occasionally campers have been harassed or assaulted by hostile locals at these deserted beaches, so be alert to trouble.

To the north lies Makalawena Beach, a pristine, white-sand strip. Park your car by the service road that's cabled off, and walk toward the old house on the beach. Find the coastal trail further *makai* and hike north for about 1.25 miles.

The hike is over lava rock, so you'll be ecstatic to reach Makalawena's clear waters, ideal for swimming, snorkeling and especially bodyboarding. Before heading back, rinse off the salt at a brackish pond behind the dunes at the southern end of the beach.

Another hidden treasure, Makole'a Beach, south of Kekaha Kai, is a small black-sand beach where you likely won't encounter another soul. If you're walking from the park, find the easy-to-navigate 'path' along the lava fields; follow the coastline and you can't lose your way. With a 4WD, turn left at the first parking lot in the park; drive for about 1000yd until you reach a path that is marked by coral and goes to the ocean; from here it's probably wise to walk rather than drive to the beach.

This beach might be less breathtakingly impressive than the others within park grounds, but black sand near Kona is rare. There's no shade, and the lava rock and black sand compound the heat.

KA'UPULEHU

Even if you're not high-rolling enough to stay at either of the two exclusive resorts located in Ka'upulehu, you can still visit the area's beautiful white-sand beaches, thanks to shoreline public access laws. Ka'upulehu's first incarnation was as a remote fishing village, accessible only by boat. After being destroyed in the 1946 tsunami, the area was abandoned until the early 1960s, when a wealthy yachter anchored offshore came up with an idea that spawned the resort movement here and for-ever changed this stretch of coast.

The Four Seasons hands out free parking passes to those visiting **Kukio Bay** beach. A mile-long coastal footpath through the lava connects the hotel to the bay via an area of reddish lava and brackish water, where turtles can be seen. A string of pristine, easily acces-sible little coves lies further south. Showers, rest rooms and drinking water are available.

Sleeping

Four Seasons Resort Hualalai (☎ 325-8000; 800-332-3442; www.fourseasons.com; 100 Ka'upulehu Dr; r $540-780, 1-bedroom ste $935-3450; ✗ ☒) Known for its high luxury and impeccable service, the Four Sea-sons is the only five-diamond resort on the Big Island. Resort guests can enjoy a PGA-tour golf course and a world-class spa. Ironically, the adjacent Ka'upulehu Beach isn't great for swimming as a steep drop in the reef creates strong rip currents.

Kona Village Resort (☎ 325-5555, 800-367-5290; www.konavillage.com; 1 Kahuwai Bay Dr; 1-r hale $775-4290, 2-r hale $965-5565; ☒) When this 82-acre hidea-way resort opened in 1965 it was so isolated that guests had to fly in. The intent to help its guests 'get away from it all' in high comfort yet relaxed style continues today. Thatched-roof *hale* on stilts have modern, luxurious interiors completely free of phones, radios, TVs and even air-con. Still as exclusive as it ever was, beachfront Kona Village is a favorite of the rich and famous. Rates include meals and a host of on-site activities.

Eating

During the high season the Four Seasons asks nonguests to call the day they plan to visit to confirm availability.

Pahu'ia (☎ 325-8000; Four Seasons Resort Hualalai; mains $25-48; ✆ 6:30-11:30am & 5:30pm-9:30pm) For high-class Hawaii regional cuisine in a formal, elegant oceanfront setting, Pahu'ia is the place. Its fresh seafood is harvested from the nearby Nelha project. Reservations required for dinner.

Hualalai Grille by Alan Wong (☎ 325-8525; Golf Clubhouse, Four Seasons Resort Hualalai; mains $30-38;

✆ 11:30am-2:30pm & 5:30-9pm) Nicknamed the '19th Hole,' the Hualalai Grille reopened under the direction of celebrity chef Alan Wong in early 2004, with signature dishes like the 'New Wave' Opihi Shooter appetizer – a tall glass of local limpets in spicy tomato water, fennel basil and *ume shiso* (Japanese plum) essences. Plus, you'll find creative fish mains and intriguing Hawaii-style versions of American classics, like the 'soup and sand-wich' appetizer with chilled red-and-yellow-tomato soup and fois gras, *kalua* pig and a grilled cheese sandwich. Reservations are recommended.

Drinking & Entertainment

Beach Tree Bar (☎ 325-8000; Four Seasons Resort Hualalai; ✆ 10am-9pm) Sip a mai tai with your toes in the sand and your eyes on the sunset. Enjoy live music from Tuesday to Saturday.

Kona Village Resort (☎ 325-5555, 800-367-5290; 1 Kahuwai Bay Dr; adult/child 3-5/child 6-12 $97/40/67; ✆ 6pm Wed & Fri) The old-world Polynesian set-ting gives an authentic feel for a spectacular show at the best commercial luau on Hawai'i. A buffet dinner and a cocktail (only one?!) are included. Reserve ahead.

KIHOLO BAY

Just south of the 82-mile marker a lookout commands a fantastic view of Kiholo Bay. With its pristine turquoise waters and shore-line fringed with coconut trees, the bay is an oasis in the lava.

An inconspicuous trail down to the bay starts about 100yd south of the 81-mile marker (look for a dirt turnout along the highway). Walk straight in for about 10ft, then veer left and follow a 4WD road, the beginning of which has been blocked off by boulders to keep vehicles out. Near the end of the trail look for a faint footpath toward the left. Allow 20 to 30 minutes total.

Kiholo Bay, almost 2 miles wide, has a lovely, large spring-fed pond called Luahi-newai at the southern end of the bay. It's re-freshingly cold and fronted by a black-sand beach, which is great for swimming when it's calm. As you walk to the freshwater pond, check out the **Queen's Bath**, a freshwater swim-ming hole that appears deceptively small but actually extends back into the rock for about 40ft. Look for a *makai* opening in the trees after you pass the gargantuan yellow estate and tennis courts. On the northern end you can actually walk across a shallow channel to a small island with white sand. In the water you might see green sea turtles.

SOUTH KOHALA COAST

The Big Island's South Kohala Coast is known throughout the islands as the Gold Coast. Some attribute the moniker to the abundant yellow tang in coastal waters, while others point out the vast number of coffers that have been filled by the resort tourism here. But likely tourism officials wanted to draw attention to the characteristic constant sunshine that makes for ideal beach weather.

Here endless, stark lava fields are beaten by that golden sunshine and made even more inhospitable by the infamous Kohala winds, known to blow lighter-weight Ironman cyclists right over. This harsh environment hardly seems like it would have attracted ancient Native Hawaiians, yet it is packed with historical trails, heiau, fishponds and petroglyph sites. It's also packed with resorts, one right after the other, each a green oasis of landscaping

and golf courses. These days locals could never afford to live here, and even Waikoloa Village – initially intended for resort employees – has been taken over by retiree transplants. To paraphrase the musician Iz (p49), how would the ancients feel about that?

WAIKOLOA RESORT AREA
pop 4800

Contrasting sharply with the unforgiving fields of lava surrounding it, the celebrated Waikoloa Resort area gets the most attention on the southern Kohala Coast. It's not just the two mega-hotels, the condo complexes, the 36 holes of golf or the notable restaurants that bring it fame. It's the Big Island's most upscale shopping mall and an endless string of events that keep Waikoloa on the tip of everyone's tongue.

Information

Big Island Visitors Bureau (☎ 886-1655, 800-648-2441; www.gohawaii.com; Suite B15, King's Shops, 250 Waikoloa Beach Dr) is helpful but can be annoyingly unbiased. General services – and a **post office** (☎ 885-6239; cnr Waikoloa Rd & Pua Melia St) – can be

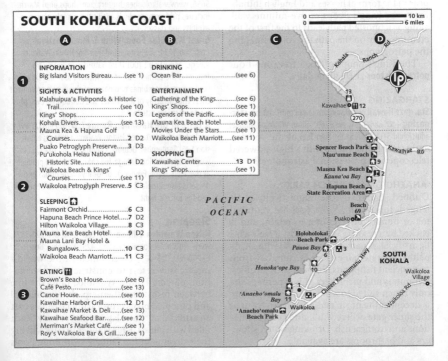

SOUTH KOHALA COAST

0 — 10 km
0 — 6 miles

INFORMATION
Big Island Visitors Bureau.......(see 1)

SIGHTS & ACTIVITIES
Kalahuipua'a Fishponds & Historic
  Trail.............................(see 10)
Kings' Shops.......................**1** C3
Kohala Divers....................(see 13)
Mauna Kea & Hapuna Golf
  Courses..........................**2** D2
Puako Petroglyph Preserve...**3** D3
Pu'ukohola Heiau National
  Historic Site....................**4** D2
Waikoloa Beach & Kings'
  Courses.........................(see 1)
Waikoloa Petroglyph Preserve..**5** C3

SLEEPING 🏠
Fairmont Orchid...................**6** C3
Hapuna Beach Prince Hotel....**7** D2
Hilton Waikoloa Village..........**8** C3
Mauna Kea Beach Hotel.........**9** D2
Mauna Lani Bay Hotel &
  Bungalows......................**10** C3
Waikoloa Beach Marriott......**11** C3

EATING 🍴
Brown's Beach House............(see 6)
Café Pesto..........................(see 13)
Canoe House.......................(see 10)
Kawaihae Harbor Grill..........**12** D1
Kawaihae Market & Deli........(see 13)
Kawaihae Seafood Bar..........(see 12)
Merriman's Market Café.......(see 1)
Roy's Waikoloa Bar & Grill....(see 1)

DRINKING
Ocean Bar..........................(see 6)

ENTERTAINMENT
Gathering of the Kings...........(see 6)
Kings' Shops........................(see 1)
Legends of the Pacific...........(see 8)
Mauna Kea Beach Hotel........(see 9)
Movies Under the Stars........(see 1)
Waikoloa Beach Marriott.....(see 11)

SHOPPING 🛍
Kawaihae Center...................**13** D1
Kings' Shops........................(see 1)

PACIFIC
OCEAN

Kohala Ranch Rd

Kawaihae ● 🏠 **13** **12**
(270)

Spencer Beach Park 🏠 **4**
Mau'umae Beach 🏠 **9**
Mauna Kea Beach 🏠 **2**
Kauna'oa Bay
Hapuna Beach 🏠 **7**
State Recreation Area

Kawaihae Rd

Beach **69**
Puako ●

Holoholokai
Beach Park 🏠
Pauoa Bay 🏠 **3**
6

SOUTH
KOHALA

Honoka'ope Bay
🏠 **10**

Waikoloa
Village ●

8 🏠 **1**
'Anaeho'omalu **11** 🏠 **5**
Bay
'Anaeho'omalu 🏠
Beach Park

Queen Ka'ahumanu Hwy

Waikoloa Rd

Waikoloa

HAWAI'I (THE BIG ISLAND)

TOP BEACHES FOR SWIMMING

- Ho'okena Beach (p227)
- White Sands Beach (p204)
- Manini'owali Beach (Kua Bay) (p231)
- Makalawena Beach (p231)
- Kukio Bay Area (p232)
- Beach 69 (p237)
- Hapuna Beach (p237)
- Kauna'oa Bay (p238)

---

found in the inland residential community of Waikoloa Village, in **Waikoloa Highlands Center** (cnr Waikoloa Rd & Paniolo Ave).

Sights & Activities

WAIKOLOA PETROGLYPH PRESERVE

A lava field etched with impressive petroglyphs, many dating back to the 16th century, is located beside the Kings' Shops. Some are graphic (humans, birds, canoes) and others cryptic (dots, lines). Western influences appear in the form of horses and English initials. From the King's Shops, a five-minute walk along a signposted path leads to the first of the etchings. Stay on the path to avoid damaging the petroglyphs.

The King's Shops offers a free, one-hour **petroglyph tour** at 10:30am daily.

STARGAZING

Stargaze Hawaii (www.stargazehawaii.com) offers **stargazing** (☎ 886-1234, ext 2760; Hilton Waikoloa Village; adult/child 5-11 $25/15; ☽ 8pm Tue) of the consistently clear Kohala skies with a high-powered telescope and professional astronomers.

'ANAEHO'OMALU BEACH PARK

Dubbed 'A Bay' by the linguistically challenged, this **beach** (☽ 6am-8pm) has required major human intervention to retain, and is backed by a resort. Consequently, it feels a little artificial. A narrow strip of sand with shady palms separates an extremely calm bay from two ancient fishponds. Popular with families, swimmers and picnickers, this is perhaps the only beach suited to windsurfing. Snorkeling is decent at the north end, directly in front of the sluice gate, where you'll find coral formations and tropical fish. Drinking water, showers and bathrooms are available.

Archaeologists have found evidence of human habitation here dating back more than 1000 years. A short footpath with interpretive plaques starts near the showers and passes fishponds, caves, ancient house platforms and a shrine.

To get here, turn left off Waikoloa Beach Dr opposite the Kings' Shops.

GOLF

Golfers will enjoy a game at the **Waikoloa Beach & Kings' Courses** (☎ 877-924-5656, King's 886-7888, beach 886-6060; www.waikoloabeachresort.com/golf.php; guests/nonguests $130/195), each with 18 holes' worth of stunning views and lava flows.

CULTURAL ACTIVITIES

The **King's Shops** (☎ 877-924-5656; www.waikoloabeachresort.com/shops.php; 250 Waikoloa Beach Dr) offers free daily cultural activities ranging from hula and ukulele classes to arts and crafts. Except for the ukulele class, most attendees are under 13. See the website for a schedule.

Festivals & Events

Great Waikoloa Ukulele Festival (☎ 877-924-5656; www.waikoloabeachresort.com/shops.php) March. Includes performances by Hawaii's top ukulele players, exhibits and classes.

Great Waikoloa Food, Wine & Music Festival (☎ 886-1234, www.dolphindays.com; Hilton Waikoloa Village; admission $100) Third Saturday in June. This festival is the culmination of the Hilton's four-day Dolphin Days event. It combines two dozen of the state's prominent chefs with an array of fine wines and boutique brews, plus world-class jazz artists.

A Taste of the Hawaiian Range (☎ 322-4892; www.ctahr.hawaii.edu/taste/; Hilton Waikoloa Village; admission $35) September-October. Celebrated Big Island chefs work magic with local range-fed meats and local produce at this food event. Producers of locally made drinks and desserts also sample their products. Portions are generous and the price is right.

Sleeping

Hilton Waikoloa Village (☎ 886-1234, 800-221-2424; www.hiltonwaikoloavillage.com; 425 Waikoloa Beach Dr; r $200-690; ☒ ☒ ☒) Once billed as the world's most costly resort to construct, the ostentatious 62-acre Hilton Waikoloa blurs the line between resort and theme park. A monorail and canopied boats cruise artificial canals past an artificial saltwater lagoon and a sandy beach filled with guests. Kids wander in packs, living their dreams in the fantasy swimming pools and 175ft waterslide. The lobby showcases a multimillion-dollar art collection of museum-quality pieces from throughout Polynesia and Asia. If you stay here, you'll be made comfortable by all the usual Hilton amenities. If you don't, this is an ideal place to witness the extravagance of Hawaiian resorts.

Waikoloa Beach Marriott (☎ 886-6789, 888-924-5656; www.waikoloabeachmarriott.com; 69-275 Waikoloa Beach Dr; r $325-535; ⊠ ⊠) The Marriott's beachside location is far superior to the Hilton's, and the Kings' Shops are within walking distance. At the time of research, the Marriot was two years into a one-year, $40-million renovation. Rooms were still available.

Eating

Merriman's Market Café (☎ 886-1700; dinner mains $17-27; ⊠ 11am-9:30pm) The Market Café serves flavorful Mediterranean-influenced dishes featuring organic island-grown produce, fresh fish caught locally, and the finest artisanal breads, cheeses and wines. The setting is casual, and lunch mains stay under $15. Though the Merriman's in Waimea (p250) is highly recommended, this location feels a bit like a tourist trap. The flavors are wonderful, but the portions are tiny and the service is shaky.

Roy's Waikoloa Bar & Grill (☎ 886-4321; mains $26-30; ⊠ 5:30-9:30pm) Renowned Roy's takes regional Hawaiian cuisine and gives it an international twist, with impressive results. Dishes like rack of lamb in a *liliko'i* Cabernet sauce, and braised beef shortribs with a honey mustard sauce, homemade poi and *lomi* tomatoes ($27.50) will knock your socks off.

In Waikoloa Village, **Waikoloa Village Market** (☎ 883-1088; Waikoloa Highlands Center; ⊠ 6am-9pm) is a fair-sized grocery store with a very basic deli. There's a **farmers market** (Waikoloa Community Church, Paniolo St; ⊠ 7-10am) every Saturday.

Entertainment

If you can afford the Kona Village luau (p232), go for that.

Legends of the Pacific (☎ 886-1234, ext 54; Hilton Waikoloa Village; adult/child 5-12 $78/39; ⊠ 6pm Tue & Fri) The Hilton's luau includes a colorful show, one cocktail and a dinner buffet with a lavish dessert selection.

Waikoloa Beach Marriott (☎ 886-6789, 888-924-5656; adult/child 6-12 $75/36; ⊠ 6pm Sun & Wed) The open bar at this luau will make the Hawaiian-style dinner buffet seem even tastier and the show even more vibrant.

Movies under the Stars (☎ 886-8811; www.waikoloa beachresort.com/shops.php; admission adult/child under 5 $5/free) Hollywood flicks are projected on a 17ft by 10ft digital screen on the lawn on the *mauka* side of King's Lake at dusk on Tuesdays. Bring something to sit on.

King's Shops (☎ 877-924-5656; www.waikoloabeach resort.com/shops.php; ⊠ shows 6pm Mon-Fri, 4pm Sat & Sun) These free performances of Hawaiian music and dance vary wildly in quality. Try to catch excellent local slack-key guitarist John Keawe.

Shopping

Kings' Shops (☎ 877-924-5656; 250 Waikoloa Beach Dr; ⊠ 9:30am-9pm) Satisfy your inner shopper at the designer boutiques (think Louis Vuitton) and cute shops at this outdoor shopping mall.

Getting There & Away

A *makai* turnoff just south of the 76-mile marker leads to the Waikoloa Resort area, containing the hotels, golf course and King's Shops. Waikoloa Village is about 8 miles *mauka* up Waikoloa Rd, which is just north of the 75-mile marker.

MAUNA LANI RESORT AREA

Like the others, the Mauna Lani Resort is home to two hotels, 36 holes of golf and condo complexes. What it has over its neighbors are significant historical sites and a refreshingly open attitude toward nonguests who wish to

---

GOLD COAST RESORT REPORT

■ **Four Seasons Resort Hualalai** (p232) Impeccable service and dining

■ **Kona Village Resort** (p232) Privacy and a taste of old Hawai'i

■ **Hilton Waikoloa Village** (opposite) Extravagant, larger-than-life playground for kids

■ **Mauna Lani Bay Hotel & Bungalows** (p236) Grounds containing ancient Hawaiian sites and a commitment to 'green' energy

■ **Fairmont Orchid** (p236) Continental style right on the beach

■ **Hapuna Beach Prince Hotel** (p238) Fun beach and the island's premier golf course

HAWAI'I (THE BIG ISLAND)

explore its trails, fishponds and formidable petroglyph preserve. Surrounded by a barren lava field, the resort is brought to life by the emerald green of its golf course and fuchsia splashes of bougainvillea.

Sights & Activities

The beach fronting the Mauna Lani Bay Hotel is protected, but the water is rather shallow; snorkelers might prefer exploring a coral reef beyond the inlet. A less frequented cove is down by the Beach Club restaurant, a 15-minute walk south. The snorkeling is great at **Pauoa Bay** in front of the Fairmont Orchid, though the hotel frowns on nonguest access.

HONOKA'OPE BAY

One mile south of the hotel, this **bay** is protected at the southern end, and it's good for swimming and snorkeling when seas are calm. Reach it either by an old coastal trail (passing a historic fishing and village site) or by taking the access road.

KALAHUIPUA'A FISHPONDS

These ancient **fishponds** lie along the beach just south of the Mauna Lani Bay Hotel, partly shaded by a grove of coconut palms and *milo* (native hardwood) trees. They are among the few still-working fishponds in Hawai'i, and are stocked, as in ancient times, with *awa* (Hawaiian milk fish). Water circulates from the ocean through traditional *makaha* (sluice gates), which allow small fish to enter but keep mature, fattened catch from leaving. You might notice fish sporadically jumping into the air and slapping down on the water, an exercise that knocks off parasites.

KALAHIPUA'A HISTORIC TRAIL

This **trail** begins on the inland side of the Mauna Lani Bay Hotel, at a marked parking lot opposite the resort's little grocery store. Pick up a free, self-guided trail map from the concierge desk.

The first part of the trail meanders through a former Hawaiian settlement dating from the 16th century, passing lava tubes once used as cave shelters and a few other archaeological and geological sites marked by interpretive plaques. Keep an eye out for quail, northern and red-crested cardinals, saffron finches and Japanese white-eyes.

The trail then skirts fishponds lined with coconut palms and continues out to the beach,

where there's a thatched shelter with an outrigger canoe and a historic cottage with a few Hawaiian artifacts. Continue southwest past the cottage to loop around the fishpond and back to your starting point – a round-trip of about 1.5 miles.

Take a break en route at the cove near the southern tip of the fishpond, where the swimming is good and a restaurant offers simple lunches.

HOLOHOLOKAI BEACH PARK

North of the Fairmont Orchid, this **beach** has a rocky shoreline composed of coral chunks and lava. While not great for swimming, the waters are fine for snorkeling during calm surf. Facilities include showers, drinking water, rest rooms, picnic tables and grills.

To get there, take Mauna Lani Dr and turn right at the rotary, then right again on the beach road immediately before the Fairmont Orchid. The park leads to the Puako petroglyphs.

PUAKO PETROGLYPH PRESERVE

With more than 3000 **petroglyphs**, this preserve is one of the largest collections of ancient lava carvings in Hawai'i and definitely worth a visit.

The human figures drawn in simple linear forms are among the oldest examples of such drawings in Hawai'i. Like all petroglyphs in Hawaii, the meaning of the symbols remains enigmatic.

From the *mauka* end of the Holoholokai Beach parking lot, a well-marked trail leads 1300yd to the preserve. The walk is easy, but good shoes are recommended. Avoid midday as the path is only partly shaded. Stay on the path to avoid damaging the petroglyphs.

Sleeping

Mauna Lani Bay Hotel & Bungalows (☎ 885-6622, 800-367-2323; www.maunalani.com; 68-1400 Mauna Lani Dr; r $430-670; 🛈 🐾) Perhaps the most impressive attributes of the Mauna Lani Hotel are the inclusion of an on-staff historian and marine curator, and that it has the greatest solar electricity–generating capacity of any luxury resort in the world. The architecture of the hotel is rather dated and the grounds sedate, but you can still count on the Mauna Lani for luxury and excellent service.

Fairmont Orchid (☎ 885-2000, 800-845-9905; www.fairmont.com/orchid; 1 N Kaniku Dr; r $569-899) At the more updated and attractive Orchid you'll find an exotically furnished lobby and lush landscaped grounds. Guest rooms have a continental elegance, while lava rocks surround an oceanfront pool. Expect impeccable service and serious pampering.

Eating & Drinking

Both hotels have several restaurants offering breakfast buffets and formal or informal lunches.

Canoe House (☎ 885-6622; Mauna Lani Bay Hotel & Bungalows; mains $27-50; ⏰ 6-9pm) Let a salad of Waipi'o Valley fern shoots and white asparagus ($12) or filet mignon with Hamakua mushrooms and green tea soba noodles ($42) tantalize your senses at the Mauna Lani's signature restaurant. Dine inside or out at this celebrated oceanfront restaurant blending the flavors of East and West.

Brown's Beach House (☎ 885-2000; Fairmont Orchid; mains $29-59; ⏰ 11:30am-2:30pm & 6-9:30pm) It's hard to say which is the superior aspect of Brown's: the flavorful cuisine highlighting Big Island produce with an emphasis on fresh seafood, or the relaxed tropical atmosphere and beach cove view. The crab-encrusted 'opakapaka (pink snapper) in sake-mirin butter with wasabi mashed potatoes ($39) wins acclaim.

Ocean Bar (☎ 885-2000; Fairmont Orchid; ⏰ 11:30am-10pm) Dig your toes into the sand and take in the sunset from your oceanfront or poolside table. The round bar with its thatched roof couldn't be more tropical, and at night fire lights up the scene. There's live music nightly.

Entertainment

Gathering of the Kings (☎ 326-4969; www.gatheringofthekings.com; Fairmont Orchid; adult/child 6-12 $99/65; ⏰ Tue & Sat) This luau retells the story of the Polynesians' journey to Hawaii through dance and drama, and features a gourmet Polynesian dinner buffet by an award-winning chef, as well as an open bar.

PUAKO

pop 430

Puako is a one-road beach town that's lucky to remain off the beaten tourist track. The town is simply a mile-long row of houses, with many marked 'shoreline access' points.

Sights & Activities

The main attraction at Puako is giant **tide pools**, set in the swirls and dips of *pahoehoe* coastline. Some pools are deep enough to shelter

live coral and other marine life. A narrow beach of pulverized coral and lava lines much of the shore. Snorkeling can be excellent off Puako, but the surf is usually too rough in winter.

For the easiest beach access, go to the south end of the village, stopping just before the 'Road Closed 500 Feet' sign. Take the short dirt road toward the water. There is no beach per se, but there is a small cove that's used for snorkeling and shore diving; be careful of the undertow. Walk a couple of minutes north to see a few petroglyphs, a board for *konane* (a game similar to checkers) chinked into the lava, and tide pools deep enough to cool off in.

Nearby, beautiful **Beach 69** (⏰ gate 7am-8pm) is a calm bay with a rock island that is great for a dip. Low, thick trees with a rope swing or two provide plenty of shade and create private pockets between them. In case you're wondering, telephone pole 69 was once the marker for the beach, hence the beach's name. Bathrooms and showers are available.

To get to Puako, turn *makai* down Puako Rd between the 70- and 71-mile markers. For Beach 69, take the first right turn off Puako Rd. An access road from Hapuna Beach State Recreation Area leads to both Puako and Beach 69.

HAPUNA BEACH STATE RECREATION AREA

Already legendary as the Big Island's most popular and accessible **beach** (⏰ gate 7am-8pm), Hapuna is also ranked among the world's best beaches by *Condé Nast Traveler*. Its clear, deep waters and broad stretch of fluffy golden sand are the picture of a classic tropical beach. Low trees separate the beach from its facilities, and a resort lies at its north end. Hapuna packs on weekends, so arrive before noon to park with ease.

When calm, Hapuna affords good swimming, snorkeling and diving. When the surf's up in winter, bodysurfers and bodyboarders get their turn. High winter surf can produce strong currents close to the shore and a pounding shorebreak, and numerous tourists unfamiliar with the water conditions have drowned here. Lifeguards are on duty.

The park has a landscaped picnic area with two pavilions, showers, drinking water and rest rooms. It's best not to leave valuables in your car.

HAWAI'I (THE BIG ISLAND)

A tiny cove with calmer water and a small sandy beach lies about five minutes' walk north of the park.

Up from the beach, the park rents A-frame **cabins** (q $20) with million-dollar views. The cabins are spread though an exposed area and are surrounded by rolling hills. They make for a comfortable stay, and have electricity, a picnic bench inside and two single-file sleeping ledges. Amenities include shared bathrooms with showers and a cooking pavilion with a stove and fridge. The nighttime land breeze can make the incessant highway noise unbelievably loud, and it whips forcefully through the screened-in cabins, so bring earplugs and a good blanket. An advanced permit is required (see p191), though the camp host will issue a same-day, one-night permit (if space is available) if you catch him during his office hours (2pm to 4pm). Tent camping is not permitted, though exceptions are sometimes made.

MAUNA KEA RESORT AREA

Mauna Kea has the esteemed role of being the granddaddy of the Kohala Coast resorts. Built in 1965 by the late Laurance Rockefeller, the Mauna Kea Beach Hotel was the first luxury hotel on the Neighbor Islands. Today the resort offers luxury accommodations and 36 holes of golf adjacent to gorgeous Hapuna Beach, not to mention a couple of beaches of its own. The turnoff is just north of the 68-mile marker.

Sights & Activities

Kauna'oa Bay (aka 'Mauna Kea Beach') might be the most visually stunning beach on the Big Island. The crescent-shaped cove has fine white sand and a gradual slope that fosters excellent swimming conditions most of the year. On the north end, snorkeling conditions are good during calm waters.

Just north of Mauna Kea Beach is delightful **Mau'umae Beach**, with soft white sand, shady trees and protected waters. Locals are proprietary about this beach, so don't overstep your welcome. To get here, go toward the Mauna Kea Beach Hotel, turn right on Kamahoi and cross two wooden bridges. Look for telephone pole 22 on the left and park. Walk down the trail to the Ala Kahakai sign and turn left toward the beach.

Stargaze Hawaii (www.stargazehawaii.com) offers **stargazing** (☎ 880-3155; Hapuna Beach Prince Hotel; adult/child 5-11 $25/15; ☽ 8pm Mon, Wed, Thu & Sun)

of the consistently clear Kohala skies with a high-powered telescope and professional astronomers.

Golfers will be itching to play the combined 36 holes of the **Mauna Kea & Hapuna Golf Courses** (☎ 882-5400; Mauna Kea course guest/nonguest $120/145, Hapuna course guest/nonguest $150/210). The first is a 72-par championship course that consistently ranks among the top 10 courses in the world, while the second has a 700ft elevation gain and was designed by Arnold Palmer and Ed Seay.

Festivals & Events

In September locals flock to the annual **Poke Contest** (☎ 880-3424; www.pokecontest.com; admission $5), which is the 'signature event' of the Hapuna Beach Prince Hotel's Aloha Festival. Over 55 professional and amateur chefs compete and sample out their concoctions – some of them quite creative – after the judging concludes.

Sleeping & Eating

Hapuna Beach Prince Hotel (☎ 880-1111, 866-774-6236; www.princeresortshawaii.com; r $295-47; ☐) The Mauna Kea Beach Hotel's impressive 'sister' hotel now has the resort all to herself. Guests can enjoy a beautiful pool right on Hapuna Beach, and entertainment including outdoor movies, live music and hula. Its handful of bars and restaurants are open to the public, and include a sushi and oyster bar and a steakhouse.

Mauna Kea Beach Hotel (☎ 882-7222, 800-882-6060; www.maunakeabeachhotel.com; 62-100 Mauna Kea Beach Dr) The Mauna Kea suffered major structural damage in the 2006 earthquake, and at the time of research had closed its doors pending renovation. Check the website for an update.

Entertainment

Mauna Kea Beach Hotel (☎ 882-5810; 62-100 Mauna Kea Beach Dr; adult/child $84/42; ☽ 6pm Tue) The acclaimed *kumu hula* (hula teacher) from North Kohala, Nani Lim, and her *halau* (hula group) perform authentic renditions of ancient and modern Hawaiian songs and dances. An open bar and a buffet of traditional and regional Hawaiian foods is included.

SPENCER BEACH PARK

Unless you have kids or are looking for the best place north of Kona to sleep under the stars, you can skip Spencer Beach Park. Its waters are calm and silty, and its small beach not the most attractive.

The park infrastructure is large, with a lifeguard station, picnic tables and a pavilion, BBQ grills, rest rooms, showers, drinking water, and both basketball and volleyball courts. The shady coastal Ala Kahakai Trail leads 10 minutes south to Mau'umae Beach (see opposite).

Camping is allowed in areas on either side of the cove; one is waterfront and under low trees, and the other is a grassy picnic area. The ground is fairly even with lots of small rocks. Prepare for wind as it can really kick up here. A county permit is required (see p193). A camp host is often onsite, and they will occasionally sell one-night permits.

The turnoff to Spencer Beach Park (and Pu'ukohola Heiau National Historic Site) is off Hwy 270, between Kawaihae and the intersection with Hwy 19.

PU'UKOHOLA HEIAU NATIONAL HISTORIC SITE

By 1790 Kamehameha the Great had conquered Maui, Lana'i and Moloka'i. However, power over his home island of Hawai'i proved to be a challenge. When told by a prophet that if he built a heiau dedicated to his war god Kuka'ilimoku atop Pu'ukohola in Kawaihae he'd rule all the islands, Kamehameha built **Pu'ukohola Heiau**, a structure that's 224ft by 100ft, with 16ft to 20ft walls.

It is believed that Kamehameha labored alongside his men in a human chain 20 miles long, transporting rocks hand to hand from Pololu Valley in North Kohala. After finishing the heiau by summer 1791, Kamehameha held a dedication ceremony and invited his rival and cousin, Keoua, the chief of Ka'u. When Keoua came ashore, he was killed and taken to the *luakini* as the first offering to the gods. With Keoua's death, Kamehameha took sole control of the Big Island, eventually ruling all the islands by 1810.

Pu'ukohola Heiau was once adorned with wooden *ki'i* and thatched structures, including an oracle tower, an altar, a drum house and a shelter for the high priest. After Kamehameha's death in 1819, his son Liholiho and powerful widow Ka'ahumanu destroyed the deity images and the heiau was abandoned.

Today, only the basic rock foundation remains, but it's still impressive and has been designated a **national historic site** (☎ 882-7218;

www.nps.gov/puhe; admission free; ☒ 7:30am-4pm). A two-minute trail to the heiau starts at the visitor center, which has brochures and a three-minute video on the site's history. Following the 2006 earthquake, entering Pu'ukohola or Mailekini Heiau (below) was prohibited (repairs to the stone structures will take several years and millions of dollars). If you arrive after 3:30pm you'll be asked to park at Spencer Beach Park and walk to the heiau along an old entrance road closed to vehicle traffic.

Just beyond Pu'ukohola Heiau are the ruins of **Mailekini Heiau**, which predates Pu'ukohola and was once used as a fort by Kamehameha. **Hale o Kapuni Heiau**, a third temple dedicated to shark gods, lies submerged just offshore; nearby, on land, you can see the stone leaning post where the high chief watched sharks bolt down offerings.

The trail leads across the highway to the site of **John Young's homestead**. Young, a shipwrecked British sailor, served Kamehameha as a military advisor and island governor. Today, all that remains are partial foundations for two of Young's buildings.

The park holds a free **cultural festival** in August, in which reenactments of processions, a royal court and battles are held, as well as demonstrations of hula and ancient crafts. There are also canoe rides and Hawaiian food sampling.

KAWAIHAE

The Big Island's second-largest deepwater commercial harbor conceals the coast in unattractive Kawaihae. You'll be shocked to find that two upscale restaurants have managed to make a name for themselves in this pit-stop hamlet of fuel tanks and cattle pens.

North Kohala has the oldest section of the island's coast, with healthy reef ecosystems, numerous lava tubes, arches and pinnacles, and uncrowded waters. **Kohala Divers** (☎ 882-7774; www.kohaladivers.com; Kawaihae Center, Hwy 270; snorkeling $59, dives $89-115) offers dive, snorkeling and whale-watching (seasonal) tours, and dive instruction and certification. Staff members are knowledgeable and friendly, and dive groups are kept small (maximum of six).

Eating & Drinking

Café Pesto (☎ 882-1071; Kawaihae Center, Hwy 270; lunch/dinner mains $11/25, small/large pizzas $11/18; ☒ 11am-9pm Sun-Thu, to 10pm Fri & Sat) Owing to its innovative Italian dishes with Asian and island flavors, this chic little café is among the Big Island's most notable restaurants. The small bar with its cool lighting, awesome panoramic oil painting and comfy lounge chairs is ideal for a pre-dinner drink. Then decide between the likes of seafood risotto with a savory sweet-chili sauce and pizza with shrimp, shiitake mushrooms, green onions and cilantro créme fraîche.

Kawaihae Seafood Bar (☎ 880-9393; Hwy 270; mains $11-23; ◷ 11am-10:30pm) The charismatic upper-floor Seafood Bar is the best spot in town for a drink, or a lighter meal than you'll find at its partner, the Harbor Grill. The long bar has a thatched cover and good ocean-themed decor. The entree salads, *poke* burger ($11), and gin-ger steamed clams ($17) are favorites.

Kawaihae Harbor Grill (☎ 882-1368; Hwy 270; break-fast $8-16, dinner $19-32; ◷ 11:30am-2:30pm & 5:30-9pm Mon & Tue, 7-11am, 11:30am-2:30pm & 5:30-9pm Wed-Sun) The Grill is housed in an early-20th-century general store building with cute interior decor, and it's a local favorite. Fresh seafood is the specialty, appearing in omelettes in the morning ($12) and tasty dishes such as a red Thai curry ($26) in the evening.

Kawaihae Market & Deli (☎ 880-1611; Kawaihae Center, Hwy 270; ◷ 4:30am-9pm Mon-Fri, 5:30am-8pm Sat & Sun) offers the standards, plus pasta and tofu salads that are better than you might expect.

NORTH KOHALA COAST

North Kohala is a detour seldom taken by overly rushed visitors to the Big Island who are determined to stick to Hawai'i Belt Rd. It starts out slow, with deforested hills covered with waving pasture grasses and few buildings. Off-shore the coast drops off more gradually here than down in Kona, promising excellent snorkeling and diving conditions.

Geologically the oldest part of the Big Island, the North Kohala Coast is rich in ancient history. Several significant historical sites can be found on the region's southern coast, including the birthplace of King Kamehameha I.

North Kohala was sugar country until the Kohala Sugar Company closed down its operations in 1975. Though it's been 30 years since Kohala's last cane was cut, the occasional strip of feral cane can still be seen along the

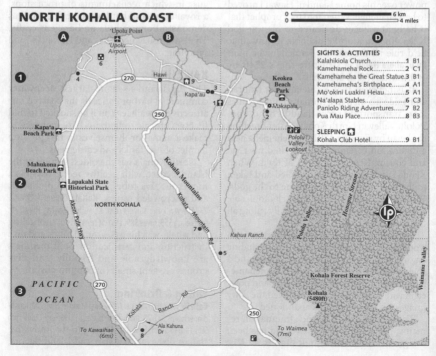

NORTH KOHALA COAST

SIGHTS & ACTIVITIES
Kalahikiola Church..................1 B1
Kamehameha Rock..................2 C1
Kamehameha the Great Statue.3 B1
Kamehameha's Birthplace.......4 A1
Mo'okini Luakini Heiau..........5 A1
Na'alapa Stables.....................6 C3
Paniolo Riding Adventures......7 B2
Pua Mau Place........................8 B3

SLEEPING
Kohala Club Hotel..................9 B1

NORTH KOHALA UPCOUNTRY RIDES

Get a feel for Hawaii's *paniolo* culture through a horseback ride or visit to one of North Kohala's upcountry ranches. The riding is open range, not nose-to-tail, and there are trotting and cantering opportunities on all the rides. Children under eight, and those under 4ft tall or over 230lb are typically not allowed on rides.

Paniolo Riding Adventures (☎ 889-5354; www.panioloadventures.com; Hwy 250; rides $89-159) Offers short, long, picnic and sunset rides over 11,000-acre Ponoholo Ranch, a working cattle ranch. Horses are all riding horses, and they're selected for the rider's experience. Boots, hats, chaps and jackets are provided free of charge.

Na'alapa Stables (☎ 889-0022; www.naalapastables.com; Kohala Ranch Rd; rides $68-88, wagon tour adult/child $36/17) Na'alapa Stables organizes rides across the pastures of the 8500-acre Kahua Ranch, affording fine views of the coast from its 3200ft elevation. Also offered is a narrated historical tour of the ranch aboard an 1860s-style farm wagon.

Evening at the Ranch (☎ 987-2108; www.eveningatkahua.com; Kohala Ranch Rd; adult/child under 12 $104/52) This evening at Kahua Ranch includes a narrated drive from the Waikoloa Resort Area (Map p233), activities such as roping and horseshoe pitching, and a telescope stargazing session. Enjoy the sunset with an open beer and wine bar, followed by a ranch-style, all-local BBQ dinner with the ranch owners, accompanied by guitar-playing paniolo. A campfire with s'mores follows. Be warned that with a 60-person maximum, the evening can feel a bit like a tour-bus excursion.

---

highway. This sugar legacy left Hawi and Kapa'au, two sweet little towns now home to artists and alternative thinkers.

The land becomes more green and lush as the highway heads east and you leave the rain shadow created by the Kohala Mountains. The angles of the land become more dramatic, and the scenery more picturesque, as Hwy 270 winds toward Pololu Valley, the jewel in North Kohala's crown.

AKONI PULE HIGHWAY

The land along the Akoni Pule Hwy (Hwy 270) remains largely undeveloped, making it quite easy to imagine the Hawai'i of old. The view of the horizon is spectacular, stretching straight and uninterrupted as far as the eye can see.

Pua Mau Place

Lose yourself in a hibiscus-flower maze and ogle bizarre bronze sculptures of animals and giant insects at these **botanic and sculpture gardens** (☎ 882-0888; www.puamau.org; Ala Kahua Dr; admission adult/child up to 10 $10/free; ☺ 9am-4pm). The 15 acres of native and exotic plants (and peacocks!) are a splash of color in a landscape stripped of much of its original vegetation. Ala Kahua Dr intersects the highway just north of the 6-mile marker.

Lapakahi State Historical Park

This **park** (☎ 882-6207; admission free; ☺ 8am-4pm, closed holidays) was a remote fishing village 600 years ago. Fish were plentiful, and the cove provided a safe canoe landing year-round. Eventually some of the villagers moved to the wetter uplands and began to farm, trading their crops for fish with those who had stayed on the coast, thereby creating an *ahupua'a* (wedge-shaped land division including seafront and mountainous interior). When the freshwater table dropped in the 19th century, the village was abandoned.

The 262-acre park encourages visitors to imagine traditional life here. An unshaded, 1-mile **loop trail** passes the remains of stone walls, house sites, canoe sheds and fishing shrines. Displays show how fishers used lift nets to catch *opelu* (pan-sized mackerel scad), a technique still practiced today, and how the salt used to preserve the fish was dried in stone salt pans. Visitors can try their hand at Hawaiian games, with game pieces and instructions laid out for *'o'o ihe* (spear throwing), *konane* and *'ulu maika* (stone bowling). Brochures are available at the trailhead.

Lapakahi's clear waters are loaded with tropical fish and are part of a marine-life conservation district. This is a historical, not recreational, park and certain areas are considered sacred. Park staff may grant permission for swimming, but check with them first.

The park is located just south of the 14-mile marker.

Mahukona Beach Park

This **park** has a rather ratty oceanfront picnic area and an abandoned landing. Once a key port for the Kohala Sugar Company, the landing was connected to sugar mills by rail. Today locals fish off it and use its ladder to get in and out of the water to swim or spearfish. Despite the name, there is no beach here.

Beyond the landing are interesting snorkeling and diving spots, although they're usually too rough in winter. Heading north, it's possible to follow an anchor chain out to a submerged boiler and the remains of a ship in about 25ft of water. You can rinse off at a shower near the ladder.

The oceanfront picnic area has portable toilets, an unkempt wooden pavilion, picnic tables and BBQ pits. Camping is allowed on the park's gently sloping grassy area with some tree cover. A county permit is required

(see p193), and campers should bring water and insect repellent.

The entrance is around the 15-mile marker. As you drive in, veer right for the landing, and left for the picnic area.

Kapa'a Beach Park

This relatively unused beach park affords access to clear waters and great snorkeling, if you venture past the rocky shore. The views of Maui can be spectacular.

The park itself is mostly parking lot, with only a falling-apart wooden picnic pavilion and portable toilets. Camping with a county permit (see p193) is allowed on uneven ground beneath low trees and amid large stones. There is only one really choice spot with a picnic table near the water.

The entrance is just north of the 16-mile marker.

HOME OF KAMEHAMEHA THE GREAT

Kamehameha the Great was born on the Big Island in 1758 near Mo'okini Luakini Heiau (opposite). As a young boy he was brought to Kealakekua Bay (p218) to live at the royal court of his uncle, Kalaniopu'u, high chief of the island.

Kamehameha became Kalaniopu'u's fiercest general, and the chief appointed him guardian of the war god, Kuka'ilimoku, the 'snatcher of land.' The deity was embodied in a coarsely carved wooden image with a bloody red mouth and a helmet of yellow feathers. Kamehameha carried an image of Kuka'ilimoku into battle with him, and according to legend it would screech out terrifying battle cries during the fiercest fighting.

Immediately after Kalaniopu'u's death in 1782, Kamehameha led his warriors against Kalaniopu'u's son, Kiwalao, who had taken the throne. Kiwalao was killed, and Kamehameha emerged as ruler of the Kohala region and one of the ruling chiefs of the Big Island.

But Kamehameha was too ambitious to share control of the islands. In 1790, with the aid of a captured foreign schooner and two shipwrecked sailors, Isaac Davis and John Young, whom he used as gunners, Kamehameha attacked and conquered the island of Maui.

Kamehameha was on Moloka'i preparing for an invasion of O'ahu when he learned that Keoua Kuahu'ula, his cousin and chief of the Ka'u region, was attacking the Hamakua Coast. Keoua boldly pillaged Waipi'o Valley (p262), the most sacred area on the Big Island and the site where Kamehameha had ceremonially received his war god a decade earlier.

As an angry Kamehameha set sail for home, Keoua's soldiers beat a quick retreat back to Ka'u. But when the withdrawing troops passed beneath the slopes of Kilauea, the volcano suddenly erupted. Toxic fumes and ash engulfed many of the warriors, who were instantly killed. In the midst of these power struggles, the prophet Kapoukahi from Kaua'i told Kamehameha that if he built a new heiau (a stone temple) to honor his war god, Kuka'ilimoku, he would become ruler of all the islands.

Kamehameha thus built Pu'ukohola Heiau (p239) in Kawaihae in 1791. Then he sent word to Keoua that his appearance was requested at the heiau for reconciliation. Keoua, well aware that this was a luakini, probably knew his fate was sealed, but he sailed to Kawaihae anyway. Upon landing, Keoua and his party became the heiau's first sacrifices. With Keoua dead, Kamehameha became sole ruler of the Big Island.

Over the next few years Kamehameha conquered all the islands except Kaua'i, over which he established suzerainty. He named the entire kingdom after his home island, Hawai'i.

Mo'okini Luakini Heiau

One of the oldest and most historically significant temples in the Hawaiian islands, this **heiau** (☎ 373-8000; admission free; ☽ dawn-dusk) sits on a grassy knoll near 'Upolu Point at the northern tip of the Big Island. The massive structure, which measures about 250ft by 125ft, with walls 6ft high, was a 'closed' heiau, reserved for *ali'i nui* (kings and ruling chiefs) for fasting, praying and offering of human sacrifices to their gods. There's a clear view of Maui and, during winter, humpback whales, from the heiau site. There are no facilities.

The heiau was dedicated to the god Ku, and built from 'sunrise to first light' by up to 18,000 'little people' passing water-worn basalt stones in complete silence from Pololu Valley – a distance of 14 miles – under the supervision of Kuamo'o Mo'okini. According to Mo'okini genealogical charts, the heiau was built around AD 480.

Five hundred years later Pa'ao, a priest from Samoa, raised the walls to 30ft and changed the altar to a scalloped shape as his *ho'okupu* (offering) to the gods. He was the first to introduce human sacrifices in an effort to stem dilution of the royal bloodlines and to enforce stricter moral codes of conduct.

In 1963 the National Park Service designated Mo'okini Luakini Heiau as Hawaii's first registered National Historic Landmark. Fifteen years later, it was deeded to the state.

About 1000yd down a dirt road below the heiau is the legendary **site of Kamehameha's birth** (opposite). As it's told, when Kamehameha was born on a stormy winter night in 1758, his mother was told by a kahuna that her son would be a powerful ruler and conquer all the islands. Upon hearing this, the ruling high chief of Hawai'i ordered all male newborns killed. Thus, after Kamehameha was taken to the Mo'okini Luakini Heiau for his birth rituals, he was spirited away into hiding in the mountains.

The current *kahuna nui* (high priestess), Leimomi Mo'okini Lum, is the seventh high priestess of the Mo'okini bloodline serving the temple. In 1978 she lifted the *kapu* that restricted access to the temple, thereby opening it to visitors. All other *kapu* that protect the sacred grounds remain in effect.

The heiau suffered damage during the October 15, 2006, earthquake (see p198), but Lum has said she doesn't want it repaired, and the state will honor her request. At the time she said: 'It has been here 1500 years. I'm not

going to change it. I'm 80. I don't look that good, but I looked good when I was 20.'

Getting There & Away

There are two routes to the heiau. The first and most convenient requires advance notice. Turn *makai* off the highway onto Old Coast Guard Station Rd, between the 18- and 19-mile markers. Follow the one-lane paved road for about a mile. Turn right onto a red-cinder road, which has two locked cattle gates that will be left open if you call ahead. An alternative route, which doesn't require advance notice, is to drive toward 'Upolu Airport then turn south on the coastal dirt road. This road can be muddy and impassable after rain. Of course, you could always walk part of either route.

HAWI

pop 940

Other than nosing through a few charming shops and galleries, there's not much to do in Hawi (hah-*vee*) proper…which is a great excuse to eat yourself silly. Hawi was once the largest of half a dozen towns in the region built to support the Kohala Sugar Company. The town's buildings, in a compact group along the highway, reflect this early-20th-century founding. Alternative-living types have transformed Hawi into a delightful place to visit, and, even if you don't stay, you must eat here. It makes a comfortable base from which to explore the lush, gorgeous scenery of the northernmost tip of the island.

Hawi has a small **visitors center** (Hwy 270) offering sketch maps and a few brochures. A post office, grocery store and gas station round out the town services. A cool and shady **park** with giant banyan trees is on Hwy 250. Behind it is the old sugar-mill tower, a remnant of the town's former mainstay.

Sleeping

Kohala Village Inn (☎ 889-0404; www.kohalavillageinn .com; 55-514 Hawi Rd; s/d $65/75, ste $100-120) In a motel-style building located right off Hwy 250, the Village Inn has simple, clean rooms a short walk from the main strip.

Eating & Drinking

For its size, Hawi has a ridiculous number of unique eateries, some of which are island bests.

Kava Kafé (☎ 889-0505; Kohala Trade Center, Hwy 270; ☽ 4:21-8:59pm) If you haven't tried kava (mildly relaxing juice of the 'awa plant), this intimate local hangout can help you out. Choose between traditional or flavors such as Maya Chocolate, made with coconut milk, ginger, chocolate, cayenne and cinnamon. On Friday there's live post-sunset tunes and an all-you-can-drink special ($10).

Short 'n' Sweet (☎ 889-1444; Kohala Trade Center, Hwy 270; panini $6.95; 🕑 9am-6pm Mon, Wed & Thu, to 8:30pm Fri & Sat, to 2pm Sun) Sweet or savory – that's the question at this quality, two-table bakery. In the morning choose between a breakfast panini or delicate, French-style croissant and pastries, or, on Sunday, eggs Benedict. Midday brings sandwiches on housemade focaccia bread and salads (often local and organic) with homemade dressings. On Friday and Saturday evening locals pack in for pizza made from scratch. As if that's not enough, the sweets are incredible. Don't miss the Kohala Crunch Bar ($4.95), which tops mac-nut brittle with bittersweet chocolate ganache and a dusting of cocoa powder.

Hula La's Mexican Kitchen (☎ 889-5668; Kohala Trade Center, Hwy 270; plates $7; 🕑 11am-8pm Mon-Fri, to 4pm Sat & Sun) This food stand will satisfy your Mexican craving with an extensive menu of fresh and yummy plates and à la carte items. Warning: the portions aren't huge and the kitchen's idea of 'greens' is a few leaves.

Aunty's Place (☎ 889-0899; Hwy 270; meals $10; 🕑 11am-4pm & 5-9pm) Gerda 'Aunty' Medeiros makes pizza all day, and traditional hearty German dinners at night, served in a casual diner setting. While the owner doesn't like to compare her 'housewife cooking' to Waimea's Edelweiss restaurant's 'hotel cooking,' she shouldn't be so modest. There's karaoke on Friday from 9:30pm until 2am.

Sushi Rock (☎ 889-5900; Hwy 270; nigiri $4-5, sushi rolls $7-10; 🕑 noon-8pm Thu-Tue) The entire island talks about personal and charming Sushi Rock. Youthful owner-chef Rio Miceli, a Hawi native, has made lasting friends through his traditional and new-wave sushi, such as his generous Rainbow Roll and the Kohala ('ahi poke, fresh papaya and cucumber, rolled in macadamia nuts). The full bar, soups, salads and grilled fish and chicken dishes also aim to please. There's live music on Friday night.

Bamboo (☎ 889-5555; Hwy 270; lunch $9-14, dinner $12-30; 🕑 11:30am-2:30pm & 6-8pm Tue-Sat, 11:30am-2:30pm Sun) Suspended Balinese umbrellas, green lights in the shape of palm trees, photo collages of Bamboo friends and twinkling white lights fill the old general store building that houses North Kohala's best restaurant. Friendly waitstaff bustle around in T-shirts, proving that there's no dress code here. Fresh, local food with vibrant flavor is the focus, and the menu's most exotic flavors are pulled off with ease. Bamboo is excellent value, so relax and get your tab started, which will be easy after you've had one of the bar's killer mai tais! Dinner here on a Friday or Saturday night, when down-home Hawaiian music (try to catch John Keawe) and hula are in full swing, may well be one of your best dining experiences on the island. Reservations are recommended.

A **farmers market** (Hwy 250; 🕑 7:30am-1pm Sat) is held in the park.

Shopping
L Zeidman Gallery (☎ 889-1400; Hwy 270; 🕑 10am-5pm Mon, to 6pm Tue-Sat, to 4pm Sun) Bowls and sculpture made from over 50 types of Hawaiian wood – most of them grown on the Big Island – are on display here. The craftsmanship standard is high, with prices to match.

KAPA'AU
pop 1160

Kapa'au, though not quite as cute as Hawi, is home to a handful of shops and galleries displaying both crafts and fine art by local artists. Being that it is North Kohala's largest town, Kapa'au's compact main drag has a few civic buildings mixed in with historical and uninspired modern architecture. As it's Kamehameha's childhood home, the June **King Kamehameha Day** festivities here have extra significance, and are celebrated with a parade and Hawaiian music, dance, and food in the park.

Information
The island's biggest and best used bookstore, **Kohala Book Shop** (☎ 889-6400; Hwy 270; 🕑 11am-5pm Mon-Sat), is also a gathering place for local authors and literary luminaries from abroad. Kapa'au also has a grocery store, two banks with ATMs, a gas station and a police station.

Sights & Activities
Kamehameha Park has a large, modern gymnasium, and everything from a ballpark to a swimming pool, all free and open to the

public. There are also picnic tables and a kiddie play structure.

KAMEHAMEHA THE GREAT STATUE

This **statue** on the front lawn of the North Kohala Civic Center may look familiar. Its lei-draped and much-photographed twin stands opposite Honolulu's 'Iolani Palace (p104).

The statue was made in 1880 in Florence by American sculptor Thomas Gould. When the ship delivering it sank off the Falkland Islands, a second statue was then cast from the original mold. The duplicate statue arrived at the islands in 1883 and took its place in downtown Honolulu. Later the sunken statue was recovered from the ocean floor and completed its trip to Hawaii. It was then sent here, to Kamehameha's childhood home. A notice board behind the statue tells the full story.

KALAHIKIOLA CHURCH

Protestant missionaries Elias and Ellen Bond built this **church** in 1855. The land and buildings on the drive in are part of the vast Bond estate, proving that missionary life wasn't one of total deprivation. Large portions of three of the church's walls crumbled in the 2006 earthquake, and the congregation immediately began fundraising to rebuild. Towering banyan trees and peaceful macadamia-nut orchards surround the church, making it a worthwhile detour.

The church is 900yd up 'Iole Rd, which is on the *mauka* side of the highway between the 23- and 24-mile markers.

KOHALA YOGA COMMUNITY CENTER

This **center** (☎ 889-0583; Sakamoto Bldg, 55-3877 Hwy 270; drop-in class $14) offers classes in yoga, pilates, dance and martial arts.

KAMEHAMEHA ROCK

According to legend, Kamehameha carried this rock up from the beach below to demonstrate his strength. Much later, when a road crew attempted to move the rock to a different location, the rock stubbornly fell off the wagon – a sign that it wanted to stay put. Not wanting to upset Kamehameha's mana, the workers left it in place. Keep an eye out for the facade of the **Tong Building**, a colorful old Chinese hall secluded in the trees above the rock.

The rock is on the *mauka* side of Hwy 270, on a curve just past a small bridge, about 2 miles east of Kapa'au.

Sleeping & Eating

Kohala Club Hotel (☎ 889-6793; www.kohala-club-hotel.com; 54-3793 Hwy 270; d $56) This inn has a staggered row of 1930s-feeling wooden summer cottages surrounded by lush tropical landscaping. The rooms are small and simple, with fairly updated fixtures (including cable TV) and wooden porches. Look for a sign suspended over a driveway on the *makai* side, south of mile marker 23.

Kohala Country Adventures Guest House (☎ 889-5663, 866-892-2484; www.kcadventures.com; d $85-125, ste $160; 🖳) Drift off to the sounds of distant waves and let birds wake you at this guesthouse on 10 acres with tropical gardens, livestock and a clear view of Maui. All three options have private entrances and decks, and homey decor. Wireless access is available in a common area with a TV, DVD player, games, a refrigerator and laundry facilities.

Kohala Rainbow Café (☎ 889-0099; Hwy 270; sandwiches & salads $8; 🕙 11am-5pm Mon-Fri) Jen's small café has tasty chicken Caesar salads, good chili and a recommended Greek wrap sandwich with organic greens. Also on the menu are fresh-fruit smoothies, deli sandwiches and soups.

MAKAPALA

The highway becomes more narrow and winding after Kapa'au, bringing the lush, green jungle closer to the road. A few single-lane bridges add to the sensation that the end of the road is near. The village of Makapala has only a few hundred residents, and few commercial buildings.

Take in the awesome mana of the North Kohala coast at the **Keokea Beach Park** (🕙 gate 7am-11pm). Tall, reddish cliffs rise above a rock-lined bay with a protected boat launch. The surf really surges with a west swell, attracting a motley crew of experienced local surfers. Swimming is sketchy due to dangerous shore breaks and strong currents. The facilities aren't in great shape, but there are BBQ grills, showers and portable toilets. A pavilion with two picnic tables on a small rise is possibly the prime picnic spot on the Leeward Coast.

An old **Japanese cemetery** is on the way down to the beach. Most of the gravestones are in kanji (Japanese script), and filled sake cups sit in front of a few.

The park is down a well-marked road, about 1 mile off the highway.

POLOLU VALLEY

Hwy 270 ends at a viewpoint overlooking secluded Pololu Valley, with a stunning backdrop of steeply scalloped coastal cliffs spreading out to the east. The lookout has the kind of strikingly beautiful angle that's rarely experienced without a helicopter tour – and it's just as stunning as the more famous Waipi'o Valley lookout.

Pololu was once thickly planted with wetland taro. The Pololu Stream fed the valley, carrying water from the remote, rainy interior to the valley floor. When the Kohala Ditch was built, it siphoned off much of the water for sugarcane and put an end to taro production. The last islanders left the valley in the 1940s, and the valley slopes are now forest-reserve land. The ditch continued to be a water source for Kohala ranches and farms, but it was rendered unusable by the 2006 earthquake. At the time of research, repair costs were still being assessed.

Sights & Activities

The shaded **Pololu Valley Trail**, from the lookout down to the mouth of Pololu Valley, takes less than 30 minutes to walk. It's steep, but switchbacks keep it from being overly strenuous, and the view is a constant reward. It's a little rocky toward the bottom, and walking sticks are often left at the trailhead. There are no facilities.

A 900m black-sand **beach** lies at the mouth of the valley and the end of the trail. The surf is usually intimidating in winter, and there can be rip currents year-round, so swimming isn't recommended. A forested rise behind the beach has a fairytale quality and trees that call out for rope swings and hammocks.

Intrepid hikers can continue to the next valley, **Honokane Nui**. Be warned that the trail is treacherously slippery and traverses private property, and it's relatively easy to get lost. It takes about two hours each way from the lookout. Follow the vague trail on the eastern side of Pololu Valley, going up the 600ft mountain and over the ridge before dropping into Honokane Nui Valley. Don't hike too close to the ocean, as strong waves are capable of sweeping you away.

Tours

Hawaii Forest & Trail (☎ 331-8505, 800-464-1993; www .hawaii-forest.com; waterfall tour adult/child under 12 $114/89, 4WD tour adult/child 6-12 $99/79) offers two tours in

the Kohala area. One is a hike along the Kohala Ditch Trail to waterfalls, and includes transportation from the Waikoloa Resort Area. The other is through the Pololu Valley in a six-wheel off-road vehicle and on foot.

WAIMEA (KAMUELA)

pop 7030

The cool, green rolling pastureland surrounding Waimea is perhaps Hawai'i's most unexpected face. This is cattle and cowboy country, and nearly all of it, including Waimea itself, is owned, run or leased by Parker Ranch, one of the largest ranches in the USA. Covering about 175,000 acres, Parker Ranch land constitutes about 10% of the Big Island and is about twice the size of Lanai.

In a familiar Hawaii story, it all began because an introduced species – seven longhorn cattle given as a gift to King Kamehameha in 1793 – reproduced to become a pest. In 1809 the king commissioned 19-year-old John Palmer Parker to thin and control the wild herd. The skillful Parker did so, and he further secured his future by marrying one of Kamehameha's granddaughters. As Parker's holdings grew, he brought three Mexican-Spanish cowboys over to better train his Hawaiian ranch hands. The *paniolos,* as the newcomers were called, also brought their guitars – and Hawaiians quickly adapted the instrument into their own distinctive and now famous 'slack-key' style.

Beyond this interesting slice of island history, Waimea offers travelers some great lodgings, first-rate art galleries and gourmet eats, including Merriman's, a forerunner in the Hawaii Regional Cuisine movement. So long as you don't mind the fog and brisk afternoon winds, Waimea makes an appealing base for exploring the nearby Kohala and Hamakua Coasts.

ORIENTATION

Waimea is also referred to as Kamuela, which is the Hawaiian spelling of Samuel; most claim it's for Samuel Parker of Parker Ranch fame. Maps usually list both names, the phone book and post office only use Kamuela, and, yes, it gets confusing.

The junction of Hwys 19 and 190 is the center of town; most businesses and sights are near it. From Hilo, Hwy 19 is commonly

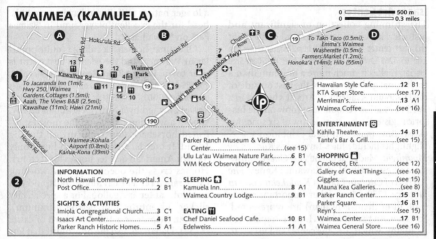

WAIMEA (KAMUELA)

Hawaiian Style Cafe..............**12** B1	
KTA Super Store...................(see 17)	
Merriman's.........................**13** A1	
Waimea Coffee...................(see 16)	

ENTERTAINMENT 🎭
Kahilu Theatre......................**14** B1	
Tante's Bar & Grill................(see 15)	

SHOPPING 🛍
Crackseed, Etc....................(see 12)	
Gallery of Great Things........(see 16)	
Giggles..............................(see 15)	
Mauna Kea Galleries.............(see 8)	
Parker Ranch Center.............**15** B1	
Parker Square.....................**16** B1	
Reyn's.............................(see 15)	
Waimea Center....................**17** B1	
Waimea General Store.........(see 16)	

INFORMATION
North Hawaii Community Hospital..**1** C1
Post Office...............................**2** B1

SIGHTS & ACTIVITIES
Imiola Congregational Church.......**3** C1
Isaacs Art Center.........................**4** B1
Parker Ranch Historic Homes........**5** A1

Parker Ranch Museum & Visitor
Center..................................(see 15)
Ulu La'au Waimea Nature Park........**6** B1
WM Keck Observatory Office.........**7** C1

SLEEPING 🛏
Kamuela Inn............................**8** A1
Waimea Country Lodge..............**9** B1

EATING 🍴
Chef Daniel Seafood Cafe..............**10** B1
Edelweiss................................**11** A1

To Tako Taco (0.5mi);
Emma's Waimea
Washerette (0.5mi);
Farmers Market (1.2mi);
Honoka'a (14mi); Hilo (55mi)

To Jacaranda Inn (1mi);
Hwy 250; Waimea
Gardens Cottages (1.5mi);
Aaah, The Views B&B (2.5mi);
Kawaihae (11mi); Hawi (21mi)

To Waimea-Kohala
Airport (0.8mi);
Kailua-Kona (39mi)

0 — 500 m
0 — 0.3 miles

HAWAI'I (THE BIG ISLAND)

---

called the Mamalahoa Hwy, though west of Hwy 190, Hwy 19 becomes Kawaihae Rd, while Hwy 190 continues as the Mamalahoa Hwy. If you've followed this, remember that, further east, a section of the 'Old Mamalahoa Hwy' intersects and parallels Hwy 19.

INFORMATION

Waimea has no town visitor center. However, the town's official website, www.kamuela .com, is a good source of information. For a more personal window into local life (with lots of interesting info on local agriculture), visit www.ahualoa.net.

Emma's Waimea Washerette (☎ 345-8213; Kawaihae Rd; ⏱ 6am-9pm) Across from Tako Taco.

North Hawaii Community Hospital (☎ 885-4444; 67-1125 Mamalahoa Hwy) Emergency services 24 hours.

Post office (☎ 885-6239; 67-1197 Mamalahoa Hwy; ⏱ 8am-4:30pm Mon-Fri, 9am-noon Sat) Address all Waimea mail to Kamuela.

SIGHTS
Parker Ranch Museum & Visitor Center

This small **museum** (☎ 885-7655; www.parker ranch.com; Parker Ranch Center, 67-1185 Mamalahoa Hwy; adult/child over 5 $7/5.50; ⏱ 9am-5pm Mon-Sat, last entry 4pm) provides a thorough account of ranch history. Displays include some fascinating Parker-family memorabilia, such as portraits, lineage charts, fancy gowns and traditional Hawaiian quilts. The re-created tack house is particularly evocative, with 100-year-old saddles and branding irons. Though it has a romantic gloss, the 25-minute movie on Parker

Ranch tells the history well and describes current ranch operations. It also includes some fantastic historic footage, such as when shipping the cattle meant driving them into the sea and lifting them with slings onto the decks of waiting steamers. In front of Parker Ranch Center, near the parking lot's main entrance, the *paniolo* statue is garlanded with brands from all of Hawai'i's ranches.

Parker Ranch Historic Homes

See how wealthy landowners lived in these two 19th-century **homes** (☎ 885-5433; www .parkerranch.com; Mamalahoa Hwy; adult/child & senior $9/7; ⏱ 10am-5pm, last entry 4pm), less than a mile south of the intersection of Hwys 190 and 19. 'Tours' consist of a 15-minute presentation, after which visitors explore the houses on their own.

Built in 1962, **Pu'uopelu** is the estate's sprawling 8000-sq-ft grand manor, which showcases the impressive collection of European and Chinese art of the last Parker Ranch owner, Richard Smart. One room celebrates Smart's theatrical performances, both on Broadway and in Europe. Next door is **Mana Hale**, a gleaming re-creation of the original 1840s home built by John Parker in the hills outside Waimea. Parker constructed it in a plain saltbox style, but his use of koa wood resulted in an extraordinarily warm and rich interior (the original was dismantled board by board and rebuilt here). Period furnishings and historic photos of the hardy-looking Parker clan round out the experience.

Isaacs Art Center

The stunning collection of significant and historic Hawaiian paintings and artifacts at this **art center** (☎ 885-5884; http://isaacartcenter.hpa .edu; 65-1268 Kawaihae Rd; admission free; ◷ 10am-5pm Tue-Sat) makes it much more a museum than a traditional gallery – one of the best outside of the Honolulu Academy of Arts. It's housed in a 1915 plantation schoolhouse (now on the historic register), whose single row of six spacious classrooms makes an ideal exhibition space. Highlights include Jules Tavernier's *Kilauea by Moonlight*, Madge Tennent's *Lei Queen Fantasia*, and especially Herb Kawainui Kane's *The Arrival of Captain Cook at Kealakekua Bay in January 1779*. Many other important artists (not all of them Hawaiian) are represented. Sales benefit the attached Hawai'i Preparatory Academy, which runs the center and uses it to teach art to its students. Don't miss it.

WM Keck Observatory Office

The lobby of this working **office** (☎ 885-7887; 65-1120 Mamalahoa Hwy; ◷ 8am-4:30pm Mon-Fri) is open to the public. It's worth visiting if you won't be going to Mauna Kea's visitor center (see p254). A computer station and video nicely overview the twin Kecks and their astronomical work, plus there are pretty photos, scale models and a telescope trained on Mauna Kea.

Church Row

Conveniently enough, Waimea's historic churches are gathered along the same street just off Mamalahoa Hwy. In the park that fronts the 'row' is a display describing all five, which include Baptist, Buddhist, Mormon and Hawaiian Christian places of worship. All hold services.

The **Imiola Congregational Church** (◷ services 9:30am) was constructed in 1857 and restored in 1976. The beautiful interior was built mainly of koa, which glows unadorned by stained glass or painted scenes. In the churchyard is the grave of missionary Lorenzo Lyons, who arrived in 1832 and spent 54 years in Waimea. Lyons wrote many of the hymns that are still sung in Hawaiian here each Sunday. Also in the garden is the church bell, which is too heavy for the church roof to support.

ACTIVITIES

Ulu La'au Waimea Nature Park, off Hwy 190, is a small green space perfect for a stroll or picnic; it's lovingly tended, and plans are to develop a longer nature trail. If you have young kids, head for the excellent playground in **Waimea Park** on Kawaihae Rd.

Of course, horseback riding is quite popular in Waimea, and the island's best outfit is near town. **Dahana Ranch Roughriders** (Map p252; ☎ 885-0057, 888-399-0057; www.dahanaranch.com; rides per 1½/2hr $60/100; ◷ 9am, 11am, 1pm & 3pm, reservations required), owned by a Native Hawaiian family, is both a working ranch and the most established horseback tour company on the Big Island. It breeds, raises, trains and uses only its own American quarter horses for its tours. Horses cross the open range of a working cattle ranch rather than follow trails, and you can trot, canter and gallop. For a special 'city slicker' adventure (four-person minimum), you can help drive a 100-head herd of cattle ($130). Dahana is also the only outfit that lets very young children (aged three and up) join in. It's located 7.5 miles east of Waimea, off Old Mamalahoa Hwy.

Parker Ranch also offers two-hour **horseback rides** (☎ 885-7655; rides $79; ◷ 8:15am & 12:15pm), for everyone aged seven and up, which focus on ranch history (you visit stone corrals and the arena), and a 1.5-hour sunset ride at 4pm.

COURSES

In early November the annual **Waimea 'Ukulele & Slack Key Institute** (☎ 885-6017; www.kahilutheatre .org/ukulele.htm) brings prominent local and international musicians together for a concert at the Kahilu Theatre (p250). A great series of workshops is also held, ranging from beginner to master classes, with opportunities for private lessons. An evening open-mike jam session (or *kanikapila*), in which students play with the masters, is free.

TOURS

It won't get your pulse racing, but Parker Ranch also offers a horse-drawn **wagon ride** (☎ 885-7655; adult/child & senior $15/12; ◷ departures every hour 10am-2pm Tue-Sat), which leaves from near the visitor center. Guides work the cowboy shtick, which is fun if you have young kids.

Foodie alert! A brand-new **Merriman's Farm and Dinner Tour** ($155 per person; ◷ 2:30pm Mon-Thu) visits two farms devoted to sustainable agriculture and ends the day with a special four-course dinner at the restaurant. For tour reservations, contact **Hawaii Forest & Trail** (☎ 331-8505; www.hawaii-forest.com).

FESTIVALS & EVENTS

Small rodeo events occur year-round on the Big Island.

Fourth of July Parker Ranch Rodeo A uniquely Waimea event, with cattle roping, bull riding, horse races and other hoopla at the Rodeo Arena.

Aloha Festivals Ho'olaule'a See http://alohafestivals .com. During the statewide Aloha Festivals in August and September, with food, games, art and crafts, and entertainment, plus the Aloha Festival Paniolo Parade, with marching bands, floats, taiko drumming and equestrian units.

Round-Up Rodeo Labor Day weekend, first Monday in September. Another whip-cracking Parker Ranch rodeo, this one lasting two days.

SLEEPING

Kamuela Inn (☎ 885-4243, 800-555-8968; www.hawaii -bnb.com/kamuela.html; 1600 Kawaihae Rd; r $60-85, ste $90-185) This motel is definitely the best deal in town. The 31 rooms aren't fancy, but they are clean and modestly attractive, all with TV and private bath. Within the complex, room sizes and situations vary; spending a little more can significantly improve your experience.

Aaah, the Views B&B (☎ 885-3455; www.aaahthe views.com; 66-1773 Alaneo St; s $85-95, d $95-105, ste $150-170) Rooms are small but views are large at this delightful B&B. The two smallest rooms share a bath. Two suites have private bath: the Garden Cottage includes a loft bed (great for kids), while the Dream Room earns the name for its breathtaking vistas, Jacuzzi tub and private outdoor shower. All rooms have cable TV, phone, fridge and microwave. Lingering on the porch by a burbling stream will lead to many 'aaahs.' Ask about weekly discounts.

Waimea Country Lodge (☎ 885-4100, 800-367-5004; www.castleresorts.com; 65-1210 Lindsey Rd; r $110-120, with kitchenette $130) This 21-room motel makes an acceptable backup if all other lodging is booked: rooms are scuffed, tired and overpriced, and they suffer from street noise, but they are clean enough and don't lack for space.

Waimea Gardens Cottages (☎ 885-8550; www .waimeagardens.com; cottages d incl breakfast $160-170; ▣) Just 2 miles west of town (near the intersection of Kawaihae Rd & Hwy 250) two charming cottages make for private, romantic getaways. Both are fully stocked with amenities. Waimea Cottage is spacious and light, with rose walls, a floral bedspread and a working fireplace. Kohala Cottage is larger, with a full kitchen and an airy, indulgent bath with

its own tiny garden. There's a three-night minimum stay.

Jacaranda Inn (☎ 885-8813; www.jacarandainn .com; 65-1444 Kawaihae Rd; r $125-150, ste $170-200) The eight romantic rooms here are indulgent, antique-filled visions, a mix of four-poster beds, opulent tiled baths, carved furniture, Jacuzzi tubs and oriental rugs over hardwood floors. No two are alike. The secluded nest of buildings is connected by hedge-lined wooden walkways. Plans for 2007 include opening a restaurant in the main house and adding some bargain rooms ($70 to $90) in an adjacent cottage.

EATING

Some of the Big Island's best eats are in Waimea, beginning with the excellent **farmers market** (⏱ 7am-noon Sat) at the Hawaiian Home Lands office, near the 55-mile marker on Hwy 19. The **KTA Super Store** (☎ 885-8866; Waimea Center, 65-1158 Mamalahoa Hwy; ⏱ 6am-11pm) has a pharmacy and *poke*.

Waimea Coffee (☎ 885-2100; Parker Sq; sandwiches $7; ⏱ 7am-5pm Mon-Fri, 8am-5pm Sat, 9am-4pm Sun) This nice coffee shop has wi-fi, espresso drinks, and a variety of wraps and sandwiches.

Tako Taco (☎ 887-1717; 65-1271 Kawaihae Rd; dishes $4-9; ⏱ 11am-8pm Mon-Sat, noon-8pm Sun) It won't put Mexico out of business, but it's hard to find disappointment in the Mexican dishes here. The pineapple-tomatillo salsa is pure heaven; pour it liberally over fresh enchiladas, fish tacos and *chili rellenos* (stuffed chillies).

Hawaiian Style Cafe (☎ 885-4295; Hayashi Bldg, 64-1290 Kawaihae Rd; dishes $6-9; ⏱ 7am-1:30pm Mon-Sat, to noon Sun) Join locals at the horseshoe-shaped counter that dominates the island's best greasy spoon: filling servings of *loco moco*, pancakes, *laulau*, poi, fried rice, burgers and more will keep you going all day. As the sign says: 'Come early. When food is *pau*…there is no more!'

Chef Daniel Seafood Cafe (☎ 887-2200; 65-1259 Kawaihae Rd; mains $13-45; ⏱ 3:30-9pm) Chef/owner

---

TOP EATS: WINDWARD SIDE

- **Merriman's** (p250)
- **Chef Daniel Seafood Cafe** (above)
- **Hilo Bay Cafe** (p278)
- **Restaurant Kaikodo** (p279)
- **Thai Thai Restaurant** (p301)

HAWAI'I (THE BIG ISLAND)

Daniel Thiebaut remade and renamed his Waimea restaurant in 2006, turning it into an eclectic gourmet destination for seafood lovers. There's now a top-notch sushi bar, a fun tapas menu (where favorite appetizers like phyllo-wrapped shrimp now live), inexpensive pastas and risottos ($13 to $21) and an extravagant selection of lobster and seafood platters ($40 and above). The rambling, remodeled historic building has never looked better.

Edelweiss (☎ 885-6800; Kawaihae Rd; dinner mains $26-32; ☺ 11am-1pm & 5-8pm Tue-Sat) Waitresses in traditional dress serve large platters of roast pork, weiner schnitzel, bratwurst, lamb and steak – with liberal sides of sauerkraut – in Edelweiss' warm (but not romantic) dining room. It's rich, hearty, accomplished German cooking that wins raves.

Merriman's (☎ 885-6822; www.merrimanshawaii .com; Opelo Plaza, 65-1227 Opelo Rd; dinner mains $30-45; ☺ 11:30am-1:30pm Mon-Fri, 5:30-9pm daily) An innovator of Hawaii Regional Cuisine, chef and owner Peter Merriman created the Big Island's first gourmet restaurant devoted to organic, island-grown produce and meats. Romance infuses the dining room, and the service is perfect, but the proof is on the plate: Hawaiian- and Asian-influenced dishes like ponzu-marinated mahimahi, wok-charred 'ahi and panko-and-lime-crusted scallops are world-class gems. For over 18 years he's been taking a torch to his signature coconut crème brûlée, and it still only wants for two spoons.

ENTERTAINMENT

Kahilu Theatre (☎ 885-6017, box office 885-6868; www .kahilutheatre.org; Parker Ranch Center, 67-1186 Lindsey Rd; admission $35-45; ☺ showtimes vary) Waimea may not be hopping with nightlife, but it enjoys a first-class year-round slate of dance, music and theater. Performers at Kahilu have included Chick Corea, Paul Taylor Dance Company, Laurie Anderson, Chanticleer and the Harlem Gospel Choir. A big draw is the annual Waimea 'Ukulele & Slack Key Institute concert (p248).

Tante's Bar & Grill (☎ 885-8942; Parker Ranch Center; ☺ 10:30am-2pm, 5-9pm Wed-Mon) Don't miss this bar on Thursday night, when guitarist 'Braddah Smitty' (Smitty Colburn) plays Hawaiian music (and locals often jam with him); it can get packed. Friday and Saturday nights are a mix of live bands and DJs.

SHOPPING

Three shopping malls line Hwy 19 through town: **Parker Ranch Center** (67-1185 Mamalahoa Hwy), where the stop signs say 'Whoa,' **Waimea Center** (65-1158 Mamalahoa Hwy), and **Parker Square** (65-1279 Kawaihae Rd). The first two have groceries and basics in addition to gift shops, while Parker Square aims for the more discriminating, upscale gift buyer.

Gallery of Great Things (☎ 885-7706; Parker Sq; ☺ 9am-5:30pm Mon-Sat, 10am-4pm Sun) Crammed with antiques, art and collectibles from Hawaii, Polynesia and Asia, this standout is guaranteed to empty your wallet.

Mauna Kea Galleries (☎ 887-2244; www.maunakea galleries.com; 65-1298 Kawaihae Rd; ☺ 11am-6pm Mon-Fri) This gallery has authentic, one-of-a-kind items and artifacts, and prices to match. But browsing is free: check out Duke Kahanamoku's surfboard, original Webber engravings (from Cook's voyage), poi pounders, movie posters, vintage aloha shirts and classic kitsch.

Reyn's (☎ 885-4493; Parker Ranch Center; ☺ 9am-5pm Mon-Sat, to 3pm Sun) If you want to dress like a local, shop at Reyn's. Its classic, understated aloha shirts (which use Hawaiian fabrics in reverse) never go out of style.

Giggles (☎ 885-2151; Parker Ranch Center; ☺ 9am-5:30pm Mon-Sat, to 3pm Sun) A must for affordable, baby- and kid-size aloha shirts and dresses, plus cool toys and rare Hawaiian Hello Kitty items.

Crackseed, Etc (☎ 885-6966; Hayashi Bldg, Kawaihae Rd; ☺ 9:30am-4:30pm Mon-Fri, 10am-4pm Sat) Searching for that unusual Chinese dried-fruit snack called 'crack seed' (see p55)? You've found it. For addicts, the shop sells *li hing* powder in bulk, plus great Hawaiian gifts.

GETTING THERE & AROUND

Waimea-Kohala Airport is south of town, but you aren't likely to fly there. From Monday to Saturday the free Hele-On Bus (p199) goes from Waimea to Kailua-Kona on its 16 Kailua-Kona route (65 minutes), and to Hilo on its 7 Downtown Hilo route (one hour 20 minutes). The bus stops at Parker Ranch Center.

The drive from Kailua-Kona is 37 very scenic miles along Hwy 190; you ascend into grassy rangeland studded with prickly-pear cacti and enjoy great coastal views. From Hilo, the drive is 51 miles along Hwy 19 around the Hamakua Coast.

Though Waimea isn't large, you need a car to get around. Parking is ample, but commuter peak times see terrible traffic jams.

AROUND WAIMEA

Kohala Forest Reserve

East of Waimea on Hwy 19, there is an excellent hike along the **Kohala Forest Reserve Trail**, which leads several miles through a forest of ohia trees and past a bamboo grove to reveal stunning views of the back of Waipiʻo Valley. The trail is usually well maintained, and it's about 2.5 miles to the first viewpoint, after which you can continue for several more miles, enjoying some of the most gorgeous scenery ever devised. This is one of the Big Island's best short hikes, but note that at the time of research it was closed due to damage from the October 2006 earthquake.

To get there, from Waimea head east on Hwy 19 for about 3 miles, then turn left (or north) on White Rd. Drive about a mile to the end of the road, park at the gate, and enter the gate on foot (closing it behind you). Walk past Waimea Reservoir; in about 1.5 miles a sign lets you know you've entered the Kohala Forest Reserve.

Old Mamalahoa Highway

If you're driving between Waimea and Honokaʻa, consider taking this portion of the Old Mamalahoa Hwy, a 10-mile detour off Hwy 19 (from Waimea, enter at the 52-mile marker; from Honokaʻa, enter at the 43-mile marker across from Tex Drive-In). This winding, unhurried road provides a soothing glimpse of surrounding ranchland, horses, and herds of cattle. For a little adventure, search out the old miner's quarry cave; it's on the inside (southern edge) of a prominent bend in the road about 4 miles from the Waimea turnoff. The overgrown entrance is hard to see, and you'll need a flashlight.

MAUNA KEA

At 13,796 ft, Mauna Kea is Hawaiʻi's highest peak, but, measured from its beginnings on the ocean floor, it adds another 15,000 ft, becoming the world's tallest mountain (a claim it essentially shares with Mauna Loa). Size, however, is just one measure of Mauna Kea's stature. Here, nature, spirituality and science have converged and sometimes conflicted in vivid, striking ways. This dormant volcano's harsh environment once sported a glacier, and it remains home to numerous endangered endemic species. Mauna Kea is also one of the holiest places in traditional Hawaiian spirituality, and on its most sacred spot – the summit – has gathered the greatest collection of major astronomical telescopes in the world.

HAWAIʻI (THE BIG ISLAND)

DETOUR: HAKALAU FOREST NATIONAL WILDLIFE REFUGE

The Hakalau Forest National Wildlife Refuge is a place few people, even locals, ever venture. This extremely remote refuge protects a portion of the state's largest koa-ohia forest, which provides habitat for endangered bird species, including the native hoary bat and Hawaiian hawk. About 7000 acres are open to public access, but only on weekends and state holidays.

This is solely a 4WD (or rugged mountain biking) adventure. From Waimea, a dirt road runs 44 miles around Mauna Kea (meeting up with the summit access road, another starting point); while most of it is reasonably well graded, a middle section is desperately unkempt. When the road's dry, a 2WD could shudder through the washboardy first 10 miles or so, and if it's rained, don't bother at all – some of the mud bogs are said to be bottomless. Once you get to the refuge, there are no facilities, signage or trails.

On Hwy 19 at the 55-mile marker near Waimea, turn south onto Mana Rd, which eventually becomes Keanakolu Rd. Initially, you pass through bucolic Parker Ranch land; several cattle grates need to be opened and closed as you go. About halfway between Waimea and Saddle Rd is a stone monument to David Douglas, the famed Scottish botanist, for whom the Douglas fir tree is named. In 1834, Douglas died under mysterious circumstances near here.

You need a permit, which you can obtain by calling or writing to the **refuge manager** (☎ 933-6915; www.fws.gov/pacificislands/wnwr/bhakalaunwr.html; 32 Kinoʻole St, Hilo, HI 96720; ☷ 8am-4pm Mon-Fri). An ideal time to visit is during the second week in October, which is National Wildlife Refuge Week, when Hawaiian ornithological experts and rangers are on hand. The easiest way to visit is with **Hawaii Forest & Trail** (☎ 331-8505, 800-464-1993; www.hawaii-forest.com; tours $160), which offers a birding adventure tour in the Hakalau refuge.

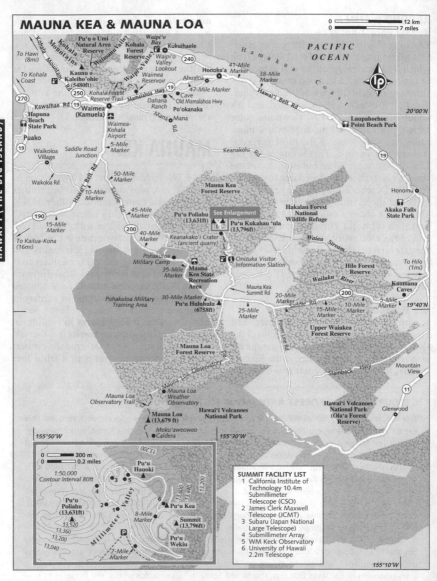

MAUNA KEA & MAUNA LOA

SUMMIT FACILITY LIST
1. California Institute of Technology 10.4m Submillimeter Telescope (CSO)
2. James Clerk Maxwell Telescope (JCMT)
3. Subaru (Japan National Large Telescope)
4. Submillimeter Array
5. WM Keck Observatory
6. University of Hawaii 2.2m Telescope

Hilo's newest museum, 'Imiloa (p272), provides a wonderful introduction to the mountain and its history, but a visit to Mauna Kea itself, particularly the summit, is an unforgettable experience. All of Hawaii lies below (not to mention 40% of earth's atmosphere) as you sail into an ocean of stars. Even though it means long pants, a winter coat, some thoughtful arrangements, and a little luck, you won't be sorry you left the beach to make the pilgrimage.

HISTORY

Mauna Kea began under the ocean, rising to become the tallest peak in Polynesia. Between 40,000 and 13,000 years ago, ice-age glaciers covered the summit, beneath which lava continued to erupt. Mauna Kea's last eruption was around 4500 years ago (it has since slid off the hot spot), and scientists consider it 'dormant.'

Certain plants and animals adapted to this unique environment. Ascending the mountain, biological zones shift from rain forest to koa-and-ohia forest to open woodland to shrubs and finally (above 11,500ft) to alpine desert. At every elevation there are numerous species endemic to Hawai'i, and some found only on Mauna Kea. Plants endemic to Mauna Kea's summit include two lichens and the dramatic Mauna Kea silversword, which takes 50 years to flower, and does so only once (for more, see p407).

Summit creatures are restricted mostly to bugs, spiders, mites and beetles. Strangest by far is the endemic *wekiu*, a bug that adapted by changing from a herbivore to a bug-eating carnivore, and by developing 'antifreeze' blood to survive the subfreezing temperatures. Further down the mountain, several of Hawai'i's endemic birds call Mauna Kea home, such as the nene and the *palila* honeycreeper, as well as the endangered Hawaiian bat, the *'ope'ape'a*.

The arrival of Polynesians on Hawai'i affected Mauna Kea hardly at all, but the mountain came to play a central role in Hawaiian cosmology. Mauna Kea is believed to be the firstborn child of the gods Wakea and Papa, who also gave birth to taro and the first

---

THE PLACE BETWEEN HEAVEN & EARTH

On Mauna Kea's summit, the first snow of winter is falling.

Near the visitor center, Ranger James Keali'i Pihana – known affectionately as 'Kimo' – is blocking the frozen road in his pickup and trying to explain to a *haole* (Caucasian) writer what Mauna Kea means to Hawaiians.

'To us, Mauna Kea is not "White Mountain," it is "the heavens." It is the "Mount of Waikea," the place between heaven and earth. The *kumulipo* tells the creation story of these islands, the first creation of man, and Mauna Kea is the center of our "Bible story."'

Beneath his stiff ranger cap, long gray hair curls over Kimo's collar. His dark eyes are intense as his thick laborer's hands gently conjure visions in the air.

'Mauna Kea is the home of the snow goddess, Poliahu, Pele's sister. Ceremonies are still conducted: equinox, solstices, first light, pray to the sun. In the old days, common people could only go up as far as the visitor center today. Lake Waiau is sacred water. Umbilical cords were put in the lake for the protection of children. My son's umbilical cord is in the lake right now.'

Officially, Kimo is Mauna Kea's resident 'Hawaiian cultural practitioner,' but he doesn't need the title. 'My authority comes from the ruling chiefs of Hawaii. I'm the conscience of the Hawaiian people up here.'

An elder and priest, a kahuna, Kimo and others walked up the mountain in 1998 to voice their deep concern over the 'golf balls' – the observatories. Sacred places and burial sites had been built on and disturbed, and new observatories were going up without communicating with or consulting Native Hawaiians.

'We found astronomers were not having respect for the mountain.' A rally was held, and Kimo says, 'I scolded all of them, from the governor on down. Our people were ready to shut the road down.'

It was a pivotal moment, and the politicians and astronomers responded. A Native Hawaiian advisory council was created, Kimo conducted 'cleansing rituals to forgive and repent,' and then he applied for a job. He now spends his days like any other ranger, but his more important duty is communicating with Hawaiian leaders about what's happening on their sacred mountain.

He says, 'There is much more cooperation today. The directors acknowledge they need to respect Hawaiian protocol. Locals are accepting of astronomy. The mountain is calm.'

As he talks, two Japanese men approach the truck; despite the weather, they still want to drive to the top. One pleads, 'We've traveled very far.'

Kimo shakes his head. 'The mountain rules' is all he offers.

On this night, Poliahu is spreading her white robe over the summit, and Kimo doesn't seem at all sad to be the one making sure no one disturbs her homecoming.

human (from whom Hawaiians and all people descend). The mountain is also considered a sacred realm of the gods (where people are not meant to live), and the summit is the place were sky and earth separated to create heaven.

Three sister goddesses call the summit home; the most famous is the snow goddess Poliahu, who lives in Pu'u Poliahu. In legends, Poliahu often competes with Pele, and their snow-and-lava tussles are a metaphorically correct depiction of Mauna Kea's geology. For Hawaiians, Mauna Kea was (and remains) a temple, a place of worship and a sacred burial site.

The arrival of Westerners in the late 1700s also meant the introduction of feral cattle, goats and sheep on Mauna Kea. By the early 20th century these animals had decimated the mountain's natural environment; animal eradication efforts, begun in the 1920s and continuing today, have helped nature to partly restore itself.

In 1960 astronomer Gerard Kuiper placed a telescope on Pu'u Poliahu and announced that 'the mountaintop is probably the best site in the world from which to study the moon, the planets and stars.' Kuiper turned out to be right.

In 1968, the same year the first Mauna Kea observatory was built, the University of Hawai'i (UH) was granted a 65-year lease to the summit area, now called the 'Mauna Kea Science Reserve.' The university leases property to others, and 13 telescopes are currently in operation, which is more than on any other single mountain. They include three of the world's largest, and their combined light-gathering power is 60 times greater than the Hubble Space Telescope.

All this building and development on such an environmentally fragile and culturally sacred place has led to heated conflicts (see p253). Today, concerted efforts are being made to balance the needs of all stakeholders on Mauna Kea, so that the environment is protected, Hawaiian culture is respected and cutting-edge astronomy continues. It's a three-sided conflict that has become common in modern-day Hawaii.

ORIENTATION & INFORMATION

The Mauna Kea Summit Rd is near mile marker 28 on Saddle Rd (for more on driving this road with a rental car, see p258). From the Saddle Rd junction, it's six paved miles to the Onizuka Visitor Information Station (see below).

Any standard car can drive this far; it takes about 50 minutes from Hilo or Waimea and 1.5 hours from Kailua-Kona. Past the visitor center, it's another 8 miles (half unpaved) and nearly 5000ft to the summit; only 4WD vehicles should be used from this point. To visit the summit without a 4WD, you need to join a Mauna Kea tour (see p257), hike, or beg a lift at the visitor center from someone with a 4WD (you might get lucky).

Note that the Mauna Kea summit is not a national, state or county park. There are no restaurants, gas stations or emergency services. Weather conditions can change rapidly, and daytime temperatures range from the 50s to below freezing. The summit can be windy, and observatory viewing rooms are just as cold as outside. Bring warm clothing, a heavy jacket, sunglasses and sunscreen. Call the **recorded hotline** (☎ 935-6268) for info on weather and road conditions.

DANGERS & ANNOYANCES

The Onizuka Visitor Information Station is at 9200 ft, and even here some visitors might experience shortness of breath and mild altitude sickness. At the 13,796ft summit, atmospheric pressure is 60% what it is at sea level, and altitude sickness is common. Symptoms include nausea, headaches, drowsiness, impaired reason, loss of balance, shortness of breath and dehydration. The only way to recover is to descend. Kids under 16, pregnant women, and those with high blood pressure or circulatory conditions should not go to the summit. Nor should you scuba dive within 24 hours of visiting Mauna Kea.

The best way to avoid altitude sickness is to ascend slowly. All hikers and travelers to the summit should stop first at the visitor center for at least 30 minutes to acclimatize before continuing.

SIGHTS
Onizuka Visitor Information Station

Officially the Onizuka Center for International Astronomy, the **center** (☎ 961-2180; www .ifa.hawaii.edu/info/vis; ◷ 9am-10pm) was named for Ellison Onizuka, a Big Island native, and one of the astronauts who perished in the 1986 *Challenger* space-shuttle disaster.

In itself, the Onizuka Visitor Information Station is rather modest, but its one room is packed with information: inside are photo displays of the Mauna Kea observatories, videos on astronomy, descriptions of discoveries made from the summit, computer feeds and virtual tours of several observatories, and exhibits of the mountain's history, ecology and geology. The rangers, interpretive guides and volunteers are extremely knowledgeable about astronomy and Mauna Kea's cultural significance, and they are eager to help with hiking and driving advice.

Plus, you can purchase (and heat in a microwave) coffee, hot chocolate and instant noodles, or munch on freeze-dried astronaut food, and there are books and gifts for sale. Several hikes are possible from the visitor center (see p256), and at night the free stargazing program is held here (see p256).

Summit Observatories

If you have a 4WD you may drive to the summit in the daytime, and you are allowed to stay until a half hour after sunset. Since vehicle headlights interfere with astronomical observation, all cars are asked to leave before nightfall. It takes about half an hour to drive the 8-mile summit road; the first 4.5 miles are gravel.

Just before the pavement begins, the area on the east side of the road is dubbed 'moon valley,' because it's where the Apollo astronauts rehearsed with their lunar rover before their journey to the real moonscape.

Just past the 6-mile marker is a parking area; below this is the trailhead to Lake Waiau and to the ancient adze quarry Keanakako'i. Getting to both takes about an hour, depending on your acclimatization. During Mauna Kea's ice age, when molten lava erupted under the glaciers, it created an extremely hard basalt, which ancient Hawaiians chipped into sharp adzes at **Keanakako'i**. These tools were fashioned on the mountain and traded throughout the islands. Entering the fragile quarry is highly discouraged.

Nearby, sitting inside Pu'u Waiau at 13,020ft, is **Lake Waiau**. This unique alpine lake is the third-highest in the USA. Thought by ancient Hawaiians to be bottomless, it is actually only 10ft deep and, despite desert conditions, never dry. Clay formed from ash holds the water, which is fed by melted snow, permafrost and less than 15in of rainfall annually. To Hawaiians, these sacred waters are considered the 'umbilical cord' (or *piko*) connecting heaven and earth, and a traditional practice is to place a baby's umbilical cord in the water to assure good health.

On the summit are the massive dome-shaped observatories, which rise up from

HAWAI'I (THE BIG ISLAND)

CHICKEN LITTLE WITH A TELESCOPE

If you're the anxious type, you probably already know what NEO stands for. No, it's not a character from *The Matrix*; it's a 'near earth object' – a large asteroid that flies a little too close to earth. Some scientists believe asteroid impacts have caused earth's mass extinctions, and one theory is that the hot spot that created Hawaii was made when an asteroid dimpled the earth's crust.

Funny thing is, faint, close (and deadly) objects are actually harder to see than cute winking stars a million light years away.

Finding, tracking and predicting the unwelcome arrival of NEOs is the main goal of the University of Hawai'i's next big telescope on Mauna Kea – Pan-STARRS. A prototype has already been tested at Maui's Haleakala National Park, and construction of the real thing begins soon – either gutting or rebuilding the observatory containing UH's 2.2m telescope (but not *adding*, astronomers are quick to note, a 14th summit observatory). 'First light,' the term for when a new telescope first opens its eye, is slated for 2010.

The Pan-STARRS telescope will contain four 1.8m mirrors, but its main distinguishing feature will be its camera resolution – which will spit out unheard-of 1.4 gigapixel images (and, yes, we hope they counted).

The plan is for the telescope to completely survey the sky three times every lunar cycle for 10 years. Ideally, this will find 90% of all potentially hazardous objects and locate 99% of all visible stars in our neighborhood of the galaxy. The telescope will also come in handy for supernova research.

To learn more about NEOs, visit http://neo.jpl.nasa.gov/neo.html. For more on Pan-STARRS, visit www.ifa.hawaii.edu.

the stark terrain like some futuristic human colony on another planet. Unfortunately, you can't see much inside the observatories. Currently only two have visitor galleries, and they're minimal: the **WM Keck Observatory visitor gallery** (www.keckobservatory.org; admission free; 10am-4pm Mon-Fri) includes a display, a 15-minute video, public bathrooms and a viewing area inside the Keck I dome; and the **University of Hawai'i 2.2m Telescope** (admission free; 9:30am-3:30pm Mon-Thu), which has displays and a view of the telescope room.

The short, 200yd trail to Mauna Kea's true summit begins opposite the University of Hawai'i telescope; it's harder than it looks, and it's not necessary to go to see the sunset. The summit is marked by a US Geological Survey (USGS) summit benchmark and a Native Hawaiian altar. Given the biting winds, high altitude and extreme cold, most people don't linger.

From the summit, the breathtaking sunsets will take your words over the horizon; look east to see 'the shadow,' or the gigantic silhouette of Mauna Kea looming over Hilo. Moonrises can be equally stunning: the high altitude can make the moon appear squashed and misshapen, or sometimes resembling a brushfire.

ACTIVITIES
Hiking
Several short walks are possible starting from the visitor center. At one end of the parking lot, you can enter an area protecting the endemic, dramatic silversword, while across from the visitor center, a 10-minute uphill hike on a well-trodden trail crests **Pu'ukalepeamoa**, a cinder cone that offers the best sunset views near the center. Several moderate hikes also begin from the summit road (see p255).

Then there is the 6-mile **Humu'ula–Mauna Kea Summit Trail**, which begins at the Kilohana picnic tables near the visitor center and climbs nonstop about 4600ft to the top of Mauna Kea. This is a daunting, very strenuous all-day hike. In addition to high altitude, steep grades, winds and changeable weather, much of the trail is over crumbled 'a'a and loose cinder, which gets tiresome.

To do this trail, start early, by dawn or soon thereafter. Most people need five to six hours to reach the summit, and eight to 10 hours for the round-trip. Get a hiking map, consult with rangers and register at the center before starting.

Park at the Onizuka Center and walk up the road to the Kilohana picnic area, then follow the **Humu'ula Trail** signs uphill. Signs continue for the first mile or so; after about an hour the summit road comes back into view on your right, and the vegetation starts to disappear. From here, red poles with reflectors help guide your way, at times weaving around cinder cones. You will also pass various spur trails; all lead back to the access road.

Most of the way you pass through the **Mauna Kea Ice Age Natural Area Reserve**. After about three hours, a sharp, short ascent takes you over a rise, and **Keanakako'i**, the adze quarry (see p255), appears off to the right; look for large piles of bluish-black chips. Do not enter or remove anything from this protected area.

After another steep mile or so you reach a four-way junction, where a 10-minute detour to the left brings you to **Lake Waiau** (see p255). Return to the four-way junction and head north (uphill) for the final push to meet the Mauna Kea Access Rd at a parking area. Suddenly the observatories are visible on the summit, and straight ahead is Millimeter Valley, nicknamed for the three submillimeter observatories you see (among them the James Clerk Maxwell Telescope). The 'trail' ends at the 7-mile marker of the access road, but the top of the mountain still snickers at you another 1.5 miles further up the road.

You didn't come this far not to reach the true summit, so soldier on till you reach the University of Hawai'i 2.2m Telescope, where the short spur trail to the summit begins (see p255).

When it's time to descend, most hikers return along the shoulder of the access road rather than retracing the trail. Though the road is 2 miles longer, it's easier on the knees and easier to follow if the light is fading. Also, it's common for hikers to get offered a lift downhill, and sticking to the road increases your chances.

Stargazing
The Onizuka Visitor Information Station (p254) offers a free stargazing program from 6pm to 10pm, weather permitting (bad weather prevents stargazing only two to three nights per month). There are no reservations, but you could call the visitor center to confirm that the program is on that evening. At 9200ft the skies are among the clearest, driest

and darkest on the planet. In fact, at the station you're above the elevation of most major telescopes worldwide. This is the *only* place you can use telescopes on Mauna Kea; there are no public telescopes on the summit. How much you'll see depends on cloud cover and moon phase. The busiest nights are Friday and Saturday.

Skiing

You brought your skis to Hawai'i, right? For a month or two (beginning in January or February), enough snow usually falls on Mauna Kea's heights to allow for winter sports. Snowboards are used more often than skis, but on a nice day the 'slopes' can get crowded with locals using surfboards, bodyboards, inner tubes, food trays – whatever! One popular tradition is to fill a truck bed with snow, drive to the beach and build a snowman.

Skiing Mauna Kea is a novelty experience, and a haphazard one. There are no groomed trails, no lifts, no patrols; exposed rocks and ice sheets are constant dangers, and the steep slopes make steering and stopping difficult. Also, commercial ski tours on Mauna Kea are prohibited; avoid any company that offers one.

TOURS

The Onizuka Visitor Information Station offers **free summit tours** (admission free; ◔ 1pm Sat & Sun), but you must provide your own 4WD transportation. No reservations are needed; simply arrive at the visitor center by 1pm to join the tour. (You can sometimes hitch a ride with a friendly person who has a 4WD, but don't count on it.) The first hour is spent watching videos about astronomy on Mauna Kea as you acclimatize, then you caravan to the summit, where you hear a talk on the history and workings of the summit telescopes. The tours then visit one or two telescopes: the University of Hawai'i's 2.2m telescope and/or WM Keck's 10m telescope. Tours depart from the summit at about 4:30pm, but most people stay for sunset and come down on their own. Pregnant women, children under 16, and those with circulatory and respiratory conditions are not allowed, and tours don't go in bad weather, so call ahead.

Subaru Telescope (☎ 934-5056; www.naoj.org /Information/Tour/Summit; ◔ 10:30am, 11:30am & 1:30pm) offers 30-minute summit tours up to 15 days per month, in English and in Japanese. You must make reservations (by internet only), and you need your own transportation to the summit.

If you prefer not to drive, a handful of companies offers sunset tours; times vary by season, but they typically start around noon, include a meal stop, arrive at the summit for about an hour at sunset, return to the Onizuka Center for stargazing, and get you home after 9pm. All require participants to be at least 16 years old, and all but Arnott's pick up from the Kona/Waikoloa/Waimea area.

Arnott's Lodge (☎ 969-7097; www.arnottslodge.com; 98 Apapane Rd, Hilo; guests/nonguests $70/100) Arnott's tour is more for hikers than stargazers. It's cheaper, leaves from Hilo and encourages hiking to the true summit, but guides don't overwhelm you with astronomy. Stargazing occurs below the visitor center using binoculars.

Hawaii Forest & Trail (☎ 331-8505, 800-464-1993; www.hawaii-forest.com; tours $170) Hosts a hot picnic dinner at a Parker Ranch outpost, and provides gloves and a parka. Guides focus on astronomy, and stargazing is conducted at the visitor center using their own telescopes.

Mauna Kea Summit Adventures (☎ 322-2366, 888-322-2366; www.maunakea.com; tours $178) Similar to Hawaii Forest & Trail, Summit Adventures has been doing this the longest (over 20 years). You get a hot meal, gloves and parka, and visitor-center stargazing through their telescopes. Book online two weeks in advance for a 15% discount.

FESTIVALS & EVENTS

Every Saturday night at 6pm the Onizuka center hosts a rotating series of lectures and events:
'The Universe Tonight' First Saturday of the month. Astronomy lecture.
University of Hawai'i Hilo Astrophysics Club Second Saturday of the month. Students assist with stargazing.
Malalo I Ka Lani Po Third Saturday of the month. Culture lecture.
University of Hawai'i Hilo music program Fourth Saturday of the month. All genres.

During big meteor showers the center staffs its telescopes for all-night star parties; call for details.

SLEEPING

At the 35-mile marker, Mauna Kea State Recreation Area maintains five simple cabins ($35 per night, Friday to Sunday only), which have three twin beds and a bunk bed, flush toilets, a kitchen, lights, electricity, a space heater and Mauna Loa views. However, they have no

RIDIN' THE SADDLE

True to its name, Saddle Rd (Hwy 200) runs along a saddle-shaped valley between the island's two highest points, Mauna Kea to the north and Mauna Loa to the south. It's a very scenic drive: sunrise and sunset bathe these majestic mountains in a gentle glow, on clear days the vistas extend forever (at least to Maui), and you pass through gorgeous varied terrain.

But this 53-mile, mostly two-lane paved road suffers a bad rap. Originally built by the military, who tenderize portions with their armored vehicles, it has long been forbidden by car-rental companies: sometimes narrowing to one lane, winding and hilly, with blind turns, no lights and frequent fog, it's been the perfect recipe for accidents.

However, its condition, and its reputation, are changing. Today, from Hilo all the way to the 35-mile marker at Mauna Kea State Recreation Area, the road is no worse than Hwy 19, which circles the island; current construction of a realignment of Saddle Rd from the 19-mile marker to the 37-mile marker will improve it further. Travel from Kona remains a bit sketchy (perhaps because of the Pohakuloa Military Training Area at the 36-mile marker): the pavement deteriorates the higher you go, and, like locals, you'll soon be hugging the middle to avoid the potholes.

Despite this, some car-rental companies have relaxed their restrictions. Both Alamo and National now allow driving on Saddle Rd, though Harper is the only company that will rent a 4WD you can take to Mauna Kea's summit. If you want to visit Saddle Rd, Mauna Kea or Mauna Loa, call the local offices of the car-rental companies to find out their current policies (see p200).

Finally, Saddle Rd contains no services or gas; before coming, fill up, check your spare tire, pack a lunch and don't forget your camera.

drinkable water (or showers), kitchens come unequipped, and nearby military maneuvers and seasonal hunting could intrude on your solitude. For reservations, contact the **Division of State Parks** (Map p268; ☎ 974-6200; www.hawaii.gov/dlnr /dsp; PO Box 936, Hilo, HI 96721; ⏲ 8am-3:30pm Mon-Fri).

GETTING THERE & AROUND

From Kona, Saddle Rd (Hwy 200) starts just south of the 6-mile marker on Hwy 190. From Hilo, drive *mauka* on Kaumana Dr, which becomes Saddle Rd (Hwy 200). All drivers should start with a full tank of gas, as there are no gas stations on Saddle Rd (for more, see above).

As described under Orientation (see p254), past the visitor center the road is suitable only for 4WD vehicles. Over half the road is gravel, sometimes at a 15% grade, and the upper road can be covered with ice. When descending, drive in low gear (or you can ruin your brakes), and pay attention for any signs of altitude sickness. Driving when the sun is low – in the hour after sunrise or before sunset – can create hazardous blinding conditions.

AROUND MAUNA KEA
Mauna Loa's Northern Flank

As much as Mauna Kea, Mauna Loa rewards those who make the effort to climb it. The unsigned Mauna Loa Observatory Rd starts

near the 28-mile marker on Saddle Rd, nearly opposite the Mauna Kea Access Rd and next to Pu'u Huluhulu (see below). The single-lane, 17.5-mile asphalt road ends at a parking area just below the weather observatory at 11,150ft. There are no visitor facilities or bathrooms. From the observatory, the Mauna Loa Observatory Trail climbs to the mountaintop.

The narrow road is passable in a standard car, but it's in terrible condition and full of blind curves. Allow an hour. The squiggled white line is to aid drivers in the fog.

HIKING

Just off Saddle Rd at the Mauna Loa road turnoff, **Pu'u Huluhulu** is a cinder cone covered with bushy foliage. An easy short hike surmounts and circles it, providing splendid mountain views in all directions, and this makes a reflective way to spend 30 minutes acclimatizing before continuing up Mauna Loa. There's a pit toilet at the trailhead.

At the end of Mauna Loa Observatory Rd is the **Mauna Loa Observatory Trail**, which is the most recommended route to the summit (for the daunting Mauna Loa Summit Trail, see p298). Make no mistake: the Observatory Trail is a difficult, all-day adventure, but few 13,000ft mountains exist that are so accessible to the average hiker. This is a rare and unforgettable experience.

Day hikers do not need a permit, but if you would like to overnight at Mauna Loa Cabin (see p299), register the day before at the Kilauea Visitor Center in Hawai'i Volcanoes National Park (see p291).

Begin hiking early, preferably by 8am; you want to be off the mountain or descending if afternoon clouds roll in. The trail is marked by cairns, which disappear in the fog. If this happens, stop hiking; find shelter in one of several small tubes and hollows along the route until you can see again, even if this means waiting till morning.

It is nearly 4 miles to the trail junction with the **Mauna Loa Summit Trail** (Map p289). Allow three hours for this gradual ascent of nearly 2000ft. If it weren't for the altitude and thin air, this would be a breeze. Instead, proceed slowly but steadily, keeping breaks short. If you feel the onset of altitude sickness (p254), descend. About two hours along, you re-enter the national park, and the lava erupts in a rainbow of colors: sapphire, turquoise, silver, ochre, orange, gold, magenta.

Once at the trail junction, the majesty of the summit's **Moku'aweoweo Caldera** over-whelms the imagination. Day hikers have two choices: proceed another 2.6 miles and three hours along the **Summit Trail** to the tippy-top at 13,677ft (visible in the distance), or explore the caldera itself by following the 2.1-mile **Mauna Loa Cabin Trail** (Map p289). For those who can stand not summiting, the second option is extremely interesting, leading to even grander caldera views and a vertiginous peek into the awesome depths of **Lua Poholo** (Map p289).

Descending takes half as long as ascending: depending on how far you go, prepare for a seven- to 10-hour hike round-trip. Bring copious amounts of water, food, a flashlight and rain gear, and wear boots, a winter coat and a cap – it's cold and windy year-round.

HAMAKUA COAST

The Hamakua Coast winds along the island's verdant northern shoreline, from the dramatic cliffs of Waipi'o Valley all the way to Hilo. A good map tells you what you need to know about the weather and terrain: innumerable

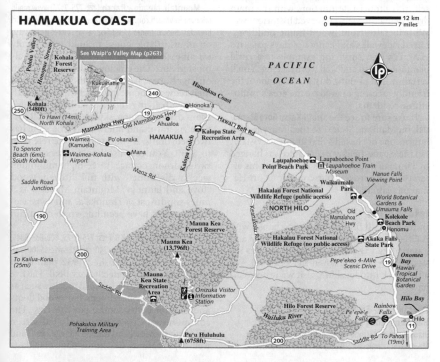

streams course down the north and east flanks of Mauna Kea, wrinkling the coastline with lush ravines and gulches, and telling a tale of rain. In an impressive engineering feat, the Hawai'i Belt Rd (Hwy 19) traverses the largest of these gulches on sweeping cantilevered bridges. All in all, it makes the best of scenic drives, and it offers wonderful opportunities to veer off the highway and get lost – in nature, and even in time, experiencing Hawai'i as it existed before the unyielding drumbeat of our modern age.

HONOKA'A
pop 2230

For most of the 20th century Honoka'a was a sugar plantation town. Immigrants came from England, China, Spain, Japan, Puerto Rico and the Philippines to work in the surrounding sugarcane fields, and a building boom in the 1920s and 1930s filled the busy main street with the era's iconic plantation-Western-style architecture. Then, in 1993, after more than 100 years as the town's economic engine, the Honoka'a Sugar Company processed its last harvest and shuttered its mill.

Today, Honoka'a is slowly remaking itself into a tourist destination, with the main draw being the well-preserved historic town. With its false-front, wood-frame buildings, raised sidewalks and echoes of days past, it's Hawai'i's best surviving example of a rural plantation town and well worth seeing. You'll certainly find nothing dusty or false about the friendly greeting offered by the area's multi-ethnic residents.

Make sure to see the small **Katsu Goto Memorial**, on Mamane St next to the library, which honors one of Hawai'i's first union activists. A Japanese cane-field worker, Goto was hanged by Honoka'a sugar bosses in 1889 for his attempts to improve labor conditions on Hamakua plantations.

Information

In town you'll find all the basics: banks with ATMs, a grocery store, a coin laundry and a **post office** (☎ 800-275-8777; 45-490 cnr Lehua St & Mamane St; ☺ 9am-4pm Mon-Fri, 8:15-9:45am Sat). For a real peek into local life, visit www.honokaa hawaii.com.

Festivals & Events

Hamakua Music Festival (☎ 775-3378; www .hamakuamusicfestival.org; Honoka'a People's Theater, Mamane St; admission $30-40) Mid-May and early October. A premier music event combining Hawaiian, jazz and classical music and gathering such world-class talents as Cedar Walton and James Moody. The festival also awards scholarships to music students islandwide, presents student workshops with visiting celebrities, and provides funding for music teachers in public schools.

Honoka'a Western Weekend (☎ 933-9772; Mamane St; admission free) Late May. An annual event that awakens the usually sleepy Mamane St with a BBQ, a parade, a country dance, a rodeo and entertainers such as local icon Melveen Leed.

Sleeping

Honoka'a makes a good base for Waipi'o Valley adventures.

Hotel Honoka'a Club (☎ 775-0678, 800-808-0678; www.hotelhonokaa.com; Mamane St; dm/s/d with shared bathroom $20/30/40, r $50-75, ste $95) The only game right in town, these plantation workers' rooms are charming in a lived-in way; expect scuffs, thin walls, and a friendly greeting from Annelle, the owner. Two end rooms with ocean views are best, while all the upstairs rooms with private bathrooms are better than the downstairs hostel. Breakfast is simple, fresh and homespun, like the place.

Mountain Meadow Ranch (☎ 775-9376; www.mountainmeadowranch.com; 46-3895 Kapuna Rd, Ahualoa; ste incl breakfast $95, cottages $135) For a private getaway, or an affordable house to hold your family for an extended stay, this 7-acre ranch is almost idyllic. The gracious owners, who train quarter horses, have turned the lower level of their redwood home into a very spacious B&B suite, with living room, tiled bath, barber's chair, dry-heat sauna, skylights, TV/VCR, wi-fi, refrigerator and microwave. The suite has two bedrooms; if you use both, the rate rises to $150. You can also book a freestanding two-bedroom cottage (three-night minimum; weekly discounts) with full kitchen, wood stove and laundry. Mountain Meadow is 3 miles southwest of Honoka'a, and so peaceful urbanites have been known to complain about the quiet.

Waipi'o Wayside B&B (☎ 775-0275, 800-833-8849; www.waipiowayside.com; Hwy 240; r incl breakfast $100-190) This gorgeously furnished 1932 plantation house makes for a perfectly cozy B&B. The five rooms aren't large, but special touches such as iron bedframes, plush linens, hardwood floors and elegant baths soothe any worries. The common room has a library and a flat-screen TV (with movies), and there's a large lanai and well-kept grounds. Full homemade breakfasts are a highlight. It's between the 3- and 4-mile markers on Hwy 240.

Eating

Fine dining it's not, but Honoka'a has a few satisfying choices. Near Honokaa Trading Company, a farmers market is held on Saturday from 7:30am.

Simply Natural Deli (☎ 775-0119; Mamane St; dishes $4-8; ☽ 8am-2:30pm Mon-Sat) Order up organic, wholesome taro pancakes, tempeh eggs, fruit smoothies and filling sandwiches at this good-vibe café.

Tex Drive-In (☎ 775-0598; Hwy 19; sandwiches & plate lunches $4-9; ☽ 7am-8pm) A *malasada* is just a donut, but Tex is famous for making them fresh, fat and delicious. They come plain (95c) or filled ($1.30). Tex also serves an above-average plate lunch, with crisp green salads and tasty renditions of the classic meats, like Korean chicken. There's also an attached gift and garden shop.

Café il Mondo (☎ 775-7711; 45-3626A Mamane St; sandwiches $6, pizza $11-13; ☽ 11am-8pm Tue-Sat) From the outside you'd think you were losing a bet, but this casual Italian restaurant serves some of the island's best pizza. Toss in oven-baked sandwiches, calzones and pasta specials, and you're definitely a winner.

Entertainment

Honoka'a People's Theater (☎ 775-0000; Mamane St; adult/child $6/3) Catch a first-run movie in this atmospheric 1930s theater (with old-school projectors in the lobby). It also hosts occasional events, including the not-to-be-missed Hamakua Music Festival (opposite).

Shopping

Honokaa Trading Company (☎ 775-0808; Mamane St; ☽ 11am-4pm) Afternoons are lost rummaging through the dusty treasures in this second-hand store. Highlights are used books on Hawaii, vintage business signs, a few true antiques and aloha shirts. Opening hours are subject to the owner's hula schedule.

Kama'aina Woods (☎ 775-7722; Lehua St; ☽ 9am-5pm Mon-Sat) This workshop creates some of the finest koa woodworking you'll find. The store also sells smaller items to go with its gems, like a koa concert ukulele.

Honokaa Marketplace (☎ 775-8255; 45-3586 Mamane St; ☽ 9:30am-5:30pm) Amazing handmade Hawaiian quilts, bright painted bedspreads and sheets.

Hamakua Fudge Shop (☎ 775-1430; 45-3611 Mamane St; ☽ 10:30am-4:30pm Mon-Sat, noon-3pm Sun) Creamy fudge ($14/lb), all made here, with unusual island variations. There's no finer use of the mac nut.

Getting There & Away

From Monday to Saturday the free Hele-On Bus (p199) arrives from Kona on the 7 Downtown Hilo route, then continues on to Hilo. From Hilo, take either the 31 Honoka'a route or the 16 Kailua-Kona route (which continues to Kona). It takes an hour from either direction.

KUKUIHAELE

pop 320

If you're on your way to Waipi'o Valley, you might stop in the tiny village of Kukuihaele for four reasons: to browse its two gift shops, mail a letter in the post office, meet your Waipi'o Valley tour or book a memorable stay in a house or B&B. Kukuihaele is about 7 miles from Honoka'a, on a loop road off Hwy 240.

Sleeping

Hale Kukui Orchard Retreat (☎ 775-7130, 800-444-7130; www.halekukui.com; 48-5460 Kukuihaele Rd; studios $145, 2-bedroom ste $180, 1-room cottages $195) These three tranquil and secluded rooms all have wonderful views and pleasing decor, but the perspective of Waipi'o from the detached cottage may make you forget your name. All have TV, phone, kitchen, private bath and even private jet tubs on the decks. Guests can pick a variety of fruit (for $5) from the surrounding orchard.

NIGHT MARCHERS

Kukuihaele means 'traveling light' in Hawaiian, and the name refers to the 'night marchers,' ghosts of Hawaiian warriors passing through, carrying torches on their way to Waipi'o Valley, which contains a hidden entrance to the netherworld. Night marchers are believed to walk through ancient battlefields on the night of Huaka'ipo (27th phase of the moon). According to legend, if you look directly at them or if you're in their way, you'll die. It's possible to survive if one of your ancestors is a marcher – or if you lie face down on the ground.

Oceanview House (☎ 775-9098, 866-492-4746; www
.hawaiioceanviewhouse.com; Hwy 240; 2-bedroom house $155)
If you're looking for a house to call your own,
this is a stellar choice. It has attractive furnishings and decor, a fully equipped kitchen,
two bedrooms, a living room, a laundry, a
TV, a phone and geckos aplenty – plus a
gorgeous view of the endless Pacific with a
peek of Waipi'o Valley. There's nothing not
to like. Don't worry, if the Cliff House below
is booked, your mate will still kiss you for
bringing them here.

Cliff House Hawaii (☎ 775-0005, 800-492-4746;
www.cliffhousehawaii.com; Hwy 240; 2-bedroom house $195)
Views? You want views? Forget about it. While
the layout and level of decor are identical to
the Oceanview House above, *your* sweeping view is like a private perch over Waipi'o.
If you love someone, bring them here –
and book *way* in advance.

Shopping

Neptune's Garden Gallery at Last Chance Store (Map
p263; ☎ 775-1343; www.neptunesgarden.net; ☒ 9am-
3:30pm Mon-Sat) New owners have turned the
Last Chance Store into a gallery for their
stained glass – much of it whimsical, some of
it stunning. They also still carry water, soda,
snacks and ice cream.

Waipio Valley Artworks (Map p263; ☎ 775-0958, 800-
492-4746; www.waipiovalleyartworks.com; ☒ 8am-5pm)
One of the better gift shop/galleries you'll
find, with lots of koa and ceramic art, plus an
excellent selection of books and prints. Several
Waipi'o tours leave from here, and the shop
sells cheap sandwiches ($5), muffins, coffee,
water and trail snacks.

WAIPI'O VALLEY

Hawaii contains many beautiful places, but a
select few pulsate like dreams sprung to life.
The largest of seven spectacular amphitheater
valleys on the windward side of the Kohala
Mountains, Waipi'o embodies the Hawaii of
fantasy: white waterfalls trickle down near-
vertical emerald cliffs (some 2000ft high), while
on the valley floor a tangle of jungle, flowering
plants and taro patches is edged with a black-
sand beach pounded by frothy azure waves. But
this evocative scene is animated by something
else. The Hawaiians call it mana, and it's hard
not to suspect more is at work here than pretty
scenery.

Most people admire the valley from the
lookout, which is the abrupt end to Hwy 240.

The valley itself contains no lodging or services, and the precipitous winding road to the
bottom requires a 4WD or two sturdy feet.
Currently, the lookout has only a parking
lot, a phone and a bathroom, but plans are
underway to expand the lookout area, add
descriptive signs and even hire a ranger.

History

In ancient times Waipi'o Valley was the political and religious center of Hawai'i and home to
the highest ali'i. Waipi'o is also the site where
Kamehameha the Great received the statue of
his fearsome war god, Kuka'ilimoku.

According to oral histories, several thousand people lived in this fertile valley before
the arrival of Westerners. Waipi'o's sacred
status is evidenced by a number of important heiau. The most sacred, Paka'alana, was
also the site of one of the island's two major
pu'uhonua (the other is now a national historical park, see p226), but today its location
has been lost.

In the 19th century Waipi'o Valley's population dropped, despite an influx of Chinese
immigrants. Nevertheless, the valley still supported schools, restaurants and churches, as
well as a hotel, a post office and a jail.

In 1946 Hawai'i's most devastating tsunami
slammed great waves far back into the valley (see p265). Coincidentally or not, no one
in this sacred place perished. But afterwards
most people resettled 'topside,' and Waipi'o
has been sparsely populated ever since.

Today, many of the valley's 50 or so residents have taro patches (most laid out in the
16th century), and you may see farmers knee-
deep in the muddy ponds. Other Waipi'o
crops include lotus root, avocados, breadfruit,
oranges, limes and *pakalolo* (marijuana).

Dangers & Annoyances

Waipi'o Stream divides the beach in half: take
care crossing it, as it is full of ankle-twisting,
slippery rocks; it's best to cross in deeper,
slower-moving water away from the surf. In
the winter rainy season the stream can swell
till it's impassable, with occasional flash floods.
In fact, all valley streams along the Windward
Coast are susceptible to flash floods; be watchful for rising waters, and wait to cross. Floods
usually subside in a few hours.

On the beach, swimming is not recommended, as there is extremely rough surf, a
tremendous undertow and hidden rocks.

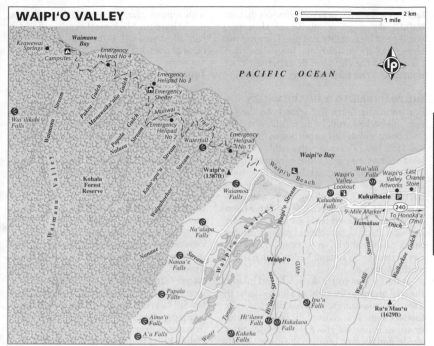

WAIPI'O VALLEY

Finally, don't drink from *any* creeks or streams without first boiling or treating the water. Feral animals roam the area, making leptospirosis a real threat (see p574).

Activities

Locals enjoy **surfing** at Waipi'o, but it's not for novices or newcomers; watch the waves for an afternoon and talk to locals before putting your board in the water. Constant rough surf makes the beach almost useless for swimming.

Most people come to Waipi'o to **hike**. Just walking into and out of the valley is adventure enough, but, if you want more, consider tackling the **Muliwai Trail**. This challenging two- or three-day trip starts from the far end of Waipi'o Valley and leads to the adjacent Waimanu Valley.

WAIPI'O VALLEY HIKE

Spending a day in Waipi'o Valley is reason enough to come to the Big Island. From the lookout a very steep, 1-mile paved road descends to the valley floor. You can jiggle-jog down the 25% grade in about 20 minutes, but

it's a 40- to 60-minute plod returning uphill; if you're lucky, someone will offer you a lift.

At the bottom, turn *mauka*; in five minutes you'll come to perfect views of ribbony **Hi'ilawe Falls**, which at over 1200ft is Hawai'i's highest free-fall waterfall. It's possible to bushwhack your way to the falls itself, but there's no trail, it's often muddy, and you risk traipsing across private land, which valley residents are less than keen on. Also, you're free to continue walking up-valley along the road, but the ever-growing number of 'Kapu – No Trespassing' signs and unfriendly dogs makes it clear that locals prefer visitors to stay nearer the beach.

Back at the main junction, turn *makai* along a muddy dirt road to reach sublime **Waipi'o Beach** in about 10 minutes. The beach is lined with graceful ironwood trees, and free-roaming horses often walk the roads and rest on the sand with you. Bucolic **Waipi'o Stream** enters the ocean (see opposite), splitting the rockier eastern strand from the sandy western end.

At the far east end it's possible to boulder for 20 minutes around the coast to **Kaluahine**

Falls (it's sometimes dry) with views of distant **Wai'ulili Falls** cascading into the sea. However, you'll need luck, agility and good timing; the large rocks are unsteady and huge waves can crash up to the cliff face. Be extremely cautious, and never take your eyes off the sea.

MULIWAI TRAIL TO WAIMANU VALLEY

For some, the Zorro-like scratch on the far cliff will beckon, and, by all means, strap on your boots and day hike a portion of the Muliwai Trail. Just 15 steep minutes yields unparalleled valley views, and more gorgeous sights await once you've crested the cliff. However, getting all the way to Waimanu Valley and back in a day is unrealistic. Depending on pace and fitness, the total, 9.5-mile hike from the Waipi'o Lookout takes six to eight hours one way. Backpackers should really consider this a two-night trip, so you can enjoy a full day in timeless Waimanu Valley, which is like a mini-Waipi'o.

At the far west end of the beach, just inland, the trail begins to the right of a locked gate; in a few feet, you come to a Na Ala Hele and state forestry sign. Proceed uphill. In 30 minutes or so, an ironwood grove provides delicious shade, and the first break in the grove signals your last and best view of Waipi'o – rest here and take it in.

After another 15 minutes in the ironwoods, the trail heads inland, into pine forest, and levels out; you've climbed over 1200ft in about a mile – whew! You quickly reach Helipad 1, and from here the trail dips in and out of stream gulches for about 5 miles. Hugged by cliffs, surrounded by forest, periodically swarmed by mosquitoes, you get only peekaboo views of the ocean until the end.

Compensating for this, in the shadiest heart of each gulch are some of the prettiest cascading rivulets imaginable; some become waterfalls, some burble in quiet pools. If treated, the water is drinkable. At Helipad 2, you are about halfway there; at Helipad 3 is a trail shelter; and soon after Helipad 4 the difficult descent into Waimanu Valley begins.

The final mile of the trail can be badly maintained and entails a steep, slippery and exposed descent of 1200ft. Fatigue (and recent rainy weather) can make this particularly treacherous, so go slow.

On weekends and holidays you may be shocked to arrive and find the camping area nearly full; local kayakers sometimes come with tons of gear. Arrive midweek and you might have the black-sand beach and waterfalls all to yourself. Either way, as the commercial goes, it's priceless.

Tours

Taking a guided tour is another popular option for getting into the valley.

Hawaiian Walkways (☎ 775-0372, 800-457-7759; www.hawaiianwalkways.com; guided hikes $95) Takes you on a hike through private land to waterfalls and pools, where you can swim.

Na'alapa Stables (☎ 775-0419; www.naalapastables .com; rides $85; ☷ departures 9:30am & 1pm Mon-Sat) This outfit also offers a 2½-hour horseback ride; children must be at least eight years old.

Waipio Ridge Stables (☎ 775-1007, 877-757-1414; www.waipioridgestables.com; rides $85-165; ☷ departures 8:45am) Horseback-riding tours follow a 2½-hour valley-rim route or go on a five-hour trot deeper into the rain forest that ends with a picnic and a swim at a hidden waterfall.

Waipio Valley Shuttle (☎ 775-7121; adult/child under 11 $45/25; ☷ departures 9am, 11am, 1pm & 3pm Mon-Sat) Runs two-hour 4WD taxi tours; will sometimes arrange dropoffs (add $10), but it depends on space (and no guaranteed pickup).

Waipi'o Valley Wagon Tours (☎ 775-9518; www .waipiovalleywagontours.com; adult/child 4-12 $55/25; ☷ departures 9:30am, 11:30am, 1:30pm & 3:30pm Mon-Sat) For a quaint experience, this 1½-hour jaunt in an open mule-drawn wagon carts visitors over rutted roads and rocky streams.

Sleeping

There is no longer any official camping in Waipi'o Valley. **Kamehameha Schools Bishop Estate** (☎ 776-1104) has stopped allowing campers on its land (which is on the near side of Waipi'o Stream), and you should respect all 'Kapu – no camping' signs. However, informal, unofficial camping still occurs on the far side of Waipi'o Stream; this is still private land, but tenters are usually tolerated in between the semipermanent local 'encampments.' There are porta-potties, but no water or other facilities. That said, Kamehameha Schools restricted camping because too many campers were abusing the beach area; the best advice is to sleep topside. Alternatively, call Kamehameha Schools and see if it allows camping again.

Backcountry camping in the Waimanu Valley is managed by the state, and is allowed by free permit for up to six nights. Facilities include fire pits and a couple of composting outhouses. Reservations are taken no more than 30 days in advance by the **Division of Forestry & Wildlife** (☎ 974-4221; www.dofaw.net; 19 E Kawaili St, Hilo, HI 96720; ✆ 7:45am-4:30pm Mon-Fri). With two weeks' notice the permit can be mailed to you.

KALOPA STATE RECREATION AREA

This 100-acre state park preserves a beautiful, rare example of a native forest, containing mainly the trees, shrubs and ferns that were already present when the Polynesians arrived. Few people venture up here, perhaps because, at an elevation of 2000ft, the Kalopa forest is cooler and wetter than the coast. However, the quiet enhances the feeling that you are stepping back in time. To get here, turn *mauka* off Hwy 19 at the Kalopa Dr sign and drive 3 miles.

Trail brochures are very informative. From the cabins a three-quarter-mile, loop **nature trail** guides you through old ohia forest, with several giant specimens. Don't miss the dramatic strangler fig, as emblematic a species as there is of the pervasive problem of invasive flora. Two native birds call the forest home, the elusive Hawaiian hawk, or *'io*, and the small brown-and-white *'elepaio*, which has a bright whistle.

For a longer hike, take the pretty **Kalopa Gulch Trail**, which enters the adjoining forest reserve and edges Kalopa Gulch for about a mile. The trail begins next to the campground entrance (get trail maps near the cabins). While the main trail is recommended and clearly marked, side trails (such as Silk Oak and Blue Gum Lanes) are badly maintained and hard to follow. Plan for a 3-mile hike.

Kalopa has three great tent sites; each is a covered concrete patio in a pretty grassy area with well-kept facilities. Rest rooms have indoor showers, and covered picnic pavilions

HAWAI'I (THE BIG ISLAND)

APRIL FOOL'S DAY, 1946

On the morning of April 1, 1946, Hawaii's worst tsunami struck without warning. Along the Big Island's Windward Coast it destroyed railroad bridges and Hilo's bayfront, and 159 people died. In Waipi'o, the water filled the valley like a bowl, but no one perished. At the plantation town of Laupahoehoe many homes and the schoolhouse were swept away, and 35 people were killed. Most of these were children who, on their way to school, had detoured to wonder at something strange – the sea was disappearing.

Survivor Bunji Fujimoto remembers: 'Somebody started yelling, "Oh, there's no water in the ocean." Being that it was April Fool's Day, half of us didn't believe what they were saying. Then, we saw the water receding out. We went down towards the park, where the monument is now, to see what's it all about.'

A crowd gathered at the shore: for 300yd or more there was only ocean bottom, with bright red moss and stranded fish flapping about. The water then filled in and receded several times.

Says survivor Joseph Ah Choy: 'We was just running back and forth when the wave come up. We go run to the grandstand. When the wave go back, we follow. When the water come up again, we run again. We had about seven or eight small kine waves coming in and out. I don't know what made me run straight from the last one.'

This time, says Fujimoto, 'the wave was like filling a cup with water, but when it reaches the brim, it doesn't stop.' As the children raced away like mad, some fell and others hid again in the grandstand. Running without stopping, Fujimoto says, 'I saw the bleachers collapse like a house of matchsticks, making terrifying cracking sounds. The other thing I remember was one of the teachers' cottages sailing through the coconut trees.'

In eerie silence, successive waves picked up people and buildings, leaving some stranded uphill while dragging everything else out to sea. Over 20 people were never found. One woman and two boys floated for nearly three days before being rescued.

Afterward, the town relocated topside. The Hamakua Coast railroad never ran again, and two years later an official tsunami-warning system was created. A memorial was erected on Laupahoehoe Point to honor the town's victims, and since then the community gathers there every April Fool's Day to eat, play music and listen to survivors 'talk story.'

The quotes above are taken from the book *April Fool's*, an award-winning oral history compiled by Laupahoehoe school students in 1996. Copies are available at the train museum (p266).

have electricity, running water and BBQ grills. In a separate area, simple but nice cabins have bunk beds, linens and blankets, hot showers, and access to a fully equipped kitchen. For permits, see p191.

LAUPAHOEHOE

pop 470

Laupahoehoe means 'leaf of pahoehoe lava,' an apt name for the extremely evocative **Laupahoehoe Point**, a flat peninsula tucked beneath cliffs that's battered relentlessly by the sea. Legend has it that Poliahu, the snow goddess, was sledding down Mauna Kea one day when her ever-jealous sister, Pele, decided to compete with her. One thing led to another, as it often does, and the goddesses were soon fighting, lava melting snow and snow freezing lava, until finally Poliahu forced Pele all the way down Mauna Kea and into the sea, leaving behind this spit of land – which, according to science, is the result of a late-stage Mauna Kea eruption.

Until 1946 the point contained a small but thriving plantation town, but that year a tsunami struck and destroyed most of it (see p265); afterward the town moved uphill. Today a monument commemorates the event, and the point is a county beach park with some of the best camping on the island (for information on permits, see p193).

The park has rest rooms, outdoor showers, water, covered pavilions and electricity. Weekends can be busy with locals and families;

midweek is quieter. You can't swim here, but the rugged coast is sure worth admiring.

Up by the highway the **Laupahoehoe Train Museum** (☎ 962-6300; www.thetrainmuseum.com; adult/child $4/2; ☷ 9am-4:30pm Mon-Fri, 10am-2pm Sat & Sun) evokes Hawai'i's long-gone railroad era – it's chock-full of nostalgic, lovingly tended ephemera, including 'Rusty' the switch engine, 'Woody' the caboose and a budding model railroad. The porch has kids' trains to play with. Continue past the museum into town, and you'll find a quiet gallery and a '50s-style diner.

Laupahoehoe is midway between Honoka'a and Hilo on Hwy 19. Near the 27-mile marker a 'Laupahoehoe Point' sign leads you down the steep winding road to the coast, while the museum is visible from the highway between the 25- and 26-mile markers.

KOLEKOLE BEACH PARK

This grassy park set dramatically beneath a highway bridge is great for an afternoon picnic. Facilities are run down, but there's nothing wrong with the trim wide lawn, Kolekole Stream or the rocky beach. Locals sometimes surf and bodyboard here, but it's not good for ocean swimming.

You can tent camp with a county permit (see p193), but weekends get crowded with picnicking families. There are better choices.

To get here, turn inland off Hwy 19 at the southern end of the Kolekole Bridge, south of the 15-mile marker.

DETOUR: OLD MAMALAHOA HIGHWAY

The Hamakua Coast is perfect for those who like exploring neglected old roads just to see what you can find. This 4-mile portion of the bypassed Old Mamalahoa Hwy certainly satisfies that itch. However, if you take this, don't miss the bridge over **Nanue Falls** on Hwy 19 between the 18- and 19-mile markers; park south of the bridge and walk back for vertiginous views of the steep gulch.

Coming from the north, turn off Hwy 19 at the 19-mile marker, following the sign for **Waikaumalo County Park**. Here, a grassy slope (with picnic area) leads to a pretty stream, which if you're so inclined is tailor-made for muddy jaunts upstream.

Driving on, Old Mam Hwy becomes a one-lane road, which dips into a series of stream gulches overhung with thick foliage; it's sometimes possible to pull over next to the bridges and explore. Out of the gulches, you pass small bucolic farms and ocean views. A little less than halfway along, keep an eye out for **Honohina Cemetery**, a historic Japanese graveyard full of crumbling, kanji-covered headstones.

The south end of the road is anchored by **World Botanical Gardens** (☎ 963-5427; www.wbgi.com; adult/child 6-12/child 13-17 $13/3/6; ☷ 9am-5:30pm), which is signed on Hwy 19 near the 16-mile marker. The fee is a bit steep for the modest gardens, even including access to the beautiful, three-tiered **Umauma Falls**, but if you're jonesing for a walk you'll get your money's worth.

HONOMU
pop 540

Like Honoka'a, Honomu is an old sugar town whose fading, false-fronted buildings could pass for an old Western movie set. It's a stop on your way to or from Akaka Falls; along the single main street you can troll for treasures in several galleries and get lunch or ice cream. The town, falls and Hwy 220 (which leads to both) are clearly signed from Hwy 19 between the 13- and 14-mile markers.

Woodshop Gallery & Cafe (☎ 963-6363; www.wood shopgallery.com; lunch dishes $7-8.50; 10:30am-5:30pm) is the largest gallery, with an excellent selection of prints, crafts and wood carvings. The small café makes a notable grilled 'ahi sandwich and serves freshly made curries and plate lunches.

AKAKA FALLS STATE PARK

The only way these impressive falls could be any easier to reach would be to put them in the parking lot – but then you'd miss the enchanting half-mile loop **trail** through the rain forest, whose varied, dense foliage includes banyan and monkeypod trees, massive philodendrons, fragrant ginger, dangling heliconia, orchids and gigantic bamboo groves.

Follow the park's advice and start by heading to the right: you come first to 100ft **Kahuna Falls**, which strikes you as the perfect Hawaiian cascade for about as long as it takes to reach its neighbor. Then, when you see 420ft **Akaka Falls**, you can swoon properly, as the water tumbles majestically down a fern-draped cliff, its spray sometimes painting a rainbow. Don't miss it.

From Hwy 19 the falls are about 4 miles inland on Hwy 220.

PEPE'EKEO FOUR-MILE SCENIC DRIVE

Between Honomu and Hilo, a 4-mile scenic loop off Hwy 19 is a majestic tropical drive; from the north, between the 10- and 11-mile markers, look for the scenic drive and Onomea Bay signs.

Stop first at **What's Shakin'** (☎ 964-3080; items $6-10; 10am-5pm), where the all-fruit smoothies 'broke da' mout.' It also has fresh sandwiches and burgers.

Similar to the Old Mamalahoa Highway (see opposite), the road crosses a string of one-lane bridges over little streams through lush jungle. In places a canopy of African tulip trees drop their orange flowers onto the road. About half a mile before the botanical gardens, a wooden bridge is a good place to stop and follow a small path to the babbling water.

Hawaii Tropical Botanical Garden (☎ 964-5233; www.htbg.com; adult/child $15/5; 9am-4pm) is an overabundantly lush nature preserve with 2500 species of tropical plants from around the world. A mile-long paved path winds amid streams, pools, pretty waterfalls, ocean viewpoints, dangling heliconia and towering palms – with flowering plant life dazzling at every step. Though almost all non-native, the gardens define 'tropical jungle' to a T, so to complain seems a quibble. For native flora, visit Kalopa State Recreation Area (p265) or the Amy Greenwell Ethnobotanical Garden (p219).

On either side of the gardens are **Na Ala Hele trailheads** leading to scenic Onomea Bay. The southern trailhead has easier parking and access, and the trails themselves connect, leading in just a few minutes to rocky coves, a stream, waterfalls and a dramatic finger of land jutting into the turtle- and shark-filled bay. Divers like this spot, but the water is usually too rough for swimming and snorkeling. (And for you nosy types: a guard and fences prevent sneaking into the botanical gardens.)

HILO

pop 40,800

Hilo has been knocked down twice by tsunamis (in 1946 and 1960), it's been threatened by Mauna Loa lava flows (most recently in 1984), and statistically it gets rained on two out of three days (earning it the title 'rainiest city in the USA') – all of which residents greet with a stoic shrug. In fact, residents don't really mind that most tourists never leave the Kona Coast beaches, and those that come usually scatter at the first drop of rain. They like being 'scruffy old Hilo town,' and wouldn't mind staying that way.

Trouble is, nothing stays the same forever (as residents well know), and visitors are starting to realize that Hilo has something the Kona Coast often lacks: character. The city's population has long been a comfortable blend of Japanese, Korean, Filipino, Portuguese, Puerto Rican, Hawaiian and Caucasian. Residents actually live, work and play in the historic, walkable downtown, and Hilo's legendary farmers

HILO

HAWAI'I (THE BIG ISLAND)

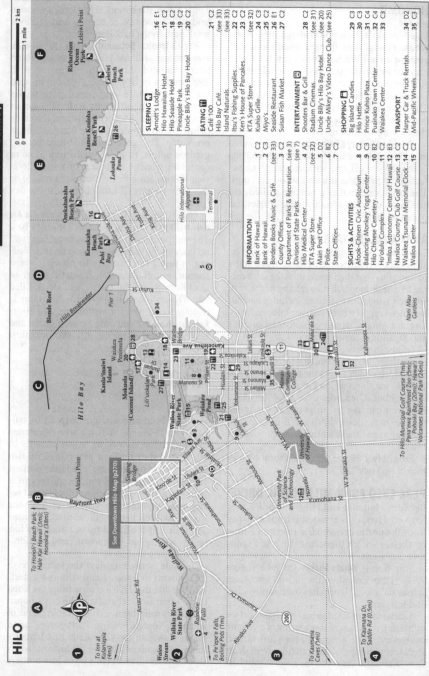

SLEEPING 🛏
Arnott's Lodge	16 E1
Hilo Hawaiian Hotel	17 C2
Hilo Seaside Hotel	18 C2
Pineapple Park	19 C2
Uncle Billy's Hilo Bay Hotel	20 C2

EATING 🍴
Café 100	21 C2
Hilo Bay Café	(see 33)
Island Naturals	(see 33)
Itsu's Fishing Supplies	22 C2
Ken's House of Pancakes	23 C2
KTA Super Store	(see 32)
Kuhio Grille	24 C3
Miyo's	25 C3
Seaside Restaurant	26 E1
Suisan Fish Market	27 C2

ENTERTAINMENT 🎭
Shooters Bar & Grill	28 C2
Stadium Cinemas	(see 31)
Uncle Billy's Hilo Bay Hotel	(see 20)
Uncle Mikey's Video Dance Club	(see 25)

SHOPPING 🛍
Big Island Candies	29 C3
Hilo Hattie	30 C3
Prince Kuhio Plaza	31 C4
Puainako Town Center	32 C4
Waiakea Center	33 C3

TRANSPORT
Harper Car & Truck Rentals	34 D2
Mid-Pacific Wheels	35 C3

INFORMATION
Bank of Hawaii	1 C2
Bank of Hawaii	2 C3
Borders Books Music & Café	(see 33)
County Offices	3 C2
Department of Parks & Recreation	(see 7)
Division of State Parks	4 A2
Hilo Medical Center	(see 32)
KTA Super Store	5 D2
Main Post Office	6 B2
Police	7 C2
State Offices	

SIGHTS & ACTIVITIES
Afook-Chinen Civic Auditorium	8 C3
Balancing Monkey Yoga Center	9 C3
Hilo Chinese Cemetery	10 B2
Ho'olulu Complex	11 C2
'Imiloa Astronomy Center of Hawaii	12 B3
Naniloa Country Club Golf Course	13 C2
Waiakea Tsunami Memorial Clock	14 C2
Wailoa Center	15 C2

market is its town hall – the place where community business, gossip and shopping get taken care of on a twice-weekly basis.

Then there's the scenery: Hilo perches on a crescent-shaped bay and is hugged by rain forests. Within an hour folks can be tripping over lava in Hawai'i Volcanoes National Park, soaking in Puna's hot springs, admiring Hamakua Coast waterfalls or stargazing on Mauna Kea.

And so outsiders have begun moving in. Top-notch galleries have infested barren storefronts; gourmet restaurants have invaded long-dead banks. Yoga studios, gift shops, museums, the busy cruise-ship port: locals are cautiously pleased but increasingly anxious about how the changes are affecting their town's character and culture. Ask about the rising cost of real estate and the traffic, and they even get downright cranky.

So, don your drabbest T-shirt and shorts, grab an umbrella and enjoy Hawai'i's best little city before the next disaster reorients the streets, be it by tsunami, lava or, worst of all, development.

HISTORY

The county capital, Hilo has a long history as a harbor town, commencing with the first Polynesian settlers who farmed, fished and traded goods along the Wailuku River. By the 1900s numerous wharves dotted the bay, a railroad connected Hilo with the Hamakua Coast, and the breakwater was under construction. From then until the middle of the 20th century Hilo was the Big Island's center of economic, commercial and political power.

The first blow to its status came on April 1, 1946, when its waterfront was destroyed by an enormous tsunami. Many communities along the coast were devastated (such as Laupahoehoe; see p265), but Hilo was hardest hit, suffering 96 fatalities and tens of millions of dollars in damage. Hilo rebuilt its waterfront, but in 1960, only 14 years later, another tsunami destroyed it again, taking 61 lives and causing $22 million in damage. This time, Hilo gave in and turned the waterfront into parks.

By now the coastal railroad was a memory, the sugar industry had peaked, and the Big Island was developing a new source of income – tourism – which was focused almost exclusively on the island's sun-drenched, sandy western shores. In the 1970s, as resorts and real-estate barons jockeyed for position and profit on the Kona and Kohala Coasts, Hilo was left behind, unable to recover and compete. With the demise of sugar in the 1980s

HAWAI'I (THE BIG ISLAND)

HILO IN...

One Day

With only a day, time your visit for the **farmers market** (p273), and allow a few hours to absorb Hilo's grandest museum, **'Imiloa** (p272). If it's sunny, enjoy a picnic lunch at pretty **Lili'uokalani Park** (p273). In the afternoon, stroll downtown Hilo's **historic buildings** (p274) and browse its **galleries** and **shops** (p280). For dinner, join the locals relaxing at **Cafe Pesto** (p279) and, if you're lucky, the **Palace Theater** (p280) will have something good scheduled.

Two Days

Today, the **Lyman Museum** (p272) calls for a crash course on Hawaiian history and, if the weather's clear, make sure to swim, snorkel, dive or surf at one of Hilo's appealing **beaches** (p274). Great short trips include the **waterfalls** (p281) along Waianuenue Ave, and **Hawaii Tropical Botanical Garden** (p267) and **Akaka Falls** (p267) along Hwy 19. For dinner, aim for the romantic and culinary delights of **Restaurant Kaikodo** (p279).

Four Days

With a third day, discover the wilds of **Puna** (p283), and, with a fourth, make sure to give an afternoon and evening to **Mauna Kea** (p251). **Hawai'i Volcanoes National Park** (p288) is much more than a Hilo day trip, but don't miss it if that's all you've got. Also, deepen your Hilo explorations by visiting the **Pacific Tsunami Museum** (p272) and the **Hawaii Plantation Museum** (p273), and experimenting with **crack seed** (p279) at Hilo Seed & Snacks and **strawberry mochi** at Two Ladies Kitchen (p279).

and 1990s, the shift in power from east to west was completed.

ORIENTATION

Hilo's charming, compact 'downtown' is about six square blocks on the southwest side of the bay: it lies between Kamehameha Ave and Kino'ole St (both parallel to the bay)

and between Waianuenue Ave and Mamo St. On the bay's southeast side, small Waiakea Peninsula is rimmed by Banyan Dr, which contains Hilo's modest hotel row. Note that most B&Bs are in residential neighborhoods closer to downtown.

From the Hamakua Coast, Hwy 19 enters Hilo from the north, passes downtown, then

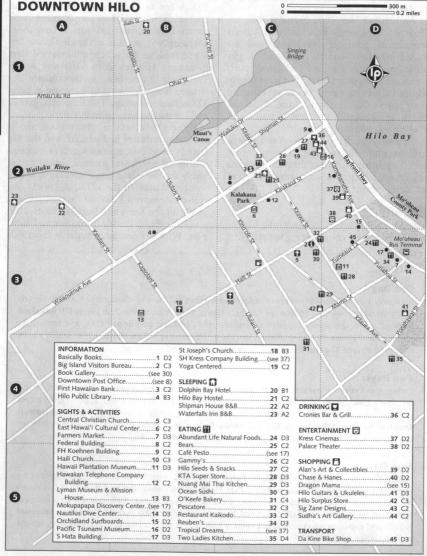

DOWNTOWN HILO

INFORMATION
Basically Books.............................**1** D2
Big Island Visitors Bureau..............**2** C3
Book Gallery................................(see 30)
Downtown Post Office..............(see 8)
First Hawaiian Bank.....................**3** C2
Hilo Public Library.......................**4** B3

SIGHTS & ACTIVITIES
Central Christian Church..............**5** C3
East Hawai'i Cultural Center.........**6** C2
Farmers Market............................**7** D3
Federal Building...........................**8** C2
FH Koehnen Building....................**9** C2
Haili Church................................**10** C3
Hawaii Plantation Museum.........**11** D3
Hawaiian Telephone Company
  Building..................................**12** C2
Lyman Museum & Mission
  House....................................**13** B3
Mokupapapa Discovery Center..(see 17)
Nautilus Dive Center...................**14** D3
Orchidland Surfboards................**15** D2
Pacific Tsunami Museum.............**16** D2
S Hata Building..........................**17** D3

St Joseph's Church......................**18** B3
SH Kress Company Building.......(see 37)
Yoga Centered...........................**19** C2

SLEEPING 🏠
Dolphin Bay Hotel......................**20** B1
Hilo Bay Hostel..........................**21** C2
Shipman House B&B....................**22** A2
Waterfalls Inn B&B.....................**23** A2

EATING 🍴
Abundant Life Natural Foods.....**24** D3
Bears..**25** C2
Café Pesto...............................(see 17)
Gammy's...................................**26** C2
Hilo Seeds & Snacks..................**27** C2
KTA Super Store........................**28** C2
Nuang Mai Thai Kitchen.............**29** C3
Ocean Sushi..............................**30** C3
O'Keefe Bakery.........................**31** C4
Pescatore.................................**32** C2
Restaurant Kaikodo...................**33** C2
Reuben's..................................**34** D3
Two Ladies Kitchen....................**35** D4

DRINKING 🍷
Cronies Bar & Grill....................**36** C2

ENTERTAINMENT 🎭
Kress Cinemas...........................**37** D2
Palace Theater...........................**38** D2

SHOPPING 🛍️
Alan's Art & Collectibles............**39** D2
Chase & Hanes..........................**40** D2
Dragon Mama..........................(see 15)
Hilo Guitars & Ukuleles..............**41** D3
Hilo Surplus Store.....................**42** C3
Sig Zane Designs.......................**43** C2
Sudha's Art Gallery...................**44** C2

TRANSPORT
Da Kine Bike Shop.....................**45** D3

meets Hwy 11 at the intersection with Banyan Dr. Hwy 11 goes south and is called Kanoele-hua Ave in town; further south, it becomes the Hawai'i Belt Rd and leads to the Puna district, Hawai'i Volcanoes National Park and Ka'u. South of the airport, Kanoelehua Ave is lined with shopping malls; this is Hilo's main retail district, complete with a Wal-Mart, a multiplex cinema and all the other big-box stores.

INFORMATION
Bookstores
Basically Books (Map p270; ☎ 961-0144, 800-903-6277; 160 Kamehameha Ave; ⏰ 9am-5pm Mon-Sat, 10am-4pm Sun) Longtime indie bookseller that specializes in maps, travel guides and Hawaiian and out-of-print titles.
Book Gallery (Map p270; ☎ 935-4943; 259 Keawe St; ⏰ 9:30am-5pm Mon-Fri, 9am-3pm Sat) Packed with great kids' and local Hawaiian books.
Borders Books Music & Café (Map p268; ☎ 933-1410; Waiakea Center, 301 Maka'ala St; ⏰ 8am-9pm Sun-Thu, to 10pm Fri & Sat) Full-service chain selling books, CDs, tons of periodicals and Starbucks coffee.

Emergency
Police (Map p268; ☎ 935-3311; 349 Kapi'olani St) For nonemergencies.
Police, Fire & Ambulance (☎ 911) For emergencies.
Sexual Assault Hotline (☎ 935-0677)
Suicide Prevention Hotline (☎ 800-784-2433)

Internet Access
For a public terminal, your best bet is the public library.

Library
Hilo Public library (Map p270; ☎ 933-8888; www .librarieshawaii.org; 300 Waianuenue Ave; ⏰ 11am-7pm Tue & Wed, 9am-5pm Thu & Sat, 10am-5pm Fri) To use the free internet terminals or take out books, you must purchase a three-month nonresident library card ($10). The pretty interior courtyard is a pleasant place to write and read.

Media
NEWSPAPERS
The *Hawaii Tribune-Herald* (www.hawaii tribune-herald.com) is the Big Island's main daily newspaper.

RADIO
The vast majority of radio stations are based in Hilo, and, due to geography, they can be heard only on the island's east side (though some simulcast on Kona stations). The website www.hawaiiradiotv.com/BigIsleRadio.html has complete listings.
KANO 91.1 FM (www.hawaiipublicradio.org) Hawai'i Public Radio featuring classical music and news.
KAPA 100.3 FM The best for current Hawaiian music, and voted the best by *Hawaii Island Journal*.
KHBC 1060AM (www.khbcradio.com) Traditional Hawaiian and old-fashioned jazz; check out longtime DJ Mel 'Mynah Bird Medeiros' 6am to 10am Monday to Saturday.
KPVS 95.9 FM If you want hip-hop, tune in to 'Da Beat.'
KWXX 94.7 FM (www.kwxx.com) Interspersed amid the pop hits are some worthwhile Hawaiian shows.

Medical Services
Hilo Medical Center (Map p268; ☎ 974-4700, ☎ emergency room 974-6800; 1190 Waianuenue Ave; ⏰ 24hr emergency) Located near Rainbow Falls.
KTA Super Store (Map p268; ☎ 959-8700; Puainako Town Center, 50 E Puainako St; ⏰ pharmacy 8am-8pm Mon-Fri, to 6pm Sat, to 5pm Sun) For prescriptions.

Money
All banks in Hilo have 24-hour ATMs.
Bank of Hawaii (Map p268) Kawili St (☎ 961-0681; 417 E Kawili St); Pauahi St (☎ 935-9701; 120 Pauahi St)
First Hawaiian Bank (Map p270; ☎ 933-2222; 120 Waianuenue Ave)

Post
Downtown post office (Map p270; ☎ 933-3014; 154 Waianuenue Ave; ⏰ 9am-4pm Mon-Fri, 12:30-2pm Sat) Conveniently located in the Federal Building downtown.
Main post office (Map p268; ☎ 933-3019; 1299 Kekuanaoa St; ⏰ 8am-4:30pm Mon-Fri, 9am-12:30pm Sat) Holds general delivery mail.

Tourist Information
Big Island Visitors Bureau (Map p270; ☎ 961-5797, 800-648-2441; www.gohawaii.com; 250 Keawe St; ⏰ 8am-4:30pm Mon-Fri) Check the website for a detailed events calendar with links.

SIGHTS
Charming, tousled, in transition, Hilo's historic, walkable downtown is an evocative mix of storm-lashed wooden storefronts, weed-filled lots and renovated establishments shining in the rain like new pennies. The weathered, early-20th-century architecture gives the city a bygone feel, but it's misleading. A tour of Hilo's museums, shops and parks reveals a town rapidly catching up with a new century.

'Imiloa Astronomy Center of Hawaii

Christened in 2006, 'Imiloa (Map p268; ☎ 969-9700; www.imiloahawaii.org; 600 'Imiloa Pl; adult/child 4-12 $14.50/7.50; ☺ 9am-4pm Tue-Sun, plus holiday Mon) is a unique, provocative look at the creation stories of two very different peoples: Native Hawaiians and modern astronomers. This unusual combination wouldn't make sense except that it embodies the story of Mauna Kea, which is central to Hawaiian mythology and is now home to the world's most important conglomeration of observatories (see p255). Comparing these stories side by side, one is struck by both their points of divergence and their remarkable synchronicities, and this gorgeous museum does an absolutely first-rate job bringing them both to life.

You begin by walking through a recreation of Mauna Kea itself. Then you are introduced to the *kumulipo*, the Hawaiian creation story (which is chanted in Hawaiian), and to wider Hawaiian culture. This is followed by bilingual exhibits (in English and Hawaiian) on the Big Bang, and descriptions of ancient Polynesian voyaging (including a scale model of the famed *Hokule'a* canoe) and modern-day astronomy on Mauna Kea. Keeping the eye-popping quotient high are videos, a 3D theater, 'Atomic Time Machines,' and an up-to-the-minute, 120-seat planetarium featuring a free, interesting 22-minute film, *Maunakea: Between Earth and Sky* (at 11am, 1pm and 2:30pm).

There's also a restaurant, a gift shop, a Hawaiian language center (call for weekend class schedules) and once-a-month astronomy presentations (call ☎ 969-9711 for reservations). Don't wait for a rainy day. 'Imiloa is one of Hawaii's most fascinating museums.

Lyman Museum & Mission House

This comprehensive **museum** (Map p270; ☎ 935-5021; www.lymanmuseum.org; 276 Haili St; adult/child 6-17 $10/3; ☺ 9:30am-4:30pm Mon-Sat) escorts you through almost the entire natural and cultural history of Hawaii in admirably succinct fashion. Geologic exhibits begin with the first volcanic cone to break the sea's surface and include great examples of lava rock – such as lava bombs, *pahoehoe* toes, Pele's tears (solidified drops of volcanic glass) and Pele's hair (fine strands of volcanic glass). You even get to walk through a 'lava tube.'

Exhibits on ancient Hawaiian life are well done, with informative displays on simple everyday tasks – such as how adzes, feather lei,

kapa, and thatched homes were made – as well as on ancient sports, religious worship and the mysteries of the *kapu* system. Other displays and special exhibits highlight the lifestyles of the islands' many immigrants, who eventually created Hawaii's multiethnic society.

Then, adjacent to the museum (and included in the admission), is the **Mission House**, which was built by the Reverend David Lyman and his wife, Sarah, in 1839. The modest house reflects the missionaries themselves; it contains many original furnishings, including Sarah Lyman's melodeon, rocking chair, china and quilts. Docents do a good job of evoking missionary life and the role the Lymans played on the Big Island; free tours leave hourly throughout the day.

Pacific Tsunami Museum

For heart-stopping drama and sheer emotion, it's hard to top this tidy **museum** (Map p270; ☎ 935-0926; www.tsunami.org; 130 Kamehameha Ave; adult/child 6-17 $7/2; ☺ 9am-4pm Mon-Sat), which brings to life the destructive horror of Pacific Ocean tsunami. Multimedia exhibits are excellent (including chilling computer simulations, videos, documentaries, dioramas and more), but it's the first-person accounts by survivors that grab you. Some docents are also Hilo tsunami survivors. Though focused on tsunami, displays amount to a de facto history of Hilo; ask for the free tsunami sites walking tour brochure.

Mokupapapa Discovery Center

The best, and surely the easiest, way to visit the long string of islands and atolls that make up the Northwestern Hawaiian Islands is to visit this **museum** (Map p270; ☎ 933-8184; www.hawaiireef noaa.gov; 308 Kamehameha Ave; admission free; ☺ 9am-4pm Tue-Sat). New in 2003, it packs a lot in a small space, describing all the islands and their abundant marine life through videos, films, displays, maps and interactive exhibits, such as a mock-up of the *Pisces V* diving submersible, with workable robotic arms. It's worth visiting just to hear the *kumulipo* (ancient chant).

East Hawai'i Cultural Center

In quiet, unassuming fashion, Hilo is becoming a bona fide art town, and for many years, the heart of Hilo's art scene has been the **East Hawai'i Cultural Center** (Map p270; ☎ 961-5711; www .ehcc.org; 141 Kalakaua St; suggested donation $2; ☺ 10am-4pm Mon-Sat), which is dedicated to promoting local artists. Diverse exhibits showcase everyone from established professionals to competent amateurs, all engaged in celebrating and digesting the Hawaiian experience. They also offer a range of workshops and classes (including painting, drawing, ukulele and hula).

Hawaii Plantation Museum

Another newcomer, this delightful, homespun **museum** (Map p270; ☎ 961-0024; www.memories ofhawaiibigisland.com; 301 Keawe St; adult/child 5-15 $6/3; ⓨ 10:30am-4:30pm Tue-Fri, 10am-3pm Sat & Sun) is dedicated to preserving Hawaii's plantation-era life. It has the slightly disheveled feel of a jumble sale with placards – and rightly so. What began as owner Wayne Subica's desire to celebrate the plantation baseball teams of his youth now expands almost daily, with residents donating their personal memorabilia to the ever-widening and diversifying collection – surprises await you at every turn. Indeed, Wayne has already outgrown his downtown Hilo location; call first to see if he's moved.

Farmers Market

Nearly 20 years old, Hilo's **farmers market** (Map p270; www.hilofarmersmarket.com; cnr Mamo St & Kamehameha Ave; ⓨ 6am-3pm Wed & Sat) is an island-wide event, as locals gather from all over (even Kona) to shop for fresh produce and catch up with friends. It's certainly Hilo's liveliest scene, with everyone mingling, tasting, buying and gossiping. Covered stalls sell the gamut of island produce, and the quality is excellent: pick up papayas, *liliko'i*, breadfruit, apple bananas, mangoes and star fruit. If you're cooking, you'll find lots of Asian greens, organic vegetables and local produce (like mushrooms from Laupahoehoe). There's prepared food, too: bento boxes (with Spam *musubi*), fresh baked breads and desserts, juices, and machete-cut coconuts for drinking. Tropical flowers can be had by the armful.

Opposite this scene, a huge number of craft and clothing stalls lay out their wares: browse for sarongs and T-shirts, rubbah slippahs and wood carvings, shell jewelry and coconut-leaf baskets. There's some wonderful stuff, but not all the crafts are authentic, so shop carefully.

Wailoa River State Park

Drive along Kamehameha Ave east of the downtown area, and the first thing you notice about this **state park** (Map p268) is its imposing

14ft, Italian-made bronze statue of Kamehameha the Great; erected in 1997, and restored with gold leaf in 2004, the statue has an outstretched arm that seems to beckon you, and actually, the park's lawns, ponds and arched bridges make a nice stroll. Spring-fed **Waiakea Pond** contains saltwater and brackish-water fish, and two **memorials** are worth seeing: a tsunami memorial dedicated to the 1946 and 1960 victims, and a Vietnam War memorial with an eternal flame.

Adjacent, the **Wailoa Center** (Map p268; ☎ 933-0416; admission free; ⓨ 8:30am-4:30pm Mon, Tue, Thu & Fri, noon-4:30pm Wed) is an eclectic, small state-run art gallery. Multicultural exhibits change monthly and the artists are local, but otherwise there's no telling what you'll find: perhaps quilts, bonsai, historical photos, Chinese watercolors or whimsical mixed media.

Banyan Drive & Lili'uokalani Park

Around tiny Waiakea Peninsula curves **Banyan Dr** (Map p268), so-named for the massive banyan trees lining it, containing Hilo's short 'hotel row.' Royalty and celebrities planted the trees in the 1930s, and plaques identify the honorees: Babe Ruth, Amelia Earhart, King George and Mrs Cecil B DeMille, among others.

Banyan Dr also skirts around the nine-hole Naniloa Golf Course (p275) and the 30-acre, Japanese-style **Lili'uokalani Park** (Map p268). This lovely green oasis is named for Hawai'i's last queen. It contains manicured lawns, saltwater ponds, patches of bamboo, quaint arched bridges, stone lanterns, pagodas and a teahouse. With 2 miles of paths and ideal views of the ocean, Hilo and (on a clear day) Mauna Kea, it's perfect for a sunset stroll, an early-morning jog or an afternoon picnic with the kids (who often bring nets to snare pond fish).

Connected to Lili'uokalani Gárdens by a footbridge is the tiny island of **Mokuola** (Map p268). Also known as 'Coconut Island,' it's a separate county park with picnic tables and swimming, and is quite popular with local anglers.

Not really on the peninsula, but fronting Kamehameha Ave on the park side, close to Manono St, is the **Waiakea Tsunami Memorial Clock** (Map p268). The clock is stuck at 1:05, the exact moment, in the predawn hours of May 23, 1960, when Hilo's last major tsunami swept ashore.

Pana'ewa Rainforest Zoo

Upon entering this modest 12-acre **zoo** (Map p281; ☎ 959-9233; www.hilozoo.com; admission free; ⊙ 9am-4pm, petting zoo 1:30-2:30pm Sat), most visitors receive a cheerful 'Hi! How are you?' from Max, the zoo's talking parrot and official goodwill ambassador. The zoo's real prize, however, is a white Bengal tiger enjoying a large grassy area. You only need an hour or two to tour the pleasantly manicured grounds, which feature several endangered Hawaiian birds, monkeys, reptiles, a pygmy hippo, and gaggles of free-roaming peacocks and chickens. Kids love it. To get here, turn off Hwy 11 at W Mamaki St, just past the 4-mile marker; the zoo is another mile west.

Historic Buildings

Compact downtown Hilo, with its historic buildings and panoramic bay, rewards wanderers; pick up a free historic sites legend at the visitor center.

Sitting on the corner of Kamehameha and Waianuenue Aves, the **FH Koehnen Building** (Map p270) is an eye-catching blue 1910 building with interior koa walls and ohia floors. East on Kamehameha at the corner of Kalakaua St, the **Pacific Tsunami Museum** (p272) occupies the 1930 First Hawaiian Bank Building, which was built by renowned Honolulu architect CW Dickey. Another block east on Kamehameha is the art-deco 1932 **SH Kress Company Building** (Map p270), which fell into disrepair in the 1980s but was restored in 1990. Along with a movie theater and shops, it now houses a 245-student public-charter school. Further east on Kamehameha Ave (near Mamo St), the 1912 **S Hata Building** (Map p270) is a fine example of renaissance-revival architecture. The US government seized the building from the original Japanese owner during WWII; after the war, the owner's daughter bought it back and restored it.

From Kamehameha Ave, Haili St is interesting. The first notable building is Hilo's 1925 **Palace Theater** (p280), which was the first deluxe playhouse on the Big Island. Over the next two blocks you pass the simple, Victorian-style **Central Christian Church** (Map p270), built by Portuguese immigrants in the early 1900s; 1859 **Haili Church** (Map p270), which wouldn't look out of place in the New England countryside; and Catholic **St Joseph's Church** (Map p270), a 1919, pink paean of Spanish-mission design. Just past St Joseph's is the 1839 **Lyman Mission House**, which is now part of the Lyman Museum (p272).

Side by side on Kalakaua St, south of Keawe St, are two striking structures. First is the **East Hawai'i Cultural Center** (p272), which served as the Hilo police station until 1975; its hipped roof and covered lanai were common features in 19th-century island homes. Next door, the handsome 1920s **Hawaiian Telephone Company Building** (Map p270) is another CW Dickey creation that displays Spanish, Italian and Californian mission influences.

Outside of downtown, on Ululani St near Ponahawai St, the **Hilo Chinese Cemetery** (Map p268) is announced by a gorgeous, green-and-red temple building. The board out front lists the names, dates and villages of the Chinese immigrants buried here.

Beaches

Hilo is no beach town, but east of Banyan Dr, 4-mile Kalaniana'ole Ave (Hwy 19) passes a string of intriguing small pockets that only the most curmudgeonly of beach bums would complain about. Depending on weather and tides, rough surf can stir up these spots, making swimming dangerous, so assess conditions carefully.

About 1.5 miles east of Banyan Dr along Kalaniana'ole Ave, across from Baker Ave, **Keaukaha Beach Park** (Map p268) on Puhi Bay is the smallest spot. A semiprotected cove is often filled with kids, and on the east side is a good beginner dive site, 'Tetsu's Ledge,' at 30ft.

Further east, **Onekahakaha Beach Park** (Map p268) should be the destination for families with small children, who can splash safely in a broad, shallow, sandy-bottomed pool (with steps) that is well protected from the surf. On calm days an unprotected cove on the Hilo side is good for snorkeling. The park has lifeguards on weekends and holidays, rest rooms, showers, grassy lawns, covered pavilions and the Hilo Horseshoe Club.

Older kids and snorkelers should aim for the next spot, **James Kealoha Beach Park** (Map p268). The east side contains a much deeper protected basin with usually calm, clear aquamarine water and pockets of white sand; it's dreamy and perfect for swimming, and sea turtles like it, too! The park's western side is open ocean and rocky; in winter, the bigger waves are popular with surfers, and locals net fish. There are rest rooms, covered pavilions, a coconut grove and weekend lifeguards.

Another mile eastward, **Leleiwi Beach Park** (Map p268) is a pretty stretch of ragged coastline. Surfers show up here too, when the waves get big enough, and it's known as the best place to shore-dive in Hilo. The entrance is a bit tricky; ask for advice at Nautilus Dive Center (right).

Just beyond Leleiwi, near the end of the road, **Richardson Ocean Park** (Map p268) has just enough black-sand beach to inspire sunbathing. So long as it's calm, swimming is fine. Snorkeling is super at the warmer, eastern end, where the lava rocks create interesting nooks and crannies; in late afternoon sea turtles often nestle here. When surf is rough, walk to the far east end to enjoy explosive waves. There are rest rooms, showers, picnic tables and a lifeguard.

North of downtown Hilo, the protected cove at **Honoli'i Beach Park** (Map p281) has Hilo's best bodyboarding and surfing, particularly for beginners. A lovely, well-tended grassy picnic area fronts the beach, with fantastic views of Hilo, plus there are rest rooms, outdoor showers and a lifeguard. Honoli'i isn't the best for swimming, as the adjacent river often muddies the waters. From Hilo, take Hwy 19 north; after the 4-mile marker, turn right onto Nahala St, then left onto Kahoa St. People park on the roadside and walk down to the park.

ACTIVITIES
Swimming
For lap swimming, the **Ho'olulu Complex** (Map p268; ☎ 961-8698) has an impressive, Olympic-sized, open-air pool (with high dive but no kiddie pool). Open swim times vary; call for hours.

Beach swimming is somewhat limited. See opposite for a description of Hilo's offerings.

Diving
The best spot near Hilo is **Leleiwi Beach** (Map p268), with depths of 10ft to 70ft, while **Pohoiki Bay** (Map pp192–3), in the nearby Puna district, is the best dive site in east Hawai'i, with depths of 20ft to 100ft. Both have an impressive variety of marine life.

They may run the only dive shop in Hilo, but the good folks at **Nautilus Dive Center** (Map p270; ☎ 935-6939; www.nautilusdivehilo.com; 382 Kamehameha Ave; scuba package from $30, dives $85-105) are reliable, friendly and generous with advice. They run a variety of dives (including a beginner's intro dive) and have PADI certification courses. For safety reasons, their lava dives are on hold indefinitely – but call to check!

Surfing
The best surfing spot near Hilo is Honoli'i Cove at Honoli'i Beach Park (Map p281), but see opposite for other spots.

Stop by **Orchidland Surfboards** (Map p270; ☎ 935-1533; www.orchidlandsurf.com; 262 Kamehameha Ave; ☺ 9am-5pm Mon-Sat, 10am-3pm Sun) for surfboard and bodyboard rentals ($20/12 per day) and to buy surf gear and clothes. Owner Stan Lawrence is an expert surfer, and he opened the Big Island's first surf shop in 1972. Check his website for surf reports and cool videos.

Golf
Golf is cheap – at least in Hilo. Check out the 18-hole **Hilo Municipal Golf Course** (Map p281; ☎ 959-7711; 340 Haihai St; Mon-Fri $29, Sat & Sun $34) or the nine-hole **Naniloa Country Club Golf Course**

HAWAI'I (THE BIG ISLAND)

HILO FOR NA KEIKI

Hilo doesn't have many dedicated kid amusements, but if it's sunny (or at least not raining) you won't lack for outdoor choices. Topping the list is Hilo's **Pana'ewa Rainforest Zoo** (opposite), just south of town; if you have young kids, time your visit for Saturday's petting zoo. Hilo also has several excellent parks in or near downtown: **Lili'uokalani Park** (p273) is the prettiest and most diverse, but **Wailoa River State Park** (p273) has plenty of space to run, and **Kalakaua Park** (Map p270) has a majestic, shady banyan tree perfect for a picnic, plus a time capsule and carp pool. And don't forget Hilo's **beaches** (opposite), which offer fun for every age. Kids can usually suffer through a visit to the **Farmers Market** (p273) if they're drinking from a fresh-cut coconut. If you visit in September, the annual **Hawai'i County Fair** (p276) is a great old-fashioned event with all the usual carnival rides and games.

Of course, if it *is* raining, well, it only costs a buck to take in a movie at downtown's **Kress Cinemas** (p280), and if you don't like what's playing there, check out **Stadium Cinemas** (p280) in Prince Kuhio Plaza, which also has a video arcade.

(Map p268; ☎ 935-3000; 9-/18-hole green fees $25/45). Hilo duffers only quit when it *really* rains.

Yoga

The attractive 'heated' **Yoga Centered** (Map p270; ☎ 934-7233; www.yogacentered.com; 37 Waianuenue Ave; drop-in class $12) studio offers mostly Ashtanga and Vinyasa (flowing sequences of poses) classes, plus the latest yoga fashions.

Run out of the owner's home, **Balancing Monkey Yoga Center** (Map p268; ☎ 936-9590; www .balancingmonkey.com; 65 Mohouli St; drop-in class $13) offers more casual, 90-minute classes in either the Ashtanga or Iyengar method.

FESTIVALS & EVENTS

For a complete listing of Big Island events, visit www.gohawaii.com.

Merrie Monarch Festival (☎ 935-9168; www.merrie monarchfestival.org; 2-night admission general/reserved $10/15) Starts Easter Sunday. Hilo's biggest event is a weeklong cultural festival that culminates with a spirited hula competition. The islands' best hula troupes vie in *kahiko* (ancient) and *'auana* (modern) categories, with a skill and seriousness that put hotel hula shows to shame. Other events include a *ho'olaule'a* (celebration), a Miss Aloha Hula contest and a parade. Tickets go on sale at the end of December and sell out within a month.

May Day Lei Day Festival (☎ 934-7010; www.hilo palace.com; admission free) On the first Sunday in May the art of lei making is celebrated with incredible displays, demonstrations, live music, hula and more at the Palace Theater.

Big Island Hawaiian Music Festival (☎ 961-5711; www.ehcc.org) Mid-July. A two-day concert featuring accomplished ukulele, steel-guitar and slack-key-guitar players from across the islands.

Aloha Festival (http://alohafestivals.com) During the August/September statewide Aloha Festival, Hilo jumps in with an outdoor concert and a festival honoring Queen Lili'uokalani.

Hawai'i County Fair September. The fair comes to town on the grounds of the Afook-Chinen Civic Auditorium (Map p268). It's pure rural nostalgia, with carnival rides, cotton candy, orchid shows and agricultural exhibits.

SLEEPING

The resorts and 'vacation rental' condos of the Kona Coast are nonexistent in Hilo. Instead, you'll find more affordable standard hotels and very comfortable, even historic, B&Bs.

Budget

Hilo Bay Hostel (Map p270; ☎ 933-2771; www.hawaii hostel.net; 101 Waianuenue Ave; dm $20, r with/without bathroom $60/50; 🖳) Put simply, this hostel is great.

Perfectly situated downtown (walkable to almost everything), it occupies an airy historic building with hardwood floors, well-maintained rooms and real character. A diverse crowd of older, international travelers and a welcoming staff keep the mood low-key, relaxed and friendly. The attractive common room has TV and internet computers ($5 per hour). Private rooms are a great deal (room 9 holds a surprise in the exterior mural).

Arnott's Lodge (Map p268; ☎ 969-7097; www.arnotts lodge.com; 98 Apapane Rd; tent sites $10, dm/r with shared bathroom $20/60, r/ste $70/130; 🖳) If you just need a bed, a shower and the company of fellow travelers (mainly backpackers), Arnott's is fine, but most rooms occupy a worn-down motel in need of TLC, hostel policies are less than welcoming, and staff can be impatient. Tents occupy a crowded open lawn and use outdoor showers. The large patio hosts social events, and there's a movie room, internet access ($6 per hour), a coin laundry, bike rentals ($2 to $5 per day), and shuttles to downtown ($3 round-trip) – a necessity if you don't have a car. Ask about free airport pickups (until 7:30pm). Overall, keep expectations minimal.

Pineapple Park (Map p268; ☎ 935-6360, 323-2224; www.pineapple-park.com; cnr Pi'ilani & Kalanikoa Sts; dm $25, r $65) Hilo's smallest hostel, Pineapple Park has shared facilities that don't allow for much modesty, dorms are basic but clean, and private rooms are attractive. It's outside of, but still walkable to, downtown. There's another location in Kona, and ask about the owners' hostel outside Mountain View. It rents kayaks.

Midrange & Top End

Uncle Billy's Hilo Bay Hotel (Map p268; ☎ 935-0861, 800-442-5841; www.unclebilly.com; 87 Banyan Dr; r $105-120; ⊠ 🖳) Unfortunately, the kitschy and wind-battered Polynesian decor that is Uncle Billy's signature doesn't extend into the rooms, which are plain and a little tired. Still, it's a decent, dependable Banyan Dr choice, but it's only a good deal if you get an internet special (available by phone if you ask); rates drop by 25% or more. The hotel's mediocre restaurant has nightly entertainment (see p280).

Hilo Seaside Hotel (Map p268; ☎ 935-0821, 800-560-5557; www.hiloseasidehotel.com; 126 Banyan Dr; r $110-130; ⊠ 🖳) Like Uncle Billy's, the Seaside offers deep internet discounts (30% to 40%) off its rack rates; don't book without them. This

Banyan Dr fixture is a warren of average, clean rooms in a motel-style complex. Given the layout, noise can be an issue; the deluxe ocean-wing rooms are the quietest (with only OK views), but you pay for it.

Dolphin Bay Hotel (Map p270; ☎ 935-1466; www .dolphinbayhotel.com; 333 Iliahi St; studios $100-110, 1-/2-bedroom units $130/150) In a residential neighborhood walkable to downtown, Dolphin Bay makes an ideal base for east Hawai'i explorations. The glowing lava-fall framing the office is your first clue that the owner loves volcanoes, and he freely shares his wealth of outdoor experience. All 18 rooms are unfussy but well-kept apartment units with full kitchens and a TV – nothing fancy, but quite comfortable. Free fresh fruit and coffee are available in the morning, along with slightly charred walking sticks.

Inn at Kulaniapia (☎ 935-6789, 866-935-6789; www .waterfall.net; d $120, cottages $175; ☐) Lose yourself at this romantic four-room B&B, which is secluded high above Hilo next to a 120ft waterfall and a swimming hole. Beautifully furnished rooms have private marble-tile bath and balcony. The Kamehameha room has the ideal waterfall view, but the expansive breakfast patio provides an airy perch for all to enjoy the lusciousness. The small cottage is stylish, with full kitchen, and guests share a hot tub. The inn is several miles north of Hilo off Amau'ulu Rd; call for directions.

Hale Kai Hawaii (☎ 935-6330; www.halekaihawaii .com; 111 Honoli'i Pali; d $125-155; ☒) For memorable views of Hilo from across the bay, book one of the four rooms here, which your friendly, artistic hosts have decorated with their own art. All rooms share a wide lanai, a hot tub and a tiny pool, and each has pretty quilts, wi-fi, a TV and a king- or queen-size bed. The generous continental breakfast is delicious. Hale Kai overlooks Honoli'i Beach Park, 5 miles north of downtown Hilo.

Hilo Hawaiian Hotel (Map p268; ☎ 935-9361, 800-367-5004; www.castleresorts.com; 71 Banyan Dr; r $160-211; ☒ ☐ ☒) Hilo's best big hotel is the Hilo Hawaiian on Banyan Dr. Rooms are pleasing – neat and clean, with a standard tropical floral decor. Ocean-view rooms really deliver, and most have a private lanai. Add in expected comforts like phone, cable TV, air-conditioning and fridge, plus a freshwater pool, internet access and a decent restaurant, and you won't be disappointed.

Waterfalls Inn B&B (Map p270; ☎ 969-3407, 888-808-4456; www.waterfallsinn.com; 240 Kaiulani St; r incl

TOP SLEEPS: WINDWARD SIDE

- **Jacaranda Inn** (p249)
- **Mountain Meadow Ranch** (p260)
- **Cliff House Hawaii** (p262)
- **Inn at Kulaniapia** (left)
- **Shipman House B&B** (below)
- **Bed & Breakfast Mountain View** (p283)
- **My Island B&B** (p300)

breakfast $150-215) The four generous rooms in this historic plantation home are opulently decorated, and the romantic aura continues with spectacular rain forest views out back. Rooms have queen- or king-size beds, TVs, wi-fi and refrigerators. It'll be hard to leave this grand old lady to begin each day's requisite sightseeing – and if you never do, who cares?

Shipman House B&B (Map p270; ☎ 934-8002, 800-627-8447; www.hilo-hawaii.com; 131 Kaiulani St; r incl breakfast $210-230) This gracious Victorian mansion, still run by Shipman heirs, stands out as Hilo's most historic and romantic option. In the public rooms, play the grand piano Queen Lili'uokalani entertained on, and admire the family's museum-quality collection of antiques and artifacts. The three mansion rooms are special experiences, but the two rooms in the 1910 guest cottage are also recommended: all have nice baths, high ceilings, vintage furnishings, hardwood floors covered with *lauhala* mats, refrigerators and kimonos. The spacious breakfast patio, with gorgeous hilltop views, hosts a hula class Wednesday night.

EATING

Hilo has a satisfying variety of dining options, from cheap local *grinds* (food) to true gourmet feasts.

Budget

Bears (Map p270; ☎ 935-0708; 106 Keawe St; items $3-5; ⏰ 5:30am-4pm Mon-Fri, to 1pm Sat, 6:30am-noon Sun) If you need an early jolt of espresso, join locals at this relaxed downtown hangout, which also serves muffins, bagels, eggs and waffles. Service is hectic but full of aloha.

Café 100 (Map p268; ☎ 935-8683; 969 Kilauea Ave; loco moco $2-5, plate lunches $5-7; ⏰ 6:45am-8:30pm Mon-Sat) This legendary drive-in popularized the *loco moco*, which is rice topped with hamburger, fried egg and brown gravy, and now available in 20 varieties. Or opt for the classic plate lunch, with sides of rice and potato-mac salad. It's fast food Hawaiian-style.

Ken's House of Pancakes (Map p268; ☎ 935-8711; 1730 Kamehameha Ave; meals $6-13; ☯ 24hr) Strand a New Jersey diner in the tropics and you get a mile-long menu filled with mac-nut pancakes, fat crab omelettes, juicy burgers and *kalua* pig dinners. In other words, it's '*ono*, bra'! Local families keep it packed night and day, and it's the perfect place to bring yours (particularly pint-sized fussy eaters).

Miyo's (Map p268; ☎ 935-2273; Waiakea Villa, 400 Hualani St; mains $7-13; ☯ 11am-2pm & 5:30-8:30pm Mon-Sat) Overlooking Waiakea Pond, Miyo's resembles a rustic Japanese teahouse. Tasty, fresh renditions of tempura, sesame chicken, beef teriyaki, donburi, sashimi and more are generously accompanied by soup, rice and salad. Call ahead to reserve a coveted window table at this local favorite. The restaurant is in the first complex of buildings adjacent to the pond as you enter Waiakea Villa.

Kuhio Grille (Map p268; ☎ 959-2336; Suite A106, Prince Kuhio Plaza; mains $8.50-17; ☯ 6am-10pm Sun-Thu, to midnight Fri & Sat) Locals needing a fix of traditional Hawaiian comfort food gather at the family-run Kuhio Grille. Its specialty is the filling 1lb *laulau* – various meats wrapped in taro leaves and steamed. However, all the Hawaiian favorites are here, such as poi, *lomilomi, kalua* pig, *haupia* and *loco moco*. Behind Prince Kuhio Plaza.

Naung Mai Thai Kitchen (Map p270; ☎ 934-7540; 86 Kilauea Ave; lunch buffet $6-7, mains $10-12; ☯ 11am-2pm, 5-8:30pm Mon-Fri, 5-9pm Sat) Nondescript outside, about as big as a minute inside, this Thai restaurant dishes up curries with a nice bite and an above-average pad thai. The buffet lunch is a bargain, and at night the intimate, softly lit space is appealing.

GROCERIES

Picnics and meals that are the stuff of legend can be assembled in Hilo. First stop is always the extensive farmers market (p273). For equally fresh ingredients from the sea, try **Suisan Fish Market** (Map p268; ☎ 935-9349; 93 Lihiwai St; ☯ 8am-5pm Mon-Fri, to 4pm Sat); it has an attention-grabbing variety of *poke* and will fry whole fish on the spot next door. **O'Keefe Bakery** (Map p270; ☎ 934-9334; www.okeefebakery.com; 374 Kino'ole St; sandwiches $6; ☯ 6am-5pm Mon-Fri, to 3pm Sat) bakes artisanal breads and cookies and makes mouth-watering sandwiches.

For organic foods, bulk grains, fruit smoothies and travel-ready salads and mains, head for **Abundant Life Natural Foods** (Map p270; ☎ 935-7411; 292 Kamehameha Ave; ☯ 8:30am-7pm Mon, Tue, Thu & Fri, 7am-7pm Wed & Sat, 10am-5pm Sun) in downtown Hilo, which also has a simple café. Bigger and with a larger selection of hot items, **Island Naturals** (Map p268; ☎ 935-5533; Waiakea Center, 303 Maka'ala St; ☯ 8:30am-8pm Mon-Sat, 10am-7pm Sun) is near the Hwy 11 malls.

For their regular groceries, Hilo shoppers prefer **KTA Super Store** Downtown (Map p270; ☎ 935-3751; 323 Keawe St; ☯ 7am-9pm, to 7pm Sun); Puainako Town Center (Map p268; ☎ 959-9111; 50 E Puainako St; ☯ 5:30am-midnight). The downtown store is as cramped as the Puainako location is enormous, but both carry an extensive selection of fresh-made *poke*, bento, sushi and other packaged and specialty items. At both, go early – the good stuff sells out fast!

Midrange

Reuben's (Map p270; ☎ 961-2552; 336 Kamehameha Ave; meals $10-15; ☯ 11am-9pm Mon-Fri, noon-9pm Sat) Talk about changes in longitude: Reuben's has the underlit, cinder-block, folding-table, bright-muraled look of a real Oaxaca cantina, and the food isn't far behind. Plates are greasy, cheesy and generous, and you'll agree that the *chillies rellenos*, fish tacos and salsa '*broke da' mout*.' Service may be slow, but that's why Mexico invented the margarita ($5).

Ocean Sushi (Map p270; ☎ 961-6625; 239 Keawe St; bento $12-14; ☯ 10am-2pm & 5-9pm Mon-Sat) Zip atmosphere, rushed service, linoleum floors – but it's still *the* place for sushi in Hilo. Rolls ($3 to $6) are inventive – using mac nuts, tropical fruit, *poke* and more – and priced so you can order a bunch. The Volcano roll wins for best California roll update.

Hilo Bay Café (Map p268; ☎ 935-4939; Waiakea Center, 315 Maka'ala St; mains $15-26; ☯ 11am-9pm Mon-Sat, 5-9pm Sun) New in 2003, Hilo Bay Café offers Hawaiian-infused gourmet cuisine that holds its own with anyone. The crab cakes are as delicious as they are tall, and the seared macadamia nut–crusted scallops are alone worth the trip. The changing menu also includes rib-eye steak, barbecued ribs, mahimahi, *poke* and more, and the short wine list makes choosing an easy task: all vintages are priced the same. The only knock is the mall setting, which despite the restaurant's stylish modern interior isn't as warmly romantic as the food deserves.

SWEETS & SNACKS

Hilo has several notable shops selling edible treats you shouldn't miss – particularly if you have a sweet tooth and an adventurous palate. The best ice cream and sorbet on the island comes from a Kawaihae creamery that produces two equally yummy premium lines: Hilo Homemade (classic single flavors) and Tropical Dreams (novel fusion flavors). Get a cone of the former at **Gammy's** (Map p270; ☎ 933-1520; 41 Waianuenue Ave; per scoop $3; ◷ 8am-7pm Mon-Sat, 10am-7pm Sun), and a scoop of the latter at **Tropical Dreams** (Map p270; ☎ 935-9109; 174 Kamehameha Ave; per scoop $2.50; ◷ 7am-5pm Mon-Thu, 10am-9:30pm Fri & Sat).

For a delicious island take on traditional Japanese *mochi* (sweet rice dessert) and *manju* (baked adzuki bean–filled cake), stop at **Two Ladies Kitchen** (Map p270; ☎ 961-4766; 274 Kilauea Ave; 8-piece boxes $6; ◷ 10am-5pm Wed-Sat). Tempting, beautifully packaged mixed boxes allow for sampling (with flavors like peach and passion fruit), but whatever you do don't pass on the specialty, strawberry *mochi*. This handmade delight is a prize possession.

A closet-sized shopfront, **Hilo Seeds & Snacks** (Map p270; ☎ 935-7355; 15 Waianuenue Ave; snacks under $5; ◷ 9:30am-5pm Mon-Fri) contains an overwhelming variety of 'crack seed,' that bizarre Chinese dried-fruit snack that some find addictive and others find – well, try some yourself. The friendly owner will explain the types: plums dried with salt, vinegar, sugar and more, some medicinal and others mild. Mango with *li hing* powder is a sweet choice.

And no visit to Hilo is complete without a stop at **Itsu's Fishing Supplies** (Map p268; ☎ 935-8082; 810 Pi'ilani St; items $2-7; ◷ 8am-5pm Mon-Fri) – yes, a fishing-supply store! – which sells Hilo's best ice shave (note: Hilo folks call it 'ice shave,' not 'shave ice'). The ice shave is hand-cranked off an ice block, scooped into a cone and topped with your choice of sweet syrups – double your pleasure and add ice cream in the middle. The hardworking owners offer a popular, fresh lunch buffet as well.

Pescatore (Map p270; ☎ 969-9090; 235 Keawe St; pizzas $13, mains $16-26; ◷ 8:30am-2pm & 5:30-9pm) The ideal neighborhood restaurant, with attentive service and quality ingredients prepared simply, Pescatore will satisfy any Italian cravings. The *'ahi* carpaccio is a star, the sausage is homemade, and the authentic fare includes *cioppino*, *fra diavolo* and eggplant parmesan.

Café Pesto (Map p270; ☎ 969-6640; 308 Kamehameha Ave; pizzas $11-18, dinner mains $16-30; ◷ 11am-9pm Sun-Thu, to 10pm Fri & Sat) Housed in a beautifully renovated historical building, Café Pesto offers a varied but accomplished menu. It started as a pizza place – and the pies remain a noteworthy specialty – but it now offers delectable risottos, fresh stir-fries, interesting pastas and more, many featuring seafood. With weekend guitarists and a lively mix of locals, a friendlier scene can't be found downtown.

Seaside Restaurant (Map p268; ☎ 935-8825; 1790 Kalaniana'ole Ave; meals $20-26; ◷ 5-8:30pm Tue-Sun, to 9pm Fri & Sat) The calling card of this local institution is that its mullet and *aholehole* (flagtail) are raised in its own fish ponds. The traditional preparation (steamed in *ti* leaves) is good, but 'Chinese-style' is a flavorful variation. If it has *moi* – order it. This reef fish was once reserved for Hawaiian royalty and it's delectably soft. The restaurant also has ocean fish and a good selection of *poke* appetizers. The view is nice, but you're here for the fish, not the so-so ambience and uneven service.

Top End

Restaurant Kaikodo (Map p270; ☎ 961-2558; www .restaurantkaikodo.com; 60 Keawe St; dinner mains $20-35; ◷ 11am-2pm Mon-Fri, 5:30-9pm nightly) You hit the trifecta with Kaikodo – where the food, service and decor are all winners. For artistic, romantic ambience, nothing in Hilo can match it. Indeed, the whole scene – the Venetian chandeliers and intimate tatami room, the former bank vault converted into a wine cellar, the chef's gourmet flourishes and seafood pirouettes (the *poke*, the bisque!), the Friday-night transformation into a mellow 'club' – seems air-lifted from San Francisco. Indeed, a few locals grumble it's not 'Hilo,' but if you love food (and your traveling companion), make reservations.

DRINKING & ENTERTAINMENT

The words 'Hilo' and 'great nightlife' don't usually rub together. Outside of the Palace Theater and a couple nightclubs, the only ones making noise at night are the coqui frogs (see p285).

Bars & Nightclubs

Shooters Bar & Grill (Map p268; ☎ 969-7069; 121 Banyan Dr; admission $5, drinks $5-7; ☺ 9pm-2am Wed, 10pm-3am Thu-Sat) Local 20-somethings who want to dance to DJ-spun tunes have two main choices: first is this Banyan Dr nightclub, which has various 'theme' nights.

Uncle Mikey's Video Dance Club (Map p268; ☎ 933-2667; www.unclemikeysnightclub.com; Waiakea Villa, 400 Hualani St; cover charge $10; ☺ 9pm-1:30am Wed, Fri & Sat) Then there's Uncle Mikey's, which is next door to Miyo's (for directions, see p278). Saturdays are best; the open-air dance floor is more interesting than Shooters.

Uncle Billy's Hilo Bay Hotel (Map p268; ☎ 935-0861; 87 Banyan Dr; live music from 6pm) Uncle Billy's restaurant features Hawaiian musical entertainment from 6pm nightly. Groups vary; currently, Sunday features a family with the best, most varied act, including *na keiki* (children) doing hula.

Cronies Bar & Grill (Map p270; ☎ 935-5158; 11 Waianuenue Ave; ☺ 11am-2am Mon-Sat) Cronies is a bright, TV-festooned sports bar with occasional live music. Its big-windowed downtown location puts it a notch above the Banyon Dr hotel bars.

Theaters & Cinemas

Palace Theater (Map p270; ☎ 934-7010, box office 934-7777; www.hilopalace.com; 38 Haili St; tickets $7) The resurrected, historic Palace Theater is Hilo's cultural crown jewel. Its eclectic programming includes arthouse and silent films (accompanied by the house organ), music and dance concerts, Broadway musicals, and various cultural festivals. Every Wednesday morning it hosts a 'Mornings at the Palace' Hawaiian cultural series ($5) with rotating programs.

Kress Cinemas (Map p270; ☎ 935-6777; 174 Kamehameha Ave; tickets $1) For a buck (!), you can enjoy second-run films at this atmospheric place.

Stadium Cinemas (Map p268; ☎ 961-3456; Prince Kuhio Plaza, 111 E Puainako St; adult/child/matinee $8:50/5.25/6) New Hollywood releases are shown at this plush, up-to-date multiplex cinema.

SHOPPING

Downtown Hilo has some of the coolest, most unique gift stores and boutiques on the island. If you're hunting local and/or fine art, the gallery scene is hopping; two are below, but check out others at the corner of Mamo St and Kilauea Ave.

Sudha's Art Gallery (Map p270; ☎ 934-0009; www.sudhaachar.com; 100 Kamehameha Ave; ☺ 11am-4pm Tue-Sat) Run by the longtime chairman of the East Hawai'i Cultural Center (p272), this gallery sells high-quality paintings, sculpture and woodworking. Upstairs, find secondhand books.

Chase & Hanes (Map p270; ☎ 934-9101; 224 Kamehameha Ave; ☺ 10am-5:30pm Mon-Fri, to 5pm Sat) Come here for more great art, jewelry, vintage signs and koa bowls.

Sig Zane Designs (Map p270; ☎ 935-7077; www.sigzane.com; 122 Kamehameha Ave; ☺ 9:30am-5pm Mon-Fri, 9am-4pm Sat) Famous state wide, Sig Zane custom designs his own fabrics and styles, lifting the humble aloha shirt and tropical-flower dress into the realm of fashion.

Hilo Hattie (Map p268; ☎ 961-3077; www.hilohattie.com; Prince Kuhio Plaza; ☺ 8:30am-6pm) Good-quality Hawaiian wear for the whole family. The wide selection of styles ranges from bright and kitschy to almost understated.

Dragon Mama (Map p270; ☎ 934-9081; www.dragonmama.com; 266 Kamehameha Ave; ☺ 9am-5pm Mon-Fri, to 4pm Sat) Luscious kimonos, unique shirts and custom-made pillows from imported Japanese fabrics.

Hilo Guitars & Ukuleles (Map p270; ☎ 935-4282; www.hiloguitars.com; 56 Ponahawai St; ☺ 10am-5pm Mon-Fri, to 4pm Sat) All musicians, budding and otherwise, should come here for top-quality ukes ($40 and up) and Hawaiian sheet music.

Big Island Candies (Map p268; ☎ 935-8890, 800-935-5510; www.bigislandcandies.com; 585 Hinano St; ☺ 8:30am-5pm) This candy factory makes stylishly packaged confections and shortbread – watch them hand-dip chocolate from behind picture windows. One visit makes short work of your gift list.

Hilo Surplus Store (Map p270; ☎ 935-6398; 148 Mamo St; ☺ 8am-5pm Mon-Sat) This vintage army surplus store is *the* place for jungle-grade machetes or a bolt of camouflage Gore-Tex. Campers will find rain gear, tents and authentic mess kits.

Alan's Art & Collectibles (Map p270; ☎ 969-1554; 202 Kamehameha Ave; ☺ 10am-4:30pm Mon & Wed-Fri, 1-4:30pm Tue, 10am-3pm Sat) Time travel through Hawai'i's past in this secondhand shop, full of coconut ashtrays, bowling trophies, Elvis posters, record albums, aloha shirts and occasional treasures.

GETTING THERE & AWAY
Air

Although most Big Island visitors fly into Kona airport, Hilo airport (Map p281) is also busy. See p199 for more information.

HAWAI'I (THE BIG ISLAND)

Bus
The principal Hilo station for the **Hele-On Bus**
(☎ 961-8744; www.co.hawaii.hi.us/mass_transit/heleonbus
.html; ⏱ 7:45am-4:30pm Mon-Fri) is at **Mo'oheau terminal** (Map p270; 329 Kamehameha Ave). All intraisland
buses originate here. Routes connect to Kona
and most towns in between, and they connect
to Pahoa and Hawai'i Volcanoes National
Park. See individual destinations for details
on specific routes to/from Hilo.

GETTING AROUND
For directions to/from the airport, see p199.

Bicycle
Biking around Hilo is fun – when it isn't
raining.
Da Kine Bike Shop (Map p270; ☎ 934-9861; 18 Furn-
eaux Lane; ⏱ 9am-6pm Tue-Fri, 9am-3pm Sat) Rents bikes
for $15 to $30 a day, and also offers island cycling tours.
Mid-Pacific Wheels (Map p268; ☎ 935-6211; 1133-C
Manono St; ⏱ 9am-6pm Mon-Sat, 11am-5pm Sun) Rents
bikes for $20 per day.

Car
Hilo is a car-oriented town. Shopping malls and
businesses usually have ample lots, while most
streets downtown allow free two-hour parking.
On most days it's easy to find a space, but the
bayfront area gets jammed during the Saturday
and Wednesday farmers market (see p273).

Public Transport
The Hele-On Bus (above) has a few intracity
routes, all free, operating Monday to Friday
only:
No 4 Kaumana Goes five times a day (from 7:35am to
2:20pm) to Hilo Public Library and Hilo Medical Center
(near Rainbow Falls).
No 6 Waiakea-Uka Goes five times a day (from 7:05am
to 3:05pm) to the University of Hawai'i at Hilo and Prince
Kuhio Plaza.
No 7 Downtown Hilo Goes a dozen times a day (from
7am to 9pm) to Aupuni Center and Prince Kuhio Plaza.

Taxi
In Hilo, call **Marshall's Taxi** (☎ 936-2654) or **Percy's
Taxi** (☎ 969-7060).

AROUND HILO
Southwest of downtown Hilo, a short drive on
Waianuenue Ave leads to three scenic waterfalls, while a 10-minute drive on Hwy 200
leads to the atmospheric Kaumana Caves. At
all, car break-ins are an occasional problem.

Rainbow Falls
Just a few minutes from Hilo, this **waterfall**
provides the sort of instant gratification that's
a godsend to parents and tour-bus operators.
The delightful cascade – whose spray winks
a rainbow in the morning when the sun is
right – can almost be seen from the parking lot. Natural beauty doesn't get any easier
than this.

The cave beneath the falls is said to have
been the home of Hina, mother of Maui.
While you can't get to the cave, a short, unpaved path leads from the left side of the parking lot to the top of the falls, where there are
some inviting pools with a rope swing. The
trail passes beneath a tremendous banyan tree,
whose thick canopy blocks the sun and whose
roots could swallow children. It's great for
little explorers, but be prepared for voracious
mosquitoes.

Pe'epe'e Falls & Boiling Pots
Two miles past Rainbow Falls along Waianuenue Ave, this **waterfall** is prettier still, a series
of dramatic falls that create swirling, bubbling
pools (or 'boiling pots'). A grassy lawn and

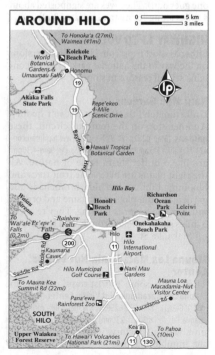

AROUND HILO
0 — 5 km
0 — 3 miles

To Honoka'a (27mi);
Waimea (41mi)

Kolekole
Beach Park
World
Botanical
Gardens &
Umauma Falls   Honomu

19

Akaka Falls
State Park   Pepe'ekeo
4-Mile
19   Scenic Drive

Hawaii Tropical
Botanical Garden

Hilo Bay

Weia
Stream   Honoli'i
Beach   Richardson
Park   Ocean
To   Park   Leleiwi
Wai'ale Pe'epe'e   Rainbow   Point
Falls   Falls
(0.2mi)   Onekahakaha
200   Beach Park
Kaumana   Hilo
Rd   11   Hilo
Saddle Rd   International
Airport
To Mauna Kea   Hilo Municipal   Nani Mau
Summit Rd (22mi)   Golf Course   Gardens
Pana'ewa   Mauna Loa
Rainforest Zoo   Macadamia-Nut
Visitor Center
Macadamia Rd

SOUTH
HILO   Kea'au   To Pahoa
(10mi)
Upper Waiakea   To Hawai'i Volcanoes   11   130
Forest Reserve   National Park (21mi)

bathrooms make this a good picnic spot. A slippery, rocky, steep trail leads down to the water itself (past an abused 'No Swimming' sign); it's very pleasant to relax here, but don't dismiss the sign. Drownings do occur.

Wai'ale Falls

Less than a mile further you'll cross a bridge in front of unsigned Wai'ale Falls, which are not on any tour-bus itinerary. An uneven, buggy, 15-minute hike through the forest (the trail begins to the right of the bridge) leads to the top of the **falls**, where lava-encased swimming holes and a view to the ocean make a wonderful retreat. Locals think so too; come midweek for the quietest experience.

Kaumana Caves

These **caves** are actually a large lava tube formed by an 1881 Mauna Loa eruption. The tube is extensive (enter the left or right opening), but it narrows periodically and lengthy explorations require some crawling; it's a much more evocative experience than Thurston Lava Tube in Hawai'i Volcanoes National Park. Bring two flashlights (in case one goes out!). The caves are signposted about 4 miles along Kaumana Dr (Hwy 200).

HIGHWAY 11 TO VOLCANO

Either as short trips from Hilo or as diversions on the way to the national park, Hwy 11 contains several reasons to stop.

Nani Mau Gardens

Unfortunately, this almost doesn't qualify. Another stop on the tour-bus circuit, these **gardens** (Map p281; ☎ 959-3500; www.nanimau.com; 421 Makalika St; adult/child 4-10 $10/5; ☗ 9am-4:30pm) are like a buffet steam table of nature. All the right plants are here – the fruit trees and blooming hibiscus, orchids, bromeliads and gardenias – but plots are so tame and orderly much of the flavor is missing. They're about 3 miles south of Hilo; from Hwy 11, turn east on Makalika St.

Mauna Loa Macadamia-Nut Visitor Center

Then again, some 'tourist traps' can be fun. **Mauna Loa Macadamia-Nut Visitor Center** (Map p281; ☎ 966-8618, 888-628-6256; www.maunaloa.com; Macadamia Rd; ☗ 8:30am-5:30pm) provides a window on a working factory, where you can watch the humble mac nut as it moves along the

assembly line from cracking to roasting to chocolate dipping and packaging. The gift shop, of course, has every variation ready for purchase, with tasters. C Brewer Co, which owns the Mauna Loa company, produces most of Hawaii's macadamia nuts. The factory is well signed about 5 miles south of Hilo; the 3-mile access road dips through acres of macadamia trees.

Mountain View

Just before Mountain View, after the 12-mile marker on Hwy 11, make sure to visit **Dan De Luz's Woods** (Map p284; ☎ 968-6607; Hwy 11; ☗ 9am-5pm). Dan is a master woodworker who takes native hardwoods such as koa, sandalwood, mango and banyan and crafts gorgeous bowls, platters and furniture. His store is an education, and his workshop is next door. Adjacent **Koa Kaffee** (Map p284; ☎ 968-1129; Hwy 11; ☗ 7am-7:30pm Wed-Sun) is a recommended home-style diner with local *grinds*.

A half mile further, coffee lovers (or addicts, if you will) should put on the brakes for the **Hilo Coffee Mill** (Map p284; ☎ 968-1333; www.hilo coffeemill.com; Hwy 11; ☗ 10am-4pm Mon-Fri), which is dedicated to supporting and promoting East Hawai'i coffee plantations. Free samples are

---

BEST WAYS TO EXPERIENCE ISLAND TIME

- Have the beach to yourself at **Makala-wena Beach** (p231)

- Camp midweek at moody **Laupahoe-hoe Point** (p266)

- Browse the **Maku'u Craft & Farmers Market** (p284) and get lost on **Puna backroads** (p286)

- Experience old Hawaii and lush scenery on the **drive from Hawi to Pololu Valley** (p243)

- Take an early-morning paddle around **Kealakekua Bay** (p222)

- Meditate alongside a Tibetan lama at **Wood Valley Temple** (p303)

- Visit island plantation days at the **Hawaii Plantation Museum** (p273)

- Drive **Chain of Craters Rd** (p294) to marvel at the lava and this growing island

offered at the counter, where coffee is treated as though it were fine wine. The Mill sells fresh coffee and espresso drinks, hot and cold, and you can buy whole beans. Visit the roaster next door to further your education; orchard tours are sometimes offered.

Within the village of Mountain View (at the 14-mile marker), **Mountain View Bakery** (☎ 968-6353; Old Volcano Rd; 🕑 7:30am-noon Mon, Tue & Thu, to 1:30pm Sat) bakes delicious glazed doughnuts and its iconic 'stone cookies,' which are indeed rock hard but tasty. It's in the yellow building.

An affordable, peaceful retreat, **Bed & Breakfast Mountain View** (Map p284; ☎ 968-6868, 888-698-9896; www.bbmtview.com; r incl breakfast $55-95) offers four comfortable rooms (two with private bathroom) in the warm home of famous Big Island artists Jane and Linus Chao. Hidden on a quiet road a mile from Hwy 11, surrounded by pretty landscaping, the Chaos' large house (built for grown kids who never stayed) is graced with their splendid art and genuine aloha.

Akatsuka Orchid Gardens

Past the 22-mile marker on Hwy 11, tour buses also pull into these **gardens** (Map p284; ☎ 967-8234, 888-967-6669; www.akatsukaorchid.com; Hwy 11; admission free; 🕑 8:30am-5pm), which are really a warehouse stuffed with perennially blooming orchids. It's a sizable collection, ready for shipping, and seeds and starters for Kona coffee plants, papaya, guava, hibiscus and bamboo orchids are for sale.

PUNA

Puna has long had a reputation as something of an outlaw community – a place where nonconformity is both prized and nurtured. This has created its own self-selecting momentum: in Puna you'll find psychedelic hippies, funky artists, New Age spiritual practitioners, alternative healers, Hawaiian sovereignty activists, *pakalolo* growers, organic farmers, off-the-grid survivalists and those who live off the land simply because they were never cut out for straight jobs to begin with.

The landscape probably has something to do with this. Containing the eastern tip of the island, Puna retains thick, unspoiled portions of sometimes hallucinatory forest and coastline, but it also lives uneasily in the shadow of Kilauea – which has periodically sent lava flows coursing across neighborhoods and towns. One settles here only by accepting wildness and impermanence as the price.

Considering all this, it is somewhat surprising that Puna is the fastest-growing district in the state. This is because it is one of the Big Island's last places where middle- and lower-middle-class Hawaiian families can still afford to buy a home. The northern half of Puna has become one unending subdivision, and in some places home prices have tripled in the last decade.

For the traveler, Puna makes a sultry, hang-loose place to ditch the guidebook, hang out and get to know local 'punatics.' In your explorations, though, respect all 'Kapu – No Trespassing' signs; some of them are meant very seriously. The heart of Puna is contained in and around the triangle made by Hwys 130, 137 and 132.

KEA'AU

pop 2010

Situated just off Hwy 11, Kea'au is Puna's largest town, and it serves the major shopping and business needs of the district's burgeoning subdivisions – Hawaiian Paradise Park, Hawaiian Beaches, Hawaiian Acres and Orchidland Estates. For travelers, it's mainly useful for fresh provisions or lunch.

Everything is either in or near the Kea'au Shopping Center, at the main crossroads; it has a laundry, an ATM, a large grocery store and a natural food store (all open daily).

Across the road, small **Kea'au Village Market** (☎ 966-4553; 🕑 9am-5pm) has outdoor stalls with fresh local produce, gift shops and friendly **Triple K Grindz** (meals $6-8; 🕑 9am-5pm Mon-Sat), grilling up tasty plate lunches.

More quick local *grinds* can be had at the original **Verna's Drive-In** (☎ 966-9288; meals $4-7.50; 🕑 6am-9pm), just past the shopping center on Hwy 130.

PAHOA

pop 960

If Puna is a state of mind, Pahoa is as close to a physical center as you'll find. It's a ramshackle, ragamuffin town with raised wooden sidewalks, peeling paint and an unkempt bohemian edge. No one's in a hurry, and you needn't be either.

HAWAI'I (THE BIG ISLAND)

HAWAI'I (THE BIG ISLAND)

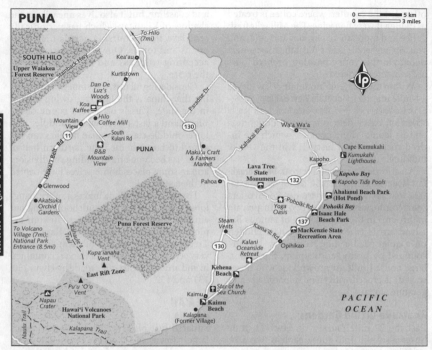

Orientation & Information

Roads in and around Pahoa are known by many names. For example, the main road through town is signposted as Pahoa Village Rd but is also called Government Main Rd, Old Government Rd, Main St, Puna Rd and Pahoa Rd – but Hwy 130 is also known as Pahoa Rd!

In town you'll find a convenience store, banks and a **post office** (☎ 965-1158; 15-2859 Pahoa Village Rd; ☒ 8:30am-4pm Mon-Fri, 11am-2pm Sat).

Next to Pahoa Village Center, **Sirius Coffee** (☎ 965-8555; Pahoa Village Rd; per 30min $2; ☒ 7am-5pm Mon-Fri, 8am-3pm Sat, 8am-3pm Sun) has internet terminals. It also has espresso coffee, and cheap sandwiches ($5).

The free Hele-On Bus (p199) goes from Hilo to Kea'au and Pahoa six times a day Monday to Friday; take the 9 Pahoa.

Sights & Activities

Join the entire Puna *'ohana* (family) at the **Maku'u Craft & Farmers Market** (☒ 8am-2pm Sun) on Hwy 130 between the 7-mile and 8-mile markers: there's hot BBQ, live music, psychic readings, jewelry, clothing, massage, art, wood

carvings – even fresh produce! The **Pahoa Farmers Market** (☒ 8am-3pm Sun), behind Luquin's, is deserted by comparison.

For swimming, don't miss the gorgeous, outdoor, Olympic-size pool at **Pahoa Community Aquatic Center** (Kauhale St; ☒ 9am-4pm), behind the Pahoa Neighborhood Facility; it's got nice showers and a separate kids' pool.

Sleeping & Eating

Island Paradise Inn (☎ 990-0234; www.vrbo.com/23179; Pahoa Village Rd; d $40-50) Smack downtown, this inn is actually a row of former plantation-worker houses that's been converted into small, clean, attractive and, above all, very affordable rooms, all with private bathroom and kitchenette. The Bamboo Room is a tiny gem; two rooms in the plantation owner's house are bigger.

Island Naturals (☎ 965-8322; 15-1403 Pahoa Village Rd; ☒ 7:30am-7:30pm Mon-Sat, 8am-7pm Sun) This natural foods store is notable for its fresh, interesting range of sandwiches, packaged salads, baked goods and hot food.

Pahoa's Village Café (☎ 965-0072; 15-2471 Pahoa Village Rd; mains $7-9; ☒ 8am-2pm Wed-Sun, 5:30-9pm

Fri & Sat) This attractive café serves a quality burger and ample plates of omelettes, crepes and waffles. Dinner specials include 'ahi and steaks.

Luquin's Mexican Restaurant (☎ 965-9990; 15-2942 Pahoa Village Rd; mains $8-15; ⊙ 7am-9pm) Everybody recommends Luquin's – not so much for the good-but-not-great Mexican food as for the scene. This Pahoa institution is a gathering place to hang out, eat, talk story and enjoy a drink or three at the cocktail bar.

Paolo's Bistro (☎ 965-7033; Pahoa Village Rd; mains $11-20; ⊙ 5:30-9pm Tue-Sun) Tablecloths and cloth napkins equal fine dining in Pahoa, as does the well-executed short menu of northern Italian fare.

Drinking & Entertainment

Shaka's (☎ 965-1133; 15-2929 Pahoa Village Rd; ⊙ from 4pm Mon-Sat) This lively, eclectic bar has pool tables and a mixed gay-and-straight crowd. DJs and live bands alternate with karaoke.

LAVA TREE STATE MONUMENT

Entering this **park** beneath its tight-knit canopy of monkeypod trees is an otherworldly experience. A short, easy loop trail passes through a tropical vision of Middle Earth, full of ferns, orchids and bamboo, and highlighting unusual 'lava trees,' which were created in 1790 when a rain forest was engulfed in *pahoehoe* from Kilauea's East Rift Zone. The lava enveloped the moisture-laden ohia trees and then receded, leaving lava molds where the destroyed trees once stood. These mossy lava shells now lie scattered like dinosaur bones, adding to the park's ghostly

aura. Then, in late afternoon, the love songs of coqui (see below) reverberate among the trees. To get here, follow Hwy 132 about 2.5 miles east of Hwy 130.

Lava Tree Tropic Inn (☎ 965-7441; www.lavatree tropicinn.com; 14-3555 Puna Rd, Pahoa; d $90-135; ☐) Next to the state monument, this B&B will appeal in style and mood to Europeans. The Hungarian owner has converted the upstairs into five comfortable rooms, sprucing them up with artistic touches while retaining a homey feel. The suite has a fun powder room, a Jacuzzi tub and a bidet. Breakfast comes with a few Hungarian treats, while Tuesday is music night in the barn. The dramatic entrance gate was also crafted by a Hungarian artist.

KAPOHO

Hwy 132 heads east until it meets Hwy 137 at what is called 'Four Corners' near Kapoho. This spot contained a farming town until Pele paid a visit in January 1960. A fissure opened up in the midst of a nearby sugarcane field; while the main flow of *pahoehoe* lava ran toward the ocean, a slower-moving offshoot of *'a'a* lava crept toward the town, burying orchid farms in its path. Two weeks later the lava entered Kapoho and buried the town. A hot-springs resort and nearly 100 homes and businesses disappeared beneath the flow. Amazingly, when the lava approached the sea at Cape Kumukahi, it parted into two flows around the lighthouse, which alone survived. Old-timers say it's because, on the eve of the disaster, the lighthouse keeper offered a meal to Pele, who had appeared in the form of an old woman, and she spared the structure.

HAWAI'I (THE BIG ISLAND)

NOISY *!£% LITTLE FROGS

Many hotels and B&Bs around Hilo and Puna provide earplugs in the nightstand. Why? Wait till dusk. That's when Hawai'i's cutest invasive pest – the coqui – makes itself heard. These tiny Puerto Rican frogs, most no bigger than a quarter, arrived on the island in 1990 and, finding no natural predators, proliferated wildly. Around Lava Tree State Monument densities are the highest in the state and twice that of Puerto Rico.

Within 2ft the coqui's sweet chirp can register between 90 and 100 decibels, and at a distance a chorus maintains 70 decibels – equivalent to a vacuum cleaner. To hear what you're in for, visit www.hear.org/AlienSpeciesInHawaii/species/frogs.

Frustrated, sleep-deprived locals would crush them in their bare hands, if only they could. Instead, the best eradication method is to spray a 16% citric acid solution, though, in the most infested places, coqui return in a few days. Another problem is that the coqui eat too many bugs, competing with native birds and possibly hurting native flowering plants.

After a few nights, you too may join local 'coquistadores' – madly spraying the forest to reclaim Hawai'i's once-quiet nights.

DETOUR: PUNA BACKROADS

The old lighthouse that Pele spared isn't much to see – just a tall piece of white-painted metal scaffolding. But it's still rewarding to head straight across 'Four Corners' from Hwy 132 and brave the rutted, 1.5-mile dirt road to the end of **Cape Kumukahi**. This is the easternmost point in the state, and the air that blows across it is the freshest in the world (so scientists say). Even better, the lava-covered cliffs are gorgeous and lonely. If you're up for some scrambling, they're an ideal place to contemplate the meeting of sky, sea and lava.

Turn left, or north, at 'Four Corners,' and time will seem to slow to a stop as you enter a teeming, ancient, vine-draped forest pulsing with mana. The dirt road leads to **Wa'a Wa'a** and is passable for standard cars, but it's cratered, narrow and twisted. Mind the numerous 'Kapu' signs (some protect sacred burial sites, others private property) and go slow. After about 2 miles it's shocking to pass new homes. After 4 miles you'll get to a boulder **beach** shaded by ironwood trees; it's possible to park here and scramble along the shore, or simply sit, have lunch and marvel.

Most visitors turn right here and continue along Hwy 137, but this area has some interesting detours (see above).

RED ROAD (HIGHWAY 137)

Scenic, winding Hwy 137 is nicknamed Red Rd because its northern portion is paved with red cinder. It's a relaxing, atmospheric drive that periodically passes beneath tunnel-like canopies of milo and *hala* (pandanus) trees.

Kapoho Tide Pools

The best snorkeling on the Big Island's windward side is this sprawling network of **tide pools**, which in 2003 were officially named the Wai Opae Tide Pools Marine Life Conservation District. Here, Kapoho's lava-rock coast is a mosaic of protected, shallow, interconnected pools containing a rich variety of sea life. It's easy to pool-hop for hours, tracking saddle wrasses, Moorish idols, butterfly fish, sea cucumbers and much more.

From Hwy 137, a mile south of the lighthouse, turn onto Kapoho Kai Dr, which winds a little and dead-ends at Wai Opae; turn left and park in the lot. There are no facilities.

Ahalanui Beach Park

This park is also called 'the hot pond' because of its main attraction – a large, spring-fed **thermal pool** set in lava rock that's deep enough for swimming. It makes for a pretty sweet bathtub: water temperatures average 90°F, cement borders make for easy access, tropical fish abound, and, though the ocean pounds the adjacent seawall, the pool remains mellow. However, while ocean waters flush the pond, some warn of a risk of bacterial infection; don't enter if you have any cuts.

The park is officially open from 7am to 7pm, but the gates are never locked and nighttime soaks are possible. The park has picnic tables, portapotties and a lifeguard daily. Don't leave valuables in your car.

Isaac Hale Beach Park

This **beach** (Hale is pronounced '*ha*-lay') at Pohoiki Bay is basically a line of parking spaces along a rocky beach with a boat ramp at one end. On weekends there's usually a frenzy of activity, as local families and teens picnic, fish, swim, surf and hang out. However, the swimming is limited due to the rough water, which makes for challenging surfing so long as you avoid the rocks.

Beyond the boat ramp a well-worn path leads past a house to a small natural hot pond that's large enough to hold a handful of folks. It's well worth searching out.

The park has portapotties and an outdoor shower, but no drinking water. Camping is allowed (for permits, see p193), but it isn't recommended, due to semipermanent squatters and lack of upkeep. However, the county has put renovating this park on its 'to-do' list, so check back for improvements.

Pohoiki Road

Past Isaac Hale, Red Rd veers left, while straight ahead is **Pohoiki Rd**, which is a good shortcut to Pahoa. It is another of Puna's shaded, mystical roads, winding through thick forest dotted with papaya orchards and wild *noni* (Indian mulberry).

If you're looking for a personalized retreat in a secluded forest (and who isn't?), Puna has two excellent choices. The smaller and more focused is **Yoga Oasis** (☎ 965-8460, 800-274-4446;

www.yogaoasis.org; 13-678 Pohoiki Rd; s/d r $75/100, cabins $125/145), which rarely hosts more than a dozen guests at a time. All rates include daily yoga and an organic breakfast, and rooms are more nicely furnished than the undeveloped setting promises; bath facilities are particularly impressive. Various retreat packages are offered. To get here, look for a driveway on your left with colorful flags over it, 2 miles up from Red Rd. (See below for info on the other retreat option.)

MacKenzie State Recreation Area

Puna does not lack for moody, mana-imbued settings, and yet another is this extensive grove of ironwood trees edging sheer, 40ft cliffs above a restless ocean. During the day, this quiet, secluded **park** makes an unforgettable picnic spot. However, while camping is allowed (for permits, see p191), occasional crime has been a problem, and staying overnight is not recommended.

Opihikao & Around

Blink and you'll miss the village of Opihikao, which is marked by a little Congregational church. The real reason travelers stop here is Puna's other notable retreat, between the 17- and 18-mile markers on Hwy 137.

Larger and more diverse, both in its clientele and its offerings, **Kalani Oceanside Retreat** (☎ 965-7828, 800-800-6886; www.kalani.com; tents s/d $30/40, r & cottages d $110-170, tree house d $260; ▣) occupies a sprawling compound that fairly hums with activity and energy. It makes a fun, communal place to stay even if you don't participate in the programs, which range from yoga, meditation and dance to alternative healing and outdoor 'adventures' such as hiking and snorkeling. The vibe is relaxed and open: some programs are geared to gay guests, and the pool and sauna are clothing optional after 3pm. An outdoor dining room (also open to nonguests) serves healthy buffet-style meals. And the rooms? All of them are simple and breezy, with bright tropical spreads and plywood floors that are covered in *lauhala* mats. The camping area is the best spot for tents in Puna. Ask about the packages.

Kehena Beach

To hang loose Puna-style, come to this tremendously beautiful **black-sand beach**. At the base of rocky cliffs, shaded by coconut and ironwood trees, folks come to doff their clothes, sunbathe, play music, meditate, party and swim. All types and persuasions mix easily – hippies, Hawaiians, gays, families, teens, seniors and tourists. Though it's not for the shy, the vibe at this nude beach is friendly. In the mornings, dolphins sometimes join the party, venturing close to shore.

Be careful in the surf, which is powerful even when the water is 'calm.' Deaths occur here every year, and you shouldn't venture beyond the rocky point at the southern end. Kehena is on Red Rd, immediately south of the 19-mile marker. From the small parking lot, a short, steep path leads down to the beach. Don't leave any valuables in your car.

Kalapana (Former Village)

As with Kapoho in 1960, so it was for Kalapana 30 years later: in 1990 a redirection of the current ongoing eruption buried most of this village, destroying 100 homes and obliterating what was once Hawai'i's most famous black-sand beach, **Kaimu Beach**.

Today Hwy 137 ends abruptly at the eastern edge of what used to be Kalapana. A few houses here were spared, and the dead-end is now two things: a modest complex catering to tourists and an outpost of the Hawaiian sovereignty movement. You can buy current lava photos and gifts, an ice shave or smoothie, and get a filling plate lunch at a branch of **Verna's Drive-In** (☎ 965-8234; meals $2-6; ☺ 10am-5pm). In the afternoon, sidle up to the outdoor **kava bar** (☺ 3-10pm), where you can try this unique concoction and rub elbows with locals. An interesting conversation starter is to ask about the adjacent billboard display promoting the establishment of the 'lawful Hawaiian government.' The display provides a full account of Hawaiian history, past and present, from a native perspective.

Finally, a short walk across the lava leads to a new **black-sand beach**, where hundreds of baby coconut palms (plant one yourself, for good luck) surround a comma of sand. The water is too rough to swim, but it's a thoughtful spot.

HIGHWAY 130

Red Rd intersects Hwy 130 (Old Kalapana Rd), which leads north to Pahoa. At the 20-mile marker the 1929 **Star of the Sea Church** (☺ 9am-4pm) is noted for the naive-style paintings that cover the walls and the trompe l'oeil mural behind the altar, whose illusion of depth is remarkably effective. Inside, displays recount the history of the church and of the area's missionaries. Plans are eventually to turn the church into a community cultural center.

At the 15-mile marker, roughly 3.5 miles south of Pahoa, there's a faded blue 'Scenic View' highway sign, but no view. Surprise! Instead, park and follow the small path, which quickly forks around a steaming, shaggy spatter cone. Here, a handful of vents has been modified into **natural steam baths**, some with wooden planks to sit on, others with tarps. Most accommodate only one or two people; look for an unoccupied vent and enjoy. Most wear bathing suits, but some don't – hey, it's Puna.

HAWAI'I VOLCANOES NATIONAL PARK

Of all the marvels that Hawaii offers, none equals the awe-inspiring majesty and raw brutal power of the two active volcanoes contained within Hawai'i Volcanoes National Park (HAVO). The entire island chain is the result of the volcanic processes on display here, which is nothing less than the ongoing birth of Hawaii.

The elder volcano is Mauna Loa, whose massive bulk slopes as gently as Buddha's belly, as if earth's largest mountain (as measured from the seafloor) were nothing more than an overgrown hill. But, at over 13,000ft, its navel is frigid year-round, an alpine desert that's snow covered in winter.

The other volcano is Kilauea. This is the park's centerpiece – the youngest and most active volcano on earth. Kilauea Caldera is the home of Pele, who must be the most accommodating goddess in the entire Hawaiian pantheon. How else to explain her tourist-ready volcano – where you can cross the steaming tops of active craters and, if you're lucky, walk right up to the flowing lava itself?

At roughly 333,000 acres (and counting), HAVO is larger than the island of Moloka'i, and its landscape is more varied – with black-lava deserts, rain forests, grassy coastal plains, snowy summits and more. The park is Hawai'i's best place for hiking and camping, with about 140 miles of trails, but you don't *have* to break a sweat: good roads circle the caldera and take in the main highlights.

Kilauea's East Rift Zone has been erupting since 1983, and it has remade this side of the island. In 1988 lava blocked the coastal road to Puna, and in 1990 it covered the entire village of Kalapana. Since that time the flows have crept further west, engulfing Kamoamoa Beach in 1994 and later claiming an additional mile of road and most of sacred Wahaula Heiau.

The center of the action is the Pu'u 'O'o Vent, a smoldering cone in the northeastern section of the park. While it occasionally erupts in geyserlike fountains, this isn't the norm. Hawai'i's shield volcanoes lack the explosive gases of other volcanoes, and so most of the time lava simply oozes and creeps along. It's the best show on the island, and, when Pele does send up dramatic curtains of fire, people stream in from everywhere to watch (as they have for over two centuries).

However, there's no telling how or even if lava will be flowing when you're here. Pele may be accommodating, but she keeps her own counsel. There's simply no predicting what will happen next in what is certainly the USA's most dynamic national park.

ORIENTATION

This vast and varied park can fill as many days as you give it, particularly if you enjoy hiking. Just past the entrance, the Kilauea Visitor Center, Volcano Art Center and Volcano House are clustered together.

The park's main road is Crater Rim Dr, which circles the moonscape of Kilauea Caldera. If you only have a few hours, spend them seeing the drive-up sites on this road. The park's other scenic drive is Chain of Craters Rd, which leads south 20 miles to the coast, ending at the site of the most recent lava activity. It's a two-hour round-trip drive without stops.

Some sites and shorter trails are accessible by wheelchair, and, as is typical, crowds gather at scenic viewpoints and dissipate quickly along the trails.

A mile from the park entrance, the village of Volcano (p300) serves park visitors with a nice selection of restaurants and accommodations.

Maps

Pele is no friend to cartographers; though generally reliable, maps have a short shelf life in this everchanging terrain. That said, the free color map given at the park's entrance is usually fine for driving around, seeing the

HAWAI'I (THE BIG ISLAND)

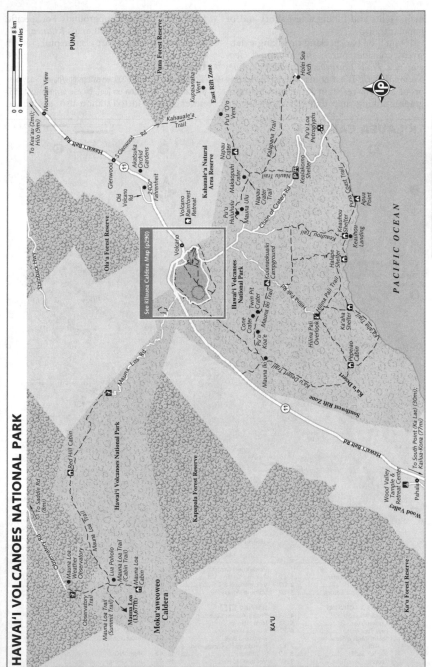

HAWAI'I VOLCANOES NATIONAL PARK

main sights and hiking a few short and/or popular trails.

If you'll be backpacking or hiking extensively, consider purchasing *National Geographic's Trails Illustrated Hawaii Volcanoes National Park*. It's a comprehensive, waterproof and rip-resistant large-format topographic hiking map that IDs most terrain features, including campgrounds. For specific hikes, the USGS 1:24,000 maps *Kilauea*, *Volcano* and *Ka'u Desert* are also helpful.

INFORMATION

The **park** (☎ 985-6000; www.nps.gov/havo; 7-day pass per car $10, per person on foot, bicycle or motorcycle $5) never closes. The toll station also sells annual

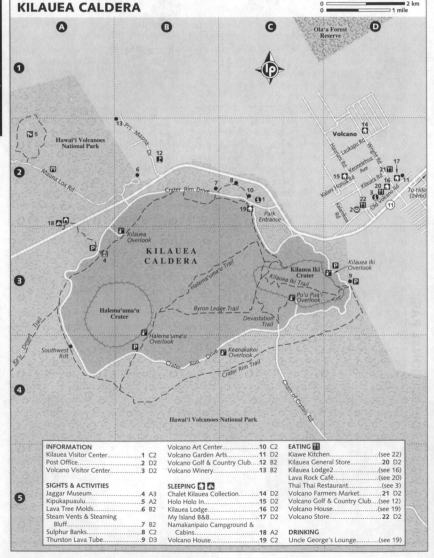

KILAUEA CALDERA

| 0 | 2 km |
| 0 | 1 mile |

HAWAI'I (THE BIG ISLAND)

park passes (HAVO only/all national parks $20/50).

Kilauea Visitor Center (Map p290; ☎ 985-6017; ⏱ 7:45am-5pm) should be your first stop. Rangers can advise you on volcanic activity, trail conditions and the best things to see based on your time. A board lists the week's guided hikes and ranger programs. Pick up trail pamphlets and junior-ranger program activity sheets ($1.25), and the excellent bookstore has a plethora of volumes and videos on volcanoes, flora, hiking, and Hawaiian culture and history. There's also an ATM, a pay phone and rest rooms.

The park's **hotline** (☎ 985-6000; ⏱ 24hr) provides daily recorded updates on park weather, road closures and lava-viewing conditions. The USGS also has eruption updates on its website (http://hvo.wr.usgs.gov). Note that the nearest gas is in Volcano village.

At 4000ft above sea level, the Kilauea Caldera area is generally 10°F to 15°F cooler than Hilo or Kona, but weather is unpredictable and microclimates can vary dramatically within the park. Plan and prepare for hot sun, dry wind, fog, chilly rain and soaking downpours, all in a day. At a minimum, bring long pants, a jacket or sweater and a rain slicker.

The free Hele-On bus (p199) leaves once a day from Hilo (at 2:40pm) and arrives at the park visitor center an hour later; take the 23 Kau.

DANGERS & ANNOYANCES

If you need reminding, the park contains active volcanoes, which create a few unusual hazards. For instance, it's entirely possible that a visit could end in your death. Statistics are of course in your favor (fatalities are *rare*), but no one – *not even the scientists* – knows what Pele will do next.

Oddly enough, hot lava is itself not the most threatening personal danger. Instead, deaths tend to occur when people venture too close to the current active flow – and wind up on unstable 'benches' of new land that collapse, or get caught in steam explosions when lava enters the ocean.

Meanwhile, hardened lava is uneven and brittle, and rocks can be glass-sharp. Thin crusts can give way over unseen hollows and lava tubes; the edges of craters and rifts crumble easily. Deep earth cracks may be hidden by plants. When hiking, abrasions, deep cuts and broken limbs are all possible.

Even more than most places, stay on marked trails and take park warning signs seriously. Don't venture off on your own. This can damage fragile areas, lead to injuries, and leave tracks that encourage others to follow.

Air quality is a constant issue. When lava meets the sea, it creates a 'steam plume,' which is a toxic cocktail of sulfuric and hydrochloric acid mixed with airborne silica (or glass particles). Also, the Pu'u 'O'o vent belches about 2000 tons of sulfur dioxide daily. Depending on the winds, all this can settle over the park as 'vog.' Even when you can't see vog, you'll taste it. Before hiking, check the visitor center's air-quality monitor, particularly if you're heading to the active flow. In addition, steam vents throughout the park can spew high concentrations of sulfuric fumes (which smell like rotten egg); Halema'uma'u Overlook (Map p290) and Sulphur Banks (Map p290) are prime spots. Given all this, people with respiratory and heart conditions, pregnant women, infants and young children should take special care when visiting.

Finally, vast areas of the park qualify as desert. Dehydration is common. Carrying two quarts of water per person is the standard advice, but bring more and keep a gallon in the trunk: you'll drink it.

If you plan to get out of your car, come prepared: bring hiking shoes or sneakers, long pants, a hat, sunscreen, water (and snacks), a flashlight with extra batteries and a first-aid kit.

SIGHTS
Crater Rim Drive

This incredible 11-mile loop road skirts the rim of Kilauea Caldera. It passes the visitor center, a museum, a lava tube, steam vents, rifts, hiking trails and views of the smoking crater that'll knock your socks off. Don't miss it. Also, since it's relatively level, it's the park's best road for cyclists. This description starts at the visitor center and goes counterclockwise.

KILAUEA VISITOR CENTER

Looking good after a 2005 refurbishment, the tidy **visitors center** (Map p290) is an excellent place to start. On the hour (from 9am to 4pm), a small **theater** shows a free 20-minute film on Kilauea, with spectacular eruption footage. Attractive new exhibits, listening stations and life-size dioramas introduce the area's geology, flora, fauna and conservation issues. Out front, rangers give regular talks around the scale model of Hawaii.

VOLCANO ART CENTER

Next door to the visitors center, inside the 1877 Volcano House lodge, this **gallery shop** (Map p290; ☎ 967-7565, 866-967-7565; www.volcanoart center.org; ☼ 9am-5pm) sells high-quality island pottery, paintings, woodwork, sculpture, jewelry, Hawaiian quilts and more. Browsing the stunning collection is as satisfying as buying (well, almost). The resident nonprofit arts organization also hosts craft and cultural workshops, music concerts, plays and dance recitals, all listed in its free bimonthly *Volcano Gazette*.

SULPHUR BANKS

Nearby, wooden boardwalks weave through steaming Sulphur Banks, where numerous **holes and rocky vents** (Map p290) have been stained yellow, orange and neon green by the hundreds of tons of sulfuric gases that are released here daily. The smoldering, foul-smelling area looks like the aftermath of a forest fire. It's possible to walk here from the art center, cross the road, visit the Steaming Bluffs (below) and loop back on a portion of Crater Rim Trail.

STEAM VENTS

At the next pull-off, these nonsulfurous steam **vents** (Map p290) make a good drive-up photo op; they are the result of rainwater that percolates down and is heated into steam by hot rocks underground. Much more evocative is the short walk to the crater rim at **Steaming Bluff**, where the magnificent crater view feels infernolike as steam from the cliffs below pours over you. Cool early mornings or cloudy afternoons showcase the steam best.

JAGGAR MUSEUM

The exhibits at this small **museum** (Map p290; ☎ 985-6049; ☼ 8:30am-5pm) are a nice complement to the visitor center: they introduce the museum's founder, the famous volcanologist Dr Thomas A Jaggar; overview the Hawaiian pantheon; and provide a deeper understanding of volcanic geology. They also sport a bank of real-time seismographs actively tracking the park's daily quota of earthquakes.

And if none of that sounds interesting, at least stop for the view of Halema'uma'u Crater and, on a clear day, Mauna Loa 20 miles away. It's crazy delicious – guaranteed to bankrupt your camera battery.

Just before you reach the museum, the **Kilauea Overlook** (Map p290) also provides a pause-worthy panorama, and a few miles beyond is the **Southwest Rift** (Map p290). This rocky fissure is more massive and long than it looks; it slices from the caldera summit here all the way to the coast and under the ocean floor.

HALEMA'UMA'U OVERLOOK

Pele's cup steams quietly now, but for at least 100 years (from 1823, when missionary William Ellis first described it), Halema'uma'u was a boiling lake of lava that alternately overflowed its banks and receded.

Such a prodigious occurrence attracted travelers from all over the world. Looking in, some saw the fires of hell, others primeval creation, but none left unmoved. Mark Twain wrote that he witnessed

> Circles and serpents and streaks of lightning all twined and wreathed and tied together…I have seen Vesuvius since, but it was a mere toy, a child's volcano, a soup kettle, compared to this.

Then, in 1924, the show ended with a flourish. The crater floor subsided rapidly, touching off a series of explosive eruptions. Boulders and mud rained down for days. When it was over, the crater had doubled in size – to about 300ft deep and 3000ft wide. Lava activity ceased and the crust cooled.

Halema'uma'u has erupted 17 times since then; it's the most active area on the volcano's summit. The last eruption was on April 30, 1982. Geologists only realized something was brewing that morning as their seismographs went haywire. The park service quickly cleared hikers from the crater floor, and before noon a half-mile fissure broke open and began spewing out 1.3 million cu yd of lava. Today, the ground is again firm, but things don't feel settled just yet.

All of the Big Island is Pele's territory, but Halema'uma'u is her home. Ceremonial hula is performed in her honor on the crater rim, and throughout the year people leave offerings

---

SACRED GROUND

Most US national parks show evidence of ancient spiritual practices. This isn't surprising. National parks are just our modern, secular way of protecting and celebrating those transcendentally beautiful landscapes that tug at our collective soul.

Hawai'i Volcanoes National Park is no different. Ancient Hawaiians regarded the volcanoes as sacred – the home of the gods – and modern-day Hawaiians continue their spiritual practices.

But there *is* a way in which this park is unique. We tend to think of landscapes as essentially unchanging, but here our senses deceive us.

It's not just the new lava pouring daily into the ocean. Consider the dates sprinkled on the park's map: many significant features are a mere 30, 20 or 10 years old. Island residents and park rangers have watched new craters being born even as their homes and treasured landscapes have been buried under the flows. Outside the park, hike over the lava around Kapoho and Kalapana, and you're walking through ghost neighborhoods.

As a result, many residents feel a relationship to the volcanoes that is intensely personal. Many react with frustration when they hear, yet again, about the superstition that Pele will visit misfortune on those who disturb or take her lava. They feel this way of putting it trivializes the point. Instead, they would like visitors not to do these things out of simple respect – for the land, for the gods, for the people who believe in them, and for the people for whom these volcanoes are children they have suffered over and watched grow before their eyes.

---

of flowers, leaf-wrapped rocks and gin to appease the goddess. The overlook is the start of the Halema'uma'u Trail (Map p290). If you venture for a half mile past the overlook you can see the 1982 lava-flow site.

DEVASTATION TRAIL

Continuing east along the road's southern portion, you pass Keanakako'i Crater and the intersection with Chain of Craters Rd. At this intersection is also a parking area for the half-mile **Devastation Trail** (Map p290); parking is also available at the trail's other end, the Pu'u Pua'i Overlook further east.

The paved, wheelchair-accessible Devastation Trail passes through the fallout area of the 1959 eruption of Kilauea Iki Crater, which decimated this portion of the rain forest. The trail is not half as dramatic as its name, however, nor does it hold a candle to the more involved Kilauea Iki Trail. The overlook does provide a fantastic vantage point into the crater, and it's a quick walk to see Pu'u Pua'i, which formed during the eruption.

THURSTON LAVA TUBE

East of the intersection with Chain of Craters Rd you enter the rain forest of native tree ferns and ohia that covers Kilauea's windward slope.

Often crowded to the extreme, this **lava tube** (Map p290) is the endpoint of an enjoyable short walk through lovely, bird-filled ohia

forest (it's a good place to spot the red-bodied 'apapane, a native honeycreeper). The lava tube itself is enormous – big enough for your car, much less yourself – and a short initial section is lighted.

Lava tubes are formed when the outer crust of a river of lava starts to harden but the liquid lava beneath the surface continues to flow through. After the flow has drained out, the hard shell remains. Eastern Hawai'i is riddled with lava tubes, but this may be the grandest example. The tube extends for quite a ways beyond the lighted area; with a flashlight it's easy to keep going – and highly recommended.

KILAUEA IKI CRATER

When Kilauea Iki (Little Kilauea) burst open in a fiery inferno in November 1959, the whole crater floor turned into a bubbling lake of molten lava. Its fountains reached record heights of 1900ft, lighting the evening sky with a bright orange glow for miles around. At its peak, it gushed out two million tons of lava an hour.

The overlook provides an awesome view of the mile-wide **crater** (Map p290), and the hike (p296) across its hardened surface is the park's most popular. One good strategy for visiting this often crowded, but scenic portion of Crater Rim Dr is to park at the Kilauea Iki Overlook and walk the Crater Rim Trail to Thurston Lava Tube and back; it's about a mile all told and easy as pie.

Chain of Craters Road

This **road** (Map p289) gets shorter all the time (most recently in 2003). It currently winds about 18 miles down the southern slopes of Kilauea Volcano, ending abruptly at the latest East Rift Zone lava flow on the Puna Coast. It's paved but curvaceous; allow 45 minutes to an hour one way without stops.

For visual drama, the road is every bit the equal of Crater Rim Dr. As you descend toward the sea, panoramic coastal vistas open before you, allowing you to admire frozen fingers of lava as they raced toward the ocean. Then, along the coast, you get to stare at those same flows from below, looking up to where they crested the cliffs and plunged across the land. Early morning and late afternoon are the best times to photograph this unique landscape, when sunlight slants off the lava.

The road takes its name from a series of small, drive-up craters that lie along the first few miles. In addition, the road provides access to several trails, a campground, petroglyphs and the ever-evolving hike to the active flow itself.

At one time, Chain of Craters Rd connected to Hwys 130 and 137 in Puna. Lava flows closed the road in 1969, but, slightly rerouted, it reopened in 1979. Then Kilauea's active flows cut the link again in 1988, burying a 9-mile stretch of the road.

HILINA PALI ROAD

The first major intersection is this 9-mile, one-lane **road** (Map p289). Four miles along this road is the small **Kulanaokuaiki Campground** (p299). The road itself is not very scenic, and it is so winding that the drive can take over 40 minutes one way. However, it ends at a **lookout** of exceptional beauty. The grassy coastal plain below will beckon hikers to descend the steep Hilina Pali Trail here, but be prepared for a full-day adventure and a grueling uphill return. Others will be content to follow the trail for 100yd and sigh rapturously.

MAUNA ULU

In 1969, eruptions from Kilauea's east rift began building a new **lava shield** (Map p289), which eventually rose 400ft above its surroundings. It was named Mauna Ulu (Growing Mountain). By the time the flow stopped in 1974, it had covered 10,000 acres of parkland and added 200 acres of new land to the coast.

It also buried a 12-mile section of Chain of Craters Rd in lava up to 300ft deep. A half-mile portion of the old road survives, and you can follow it to the lava flow by taking the turnoff on the left, 3.5 miles down Chain of Craters Rd. Just beyond this is Mauna Ulu itself.

The easy **Pu'u Huluhulu Overlook Trail**, a 2-mile round-trip hike, begins at the parking area (which is also the trailhead for Napau Crater Trail, p297). The overlook trail ends at the top of a 150ft cinder cone, which is like a crow's nest on a clear day: the vista nets Mauna Loa, Mauna Kea, Pu'u 'O'o vent, Kilauea, the East Rift Zone and the ocean beyond. Just before you is the steamy teacup of Mauna Ulu crater. Nothing stops hikers from checking this out, but the park service would prefer if you didn't. The rim is fragile, for one, but also, rangers who watched it being born feel almost parentally protective.

KEALAKOMO

About halfway along the road is this covered **shelter** (Map p289; it's nicknamed 'pizza hut' for the shape of its roof) with picnic tables and a commanding view of the coastline. The trailhead for the Naulu Trail is across the road. After Kealakomo, the road descends long, sweeping switchbacks, some deeply cut through lava flows.

PU'U LOA PETROGLYPHS

The gentle Pu'u Loa Trail leads less than a mile to the largest concentration of ancient petroglyphs in the state. At **Pu'u Loa** (Map p289), early Hawaiians chiseled more than 20,000 drawings into *pahoehoe* lava. Given the setting, it's easy to see why this spot might have been considered sacred. There are abstract designs, animal and human figures, as well as thousands of dimpled depressions (or cupules) that were receptacles for umbilical cords. Placing a baby's umbilical stump inside a cupule and covering it with stones was meant to bestow health and longevity on the child.

The parking area and trailhead are signed between the 16- and 17-mile markers. At the site, stay on the boardwalk at all times – not all the petroglyphs are obvious, and you are likely to trample (and damage) some if you walk over the rocks.

HOLEI SEA ARCH

Near the end of the road, across the ranger station, is this **sea arch** (Map p289). This rugged section of the coast has sharply eroded lava cliffs, called Holei Pali, which are constantly being pounded by the crashing surf. The high rock arch, carved out of one of the cliffs, is impressive, although the wave action of Namakaokahai, goddess of the sea and sister to Pele, has numbered its days.

THE END OF THE ROAD

Chain of Craters Rd ends abruptly wherever hardened lava covers the road. This is the starting point for hikes to see the active flow (see p297). At road's end you'll find rangers (till 9pm daily), an information board with a four-minute safety video, portable toilets and a **snack shack** (☺ noon-6pm, in theory) selling bottled water, candy and batteries.

Mauna Loa Road

If you really want to escape the crowds, consider exploring 11.5-mile Mauna Loa Rd, which begins off Hwy 11 outside the park entrance. The first turnoff leads to some neglected **lava tree molds** (Map p290), deep tube-like apertures formed when a lava flow engulfed the rain forest. Then, after a mile, there is a picnic area (with toilets) and just beyond this is **Kipukapuaulu** (Map p290), which is informally known as 'Bird Park.' This unique 100-acre sanctuary (or 'Special Ecological Area') protects an island of ancient forest containing rare endemic plants, insects and birds. About 400 years ago a major Mauna Loa lava flow buried the land here, but Pele split the flow and saved this small island of vegetation; in Hawaiian these are known as a *kipuka*.

An easy 1-mile loop trail through the forest makes for a very meditative walk, particularly in the morning surrounded by birdsong. You'll see lots of koa trees and pass a lava tube where a unique species of big-eyed spider was discovered in 1973.

About 1.5 miles past Bird Park, Mauna Loa Rd passes another *kipuka* (Kipuka Ki), and 2 miles later the road narrows to one lane. Go slow; it's winding, with lots of blind curves. Along the way are several places to pull over to admire the views and trails to explore – it's a wonderful diversion. By the end of the road, you've ascended to 6662ft; this is the start of the extremely difficult **Mauna Loa Trail** (p298) to the summit. Wander down the trail a few dozen yards for expansive southern vistas that include the smoking Kilauea Caldera far below.

ACTIVITIES

Hiking is the park's main activity, and there are trails to suit all abilities and most desires. Ranger-led walks occur daily and typically don't last longer than an hour; visit the visitor center (p291) for a list (the Wednesday trip to Pua Po'o lava tube is highly recommended). Or join a guided hike with outdoor-adventure companies Hawaii Forest & Trail or Hawaiian Walkways (p197).

Otherwise, cyclists can enjoy circumnavigating Kilauea Caldera along Crater Rim Dr, and mountain-bikes are allowed on a few firebreak roads, such as Escape Rd past Thurston Lava Tube. Helicopter tours are also popular (see p201).

Hiking

If variety is the spice of life, park trails make a tasty feast. You can hike to secluded beaches or the snowcapped 13,677ft summit of Mauna Loa; through lush native rain forests or barren lava wastelands; across the hardened top of the world's most active volcano or to the glowing source of its current eruption.

There are excellent trails of every length and level of difficulty. Plus, many trails intersect, allowing the flexibility to design your own routes. Most of the park is accessible to day hikers, while most backcountry destinations require only a single overnight. However, if you wish, you can wander backcountry trails for days.

BEST HIKES

■ **Mauna Loa's Observatory Trail** (p258) Visit the majestic summit of the world's largest volcano

■ **Waipi'o Valley Trail** (p263) This valley is a dream come to life

■ **Kilauea Iki Trail** (p296) Encapsulates the wonder of Hawai'i Volcanoes National Park

■ **Napau Crater Trail** (p297) Rain forests, immense craters and the active Pu'u 'O'o vent

■ **Hike to hot lava** (p297) Easy or hard, hiking to hot lava leaves you speechless

■ **Pololu Valley Trail** (p246) Reach a black-sand beach hugged by emerald cliffs

---

If you're interested in overnight back-packing, note that backcountry camping is limited and entirely first come, first served; backcountry trails contain hiking shelters, simple cabins or primitive campgrounds. All have pit toilets. Bring a stove, as open fires are prohibited. Almost no freshwater is available anywhere; some campgrounds have catchment water (always treat before drinking), and the visitor center posts a daily log of water levels. Overnight hikers must get a free permit (and register) at the visitor center no sooner than the day before their hike; each site has a three-day limit.

Below are some of the most popular and/or recommended day hikes, along with a few backcountry possibilities and variations. Some of the park's shortest hikes are mentioned above in the descriptions of the park's main roads.

KILAUEA IKI TRAIL

If you only have time for one hike, choose this one. It's the park's most popular trail (Map p290) and for good reason – it captures all the summit's drama and beauty in one manageable, moderate, 4-mile, two-hour package.

The trail is a loop, with multiple start points and trail junctions (making the hike easy to expand). A good strategy is to park at Kilauea Iki Overlook (to avoid the Thurston Lava Tube madness) and proceed counterclockwise along the crater rim. Passing through an ohia forest, you can admire the mile-long lava bathtub below before descending into it.

After almost a mile you descend onto Waldron Ledge; multiple trail junctions allow for explorations of the main caldera rim, or extend your loop by connecting with the Halema'uma'u and Byron Ledge Trails for an all-day adventure. Either way, once you reach the west end of the crater (oh, the view!), descend 400ft to the crater floor.

Across the *pahoehoe* crust the trail can get indistinct, but it's not hard to follow; *ahu* (or cairns) aid navigation. When you pass the vent beneath the Pu'u Pua'i cinder cone, respect park caution signs. After all, molten magma is a mere 230ft below the surface here (less than a football field). Once you reach the crater's east end, your only choice is to ascend 400ft up the switchbacks. On the rim again, explore Thurston Lava Tube on your return to the Kilauea Iki Overlook.

HALEMA'UMA'U TRAIL

If you have more time (about four to five hours), this 7-mile loop (Map p290) is extremely rewarding. It starts near Volcano House (p299), quickly passes through ohia forest, and spends the bulk of its time traversing the ragged blankets of lava that cover Kilauea Caldera. The trail is completely exposed; depending on the weather, it'll be hot and dry or chillingly damp. Bring lots of water.

You may think that lava is lava, but this hike will change your mind. You pass numerous flows – some old (1885) and some new (1982) – and the diversity is astonishing, as is the overall effect of the otherworldly landscape. Nearly 3 miles from the start, the trail ends at the steaming Halema'uma'u Overlook (see p292). Ask Pele's blessing, and return on the Byron Ledge Trail, which allows for easy peeks of or a side trip into Kilauea Iki Crater.

CRATER RIM TRAIL

This 11.5-mile trek (Map p290) circles the summit, running roughly parallel to Crater Rim Dr (p291) – if you do the whole thing, plan for five or six hours, but many people hike only portions. Overall, the trail is mostly level. On the north side, the trail is busiest as it skirts the view-licious crater rim, while on the south side, it runs outside the paved road (and away from caldera views) and you likely will see no one. Lots of side trips are possible, and you pass through a wide variety of terrains; one of the most beautiful sections is the forested southeast portion. Note that it's acceptable – for hikers doing one-way hikes, either here or elsewhere – to hitch a ride to/from a trailhead, but it's best to park at the end and hitch to the start, so you hike *to* your car.

MAUNA IKI TRAIL

For solitude in a mesmerizing lava landscape, take this trail (Map p289) into the Ka'u Desert, but start from the north, along what is sometimes labeled the Footprints Trail. From this approach, the trailhead access is easier, your initial commitment is low and variations allow great extensions of your route. This hike can be an easy 3.5-mile sampling, a moderate 7- to 8-mile afternoon or an 18-mile overnight backpack.

On Hwy 11 between the 37- and 38-mile markers, look for the 'Ka'u Desert Trailhead' parking area. Start early, as midday can be brutally hot and dry. Initially, the trail is very clear, level and partly paved, threading through sand-covered *pahoehoe* flows. In 20 minutes you reach a structure protecting ancient footprints preserved in hardened ash. More footprints exist in the surrounding rock; look carefully so as not to walk on them.

Past the hut, the trail is marked by easy-to-follow cairns. As you gradually ascend, views expand, with gentle giant Mauna Loa behind and the immense Ka'u Desert in front. After 1.8 miles you crest the rise at **Mauna Iki** (and the trail junction) and stand likely alone in the middle of a vast lava field.

From here, backpackers will turn right, following the Ka'u Desert Trail over 7 miles to Pepeiao Cabin. Day hikers can turn left, following the Ka'u Desert Trail for 1232yd to the junction with the official Mauna Iki Trail, which runs another 6.3 miles to Hilina Pali Rd (the other starting point). Hiking about halfway along the Mauna Iki Trail, to Pu'u Koa'e, makes a good endpoint.

The lava terrain is noticeably more intense and wild as you continue, with vivid colorful rents, collapsed tubes and splatter cones; in cracks you can find piles of golden Pele's hair. The discoveries are almost endless.

NAPAU CRATER TRAIL

The Napau Crater Trail (Map p289) is perhaps the most varied and satisfying all-day hike in the park. It passes lava fields, immense craters and thick forest, and it ends with spectacular views of Pu'u 'O'o, the source of Kilauea's current eruption. Depending on route and pace, it's a 14- to 18-mile adventure that can take seven to 11 hours (round-trip). Backcountry camping is available if you prefer to do this as an overnight. Note that this is the only day hike that requires a permit; all hikers should register at the visitor center before heading out.

Rather than taking the Napau Crater Trail from its trailhead (the same one as for Pu'u Huluhulu Overlook Trail, p294), you'll save about 4 miles and several hours round-trip

HAWAI'I (THE BIG ISLAND)

HOT LAVA

You didn't come all this way not to see an active volcano do its stuff. After a day or two in the park, after all the talk of dangers and goddesses and geologic marvels, you just want to see some good-ol' red-hot molten lava. And if you're lucky, you will.

Since 1983 Kilauea has been continuously erupting, with only short pauses. The site of the eruption shifts, and there's no predicting where the lava will be (or even if it will be) flowing when you're here. At times lava crosses Chain of Craters Rd, and at others getting to the active flow requires a several-mile, several-hour hike from road's end (for facilities here, see p295). Whatever the hike, the best strategy is to come during daylight and stay through sunset, when the surreal orange lava glow illuminates the night and can shimmer on the distant hillside.

The National Park Service facilitates lava visits (for flow updates, call ☎ 985-6000 or visit http://hvo.wr.usgs.gov/kilauea/update/main.html), and you can join a private guided tour (p197). Using temporary reflectors and blinking lights, rangers mark routes to safe viewing areas as well as routes that lead close to the flow. Their paramount concern is safety: talk to rangers before hiking, and come prepared. During the day the black lava is hot and dry; after dark, the insane, Mordor-like terrain (an extraordinary experience in itself) becomes doubly treacherous. It may rain, or the toxic steam plume could blow over you. Wear boots, pants and a hat, and bring rain gear, a walking stick, gloves, two flashlights, a first-aid kit, lots of water and food. Oh, and your camera (with extra batteries).

Like moths to a flame, some people try to get as close to the flow as possible. Dangerous? You bet. When molten 2100°F rock meets the sea it can explode, creating showers of scalding water and lava chunks. New ledges or benches of lava can collapse without warning. In 1993 a bench collapse killed one person and seriously injured a dozen others; in 2000, two people were found scalded to death. In the excitement of the moment, don't forget to respect Kilauea's unpredictable power.

Even for people who live here, seeing the lava never gets old. Witnessing such an elemental act of creation inspires profound awe, and watchers sometimes stand in silent reverence through the night. It's often promised, and here it's true: this is a once-in-a-lifetime experience.

(and lose nothing in scenery) if you begin on the Naulu Trail, which leaves from Kealakomo (p294) on Chain of Craters Rd. This route is described here.

For the first hour, you hike mostly sinuous, leathery *pahoehoe* lava, following sometimes difficult-to-see cairns. Then you enter some trees and (surprise!) stumble across paved portions of the old Chain of Craters Rd, which was buried in a 1972 eruption. Follow the pavement (complete with dashed white line) past the junction with the unmaintained **Kalapana Trail**.

After a quick sprint across some *'a'a* (which is exactly what you'll say if you trip), you enter moody fern-and-ohia forest; in less than a mile is the Napau Crater Trail junction – turn right.

Keep an eye on your left for openings to view the mile-wide Makaopuhi Crater. About 30 minutes later, low lava rock walls indicate the site of an old *'pulu* factory.' *Pulu* is the golden, silky 'hair' found at the base of *hapu'u* (tree fern) fiddlehead stems. Ancient Hawaiians used *pulu* to embalm their dead, and in the late 1800s *pulu* was exported as mattress and pillow stuffing, until it was discovered that it eventually turned to dust.

You may think you're near the airport – considering the helicopter traffic – but in fact you're 10 minutes from the primitive **campground** (with pit toilet). Definitely take the spur to the Napau Crater **overlook** (to see steaming Pu'u 'O'o), then negotiate the confused tangle of paths near the campsites and pick up the trail to **Napau Crater** itself. The surreal terrain here, past hummocks, vents and tree molds, is wondrous.

Carefully descend the ragged gravelly switchbacks and continue across and out of Napau Crater; the trail then drags you another 2 miles or so across a shattered, shocking landscape beneath gaping **Pu'u 'O'o**. Only go as close as the sign and common sense indicate. On the side of the vent the lava crust is thin, gassy and very dangerous; tremendous cinder cone collapses can occur without warning.

KAHAUALE'A TRAIL

You may hear or read a lot of conflicting advice about this trail (Map p289), which is the shortest route to the Pu'u 'O'o vent. It started as an 'unofficial,' unmaintained pig-hunter's trail, and because it's outside national-park boundaries (but reaches the vent) park rangers once discouraged using it. Today, however, the county 'officially' recognizes the trail with a spiffy trailhead sign, and HAVO rangers won't tell you not to go. But the question remains: should you?

The real problems with this 4.2-mile trail concern its condition and the safety of your car. Despite the reassuring route map on the trailhead sign, the trail is poorly maintained: there are numerous confusing spurs, and when it's wet, it's a muddy slog. When it's dry, some people enjoy and recommend it; the forest is indeed beautiful and certainly uncrowded. Once the forest ends, cairns and reflectors help mark the route another mile closer to the vent. Allow six to seven hours round-trip.

And your car? To reach the trail from HAVO, take Hwy 11 toward Hilo and turn south on S Glenwood Rd (just past the 20-mile marker) for 3 miles; continue straight for another mile on a deeply rutted dirt road (called Captains Dr) until you dead end at the trail sign. Park past the abandoned cars and among the fresh piles of broken glass.

Best advice? Come with a local in their car, or forget it.

MAUNA LOA TRAIL

Reaching the summit of 13,677-ft Mauna Loa is a sublime experience, one that most everyday hikers would rank as one of the best treks of their lives. However, if you're an everyday hiker, you don't want to get there by way of the 19-mile Mauna Loa Trail (Map p289) that leaves from the end of the park's Mauna Loa Rd. Everyday hikers should instead tackle the 6.5-mile Observatory Trail (p258), which is accessed from Saddle Rd and leaves from the Mauna Loa Weather Observatory.

If you fall within that smaller class of extremely fit, elite hikers – for whom the easy way is no way at all – this is your trail. It ascends over 6000ft, and, while it is not technically challenging, due to the high elevation and frequent subarctic conditions it takes at least three and usually four days. Two simple cabins with mattress-covered bunks, pit toilets and catchment water (which must be treated) are located on the route; the first cabin sleeps eight, the second 12, and they are available on a first-come, first-served basis. Get a free backcountry permit, advice and water-level updates at the Kilauea Visitor Center (p291) the day before your hike.

Typically, the first day is spent hiking 7.5 miles to Pu'u 'Ula'ula at 10,035ft, where **Red Hill Cabin** is located. The next day is spent hiking 9.5 miles to Moku'aweoweo Caldera, and another 2 miles to **Mauna Loa Cabin** at 13,250ft; from here you can admire the summit directly across the caldera. On the third day, you hike nearly 5 miles around the caldera to reach the summit and return for a second night at Mauna Loa Cabin. On the fourth day, you descend.

Now, the fun part: altitude sickness is common, even expected; going slowly aids acclimatization. Nighttime temperatures are below freezing. Storms may bring snow, blizzards, whiteouts, rain and fog, all of which can obscure the *ahu* (cairns) that mark the trail, making it impossible to follow. And don't forget that Mauna Loa is still active. It could erupt.

PUNA COAST TRAILS
Three main trails (Map p289) take hikers down to the Puna Coast: the **Hilina Pali**, **Keauhou** and **Puna Coast Trails**. These trails start from vastly different places, but they each eventually intersect (with each other and even more trails), and they lead to four separate backcountry campgrounds or shelters. Because of steep elevation changes and distance, these trails are most commonly done as overnight backpacks. But this is also because, once you see the grassy, wind-swept coast, you won't want to leave. Talk to rangers for advice on the best route based on your time and to check water-catchment levels at the shelters.

For day hikers, the shortest and most interesting trail is Hilina Pali, which leaves from the end of **Hilina Pali Rd** (p294). But don't make this the first hike of your trip: it descends 2200ft in 3.5 miles, including an initial cliffside tumble of about 1300ft in under 2 miles. Once at the bottom of the cliff, veer right on **Ka'aha Trail** for the shortest route to the coast.

FESTIVALS & EVENTS
Regular park programs include **After Dark in the Park** (Kilauea Visitor Center Auditorium; admission free; ✷ 7pm Tue), a series of free talks by experts on cultural, historic and geological matters, held two or three times monthly.

The **Volcano Art Center** (☎ 967-8222; www.volcanoartcenter.org) hosts a full slate of events year-round. The following annual events are free with park admission.

Na Mea Hawaii Hula Kahiko Series Four times throughout the year, free hula *kahiko* performances are held outdoors overlooking Kilauea Caldera.
Annual Spring Dance Concert Last weekend in March. An event hosted by the Volcano Art Center, presenting works by Big Island choreographers and dancers.
Kilauea Volcano Wilderness Runs Late July. This popular marathon is actually four separate events: a 10-mile run around the rim of Kilauea Caldera; both a 5-mile run and a 5-mile walk that go down into Kilauea Iki Crater; and a 26-mile marathon through the Ka'u Desert. Call ☎ 985-8725 for details.
Aloha Festivals Ka Ho'ola'a o Na Ali'i (http://aloha festivals.com) Don't miss this brilliant Native Hawaiian royal court procession on the Halema'uma'u Crater rim, with ceremonial chanting and hula, during the August/September Aloha Festival.

SLEEPING
Accommodation options within the national park are limited; nearby Volcano village (p300) has more choices.

Camping
The park has two first-come, first-served drive-up campgrounds that are the right price – free! Facilities are well kept; expect nights to be crisp and cool. The only time the sites get full are busy holiday weekends.

Kulanaokuaiki Campground (Map p289; Hilina Pali Rd) About 4 miles along Hilina Pali Rd, this secluded, quiet, eight-site campground has pit toilets and picnic tables, but no water.

Namakanipaio Campground & Cabins (Map p290; ☎ cabin bookings 967-7321; cabins d $50, extra person $8) Between the 32- and 33-mile markers off Hwy 11, 3 miles west of the visitor center, this campground's two pleasant grassy meadows fill with as many tents as they'll hold. It lacks privacy, but nice facilities include rest rooms, water, fireplaces, picnic tables and a covered pavilion. Adjacent to the campground, but with access to a separate bathroom (with showers), are 10 windowless, plywood A-frame cabins with a double bed, two single bunks, grills, picnic tables and electric lights, but no power outlets or heating. Volcano House takes bookings and provides linens, but bring a sleeping bag – it gets cold!

Top End
Volcano House (Map p290; ☎ 967-7321; www.volcano househotel.com; 1 Crater Rim Dr; r $95-225) Perched on the rim of Kilauea Caldera, Volcano House has a venerable history, but its accommodations

are simply average, well-kept hotel rooms with louvered wooden blinds and pink spreads. Splash out for a deluxe view room, though, and there's no disappointment – these take in the whole steaming thing (even if the view disappears after dark). Avoid the cheapest Ohia Wing rooms; they're below ground and poorly ventilated. Reserve far in advance.

EATING & DRINKING

The restaurant at **Volcano House** (Map p290; ☎ 967-7321; www.volcanohousehotel.com; 1 Crater Rim Dr; buffet breakfast & lunch $12-15, dinner mains $15-27; ☺ 7-10:30am, 11am-2pm, 5:30-9pm) serves a cafeteria-quality buffet for breakfast and lunch. Dinner plates match what you'd expect at your uncle's second wedding – though the dining-room view is a knockout. There's a snack bar during the day if you want something small, and at night the decidedly unatmospheric **Uncle George's Lounge** (☺ 4:30-9pm) has a full bar.

GETTING THERE & AROUND

The national park is 29 miles (about 40 minutes) from Hilo and 97 miles (2½ hours) from Kailua-Kona. From either direction, you'll drive on Hwy 11. Volcano village is a mile east of the park entrance.

AROUND HAWAI'I VOLCANOES NATIONAL PARK
Volcano
pop 2230

The village of Volcano is a mystical place of giant ferns, giant *sugi* (Japanese evergreen) and ohia trees full of puffy red blossoms. Many artists and park employees enjoy the seclusion here.

INFORMATION

The teensy **Volcano Visitor Center** (Map p290; ☎ 985-7422; Old Volcano Rd; ☺ 8am-5pm) is usually staffed; when it is, staff members will help book you a room. The visitor center and a laundromat are located next to Thai Thai Restaurant. Down the street is the **post office** (Map p290; ☎ 967-7611; 19-4030 Old Volcano Rd; ☺ 7:30am-3:30pm Mon-Fri, 11am-noon Sat).

SIGHTS & ACTIVITIES

The friendly, attractive **Volcano Winery** (Map p290; ☎ 967-7772; www.volcanowinery.com; 35 Pi'i Mauna Dr; ☺ 10am-5:30pm) offers free tastings of its six vintages. Two mix in jaboticaba berries and another uses guava for sweet, unusual variations.

A rich honey wine is almost like mead. Who knew Hawai'i had a wine country?

Come early to glass-blowing studio **2400° Fahrenheit** (Map p289; ☎ 985-8667; www.2400F.com; Old Volcano Rd; ☺ 10am-4pm Thu-Mon) and watch artists Michael and Misato Mortara create their mind-boggling glass bowls and vases. A tiny gallery displays finished pieces. It's outside of Volcano on Hwy 11, near the 24-mile marker.

You see artist Ira Ono's voluptuous masks everywhere. His gallery, **Volcano Garden Arts** (Map p290; ☎ 967-7261; www.volcanogardenarts.com; 19-3834 Old Volcano Rd; ☺ 10am-4pm Tue-Sun) – packed with other artists and including a small 'café' – is central to the recent upswing in the Volcano art scene.

The 18-hole **Volcano Golf & Country Club** (Map p290; ☎ 967-7331; Pi'i Mauna Dr; green fees before/after noon $66/50) has majestic links sitting beneath Mauna Kea and Mauna Loa.

Sleeping

Volcano has a preponderance of nice B&Bs and vacation homes. **Volcano Gallery** (☎ 800-908-9764; www.volcanogallery.com) is a locally managed rental agency listing over two dozen good properties, most in the $145 to $165 range.

BUDGET

Holo Holo In (Map p290; ☎ 967-7950; www.enable.org /holoholo; 19-4036 Kalani Honua Rd; dm $18, r $45-60; ☐) Don't be put off by this small hostel's exterior. Inside, the two six-bed dorms and four private rooms are meticulously cared for, sizable and pleasant. The kitchen is nicely equipped, and there's a laundry. It's a quiet, homey place tended by a gracious host.

MIDRANGE & TOP END

My Island B&B (Map p290; ☎ 967-7216; www.myisland innhawaii.com; 19-3896 Old Volcano Rd; s $65-95, d $80-115, house d $155) Set among acres of gorgeous, land-scaped rain-forest gardens, this historic 1886 house is now a European-style B&B. The friendly, knowledgable hosts serve a lovely breakfast and prepare you well for your park visits – Gordon is a colorful raconteur who has written several books on Hawaii. The three main-house rooms also have character but are small (two share a tiny bathroom with a redwood-and-copper tub!); two studio rooms in a separate building have TV and kitchenette; and, nearby, the three-bedroom, two-bathroom, fully-equipped Deck House makes an ideal roost for families.

Kilauea Lodge (Map p290; ☎ 967-7366; www.kilauea lodge.com; Old Volcano Rd; incl breakfast r $150-165, cottages d $165-190) At Volcano's most attractive property, rooms are a vision of upscale country romance, with working fireplaces, cozy quilts, rockers and bathroom skylights. Only cottages have TV and phone, but all guests can soak in the gorgeous hot tub set in paradisical gardens. Kilauea Lodge also features a fine restaurant (see right).

Volcano Rainforest Retreat (Map p289; ☎ 985-8696, 800-550-8696; www.volcanoretreat.com; 11-3832 12th St; cottages d incl breakfast $140-260) With its spiritual focus and unusual, gorgeous cedar structures, this is not your typical B&B. Artfully positioned among trees, four plush private cottages maximize your experience of nature, some with outdoor showers and Japanese-style soaking tubs. Adding to the northern California vibe, massage, Reiki healing and guided spiritual retreats are also offered. Reserve far in advance.

Chalet Kilauea Collection (☎ 967-7786, 800-937-7786; www.volcano-hawaii.com; Wright Rd) With three B&Bs (and five vacation homes; call for details), Chalet Kilauea has something for everyone. The Inn at Volcano ($160 to $400) is the flagship property: it's the place for honeymooners and couples seeking indulgent pampering and opulent, luxurious furnishings; go all out with the jaw-dropping Forest Suite. Taking it down two notches, Lokahi Lodge ($110 to $170) provides nice but simpler country charms, and Volcano B&B ($55 to $80) is an acceptable no-frills option. All come with a breakfast that is calibrated to the rate.

Eating

Volcano hosts a fantastic **farmers market** (Map p290; Cooper Community Center, Wright Rd; ☑ 6:30-9:30am Sun), with good produce, crafts and even a used-book sale; it's a real community event.

Lava Rock Café (Map p290; ☎ 967-8526; Old Volcano Rd; mains $7-10; ☑ 7:30am-5pm Mon, to 9pm Tue-Sat, to 4pm Sun) Located behind Kilauea General Store, this basic diner is nothing special, but it's the favored spot for breakfast or a burger. Kids' menu available.

Volcano Golf & Country Club (Map p290; ☎ 967-7331; Pi'i Mauna Dr; meals $5-9; ☑ restaurant 8am-3pm) Locals come here for affordable lunch specials ($6), fresh mahimahi burgers and the low-key atmosphere.

Thai Thai Restaurant (Map p290; ☎ 967-7969; 19-4084 Old Volcano Rd; mains $12-17; ☑ 4-9pm) The owners get their spices directly from Thailand, and they make perhaps the island's best Thai cuisine. Mahimahi curry is the specialty, the pad thai is excellent, and portions are generous. Considering the heat of 'medium hot,' we're guessing 'Thai hot' would impress Pele.

Kiawe Kitchen (Map p290; ☎ 967-7711; cnr Old Volcano & Haunani Rds; pizzas $16, mains $20-24; ☑ noon-2:30pm & 5:30-9pm) This pleasant café with outdoor seating offers dependable versions of shrimp scampi, mahimahi and rib-eye steak, plus thin-crust pizza and Big Island microbrews. It's a local favorite that comes with a friendly atmosphere.

Kilauea Lodge (Map p290; ☎ 967-7366; www.kilauea lodge.com; Old Volcano Rd; mains $25-35; ☑ 5:30-9pm) Kilauea Lodge strikes the right upscale rustic notes with its vaulted beam ceiling, wooden floors and historic stone fireplace. The kitchen prepares gourmet versions of mostly German comfort food: *hasenpfeffer* (braised rabbit), venison, antelope filet, sausage and sauerkraut, and Parker Ranch steaks. Sauces are rich, and plates aren't insulted with a token slice of papaya. If you're in the mood for the menu, Kilauea Lodge is as good as you'll find on the Big Island. Reservations advised.

For groceries, pickings are slim at both **Volcano Store** (Map p290; ☎ 967-7210; cnr Old Volcano & Haunani Rds; ☑ 5am-7pm) and **Kilauea General Store** (Map p290; ☎ 967-7555; Old Volcano Rd; ☑ 7am-7:30pm Mon-Sat, to 7pm Sun). The best trail lunch will be leftovers from the night before (Hint: think Thai).

KA'U

Landscapes in the Ka'u district vary from lush foothills to vast expanses of hardened lava, bucolic pastureland to groves of macadamia nuts and island-favorite Ka'u oranges. Few live in this rural area, with only 5000 people spread over three towns.

For most travelers the attraction to Ka'u lies mainly in the chance to set foot on the southernmost point in the USA. But those who seek experiences off the beaten path will find reward in the remote, secluded beaches and in the legacy of Ka'u's sugar-plantation past. The more spiritually inclined will welcome the opportunity to meditate alongside a Tibetan lama.

HAWAI'I (THE BIG ISLAND)

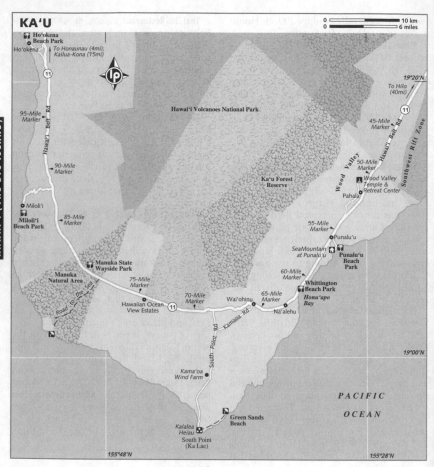

The mana found in the raw and windy southernmost tip of the island is powerful. It is considered to be the landing point of the first Polynesians to set foot on Hawaiian soil, which is remembered in the local saying, *Aha' la i ka pupuhi* ('travel with the speed of the wind').

PAHALA

pop 1400

Pahala doesn't have a thing going on, but it is *the* spot in these parts for a fresh *malasada*, and it makes for a pretty pleasant stop. Ka'u Agribusiness once had 15,000 acres of cane planted for 15 miles in either direction, but the mill's closure in 1996 turned Pahala into a former sugar town. The company has since

replaced the cane with groves of macadamia-nut trees. For a look at some of the charming early-20th-century **plantation homes**, cruise Maile St and Pikake St.

Pahala's only shopping center holds the town's café, a market, a post office and a bank with an ATM. Nearby are a gas station and the **Ka'u Hospital** (☎ 928-8331; www.kau.hhsc.org; Kamani St).

Sleeping & Eating

Hale o Luna (☎ 928-8144; www.pahala.info; r $89, house $149; 🖵) One look at this centrally located, beautifully restored 1936 plantation house and you'll begin inventing reasons to extend your stay. Polished antiques and richly colored carpets stand on gleaming hardwood floors.

Original artwork and shelves of books and games give an intellectual air. Each of the two bedrooms has luxurious bedding and a private bathroom. The retro kitchen is completely stocked and big enough to have a party in. Every detail is in the best of taste, and, wow, what a bargain.

Pahala Town Cafe (☎ 928-8200; Pikake St; meals $4-8; ⏰ 7am-7:30pm) Being the only eatery, this sterile café feels the need to be it all. Soups, salads and wraps are all on the extensive menu, but it's best to stick to what it does best: plate lunches, burgers and fried things. The gigantic *malasada* with optional fillings are the only breakfast item.

Shopping

Pahala Plantation Store (☎ 928-9811; 96-3207 Maile St; ⏰ 8am-6pm Mon, Tue, Thu & Fri, to noon Wed) Housed in a historic bank building, this little shop sells local products, books and interesting gifts. Inquire here about renting restored plantation cottages.

Getting There & Away

Pahala is on the *mauka* side of Hwy 11. Its northern entrance is up Kamani St, south of the 51-mile marker. Southern access is via

Maile St (aka Pine Tree Lane), north of the 53-mile marker. From Maile St, turn left up Pikake St to reach the shopping center.

PUNALU'U
pop 880

Once a major Hawaiian settlement, today Punalu'u is home to a popular beach park and SeaMountain, Ka'u's only condo complex. At the time of research, locals were distraught over SeaMountain's threat to develop untouched areas surrounding the beach park, and the area's future was unclear.

Punalu'u Beach Park provides easy access to a pretty little bay with a black-sand beach famous for basking green sea turtles. The turtles are both endangered and very sensitive to human disturbance – don't approach them. Punalu'u is one of the few beaches where rare hawksbill turtles lay their eggs, so take caution not to disturb their sandy nests.

The most popular part of the beach is the northern pocket, lined with coconut palms and backed by a duck pond. The ruins of the Pahala Sugar Company's old warehouse and pier lie slightly to the north. The Kane'ele'ele Heiau ruins sit on a small rise. Most days, the waters are not ideal for swimming, and it's

HAWAI'I (THE BIG ISLAND)

DETOUR: WOOD VALLEY

If you're into temples, the Tibetan Buddhist **Wood Valley Temple & Retreat Center** (Nechung Dorje Drayang Ling; Map p302; ☎ 928-8539; www.nechung.org; admission $5; ⏰ 10am-5pm) outside of Pahala is worthy of a detour. The small temple is decoratively painted in colorful detail, as Tibetan Buddhists are prone to do, and is striking against the backdrop of the center's lush, 25-acre property. Tibetan Buddhists are also prone to ornate altars, and Wood Valley's falls right into line. As if all of this weren't exotic enough, peacocks roam freely through the grounds. The relaxing property of the valley's silence is enhanced by the constant sounds of birds and humming insects.

The temple was built around 1902 by Japanese sugarcane laborers who lived throughout the valley. Later abandoned, it was rediscovered in the early 1970s by an anthropologist. In 1973 a Tibetan lama, Nechung Rinpoche, established it in the Tibetan Buddhist tradition. In 1980 the Dalai Lama visited to dedicate the temple, and he returned for a visit in 1994. Many well-respected Tibetan lamas conduct programs here every year.

Visitors are welcome to attend daily chanting and meditation sittings at 8am and 6pm (it might be just you and the Rinpoche!) or visit the temple and gift shop. In addition to a regular schedule of Buddhist teachings, Wood Valley also hosts nondenominational retreats.

For a personal retreat, plan a short stay in the center's cheerfully painted **guesthouse** (dm/s/d with shared bathroom $40/50/75). Guests have the run of the building, which has a full kitchen and a screened-in dining area and lanai with lush views, as well as several reading nooks. None of the rooms is spacious, and the four-bed dorm rooms are not for the claustrophobic. Private rooms are colorfully or thematically decorated and charming in a low-budget way. Things can feel quite damp following prolonged rains, yet mustiness is magically kept to a minimum. A two-night minimum stay is required, though occasionally a one-night stay is accepted for an additional $20.

To get here, follow Pikake St about 4 miles inland from Pahala's shopping center (see opposite).

HAWAI'I (THE BIG ISLAND)

fun to watch *malihini* (newcomers) braving the icy, spring-fed waters. Fierce rip currents pull seaward near the pier.

The park has several picnic pavilions, rest rooms, showers and drinking water, and is spread over a grassy rise just above the crashing waves. Camping is allowed anywhere throughout the grassy picnic area with a county permit (p460). The area is very exposed, and there's one low area should the winds really pick up. Benign local teens often congregate in the parking lot at night and blare their stereos. Come daybreak, the park quickly becomes overrun with picnickers and even tour buses.

SeaMountain's **golf course** (☎ 928-6222; green fees $46-49; ☽ 7am-6pm) has ocean views from each of its 18 holes.

There are two turnoffs for Punalu'u between the 56- and 57-mile markers. Both are well signposted for either SeaMountain or Punalu'u Park.

WHITTINGTON BEACH PARK

This small beach park has tide pools to explore and the cement pilings of an old pier, which was used for shipping sugar and hemp until the 1930s. The ocean is usually too rough for swimming and, despite the name, there is no beach. Green sea turtles can sometimes be seen offshore. Apparently they've been frequenting these waters for some time, as the bay's name is Honu'apo (Caught Turtle).

Bathrooms with no potable water and sheltered picnic pavilions without good views are grouped together near a pretty, pondlike inlet and a group of tall coconut palms. Camping on the grass throughout the park is allowed with a county permit (p460). The park is far enough from the highway to be quiet and feel a little isolated. Unless you prefer solitude, camping at Punalu'u might feel safer.

The turnoff for the park is between the 60- and 61-mile markers. Look for a stop sign and a brown park sign on the *makai* side of Hwy 11, just below the rise to the Honu'apo Bay lookout.

NA'ALEHU

pop 920

A town of just a few blocks, Na'alehu milks its title of 'The Southernmost Town in the USA' for all it's worth. Towering banyan trees, a colorful old theater building and early-20th-century homes set back from the road lend Na'alehu a potent historical feeling and make for pretty scenery.

This, Ka'u's commercial and religious center, has a grocery store, a gas station, an ATM, a post office, a police station and no fewer than six churches. Leave your shoes at the door at **Na'alehu Main Street** (cnr Hwy 11 & Ka'alaiki Rd; per hr $3; ☽ 1-5pm Mon-Fri), a community internet café run by volunteers.

Eating

Punalu'u Bakeshop (☎ 929-7343; cnr Hwy 11 & Ka'alaiki Rd; deli items $4-7; ☽ 9am-5pm) This, the island's best-known sweet bread bakery, is Na'alehu's major tourist attraction, and it's a mandatory tour-bus stop. Its sweet bread comes plain or in the brightly colored flavors of guava, *liliko'i* or taro. Snack on a pastry or *malasada*, or grab a salad or sandwich to go from the deli (steer clear of the mediocre plate lunches). A small lawn bordered by flower beds out back is prime for picnicking.

Hana Hou (☎ 929-9717; Spur Rd; plate lunches $9-14, mains $15; ☽ 8am-3pm Mon-Wed, to 8pm Thu & Sun, to 9pm Fri & Sat) Of the two restaurants in town, there's really no question: Hana Hou is the spot. On the *makai* side of Hwy 11, this friendly diner serves up 'real food for a decent price' with no holds barred on flavor. Its menu sports the usual meat and fish plates, along with extras like stir-fries and chicken parmesan. Asian-inspired sauces and macadamia-nut crusts spice up the nightly specials. Tables sport Hawaiian-print runners, and paper cranes hang from the ceiling. The chock-full dessert case won't let you leave without.

A **farmers market** (Hwy 11; ☽ 8am-noon Wed & Sat) is held across from the theater.

WAI'OHINU

A place between here and there, green Wai'-ohinu is little more than an annex of Na'alehu. Its landmark **Mark Twain monkeypod tree** (Hwy 11) was planted by the author in 1866 and fell in a 1957 hurricane. Hardy new trunks have sprung up and replaced it, backed by a macadamia-nut orchard.

Sleeping

Shirakawa Motel (☎ 929-7462; www.shirakawamotel .com; 95-6040 Hwy 11; s/d $45, r with kitchenette $55-65) Two single-story blocks of dark rooms backed by a steep, lush hillside offer a worn-down but adequate budget option. Bathrooms are laughably tiny, with sinks located inside the room. The place is still family run, and the longtime owners can tell you all about the Big Island 'back in the day' if you get on their good side.

Macadamia Meadows B&B (☎ 929-8097, 888-929-8118; www.macadamiameadows.com; d incl breakfast $89-129, ste $139; ☑) Just a half-mile south of town, a family of friendly macadamia-nut farmers rents rooms on the ground floor of their contemporary home. The decor in the rooms is nothing special, but they're are spacious and clean, with private entrances, lanai, cable TV, a microwave and a refrigerator. Guests receive a free tour of the surrounding orchard, and there's a tennis court onsite.

Hobbit House B&B (☎ 929-9755; www.hi-hobbit .com/Hawaii/bnb; ste $170) With its mushrooming roof, and windows and supports fashioned from lacquered tree branches, whimsical Hobbit House looks positively medieval. The ground-floor guest suite has exposed beam ceilings, a full kitchen and a romantic antique bedroom set. A panoramic ocean view can be enjoyed from every living-room window or the double-wide Jacuzzi bathtub. Preventing this place from being truly sublime is the underfurnished living room, some outdated fabrics and decor, and the gray industrial carpet throughout. The hosts are especially personable and familiar with the island, and they power the place with alternative energy. The steep and rough half-mile journey up requires careful driving.

SOUTH POINT

South Point is the southernmost point in the USA and a national historic landmark. In Hawaiian, it's known as Ka Lae, which means simply The Point. South Point combines bright green grassy fields with dark lava cliffs and a turbulent turquoise ocean. This rugged coastline is the site where the first Polynesians landed, in desperate straits by some accounts. Much of the area now falls under the jurisdiction of Hawaiian Home Lands. There are no facilities.

To get here, take South Point Rd between the 69- and 70-mile markers. The 10-mile road is mostly one lane, so be sure to give the *shaka* (Hawaiian hand greeting) if someone waves you ahead.

Sights
KAMA'OA WIND FARM
The winds are bracing here, as evidenced by tree trunks bent almost horizontal. After a few miles of scattered houses, macadamia-nut farms and grassy pastureland, you'll see the rows of high-tech windmills composing the **wind farm**. Each of these wind-turbine generators can produce enough electricity for 100 families. Theoretically, the state could produce more than enough electricity to meet its needs by using wind-energy conversion, but the wind farm is currently not operating at capacity.

About 4 miles south of the wind farm are the abandoned buildings of a Pacific Missile Range Station. Until 1965 missiles shot from California to the Marshall Islands in Micronesia were tracked here.

When the road forks, veer right for Ka Lae and left for Green Sands Beach.

KA LAE
The confluence of ocean currents just offshore makes this one of Hawai'i's most bountiful fishing grounds. Locals fish off the craggy cliff, with some of the bolder ones leaning out over steep lava ledges. Land ruins here include **Kalalea Heiau**, classified as a *ko'a* (a small stone pen designed to encourage fish and birds to multiply). Look inside for a well-preserved fishing shrine where ancient Hawaiians left offerings to Ku'ula, the god of fishermen.

An outcropping on the heiau's western side has numerous **canoe mooring holes** that were drilled long ago into the lava rock. Strong currents would pull the canoes out into deep, turbulent waters where the enterprising ancient Hawaiians could fish, still tethered to the shore, without getting swept out to sea.

The wooden platforms built on one section of cliff have hoists and ladders for the small boats anchored below. You may see a *honu* (green sea turtle) or two gliding around in the relatively calm water here. Locals boast of **cliff jumping** here.

There's a large *puka* (hole) in the lava directly behind the platforms where you can watch water rage up the sides and recede again with incoming waves. Keep an eye out for it, as it's not obvious until you're almost on top of it.

Walk down past the light beacon and continue along the wall to finally reach the southernmost point in the USA. There are no markers here, no souvenir stands, just crashing surf and lots of wind.

BEST SPLURGE ACTIVITIES

■ A nighttime **snorkel or dive with manta rays** (p205)

■ A **Mauna Kea sunset and stargazing tour** (p257)

■ The island's highest-quality **luau** (p232)

■ An open-door aerial lava tour with **Paradise Helicopters** (p201)

■ Riding horses and driving cattle at **Dahana Ranch** (p248)

■ A day on the high seas on Fairwind's **Hula Kai** (p205)

■ An evening at **Mamalahoa Hot Tubs & Massage** (p220)

GREEN SANDS BEACH

Few can resist a peek at this **beach**, also known as Papakolea. It was formed by semiprecious olivine (a type of volcanic basalt) crystals eroded from the cliffs of the ancient littoral cone and worn smooth by a relentless and pounding surf. The olivine sand is mixed with black sand, and appears a dull olive green. You can swim here, but waves are strong and pound the shore at full force. Pick a calm day to visit, for the beach can be flooded during high surf or overly windy conditions.

A parking lot for the beach is marked by a sign. Should a local attempt to charge you for 'secure parking,' decline on the basis that no one can legally charge 'admission' to the public-access shoreline. Local police advise against leaving valuables in your car.

From here, passing the Kaulana boat ramp, it's a 2.5-mile hike along a rutted dirt road to the beach. If you have a high-riding 4WD you could drive in, but the road is rough and it'll probably take about 25 minutes. It's a gentle and beautiful – though windy – hike. A scramble down some cliffs is required to reach the beach.

It's doubtful you'll have the place to yourself, so if you're after total solitude, try the Road to the Sea (see right).

HAWAIIAN OCEAN VIEW ESTATES

pop 2180

Hawaiian Ocean View Estates (HOVE) is a huge subdivision established in the 1950s and set among desolate lava fields. This area is one of the last sunny expanses of land in Hawai'i to be totally free of resorts, most probably due to the harsh terrain and lack of beaches. Controversial development proposals occasionally pop up, but so far all have been defeated, to the relief of island environmentalists. Land is cheap and the area feels isolated and economically depressed. Any local will tell you that crystal methamphetamine is produced here and drugs are a major problem.

A gas station, a grocery store and a little café are located in a scruffy shopping center on the *makai* side. Turning *mauka* on Lotus Blossom Rd brings you to **Ocean View Pizzeria** (☎ 929-9677; Ocean View Town Center; pizzas small/large $11/15, sandwiches $5-6.50; ☽ 11am-7pm Sun-Thu, to 8pm Fri & Sat), the most recommended eatery in town (which isn't saying much). It makes submarine sandwiches and killer milkshakes in addition to pizza.

Nearby, **Anuenue Natural Foods** (☎ 929-7550; Ocean View Town Center; ☽ 9am-5:30pm Mon-Fri, to 5pm Sat, 11am-4pm Sun) has a decent bakery, deli and hot lunch bar (from 11am) and a good selection of health foods.

There are a couple of B&Bs in town, but, really, you'd rather stay elsewhere.

ROAD TO THE SEA

The Road to the Sea is hardly traveled, and it's no wonder: the unpaved **4WD-only road** crosses loose lava rock, ledges and cracks. If you brave the journey, however, you'll likely have the beaches to yourself. Be warned that whipping winds can turn sand into an airborne exfoliant on especially gusty days, and the water is often rough.

To get here, turn *makai* at the row of three mailboxes between the 79- and 80-mile markers and set your odometer. Another landmark is the 'Ka Ulu Malu Shady Grove Farm' sign. The road is private, and barking dogs might give you a chase.

From here you'll cross 6 miles over a rudimentary, seemingly never-ending lava road. To reach the first and smaller of the two beaches takes 30 minutes, if you drive slowly, although it can be done in 20 minutes, if you're comfortable on rough terrain.

To reach the second beach, drive a half mile back inland. Skip the first left fork that appears (it's a dead end) and take the second left fork. Look for arrows that are painted on the lava rock. The road heads inland before heading toward the shore again, and the course isn't always apparent. There are many places where you can lose traction or get lost. Almost a mile from the fork you'll reach a red *pu'u* (hill). Park here and walk down to the ocean. If you decide to walk the whole distance, it's about 1.5 miles. Bring as much water as you can carry, as it's hot and shadeless.

Neither beach is named, but both have exquisite black-and-green sand, similar to Green Sands Beach. The looming cliffs here are stunning, and low tide presents intriguing beach-trekking possibilities.

Maui

According to legend the other Hawaiian islands didn't even exist until the prankish demigod Maui snagged his fishhook on the ocean floor and yanked them above the surface. Maui has been making a splash ever since.

Check those travel magazine reader polls ranking the world's best islands and guess what comes to the top? Maui is the dream date of honeymooners, the darling of celebrities, the siren call for artists and spiritual seekers. Dang! Everybody wants to be here.

The beaches themselves are reason enough for all this excitement, but things really take off once you get your toes wet. The old sugarcane town of Pa'ia got dubbed the 'world windsurfing capital' years ago and Kanaha kiteboarders are etching out a place on the map today. Snorkeling is phenomenal. Hoist your surfboard over your head, put on your diving gear or jump in a kayak – it's all here. And whale watching on Maui is as good as it gets.

Maui's diversity is part of its allure. You can camp under the moon in a volcanic crater, trek through the rain forest to a hidden waterfall or stroll the streets of an old whaling town. Make your base in hip New Age communities with inviting B&Bs, yoga studios and vegetarian restaurants, or drench yourself at beachside resorts with five-star dining and indulgent spas. Once you've soaked up enough sun, head for the cool green hills of Upcountry Maui or go bask in aloha in the old Hawaiian town of Hana.

HIGHLIGHTS

- Snorkel eye to eye with turtles at **Malu'aka Beach** (p367)
- Catch the outrigger launch at Lahaina's **International Festival of Canoes** (p324)
- Trek the rain forest to 400ft **Waimoku Falls** (p382)
- Treat your sweet tooth to cream puffs at **Komoda Store & Bakery** (p397)
- Sail among breaching **humpback whales** (p324)
- Enjoy the aloha at the **Old Lahaina Luau** (p328)
- Hike the crunchy cinder floor of **Haleakala Crater** (p408)
- Twist and turn 38 glorious miles down the **Hana Hwy** (p373)
- Fly across **Kanaha** (p348) on a sailboard
- Feast on island grinds (food) at Lahaina's **Aloha Mixed Plate** (p326)

| POPULATION: 120,000 | AREA: 728 SQ MILES | OFFICIAL FLOWER: LOKELANI |

CLIMATE

If beach, beach, beach is all you ever think about, hightail it to Maui's west coast, which shines with hot, dry, sunny conditions from Kapalua at the north end to Makena at the south. Hana and the jungly eastern side of the island pick up much more rain. Annual rainfall averages 15in along the west coast and 69in in Hana. The Upcountry slopes beneath Haleakala commonly have intermittent clouds, making for a cooler, greener respite and ideal conditions for land-based activities, like hiking. Maui's rainiest months are between December and March.

Temperatures vary more with elevation and location than with season. Daytime highs on Maui vary only about 7°F between summer and winter, and coastal waters are always warm. Average daily temperatures in August hover around 80°F in Lahaina, Kihei or Hana, but only 50°F at Haleakala summit. The lowest temperature ever recorded on Maui was 14°F at the summit of Haleakala, where overnight lows dip below freezing and the volcano even gets an occasional winter snowcap.

See p556 for more climate information and climate charts. For an islandwide recorded weather forecast, call ☎ 877-5111. For a more extensive marine forecast, including surf conditions, call ☎ 877-3477.

NATIONAL, STATE & COUNTY PARKS

Let's start at the top. The undisputed star of Maui's parks, Haleakala National Park (p403) embraces the lofty volcanic peaks that gave rise to east Maui. With its extraordinary landscape of red cinder cones and gray lava, the park offers one-of-a-kind hiking and sightseeing, good birding and some of the best camping on Maui. The park's summit section (p403) contains awesome Haleakala volcano and most of the major sights. But this is a park with two faces, the lush coastal side standing in sharp contrast to the barren, lunarlike crater of Haleakala. In the park's Kipahulu section (p381) south of Hana, you can hike to towering waterfalls, swim in cascading pools and visit ancient Hawaiian archaeological sites.

A standout among the state parks is 'Iao Valley State Park (p353), whose towering green pinnacle rises from the valley floor so gloriously that it makes the cover of travel magazines.

For the ultimate stretch of unspoiled beach, head to Makena State Park (p368), the northern portion of which is a haunt for nude sunbathers. The most interesting oceanside park with camping is Wai'anapanapa State Park (p377), which sits on a gem of a black-sand beach north of Hana and has lava caves and a coastal trail to explore. If you want to discover a dreamy cloud forest, head Upcountry to Polipoli Spring State Recreation Area (p401), where a lightly trodden network of trails winds beneath lofty trees.

County parks center around the beaches and include some hot places, like Kanaha Beach Park (p347) and Ho'okipa Beach Park (p370) for windsurfing and kiteboarding.

Camping
NATIONAL PARKS

For the best camping on Maui, head to Haleakala National Park. Drive-up camping is available in both the summit (p410) and Kipahulu (p383) sections of the park, and no fees, reservations or permits are required. Haleakala also offers free backcountry camping on the crater floor with a permit, as well as high-demand $75 cabin rentals (p410).

STATE PARKS

Polipoli (p402) and Wai'anapanapa (p377) state parks both have campsites and cabins. Polipoli, deep in the rainforest, has one primitive cabin at the end of a rough access road that usually requires a 4WD vehicle. If you're not a pig hunter, you'll find the dozen beachside cabins at Wai'anapanapa, just north of Hana, more to your taste. Book well in advance to avoid disappointment!

Camping permits are required for state parks. Tent camping costs $5 per day per site and cabins cost $45 to $55. For permits and cabin reservations, contact the **Division of State Parks** (☎ 984-8109; www.hawaii.gov/dlnr/dsp; Room 101, State Office Bldg, 54 S High St, Wailuku, HI 96793; ⏰ 8am-3:30pm Mon-Fri).

COUNTY PARKS

Kanaha Beach Park (p347), just north of Kahului airport, allows camping Thursday through Monday; Papalaua Beach Park (p332), on Hwy 30 south of Lahaina, allows camping Friday through Wednesday. Camping is limited to three consecutive nights. Permits cost $3 per adult per day (50¢ for children under 18), and are available by mail or in person from the **Department of Parks & Recreation** (☎ 270-7389; www.co.maui.hi.us; 700 Halia Nakoa St, Wailuku, HI 96793;

MAUI

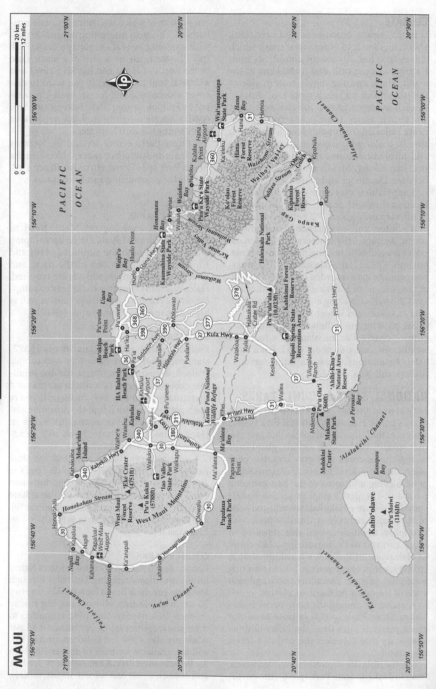

⏰ 8am-noon & 12:30-4pm Mon-Fri), at the War Memorial Complex at Baldwin High School.

ACTIVITIES

Here's where the real adventure begins. Sure, it might be fun to melt away a day on one of Maui's sundrenched beaches, but there's no need to stop there: an oceanful of action is just a sandal shuffle away. Maui has great conditions for virtually anything to do with the water, from snorkeling to kiteboarding, and the surfing and windsurfing here is the stuff of legends.

When your waterlogged body has had enough, there's a plethora of things to do on land. Maui's hiking trails go to some incredible places. And if knocking around a little white ball is your thing, would-be Tigers can stalk the very greens where the real Tiger plays.

Only a few activities require planning before landing on Maui. Most of the time you can just show up, look around and decide. And if you want to try something new for the first time, pros waiting in the wings offer instructions on everything from kiteboarding to tennis swings. Details on gear rentals, lessons and specific locations for each activity are found in the destination sections.

Water Activities

SURFING

Maui's surfing spots are legendary. See the boxed text (p313) for details.

WINDSURFING

This sport reaches its peak on Maui. Ho'okipa Beach (p370), near Pa'ia, hosts top international windsurfing competitions. The wind and waves combine at Ho'okipa in such a way that makes gravity seem arbitrary. Ho'okipa is for experts only, though, as hazards include razor-sharp coral and dangerous shorebreaks. For kick-ass wind without taking your life in your hands, the place to launch is Kanaha Beach (p347) in Kahului, but avoid the busy weekends when the water becomes a sea of sails.

Overall, Maui is known for its consistent winds. Windsurfers can find action in any month, but as a general rule the best wind is from June to September and the flattest spells are from December to February.

At Ma'alaea Bay (p354), where the winds are usually strong and blow offshore to-ward Kaho'olawe, conditions are good for advanced speed sailing. In winter, on those occasions when *kona* (leeward) winds blow, the Ma'alaea–Kihei area is often the only place windy enough to sail.

Most windsurfing shops are based in Kahului and handle rentals, give lessons, sell windsurfing gear, and even book package tours that include gear, accommodations and car.

SNORKELING

Don a mask and fins and a whole other world opens up. The waters around Maui harbor are a kaleidoscope of colorful fish, coral and honkin' big sea turtles. For great snorkeling from the beach, prime spots include Malu'aka Beach, dubbed 'Turtle Beach' (p367), in Makena; 'Ahihi-Kina'u Natural Area Reserve (p369), south of Makena; Ulua Beach (p363) in Wailea; Pu'u Keka'a (p333), aka Black Rock, in Ka'anapali; Kapalua Bay (p340); and, in summer, Slaughterhouse Beach and Honolua Bay (p341), north of Kapalua.

Snorkelers should get an early start, as not only does the first half of the morning offer the calmest water conditions but at some of the more popular places crowds begin to show by 10am. Snorkeling gear can readily be rented at reasonable prices from dive shops or at more inflated prices from hotel beach huts.

The hottest spot for snorkeling cruises is to the largely submerged volcanic crater of Molokini, off Maui's southwest coast. Half of the crater rim has eroded away, leaving a crescent-moon shape that rises 160ft above the ocean surface. A coral reef extends outward from Molokini, providing excellent snorkeling. Scores of boats set out daily from Ma'alaea and Lahaina harbors. Boats are usually out from about 7am to noon and charge $40 to $50 per person, including drinks and snorkeling gear. Competition is fierce, so discounts are easy to come by. Forget those cheaper afternoon cruises, as the wind makes for choppy waters and lousy visibility later in the day.

SCUBA DIVING

While snorkelers hang in the shallow waters of Molokini, divers get to explore the submerged crater's deep back wall where the thrills include steep ledges, manta rays and white-tipped reef sharks. The other prime dive destination is Cathedrals (p423), off Hulopo'e Beach on the island of Lana'i, which takes its

MAUI

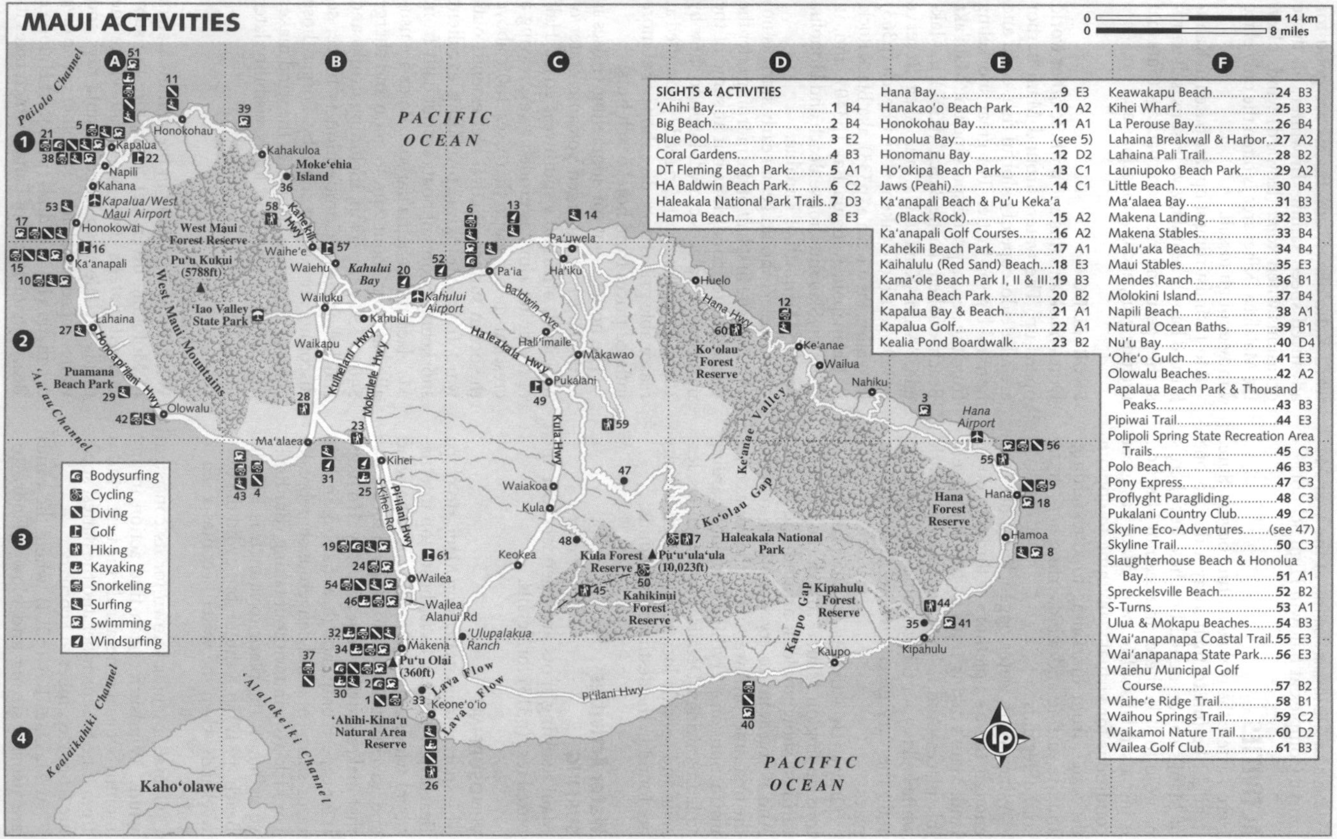
MAUI ACTIVITIES
0 14 km
0 8 miles
A B C D E F
1 2 3 4
SIGHTS & ACTIVITIES
'Ahihi Bay 1 B4
Big Beach 2 B4
Blue Pool 3 E2
Coral Gardens 4 B3
DT Fleming Beach Park 5 A1
HA Baldwin Beach Park 6 C2
Haleakala National Park Trails 7 D3
Hamoa Beach 8 E3
Hana Bay 9 E3
Hanakao'o Beach Park 10 A2
Honokohau Bay 11 A1
Honolua Bay (see 5)
Honomanu Bay 12 D2
Ho'okipa Beach Park 13 C1
Jaws (Peahi) 14 C1
Ka'anapali Beach & Pu'u Keka'a (Black Rock) 15 A2
Ka'anapali Golf Courses 16 A2
Kahekili Beach Park 17 A1
Kaihalulu (Red Sand) Beach 18 E3
Kama'ole Beach Park I, II & III 19 B3
Kanaha Beach Park 20 B2
Kapalua Bay & Beach 21 A1
Kapalua Golf 22 A1
Kealia Pond Boardwalk 23 B2
Keawakapu Beach 24 B3
Kihei Wharf 25 B3
La Perouse Bay 26 B4
Lahaina Breakwall & Harbor 27 A2
Lahaina Pali Trail 28 B2
Launiupoko Beach Park 29 A2
Little Beach 30 B4
Ma'alaea Bay 31 B3
Makena Landing 32 B3
Makena Stables 33 B4
Malu'aka Beach 34 B4
Maui Stables 35 E3
Mendes Ranch 36 B1
Molokini Island 37 B4
Napili Beach 38 A1
Natural Ocean Baths 39 B1
Nu'u Bay 40 D4
'Ohe'o Gulch 41 E3
Olowalu Beaches 42 A2
Papalaua Beach Park & Thousand Peaks 43 B3
Pipiwai Trail 44 E3
Polipoli Spring State Recreation Area Trails 45 C3
Polo Beach 46 B3
Pony Express 47 C3
Proflyght Paragliding 48 C3
Pukalani Country Club 49 C2
Skyline Eco-Adventures (see 47)
Skyline Trail 50 C3
Slaughterhouse Beach & Honolua Bay 51 A1
Spreckelsville Beach 52 B2
S-Turns 53 A1
Ulua & Mokapu Beaches 54 B3
Wai'anapanapa Coastal Trail 55 E3
Wai'anapanapa State Park 56 E3
Waiehu Municipal Golf Course 57 B2
Waihe'e Ridge Trail 58 B1
Waihou Springs Trail 59 C2
Waikamoi Nature Trail 60 D2
Wailea Golf Club 61 B3
Bodysurfing
Cycling
Diving
Golf
Hiking
Kayaking
Snorkeling
Surfing
Swimming
Windsurfing
PACIFIC OCEAN
PACIFIC OCEAN
Pailolo Channel
'Au'au Channel
'Alalakeiki Channel
Kealaikahiki Channel
Kaho'olawe
Honokohau
Kapalua
Napili
Kahana
Kapalua/West Maui Airport
Honokowai
Ka'anapali
Lahaina
Honoapi'ilani Hwy
Puamana Beach Park
Olowalu
West Maui Forest Reserve
Pu'u Kukui (5788ft)
West Maui Mountains
'Iao Valley State Park
Kahakuloa
Moke'ehia Island
Kahekili Hwy
Waihe'e
Waiehu
Wailuku
Waikapu
Ma'alaea
Kahului Bay
Kahului
Kahului Airport
Kuihelani Hwy
Mokulele Hwy
Kihei
S Kihei Rd
Pi'ilani Hwy
Wailea
Wailea Alanui Rd
Makena
Pu'u Olai (360ft)
Keone'o'io
Lava Flow
Lava Flow
'Ahihi-Kina'u Natural Area Reserve
'Ulupalakua Ranch
Pa'ia
Baldwin Ave
Hali'imaile
Haleakala Hwy
Pukalani
Makawao
Pa'uwela
Ha'iku
Kula Hwy
Waiakoa
Kula
Keokea
Kula Forest Reserve
Pu'u'ula'ula (10,023ft)
Kahikinui Forest Reserve
Haleakala National Park
Ko'olau Gap
Ke'anae Valley
Ko'olau Forest Reserve
Huelo
Hana Hwy
Ke'anae
Wailua
Nahiku
Hana Airport
Hana
Hana Forest Reserve
Hamoa
Kipahulu Forest Reserve
Kaupo Gap
Kaupo
Kipahulu
Pi'ilani Hwy

name from its intriguing underwater caverns, arches and connecting passageways.

Most dive operators on Maui offer a full range of dives, as well as refresher and advanced certification courses. Book directly, and don't monkey around with activity desks.

Maui Dive Shop (☎ 800-542-3483; www.mauidive shop.com; dives from $90, courses from $350) is a reliable operation with branches around the island, including in Kihei, Lahaina, Wailea and Kahana. The shop offers a handy free magazine that details Maui's best diving and snorkeling spots.

KAYAKING

On Maui, kayakers really get an adventure. The most popular spot is Makena (p367), an area rich with marine life, including sea turtles and humpback whales (in winter). Unspoiled La Perouse Bay (p369), a marine preserve south of Makena, is the best place for kayakers to see schools of spinner dolphins. Another good spot for kayaking in the calmer summer season is Honolua-Mokule'ia Bay Marine Life Conservation District (p341), north of Kapalua, where there are also lots of turtles and possibilities for dolphin sightings. Keep in mind that water conditions on Maui are usually clearest and calmest early in the morning, so that's an ideal time to head out.

If you have experience, you can rent a kayak and paddle your own path. Otherwise, join a guided tour – they'll show you the ropes before taking off.

SWIMMING

Maui makes a credible claim to being the best Hawaiian island when it comes to beaches. The northwest coast from Ka'anapali (p333) to Honolua Bay (p341) and the southwest coast from Kihei (p356) through Wailea (p363) to Makena (p367) harbor scores of sandy beaches with good year-round swimming conditions. The windward northern and eastern coasts are generally rough for swimming in winter but quieten down in summer.

KITEBOARDING

Kiteboarding has taken off big time. If you want to try your hand at the sport, there's no better place than Maui. All the action centers at 'Kite Beach,' the western end of Kanaha Beach Park (p347) in Kahului.

Land Activities

HIKING

Hikers on Maui can choose from an amazing diversity of trails that traverse coastal deserts, bamboo forests and lush green jungles. Hands down the most extraordinary trails are in Haleakala National Park (p403), where hikes ranging from half-day walks to quad-busting multiday treks meander across the moonscape of Haleakala Crater. In the Kipahulu section of the national park, south of Hana, a trail leads up past terraced pools ideal for a dip and on to the towering waterfalls that feed them.

In Maui's Upcountry, Polipoli Spring State Recreation Area (p401) has an extensive trail system in cloud forest, including the daylong

---

MAUI SURF BEACHES & BREAKS *Jake Howard*

While there are hippie holdouts from the 1960s who believe the spirit of Jimi Hendrix roams the Valley Isle's mountains, today Maui's beaches are where most of the island's action is found. On the north shore, near the town of Ha'iku (p398), is the infamous big-wave spot known as **Peahi**, or **Jaws**. Determined pro surfers, such as Laird Hamilton, Dave Kalama and Derrick Doerner, have helped put the planet's largest, most perfect wave on the international map, appearing in everything from American Express commercials to mutual fund ads. Jaws' waves are so high that surfers must be towed into them by WaveRunners.

Not into risking your life on your vacation? No worries, there are plenty of other waves to ride. Maui's west side, especially around **Lahaina** (p317), offers a wider variety of surf. The **Lahaina Breakwall and Harbor**'s fun reef breaks cater to both beginner and intermediate surfers. To the south is **Ma'alaea Pipeline**, a fickle right-hand reef break that is often considered one of the fastest waves in the world. On the island's northwest corner is majestic **Honolua Bay**. This right point break works best on winter swells and is considered one of the premier points not just in Hawaii, but around the world.

Gentler shorebreaks good for bodysurfing can be found around **Pa'ia** (p369), **Kapalua** (p340) and the beaches between **Kihei** (p356) to **Makena** (p367).

Skyline Trail that connects with Haleakala summit.

North of Wailuku is the lofty Waihe'e Ridge Trail (p343), which penetrates deep into the misty West Maui Mountains. Near Ma'alaea Bay, the challenging Lahaina Pali Trail (p355) follows an old footpath on the drier western slope of the same mountain mass.

Several pull-offs along the Hana Hwy (p373) offer short nature walks that lead to hidden waterfalls and unspoiled coastal views. A longer coastal trail between Wai'anapanapa State Park (p377) and Hana Bay follows an ancient Hawaiian footpath past several historic sights, as does the Hoapili (King's Hwy) Trail (p369) from La Perouse Bay on the other side of the island.

The **Sierra Club** (☎ 573-4147; www.hi.sierraclub.org /maui) sponsors guided hikes led by naturalists to various places on Maui, mostly on Saturday. Nonmembers are asked to pay $5 each; carpooling to trailheads may be available.

CYCLING & MOUNTAIN BIKING
If you want to take off on a mountain-bike, head to the Upcountry. Experienced downhill riders will find unparalleled thrills on the wilderness Skyline Trail (p402), which leads from Haleakala National Park into Polipoli Spring State Recreation Area. Much less adventurous, but hugely more popular, is the guided Haleakala sunrise bike ride (p410) from the volcanic summit down to the coast, which requires barely a pedal. Diehard cyclists do it the other way, biking solo up the mountain to the summit – a calf-quivering workout worthy of applause.

HORSEBACK RIDING
As you might expect on an island with a wealth of ranch land, Maui has some excellent trail rides. The most unusual ride, offered by Pony Express (p400), meanders down into the barren hollows of Haleakala Crater via Sliding Sands Trail. Top-notch rides that take in greener pastures start from Makena (p369) and Kipahulu (p384).

GOLF
With scenic ocean vistas and emerald mountain slopes, golfing just doesn't get much better. The most prestigious of all of Maui's courses is the Plantation Course at Kapalua (p342), which kicks off the annual PGA tour. Only slightly less elite are the championship greens at Wailea (p365) and Ka'anapali (p335).

At the other end of the spectrum, you can enjoy a fun round at the friendly Waiehu Municipal Golf Course (p343) and at lesser-known country clubs elsewhere around the island. Pick up the free tourist magazine *Maui Golf Review* for in-depth course profiles and tips on playing specific holes.

TENNIS
The county maintains tennis courts in several towns, which are free to the public on a first-come, first-served basis. Numerous hotels and condos also have tennis courts for their guests. If you're looking to hone your game, you'll find world-class tennis clubs in Wailea (p365) and Kapalua (p342).

GETTING THERE & AWAY
Air
Most travelers disembark in central Maui at Kahului, which has the busiest airport in Hawaii outside Honolulu. North of Lahaina in west Maui, Kapalua airport is a small airport serviced by prop planes and commuter aircraft. Tiny Hana airport sees only a few flights a day, all by prop plane.

Hana airport (HNM; ☎ 248-8208) A single terminal off the Hana Hwy, about 3 miles north of Hana in east Maui.

Kahului International Airport (OGG; ☎ 872-3830) For information on getting to and from Kahului's airport, see opposite. There's a small visitor information desk (☎ 872-3893; ⏱ 7:45am to 9:45pm) in the baggage-claim area. Nearby are courtesy phones for contacting accommodations and ground transportation, plus racks upon racks of free tourist magazines and brochures. Near the departure gates are newsstands, gift shops, ATMs, a coffee shop, a restaurant and a cocktail lounge.

Kapalua airport (JHM; ☎ 669-0623) The terminal is off Hwy 30, about midway between Kapalua and Ka'anapali, within easy reach of Lahaina.

Several airlines provide direct flights from the US mainland to Maui, including **Hawaiian Airlines** (☎ 800-367-5320; www.hawaiianair.com) and **Aloha Airlines** (☎ 800-367-5250; www.alohaairlines.com), both of which also offer a full schedule of daily flights between Maui and the other Hawaiian islands. See p566 for airline contact details and more information on flights to Maui from the mainland and abroad. See p568 for more on interisland flights.

Boat

Interisland ferries to Moloka'i and Lana'i depart from Lahaina Harbor. For information on ferry schedules and ticket prices, see p433 for sailings of the *Moloka'i Princess* to Molokai and p416 for Expeditions' handy Maui–Lana'i ferry. For information on the Hawaii Superferry, see p570.

GETTING AROUND

If you really want to explore Maui thoroughly, and reach off-the-beaten-path sights, you'll need to have your own wheels. Public transportation is limited to the main towns and tourist resorts.

Be aware that most main roads on Maui are called highways whether they're busy four-lane thoroughfares or just quiet country roads. What's more, islanders refer to highways by name, rarely by number. If you ask someone how to find Hwy 36, chances are they're going to stare at you blankly – ask for the Hana Hwy instead.

The best map for getting around is the encyclopedic *Ready Mapbook of Maui County*, but it's bulky. A good lightweight, foldout map is Nelles' *Maui, Molokai & Lanai*. The colorful Franko's *Maui, the Valley Isle* features water sports and is sold at dive shops; it's waterproof and rip resistant.

To/From the Airports

An airport transfer service, **Executive Shuttle** (☎ 669-2300, 800-833-2303), offers competitive fares and good service. The one-way trip from Kahului airport to Wailuku costs $19, to Kihei $26, to Wailea $29, to Lahaina $36 and to Kapalua $50. Executive has a courtesy phone in the baggage-claim area, but you can also make a reservation in advance to speed things along.

Kahului airport's taxi dispatchers are near the exit of the baggage-claim area. Approximate fares to Wailuku cost $15, to Kihei $30, to the Pa'ia–Ha'iku area $25 to $35 and to Lahaina $60.

Taxi fares from the Kapalua airport average $15 to Ka'anapali and $20 to $30 to most other places along the west Maui coast. Many resorts on the Ka'anapali coast offer free shuttles to/from Kapalua airport.

Bicycle

Cyclists on Maui face a number of challenges: narrow roads, heavy traffic, an abundance of hills and mountains, and the same persistent winds that so delight windsurfers.

Maui's stunning scenery may entice hardcore cyclists, but casual riders hoping to use a bike as a primary source of transportation around the island may well find such conditions daunting.

Getting around by bicycle within a small area can be a reasonable option for the average rider, however. For example, the tourist enclave of Kihei is largely level and now has cycle lanes on two main drags, S Kihei Rd and the Pi'ilani Hwy.

The full-color *Maui County Bicycle Map* ($6), available from bicycle shops, shows all the roads on Maui that have cycle lanes and gives other nitty-gritty details. Consider it essential if you intend to do your exploring by pedal power. For information on bicycle rentals, see specific destinations around the island.

Bus

With the exception of O'ahu, Maui has Hawaii's most extensive public bus system. But don't get too excited – the buses can take you between the main towns, but they're not going to get you to many prime out-of-the-way places, such as Haleakala National Park, Hana or Makena's Big Beach. And some of the buses, such as the one between Ma'alaea and Lahaina, make a direct beeline, passing trailheads and beaches without stopping.

Maui Bus (www.mauicounty.gov/bus) Roberts Hawaii (☎ 871-4838); Maui County (☎ 270-7511), the island's public bus system, operates several routes, each of them daily. The main routes run once hourly throughout the day and several have schedules that dovetail with one another for convenient connections. The handiest buses for visitors are the routes Kahului–Lahaina, Kahului–Wailea, Kahului–Wailuku, Ma'alaea–Kihei, Lahaina–Ka'anapali and Ka'anapali–Napili. Fares are just $1 per ride. There are no transfers, however, so if your journey requires two separate buses, you'll have to buy a new ticket when you board the second bus. Monthly passes ($45) are also available.

Maui Bus also operates a couple of loop routes around Wailuku and Kahului, serving two dozen stops, including all of the major shopping centers, the hospital and government offices. These buses are mainly geared for local shoppers, but are provided free to everyone – just hop on.

All buses allow you to carry on only what fits under your seat or on your lap, so forget the surfboard.

In addition to the public buses, free resort shuttles take guests between hotels and restaurants in the Ka'anapali and Wailea areas.

Car & Motorcycle

See p571 for more information on the national car-rental chains, including their toll-free numbers and websites. **Alamo** (☎ 871-6235), **Avis** (☎ 871-7575), **Budget** (☎ 871-8811), **Dollar** (☎ 877-7227), **Hertz** (☎ 877-5167) and **National** (☎ 871-8851) all have booths at Kahului airport. Alamo, Avis, Budget, Dollar and National also have offices on Hwy 30 in Ka'anapali and will pick you up at Kapalua airport. Dollar is the only rental agency serving Hana airport.

In addition to the national chains, there are a few local car-rental agencies on the island. See p363 in Kihei and p329 in Lahaina for details. For information on renting motorcycles, see p363 in Kihei and p329 in Lahaina.

Taxi

Companies with service throughout the island include **Royal Sedan & Taxi Service** (☎ 874-6900) and **Sunshine Cabs of Maui** (☎ 879-2220).

Tours

If you don't have your own transportation, you can take in the island's attractions by joining a guided tour.

DRIVING DISTANCES & TIMES

Average driving times and distances from Kahului are as follows. Naturally allow more time during morning and late afternoon rush hours.

Destination	Miles	Time
Haleakala Summit	36	1½hr
Hana	51	2hr
Kapalua	32	1hr
Kihei	12	25min
La Perouse Bay	21	50min
Lahaina	23	45min
Makawao	14	30min
Makena	19	40min
'Ohe'o Gulch (via Hana)	61	2¾hr
Pa'ia	7	15min
Wailuku	3	15min

BOAT

Maui has enough dinner cruises, sunset sails and charter sailboats to fill a book. Most leave from Lahaina and Ma'alaea Bay, although a few depart from south Maui.

The best tours are the whale-watchers, which operate from December to mid-May, when the humpbacks are hanging around Maui's west-coast waters. Recommended is the nonprofit **Pacific Whale Foundation** (☎ 249-8811, 800-942-5311; www.pacificwhale.org), which operates naturalist-led tours from Ma'alaea and Lahaina. Trips include whale watching in season, as well as wild dolphin ecoadventures and snorkel tours year-round. Some of the proceeds benefit marine-conservation projects.

For snorkel and dive tours to Molokini crater, see p311.

BUS & VAN

The most popular tours are the drive to Hana, which runs down the Hana Hwy and includes Kipahulu, and the trip to Haleakala National Park. Both are full-day tours. The going rate for the Haleakala tour is about $70/40 per adult/child under 12. For the Hana trip, it's about $90/60 per adult/child under 12. Because of the narrow, winding road conditions, both of these trips are done in minivans or half-sized buses, so the tours tend to be more personal and less crowded than those found elsewhere.

'Ekahi Tours (☎ 877-9775, 888-292-2242; www.ekahi .com) is a family-run operation that organizes a variety of personalized tours focusing as much on Hawaiian culture as sightseeing, including a tour of Kahakuloa village (per adult/child under 12 $80/60) that offers a visit to a working taro patch.

Other reliable operators:

Polynesian Adventure Tours (☎ 877-4242, 800-622-3011; www.polyad.com)

Roberts Hawaii (☎ 539-9400, 800-831-5411; www .robertshawaii.com)

Valley Isle Excursions (☎ 661-8687, 877-871-5224; www.tourmaui.com)

HELICOPTER

Numerous helicopter companies take off from the Kahului heliport for trips around the island. Some cross the channel and tour Moloka'i's spectacular north shore as well.

Companies advertise in the free tourist magazines, which are available everywhere,

MAUI...

In Three Days
On day one take a walking tour of the old whaling town of **Lahaina** (below), lunch on seafood at a waterfront restaurant and treat yourself in the evening to the **Old Lahaina Luau** (p328). Begin day two snorkeling with turtles at **Malu'aka Beach** (p367), followed by a picnic at glorious **Big Beach** (p368). In the afternoon hit **'Iao Valley State Park** (p353) and then head to **Pa'ia** (p369), with its eclectic cafés and shops. Set the alarm early on day three for the drive to **Haleakala National Park** (p403) to catch the sunrise and hike into the crater; reward your effort with a sunset dinner at **Mama's Fishhouse** (p373).

In Five Days
Give yourself a full day to enjoy the jaw-droppingly beautiful **Road to Hana** (p373). Bring it back to the water on day five, taking a whale-watching **cruise** (p324) in the morning and letting the wind sail you across **Kanaha Beach** (p347) in the afternoon.

In One Week
With one week you've got time to explore the **Upcountry's** (p393) gardens and cloud-forest trails, **kayak** (p359) along the south Maui coast, take a snorkel or dive outing to **Molokini** (p311), and catch a Hawaiian music concert at the **Maui Arts & Cultural Center** (p348).

Alternative Maui
Starting by booking a room at **Hale Akua Shangri-la** (p374) in Huelo. Join in morning meditation at the **Maui Tibetan Buddhist Dharma Center** (p371) in Pa'ia. Catch a yoga class or let your chi flow in an ecstatic dance session at **Studio Maui** (p398). Breathe in some aromatherapy on a tour of the **Ali'i Kula Lavender Farm** (p400) and follow it up with a visit to Maui's spiritual power point, **Haleakala summit** (p407). Finally, head to Hana for a night in a yurt and a relaxing massage in a garden setting at **Luana Spa Retreat** (p380).

MAUI

and prices are competitive. Typical 30-minute tours of the West Maui Mountains cost around $125 and one-hour circle-island tours cost about $250. Be aware that not every seat is a window seat; ask about seating policies before making reservations to avoid disappointment.

Some established companies:
Alex Air (☎ 871-0721)
Blue Hawaiian (☎ 871-8844)
Sunshine Helicopters (☎ 871-6135)

LAHAINA

pop 18,000
With its mountain backdrop and breezy seaside setting, Lahaina has been a magnet for travelers since ancient times. Much of what Maui has to offer reaches its peak in this old town, which still takes its appearance from its whaling-era past. The island's top chef-driven restaurants, Maui's finest luau and its largest collection of historic sites are all found here –

and that's just for starters. Maui's hottest festivals are held in the heart of Lahaina – some so huge they literally take over the entire mile-long waterfront. And should you want to take some of the fun out onto the water, a harborful of cruises, whale-watcher boats and dive trips are just steps away.

In the evening a magnificent ball of fire descends upon the harbor, casting a glow over the neighboring island of Lana'i. Nearly every dinner restaurant along shoreline Front St boasts a stellar sunset view – sit back with a frosty drink and have yourself a Kodak moment.

HISTORY
Lahaina has long been at the heart of the action. In ancient times it housed a royal court for high chiefs and it was the breadbasket – or, more accurately, the breadfruit basket – of west Maui. After Kamehameha the Great unified the islands he chose Lahaina as his base, and the capital remained there until 1845. The first Christian missionaries arrived in the 1820s and within a decade Hawaii's first stone

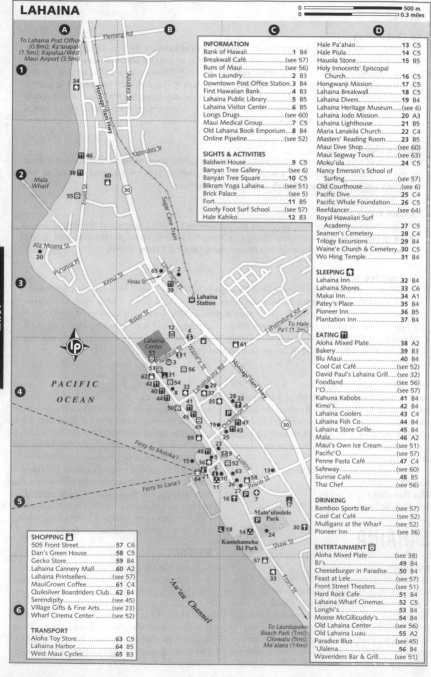

LAHAINA

0 — 500 m
0 — 0.3 miles

To Lahaina Post Office
(0.8mi); Ka'anapali
(1.5mi); Kapalua/West
Maui Airport (3.5mi)

Fleming Rd

Mala
Wharf

PACIFIC
OCEAN

Ferry to Moloka'i

Ferry to Lana'i

'Au'au Channel

To Launiupoko
Beach Park (1mi);
Olowalu (5mi);
Ma'alaea (14mi)

Malu'uluolele
Park

Kamehameha
Iki Park

MAUI

INFORMATION
Bank of Hawaii.........................1 B4
Breakwall Café.................(see 57)
Buns of Maui...................(see 56)
Coin Laundry.........................2 B3
Downtown Post Office Station.3 B4
First Hawaiian Bank................4 B3
Lahaina Public Library..........5 B5
Lahaina Visitor Center...........6 B5
Longs Drugs.....................(see 60)
Maui Medical Group.............7 C5
Old Lahaina Book Emporium...8 B4
Online Pipeline.................(see 52)

SIGHTS & ACTIVITIES
Baldwin House.......................9 C5
Banyan Tree Gallery.........(see 6)
Banyan Tree Square.............10 B4
Bikram Yoga Lahaina..........(see 51)
Brick Palace.......................(see 5)
Fort...................................11 B5
Goofy Foot Surf School.....(see 57)
Hale Kahiko.......................12 B3

SHOPPING
505 Front Street.................57 C6
Dan's Green House..............58 C5
Gecko Store........................59 B4
Lahaina Cannery Mall.........60 A2
Lahaina Printsellers.........(see 57)
MauiGrown Coffee...............61 C4
Quiksilver Boardriders Club..62 B4
Serendipity.....................(see 45)
Village Gifts & Fine Arts....(see 23)
Wharf Cinema Center........(see 52)

TRANSPORT
Aloha Toy Store...................63 C5
Lahaina Harbor...................64 B5
West Maui Cycles.................65 B3

Hale Pa'ahao.......................13 C5
Hale Piula..........................14 C5
Hauola Stone......................15 B5
Holy Innocents' Episcopal
  Church............................16 C5
Hongwanji Mission...............17 C5
Lahaina Breakwall...............18 C5
Lahaina Divers....................19 B4
Lahaina Heritage Museum....(see 6)
Lahaina Jodo Mission..........20 A3
Lahaina Lighthouse.............21 B5
Maria Lanakila Church.........22 C4
Masters' Reading Room.........23 B5
Maui Dive Shop.................(see 60)
Maui Segway Tours...........(see 63)
Moku'ula...........................24 C5
Nancy Emerson's School of
  Surfing..........................(see 57)
Old Courthouse.................(see 6)
Pacific Dive.......................25 C5
Pacific Whale Foundation.....26 C5
Reefdancer.....................(see 64)
Royal Hawaiian Surf
  Academy.........................27 C5
Seamen's Cemetery.............28 C4
Trilogy Excursions...............29 B4
Waine'e Church & Cemetery..30 C5
Wo Hing Temple..................31 B4

SLEEPING
Lahaina Inn........................32 B4
Lahaina Shores...................33 C6
Makai Inn..........................34 A1
Patey's Place......................35 B4
Pioneer Inn........................36 B5
Plantation Inn....................37 B4

EATING
Aloha Mixed Plate...............38 A2
Bakery...............................39 B3
Blu Maui...........................40 B4
Cool Cat Café...................(see 52)
David Paul's Lahaina Grill...(see 32)
Foodland.........................(see 56)
I'O.................................(see 57)
Kahuna Kabobs...................41 B4
Kimo's..............................42 B4
Lahaina Coolers...................43 C4
Lahaina Fish Co..................44 B4
Lahaina Store Grille.............45 B4
Mala................................46 A2
Maui's Own Ice Cream.......(see 51)
Pacific'O.........................(see 57)
Penne Pasta Café.................47 C4
Safeway..........................(see 60)
Sunrise Café.......................48 B5
Thai Chef........................(see 56)

DRINKING
Bamboo Sports Bar.............(see 57)
Cool Cat Café...................(see 52)
Mulligans at the Wharf.......(see 52)
Pioneer Inn.....................(see 36)

ENTERTAINMENT
Aloha Mixed Plate..............(see 38)
BJ's.................................49 B4
Cheeseburger in Paradise.....50 B4
Feast at Lele....................(see 57)
Front Street Theaters.........(see 51)
Hard Rock Cafe....................51 B4
Lahaina Wharf Cinemas.......52 C5
Longhi's............................53 B4
Moose McGillicuddy's...........54 B4
Old Lahaina Center...........(see 56)
Old Lahaina Luau.................55 A2
Paradice Bluz..................(see 45)
'Ulalena...........................56 B4
Waveriders Bar & Grill.......(see 51)

church, first missionary school and first printing press were all in place in Lahaina.

In time Lahaina became the dominant port for whalers, not only in Hawaii but for the entire Pacific. The whaling years reached their peak in Lahaina in the 1840s, with hundreds of ships pulling into port each year. The town took on the whalers' boisterous nature, opening dance halls, bars and brothels. When the whaling industry fizzled in the 1860s, Lahaina became all but a ghost town. In the 1870s sugarcane came to Lahaina and it remained the backbone of the economy until tourism took over in the 1960s.

ORIENTATION

The focal point of Lahaina is its bustling small-boat harbor, backed by the old Pioneer Inn and Banyan Tree Sq. The main drag and tourist strip is Front St, which runs along the shoreline.

INFORMATION
Bookstores
Old Lahaina Book Emporium (☎ 661-1399; 834 Front St; ⊙ 10am-9pm Mon-Sat, to 6pm Sun) Bookworms, you're in for a feast at Maui's finest independent bookstore; new and used volumes, plus vintage Hawaiiana.

Emergency
Police (☎ 244-6400) For nonemergencies.
Police, Fire & Ambulance (☎ 911)

Internet Access
Breakwall Café (☎ 661-7220; 505 Front St; per 1st 10min $2, additional 10min $1; ⊙ 9am-5pm Mon-Sat) Quiet setting, good espresso and if you have your own laptop, wi-fi is free.
Buns of Maui (☎ 661-5407; Old Lahaina Center, 880 Front St; per min 8¢; ⊙ 7:30am-8:30pm) Only four computers, but you can't beat the price at this little café named for its yummy cinnamon rolls.
Online Pipeline (☎ 661-5575; 658 Front St; per min 10¢; ⊙ 9am-9pm, to midnight Fri & Sat) At the rear of Lahaina Wharf Cinemas. A roomful of speedy stations and no waits, though it can get noisy with gamers.

Laundry
Coin laundry (Limahana Pl; ⊙ 24hr) Opposite the bakery.

Libraries
Lahaina Public Library (☎ 662-3950; 680 Wharf St; ⊙ noon-8pm Tue, 9am-5pm Wed & Thu, 10:30am-4:30pm Fri & Sat)

Media
Lahaina News (☎ 667-7866; www.lahainanews.com) This free weekly, easily found around town, has the scoop on Lahaina's entertainment scene as well as local issues.

Medical Services
The Maui Memorial Medical Center in Wailuku (p350) is the nearest hospital in case of emergencies.
Longs Drugs (☎ 667-4384; Lahaina Cannery Mall, 1221 Honoapi'ilani Hwy; ⊙ 7am-midnight) Lahaina's largest pharmacy.
Maui Medical Group (☎ 249-8080; 130 Prison St; ⊙ 7:30am-9pm Mon-Fri, 8am-noon Sat & Sun) This clinic handles nonemergencies.

Money
Both banks have 24-hour ATMS.
Bank of Hawaii (☎ 661-8781; Old Lahaina Center, 880 Front St)
First Hawaiian Bank (☎ 661-3655; 215 Papalaua St)

Post
Downtown post office station (Old Lahaina Center, 32 Papalaua St; ⊙ 8:15am-4:15pm Mon-Fri) Central if you're in town, but longer lines and fewer parking spaces than Lahaina Post Office.
Lahaina post office (☎ 661-0904; 1760 Honoapi'ilani Hwy, Lahaina, HI 96761; ⊙ 8:30am-5pm Mon-Fri, 9am-1pm Sat) You'll have to go a couple of miles north of town near the Lahaina Civic Center to pick up general-delivery mail (held 30 days) sent to Lahaina.

Tourist Information
Lahaina Visitor Center (☎ 667-9193; www.visit lahaina.com; 648 Wharf St; ⊙ 9am-5pm) The cashier desk at the gift shop in the Old Courthouse doubles as the visitor information center and distributes a free Lahaina pocket guide.

SIGHTS
Many of Lahaina's top sights are clustered around the harbor, and most of the rest are either on Front St or within a couple of blocks of it. This makes Lahaina an ideal town to explore on foot. See p322 for a recommended walking tour.

Banyan Tree Square
You know a tree has stature when throngs of townsfolk gather each year to celebrate its birthday! Marking the center of Lahaina, this awesome banyan tree sprawls across the entire square and ranks as the largest banyan tree in the USA. Planted as a seedling

MAUI

on April 24, 1873 to commemorate the 50th anniversary of missionaries in Lahaina, the tree has become a virtual forest unto itself, with 16 major trunks and scores of horizontal branches reaching across the better part of an acre. It attracts playful kids who swing Tarzan-style on the aerial roots and meditative types seeking a break from the crowds on Front St.

Old Courthouse

Seaside of the banyan tree stands Lahaina's **old courthouse** (648 Wharf St), built in 1859. The location overlooking the bustling harbor was no coincidence. Smuggling was so rampant during the whaling era that officials deemed this the ideal spot to house the customs operations, the courthouse and the jail – all neatly wrapped into a single building. It also held the governor's office, and in 1898 the US annexation of Hawaii was formally concluded here.

The old jail in the basement has been turned into the **Banyan Tree Gallery** (☎ 661-0111; ⏱ 9am-5pm) and the cells that once held drunken sailors now display fine artwork. It's a fun place to walk through. One of the cells displays fascinating period photos showing the courthouse and banyan tree as they looked a century ago. All the art, jewelry and woodwork on sale here are creations of island artists who operate the gallery as a cooperative.

The inspired **Lahaina Heritage Museum** (☎ 667-1959; admission free; ⏱ 9am-5pm), operated by Lahaina Town Action Committee volunteers, displays changing exhibits that celebrate Lahaina's culture and history. The focus could be on anything from ancient Hawaiian society to 19th-century whaling, but whatever it is it's well worth the climb to the 2nd floor to check it out.

Wo Hing Temple

This two-story **temple** (☎ 661-5553; 858 Front St; admission $1; ⏱ 10am-4pm) opened in 1912 as a meeting hall for the Chinese benevolent society Chee Kung Tong. It provided Chinese immigrants a place to preserve their cultural identity, celebrate festivities and socialize in their native tongue.

After WWII Lahaina's ethnic Chinese population spread far and wide and the temple fell into decline. It was restored and turned into a museum in 1984. Inside you'll find period photos, a ceremonial dancing-lion costume and a Taoist shrine.

Whatever you do, don't miss the tin-roof cookhouse out back, which holds a little theater showing fascinating films of Hawaii shot by Thomas Edison in 1898 and 1906, soon after he invented the motion-picture camera. These grainy B&W shots capture poignant images of old Hawaii, with *paniolo* (Hawaiian cowhands) running their cattle, cane workers in the fields and everyday street scenes. Take a look at the wall behind the screen to find a collection of opium bottles unearthed during an excavation of the grounds.

Hale Pa'ahao

Hale Pa'ahao (which means Stuck-in-Irons House), Lahaina's old **prison** (☎ 667-1985; cnr Prison & Waine'e Sts; admission free; ⏱ 10am-4pm Mon-Sat), was built in 1852 by convicts who dismantled the old harborside fort and carted the stones here to construct the 8ft-high prison walls.

Inside one of the whitewashed cells you'll find an 'old seadog' mannequin spouting a recorded description of 'life in this here calaboose.' Another cell displays a list of arrests for the year 1855. The top three offenses were drunkenness (330 arrests), adultery and fornication (111), and 'furious riding' (89). Other wayward transgressions of the day included profanity, lascivious conduct, aiding deserting sailors and drinking '*awa* (kava moonshine).

Baldwin House

The oldest Western-style building in Lahaina is the **Baldwin House** (☎ 661-3262; 696 Front St; adult/family $3/5; ⏱ 10am-4pm), erected in 1834 by Reverend Dwight Baldwin, a missionary doctor. It served as both his home and Lahaina's first medical clinic. The coral and rock walls are a hefty 24in thick, which keeps the house cool year-round. The exterior walls are now plastered over, but you can get a sense of how they originally appeared by looking at the Masters' Reading Room next door.

Think your flight to Hawaii was long? It took the Baldwins 161 days to get here from their native Connecticut. These early missionaries traveled neither fast nor light, and the house still holds the collection of china and furniture they brought with them around the Horn. Also on display are some fine Hawaiian quilts and period clothing.

Waine'e Church

The first stone church in Hawaii, **Waine'e Church** (535 Waine'e St), was built in 1832 and cursed with a run of bad luck. First the steeple collapsed in 1858, then in 1894 royalists enraged that the minister supported Hawaii's annexation torched it to the ground. A second church, built to replace the original, burned in 1947, and the third was blown away in a storm a few years later. One might get the impression that the old Hawaiian gods didn't take kindly to the house of this foreign deity! The fourth version, however, has been standing since 1953 and still holds regular Sunday services.

The adjacent **cemetery** holds as much intrigue as the church. Here lie several notables: Governor Hoapili, who ordered the original church built; Queen Keopuolani, a wife of Kamehameha I; and Reverend William Richards, Lahaina's first missionary.

Library Grounds

At first glance you might not see much but a closer look reveals a treasure trove of obscure sights. The grounds of the **Lahaina Public Library** (☎ 662-3950; 680 Wharf St; ☺ noon-8pm Tue, 9am-5pm Wed & Thu, 10:30am-4:30pm Fri & Sat) were once the site of a royal taro field; Kamehameha III occasionally toiled in the mud here to instill in his subjects the dignity of labor.

Here, too, sat the first Western-style building in Hawaii, the **Brick Palace**, erected by Kamehameha I around 1800 so he could keep watch on arriving ships. Despite the grand name, this 'palace' was a simple two-story structure built by two ex-convicts from Botany Bay. All that remains today is the excavated foundation, on the *makai* (seaward) side of the library.

Walk to the nearby shoreline to see the **Hauola Stone**, a flat seat-shaped rock that the ancient Hawaiians believed emitted healing powers to those who sat upon it. To spot this water-worn stone, look to the right as you face the ocean – it's just above the water's surface, the middle of three lava stones. In the 14th and 15th centuries royal women sat on the stone while giving birth to the next generation of chiefs and royalty.

About 100ft to the south stands the **Lahaina Lighthouse**, which lays claims to being the oldest lighthouse in the Pacific. Commissioned in 1840 to aid whaling ships pulling into Lahaina, it shone with a beam fueled by sperm-whale oil. The current structure dates from 1916.

Hale Kahiko

The three thatched houses at **Hale Kahiko** (Lahaina Center, 900 Front St; admission free; ☺ 9am-6pm) replicate part of an ancient Hawaiian village. The location at the back of a shopping center isn't without its irony, but the site nonetheless offers an insightful glimpse of Hawaiian life before Western development swept the landscape.

The buildings are authentically constructed of ohia-wood posts, native pili grass thatch and coconut-fiber lashings. The grounds are planted in native flora that Hawaiians relied upon for food and medicinal purposes. Each *hale* (house) had a different function; one was used as family sleeping quarters, one as a men's eating house, and the third as a workshop where women made tapa. Inside you'll find gourd containers, woven baskets, poi pounders and other essentials of Hawaiian life.

Hale Pa'i

The cottage at the side of Lahainaluna High School, **Hale Pa'i** (☎ 667-7040; 980 Lahainaluna Rd; admission by donation; ☺ 10am-4pm Mon-Fri), housed Hawaii's first printing press. Although its primary mission was making the Bible available to Hawaiians, the press also produced other works, including the first Hawaiian botany book and, in 1834, Hawaii's first newspaper. Heavily used, the original Ramage press wore out in the 1850s, but several of the items printed from it are still on display. Should you want to try your hand as a 19th-century pressman, a replica of the original equipment can be used to hand-press your own copy of a page from the first Hawaiian primer. Reprints of amusing 'Temperance Maps' ($5) drawn by an early missionary to illustrate the perils of drunkenness make unique souvenirs.

Lahaina Jodo Mission

Enjoy a meditative moment at this **Buddhist mission** (12 Ala Moana St), where a 12ft-high bronze Buddha sits serenely in the courtyard looking out across the Pacific toward its homeland in Japan. The grounds contain a lofty pagoda and a 3-ton temple bell, Hawaii's largest, which is rung 11 times at 8pm daily.

ACTIVITIES

Lahaina is not known for its beaches, which are generally shallow and rocky. For swimming and snorkeling, head up the coast to

MAUI

RIGHTEOUS & ROWDY

Lahaina owes much of its period appearance to two diametrically opposed groups of New Englanders who landed in the 1820s. In 1823 William Richards, Lahaina's first missionary, converted Maui's native governor, Hoapili, to Christianity and persuaded him to pass laws against 'drunkenness and debauchery.' After months at sea sailors weren't looking for a prayer service when they pulled into port – to them there was 'no God west of the Horn.' Missionaries and whalers almost came to battle in 1827 when Governor Hoapili arrested a whaler captain for allowing women to board his ship. The crew retaliated by shooting cannonballs at Richards' house. The captain was released, but laws forbidding liaisons between seamen and Hawaiian women remained in force.

It wasn't until Governor Hoapili's death in 1840 that laws prohibiting liquor and prostitution were no longer enforced and whalers began to flock to Lahaina. Among the sailors who roamed Lahaina's streets was Herman Melville, who later penned *Moby Dick*.

---

neighboring Ka'anapali (p333). For boat tours, whale watching and other cruises, see p324.

Diving

Dive boats leave from Lahaina Harbor, with programs suited for all levels.

Lahaina Divers (☎ 667-7496, 800-998-3483; www.lahainadivers.com; 143 Dickenson St; 2-tank dives from $125; ☺ 6am-8pm), Maui's first PADI five-star center, offers a full menu of dives, from advanced night dives to 'discover scuba' dives for noncertified divers. The latter goes out to a reef thick with green turtles and makes a great intro to the sport.

Maui Dive Shop (☎ 661-5388, 800-542-3483; www.mauidiveshop.com; Lahaina Cannery Mall, 1221 Honoapi'ilani Hwy; dives from $90, courses from $350; ☺ 8am-9pm) is another reliable full-service operation with a dive geared for everyone.

Check out **Pacific Dive** (☎ 667-5331; www.pacificdive.com; 150 Dickenson St; shore dives from $59; ☺ 8am-5pm) if you just want an inexpensive dive from the beach.

Surfing

Lahaina makes a good spot to pick up surfing for the first time, with gentle waves and ideal conditions for beginners. The section of shoreline known as **Lahaina Breakwall**, north of Kamehameha Iki Park, is a favorite spot for novice surfers. Surfers also take to the waters just offshore from Launiupoko Beach Park (p330).

Several places in Lahaina offer surfing lessons for beginners. Most guarantee you'll be able to ride a wave after a two-hour lesson, or there's no charge. Rates vary depending upon the number of people in the class and the length of the lesson, but for a two-hour lesson

expect to pay about $55 in a small group, $150 for a private lesson.

Goofy Foot Surf School (☎ 244-9283; www.goofyfootsurfschool.com; 505 Front St; ☺ 7:30am-9pm Mon-Sat) does a fine job of combining fundamentals with fun. In addition to lessons, it runs daylong surf camps and rents boards to experienced surfers.

Besides honing a fine reputation for its instruction, **Royal Hawaiian Surf Academy** (☎ 276-7878; 117 Prison St; ☺ 8am-5pm) has the coolest T-shirts. Look familiar? MTV focused its lens on Royal Hawaiian's surf instructors for its 2007 *Living Lahaina* reality series.

Nancy Emerson, who was winning international surfing contests by the time she was 14, runs **Nancy Emerson's School of Surfing** (☎ 244-7873; www.mauisurfclinics.com; 505 Front St; ☺ 8am-5pm), the oldest surfing school on the island.

Yoga

If it's time to stretch and breathe deeply, bring your mat and pop in to **Bikram Yoga Lahaina** (☎ 250-1120; www.bikramyoga.com; Lahaina Center, 900 Front St; class $15; ☺ schedule varies). Classes include a daily morning session at 8am (9am Sunday).

WALKING TOUR

Explore Lahaina's fascinating past on this walking tour that takes you to a run of pivotal historical sites.

Stroll around **Banyan Tree Sq (1; p319)**, investigate the old courthouse (p320) and enjoy the view from the harbor before starting your walk at the west side of the square. The four cannons on the waterfront opposite the courthouse were raised from an 1816 shipwreck; in a comical twist, they now point at Lahaina's

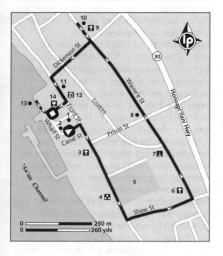

small-boat harbor, which is jam-packed with sunset sailboats and windjammers.

At the corner of Wharf and Canal Sts, you'll see a reconstructed section of coral wall from an 1832 **fort (2)** built to keep rowdy whalers in line. Each day at dusk a Hawaiian sentinel beat a drum to alert sailors to return to their ships. Those who didn't make it back in time ended up imprisoned in the fort. In 1854 the fort was dismantled and its coral blocks were used to build the new prison.

Continue up Canal St, which takes its name from the canal system that once ran through Lahaina. An enterprising US consul officer built the canal in the 1840s to allow whalers easier access to freshwater supplies – for a fee, of course. The canal turned into a breeding ground for mosquitoes, so it was eventually filled in. The mosquito, incidentally, was introduced to Hawaii via the water barrels the whalers brought from North America.

Turn right on Front St to reach **Holy Innocents' Episcopal Church (3**; 561 Front St), which has an interior splashed in a Hawaiiana motif, including paintings on the koa altar depicting a fisher in an outrigger canoe and Hawaiian farmers harvesting taro. Until the turn of the

20th century, the church property was the site of a vacation home belonging to Hawaii's last monarch, Queen Lili'uokalani.

Just south of the church you'll find a grassy building foundation, all that remains of **Hale Piula (4)**, Lahaina's halfhearted attempt at a royal palace. The construction was abandoned in the 1830s because Kamehameha III preferred to sleep in a Hawaiian-style thatched house. When it came to stones, Hawaiians were the ultimate recyclers and the palace was dismantled, the stone blocks used to build the harborside courthouse.

Across the street is **Malu'uluolele Park (5)**, which once contained a pond with a central island, Moku'ula, that was home to ancient kings and the site of an ornate burial chamber. Despite its history, the pond was buried, and today it's a county park with basketball courts, tennis courts, a baseball field and not a hint of its fascinating past.

Turn left on Shaw St, then left on Waine'e St to reach **Waine'e Church (6**; p321). Stroll the old cemetery adjacent to the church, where several of the most important figures in 19th-century Maui are buried. Evocative inscriptions and photo cameos adorn many of the old tombstones.

Next up, as you continue north, is **Hongwanji Mission (7**; 551 Waine'e St), a Buddhist temple dating to 1904. You'll find one of Lahaina's more notorious sights, **Hale Pa'ahao (8**; p320), on the corner of Prison St. Here you can take a peek into the old prison cells where drunken whalers once served time for debauchery.

Continue north along Waine'e St to Dickenson St to reach **Maria Lanakila Church (9)**, Maui's first Catholic church, which dates to 1846 and has a tile-work portrait of Father Damien. Adjacent to the church is the **Seamen's Cemetery (10)**, which despite its name has only one seaman's tombstone that can be identified. However, historical records indicate that numerous sailors from the whaling era were buried here, including a shipmate of Herman Melville's from the *Acushnet*.

From here, walk down Dickenson St toward the harbor. On the corner of Front and Dickenson Sts is the **Masters' Reading Room (11)**, which during Lahaina's whaling heyday served as an officers club. From here captains could keep an eye on rabble-rousing in the harbor across the road. The original construction of coral and stone block remains intact, and it's now home to the Lahaina Restoration

MAUI

LAHAINA FOR NA KEIKI

Kids will find some fun sights, beginning with that awesome **banyan tree** (p319), whose dangling aerial roots invite at least one Tarzan-style swing. The **Sugar Cane Train** (below) makes a popular family outing, especially for the little ones. Or let *na keiki* (children) try their hand at surfing, taking a lesson from kid-friendly **Goofy Foot Surf School** (p322). And there are plenty of other water activities, including wintertime **whale-watching cruises** (below). Head to neighboring **Ka'anapali** (p333) for fun on the beach and good snorkeling.

Foundation, the group instrumental in preserving Lahaina's historical sites. Next door is the **Baldwin House** (12; p320), a former missionary home turned museum.

Cross the road to return to the harbor, stopping to view the **Brick Palace** (13; p321) and the Hauola Stone (p321), waterfront sights at the rear of the library.

Cap off your tour with a cold drink at the atmospheric **Pioneer Inn** (14; p327), the most prominent landmark on the harborfront. For half a century this veranda-wrapped building was Lahaina's only hotel; Jack London once slept here. It's got a whaling-era atmosphere, with swinging doors, ship figureheads and signs warning against womanizing in the rooms. Actually, the inn was built in 1901, long after the whaling days ended, but nobody seems to notice or care.

TOURS

Lahaina Harbor brims with catamarans and other vessels catering to the tourist trade. You'll find scores of day cruises, from whale-watchers and glass-bottomed boats to daylong sails to Lana'i.

Atlantis Submarine (☎ 667-2224, 800-548-6262; www.atlantisadventures.com; adult/child under 12 $84/42) See the world from a porthole aboard this 65ft sub that dives to a depth of 130ft to see coral, tropical fish and the sunken *Carthaginian*, a sailing brig that played a leading role in the 1965 movie *Hawaii*. Tours depart from 9am to 2pm from Lahaina Harbor.

Maui Segway Tours (☎ 662-0888; www.mauisegway tours.com; 640 Front St; 2hr tour $79; ⊙ 8am-5pm) Geek alert: sightseeing tours via a Segway scooter leave opposite Banyan Tree Sq, go as far as Mala Wharf and take

in Lahaina's historical sights. Ah, c'mon, you know you've always wanted to try one...

Pacific Whale Foundation (☎ 879-8811, 800-942-5311; www.pacificwhale.org; 612 Front St; adult/child 7-12 $32/16; ⊙ 6am-6pm) This nonprofit foundation offers several cruises, all with a bent on learning more about the marine environment. In winter its whale-watchers sail out of Lahaina Harbor several times daily. In the unlikely event you don't spot whales, your next trip is free – and kids under six years are always free.

Reefdancer (☎ 667-2133; Lahaina Harbor; adult/child 7-12 per 1hr $33/19, 1½hr $45/25) A cheaper alternative to the submarine, this glass-bottomed boat has a submerged lower deck lined with underwater viewing windows. Departures are from 10am to 2:15pm.

Sugar Cane Train (☎ 667-6851; www.mauisteamtrain .com; 975 Limahana Pl; adult/child 3-12 $20/14; ⊙ 10am-4pm) Fully restored, the century-old steam train that once carried cane from the fields to Lahaina's sugar mill now carries tourists on a 30-minute ride between Lahaina and Ka'anapali. The ride's a bit pokey and there's not really much to see, but kids will love it and steam-train buffs will no doubt want to hop aboard.

Trilogy Excursions (☎ 661-4743, 888-225-6284; www .sailtrilogy.com; 180 Lahainaluna Rd; adult/child 3-15 $179/90) This top-notch family-run operation specializes in ecofriendly catamaran tours that let you get your feet wet. The early daylong (6am to 4pm) trip from Lahaina to Lana'i's Hulopo'e Beach includes a BBQ lunch, volleyball on the beach and snorkeling time, or catch the 10am boat that adds on dinner and sails back to Lahaina at sunset. In winter there's whale watching along the way and you can spot spinner dolphins year-round. Save 10% by booking online.

FESTIVALS & EVENTS

Mauians love a party and Lahaina is party central. The top festivals draw huge crowds, with Front St closed to traffic during the events. For updated details on Lahaina festivities, contact the **LahainaTown Action Committee** (☎ 667-9194; www.visitlahaina.com).

Chinese New Year Lahaina welcomes the lunar new year – on a weekend between mid-January and mid-February – with a street festival on Front St, complete with colorful lion dances, martial-arts demos and an explosion of firecrackers.

Ocean Arts Festival The migration of humpback whales is the theme of these festivities celebrated on the second weekend in March at Banyan Tree Sq with Hawaiian music, hula and games.

Banyan Tree Birthday Party Branch out a bit! Lahaina's favorite tree gets a two-day birthday party, complete with a frosted cake and a serenade by island musicians. It's held on the weekend closest to April 24.

International Festival of Canoes (www.mauicanoe fest.com) Maui's premier cultural event draws master carvers from around the Pacific who descend on Lahaina to carve outrigger canoes. The whole log-to-launch process takes place right in the town center, beginning in mid-May. The event ends on the last Saturday in May with the Parade of Canoes down Front St and ceremonial launchings from Kamehameha Iki Park. Festivities include Hawaiian music and island grinds. Don't miss it.

Kamehameha Celebration Native Hawaiians on horseback, marching bands and floral floats take to Front St to honor King Kamehameha the Great on this public holiday in mid-June.

Fourth of July Bands perform tunes on the lawn of the public library from 6pm and fireworks light up the sky over the harbor at 8pm.

A Taste of Lahaina At Maui's biggest culinary blast, held in early September, the island's top chefs strut their stuff, offering tastings of their signature dishes to festivalgoers. In addition to the food booths, there's a country store selling those 'secret ingredients' that chefs rely on, and a beverage garden. And it's not just a foodies' fest. Music has come into its own in this annual event, attracting the island's best musicians and turning it into an upbeat party scene.

Halloween in Lahaina The biggest bash of them all, dubbed 'Mardi Gras of the Pacific,' attracts a whopping 30,000 revelers to a street festival of music, dancing and costume contests on October 31. All the action is on Front St. Forget parking; take a bus or taxi to this one.

Holiday Lighting of the Banyan Tree Lahaina lights Hawaii's biggest tree on the first weekend in December with thousands of colorful lights, accompanied by music and a craft show. And, of course, Santa will be there for the *keiki*.

SLEEPING

Despite the flood of tourists that fill its streets, Lahaina doesn't have that many places to stay. All of west Maui's resort hotels are to the north. The nearest campground (p332) is in Olowalu, 5 miles south of town. See p332 for midrange B&Bs between Lahaina and Ka'anapali.

Budget

Patey's Place (☎ 667-0999; www.alternative-hawaii.com /affordable/maui.htm; 761 Waine'e St; dm $25, s/d $65/75, with shared bathroom $45/55; P 💻) Lahaina's only hostel, Patey's occupies an aging building, offering basic accommodations. It has separate dorms for men and women. There are also private rooms, but unless you need to be in Lahaina, you'll find better value elsewhere on the island. Guests have access to a common

kitchen, coin-operated laundry facilities and internet facilities ($6 per hour).

Midrange

Makai Inn (☎ 662-3200; www.makaiinn.net; 1415 Front St; r $95-156; P) A 20-minute walk from the town center, this family-run place is a gem. Although it's an older condo complex, the rooms are bright and breezy, with oceanfront lanai and Hawaiian decor throughout. The tropical garden in the central courtyard would be the envy of any top-end resort. All units have full kitchens. The main price difference is the distance from the ocean, but even the cheapest option is a mere stone's throw from the water.

Lahaina Inn (☎ 661-0577, 800-669-3444; www .lahainainn.com; 127 Lahainaluna Rd; r incl breakfast $105-120, ste $150; P 🐾) History buffs, you're in for a treat. Crazy Shirts founder Rick Ralston spent millions restoring this century-old streetside inn to its original character. Rooms are small but delightfully atmospheric, with Hawaiian quilts and antique furnishings. To keep the period ambience intact, rooms are sans TV. Parking costs $5.

Pioneer Inn (☎ 661-3636, 800-457-5457; www.pioneer innmaui.com; 658 Wharf St; r $135-175, ste $165-185; 🐾 💻) It can be noisy from the traffic and raucous bar, but this historic two-story hotel couldn't be more in the middle of the action. Unfortunately, the funky old harbor-front rooms for which the inn was famous are gone. Instead, small motel-style rooms face the busy streets. Considering the size of the rooms and the less-than-soundproof walls, it's pricey unless you find an online deal.

Plantation Inn (☎ 667-9225, 800-433-6815; www .theplantationinn.com; 174 Lahainaluna Rd; r incl breakfast $160-225, ste $235-265; P 🐾 💻) Encompassing a quiet courtyard, this two-story Victorian-style inn radiates period elegance. Its plantation charm is accented with rocking chairs on the porch, four-poster beds in the rooms and antiques throughout. Breakfast is provided at Gerard's, the inn's upscale French restaurant.

Lahaina Shores (☎ 661-3339, 800-642-6284; www .lahainashores.com; 475 Front St; studios/1 bedroom from $200/275; P 🐾 💻) The only oceanfront condo complex in central Lahaina that's run like a hotel. Guests are within a stone's throw of Lahaina's top restaurants, and the beach out back has nighttime entertainment and good conditions for beginner surfers. The units are

MAUI

roomy, and even the studios have full kitchen and lanai. Parking costs $3.

EATING

Lahaina teems with wonderful places to eat. Whether you're looking for local grinds or five-toque nouvelle cuisine, it's all here. Just be aware that as so many folks staying in Ka'anapali pour into Lahaina at dinnertime, the traffic often jams up, so give yourself extra time and call ahead to make reservations.

Budget

Bakery (☎ 667-9062; 991 Limahana Pl; snacks $1.50-5.50; ☯ 5:30am-1pm Mon-Fri, to noon Sat) Don't be deterred by its stark warehouse appearance – on the other side of the rickety screen door you'll find superb French breads, flaky pastries, huge pizza slices and tasty sandwiches made to order.

Maui's Own Ice Cream (☎ 667-2663; Lahaina Center, 900 Front St; s dip $3; ☯ 11am-10pm Mon-Fri, 1-10pm Sat, noon-5pm Sun) Tip a cone to Maui-made Rose-lani ice cream in luscious tropical flavors, like chocolate macadamia nut and passion fruit sorbet.

Aloha Mixed Plate (☎ 661-3322; 1285 Front St; plates $4-14; ☯ 10:30am-10pm) Hands down, the best place on Maui to enjoy a Hawaiian-style meal in a beachside setting. Go local with the Hawaiian plate lunch brimming with *kalua* (traditional method of cooking in an underground pit) pig, *lomilomi* salmon (minced, salted salmon, diced tomato and green onion) and other taste treats. And then there are the award-winning coconut prawns – order them as a *pupu* (snack or appetizer) or as part of a mixed plate, but don't go away without trying them.

Sunrise Café (☎ 661-8558; 693-A Front St; mains $6-11; ☯ 6am-4pm) Sit on the little lanai and watch the morning harbor action at this cozy hole-in-the-wall. Locals rave about the eggs, Portuguese sausage and fruit plate ($7), and Sunrise also makes good breakfast burritos and decadent chocolate pancakes. At lunch it's salads and sandwiches.

Penne Pasta Café (☎ 661-6633; 180 Dickenson St; mains $7-15; ☯ 11am-9:30pm Mon-Fri, 5-9:30pm Sat & Sun) It's a simple place on a side street rather than the main drag, but that helps keep prices low, and you can dine alfresco at streetside tables. Think Italian without the hefty calories – fresh salads, tasty flatbread pizzas, gluten-free brown-rice pasta are the highlights. All in all, it's excellent value.

Cool Cat Café (☎ 667-0908; Wharf Cinema Center, 658 Front St; meals $8-12; ☯ 11am-10pm) Maui's top-rated burger, hand-patted 100% Angus beef, with the price depending on how you want to load it up. The open-air café, on the 3rd floor, overlooks Banyan Tree Sq.

Kahuna Kabobs (☎ 661-9999; 884 Front St; meals $8-14; ☯ 9am-9:30pm) Tucked into a courtyard off Front St, this popular local eatery attracts surfers with its killer wrapped-'ahi (yellowfin tuna) sandwich and teriyaki kebabs. Vegetarians won't be disappointed with the 'veggie hipster' falafel wrap. Order at the window and chow down at one of the shaded café tables.

Lahaina Store Grille (☎ 661-9090; 744 Front St; mains $9-30; ☯ 11am-10pm, oyster bar till midnight) Classy and contemporary, this grill and oyster bar specializes in briny delights from the sea. Tequila-glazed shrimp, raw oysters, *poke* (cubed raw fish mixed with shoyu, sesame oil, salt, chili pepper, inamona or other condiments) – you name it, they've got it. Come after 5pm when the rooftop garden opens and watch the lights twinkle over Lahaina.

Thai Chef (☎ 667-2814; Old Lahaina Center, 880 Front St; mains $10-16; ☯ lunch 11am-2pm Mon-Fri, dinner from 5pm daily) Hidden in the back of a shopping center, the place looks like a dive from the outside, but the food is incredible. Start with the fragrant ginger coconut soup and the crispy spring rolls and then move on to savory curries that explode with flavor. Plenty of luscious choice for vegetarians and carnivores alike.

Foodland (☎ 661-0975; Old Lahaina Center, 880 Front St; ☯ 6am-midnight) and **Safeway** (☎ 667-4392; Lahaina Cannery Mall, 1221 Honoapi'ilani Hwy; ☯ 24hr) super-markets both have delis that sell all you need for a picnic lunch.

Midrange

Lahaina Coolers (☎ 661-7082; 180 Dickenson St; break-fast & lunch $7-13, dinner mains $12-25; ☯ 8am-2am) Whether you swing by early in the morning or after the dance floor has emptied, this ec-lectic open-air restaurant always has a crowd. You can mix and match an endless variety of omelette options and opt to have breakfast any time of the day. Other top choices include the tasty *kalua* pig tacos, creative pizzas and Kula green salads.

Kimo's (☎ 661-4811; 845 Front St; lunch $8-13, dinner $17-29; ☯ 11am-10:30pm) At this Hawaiian-style standby, you'll not only find reliable food and a fine water view, but the place is large and lively enough that the kids can relax and be themselves. All the usual fresh fish, steak and chicken dinners come with warm carrot muffins and a Caesar salad. Lunch covers the gamut, from sandwiches and salads to the catch of the day.

Lahaina Fish Co (☎ 661-3472; 831 Front St; lunch $9-15, dinner $13-29; ⏰ 11am-10pm) Sit on the deck above crashing waves and enjoy some of Lahaina's freshest fish. And there's no slack on the serving size either – so it's little wonder this place packs a crowd. Lots of fish preparations to choose from, but if you want to walk away with the best value, order the fish-and-chips for just $13. Come early for a good table at sunset.

Blu Maui (☎ 661-9491; 839 Front St; lunch $11-15, dinner $15-30; ⏰ 10:30am-9:30pm) In a town that abounds in ocean views, this smart restaurant, which literally hangs over the water, takes first prize. A breezy blue and white decor and a solid Mediterranean-influenced menu also separate it from the pack. Crispy calamari, classic Greek salads and grilled lamb offer an interesting alternative to the more typical surf and turf menus along Front St.

Mala (☎ 667-9394; 1307 Front St; mains $14-30; ⏰ 11am-10pm Mon-Fri, 9am-10pm Sat, 9am-9pm Sun) It may be a new kid on the block, but this waterfront bistro is already winning awards. Mala fuses Spanish and Pacific influences in dishes like 'opakapaka (pink snapper) ceviche and black-bean Manila clams in a ginger sauce. Save room for the delightfully decadent 'caramel miranda' dessert. The best time to come is at night, when the tiki torches on the ocean lanai add a romantic touch.

Top End

Pacific'O (☎ 667-4341; 505 Front St; lunch $13-16, dinner $26-36; ⏰ 11am-4pm & 5:30-10pm) Terrific contemporary cuisine pair with a renowned wine list at this stylish seaside restaurant. The menu is bold and innovative – where else can you try a crispy coconut roll with seared scallops and arugula pesto? Lunch is a tamer affair, with salads and sandwiches, but the same in-your-face ocean view. Live dinnertime jazz on the weekends cranks the hip atmosphere up a notch.

I'O (☎ 661-8422; 505 Front St; mains $28-36; ⏰ 5:30-10pm) Lahaina's hottest fine-dining waterfront restaurant is chef James McDonald's cutting-edge venture into nouveau Hawaiian cuisine. It shares the same view as its adjacent sister

---

IT'S PERFECTLY CLEAR

Here's a riddle: what starts a mile under the waves, costs $35 a bottle and will give you a head-spinning high?

It's Ocean, a new distilled-on-Maui vodka made with desalinated water drawn from the depths of the ocean. It's become the hottest spirit in Maui bars and fine restaurants. Order it up, or buy a bottle in local stores. Passion-fruit screwdriver, anyone?

---

operation, Pacific'O, but the menu doesn't drift quite as far and wide. Standouts include the crab cakes with goat cheese, seared fresh catch in lobster curry and 'cowboy ribs' with mango butter. If you dine early, you'll overhear the Feast at Lele luau (p328) on the beach below. Fierce martini menu, too.

David Paul's Lahaina Grill (☎ 667-5117; 127 Lahainaluna Rd; mains $28-41; ⏰ from 6pm; 🥄) The darling of gourmet magazines, this sophisticated restaurant in historic Lahaina Inn superbly blends local ingredients with tastes from Europe and the Pacific Rim. Standouts include Kona coffee–roasted rack of lamb and 'opakapaka in lobster-champagne sauce. Although the food gets rave reviews, service can be rushed, so be prepared to hold on to your plates.

DRINKING

Aloha Mixed Plate (☎ 661-3322; 1285 Front St; ⏰ 10:30am-10pm) This is the Hawaii you came to find. Off the main drag, at the north side of town, this beachside shack is pure fun. Let the sea breeze whip through your hair while lingering over a rainbow-colored tropical drink – come between 2pm and 6pm and they're half price. And at sunset you'll be able to hear Old Lahaina Luau's music beating next door.

Pioneer Inn (☎ 661-3636; 658 Wharf St; ⏰ 11am-10pm) This century-old landmark, with its whaling-era atmosphere and harborside veranda, makes for great people watching. Easily the most popular place for a drink in Lahaina. Guitarists playing soft rock or country music add to the mood at sunset.

Bamboo Sports Bar (☎ 667-0361; 505 Front St; ⏰ 11am-2am) Known as the place 'where locals hang loose,' this is where everyone, tourists and islanders alike, comes to watch sports on big-screen TV, shoot a game of pool and down a few cold beers along with Asian-style *pupu.*

Cool Cat Café (☎ 667-0908; Wharf Cinema Center, 658 Front St; ☼ 11am-10pm) The breezy open-air setting and cool '50s decor would make Elvis and Marilyn feel right at home. Whether you're looking for fountain drinks or hard-hitting cocktails, this is the perfect spot to whet the whistle as the sun sets over the harbor. Happy hour and live music at sunset.

Mulligans at the Wharf (☎ 661-8881; Wharf Cinema Center, 658 Front St; ☼ 11am-midnight) Lahaina's Irish pub has something for everyone – sports TV, Irish ales and live music. Happy hour is from 4pm to 6pm and again from 10pm through midnight.

ENTERTAINMENT

Much of what's happening on the island after dark happens in Lahaina, with Front St the center of the action. Check the free weeklies *Lahaina News* and *Maui Time*, both of which have extensive entertainment listings. Typically, nightspots in Lahaina don't have a cover charge unless there's a big-name performer. In addition to the places listed here, many of Lahaina's waterfront restaurants have live music at dinnertime.

Nightclubs

Moose McGillicuddy's (☎ 667-7758; 844 Front St) This place attracts the party crowd, out to drink and dance till they drop. With its two dance floors, Moose hops with DJs nightly and live music on weekends. Happy hour (3pm to 6pm) features piña coladas for a mere $2.

Waveriders Bar & Grill (☎ 661-1200; Lahaina Center, 900 Front St) Surfers and the 20-something crowd cruise in here for the nightly live music scene, which covers the gamut of styles from hip-hop to rock.

Cheeseburger in Paradise (☎ 661-4855; 811 Front St) You can hear the music a block away from this energetic open-air place on the waterfront. No surprise, the music's Jimmy Buffett style, and the setting is pure tropics from the rattan decor to the frosty margaritas. Live soft rock from 4:30pm to 10:30pm nightly.

Paradice Bluz (☎ 667-5299; 744 Front St) The dark interior of this cool jazz house sports black leather couches and red brick walls hung with paintings of legendary jazz greats. The music is jazz, blues, funk and R&B, with most of the live action on Friday and Saturday nights.

BJ's (☎ 661-0700; 730 Front St) This place boasts an ocean view and live music from 7:30pm to 10pm nightly. Incidentally, this was where the legendary 1970s Blue Max club partied.

Hard Rock Cafe (☎ 667-7400; Lahaina Center, 900 Front St) There's not much that's Hawaiian about this rock-themed chain restaurant, but it does get jiggy to the island's best reggae on Monday from 10pm.

Longhi's (☎ 667-2288; 888 Front St) This upscale Italian restaurant with its art deco decor and koa-wood dance floor has live music and dancing on Tuesday and Friday nights from 9:30pm. It tends to draw an older, well-heeled crowd.

Luau, Hula & Theater

You'll find some of the best shows on the island right here in Lahaina. Its two luau have few rivals anywhere in Hawaii (reservations are essential) and catching one is a sure bet to highlight a vacation.

Old Lahaina Luau (☎ 667-1998; www.oldlahainaluau .com; 1251 Front St; adult/child under 12 $85/55; ☼ 5:15-8:15pm) This is the real deal. Simply put, no other luau on Maui comes close to matching this one for its authenticity and all-around aloha. The hula troupe is first-rate and the feast is terrific, with high-quality Hawaiian fare and none of the long lines you'll find at a resort-hotel luau. It's held on the beach at the north side of town.

Feast at Lele (☎ 667-5353; www.feastatlele.com; 505 Front St; adult/child under 12 $99/69; ☼ 6-9pm) Cooked up by the award-winning chef at I'O restaurant, this Polynesian luau is an intimate beachside affair. Dance performances in Hawaiian, Maori, Tahitian and Samoan styles are each matched to a food course. With the Hawaiian music, you're served *kalua* pork and taro; with the Maori, duck salad with poha berry dressing; and so on. A true gourmet feast.

'Ulalena (☎ 661-9913; www.ulalena.com; Old Lahaina Center, 880 Front St; adult $48-68, child under 12 free with adult; ☼ 6:30pm Tue-Sat) Along the lines of a Cirque du Soleil–style show, this extravaganza has its home at the 700-seat Maui Theatre. The theme is Hawaiian history and storytelling; the medium is modern dance, brilliant stage sets, acrobats and elaborate costumes. All in all, an entertaining, high-energy performance.

And then there's free hula at the shopping centers. **Lahaina Cannery Mall** (☎ 661-5304; 1221 Honoapi'ilani Hwy), at the north side of town, presents hula shows at 1pm Saturday and Sun-

---

ART NIGHT

Art aficionados, this one's for you. Every Friday night is 'Art Night' in Lahaina. Dozens of galleries have openings, some with entertainment, wine and hors d'oeuvres. It's a great time to stroll the Front St art scene, meet artists and nibble a little cheese. The action's from 7pm to 10pm and it's all free – that is, unless you see a little treasure that catches your fancy.

---

day and 7pm Tuesday and Thursday. **Lahaina Center** (900 Front St) has hula shows at 2:30pm Wednesday and at 3:30pm Friday.

Cinemas

Two multiscreen theaters show first-run movies: **Lahaina Wharf Cinemas** (Wharf Cinema Center, 658 Front St) and **Front Street Theaters** (Lahaina Center, 900 Front St). For show times at either, call ☎ 249-2222.

SHOPPING

Art galleries, souvenir shops and boutiques run thick along Front St between the harbor and Papalaua St. And you'll find lots of shops under one roof at the **Wharf Cinema Center** (☎ 661-8748; 658 Front St) and **Lahaina Cannery Mall** (☎ 661-5304; 1221 Honoapi'ilani Hwy).

Banyan Tree Gallery (☎ 661-0111; 648 Wharf St) The nonprofit collective Lahaina Arts Society represents more than 100 island artists at this extensive gallery. The works run the gamut from avant-garde paintings to traditional weavings. Many of Maui's best-known artists got their start here, and there are some gems among the collection, so it's a good place to start your browsing.

Village Gifts & Fine Arts (☎ 661-5199; cnr Front & Dickenson Sts) This little shop in the Masters' Reading Room sells prints, wooden bowls and silkscreened fabrics, with a portion of the proceeds supporting the Lahaina Restoration Foundation.

Gecko Store (☎ 661-1078; 703 Front St) Everything sold here – T-shirts, toys, jewelry, you name it – crawls with friendly Hawaiian geckos. You'll be amazed at what geckos can do.

Dan's Green House (☎ 661-8412; 133 Prison St) Looking for an unusual souvenir? Dan's specializes in 'fuku-bonsai' – a mini-tree only a few inches high with its roots grown around a Hawaiian lava rock.

MauiGrown Coffee (☎ 661-2728; 277 Lahainaluna Rd; 6:30am-5pm Mon-Sat) On the mountain side of the highway, next to the former sugar mill's smokestack, this shop sells west Maui's newest homegrown crop, Ka'anapali Estate coffee. Buy it by the pound, or test it by the cup.

Quiksilver Boardriders Club (☎ 661-3505; 849 Front St) Whether you're a surfer looking for a board or just want to buy new threads with hip surfing motifs, Quiksilver is the place.

Lahaina Printsellers (☎ 667-5815; 505 Front St) Hawaii's largest purveyor of antique maps, including fascinating originals dating back to the days of Captain Cook; also sells affordable reproductions.

Serendipity (☎ 667-7070; 752 Front St) Brilliant sarongs and classy tropical wear for women, several notches above the competition.

GETTING THERE & AWAY

The Honoapi'ilani Hwy (Hwy 30) connects Lahaina with Ka'anapali and points north, with Ma'alaea to the south and Wailuku to the east. Ferries to Lana'i (p416) and Moloka'i (p433) dock at Lahaina Harbor.

GETTING AROUND
To/From the Airport

To get to Lahaina from the airport (p314) in Kahului, take Hwy 380 south to Hwy 30; by car or taxi, the drive takes about 45 minutes. Most visitors rent cars at Kahului airport, then drive to Lahaina; see p316. For information on taxi service from the airport, see p316.

Bicycle

For bike rental visit **West Maui Cycles** (☎ 661-9005; 1087 Limahana Pl; bicycles per day $20-50; 9:30am-5pm Mon-Sat, 10am-4pm Sun), which has quality road performance and mountain-bikes, as well as cheaper cruisers that are fine for just kicking around town.

Bus

The **Maui Bus** (www.mauicounty.gov/bus) connects Kahului and Lahaina ($1, one hour) with a stop at Ma'alaea, where connections can be made to Kihei and Wailea. Another route connects Lahaina and Ka'anapali ($1, 30 minutes). Both routes depart from the Wharf Cinema Center hourly from 6:30am to 8:30pm.

Car & Motorcycle

If it's got two wheels and a motor, you can bet you'll find it at **Aloha Toy Store** (☎ 662-0888; 640

Front St; 8am-5pm), which rents mopeds ($65 per day), Kawasaki motorcycles ($119) and Harleys ($149), and even offers tours (p324) on Segways.

PARKING
Much of Front St has free on-street parking, but there's always a line of cruising cars competing for spots. Your best bet is the large parking lot at the corner of Front and Prison Sts, where there's free public parking with a three-hour limit. There are also a few private parking lots, averaging $5 per day, with the biggest one being Republic Parking on Dickenson St. Otherwise, park at one of the shopping centers and get your parking ticket validated for free by making a purchase.

Taxi
For a taxi, call **Ali'i Cab** (661-3688), **LA Taxi** (661-4545) and **Paradise Taxi** (661-4455), which operate out of Lahaina.

WEST MAUI

Backed by pleated mountains and fronted by a sea full of adventures, west Maui lures more visitors than any other part of the island. It lays claim to gorgeous beaches, exceptional restaurants and the legendary whaling town of Lahaina (p317).

A 10-mile stretch of beachside resorts runs north from flashy Ka'anapali to exclusive Kapalua, home to one of the nation's top golf courses. In addition to megahotels and waterfront condos, the honeymoon crowd will find romantic inns and intimate B&Bs.

Surfers, snorkelers and divers, gear up – there's top-notch action along this coast. Not that you need to jump in to appreciate everything that happens in the water. West Maui is whale-watch central, home to a fleet of sailboats offering unforgettable cruises. Or just book one of those seaside condos and watch the whales cruise by as you lounge on your balcony and sip a mai tai (alcoholic drink made from rum, grenadine, and lemon and pineapple juices).

LAHAINA TO MA'ALAEA
The stretch between Lahaina and Ma'alaea offers fine mountain scenery, but during winter everyone is craning their necks toward the water as they drive along the highway. This is the road that gave rise to Maui's popular bumper sticker 'I brake for whales.' During winter humpback whales occasionally breach as close as 100yd from the coast. Forty tons of leviathan suddenly exploding straight up through the water can be a real showstopper! Unfortunately, some drivers whose heads are drawn oceanward by the sight hit their brakes and others don't, making for high rear-ender potential. Beach parks and pull-offs along the road offer some great vantages for watching the action.

Puamana & Launiupoko Beach Parks
Shady **Puamana Beach Park**, about 1.5 miles south of Lahaina, is rocky but it sometimes has good conditions for beginning surfers – otherwise it's mostly a quick stop for a seaside view, particularly at sunset.

Better yet is **Launiupoko Beach Park**, where even the rest rooms glow with murals of young surfers hitting the waves. The south side of the beach has small waves ideal for beginning surfers, while the north side ratchets it up a notch for those who have honed their skills. Not that surfing is all that happens here – keiki have a blast wading in the large rock-enclosed shoreline pool and good picnic facilities make it an ideal spot for families. Launiupoko is at the traffic lights at the 18-mile marker.

Olowalu
The West Maui Mountains form a scenic backdrop, giving Olowalu its very name, which means 'many hills' in Hawaiian. The tiny village is marked by the Olowalu General Store and a fine chef-driven French restaurant, both at the 15-mile marker.

SIGHTS & ACTIVITIES
When the ocean is calm, **snorkelers** take to the water near the 14-mile marker. The coral reef is large and shallow, so the potential is there, but it's often silty and 'Sharks May Be Present' signs lining the beach may give would-be snorkelers pause.

A dirt road starting behind the general store leads to the **Olowalu Petroglyphs**. Go around the north side of the store, park just beyond the water tower and look for the signposted gate. A quarter-mile walk leads up this hot, open road to the petroglyphs. It's easy to follow; just keep the cinder cone straight ahead of you as you go. As with most of Maui's extant petroglyphs, these figures are carved into the

WEST MAUI

0 —————— 5 km
0 —————— 3 miles

A **B** **C** **D**

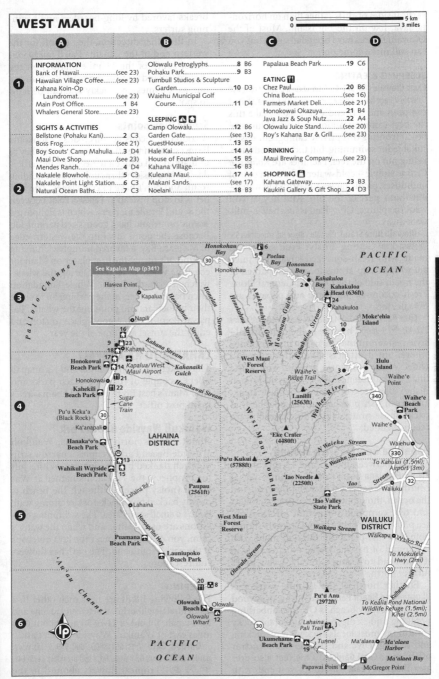

See Kapalua Map (p341)

vertical sides of cliffs rather than on horizontal lava, like on the Big Island. Most of the Olowalu figures have been damaged, but you can still make some out.

SLEEPING & EATING

Camp Olowalu (☎ 661-4303; www.campolowalu.com; 800 Olowalu Village Rd; campsite per person $10) Oceanfront camping and a friendly caretaker make this the best camping option in west Maui. The beach fronting this private campground isn't suitable for swimming, but there's good snorkeling out on the reef. Facilities are *Robinson Crusoe* simple – cold-water showers, a pair of outhouses, picnic tables and drinking water – but that's part of the fun. And hey, if you want to splurge, Chez Paul is just half-a-mile walk away.

Olowalu Juice Stand (Olowalu Village Rd; smoothies $5; ❤️ 9am-5pm) Getting thirsty? Fruit smoothies made with fresh-squeezed sugarcane juice are whipped up at this food truck parked at the north side of the Olowalu General Store. Fresh coconuts, pineapple and papayas are for sale, too.

Chez Paul (☎ 661-3843; 820 Olowalu Village Rd; mains $32-44; ❤️ 5-9pm) This fine French provincial–style restaurant may be in the middle of nowhere, but it attracts diners from far and wide. While old-world artwork and white linen add ambience, it's the classic French dishes like rack of lamb, béarnaise steak, and fresh fish poached in champagne that packs those pretty tables. Reservations are recommended.

Papalaua Beach Park & Around

Midway between the 11- and 12-mile markers is **Papalaua Beach Park**, a nothing-special county park squeezed between the road and the ocean, though it does have firepits, toilets and tent camping (for permit information, see p309) under kiawe trees. Campers should note that this place can buzz all night with the sound of passing traffic – better to skip it and head to Camp Olowalu, a few miles further north.

Further north at the 12-mile marker is **Ukumehame Beach Park**. Shaded by ironwood trees, this sandy beach is OK for sunbathing or taking a quick dip, but because of the rocky conditions most locals stick with picnicking and fishing. Dive and snorkel boats anchor offshore at **Coral Gardens**. This reef also creates **Thousand Peaks** toward its west end, with

breaks favored by long-boarders and beginning surfers.

In the other direction, the pull-off for the western end of the Lahaina Pali Trail (p355) is just south of the 11-mile marker, on the *mauka* (inland) side of the road. Keep an eye out, as it comes up quickly and can be hard to spot.

Scenic Viewpoints

A couple of inconspicuous roadside lookouts lie just south of the 10-mile marker, but they're unmarked and difficult to negotiate in traffic – don't even consider them unless you're heading south and don't have to cross lanes. The best bet is to stop instead at **Papawai Point** between the 8- and 9-mile markers, which is signposted 'scenic point' and has a good-sized parking lot. Because the point juts into the western edge of Ma'alaea Bay, a favored humpback nursing ground, it's one of the best places on Maui for coastline whale watching. During the whale-watch season, the Pacific Whale Foundation often has volunteers at the parking lot to share their binoculars and point out the whales. Papawai Point is also a good place to stop and enjoy the sunset any time of the year.

LAHAINA TO KA'ANAPALI

The stretch between Lahaina and Ka'anapali offers a couple of roadside beach parks and west Maui's best B&Bs and the Lahaina area's main post office.

Wahikuli Wayside Beach Park

About 2 miles north of Lahaina, Wahikuli Wayside Beach Park occupies a narrow strip of beach flanked by the highway. With a gift for prophecy, the Hawaiians named it Wahikuli (noisy place). Although the beach is mostly backed by a black-rock retaining wall, there's a small sandy area. The swimming conditions are usually fine, and when the water's calm, you can snorkel near the lava outcrops at the park's south end. The park has showers and rest rooms.

SLEEPING

The following B&Bs are near each other in a residential neighborhood between Lahaina and Ka'anapali, inland of Hwy 30 and about 0.25 miles east of Wahikuli Wayside Beach Park.

Garden Gate (☎ 661-8800, 800-939-3217; www .gardengatebb.com; 67 Kaniau Rd; r incl breakfast $119-149; Ⓟ ❤️ Ⓡ) Tropical flowers abound in the central courtyard of this guesthouse, which makes a good alternative should the other two neighborhood B&Bs be full. The rooms are modern with the expected amenities, but swing for the pricier ones and you'll add on upper-floor ocean views, spacious lanai and Jacuzzis – well worth the additional $30.

GuestHouse (☎ 661-8085, 800-621-8942; www .mauiguesthouse.com; 1620 'Ainakea Rd; s/d incl breakfast $129/149; P 🔀 🖵 🖳) You can't get much cushier than this, with amenities that put the nearby resorts to shame. Each room has a 42in plasma TV, a hot tub, ultracomfortable mattresses and private lanai. Stained-glass windows and rattan furnishings reflect a Hawaiian motif. Long-distance calls, online computer use, wi-fi and beach-gear supplies are all free. Guests have access to a fully equipped kitchen and laundry facilities.

House of Fountains (☎ 667-2121, 800-789-6865; www.alohahouse.com; 1579 Lokia St; r incl breakfast $140-170; P 🔀 🖳) With rich koa woods, Hawaiian handicrafts, even an outrigger canoe hanging from the ceiling, it's no surprise why this place won the visitors bureau award as *the* most Hawaiian B&B in the entire state. In addition to the museum-quality Hawaiiana collection, you'll find well-equipped rooms with queen beds, refrigerators, DVD players and phones. German is spoken here and a breakfast of Hawaiian-grown goodies is provided.

Hanaka'o'o Beach Park

This long, sandy beach extending south from Ka'anapali Beach Resort has a sandy bottom and water conditions that are usually quite safe for swimming. However, southerly swells, which sometimes develop in summer, can create powerful waves and shorebreaks, while the occasional *kona* storm can kick up rough water conditions in winter. Snorkelers head down to the second clump of rocks on the south side of the park, but it really doesn't compare with sites further north. The park has full facilities and a lifeguard. Hanaka'o'o Beach is also called 'Canoe Beach,' as west Maui outrigger canoe clubs practice here in the late afternoons.

KA'ANAPALI
pop 1375
West Maui's premier beach resort, Ka'anapali extends along 3 miles of sandy beach with views across the 'Au'au Channel to Lana'i and Moloka'i. With a dozen oceanfront hotels, two 18-hole golf courses and an oceanful of water activities, Ka'anapali offers all the trappings of resort vacationing.

It's hard to imagine the area was nothing but cane fields until the late 1950s, when sugar giant Amfac pulled 600 acres out of production, earmarked the land for development and transformed it into Hawaii's first major resort outside of Waikiki. Ka'anapali is certainly not a 'getaway' in the sense of avoiding the crowds, but it has its quieter niches, especially at the northern end of the resort.

Sights
KA'ANAPALI BEACH
The generous long sandy strand fronting the Ka'anapali resort hotels is the busiest stretch of beach on the west Maui coast. Dubbed 'Dig Me Beach' for all the well-waxed strutting that takes place here, it's a vibrant scene with surfers, bodyboarders and parasailers decorating the water, and sailboats pulling up on shore.

Check with the hotel beach huts before jumping in, however, as water conditions vary with the season and currents along sections of the beach can be strong. A coral reef runs from the southern end of the Westin down to the Hyatt and in calm weather it provides decent snorkeling.

Still, you'll find the best underwater sights off **Pu'u Keka'a**, also known as Black Rock, the lava promontory that protects the beach in front of the Sheraton. First-time snorkelers will be happy with the coral and fish at the protected southern side of Pu'u Keka'a, but the real prize is the horseshoe cove cut into the tip of the rock, where there's more pristine coral, abundant tropical fish and the occasional turtle. There's often a current to contend with off the point, which can make getting to the cove a little risky, but when it's calm you can swim right around into

---

BEST BEACHSIDE DINING

- For breakfast: **Gazebo Restaurant** (p340), Napili
- For lunch: **Aloha Mixed Plate** (p326), Lahaina
- For *pupu*: **Hula Grill & Barefoot Bar** (p336), Ka'anapali
- For dinner: **Pacific'O** (p327), Lahaina

MAUI

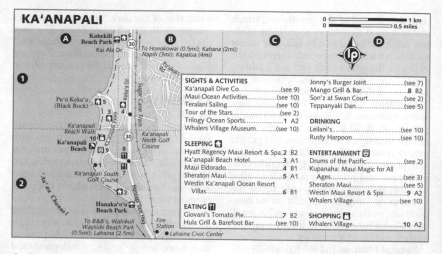

the horseshoe. Pu'u Keka'a is also a popular shore-dive spot. If you want to see what the horseshoe cove looks like, take the short footpath to the top of the rock, where you can peer right down into it.

The resort hotels offer free beach parking, but the number of spaces allotted are so limited they commonly fill by mid-morning. If you don't find a space, a good alternative is to park for free at Kahekili Beach Park to the north or at Hanaka'o'o Beach Park to the south and stroll along the shore.

KAHEKILI BEACH PARK
Backed by swaying palms, this idyllic golden-sand beach is Ka'anapali's jewel. It has fantastic snorkeling and although it's open ocean, the water is usually calm and perfect for swimming. And unlike the main Ka'anapali strip, there are no crowds, access is easy and there's plenty of free parking. The park has showers, rest rooms, a covered picnic pavilion and BBQ grills, making it a fine place for a beachside picnic.

Snorkelers can swim north to Honokowai Point and then ride the mild current, which runs north to south, all the way back. Not only do these waters harbor an excellent variety of fish, but sea turtles thrive here as well.

The wide beach is also ideal for strolling. A boardwalk connects Kahekili Beach Park to Pu'u Keka'a at Ka'anapali Beach. Or you could walk north along the beach for about 20 minutes to Honokowai Point and have lunch in the village.

The park is at the north side of Ka'anapali. From the Honoapi'ilani Hwy, turn west past the 25-mile marker onto Kai Ala Dr (opposite Pu'ukoli'i Rd), then bear right.

WHALERS VILLAGE MUSEUM
Fascinating exhibits are in store for the visitor at this superb whaling **museum** (☎ 661-5992; Level 3, Whalers Village, 2345 Ka'anapali Pkwy; admission free; ⏰ 9:30am-10pm). Authentic period photographs, whaling ship logs and detailed interpretive boards sound the depths of whaling history. It's all rounded out with exhibitions of harpoons, whale jawbones and a wild array of scrimshaw.

BRAVE SOULS

According to traditional Hawaiian beliefs, Pu'u Keka'a, the westernmost point of Maui, is a place where the spirits of the dead leap into the unknown to be carried to their ancestral homeland.

The rock is said to have been created during a scuffle between the demigod Maui and a commoner who questioned Maui's superiority. Maui chased the man to this point, then froze his body into stone and cast his soul out to sea.

A different kind of soul jumps into the water today. You'll often find a line of daring teens waiting for their turn to leap off the rock for a resounding splash into the cool cove below.

In the 19th century whales were considered a 'floating gold mine' of oil, spermaceti, blubber and baleen. A lot of the character of the whalers comes through here, and you'll get a feel for how rough and dirty the work really was. Wages were so low that sailors sometimes owed the ship money by the time they got home and had to sign up for another four-year stint just to pay off the debt. No wonder so many jumped ship when they reached Maui! Films on whales run continuously in a little theater next to the museum shop, which sells excellent scrimshaw carvings.

Interest piqued? You'll find a full-size **sperm whale skeleton** hanging at the front entrance to the shopping center to round out the experience.

KA'ANAPALI BEACH WALK

Enjoy the eye candy on this mile-long walk that runs between the Hyatt and the Sheraton, the opulent hotels that anchor the ends of Ka'anapali Beach. Just steps from the lively beach scene, two hotels along the walk worth a detour are the Hyatt and the Westin for their dazzling garden statuary and landscaping replete with free-form pools, rushing waterfalls and swan ponds. A walk through the Hyatt's rambling lobbies is like museum browsing – the walls hang with everything from heirloom Hawaiian quilts to meditative Buddhas and Papua New Guinea war shields.

At the southern end of the walk the graceful 17ft-high bronze sculpture *The Acrobats*, a work by Australian John Robinson, makes a dramatic silhouette against the sunset. If you walk along the beach in the early evening, you'll often be treated to entertainment, most notably from the beachside restaurants at Whalers Village (p337) and from the Hyatt, which holds its luau (p337) on the oceanfront.

Activities
WATER ACTIVITIES

Trilogy Ocean Sports (☎ 667-6816; Ka'anapali Beach Walk; ☽ 8am-5pm), in a beach hut in front of the Marriott, offers two-hour surfing lessons ($69) and rents snorkel sets and bodyboards for $15 a day.

Ka'anapali Dive Co (☎ 667-4622; www.kaanapali diveco.com; Westin Maui Resort & Spa; one-tank dive $65; ☽ 9am-5pm) offers beach dives to certified divers and an introductory dive ($89) for nov-ices that starts with instruction in a pool and ends with a guided dive from the beach.

Maui Ocean Activities (☎ 667-2001; www.mauiwater sports.com; Whalers Village, 2345 Ka'anapali Pkwy; kayak/ surfboard rental 1hr $15; ☽ 8am-4pm) has kayak and surfboard rentals; gives 1½-hour surfing ($59) and windsurfing lessons ($69); and rents 14ft hobie cats for $55 an hour.

Teralani Sailing (☎ 661-1230; www.teralani.net; Whalers Village, 2345 Ka'anapali Pkwy; outings $59-89) offers a variety of sails to match the season, including morning snorkel sails, sunset sails and whale-watch outings. Opening hours vary.

LAND ACTIVITIES

Ka'anapali Golf Courses (☎ 661-3691; www.kaanapali -golf.com; 2290 Ka'anapali Pkwy; green fees $170-205, after 1pm $85-110; ☽ first tee time 6:30am) consists of two courses. The more demanding Ka'anapali North Golf Course, designed by Robert Trent Jones, is tournament grade with greens that emphasize putting skills. The Ka'anapali South Golf Course is a bit shorter and more of a resort course. The setting (bordering condos and the road) isn't as tranquil as the courses in Kapalua, but it tends to be less windy down this way and the rates are a relative bargain.

Treat yourself to stellar stargazing at the Hyatt resort's rooftop **Tour of the Stars** (☎ 667-4727; 200 Nohea Kai Dr; admission $25-30). These astronomy programs, using a 16in-diameter telescope, are limited to 14 people and held at 8pm, 9pm and 10pm on clear nights. If you're with your honey, opt for the couples-only 'romance tour' at 11pm Friday and Saturday, which rolls out champagne and chocolate-covered strawberries.

Courses

Whalers Village (☎ 661-4567; www.whalersvillage.com; 2435 Ka'anapali Pkwy) offers lei-making classes, hula lessons and the like. Look for the schedule, which changes throughout the year, in the shopping center's free magazine.

Festivals & Events

Maui Onion Festival (www.whalersvillage.com) This festival highlights everything that can be done with Maui's celebrated onions. Held at Whalers Village on the first weekend in August, things heat up with raw onion-eating contests (participants get free breath mints!) and cooking demonstrations by Maui's best chefs.

Maui Chefs Present (www.visitlahaina.com) Gourmands have their day on the first Friday in September at the Hyatt Regency Maui Resort & Spa, when celebrity chefs whip up dozens of dishes under the stars. It's a precursor event for the illustrious A Taste of Lahaina festival (p324).

Na Mele O Maui Song & Art Competition (www .kaanapaliresort.com) At the Hyatt Regency Maui Resort & Spa in mid-December, the 'Song of Maui' features childrens' choral groups singing Native Hawaiian music with themes like 'The Queen's Garden' (Queen Lili'uokalani, Hawaii's last monarch, was a renowned music composer and advocate of Hawaiian pride). Lots and lots of aloha at this one.

Sleeping

All the following accommodations are either on the beach or within walking distance of it. In addition to these resorts, there are recommendable B&Bs (p332) nearby between Ka'anapali and Lahaina.

Ka'anapali Beach Hotel (☎ 661-0011, 800-262-8450; www.kbhmaui.com; 2525 Ka'anapali Pkwy; r incl breakfast from $210; P ☒ ☒) The place to go Hawaiian style! This granddaddy of Ka'anapali's resort hotels scored an enviable location on a gorgeous stretch of beach. Sure the rooms show their age, but the place abounds in aloha in so many ways, including free guest lessons in ukulele, hula and lei-making. And it's the smallest of the resorts along the entire beach – which adds to the pleasant low-key atmosphere.

Maui Eldorado (☎ 661-0021, 800-688-7444; www .outrigger.com; 2661 Keka'a Dr; studios/1-bedroom units from $279/329; P ☒ ☒) A golfer's haven, you can step off your lanai and onto the fairways at this condo complex bordering the golf course. Best deal are the studios, which are very large and have kitchens set apart from the bedroom area. Don't bother paying extra for the ocean view – this one's all about the greens.

Hyatt Regency Maui Resort & Spa (☎ 661-1234, 800-233-1234; www.maui.hyatt.com; 200 Nohea Kai Dr; r from $380; P ☒ ☒) You'll be struck by the lavishness of this place as soon as you step into the lobby atrium with its orchids, palm trees and extravagant artwork. But don't think that makes it highbrow. The Hyatt is heaven for kids, with parrots in the palms and an awesome pool of swim-through grottos and towering water slides. For grown-ups, there's a swim-up bar and a pampering full-service spa.

Sheraton Maui (☎ 661-0031, 866-716-8109; www .sheraton-maui.com; 2605 Ka'anapali Pkwy; r from $415; P ☒ ☒) This sleek resort breathes elegance and enjoys a prime beach location, smack in front of Pu'u Keka'a (Black Rock). The rooms

have rich wood tones and Hawaiian prints, and the grounds have night-lit tennis courts, a fitness center and a lava-rock swimming pool that kids will dig. Online deals can sometimes ease the price bite.

Westin Ka'anapali Ocean Resort Villas (☎ 921-4654; www.westin.com/kaanapalivillas; 6 Kai Ala Dr; studios from $520; P ☒ ☒) This new condo-style resort enjoys a super location at the quieter north end of Ka'anapali where the waters are calmer and the crowds thin out. All rooms have full kitchens, marble baths with whirlpool tubs and free high-speed internet. Book online and the prices drop from the stratosphere by 35%.

Eating

BUDGET

Whalers Village (☎ 661-4567; www.whalersvillage .com; 2435 Ka'anapali Pkwy) This shopping center has a small basement-level food court, with Chinese fast food, pizza-by-the-slice, burgers and shave ice.

Jonny's Burger Joint (☎ 661-4500; 2291 Ka'anapali Pkwy; burgers $6-10; ☒ 11:30am-2am) Shoot a game of pool while your burger is flipped at this combo eatery-bar at the entrance to Ka'anapali. The huge burgers, served with caramelized Kula onions, are among the best you'll find on Maui.

MIDRANGE

Mango Grill & Bar (☎ 667-1929; 2290 Ka'anapali Pkwy; mains $6-24; ☒ 7:30am-9:30pm) Overlooking the golf course, Mango brings them in with huge servings and a menu that covers the gamut from local grinds to New York steak. People come from miles around for the breakfast fare, especially the French toast smothered in tropical fruits.

Hula Grill & Barefoot Bar (☎ 667-6636; Whalers Village, 2345 Ka'anapali Pkwy; grill menu $8-18, dinner mains $19-30; ☒ 11am-10:30pm) The top choice for beachside atmosphere. Watch the swimsuit parade pass by as you dine under coconut-frond umbrellas on creative *pupu*, like spicy coconut calamari or crab and mac-nut wontons. Dinner kicks it up a notch with kiawe-grilled steaks and Sichuan-screamin' sesame *'opakapaka*.

Giovani's Tomato Pie (☎ 661-3160; 2291 Ka'anapali Pkwy; mains $11-22; ☒ 5-9:30pm) This family-friendly restaurant near the highway offers solid, reasonably priced Italian fare with something for everyone. Adults can dine on antipasto and parmigiana, while the kids munch away on buffalo wings and pizza.

Son'z at Swan Court (☎ 667-4506; Hyatt Regency Maui Resort & Spa, 200 Nohea Kai Dr; mains $28-46; ☯ 5-10pm) Between the waterfalls, the swan pond and tiki torches, this is hands-down Ka'anapali's most romantic dinner choice. In addition to the expected fine-dining steak and lobster menu, there are plenty of island touches, like Maui goat cheese ravioli. Incredible wine list, too.

TOP END

Teppanyaki Dan (☎ 661-0031; Sheraton Maui, 2605 Ka'anapali Pkwy; dinner $35-50; ☯ 6-9:30pm Tue-Sat) Chefs let the knives fly as they cook traditional teppanyaki meals right at your table. The only difference from dining in Tokyo is that here the ingredients are fresh Hawaiian. Choose from seafood options, like Kona lobster or hibachi butterfly fish, or go for the juicy steak.

Drinking

Leilani's (☎ 661-4495; Whalers Village, 2345 Ka'anapali Pkwy; ☯ 11am-midnight) This open-air bar right on the beach is a good place to have a few drinks while catching a little sunshine. It also has a good grill and *pupu* menu.

Rusty Harpoon (☎ 661-3123; Whalers Village, 2345 Ka'anapali Pkwy) Long happy hours (2pm to 6pm and 10pm to 1:30am) and hard-hitting daiquiris attract the crowds, as do the big-screen sports TVs.

Entertainment

There's always something happening at the Ka'anapali hotels, ranging from music in the lounges and restaurants to luau and hula shows.

HULA & LIVE MUSIC

Ka'anapali Beach Hotel (☎ 661-0011; 2525 Ka'anapali Pkwy) 'Maui's most Hawaiian hotel' cheerfully entertains anyone who chances by between 6:30pm and 7:30pm with a free hula show. There's also music and dancing nightly in the hotel's Tiki Courtyard.

Sheraton Maui (☎ 661-0031; 2605 Ka'anapali Pkwy) Beachside torch-lighting and a cliff-diving ceremony from Pu'u Keka'a take place at sunset, followed by music with hula dancing from 6pm to 8pm at the hotel's Lagoon Bar.

Hyatt Regency Maui Resort & Spa (☎ 661-1234; 200 Nohea Kai Dr) There's a free torch-lighting ceremony at 6:15pm, followed by Hawaiian music until 9:30pm in the Weeping Banyan Lounge.

Westin Maui Resort & Spa (☎ 667-2525; 2365 Ka'anapali Pkwy) The hotel's poolside bar and grill has live Hawaiian music from 3pm to 9pm.

Whalers Village (☎ 661-4567; 2435 Ka'anapali Pkwy) Ka'anapali's shopping center puts on live Hawaiian music, hula and Polynesian dance performances from 6:30pm to 8pm on Monday and Wednesday.

Both **Leilani's** (☎ 661-4495; Whalers Village, 2345 Ka'anapali Pkwy; ☯ 11am-midnight) and **Hula Grill & Barefoot Bar** (☎ 667-6636; Whalers Village, 2345 Ka'anapali Pkwy; ☯ 11am-10:30pm), adjacent beachside at Whalers Village, have live guitar music throughout the afternoon and evening.

LUAU & DINNER SHOWS

Drums of the Pacific (☎ 667-4727; Hyatt Regency Maui Resort & Spa, 200 Nohea Kai Dr; adult/child 6-12 $86/45; ☯ 5-8pm) Ka'anapali's best luau includes an *imu* ceremony (the unearthing of a roasted pig from an underground oven), an open bar, a Hawaiian-style buffet dinner, and a flashy South Pacific dance and music show.

Kupanaha: Maui Magic for all Ages (☎ 661-0011; Ka'anapali Beach Hotel, 2525 Ka'anapali Pkwy; adult/child 6-12 $79/29; ☯ Tue-Sat) Illusionists take a Hawaiian slant adding legends through hula and chants to the usual magic at this dinner show.

Shopping

You'll find more than 50 shops at **Whalers Village** (☎ 661-4567; 2435 Ka'anapali Pkwy; ☯ 9:30am-10pm) shopping center:

ABC store (☎ 667-9700) For beach mats, sunblock and sundries.

Honolua Surf (☎ 661-5455) The place to pick up Maui-style board shorts and other casual beachwear.

Honolua Wahine (☎ 661-3253) Get your bikinis here.

Martin & MacArthur (☎ 661-0088) Museum-quality Hawaiian-made wood carvings, paintings and other crafts.

Na Hoku (☎ 667-5411) One of Hawaii's oldest jewelers, specializes in Hawaiian floral and marine life designs.

Sand People (☎ 662-8785) Eclectic island-made souvenirs, from papaya soap to T-shirts.

Getting There & Around

The **Maui Bus** (www.mauicounty.gov/bus) connects the Whalers Village shopping center in Ka'anapali with the Wharf Cinema Center in Lahaina hourly from 6:30am to 8:30pm, and north up the coast to Kahana and Napili hourly from 6am to 8pm.

The free **Ka'anapali Trolley** (☎ 667-0648) runs between the Ka'anapali hotels, Whalers Village and the golf course about every 20 minutes between 10am and 10pm.

HONOKOWAI

pop 3000

Honokowai is condoville, no doubt about it. But don't write the place off – it's convenient, affordable and low-rise, and the ocean views are every bit as fine as in the upscale resorts to the south. The condominiums here are on a more intimate scale, many perched right on the waterfront, with louvered windows that let in the sea breeze. And an influx of fresh faces is giving the town a new hipper dining scene.

Orientation

North of Ka'anapali, the road forks. If you want to zip up to the northern beaches, bypassing the condos and resorts, the main road is Honoapi'ilani Hwy (Hwy 30), which has a bicycle lane. The parallel shoreline road is Lower Honoapi'ilani Rd, which leads into Honokowai.

Sights & Activities

Honokowai Beach Park, in the center of town, is good for picnics, but it's largely lined with a submerged rock shelf and has poor swimming conditions with shallow waters. Water conditions improve at the south side of town, and you can walk along the shore down to the glorious **Kahekili Beach Park** that marks the northern end of Ka'anapali – rent a snorkel from **Boss Frog** (☎ 665-1200; 3636 Lower Honoapi'ilani Rd; per day from $2; 8am-5pm) before you set off.

Sleeping

Kuleana Maui (☎ 669-8080, 800-367-5633; www.kuleana resorts.com; 3959 Lower Honoapi'ilani Rd; 1-/2-bedroom units from $135/225;) For Honokowai, this is one of the larger condominium complexes, but it's nicely spread out on several acres of palm-shaded grounds and the price makes it good value. The room amenities are generous, with full kitchens and entertainment centers.

Hale Kai (☎ 669-6333, 800-446-7307; www.halekai .com; 3691 Lower Honoapi'ilani Rd; 1-/2-/3-bedroom units $145/195/295;) This cheery old-fashioned condo is so close to the water's edge that guests can literally step off their lanai and onto the beach. The place abounds in Hawaiian

accents from the room decor to the lava-rock exterior. If you have a group, go for the three-bedroom corner unit, which has a cool loft, wraparound ocean-view windows and all the character of a Hawaiian beach house.

Makani Sands (☎ 669-8223; www.makanisands.com; 3765 Lower Honoapi'ilani Rd; 1-/2-bedroom units $165/250;) Friendly and quiet, Makani Sands is another shoreline hugger where you can watch whales swim by from your lanai. Units in this small condo complex have an agreeable island tone with Hawaiian prints on the wall and tropical furnishings. Rates drop 10% for weekly stays.

Noelani (☎ 669-8374, 800-367-6030; www.noelani -condo-resort.com; 4095 Lower Honoapi'ilani Rd; studios $157, 1-/2-/3-bedroom units from $197/290/357;) Aloha atmosphere, plenty of palm trees and two heated pools add to the allure at this impeccably maintained condo complex. Each unit is right on the shore and you can listen to the surf from your ocean-facing lanai. All have an extra sofa bed, and all but the studios have a washer-dryer.

Eating

Java Jazz & Soup Nutz (☎ 667-0787; Honokowai Marketplace, 3350 Lower Honoapi'ilani Rd; breakfast & lunch $5-11, dinner $10-33; 6am-9pm Mon-Sat, to 5pm Sun) This hip, arty café has a menu as eclectic as its decor. Breakfast packs a crowd that feasts on everything from bagels to frittata, lunch features gourmet sandwiches and Mexican fare, while dinner leans into Mediterranean-influenced cuisine. Plenty of vegetarian options, too.

Farmers Market Deli (☎ 669-7004; 3636 Lower Honoapi'ilani Rd; salad bar per lb $6.50; 7am-7pm) Great place to pick up healthy take-out fare. The salad bar includes organic goodies and some hot veggie dishes, the smoothies ($4) are first-rate and Maui-made ice cream is sold by the scoop ($2.50). Take it across the street to the beach and have yourself a picnic.

Honokowai Okazuya (☎ 665-0512; 3600 Lower Honoapi'ilani Rd; mains $8-12; 10am-9pm Mon-Sat) Takeout takes on class at this Japanese-style plate-lunch eatery that knows how to whip up heavenly sauces. The house-special mahi-mahi (a mild white-fleshed fish) lemon caper sauté is a sure bet, or go Japanese with the chicken *katsu don* poached in a sweet soy sauce and served on rice. A narrow strip of stools lines the wall if you want to chow down on the spot.

KAHANA

pop 2200

Kahana, the stretch extending north of Honokowai, boasts million-dollar homes, upscale beachfront condominium complexes and Maui's only microbrewery. It's a popular place to head for a night out.

Information

The **Kahana Gateway** (4405 Honoapi'ilani Hwy) shopping center has a gas station, **Bank of Hawaii** (☎ 669-3922), **Kahana Koin-op Laundromat** (☎ 669-1587; ☯ last wash 8pm) and **Whalers General Store** (☎ 669-3700; ☯ 6:30am-11pm) for basic groceries and sundries. Visit **Hawaiian Village Coffee** (☎ 665-1114; Kahana Gateway, 4405 Honoapi'ilani Hwy; per min 20¢; ☯ 6am-9pm) for internet access on its computer, or take advantage of free wi-fi on yours.

Sights & Activities

The sandy **beach** that fronts the village has reasonable swimming conditions. For snorkeling, a good area is along the rocky outcropping at the north side of the Kahana Sunset condos. You can park at the seaside **Pohaku Park** and walk north a couple of minutes to access the beach. Pohaku Park itself has a gnarly offshore break called S-Turns that attracts lots of surfers. **Maui Dive Shop** (☎ 669-3800; Kahana Gateway shopping center, 4405 Honoapi'ilani Hwy, dives/courses from $90/350; ☯ 8am-9pm) offers a full range of dives, and rents and sells quality snorkel gear.

Sleeping

Kahana Village (☎ 669-5111, 800-824-3065; www.maui.net/~village/kahana.html; 4531 Lower Honoapi'ilani Rd; 2-/3-bedroom units from $290/330; ☯ ☯) If you're traveling with the family, the spacious units here will give you plenty of elbow room. There's no skimping. From the furnishings to the generous amenities, everything about this place is top end. High-speed internet and long-distance calls (yes, even international) are free. Kids will dig the turtle murals in the pool, parents the Jacuzzi.

Eating & Drinking

Hawaiian Village Coffee (☎ 665-1114; Kahana Gateway, 4405 Honoapi'ilani Hwy; ☯ 6am-9pm) Check your email while you sip a cup of island-grown coffee. The shop also sells Maui-made ice cream and good light café fare, like bagels and quiche.

China Boat (☎ 669-5089; 4474 Lower Honoapi'ilani Rd; mains $9-33; ☯ 11:30am-2pm & 5-10pm) West Maui's best Chinese fare comes at affordable prices, with a full menu of Mandarin and Szechwan favorites. Start with the hot-and-sour soup and move on to crispy duck, or splurge on the lobster in a tasty kung pao sauce. Everything's prepared without MSG.

Maui Brewing Company (☎ 669-3474; Kahana Gateway, 4405 Honoapi'ilani Hwy; lunch $10-12, dinner mains $19-36; ☯ 11am-1:30am) This microbrewery sports a classy pub atmosphere with a glass wall overlooking the brewing operation. The food goes way beyond the usual pub menu, with oysters on the half shell, Cajun crab cakes and raspberry-glazed duck. Beers range from the light, crisp Honolua lager to Wild Hog, a robust, full-bodied black stout with a creamy finish – sample them all with six 3oz glasses ($6). Live music nightly.

Roy's Kahana Bar & Grill (☎ 669-6999; Kahana Gateway, 4405 Honoapi'ilani Hwy; mains $26-33; ☯ 5:30-10pm) A branch of Roy Yamaguchi's renowned empire, the restaurant centers around an exhibition kitchen and rakes in a crowd with its outstanding Hawaii Regional Cuisine. Specialties include sashimi-like blackened 'ahi and hibachi-grilled miso steak. The hot chocolate soufflé is pure decadence – ask for two spoons and share it with a friend.

NAPILI

pop 1600

Somewhat ironically, Napili owes its low-key appeal to its early history of resort development. Its largest hotel, Napili Kai Beach Resort, was built in 1962 as Maui's first hotel north of Ka'anapali. To protect the bay, as

---

TOP FIVE PLACES TO SPOT WHALES

- From the deck of the **Hawaiian Islands Humpback Whale National Marine Sanctuary** (p357), Kihei
- At **Papawai Point** (p332), along the highway between Ma'alaea and Lahaina
- Along the **Wailea Beach Walk** (p365), Wailea
- Aboard a **whale-watching cruise** (p324)
- From the **lanai** of your hotel room overlooking any west-facing Maui beach

MAUI

well as its investment, Napili Kai organized neighboring landowners and persuaded the county to pass a zoning bylaw restricting all Napili buildings to the height of a coconut tree. The law passed in 1964, long before the condo explosion took over the rest of west Maui, and as a result Napili has preserved a cozy scale that's been lost elsewhere.

Sights & Activities
Beautiful **Napili Beach** curves gently with deep golden sands, offering excellent swimming and snorkeling when it's calm. Big waves occasionally make it into the bay in winter, and when they do it's time to break out the skimboards – the steep drop at the beach provides a perfect run into the surf.

Sleeping
Hale Napili (☎ 669-6184, 800-245-2266; www.halenapili .com; 65 Hui Dr; studios from $145, 1-bedroom units from $215) A great choice, with thoroughly local accents from the friendly Hawaiian manager to the tropical decor. The beautifully kept units are roomy, all face the ocean and have full kitchens. The beach is – literally – just out the door. With only 18 units, it books up quickly.

Outrigger Napili Shores (☎ 669-8061, 800-688-7444; www.outrigger.com; 5315 Lower Honoapi'ilani Rd; studios from $219, 1-bedroom units $275; ☐) This condo complex boasts a palm-filled resort setting with solar-heated pools, a hot tub and lawn croquet. Two of Napili's top restaurants are right on the grounds. For Napili, the prices are reasonable, and you can often find good discounts on its website.

Napili Kai Beach Resort (☎ 669-6271, 800-367-5030; www.napilikai.com; 5900 Lower Honoapi'ilani Rd; r/studios from $220/275, 1-/2-bedroom ste from $415/600; ☒ ☐) Spread across several acres, this resort perched above the northern end of Napili Bay offers classic appeal and fills with return visitors. The units, which tastefully blend Polynesian decor with Asian touches, have ocean-view lanai, high-speed internet and, in most cases, kitchenettes. Deals include a fifth night free.

Eating
Gazebo Restaurant (☎ 669-5621; Napili Shores, 5315 Lower Honoapi'ilani Rd; meals $6-11; ☒ 7:30am-2pm) This open-air seaside restaurant has an unbelievable setting and damn good food. Sweet tooths will salivate over the white chocolate mac-nut pancakes, and the chockful omelettes

have few rivals anywhere. Big salads, hearty sandwiches and flavorful lunch plates, too. Get there when it opens to beat the breakfast queue.

Fish & Poi (☎ 442-3700; Napili Shores, 5315 Lower Honoapi'ilani Rd; mains $13-21; ☒ 11am-9pm Tue-Sun) Teak furnishings and a view of a koi pond set the mood. Hawaiian comfort food goes upscale here with crab cakes in mango dipping sauce, tempura-style fish-and-chips and chicken-papaya salad. Kids will like the *na keiki* menu of burgers and grilled cheese, and parents will like the price (from $3).

Sea House Restaurant (☎ 669-1500; Napili Kai Beach Resort, 5900 Lower Honoapi'ilani Rd; dinner mains $18-32; ☒ 5:30-9pm) Alfresco seaside dining is enhanced by tiki torches and an extensive selection of Pacific and American fare. Stick with the seafood and you won't go wrong. A good choice is the coconut shrimp with Thai chili sauce or go purely Hawaiian with taro-crusted sea bass.

Entertainment
Napili Kai Beach Resort (☎ 669-6271; 5900 Lower Honoapi'ilani Rd; adult/child 6-12 $10/5; ☒ 5-6:30pm Tue) The resort hosts a culturally rich hula show performed by a local *na keiki* troupe. Definitely worth your time.

KAPALUA & AROUND
pop 600

Kapalua, nestled in pineapple fields and overlooking beautiful beaches, is the most exclusive resort development in Maui. There's not a golfer worth their salt that doesn't know of Kapalua. As Maui's premier golf destination, Kapalua takes top billing as the site of the PGA Tour's opening tournament of the year. Golf certainly isn't the only thing Kapalua has going for it, but it is, after all, the resort's *raison d'être*.

Despite its trio of top-rated golf courses, Kapalua has managed to stay green with the environment. The courses are certified by Audubon International as 'cooperative sanctuaries,' meaning they meet strict standards for restricted water and pesticide use, and maintain a landscape that provides habitat for wildlife.

Sights
KAPALUA BEACH
This picture-perfect beach gets the seal of approval! Not only do tourists sun on the

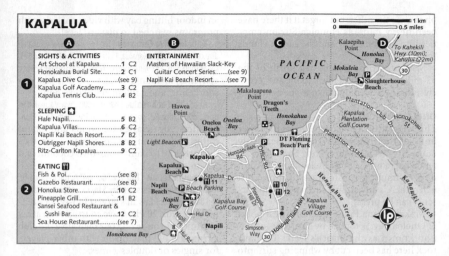

KAPALUA

SIGHTS & ACTIVITIES
Art School at Kapalua.............1 C2
Honokahua Burial Site..........2 C1
Kapalua Dive Co.................(see 9)
Kapalua Golf Academy.........3 C2
Kapalua Tennis Club.............4 B2

ENTERTAINMENT
Masters of Hawaiian Slack-Key
  Guitar Concert Series......(see 9)
Napili Kai Beach Resort.......(see 7)

SLEEPING
Hale Napili.........................5 B2
Kapalua Villas.....................6 C2
Napili Kai Beach Resort........7 B2
Outrigger Napili Shores.........8 B2
Ritz-Carlton Kapalua............9 C2

EATING
Fish & Poi..........................(see 8)
Gazebo Restaurant..............(see 8)
Honolua Store.....................10 C2
Pineapple Grill....................11 B2
Sansei Seafood Restaurant &
  Sushi Bar.........................12 C2
Sea House Restaurant.........(see 7)

beach here, but endangered monk seals sometimes haul out to snooze the afternoon away on the soft white sand.

And what good taste they have, too. This crescent-shaped beach, with its clear view of Moloka'i across the channel, offers everything you need for a day at the beach. Long rocky outcrops at both ends of the bay make Kapalua Beach the safest year-round swimming spot on this coast. You'll find good snorkeling on the right side of the beach, with lots of large tangs, butterfly fish and orange slate-pencil sea urchins.

Take the drive immediately north of Napili Kai Beach Resort to get to the beach parking area, where there are rest rooms and showers. Look for the tunnel that leads from the parking lot north to the beach.

DT FLEMING BEACH PARK
Surrounded by ironwood trees and adjacent to an old one-room schoolhouse, this long, sandy beach feels like an outpost from another era. Experienced surfers and bodysurfers find good wave action here, especially in winter. The shorebreaks can be tough, however, and this beach is second only to Ho'okipa for injuries. It also has powerful currents, so check with the lifeguard before jumping in. The reef on the right is good for snorkeling when it's very calm.

Fleming, which takes its name from the Scotsman who developed the area's pineapple industry, has rest rooms, picnic facilities and showers. The access road is off Honoapi'ilani

Hwy (Hwy 30), immediately north of the 31-mile marker.

SLAUGHTERHOUSE BEACH & HONOLUA BAY
Amazing water conditions here. It can be tranquil and flat as a lake, or savage with incredible surf, depending on the season. But no matter its mood, it's always ideal for some sort of action.

Slaughterhouse Beach (Mokule'ia Bay) and Honolua Bay are separated by the narrow Kalaepiha Point and together form the Honolua-Mokule'ia Bay Marine Life Conservation District.

Honolua Bay faces northwest and when it catches the winter swells it has some of the most awesome surfing anywhere in the world. It's so good its been cover material for surfing magazines.

Slaughterhouse Beach is a first-rate bodysurfing spot during the summer. Its attractive white-sand crescent is good for sunbathing and exploring – look for glittering green olivine crystals in the rocks at the south end of the beach.

In summer snorkeling is excellent in both bays, thanks in part to prohibitions on fishing in the preserve. As an added treat, spinner dolphins sometimes hang near the mouth of the bays, swimming just beyond snorkelers. Both sides of Honolua Bay have good reefs with abundant coral, while the midsection of the bay has a sandy bottom. When it's calm, you can snorkel around Kalaepiha Point from

MAUI

one bay to the other, but forget it if there have been heavy rains, as Honolua Stream empties into Honolua Bay and the runoff clouds the water.

Slaughterhouse Beach, just north of the 32-mile marker, has public parking and a concrete stairway leading down to the beach.

ONELOA BEACH

This wide, white-sand beach fronts the lower links of the Ironwoods golf course. Aptly named (Oneloa means 'Long Sand'), it extends half a mile along Oneloa Bay. On calm days swimming is safe close to shore, but when there's any sizable surf, strong rip currents can be present.

Makaluapuna Point, the northwest point of Oneloa Bay, is topped by a curious formation known as the **Dragon's Teeth**. The lava rock here has been cut by whipping surf into 3ft-high spikes that bear an uncanny resemblance to pointed teeth. It's a fun site to walk to and only takes about 15 minutes return. En route you'll pass the Honokahua burial site, a 13.6-acre native burial ground; you can skirt along the outside of this area but don't enter any sites marked 'Please Kokua,' which are easily visible islets of overgrown native vegetation bordering manicured golf greens.

To get to the Makaluapuna Point end of the beach, drive north to the end of Lower Honoapi'ilani Rd, past the Ritz, where you'll find beach parking and a monument giving details on the burial site. The trail to the Dragon's Teeth leads from the monument along the north edge of the golf course.

Activities

Kapalua Golf (☎ 669-8044, 877-527-2582; www.kapalua maui.com; 2000 Village Rd; Village/Bay/Plantation course green fees before 2pm $195/210/295, after 2pm $90/100/125; ᗌ first tee 7am) comprises three of the island's top championship golf courses. The Village is Kapalua's stunning mountain course, rising from sea level to nearly 800ft in the first six holes. The Bay course is the tropical ocean course, meandering through palms past a lava peninsula. The challenging Plantation course sweeps over a rugged landscape of hills and deep gorges.

Want to hone your golf skills? **Kapalua Golf Academy** (☎ 669-6500; 1000 Office Rd; 1hr clinic $30, lessons per hr $110; ᗌ 7am-6pm), staffed by PGA pros, is Hawaii's top golf academy. Facilities include an indoor hitting bay with video analysis, with programs matched to players' levels.

Kapalua Dive Company (☎ 669-3448; www.kapalua dive.com; Ritz-Carlton Kapalua, 1 Ritz-Carlton Dr; dives from $75, kayak tours $70; ᗌ 9am-5pm) offers a range of water activities, including kayak tours that take you snorkeling, and a full menu of dive outings.

Art School at Kapalua (☎ 665-0007; www.kapaluaart .com; 800 Office Rd; yoga $15; ᗌ office 10am-4pm Mon-Fri) offers yoga classes for adults and lots of things to keep na keiki occupied, from toddler art time to paint-your-own coconut and ceramics.

Kapalua Tennis Club (☎ 669-5677; 100 Kapalua Dr; resort guests/nonguests per day $14/16, racquet rental $6; ᗌ 8am-6pm) is Hawaii's largest full-service tennis club, with 20 Plexipave courts and an array of clinics. If you're on your own, give the club a ring and it'll match you with other players for singles or doubles games.

Tours

Maui Pineapple Company (☎ 669-6201; 2½-hr tours $30; ᗌ tours 9:30am & 12:30am Mon-Fri) opens its fields for pineapple-plantation tours led by seasoned workers, who will give you the lowdown on pineapple growing and its history. Reservations are required, as are covered shoes. The price includes picking your own pineapple to take home.

Festivals & Events

Mercedes-Benz Championship (www.pgatour.com) Watch Tiger and friends tee off at the PGA Tour's season opener in early January at the Plantation course, vying for a $5.5 million purse.

Celebration of the Arts (www.celebrationofthearts .org) This festival in early April at the Ritz-Carlton celebrates traditional Hawaiian culture with workshops, hula demonstrations, arts and music.

Kapalua Wine & Food Festival (www.kapaluamaui. com) Held over four days in mid-July at the Ritz-Carlton, this culinary extravaganza features renowned winemakers and Hawaii's hottest chefs in cooking demonstrations and wine tastings.

Billabong Pro Maui (www.kapalua.maui.com) This annual women's title race, held at Honolua Bay when the surf's up in mid-December, showcases the world's top wahine (female) surfers. And as the final event of the surfing professionals World Championship Tour, it may determine the world's champ. One awesome show.

Sleeping

Kapalua Villas (☎ 669-8088, 800-545-0018; www .kapaluavillas.com; 500 Office Rd; 1-/2-bedroom units from

$289/399; ⊠ 🐶) If you have a small group, this is the way to go. Three luxury condominium complexes comprise the Kapalua Villas, with some units on the golf course and others overlooking the beach. The one-bedroom units sleep up to four, the two-bedroom units sleep six. Amenities include free tennis and discounted golf.

Ritz-Carlton Kapalua (☎ 669-6200, 800-262-8440; www.ritzcarlton.com; 1 Ritz-Carlton Dr; r incl breakfast from $375; ⊠ 🐶) This luxe hotel's low-keyed elegance attracts the exclusive golf crowd. On a hillside fronting the greens and the sea, the hotel has a heated multilevel swimming pool shaded by palm trees, a spa and a fitness club. Rooms have oversized marble bathrooms, goose-down pillows…you get the picture.

Eating
Sansei Seafood Restaurant & Sushi Bar (☎ 669-6286; 600 Office Rd; sushi $3-15, mains $17-32; ☽ 5-10pm Sun & Mon, 5:30-10pm Tue-Sat) Although Sansei gets lots of attention for its innovative sushi, don't overlook the non-sushi house specials, which are designated on the menu with an octopus. The tempura rock shrimp in garlic aioli flawlessly blends Japanese and French flavors and the spicy dungeness crab ramen with truffle broth is another winner. Order before 6pm and all food is discounted 25%.

Honolua Store (☎ 669-6128; 502 Office Rd; lunches $5-6; ☽ store 6am-8pm, deli to 2:30pm) A nod to normalcy in the midst of lavish exclusiveness, this old general store has a cafeteria-style deli serving sandwiches and local food (takeout only), like stew and fried chicken.

Pineapple Grill (☎ 669-9600; Kapalua Bay Golf Course clubhouse; lunch $10-16, dinner mains $27-39; ☽ 11am-2pm & 5-10pm) Hot and fresh off the grill, this smart place is edging out the competition with its innovative fusion fare. Tantalize the tastebuds with the likes of lobster-coconut bisque and Maui-coffee roasted duck breast. A well-matched wine list and a grand hilltop view make this a prime dining choice. Come before 6pm to take advantage of the three-course ($32) sunset dinner specials.

Entertainment
Masters of Hawaiian Slack-Key Guitar Concert Series (☎ 669-3858; www.slackkey.com; Ritz-Carlton Kapalua; admission $40) Top slack-key guitarists Cyril Pahinui, Ledward Kaapana and Dennis Kamakahi are monthly guests at this exceptional concert series, and George Kahumoku Jr, a slack-key legend in his own right, is the weekly host. The cozy theater has only 125 seats, so call ahead for reservations. Performances are at 6pm and 8:30pm Wednesday.

KAHEKILI HIGHWAY
The road around the 'top' of the island meanders into a slice of rural Hawaii that hasn't changed its face for tourism.

In fact, it's hard to imagine that trendy west Maui could hold such unspoiled countryside. It's kept in its pastoral state thanks to the Kahekili Hwy ('highway' – ha!), which narrows to little more than the width of a driveway, keeping construction trucks at bay. Not for the faint of heart, parts of the road are so narrow that traffic slows down to just 5mph as it wraps around hairpin curves.

It's about 22 miles in all from the southern end of the road at Wailuku to its northern end in Honokohau. Like its counterpart to the south (the Pi'ilani Hwy around the southern flank of Haleakala), the Kahekili Hwy (Hwy 340) is shown either as a black hole or an unpaved road on most tourist maps. Truth be told, it's paved the entire way – the car-rental companies just don't want you on it.

The stretch between Honokohau and Kahakuloa is two lanes and easygoing, while the section between Kahakuloa and Waihe'e is mostly one lane (with two-way traffic) and has a few hair-raising cliffside sections without shoulders. The posted speed limit on this section maxes out at 15mph, but taking it slowly is the whole point anyway. Allow at least 1½ hours, not counting stops, and gas up before starting out.

Waiehu & Waihe'e
Waiehu Beach Rd turns into Kahekili Hwy at the northern end of Wailuku and heads through the little towns of Waiehu and Waihe'e. The county-run **Waiehu Municipal Golf Course** (☎ 243-7400; 200 Halewaiu Rd; greens fee $45, optional cart $16), near the shore, is an affordable and easily walkable course.

The lightly trodden **Waihe'e Ridge Trail** follows a ridgetop deep into the West Maui Mountains, rewarding hikers with breathtaking views along the way. Take the one-lane paved road that starts on the inland side of the highway just south of the 7-mile marker and leads up to the Boy Scouts' Camp Mahulia. The drive winds through open pasture, so keep an eye out for cattle that mosey across the road. The trailhead, marked with a Na Ala Hele sign, is a mile up on the left just before the camp. There's a little parking area beside the trailhead.

The well-defined trail is 3 miles one way and takes about three hours for the roundtrip. It crosses forest reserve land, and though it's a bit steep, it's a fairly steady climb and not overly strenuous. Consider packing a lunch, as there's a picnic spot with an unbeatable view waiting at the end.

Starting at an elevation of 1000ft, the trail climbs a ridge, passing from pasture to cool forest. Guava trees and groves of rainbow eucalyptus are prominent along the way, and if you look closely you can usually find thimbleberries. From the 0.75-mile post, panoramic views open up with a scene that sweeps clear down to the ocean along the Waihe'e Gorge and deep into pleated valleys. As you continue on, you'll enter ohia forest with native birds and get distant views of waterfalls cascading down the mountains. The ridgetop views are similar to those you'd see from a helicopter, though the stillness along this route can be appreciated only by those on foot. The trail ends at the 2563ft peak of Lanilili, where you'll enjoy great views in all directions.

Waihe'e to Kahakuloa

Back on the highway, near the 7-mile marker, **Mendes Ranch** (☎ 871-5222; www.mendesranch.com; 3530 Kahekili Hwy; 2hr ride $110; ☻ rides 8:15am & 12:15pm), a working cattle ranch, offers *paniolo*-style horseback rides past sea cliffs and waterfalls.

Next you'll pass a **waterfall** on the left, rain permitting. For another view, stop at the pull-off about 170yd north of the 8-mile marker and look down into the ravine below to see a picture-perfect waterfall framed by double pools.

Continuing around beep-as-you-go hairpin turns, the highway gradually levels out atop sea cliffs. Before the 10-mile marker is **Turnbull Studios & Sculpture Garden** (☎ 244-9838; ☻ 10am-5pm Tue-Fri), where you can view Bruce Turnbull's grand bronze and wood creations, as well as the works of other area artists…very cool stuff.

Just before the 14-mile marker, the hilltop **Kaukini Gallery & Gift Shop** (☎ 244-3371; ☻ 10am-5pm) has works by island artists, with watercolors, native-fiber baskets, pottery and much more. There's a soda machine here, too, and a good bird's-eye view of Kahakuloa village from the grounds.

Kahakuloa Village

Remote and quintessentially Hawaiian, Kahakuloa sits at the base of a tidy valley embraced by sea cliffs standing like sentinels on either side of the bay. Although it contains only a few dozen homes, Kahakuloa (Tall Lord) has two churches. The little tin-roof **Catholic mission** sits hillside at the southern end of town, just off the road, and the **Protestant church**, sporting a green wooden exterior and red-tile roof, hunkers down on the valley floor further north. The town doesn't have any shops, but villagers set up roadside stands selling shave ice, fruit and '*ono* (delicious) banana bread.

Heading up out of the valley a pull-off above the northern edge of town provides a bird's-eye view of the village and the surrounding coast. The rise on the south side of Kahakuloa Bay is **Kahakuloa Head** (636ft), once one of chief Kahekili's favorite cliff-diving spots. As you climb out of the valley, the terrain is hilly, with rocky cattle pastures punctuated by tall sisal plants. At a number of pull-offs, you can stop and explore. Lush pastures beg you to traipse down the cliffs and out along the rugged coastline.

Bellstone & Ocean Baths

That huge boulder with concave marks on the inland side of the road just past the 16-mile marker is **Pohaku Kani**, a bellstone. If you hit it with a rock on the Kahakuloa side, where the deepest indentations are, you might be able to get a hollow sound. It's pretty resonant if you hit it right, though it takes some imagination to hear it ring like a bell.

Just opposite, a couple of vague 4WD tracks lead off toward the coast. Park and head right (south) to reach an overlook; from there you can plan how to navigate your way down the lava cliffs to the **natural ocean baths** at the ocean's edge. Bordered by lava rock and encrusted with olivine minerals, incredibly clear pools sit in the midst of roaring surf. Some have natural steps, but if you're tempted to go in, size it up carefully – people unfamiliar with the water conditions here have been swept into the sea and drowned. If the area is covered in silt from recent storm runoffs, or the waves look too high, forget about it – it's dangerous.

Nakalele Point

From roadside pull-offs between the 38- and 39-mile markers, a brief walk leads out to a **light station** at the end of Nakalele Point. The coastline here has interesting pools, arches and other formations worn out of the rocks by the pounding surf. Continue walking along the coast (there's no trail) for another 15 minutes until you reach the impressive **Nakalele Blowhole**; if you see only a little sputtering, that's because you haven't found the *big* blowholes – keep going. During winter you can sometimes spot humpbacks breaching offshore.

As you continue north along the highway, Moloka'i comes into view, and the scenery is very lush on the way to **Honokohau Bay**, the furthest point north on Maui.

CENTRAL MAUI

Central Maui is the least touristed section of Maui, though the one everyone passes through. The airport is here. The main harbor is here. And all highways lead to Kahului, the commercial heart of the island. If you need a mega-shopping fix or have business to attend to, Kahului is probably where you're heading.

Not that this area is without its visitor attractions – far from it. Wind-whipped Kanaha Beach Park has morphed into the hottest kiteboarding Mecca in Hawaii, and both Kanaha and Ma'alaea have primo windsurfing, too. Central Maui claims the island's two waterbird sanctuaries and what may well be the world's top tropical aquarium. And each day a line of cars winds its way up to the emerald jewel of 'Iao Valley State Park. Wailuku, the sleepier end of it all, will appeal to those who like to poke around dusty antique shops and rub shoulders with the locals at neighborhood eateries.

KAHULUI

pop 20,150

Since it's home to the island's gateway airport, nearly everyone's first glimpse of Maui is of Kahului. Brace yourself – it's not going to be a paradisiacal scene. Kahului is a utilitarian, work-a-day town with industrial warehouses, strip malls and traffic congestion. You'll probably be relieved to be heading on to greener pastures or sunnier beaches, but after you

settle in, do come back and take a second look. There are hidden gems to be uncovered: mingle with easygoing locals at the Saturday morning swap meet, let the wind carry you across the waves at Kanaha Beach or catch a slack-key guitarist performing on the lawn of the Maui Arts & Cultural Center. Kahului is more than just the island's shopping center.

History

Fronted by the island's deepwater port, Kahului has long been the commercial heart of Maui. In the 1880s it became headquarters to Hawaii's first railroad, built to haul sugar from the refineries to the harbor. In 1900 an outbreak of bubonic plague hit Kahului, and the settlement that had grown up around the harbor was purposely burned to the ground.

Present-day Kahului is a planned community developed in the early 1950s by the Alexander & Baldwin sugar company. It was called 'Dream City' by cane workers, who had long dreamed of moving away from the dusty mill camps into a home of their own. These first tract houses are still found at the southern end of town.

Orientation

The airport is on the east side of town, connected to central Kahului by Keolani Pl, which leads to both the Haleakala Hwy (Hwy 37) and the Hana Hwy (Hwy 36). Ka'ahumanu Ave (Hwy 32) is Kahului's main artery, connecting the town to neighboring Wailuku (p350). Dairy Rd, to the south, links to both Lahaina (take Hwy 380) and Kihei (take Hwy 311).

Information

Bank of Hawaii (☎ 871-8250; 27 S Pu'unene Ave) Convenient location and a 24-hour ATM.

Borders Books & Music Café (☎ 877-6160; Maui Marketplace, 270 Dairy Rd; ⏱ 9am-10pm Sun-Thu, to 11pm Fri & Sat) Good selection of maps, Hawaiiana books and international newspapers.

Kahului Public Library (☎ 873-3097; 90 School St; ⏱ 1-8pm Tue, 10am-5pm Wed-Sat)

Kinko's (☎ 871-2000; Dairy Center, 395 Dairy Rd; per min 20¢; ⏱ 7am-10pm Mon-Fri, 9am-9pm Sat, 9am-6pm Sun) Fast internet access with no minimums.

Longs Drugs (☎ 877-0041; Maui Mall, 70 E Ka'ahumanu Ave; ⏱ 7am-midnight) The town's largest pharmacy, with both over-the-counter and prescription drugs.

MAUI

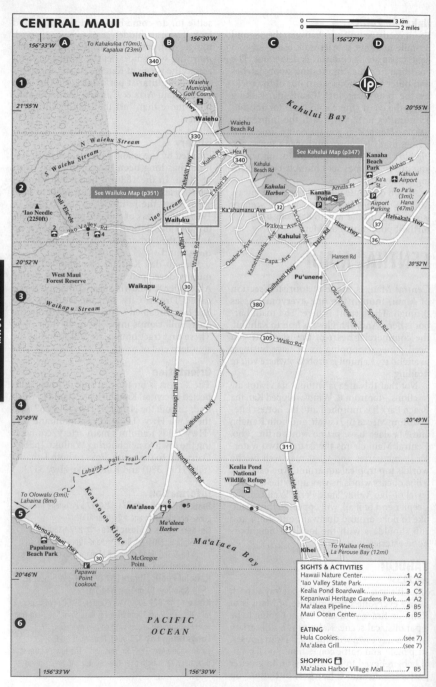

CENTRAL MAUI

MAUI

SIGHTS & ACTIVITIES

Hawaii Nature Center	1	A2
'Iao Valley State Park	2	A2
Kealia Pond Boardwalk	3	C5
Kepaniwai Heritage Gardens Park	4	A2
Ma'alaea Pipeline	5	B5
Maui Ocean Center	6	B5

EATING

Hula Cookies	(see 7)	
Ma'alaea Grill	(see 7)	

SHOPPING

Ma'alaea Harbor Village Mall	7	B5

Maui Visitors Bureau (☎ 872-3893; www.visitmaui
.com; Kahului airport; ☉ 7:45am-9:45pm) Has a staffed
booth in the airport's arrivals area. Pick up free tourist
magazines and brochures from the racks nearby.

Post office (☎ 871-2487; 138 S Pu'unene Ave, Kahului,
HI 96732) General delivery mail is held 30 days.

Sights

KANAHA BEACH PARK

When the winds pick up this mile-long beach
is surf city with hundred of colorful sails rip-
ping across the waves. Both windsurfing and
kiteboarding are so hot here that the beach
has been divvied up, with kiteboarders con-
verging at the southwest end and windsurfers
hitting the water at the northeast end. Kanaha
Beach is the best place in Maui for beginners

to learn both sports, and most windsurfing
and kiteboarding shops (p348) give their lessons here.

There's a section in the middle of the beach
roped off for swimmers, but this place is really
all about wind power. You'll find rest rooms,
showers and shaded picnic tables.

To get there, look for the shoreline access
sign down by the car-rental lots at the airport,
or if you're coming from downtown Kahului
take Amala Pl.

KANAHA POND BIRD SANCTUARY

Just beyond Hwy 37, near its junction with Hwy
36, **Kanaha Pond** (admission free; ☉ dusk-dawn) provides a haven for rare Hawaiian birds, including
the endangered black-necked stilt, a wading

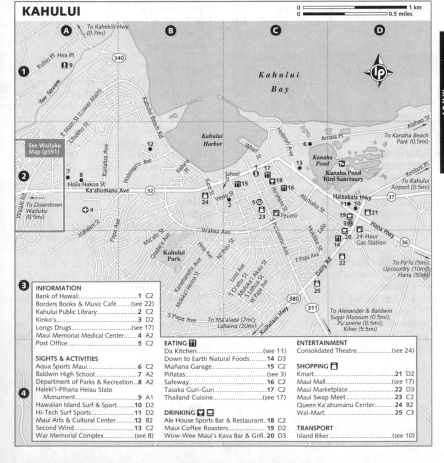

KAHULUI

bird with long orange legs that feeds along the pond's marshy edges. Even though this graceful bird has a population of just 1500 in the entire state, you can count on spotting it here.

An observation deck just a short walk beyond the parking lot offers the ideal lookout for spotting stilts, coots, ducks and black-crowned night herons. Close the gate and walk into the preserve quietly; you should be able to make several sightings right along the shoreline.

It's possible to hike on the sanctuary's service roads from September to March – when the birds aren't nesting – by obtaining a free permit from the **Department of Land & Natural Resources** (☎ 984-8100; Room 101, State Office Bldg, 54 S High St, Wailuku; ⊙ 7:45am-4:30pm Mon-Fri).

MAUI ARTS & CULTURAL CENTER
Maui's pride and joy, the $32 million **Maui Arts & Cultural Center** (MACC; ☎ 242-2787, tour reservations ext 228; www.mauiarts.org; 1 Cameron Way; admission free; ⊙ tour 11am Wed) is the island's premier concert venue. Free tours (reservations required) include both the concert halls and the grounds, which have the remains of a heiau. The center's **Schaefer International Gallery** (⊙ 11am-5pm Tue-Sun) has changing exhibits of works by both island and international artists.

Activities
WINDSURFING
Windswept Kahului is the base for Maui's main windsurfing operations. Board-and-rig rentals start around $50/300 per day/week. Introductory windsurfing classes last a couple of hours and cost around $85. The business is competitive, so ask about discounts. Shops that sell and rent gear and arrange lessons:
Hawaiian Island Surf & Sport (☎ 871-4981, 800-231-6958; www.hawaiianisland.com; 415 Dairy Rd; ⊙ 8:30am-6pm)
Hi-Tech Surf Sports (☎ 877-2111; www.htmaui.com; 425 Koloa St; ⊙ 9am-6pm)
Second Wind (☎ 877-7467, 800-936-7787; www .secondwindmaui.com; 111 Hana Hwy; ⊙ 9am-6pm Mon-Sat, 10am-5:30pm Sun)

KITEBOARDING
Kiteboarding has taken off big-time in Kahului. The action centers on Kite Beach, the southwest end of Kanaha Beach Park – go down and see what it's all about if you're thinking of giving it a fly. **Aqua Sports Maui** (☎ 242-8015; www.mauikiteboardinglessons.com; 96 Amala

Pl; 4hr intro course $240; ⊙ 8:30am-5pm) offers custom kiteboarding instruction tailored to your learning style.

Festivals & Events
Neil Pryde Slalom (www.mauiwindsurfing.org) Top windsurfers take to the waves at this windsurfing slalom competition at Kanaha Beach Park in mid-June.
Ki Ho'alu Slack-Key Guitar Festival (www.mauiarts .org) Held at the Maui Arts & Cultural Center in late June, this festival showcases big-name slack-key guitarists from throughout the state. A real cool scene with both old-time music and jazzed-up contemporary picking. And there are plenty of food booths selling local grinds, so plan to spend the day.
US Windsurfing Nationals (www.mauinationals.com) Held for a week in early August, this event consists of several windsurfing races for different levels and ages. Lots of action in the water.
Maui Marathon (www.mauimarathon.com) This 26.2-mile race held in mid-September begins at Queen Ka'ahumanu Center.

Sleeping
Kanaha Beach Park allows camping (see p309 for permits and fees), but the campsites are located right beneath Kahului airport's flight path with planes rumbling overhead from dawn to midnight. It's not only a noisy option, but folks down-and-out on their luck hang out here and personal safety is also an issue. Bottom line: there are better places to camp (see p309).

Eating
BUDGET
Down to Earth Natural Foods (☎ 877-2661; 305 Dairy Rd; ⊙ 7am-9pm Mon-Sat, 8am-8pm Sun) For health food or goodies to take to the beach, you'll find Maui's largest selection here, including a full deli with hot and cold dishes and an excellent salad bar.

Tasaka Guri-Guri (☎ 871-4513; Maui Mall, 70 E Ka'ahumanu Ave; scoop/quart 50¢/$5; ⊙ 10am-6pm Mon-Sat, to 8pm Fri, to 4pm Sun) For the coolest treat in town join the crowd at this hole-in-the-wall shop dishing up tangy homemade tropical sherbets. The *guri-guri*, as it's called, is so popular that locals pick up quarts on the way to the airport to take to friends when they go off-island.

Piñatas (☎ 877-8707; 395 Dairy Rd; mains $5-10; ⊙ 10:30am-8pm Mon-Sat, from 11am Sun) Simple and cheery, this serape-draped cantina won the *Maui News* readers poll for the best Mexican

TOP FIVE VEGETARIAN EATS

- **Fresh Mint** (p373) in Pa'ia
- **Veg Out** (p399) in Ha'iku
- **A Saigon Cafe** (p352) in Wailuku
- **Java Jazz & Soup Nutz** (p338) in Honokowai
- **Down to Earth Natural Foods** (opposite) in Kahului

food on Maui. The surfer's favorite is the 'kitchen sink burrito,' oversized and stuffed with beef, beans, guacamole, sour cream and just about everything else you'd find in a Mexican kitchen but the sink.

Da Kitchen (☎ 871-7782; 425 Koloa St; plate lunches $7-12; ☒ 9am-9pm) Tropical decor, friendly staff and unbeatable local grinds combine to make this a favorite with islanders. The *kalua* pork is, as they say, 'so tender it falls off da bone' and the more expensive plate lunches are big enough to feed two. Expect a crowd at lunch but don't be deterred, as the service is quick.

Thailand Cuisine (☎ 873-0225; Maui Mall, 70 E Ka'ahumanu Ave; mains $9-15; ☒ 10:30am-3:30pm & 5-9:30pm) The solid menu of well-prepared Thai dishes includes aromatic Panang curries redolent with lime and sweet basil, and a spicy vegetarian 'evil prince tofu' that will fire up your tastebuds. Cool it all down with a dish of homemade coconut ice cream.

If you need groceries, **Safeway** (☎ 877-3377; 170 E Kamehameha Ave; ☒ 24hr) supermarket is in the town center.

MIDRANGE

Mañana Garage (☎ 873-0220; 33 Lono Ave; lunch $10-15, dinner $19-30; ☒ 11am-9pm Mon-Tue, 11am-10:30pm Wed-Sat; ☒) A favorite venue with the theater crowd, this sizzling place sports a splashy Caribbean decor and delicious Latin-influenced dishes. The blackened-fish tostada and guava-glazed barbecued ribs are Hawaiian-accented house specials. Vegetarians can spice it up with the roasted veggie enchiladas accompanied by mole dulce. There's live salsa and Hawaiian music a few nights a week – call for the schedule.

Drinking

Wow-Wee Maui's Kava Bar & Grill (☎ 871-1414; 333 Dairy Rd; ☒ 6am-9pm Sun-Thu, to midnight Fri & Sat) This hip café is the place to try kava (also called *'awa* in Hawaiian) drinks served in a coconut

shell. Mildly intoxicating, this spicy elixir (yes, it's legal) is made from the roots of the *Piper methysticum* plant and was a favored ceremonial drink in old Hawaii.

Maui Coffee Roasters (☎ 877-2877; 444 Hana Hwy; ☒ 7am-6pm Mon-Fri, 8am-5pm Sat, 8am-2:30pm Sun) The island's best coffee deal will set you back just 65¢ a cup at this laid-back shop where locals linger over java and pastries while surfing the net on free wi-fi.

Ale House Sports Bar & Restaurant (☎ 877-9001; 355 E Kamehameha Ave) This high-energy place attracts mainland expats who come in droves to watch major league baseball and football games on a wall of TVs. And to make sure everyone shows up, it offers $2.50 drafts whenever a big game is on.

Entertainment

Maui Arts & Cultural Center (MACC; ☎ box office 242-7469; www.mauiarts.org; 1 Cameron Way) There's always something happening at this state-of-the-art entertainment complex, which boasts two indoor theaters and a large outdoor amphitheater, all with excellent acoustics. As Maui's main venue for music, theater and dance, it hosts everything from ukulele jams to touring rock bands. Check its online schedule to see what's in the lineup during your stay.

Consolidated Theatre (☎ 875-4910; Queen Ka'ahumanu Center, 275 Ka'ahumanu Ave) Shows first-run movies.

Shopping

Kahului has Maui's big-box discount chains and the lion's share of its shopping malls. Mainland discount stores like **Wal-Mart** (☎ 871-7820; 1011 Pakaula St; ☒ 6am-11pm) and **Kmart** (☎ 871-8553; 424 Dairy Rd; ☒ 8am-11pm) are all on or near Dairy Rd. The island's two largest malls, **Queen Ka'ahumanu Center** (☎ 877-4325; 275 Ka'ahumanu Ave; ☒ 9:30am-9pm Mon-Fri, to 7pm Sat, 9:30am-5pm Sun) and the **Maui Marketplace** (☎ 873-0400; 270 Dairy Rd; ☒ most stores 10am-9pm Mon-Sat, to 7pm Sun), are nearby.

Maui Swap Meet (☎ 877-3100; Pu'unene Ave; admission 50¢; ☒ 5:30am-1pm Sat) Skip the mall and head to this quintessential island scene where you buy direct from craftspeople and local farmers. You'll not only find fresh organic Hana fruits, Kula veggies and homemade banana bread, but it's a fun place to souvenir shop for everything from Hawaiian quilts to Maui designed T's. This place glows with aloha and the prices are unbeatable.

MAUI

Getting There & Around

TO/FROM THE AIRPORT

Most visitors pick up rental cars (p316) at Kahului airport. See p315 for shuttle and taxi information.

BICYCLE

Island Biker (☎ 877-7744; 415 Dairy Rd; per day/week $40/140; ☺ 9am-5pm Mon-Fri, to 3pm Sat) rents quality mountain-bikes and road-racing bikes.

BUS

The **Maui Bus** (www.mauicounty.gov/bus) connects Kahului with Ma'alaea, Kihei, Wailea and Lahaina; each route costs $1 and runs hourly. There are also free hourly buses that run around Kahului and connect to Wailuku.

HALEKI'I-PIHANA HEIAU STATE MONUMENT

One of Maui's most important historical sites, **Haleki'i-Pihana Heiau** (Map p347; Hea Pl; admission free; ☺ sunrise-sunset) holds the remains of two adjoining temples atop a knoll with a commanding view of central Maui.

The site was the royal court of Kahekili, Maui's last ruling chief, and the birthplace of Keopuolani, wife of Kamehameha the Great. After his victory at the battle of 'Iao in 1790, Kamehameha came to this site to worship his war god Ku, offering the last human sacrifice on Maui.

Haleki'i (House of Images), the first heiau, has stepped stone walls that tower above 'Iao Stream, which was the source for the stone used in construction. The pyramidlike mound of **Pihana Heiau** (Gathering Place of Supernatural Beings) is a five-minute walk beyond, but a thick overgrowth of kiawe makes it harder to discern. Much larger than Haleki'i, Pihana was the temple used for human sacrifices.

Although it's all but abandoned, a certain mana still emanates from the site. To imagine it all through the eyes of the Hawaiians 200 years ago, ignore the surrounding industrial warehouses and tract homes and concentrate instead on the wild ocean vistas.

To get to the monument, two miles northeast of central Wailuku, take Waiehu Beach Rd (Hwy 340) and turn inland onto Kuhio Pl three-quarters of a mile south of the intersection of Hwys 340 and 330. Then take the first left onto Hea Pl and drive up through the gates. The site is less than half a mile from Hwy 340.

WAILUKU

pop 12,300

Wailuku offers a curious juxtaposition of old and new. As the county capital, its central area has a modern facade marked by midrise office buildings. The backstreets are far more earthy with a mishmash of pawnshops, galleries and antique shops that make for interesting browsing.

Although there aren't a lot of tourists in town, Wailuku offers a bevy of historic sites. Among those listed on the National Register of Historic Places are the Bailey House Museum, Ka'ahumanu Church and the 'Iao Theatre. And thanks to the combination of low rent and hungry government employees, Wailuku has several good eating options at prices that shame Maui's more touristed towns.

Information

The county and state office buildings are adjacent on S High St, near its intersection with Main St.

First Hawaiian Bank (☎ 877-2377; 27 N Market St)

Maui Memorial Medical Center (Map p347; ☎ 244-9056; 221 Mahalani St; ☺ 24hr) This is the island's main hospital, with 24-hour emergency services. It is in the eastern suburbs of Wailuku.

Maui Visitors Bureau (MVB; ☎ 244-3530, 800-525-6284; www.visitmaui.com; 1727 Wili Pa Loop; ☺ 8am-4:30pm Mon-Fri) Essentially an administrative office – you'll find better information and more brochures at the airport booth (p345).

Post office (☎ 244-1653; 250 Imi Kala St; ☺ 8am-4:30pm Mon-Fri, 9am-noon Sat)

Dangers & Annoyances

One caution: the town can get rough at night. The public parking lot on W Main St is an after-dark hangout rife with drug dealing and fights that gets more police calls than any other spot on Maui.

Sights

BAILEY HOUSE MUSEUM

The 1833 home of missionary Edward Bailey has been converted into a worthwhile **museum** (☎ 244-3326; 2375 W Main St; adult/child under 12 $5/1; ☺ 10am-4pm Mon-Sat) highlighting local history. The second story remains much the same as it was in missionary days, decorated with antiques and some of the works that Bailey, an accomplished engraver, created.

But it's the Hawaiian section on the ground floor that's the real prize. The museum boasts

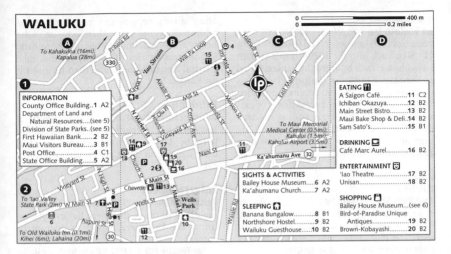

WAILUKU

0 — 400 m
0 — 0.2 miles

To Kahakuloa (16mi);
Kapalua (28mi)

INFORMATION
County Office Building..**1** A2
Department of Land and
  Natural Resources....(see 5)
Division of State Parks..(see 5)
First Hawaiian Bank......**2** B2
Maui Visitors Bureau.....**3** B1
Post Office....................**4** C1
State Office Building......**5** A2

To 'Iao Valley
State Park (2mi)

To Old Wailuku Inn (0.1mi);
Kihei (6mi); Lahaina (20mi)

To Maui Memorial
Medical Center (0.5mi);
Kahului (1.5mi);
Kahului Airport (3.5mi)

Ka'ahumanu Ave **32**

SIGHTS & ACTIVITIES
Bailey House Museum....**6** A2
Ka'ahumanu Church.......**7** A2

SLEEPING
Banana Bungalow............**8** B1
Northshore Hostel...........**9** B1
Wailuku Guesthouse.....**10** B2

EATING
A Saigon Café...............**11** C2
Ichiban Okazuya...........**12** B2
Main Street Bistro.........**13** B2
Maui Bake Shop & Deli.**14** B2
Sam Sato's...................**15** B1

DRINKING
Café Marc Aurel...........**16** B2

ENTERTAINMENT
'Iao Theatre.................**17** B2
Unisan.........................**18** B2

SHOPPING
Bailey House Museum....(see 6)
Bird-of-Paradise Unique
Antiques......................**19** B2
Brown-Kobayashi..........**20** B2

a superb collection of handcrafted bowls made from native woods and other ancient artifacts, including stone adzes, feather lei and tapa cloth. There's also a display of spears, shark-tooth daggers and other weapons similar to those used in the bloody battles at nearby 'Iao Valley.

Don't miss the 10ft redwood surfboard that belonged to surfing legend Duke Kahanamoku and the koa fishing canoe (c 1900), which are in an open-air exhibit at the right side of the parking lot.

KA'AHUMANU CHURCH
The oldest Congregational church in Maui, **Ka'ahumanu Church** (cnr Main & High Sts) dates to 1832 and takes its name from Queen Ka'ahumanu, who cast aside the old gods and burned temple idols, allowing Christianity to flourish. She visited Wailuku and in her ever-humble manner requested that the church bear her name.

Missionary Edward Bailey built the church atop a former heiau site and royal compound. The old clock in the steeple, brought around the Horn in the 19th century, still keeps accurate time. Hymns are sung in Hawaiian at Sunday morning services, but at other times it's a look-from-outside site, as the church is usually locked.

Festivals & Events
The **Maui County Fair** (www.mauicountyfair.com) is held in late September at the War Memorial Complex. This venerable annual fair has agri-cultural exhibits, amusement rides, ethnic foods and a dazzling orchid display.

Sleeping
BUDGET
Wailuku's two hostels are in older, termite-gnawed buildings that occasionally get a fresh coat of paint but are otherwise spartan. Because of frequent staffing changes it's hard to predict what your experience will be like. Best advice: size up the places when you arrive and don't dish out money for a lengthy stay in advance.

Banana Bungalow (☎ 244-5090, 800-846-7835; www .mauihostel.com; 310 N Market St; dm $26, s/d with shared bathroom $54/65; ▯) The dorms are cramped, but on the plus side amenities include a backyard hot tub and BBQ facilities, coin laundry, shed for storing windsurfing gear, free airport shuttle and island tours.

Northshore Hostel (☎ 986-8095, 866-946-7835; www.northshorehostel.com; 2080 E Vineyard St; dm $25, s/d with shared bathroom $50/65; ▯) The smaller of the two hostels, it has fewer offerings and is typically the last resort. There is a common kitchen plus gear storage.

Wailuku Guesthouse (☎ 877-986-8270; www.wailuku house.com; 210 S Market St; r $69-85; ▣) In a better part of town than the hostels, this affordable family-run guesthouse offers Hawaiian-style hospitality with simple, clean rooms, each with their own bathroom and private entrance. There's a refrigerator and coffeemaker in the rooms, and guests have access to a BBQ and pool in the garden.

MAUI

MIDRANGE

Old Wailuku Inn (☎ 244-5897, 800-305-4899; www
.mauiinn.com; 2199 Kaho'okele St; r incl breakfast $140-190;
☒) Step back into the 1920s in this elegant
period home, built by a wealthy banker. Listed
on the State Register of Historic Places, this
authentically restored inn retains the antique
furniture and native hardwood floors of earlier times, while discreetly adding modern
amenities. Each room is unique, but all are
large and comfy with traditional Hawaiian
quilts warming the beds.

Eating

BUDGET

Maui Bake Shop & Deli (☎ 242-0064; 2092 Vineyard
St; snacks $2-5; ☺ 6am-2:30pm Mon-Fri, 7am-1pm Sat)
Wailuku's most central bakery is a family
operation that makes fancy French pastries
and tasty croissant sandwiches.

Sam Sato's (☎ 244-7124; 1750 Wili Pa Loop; mains $5-8;
☺ 7am-2pm Mon-Sat) Don't even think of coming
during the noon rush – islanders flock here
from far and wide for the dry noodles (not
really dry, but cooked with a soy-based sauce)
and saimin noodle soups that are the specialties at this bustling eatery. Sato's also makes
manju (Japanese cakes filled with sweet bean
paste), which Honolulu residents rave about
and are sold at the counter until 4pm.

Ichiban Okazuya (☎ 244-7276; 2133 Kaohu St; mains
$6-7; ☺ 10am-2pm & 4-7pm Mon-Fri) Little more than
a tin-roofed shed, this place tucked behind
the government buildings has been dishing
out tasty Japanese-style plate lunches to office
workers for half a century, so you'd better believe it has the recipes down pat. It's takeout,
but there's an inviting picnic table shaded by
an old mango tree out back.

MIDRANGE

Main Street Bistro (☎ 244-6816; 2051 Main St; mains
$6-14; ☺ 11am-2:30pm Mon-Fri) Upbeat decor
and sumptuous bistro fare make a winning
combination at this downtown eatery that's
a favorite of the business-lunch crowd. Innovative salads and sandwiches, juicy steaks and
tempting dishes like pan-roasted fresh catch
with asparagus shore up the menu. Save room
for the homemade banana cream pie.

A Saigon Café (☎ 248-9560; cnr Main & Kaniela Sts;
mains $7-20; ☺ 10am-9:30pm Mon-Sat, to 8:30pm Sun)
Follow the locals to this backstreet gem serving the finest Vietnamese fare on Maui. Start
with the Buddha rolls, a delightful combin-

ation of tofu, veggies and fresh basil served
with spicy peanut sauce, then move on to the
hearty *pho* noodle soup or one of the aromatic
lemongrass curries. It's tricky to find: take
Central Ave to Nani St and then turn south
on Kaniela St.

Drinking

Café Marc Aurel (☎ 244-0852; 28 N Market St; ☺ 7am-at
least 9pm Mon-Sat) Organic espresso and foamy
lattes by day, and a wine bar with jazz and
belly dancing at night are on tap at this hip
café.

Entertainment

Unisan (☎ 244-4550; 2102 Vineyard St) The main
nightspot in town, this place has everything
from karaoke to jazz, as well as open-mike
comedy.

'Iao Theatre (☎ 242-6969; N Market St) Beautifully
restored after years of neglect, the 1928 art-
deco theater that once hosted such big names
as Sinatra and Bob Hope is now the venue for
community theater productions.

Shopping

Bailey House Museum (☎ 244-3326; 2375 W Main St)
The gift shop here sells fine local crafts and a
good selection of books about Maui.

Brown-Kobayashi (☎ 242-0804; 38 N Market St)
Museum-quality Asian antiques.

Bird-of-Paradise Unique Antiques (☎ 242-7699;
56 N Market St) Poke around here for vintage
Hawaiiana.

Getting There & Around

The **Maui Bus** (www.mauicounty.gov/bus) runs free
buses between Wailuku and Kahului hourly
from 7:30am to 8:30pm. Wailuku stops include the state office building, the Maui Memorial Medical Center and the post office.

'IAO VALLEY ROAD

Filled now as it is with tour buses and picnickers, it's hard to imagine 'Iao Valley was once
the site of Maui's bloodiest battle. In 1790
Kamehameha the Great invaded Kahului by
sea and routed the defending Maui warriors
up into precipitous 'Iao Valley. Those unable
to escape over the mountains were slaughtered
along the stream. The waters of 'Iao Stream
were so choked with bodies that the area was
called Kepaniwai (Dammed Waters).

'Iao Valley Rd follows that same streamside
route, but today it's a pretty drive up to 'Iao

Valley State Park and Maui's most photographed landmark, 'Iao Needle.

Kepaniwai Heritage Gardens Park

Two miles west of Wailuku, this family-oriented **park** ('Iao Valley Rd; ☉ 7am-7pm) pays tribute to Hawaii's varied ethnic heritage. Among the highlights are a traditional Hawaiian *hale*, a New England-style missionary home, a Filipino farmer's hut, Japanese gardens with stone pagodas and a Chinese pavilion with a statue of revolutionary hero Sun Yat-sen (who, incidentally, briefly lived on Maui). 'Iao Stream runs through the park, bordered by picnic shelters with BBQ pits. The place is cheerfully alive with families picnicking here on weekends.

At the west end of the park is the **Hawaii Nature Center** (☎ 244-6500; 875 'Iao Valley Rd; adult/child 5-12 $6/4; ☉ 10am-4pm), a nonprofit educational facility with kid-oriented exhibits. The center also leads two-hour **rain-forest walks** (adult/child 5-12 $30/20); reservations are required.

At a bend in the road a half-mile after Kepaniwai County Park, you'll likely see a few cars pulled over and their occupants staring off into Pali 'Ele'ele, a gorge on the right where a **rock formation** has eroded into the shape of a profile. Some legends associate it with a powerful *kahuna* (priest) who lived here during the 1500s, but today it bears an uncanny resemblance to former President John F Kennedy. If parking is difficult here, just continue on to 'Iao Valley State Park, as it's only a couple of minutes' walk from the viewing site back to the viewing site.

'Iao Valley State Park

If you've seen just one photograph of Maui's lush interior, odds are it was of 'Iao Needle, the green pinnacle that provides the focal point for **'Iao Valley State Park** (admission free; ☉ 7am-7pm). Nestled in the mountains, 3 miles west of central Wailuku, this park extends clear up to Pu'u Kukui (5788ft), Maui's highest and wettest point.

'IAO NEEDLE

The rock pinnacle that rises straight up 2250ft takes its name from 'Iao, the beautiful daughter of Maui. 'Iao Needle is said to be 'Iao's clandestine lover, captured by Maui and turned to stone. A monument to love, this is truly the big kahuna, the ultimate phallic symbol.

Whether you believe in legends or not, this place looks like something from the pages of a fairy tale. Clouds rising up the valley form an ethereal shroud around the top of 'Iao Needle. With a stream meandering beneath and the steep cliffs of the West Maui Mountains in the backdrop, it's a picture-postcard scene. Just a few minutes' walk from the parking lot, you'll reach a bridge where most people snap their photos of the needle. A better idea is to take the walkway just before the bridge that loops downhill by the stream; this leads to the nicest photo angle, one that captures the stream, bridge and 'Iao Needle together.

TRAILS

After you cross the bridge you'll come to two short trails that start opposite each other. Both take just 10 minutes to walk and shouldn't be missed. The upper path leads skyward up a series of steps, ending at a sheltered lookout with a closeup view of 'Iao Needle. The lower path leads down along 'Iao Stream, skirting the rock-strewn streambed past native hau trees with their fragrant hibiscus-like flowers. Look around and you'll be able to spot fruiting guava trees as well.

PU'UNENE

Pu'unene is all about sugar. Vast fields of sugarcane expand out from the Hawaiian Commercial & Sugar (C&S) Company's mill that sits smack in the center of the village. If you happen to swing by when the mill is boiling down the sugarcane, the air hangs heavy with the sweet smell of molasses.

No surprise here, Pu'unene's main attraction is the **Alexander & Baldwin Sugar Museum** (☎ 871-8058; cnr Pu'unene Ave & Hansen Rd; adult/child 6-17 $5/2; ☉ 9:30am-4:30pm Mon-Sat, also Sun Jul & Aug), an intriguing little collection in the former home of the mill's superintendent. Exhibits

---

DETOUR: OLD PU'UNENE

A little slice of a bygone plantation village is hidden behind the sugar mill in Pu'unene. There, a long-forgotten church lies abandoned in a field of waving cane, across from the village's old schoolhouse. But the place isn't a ghost town. Out back, just beyond the school, is an old shack that's served as a used bookstore since 1913. It's a bit musty and dusty, but still sells books for a mere dime. To get there turn off Mokulele Hwy (Hwy 311) onto Hansen Rd and take the first right onto Old Pu'unene Ave, continuing past the old Pu'unene Meat Market building (c 1926) and the mill. Turn left after half a mile, just past a little bridge. Just before the pavement ends, turn right and drive behind the old school to reach the bookstore.

---

give the skinny on the sugarcane biz and include a working scale model of a cane-crushing plant.

Most interesting, however, are the images of people. The museum traces how Samuel Alexander and Henry Baldwin gobbled up vast chunks of Maui land, how they fought tooth and nail with an ambitious Claus Spreckels to gain access to Upcountry water, and how they dug the extensive irrigation systems that made large-scale plantations viable.

Representing the other end of the scale is a turn-of-the-20th-century labor contract from the Japanese Emigration Company stating that the laborer shall be paid $15 a month for working the fields 10 hours a day, 26 days a month.

KEALIA POND NATIONAL WILDLIFE REFUGE

A bird-watcher's oasis, the **Kealia Pond NWR** (☎ 875-1582; Mokulele Hwy; ☼ 7:30am-4pm Mon-Fri) harbors native waterbirds year-round and hosts migratory ducks and shorebirds from

---

TAKE THE BOARDWALK

The coastal dunes nestling Kealia Pond provide not only a fragile habitat for native waterbirds but also a nesting site for the endangered hawksbill sea turtle. Until now the dunes, and the wonders of nature they harbor, have been largely inaccessible, but in 2007 an elevated boardwalk extending along 2200ft of marsh was opened, providing one of the finest nature walks on Maui. Interpretive plaques and benches along the way offer opportunities to stop and enjoy the splendor, and in winter you might also be able to spot passing offshore humpback whales. The boardwalk begins on N Kihei Rd near the 2-mile marker.

October to April. In the rainy winter months Kealia Pond swells to more than 400 acres, making it one of the largest natural ponds in Hawaii. In summer it shrinks to half the size, giving it a skirt of crystalline salt (Kealia means 'salt-encrusted place').

You can view the pond from the boardwalk (see boxed text, left) on N Kihei Rd, as well as from the refuge's visitor center off Mokulele Hwy at the 6-mile marker. In both places, you're almost certain to spot wading Hawaiian black-necked stilts, Hawaiian coots and black-crowned night herons – all native waterbirds that thrive in this sanctuary. The visitor center occupies an abandoned catfish farm with footpaths atop the walls that separate the old fishponds, a layout that allows you to get very close to the birds, and this is also the best place to see wintering osprey, a majestic fish hawk that dive-bombs for its prey in the fishponds.

MA'ALAEA BAY
pop 450

Ma'alaea Bay borders the south side of the plains that run between the great rises of Haleakala and the West Maui Mountains. Prevailing trade winds from the north funnel between these two mountain masses, giving Ma'alaea the strongest winds on the island. By midday you'll need to hold on to your hat.

Sights

Dedicated to Hawaii's dazzling marine life, **Maui Ocean Center** (☎ 270-7000; www.mauioceancenter.com; 192 Ma'alaea Rd; adult/child 3-12 $22/15; ☼ 9am-6pm Jul & Aug, to 5pm Sep-Jun) is the largest tropical aquarium in the USA. Kids love the place but adults will also be blown away by the brilliant fish and coral here.

Exhibits start with creatures of shallow intertidal waters and progress into deep ocean life. The center filters seawater from the adjacent bay through its tanks, providing a nutrient-rich environment that allows coral (it boasts the world's largest aquarium collection) and fish to thrive. The extensive 'living reef' section focuses on the sealife you'd spot snorkeling in Hawaii, with displays identifying rainbow-colored wrasses, menacing moray eels and other tropical fish.

Most spectacular of all is the enormous open ocean tank with a 54ft glass tunnel that allows you to walk right through the center of the tank as schools of fish, gliding eagle rays and menacing tiger sharks encircle you. It's as close as you'll get to being underwater without donning dive gear. The 'Hawaiians and the sea' exhibit offers insights into ancient fishing techniques, including fishpond aquaculture. For a meditative experience, don't miss the mesmerizing column of free-floating jellyfish, a sort of living lava lamp. Elsewhere are interactive displays on whales, as well as a fun touch pond for kids and a sea turtle pool where injured turtles are treated for eventual release into the wild.

Activities

WINDSURFING & SURFING

Wicked winds from the north shoot straight out toward Kaho'olawe, creating some of the best **windsurfing** conditions on Maui. In winter, when the wind dies down elsewhere, windsurfers still fly along Ma'alaea Bay.

The bay also has a couple of hot surfing spots. The **Ma'alaea Pipeline**, south of the harbor, freight-trains right and is the fastest surf break in all Hawaii. Summer's southerly swells produce huge tubes. Ma'alaea Bay is fronted by a continuous 3-mile stretch of sandy **beach**, running from Ma'alaea Harbor south to Kihei,

---

DAREDEVILS PLUNGE

If the idea of swimming in a tank full of sharks sounds like a thrill, then this might be for you. Divers at **Maui Ocean Center** (☎ 270-7000; dive $199; ☯ dives 8:30am Mon, Wed & Fri) take daredevils on a dive into a 750,000-gallon deep-ocean pool where they swim with large fish, rays and, yes, even full-grown sharks. You must be at least 15 years old and a certified diver to take the plunge. There's a limit of just four divers a day, so advance reservations are essential.

---

which can be accessed at several places along N Kihei Rd.

HIKING

Hilltop views of Kaho'olawe and Lana'i are in store along the **Lahaina Pali Trail**, which follows an ancient footpath as it zigzags steeply up through native dryland. After the first mile it passes into open, sun-baked scrub, from where you can see Haleakala and the fertile central plains. Ironwood trees precede the crossing of Kealaoloa Ridge (1600ft), after which you descend through Ukumehame Gulch. Look for stray petroglyphs and *paniolo* graffiti. Stay on the footpath all the way down to Papalaua Beach and don't detour onto 4WD roads. The 5.5-mile trail should take about 2½ hours each way.

You can hike in either direction, but starting off early from the east side of the mountains keeps you ahead of the blistering sun. The trailhead access road, marked by a Na Ala Hele sign, is on Hwy 30, about 100yd south of the intersection of Hwy 380. If you prefer to start at the west end or want to have a ride waiting for you when you finish, the trailhead is 200yd south of the 11-mile marker on Hwy 30.

Eating

Ma'alaea Harbor Village Mall, the shopping center adjacent to the Maui Ocean Center, has several eateries.

Hula Cookies (☎ 243-2271; Ma'alaea Harbor Village Mall; snacks $2-4; ☯ 10am-6pm Mon-Sat, to 5pm Sun) Have you been good? Reward the inner child in you with fresh-made cookies and island-made ice cream chockful of macadamia nuts, coconut and mango.

Ma'alaea Grill (☎ 243-2206; Ma'alaea Harbor Village Mall; lunch $7-15, dinner $17-33; ☯ 10:30am-3pm Mon, to 9pm Tue-Sun) This place has it all: a fantastic harbor view, attentive service and excellent food. Fresh seafood, organic salads and tasty focaccia sandwiches shore up the menu. At dinner the blackened mahimahi with fresh papaya salsa and the coconut-fried shrimp are favorites. And it's family friendly, with a $5 kids menu.

Getting There & Away

Located at a crossroads, Ma'alaea has good connections to the rest of Maui's public bus system. The **Maui Bus** (www.mauicounty.gov/bus) connects Ma'alaea Harbor Village shopping center with Lahaina, Kahului, Kihei and Wailea. Service depends on the route, but buses ($1) operate hourly from around 6am to 8pm.

SOUTH MAUI

South Maui serves up an alluring combination of reliably sunny weather and fab beaches. There are more water adventures to be had here than anyplace else on Maui. Snorkel coral reefs teeming with turtles, kayak remote bays frequented by dolphins, take off in an outrigger canoe – the list goes on and on.

The three communities that make up south Maui each have their own distinct personality and appeal. Kihei offers the ultimate family-friendly vacation scene, with scores of condos along an endless stretch of beach. Wailea takes it upscale, with tony resorts and designer golf courses. Makena marks the quieter end of it all, with undeveloped beaches and untamed scenery.

KIHEI
pop 19,850

With 6 miles of sun-kissed beaches, it's no secret why Kihei has boomed into the island's largest tourist destination. Yes, much of the coast is willy-nilly with condos, eateries and shopping centers, but then again it's got everything one needs for a seaside vacation. And the town's done a lot to mitigate some of the binge building of the past, adding walking

---

MAUI FOR NA KEIKI

Na keiki (children) love a day at the beach, so what better place to start than in the water?

■ Take a Hawaiian-style canoe ride from **Polo Beach** (p364).

■ Get a close-up look at whales on a **whale watching cruise** (p324).

■ Be dazzled by sharks and stingrays at the walk-through tank at **Maui Ocean Center** (p354).

■ Don a mask and meet a turtle up close at **Turtle Beach** (p367).

■ Refresh with a rainbow-striped shave ice at **Local Boys Shave Ice** (p361).

---

and cycling paths and restricting new development. Truth be told, Kihei has plenty of advantages over some of Maui's ritzier destinations. The abundance of rooms makes Kihei's rates a relative bargain, the bar and club scene hops, and Kihei's dining has finally come into its own.

Orientation

The Pi'ilani Hwy (Hwy 31) runs parallel to and bypasses the start-and-stop traffic of S Kihei Rd. Half a dozen crossroads connect the two, making it easy to zip in and out of Kihei efficiently. Bike lanes run along the Pi'ilani Hwy and S Kihei Rd, but cyclists need to be cautious of inattentive drivers making sudden turns across the lanes.

Information

Bank of Hawaii (Map p357; ☎ 879-5844; Azeka Mauka, 1279 S Kihei Rd)

Coffee Store (Map p357; ☎ 875-4244; Azeka Mauka, 1279 S Kihei Rd; per min 20¢; ☺ 6:30am-8pm Mon-Sat, to 5pm Sun)

Cyberbean Internet Café (Map p358; ☎ 879-4799; Kihei Town Center, 1881 S Kihei Rd; per min 20¢; ☺ 7am-9pm Mon-Sat, 8am-8pm Sun) Several computers, no waiting.

Kihei Police District Station (Map p358; ☎ 244-6400; Kihei Town Center, 1881 S Kihei Rd; ☺ 7:45am-4:30pm Mon-Fri)

Lipoa Laundry Center (Map p357; Lipoa Center, 40 E Lipoa St; ☺ 8am-9pm Mon-Sat, to 5pm Sun)

Longs Drugs (Map p357; ☎ 879-2033; 1215 S Kihei Rd; ☺ 7am-midnight) Kihei's largest pharmacy.

Post office (Map p357; ☎ 879-1987; 1254 S Kihei Rd)

Urgent Care Maui Physicians (Map p357; ☎ 879-7781; 1325 S Kihei Rd; ☺ 7am-10pm) This clinic accepts walk-in patients.

Sights

In terms of swimming beaches, the further south you go, the better it gets. At the northern end of Kihei, swimming is not advised, but kayaking is good in the morning and windsurfers set off in the afternoon. For the best snorkeling in Kihei, head to Keawakapu Beach.

KEAWAKAPU BEACH

There's a lot to like about this beach, which stretches from the southernmost part of Kihei to Wailea's Mokapu Beach. Not only is Keawakapu Beach (Map p358) less crowded than Kihei's roadside beaches but it offers a

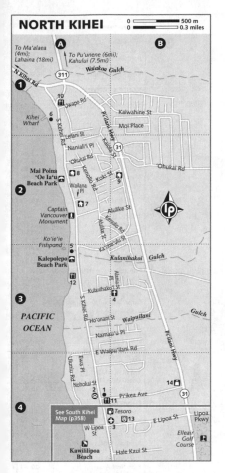

NORTH KIHEI

parking can be found at the side of Mana Kai Maui.

KAMA'OLE BEACH PARKS

Kama'ole is one long beach divided into three sections (Kam I, II and III; Map p358) by rocky points. All three are lovely golden-sand beaches with full facilities, including lifeguards.

Water conditions vary with the weather, but swimming is usually good. For the most part, these beaches have sandy bottoms with a fairly steep drop, which tends to create good conditions for bodysurfing, especially in winter.

For snorkeling, the south end of Kama'ole Beach Park III has some nearshore rocks harboring a bit of coral and a few colorful fish.

HAWAIIAN ISLANDS HUMPBACK WHALE NATIONAL MARINE SANCTUARY

The **marine sanctuary headquarters** (Map p357; ☎ 879-2818, 800-831-4888; www.hawaiihumpbackwhale.noaa.gov; 726 S Kihei Rd; ☺ 10am-4pm Mon-Fri) is a great place to get acquainted with Hawaii's spectacular

stellar view, and during winter humpback whales come quite close to shore.

With its cushiony soft sand, it's a favorite place for people doing sunrise yoga and wake-up strolls and it's also a good spot for a sunset swim. Mornings are the best time for snorkeling; head to the rocky outcrops that form the northern and southern ends of the beach.

There are three beach access points, all with outdoor showers. To get to the south end, go south on S Kihei Rd until it dead-ends at a beach parking lot. Near the middle of the beach, there's a parking lot at the corner of Kilohana and S Kihei Rd; look for a blue shoreline access sign on the *makai* side of the street. At the northern end, beach

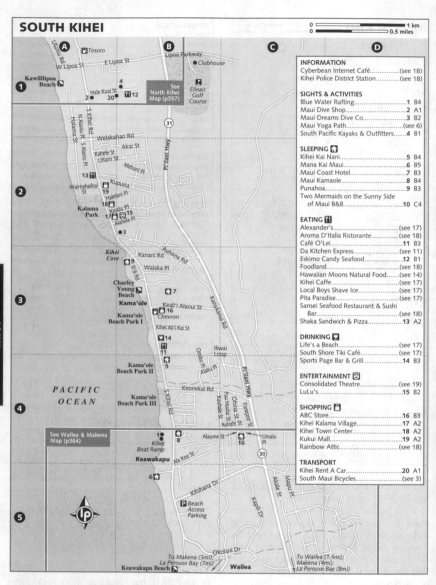

SOUTH KIHEI

0 ———————— 1 km
0 ———————— 0.5 miles

marine life. The building overlooks an ancient fishpond that's under restoration and the oceanfront lookout is ideal for sighting the humpback whales that frequent the bay during winter. There's even a free telescope set up for viewing. Displays on whales and sea turtles offer interesting background on the creatures you might spot here. And there's always a whale

poster or other free handout available for the kids. Want to take it deeper? Swing by at 11am on Tuesday for the center's '45 Ton Talks' on whales.

KALEPOLEPO BEACH PARK
Children love to play in the calm, shallow waters at this beach park (Map p357), which

---

DETOUR: CHARLEY YOUNG BEACH

Hidden off a side street, this neighborhood beach (Map p358) is the least touristed strand in Kihei. It's a real jewel in the rough, broad and sandy, and backed by wispy ironwood trees. You're apt to find fishers casting their lines, families playing volleyball and someone strumming a guitar. It also has some of the better bodysurfing waves in Kihei. Beach parking is on the corner of S Kihei Rd and Kaiau Pl. To get to the beach, simply walk to the end of Kaiau Pl and follow the steps down the cliff.

---

borders the south side of the Hawaiian Islands Humpback Whale National Marine Sanctuary headquarters. The swimming area is essentially a big pool, because the waters are encircled by the stone walls of **Ko'ie'ie Fishpond** (Map p357). The most intact fishpond remaining on Maui, Ko'ie'ie was built in the 16th century to raise mullet for the *ali'i* (royalty). The 3-acre fishpond is on the National Register of Historic Places.

MAI POINA 'OE IA'U BEACH PARK

This long sandy beach (Map p357) at the northern end of Kihei has full facilities. Sunbathing is good in the morning before the wind picks up, while windsurfing is best in the afternoon. Windsurfing lessons are given here, and outrigger canoes and kayaks launch from the beach.

KALAMA PARK

A retaining wall runs along the shoreline, so most of the action here is for landlubbers. This expansive park (Map p358) has ball fields, tennis and volleyball courts, a skateboard park, a playground, picnic pavilions, rest rooms and showers.

DAVID MALO'S CHURCH

Philosopher David Malo, who built this church in 1853, was the first Hawaiian ordained to the Christian ministry and coauthor of Hawaii's first constitution. While most of Malo's original church was dismantled, a 3ft-high section of the walls still stands beside a palm grove. Pews are lined up inside the stone walls, where open-air services are held at 9am on Sunday by **Trinity Episcopal Church-by-the-Sea** (Map p357; 100 Kulanihako'i St).

Activities

DIVING & SNORKELING

Maui Dive Shop (Map p358; ☎ 879-3388; www.mauidiveshop.com; 1455 S Kihei Rd; dives/courses from $90/350; ☷ 6am-9pm), the main outlet of this islandwide diving chain, is a good spot to rent or buy water-sports gear, including bodyboards, snorkels, fins and wet suits.

Maui Dreams Dive Co (Map p358; ☎ 874-5332, 888-921-3483; www.mauidreamsdiveco.com; 1993 S Kihei Rd; two-tank dives/courses from $89/300; ☷ 7am-6pm), a family-run, five-star PADI outfit, gets enthusiastic reviews for its personal attention and environmentally friendly approach.

Blue Water Rafting (Map p358; ☎ 879-7238; www.bluewaterrafting.com; Kihei Boat Ramp; Molokini/Kanaio trip $45/90; ☷ 9am-5pm) has a Molokini Express trip that's perfect for those who want to zip out to the crater, snorkel and be back within two hours. An adventurous half-day trip heads southward to snorkel remote coves along the Kanaio coast.

KAYAKING & CANOEING

South Pacific Kayaks & Outfitters (Map p358; ☎ 875-4848, 800-776-2326; www.southpacifickayaks.com; 95 Hale Kuai St; 1-/2-person kayaks per day $40/50, tours $65-99;

TOP 10 BEACHES

- **Ulua Beach** (p363) for morning snorkeling and afternoon bodysurfing
- **Ho'okipa Beach** (p370), where experts head for primo surfing and windsurfing
- **Kanaha Beach** (p347) for kickin' kiteboarding and intermediate windsurfing
- **Kahekili Beach** (p334), Ka'anapali's least-crowded snorkeling and swimming spot
- **Honolua Bay** (p341) for surfing in winter, snorkeling in summer
- **Kapalua Bay** (p340), a beauty anytime for snorkeling and swimming
- **Big Beach** (p368) for long beach strolls, bodyboarding and bodysurfing
- **Malu'aka Beach** (p367), the best place to snorkel with turtles
- **Little Beach** (p368), haunt of the clothing-optional crowd
- **Wai'anapanapa Beach** (p377), Maui's most stunning black-sand beach

MAUI

⊙ 6am-9pm) is a long-established operation, and leads kayak-and-snorkel tours in the 'Ahihi-Kina'u Natural Area Reserve vicinity. It also rents kayaks for those who want to go off on their own, and will deliver them to Makena Landing (p367).

Kihei Canoe Club (Map p357; www.kiheicanoeclub .com; Kihei Wharf; donation $25) invites visitors to share in the mana by joining members in paddling their outrigger canoes on Tuesday and Thursday mornings. No advance registration is necessary; just show up at the wharf at 7:30am. The donation helps offset the cost of maintaining the canoes and entitles you to join them each Tuesday and Thursday for the rest of the month.

YOGA

If you need to loosen up after a long flight, **Maui Yoga Path** (Map p358; ☎ 874-5545; 2960 S Kihei Rd; class $17; ⊙ 9am) has sessions at Mana Kai Maui resort that focus on the relaxing stretches and breathing exercises of Iyengar yoga.

Festivals & Events

Whale Day Parade & Celebration (www.great mauiwhalefestival.com) Kihei's top family-oriented festival, this big bash celebrates Maui's humpback whales with live entertainment and dancing all day, a parade, local crafts and food booths. Fun things for kids include a whale regatta (Maui's version of a rubber duck race), a children's carnival and storytelling. It's held at Kalama Park, next to the big whale statue, on a Saturday in mid-February.

Maui Ohana Pride (www.mauigayinfo.com) Maui's Gay & Lesbian Organization and supporters get together to celebrate at Kalama Park on the first Sunday in June, with drag races (kings and queens), a free BBQ dinner and

---

TOP FIVE WAYS TO PLUG IN

- ▣ To local issues: **Maui News** (www.mauinews.com)
- ▣ To the environmental scene: **Sierra Club** (www.hi.sierraclub.org/maui)
- ▣ To the island art scene: **Art Guide Maui** (www.artguidemaui.com)
- ▣ To Maui's gay community: **www.pridemaui.com**
- ▣ To listen to a live audio feed of whales off the coast of Kihei: **The Whalesong Project** (www.whalesong.net)

---

volleyball on the beach. Everyone heads over to Hapa's to end it all with a big dance party.

Sleeping

In Kihei, hotels and B&Bs can be counted on one hand while condos line up cheek to jowl. Some condominium complexes maintain a front desk or a daytime office that handles bookings, but others are booked only via rental agents. In many places along S Kihei Rd the traffic is noisy, so when you book, avoid rooms close to the road.

The following rental agents handle Kihei condos:

Bello Realty (☎ 879-3328, 800-541-3060; www.bellomaui.com)

Kihei Maui Vacations (☎ 879-7581, 800-541-6284; www.kmvmaui.com)

Resort Quest Maui (☎ 879-5445, 866-774-2924; www.resortquestmaui.com)

BUDGET

Ocean Breeze Hideaway (Map p357; ☎ 879-0657, 888-463-6687; www.hawaiibednbreakfast.com; 435 Kalalau Pl; r incl breakfast $80-95; 🐾) The friendly hosts know how to make guests feel at home at this B&B, with two comfortable rooms, one with a queen bed and ceiling fans, the other with a king bed and air-con. Each has a private entrance and refrigerator.

MIDRANGE

Nona Lani Cottages (Map p357; ☎ 879-2497, 800-733-2688; www.nonalanicottages.com; 455 S Kihei Rd; r $100, cottages from $120) The scent of plumeria fills the air and the hosts make lei from the flowers grown on the grounds. Rooms in the main house are super comfy. The cottages are delightfully old-fashioned, simple but with all the necessities, and they sleep up to four. Opt for one of the rear cottages to avoid traffic sounds. In high season rooms have a four-night minimum, cottages a seven-night minimum.

Two Mermaids on the Sunny Side of Maui B&B (Map p358; ☎ 874-8687, 800-598-9550; www.twomermaids .com; 2840 Umalu Pl; studios/1-bedroom units incl breakfast $110/135; 🐾 🐕) The two women that operate this B&B have added many friendly personal touches. The units have kitchenettes and cheerful tropical decor, a breakfast of organic island fruit is provided and families are welcome – the backyard pool has a shallow section just for kids. One of the owners is a justice of the peace, who can provide wedding packages for a getaway honeymoon.

Maui Sunseeker (Map p357; ☎ 874-3131, 800-399-3885; www.mauisunseeker.com; 551 S Kihei Rd; studios $120-170) Catering to gay and lesbian travelers, this place consist of two adjacent properties. Opt for the rear one, known formerly as Wailana Inn, as its studios beam with tasteful decor that outshines other places in this price range. Amenities include kitchenette and lanai, and there's a clothing-optional rooftop deck with a hot tub and broad ocean views.

Kihei Kai Nani (Map p358; ☎ 879-9088, 800-473-1493; www.kiheikainani.com; 2495 S Kihei Rd; 1-bedroom units $139; ❁ 🏊) This low-rise complex, located opposite Kamaʻole Beach Park II, has roomy one-bedroom units. Don't be fooled by the affordable price; this inviting place has well-equipped units with private lanai. Guests gather around the BBQ grills for evening cookouts – a great way to meet the neighbors.

Mana Kai Maui (Map p358; ☎ 879-2778, 800-367-5242; www.crhmaui.com; 2960 S Kihei Rd; r/1-bedroom units from $145/245; ❁ 🏊) Perched on a point overlooking Keawakapu Beach, this complex is tops for sunset views and whale watching. And you can swim and snorkel from the beach right outside the door. You'll find all the conveniences of a condo as well as the pluses of a hotel, with a front desk and a full-service restaurant. Pay the extra $20 for an ocean-view unit.

Punahoa (Map p358; ☎ 879-2720, 800-564-4380; www.punahoabeach.com; 2142 Iliʻili Rd; studios/1-bedroom units $150/231). Watch the sun set from your lanai at this cozy 15-unit condo set smack on a beautiful beach. It's on a quiet side road, with good surfing and swimming a sandal shuffle away. The units have fully equipped kitchens and everything else you'd find in the larger condo complexes. The only difference is, instead of a pool, you've got an ocean.

Maui Kamaole (Map p358; ☎ 874-5151, 800-367-5242; www.crhmaui.com; 2777 S Kihei Rd; 1-/2-bedroom units from $200/245; ❁ 🏊) Bougainvillea draped over the balconies and birdsong in the gardens set the tone at this luxurious condo. Everything is low rise, the units are spacious and the quiet location off Kamaole Beach Park III is primo. There's little wonder the place has a loyal following of return guests. Unbeatable value for such cushy digs.

TOP END

Maui Coast Hotel (Map p358; ☎ 874-6284, 800-895-6284; www.mauicoasthotel.com; 2259 S Kihei Rd; r/ste from $245/275; ❁ 🏊) This modern seven-story hotel has large well-appointed rooms. It's set back from the road, away from the traffic, and offers complimentary internet access, laundry facilities and tennis courts. Ask about fifth-night-free deals or book online and get a free rental car at the regular room rate.

Eating

Although most visitors to Kihei have condo kitchens, Kihei's evolving dining scene is too good to pass up.

BUDGET

Local Boys Shave Ice (Map p358; Kihei Kalama Village, 1913 S Kihei Rd; shave ice $4; ⏱ 10am-9pm) Up for a cool treat? This stall conveniently located opposite Kalama Park dishes up shaved ice drenched in a rainbow of sweet syrups.

Kihei Caffe (Map p358; ☎ 879-2230; 1945 S Kihei Rd; mains $5-10; ⏱ 5am-2pm) If jet lag has you up before sunrise, head here. Breakfast burritos and eggs in every conceivable preparation highlight the menu. Best of all, the eye-popping coffee comes with a free refill.

Da Kitchen Express (Map p358; ☎ 875-7782; Rainbow Mall, 2439 S Kihei Rd; meals $7-10; ⏱ 9am-9pm) It's all about the plate lunches – tasty and huge – at this quintessentially Hawaiian diner. The local favorite is Da Lau Lau Plate (with steamed pork wrapped in taro leaves), but you won't go wrong with any choice, from teriyaki chicken to *loco moco* (a dish of rice, fried egg and hamburger patty topped with gravy).

Hawaiian Moons Natural Foods (Map p358; ☎ 875-4356; Kamaʻole Beach Center, 2411 S Kihei Rd; ⏱ 8am-9pm) sells all sorts of healthy food and has a salad bar (per lb $6.50) that would make a nice light picnic lunch. Kihei has two 24-hour supermarkets: **Foodland** (Map p358; ☎ 879-9350; Kihei Town Center, 1881 S Kihei Rd) and **Safeway** (Map p357; ☎ 891-9120; Piʻilani Village, 277 Piʻikea Ave). **Kihei Farmers Market** (Map p357; 61 S Kihei Rd; ⏱ 1:30-5:30pm Mon, Wed & Fri) is a good place to pick up fruits and vegetables.

MIDRANGE

Yorman's by the Sea (Map p357; ☎ 874-8385; Menehune Shores, 760 S Kihei Rd; breakfast & lunch $5-10, dinner $20-36; ⏱ 7:30am-10pm) Don't expect locals to let this one out of the bag. Kihei's best-kept secret, Yorman's overlooks an ancient fishpond and has an amazing water view. The food hails from the US South, with the likes of pork chops and pecan-crusted chicken. A jazz band (with owner Yorman Williams on bass) plays

MAUI

in the evening. Or swing by for Sunday brunch when there's live ukulele music.

Shaka Sandwich & Pizza (Map p358; ☎ 874-0331; 1770 S Kihei Rd; mains $6-21; ☜ 10:30am-9pm) Here you'll find Maui's best pizza, including a sweet Hawaiian version topped with ham and Maui-grown pineapple. Good cheesesteak sandwiches, too.

Stella Blues (Map p357; ☎ 874-3779; Azeka Mauka, 1279 S Kihei Rd; breakfast $6-10, lunch & dinner $8-26; ☜ 7:30am-midnight) You'll find a good meal here any time of the day. The jalapeño-laden Mexican omelette will jump-start your morning, or go Hawaiian with banana mac-nut pancakes. Lunch is built around specialty salads and sandwiches, while dinner leans into a seafood and steak menu.

Eskimo Candy Seafood (Map p358; ☎ 891-8898; 2665 Hale Kuai St; meals $7-16; ☜ 10:30am-7pm Mon-Fri) A real find on a side street between the beach and the highway, Eskimo Candy is essentially a fish market with a take-out counter and a couple of tables. Delicious fresh 'ahi and Kula veggie wraps, decent fish tacos and excellent *poke*.

Pita Paradise (Map p358; ☎ 875-7679; Kihei Kalama Village, 1913 S Kihei Rd; mains $7-20; ☜ 11am-9:30pm) Enjoy Mediterranean fare at this patio café. The lamb kebab with herb-roasted potatoes is a great choice and the baklava ice cream is to die for. It also serves an excellent Greek salad and there's a kids menu.

Alexander's (Map p358; ☎ 874-0788; Kihei Kalama Village, 1913 S Kihei Rd; meals $8-13; ☜ 11am-9pm) *The* place for fish-and-chips, made with your choice of mahimahi, 'ahi or *ono* (wahoo). The fried fare is a bit greasy but the grilled fish is absolute perfection. The food is prepared for takeout, or eat at the picnic tables at the side.

Aroma D'Italia Ristorante (Map p358; ☎ 879-0133; Kihei Town Center, 1881 S Kihei Rd; mains $9-20; ☜ 5-9pm) Double-dare you to walk by at dinnertime and not be pulled in by the temping aromas wafting out the door! This place has it all – classy service, old-world decor and a chef-owner who relies upon her traditional family recipes to create delicious pasta dishes.

Horhito's Mexican Cantina (Map p357; ☎ 891-6394; Lipoa Center, 41 E Lipoa St; combo plates $11-14; ☜ 5pm-at least 10pm) This is the real deal, with an accomplished Mexican chef, friendly staff and generous servings. Best of all, they don't skimp on the spices. If you're not up for traditional Mex fare, try the 'surf wraps' loaded with fresh fish and served with potatoes.

Sansei Seafood Restaurant & Sushi Bar (Map p358; ☎ 879-0004; Kihei Town Center, 1881 S Kihei Rd; appetizers $3-15, mains $17-32; ☜ 5:30-10pm Tue-Sat, 5-10pm Sun & Mon) This is the busiest place in town, but worth the wait for a table. The innovative appetizer menu rolls out everything from traditional sashimi to lobster ravioli. Hot Eurasian fusion dishes include the likes of Peking duck in a foie gras demi. And despite its loyal following, Sansei offers deals – come between 5:30pm and 6pm and all food is discounted by 25%.

Café O'Lei (Map p358; ☎ 891-1368; Rainbow Mall, 2439 S Kihei Rd; dinner $17-39; ☜ 10:30am-10pm Tue-Sun) Sophisticated atmosphere, superb food and honest prices separate this place from other upscale Kihei dining spots. For a tangy treat, try the sesame-seared 'ahi. There are also creative salads using organic local greens, unbeatable lunch deals for under $10 and a sushi chef after 4:30pm. And don't miss the martinis.

Drinking

Kihei Kalama Village (Map p358; 1913 S Kihei Rd), opposite Kalama Beach, houses the main cluster of Kihei's watering holes. Following are two favorites:

Life's a Beach (☎ 891-8010) A brightly painted, Bob Marley–lovin' shack with neon palm trees, live music, DJs and a breezy beach view.

South Shore Tiki Lounge (☎ 874-6444) Down your beers here while shooting some pool under the watchful eye of a tiki god.

Sports Page Grill & Bar (Map p358; ☎ 879-0602; Kama'ole Beach Center, 2411 S Kihei Rd) If life won't be complete without the playoffs on the big screen, come here.

Entertainment

Hapa's Night Club (Map p357; ☎ 879-9001; Lipoa Center, 41 E Lipoa St; admission $5-8; ☒) If you're looking to hit the dance floor, Hapa's has the best scene on Maui. The place rocks on Monday to the guitar work of local legend Willie K; hosts the gay community on 'ultra fab' Tuesday; has a DJ on Wednesday; and comes up with anything from salsa to reggae on other nights.

LuLu's (Map p358; ☎ 879-9944; 1941 S Kihei Rd) No problem finding LuLu's – you can hear this boisterous place a mile away. Ultracasual, it's got a kitsch-cluttered bar where drinks flow freely and the music rocks from Wednesday to Saturday nights.

Bocalino (Map p357; ☎ 874-9299; Azeka Mauka, 1279 S Kihei Rd) Sip the perfect martini while listening to live Hawaiian music at this bistro bar; music from 10pm to 1am nightly.

Yorman's by the Sea (Map p357; ☎ 874-8385; Menehune Shores, 760 S Kihei Rd; ☟ 7:30am-10pm) If jazz is your thing, Yorman's is your place.

Consolidated Theatre (Map p358; ☎ 875-4910; Kukui Mall, 1819 S Kihei Rd) This multiscreen cinema shows first-run movies.

Shopping

Kihei's largest shopping center, **Pi'ilani Village** (Map p357; 225 Pi'ikea Ave), has scores of stores, including **Tropical Disc** (☎ 874-3000), where there's a fine selection of Hawaiian tunes and headphone setups for previewing releases, and **Crazy Shirts** (☎ 875-6440), with a good selection of quality Hawaiian-motif shirts.

Kihei Kalama Village (Map p358; 1913 S Kihei Rd) Kihei overflows with souvenir shops of all sorts, the most interesting being Kihei Kalama Village, opposite Kalama Park, which has a collection of stalls selling cheapo T-shirts, sarongs and jewelry.

ABC store (Map p358; ☎ 879-6305; 2349 S Kihei Rd; ☟ 6am-11pm) This tourist-oriented convenience store sells liquor, cheap beach mats, suntan lotion and other practical beach items.

Rainbow Attic (Map p358; ☎ 874-0884; Kihei Town Center, 1881 S Kihei Rd) Good collection of quality second-hand aloha shirts.

Getting There & Around
BICYCLE
South Maui Bicycles (Map p358; ☎ 874-0068; 1993 S Kihei Rd; per day $22-60, per week $99-250; ☟ 10am-6pm Mon-Sat) rents top-of-the-line Trek road bicycles as well as basic around-town bikes.

BUS
The **Maui Bus** (www.mauicounty.gov/bus) company serves Kihei with two bus routes. One route connects Kihei with Wailea and Ma'alaea; stops include Kama'ole Beach III, Pi'ilani Village shopping center, and Uwapo and S Kihei Rds. The other route primarily serves the northern half of Kihei, with a half-dozen stops along S Kihei Rd. Both routes operate hourly from around 5:30am to 7:30pm and cost $1.

CAR & MOTORCYCLE
A family-owned operation, **Kihei Rent A Car** (Map p358; ☎ 879-7257, 800-251-5288; www.kiheirentacar.com; 96 Kio Loop; per day/week from $25/160) rents cars and jeeps to 21-year-olds, accepts cash deposits and includes free mileage.

Hula Hogs (Map p357; ☎ 875-7433, 877-464-7433; www.hulahogs.com; 1279 S Kihei Rd; per day from $105) are the folks to see if you want to pack your saddlebags and tour Haleakala and the rest of Maui on a Harley-Davidson Road King. Helmets and rain gear are included.

WAILEA
pop 5200
Wailea is oh so well heeled. Don't even bother looking for a gas station or fast-food joint. Wailea is all about swank beachfront hotels, low-rise condo villas, emerald golf courses and a tennis club so chic it's dubbed 'Wimbledon West.'

One look at Wailea's beaches and it's easy to see why it's become such hot real estate. The golden-sand jewels along the Wailea coast are postcard material offering good swimming, snorkeling and sunbathing. So grab a beach mat, pack the snorkel and enjoy the good life.

Orientation & Information
If you're heading to Wailea from Lahaina or Kahului, be sure to take the Pi'ilani Hwy (Hwy 31) and not S Kihei Rd, which can be a slow drive through congested traffic. Wailea's main road is Wailea Alanui Dr, which turns into Makena Alanui Dr after Polo Beach and continues south to Makena.

The **Shops at Wailea** (3750 Wailea Alanui Dr; ☟ 9:30am-9pm) has an ATM, as do many of the hotels.

Sights
Wailea's beaches begin with the southern end of Keawakapu Beach in Kihei and continue south toward Makena. All of the beaches that are backed by resorts have public access, with free parking, showers and rest rooms.

ULUA & MOKAPU BEACHES
Ulua Beach is such a gem that brides and grooms march down here on Saturdays to tie the knot. With Kaho'olawe and Molokini as a backdrop, and a straight-on sunset view, it's no secret why the place is so popular.

But to be really dazzled, don a mask and hit the water. Ulua Beach has Wailea's best easy-access snorkeling. Head straight for the coral at the rocky outcrop on the right side of Ulua Beach, which separates it from its twin to

WAILEA & MAKENA

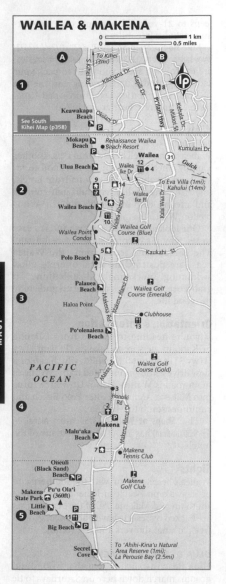

0 ——————— 1 km
0 ——————— 0.5 miles

SIGHTS & ACTIVITIES

Hawaiian Sailing Canoe Adventures	1 A3
Keawala'i Congregational Church	2 A4
Makena Landing	3 B4
Maui Ocean Activities	(see 6)
Wailea Tennis Club	4 B2

SLEEPING 🏠

Fairmont Kea Lani	5 A3
Grand Wailea Resort Hotel & Spa	6 A2
Maui Prince Hotel	7 A4
Pineapple Inn Maui	8 B1
Wailea Marriott Resort	9 A2

EATING 🍴

Ferraro's	10 A2
Jawz Tacos	11 A5
Joe's Bar & Grill	12 B2
Longhi's	(see 14)
SeaWatch	13 B3
Waterfront Deli	(see 14)

ENTERTAINMENT

Four Seasons Resort	(see 10)
Wailea Marriott Resort	(see 9)

SHOPPING 🛍

Blue Ginger	(see 14)
Honolua Surf Co	(see 14)
Martin & MacArthur	(see 14)
Maui Waterwear	(see 14)
Na Hoku	(see 14)
Shops at Wailea	14 B2

WAILEA BEACH

The largest and widest of Wailea's beaches is backed by both the Four Seasons and the Grand Wailea resorts, so it's no surprise that the bulk of Wailea's vacationers get their tans there.

The beach slopes gradually, making it a good swimming spot. When the water's calm, there's snorkeling around the rocky point on the south side of the beach. Divers entering the water at Wailea Beach can follow an off-shore reef that runs down to Polo Beach. At times there's a gentle shorebreak suitable for bodysurfing. The beach access road runs between the Four Seasons and Grand Wailea resorts.

POLO BEACH

Although fronted by a condo development and the Fairmont Kea Lani, the south end of Polo Beach is seldom crowded.

When there's wave action, bodyboarders and bodysurfers usually find a good shorebreak here. When the waters are calm, the rocks at the northern end of the beach are good for snorkeling. At low tide, the lava outcropping at the southern end of the beach has

the north, Mokapu Beach. Snorkeling is best in the morning before the winds pick up and the crowds arrive. When the surf's up, forget snorkeling – go bodysurfing instead.

Ulua Beach is between the Wailea Marriott Resort and the Renaissance Wailea Beach Resort; take the first road south of the Renaissance to get to the beach parking lot.

some interesting little tide pools that harbor spiny sea urchins and small fish.

To get to Polo Beach, turn down Kaukahi St after the Kea Lani. There's a beach parking lot on the right, near the end of the road.

PALAUEA BEACH

This untouristed sandy stretch just to the south of Polo Beach attracts locals who come to surf and bodyboard. Kiawe trees block the view of the beach from the roadside, but you can find it easily by looking for the line of cars along Makena Rd.

PO'OLENALENA BEACH

Beyond all the development of the Wailea resort strip lies this lovely long crescent with two Hawaiian names: Po'olenalena Beach and Paipu Beach.

This beach is well used by local families on weekends, but it's rarely crowded and the shallow, sandy bottom and calm waters make for excellent swimming. There's good snorkeling off both the southern and northern lava points. **Haloa Point**, a bit further north, is a popular scuba-diving spot.

The beach parking lot is on Makena Alanui Rd, a half-mile south of its intersection with Makena Rd. The only facilities consist of a pit toilet.

WAILEA BEACH WALK

For a delightful stroll, take the 1.3-mile shoreline path that connects Wailea's beaches and the resort hotels that front them. Running from the Renaissance Wailea Beach Resort to the Fairmont Kea Lani, the undulating path winds above jagged lava points and back down to the sandy shore.

The walk is a winner any time of the year, but in winter it's one of the best walks in all of Hawaii for spotting humpback whales – on a good day you may be able to see more than a dozen of them frolicking in the waters offshore. Forgot your binoculars? Just drop a coin in the telescope in front of the Wailea Marriott Resort.

Some of the luxury hotels you'll pass along the walk are worth strolling through as well, most notably the Grand Wailea Resort, which is adorned with $30 million worth of artwork. In front of the Wailea Point condos are the foundations of three Hawaiian house sites dating to AD 1300; this is also a fine spot to watch the sun set.

Activities

WATER ACTIVITIES

Maui Ocean Activities (☎ 667-2001; www.mauiwater sports.com; Grand Wailea Resort, 3850 Wailea Alanui Dr; snorkel/kayak rental per hr $8/15; � 8am-4pm) has watersports rentals and gives surfing lessons ($69) and windsurfing lessons ($90).

Hawaiian Sailing Canoe Adventures (☎ 281-9301; www.mauisailingcanoe.com; 2hr tour $79; � tour 10am) takes you on a tour of the coast aboard a Hawaiian-style outrigger canoe while sharing insights into Native Hawaiian traditions. Tours depart from Polo Beach.

LAND ACTIVITIES

Wailea Golf Club (☎ 875-7450, 800-332-1614; www.wailea golf.com; 100 Golf Club Dr; green fees $155-200; � 1st tee 7am) consists of three championship courses. The Emerald course is a tropical garden that consistently ranks top; the rugged Gold course takes advantage of volcanic landscapes; and the Blue course is marked by an open fairway and challenging greens.

Wailea Tennis Club (☎ 879-1958, 800-332-1614; www.waileatennis.com; 131 Wailea Ike Pl; court fees $30-60; � 7am-7pm) is an award-winning complex with 11 Plexipave courts, a dress code, lessons, clinics and equipment rentals.

Festivals & Events

Lots of Hollywood celebs show up for the **Maui Film Festival** (www.mauifilmfestival.com), a five-day extravaganza in mid-June. Movies are screened outdoors under the stars at various locations around Wailea, including at the 'SandDance Theater' right on Wailea Beach.

Sleeping

Pineapple Inn Maui (☎ 298-4403, 877-212-6284; www.pineappleinn.com; 3170 Akala Dr; r/cottages $129/185; ☒ ☒) A class act at affordable prices – this little boutique inn has rooms that are as nice as at the exclusive resorts. It's not on the water, but every room has an ocean-view lanai and you can watch the sunset from the pool. The rooms have kitchenettes – for serious cooking, consider the sweet two-bedroom cottage, which has a full kitchen.

Wailea Marriott Resort (☎ 879-1922, 800-367-2960; www.waileamarriott.com; 3700 Wailea Alanui Dr; r from $350; ☒ ☒) Wailea's first hotel, this place scored a prime oceanfront location between two of Wailea's loveliest beaches. It's also the smallest and most Hawaiian of the resorts with koi ponds, palm trees and tropical decor. Although

MAUI

it's an older property, a $70-million renovation has upgraded it thoroughly, adding a spa and modern amenities.

Fairmont Kea Lani (☎ 875-4100, 800-659-4100; www .kealani.com; 4100 Wailea Alanui Dr; ste/oceanfront villa from $475/1300; ✖ ❧) If you want to star gaze Hollywood style, head to this swank resort. With its Moorish-style architecture, the resort resembles something out of *Arabian Nights*, but what really draws the rich and famous is the privacy. The villas even have their own plunge pools. Of course, everyone does eventually come down to the beach.

Grand Wailea Resort Hotel & Spa (☎ 875-1234, 800-888-6100; www.grandwailea.com; 3850 Wailea Alanui Dr; r from $500; ✖ ❧) Maui's most extravagant resort – the lobbies are replete with bronze sculptures, while the grounds are all tropical gardens and spouting fountains. Some of it has a chic Hawaiiana motif; all of it is unabashedly opulent. A 2000ft-long system of water slides and waterfall grottoes will thrill kids of any age. The place is family-friendly with a full schedule of activities for kids – not that they'll ever want to leave the pool.

Eating

Waterfront Deli (☎ 891-2039; Shops at Wailea, 3750 Wailea Alanui Dr; meals $5-10; ❧ 7am-8pm) Wailea's sole budget option, this deli inside the Whalers General Store serves up sandwiches on bread it bakes fresh. Choices range from mainland standards, like the hot corned-beef Reuben to Maui taro burgers. It's a good stop on the way to the beach – it even boxes up picnic lunches.

Longhi's (☎ 891-8883; Shops at Wailea, 3750 Wailea Alanui Dr; breakfast & lunch $6-18, dinner $24-40; ❧ 8am-10pm) This award-winning restaurant is a favorite at breakfast, when it bakes its own pastries and serves a knockout Italian frittata. Lunch revolves around sandwiches and pasta dishes, while at dinner Longhi's grills up Wailea's best steaks. There are lots of seafood options as well.

SeaWatch (☎ 875-8080; 100 Wailea Golf Club Dr; breakfast & lunch $9-15, dinner $25-34; ❧ 8am-10pm) Head up here to the golf course if you want to escape the hotel scene. At breakfast the crab-cake eggs Benedict sizzles. At other times you'll find tasty sandwiches, salads and seafood. Dine on the veranda for a panoramic ocean view across the fairway.

Joe's Bar & Grill (☎ 875-7767; 131 Wailea Ike Pl; mains $22-38; ❧ 5:30-9:30pm) Run by the owners of the famed Hali'imaile General Store, Joe's has become celebrated in its own right. The emphasis is on solid American standards, like the slow roast beef prime rib or the fresh catch served with honey butter and whipped potatoes. Go Hawaiian for dessert, with a decadent pineapple cake topped with glazed macadamia nuts.

Ferraro's (☎ 891-8883; Four Seasons Resort, 3900 Wailea Alanui; lunch $17-25, dinner $36-50; ❧ 11am-9pm) No other place in Wailea even comes close to this breezy restaurant for atmospheric seaside dining. Lunch strays into fun selections, like *kalua* pig quesadillas with mango poi, while dinner gets more serious, offering a solidly Italian menu with wood-fired bruscetta, lobster risotto and wonderful pesto dishes.

Entertainment

All of the Wailea hotels have some sort of live music, most often jazz or Hawaiian, in the evening.

Four Seasons Resort (☎ 874-8000; 3900 Wailea Alanui) The lobby lounge has Hawaiian music and hula performances from 5:30pm to 8:30pm nightly and a mix of jazz, slack-key and flamenco guitar later in the evening.

Wailea Marriott Resort (☎ 879-1922; 3700 Wailea Alanui; adult/child 6-12 $85/42; ❧ 5-8pm Mon, Thu, Fri & Sat) It's a bit of a tourist-resort-luau-cliché but the Marriott still runs the best luau this side of Lahaina, and it's right on the oceanfront lawn.

Shopping

Shops at Wailea (☎ 891-6770; 3750 Wailea Alanui Dr; ❧ 9:30am-9pm) This two-story shopping center has dozens of shops, most flashing names like Prada and Gucci, but there are some good local names here, too:

Blue Ginger (☎ 891-0772) Women's clothing in cheery colors and tropical motifs.

Honolua Surf Co (☎ 891-8229) Hip surfer-motif T-shirts, shorts and aloha shirts.

Martin & MacArthur (☎ 891-8844) Top-quality Hawaiian-made wood carvings, paintings and other crafts.

Maui Waterwear (☎ 891-1939) A full line of tropical swimwear.

Na Hoku (☎ 891-8040) Hawaiian jeweler specializing in island floral and marine life designs.

Getting There & Around

The **Maui Bus** (www.mauicounty.gov/bus) operates between Wailea and Kahului hourly until 8:30pm. The first bus leaves the Shops at

Wailea at 6:30am and runs along S Kihei Rd before heading up to the Pi'ilani Village shopping center and Ma'alaea. From Ma'alaea you can connect to buses bound for Lahaina.

A free **shuttle bus** (☎ 879-2828) runs around the Wailea resort every 30 minutes from 6:30am to 6pm, stopping at the Grand Wailea and Four Seasons resorts, the Shops at Wailea and the golf courses.

MAKENA
pop 475

Makena is where untamed south Maui begins. Sitting beneath the slopes of Upcountry's 'Ulupalakua Ranch, Makena Bay was once used to load cattle bound for Honolulu markets. When that stopped in the 1920s, Makena became a real sleeper. In the 1980s the ranch sold off an 1800-acre plot that now houses the Maui Prince Hotel and its golf course, but the rest of Makena belongs to the free at heart.

Its crystal-clear waters offer a mixed plate of aquatic adventures with phenom snorkeling, kayaking and bodysurfing. The beaches are nothing short of glorious. The king of them all, Big Beach, is an immense sweep of glistening sand and a prime sunset-viewing locale.

The secluded cove at neighboring Little Beach is Maui's most popular nude beach.

Sights & Activities
MAKENA BAY
This is a kickin' bay for water activities. There's no better place on Maui for kayaking and when seas are calm snorkeling is good along the rocks at the south side of **Makena Landing**, the boat launch that's the center of the action; there are also showers and toilets here. Makena Bay is also a good place for shore dives; divers will want to head to the north side of the bay.

Kayak-rental companies deliver kayaks here – see South Pacific Kayaks (p359) – you can either head off on your own or join one of its tours. Although the norm is to make arrangements in advance (there are no shops here), if there's an extra kayak on the trailer, you might be able to arrange something at the last minute on the spot. Paddle your kayak south along the lava coastline to Malu'aka Beach, where green sea turtles abound.

South of the landing is the **Keawala'i Congregational Church**, one of Maui's earliest missionary churches. The current building was erected in 1855 with 3ft-thick walls made of burnt coral rock. Don't miss the adjacent graveyard, which has old tombstones adorned with cameo photographs, many of Hawaiian cowboys laid to rest in the 1920s. Makena Rd ends shortly after the church at a cul-de-sac on the ocean side of Maui Prince Hotel.

MALU'AKA BEACH
Forget the official name – everyone just calls this 'Turtle Beach.' Snorkelers and kayakers flock here to see the sea turtles that frequent this golden-sand beach fronting the Maui Prince Hotel. You'll find fantastic coral about 100yd out. Sea turtles feed along the coral and often swim within just feet of the snorkelers. The best action is at the south end of the beach, but you won't have any problem finding it, since that's where everyone else will be.

There are beach parking lots, rest rooms and showers at both ends of the beach. At the north side, there's the lot opposite Keawala'i Congregational Church. Or, after driving south past the Maui Prince Hotel, take the first sharp right, where there's additional parking for about 60 cars.

MAUI

MAKENA STATE PARK

This grand park wraps three beaches in one, and should be high on every traveler's itinerary. Its crowning glory, Big Beach, is the sort of scene that people conjure up when they dream of a Hawaiian beach – beautiful and expansive, with virtually no development on the horizon. Although it's a state park, Makena remains in a natural state, with no facilities except for a couple of pit toilets and picnic tables.

Oneuli (Black Sand) Beach

Look for the first Makena State Park access sign and the dirt road leading to this little salt-and-pepper-sand beach. A lava shelf along the shoreline means that it is not good for swimming, but families come here on the weekends for fishing and picnics. Kayakers take to the water here as well, and it can be a good spot for seeing turtles poking their heads out of the water as they feed along the shore.

Big Beach

The Hawaiian name for Big Beach is Oneloa, literally 'Long Sand.' And indeed the golden sands stretch for the better part of a mile and are as broad as they come. The waters are a beautiful turquoise. When they're calm you'll find kids bodyboarding here, but at other times the breaks belong to experienced bodysurfers, who get tossed wildly in the transparent waves.

In the late 1960s this was the site of an alternative-lifestyle encampment that took on the nickname 'Hippie Beach.' The tent city lasted until 1972, when police finally evicted everyone. More than a few of Maui's now-graying residents can trace their roots on the island to those days.

The turnoff to the main parking area is a mile beyond the Maui Prince Hotel. A second parking area lies a quarter of a mile to the south. You can also park alongside the road and walk in; watch out for kiawe thorns in the woods behind the beach. Thefts and broken windshields are unfortunately commonplace; do not leave anything valuable in your car.

Little Beach

Little Beach, also known as Pu'u Ola'i Beach, is south Maui's *au naturel* beach (though nudity is officially illegal). Hidden by a rocky outcrop

that juts out from Pu'u Ola'i, the cinder hill that marks the north end of Big Beach, most visitors don't even know Little Beach is there. But take the short trail up the rock that links the two beaches and bam, there it is, spread out in front of you. The crowd is mixed, about half gay and half straight.

Little Beach fronts a sandy cove that usually has a gentle shorebreak ideal for bodysurfing and bodyboarding. When the surf's up, you'll find plenty of local surfers here as well. When the water's calm, snorkeling is good along the rocky point.

SECRET COVE

Well, once it was secret. Now a favorite for getaway weddings, it's a toss-up whether you'll have this little pocket cove all to yourself or it'll be packed to the brim with tuxes and tulle. But this lovely postcard-size beach of golden sand with a straight-on view of Kaho'olawe is certainly worth a peek.

The cove is a quarter-mile after the southernmost Makena State Park parking lot. The entrance is through an opening in a lava-rock wall, marked with a blue-and-white shoreline sign just south of house No 6900.

Festivals & Events

The **Xterra World Championship** (www.xterraplanet .com), held in late October at the Maui Prince Hotel, is a major off-road triathlon that begins with a 1-mile swim, follows with an 6.8-mile trail run and tops off with a grueling 18.65-mile bike ride up the slopes of Haleakala.

Sleeping & Eating

Maui Prince Hotel (☎ 874-1111, 800-321-6248; www .mauiprince.com; 5400 Makena Alanui Dr; r from $350; ✖ ⧉) It looks like a fortress from the outside, but the interior incorporates a fine sense of Japanese aesthetics. The five-story hotel surrounds a courtyard with waterfalls, running streams, carp ponds and raked-rock gardens. All of the 310 rooms have at least partial ocean views. It also has a well-regarded Japanese dinner restaurant.

Jawz Tacos (Makena State Park; snacks $3-9; ☾ 11am-3:30pm) This food truck parks in the northernmost Big Beach parking lot selling mahimahi tacos, burritos and shave ice. Other vendors selling cold coconuts, pineapples and the like can be found along Makena Alanui Dr opposite Big Beach.

BEYOND MAKENA

Makena Rd continues as a narrow paved road for 3 miles after Makena State Park. The road goes through the 'Ahihi-Kina'u Natural Area Reserve before deadending at La Perouse Bay.

Sights & Activities

'AHIHI-KINA'U NATURAL AREA RESERVE

This rugged 2045-acre preserve includes the protected waters of 'Ahihi Bay and Cape Kina'u, created when Maui's last lava flow spilled out to the sea in 1790. Here you'll find all the *'a'a* (rough, jagged lava) you could ever want to see.

Snorkeling is great in the reserve. Just about everyone heads to the little roadside cove 170yd south of the first reserve sign – granted it offers decent snorkeling, but there are better, less-crowded options. Instead, drive 350yd past the cove and look for a large clearing on the right. Park here and follow the coastal footpath south for five minutes to reach a black-sand beach with fantastic coral, clear water and few visitors. Enter the water from the left side of the beach where access is easy, snorkel in a northerly direction and you'll immediately be over awesome coral gardens teeming with an amazing variety of fish. Huge rainbow parrotfish abound here and it's not unusual to see turtles, and the occasional reef shark (generally harmless) as well.

LA PEROUSE BAY

In addition to the raw natural beauty of this place, La Perouse Bay is steeped in a rich history. It was at La Perouse that the first Westerners set foot on Maui. When the French explorer Jean François de Galaup La Perouse landed here in 1786, scores of Hawaiians from the village of Keone'o'io came out to greet him. The remains of the ancient village – mainly house and heiau platforms – can be seen scattered among the lava patches. A **monument** to La Perouse, for whom the bay is named, is located at the end of the road.

This is also a great place to see spinner dolphins, which commonly come into the bay during the early part of the day. The waters are rough and challenging, but expert kayakers and divers sometimes give it a go, and the sealife is amazing. However, strong offshore winds put snorkeling and swimming out of the question.

Makena Stables (☎ 879-0244; www.makenastables .com; trail ride $145; ☻ 8-11:30am Mon-Sat), located just before the road ends, offers morning-long horseback rides up the slopes of 'Ulupalakua Ranch led by a Maui-born cowboy whose stories are as fascinating as the terrain.

From La Perouse Bay, it's possible to continue on foot along the **Hoapili (King's Hwy) Trail**. This ancient path follows the coastline across jagged lava flows (wear your hiking boots). It's a dry area with no water and little vegetation, so it can get very hot. The first part of the trail is along the sandy beach at La Perouse Bay. Right after the trail emerges onto the lava fields, it's possible to take a spur trail for three-quarters of a mile down to the light beacon at the tip of Cape Hanamanioa. Alternatively, walk inland to the Na Ala Hele sign and turn right onto the King's Hwy as it climbs through rough *'a'a* lava inland for the next 2 miles before coming back to the coast to an older lava flow at Kanaio Beach. The area is fragile and much studied.

NORTH SHORE & EAST MAUI

East Maui begins in the windsurfing haven of Pa'ia and flows south down the winding coastal road to the tranquil village of Hana, the most celebrated drive in Hawaii. And it doesn't stop there. After Hana, the road continues to the cool pools of 'Ohe'o Gulch, in the coastal Kipahulu section of Haleakala National Park, and becomes an adventurous romp around the south side of the island.

PA'IA

pop 2500

Pa'ia is all about rebirth. Once a thriving sugar town, a century ago it boasted 10,000 residents living in plantation camps above the now-defunct Pa'ia sugar mill.

During the 1950s there was an exodus to Kahului, shops closed and Pa'ia began to collect cobwebs. It was virtually a ghost town a decade later when hippies seeking paradise landed here. In the early 1980s windsurfers discovered nearby Ho'okipa Beach, and Pa'ia broke onto the map as the 'windsurfing capital of the world.'

The old wooden storefronts that at one time housed grain stores and mom-and-pop

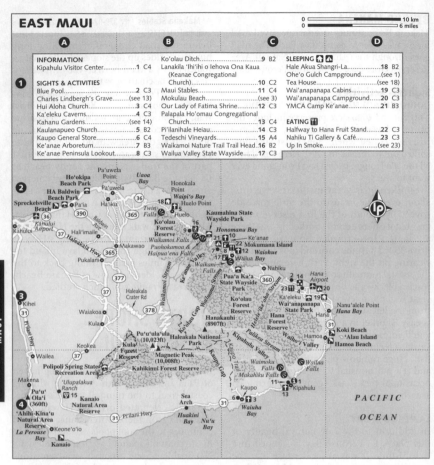

EAST MAUI

INFORMATION		Ko'olau Ditch.....................................9 B2	SLEEPING 🏠 🛖
Kipahulu Visitor Center.............1 C4		Lanakila 'Ihi'ihi o Iehova Ona Kaua	Hale Akua Shangri-La.................18 B2
		(Keanae Congregational	Ohe'o Gulch Campground...........(see 1)
SIGHTS & ACTIVITIES		Church)..10 C2	Tea House......................................(see 18)
Blue Pool..................................2 C3		Maui Stables................................11 C4	Wai'anapanapa Cabins................19 C3
Charles Lindbergh's Grave........(see 13)		Mokulau Beach..........................(see 3)	Wai'anapanapa Campground......20 C3
Hui Aloha Church.....................3 C4		Our Lady of Fatima Shrine........12 C4	YMCA Camp Ke'anae...................21 B3
Ka'eleku Caverns.....................4 C3		Palapala Ho'omau Congregational	
Kahanu Gardens.......................(see 14)		Church..13 C4	EATING 🍴
Kaulanapueo Church................5 B2		Pi'ilanihale Heiau.......................14 C4	Halfway to Hana Fruit Stand......22 C3
Kaupo General Store................6 C4		Tedeschi Vineyards....................15 A4	Nahiku Ti Gallery & Café............23 C3
Ke'anae Arboretum..................7 B3		Waikamoi Nature Trail Trail Head..16 B2	Up In Smoke...............................(see 23)
Ke'anae Peninsula Lookout.......8 C3		Wailua Valley State Wayside......17 C3	

---

grocers now host New Age galleries, surf shops and an ever-growing variety of scrumptious restaurants. The accents, flavors and scents of today's Pa'ia reflect an international potpourri of influences and people, creating a destination like no other on Maui.

Orientation

The Hana Hwy (Hwy 36) runs straight through the center of Pa'ia. This is the last real town before Hana and the last place to gas up your car, but that's never a problem as there's a 24-hour gas station in town. Pa'ia is also a link to the Upcountry via Baldwin Ave, which runs to Makawao passing the old sugar mill en route. Everything in town is within walking distance.

Information

Bank of Hawaii (☎ 579-9511; 35 Baldwin Ave) Has a 24-hour ATM.

Livewire Café (☎ 579-6009; 137 Hana Hwy; per min 15¢, 20-min minimum; ⏲ 6am-10pm) Great place to surf the internet – lots of stations, no wait.

Pa'ia Laundromat (129 Baldwin Ave; ⏲ 5am-8pm)

Post office (☎ 579-8866; 120 Baldwin Ave; ⏲ 8:30am-4:30pm Mon-Fri, 10:30am-12:30pm Sat)

Sights

HO'OKIPA BEACH PARK

Ho'okipa reigns supreme as the world's premier windsurfing beach, with strong currents, dangerous shorebreaks and razor-sharp coral offering the ultimate challenge. It is to topnotch windsurfers what Everest is to climbers.

The beach is also one of Maui's prime surfing spots. Winter sees the biggest waves for board surfers, and summer has the most consistent winds for windsurfers. To prevent intersport beefs, surfers typically hit the waves in the morning and the windsurfers take over during the afternoon.

The action in the water is suitable for experts only. But a hilltop perch overlooking the beach offers spectators a bird's-eye view of the world's top windsurfers doing their death-defying stuff. Ho'okipa is just before the 9-mile marker; to reach the lookout above the beach take the driveway at the east side of the park.

HA BALDWIN BEACH PARK

Bodyboarders and bodysurfers take to the waves at this big county park about a mile west of Pa'ia, at the 6-mile marker. The wide sandy beach drops off quickly and when the shorebreak is big unsuspecting swimmers can get slammed soundly. If you see lots of bodysurfers in the water, it's probably big! Showers, rest rooms, picnic tables, and a well-used baseball and soccer field round out the facilities. The park has a reputation for drunken nastiness after the sun sets but it's typically fine in the daytime when there's a lifeguard on duty.

SPRECKELSVILLE BEACH

Extending west from HA Baldwin Beach, Spreckelsville is a good walking beach but its near-shore lava shelf makes it less than ideal for swimming. The rocks do, however, provide protection for young kids. If you walk to the center of the beach, you'll come to a section dubbed 'baby beach' where local families take the little ones to splash.

To get there, turn toward the ocean on Nonohe Pl, then take the last left before entering the Maui Country Club.

TAVARES BEACH

The best choice for swimming in the Pa'ia area, this sandy beach attracts lots of families on weekends but is seldom crowded during the week. A submerged rocky lava shelf runs parallel to the beach about 25ft from the shore and is shallow enough for swimmers to scrape over. Once you know it's there, the rocks are easy to avoid, so take a look before jumping in. The beach parking lot is at the first shoreline access sign on the Hana side of the 7-mile marker. There are no facilities.

Activities

At **Hana Hwy Surf** (☎ 579-8999; 65 Hana Hwy; surfboards/bodyboards per day $20/10; ☼ 9am-6pm Mon-Sat, 10am-5pm Sun), Pa'ia's surfing headquarters, the staff even have a daily recorded surf report.

Simmer (☎ 579-8484; www.simmerhawaii.com; 137 Hana Hwy; sailboards per day/week $44/280; ☼ 10am-6pm) is all about windsurfing and handles everything from repairs to top-of-the-line gear rentals. Cool sportswear, too.

You can join in morning meditation, yoga sessions and various other spiritual activities at **Maui Tibetan Buddhist Dharma Center** (☎ 579-8076;

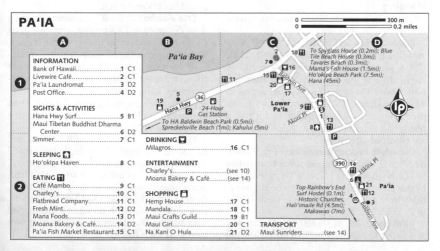

MAUI

---

007 ON MAUI

Big-wave riding, which reaches its pinnacle on Maui's north shore, has made a splash in Hollywood. The opening scene of the 20th James Bond thriller, *Die Another Day*, features famed Hawaii surfer Laird Hamilton tearing across a monstrous wave at Jaws, which in winter boasts the planet's biggest, baddest barrels. The waves are so insanely awesome, the only way for surfers to reach them is to be towed out by a specialized jet-ski. Hamilton, in a camouflaged wetsuit with night-vision goggles, played the role of Bond riding treacherous surf to reach his assassination assignment off the North Korean coast.

---

www.mauidharmacenter.org; 81 Baldwin Ave; 🕑 6:30am-6:30pm), in the center of town.

Festivals & Events

Aloha Classic Wave Championships (www.maui windsurfing.org) This major international tournament brings the world's best sailboarders out to one-up the competition at Ho'okipa Beach during a week in November. Get there early to get a parking space overlooking the beach. It doesn't get any better than this.

High-Tech/Lopez Split Surfbash (www.mauisurf ohana.org) Maui's largest surf contest takes place at Ho'okipa Beach on the last weekend in November or the first weekend in December, with competing short-boarders, long-boarders and bodyboarders.

Sleeping

Although Pa'ia has no hotels, there are several decent sleeping options.

Rainbow's End Surf Hostel (☎ 579-9057; www .mauigateway.com/~riki; 221 Baldwin Ave; dm/r $25/65; 🖳) A surfer motif and simple clean rooms are in store at this small hostel, 10-minutes' walk from Pa'ia center. Guests have access to a kitchen, shared TV room and free wi-fi. It's predominately a surfer crowd, but it's in a residential neighborhood, so quiet-time rules are enforced after 10pm.

Chameleon Vacation Rentals Maui (☎ 575-9933; 866-575-9933; www.donnachameleon.com; r & cottages from $65) Only smoke-free places to stay are offered by this ecominded operation that books everything from oceanfront cottages to rustic cabins in Pa'ia and Ha'iku.

Ho'okipa Haven (☎ 579-8282, 800-398-6284; www .hookipa.com; 62 Baldwin Ave No 2A; r & cottages from $85)

This established vacation rental service books scores of places in the greater Pa'ia area and often offers last-minute specials online.

Blue Tile Beach House (☎ 579-6446, 888-579-6446; www.beachvacationmaui.com; 459 Hana Hwy; r incl breakfast $90-150, ste $250) You could jump off the balcony and right into the water at this exclusive house overlooking Tavares Beach. Sleeping options range from a small straightforward room to the spacious honeymoon suite with wraparound ocean-view windows and a four-poster bed. All six rooms share a living room with fireplace and a full kitchen.

Spyglass House (☎ 579-8608, 800-475-6695; www .spyglassmaui.com; 367 Hana Hwy; r $110-170) Right on the ocean at the end of a private road, this eclectic place is loaded with character, from its porthole windows to its seaside hot tub. It was once a favorite haunt of LSD guru Timothy Leary. Today the Spyglass attracts mostly surfers and families who prefer salt spray to resort glitter. Guests have access to a kitchen and BBQ grills.

Eating

Any excuse for stopping in Pa'ia around mealtime will do – the food is almost universally wonderful. Nothing better awaits you in Hana, so grab your picnic supplies before heading onward.

BUDGET

Mana Foods (☎ 579-8078; 49 Baldwin Ave; 🕑 8:30am-8:30pm) A substantial health food store, with everything from organic produce to fresh-baked breads and a deli.

Café Mambo (☎ 579-8021; 30 Baldwin Ave; mains $6-16; 🕑 8am-9pm) This upbeat, arty café adds a splash of innovation to everything it does. Breakfast, served until noon, features create-your-own omelettes. At other times choose from fragrant Moroccan stews, mouth-watering *kalua* duck fajitas and tempting vegetarian selections. Mambo also packs box lunches in coolers for the road to Hana (for two people $17).

Flatbread Company (☎ 579-8989; 89 Hana Hwy; mains $7-19; 🕑 5-10pm) Wood-fired pizzas made with organic sauces, nitrate-free pepperoni, Kula onions – you'll never stop at a chain pizza house again. Lots of fun combinations, from vegan to kiawe-smoked ham and organic pineapples. Start with mesclun salad topped with Surfing Goat Dairy chevre – Maui-grown flavors at their finest!

Fresh Mint (☎ 579-9144; 115 Baldwin Ave; mains $8-13; ◷ 5-9pm) Authentic Vietnamese fare, but totally veg, the chef-owner of this place takes pride in her artistically presented dishes. Even meat eaters will be blown away by the way soy takes on the flavors and texture of the foods they substitute – if in doubt, just try the spicy ginger soy beef. For dessert, don't miss the mango tapioca.

Charley's (☎ 579-9453; 142 Hana Hwy; mains $8-19; ◷ 7am-midnight) Got a hankering for breakfast in the afternoon? No problem here. Charley's will whip you up island-fresh eggs any time of the day. The eggs Benedict with sautéed spinach and mushrooms is simply *ono*. The burgers, steaks and pizzas don't disappoint either.

Pa'ia Fish Market Restaurant (☎ 579-8030; 110 Hana Hwy; meals $9-15; ◷ 11am-9:30pm) Come mealtime the tables here are packed like sardines. Fish just doesn't get any fresher than this – you even get to see your options on display at the counter, where the day's catch is lined up. The local favorite is fish-and-chips, but the menu includes plenty of other tempting fish preparations, from wine-sautéed to unbeatable tacos.

MIDRANGE

Moana Bakery & Café (☎ 579-9999; 71 Baldwin Ave; breakfast & lunch $7-15, dinner $12-33; ◷ 8am-3pm Sun-Tue, 8am-9pm Wed-Sat) Since Moana's French pastry master left to start his own restaurant, the pastries here have lost their edge, but everything else remains right on at this hip restaurant. The blackened *'ahi* wrap sandwich served with mango-pineapple salsa and Moloka'i sweet potatoes is a sure winner.

TOP END

Mama's Fish House (☎ 579-8488; 799 Poho Pl; mains $34-50; ◷ 11am-2:30pm & 5-9:30pm) Maui's most celebrated seafood restaurant pairs a fine ocean view with impeccably prepared fish. Just what's on the menu depends on the day's catch, but you'll always find superb options. For a local favorite bursting with Hawaiian flavor, order either the *'opakapaka* or the *onaga* (mild-tasting red snapper) sautéed in coconut milk and served with grilled bananas. When the beachside tiki torches are lit at dinner the scene is oh-so-romantic. Mama's is at Ku'au Cove, along the Hana Hwy, and is 2 miles east of Pa'ia center. Reservations are essential.

Drinking & Entertainment

Milagros (☎ 579-8755; 3 Baldwin Ave; ◷ 8am-10pm) *The* spot for a late-afternoon beer or the perfect margarita. The sidewalk tables are perched perfectly for watching all the action on Pa'ia's busiest corner.

Charley's (☎ 579-9453; 142 Hana Hwy) A hangout of country-music icon Willie Nelson when he's on the island (he lives on the outskirts of Pa'ia), Charley's has live music and dancing most nights.

Moana Bakery & Café (☎ 579-9999; 71 Baldwin Ave) If jazz is your thing, this is your place, with live music Wednesday to Saturday nights.

Shopping

Lots of cool shops and a laid-back atmosphere add up to fun browsing.

Maui Crafts Guild (☎ 579-9697; 43 Hana Hwy) One of the island's best galleries, this collective of Maui artists and craftspeople sells everything from pottery and jewelry to handpainted silks and natural-fiber baskets. It's on the *makai* side of the road as you come into town from Kahului.

Na Kani O Hula (☎ 573-6332; 105 Baldwin Ave) Producing instruments for hula *halau* (troupes), the shop sells *'uli'uli* (feather-decorated gourd rattles), bamboo nose flutes and more – any of which would make for a fascinating souvenir.

Hemp House (☎ 579-8880; 16 Baldwin Ave) OK, it's Pa'ia – you know there'd be a place selling hemp clothing, hemp lotion and even hemp Frisbees.

Mandala (☎ 579-9555; 29 Baldwin Ave) Check out the lightweight cotton and silk clothing, Buddhas and Asian crafts at this diverse shop.

Maui Girl (☎ 579-9266; 12 Baldwin Ave) Get your itty-bitty bikinis here.

Getting Around

You can rent Trek mountain-bikes at **Maui Sunriders** (☎ 579-8970; www.mauibikeride.com; 71 Baldwin Ave; per day/week $30/90; ◷ hours vary). The price includes a bike rack, so a travel companion could drop you off at the top of Haleakala, or anywhere else, to cycle a one-way route.

THE ROAD TO HANA

Get ready for an adventure. Simply put, this breathtaking drive has few rivals anywhere on the planet. Narrow and serpentine, the Hana Hwy is a cliff-hugger that winds between jungly valleys and razor-edge cliffs, curling

MAUI

MAUI

TOP FIVE HANA TRIP TIPS

- Beat the crowd – get a sunrise start.
- Fill up the tank in Pa'ia; the next gas station isn't until Hana.
- Bring a picnic and plenty to drink.
- Wear a bathing suit under your clothes so you're ready for impromptu swims.
- Pull over to let local drivers pass.

---

around more than 600 twists and turns along the way. One-lane bridges mark dozens of waterfalls, some gentle and inviting, others so sheer they kiss you with spray as you drive past.

The valleys along the way are a virtual Garden of Eden. The scent of wild ginger sweetens the air, and even the trees burst into flower, adding splashes of orange to the verdant rain forests. Best of all, you don't have to enjoy it all from the inside of a car – there are plenty of opportunities to swim beneath a waterfall, stroll in the forest and explore other wonders along the way. The key thing here is not to cut yourself short. Get on the road early and you'll have plenty of time to make your own adventure.

Twin Falls

At Hwy 36's intersection with Hwy 365, just after the 16-mile marker, the Hana Hwy changes numbers to Hwy 360 and the mile markers begin again at zero.

After the 2-mile marker on Hwy 360, a parking area on your right next to a fruit stand marks the start of the trailhead to Twin Falls. The walk to the falls takes approximately 30 minutes return and is nice enough if you're based in the area, but if you're on the way to Hana, don't bother to stop here now – there are better waterfalls further down the road.

Huelo

Huelo Rd, a one-lane road a half-mile past the 3-mile marker, leads down to **Kaulanapueo Church**, which was constructed of coral in 1853 and named for the pueo (owls) that once thrived in the surrounding forest. The tin-roofed church is often locked, however, so if you're short on time, this one can be saved for another day.

SLEEPING

Hale Akua Shangri-La (☎ 572-9300, 888-368-5305; www.haleakua.com; Huelo Rd; r $60-300; 🐾) Wake up to a sunrise seaview all the way to Hana at this cliffside garden of Eden. Spread over 5 acres, Shangri-La offers Maui's most cosmic getaway. Accommodations range from a simple poolside room to an ultraromantic Balinese cottage. All guests have access to a clothing-optional hot tub, swimming pool, kitchen facilities, morning yoga classes and lots of meditative spaces.

Tea House (☎ 572-5610; www.mauiteahouse.com; Huelo Rd; 1-bedroom cottages $130) Another hidden Huelo jewel, this Asian-style cottage is built with walls recycled from a Zen temple. The place is so secluded that it's off the grid, and uses its own solar power to stoke up the lights. Guests have a small kitchen and an open-air bath in a redwood gazebo. Meditate at a Tibetan-style stupa with a spectacular ocean view.

Ko'olau Forest Reserve

Hold on to your hat – now the real fun begins! As the highway snakes along the edge of the Ko'olau Forest Reserve, the jungle takes over with a one-lane bridge and waterfall offering drama around every other bend. Ko'olau, which means 'windward,' catches the rain clouds and squeezes out about 80in of rain annually along the coast and a mighty 200in to 300in up the slopes. No surprise – that makes for awesome waterfalls as the rainwater rushes down the reserve's abundant gulches and streams.

Paralleling the highway is the **Ko'olau Ditch**, a century-old system that carries up to 450 million gallons of water a day through 75 miles of ditches and tunnels from the rain forest to the dry central plains of Maui. If you want to take a closer look at the Ditch, stop at the small pull-off just before the bridge that comes up immediately after the 8-mile

---

HEAVENLY DRIVE

Hawaiians cherished the beauty along the north shore long before the first Model-T came barreling down the road. So it's no surprise the 54 bridges to Hana have 54 poetic Hawaiian names taken from the streams and gulches they cross – names like Heavenly Mist, Prayer Blossoms and Reawakening.

---

marker. Just 50ft above the road you can see a hand-hewn stone-block section of the ditch on your right.

After the village of **Kailua**, home to the workers who maintain the ditch, you'll be treated to a splash of color as you pass groves of painted eucalyptus trees with rainbow-colored bark.

Waikamoi Trail & Waterfalls

A half-mile past the 9-mile marker, a wide dirt pull-off provides space for a few cars to park below the **Waikamoi Nature Trail**. This peaceful 30-minute trail loops through tall trees with wonderful fresh scents and lots of birdsong. The grand reddish trees covered with climbing philodendron vines are *Eucalyptus robusta*. The ridge at the top of the trail provides a fine view of the winding Hana Hwy.

The next few sights come up quickly, so keep a keen eye out. **Waikamoi Falls** is at the bridge just before the 10-mile marker. The lower waterfall has a pool and it's possible to walk a short way up to a higher waterfall, but the rocks can be slippery, and the bottom one is prettier anyway. Past Waikamoi, bamboo grows almost horizontally out from the cliffs, creating a canopy effect over the road.

Immediately after the 11-mile marker you will pass **Puohokamoa Falls**, another zenlike waterfall. This one doesn't have any public access, but you can get a view of it right from the bridge.

If you're ready for a dip, **Haipua'ena Falls**, half a mile after the 11-mile marker, provides a gentle waterfall with an Eden-like pool deep enough for swimming. Most people don't know this one's here, as you can't see the pool from the road. There's space for a couple of cars on the Hana side of the bridge. To reach the falls, just walk 100yd upstream.

A perfect place to break out the picnic is **Kaumahina State Wayside Park**, which comes

up shortly after the 12-mile marker. And it has clean rest rooms, making it a much-appreciated stop right about now. A short walk up the hill past the rest rooms will reward you with a view of the striking coastal scenery that awaits to the south.

Honomanu Bay

For the next several miles, the scenery is absolutely stunning, opening up to a new vista as you turn round each bend. If it's been raining recently, you can expect to see waterfalls galore crashing down the mountains.

Just after the 14-mile marker, an inconspicuous road heads down to Honomanu Bay and a rocky black-sand beach used mostly by surfers and fishers. The water's usually too turbulent for swimming, but on very calm days it's possible to snorkel here.

Ke'anae

You've made it halfway to Hana! Ke'anae Valley, which extends down from the Ko'olau Gap in Haleakala Crater, radiates green thanks to 150in of rain yearly. Ke'anae Peninsula was formed by a later eruption of Haleakala that gushed through the Ko'olau Gap straight down Ke'anae Valley and into the ocean. Outlined by its black-lava shores, Ke'anae Peninsula still wears its birthmark around the edges. Unlike its rugged surroundings, the peninsula is very flat, like a leaf floating on the water.

Time for a stretch? **Ke'anae Arboretum**, three-quarters of a mile past the 16-mile marker, follows a stream bed past an array of shady trees. Coolest of all are the painted eucalyptus trees and the golden-stemmed bamboo, whose green stripes look like the strokes of a Japanese *shodo* artist. The path, which takes about 20 minutes to walk, passes ginger and other fragrant plants before ending at taro patches.

See a slice of 'Old Hawaii' by taking the road leading down to Ke'anae Peninsula, just beyond Ke'anae Arboretum. Ke'anae is a quiet little village where colts and goats roam freely. **Lanakila 'Ihi'ihi o Iehova Ona Kaua** (Ke'anae Congregational Church), built in 1860, is a half-mile from the Hana Hwy. This is one church made of lava rocks and coral mortar whose exterior hasn't been covered over with layers of whitewash, and rather than being locked tight, you'll find open doors and a guest book. The road ends at a scenic coastline of jagged black rock and pounding waves. The rock

MAUI

island off the coast is **Mokumana Island**, a seabird sanctuary.

Back up on the Hana Hwy, there's a good view of Ke'anae village, with its squares of planted taro fed by Ke'anae Stream, at **Ke'anae Peninsula Lookout**, an unmarked pull-off just past the 17-mile marker on the *makai* side of the road; look for the yellow tsunami speaker.

SLEEPING

YMCA Camp Ke'anae (☎ 248-8355; www.mauiymca .org; 13375 Hana Hwy; campsite or dm $17, cottages $125) When they're not tied up by groups, the Y's cabins, on a knoll overlooking the coast, are available to individuals as hostel-style dorms. You'll need your own sleeping bag, and cooking facilities are limited to simple outdoor grills. Another option is pitching your tent on the grounds. The Y also has two cottages, each with full facilities, two bedrooms and a lanai with spectacular ocean views. The camp is between the 16- and 17-mile markers.

Wailua

Shortly after the Ke'anae Peninsula Lookout, you'll pass a couple of roadside fruit stands. Best is **Halfway to Hana** (☎ 248-8301; ☽ 8:30am-4pm), south of the 17-mile marker, which sells banana bread baked fresh every morning, as well as fruit slices, shave ice and cool drinks.

Take Wailua Rd *makai* a quarter mile after the 18-mile marker to reach **Our Lady of Fatima Shrine**. Also known as the Coral Miracle Church, this blue-and-white chapel was built in 1860 using coral from a freak storm that deposited the material onto a nearby beach. After the church was completed, another rogue storm hit the beach and swept all the leftover piles of coral back into the sea…or so the story goes. The current congregation now uses **St Gabriel's Mission**, the newer church out front.

From Wailua Rd you can also get a peek of the long cascade of **Waikani Falls** if you look back up toward the Hana Hwy. Wailua Rd dead ends a half mile down, though you won't want to go that far, as blocked-off driveways prevent cars from turning around.

Waysides

Back on the Hana Hwy, just before the 19-mile marker, **Wailua Valley State Wayside** lookout comes up on the right. It provides a broad

---

> **DETOUR: NAHIKU**
>
> Get a glimpse of a rural life in the village that once encompassed Hawaii's only rubber plantation. The plantation folded in 1916, but some of the old rubber trees can still be seen along the road, half-covered in a canopy of climbing vines. Be forewarned, the road is one lane the entire way and passing traffic requires pulling over and backing up – so this is not a detour for the faint of heart. The turnoff onto the unmarked Nahiku Rd is just east of the 25-mile marker. After winding down 2.5 miles you'll reach the village center with its brightly painted church and smattering of old wooden houses.

---

view into Ke'anae Valley, which appears to be a hundred shades of green. You can see a couple of waterfalls, and on a clear day look up at Ko'olau Gap, the break in the rim of Haleakala Crater. If you climb up the steps to the right, you'll find a good view of Wailua Peninsula, but there's an even better view of it at the large paved **pull-off** 0.25 miles down the road.

Halfway between the 22- and 23-mile markers, **Pua'a Ka'a State Wayside Park** centers around a tranquil waterfall and a pool large enough for swimming. The park also has rest rooms and shaded streamside picnic tables.

EATING

Nahiku Ti Gallery & Café (☎ 248-8800; ☽ 6am-5:30pm) Before the 29-mile marker, Nahiku Ti serves Maui-grown coffee, smoothies and simple pastries.

Up in Smoke (snacks $3-6; ☽ 10am-5pm Fri-Wed) The bustling BBQ stand next door to Nahiku Ti is the place to try smoked breadfruit and *kalua* pig tacos.

'Ula'ino Road

This road leads *makai* from the Hana Hwy, just south of the 31-mile marker, to three worthwhile sights. The Ka'eleku Caverns are on the paved part of the road, half a mile from the Hana Hwy. The other sights on this road can be a bit more challenging to reach. Even when it's very dry, you probably won't be able to go the entire 3 miles of 'Ula'ino Rd without a 4WD, but you can usually get as far as Kahanu Gardens.

KA'ELEKU CAVERNS

You don't need to be a geology buff to get off on these mammoth **caves** (☎ 248-7308; www .mauicave.com; admission $11.95; ☽ 10:30am-4:30pm Mon-Sat), formed by ancient lava flows. The caves are so formidable that they once served as a slaughterhouse – 17,000lb of cow bones had to be removed before they were opened to tourists! Winding your way through the extensive underground lava tubes you'll find a unique ecosystem of stalactites and stalagmites. Most people take about an hour to explore. The admission includes use of flashlights and hard hats. Bring a sweater – it's cool down under.

KAHANU GARDENS

These remarkable **gardens** (☎ 248-8912; www .ntbg.org; self-guided tour adult/child under 12 $10/free; ☽ 10am-2pm Mon-Fri) cover 122 acres of ethnobotanical wonders, including the world's largest breadfruit tree collection. Operated by the National Tropical Botanical Garden, which is dedicated to the conservation of rare and medicinal plants, Kahanu Gardens features collections from the tropical Pacific. Most interesting is the canoe garden, landscaped with plants brought to Hawaii by early Polynesian settlers.

The grounds are also the site of **Pi'ilanihale Heiau**, the largest temple in Hawaii, with a stone platform reaching 450ft in length. The history of this astounding heiau is shrouded in mystery, but there's no doubt that it was an important religious site for Hawaiians. Archaeologists believe construction began as early as AD 1200 and the heiau was built in sequences. The final grand scale was the work of Pi'ilani (the heiau's name means House of Pi'ilani), the 14th-century Maui chief who is also credited with the construction of many of the coastal fishponds in the Hana area.

The gardens and heiau, on Kalahu Point, are 1.5 miles down 'Ula'ino Rd. The road is crossed by a streambed immediately before reaching the gardens; if it's dry you should be able to drive over it OK, but if it's been raining heavily don't even try.

BLUE POOL

Past Kahanu Gardens, 'Ula'ino Rd quickly becomes rough. Major dips in the road pass over another streambed that clearly calls for 4WD vehicles, especially if it has been raining hard recently. You may have to park off to the side of the road and walk the final mile to the coast.

When you get to the water's edge, turn left and strike out across the beach boulders for five minutes or so until you see the broad cascading waterfall and its crystal-blue pool. The Blue Pool is of spiritual significance to Native Hawaiians. Be sure to stop and read the signboard on 'Ula'ino Rd, opposite Ka'eleku Caverns, which the local *'ohana* (family) has posted with guidelines on visiting the site.

Wai'anapanapa State Park

This coastal park offers a sparkling potpourri of sights, from jet-black sands and sea arches to cool caves and ancient burial sites. If you're lucky, you might even spot a monk seal sunning along the shore.

The park's **black-sand beach** drops quickly and the water is best suited for strong swimmers. Powerful rips are the norm, but when it's very calm the area around the sea arch offers good snorkeling. Check it out carefully, though, as people have drowned here.

Don't miss the pair of lava-tube **caves**, a five-minute walk from the parking lot. The garden-like exteriors are draped with ferns, while the interiors harbor deep pools. Wai'anapanapa means 'glistening waters,' and its mineral waters are said to rejuvenate the skin. On certain nights of the year, the waters in the caves turn red. Legend says it's the blood of a princess and her lover who were killed in a fit of rage by the princess's jealous husband after he found them hiding together here. Less romantic types attribute the phenomenon to swarms of tiny bright-red shrimp called *'opaeula,* which occasionally emerge from subterranean cracks in the lava.

A **coastal trail** leads south 2.5 miles from the park to Kainalimu Bay, just north of Hana Bay, offering splendid views along the way. Shortly beyond the park cabins the trail passes blowholes and burial grounds before reaching temple ruins. As the trail fades, keep following the coast over old lava fields. Once you reach the boulder-strewn beach at Kainalimu Bay, it's about a mile further to Hana center.

The road into Wai'anapanapa State Park is just after the 32-mile marker, half a mile south of the turnoff to Hana airport. The road ends at Pailoa Bay, above the park's black-sand beach.

SLEEPING

Fall asleep to the lullaby of the surf at one of the park's campsites on a shady lawn near the beach. There is one caveat – this is the rainy side of the island, so it can get wet at any time. The park also has a dozen housekeeping cabins that are extremely popular and usually book up months in advance. See p309 for details on permits, fees and reservations.

HANA
pop 1855

After the incredible drive getting to Hana, some visitors are surprised to find the town is, well, a bit of a sleeper.

Hana doesn't hit you with a bam. Except for that flustered cluster of daytrippers in the center of town who have unfolded themselves from their cars to ask 'Is this it?,' the town is quiet. Cows graze lazily in green pastures stretching up the hillsides. Neighbors chat over plate lunches at the beach. Even at Hana's famed hotel, the emphasis is on relaxation.

What Hana has to offer is best appreciated by those who stop and unwind. Visitors who stay awhile will experience an authentic slice of aloha in this one-of-a-kind town.

On an island that booms with mainland influences, Hana's isolation is worshipped religiously. That long and winding road that separates Hana from the central part of the island also contributes to its preservation as one of the few real Hawaiian communities left in the state. The majority of its residents have Hawaiian blood and a strong sense of 'ohana. If you listen closely, you'll hear the words 'auntie' and 'uncle' a lot. And although it's a tight community, Hana's not a closed one. Over the years a handful of celebrities, including George Harrison and Kris Kristofferson, have bought homes here and had an active presence in the community. Stick around – there's a lot more than first meets the eye.

History

It's hard to imagine little Hana as the epicenter of Maui but this village produced many of ancient Hawaii's most influential *ali'i*. Hana's great 14th-century chief Pi'ilani marched from here to conqueror rivals in Wailuku and Lahaina, and become Maui's first unified leader. The paths he took became such vital routes that even today half of Maui's highways still bear his name.

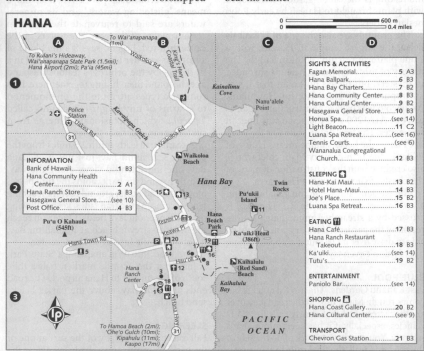

HANA

| 0 | 600 m |
| 0 | 0.4 miles |

To Wai'anapanapa (1mi)

To Kulani's Hideaway, Wai'anapanapa State Park (1.5mi); Hana Airport (2mi); Pa'ia (45mi)

King's Hwy Coastal Trail

Waikoloa Rd

Kainalimu Cove

Nanu'alele Point

Police Station

Uakea Rd

Kawaiipapa Gulch

Waikoloa Rd

Waikoloa Beach

Hana Bay

Twin Rocks

Pu'ukii Island

Pu'u O Kahaula (545ft)

Keawa Pl

Keanini Dr

Hana Beach Park

Ka'uiki Head (386ft)

Hana Town Rd

Hau'oli St

Hana Ranch Center

Kaihalulu (Red Sand) Beach

Kaihalulu Bay

Mill Rd

Hana Hwy

To Hamoa Beach (2mi); 'Ohe'o Gulch (10mi); Kipahulu (11mi); Kaupo (17mi)

PACIFIC OCEAN

INFORMATION
Bank of Hawaii.....................1	B3
Hana Community Health	
Center..............................2	A1
Hana Ranch Store...............3	B3
Hasegawa General Store.......(see 10)	
Post Office.........................4	B3

SIGHTS & ACTIVITIES
Fagan Memorial...................5	A3
Hana Ballpark.....................6	B3
Hana Bay Charters...............7	B2
Hana Community Center.......8	B3
Hana Cultural Center............9	B2
Hasegawa General Store.......10	B3
Honua Spa.........................(see 14)	
Light Beacon......................11	C2
Luana Spa Retreat................(see 16)	
Tennis Courts.....................(see 6)	
Wananalua Congregational	
Church............................12	B3

SLEEPING
Hana-Kai Maui.....................13	B2
Hotel Hana-Maui..................14	B3
Joe's Place.........................15	B2
Luana Spa Retreat................16	B3

EATING
Hana Café..........................17	B3
Hana Ranch Restaurant	
Takeout...........................18	B3
Ka'uiki.............................(see 14)	
Tutu's..............................19	B2

ENTERTAINMENT
Paniolo Bar........................(see 14)	

SHOPPING
Hana Coast Gallery...............20	B2
Hana Cultural Center............(see 9)	

TRANSPORT
Chevron Gas Station.............21	B3

The landscape changed dramatically in 1849 when ex-whaler George Wilfong bought 60 acres of land to plant sugarcane. Hana went on to become a booming plantation town, complete with a narrow-gauge railroad connecting the fields to the Hana Mill. In the 1940s Hana could no longer compete with larger sugar operations in central Maui and the mill went bust.

Enter San Francisco businessman Paul Fagan, who purchased 14,000 acres in Hana in 1943. Starting with 300 Herefords, Fagan converted the cane fields to ranch land. A few years later he opened a six-room hotel as a getaway resort for well-to-do friends and brought his minor-league baseball team, the San Francisco Seals, to Hana for spring training. That's when visiting sports journalists gave the town its moniker, 'Heavenly Hana.' Today Hana Ranch remains the backbone of Hana's economy and its hillside pastures graze some 2200 head of cattle worked by *paniolo*.

Orientation & Information

Hana closes up early. If you're going to be heading back late, get gas in advance – the sole gas station, **Chevron** (☎ 248-7671; cnr Mill Rd & Hana Hwy; ☷ 7am-7:30pm), has limited opening hours.

Hana Ranch Center (Mill Rd) is the commercial center of town. It has a **post office** (☎ 248-8258); a tiny **Bank of Hawaii** (☎ 248-8015; ☷ 3-4:30pm Mon-Thu, to 6pm Fri); and the **Hana Ranch Store** (☎ 248-8261; ☷ 7am-7:30pm), which sells groceries, liquor and general supplies. There's no ATM at the bank, but **Hasegawa General Store** (☎ 248-8231; 5165 Hana Hwy; ☷ 7am-7pm Mon-Sat, 8am-6pm Sun) has one. The **Hana Community Health Center** (☎ 248-8294; 4590 Hana Hwy; ☷ 8am-5pm) is at the north side of town.

Sights
HANA BEACH PARK

Every town has a focal point and in Hana this bayside park is action central. People come here to take the kids for a splash, to picnic on the beach, to strum their ukulele with friends. The **black-sand beach** on the south side of the park has a snack bar, showers, rest rooms and picnic tables.

When water conditions are very calm, snorkeling and diving are good out in the direction of the light beacon. Currents can be strong, and snorkelers shouldn't venture beyond the beacon. Surfers head to **Waikoloa Beach**, at the northern end of the bay.

HANA CULTURAL CENTER

Absorb a little local history at this down-home **museum** (☎ 248-8622; www.hookele.com/hccm; 4974 Uakea Rd; admission $2; ☷ 10am-4pm) displaying Hawaiian artifacts, wood carvings and quilts. And don't miss the four authentically reconstructed thatched *hale* at the side of the museum, which can be seen even if you arrive outside of opening hours.

The grounds also contain a three-bench, c 1871 **courthouse**. Although it looks like a museum piece, the court is still used on the first Tuesday of each month; a judge shows up to hear minor cases, such as traffic violations, sparing Hana residents the need to drive all the way to Wailuku.

KAIHALULU (RED SAND) BEACH

A favored haunt of nude sunbathers, this little cove on the south side of Ka'uiki Head owes its sand to the red cinder hill and its turquoise waters to Hana's pollution-free remoteness. The cove is partly protected by a lava outcrop, but the currents can be powerful when the surf is up. Water drains through a break on the left side, which should be avoided. Your best chance of finding calm waters is in the morning.

The path to the beach is at the end of Uakea Rd beyond the ballpark. It starts across the lawn at the lower side of the Hana Community Center, where a steep 10-minute trail continues down to the beach. En route you'll pass an overgrown Japanese cemetery, a remnant of the sugarcane days.

HASEGAWA GENERAL STORE

In its previous incarnation, this century-old **general store** (☎ 248-8231; 5165 Hana Hwy; ☷ 7am-7pm Mon-Sat, 8am-6pm Sun) was Hana's best-known sight. After the original place burned down in 1990, it relocated under the rusty tin roof of the town's old theater building. Some of its character was lost along with its eclectic inventory, but the store still haphazardly packs just about everything from bags of poi and aloha dolls to the record that immortalized the store in song.

WANANALUA CONGREGATIONAL CHURCH

Erected in 1838 to replace the congregation's original grass church, this **edifice** (cnr Hana Hwy & Hau'oli St) with its hefty rock walls resembles an ancient Norman church. Take a close look and you'll notice that the rock is cut from lava. Also noteworthy is the little cemetery at the side, where the graves are randomly laid out rather than lined up in rows. Even at rest, Hana folks like things casual.

FAGAN MEMORIAL
Paul Fagan often ended his day with a walk up Lyon's Hill to enjoy the view at sunset – and you might want to see for yourself why! The hill is now topped with a **memorial cross** (Hana Town Rd) to Fagan that's Hana's most dominant landmark. The 15-minute trail up Lyon's Hill starts opposite Hotel Hana-Maui.

Activities
Hana Bay Charters (☎ 248-4999, 800-471-8082; www .hanabaycharters.com; Uakea Rd; tours $79-139; ☺ tours 8am & noon) offers adventurous snorkel tours into secluded bays frequented by spinner dolphins, sea turtles and colorful fish.

If you prefer to be coddled, the posh **Honua Spa** (☎ 270-5290; Hotel Hana-Maui, 5031 Hana Hwy; treatments $70-185; ☺ 9am-8pm) can pamper you with Hawaiian *lomolomi* massages, hot stone rubs and ginger scrubs. **Luana Spa Retreat** (☎ 248-8855; 5050 Uakea Rd; treatments $40-155; ☺ by appointment) offers massages and body treatments in a Hawaiian-style open-air setting.

Hana Ballpark has some public **tennis courts**. Other activities, including **horseback rides** and **kayaking**, can be arranged through Hotel Hana-Maui.

Festivals & Events
East Maui Taro Festival (www.tarofestival.org) Held on a weekend in late March or early April at Hana Ballpark, this is the town's big annual bash. It's one of the most authentically Hawaiian events in the state, with poi-making demonstrations, outrigger canoe races, a taro pancake breakfast and hula dancing. Some of Hawaii's best ukulele players and slack-key guitarists show up to share their music with friends. It's a great time to be in Hana, but be sure to book your accommodations well in advance.
Hana Relays (www.virr.com) The ultimate relay road race, it follows the untamed Hana Hwy 52 breathtaking miles from Kahului to Hana Ballpark. It's held on the second Saturday in September.

Sleeping
In addition to the following accommodations options, there are cabins and tent camping avaibale at Wai'anapanapa State Park (p377), just to the north of Hana, and camping at 'Ohe'o Gulch (p383), about 10 miles south near Kipahulu.

BUDGET
Joe's Place (☎ 248-7033; www.joesrentals.com; 4870 Uakea Rd; r with shared/private bath $45/55) As long as you don't expect anything fancy you'll be happy at Hana's only nod to the budget traveler. The dozen rooms are basic but clean, and you can chat with fellow travelers as you grill dinner on the barbie. Guests also have a shared TV den and use of a kitchen.

MIDRANGE
Kulani's Hideaway (☎ 248-8234; www.kulanishideaway .com; Wai'anapanapa Rd; 1-/2-bedroom units $80/160) On the doorstep of Wai'anapanapa State Park, this sparkling two-unit hideaway pairs all the comforts of home with ready access to the park's natural wonders. Just a few minutes' walk to the park and a five-minute drive to town, the units have full kitchens so you can avoid Hana's sky-high dinner prices. And there's no minimum stay.

Luana Spa Retreat (☎ 248-8855; www.luanaspa.com; 5050 Uakea Rd; d $110) If you've never stayed in a yurt, here's the perfect opportunity. On a hill overlooking Hana Bay, this unique charmer is a cross between camping and a cottage. The yurt sports a well-equipped kitchenette, a comfy queen bed and even a stereo with Hawaiian music. Shower outdoors in a bamboo enclosure, enjoy the scent of native flowers – all in all, this is *aloha 'aina* (love of the land) at its finest.

Hana Kai-Maui (☎ 248-8426, 800-346-2772; www .hanakai.com; 1533 Uakea Rd; studios $145-175, 1-bedroom units $165-255) Listen to the surf crash from your lanai at this well-run oceanfront condominium complex. A sandy beach is just a stone's throw away. For the best ocean views request a top-floor corner unit.

TOP END
Hotel Hana-Maui (☎ 248-8211, 800-321-4262; www .hotelhanamaui.com; 5031 Hana Hwy; r $425-495, cottages $575-1425; ⛲) Maui's first and foremost getaway hotel, this pampering place breathes tranquility. Everything's airy and open, rich with Hawaiian accents, from island art in the lobby to hand-stitched quilts on the beds. Rooms have old-fashioned comforts with hardwood floors and French doors opening to trellised patios. Delightfully absent are electronic gadgets – sans even alarm clocks! If that's not relaxing enough, there's complimentary yoga and a full-service spa offering Hawaiian massage and seaweed wraps.

Eating

Hana has just a couple of stores with limited grocery selections, so if you're staying awhile it's best to stock up in Kahului before heading down.

Tutu's (☎ 248-8224; Hana Beach Park; snacks $3-8; ✍ 8:30am-4pm) The quintessential beach grill, Tutu's serves up the expected menu of shave ice, plate lunches and burgers. Just grab a table on the sand and you've got yourself an instant picnic at Hana's favorite family beach.

Hana Café (5050 Uakea Rd; meals $5-10; ✍ 10am-4pm) You'll find a local crowd at this hidden gem set back from the road opposite Hana Ballpark. It's little more than a lunchwagon, but it serves café fare on par with Maui's finest, including organic salads, scrumptious carrot-coconut soup and foamy lattes. On Sunday there's homemade Thai food worth lining up for.

Hana Ranch Restaurant Takeout (☎ 248-8255; Hana Ranch Center, Mill Rd; meals $6-12; ✍ 6:30am-4pm Wed, Fri & Sat, 6:30am-7pm Sun-Tue & Thu) Busiest spot in town, and for good reason. Everybody comes for the mammoth burgers made of free-range Hana cattle – it doesn't get any fresher than this. Vegetarians aren't left out either; the taro burger offers a slice of Maui before ranching took hold. Good breakfast fare and plate lunches, too. Oh, and did we mention the ocean-view picnic tables?

Ka'uiki (☎ 248-8211; Hotel Hana-Maui, 5031 Hana Hwy; prix fixe lunch $32, dinner $57; ✍ 11:30am-2:30pm & 6-9pm) This is the place for a splurge. The menu emphasizes seafood, meats and produce from Hana's waters and farms; some of the dishes are prepared with a Hawaiian accent, others with an Asian influence. Best deal is the three-course prix fixe menu, with yummy options like fresh catch with ginger aioli and fern tempura.

Drinking & Entertainment

Paniolo Bar (☎ 248-8211; Hotel Hana-Maui, 5031 Hana Hwy; ✍ 10am-9pm) A classy place to enjoy a drink, this open-air bar at Hotel Hana-Maui often has live Hawaiian music in the evening.

Shopping

Hana Coast Gallery (☎ 248-8638; 5031 Hana Hwy; ✍ 9am-5pm) Stop by this gallery located at the north side of Hotel Hana-Maui even if you are not shopping for anything, just to see the museum-quality wooden bowls, paintings and Hawaiian featherwork.

Hana Cultural Center (☎ 248-8622; 4974 Uakea Rd; ✍ 10am-4pm) The town's museum has a gift shop with a selection of local crafts.

BEYOND HANA

South from Hana, the road changes its name to the Pi'ilani Hwy and winds down to Kipahulu, passing 'Ohe'o Gulch, the southern end of Haleakala National Park. This incredibly lush stretch is perhaps the most beautiful part of the entire drive. Between the hairpin turns, one-lane bridges and drivers trying to take in all the sights, it's a slow-moving 10 miles, so allow yourself at least 45 minutes. Along the way you'll see orchids growing out of the rocks and waterfalls cascading down the cliffs. Most spectacular of all is **Wailua Falls**, which appears soon after the 45-mile marker, dropping an awesome 100ft just beyond the road.

Haneo'o Road Loop

It's well worth a detour off the highway to take this 1.5-mile loop, which skirts a scenic coastline. The turnoff onto Haneo'o Rd is just before the 50-mile marker.

Koki Beach, at the base of a red cinder hill less than a half-mile from the start of the loop, attracts local surfers, though submerged rocks and strong currents make it hazardous for newcomers. The beach has chocolate-brown sand, much of which washes away in winter, leaving a rocky shoreline.

The offshore isle topped by a few coconut palms is **'Alau Island**, a seabird sanctuary. The trees were planted years ago by Hana residents to provide themselves with coconut milk while fishing from the island.

A little further is **Hamoa Beach**, whose lovely gray sands are used by Hotel Hana-Maui, but are open to all. Author James Michener once called it the only beach in the North Pacific that actually looked as if it belonged in the South Pacific. When surf's up, surfers and bodyboarders flock to the waters, though be aware of rip currents. When seas are calm, swimming is good in the cove. Public access is down the steps just north of the hotel's bus-stop sign. Facilities include showers and rest rooms.

'Ohe'o Gulch

The southern end of **Haleakala National Park** (admission per car per 3 days $10; ✍ 24hr) dips down into the lush Kipahulu area. There's no access

MAUI

between this section of the park and the main Haleakala summit area (p403), so your visit to the cindery summit will need to wait for another day. But hold onto your ticket, because it's good for both sections of the park. The crowning glory of the Kipahulu section is 'Ohe'o Gulch with its magnificent waterfalls and wide pools, each one tumbling into the next one below. When the sun shines, these cool glistening pools make great swimming holes.

HISTORY

Back in the 1970s 'Ohe'o Gulch was dubbed the 'Seven Sacred Pools' as part of a tourism promotion and the term still floats around freely, much to the chagrin of park officials. It's a complete misnomer since there are 24 pools in all, extending from the ocean to Waimoku Falls, and they were never sacred – but they certainly are divine. The waters once supported a sizable Hawaiian settlement of farmers who cultivated sweet potatoes and taro in terraced gardens beside the stream. Archaeologists have identified the stone remains of more than 700 ancient structures at 'Ohe'o.

One of the expressed intentions of Haleakala National Park is to manage its Kipahulu area 'to perpetuate traditional Hawaiian farming and ho'onanea' – a Hawaiian word meaning to pass the time in ease, peace and pleasure. So kick back and have some fun!

INFORMATION

The national park's **Kipahulu Visitor Center** (☎ 248-7375; www.nps.gov/hale; ☺ 9am-5pm) offers a thin menu of visitor programs, depending on the season and the staff available. The mainstay is short cultural history talks usually given on the half hour between 12:30pm and 3:30pm. You'll find rest rooms at the parking lot and bottles of drinking water can be purchased at the visitor center. Food and gas are not available.

SIGHTS & ACTIVITIES
Lower Pools

Even if you're tight on time, you've got to take this 20-minute stroll! The **Kuloa Point Trail**, a half-mile loop, runs from the visitor center down to the lower pools and back. At the junction with Pipiwai Trail go right. A few minutes down, you'll come to a broad grassy knoll with a gorgeous view of the Hana coast. On a clear

day you can see the Big Island, 30 miles away across 'Alenuihaha Channel. This would be a fine place to break out a picnic lunch.

The large freshwater pools along the trail are terraced one atop the other and connected by gentle cascades. Their cool waters are refreshingly brisk. The second big pool below the bridge is a favorite swimming hole. Although the water is usually calm, heavy rains falling far away on the upper slopes can bring a sudden torrent here at any time. If the water starts to rise, get out immediately. Several people have been swept out to sea from these pools by flash floods. Slippery rocks and unseen submerged ledges are other potential hazards, so check carefully before jumping in.

And here's something quirky: 'Ohe'o Gulch is home to a rare goby fish called *'o'opu*, which spends the first stages of its life in the ocean, but returns to breed in the upper stream. The fish, which has a face that resembles a frog, works its way up the chain of pools and waterfalls by using its front fins as suction cups as it climbs the rocks.

Waterfall Trails

The **Pipiwai Trail** runs up the 'Ohe'o streambed, rewarding hikers with picture-perfect views of the upper falls. The trail starts on the *mauka* side of the visitor center and leads up to Makahiku Falls (0.5 miles) and Waimoku Falls (2 miles). Or take a little shortcut by picking up the trail from the pedestrian crossing at the highway. To see both falls, allow about two hours return. The upper section is muddy, but boardwalks cover some of the worst bits.

Along the path, you'll pass large mango trees and patches of guava before coming to an overlook after about 10 minutes. **Makahiku Falls**, a long bridal-veil waterfall that drops into a deep gorge, is just off to the right. Thick green ferns cover the sides of 200ft basalt cliffs where the fall cascades – a very rewarding scene for such a short walk.

Continuing along the main trail, you'll walk beneath old banyan trees, cross Palikea Stream (killer mosquitoes thrive here) and enter the wonderland of the **Bamboo Forest**, where thick groves of trees bang together musically in the wind. Beyond them is **Waimoku Falls**, a thin, lacy 400ft waterfall dropping down a sheer rock face. When you come out of the first grove, you'll see the waterfall in the distance. Forget swimming under Waimoku

Falls – its pool is shallow and there's a danger of falling rocks.

If you want to take a dip, you'll find better pools along the way. About 100yd before Waimoku Falls, you'll cross a little stream. If you go left and work your way upstream for 10 minutes, you'll come to an attractive waterfall and a little pool about neck deep. There's also an inviting pool in the stream about halfway between Makahiku and Waimoku Falls.

TOURS

For fascinating insights into the area's past, join one of the free hour-long ethnobotanical tours led by **Kipahulu Ohana** (www.kipahulu.org), a collective of Native Hawaiian farmers who have restored ancient taro patches within the park. The tours are given at 1pm on the first Tuesday of the month, departing from the park's visitor center.

SLEEPING

The national park maintains a primitive campground a quarter of a mile southeast of the Kipahulu Visitor Center. The campground is Hawaiian style – a huge open pasture set amid the stone ruins of an ancient village. You'll find some incredible places to pitch a tent on grassy cliffs right above the coast and the pounding surf. Bring mosquito repellent and gear suitable for rainy conditions.

In winter you'll usually have the place to yourself, and even in summer there's typically enough space to handle everyone who shows up. Facilities include pit toilets, picnic tables and grills but *no* water. Permits aren't required. Camping is free but limited to three nights each month.

GETTING THERE & AWAY

A lot of people leave the 'Ohe'o Gulch area in mid-afternoon to head back up the Hana Hwy. Some of them, suddenly realizing what a long trek they have ahead, become very impatient drivers.

You might want to consider leaving a little later, which would give you more time to sightsee and enable you to avoid the rush. Getting caught in the dark on the Hana Hwy does have certain advantages. You can see the headlights of oncoming cars around bends that would otherwise be blind, and the traffic is almost nonexistent.

There are no shortcuts back, but there's usually another option. From Kipahulu, the

Pi'ilani Hwy (don't be misled by the term 'highway' – it's just a dirt road in places) heads west through Kaupo to the Upcountry. It's usually passable, but not always, and it shouldn't be done in the dark. Also, be aware that it's going to take as long as going back up the Hana Hwy, so if you opt for the Pi'ilani Hwy, take it as an adventure, not a time-saver. The Kipahulu Visitor Center posts the road conditions.

For details on the drive, see the Pi'ilani Hwy section (p384).

Kipahulu

Less than a mile south of 'Ohe'o Gulch lies the little village of Kipahulu. It's hard to imagine, but this sedate community was once a bustling sugar-plantation town complete with its own mill. After the mill closed in 1922, unsuccessful attempts were made to grow pineapples and then ranching took hold in the late 1920s. Today mixed among modest homes are a scattering of exclusive estates, including the former home of the famed aviator Charles Lindbergh.

Fruit stands are set up here and there along the roadside; some are attended by elderly women who string lei and sell bananas and woven *lauhala* (pandanus-leaf) hats. This is the end of the line for most day visitors who have pushed beyond Hana.

SIGHTS

Charles Lindbergh, who relished his privacy during the final years of his life, moved to remote Kipahulu in 1968. Following his death from cancer in 1974, Lindbergh was buried in the graveyard of **Palapala Ho'omau Congregational Church**. The inscription he selected for his simple grave (If I take the wings of the morning and dwell in the uppermost parts of the sea…) is taken from Psalm 139.

The church with its 26in-thick walls and simple wooden pews dates from 1864. Look at its window painting of a Polynesian Christ draped in the red and yellow feather capes that were worn only by Hawaii's highest chiefs.

Lindbergh's spirit (and his desire to be out of the public eye) may still be at play, because many would-be visitors fail to find his grave, getting the location mixed up with St Paul's Church, which sits on the highway three-quarters of a mile south of Oheo. The dirt drive to Palapala Ho'omau church is half a mile beyond that, on the *makai* side of the road immediately after the 41-mile marker.

MAUI

LINDBERGH'S LAST FLIGHT

When Charles Lindbergh and his wife, the aviatrix and poet Anne Morrow Lindbergh, first began visiting Maui in the 1960s, they were captivated by its beauty. Sam Pryor, a friend who lived at 'Ohe'o Gulch, sold them a little plot of Kipahulu rain forest and they built the cliffside home they christened Argonauta in 1971. The Historic Hawai'i Foundation is currently trying to restore and move Argonauta and Anne's writer's cottage within the boundaries of the national park.

It seems that all his life Charles Lindbergh had been seeking the privacy that only Hana could provide. After making the first ever nonstop solo flight across the Atlantic in 1927, this shy man was catapulted into the limelight. During a goodwill tour to Mexico he met Anne Morrow and married her in 1929. A few years later, the famous couple's 20-month-old son was kidnapped and later found dead, during which time they were constantly hounded by the press. Charles' controversial political actions before WWII, which included accepting a Nazi medal of honor and speaking out against US voluntary involvement in the war before Pearl Harbor, earned them further notoriety.

Toward the end of his life Charles frequently retreated to his Hana home, re-emerging into public life only as a spokesperson for the conservation movement, particularly of endangered humpback and blue whales. When he learned that he was dying of cancer in 1974, Lindbergh said, 'I'd rather spend two days on Maui than two months in this hospital in New York City.' He immediately flew back to the island and died a few days later, on August 26, 1974.

Charles Lindbergh is buried in the graveyard of Palapala Ho'omau Congregational Church. His simple grave is surrounded by lava rocks, just as he designed it, and sits under a plum tree. He lies buried in a eucalyptus coffin dressed in his favorite work clothes, a plaid shirt and khakis, plus a Hudson's Bay blanket. The gravestone inscription, 'If I take the wings of the morning/And dwell in the uttermost parts of the sea,' is incomplete. The next verse of Psalm 139 is 'Even there shall thy hand lead me/And thy right hand shall hold me.' Anne Morrow Lindbergh died on February 7, 2001, at her home in rural Vermont.

The grave is adjacent to the church, and is surrounded by lava rocks and a little fence.

ACTIVITIES

Native Hawaiian-owned **Maui Stables** (☎ 248-7799; www.mauistables.com; 3hr ride $150; ☺ departures 9am & 12:30pm), between the 40- and 41-mile markers, offers trail rides that delve into local legends while climbing the scenic slopes above Kipahulu.

PI'ILANI HIGHWAY

The most remote stretch of road on Maui, the Pi'ilani Hwy travels 25 ruggedly scenic miles between Kipahulu and 'Ulupalakua Ranch as it skirts along the southern flank of Haleakala.

Diehards will love this road, while the more timid may wonder what they've gotten themselves into in these lonesome boonies. Signs such as 'Motorists assume risk of damage due to presence of cattle' and 'Narrow winding road, safe speed 10mph' give some clues that this is not your typical highway. But those who do venture onward can beat their own path to unnamed beaches and ancient heiau before heading back toward civilization.

The hardest part is finding out if the road is currently open and passable, although it usually is. Many tourist maps mark it as impassable, and car-rental agencies say that just being on it is a violation of their contract.

The road winds like a drunken cowboy but most of it is paved. The only real tricky section is 5 unpaved miles around Kaupo. Depending on when it was last graded, you can usually make it in a regular car, though it may rattle your bones. But after hard rains, streams flow over the road, making passage difficult, if not dangerous. A 4WD vehicle, or at least a high-riding car, will minimize your chances of bottoming out.

Flash floods sometimes wash away portions of the road, making it impossible to get through until it's repaired. The **county public works department** (☎ 248-8254; ☺ 6:30am-3pm Mon-Fri) fields calls about road conditions, or ask at the **Kipahulu Visitor Center** (☎ 248-7375; ☺ 9am-5pm) at 'Ohe'o Gulch.

(Continued on page 393)

Voices from the Islands

Young hula dancer of the Na Mea Hula O Kahi-kinaokalalani dance group, Waikiki (p151)

ANN CECIL

O'AHU INTERVIEW
Food Memories of Hawaii

NAME	Lesa Griffith
AGE	43
OCCUPATION	Writer and editor
RESIDENCE	Honolulu

'I grew up eating my grandmother's home-style Japanese dishes, many of which were the precursors of today's East-West fusion. But my palate got international training when I lived in Africa, the Middle East, New York City and Hong Kong.'

I grew up in the Manoa Valley of Honolulu. My strongest childhood memories of food are of my grandmother's *oyaku donburi* (a chicken and egg casserole) and, embarrassing to say, cheeseburgers and orange freezes from Chunky's, a greasy drive-in that doesn't exist anymore.

Yes we did have Spam in the pantry. My mother would use it like bacon or mix it in with fried rice or saimin. Occasionally she'd do a Spam 'roast,' baked in a mustard and brown-sugar sauce. I loved it. She and I would never cook those things today; the general concept of nutrition was completely different 35 years ago.

Hawaii is the champion of potluck. In my family, cousin Iris brings her Chinese salad, cousin Linda brings *furikake*-crusted salmon in teriyaki sauce, and great aunt Kikuchan makes a Jell-O salad. I'm half haole (Caucasian) and half Japanese; a combination we call *hapa* here.

My Hawai'i food epiphany came when I first tried *pa'i 'ai* (taro that is pounded but not watered down into poi). It was thick and slightly sweet with so much more flavor than poi. I also love how all the island cuisines are fused into what's known as Hawaiian Regional Cuisine and how chefs like Hiroshi Fukui make *haute*, playful reworkings of common dishes.

AS RELATED TO CHINA WILLIAMS

Tropical fruits at luau (Hawaiian feast), O'ahu (p151)

LINDA CHING

Pounding poi (taro root; p56) at the Taro Festival, Waialua (p181)
ANN CECIL

PLACES TO EXERCISE YOUR PALATE

Hiroshi Eurasian Tapas (p125) Food follows an arc with playful interpretations of Japanese country-style dishes.

Nico's at Pier 38 (p135) High-quality fish dishes at plate-lunch prices.

Town (p128) A stage for local and organic ingredients from O'ahu and Neighbor Islands.

Fishmonger at a market in Wailuku (p350), Maui.
ALISON WRIGHT

MAUI INTERVIEW
Whale Tales

NAME	Allen Tom
AGE	Mid-40s
OCCUPATION	Pacific Islands Regional Director, National Marine Sanctuaries
RESIDENCE	Kula

I like to go to places to see something unique. People go on an African safari to see elephants and lions. On Maui it's whales.

Do people realize Hawaii is the best place in the world to see whales from shore? If you get seasick you don't even have to get on a boat. You can just sit on the beach in Maui in winter and see a whale. You can go snorkeling and hear a whale, even feel the vibrations in the water. It's a life-changing experience for many people.

Maui is great. The beaches are free, clean, you can find parking. There are a zillion places to snorkel, with myriad fish. Unlike other places where they are hunted, sea turtles here don't swim away. It's a great way to learn about the marine environment. You get it all in one package.

AS RELATED TO NED FRIARY & GLENDA BENDURE

WHALE SAFARIS

Ulua Beach (p363) The access is easy, the snorkeling is good, and this is one of the beaches where whales come in so close you might actually hear them in the water.

Wailea Beach Walk (p365) This 1¼-mile walk along the Wailea coast offers unbeatable vantage points for watching passing humpback whales.

Whale-watching cruises (p324) The boats know all the best spots, and offer a close-up view of humpbacks demonstrating their hulking presence in leaps and bounds.

Breaching humpback whale off Maui (p316)

KARL LEHMANN

MOLOKA'I INTERVIEW
Paddling Ocean Swells

NAME	Camie Kimball
AGE	54
OCCUPATION	Teacher
RESIDENCE	Kawela

My husband taught me about outrigger canoeing, and at the time that I started, over 25 years ago, there weren't that many women doing it.

I've crossed the Kalohi Channel to O'ahu in one- and two-person outrigger canoes, as well as part of a six-woman team. Outrigger canoeing has become a high-school sport, and I've coached youth teams as well.

Moloka'i's South Shore is where we usually practice, either inside the reef when the tide is high, or outside it, but you've got to be ready for high winds. Heading downwind in a one-person canoe makes it possible to surf down the backside of the surf swells, which is real fun. It's really great to get out on the ocean, and during part of the year you could come upon whales.

Our island doesn't own its own *koa* wood canoe, which is required to compete in state regattas, but we just got a *koa* log from the Big Island. From it, a group including local youth and a master carvesman is going to carve a 40ft canoe for Moloka'i.   AS RELATED TO MOLLY GREEN

TAKE TO THE SEA

Kawakiu Beach (p454) In the summer, the waters at Moloka'i's West End beaches go calm and glassy, and Kawakiu Beach's clear waters become an ideal snorkeling spot.

Northern Coast (p450) Moloka'i's wild and uninhabited northern coast is home to the world's highest sea cliffs. Chartering a boat is the best way to take in their green, velvety magic and silvery waterfalls.

Pala'au barrier reef (p431) Hawaii's longest barrier reef handily creates a calm water zone to paddle along with the wind ruffling your hair and Moloka'i's spectacular coastline stretching out in front of you.

Papohaku Beach (p455) is the longest beach on Molokai's west end.
JAMES MARSHALL

BIG ISLAND INTERVIEW
A Changing Culture

NAME	Bobby Camara
AGE	59
OCCUPATION	Naturalist
RESIDENCE	Volcano

'The word "aloha" has become commercialized and trivialized. I save it for close friends. Aloha exemplifies the best in people.'

My great-grandparents came to the Kingdom of Hawaii in the 1880s from Madeira and the Azores to work on sugar plantations. Growing up in Honoka'a, a plantation town, was probably like growing up in any small working-class community – that simple life.

I have such wonderful memories. I remember Kailua-Kona without traffic lights or paved roads. Things were so much calmer. Now there are traffic jams miles long, and housing costs are out of sight. Affordable housing is a big issue – and housing where the jobs are. People commute hours a day from Puna or Hilo to Kona.

Food is a big part of local culture. At weddings, funerals and baby luau, hundreds can be invited – and everyone gets fed. There's a saying that people don't eat till they're full, they eat till they're tired. Now though, you can call a caterer, and don't spend four days cooking.

Food and cultural customs often separate locals from newcomers. Recent arrivals often don't take the time to learn about this place and local people. It's not like it was before, with lots of different kinds of people together in a small town. Now there's a bigger separation between 'us' and 'them.'

The idea that Hawaii is a 'paradise' is silly. We all work and pay bills. I'll admit though that our geography is spectacular and our cultures are unique. I truly can't live anywhere else.

AS RELATED TO JEFF CAMPBELL

Hapuna Beach (p237), South Kohala Coast, Big Island

KARL LEHMANN

Making offerings to the Fire Goddess, Pele (p34), Halema'uma'u Crater (p292), Big Island
ANN CECIL

Hiking the Kilauea Iki Crater (p293) in Hawaii Volcanoes National Park, Big Island
SCOTT DARSNEY

BOBBY'S BIG ISLAND FAVORITES

Kilauea Caldera (p288) No Big Island visit is complete without a visit to the still-active volcanic home of Pele, revered by many as the creator of all Hawaii.

Kohala Mountain Road (Map p240) As you travel south down this scenic road, descending from the Kohala Mountains, siblings Mauna Kea, Mauna Loa and Hualalai pose together for a classic Hawai'i snapshot.

North Kona Coast beaches (p231) North of Kona international airport is a string of near-perfect, white-sand beaches: Mahai'ula, Manini'owali, Makalawena and others.

KAUA'I INTERVIEW
Fields of Green

NAME	Lyndsey Haraguchi-Nakayama
AGE	28
OCCUPATION	Taro farmer and taro entrepreneur
RESIDENCE	Hanalei

I grew up in the mud, in the taro patch. When I was little, I carried a flag in the fields so people could find me. My dad had me driving a tractor from age six and I needed props to reach the pedals.

People wonder why I can't surf when I'm from Hanalei (p507). Some of my classmates, including Bruce Irons, are now professional surfers. But I was a tomboy and enjoyed working outside. I had no time to watch TV or go shopping.

Our farm is located on an ancient Hawaiian *ahupua'a* (land division from mountain to sea) where taro was grown. My great-great-grandfather farmed rice; my grandfather returned to farming taro. The land has gone full circle, from taro to rice to taro again.

I left Kaua'i to attend UH Manoa and work in Honolulu. In 2005 I returned with my husband. I am the fifth generation to farm the land. A farmer's life is hard. We're flooded three or four times a year. We're at the mercy of the weather and market prices. We have no pay rises or long weekends. A farmer needs to be stubborn. You definitely don't do it for the money.

AS RELATED TO LUCI YAMAMOTO

ECOFARM TOURS

Blair Estate Organic Coffee Farm (p492) Coffee is Les Drent's passion, and his small, organic coffee farm is delicious testament to it. Understand what's involved in your morning brew.

Gay & Robinson Sugar Mill Tour (p536) The last remaining sugar company on Kaua'i, Gay & Robinson cane fields still thrive. Explore the vast ranchland even more by ATV (all-terrain vehicle).

Ho'opulapula Haraguchi Rice Mill Tour (p510) Step back in time and learn about a family's tradition of rice and taro farming. Set in the Hanalei National Wildlife Refuge, you'll also see native birds and waterfowl.

Patchwork of taro crops on Kaua'i (p507)
PETER HENDRIE

(Continued from page 384)

The best way to approach the drive is with an early-morning start, when the road is so quiet you'll feel like the last soul on earth. Take something to munch and plenty to drink, and check your oil and spare tire. It's a long haul to civilization if you break down, and the tow charge can run to hundreds of dollars. Gas stations and other services are nonexistent between Hana and the Upcountry.

Kaupo

As the road winds around from Kipahulu, it skirts the edge of rocky cliffs and passes big mango trees, banyans and *wiliwili* trees with red tiger-claw blossoms. Then you'll see increasing numbers of *hala* (pandanus) and guava trees as the road bottoms out into gravel.

The village of Kaupo is around the 35-mile marker. However, don't expect a developed village in any sense of the word, as Kaupo is a scattered community of *paniolo*, many of them fourth-generation ranch hands who work the Kaupo Ranch. The only lowlands on this section of coast, Kaupo was once heavily settled and is home to three ancient heiau and two 19th-century churches. Kaupo Ranch cattle were once shipped from a landing in the bay, and you can still see steps leading down into the water on a rock jutting out into the ocean.

Loaloa Heiau, Kaupo's largest temple, is a registered national historical monument. All three heiau sites are *mauka* of the **Hui Aloha Church**, which is three-quarters of a mile east of Kaupo General Store. This picturesque white-washed church, built in 1859, sits on the rocky black-sand **Mokulau Beach**, an ancient surfing site. Mokulau, meaning 'many small islands,' is named for the rocks just offshore.

Kaupo General Store (☎ 248-8054; ☷ 10am-5pm Mon-Sat), on the east side of the gap, is 'the only store for 20 miles' and sells snacks and drinks, but opening hours can be a bit flexible, so it's best not to count on it.

Kaupo to 'Ulupalakua Ranch

Past Kaupo village, you'll be rewarded with awesome views of Kaupo Gap, a large opening in the rim of majestic Haleakala. Then *makai* of the 31-mile marker, a very rough but short 4WD road passes through a gate and runs down to the ocean at **Nu'u Bay**, favored by locals for swimming when the water is calm.

Spinner dolphins sometimes play offshore. If you're tempted to hit the water here, stay within the bay, as strong currents and riptides inhabit the open ocean beyond.   .

After another mile, there's a wide turnoff on the *mauka* side of the highway. From here you can walk to dramatic **Huakini Bay**, where you can sit on smooth boulders and watch the violent surf. As the road continues, it runs in and out numerous gulches and crosses a few bridges, edging closer to the coast. Striations of lava testify to centuries of volcanic upheaval.

After the 29-mile marker, keep an eye out for a natural lava **sea arch**. Continue driving until it disappears from sight, then spot a turnout on the *makai* side. You can park here and take the worn footpath down through pastoral green fields to the cliff's edge to see the arch close up and blowholes spouting along the coast.

A few miles south of 'Ulupalakua Ranch, the road crosses an expansive **lava flow**, dating from 1790, Haleakala's last-gasp eruption. This flow, part of the Kanaio Natural Area Reserve, is the same one that covers the La Perouse Bay area (p369). It's still black and barren all the way down to the sea.

Just offshore is the crescent island of Molokini with Kaho'olawe beyond. On a clear day you can even see the Big Island popping its head up above the clouds. There's such a wide-angle view that the ocean horizon is noticeably curved, and sunsets are bewitching.

As you approach Tedeschi Vineyards, groves of fragrant eucalyptus trees replace drier and scrubbier terrain. It's open rangeland here; cattle graze beside the road and occasionally mosey across in front of you.

UPCOUNTRY

Upcountry proves that Maui has a lot more to offer than just a day at the beach. These cool slopes curving around the western flank of Haleakala are carpeted with bountiful gardens and rolling pastures. And you can take in the magnificent scenery from lots of fun angles – zipline across deep gorges, paraglide down the hillsides, hike through a lofty cloud forest or barrel down from the summit on a mountain-bike. The yoga scene has also mushroomed in these hills, adding new vigor to sleepy towns like Ha'iku.

Not that you have to stretch your quads to have fun here. Check out the art scene that's

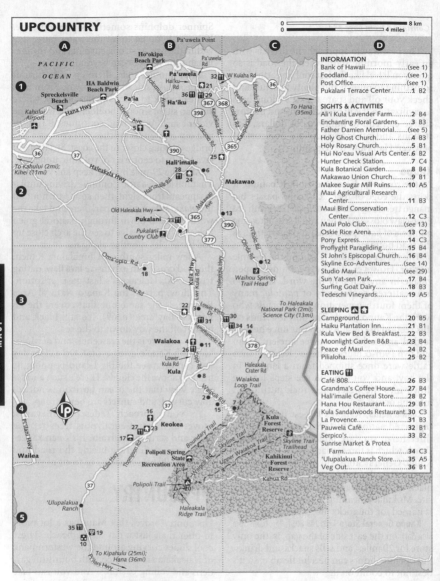

UPCOUNTRY

0 ————————— 8 km
0 ————————— 4 miles

opened up shop in the old cowboy town of Makawao, soak up the fragrant scents at the lavender farm in Kula or go tip a glass at the winery at 'Ulupalakua Ranch. A handful of gourmet chefs have escaped the resort bustle and opened up restaurants in the most unexpected places, so get out there and explore. The Upcountry area is much more than just a pass-through on the way to the Haleakala National Park.

HIGHWAY 390: PA'IA TO MAKAWAO

Baldwin Ave (Hwy 390) rolls along uphill for seven winding miles between Pa'ia (p369) and Makawao, starting amid feral sugarcane fields and then traversing pineapple fields interspersed with little open patches where cattle graze.

Churches

Two churches grace Baldwin Ave. **Holy Rosary Church** (945 Baldwin Ave), with its memorial statue of Father Damien, comes up first on the right, and the attractive **Makawao Union Church** (1445 Baldwin Ave), a stone-block building with stained-glass windows, is further along on the left. Makawao Union Church, built in 1916, is on the National Register of Historic Places.

Hui No'eau Visual Arts Center

Past Hali'imaile Rd, just after the 5-mile marker, is Kaluanui, the former plantation estate of sugar magnates Harry and Ethel Baldwin, which now houses the **Hui No'eau Visual Arts Center** (☎ 572-6560; www.huinoeau.com; 2841 Baldwin Ave; admission free; ☒ 10am-4pm). Famed Honolulu architect CW Dickey designed the two-story plantation home with Spanish-style tile roof in 1917. The prestigious arts club founded here in the 1930s offers classes in printmaking, pottery, woodcarving and other visual arts. You're welcome to visit the gallery, which exhibits topnotch local artists, and walk around the grounds, which include stables turned into art studios. The gift shop sells quality ceramics, glassware and original prints.

Hali'imaile

pop 900

Hali'imaile is a little pineapple town in the midst of an expansive plantation. Its name, which means 'fragrant twining shrub,' comes from the *maile* plants used for lei-making that covered the area before pineapple took over. The heart of town – actually the only commercial business in town – is the old general store (c 1918) that's been turned into Upcountry's top restaurant.

Hali'imaile Rd runs through the town, connecting Baldwin Ave (Hwy 390) with the Haleakala Hwy (Hwy 37).

SLEEPING & EATING

Peace of Maui (☎ 572-5045, 888-475-5045; www.peace ofmaui.com; 1290 Hali'imaile Rd; s/d with shared bathroom $50/55, 2-bedroom cottages $120; ☐) This aptly named place, spread over 2 acres in quiet Hali'imaile, is an unbeatable budget option. Rooms in the main house are small but comfortable, each with refrigerator and TV. Guests can access a fully equipped kitchen and living room with an online computer. At night you can gaze at the stars from the hot tub. The cottage, which can sleep up to six, is pure luxury, complete with an ocean-view lanai.

Hali'imaile General Store (☎ 572-2666; 900 Hali'imaile Rd; lunch $10-22, dinner $23-34; ☒ 11am-2:30pm Mon-Fri, 5:30-9:30pm daily) Owner-chef Bev Gannon was one of the original forces behind the Hawaii Regional Cuisine movement and a steady flow of in-the-know diners beat a track to this tiny village to feast on her inspired creations. Even lunch is a treat with blackened 'ahi wraps and ginger-chili duck tostadas, but the real heavy hitters come out at dinner. The atmospheric setting, with its high ceilings and plantation-era decor, is nearly as interesting as the food.

MAKAWAO

pop 6330

Lined with Old West–style wooden buildings and bordered by cattle pastures, Makawao proudly reflects its *paniolo* history. If you want to see what a real Hawaiian rodeo is all about, swing by on the Fourth of July, when Makawao's streets fill with cowhands parading on horseback wearing *palaka* (checked shirts) and festive lei.

But that's just one side of the place. Many of the old shops that once sold saddles and cattle feed now have artsy new tenants who have turned Makawao into a happening art center. You'll find many fine studios in town selling the works of painters and sculptors who have escaped frenzied scenes elsewhere to set up shop in the tranquil hills around Makawao.

All in all, this is one fun town to explore. It's got a delightful mix of age-old mom-and-pop stores thriving next to artist-run galleries and chic boutiques.

Orientation & Information

Most everything is within a few minutes' walk of the main intersection, where Baldwin Ave (Hwy 390) meets Makawao Ave (Hwy 365), including the **post office** (☎ 572-0019; 1075 Makawao Ave) and **public library** (☎ 573-8785; 1159 Makawao Ave; ☒ noon-8pm Mon & Wed, 9:30am-5pm Tue, Thu & Sat). There's an ATM at the **Minit Stop** (☎ 573-9295; 1100 Makawao Ave; ☒ 5am-11pm) gas station.

Sights & Activities

OLINDA ROAD

Scenic back roads head out in almost every direction from Makawao. The best of all is

MAUI

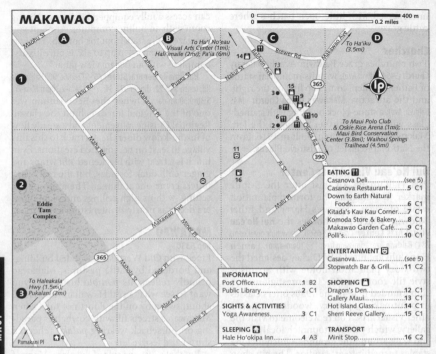

MAKAWAO

EATING
Casanova Deli	(see 5)
Casanova Restaurant	5 C1
Down to Earth Natural Foods	6 C1
Kitada's Kau Kau Corner	7 C1
Komoda Store & Bakery	8 C1
Makawao Garden Café	9 C1
Polli's	10 C1

ENTERTAINMENT
| Casanova | (see 5) |
| Stopwatch Bar & Grill | 11 C2 |

INFORMATION
| Post Office | 1 B2 |
| Public Library | 2 C1 |

SIGHTS & ACTIVITIES
| Yoga Awareness | 3 C1 |

SLEEPING
| Hale Ho'okipa Inn | 4 A3 |

SHOPPING
Dragon's Den	12 C1
Gallery Maui	13 C1
Hot Island Glass	14 C1
Sherri Reeve Gallery	15 C1

TRANSPORT
| Minit Stop | 16 C2 |

Olinda Rd, which picks up in town where Baldwin Ave leaves off, drifting up past the **Oskie Rice Arena**, where rodeos are held, and the **Maui Polo Club**, which holds matches on Sunday afternoons in the fall. From here the winding road is little more than a path through the forest, with knotty tree roots as high as your car caressing the roadsides. The air is rich with the spicy fragrance of eucalyptus trees and occasionally there's a clearing with an ocean vista. Four miles up from town, past the 11-mile marker, is the **Maui Bird Conservation Center** (closed to the public), which breeds nene (native Hawaiian goose) and other endangered birds. To make a loop, turn left onto Pi'iholo Rd near the top of Olinda Rd and wind back down into town.

WAIHOU SPRINGS TRAIL
If you're up for a walk in the woods, take this peaceful trail, which begins 4.75 miles up Olinda Rd from central Makawao. The forest is amazingly varied, having been planted by the US Forest Service in an effort to determine which trees would produce the best quality lumber in Hawaii. The trail, which begins on a soft carpet of pine needles, passes Monterey cypress and eucalyptus as well as orderly rows of pine trees. After 0.7 miles, you'll be rewarded with a view clear out to the ocean, and up to this point it's easy going. It's also possible to continue steeply downhill for another quarter-mile to reach Waihou Springs, but that part of the trail can be a muddy mess.

YOGA
Yoga Awareness (☎ 573-7771; www.yogaawareness.com; 3660 Baldwin Ave; class $20; ⊙ 8:30am-7:30pm) welcomes visitors to join the regulars in one of its daily group yoga classes.

Festivals & Events
Upcountry Fair Traditional agricultural fair with a farmers market, arts and crafts, chili cookoff, *keiki* games and good ol' country music; held on the second weekend in June at the Eddie Tam Complex.
Makawao Rodeo More than 300 *paniolo* show up at the Oskie Rice Arena on the weekend closest to Independence Day (July 4) to compete in roping and riding competitions at Hawaii's premier rodeo. Qualifying events occur all day on Thursday and Friday to determine who's left to compete for the big prizes over the weekend. If you're looking for

---

BUMPY RIDE

One of the hottest topics on Maui revolves around the bicycle tours downhill from Haleakala National Park to the coast. In the past decade the number of commercial vans carting cyclists to the top of Haleakala to catch the sunrise has more than doubled. Not only has it made for a congested sunrise experience – with as many as 1000 people huddled at the crater overlooks – but it's brought an outcry from Mauians who feel the bike traffic is overrunning their small communities.

Part of the thrill for cyclists – well, seeing how there's no real pedaling involved in a downhill cruise, perhaps the only thrill – is maneuvering the hairpin twists and turns on the Upcountry's narrow roads.

But for Upcountry residents who travel these 'highways' for more mundane reasons, such as getting to work, it's a frustration. When a line of cyclists is ahead, drivers are forced to slow to a crawl, waiting for the group to pull over to let them pass. The roads have few shoulders, so the wait can be a long one. And, of course, once one group of cyclists is passed, there's the next one. 'Road rage' has made it into the vernacular in the otherwise mellow Upcountry.

Just about everyone, including the tour operators, agree the situation needs a fix. The national park recently cut the number of cycle tour vans allowed at sunrise from 30 to 19. A group called the Upcountry Citizens for Bike and Traffic Safety would like to take things even further. It notes that many people taking the tours haven't ridden a bike in years, and cites accident reports showing ambulance calls for injured downhill cyclists averages a few times a week, mostly from falls. The group is pushing for more restrictions, including the elimination of the van that follows each group of cyclists, which prevents cars from passing, and better education for would-be cyclists.

Winding Baldwin Ave, the last leg of many of the cycle tours, has been a particular bone of contention, since it's the busy link between Makawao and Pa'ia. Cars and cyclists now vie for the same narrow road space, but plans are underway for a separate cycle route paralleling 6 miles of Baldwin Ave. The state has approved $5 million for the cycle path and the pineapple company that owns the land the path would use is supportive. It's a start.

---

excitement on Friday night, head up to the arena to see the daredevil bull-riding bash.

Paniolo Parade Held on the Saturday morning closest to July 4, this festive parade goes right through the heart of Makawao; park at the rodeo grounds and take the free shuttle to the town center.

Sleeping

Hale Ho'okipa Inn (☎ 572-6698; www.maui-bed-&-breakfast.com; 32 Pakani Pl; r incl breakfast $125-145, 2-bedroom ste $160-175) Within walking distance of the town center, this historic craftsman-style house built in 1924 has four inviting

---

TOP FIVE FESTIVALS & EVENTS

- **International Festival of Canoes** (p324) in Lahaina
- **Makawao Rodeo** (opposite) in Makawao
- **East Maui Taro Festival** (p380) in Hana
- **Ki Ho'alu Slack-Key Guitar Festival** (p348) in Kahului
- **A Taste of Lahaina** (p324) in Lahaina

---

guest rooms furnished with antiques. Most romantic is the 'rose room,' with its own lanai entrance and a claw-foot bathtub.

Eating

BUDGET

Down to Earth Natural Foods (☺ 572-1488; 1169 Makawao Ave; ☺ 8am-8pm) It says something about a town when its biggest grocer is a health food store. You'll find everything from organic produce to takeout sandwiches.

Komoda Store & Bakery (☎ 572-7261; 3674 Baldwin Ave; pastries 70¢-$2; ☺ 7am-5pm Mon, Wed, Thu & Fri, to 2pm Sat) Justifiably famous throughout the islands for its mouth-watering cream puffs and *liliko'i* (passion fruit) malasadas, this generations-old family bakery makes the perfect morning stop. And the emphasis is on mornings 'cause it often sells out by noon. Don't miss it.

Casanova Deli (☎ 572-0220; 1188 Makawao Ave; mains $4-7; ☺ 7am-6pm Mon-Sat, 8:30am-6pm Sun) Makawao's best breakfast option, this Italian deli has buttery croissants, fluffy omelettes and strong coffee, as well as hot sandwiches and Greek salads. Take it all out on the roadside deck and watch the world flow by.

MAUI

Kitada's Kau Kau Corner (☎ 572-7241; Baldwin Ave; meals $4-8; ⏲ 6:30am-1:30pm Mon-Sat) In a funky old building on the main drag, Kitada's has been making Makawao's favorite saimin for the better part of a century. If you're not up for slurping noodles, this little shop grills up a good hamburger, too.

Makawao Garden Café (☎ 573-9065; 3669 Baldwin Ave; mains $6-10; ⏲ 11am-4pm) If you're in the mood for a taro salad or perhaps fresh mahimahi on homemade focaccia, seek out this owner-run café tucked into a courtyard at the north end of Baldwin Ave. *The* place to have lunch on a sunny day.

MIDRANGE
Polli's (☎ 572-7808; 1202 Makawao Ave; mains $8-20; ⏲ 7am-10pm Mon-Sat, 8am-10pm Sun) Locals flock to this old standby Tex-Mex restaurant to down a few *cervezas* (beers) while munching away on nachos, tacos and sizzling fajitas. Nonstop surf videos and plenty of spirited chatter keep the scene high energy.

Casanova Restaurant (☎ 572-0220; 1188 Makawao Ave; pizza $12-20, mains $22-28; ⏲ 5-10pm) The one Makawao restaurant that lures diners up the mountain, Casanova offers good Italian fare, classy service and well-paired wines. The menu ranges from unbeatable wood-fired pizzas and zesty pasta dishes to filet mignon smothered in wild mushrooms. Request a rear table overlooking the gardens.

Entertainment
Casanova (☎ 572-0220; 1188 Makawao Ave) East Maui's hottest music spot, Casanova has live music several nights a week, anything from ska and funk to steel guitar and *paniolo* country-style music.

Stopwatch Bar & Grill (☎ 572-1380; 1127 Makawao Ave) For the quintessential local scene, swing by this friendly sports bar, which brings in Upcountry musicians like the Haiku Hillbillys on Friday and Saturday nights. Any other time it's all about sports TV.

Shopping
Makawao is chock-full of interesting shops. Start your exploration by wandering down Baldwin Ave starting at its intersection with Makawao Ave.

Gallery Maui (☎ 572-8092; 3643 Baldwin Ave) The standout in a town full of galleries, this shop carries the works of 20 island painters, sculptors and woodcrafters.

Hot Island Glass (☎ 572-4527; 3620 Baldwin Ave) Watch glassblowers spin their red-hot creations from 10:30am to 4pm at Maui's oldest handblown glass studio.

Sherri Reeve Gallery (☎ 572-8931; 3669 Baldwin Ave) Island artist Sherri Reeve paints floral watercolors in a pastel palette on everything from T-shirts to full-size canvasses.

Dragon's Den (☎ 572-2424; 3681 Baldwin Ave) Get your Chinese herbs, crystals and jade heart stones here.

HA'IKU
pop 4500

If the bustle of the beachside resorts isn't for you, Ha'iku offers an up-and-coming alternative scene.

Ha'iku's roots are in sugar cane. Alexander & Baldwin grew their first 12 acres of the sweet stuff right here in 1869, and the village once had both a sugar mill and a pineapple cannery. Today the old cannery building is once again the heart of the community, housing Maui's hippest yoga studio, several surfboard shops and a couple of good eateries.

Ha'iku is a spread-out community, stretching from the foothills of Makawao down to the Hana Hwy on the coast. It could make a good central base for exploring all of Maui, with most destinations on the island within easy driving distance.

Activities
Studio Maui (☎ 575-9390; www.thestudiomaui.com; Ha'iku Marketplace, 810 Ha'iku Rd; classes $17; ⏲ 7:30am-10pm) attracts a high-energy, good-karma crowd with a full schedule of yoga classes from anusara basics to power-flow yoga, as well as ecstatic dance, tango and more.

Sleeping
Pilialoha (☎ 572-1440; www.pilialoha.com; 2512 Kaupakalua Rd; s/d incl breakfast $110/130) For a delightful stay in the countryside, this is as good as it gets. Set in a tranquil eucalyptus grove, the split-level two-bedroom cottage is a charmer with hardwood floors and cheery decor. But the real star is the attention to detail – from the fresh-cut roses on the table to the Hawaiian music collection and cozy quilts on the beds, the hosts know what Hawaiian hospitality is all about.

Haiku Plantation Inn (☎ 575-7500, www.haikuplantation.com; 555 Ha'iku Rd; r incl breakfast $129-159) Graceful period touches set the tone at this 1870s home turned B&B, with antique furnishings throughout. Even the breakfast table is set with vintage tableware. Chat in the evenings with fellow guests in the sitting room where the plantation doctor who built this house once met patients. The inn also has a relaxing hot tub.

Eating

Veg Out (☎ 575-5320; Ha'iku Town Center, 810 Kokomo Rd; mains $4-9; ☟ 10:30am-7:30pm Mon-Fri, 11:30am-7:30pm Sat & Sun) Tucked inside a former warehouse, this casual vegetarian eatery serves up a killer burrito with hot tofu, beans and pineapple salsa to the sounds of Ravi Shankar. Pesto goat-cheese pizza, taro burgers and veggie wraps also satisfy.

Pauwela Café (☎ 575-9242; 375 W Kuiaha Rd; mains $7-10; ☟ 7am-2:30pm Mon-Sat, to 1pm Sun) A good spot to head at lunch, this neat place with half a dozen tables makes generous wrapped meat sandwiches, hearty salads and tempting desserts.

Hana Hou Restaurant (☎ 575-2661; Ha'iku Marketplace; 810 Ha'iku Rd; mains $8-17; ☟ 4:30-9pm Mon-Thu, 11am-9pm Fri-Sun) In pidgin the name means 'do it again,' and sure enough, people come back again and again for the backyard BBQ served at picnic tables. You can go Hawaiian with poi, *kalua* pork and *laulau* (bundles of pork or beef with salted fish that are wrapped in leaves and steamed) or sit down to burgers and beer.

PUKALANI & AROUND

pop 7380

The gateway to the Upcountry, Pukalani (Heavenly Gate) is the place to grab a quick bite and gas up on the way to Haleakala.

Orientation & Information

Upcountry's largest town, Pukalani is 2 miles from Makawao along Hwy 365. If you're coming from Kahului, take the Haleakala Hwy (Hwy 37), which climbs through cane fields before reaching Pukalani. To reach the business part of town, take the Old Haleakala Hwy exit, where the bypass highway begins. Old Haleakala Hwy is Pukalani's main street.

Pukalani Terrace Center (cnr Old Haleakala Hwy & Pukalani St) has a coin laundry, a **post office** (☎ 572-0019) and a **Bank of Hawaii** (☎ 572-7242) with a 24-hour ATM. A couple of gas stations are on the Old Haleakala Hwy.

Sights & Activities
SURFING GOAT DAIRY

The goats at this 42-acre **farm** (☎ 878-2870; www .surfinggoatdairy.com; 3651 Oma'opio Rd; admission free, tour $4; ☟ 10am-5pm Mon-Sat, to 2pm Sun) are playful but, no, they don't really ride the waves. They are, however, the source of all that luscious chevre cheese adorning the menus of Maui's top restaurants. The little store here carries an amazing variety of these creamy treats: for island flavor try the mango supreme. Not everything is geared to the connoisseur – your kids will love meeting the goat kids up close in a fun 20-minute dairy tour (minimum three people).

PUKALANI COUNTRY CLUB

A mile west of Pukalani Terrace Center, this **golf course** (☎ 572-1314; www.pukalanigolf.com; 360 Pukalani St; greens fees $53-68; ☟ 7am-6:30pm) has 18 holes of smooth greens with sweeping views.

Eating

Foodland (☎ 572-0674; Pukalani Terrace Center, cnr Old Haleakala Hwy & Pukalani St; ☟ 24hr) This supermarket is a convenient stop for those heading up the mountain for the sunrise, or coming down for supplies – there's a good sushi shop inside it as well.

Serpico's (☎ 572-8498; cnr Aewa Pl & Old Haleakala Hwy; meals $5-12; ☟ 11am-10pm) In the center of Pukalani, opposite McDonald's, this casual Italian eatery makes real New York–style pizzas and pasta dishes, and it makes them well. If you're in a hurry, there's always a $5 pizza lunch special.

KULA

pop 9730

Think of Kula as one big garden, and you won't be far off. The very name Kula is synonymous with the fresh veggies on any Maui menu worth its salt. So bountiful is Kula's soil, it produces most of the onions, lettuce and strawberries grown in Hawaii and almost all of the commercially grown proteas.

The magic is in the elevation. At 3000ft, Kula's cool nights and sunny days are ideal for growing all sorts of crops. Kula's farmers first gained fame during the California gold rush of the 1850s, when they shipped so many potatoes to West Coast miners that Kula became known as 'Nu Kaleponi,' the Hawaiian pronunciation for New California. In the late 19th century Portuguese and Chinese immigrants

MAUI

who had worked off their contracts on the sugar plantations also moved up to Kula and started small farms, giving Kula a multicultural face.

Sights

If you want to take a closer look at Kula's blooms, several walk-through gardens are open to visitors, and each has its own special appeal.

ALI'I KULA LAVENDER FARM

Up for a little aromatherapy? Maybe it's time to immerse yourself in the soothing scents at **Ali'i Kula Lavender Farm** (☎ 878-8090; www.mauikulalavender.com; 1100 Waipoli Rd; admission free; ☺ 9am-4pm). More than 30 varieties of lavender blanket the hillside – stroll the garden paths and feel your whole body relax. Then sit for a spell with a glass of lavender lemonade ($3), or browse the gift shop for lavender-scented bath gels and creams. You can also join a Lavender Garden Tea Tour ($35; call for reservations) and get the skinny on all things lavender, including a sampling of lavender scones and tea.

MAUI AGRICULTURAL RESEARCH CENTER

This 20-acre **garden** (☎ 878-1213; 424 Mauna Pl; admission free; ☺ 7am-3:30pm Mon-Thu) perched above Waiakoa village is under the jurisdiction of the University of Hawai'i. It's here that Hawaii's first proteas, natives of South Africa, were established in 1965. You can walk through rows of their colorful descendants, as well as new hybrids under development. Named for the Greek god Proteus, who was noted for his ability to change form, the varieties on display here are amazingly diverse – some look like oversized pincushions, others like feathers and still others have spinelike petals. Nursery cuttings from the plants here are distributed to protea farms across Hawaii, which in turn supply florists as far away as Europe.

To get here, follow Copp Rd (between the 12- and 13-mile markers on Hwy 37) for half a mile and turn left on Mauna Pl.

KULA BOTANICAL GARDEN

Pleasantly overgrown and shady, this mature **garden** (☎ 878-1715; 638 Kekaulike Ave; adult/child 6-12 $7.50/2; ☺ 9am-4pm) has walking paths that wind through acres of theme plantings, including native Hawaiian specimens and a 'taboo garden' of poisonous plants. Because a stream

runs through it, the garden supports a wider variety of vegetation than you'll find in other Kula gardens – the whole place is an explosion of color.

ENCHANTING FLORAL GARDENS

Sunny and open, this roadside **garden** (☎ 878-2531; 2505 Kula Hwy; adult/child 6-12 $7.50/1; ☺ 9am-5pm) near the 10-mile marker has wide paved paths for easy strolling. The garden features both tropical and cool-weather flowers, presented a bit like an oversized home garden, with neat orderly rows of colorful blooms.

HOLY GHOST CHURCH

The octagonal **Holy Ghost Church** (☎ 878-1261; Lower Kula Rd; ☺ 8am-5pm), a hillside landmark in Waiakoa, is on the National Register of Historic Places. Built in 1895 by Portuguese immigrants, the church features a beautifully ornate interior that looks like it came right out of the Old World, and indeed much of it did. The altar was carved by renowned Austrian woodcarver Ferdinand Stuflesser and shipped in pieces around the Cape of Good Hope. Finding the church is easy, as the distinctive white building is readily visible from the highway.

Activities

Pony Express (☎ 667-2200; www.ponyexpresstours.com; Haleakala Crater Rd; trail rides $95-195; ☺ 8am-5pm) offers a variety of horseback rides, beginning with easy nose-to-tail walks across a working cattle ranch. But the real prize is the trail rides into the national park's Haleakala crater, which start at the crater summit and follow Sliding Sands Trail, offering jawdropping scenery en route. Pony Express is on Hwy 378, 2.5 miles up from Hwy 377.

There's no better way to unleash your inner Tarzan than by soaring above the forest floor with **Skyline Eco-Adventures** (☎ 878-8400; www.skylinehawaii.com; Haleakala Crater Rd; 1½hr outing $79; ☺ departs 8:30am, 9:30am, 11:30am, 12:30pm, 2pm & 3pm), so don your hard hat, strap up to the zipline and let it fly. You glide freestyle along cables strung over five gulches – the hardest part is stepping off the platform for the first zip, but the rest is pure exhilaration. An half-mile hike and a suspension bridge are tossed in for good measure. One tip: reserve early, as it often books up weeks ahead.

If the Skyline ziplines don't get you high enough, try surfing the sky with **Proflyght**

Paragliding (☎ 874-5433; www.paraglidehawaii.com; Waipoli Rd; paraglide $75; ☒ varies with weather). On this one, you strap into a paraglider with a certified instructor and take a running jump off the cliffs beneath Polipoli Spring State Recreation Area for a 1000ft descent with a bird's-eye view the entire way.

Festivals & Events

The **Holy Ghost Feast**, held at the Holy Ghost Church on the last Saturday and Sunday in May, celebrates Kula's Portuguese heritage and provides a great opportunity for visitors to enjoy the aloha of Upcountry folk. This family-oriented event has games, craft booths, a farmers market and a free *laulau* meal (with the local addition of Portuguese sweetbread) to everyone who comes.

Sleeping

Kula View Bed & Breakfast (☎ 878-6736; 600 Holopuni Rd; studios incl breakfast $115) The host knows the Upcountry like the back of her hand and provides everything you'll need for a good stay, including warm jackets for the Haleakala sunrise. The studio unit sits atop her country home and offers sunset ocean views. Breakfast includes fruit from the backyard and home-made muffins.

Eating

Sunrise Market & Protea Farm (☎ 878-1600; Haleakala Crater Rd; simple eats $3-6; ☒ 7:30am-4pm) Stop here, a quarter of a mile up from the intersection of Hwys 378 and 377, to pick up some post-sunrise java, breakfast burritos and fruit salads. Then take a stroll out back to view the protea garden.

Café 808 (☎ 878-6874; Lower Kula Rd, Waiakoa; mains $4-9; ☒ 6am-8pm) Its motto, 'The Big Kahuna of Local Grinds,' says it all. This eatery, a quarter-mile south of the Holy Ghost Church, offers a wall-size chalkboard of all things local, from banana pancakes to carb-heavy, gravy-dripping *loco moco*.

Kula Sandalwoods Restaurant (☎ 878-3523; 15427 Haleakala Hwy; mains $7-12; ☒ 7:30am-3pm) The owner-chef earned her toque from the prestigious Culinary Institute of America. At breakfast she serves up a knockout eggs Benedict. Lunch moves into specialty salads and innovative sandwiches on foccacia bread. Heady espresso, too. The restaurant is less than a mile north of Haleakala Crater Rd.

La Provence (☎ 878-1313; 3158 Lower Kula Rd, Waiakoa; pastries $2-4, mains $8-20; ☒ 7am-9pm Wed-Sun) This sunny courtyard restaurant pairs mouthwatering French pastries with Kula treats, like goat-cheese salad on fresh-picked greens. In the evening bring your own beer and enjoy a gourmet pizza hot out of the brick oven. Hard to find but worth the effort: look for the low-key sign on the Kula Hwy as you approach Waiakoa.

POLIPOLI SPRING STATE RECREATION AREA

Crisscrossed with lightly trodden hiking and biking trails, this cloud forest on the western slope of Haleakala takes you deep off the beaten path. When the clouds are heaviest, visibility is measured in feet. Except for the symphony of bird calls, everything around you is still.

It's not always possible to get all the way to the park without a 4WD, but it's worth driving part of the way for the view.

Access is via Waipoli Rd, off Hwy 377, just under 0.5 miles before its southern intersection with the Kula Hwy (Hwy 37). Waipoli is a narrow, switchbacking one-lane road through groves of eucalyptus and open rangeland. Layers of clouds often drift in and out; when they lift, you'll get panoramic views across

MAUI

A LONG DAY

As the legend goes, the goddess Hina was having problems drying her tapa cloth because the days were too short. Her son Maui, the trickster demigod for whom the island is named, decided to take matters into his own hands. One morning he went up to the mountaintop and waited for the sun. As it came up over the mountain Maui lassoed the rays one by one and held tight until the sun came to a sliding halt. When the sun begged to be let go, Maui demanded that as a condition for its release it hereafter slow its path across the sky. The sun gave its promise, the days were lengthened and the mountain became known as Haleakala, 'House of the Sun.' To this day there are about 15 more minutes of daylight at Haleakala than on the coast below.

green rolling hills to the islands of Lana'i and Kaho'olawe.

The road has some soft shoulders, but the first 6 miles are paved. After the road enters the Kula Forest Reserve, it reverts to dirt. When it's muddy, the next four grinding miles to the campground are not even worth trying in a standard car.

The whole area was planted during the 1930s by the Civilian Conservation Corps (CCC), a Depression-era work program. Several of the trails pass through old CCC camps and stands of redwood, cypress, cedar and pines.

Activities

WAIAKOA LOOP TRAIL

The trailhead for the Waiakoa Loop Trail starts at the hunter check station, 5 miles up Waipoli Rd, which is all paved. Walk 0.75 miles down the grassy spur road on the left to a gate marking the trail. The hike, which starts out in pine trees, makes a 3-mile loop. You can also connect with the Upper Waiakoa Trail at a junction about a mile up the right side of the loop.

UPPER WAIAKOA TRAIL

The Upper Waiakoa Trail is a strenuous 7-mile trail that begins off Waiakoa Loop at an elevation of 6000ft, climbs 1800ft, switchbacks and then drops back down 1400ft. It's stony terrain, but it's high and open, with good views. Bring plenty of water.

The trail ends on Waipoli Rd between the hunter check station and the campground. If you want to start at this end of the trail, keep an eye out for the trail marker for Waohuli Trail, as the Upper Waiakoa Trail begins across the road.

BOUNDARY TRAIL

This 4-mile marked and maintained trail begins about 200yd beyond the end of the paved road. Park to the right of the cattle grate that marks the boundary of the Kula Forest Reserve. It's a steep downhill walk that crosses gulches and drops deep into woods of eucalyptus, pine and cedar, as well as a bit of native forest. In the afternoon the fog generally rolls in and visibility fades.

SKYLINE TRAIL

This otherworldly trail is the major link in a hiking route that begins at a lofty elevation of 9750ft in Haleakala National Park and leads down to Polipoli campground at 6200ft, a total distance of 8.5 miles. It takes about four hours to walk.

To get to the trailhead, go past Haleakala summit and take the road to the left just before Science City (p407). The Skyline Trail, which is actually a dirt road used to maintain Polipoli Spring State Recreation Area, starts in open terrain made up of cinders and craters. After 3 crunchy miles, it reaches the tree line (8500ft) and enters native *mamane* (a native tree with bright yellow flowers) forest. In winter *mamane* is heavy with flowers that look like sweet-pea blossoms.

There's solitude on this walk. If the clouds treat you kindly, you'll have broad views all the way between the barren summit and the dense cloud forest. Eventually the trail meets the Polipoli access road, where you can either walk to the paved road in about 4 miles, or continue via the **Haleakala Ridge Trail** and **Polipoli Trail** to the campground. If you prefer treads to hiking boots, the Skyline Trail is also a fun adventure on a mountain-bike.

Sleeping

Staying in Polipoli is all about roughing it.

Tent camping is free, but requires a permit from the state. Facilities are primitive, with rest rooms but no showers or drinking water. Fellow campers are likely to be pig hunters. Otherwise the place can be eerily deserted, and damp. Come prepared – this is cold country, with winter temperatures frequently dropping below freezing at night.

The park also has one housekeeping cabin. Unlike other state park cabins, this one has gas lanterns and a wood-burning stove but no electricity or refrigerator. See p309 for details on permits and reservations.

KEOKEA

Around the turn of the 20th century, Keokea was home to Hakka Chinese who farmed the remote Kula region. Modest as it may be, Keokea is the last real town before Hana if you're swinging around the southern part of the island. The sum total of the town center consists of a coffee shop, an art gallery, a gas pump and two small stores, the Ching Store and the Fong Store.

Sights

The village's green-and-white **St John's Episcopal Church** was built in 1907 to serve the Chinese community, and it still bears its name in

Chinese characters. For a time Sun Yat-sen, father of the Chinese nationalist movement, lived on the outskirts of Keokea. A statue of Sun Yat-sen and a small **park** dedicated to him can be found along the Kula Hwy (Hwy 37) beyond Grandma's Coffee House. The park has picnic tables and great views of west Maui and its hillside windmills.

Sleeping & Eating

Moonlight Garden B&B (☎ 878-6977, 866-878-6297; www.mauimoonlightgarden.com; 8980 Kula Hwy; 1-/2-bedroom cottages $125/130) Quiet and secluded, yet within walking distance of the village center, these two freestanding cottages sit amid the fruit trees of a small farm. The cottages are spacious with full kitchens and a cheerful Hawaiian decor, while the views from the decks sweep clear out to the sea. Stargazing is heavenly.

Grandma's Coffee House (☎ 878-2140; 9232 Kula Hwy; pastries $2-5, deli fare $6-10; ☺ 7am-5pm) This downhome café has homemade pastries, sandwiches and fresh dark-roasted Maui coffee. Grandma's family has been growing coffee beans in Keokea since 1918. Take your goodies out on the patio and you can eat right under the coffee trees. Grandma's is also a good place to pick up picnic fare if you're headed around the Pi'ilani Hwy to Hana.

'ULUPALAKUA RANCH

A holdout from an earlier era, 'Ulupalakua Ranch was established in the mid-19th century by James Makee, a whaling captain who jumped ship and befriended Hawaiian royalty. King David Kalakaua, the 'Merrie Monarch,' was a frequent visitor who loved to indulge in late-night rounds of poker and champagne. The 20,000-acre ranch is still worked by *paniolo* (note the sign on the ranch store warning cowboys to wipe the shit off their boots before entering!) and has some 6000 head of cattle, as well as a small herd of Rocky Mountain elk.

Hwy 37 winds south through ranch country offering good views of Kaho'olawe and the little island of Molokini.

Sights

Tedeschi Vineyards (☎ 878-6058; www.mauiwine.com; Kula Hwy; tours & tastings free; ☺ 9am-5pm, tours 10:30am & 1:30pm) offers tastings of its products in the old cottage where King David Kalakaua once

slept. These homegrown wines cover a wide gamut. Back in the 1970s, while waiting for its first grape harvest, the winery decided to take advantage of Maui's abundant pineapple. Today its biggest hit is the sweet Maui Splash, a pineapple and passion fruit dessert wine. Less of a splash are the grape wines. Attached to the tasting room and gift shop is a fascinating little **exhibit** on ranch history. Free tours of the grounds and the winery operation are given twice a day.

Opposite the winery, you can see the stack remains of the **Makee Sugar Mill**, built in 1878.

Eating

'Ulupalakua Ranch Store (☎ 878-2561; burgers $7-8; ☺ grill 11am-1:30pm, store 9am-5pm) Opposite the ranch headquarters, 5.5 miles south of Keokea, this store has a deli and lunchtime grill featuring the ranch's own hormone-free beef and elk burgers. The store also sells tourist fare such as cowboy hats and souvenir T-shirts. Say howdy to the life-sized wooden cowboys on the front porch carved by a former ranchhand.

Getting There & Away

After the vineyard, it's another 25 dusty, bumpy miles to Kipahulu along the spectacular Pi'ilani Hwy (p384).

HALEAKALA NATIONAL PARK

Get ready for an otherworldly experience – Haleakala's astonishing volcanic landscape so resembles a lunar surface that astronauts practiced mock lunar walks here before landing on the moon.

You simply haven't seen Maui, or at least looked into its soul, until you've made the trek up to the top of this awe-inspiring mountain. Its appeal is magnetic: ancient Hawaiians came to the summit to worship, Mark Twain praised its healing solitude, and visitors of all walks still find mystic experiences here.

Often referred to as the world's largest dormant volcano, the floor of Haleakala measures a colossal 7.5 miles wide, 2.5 miles long and 3000ft deep. In its prime, Haleakala reached a height of 12,000ft before water erosion carved out two large river valleys that eventually eroded into each other to form

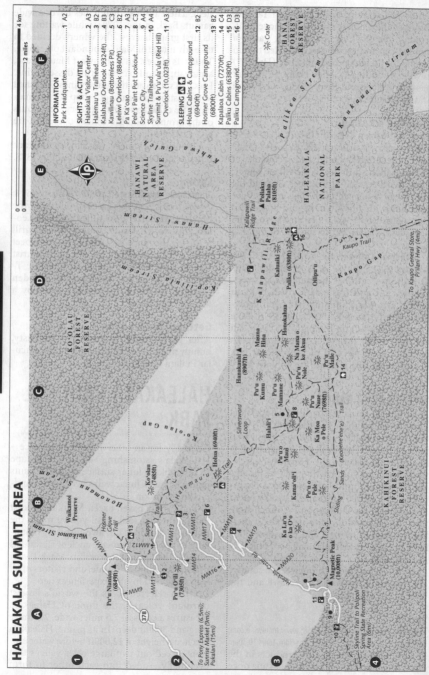

HALEAKALA SUMMIT AREA

Crater

Haleakala crater. Technically, as geologists like to point out, it's not a true 'crater,' but to sightseers that's all nitpicking. Valley or crater, it's a phenomenal sight like no other in the US National Park system.

Lookouts on the crater's rim provide breathtaking views of Haleakala's volcanic surface. But there's a lot more to Haleakala than just peering down from on high. With a pair of hiking boots you can walk down into the crater on crunchy trails that meander around cinder cones, or saddle up and mosey down onto the crater floor on horseback. For the ultimate adventure, bring a sleeping bag and spend the night.

The best conditions for viewing the crater are in the morning. Later in the day warm air generally forces clouds higher and higher until they pour through the two gaps in the crater's rim and then fill the crater itself.

Haleakala National Park stretches from the summit here all the way down to the pools of 'Ohe'o Gulch (p381) in the park's Kipahulu section on the coast south of Hana. There are separate entrances to both sections of the park, but there's no passage between them.

INFORMATION

Haleakala National Park (www.nps.gov/hale; 3-day entry pass per car $10, per person on foot, bicycle or motorcycle $5) never closes, and the pay booth at the park entrance opens before dawn to welcome the sunrise crowd. If you plan several trips, or are going on to the Big Island, consider buying an annual pass ($25), which covers all of Hawaii's national parks.

The park's **headquarters** (☎ 572-4400; ☺ 8am-4pm), less than a mile beyond the entrance, is the place to pick up brochures, buy nature books and get camping permits. There are no views at park headquarters; this is simply an information and rest room stop. So once you've taken care of your more earthly needs, hop back into the car and continue on to reach the real wonders.

You can get drinking water at park headquarters and at the visitor center, but no food is sold in the park. Bring something to eat, particularly if you're going up for the sunrise; you don't want a growling stomach to send you back down the mountain before you've had a chance to explore the sights.

It's a good idea to check weather conditions (☎ 877-5111) before driving up, as it's not

MAUI

DAYBREAK ON THE MOUNTAIN

For centuries people have been making the pilgrimage up to Haleakala to watch the majestic sunrise. It's an experience that can border on the mystical. But let's be honest – a rained-out sunrise is an anticlimactic event after getting yourself out of bed at 3am for a long drive, so check out the weather report the night before to calculate your odds of having a good experience (see p406).

Plan to arrive at the summit an hour before the actual sunrise; that will guarantee you a parking space and time to see the world awaken. Around that point the night sky begins to lighten and turn purple-blue, and the stars fade away. Ethereal silhouettes of the mountain ridges appear. The gentlest colors show up in the fragile moments just before dawn begins. The undersides of the clouds lighten first, accenting the night sky with pale silvery slivers and streaks of pink.

About 20 minutes before sunrise, the light intensifies on the horizon in bright oranges and reds, much like a sunset. Turn around for a look at Science City (p407), whose domes turn a blazing pink. For the grand finale, the moment when the disk of the sun appears, all of Haleakala takes on a fiery glow. It feels like you're watching the earth awaken.

Come prepared – it's going to be c-o-l-d! Temperatures hovering around freezing and a biting wind are the norm at dawn and there's often a frosty ice on the top layer of cinders, which crunch underfoot. If you don't have a winter jacket or sleeping bag to wrap yourself in, be sure to bring a warm blanket from your hotel. However many layers of clothes you can muster, you won't regret it.

The best photo opportunities occur before the sun rises. Every morning is different, but once the sun is up, the silvery lines and the subtleties disappear.

And if you just can't manage to get up that early, sunsets at Haleakala have inspired poets as well.

uncommon for it to be cloudy at Haleakala when it's clear on the coast. Or go straight to the crater webcam at **Haleakala Crater Live Camera** (http://koa.ifa.hawaii.edu/crater).

DANGERS & ANNOYANCES

At 10,000ft the air is relatively thin, so expect to tire more quickly, particularly if you're hiking. The higher elevation also means that sunburn is more likely.

The weather at Haleakala can change suddenly from dry, hot conditions to cold, windswept rain. Although the general rule is sunny in the morning and cloudy in the afternoon, fog and clouds can blow in at any time, and the windchill can quickly drop below freezing.

If you're going off the beaten path, be prepared. Hikers without proper clothing risk hypothermia. Remember the climate changes radically as you cross the crater floor. In the 4 miles between Kapalaoa and Paliku cabins, rainfall varies from an annual average of 12in to 300in! Take warm clothing in layers, sunscreen, rain gear, a first-aid kit and lots of water.

SIGHTS

For information on driving on Haleakala Crater Rd, see p411.

Hosmer Grove

Hosmer Grove, off a side road just after the park's entrance booth, is primarily visited by campers and picnickers, but it's also worth a stop for its half-mile loop trail (p409) that begins at the edge of the campground. The whole area is sweetened with the scent of eucalyptus and alive with the red flashes and calls of native birds.

Waikamoi Preserve

This windswept native cloud forest supports one of the rarest ecosystems on earth. Managed by the Nature Conservancy, the 5230-acre Waikamoi Preserve provides the last stronghold for 76 species of native plants and forest birds. You're apt to spot the *'i'iwi*, the *'apapane* and the yellow-green *'amakihi* flying among the preserve's koa and ohia trees. You might also catch a glimpse of the yellow-green *'alauahio* (Maui creeper) or the *'akohekohe* (Maui parrotbill), both endangered species found nowhere else.

The only way to see the preserve is to join a **guided hike**. The National Park Service offers free three-hour, 3-mile guided hikes

that enter the preserve from Hosmer Grove campground at 9am on Monday and Thursday. It's best to make reservations, which you can do up to one week in advance by calling ☎ 572-4459. Expect wet conditions; bring rain gear.

Leleiwi Overlook

Leleiwi Overlook (8840ft) is midway between park headquarters and the summit. From the parking lot, it's a five-minute walk across a gravel trail to the overlook, from where you can see the West Maui Mountains and both sides of the isthmus connecting the two sides of Maui. The trail has plaques identifying native plants, including the silver-leafed *hinahina*, found only at Haleakala, and the *kukae-nene*, a member of the coffee family.

In the afternoon, if weather conditions are right, you might see the **Brocken specter**, an optical phenomenon that occurs at high elevations. Essentially, by standing between the sun and the clouds, your image is magnified and projected onto the clouds. The light reflects off tiny droplets of water in the clouds, creating a circular rainbow around your shadow.

Kalahaku Overlook

Whatever you do, don't miss this one. Kalahaku Overlook (9324ft), about a mile above Leleiwi Overlook, offers a bird's-eye view of the crater floor and the ant-sized hikers on the trails snaking around the cinder cones below. At the observation deck, information plaques provide the skinny on each of the volcanic formations that punctuate the crater floor.

The *'ua'u* (Hawaiian dark-rumped petrel) nests in burrows in the cliff face at the left side of the observation deck between May and October. Even if you don't spot the birds, you can often hear the parents and chicks making their unique clucking sounds. Of the fewer than 2000 *'ua'u* remaining today, most nest right here at Haleakala, where they lay just one egg a year. These seabirds were thought to be extinct until sighted again in the crater during the 1970s.

A short trail below the parking lot leads to a field of silversword (*'ahinahina*), from seedlings to mature plants.

Haleakala Visitor Center

The **visitor center** (☼ sunrise-3pm) on the rim of the crater (9745ft), half a mile below the actual summit, is the park's main viewing spot. The

---

A GLOWING SUCCESS

Goats ate them by the thousands. Souvenir collectors pulled them up by their roots. They were even used to decorate parade floats, for cryin' out loud. It's a miracle any of Haleakala's famed silverswords were left at all.

It took a concerted effort to bring them back from the brink of extinction, but Haleakala visitors can once again see this luminous relative of the sunflower in numerous places around the park.

The silversword ('ahinahina) takes its name from its elegant silver spiked leaves, which glow with dew collected from the clouds. The plant lives up to 25 years before blooming for its first and last time. In its final year its shoots up a flowering stalk that can reach as high as 9ft. During summer the stalk flowers gloriously with hundreds of maroon and yellow blossoms. When the flowers go to seed in late fall, the plant makes its last gasp and dies.

Today the silversword survives solely because its fragile natural environment has been protected. After years of effort, the National Park Service has finished fencing the entire park with a 32-mile-long fence to keep out feral goats and pigs. You can do your part by not walking on cinders close to the plant, which damages the silversword's shallow roots that radiate out several feet just inches below the surface.

---

center has displays on Haleakala's volcanic origins and details on what you're seeing on the crater floor 3000ft below. Books, postcards and bottled water are for sale, and there are rest rooms here.

By dawn the parking lot fills up with everyone coming to see the sunrise show, and it pretty much stays packed all day. Leave the crowds behind by taking the 10-minute hike up **Pa Ka'oao**, which begins at the east side of the visitor center and provides stunning views of the crater.

Haleakala Summit

PU'U'ULA'ULA (RED HILL) OVERLOOK
Congratulations! The 37-mile drive from sea level to the 10,023ft summit of Haleakala you've just completed is the highest elevation gain in the shortest distance anywhere in the world. As a matter of fact, it's so high that you need to be cautious if you've come up in the late afternoon in winter, as a sudden rainstorm at this elevation can result in ice-coated roads.

Perched atop Pu'u'ula'ula, Maui's highest point, the summit building provides a top-of-the-world panorama from its wraparound windows. On a clear day you can see the Big Island, Lana'i, Moloka'i and even O'ahu. When the light's right, the colors of the crater from the summit are nothing short of spectacular, with an array of grays, greens, reds and browns. Brief natural and cultural history talks are given at the summit at 9:30am, 11:15am and 12:30pm.

Dozens of silversword have been planted at the overlook, making this the best place to see these luminous silver-leafed plants in various stages of growth.

MAGNETIC PEAK
The iron-rich cinders in this flat-top hill, which lies immediately southeast of the summit, in the direction of the Big Island, pack enough magnetism to play havoc with your compass. Modest looking as it is, it's also – at 10,008ft – the second-highest point on the island of Maui.

Science City
On the Big Island's Mauna Kea, scientists study the night sky. Here at Haleakala, appropriately enough, they study the sun. Science City, just beyond the summit, is off-limits to visitors. It's under the jurisdiction of the University of Hawai'i, which owns some of the domes and leases other land for a variety of private and government research projects.

Department of Defense–related projects here include laser technology associated with the 'Star Wars' project, satellite tracking and identification, and a deep-space surveillance system. The Air Force's Maui Space Surveillance System (MSSS), an electro-optical state-of-the-art facility used for satellite tracking, is the largest telescope anywhere in use by the Department of Defense. The system is capable of identifying a basketball-size object in space 22,000 miles away.

The Faulkes Telescope, a joint University of Hawai'i and UK operation, is dedicated to raising interest in astronomy among students, with a fully robotic telescope that can be controlled in real time via the internet from classrooms in both Britain and Hawaii.

ACTIVITIES

All park programs offered by the National Park Service are free. Ranger-led **walks** through Waikamoi Preserve (p406) are held throughout the year. Evening **stargazing programs** are offered between May and September, when the weather is warm enough. For information about **horseback rides** into the crater, see p400 .

Hiking

Hiking is awesome in the park. There are 30 miles of trail, ranging from short nature walks to treks that take a few days. Those who hike the crater will discover a completely different angle on Haleakala's lunar landscape. Instead of peering down from the rim, you'll be craning your neck skyward at the walls and towering cinder cones. You'll be a world away from anyplace else. The crater is a remarkably still place. Cinders crunching underfoot are often the only sound, except for the occasional bark of a pueo (Hawaiian owl) or honking of a friendly nene.

To protect Haleakala's fragile environment, keep to established trails and don't be tempted off them, even for well-trodden shortcuts through switchbacks.

If you're planning just one full-day outing, and you're in good physical shape, recommended is the 11.2-mile hike that starts down Sliding Sands Trail and returns via Halemau'u Trail. It goes across the crater floor, taking in both a cinder desert and a cloud forest, showcasing the park's amazing diversity. Get an early start.

SLIDING SANDS (KEONEHE'EHE'E) TRAIL

Sliding Sands (Keonehe'ehe'e) Trail starts at the south side of the visitor-center parking lot at 9740ft and descends steeply over loose cinders down to the crater floor. If you take this hike after catching the sunrise, you'll walk directly into a gentle warmish wind and the rays of the sunshine. The trail leads 9.5 miles to the Paliku cabins and campground, passing the Kapalaoa cabin at 5.8 miles after roughly four hours.

The first 6 miles of the trail follow the south wall. There are great views on the way down, but virtually no vegetation. About 2 miles down (at 1400ft), a steep spur trail leads past silversword plants to **Ka Lu'u o ka O'o** cinder cone, about a half-mile north. Four miles down, after an elevation drop of 2500ft, the trail intersects with the first of three spur trails leading north into the cinder desert, which after about 1.5 miles meets the Halemau'u Trail.

As you strike out across the crater floor for 2 miles to Kapalaoa, verdant ridges rise on your right, eventually giving way to ropy *pahoehoe* (smooth-surfaced lava). From Kapalaoa cabin to Paliku, the descent is gentle and the vegetation gradually increases. Paliku (6380ft) is beneath a sheer cliff at the eastern end of the crater. In contrast to the crater's barren western end, this area receives heavy rainfall, with ohia forests climbing the slopes.

HALEMAU'U TRAIL

If you're not up for a long hike, consider doing just part of the Halemau'u Trail. Even hiking just the first mile gives a fine view of the crater with Ko'olau Gap to the east, and it's fairly level up to this point. If you were to continue on the trail, descending 1400ft along 2 miles of switchbacks, then walk across the crater floor to Holua cabin and campground, the 7.5-mile return would make a good day hike. But start early before the afternoon clouds roll in and visibility vanishes.

At 6940ft, **Holua** is one of the lowest areas along this hike, and you'll see impressive views of the crater walls rising a few thousand feet to the west. A few large **lava tubes** here are worth exploring: one up a short, steep cliff behind the cabin, and the other a 15-minute detour further along the trail.

If you have the energy, push on just another mile to the colorful cinder cones, being sure to make a short detour onto the **Silversword Loop**, where you'll see these plants in various stages of growth. If you're here during the summer, you should be able to see the plants in flower, with their tall stalks ablaze with hundreds of maroon and yellow blossoms. But be careful – half of all silverswords today are trampled to death as seedlings, mostly by careless hikers who wander off trails. The trail continues another 6.3 miles to the Paliku cabins.

The trailhead to Halemau'u is 3.5 miles above park headquarters and about 6 miles below the Haleakala Visitor Center. There's a fair chance you'll see nene in the parking lot. If you're camping at Hosmer Grove, you can take the little-known, unexciting **Supply Trail** instead, joining the Halemau'u Trail at the crater rim after 2.5 miles.

EXPLORING THE CINDER DESERT

Almost all hiking trails lead to the belly of the beast. There's no way to see this amazing area without backtracking. Three major spur trails connect Sliding Sands Trail, from near Kapalaoa cabin, with the Halemau'u Trail between Paliku and Holua cabins. As the trails are not very long, if you're camping you may have time to do them all.

The spur trail furthest west takes in many of the crater's most kaleidoscopic cinder cones, and the viewing angle changes with every step. If you prefer stark, black and barren, both of the other spur trails take you through 'a'a (rough, jagged lava) and pahoehoe lava fields, with the one furthest east lying splattered with rust-red cinders.

All three trails end up on the north side of the cinder desert near **Kawilinau**, also known as the Bottomless Pit. Legends say the pit leads down to the sea, though the National Park Service says it's just 65ft deep. Truth be told, there's not much to see, as you can't really get a good look down the narrow shaft. Don't miss the short loop trail to sit for a while in the saddle of **Pele's Paint Pot Lookout**, the crater's most jaw-dropping vantage point.

KAUPO TRAIL

The most extreme of Haleakala's hikes is the Kaupo Trail, which starts at the Paliku campground and leads down to Kaupo on the southern coast. Be prepared for ankle-twisting conditions, blistered feet, intense tropical sun and torrential showers. Your knees will take a pounding as you descend more than 6100ft over 8.6 miles.

The first 3.7 miles of the trail drop 2500ft in elevation before reaching the park boundary. It's a steep rocky trail through rough lava and brushland, with short switchbacks alternating with level stretches. From here you'll be rewarded with spectacular ocean views.

The last 4.9 miles pass through Kaupo Ranch property on a rough jeep trail as it descends to the bottom of Kaupo Gap, exiting into a forest where feral pigs snuffle about. Here trail markings become vague, but once you reach the dirt road, it's another 1.5 miles to the end at the east side of the Kaupo General Store.

The 'village' of Kaupo (p393) is a long way from anywhere, with light traffic. Still, what traffic there is – largely sightseers braving the circle-island road and locals in pickup trucks – moves slow enough along Kaupo's rough road to start conversation. If you have to walk the final stretch, it's 8 miles to the 'Ohe'o Gulch campground.

Because this is such a strenuous and remote trail, it's not advisable to hike it alone. Note that no camping is allowed on Kaupo Ranch property, so most hikers spend the night at the Paliku campground and then get an early start.

HOSMER GROVE TRAIL

Anyone who is looking for a little greenery after hiking the crater will love this shaded woodland walk, and birders wing it here as well.

The half-mile loop trail starts at Hosmer Grove campground, three-quarters of a mile south of park headquarters, in a forest of lofty trees. The exotics in Hosmer Grove were introduced in 1910 in an effort to develop a lumber industry in Hawaii. Species include fragrant incense cedar, Norway spruce, Douglas fir, eucalyptus and various pines. Although the trees adapted well enough to grow, they didn't grow fast enough at these elevations to make tree harvesting practical. Thanks to this failure, today there's a park here instead.

After the forest, the trail moves into native shrubland, with 'akala (Hawaiian raspberry), mamane, pilo, kilau ferns and sandalwood. The 'ohelo, a berry sacred to the volcano goddess Pele, and the pukiawe, which has red and white berries and evergreen leaves, are favored by nene.

Listen for the birdcalls of the native 'i'iwi and 'apapane, both sparrow-size birds with bright red feathers that are fairly common here. The 'i'iwi has a very loud squeaking call, orange legs and a curved salmon-colored bill. The 'apapane, a fast-moving bird with a black bill, black legs and a white undertail, feeds on the nectar of ohia flowers, and its wings make a distinctive whirring sound.

MAUI

Cycling

Each morning before dawn, hoards of cyclists gather at the top of Haleakala for the thrill of coasting 38 miles down the mountain, with a 10,000ft drop in elevation.

Generally, it's an all-day affair (eight to 10 hours), starting with hotel pickup at around 2:30am, a van ride up the mountain for the sunrise and about 3½ hours of biking back down. It's not a nonstop cruise, as cyclists must periodically pull over for cars following behind, and the primary exercise is squeezing the brakes – you'll need to pedal only about 400yd on the entire trip!

With as many as 1000 people biking down the mountain each day, it's a competitive market. The going rate is around $100, which includes bike, helmet, transportation and meals. Bikes are generally modified with special safety brakes, and each group is followed by an escort van. Pregnant women, children under 12 and those shorter than 5ft tall are usually not allowed to ride, but exceptions are not unknown. Keep in mind that the road down Haleakala is narrow and winding with lots of blind curves, and there are no bike lanes.

Cruiser Phil's (☎ 893-2332, 877-764-2453; www .cruiserphil.com), **Maui Downhill** (☎ 871-2155, 800-535-2453; www.mauidownhill.com), **Maui Mountain Cruisers** (☎ 871-6014, 800-232-6284; www.mauimountaincruisers .com) and **Mountain Riders** (☎ 242-9739, 800-706-7700; www.mountainriders.com) all offer the sunrise bike tour.

In addition to the guided tours, other companies will rent you a mountain-bike with assorted gear, give you a van ride to Haleakala summit and then leave you on your own to bike down at your own pace. Be careful on the road if you choose this option. Drivers are almost certain to notice a pack of two-dozen yellow-rainsuit-clad bikers, but a single cyclist is less visible. The going rate is around $65. Companies offering this 'unguided' option include **Haleakala Bike Co** (☎ 575-9575, 888-922-2453; www.bikemaui.com) and **Maui Sunriders** (☎ 579-8970, 866-500-2453; www.mauibikeride.com).

For the downside of cycling this route, see the boxed text, p397.

SLEEPING

To spend the night at Haleakala is to commune with nature. All of the camping options are primitive; none have electricity or showers. Backcountry campgrounds have pit toilets

and limited nonpotable water supplies that are shared with the crater cabins. Water needs to be filtered or chemically treated before drinking; conserve it, as water tanks occasionally run dry. Fires are allowed only in grills and in times of drought are prohibited entirely. You must pack in all your food and supplies and pack out all your trash.

Keep in mind that sleeping at an elevation of 7000ft is not like camping on the beach. You need to be well equipped – without a waterproof tent and a winter-rated sleeping bag, forget it.

Camping

Wake up to the sound of birdsong at Hosmer Grove campground, the park's sole drive-up campground. Surrounded by lofty trees and adjacent to one of Maui's best birding trails, this campground at an elevation of 6800ft tends to be a bit cloudy but a covered picnic pavilion offers shelter if it starts to rain. Campers will also find grills, toilets and running water. Camping is free on a first-come, first-served basis. No permit is required, though there's a three-day camping limit per month. It's busier in summer than in winter and is often full on holiday weekends. The campground is just after the park entrance booth.

For hikers, two **backcountry campgrounds** lie in the belly of Haleakala Crater. The easiest to reach is at Holua, 3.7 miles down the Halemau'u Trail. The other is at Paliku, below a rain-forest ridge at the end of Halemau'u Trail. Weather can be unpredictable at both. Holua is typically dry after sunrise, until clouds roll back in the late afternoon. Paliku is in a grassy meadow, with skies overhead alternating between stormy and sunny.

Permits (free) are required for crater camping. They are issued at park headquarters on a first-come, first-served basis between 8am and 3pm on the day of the hike. Camping is limited to three nights in the crater each month, with no more than two consecutive nights at either campground. Because only 25 campers are allowed at each site, permits can go quickly when larger parties show up, a situation more likely to occur in summer.

Cabins

Three **rustic cabins** (per cabin with 1-12 people $75) dating from the 1930s lie along trails on the crater floor at Holua, Kapalaoa and Paliku. Each has a wood-burning stove, two propane burners, cooking utensils, 12 bunks with sleeping pads (but no bedding), pit toilets, and a limited supply of water and firewood.

Hiking distances to the cabins from the crater rim range from 4 miles to 9 miles. The driest conditions are at Kapalaoa, in the middle of the cinder desert off the Sliding Sands Trail. Those craving lush rain forest will find Paliku serene. Holua has unparalleled sunrise views. There's a three-day limit per month, with no more than two consecutive nights in any cabin. Each cabin is rented to only one group at a time.

The challenge here is the demand, which is so high that the National Park Service holds a monthly lottery to award reservations! To enter, your reservation request must be received two months prior to the first day of the month of your proposed stay (eg requests for cabins on any date in July must arrive before May 1). Your chances increase if you list alternate dates within the same calendar month and choose weekdays rather than weekends.

Only written (no phone) reservation requests (Haleakala National Park, PO Box 369, Makawao, HI 96768, Attn: Cabins) are accepted for the lottery. Include your name, address, phone number, specific dates and cabins requested. Only winners are notified.

If you miss the lottery, don't write the cabins off. Cancellations often result in last-minute vacancies, and occasionally occur a few weeks in advance as well. You can check for vacancies in person at park headquarters at any time, but calls (☎ 572-4459) regarding cancellations are accepted only between 1pm and 3pm, and you'll need to have a credit card handy to secure the cabin. As an added boon, if you get a vacancy within three weeks of your camping date, the cabin fee drops to $60 a day.

GETTING THERE & AROUND

Haleakala Crater Rd (Hwy 378) twists and turns for 11 miles from Hwy 377 near Kula up to the park entrance, and another 10 miles to Haleakala summit. It's a good paved road all the way, but it's steep and winding. You don't want to rush it, especially when it's dark or foggy. Watch out for cattle wandering freely across the road.

The drive to the summit takes about 1½ hours from Pa'ia or Kahului, two hours from Kihei and a bit longer from Lahaina. If you need gas, fill up the night before, as there are no services on Haleakala Crater Rd.

On your return from the summit, you'll see all of Maui unfolding below, with sugarcane and pineapple fields creating a patchwork of green on the valley floor. The highway snakes back and forth, and in some places as many as four or five switchbacks are in view all at once. Put your car in low gear to avoid burning out your brakes.

Be careful of cyclists. If you're behind a group of them, be patient – they'll eventually pull over to allow cars to safely pass. Note that bicycles are allowed to travel only on paved roads within the park, so as not to disturb the fragile ecosystem.

MAUI

KAHO'OLAWE

Seven miles southwest of Maui, the sacred but uninhabited island of Kaho'olawe (sometimes referred to as Kanaloa) has long been central to the Hawaiian-rights movement. Many consider the island a living spiritual entity, a *pu'uhonua* (refuge) and *wahi pana* (sacred place).

Yet for nearly 50 years, from WWII to 1990, the US military used Kaho'olawe as a bombing range. Beginning in the 1970s, liberating the island from the military became a rallying point for a larger resurgence of Native Hawaiian pride. Today, the bombing has stopped, the navy is gone, and healing the island is considered both a symbolic act and a concrete expression of Native Hawaiian sovereignty.

Kaho'olawe is 11 miles long and 6 miles wide, with its highest point the 1482ft Luamakika. The island and its surrounding waters are now a reserve that is off-limits to the general public because of the wealth of unexploded ordinance that remains on land and in the sea.

PATHWAY TO TAHITI

The channel between Lana'i and Kaho'olawe, as well as the westernmost point of Kaho'olawe itself, is named Kealaikahiki, meaning 'pathway to Tahiti.' When early Polynesian voyagers made the journey between Hawaii and Tahiti, they lined up their canoes at this departure point.

However, Kaho'olawe was much more than an early navigational tool. Over 540 archaeological and cultural sites have been identified. They include several heiau (an ancient stone temple) and ku'ula (fishing shrine) stones dedicated to the gods of fishers. Pu'umoiwi, a large cinder cone in the center of the island, contains one of Hawaii's largest ancient adze quarries.

A PENAL COLONY

In 1829, Ka'ahumanu, the Hawaiian prime minister, put forth her Edict of 1829, which declared that Catholics were to be banished to Kaho'olawe. Whether because of this or by coincidence, beginning in 1830, Kaulana Bay, on the island's northern side, served as a penal colony for men accused of such crimes as rebellion, theft, divorce, breaking marriage vows, murder and prostitution. History does not say if Catholics were included, and the penal colony was shut down in 1853.

INTO THE DUST BOWL

Kaho'olawe, now nearly barren, was once a lush, green and forested island.

Considering it good for stock raising, in 1858 the territorial Hawaiian government leased the entire island to ranchers. None was successful, and sheep, goats and cattle were left to run wild. By the early 1900s, tens of thousands of sheep and goats had denuded the better part of the island, turning it into an eroded dusty wasteland (even today, Kaho'olawe looks hazy from dust when seen from Maui).

From 1918 to 1941, Angus MacPhee, a former ranch manager on Maui, ran Kaho'olawe's most successful ranching operation. Granted a lease on the grounds to get rid of the goats, MacPhee rounded up and sold 13,000 goats, and then built a fence across the width of the entire island to keep the remaining goats at one end. He then planted grasses and ground cover and started raising cattle. It wasn't easy, but MacPhee, unlike his predecessors, was able to turn a profit.

TARGET PRACTICE

The US military had long felt that Kaho'olawe had strategic importance. In early 1941, it subleased part of the island from MacPhee for bombing practice. Following the December 7, 1941, Pearl Harbor attack, martial law was declared in Hawaii and the military took control of Kaho'olawe entirely. Until the war's end, it used it to practice for invasions in the Pacific theater; in addition to ship-to-shore and aerial bombing, it tested submarine torpedoes by firing them at shoreline cliffs. It is estimated that of all fighting that took place during WWII, Kaho'olawe was the most bombed island in the Pacific.

After the war, bombing practice continued. In 1953, President Eisenhower signed a decree giving the US navy official jurisdiction over Kaho'olawe, with the stipulation that when Kaho'olawe was no longer 'needed,' the unexploded ordinance would be removed and the island would be returned to Hawaiian control 'reasonably safe for human habitation.'

THE KAHO'OLAWE MOVEMENT

In the mid-1960s Hawaii politicians began petitioning the federal government to cease its military activities and return Kaho'olawe to the state of Hawaii. In 1976, a suit was filed against the navy, and in an attempt to attract greater attention to the bombings, nine Native Hawaiian activists sailed across and occupied the island. Despite their arrests, more occupations followed.

During one of the 1977 crossings, group members George Helm and Kimo Mitchell mysteriously disappeared in the waters off Kaho'olawe. Helm had been an inspirational Hawaiian-rights activist, and with his death the Protect Kaho'olawe 'Ohana movement arose. Helm's vision of turning Kaho'olawe into a sanctuary of Hawaiian culture became widespread among islanders.

In 1980, in a court-sanctioned decree, the navy reached an agreement with Protect Kaho'olawe 'Ohana that allowed them regular access to the island. The decree restricted the navy from bombing archaeological sites. In 1981 Kaho'olawe was added to the National Register of Historic Places as a significant archaeological area. For nearly a decade, the island had the ironic distinction of being the only such historic place being bombed by its government.

In 1982 the 'Ohana began to go to Kaho'olawe to celebrate *makahiki*, the annual observance to honor Lono, god of agriculture and peace (this celebration continues today). That same year – in what many Hawaiians felt was the ultimate insult to their heritage – the US military offered Kaho'olawe as a bombing target to foreign nations during biennial Pacific Rim exercises.

The offer and the exercises brought what was happening to Kaho'olawe to worldwide attention. International protests over the bombings grew, and New Zealand, Australia, Japan and the UK decided to withdraw from the Kaho'olawe exercises. The plan was scrapped.

In the late 1980s Hawaii's politicians became more outspoken in their demands that Kaho'olawe be returned to Hawaii. Then, in October 1990, as Hawaii's two US senators, Daniel Inouye and Daniel Akaka, were preparing a congressional bill to stop the bombing, President George Bush issued an order to immediately halt military activities.

THE NAVY SETS SAIL

In 1994, the US navy finally agreed to clean up and return Kaho'olawe to Hawaii. In a Memorandum of Understanding, the US navy promised to work until 100% of surface munitions and 30% of subsurface munitions were cleared. However, the catch was that the federally authorized cleanup would end in 10 years, regardless of the results (and regardless of Eisenhower's original promise).

Ten years later, after spending over $400 million, the navy's cleanup ended, and Kaho'olawe was transferred to the state. The government estimated that only 70% of surface ordinance and a mere 9% of subsurface ordinance had been removed.

The same year, in 2004, Hawaii established the **Kaho'olawe Island Reserve Commission** (KIRC; www.kahoolawe.hawaii.gov) to manage access and use of the island, preserve its archaeological areas and restore its habitats. KIRC's mandate is unique in state law, for it calls for the island to be 'managed in trust until such time and circumstances as a sovereign Native Hawaiian entity is recognized by the federal and state governments.' No such entity was then or is now so recognized, but KIRC works in the belief that one day a sovereign Native Hawaiian government will be, and this island will then become theirs.

HELPING THE 'OHANA

Working with KIRC as official stewards of Kaho'olawe, **Protect Kaho'olawe 'Ohana** (PKO; www .kahoolawe.org) conducts monthly visits to the island to pull weeds, plant native foliage, build infrastructure, clean up historic sights, conduct Hawaiian rituals and honor the spirits of the land. It welcomes respectful volunteers who are ready to help (not just sightsee). Visits last four to five days during or near the full moon; volunteers pay a $100 fee, which covers all food and transportation to the island. You'll need to bring your own sleeping bag, tent and personal supplies. PKO's website lists full details, schedules and contact information.

Lana'i

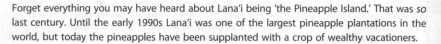

Forget everything you may have heard about Lana'i being 'the Pineapple Island.' That was *so* last century. Until the early 1990s Lana'i was one of the largest pineapple plantations in the world, but today the pineapples have been supplanted with a crop of wealthy vacationers.

It all started when Castle & Cooke, which owns 98% of the island, rebranded Lana'i 'The Private Island' and built two exclusive resorts with designer golf greens, one in the cool uplands and the other overlooking the island's finest beach. The 'new' Lana'i made it onto the jet-set map after billionaire Bill Gates rented out every room in both resorts for his wedding day.

The heart of the island is Lana'i City, the old plantation town that was built during the pineapple era. It's home to nearly all of the island's local community and still retains much of its small-town charm. Step into any of the mom-and-pop eateries surrounding its pine-studded central square and you'll find some of the friendliest people on the planet.

Explorers who venture past town will find scores of red-dirt roads, a handful of archaeological sights, and acres and acres of solitude.

Don't fret if your budget isn't in the four-figures-a-day category. A couple of small guesthouses and Lana'i's original 12-room lodge offer a more down-home side. And a great way to get a taste of Lana'i's water wonders is to simply hop a ferry or take a snorkeling cruise from Maui.

HIGHLIGHTS

- Snorkel the unspoiled waters at **Hulopo'e Beach** (p423).
- Savor Cajun cooking at **Henry Clay's Rotisserie** (p422).
- Talk story with the locals at **Dole Park** (p419).
- Trek the **Munro Trail** (p426) atop the island's spine.
- Get lost on **Shipwreck Beach** (p424)
- Spend a night in the old-fashioned **Hotel Lanai** (p421).
- Aim for a hole-in-one at the **Challenge at Manele** (opposite).
- Pedal a mountain-bike to **Garden of the Gods** (p426).
- Reminisce about the good ol' days at the **Pineapple Festival** (p420).
- Explore the underwater wonders at **Cathedrals** (opposite).

★ Shipwreck Beach

★ Garden of the Gods

Dole Park ★ ★ ★ Munro Trail
Lana'i City

Manele Bay ★ ★ Hulopo'e Beach
★
Cathedrals (Hulopo'e Bay)

| ■ POPULATION: 3300 | ■ AREA: 140 SQ MILES | ■ OFFICIAL FLOWER: KAUNA'OA |

CLIMATE

At an elevation of 1620 ft Lana'i City enjoys a mild climate with average temperatures of 66°F in winter and 73°F in summer. Bring a jacket if you're coming in winter, when nighttime temperatures dip to around 50°F. Rainfall, which is heaviest in winter, averages around 40in annually in Lana'i City and 15in along the coast. When it's overcast in Lana'i City, chances are that Hulopo'e Beach will be sunny.

ACTIVITIES

Lana'i has no national, state or county parks, but its finest beach, Hulopo'e Beach, is run by the Lana'i Company as a public park open to all.

Almost all organized activities on the island are coordinated through the resorts. These include tennis, horseback riding, golf and scuba diving.

Water Activities

Snorkeling and swimming are fantastic at Hulopo'e Beach (p423), and if you're there in the morning you can often watch dolphins frolicking just offshore.

Diving reaches its peak at the nearby **Cathedrals**, whose crystal-clear waters and grottoes harbor an abundance of colorful marine life. **Trilogy Lana'i Ocean Sports** (☎ 565-7227; www.visitlanai.com; 1036 Lana'i Ave, Lana'i City; beach dive $95, 2-tank boat dive $169; ☒ 7am-7pm) can organise everything you will need for

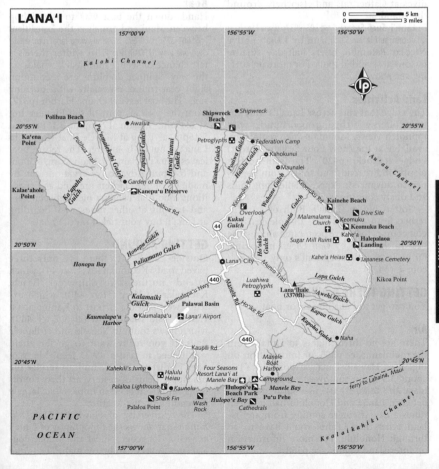

LANA'I SURF BEACHES & BREAKS *Jake Howard*

When it comes to surfing, Lana'i doesn't enjoy quite the bounty of waves as some of the other islands. Because rain clouds get trapped in the high peaks of Maui and Moloka'i there's very little rain on Lana'i, and thus far fewer reef passes have been carved out by runoff.

Yet on the south shore the most consistent surf comes in around the **Manele Point** area (p422), where the main break peels off the tip of Manele and into **Hulopo'e Bay**. Shallow reef and submerged rocks make this a dangerous spot at low tide or in smaller surf conditions; it's probably ideal on a double overhead swell. Not too far away from here, located in front of a deserted old Hawaiian settlement, is a spot called **Naha** (also known as Stone Shack). It offers a fun two-way peak, but does close out when it gets bigger.

Across the island, the north shore's wide-open **Polihua Beach** (p425) is the longest and widest sandy beach on Lana'i. Be careful of the current here, affectionately dubbed 'the Tahitian Express.' The water flowing between Moloka'i and Lana'i in the Kalohi Channel has driven many a ship into the reef, and it could easily take you on a trip to Tahiti if you're not careful.

---

dives at Cathedrals and elsewhere around the island.

Lana'i Surf Safari (☎ 306-9837; www.lanaisurf safari.com; surf lesson $185), run by Lana'i native Nicolas Palumbo, offers half-day surfing lessons at secluded spots. For more on surfing see above.

Land Activities

The ridge that cuts across Lana'i's hilly interior offers good hiking opportunities with topnotch views. Mountain-bike rentals are available at the (now Four Seasons resort) Lodge at Koele (p420). The island offers plenty of dirt roads and trails, from beginner to advanced; expect challenging hills and dusty conditions.

Golf is big on Lana'i. Both of Lana'i's resorts feature world-class 18-hole designer golf courses that have been rated among the best in the USA by *Golf Digest* magazine. Or go local-style at Hawaii's only free golf course (p420).

GETTING THERE & AWAY

You can get to Lana'i by air or boat.

Air

There are no direct flights to Lana'i from the mainland; see p566 for information on flights to Hawaii. Lana'i airport (LNY) is about 3.5 miles southwest of Lana'i City. **Island Air** (☎ 800-323-3345; www.islandair.com) flies between Lana'i and Honolulu half a dozen times a day; if you're coming from any island other than O'ahu, you'll have to go through Honolulu. For more information on interisland flights, see p568.

Boat

Hands-down the best way to island hop between Maui and Lana'i is the **Expeditions** (☎ 661-3756, 800-695-2624; www.go-lanai.com; adult/ child one way $25/20) ferry. In winter there's a fair chance of seeing humpback whales on the way. Spinner dolphins are a common sight year-round, especially with morning sails. The boat leaves Lahaina Harbor (p317) from the pier in front of the Pioneer Inn at 6:45am, 9:15am, 12:45pm, 3:15pm and 5:45pm, arriving at Manele Boat Harbor in Lana'i about an hour later. The return boat leaves Lana'i at 8am, 10:30am, 2pm, 4:30pm and 6:45pm. Advance reservations can be made by phone. Tickets are sold at Expeditions' booth at Lahaina pier between 6am and 4:45pm; at other times, or if boarding at Lana'i, buy your ticket on the boat.

GETTING AROUND

Outside Lana'i City there are only three paved roads: Keomuku Rd (Hwy 44), which extends northeast to Shipwreck Beach; Kaumalapa'u Hwy (Hwy 440), which extends west past the airport to Kaumalapa'u Harbor; and Manele Rd (also Hwy 440), which flows south to Manele and Hulopo'e Bays. If you really want to go far afield you'll need to rent a 4WD Jeep. Many of Lana'i's dirt roads were built to service the pineapple fields of yesteryear; their conditions vary from good to impassable, largely depending on the weather.

The University of Hawai'i's *Moloka'i/ Lana'i* map shows the topography of Lana'i as well as its geographical and archaeological sites. A very handy free map, *The Island*

LANA'I...

In Two Days

Start your first day swimming and snorkeling at **Hulopo'e Beach** (p423) or diving at nearby **Manele Bay** (p423). In the afternoon take a stroll around **Lana'i City** (p418) and watch the sun set over the majestic Norfolk pines at Dole Park. On the second day rent a mountain-bike or put on your hiking boots and head up the **Munro Trail** (p426) for a panoramic view of everything Lana'i has to offer.

In Four Days

Do a little beachcombing along **Shipwreck Beach** (p424) or maybe play a round of golf on the stunning greens of the **Experience at Koele** (p420), then take the evening to **Henry Clay's Rotisserie** (p422). On day four get out there and really explore – visit the **Garden of the Gods** (p426), the **Luahiwa Petroglyphs** (p425) and the ancient village of **Kaunolu** (p427).

Daytripping from Maui

Take the early morning **ferry** (opposite) from Lahaina and keep an eye out for schools of dolphins as the boat approaches **Manele Bay** (p423). Hop the shuttle into town, rub elbows with the locals over breakfast at **Blue Ginger Café** (p421) and catch the sights in **Lana'i City** (p418). In the afternoon, snorkel at **Hulopo'e Beach** (p423) before heading back to Maui on the sunset ferry.

---

of Lana'i – which shows Lana'i City, the grounds of the two resorts and the island's main roads – can be picked up free at the hotels. Lana'i City Service (below) provides customers with its *Jeep Safari Drive Guide*, a basic sketch map with off-road directions to major sights.

To/From the Airport

The resorts provide a shuttle-van service (right) that meets guests at the airport and ferry dock. Nonguests can use the shuttle for a fee, or call a taxi (p418) in advance of your arrival.

Car

The only car-rental company on the island, **Lana'i City Service** (☎ 565-7227, 800-533-7808; 1036 Lana'i Ave, Lana'i City; ☼ 7am-7pm), is an affiliate of Dollar (p571). Having a monopoly on Lana'i translates into steep prices. Unlike Dollar affiliates on other islands, this one requires a one-day deposit to make a booking. Economy cars rent for $65 a day, 4WD Jeep Wranglers for $139. Both can be in short supply and sometimes need to be booked more than a week in advance. Customers arriving by air can use the red airport courtesy phone for free pickups.

While Lana'i has many dirt roads in fine condition, Lana'i City Service restricts all its cars to paved roads – only the 4WD Jeeps

may be driven on dirt roads. Even then, the company decides on a day-to-day basis which dirt roads you can and can't drive on, depending on the weather and the current condition of the ruts and washouts. Keep in mind if you do go off the beaten path and get stuck, it can be a long walk back to town and you can expect to pay an exorbitant amount in towing and repair fees.

Shuttle

The resort shuttle van goes between the Manele Bay hotel, Hotel Lanai and the Lodge at Koele, as well as to the airport and ferry dock. Shuttles run about every 30 minutes throughout the day in peak season, hourly in the slower months. The first usually heads out about 7am, the last around 11pm. Anyone can use the shuttle for a daily fee of $25.

DRIVING DISTANCES & TIMES

From Lana'i City

Destination	Miles	Time
Garden of the Gods	6	25 min
Hulopo'e Beach	8	25 min
Kaumalapa'u Harbor	7	20 min
Keomuku	8	25 min
Lana'i Airport	3.5	15 min

LANA'I

People taking the Expeditions ferry can also opt to buy a $10 shuttle ticket at the ferry booth in Lahaina good for a return trip between Manele Bay and Lana'i City.

Taxi

Rabaca's Limousine Service (☎ 565-6670) charges $10 per person between the airport and Lana'i City, and $10 per person between Manele Bay and Lana'i City, the latter with a two-person minimum.

LANA'I CITY

pop 3000

Don't be fooled by the name, the nearest real city is an island away. This friendly little place is a rare vestige of small-town Hawaii that's been lost on other islands. You won't find any traffic lights (or traffic for that matter) and the term 'fast food' wouldn't even register here. Everything about this town says turn back the clock and unwind.

Lana'i City's main square, surrounded by tin-roofed houses and shops, looks much the same as it did during its plantation days. But make no mistake about it, the town is not a museum piece. Some things are changing but despite all that's happened on Lana'i since the pineapples were plowed under, this town has managed to retain much of its heritage. Walk around, soak up the flavor, catch a crimson sunset silhouetted against the lofty pine trees – there's still something special here.

HISTORY

Lana'i is the only Hawaiian island where the largest town is in the highlands and not on the coast. Not only is Lana'i City the largest town, but for most of the 20th century all but a handful of all Lana'ians lived right in Lana'i City.

The town was built in the 1920s as a plantation town for the field workers and staff of Jim Dole's Hawaiian Pineapple Company. The first planned city in Hawaii, Lana'i City was built in the midst of the pineapple fields, with shops and a theater surrounding the central park, rows of plantation houses lined up beyond that and a

---

A TOWN WORTH SAVING

Guess what's made the most endangered list?

According to the Historic Hawai'i Foundation, the leading advocate for cultural and historic preservation in the state, the entire town of Lana'i City is now one of the most endangered places in Hawai'i. Every year the group nominates a short list of historic places in the islands that are most threatened by neglect, insufficient funding or development. Generally the list includes crumbling churches and termite-eaten theaters, but never before has an entire community made the rolls.

Ever since pineapple production was phased out on Lana'i, people have wondered what the fate of Lana'i City would be and if a plantation town without a plantation could maintain its sense of identity.

When Castle & Cooke turned Lana'i's pineapple fields into resort golf greens in the early 1990s, the island underwent some earth-shaking changes. First came the building of two new resorts. And not just simple hotels, but truly fancy digs with world-class golf courses, luxury accommodations, a posh spa and a private-island mystique designed to lure high-spenders to Lana'i. Next came the multimillion-dollar homes. And now the first plush oceanfront condominium project, set right on the designer golf-course at Manele Bay, has opened with condo units selling for a cool $2.5 million each.

Change is now spilling into town itself. It's not just the new apartment complexes being constructed on the edge of Lana'i City, it's also the inevitable gentrification that comes along with an influx of new money. Preservationists point to the fact that some plantation-era landmarks, including the old post office and the old fire station, have already been demolished in favor of modern facilities.

But if groups like the Historic Hawai'i Foundation and the homegrown Lana'ians for Sensible Growth manage to rouse enough community support, all of Lana'i City may become a protected historic district. If not, the Lana'i City everyone knows and loves may continue to slip away, altering its face one building at a time.

LANA'I CITY

0 ————————————— 400 m
0 ————————————— 0.2 miles

To Koloiki Ridge Trail (0.1mi);
Stables at Koele (0.3mi);
Munro Trailhead (0.4mi);
Garden of the Gods (5.9mi);
Shipwreck Beach (8.4mi)

INFORMATION	
Bank of Hawaii...........................1	B3
Lana'i City Service (Car Rental)....2	C4
Lana'i Community Hospital.........3	B3
Lana'i Visitors Bureau................4	B3
Launderette Lana'i.....................5	B3
Police Station...........................6	B4
Post Office...............................7	B3

SIGHTS & ACTIVITIES	
Experience at Koele................(see 15)	
Hawaiian Church.......................8	A3
Lanai Company..........................9	B3
Lana'i Culture & Heritage Center.10	B3
Lana'i Gym..............................11	A3
Trilogy Lana'i Ocean Sports......(see 2)	

SLEEPING	
Dreams Come True...................12	C4
Hale Moe................................13	C5
Hotel Lanai.............................14	B3
Lodge at Koele (Four Seasons	
Resort Lana'i)......................15	B1

EATING	
Blue Ginger Café......................16	B3
Canoes Lana'i..........................17	B3
Coffee Works...........................18	B3
Henry Clay's Rotisserie.........(see 14)	
Pele's Other Garden.................19	B4
The Dining Room.................(see 15)	

ENTERTAINMENT	
Lana'i Theatre..........................20	B3

SHOPPING	
Dis 'N Dat...............................21	B3
Gifts With Aloha......................22	B3
Richard's Shopping Center........23	B3

TRANSPORT	
Lana'i City Service (Gas)............(see 2)	

Keomuku Hwy

Cavendish
Golf Course

Kaumoa Dr

Waialua Pl

Ehuarui Cir
Caldwell Ave
Fraser Ave
Houston St
Gay St
Ilima Ave
Jacaranda St
5th St
3rd St
4th St
Korle St
Mahana St
Nani St
Lana'i Ave
Alapa St
Purilani Pl

6th St

7th St

Dole
Park

8th St

9th St

Queens Ave

10th St

Awalua Ave
Fraser Ave
10th St
11th St

Padwa Ln
Olapa St
12th St

Muku Pl
Jasmine Dr
Queens Ave
13th St

Akahi Pl

Kaumalapa'u Hwy

Kualua Pl

Akolu Pl

To Lana'i Airport (4.5mi);
Kaumalapa'u Harbor (7.5mi)

To Luahiwa Petroglyphs (4mi);
Munro Trail End (5mi);
Manele Bay (8mi)

LANA'I

pineapple-processing plant on the edge of it all. Fortunately it was done with a little pizzazz. Dole hired New Zealander George Munro, a naturalist and former ranch manager, to oversee much of the work, and he planted the tall Norfolk and Cook Island pines that give the town its green character.

ORIENTATION

The town is laid out in a sensible grid pattern, and almost all shops and services border Dole Park, which marks the center of town. Most activities take place about a mile north of the park at or near the Lodge at Koele. Everyone knows this hotel as the Lodge at Koele, though officially it's been rebranded 'Four Seasons Resort at Lana'i, the Lodge at Koele.'

INFORMATION

There's no local daily newspaper, but community notices, including rental housing ads and the movie theater schedule, are posted on bulletin boards outside the post office and grocery stores.

Bank of Hawaii (☎ 565-6426; 460 8th St) Has a 24-hour ATM.

Lana'i Community Hospital (☎ 565-6411; 628 7th St) Offers 24-hour emergency medical services.

Lana'i Visitors Bureau (☎ 565-7600, 800-947-4774; www.visitlanai.net; 431 7th St; ⊙ 9am-5pm Mon-Fri)

Launderette Lana'i (☎ 565-7628; cnr Fraser & 7th Sts; ⊙ 6am-9pm) Self-service coin laundry.

Post office (☎ 565-6517; 620 Jacaranda St; ⊙ 9am-4:30pm Mon-Fri, 10am-noon Sat)

SIGHTS

'Sights' are pretty light on the ground, but the whole town is fun to stroll around. Visit the volunteer-run **Lana'i Culture & Heritage Center** (☎ 565-3240; 111 Lana'i Ave; admission free; ⊙ noon-2pm Mon, 9-11am & noon-2pm Tue-Fri) for a peek into Lana'i's past. If you happen to be here on Sunday morning, swing by the **Hawaiian church** and you'll be serenaded with choir music.

ACTIVITIES

The public recreation complex, which includes **Lana'i Gym** (☎ 565-3939; cnr Fraser Ave & 7th St; ⊙ 8am-4:30pm Mon & Thu-Sat), has a 75ft-long pool, a basketball court and a couple of tennis courts, all free of charge. The **activities desk** (☎ 565-7300; ⊙ 6:30am-6:30pm) at the Lodge at Koele rents mountain-bikes for $8/40 per hour/day.

Golf

Designed by Greg Norman, the **Experience at Koele** (☎ 565-4653; fees $185-240; ⊙ 8am-6:30pm) offers world-class golfing with knockout vistas along the way. And it's as challenging as it is beautiful, with a signature 17th hole dropping 250ft to a wooded ravine.

A world away and just below the manicured greens of Koele lies the **Cavendish Golf Course**, a nine-hole course where the locals tee off. It's open to all, free of dress codes and fees, although there is a donation box where visitors can drop in a few greenbacks.

Hiking

The **Koloiki Ridge Trail**, a 5-mile return hike, leads up to one of the most scenic parts of the **Munro Trail** (p426). It takes about 2¾ hours return and offers bird's-eye views of remote valleys, Maui and Moloka'i.

The trail begins at the rear of the Lodge at Koele on the paved path that leads to the golf clubhouse. From there, follow the signposted path uphill past Norfolk pines until you reach a hilltop bench with a plaque bearing the poem 'If' by Rudyard Kipling. Enjoy the view and then continue through the trees until you reach a chain-link fence. Go around the right side of the fence and continue up the hillside toward the powerlines. At the top of the pass, follow the trail down through a thicket of guava trees until you reach an abandoned dirt service road, which you'll turn left on. You'll soon intersect with the Munro Trail; turn right on it and after a few minutes you'll pass Kukui Gulch, named for the candlenut trees that grow there. Continue along the trail until you reach a thicket of tall sisal plants; about 50yd after that bear right to reach Koloiki Ridge, where you'll be rewarded with panoramas.

Horseback Riding

If you prefer to see Lana'i from a saddle, the **Stables at Koele** (☎ 565-7300; rides $50-260; ⊙ 7am-5pm) offers everything from a 1½-hour trail ride that takes in sweeping views of Maui to a four-hour private ride catered to your interest. And if the *keiki* are ready to cowboy down too, pony rides are available for just $10 per 10 minutes.

FESTIVALS & EVENTS

Lana'i's main bash, the **Pineapple Festival** (www.visitlanai.net), is held on the first Saturday in July to celebrate the island's pineapple past with local grinds, games and live music at Dole Park. If you happen to be here on the first Wednesday of any month, join the townsfolk at Dole Park for **Stars Under the Stars**, a free showing of classic movies outdoors on a 20ft screen.

SLEEPING
Midrange

Hale Moe (☎ 565-9520; www.staylanai.com; 502 Akolu Pl; r incl breakfast $90-100) Commodious rooms and an ocean-view lanai are just part of

---

PINEAPPLES ARE HISTORY

Before pineapple magnate Jim Dole arrived in the 1920s, several ventures on Lana'i, including an attempt to turn part of the dusty island into sugarcane fields, went bust for lack of water.

But Dole, whose Hawaiian Pineapple Company was already making big bucks on O'ahu, decided Lana'i was ripe for pineapples. In 1922 he paid $1.1 million for Lana'i – a mere $12 an acre – and then poured millions of dollars into turning it into one big plantation island. He built Lana'i City, dredged Kaumalapa'u Bay to make it a deepwater harbor, put in roads and water systems, cleared the land and planted pineapples. By the end of the 1920s, production was in full swing and Lana'i was producing nearly 25% of the world's pineapple crop. Dole made a fortune canning the fruit and marketing it back in the States. Although it took a nosedive during the Great Depression, the pineapple industry bounced back and was the backbone of Lana'i's economy for nearly 70 years.

Lana'i's heyday as the world's largest pineapple plantation is history now. Don't even bother looking for the spiky fruit – Lana'i now imports pineapple!

---

the appeal at this contemporary home on the south side of town. Those traveling in numbers can opt to rent the whole three-bedroom house, which sleeps up to eight, for $300.

Dreams Come True (☎ 565-6961, 800-566-6961; www.dreamscometruelanai.com; 547 12th St; r $112, 4-bedroom house $450) This spruced-up plantation house fuses antiques-laden charm with cozy comforts like Jacuzzi baths. Guests have access to a well-equipped kitchen and the yard abounds with fruit just waiting to be picked.

Hotel Lanai (☎ 565-7211, 800-795-7211; www.hotellanai.com; 828 Lana'i Ave; r $125-145, cottage $185) Sitting on the porch here and watching the sun set on Lana'i City is like stepping back to another era. Built by Jim Dole in 1923 to house plantation guests, this rustic 10-room lodge retains its original charm, with pedestal sinks and patchwork quilts. It's all very engaging, but those old walls are thin, so request a room away from the bustling restaurant. If you need more space, there's an atmospheric cottage with a four-poster bed at the rear of the property.

Hawaii Beachfront Vacation Homes (☎ 247-3637; www.hibeach.com; per day/week from $135/750) If you want your own two-bedroom plantation-style home in Lana'i City, contact these folks to get set up.

Top End

Lodge at Koele (Four Seasons Resort Lana'i; ☎ 565-7300, 800-321-4666; www.fourseasons.com/koele; 1 Keomuku Hwy; r/ste from $335/755; ❷ ☎) As if it weren't already cushy enough, the lodge is fresh off a $50 million upgrade to brand it a Four

Seasons resort. Rooms pack more amenities and bigger TVs, but it's still the pampering service that's the hallmark here. Set on a rise above town, the lodge affects the aristocratic demeanor of an English country estate, complete with afternoon tea, lawn bowling and croquet. The 'great hall' lobby brims with antiques and boasts Hawaii's two largest stone fireplaces.

EATING
Budget & Midrange

Coffee Works (☎ 565-6962; 604 'Ilima Ave; snacks $2-4; ✆ 5am-4pm Mon-Fri, 10am-6pm Sat & Sun) The best place on the island to get your java fix. Along with Kona coffee and jolting espressos, you'll find yummy carrot cake.

Canoes Lana'i (☎ 565-6537; 419 7th St; breakfast $5-9; ✆ 6:30am-1pm Thu-Tue) Sit at the counter and watch the bacon sizzle on the grill at this local eatery that serves breakfast until closing. In addition to the usual omelette and pancake menu, it's got carb-heavy island favorites like fried rice and *loco moco* (rice, fried egg and hamburger topped with gravy).

Blue Ginger Café (☎ 565-6363; 409 7th St; breakfast & lunch $5-8, dinner $8-15; ✆ 6am-8pm, to 9pm Fri & Sat) Whether you just want a tasty pastry or need to quell a growling stomach, this friendly bakery-café will fill the bill. Don't be put off by the cement floors and plastic chairs, the food here is first-rate, and at night it kicks it up a notch with dishes like shrimp scampi or fresh mahimahi smothered in capers.

Pele's Other Garden (☎ 565-9628; cnr 8th & Houston Sts; lunch $5-8, dinner $10-19; ✆ 10am-2:30pm &

LANA'I

TOP THREE NIGHTLIFE OPTIONS

- Sip a drink at **Henry Clay's Rotisserie** (below) bar (go early; last call is at 9pm)
- Stroll outdoors and look up at the stars.
- Hmm, let's see...got a deck of cards?

5-9pm Mon-Sat) Gourmet pizzas, organic salads and hot sandwiches, such as grilled chicken breast with melted Swiss cheese, are in store at this cheery Italian-style deli and bistro. Grab one of the tables out on the front porch, then sit back and watch the traffic trickle by.

Top End

Henry Clay's Rotisserie (☎ 565-4700; Hotel Lanai, 828 Lana'i Ave; mains $20-32; ☽ 5:30-8:30pm Wed-Sun) The restaurant's namesake chef shows off his New Orleans roots with memorable Cajun dishes like seafood gumbo and duck confit with garlic cassoulet. The fireplaced dining room, which dates to 1923, glows with period charm. Save room for the old-fashioned pecan pie.

The Dining Room (☎ 565-7300; Lodge at Koele, 1 Keomuku Hwy; mains $45-55; ☽ 6-9:30pm) You know a place recognizes its niche as the top restaurant when it calls itself *The* Dining Room. And indeed, this is the island's top spot for a fancy dinner out. Think French country-style cuisine with a Hawaiian twist, with the likes of seared quail, macadamia-crusted venison and Kona lobster with caviar.

DRINKING & ENTERTAINMENT

Lana'i shuts the lights out early, but the Lodge at Koele has a pianist playing in its 'great hall' from 7pm to 10pm. The bar at Henry Clay's Rotisserie occasionally has a local band. **Lana'i Theatre** (☎ 565-7500; 456 7th St), the island's cozy cinema, shows first-run feature films.

SHOPPING

About a dozen shops and galleries encircle Dole Park, so stroll around and see what catches your fancy.

A good place to start is **Gifts with Aloha** (☎ 565-6589; 363 7th St; ☽ 9:30am-6pm Mon-Sat), which has everything from aloha shirts to Hawaiian music CDs and ukuleles. Also check out **Dis 'N Dat** (☎ 565-9170; 418 8th St; ☽ 10am-5:30pm Mon-Sat), a fun shack with an eclectic collection. For a general store, **Richard's Shopping Center** (☎ 565-6047; 434 8th St; ☽ 8am-7pm Mon-Sat) carries everything from groceries and wine to T-shirts and sandals.

GETTING THERE & AROUND

The resort shuttle (p417) stops at Hotel Lanai and the Lodge at Koele. Lana'i's only car-rental office (p417) is in town.

MANELE & HULOPO'E BAYS

If you want to snorkel, dive or just spend a day at the beach, head to these adjacent bays, 8 miles south of Lana'i City. Crescent-shaped Manele Harbor provides a protected anchorage for sailboats and other small craft. From the harbor, it's just a 10-minute walk to Hulopo'e Beach.

Manele and Hulopo'e Bays are part of a marine life conservation district, which

---

DETOUR: LUAHIWA PETROGLYPHS

Lana'i's highest concentration of ancient petroglyphs are carved into three dozen boulders spread over three dusty acres on a remote slope overlooking the Palawai Basin.

To get to this seldom visited site, head south from Lana'i City along Manele Rd. Midway between the 7- and 8-mile markers, turn left onto Ho'ike Rd, the wide dirt road that comes up immediately after a roadside shed. Head for the water tower on the ridge, taking a sharp left after 1 mile. Stay on this road for half a mile and then take the jog to the right. About a third of a mile down, you'll come to a large cluster of boulders on the right. Park off to the side and walk up to the boulders.

Many of the rock carvings are quite weathered, but you can still make out linear and triangular human figures, dogs and a canoe. Other than gusts of wind, the place is eerily quiet. You can almost feel the presence of the ancients here – honor their spirits and don't touch the fragile carvings.

prohibits the removal of coral and restricts many fishing activities, all of which makes for great snorkeling and diving. Water activities can be dangerous during *kona* (leeward) storms, when winds produce strong currents and swells.

MANELE HARBOR

During the early 20th century, cattle were herded down to Manele Bay for shipment to Honolulu. These days it's the jump-off point for tourists coming from Maui on the ferry (p416) or on one of Trilogy's snorkeling cruises (p324). If you want to do a little land exploration you'll find the remains of a cattle chute by walking around the point at the end of the parking lot. Stone ruins from a fishing village are up on the hill above the parking lot, though they're largely overgrown with thorny kiawe.

But the real thrills here are beneath the surface. Coral is abundant near the cliff sides, where the bottom quickly slopes off to about 40ft. Beyond the bay's western edge, near Pu'u Pehe rock, is **Cathedrals** (Map p415), the island's most spectacular dive site with arches and grottoes. Harbor facilities include drinking water, picnic tables, a little eatery, rest rooms and showers.

HULOPO'E BEACH

Lana'i may have only one easy-access beach, but what a beauty it is. Everybody loves it – locals taking the kids for a swim, tourists on daytrips from Maui, and the spinner dolphins who frequent the bay during the early morning hours.

This gently curving white-sand beach is long, broad and protected by a rocky point to the south. The Four Seasons Resort Lana'i at Manele Bay sits on a low seaside terrace on the north side. Even with the hotel presence the beach is so big it never gets crowded. Generally, the most action occurs when the tour boats pull in from Maui at midday .

For the best **snorkeling**, head to the left side of the bay, where there's an abundance of coral and reef fish. To the left just beyond the sandy beach, you'll find a low lava shelf with tide pools worth exploring. Here, too, you'll find a protected shoreline splash pool ideal for children, with cement steps leading

---

LANA'I FOR NA KEIKI

The kids will love Hulopo'e Beach (left), where there are some cool tide pools and a protected splash pool for the little ones, and an oceanful of great snorkeling for older kids. Other activities for children are centered at the resorts. The Stables at Koele (p420) has pony rides. **Pilialoha Keiki Camp** (☎ 565-2398, ext 2399; per day $60; ⏱ 9am-5pm), a day program for kids aged 5-12 at the Four Seasons Resort Lana'i at Manele Bay, packs in games, crafts and beach outings.

---

down to it. This lovely beach park has water fountains, picnic tables, solar-heated showers and rest rooms.

PU'U PEHE

From Hulopo'e Beach, a short path leads south to the end of the point that separates Hulopo'e and Manele Bays. The point is actually a volcanic cinder cone that's sharply eroded on its seaward edge. The lava has rich rust-red colors with swirls of gray and black, and its texture is bubbly and brittle – so brittle that huge chunks of the point have broken off and fallen onto the coastal shelf below.

Pu'u Pehe is the name of the cove to the left of the point as well as the rocky islet just offshore. This islet, also called Sweetheart's Rock, has a tomblike formation on top that figures into Hawaiian legend (see below).

LOVE TO THE END

It's said that an island girl named Pehe was so beautiful that her lover decided to make their home in a secluded coastal cave, lest any other young men in the village set eyes on her. One day when he was up in the mountains fetching water, a storm suddenly blew in and by the time he rushed back down, powerful waves had swept into the cave, drowning Pehe. The lover carried Pehe's body to the top of Pu'u Pehe, where he erected a tomb and laid her to rest. Immersed in grief, he then jumped into the surging waters below and was dashed back onto the rock, joining his lover in death.

GOLF

The **Challenge at Manele** (☎ 565-2222; guests/non-guests $190/240; ⏱ 7:10am-6:30pm), designed by Jack Nicklaus, offers spectacular hole plays along seaside cliffs, and receives high ratings from golf enthusiasts.

SLEEPING

Four Seasons Resort Lana'i at Manele Bay (Map p415; ☎ 565-3800, 800-321-4666; 1 Manele Bay Rd; www .fourseasons.com/manelebay.com; r from $395; ❄ ⌘) Tropical lobbies adorned with artwork and acres of gleaming marble set the tone at this luxury hotel perched above the island's finest beach. Rooms overlook sculptured gardens, koi ponds or the ocean. In addition to top-rated golf and the beach, the resort has tennis courts and the indulgent Spa at Manele. Ask about golf packages and fourth-night-free deals.

Camping is allowed on the lawn above Hulopo'e Beach. Pick up permits from the **Lanai Company** (☎ 565-2970; 111 Lana'i Ave, Lana'i City; campsite $20). Sometimes you can get permits without advance reservations if the campground's not full – but keep in mind it's commonly booked up weeks in advance, especially during summer and on weekends throughout the year. The maximum stay is three nights.

EATING

Harbor Café (Manele Small Bay Harbor; lunch $5-8; ⏱ 7am-2:30pm) What would a day at the beach be without a plate lunch? This simple harborside café is where the locals who work at the resort head for an affordable bite. Their bacon-teri cheeseburger really hits the spot. Shave ice and ice cream too.

Ocean Grill (☎ 565-7700; Four Seasons Resort Lana'i at Manele Bay; lunch $10-18; ⏱ 11am-5pm) Dine like a millionaire on vacation at this poolside resort restaurant serving *kalua* pork quesadillas, leafy salads and creative sandwiches.

TOP THREE SPLURGES

- Dinner and drinks at the **Dining Room** (p422)
- Hot stone massage at the **Spa at Manele** (above)
- **Fireplace suite** (p421) at the Four Seasons Resort Lana'i, the Lodge at Koele

---

Hulopo'e Court (☎ 565-7700; Four Seasons Resort Lana'i at Manele Bay; breakfast buffet $24, dinner mains $28-40; ⏱ 7-11am & 6-9:30pm) A memorable way to start your day is with a lavish buffet at this open-air restaurant. At dinner there's everything from the expected rack of lamb to steamed seafood *laulau* (fish wrapped in taro and *ti* leaves and steamed) with Moloka'i sweet potatoes. The grand setting includes showy chandeliers, ornate Chinese vases and a fine ocean view.

DRINKING & ENTERTAINMENT

The Manele Bay hotel lounge, **Hale Ahe Ahe** (⏱ 5-11pm), is the place to have a drink or shoot a game of pool. If you're around at sunset, catch the hotel's torch-lighting ceremony.

KEOMUKU ROAD

Keomuku Rd (Hwy 44) heads north from Lana'i City into cool upland hills where fog drifts above grassy pastures. Along the way, impromptu overlooks offer straight-on views of the undeveloped southeast shore of Moloka'i and its tiny islet Mokuho'oniki, in marked contrast to Maui's glittering high-rises in Ka'anapali off to your right.

As the road gently slopes down to the coast, the scenery is punctuated by peculiar rock formations sitting atop the eroded red earth, similar to those at Garden of the Gods. Further along, a shipwreck comes into view. After 8 miles, the paved road ends near the coast. To the left, a dirt road leads to Shipwreck Beach, while turning right onto Keomuku Rd takes you to Keomuku Beach or, for the truly intrepid, all the way to Naha.

SHIPWRECK BEACH

If you're up for a hardy beach walk, this windswept beauty extending 9 miles along Lana'i's northeast shore is where you want to be. The beach takes its name from the many ships that its tricky reef has snared. Not surprisingly, it's fun for beachcombing, with lots of sun-bleached driftwood, some pieces still bearing witness to their past – hulls, side planks, perhaps even a gangplank if your imagination is active.

Start by taking the dirt road that runs north from the end of Hwy 44, park about

---

FISHING LINE, BRAH?

Up on the slopes at Shipwreck Beach, you'll see beach morning glory entwined with a plant that looks like yellow-orange fishing line. Look closer: this is Lana'i's official flower, a leafless parasitic vine called *kauna'oa*. Lana'ians braid the plant's skinny stems to make lei.

---

half a mile in and then walk onto the beach, continuing past some old wooden beach shacks used by fisherfolk.

As you proceed it's likely to be just you and the driftwood, the sand gradually changing colors. In some places, it's a colorful, chunky mixture of rounded shells and bits of rock that look like some sort of beach confetti.

After walking north for about a mile, you'll reach the site of a former lighthouse on a lava-rock point, though only the cement foundation remains. From here you'll get a good view of a rusting **WWII liberty ship** (cargo ship) that's wrecked on the reef.

Petroglyphs

From the lighthouse foundation, trail markings lead directly inland about 100yd to a cluster of fragile petroglyphs. The simple figures are etched onto large boulders on the right side of the path. Keep your eyes open here – sightings of wild mouflon sheep on the inland hills are not uncommon. Males have curled-back horns, and dominant ones travel with a harem.

Shipwreck in Awalua

The lighthouse site is the turn-around point for most people but it's possible to walk another 6 miles all the way to Awalua, where there's another shipwreck. The hike is windy, hot and dry (bring drinking water!), although the further down the beach you go, the prettier it gets.

KEOMUKU TO NAHA

Keomuku Beach, a barren shoreline stretch running from Kahokunui south to Halepalaoa Landing, is best suited for those scratching for something different to do. There's not really much to see other than a few marginal historical sites, scattered groves of coconuts and lots of kiawe trees.

Keomuku Rd, the 4WD-only dirt road that heads southward from the end of Hwy 44, is likely to be either dusty or muddy, but if you catch it after it's been graded, it's not too bad. Going the full 12 miles down to Naha, at the end of the road, can take as long as two hours one way when the road is rough, half of that when conditions are better.

Maunalei to Keomuku

Less than a mile down the road is **Maunalei**. An ancient heiau (stone temple) sat there until 1890 when the Maunalei Sugar Company dismantled it and used the stones to build a fence. Shortly after the temple desecration, the company's wells started to draw saltwater, which doomed the operation.

Another 4 miles further along is **Keomuku**, the center of the short-lived sugarcane plantation. There's little left to see other than the reconstructed **Ka Lanakila o Ka Malamalama Church**, which was originally built in 1903. The ruins of a couple of fishponds lie along the coast, but they're not easily visible from the road.

Kehe'a to Naha

Another heiau at **Kehe'a**, 1.5 miles south of Keomuku, was also dismantled by Maunalei Sugar, this time to build a railroad to transport the sugarcane to **Halepalaoa Landing**, south of Kehe'a. From here the road to **Naha** gets rougher and doesn't offer much for the effort, but should you want to continue, it's about 4 miles further.

ROAD TO GARDEN OF THE GODS

Sights in northwestern Lana'i are reached via the dirt road, Polihua Rd, that commences between the Lodge at Koele's tennis courts and stables. The stretch of road leading to Kanepu'u Preserve and the Garden of the Gods is a fairly good, albeit dusty, route that generally takes about 20 minutes from town. To travel onward to Polihua Beach is another matter again, however; the road to the beach is rocky, narrow and suitable only for a 4WD, and even at that it's sometimes impassable. Depending on when the road was last graded, the trip

LANA'I

could take anywhere from 20 minutes to an hour.

KANEPU'U PRESERVE

The 590-acre Kanepu'u Preserve is the last native dryland forest of its kind across all Hawaii. Just 5 miles northwest of Lana'i City, the forest is home to 49 species of rare native plants, including the endangered *'iliahi* (Hawaiian sandalwood) and *na'u* (fragrant Hawaiian gardenia). You'll get a close-up look at many of them on the self-guided interpretive trail, which takes just 10 minutes to walk.

Dryland forests once covered 80% of Lana'i until introduced goats, deer and pigs made a feast of the foliage, leaving many native species near-extinct. Credit for saving this slice of the forest goes to ranch manager George Munro, who fenced hoofed animals out in the 1920s. In 1991 the Dole company granted the Nature Conservancy oversight of the forest in perpetuity.

GARDEN OF THE GODS

Think rocks, not green. Instead of flowers you'll find a dry, barren landscape of strange wind-sculpted rocks in ocher, pink and sienna. The colors change with the light – pastel in the early morning, rich hues in the late afternoon. How godly the garden appears depends on one's perspective. Some people just see rocks, while others find the formations hauntingly beautiful.

POLIHUA BEACH

This broad, 1.5-mile-long white-sand beach at the northwestern tip of the island takes its name from the green sea turtles that nest here. Polihua means 'eggs in the bosom.' Although the beach itself is gorgeous, strong winds kicking up the sand often make it uncomfortable, and water conditions can be treacherous.

TOP THREE WATER ADVENTURES

- Take a private **surfing lesson** (p415) from a local surfer.
- Dive the dramatic grottoes at **Cathedrals** (p415).
- Go eye to eye with a rainbow parrotfish at **Hulopo'e Beach** (p423).

MUNRO TRAIL

This exhilarating 8.5-mile adventure can be hiked, mountain biked or negotiated in a 4WD vehicle. For the best views, get an early start. Those hiking or biking should be prepared for steep grades and allow a whole day. If you're driving and the dirt road has been graded recently, give yourself two to three hours. However, be aware the road can become very muddy after heavy rain and Jeeps often get stuck. It's best to consider this as a fair-weather outing. Drivers also need to watch out for sheer drop-offs.

To start, head north on Hwy 44. About a mile past the Lodge at Koele, turn right onto the paved road that ends in half a mile at the island's **cemetery**. The Munro Trail starts left of the cemetery, passing through eucalyptus groves and climbing the ridge where the path is studded with Norfolk pines. These trees, a species that draw moisture from the afternoon clouds and fog, were planted in the 1920s as a watershed by naturalist George Munro, after whom the trail is named.

Before the Munro Trail was upgraded to a dirt road, it was a footpath. It's along this trail that islanders tried to flee Kamehameha the Great when he went on a rampage in 1778. Lana'ians made their last stand just above Ho'okio Gulch, about 2.5 miles from the start of the trail.

The trail looks down on deep ravines cutting across the east flank of the mountain, and passes **Lana'ihale** (3370ft), Lana'i's highest point. On a clear day, you can see all the inhabited Hawaiian Islands, except for distant Kaua'i and Ni'ihau, along the route. Stay on the main trail, descending 6 miles to the central plateau. Keep the hills to your left and turn right at the big fork in the road. Once you hit the cattle grate, pavement is close. The trail ends back on Manele Rd (Hwy 440) between Lana'i City and Manele Bay.

KAUMALAPA'U HIGHWAY

Kaumalapa'u Hwy (Hwy 440) connects Lana'i City to the airport before ending at Kaumalapa'u Harbor, the island's deepwater shipping harbor.

KAUNOLU

Perched on a majestic bluff at the southwestern tip of the island, the ancient fishing village of Kaunolu thrived until its abandonment in the mid-19th century. The waters of Kaunolu Bay were so prolific that even royalty came here to cast their nets.

Now overgrown and all but forgotten, Kaunolu boasts the largest concentration of stone ruins on Lana'i. A gulch separates the two sides of the bay, with remnants of former house sites on the eastern side, obscured by thorny kiawe. The stone walls of **Halulu Heiau** at the western side of the gulch still dominate the scene. The temple once served as a *pu'uhonua* (place of refuge), where taboo breakers fled to elude their death sentences.

Northwest of the heiau, a natural stone wall runs along the perimeter of the sea cliff. Look for a break in the wall at the cliff's edge, where there's a sheer 80ft drop known as **Kahekili's Jump**. The ledge below makes diving into the ocean a death-defying thrill, but is recommended for professionals only. In days past, Kamehameha the Great would test the courage of upstart warriors by having them leap from this spot. More recently, it has been the site of world-class Red Bull cliff-diving championships.

To get to Kaunolu, follow Kaumalapa'u Hwy (Hwy 440) past the airport, turning left at your first opportunity onto the road that circles around the south side of the airport. The turnoff to Kaunolu is marked by a yellow water pipe; turn right onto the dirt road, which leads south in the direction of the Palaloa lighthouse. The road washes out after rain storms so expect ruts deep enough to swallow a jeep, but you may be able to make it part of the way and walk the last mile or so.

Moloka'i

If wild, remote wilderness is your style, or you're interested in seeing how Hawaiians live, then you are in for a treat. This sparsely populated island way off most people's radar is a powerful place. And it is partly this inherent power that has helped Moloka'i remain such a secret destination.

The tiny community is completely interconnected, and the *kapuna* (elders) have taken their task to preserve and pass on traditional culture seriously.

Fishing, hunting, farming and ranching are big on this rural island, and people remain very connected to the land of their ancestors. Almost half of the population here claims Native Hawaiian ancestry.

If you're after a Hawai'i spruced up for tourism, Moloka'i is not your place. An active anti-development movement has kept tourism infrastructure to a minimum here – with only one 'resort' and two hotels to be counted, and cruise ships far from its shores.

But don't be turned off, 'The Friendly Isle' is receptive to visitors, especially those showing an interest in Hawaiian ways and genuine *aloha 'aina* (love of the land).

And the land is the reason to visit Moloka'i, with its secluded beaches, stunning green valleys, cascading falls and towering sea cliffs. There are endless ways to enjoy the outdoors here.

Experience the Hawaii of 50 years ago – visit Moloka'i.

HIGHLIGHTS

- Gaze down an impenetrable valley from the **Waikolu Lookout** (p444)
- Get wet at **Dixie Maru Beach** (p455)
- Watch the sun sink from remote **Mo'omomi Beach** (p447)
- Descend 1400 steps to the historical **Kalaupapa Peninsula** (p448)
- Enjoy local tunes and a sunset mai tai at **Hula Shores** (p438) at Kaunakakai
- Shock family with a **Post-a-nut** (p447) from Ho'olehua
- Hike through another world in the **Kamakou Preserve** (p444)
- Swim under the beautiful **Moa'ula Falls** (p442)
- Cruise the **world's highest sea cliffs** (p450)
- Paddle the **Pala'au Barrier Reef** (p432)

Mo'omomi Beach ★ | Kalaupapa Peninsula ★ | World's Highest Sea Cliffs ★
Dixie Maru Beach ★ | Ho'olehua ★ | Kamakou Preserve & Waikolu Lookout ★ | Moa'ula Falls ★
Kaunakakai ★ | ★ Pala'au Barrier Reef

| ■ POPULATION: 7404 | ■ AREA: 260 SQ MILES | ■ OFFICIAL FLOWER: WHITE KUKUI BLOSSOM |

CLIMATE

At Kaunakakai, the average daily temperature is 70°F in winter and 78°F in summer. The average annual rainfall is 14in. Still, these statistics say nothing of Moloka'i's microclimates. The east coast sees more rain and wind than Kaunakakai, with the most rain falling in Halawa Valley. Central Moloka'i at lower elevations is pretty sheltered from wind, while upper elevations get the most rain on the island. The West End sees little rain, but is exposed to the wind. For more climate info, see p556.

For the National Weather Service's recorded weather and marine forecasts, call ☎ 552-2477.

NATIONAL, STATE & COUNTY PARKS

A visit to the stunning Kalaupapa Peninsula, and a tour of the leprosy settlement there, all within Kalaupapa National Historical Park (p448), should not be missed. Lush Pala'au State Park (p448) promises a fantastic view and a walk in the woods. The county's Papohaku Beach Park (p455) makes for a great barbecue spot, while One Ali'i Beach Park (p436) is less inspirational.

Camping

Moloka'i's number-one place to camp, in terms of space, setup and scenery, is the county's Papohaku Beach Park (p455) on the West End. The next best would be church-owned Waialua Pavilion & Campground (p441) in East Moloka'i.

Camping at the county's windy, side-of-the-road One Ali'i Beach Park (p437) and

soggy grounded, isolated, Pala'au State Park (p448) should be left as last resorts. At press time, the Pala'au campground was closed for construction for an undetermined period. The site up near the Waikolu Lookout (p444) in the Kamakou Area is only convenient for those exploring the park in some depth. Free permits for up to five consecutive nights are issued through the mail by the **Department of Land & Natural Resources, Division of Forestry & Wildlife Office** (☎ 984-8100; Room 101, 54 South High St, Wailuku, HI 96793) on Maui. No permits are issued on Moloka'i, though you could try speaking with a park employee if you run into one.

Ki'owea Beach Park, beside the Kapua'iwa Coconut Grove (p436), would be sweet for camping, but permits are only issued in person by the **Hawaiian Homelands** (☎ 560-6104; permits $20) on Moloka'i, and it consistently books one year in advance.

State permits (up to five-day stay $5) are obtained from the State Park Division district office on Maui (p309), and cannot be obtained on Moloka'i. That said, if you're in a pinch, it's worth dropping by the **state-park caretaker's home** (☎ 567-6923), immediately north of the mule stables on Hwy 470.

County permits (adult/child under 18 $3/50¢) are issued by the **Department of Parks & Recreation** (Map p435; ☎ 553-3204; www.co.maui.hi.us; Mitchell Pauole Center, Ainoa St, Kaunakakai; ◷ 8am-1pm & 2:30-4pm Mon-Fri), either by mail or in person. Permits are limited to three consecutive days in one park, with a yearly maximum of 15 days.

If you forget a piece of camping equipment, Molokai Fish & Dive (p433) stocks plenty.

MOLOKA'I SURF BEACHES & BREAKS *Jake Howard*

What Moloka'i, one of the most breathtaking islands in Hawaii if not the entire Pacific, possesses in beauty, it lacks in waves. Unfortunately, due to shadowing from the other islands, there just isn't much in the way of consistent surf. Yet when the surf's up, keep in mind that the Friendly Isle encompasses the ideals of 'old Hawaii' in which family remains the priority, so remember to smile a lot and let the locals have the set waves.

On the western end of Moloka'i, winter swells bring surf anywhere between 2ft and 10ft (and, very rarely, 15ft). The break known as **Hale O Lono** is one such exposed area. It comprises several fun peaks and is the starting point for the annual 32-mile of the Moloka'i-to-O'ahu outrigger and paddleboard races. On central Moloka'i's north shore, there are decent waves to be had at Mo'omomi Bay (p447). Being an archaeological site, entry into the area is dependent on approval from the Department of Hawaiian Home Lands. For information ask at the airport when you arrive. **Tunnels**, on the southern side of Pu'u o Kaiaka (p454) to the west, is a popular break for bodysurfing and bodyboarding, and is also the only sand-bottom spot on the island.

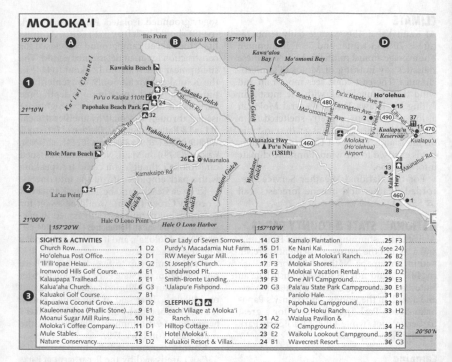

ACTIVITIES

Moloka'i has wild ocean waters, rough trails, remote rainforests and a burgeoning number of outdoor adventures. You can rent gear, go on (or tailor) tours (p432), and get activity information from the two general outfitters here, Moloka'i Outdoors (p436) and Molokai Fish & Dive (p436).

Water Activities

During the summer, waters are calm on the north and west shores, and made rough by the persistent trade winds on the south shore outside of the Pala'au barrier reef. Plan on getting out early, before the winds pick up. Winter storms make waters rough all around the island (outside of the reef), but, even so, the calm days between winter storms can be the best times to get out on the water.

SWIMMING

Most year-round spots for a swim are on the northeastern coast, with a cove at the 21-mile marker (p441) and Puko'o (p441) being the best. At the very eastern tip, Halawa Beach (p442) is good when seas are calm. On the

West End, Dixie Maru Beach (p455) is good for a dip almost all year, while Kawakiu Beach (p453) is only good in the summer.

FISHING

The sportfishing is incredible in Moloka'i waters, especially around the Penguin Banks of the southwestern tip. Bait casting is good on the southern and western shores, and torch fishing lives on in Kaunakakai's shallow waters. Boats dock and leave from the Kaunakakai Wharf. For boat charters, see p432.

KAYAKING

The northeastern shore, sheltered by the reef, is best for kayaking. At the very tip, Halawa Beach (p442) is a good launching point when seas are calm. In the summer, expert paddlers can venture around to the northern shore for a gander at the world's tallest sea cliffs (p450). Note that rental car companies do not allow kayaks to be carried atop their vehicles. Outfitters will deliver kayaks for fees ranging from $20 to $50. For kayak tours, see p432.

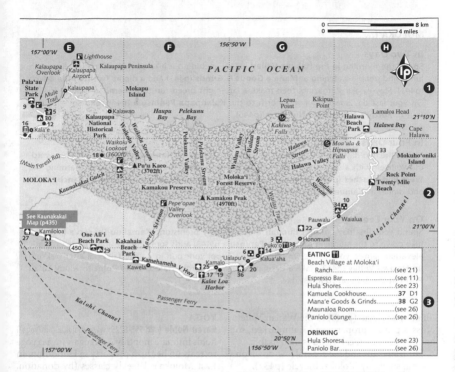

SURFING

When it's breaking, the stretch from Rock Point (p441) to Halawa Beach (p442) on the east end, and Kepuhi Beach on the West End are reliable spots. Leave Kawakiu Beach's winter waves to the experts. For secret spots, see the boxed text, p429. **Molokai Surf** (Map p435; ☎ 553-5093; Kamehameha V Hwy, Kaunakakai; ☑ 9:30am-5pm Mon-Sat) is a well-stocked shop. Moloka'i Outdoors (p432) and Molokai Fish & Dive (p432) can arrange surf lessons.

SNORKELING & SCUBA DIVING

Moloka'i's 32-mile Pala'au barrier reef – Hawaii's longest – lies along the south side of the island, promising good snorkeling and excellent diving in uncrowded waters all year long, when conditions allow. To reach the good spots, you'll need a boat. During the summer, the West End beaches are easily accessible, magical spots for snorkeling, with clear, flat waters. Here, Dixie Maru Beach (p455) and the rocks at Kawakiu Beach (p454) are both prime spots. Due to the prevailing weather conditions, diving is rare. For boat charters, see p432.

WINDSURFING & KITESURFING

Moloka'i has plenty of wind – advanced surfers can harness it in the Pailolo and Ka'iwi Channels. Moloka'i Outdoors (p436) offers windsurf lessons (two-hour lesson $50) in the summer.

WHALE WATCHING

Catch a glimpse of humpback whales breaching from December to March or April. For boat charters, see p432.

Land Activities

HIKING

Like the island itself, the hiking here is pristine, remote and rugged, with little traffic. Moloka'i's most-hiked trail is the stunning and dramatic descent to the Kalaupapa Peninsula (p448). The Nature Conservancy's Kamakou Preserve (p444) features unique rain-forest hikes in the island's untamed interior and out to scenic valley overlooks. At low tide, it's possible to do some beach walking from Hale O Lono Point (p452) to La'au Point. Hiring a guide is required to hike to the falls in lush Halawa Valley (p442). The Wailau Trail from

MOLOKA'I...

In Two Days
Spend the morning in the **Halawa Valley** (p442), including a hike to the waterfall. Follow with lunch and people-watching at **Mana'e Goods & Grinds** (p441) and a dip at **Twenty Mile Beach** (p441). Stay awake stargazing, then make a late-night bread run to **Kanemitsu Bakery** (p437). On your last day, make your way north to the **Kalaupapa Peninsula** (p448) and squeeze in a visit to **Purdy's Macadamia Nut Farm** (p446).

In Four Days
Follow the two-day itinerary, then spend your third day in the **Kamakou Preserve** (p444), rewarding yourself with a sunset cocktail at **Hula Shores** (p438). The next morning, nose around the **West End beaches** (p455), followed by an afternoon horseback ride at **Moloka'i Ranch** (p451) and dinner at **Kamuela Cookhouse** (p446), then take a ferry on to Maui.

On Your Feet
Spend your first day cruising through the seemingly prehistoric **Kamakou Preserve** (p444). A hike down to the stunning **Kalaupapa Peninsula** (p448) adds some culture and a more dramatic elevation gain to your game. On the third day, cool your bod in a waterfall pool after trekking up **Halawa Valley** (p442). Take a desolate beach walk from **Hale O Lono Point** to windy **La'au Point** at low tide on your last day.

'Ili'ili'opae Heiau (p440) to the Wailau Valley crosses private property and is unmarked, so going without a local friend is inadvisable.

For trail maps and the general low-down on hiking, swing by Molokai Bicycle (p434).

MOUNTAIN BIKING & CYCLING
There are over 40 miles of mountain biking trails on Moloka'i. The roads of the thick Moloka'i Forest Reserve (p444) are prime for mountain biking, as are trails on the arid West End, many with ocean views. Technically, the Moloka'i Ranch charges a $20 fee to ride on its property. As for cycling, pretty much all of Moloka'i's paved highways would make for a scenic ride, especially the northeastern end of Hwy 460. For trail maps and the general low-down, visit Molokai Bicycle (p434); see opposite for tours.

HORSEBACK RIDING
Horseback riding on the lush north shore is possible at Pu'u O Hoku Ranch (right) or saddle up on the wide open range at the Moloka'i Ranch (p451).

GOLF
The nine-hole Ironwood Hills Golf Club (p447) is such a honey you'll want to play it twice. There's also a more formal 18-hole Kaluakoi Golf Course (p454).

YOGA
Karen Noble (☎ 558-8225; www.molokai.com/yoga/) holds intimate monthly Ashtanga Vinyasa yoga retreats on her lush property in Honomuni in East Moloka'i. Weekly classes (by donation, $10 to $20 per class) are also offered, as are private retreats. Jump right into the ocean after finishing class in the open-air pavilion.

TENNIS
You don't need whites for the free, public tennis courts at the Mitchell Pauole Center (p436). Wavecrest Resort (p440) and Paniolo Hale (p454) condo complexes also have courts.

Tours
There is not a place on Moloka'i you can't take a tour to. Tours often have at least a three-person minimum, and booking ahead is advised. Most charter boats and small-time tour operators don't maintain offices. Book ocean outings for the first day of your stay to allow for rescheduling should conditions become unfavorable. For details on hikes led by the Nature Conservancy, see Tours (p445 and p447).

OPERATORS
For any activity Moloka'i's two major tour operators don't offer directly, they can contact someone who does. But remember, the more directly you book, the lower the price.

Molokai Fish & Dive (Map p435 ☎ 553-5926, 866-282-3483; www.molokaifishanddive.com; Ala Malama Ave, Kaunakakai; ☑ 8am-6pm Mon-Sat, to 2pm Sun) Offers kayaking ($89) and downhill-biking ($59) tours and a plumeria (frangipani) farm tour that includes lei making (adult/child $25/12). Pricey cultural hikes (per person $75) are led by local historian Lawrence Aki (for a list, see www.gomolokai.com). Horseback rides and targeting on Moloka'i Ranch are also offered (see p451). It runs scuba diving (2/3 tank $135/275), snorkeling, fishing and whale-watching excursions, as well as sunset and north shore sea-cliff cruises, either on its own twin-power Hobie Cat *Amalua* or in conjunction with boat charter outfits.

Molokai Off-Road Tours & Taxi (☎ 553-3369) offers half-/full-day highway tours ($75/95), as well as biking, kayaking and hiking tours. It no longer goes off-road.

Moloka'i Outdoors (Map p435; ☎ 553-4477, 877-553-4477; www.molokai-outdoors.com; 2nd fl, Moloka'i Center, Ala Malama Ave, Kaunakakai; ☑ 8:30am-4pm Mon, Wed & Thu, to 5pm Tue, Fri & Sat, 3-6pm Sun) This business offers a slew of water and land activities led by friendly islanders, including driving tours. Unique tours include a sunset paddle down the east coast, landing at the Hotel Moloka'i bar ($48), and visits to Moloka'i's farms (per person $70). Its boat tours are offered in conjunction with local charter outfits.

BOAT CHARTERS

Much of the Moloka'i coastline is only accessible by boat. The wild beauty of the impenetrable north-shore, home to the world's tallest sea cliffs (p450), is unforgettable. Boat charters generally leave from Kaunakakai Wharf and, if you're traveling in a group, can be tailored to your desires. Try one of these personable outfits:

Alyce C Sportfishing Charters (☎ 558-8377; www.alycecsportfishing.com) Half-day fishing charters start at $350, with a captain who knows where the fish are, and shares the catch in manageable fillets. Joe Reich has over 30 years of experience and also does whale-watching jaunts and round-island runs for $600.

Fun Hogs Sportfishing (☎ 567-6789; www.molokai fishing.com) Fish your heart out (4/6/8 hours $400/500/600) on *The Ahi,* a 27ft sportfishing boat. Snorkeling and whale watching (per person $65) are also offered. Personable Mike Holmes has 15 years of experience on Moloka'i, and has a two-person minimum.

Gypsy Sailing Adventures (☎ 553-4328; www.gypsy sailingadventures.com) New to Moloka'i, but with years of experience in Hawaiian waters, professional Richard and his 33ft catamaran *Star Gypsy* will take you on half-day ($300) or full-day ($550) cruises to snorkel, see dolphins or whale watch (per person $75).

Ma'a Hawai'i – Moloka'i Action Adventures (☎ 558-8184) Friendly Moloka'i native Walter Naki offers deep-sea fishing (half-day $400), whale watching and north-shore tours (per person $125), usually with a four-person minimum. This Hawaiian activist will also take you spear fishing or bow hunting.

GETTING THERE & AWAY

If you have time, taking the ferry from Maui is a more sociable and scenic experience than flying – the afternoon boat catches the sunset almost year-round, and in winter, breaching whales glorify the scene.

Air

Moloka'i (Ho'olehua) Airport (MKK; ☎ 567-6140; www .hawaii.gov/dot/airports/molokai/mkk) is pretty teeny: you claim your baggage on a long bench. Here off-island papers are sold, and there's a **visitor information desk** (☎ 567-6361) that is occasionally staffed.

Island Air (☎ 567-6115, 800-652-6541; www.islandair .com) operates all flights to Moloka'i, including those booked through Aloha or Hawaiian Airlines. It has eight daily flights between Moloka'i and Honolulu (25 minutes), and two between Kahului, Maui and Moloka'i (25 minutes).

Go! (☎ 888-435-9462; www.iflygo.com) has recently commenced service to Moloka'i.

Hop on a scheduled commuter flight, or charter your own flight with these puddle-jumpers. Cruising at around 1000ft, they are like a budget traveler's aerial tour:

George's Aviation (☎ 834-2120, outside Hawaii 866-834-2120; www.georgesaviation.com) Runs a daily flight between Honolulu and Moloka'i (one way/return $65/95) and Kahului and Moloka'i (one way/return $70/110) on Monday, Friday and Sunday.

Molokai Air Shuttle (☎ 567-6847, on O'ahu 545-4988) Runs six to eight flights daily between Honolulu and Moloka'i (Monday to Thursday one way/return $50/100, Friday to Sunday one way/return $65/110).

Pacific Wings (☎ 567-6814, 888-575-4546; www .pacificwings.com) Operates six flights between Honolulu and Moloka'i (one way $29), and one flight daily between Kahului and Moloka'i (one way $29).

Paragon Air (☎ 866-946-4744, on Maui 244-3356; www.paragon-air.com) Flies between Maui, Moloka'i and Kahului.

Boat

Molokai Ferry (Lahaina Cruise Company; ☎ 866-307-6524; www.molokaiferry.com; adult/child 4-12 $40/20) operates a morning and late-afternoon ferry between Lahaina (Maui) and Moloka'i's Kaunakakai

MOLOKA'I

Wharf. The 90-minute crossing through the Pailolo Channel can get choppy – likely why it's nicknamed Pakalolo Channel ('Marijuana Channel;' marijuana is proven to ease nausea). Buy tickets online, by phone or on the *Molokai Princess* a half-hour before departure.

GETTING AROUND

Renting a car here is essential, if you intend to fully explore the island. All of Moloka'i's highways and primary routes are good, paved roads.

Exploring unmarked roads is not advisable. Folks aren't too keen on strangers cruising around on their private turf and can get skittish. On the other hand, if there's a fishpond you want to see, and someone's house is between the road and the water, it's usually easy to strike up a conversation and get permission to cross. If you're lucky they might even share a little local lore and history with you, particularly the old-timers.

The University of Hawaii's joint *Moloka'i/Lana'i* map shows Moloka'i's topography; it's sold at stores in Kaunakakai. A more user-friendly lightweight fold-out map is Nelles' *Maui, Molokai, Lanai*. The bulky *Ready Mapbook of Maui County*, which includes coverage of Moloka'i and Lana'i, is an invaluable resource for adventurers.

To/From the Airport & Ferry

Two national car-rental chains are represented at the airport. Dollar provides free transportation between the ferry and the airport for its clients. Island Kine Auto Rental and Moloka'i Outdoors also do free transfers for clients between their offices and the airport or ferry. See right for more details on rental cars.

A taxi (see right) from the airport costs about $18 to Kaunakakai, $22 to the West End. Moloka'i Outdoors (p436) runs shuttles from the airport to Kaunakakai (per person $14), or Moloka'i Ranch and West End condominiums (per person $15), with a two-person minimum. **Molokai Off-Road Tours & Taxi** (☎ 553-3369) does the same for about double the price with no minimum. Make arrangements prior to arrival.

Bicycle

Molokai Bicycle (Map p435; ☎ 553-3931, 800-709-2453; www.bikehawaii.com/molokaibicycle; 80 Mohala St, Kaunakakai; ☾ 3-6pm Wed, 9am-2pm Sat) is a knowledgable shop renting out rigid and front-suspension mountain-bikes (per day $15 to $32, per week $70 to $148) and road bikes (per day $26 to $32, per week $148). Rentals include helmet, lock and water bottle. Car racks and child carriers and trailers are also rented. The owner, a school teacher, can meet clients outside of shop hours, and provide the inside scoop on biking, hiking and camping on Moloka'i. It's possible to arrange to pick up a bike at the airport or ferry. Fish & Dive (bikes per day $35 to $75) also rents rigid and full-suspension mountain-bikes. Rentals include maps, a pump and spare tube.

Car

Keep in mind that rental vehicles are technically not allowed 'off-road,' meaning any unpaved surface, and there can also be restrictions on camping. If you intend to explore more remote parts of the island, you'll at least need a vehicle with high clearance, and maybe even a 4WD. Book well in advance, especially if planning a weekend visit. There are gas stations in Kaunakakai and Maunaloa.

Budget (☎ 567-6877) and **Dollar** (☎ 567-6156, -6157) both have offices at the airport. See p571 for toll-free reservation numbers and general rental information.

Island Kine Auto Rental (Map p435; ☎ 553-5242, 866-527-7368; www.molokai-car-rental.com; 242 Ilio Rd, Kaunakakai; ☾ 7am-7pm), a local outfit in the northeast of Kaunakakai, rents out shiny compacts, jeeps, trucks and vans, including 4WDs. If you plan to off-road, there's a $50 to $75 fee, as well as a cleaning fee.

Moloka'i Outdoors (p436) rents older model cars, jeeps and vans, including 4WDs, from $24 to $65 per day.

Taxi

Both **Mid-nite Taxi** (☎ 553-5652) and **Hele Mai Taxi** (☎ 336-0967) service Moloka'i.

ROAD DISTANCES FROM KAUNAKAKAI		
Destination	Miles	Time
Halawa Valley	27	1½hr
Ho'olehua Airport	6.5	10min
Kalaupapa Trailhead	10	20min
Maunaloa	17	30min
Papohaku Beach	21.5	45min
Puko'o	16	20min
Twenty Mile Beach	20	30min

KAUNAKAKAI

pop 2726

Traffic moves slowly on the main drag in Kaunakakai, or 'town' as it's called locally. Drivers wave to neighbors, and stop for those backing out of parking places. No one is in a hurry. Shoppers weave along dusty Ala Malama Ave, ducking into buildings with run-down wooden false fronts that have a Wild West quality, and no flash whatsoever. Kaunakakai sits sheltered in a little divot in the mountains, protecting it from Moloka'i's pervasive winds.

INFORMATION

Emergency

Police, Fire & Ambulance (☎ 911)

Internet Access

Outpost (☎ 553-3377; 70 Makaena Pl; 🕑 9am-6pm Mon-Thu, to 4pm Fri, 10am-5pm Sun) Wi-fi access by donation, though there's almost no seating.

Stanley's Coffee Shop Gallery (☎ 553-9966; Ala Malama Ave; per 10min $1; 🕑 6am-4pm Mon-Fri) Faxes and printing too.

Laundry

Friendly Isle Laundromat (Kaunakakai Pl; 🕑 7am-9pm)

Laundramat (Makaena Pl; 🕑 7am-9pm) Bring your own soap to this oddly spelled place.

Media

In lieu of a daily newspaper, bulletin boards (on- and offline) around Kaunakakai are the prime source of news and announcements.

Molokai Advertiser-News (☎ 558-8253; www.molokaiadvertiser-news.com) Free weekly published on Wednesday.

Molokai Dispatch (☎ 552-2781; www.themolokaidispatch.com) Free weekly with an activist slant published each Thursday; watch the events calendar for local happenings.

Molokai Island Times (☎ 553-4443; www.molokaitimes.com) Free weekly published on Wednesday.

Medical Services

Molokai Drugs (☎ 553-5790; Molokai Professional Bldg, Kamoi St; 🕑 8:45am-5:45pm Mon-Fri, to 2pm Sat) Sells books, magazines and maps, along with pharmaceuticals.

Molokai General Hospital (☎ 553-5331; 280 Puali St; 🕑 24hr) Emergency services.

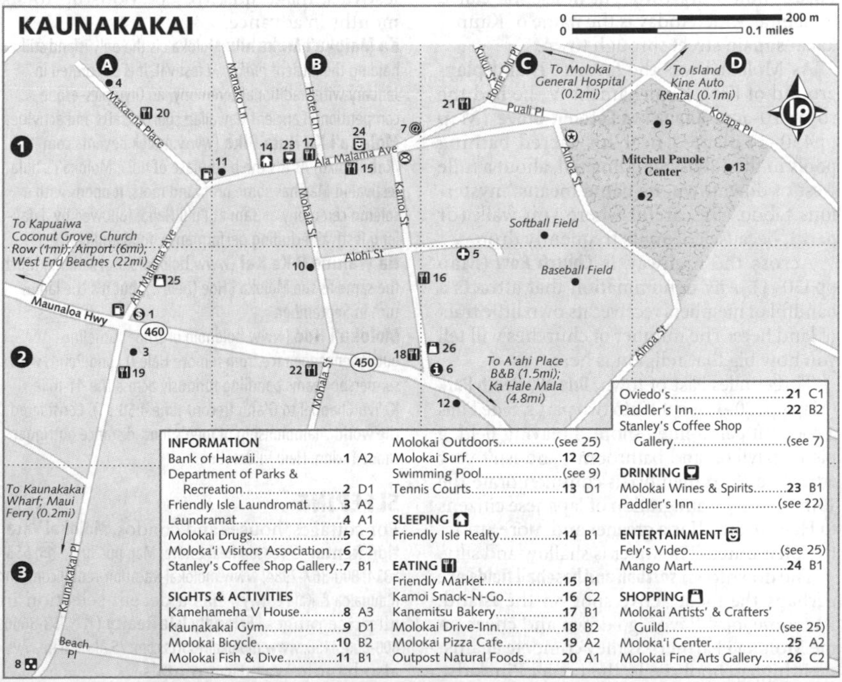
KAUNAKAKAI
0 200 m
0 0.1 miles
A
B
C
D
1
2
3
Makaena Place
Manako Ln
Hotel Ln
Kukui St
Home Olu Pl
To Molokai General Hospital (0.2mi)
To Island Kine Auto Rental (0.1mi)
Puali Pl
Kolapa Pl
Ala Malama Ave
Ainoa St
Mohala St
Kamoi St
Mitchell Pauole Center
Softball Field
Alohi St
Baseball Field
To Kapuaiwa Coconut Grove, Church Row (1mi); Airport (6mi); West End Beaches (22mi)
Ala Malama Ave
Maunaloa Hwy
460
450
To A'ahi Place B&B (1.5mi); Ka Hale Mala (4.8mi)
To Kaunakakai Wharf; Maui Ferry (0.2mi)
Kaunakakai Pl
Beach Pl
INFORMATION
Bank of Hawaii....1 A2
Department of Parks & Recreation....2 D1
Friendly Isle Laundromat....3 A2
Laundramat....4 A1
Molokai Drugs....5 C2
Moloka'i Visitors Association....6 C2
Stanley's Coffee Shop Gallery..7 B1
SIGHTS & ACTIVITIES
Kamehameha V House....8 A3
Kaunakakai Gym....9 D1
Molokai Bicycle....10 B2
Molokai Fish & Dive....11 B1
Molokai Outdoors....(see 25)
Molokai Surf....12 C2
Swimming Pool....(see 9)
Tennis Courts....13 D1
SLEEPING
Friendly Isle Realty....14 B1
EATING
Friendly Market....15 B1
Kamoi Snack-N-Go....16 C2
Kanemitsu Bakery....17 B1
Molokai Drive-Inn....18 B2
Molokai Pizza Cafe....19 A2
Outpost Natural Foods....20 A1
Oviedo's....21 C1
Paddler's Inn....22 B2
Stanley's Coffee Shop Gallery....(see 7)
DRINKING
Molokai Wines & Spirits....23 B1
Paddler's Inn....(see 22)
ENTERTAINMENT
Fely's Video....(see 25)
Mango Mart....24 B1
SHOPPING
Molokai Artists' & Crafters' Guild....(see 25)
Moloka'i Center....25 A2
Molokai Fine Arts Gallery....26 C2

MOLOKA'I

Money

Banks with 24-hour ATMs are one of Kaunakakai's few concessions to the modern world. **Bank of Hawaii** (☎ 553-3273; Ala Malama Ave) is the largest.

Post

Post office (☎ 553-5845; Ala Malama Ave)

Tourist Information

Moloka'i Visitors Association (MVA; ☎ 553-3876, on O'ahu 800-800-6367; www.molokai-hawaii.com; 2 Kamoi St) Efficient office has good accommodations information and the lowdown on goings on.

SIGHTS

The days when pineapples were loaded at **Kaunakakai Wharf** are gone, but the harbor still hums. A commercial interisland barge chugs in, skippers unload catches of mahimahi (white-fleshed fish), and a buff guy paddles his outrigger canoe. At dusk, the scene becomes sun-kissed. A roped-off area with a floating dock provides a kiddie swim area. On the west side of the wharf, near the canoe shed, are the stone foundations of oceanfront **Kamehameha V house**, now overgrown. The house was called 'Malama,' which today is the name of Kaunakakai's main street through town.

As Moloka'i was the favorite island playground of King Kamehameha V, he had the royal 10-acre **Kapua'iwa Coconut Grove** (Map pp430–1) planted near his sacred bathing pools in the 1860s. Standing tall, about a mile west of downtown, its name means 'mysterious taboo.' Be careful where you walk (or park), because coconuts frequently drop.

Across the highway is **Church Row** (Map pp430–1). Any denomination that attracts a handful of members receives its own little tract of land here. The number of churches will tell you how big that religion is here.

Three miles east of town, **One Ali'i Beach Park** (Map pp430–1) is split into two parks. Side I has a coconut palm–lined shore, a playing field, a picnic pavilion and bathrooms, and isn't very attractive. Two memorials commemorate the 19th-century immigration of Japanese citizens to Hawaii. Side II is a greener and more attractive picnic area. The water is shallow and silty.

The downtown **softball and baseball fields** are perhaps the most active spot on the island. For some local flavor, go down and cheer on the Moloka'i Farmers as they compete against their high-school rivals, the Lana'i Pinelads.

ACTIVITIES

While activities in Kaunakakai proper are limited, it is *the* place to rent gear or arrange tours.

Molokai Fish & Dive (☎ 553-5926, 866-282-3483; www.molokaifishanddive.com; 61 Ala Malama Ave; ☼ 8am-6pm Mon-Sat, 8am-2pm Sun) rents out snorkel kits ($10), bodyboards ($8), surfboards ($25 to $40) kayaks (single/double $30/42) and rods and reels ($10 to $14). It also sells camping equipment, rents bikes and runs tours (see p432).

Moloka'i Outdoors (☎ 553-4477, 877-553-4477; www.molokai-outdoors.com; 2nd fl, Moloka'i Center, Ala Malama Ave; ☼ 8:30am-4pm Mon, Wed & Thu, 8:30am-5pm Tue, Fri & Sat, 3-6pm Sun) rents windsurfing boards, tennis rackets and baby joggers, in addition to everything Fish & Dive rents. See p432 for its list of tours.

Kaunakakai Gym (☎ 553-5141; Mitchell Pauole Center; ☼ 11am-3pm Mon-Fri, 10am-3pm Sat) has an indoor swimming pool. There are also two outdoor tennis courts, free to the public. You're not likely to have to fight the crowds for a court.

FESTIVALS & EVENTS

If planning a visit during these culture-rich festivals, make hotel reservations up to six months in advance.

Ka Moloka'i Makahiki Moloka'i is the only island still holding the ancient *makahiki* festival. It is celebrated in January with traditional ceremony, an Olympics-esque competition of ancient Hawaiian sports, crafts and activities.

Moloka'i Ka Hula Piko (www.molokaievents.com /kahulapiko) As it's the birthplace of hula, Moloka'i's hula festival in May has some profound roots. It opens with a solemn ceremony at 3am at Pu'u Nana, followed by a day-long festival including performance, food and crafts.

Na Wahine O Ke Kai (www.holoholo.org/wahine) Much the same as the Moloka'i Hoe (below), but it's the ladies' turn in September.

Moloka'i Hoe (www.holoholo.org/hoe) Grueling outrigger canoe race from remote Hale O Lono Point, with six-person teams paddling furiously across the 41-mile Ka'iwi Channel to O'ahu (record time 4:50:31). Considered the world championship of men's long-distance outrigger canoe racing. Held in October.

SLEEPING

For cottages, houses and condos, **Molokai Vacation Rental** (Swenson Real Estate; Map pp430-1; ☎ 553-8334, 800-367-2984; www.molokai-vacation-rental.com; cnr Maunaloa & Kala'e Hwys) has a decent selection in all price ranges. **Friendly Isle Realty** (☎ 553-3666, 800-600-4158; www.molokairesorts.com; 75 Ala Malama Ave) also handles vacation rentals.

Budget

Camping is permitted on the right-hand side of the bathrooms at **One Ali'i Campground** (opposite) but drawbacks include strong winds, no privacy from the highway and late-night carousing. See p429 for permit details.

Midrange

A'ahi Place Bed & Breakfast (☎ 553-8033; www .molokai.com/aahi; backpacker's cabins $35, cabins incl breakfast $85) This very simple, clean cedar cottage is in a small subdivision, 1 mile east of Kaunakakai. Kind of like a camp cabin (with lots of wood and indirect light), this place has a full kitchen, two full-sized beds, a washing machine and garden lanai (patio). It's an open space best suited for one or two people. A simpler 'backpacker's' cabin is also available. Book two to three months in advance.

Ka Hale Mala (☎ /fax 553-9009; www.molokai-bnb.com; apt with/without breakfast $90/80) Enjoy the spaciousness of a 900-sq-ft, one-bedroom apartment with a fully equipped kitchen and living room with exposed-beam ceiling, with the benefit of a hot, gourmet breakfast. The two-floor house is surrounded by greenery (including fruit trees) thick enough to allow for total privacy. You can park right outside the private entrance to the ground-floor space, which is convenient for the mobility impaired. Cheryl, the friendly host, is a fount of local information and lives right upstairs. The space can sleep four, which can work out to be economical for a small group. It's about 5 miles east of Kaunakakai.

Hotel Moloka'i (Map pp430-1; ☎ 553-5347, reservations 800-535-0085; www.hotelmolokai.com; Kamehameha V Hwy; r $115-155, with kitchenette $175; 🏊) Gardens surround a compact group of two-story Polynesian-style buildings, angled to take advantage of the trade winds. Depending on the type, rooms can be spacious and have large lanai (or on the ocean-front for $10 extra), and all have ceiling fans and attractive tropical fabric accents. Upper floors have slanted walls and woven pandana-plant ceilings. The exterior of the hotel looks dated, and some of the interior furnishings are quite worn, making sunset cocktails at the hotel bar perhaps the best aspect of staying here.

Top End

Molokai Shores (Map pp430-1; ☎ 553-5954, reservations 800-535-0085; www.marcresorts.com; Kamehameha V Hwy; 1 bedroom units $124-190, 2-bedroom units $150-250; 🏊) The spacious, green grounds surrounding these three-story apartment blocks edged with flowering plants are this condo complex's best attribute. There's a barbecue area with picnic tables, a pool and even a putting green, all with an ocean view. All the units have a full kitchen, cable TV, lanai and ceiling fans, though they are individually owned, and some have atrocious 70s decor. The 3rd-floor digs have high cathedral ceilings.

EATING

Let it be known that you don't visit Moloka'i for the food. Renting a condo with kitchen facilities is a workable solution for food lovers. Keep in mind that the island's best restaurant is up in Kualapu'u, and its best lunch counter is out east.

Budget

Kamoi Snack-N-Go (☎ 553-5790; Molokai Professional Bldg, Kamoi St; scoops $2; ⏱ 10am-9pm Mon-Fri, 9am-9pm Sat, noon-9pm Sun) This convenience store is loaded with snacks and drinks and, more importantly, Honolulu-made Dave's ice cream. The Hawaiian Mud Pie and lychee flavors are stand-outs. There are daily specials – Monday is two-for-one scoops.

Kanemitsu Bakery (☎ 553-5855; Ala Malama Ave; ⏱ 5:30am-6:30pm Wed-Mon) Continue your sugar buzz at this dingy bakery responsible for the Moloka'i sweet bread and lavosh sold statewide. Its pastries, *malasada* (Portuguese doughnuts) and cookies are decent, and the cinnamon apple crisp ($1) is a favorite. Skip the attached restaurant. Every night but Monday, slip down the alley to the bakery's back door at 10pm and buy hot loaves sliced open with one of five spreads from the taciturn baker.

TOP FIVE EATS

- **Kamuela Cookhouse** (p446) for dinner specials with a touch of the gourmet, and prime-rib night
- **Mana'e Goods & Grindz** (p441) for great burgers and fresh-fish plate lunches under shady trees
- **Paddler's Inn** (p438) for an honest, good-value meal with no surprises
- **Hula Shores** (p438) for an open-air breakfast with a view of Lana'i
- **Oviedo's** (p438) for the best Filipino food in Hawaii

MOLOKA'I

Stanley's Coffee Shop Gallery (☎ 553-9966; Ala Malama Ave; sandwiches $3.50-6.25; ⏱ 6:30am-4pm Mon-Fri, to 2pm Sat) An Italian espresso machine pumps out the best coffee in town at this atmospheric diner-turned-coffee shop with white leather booths and walls loaded with oil paintings in gilded frames. The sandwiches and salads are all right, and the muffins are best when hot, but avoid the microwaved breakfast sandwiches.

Molokai Drive-Inn (☎ 553-5655; Kamehameha V Hwy; meals $3-7; ⏱ 6am-10pm) The Drive-Inn is always packed with folks picking up plate lunches, and greasy burgers and fries. The menu includes some odd-ball items like oxtail soup ($6.50), taco salad ($4), Thai spring rolls ($2.50) and, the old stand-by, fried saimin (ramen) noodles with veggies ($4.25). Serious talking story and gossip entertains while you wait.

Midrange

Molokai Pizza Cafe (☎ 553-3288; Kaunakakai Pl; meals $8-15, pizzas $9-14; ⏱ 10am-10pm Mon-Thu, to 11pm Fri & Sat, 11am-10pm Sun) Order at the counter or have a seat in the frigid, sterile dining room, at this pizza restaurant offering everything from salad and sub sandwiches to burgers and pasta. Wednesday is Mexican nights, which pulls in a small crowd. Don't bother with dessert.

Oviedo's (☎ 553-5014; Ala Malama Ave; plate lunch $9.50; ⏱ 10am-5:30pm Mon-Fri, to 4:30 Sat & Sun) The portions at this old-fashioned Filipino lunch counter are large enough to share. Bring your own veggies though because you aren't going to find many here.

Paddler's Inn (☎ 553-5256; 10 Mohala St, mains $14; ⏱ 6:30am-8:30pm) Filling a vacant niche, Paddler's Inn offers meals in a traditional restaurant setting. Basic egg and pancake plates are on the breakfast menu. For lunch and dinner, choose between sandwiches ($8.50), burgers ($8) and steak and seafood plates, with veggie stir-fry and chicken cordon bleu being the most unusual. Photos from the local paddling scene and the bar's noisy TV almost succeed in creating a sports-bar feeling here.

Hula Shores (Map pp430-1; ☎ 553-5347; Hotel Moloka'i, Kamehameha V Hwy; breakfast & lunch $5-9, dinner $14-20; ⏱ 7-10:30am & 11am-2pm daily, 6-9pm Sat-Thu, 4-9pm Fri) No one in town is very impressed with Hula Shores, but in the end, it's hard to deny Moloka'i's most-atmospheric restaurant. Breakfast is its strongest meal, with banana and/or mac (macadamia) nut pancakes and build-your-own omelettes on offer. At lunch you can order burgers and sandwiches, while

the dinner menu has the usual suspects as well as coconut shrimp and mac nut and *liliko'i* (passion fruit) chicken. Really, it's the lapping waves and tiki torches that make this place.

Groceries

Of Moloka'i's two grocery stores, **Friendly Market** (☎ 553-5595; Ala Malama St; ⏱ 8:30am-8:30pm Mon-Fri, to 6:30pm Sat) has the best selection, though the other is open on Sunday mornings. Dusty little **Outpost Natural Foods** (☎ 553-3377; 70 Makaena Pl; ⏱ 9am-6pm Mon-Thu, to 4pm Fri, 10am-5pm Sun) has some organic produce, and a fairly good selection of pricey packaged and bulk health foods. Its **deli** (⏱ 10am-3pm Mon-Fri) makes yummy and wholesome vegetarian burritos, sandwiches, burgers and salads.

DRINKING & ENTERTAINMENT

Unless you're going to the movies (see p453) there's not much to do on Moloka'i after you watch the sun go down.

Paddler's Inn (☎ 553-5256; 10 Mohala St; ⏱ 11-2am) The indoor bar is more attractive than the outdoor at Paddlers, though both have twinkling lights and locals glued to televised sports events. There's a daily happy hour from 4pm to 5pm, and occasionally live music shows out back.

Hula Shores (Map pp430-1; ☎ 553-5347; Hotel Moloka'i, Kamehameha V Hwy; ⏱ 10am-10:30pm) This poolside bar is Moloka'i's top spot for a sunset drink, replete with daily happy hour from 4pm to 6pm and live Hawaiian music nightly. Local *kapuna* (elders) gather around a table to play Hawaiian music on 'Aloha Fridays' from 4pm to 6pm – don't miss it. On Thursdays from 8pm to 10:30pm there's karaoke.

Molokai Wines & Spirits (☎ 553-5009; Ala Malama Ave; ⏱ 9am-8pm Sun-Thu, to 9pm Fri & Sat) The wide

---

PRETEND YOU LIVE HERE

You've probably noticed that most of what there is to do on Moloka'i happens outdoors, often in remote places. So how do you get down with the local folks, ie talk some story and really get a feel for what life is like here? Grab a paper and pore through it, looking for school benefits, church events or 4-H livestock competitions. Then go buy some crafts, get a taste of some home cooking, or cheer on your favorite heifer. You'll be supporting the local community and will likely make new friends in the process.

assortment of imported beers, Hawaiian micro-brews and inexpensive wines is impressive.

Mango Mart (☎ 553-8170; Ala Malama Ave; 8am-8pm Mon-Sat, to 6pm Sun) requires a credit card and ID to rent a DVD or VHS, while **Fely's Video** (Ground fl, Molokai Center, 110 Ala Malama Ave; 9am-5:30pm Mon-Sat) operates on trust. Both charge around $3.25.

SHOPPING

Saturday Market (Ala Malama Ave; 8am-3pm) Browse local crafts, try new fruits, and pick up some flowers at this weekly market in front of the Moloka'i Center. The majority of the vendors are present from 9am to 1pm.

Molokai Fish & Dive (☎ 553-5926, 866-282-3483; 61 Ala Malama Ave; 8am-6pm Mon-Sat, to 2pm Sun) Racks upon racks of island souvenirs are sold here, plus postcards, books and maps. It also stocks water-sports gear, fishing tackle, sunscreen and almost anything else you might need on Moloka'i.

Of the two local artists' galleries, **Molokai Fine Arts Gallery** (☎ 553-8520; 2 Kamoi St; 9am-5pm Mon-Sat) has higher quality work than **Molokai Artists' & Crafters' Guild** (☎ 553-8520; 2nd fl, Molokai Center, 110 Ala Malama Ave; 9:30am-5pm Mon-Fri, 8:30am-2:30pm Sat). Both stock handcrafted jewelry, lots of lei, paintings, photography, wood carving, etched glassware, pottery and Hawaiian instruments.

GETTING THERE & AROUND

Kaunakakai is a walking town, but **Mid-nite Taxi** (☎ 553-5652) and **Hele Mai Taxi** (☎ 336-0967) service Moloka'i, should you need one. **Rawlin's Chevron** (☎ 553-3214; cnr Hwy 460 & Ala Malama Ave; 6:30am-8:30pm Mon-Thu, to 9pm Fri & Sat, 7am-6pm Sun) has credit card-operated pumps, making it the only round-the-clock gas station on the island.

EAST MOLOKA'I

To an eye that appreciates grassy pastures, sweet old-style homes and craggy ocean cliffs, Moloka'i's eastern end is perhaps its most visually stimulating section. The tall green mountains reach like a backbone out to the eastern tip of the island, leaving a strip of flat land along the seafront that grows more and more narrow as the highway continues east. You'll find your speedometer gradually dropping as you take this 27-mile drive, getting caught up in the scenery and slowed by school kids dashing across the road and dogs crashed out in the middle of your lane.

Picturesque churches with tall steeples, an impressive heiau, ancient fishponds and a few historical sites will have you in and out of your car. Take an extended break for lunch or ice cream in Puko'o, and watch the characters come and go. Nap off your carb-coma on Twenty Mile Beach, and then go for a swim around the 21-mile marker.

Refreshed, you're ready to take on the winding, one-lane road, as it passes ocean cliffs and incredible views of Maui. The road then turns inland, the terrain grows lush, and you pass through ancient groves of primary forest before arriving at steep and lush Halawa Valley and its cascading falls.

The majority of Moloka'i's vacation rentals and B&Bs are on this southeastern stretch of the coast. There is no gas after Kaunakakai, so check your gauge before setting out.

KAWELA

Kakahaia Beach Park is a grassy strip wedged between the road and sea in Kawela, shortly before the 6-mile marker. It has a couple of picnic tables, and is a peaceful spot for a leg stretch or snack. This park is the only part of **Kakahai'a National Wildlife Refuge** (http://pacific islands.fws.gov/) open to the public. Most of the 40-acre refuge is inland from the road. It includes marshland, with a dense growth of bulrushes and an inland freshwater fishpond that has been expanded to provide a home for endangered birds, including the Hawaiian stilt and coot.

MOLOKA'I FOR NA KEIKI

Moloka'i isn't the most kid-friendly destination. Rough waters much of the year and few diversions mean children can become bored easily. But here are some ideas:

- **Fly a kite** (p453) The Big Wind Kite Factory offers free sport kite flying lessons.
- **Make lei** (p432) Tour a local plumeria (frangipani) farm.
- **Rent a house** (p436) Provides running-around room, plus a TV and VCR usually.
- **Ride horses** (p441) Roam the range at an organic farm.
- **Twenty Mile Beach** (p441) These shallow waters are protected from currents and waves.

MOLOKA'I

KAMALO

Only two of the four Moloka'i churches that missionary and prospective saint, Father Damien, built outside of the Kalaupapa Peninsula are still standing. One of them is **St Joseph's Church**, a small village about 10 miles east of Kaunakakai (the other is Our Lady of Seven Sorrows, right). This simple, one-room wooden church, dating from 1876, has a steeple and a bell, five rows of pews and some of the original wavy glass panes. A lei-draped statue of Father Damien and a little cemetery are beside the church.

Just over three-quarters of a mile after the 11-mile marker, a small sign, on the *makai* (seaward) side of the road, notes the **Smith-Bronte Landing**, the site where pilot Ernest Smith and navigator Emory Bronte safely crash-landed their plane at the completion of the world's first civilian flight from the US mainland to Hawaii. The pair left California on July 14, 1927, destined for O'ahu and came down on Moloka'i 25 hours and two minutes later. A little memorial plaque is set among the kiawe trees and grasses, in the spot where they landed.

Nearby, tucked back on a gorgeous 5-acre lot, the cottage at the **Kamalo Plantation** (☎ 558-8236; www.molokai.com/kamalo; d cottages incl breakfast $95) affords privacy in a garden setting shaded by towering trees. The full kitchen, barbecue and table on the lanai make it feel like home. The cottage is on the dark side, and casually furnished, but the peaceful surroundings are a real treat. The helpful owners are long-time island residents, and have a huge pack of smiling dogs that look after the property. These friendly folks also rent out the secluded **Moanui Beach House** (2-bedroom house $150) up the road. The A-frame house has cathedral ceilings, great beds and a newly renovated kitchen. Here you can step off the lanai and drag one of the house kayaks down to the ocean, while taking in incredible views of Maui.

'UALAPU'E

A half mile beyond Wavecrest Resort condo development, at the 13-mile marker, you'll spot **'Ualapu'e Fishpond** on the *makai* side of the road. This fishpond has been restored and restocked with mullet and milkfish, two species that were raised here in ancient times. After this, look to your left for the defunct **Ah Ping Store** and its old gas pump at the roadside. This classic building, of faded green wood with a red tin roof, was a Chinese-owned grocery store in the 1930s.

With a striking view of green mountains rising up behind, and the ocean lapping gently out front, the **Wavecrest Resort** (www.wavecrestaoao.com; 1-bedroom units per day/week $75/550, 2-bedroom units $125/750; ☒) enjoys a quiet location secluded from the highway. There's no beach out front, but there are tennis courts on-site and attractive grounds dotted with flowers. Each condo has a roomy living room with a sofa bed, a full kitchen, an entertainment center and lanai. Breezes blow right through the oceanfront units, which enjoy great views of Maui and Lana'i. Units are rented either directly from the owners via the website, or through Molokai Vacation Rentals or Friendly Isle Realty (p436).

KALUA'AHA

The village of Kalua'aha is less than 2 miles past Wavecrest. The ruins of **Kalua'aha Church**, Molokai's first Christian church, are a bit off the road and inland but just visible, if you keep an eye peeled. It was built in 1844 by Moloka'i's first missionary, Harvey R Hitchcock. **Our Lady of Seven Sorrows** (☺ service 7:15am Sun) is a church a quarter of a mile past the Kalua'aha Church site. The present Our Lady of Sorrows is a reconstruction from 1966 of the original woodframe building, constructed in 1874 by the missionary Father Damien. From the church parking lot, a fine view of an ancient **fishpond** and the hazy high-rise–studded shores of west Maui provide an incongruous backdrop.

'ILI'ILI'OPAE HEIAU

'Ili'ili'opae is Moloka'i's biggest and best-known heiau, and is thought to be the second largest in Hawaii. It also might possibly be the oldest religious site in the state. Over 300ft long and 100ft wide, the heiau is about 22ft high on the eastern side, and 11ft high at the other end. The main platform is strikingly level. Historians believed the original heiau may have been three times its current size, reaching out beyond Mapulehu Stream.

Once a *luakini* (temple of human sacrifice), 'Ili'ili'opae is today silent except for the chittering of birds. African tulip trees line the trail to the site, a peaceful place filled with mana (spiritual power), whose stones still seem to emanate vibrations of a dramatic past. Remember, it's disrespectful to walk across the top of the heiau. In doing so you may succumb to heat exhaustion, too, and risk twisting an ankle.

Visiting this heiau is a little tricky, since it's on private property. The best idea is to park on the highway (to avoid upsetting the neighbors) and walk up the short dirt driveway. Pass the round about around a patch of trees, and continue up the rocky road. Soon after, you'll see a trail on the left-hand side, opposite a house, that'll take you across a streambed. Head to the steps on the northern (right) side of the heiau.

The turnoff is on the *mauka* (inland) side of the highway, just over half a mile past the 15-mile marker, immediately after Mapulehu Bridge.

PUKO'O

Puko'o was once the seat of local government (complete with a courthouse, a jail, a wharf and post office) but the center of island life shifted to Kaunakakai, when the plantation folks built that more centrally located town. Nowadays, Puko'o is a sleepy, slow-paced place just sitting in a bend on the road (near 'Ili'ili'opae Heiau), but has little surprises like the cozy **beach** accessible just before the store, near the 16-mile marker. Take the short, curving path around the small bay, where fish leap out of the water, and you'll come to a sweet beach with swimmable waters, backed by kiawe and ironwood trees.

Sleeping & Eating

The incredible panoramic ocean views and surrounding green fields will cause you to instantly slow your pace at the one-bedroom **Hilltop Cottage** (☎ 558-8161, cell phone 336-2076; www .molokaihilltopcottage.com; Kamehameha V Hwy; d cottages 2-nights $450; ⬛). Sunbathe or stargaze on the wraparound lanai that's almost as big as the living space, or let the breeze blow you into the attractively decorated living room. The kitchen couldn't be any more well-stocked, and the onsite washer will keep those queen-size sheets constantly fresh.

Don't miss the chance to eat at **Mana'e Goods & Grindz** (☎ 558-8498; Kamehameha V Hwy; sandwiches $3-5.50, plates $7-8.50; ⏱ store 8am-5pm daily, counter 9am-5pm Mon-Fri, 8am-5pm Sat & Sun). The grill makes sandwiches and burgers (try the *'ahi* burger) that aren't too greasy, and *'ono* (delicious) plate lunches that are the island's best. Tall trees and green surroundings make this one of Moloka'i's prettiest places to chow down. The attached market is small though well-stocked and rents DVDs. It's near the 16-mile marker

WAIALUA

If you don't slow down, you'll miss wee Waialua, a little roadside community just past

the 19-mile marker. The attractive **Waialua Congregational Church**, which marks the center of the village, was built of stone in 1855. Nearby Waialua Beach is the site of Moloka'i's *na keiki* (children's) surf competitions.

About 1200yd after the 19-mile marker, begin looking for the remains of a stone chimney, a remnant of the **Moanui Sugar Mill**, which processed sugar until the mill burned down in the late 1800s. The ruins are about 50ft inland from the road, just before a stand of tall ironwood trees. Onward north from there, the road is spaghetti-thin, winding its way through land forlorn and mysterious, with the turquoise surf and a large fish pond just below.

If you want beach over this way, look no further than the 20-mile marker, from where a stretch of white sand called **Twenty Mile Beach** pops up right along the thin roadside. There are pull-offs for parking. Protected by the barrier reef, waters are calm, but at low tide can be too shallow for much more than a splash.

The pointy clutch of rocks sticking out, as the road swings left before the 21-mile marker, is called, appropriately enough, **Rock Point**. This popular surf spot is the site of local competitions and it's the place to go if you're looking for east-end swells. For our money, the best swimming out here is about 500yd beyond the 21-mile marker.

Sleeping

Waialua Pavilion & Campground (☎ 558-8150; jsimms@aloha.net; Kamehameha V Hwy; site per person $10) The Church maintains a grassy, oceanfront area with barbecue grills, bathrooms and showers, though little privacy from the highway. A pavilion with full kitchen is rented separately. Reserve in advance; ask for Joanne.

Dunbar Beachfront Cottages (☎ 558-8153, 800-673-0520; www.molokai-beachfront-cottages.com; 2-bedroom cottages $170) The layout and furnishings are simple and functional at these two vacation cottages on secluded private beaches in Kainalu, around the 18-mile marker. Each cottage sleeps four people and comes with a fully equipped kitchen, TV, VCR, ceiling fans, a laundry, lanai and barbecue grills. The Pu'unana unit sits up high and has lots of windows taking in the delicious sea views.

WAIALUA TO HALAWA

After the 21-mile marker, the road starts to wind upwards. This is where the driving starts to get hairy and the vistas more varied. Tall grasses right at the edge threaten to reclaim the road, while ironwood trees and spiky sisal plants dot the surrounding hills. A bike ride here would be awesome. It's a good paved road – the problem is there's not always enough of it. In places, including some cliff-hugging curves, this road is only wide enough for one car, and you'll need to do some horn tooting. The road levels out just before the 24-mile marker, where there's a view of the bulbous islet of **Mokuho'oniki**, a seabird sanctuary.

The fenced grassland in this area is part of **Pu'u O Hoku Ranch** – at 14,000 acres, it's Molokai's second-largest ranch. Founded by Paul Fagan of Hana, the name means 'where hills and stars meet' – Jimmy Stewart and JFK are among the famous faces to have visited here. This is a certified organic farm growing tropical fruits and *'awa* (kava).

A hidden grove of sacred *kukui* (candlenut trees) on the ranch property marks the grave of the prophet Lanikaula, a revered 16th-century *kahuna* (priest, healer or sorcerer). One of the reasons the battling armies of Maui and O'ahu steered clear of Moloka'i for centuries was the powerful reputations of *kahuna* like Lanikaula, who were said to have been able to pray their enemies to death. Many islanders claim to have seen the night lanterns of ghost marchers bobbing along near the grove.

The ranch offers guided **horseback riding** (☎ 558-8109; www.puuohoku.com; 1hr/2hr rides $55/75) through wooded trails and windswept pastures. It's 4-hour ride to the beach for snorkeling ($120) is terrific in the winter, when humpback whales are migrating. There's a two-person minimum, and making reservations 24 hours in advance is appreciated.

After passing the 25-mile marker, the jungle closes in, and the scent of eucalyptus fills the air. About 1.25 miles after the 25-mile marker, there's a turnoff with a panoramic view of Halawa Valley and Moa'ula and Hipuapua Falls; walk down the road a bit more for an even better vista. In the winter, this is a good place to watch for whales breaching.

There are lots of 'beep as you go' hairpin bends on the one-lane road that leads down to the valley, but the road is in good condition and the incline is reasonably gradual. No worries.

Sleeping & Eating

Pu'u O Hoku Ranch (☎ 558-8109; www.puuohoku.com; 2-bedroom cottages per day/week $140/840; 4-bedroom house $180/1080, extra guest per night $20; 🖳) For true East

End seclusion, book a stay in one of the ranch's rustic cabins with a full kitchen. The Cottage has an enclosed lanai and honey-colored bamboo furniture. The larger Grove House has a stone fireplace and Balinese furnishings, and is perfect for a family getaway. Both enjoy the ranch's incredible views and are surrounded by towering trees and rolling grassland. Also available is an entire lodge, with a fireplace, a swimming pool and sleeping accommodations for 22. Rates are based on two- and four-person occupancy for the cottage or house, respectively; two-night minimum stay required.

A barren store at the ranch gate sells kava, a few snacks and sodas.

HALAWA VALLEY

Halawa Valley enjoys end-of-the-road isolation – which residents guard jealously – and stunningly gorgeous scenery. Little remains of its three heiau sites, two of which are thought to have been *luakini*, and you'll probably feel the charge down here. In the mid-19th century, the fertile valley had a population of about 500 and produced most of Moloka'i's taro, as well as many of its melons, gourds and fruits. Taro production declined over the years, coming to an abrupt end in 1946, when a massive tsunami swept up Halawa Valley, wiping out the farms and much of the community. A second tsunami washed the valley clean in 1957. Only a few families now remain.

Sights & Activities

It's possible to swim at the base of the 250-foot, twin **Moa'ula and Hipuapua Falls**, which cascade down the back of this lush valley. They are reached via a straightforward 2-mile trail lined with historical sites. To protect these sites, and because the trail crosses private property, visiting the falls requires hiring a local guide. The $75 per person fee is inappropriately high, but consider it a donation to the local economy. For indepth historical explanation, go with Lawrence Aki, a third-generation valley resident. He books through Molokai Fish & Dive (see p436). For a tour for the senses, go with valley resident **Kalani Pruet** (☎ 336-1149; kalanipruet@yahoo.com), who concludes his tours with a visit to his flower farm and a smoothie made from fruit he gathers along the hike. Prepare for voracious mosquitoes.

Halawa Beach was a favored surfing spot for Moloka'i chiefs, and remains so today for local kids. This beach park has double coves separated by a rocky outcrop, with the north side a bit more protected than the south. When the water is calm, there's good swimming and folks launch sea kayaks here, but both coves are subject to dangerous rip currents when the surf is heavy. There can also be strong currents whenever Halawa Stream, which empties into the north cove, is flowing heavily.

Up from the beach, green Halawa Beach Park has picnic pavilions, rest rooms and running water – treat water before drinking. Although gorgeous, there's an eerie, foreboding quality here and locals may show some hostility to outsiders.

Sunday services are still occasionally held in Hawaiian at the valley's absolutely adorable green-and-white **church**, where visitors are welcome anytime (the door remains open).

CENTRAL MOLOKA'I

Central Moloka'i takes in the Ho'olehua Plains, which stretch from Mo'omomi Beach in the west to the former plantation town of Kualapu'u. Extraordinarily fitting for the heart of Moloka'i, this part of the island also has forested interiors leading to Kamakou Preserve, a unique rain forest that includes the island's highest mountain. On the north side of central Moloka'i is Kalaupapa Peninsula, the site of Hawaii's infamous leprosy colony.

Certainly the most trodden route in central Moloka'i is the drive up Hwy 460, past the Kamakou Preserve mountain-road turnoff, and onto Hwy 470, past the coffee plantation, restored sugar-mill museum, mule stables and the trailhead down to Kalaupapa Peninsula. The road ends at Pala'au State Park, site of the Kalaupapa Overlook, where you'll find one of the most captivating views on Moloka'i.

KAMAKOU AREA

If you can help it, do not leave Moloka'i without spending time in The Nature Conservancy's Kamakou Preserve, or at least a trip up to the Waikolu lookout. Exploring this secret side of Moloka'i will be an experience you will never forget. It's not just the chance to gaze down two deep valleys on the island's stunning and impenetrable northern side that makes this area so worthwhile. It's also the opportunity to explore a near-pristine rain forest that is home to more than 250 native plants (over 200 endemic) and some

BRINGING HOME THE BACON

The hunting on Moloka'i is done mostly for a good reason. The animals hunted cause deforestation, and subsequent sediment build-up on the reefs, which stifles and kills living coral.

Hawaiians have a long tradition of hunting feral pigs, and here on Moloka'i, it's still done the old-school way: hunting dogs chase down and surround the pig, nipping at it, until the hunter grabs the pig's back leg and thrusts a knife between the shoulder blades into its heart. As for feral goats, the Nature Conservancy's helicopter drops hunters in remote parts of the mountains, then scares the goats toward the hunters, who do their best to take them out.

The Axis deer roaming the island are descendants of eight deer sent from India in 1868 as a gift to King Kamehameha V. There's nothing unusual about the way their population is kept in check: the good ol' rifle. Hunting wild turkey, pheasant, quail and partridge is also rather common.

of Hawaii's rarest birds. The heights you'll reach are not the 4961ft of Kamakou Peak, the island's highest peak, but they are high and wet enough to create a landscape that is like something from prehistoric times.

The steep mountains here effectively prevent rain clouds from entering Moloka'i's central plains (they can also keep people out of the area, so a 4WD is essential). Incredibly, more than 60% of Moloka'i's water supply comes from these forests. In the 1960s a 5-mile-long tunnel was bored into the west side of Waikolu Valley. It now carries up to 28 million gallons of water daily to the Kualapu'u Reservoir.

Hawaiian women used to hike up to the top of Kamakou to bury their afterbirth. According to folklore, this ritual would lead the newly born children to reach great heights in life. These days, the few islanders that do come to the forest come to pick foliage for lei, as well as to hunt (see the boxed text, above).

Orientation

About 5.5 miles after you turn off the highway onto Maunahui Rd, you'll cross into the Moloka'i Forest Reserve. A short loop road on the left leads to a former Boy Scout camp that's now used by The Nature Conservancy. After

MOLOKA'I

a further 1.5 miles, there's an old water tank and reservoir off to the left. Another 2 miles brings you to the Sandalwood Pit, and one mile past that to Waikolu Lookout and boundary of the Kamakou Preserve.

Moloka'i Forest Reserve

As you climb and enter the Moloka'i Forest Reserve, the landscape starts off shrubby and dusty, becoming dark, fragrant woods of tall eucalyptus, with patches of cypress and Norfolk pines. Don't bother heading down the roads branching off Maunahui Rd, as the scenery will be exactly the same. Although there's no evidence of it from the road, the Kalamaula area was once heavily settled. It was here that Kamehameha the Great (Kamehameha I) knocked out his two front teeth in grieving the death of a female high chief, whom he had come to visit.

If you're up for talking story with a long-time island character, and checking out his unique (and not cheap) work, stop in on **Robin the woodcarver**. You'll see his gates on the left.

SANDALWOOD PIT

A few miles on you'll pass the centuries-old Sandalwood Pit (Lua Na Moku 'Iliahi), nothing more than a grassy depression on the left side of the road. In the early 19th century, shortly after the lucrative sandalwood trade began, the pit was hand dug to the exact measurements of a 100ft-long, 40ft-wide and 7ft-deep ship's hold, and filled with fragrant sandalwood logs cleared from the nearby forest.

In the frenzy to make a quick buck to pay for alluring foreign goods, the *ali'i* (royalty) forced the *maka'ainana* (commoners) to abandon their crops and work the forest. When the pit was full, the wood was strapped onto the backs of the laborers, who hauled it down to the harbor for shipment to China. The sea captains made out like bandits, while Hawai'i was stripped of its sandalwood forests. After all the mature trees were cut down, the *maka'ainana* pulled up virtually every new sapling, in order to spare their children the misery of another generation of forced harvesting.

WAIKOLU LOOKOUT

At 3600ft, Waikolu Lookout provides a view into the steep Waikolu Valley and out to the ocean beyond, whose depth and beauty will take your breath away. If it's been raining recently, you'll be rewarded with the numerous waterfalls streaming down the cliff sides and filling the valley with their sound. Waikolu means 'three waters' – presumably named for the three drops in the main falls at the back of the valley. Morning is best for clear views, but if it's foggy, have a snack at the picnic bench and see if it clears.

The wide, grassy **Waikolu Lookout campground** is directly opposite the lookout. If you can bear the mist and cold winds that sometimes blow up from the canyon, especially during the afternoon and evening, this could make a base camp for hikes into the preserve. The site has a picnic pavilion, and the park is working on a bathroom, but the project doesn't look like it is moving too quickly. Bring water. No open fires are allowed and camping permits are required (see p429).

Kamakou Preserve

In 1982 Moloka'i Ranch conferred on the Nature Conservancy the rights to manage the Kamakou Preserve, which starts immediately beyond the Waikolu Lookout. Its 2774 acres of native ecosystems include cloud forest, bogs, shrub land and habitat for many endangered plants and animals.

Much of the preserve is forested with *'ohi'a lehua*, a native tree with fluffy red blossoms, whose nectar is favored by native birds. It is home to two rare avian species that live only on Moloka'i, the Moloka'i creeper and Moloka'i thrush, as well as the bright red *'apapane* (Hawaiian honeycreeper), yellow-green *'amakihi* (native bird) and pueo (Hawaiian owl). Other treasures include tree ferns, native orchids and silvery lilies.

The Nature Conservancy asks visitors to sign in and out at the preserve entrance. Check out the sign-up sheet, where visitors write short entries on everything from car breakdowns to trail conditions and bird sightings. Occasionally, portions of the preserve are closed and posted notices will communicate this.

Pepe'opae Trail is Kamakou's main attraction. Almost the entire mile-long trail is along an extremely narrow boardwalk that feels at times like tightrope walking. It is covered with a coarse metal grating to prevent hikers from slipping, but you should still wear shoes with a good grip. The hike is through a nearly undisturbed Hawaiian montane bog, a miniature forest of stunted trees and dwarfed plants that feels like a world you've never before visited. This bog receives about 180in of rain each year, making it one of the wettest regions in the Hawaiian Islands. The trail ends at the **Pelekunu Valley Overlook**, where you'll enjoy a valley view of fantastic depth, and, if it's not foggy, the ocean beyond.

There are two ways to reach the Pepe'opae Trail. The easiest is to walk or 4WD from Waikolu Lookout about 2.5 miles along the main jeep road to the main trailhead. It's a nice forest walk that takes just over an hour. When in doubt, stay to the left. Exploring the side roads by car is not advised as getting stuck is practically assured. At the top of the road a sign marks the start of the trail.

The second and far rougher way is to take the **Hanalilolilo Trail**. This trail, which is muddy and poorly defined, begins on the left side of the road about five minutes' walk past the Waikolu Lookout, shortly after entering the preserve. The Hanalilolilo Trail climbs 500ft through a rain forest of moss-covered ohia trees and connects with the Pepe'opae Trail after 1.5 miles. Head left on the Pepe'opae Trail, and it's about a half-mile walk up to the Pelekunu Valley Overlook. Give yourself a good half-day to complete the round-trip hike.

Bring rain gear, as the trails in this rainforest preserve can be very muddy.

TOURS

Excellent monthly hikes with the **Nature Conservancy** (☎ 553-5236; Molokai Industrial Park, 23 Pueo Pl; www.nature.org/hawaii; suggested donation $25; ✆ 1st or 2nd Sat of the month) offer insights into the preserve's history and ecology. Transportation is provided to/from the preserve. Hikes have an eight-person maximum, and tend to book up around four months in advance. Also ask about volunteer workdays, if you're seriously interested.

Getting There & Away

Kamakou is protected in its wilderness state in part because the rutted dirt road leading to it makes it hell to reach. In dry weather, it can be possible to make it to the lookout in a two-wheel drive with good clearance, but if it's been raining at all, it's not advisable to try. In places where the road is narrow, a stuck car can block the whole road and it's ugly trying to maneuver out of that mud – especially due to drop-offs at the road's edge. During the winter (the rainy season) the road tends to get progressively more rutted until it's regraded in summer. If you want to drive all the way to

the Pepe'opae Trailhead, a 4WD is essential, and that's not just cover-your-ass guidebook jive. Even with a 4WD, if you're not used to driving in mud and on steep grades, the final section of the road can be challenging

If your group is small and you are charming, try dropping by the Nature Conservancy office (see left) and asking about catching a ride up in the back of a work truck. Alternately, **Richard Davis** (☎ 567-9136; per person $25) will take you up on ATVs and give you time to walk the trail. Ride on his ATV or drive your own.

If you decide to drive, give the Nature Conservancy a call first to check on road conditions. The turn-off for the Kamakou Area is between the 3- and 4-mile markers on Hwy 460, immediately east of the Manawainui Bridge. The paved turn-off is marked with a sign for the Homelani Cemetery. The pavement quickly ends, and the road deteriorates as it goes. The 10-mile drive from the highway to Waikolu Lookout takes about 45 minutes to drive, depending on road conditions.

KUALAPU'U

Kualapu'u is the name of both a 1017ft hill, and the little village at a crossroads that has grown up nearby. At the base of the hill is the world's largest rubber-lined reservoir, which has a capacity of up to 1.4 billion gallons of water piped in from the rainforests of eastern Moloka'i. The reservoir is the only source of water for the Ho'olehua Plains and the dry West End.

RAINY MOLOKA'I

- Catch a matinee at **Maunaloa Town Cinemas** (p453)
- Hang out with a cup of joe at **Stanley's coffee shop & gallery** (p437)
- Treat yourself to a **spa treatment** at The Lodge (p452)
- Hunt for one-of-a-kind finds at the **Plantation Gallery** (p453)
- Try one of everything at **Kanemitsu Bakery** (p437)
- Catch the game with a beer at **Paddler's Inn** (p438)
- Hole up with a **movie rental** (p438)
- Get wet!

Del Monte set up headquarters here in the 1930s, and Kualapu'u developed into a pineapple-plantation town. The center of Del Monte's activities covered the spread between Kualapu'u and the nearby Ho'olehua homesteads. The pineapple ruled for nearly 50 years, until Del Monte pulled out of Moloka'i in 1982, and the economy crumbled.

While farm equipment rusted in overgrown pineapple fields, small-scale farming began developing more intensively: watermelons, dryland taro, macadamia nuts, sweet potatoes, seed corn, string beans and onions. The soil is so rich here, some feel Moloka'i has the potential to be Hawaii's 'breadbasket.' Even so, plantation mentality is difficult to shake, and the economy was in need of a cash crop. In 1991 coffee saplings were planted on formerly fallow pineapple fields, and now cover some 600 acres.

Stop by **Moloka'i Coffee Company** (☎ 567-9064, 567-9490; www.molokaicoffee.com; cnr Hwys 470 & 490; ☺ 8am-5pm Mon-Fri, to 4pm Sat, to 2pm Sun) gift store for free samples of several types of its rich Moloka'i brews. It offers a **Morning Espresso Walking Tour** (adult/child $20/10; ☎ 10am Mon-Fri, 11am Sat & Sun) and a **Coffee Beans Tour** (adult/child $35/10; ☎ 8am & 1pm Mon-Fri) in a mule-drawn wagon through their 255-acre farm. Both tours include a 7oz bag of coffee, a processing explanation and an activity book for kids, and are weather permitting.

Eating & Drinking

Kamuela Cookhouse (☎ 567-9655; Hwy 490; breakfast & lunch $4-8.50, dinner $8-18; ☺ 7am-8pm Tue-Sat, to 2pm Mon) The food at this down-home café is hands down Moloka'i's best value, and likely its tastiest too. You might doubt that such a funky little place, with plastic folding chairs and the local radio blaring, would be capable of pulling off the likes of crusted 'ahi (yellowfin tuna) in a lime cilantro sauce ($18) or 'opakapaka (pink snapper) in a lilikoi sauce ($18). But leave your doubts at the swinging screen door. The place is packed on Thursdays, for baby back ribs in a homemade guava BBQ sauce and live music. Save room for the mac-nut and chocolate-chip pie ($3.50), if you can. No credit cards are accepted, and you've got to bring your own alcohol.

Espresso Bar (☎ 567-9241; cnr Hwys 470 & 490; snacks $2-5; ☺ 7am-4pm Mon-Fri, 8am-4pm Sat, to 2pm Sun) Moloka'i Coffee Company's café sells simple sandwiches, salads and bagels, Danishes, plus any coffee drink you might desire, at fair prices. Cooling off on the deck after the Kalaupapa Peninsula hike is highly recommended.

The view over the parking lot isn't great, but your options are seriously limited up here!

HO'OLEHUA

Ho'olehua is the dry plains area that separates eastern and western Moloka'i. Here, in the 1790s, Kamehameha the Great trained his warriors in a year-long preparation for the invasion of O'ahu.

Ho'olehua was settled as an agricultural community in 1924, as part of the first distribution of land under the Hawaiian Homes Commission Act, which made public lands available to Native Hawaiians. By 1930, more than half of Moloka'i's ethnic Hawaiian population was living on homesteads.

The first homestead was attempted closer to the coast, at Kalaniana'ole, but it failed when the well water – pumped to irrigate crops – turned brackish. Many of those islanders then moved north to Ho'olehua, where homesteaders were already planting pineapple, a crop that required little water.

As the two giants Dole and Del Monte established operations in Moloka'i, homesteaders found it increasingly difficult to market their own pineapples and were eventually compelled to lease their lands to the plantations. Today, a more reliable water supply allows the cultivation of more diversified crops, including coffee, sweet potato, papaya and herbs. The wheels of government turn slowly, but Hawaiians continue to receive land deeds in Ho'olehua in accordance with the Hawaiian Homes Act.

Sights & Activities
PURDY'S MACADAMIA NUT FARM

The Purdy family runs the best little **macadamia-nut farm tour** (☎ 567-6601; www.molokai-aloha.com/mac nuts; admission free; ☺ 9:30am-3:30pm Mon-Fri, 10am-2pm Sat, tours on the hour 10am-3pm) in all of Hawaii. Unlike tours on the Big Island that focus on processing, Tuddie Purdy takes you into his orchard and personally explains how the nuts grow. Purdy's 1.5 acres of mature trees are nearly 75 years old and grow without pesticides, herbicides, or fertilizers.

Everything is done in quaint Moloka'i style: you can crack open macadamia nuts on a stone with a hammer, and sample macadamia blossom honey scooped up with slices of fresh coconut. Macadamia nuts and honey are for sale.

To get to the farm, turn right onto Hwy 490 from Hwy 470. After 1 mile, take a right onto

Lihi Pali Ave, just before the high school. The farm is a third of a mile up, on the right.

POST-A-NUT

Gary, the friendly postmaster of the **Ho'olehua post office** (☎ 567-6144; Pu'u Peelua Ave) stocks baskets of free, unhusked coconuts that can be addressed and mailed off as a unique (even edible!) 'postcard' for $6 to $9 domestic. International mailing is also possible.

MO'OMOMI BEACH

This remote beach, located on the western edge of the Ho'olehua Plains, is ecologically unique. Managed by the Nature Conservancy, it stands as one of the few undisturbed, coastal sand-dune areas left in Hawaii. Among its native grasses and shrubs are at least four endangered plant species that exist nowhere else on earth. It is one of the few places in the populated islands where green sea turtles still find suitable breeding habitat. Evidence of an adze quarry and the fossils of a number of long-extinct Hawaiian birds have been unearthed here, preserved over time by Mo'omomi's arid sands.

Mo'omomi is not lushly beautiful, but windswept, lonely and wild. In short, totally enchanting and worth the trouble it takes to get there. Follow Farrington Ave west, past the intersection with Hwy 480, until the paved road ends. Mo'omomi Ave, which is sometimes an alternate route, is usually closed and signposted as such.

From there, it's 2.5 miles further along a red-dirt road that is in some areas quite smooth and in others deeply rutted. In places, you may have to skirt the edge of the road and straddle a small gully. It's ordinarily passable in a standard car, although the higher the vehicle the better. It's definitely best to have a 4WD. After rain, it quickly becomes muddy.

If it gets too rough, there's a pull-off halfway down this last stretch where you can park. If you get lost in the maze of dirt roads, just keep heading toward the sea and look for the picnic pavilion that announces you've found **Mo'omomi Bay**, with a little sandy beach used by sunbathers. The rocky eastern point, which protects the bay, provides a fishing perch, and further along the bluffs, a sacred ceremony might be under way. The picnic pavilion, belonging to the Hawaiian Home Lands, has toilets, but no drinking water.

The broad, white-sand beach that people refer to as Mo'omomi is not here – it's at

Kawa'aloa Bay, a 20-minute walk further west. The wind, which picks up steadily each afternoon (brace yourself), blows the sand into interesting ripples and waves. The narrower right side of Kawa'aloa Bay is partially sheltered; however, the whole bay can be rough when the surf is up, making swimming unwise.

You'll likely have Kawa'aloa to yourself, but if you don't, there are other sandy coves. Most of the area that is west of here is open ocean with strong currents. The high hills running inland are actually massive sand dunes – part of a mile-long stretch of dunes that back this part of coast. The coastal cliffs, which have been sculptured into jagged abstract designs by wind and water, are made of sand that has petrified due to Mo'omomi's dry conditions. The entire stretch of coast makes a superb spot to watch the sun set, coloring the cliffs in successive shades of golden green.

Because of the fragile ecology of the dunes, visitors should stay along the beach and on trails only. Visitors are not allowed to take any natural objects, including flora, rocks and coral. Foot access is allowed without a permit via the route described, although visitors with a 4WD vehicle can also get a gate key from the Nature Conservancy and drive directly to Kawa'aloa Bay (a permit application and $25 key deposit are required).

Tours

The **Nature Conservancy** (☎ 553-5236; www.nature .org/hawaii; Molokai Industrial Park, 23 Pueo Pl; suggested donation $25) leads excellent monthly guided hikes of Mo'omomi on the fourth of the month. Transportation is provided to and from the preserve. Reservations are required and spots fill up months in advance.

KALA'E

Four miles northeast of Hwy 460 is the sugar mill built by Rudolph W Meyer, an entrepreneurial German immigrant. Meyer was en route to the California gold rush when he stopped off on the islands, married a member of Hawaiian royalty and landed a tidy bit of property in the process. He occupied himself growing potatoes and cattle for export, and serving as overseer of the Kalaupapa leprosy settlement and as manager of King Kamehameha V's ranch lands. In 1876, when a new reciprocity treaty gave Hawaiian sugar planters the right to export sugar duty-free to the US, Meyer turned his lands over to sugar, and built the mill. It operated for only a decade.

Sights & Activities
RW MEYER SUGAR MILL

The mill, which is on the National Register of Historic Places, is the last of its kind. A lot of time and money has gone into authentic restorations, including the rebuilding of a 100-year-old steam engine, a mule-powered cane crusher, and other rusting machinery abandoned a century ago.

The **museum** (☎ 567-6436; adult/concession $2/1; ⏲ 10am-2pm Mon-Sat), beside the parking lot, contains a small display of Moloka'i's history with period photos, a few Hawaiiana items and a 10-minute video. Meyer and his descendants are buried in a little family plot out back.

This is also the Moloka'i campus for **Elderhostel** (☎ 877-426-8056; www.elderhostel.com) educational travel programs for seniors.

IRONWOOD HILLS GOLF COURSE

There are no polo shirts here, just a delightfully casual **golf course** (☎ 567-6000; green fee 9/18 holes $18/24; ⏲ 8am-5pm Mon, Wed, Fri, Sat & Sun, ⏲ 7:30am-5pm Tue & Thu), with crabgrass growing in the sand traps and local golfers who actually look like they're having fun.

PALA'AU STATE PARK

This green state park, at the end of Hwy 470, has a lookout over the Kalaupapa Peninsula, a sacred historical site and groves of wind-whispering ironwood and paper-bark eucalyptus trees. It makes for a pleasant place to picnic or make a quick stop, as the sites are just a couple of minutes from the parking lot. The lookout is best visited before you head down to the peninsula itself.

Sights & Activities
KALAUPAPA OVERLOOK

The Kalaupapa Overlook provides a scenic overview of the Kalaupapa Peninsula from the edge of a 1600ft cliff. Because of the angle of the sun, the best light for photography is usually from late morning to mid-afternoon.

The lighthouse, at the northern end of the peninsula, once boasted the most powerful beam in the Pacific. The 700,000-candlepower Fresnel crystal lens cast its light until 1986, when it was taken down and replaced by an electric light beacon.

Interpretive plaques identify significant landmarks below and explain Kalaupapa's history as a leprosy colony. The village where all of Kalaupapa's residents live is visible, but Kalawao, the original settlement and site of Father Damien's church and grave, is not.

Kalaupapa means 'flat leaf,' an accurate description of the lava-slab peninsula that was created when a low shield volcano poked up out of the sea, long after the rest of Moloka'i had been formed. The dormant Kauhako Crater, visible from the overlook, contains a little lake that's more than 800ft deep. At 400ft, the crater is the highest point on the Kalaupapa Peninsula.

There's a vague **trail** of sorts that continues directly beyond the last plaque at the overlook. The path, on a carpet of soft ironwood needles, passes through diagonal rows of trees planted during a Civil Conservation Corps (CCC) reforestation project in the 1930s. Simply follow this trail for 20 minutes or so until it peters out.

KAULEONANAHOA

Kauleonanahoa (the penis of Nanahoa) is Hawaii's premier **phallic stone**, poking up in a little clearing inside an ironwood grove. The legend goes that Nanahoa hit his wife Kawahuna in a jealous rage and when they were both turned to stone, he came out looking like this. Nature has endowed it well, it's been confirmed that it's been 'carved to some extent.' Reputedly, women who bring offerings of lei and dollar bills to the rock cock and stay overnight here return home pregnant.

Sleeping

Camping is allowed in a peaceful grassy field a quarter of a mile before the overlook, with a picnic pavilion and a portable toilet. It rains a lot here and outside of the summer dry season, your tent will likely be drenched by evening showers. See p429 for permit information.

KALAUPAPA NATIONAL HISTORICAL PARK

The isolation of the wildly beautiful Kalaupapa Peninsula is part of what makes it so intriguing. It is surrounded on three sides by some of Hawaii's roughest and most shark-infested waters, and on the fourth by the world's highest sea cliffs. This remoteness is the reason it was chosen to serve as a leprosy settlement for more than a century. Still home to leprosy patients, the peninsula has been designated a national historical park and is managed by the Hawaii Department of Health and the **National Park Service** (www.nps.gov/kala). Still remote, the only way to get there is by foot, plane or mule.

A tour of the park at the bottom of the cliffs is Moloka'i's principal attraction. Though getting in and out of the tour bus is a bit tedious, learning about the history of this area combined with the adventure of arriving there (the bus only runs at the bottom and you walk or take a mule to get there) makes for a unique experience. Arriving via the trail is highly recommended, as you'll be treated to the sound of crashing surf and views of the steep emerald velvet *pali* (cliffs) the whole way down.

HISTORY

Ancient Hawaiians used Kalaupapa as a refuge when caught in storms at sea. The peninsula held a large settlement at the time of early Western contact, and the area is rich in archaeological sites, currently under investigation. A major discovery in 2004 indicated that Kalaupapa heiau had major ritual significance, with possible astronomical purposes.

In 1835 doctors in Hawaii diagnosed the state's first case of leprosy, one of many diseases introduced by foreigners. Before modern medicine, leprosy manifested itself in dripping, foul-smelling sores. Eventually, patients experienced loss of sensation and tissue degeneration that could lead to small extremities becoming deformed or falling off altogether. Blindness was common. Alarmed by the spread of the disease, King Kamehameha V signed into law an act that banished people with leprosy to Kalaupapa Peninsula, beginning in 1865.

Hawaiians call leprosy *mai ho'oka'awale,* which means 'separating sickness,' a disease all the more dreaded because it tore families apart. Some patients arrived at the peninsula in boats, whose captains were so terrified of the disease and the rough waters they would not land, but instead dropped patients overboard. Those who could, swam to shore; those who couldn't perished.

Once the afflicted arrived on Kalaupapa Peninsula, there was no way out, not even in a casket. The original settlement was in Kalawao, at the wetter eastern end of the peninsula.

Early conditions were unspeakably horrible, with the strong stealing rations from the weak and women forced into prostitution or worse. Lifespans were invariably short, and desperate.

Father Damien (Joseph de Veuster), a Belgian priest, arrived at Kalaupapa in 1873. He wasn't the first missionary to come, but he was the first to stay. What Damien provided most of all was a sense of hope. The priest, a talented carpenter, put up more than 300 simple houses – each little more than four walls, a door and a roof. Damien also nursed the sick, wrapped bandages on oozing sores, hammered coffins and dug graves. On average, he buried one person a day. In 1888, he installed a water pipeline over to the sunny western side of the peninsula, and the settlement moved from Kalawao to where it remains today.

Damien's work inspired others. Brother Joseph Dutton arrived in 1886 and stayed 44 years. In addition to his work with the sick, he was a prolific writer who kept the outside world informed about what was happening in Moloka'i. Mother Marianne Cope arrived a year before Damien died. She stayed 30 years, helping to establish a girls' home and encouraging patients to live life to the fullest. She is widely considered to be the mother of the hospice movement. Damien died in 1889 at the age of 49. In 1995 he was beatified by Pope John Paul II and is now a candidate for sainthood. Check out the film *Molokai: The Story of Father Damien.*

Over the years, some 8000 people have come to the Kalaupapa Peninsula to live out their lives. The same year that Father Damien arrived, a Norwegian scientist named Dr Gerhard Hansen discovered *Mycobacterium leprae,* the bacteria that causes leprosy, thus proving that the disease was not hereditary, as was previously thought. Even in Damien's day, leprosy was one of the least contagious of all communicable diseases: only 4% of human beings are even susceptible to it.

In 1909 the US Leprosy Investigation Station opened at Kalawao. However, the fancy hospital was so out of touch – requiring the patients to sign themselves in for two years, live in seclusion and give up all Hawaiian-grown food – that even in the middle of a leprosy colony, it attracted only a handful of patients. It closed a few years later.

Since the 1940s sulfa antibiotics have successfully treated and controlled leprosy, but

MOLOKA'I

the isolation policies in Kalaupapa weren't abandoned until 1969. Today, fewer than 100 patients live on Kalaupapa Peninsula, most senior citizens (at the time of research, the youngest was 67, the oldest 92). They are, of course, free to leave, but they choose to stay. Many rightly feel this is their only home, and have long fought against being bought out by the government and displaced from their land.

While the state of Hawaii officially uses the term 'Hansen's Disease' for leprosy, many Kalaupapa residents consider that to be a euphemism that fails to reflect the stigma they have suffered and continue to use the old term 'leprosy.' The degrading appellation 'leper,' however, is offensive to all. 'Patient' is preferred.

INFORMATION

Old state laws requiring everyone who enters the settlement to have a 'permit,' and be at least 16 years old, are no longer a medical necessity, but they continue to be enforced in order to protect the privacy of the patients. There's no actual paper permit. Your reservation with Damien Tours or Molokai Mule Ride acts as your permit. Only guests of Kalaupapa residents are allowed to stay overnight. That said, you *can* hike down to the base of the cliffs and play on the beach, located outside the settlement, without prior arrangement.

SIGHTS & ACTIVITIES

The deserted, sensuous **beach** at the bottom of the trail has stunning *pali* views and hostile surf, undertow and some say sharks, so take care. Here you'll find pristine cocoa-colored sand and *opihi* (edible limpet) the size of silver dollars. It's imperative to be respectful of this special place: you cannot venture beyond the beach unless you're on a tour.

On typical tours, the village looks nearly deserted; the sights are mainly cemeteries, churches and memorials. Visitors are not permitted to photograph the residents. A park **visitor center** displays items used by former residents and has books and films for sale.

St Philomena Church (better known as Father Damien's Church), in Kalawao, was built in 1872. You can still see where Damien cut open holes in the floor so that the sick, who needed to spit, could attend church without shame. The graveyard at the side contains Damien's gravestone and original burial site, although his body was exhumed in 1936 and returned to Belgium. In 1995, his right hand was reinterred here.

The amazing view from Kalawao could be reason enough to visit the peninsula. It gives you a glimpse of the **world's highest sea cliffs**, measuring 3300ft, with an average gradient of 58 degrees, folding out in successive verdant ripples reaching eastward. This is your lunch spot and a favorite movie location: *Jurassic Park II* and *III, Robert Louis Stevenson* and *Mark Twain* were all shot here. This impenetrable section of the northern shore contains two majestic valleys and **Kahiwa Falls**, the state's longest waterfall. For a closer look, take a boat tour out of Kaunakakai (see p432).

TOURS

Everyone who comes to the Kalaupapa Peninsula, must visit the settlement with **Damien Tours** (☎ 567-6171; tours $40; ☾ Mon-Sat). Reservations must be made in advance (call between 4pm and 8pm). Tours last 3½ hours, are done by bus and are uncomfortably rushed due to the outbound airplane schedule. Bring your own lunch. Richard Marks, who runs Damien Tours, is a wry storyteller, opinionated oral historian and the third generation of his family to live on Kalaupapa.

Mule Rides

Molokai Mule Ride (☎ 567-6088, 800-567-7550; www .muleride.com; $165; ☾ Mon-Sat) is the only mule outfitter, and offers one of the best-known outings in the islands. While the mules move none too quickly, there's a certain thrill in trusting your life to these sure-footed beasts. Tours include a short riding lesson from real *paniolo* (Hawaiian cowboys) and lunch. Make reservations well in advance. Round-trip airport transfers are $18 per person (two-person minimum).

GETTING THERE & AWAY

The mule trail down the *pali* is the only land route to the peninsula, either on foot or by the mule rides. It is possible to combine hiking and flying.

Air

The beauty of flying in on these small prop planes is the aerial views of the *pali* and towering waterfalls. Passengers must first book a tour with Damien Tours before buying air tickets.

Pacific Wings (☎ 567-6814, on Maui 873-0877, 888-575-4546; www.pacificwings.com; one way/return $97/194) runs a flight daily from Honolulu, Maui and Kaunakakai.

Paragon Air (on Maui ☎ 244-3356, 866-946-4744; www.paragon-air.com) flies between Maui, Kaunakakai and Kalaupapa, and offers all sorts of packages.

Foot

The trailhead is on the east side of Hwy 470, just north of the mule stables, and marked by the Pala'au park sign and parked Kalaupapa employee cars. Your car will be safest parked across from the mule stables. The 3-mile trail has 26 switchbacks, 1400 steps and drops 1664ft in elevation from start to finish. It's best to begin hiking by 8am, before the mules start to go down, to avoid walking in fresh dung, though you have no choice on the return trip. Allow an hour and a half to descend comfortably. It can be quite an adventure after a lot of rain, though the rocks keep it from getting impossibly muddy.

WEST END

Once you pass the airport, Hwy 460 starts to climb up through dry, grassy rangeland without a building in sight. The long mountain range that begins to form on your left past the 10-mile marker is Maunaloa, which means 'long mountain.' Its highest point, at 1381ft, is Pu'u Nana.

The West End is a powerful place in Hawaiian history and culture. Pu'u Nana is the site of Hawaii's first hula school, and the Maunaloa Range was also once a center of sorcery. Nearby Hale O Lono Harbor to the south is the launching site for two long-distance outrigger canoe races. Almost all of the West End is owned by Moloka'i Ranch, and access to anything off the main roads that isn't a beach is at their whim, requiring special permission. You can imagine locals are not pleased with this arrangement.

The dry weather and the presence of some of Moloka'i's best beaches combine to create Moloka'i's most ideal location for resort development. Present-day Maunaloa town is centered around two high-end accommodations, and the Kaluakoi Resort Area is home to several retiree condominium complexes.

HISTORY

During the 1850s, Kamehameha V acquired the bulk of Moloka'i's arable land, forming Moloka'i Ranch, but overgrazing eventually led to the widespread destruction of native vegetation and fishponds. Following his death, the ranch became part of the Bishop Estate, which quickly sold it off to a group of Honolulu businesspeople.

A year later, in 1898, the American Sugar Company, a division of Moloka'i Ranch, attempted to develop a major sugar plantation in central Moloka'i. The company built a railroad system to haul the cane, developed harbor facilities, and installed a powerful pumping system to draw water. However, by 1901 the well water used to irrigate the fields had become so saline that the crops failed. The company then moved into honey production on such a large scale that at one point Moloka'i was the world's largest honey exporter. In the mid-1930s, however, an epidemic wiped out the hives and the industry. Strike two for the industrialists.

Meanwhile, the ranch continued its efforts to find *the* crop for Moloka'i. Cotton, rice and numerous grain crops all took their turn biting Moloka'i's red dust. Finally, pineapple took root as the crop most suited to the island's dry, windy conditions. Plantation-scale production began in Ho'olehua in 1920. Within 10 years, Moloka'i's population tripled, as immigrants arrived to toil in the fields.

In the 1970s, overseas competition brought an end to the pineapple's reign on Moloka'i. Dole closed its operation in 1976, and the other island giant, Del Monte, later followed suit. These closures brought hard times and the highest unemployment levels in the state. Then cattle raising, long a mainstay, suddenly collapsed as, due to a controversial state decision in 1985, every head of cattle on Moloka'i was destroyed after an incidence of bovine tuberculosis. The majority of the 240 smaller cattle owners then called it quits.

The Moloka'i Ranch still owns some 64,000 acres – about 40% of the island – and more than half of the island's privately held lands. With 8000 head of cattle, Moloka'i Ranch is today the second-largest working cattle ranch in the state. Even so, tourists are its main cash crop, which has repeatedly brought it into conflict with the local community (see the boxed text, p452).

MAUNALOA
pop 230

Several years ago, the Moloka'i Ranch bulldozed the old plantation town of Maunaloa, leveling all but a few buildings. New buildings mimicking old, plantation-style homes

A TROUBLED RELATIONSHIP

Even before Moloka'i Ranch began efforts to develop its lands on the West End in the 1970s, local people weren't so fond of the company. They resented the ranch for restricting access to land, which in turn restricted a number of traditional outdoor activities and visitation to sacred cultural and historical sites.

By 1975 feelings had mounted to such a degree that people took to the streets, marching from Mo'omomi Beach to Kawakiu Beach to demand access to private, and heretofore forbidden, beaches on the West End. The protest was successful and convinced Moloka'i Ranch to provide public access to Kawakiu.

In the 1990s the ranch operated a small wildlife-safari park, where many shutterbug tourists snapped pictures of exotic animals, and trophy hunters paid $1500 a head to shoot African eland and blackbuck antelope. Rumors abound of how local activists, long resistant to the type of tourist-oriented development that has all but consumed neighboring Maui, made life so difficult for the ranch that the safari park was shut down.

The newest owners of Moloka'i Ranch – an international group flying under the banner of Molokai Properties – are taking a different tack, trying to engage, rather than isolate, the local community. Realizing that local activists will never back down, the ranch realized that in order to develop, they had to cede.

In 2006 the ranch began laying plans to turn La'au Point into a luxury subdivision with 200 one-acre lots. In return, it plans to transfer the title to cultural sites and recreational areas amounting to 26,000 acres to a newly created Moloka'i Land Trust, essentially turning it into public land. It would also perpetually give up the right to develop another 24,000 acres of its own lands. Molokai Properties would give half the spoils from the development to the Moloka'i Land Trust, and use the rest to reopen the Kaluakoi Hotel. This is one of the hottest issues of debate on the island.

were erected. This drove up rents and forced out some small businesses, again provoking the ire of island residents. The result is a gathering of uniform dark-green buildings, and a town devoid of any character. Maunaloa exists merely to serve the guests of the ranch's two hotels here, with most of those living in the area also working for the ranch.

Built in the 1920s by Libby, McNeill & Libby, the original plantation town was the center of the company's pineapple activities on Moloka'i. Dole, which acquired Libby, McNeill & Libby in 1972, closed down operations in Maunaloa in 1975.

Information

Maunaloa has a **post office** (☎ 552-2852) and the only **gas station** (⏰ 6:30am-1pm Mon, Tue & Thu, 8:30am-3pm Wed & Fri, 9:30-2pm Sat) outside of Kaunakakai.

Sights & Activities

Molokai Fish & Dive operates a number of daily activities in the Maunaloa area. Reservations can be made at its **desk** (☎ 552-0184; 100 Maunaloa Hwy; ⏰ 9:30am-12:30pm) inside the Moloka'i Ranch Headquarters building, or through its shop in Kaunakakai.

The guided **horseback ride** (two-hour ride $85) is along the Kaupoa Beach Trail, with ocean and Lana'i views and visits to historical sites. With a two-person minimum, this is a romantic option for couples. For the more adventurous, there's a **paniolo roundup** (two-hour ride $85), complete with barrel racing, pole vending and cattle herding.

A **gravity bike ride** ($59) takes you 1100ft down to Kaupoa Beach on a mountain-bike. Then ride or ride shuttle back up to Maunaloa town.

Other activities include **3-D archery** ($37), **pellet marksmanship** ($37) and **clay shooting** (50 rounds $75).

From Maunaloa, a dirt road leads down to forlorn **Hale O Lono Point**, the launching point of many a paddling race to O'ahu.

Sleeping

An hourly shuttle connects the following two installations from 8am to 9pm.

Beach Village at Moloka'i Ranch (☎ 660-2824, reservations 888-627-8082; www.molokairanch.com; Kaupoa Beach; r $160-210) For some high-class camping and serious seclusion, settle into one of the 'tentalows' on remote Kaupoa Beach. Each identical 'complex,' has two canvas tents and bathroom, with a hot shower and composting toilet, on a broad wooden deck. Though very relaxing, the Beach Village is of questionable value. The grounds are natural almost to the point of being boring, and no recreation equipment of any kind is available. Waters here are rarely calm enough to enjoy outside of summer. And finally, the tents are extremely cramped and the shower and toilet have only partial roofs! It's a 20-minute drive from Maunaloa town.

Lodge at Moloka'i Ranch (☎ 660-2824, reservations 888-627-8082; www.molokairanch.com; 100 Maunaloa Hwy; r $210-290; 🔀 🖵 🕿) The lobby at the Lodge has the feel of a cozy ranch-house living room, with a tall stone fireplace, thick wood beams, a wagon-wheel chandelier and comfy couches everywhere. It overlooks miles of rolling pastureland and the blue ocean beyond. The rooms are luxurious but carry on the rustic theme with quilts, distressed wood furniture, and old-fashioned bathrooms with claw-foot tubs and braided mats. The onsite spa, Infinity pool and hammocks slung about will leech the stress right from you.

Eating

The food at the Moloka'i Ranch plays the part of higher cuisine, but you'll find it just doesn't deliver on flavor. The value is questionable, but when you're way out here, you just gotta eat.

Paniolo Lounge (☎ 660-2824; Lodge at Moloka'i Ranch; light meals $5-12; 🕑 10am-9pm) Soups, salads and sandwiches are served at cocktail tables on a wrap-around lanai with excellent views. There is a daily hot meal special for $17.

Maunaloa Room (☎ 660-2824; Lodge at Moloka'i Ranch; breakfast $4-12, dinner $21-28; 🕑 7-10am daily, 6-9pm Mon-Sat, 5-9pm Sun) A limited menu of hearty dishes such as smoked meatloaf with caramelized onions, roasted peppers and garlic mashed potatoes ($24) are served in a sedate dining room. On Wednesday evenings there is a pasta buffet ($20) and on Sundays, an Asian buffet ($21).

Beach Village at Moloka'i Ranch (☎ 660-2824; Kaupoa Beach; buffet per adult/child under 12 $31/free; 🕑 Fri & Sat) Nighttime lends a little magic to the plain, oceanfront dining area at Beach Village. Two weekly all-you-can-eat dinner buffets take place here. Fridays have a Hawaiian

theme, including *kalua* pig (a luau dish), poi (fermented taro) and *'ahi poke* (cubes of flavored, raw, yellowfish tuna). Saturdays are more American-style, with prime rib, chicken, fish and stuffed potatoes. Reservations are required, and bring your own alcohol.

For groceries, **Maunaloa General Store** (🕑 8am-6pm Mon-Sat, to noon Sun) has a limited selection of pricey groceries and alcohol.

Entertainment

Enjoy a sunset drink and *pupu* (snack) at the Lodge's genteel **Paniolo Bar** (🕑 10am-10pm). There's live music on Friday and Saturday nights, and on Sunday afternoons, the *kapuna* (elders) come together and play music. The tiny **Maunaloa Town Cinema** (☎ 552-2707, 552-2616; 1 Maunaloa Hwy; adult/child $6.50/4.25) shows first-run movies.

Shopping

Big Wind Kite Factory & Plantation Gallery (☎ 552-2364; www.molokai.com/kites; 120 Maunaloa Hwy; 🕑 8:30am-5pm Mon-Sat, 10am-2pm Sun) The island's most interesting shop makes and sells colorful windsocks and kites in all shapes and styles, including island-influenced designs. Free sport kite–flying lessons are available upon request. The adjoining shop sells spoils from the owners' travels through Southeast Asia, including clothing, mobiles, carvings and jewelry. Moloka'i's best book selection (including used novels) and constellation guides are also found here.

KALUAKOI RESORT AREA

In this 165-acre resort area, untouched grassy hills slope down toward a strip of developed land along the oceanfront. Two condominium complexes and a closed hotel front a beautifully wild white-sand beach, with two similar beaches not far away. An 18-hole golf course adds some emerald green to the scene.

In the 1970s, Moloka'i Ranch joined with Louisiana Land & Exploration Company to form the Kaluakoi Corporation, which proposed developing western Moloka'i into a major suburb of Honolulu, complete with a ferry service. The plan called for 30,000 private homes on the heretofore uninhabited west coast. A vocal antidevelopment movement boomed quicker than the buildings could, however, and the plan was scrapped.

In its place, a somewhat more modest plan was hatched for the development of Kaluakoi Resort but, after construction, it never really got off the ground. The 290-room Kaluakoi

Hotel had such a low occupancy rate that part of it was turned into condos. Things worsened after September 11, 2001. The house lots have been subdivided, but fewer than 100 houses have been built.

Later, mismanagement by a Japanese corporation effectively ran the hotel and its golf course into the ground. Moloka'i Ranch subsequently bought most of the resort property, turned the course from brown to green and started laying plans to re-open the hotel.

The turnoff for the resort area and the main West End beaches is at the 15-mile marker with a low rock wall on either side.

Sights & Activities

KAWAKIU BEACH

The northernmost of Kaluakoi's beaches, Kawakiu Beach is a broad crescent beach of white sand and bright turquoise waters. To get there, turn off Kaluakoi Rd onto the road to the Paniolo Hale condos, but instead of turning left down to the condos, continue straight toward the golf course. Where the paved road ends, there's space to pull over and park, just before crossing the greens. You'll come first to a rocky point at the southern end of the bay. Before descending to the beach, scramble around up here for a scenic view of the coast, south to Papohaku Beach and north to 'Ilio Point.

When seas are calm, usually in summer, Kawakiu is generally safe for swimming. When the surf is rough, there are still areas where you can at least get wet. On the southern side of the bay, there's a small, sandy-bottomed wading pool in the rocks. The northern side has an area of flat rocks over which water slides, to fill up a shallow shoreline pool. Outside of weekends, you may well have the place to yourself.

MAKE HORSE BEACH

To the south, Make Horse Beach supposedly takes its name from days past, when wild horses were run off the tall, dark cliff on its northern end. *Make* (mah-*kay*) means 'dead.' This pretty, tiny white-sand cove is a local favorite, and more secluded than Kepuhi. It's an idyllic spot for sunbathing and sunset, but usually not for swimming. On the calmest days, daredevils leap off the giant rock ledge at the beach's southern end.

To get here, turn off Kaluakoi Rd onto the road to the Paniolo Hale condos and then turn left toward the condo complex. You can park just beyond the condos and walk, or follow the dirt road heading off to the right for a quarter of a mile to a parking area. From there, cross the golf course to the beach.

KEPUHI BEACH

This beach is a rocky, white-sand stretch in front of the defunct Kaluakoi Hotel. Swimming conditions are usually dangerous here. Not only can there be a tough shorebreak but strong currents can be present even on calm days. During winter, the surf breaks close to shore, crashing in waves that are half water, half sand. Experienced surfers take to the northern end of the beach.

A five-minute hike up to the top of **Pu'u o Kaiaka**, a 110ft-high promontory at the southern end of Kepuhi Beach, rewards strollers with a nice view of Papohaku Beach. At the top, you'll find the remains of a pulley that was once used to carry cattle down to waiting barges for transport to O'ahu slaughterhouses. There was also a 40ft heiau on the hilltop until 1967, when the US army bulldozed it. To get to the parking lot, turn off Kaluakoi Rd onto Kaiaka Rd, proceeding a half-mile to the road's end.

KALUAKOI GOLF COURSE

Take in views of Moloka'i's finest beaches with your 18 holes at this **golf course** (☎ 552-0255; green fee $80; ☼ 7:30am-4pm).

Sleeping & Eating

Units in these condominium complexes are rented either directly from the owners (try www.molokai-condos.com) or through Molokai Vacation Rentals or Friendly Isle Realty (p436).

Paniolo Hale (studios from $95, 1-bedroom units from $120; ☜) Large trees shade this complex within a short walk of Make Horse Beach, giving it a hidden, secluded air. Each unit has a long, screened-in lanai overlooking the quiet grounds, and is spacious and bright with hardwood floors. The furnishings are attractive with tropical prints used in good taste. A good-looking place overall, with tennis courts to boot.

Ke Nani Kai (www.knkrentals.com; Kaluakoi Rd; 1-/2-bedroom units from $115/145; ☜) Set on manicured grounds adjacent to superlative Papohaku Beach and nine holes of golf, the best of these condos are arguably the nicest on Moloka'i. Each has a full kitchen, lanai, washer and dryer, a bathroom with a tub and cable TV; most have a sofa bed in the living room, making this an economical option for small groups. For $20 more you get (distant, partial) ocean views.

Kaluakoi Resort & Villas (☎ 552-2721, 800-367-5004; www.castleresorts.com; 1131 Kaluakoi Rd; studios/1-bedroom units from $135/160; 🏊) A section of the now defunct Kaluakoi Hotel was converted into vacation rentals, but being surrounded by abandoned buildings does nothing for the atmosphere. The buildings in use all have good views over the golf course and the beach, but it's hard to shake the eerie feeling around the complex. None has a full kitchen.

Near the old Kaluakoi Hotel's pool, **West End Sundries** (☉ 8am-6pm) 'rents' VHS and sells ice cream and super-basic food supplies at inflated prices. You're better off heading for Kaunakakai or Maunaloa.

WEST END BEACHES

The West End beaches, together with those in the Kaluakoi Resort area, are Moloka'i's most celebrated. From this stretch of coast the twinkling lights of O'ahu are just 26 miles away. The view is of Diamond Head to the left, Makapu'u Point to the right. You can, reportedly, see the famous 'green flash' (the green color results from atmospheric refraction of the setting or rising sun) during sunset here.

To get to the West End beaches, take the turnoff for the Kaluakoi Resort Area at the 15-mile marker (marked by a low rock wall on either side). Pass the golf course and follow Pohakuloa Rd south.

Papohaku Beach Park

Beautiful Papohaku Beach lays claim to being Hawaii's longest beach. It's 2.5 miles of quintessential paradise and vast enough to hold the entire population of Moloka'i without getting crowded. There's seldom more than a handful of beachgoers, even on sunny days, and at times you can walk the shore without seeing another soul. With fluffy orange sands gleaming in the sun, and wisps of rainbows tossed up in the crashing surf, it's a gorgeous place for barefoot strolling.

So where is everybody? Well, for one, it can be windy, with gusts of sand continually smacking you in the face. But the main drawback is the water itself, which is usually too treacherous for swimming. Though backed by low trees, there's not a lick of shade. The first access point, which is the most developed of the seven turnoffs from Kaluakoi and Pohakuloa Rds with parking lots, is Papohaku Beach Park, a grassy park with picnic facilities, run-down bathrooms and showers. There's no view of the beach from the picnic area, but a stretch of trees shelter it from the wind and it'd be a great place to throw a Frisbee around.

A third access point, at the end of Papapa Pl, provides southern access to Papohaku Beach. The large concrete tunnel at the south end of the beach was used to load sand onto barges for shipping to Honolulu. The sand was used in construction, and in building up Waikiki beaches until environmental protection laws stopped sand-mining operations in the early 1970s.

SLEEPING

The beach park is the prime place on Moloka'i to sleep under the stars. Camping is allowed on the **Papohaku Campground** (in the southern half of the park), which is divided into two sections. One section is watered by timed sprinklers from Sunday to Wednesday, the other from Thursday to Saturday. The camping area is grassy, level and shaded by a grove of trees, with picnic tables throughout. Secure your tent carefully, as the wind sometimes blows with hardy gusts.

The campground is often peaceful – the surf lulling you to sleep, and the birds waking you up. However, boisterous families with young kids and pick-up trucks move in here, especially on weekends. The beach also attracts down-and-outers, but a security guard is around to check for permit violators until about 1am. See p429 for information on camping permits.

Dixie Maru

The next three beach-access points lead to rocky coastline, suitable for fishing. At the end of the road is a small, round inlet which the ancient Hawaiians knew as Kapukahehu. It is now called Dixie Maru, after a ship that went down in the area long ago. Dixie Maru is the most protected cove on the west shore, and the most popular **swimming** and **snorkeling** area. The waters are generally calm, except when the surf is high enough to break over the mouth of the bay. The orange sand is a confetti mix of waterworn coral bits and small shells. If you're up for just finding your way as you go, it's possible to hike south along the coast to La'au Point.

NI'IHAU

Nicknamed the 'Forbidden Island,' Ni'ihau remains an intriguing mystery due to its private owner-ship and unique isolation. Accessible only to its owners, its Native Hawaiian residents, govern-ment officials, occasional US Navy personnel, and invited guests, Ni'ihau is the last bastion of traditional Native Hawaiian culture.

HISTORY

Captain Cook anchored off Ni'ihau on January 29, 1778, two weeks after 'discovering' Hawaii. Cook noted in his log that the island was lightly populated and largely barren – a description still true today. His visit was short, but it had a lasting impact. Cook introduced two things to Ni'ihau that would quickly change the face of Hawaii. He left two goats, the first of the grazing animals that would devastate the island's native flora and fauna. And his men introduced syphilis, the first of several Western diseases that would strike the Hawaiian people.

In 1864 Elizabeth Sinclair, a Scottish widow who was moving from New Zealand to Vancouver when she got sidetracked in Hawai'i, bought Ni'ihau from King Kamehameha V for $10,000 in gold. He originally tried to sell her the 'swampland' of Waikiki, but she passed it up for the 'desert island.' Interestingly, no two places in Hawaii today could be further apart, either culturally or in land value. Mrs Sinclair brought the first sheep to Ni'ihau from New Zealand and started the island's longstanding, but now defunct, ranching operation.

Today the island is owned by Mrs Sinclair's great-great-grandsons Keith and Bruce Robinson, brothers who also own a vast expanse of sugarcane land on Kaua'i. The Robinsons are highly protective of Ni'ihau's isolation and its people. In a benevolent, privatized example of socialism, they have diverted funds from their sugar company (see p536) on Kaua'i to provide Ni'ihauans with shelter, food staples and medical care, and higher education.

The Robinsons, who live on Kaua'i, are unpretentious outdoorsmen, fluent in Native Hawaiian. Keith Robinson, who worked for years in ranching and fishing, is often found in red-dirt-covered jeans, driving a beat-up pickup or doing heavy labor to save endangered plants. Bruce Robinson, whose wife is Ni'ihauan, holds top management positions in the family businesses – while also lead-ing hunting tours (see Ni'ihau Safaris, opposite) and efforts to safeguard Ni'ihau's monk seals.

POPULATION & LIFESTYLE

Ni'ihau's population is predominantly Native Hawaiian. Over the years, the island's population has dropped from 600 in the early 1980s, to 230 in the 1990 Census, to 160 a decade later.

Residents are known for being humble, generous and mellow, and most live in Pu'uwai (mean-ing 'heart' in Hawaiian), a settlement on the dry western coast. The lifestyle is extremely rustic, with no sense of hurry or on-the-dot punctuality. The island has no paved roads, no airport, no phones and no running water. Rainfall is collected in catchments, and toilets are in outhouses. While there is no island-wide electricity, homes have electricity generators and TV. Alcohol and firearms are banned, and a code of ethics advocates monogamy.

Ni'ihau is the only island where the primary language is still Hawaiian. Business is conducted in Hawaiian, as are Sunday church services. Ni'ihau has a two-room schoolhouse where three teachers hold classes from kindergarten through 12th grade for the island's 50 students. Although courses are taught solely in Hawaiian up to the fourth grade, students learn English as a second language and most are bilingual (and speak pidgin-free English).

Despite the isolation, residents are not unacquainted with the outside world. Supply boats bring soda pop as well as poi (traditional starch of steamed, mashed taro), and the island has more dirt bikes than outrigger canoes. Ni'ihau residents are free to go to Kaua'i or even Las Vegas to shop, drink a few beers or just hang out. But they cannot bring friends from other islands back home with them. If Ni'ihauans marry people from other islands, or if the Robinsons view particular residents as undesirable, they are rarely allowed to return.

GEOGRAPHY & ENVIRONMENT

Ni'ihau is the smallest of the inhabited Hawaiian Islands: 18 miles long and 6 miles at the wid-est point, with a total land area of almost 70 sq miles, including 45 miles of coast. The island is slightly over 17 miles southwest of Kaua'i. The climate is warm, windy and semiarid, with a relatively extreme temperature range, from 42 to 110°F in the shade. Ni'ihau rainfall averages a scant 12in annually because the island is in Kaua'i's rain shadow. Its highest peak, Paniau, is only 1250ft tall and cannot generate trade wind–based precipitation.

Ni'ihau's 865-acre Halali'i Lake is the largest in Hawaii, but even during the rainy winter season, it's only a few feet deep. In summer, it sometimes dries up to a mud pond.

Almost 50 endangered monk seals live on Ni'ihau, and about half of all Hawaii's endangered *'alae ke'oke'o* (coots) breed here. Introduced creatures proliferate: there's an estimated 6000 feral pigs, plus wild sheep, goats and turkeys. Ni'ihau waters have suffered depletion by outside sport and commercial fishers who sail in to fish and pick *opihi* (an edible limpet) from the island's shorebreaks.

Unique to the island are Ni'ihau shells: lustrous, warm-hued and delicate sea jewels strung into exquisite and coveted lei costing anywhere from $125 to $25,000. In late 2004, Governor Linda Lingle signed a bill mandating that only items made of 100% Ni'ihau shells and crafted entirely in Hawaii can carry the Ni'ihau label.

ECONOMY & POLITICS

The island economy has long depended on Ni'ihau Ranch, the sheep and cattle business owned by the Robinsons. But it was always a marginal operation on windy Ni'ihau, with droughts devastating herds. In 1999 Ni'ihau Ranch closed, putting most of the island's inhabitants on federal welfare.

Since then, the Robinsons have focused on two income and employment sources: the military and tourism. Since 1999, military special operations forces have been leasing sites on the uninhabited southern end of the island to stage periodic training maneuvers. The operations are small-scale, typically with teams of a dozen soldiers practicing mock rescue operations. The Robinsons have also pushed for Ni'ihau's participation in major Navy missile-testing, which is considered less invasive than overgrazing by sheep or major tourism.

Realistically, however, tourism is the only other obvious option. Thus the Robinsons started offering helicopter and hunting safari tours. Neither is a booming moneymaker, probably due to the steep tour prices and the low-key Robinsons' ambivalence about opening the island to tourists. They publicize the tours mainly by word-of-mouth, with only minimal advertising.

While most Ni'ihauans seem content with their lifestyle, outsiders have been critical. Some Native Hawaiians living on other islands see the Robinsons as colonialists and believe inhabitants should be granted their own land and self-determination, particularly to oppose a military presence. If granted independence, however, economic survival would remain tenuous and risk becoming even more so.

A weekly supply boat travels between Kaua'i and Ni'ihau. It docks on Kaua'i at Kaumakani, where the Robinsons live and base their businesses, including Ni'ihau Ranch. Kaumakani is also home to a settlement of Ni'ihauans who chose to live on Kaua'i, though many of them still work for the Robinsons. Politically, Ni'ihau falls under the jurisdiction of Kaua'i County. Interestingly, George W Bush got 39 of 40 votes cast in the 2004 US Presidential election.

VISITING NI'IHAU

Although outsiders are not allowed to visit Ni'ihau on their own, the Robinsons offer pricey helicopter flights and hunting excursions:

Ni'ihau Helicopters (☎ 877-441-3500; http://homepages.hawaiian.net/niihauisland/index.html; PO Box 690370, Makaweli, HI 96769; per person $325) The pilot flies over much of Ni'ihau but avoids the population center of Pu'uwai village; the tour stops at a beach (location depends on weather) for lunch and awesome snorkeling. The helicopter, an Agusta 109A, is not one of the big-window type of choppers used on other aerial tours. Tours must be arranged well in advance. Half-day tours take off from Burns Field on Kaua'i.

Ni'ihau Safaris (☎ 877-441-3500; http://homepages.hawaiian.net/niihauisland/index.html; PO Box 690370, Makaweli, HI 96769; per hunter/observer $1650/400) Provides everything you'll need (rifle, license, transportation, guide, preparation and shipping of trophies) to hunt Polynesian boar and feral sheep mostly, but also wild eland, Barbary sheep and wild oryx. Organizers promote this as 'useful harvesting of game' (due to overpopulation and overgrazing) and obey norms of free-chase hunting.

Dive outfits on Kaua'i offer scuba diving tours to the waters around Ni'ihau; a typical three-tank dive costs around $280. See p462 for more information.

Kaua'i

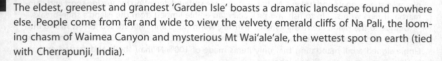

The eldest, greenest and grandest 'Garden Isle' boasts a dramatic landscape found nowhere else. People come from far and wide to view the velvety emerald cliffs of Na Pali, the looming chasm of Waimea Canyon and mysterious Mt Wai'ale'ale, the wettest spot on earth (tied with Cherrapunji, India).

Predominantly rural, Kaua'i is the least populated of the major four islands. Along the sole coastal highway, you'll find only small towns (none with more than 10,000 residents) and low-rise buildings. High-rises, meaning any structure taller than a coconut tree, are prohibited. There are only three public high schools and three movie theaters – and, among born-and-bred Kaua'ians, little heed for yuppie trappings like luxury cars and designer clothes.

Hurricane 'Iniki, which devastated the island in 1992, remains a vivid milestone tragedy in locals' collective memory. But its effects seem largely to have been overcome. Today tourism and real estate are booming. Despite concerns about rampant traffic and infrastructure inadequacies, the three major resort areas – Po'ipu, Princeville and the 'Coconut Coast' – continue to sprout new condos and time-shares. As for residential real estate, much of Kaua'i land is now affordable only to wealthy second-home owners and mainland transplants.

On Kaua'i, natural wonders easily trump human-made ones. Here, forget about shopping and skyscrapers and nightlife. This is an island proud of its island roots.

HIGHLIGHTS

- Traverse the misty native bogs of **Alaka'i Swamp** (p547)
- Identify native flora at **Limahuli Garden** (p514)
- Hike the phenomenal **Kalalau Trail** (p516)
- Bum around surf town **Hanalei** (p507)
- Explore the mammoth **Waimea Canyon** (p542)
- Let loose and go **ziplining** (p471) near Lihu'e
- Frolic with or without kids at **Lydgate Beach Park** (p479)
- Get a bird's-eye view on a **helicopter** (p466)
- Discover remote beaches along the **Maha'ulepu Heritage Trail** (p524)
- Meet local artists at **Hanapepe Art Night** (p535) on Fridays

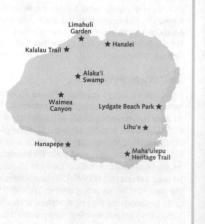

★ Limahuli Garden
★ Kalalau Trail
★ Hanalei
★ Alaka'i Swamp
★ Waimea Canyon
★ Lydgate Beach Park
★ Lihu'e
★ Hanapepe
★ Maha'ulepu Heritage Trail

■ POPULATION: 63,000 ■ AREA: 555 SQ MILES ■ OFFICIAL FLOWER: MOKIHANA

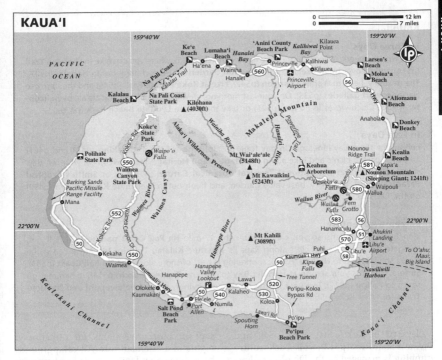

KAUA'I

CLIMATE

Does Kaua'i live up to its rainy reputation? Yes, but rainfall really varies by location and season. The South Shore and especially the Westside tend to be dry and sunny, while the North Shore and Eastside see regular showers. The biggest factor is elevation and precipitation increases as you head *mauka* (inland). Mt Wai'ale'ale (5148ft), almost smack in the middle of the island, is considered the wettest place on earth, averaging 460in of rain annually. Since the island is only 33 miles wide and 25 miles long, it's easy to escape to your preferred climate.

Seasonally, winter means guaranteed rain, particularly on the North Shore, where flooding is a fact of life. But, except during storms, sunny spells and balmy temperatures ease the rainy-day blues. Remember, no rain, no rainbows!

The National Weather Service provides recorded **local weather information** (☎ 245-6001) and **marine forecasts** (☎ 245-3564). See the Directory (p556) for more information.

STATE & COUNTY PARKS

Look at a map of Kaua'i and you'll see vast swaths of undeveloped land. The island is predominantly rural – hikers, campers and mountain bikers have no shortage of wilderness to explore.

Must-see state parks include the two Westside standouts, Waimea Canyon (p542) and Koke'e (p545) State Parks. Surrounding the awesome chasm of Waimea Canyon, the two parks are adjacent and blend into one vast terrain of steep cliffs and native forests. Hiking trails abound, but some trailheads are accessible only by 4WD.

Na Pali Coast State Park is another headliner, as the steep, slippery Kalalau Trail (p516) is now practically de rigueur. For kids, Lydgate Beach Park (p479) offers playgrounds and shallow swimming ponds.

Many excellent beaches sit on county parkland and the best are Ha'ena Beach Park (p514), Hanalei (Black Pot) Beach Park (p509), 'Anini Beach Park (p501) and Salt Pond Beach Park (p534).

CAMPING
State Parks
State park campgrounds can be found at Na Pali Coast State Park (Hanakapi'ai and Kalalau

KAUA'I

KAUA'I...

In Three Days

Start with the peerless North Shore drive to **Ke'e Beach** (p515), where you can hike the **Kalalau Trail** (p516) and recover by snorkeling. Visit **Limahuli Garden** (p514) and hang out in **Hanalei** (p507). The next day, head to **Waimea Canyon** (p542), hike at **Koke'e State Park** (p545) and then browse **Hanapepe art galleries** (p535). On your last morning, view inaccessible Mt Wai'ale'ale by **helicopter** (p466). Catch waves in **Po'ipu** (p521) or take the kids to **Lydgate Beach Park** (p479).

In Five Days

Follow the three-day itinerary. On day four, go **ziplining** (p471) or **kayaking** (p471 and p481) and then pack a picnic and hike along the **Maha'ulepu Heritage Trail** (p524). On your last day, see tropical flora at the **National Tropical Botanical Garden** (p521) or at **Smith's Tropical Paradise** (p479), a low-key, best-value garden, and hang out in lively little **Kapa'a** town (p490) on the Eastside.

Extreme Adventure

Plan for a summer trip so you can conquer the 17-mile **Na Pali Coast paddle** (p510). If not, navigate the sheer Na Pali cliffs along Kaua'i's signature **Kalalau Trail** (p516). Advanced scuba divers should head to **Ni'ihau** (p524); snorkeling is best offshore along the **Na Pali Coast** (p533). Surfers: winter is your season at **Hanalei Bay** (p508) and **Tunnels Beach** (p514); in summer go south to **Po'ipu** (p521). Test your mettle on the unnervingly steep **Awa'awapuhi and Nu'alolo Trails** (p547) at Koke'e State Park.

Valleys; p516), Koke'e State Park (p549) and Polihale State Park (p542), while backcountry camping is managed by the Division of Forestry & Wildlife around Waimea Canyon State Park (p545) and Koke'e State Park (p549).

State park permits (between $5 and $10 per campsite per night) are required. Camping is limited to five consecutive nights within a 30-day period and not more than two consecutive nights in Hanakapi'ai Valley.

You can obtain permits in person or by mail from the **Division of State Parks** (Map p472; ☎ 274-3444; www.hawaii.gov/dlnr/dsp; Department of Land & Natural Resources, Room 306, 3060 Eiwa St, Lihu'e, HI 96766; ☻ 8am-3:30pm Mon-Fri) and at state park offices on other islands. Apply months in advance.

For remote backcountry camping in Waimea Canyon, there is no charge. The **Division of Forestry & Wildlife** (Map p472; ☎ 274-3433; www.hawaiitrails .org; Department of Land & Natural Resources, Room 306, 3060 Eiwa St, Lihu'e, HI 96766; ☻ 8am-4pm Mon-Fri) issues free, backcountry camping permits for four sites in Waimea Canyon and two sites (Sugi Grove and Kawaikoi) in the Koke'e State Park area.

County Parks

Camping is available at seven county parks and permits cost $3 per night per adult camper (children under 18 free). You can

stay six consecutive nights, for a total of 60 nights in a calendar year. All campgrounds have showers and toilets, and most have covered picnic pavilions and BBQ grills.

Each site is closed one day a week for cleaning and for preventing permanent squatting. Check www.kauai.gov (go to 'Licenses & Permits' and then to 'Camping Permits') for details.

Permits are issued in person or by mail (at least one month in advance) at the **Division of Parks & Recreation** (Map p472; ☎ 241-4463; www .kauai.gov; Lihu'e Civic Center, Division of Parks & Recreation, Suite 150, 4444 Rice St, Lihu'e, HI 96766). Permits are issued between 8:15am and 4pm Monday to Friday.

ACTIVITIES

There's no excuse for staying indoors on Kaua'i (rain or shine!). Here, there is a range of outdoor activities suited to elite athletes and vacation dabblers alike.

Water Activities

Note seasonal changes in surf conditions: North Shore and Westside beaches are most hazardous around winter (October to April), when South Shore and Eastside beaches are quite calm. The pattern reverses in summer.

Before jumping in, familiarize yourself with Kaua'i's beaches at www.kauaiexplorer.com and request a free copy of the *Kaua'i Beach Safety Guide* from **Kaua'i Visitors Bureau** (Map p472; ☎ 245-3971, 800-262-1400; www.kauaidiscovery.com; Suite 101, 4334 Rice St, Lihu'e). **Franko's Dive Map of Kaua'i** ($7) identifies top diving, snorkeling, surfing and kayaking sites.

KAYAKING
River Kayaking
Kayaking the Wailua River is so popular, it's spurred a whole industry here. The river is strictly monitored against overuse, and guided kayaking tours (p481) are encouraged. A less-trafficked alternative is the Hule'ia River, near Lihu'e (p471).

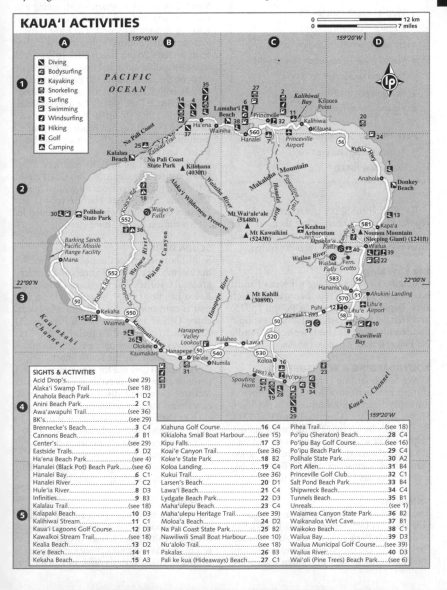

KAUA'I ACTIVITIES

BEACHES WITH LIFEGUARDS ON DUTY

Lifeguard staffing is subject to change, so call the **Ocean Safety Bureau** (☎ 241-6506) to confirm this information.

Full-Time

- Lydgate Beach Park (p479)
- Po'ipu Beach Park (p521)
- Hanalei Beach Park Pavilion (p509)
- Wai'oli (Pine Trees) Beach Park (p509)
- Salt Pond Beach Park (p534)
- Kealia Beach (p494)
- Kekaha Beach Park (p541)

Part-Time or Seasonal

- Anahola Beach Park (p495)
- Wailua Bay (p481)

Kaua'i's North Shore rivers are much less regulated and you can enjoy them at your leisure. Hanalei River (p509) and Kalihiwai Stream (p501) are highly recommended.

Sea Kayaking

Officially, all sea kayaking off Kaua'i must be done as part of a tour because of rough surf. Beginners can learn in Po'ipu (p525) and Hanalei (p509), while fit athletes should do the unforgettable (summer only) 17-mile Na Pali endurance paddle (p510).

BODYBOARDING & BODYSURFING

While bodyboarding is less glamorous than surfing, pros perform wild stunts and novices can enjoy the sport from day one. On the South Shore, try Po'ipu (Sheraton) Beach (p521), Brennecke's Beach (p522) and, for the skilled, Shipwreck Beach (p522). Newbies should start at Kalapaki Beach (p469) near Lihu'e, while experts can test themselves at Kealia Beach (p494) and Hanalei Bay (p508) near the pavilion.

SWIMMING

You can find protected swimming lagoons year-round at Lydgate Beach Park (p479), Salt Pond Beach Park (p534) and 'Anini Beach Park (p501). On the North Shore, swimming is feasible only in summer, when waters are calm at Ke'e Beach (p515) and Hanalei Bay (p508). In winter, when giant swells pound the North Shore, head to the South Shore, especially Po'ipu (Sheraton) Beach (p521) and, especially for children, Po'ipu Beach Park (p521).

SNORKELING

Snorkeling is an everyman sport, giving everyone, young and old, the chance to explore Kaua'i's underwater world. The most convenient snorkeling is found right offshore: the best spots include Po'ipu Beach Park (p521), with dense fish populations and frequent turtle spottings, on the South Shore; Salt Pond Beach Park (p534), with shallow waters, on the Westside; Lydgate Beach Park (p479), for a protected lagoon perfect for kids, on the Eastside; and Ke'e Beach (p515) and Tunnels Beach (p514), for the most spectacular setting (both above and below water), on the North Shore.

Your snorkeling options multiply if you take a cruise. The scenic Na Pali Coast circuit is the star; tours leave from Port Allen (p533), Kikialoha Small Boat Harbor (p541) and Hanalei Bay (p510), which is recommended for maximum North Shore viewing.

SCUBA DIVING

South Shore waters see the most diving activity, but North Shore reefs at Tunnels and Cannons are local favorites. The top shore-diving site is Koloa Landing (p523), a great beginner spot that is conveniently located and allows easy entry. Others are Po'ipu Beach Park (p521), Ke'e Beach (p515) and Tunnels Beach (p514). Boat dives widen your options, with the majority of sites are along the South Shore.

The hottest dive site for experienced divers, perhaps statewide, is Ni'ihau (p456), which features deep wall dives, lava formations, caves, plentiful marine life (including pelagics such as sharks) and crystal-clear waters. The often-choppy crossing between Kaua'i and Ni'ihau takes about 2½ hours and is doable only in summer.

For outfits, see listings in the Kapa'a (p490), Koloa (p519) and Po'ipu (p524) sections.

FISHING

Fishing is a mainstay sport among locals. If you're an avid fisher at home, you'll enjoy deep-sea fishing off Kaua'i, where you can sail to depths over 6000ft within an hour at trolling speed. The day's offshore catch varies

KAUA'I SURF BEACHES & BREAKS
Jake Howard

The Garden Isle is one of Hawaii's most challenging islands for surfers. On the North Shore, a heavy local vibe is pervasive; though **Hanalei Bay** (p508) offers some of the best waves among the islands, it is also one of the most localized. With Princeville Resort overlooking the break, residents may be a bit more understanding of out-of-towners in the water at Hanalei than at other North Shore spots, but surfing with respect is a must. Between localism and the inaccessibility of the Na Pali Coast, not to mention a sizable tiger shark population, you may want to pass on surfing the North Shore.

As a general rule, surf tourism is relegated to the South Shore around Po'ipu (p521). Chances are good that you'll be staying in this popular area anyway, which is perfect because there are some fun waves to be had here. Breaking best in the summer on south swells, spots like **BK's**, **Acid Drop's** and **Center's** challenge even the most advanced surfers. First-timers can get their feet wet at nearby **Brennecke's** (p522). Only bodyboarding and bodysurfing are permitted here – no stand-up surfing – and it's a great place to take the family.

On the Northeast Coast, **Unreals** breaks at Anahola Bay. It's a consistent right point that can work well on easterly wind swell, when *kona* (leeward) winds are offshore.

Surfing lessons and board hire are available mainly in Hanalei (p510) and in Po'ipu (p525). To find the swells, call the **surf hotline** (☎ 335-3720).

among giant marlin and tuna, and midweight fish such as mahimahi and *ono* (wahoo). Inshore catches include *uku* (gray snapper), *ulua* (jack), *kaku* (barracuda) and *kamanu* (rainbow runner).

Charter fishing boats depart mainly from Nawiliwili Small Boat Harbor (p469), Port Allen (p531) and 'Anini (p501).

Land Activities
HIKING

Hiking runs the gamut, from easy walks to precarious treks, over varied types of terrain. The greatest concentration of Kaua'i trails is on state forest-reserve land around Waimea Canyon State Park (p544) and Koke'e State Park (p546). Hike the Pihea Trail to the Alaka'i Swamp Trail (p547) for a look at pristine native forestland, or brave the steep Awa'awapuhi Trail (p547) for breathtaking cliff views.

On the North Shore, the Kalalau Trail (p516) offers a close-up of the peerless Na Pali Coast, while the Eastside boasts scenic mountainous trails (p482) conveniently located near towns.

The majority of Kaua'i's trails are managed by **Na Ala Hele** (Map p472; ☎ 274-3442; www.hawaiitrails .org; Department of Land & Natural Resources, Division of Forestry & Wildlife, Room 306, 3060 Eiwa St, Lihu'e, HI 96766; map $6), a statewide trails program, which offers a detailed topographic map and invaluable firsthand information

The remainder of public trails – which essentially means the Kalalau Trail and the Koke'e State Park trails nearest Waimea Canyon Dr (ie Cliff Trail, Canyon Trail and Halemanu-Koke'e Trails; see p546) – are managed by the **Division of State Parks** (Map p472; ☎ 274-3444; www.hawaii.gov/dlnr/dsp; Department of Land & Natural Resources, Room 306, 3060 Eiwa St, Lihu'e, HI 96766).

Hiking Tours
The **Sierra Club** (☎ 651-0682; www.hi.sierraclub.org/kauai/ kauai.html) leads guided hikes (suggested donation $3) ranging from beach clean-up walks to rigorous overnighters. Koke'e Natural History Museum also offers guided Wonder Walks (p546) in summer for a nominal donation.

For the ultimate learning experience, hike with geologist Chuck Blay's team, **Kaua'i Nature Tours** (☎ 742-8305; 888-233-8365; www.kauainaturetours .com; PO Box 549, Koloa, HI 96756; tours adult $82-97, child under 13 $45-64).

GOLF
While Kaua'i has only nine courses, half consistently rank among the state's best. In 2005 *Golf Digest* ranked Princeville's Prince Course (p504) number one in the state, with Kaua'i Lagoons' Kiele Course (p471) at number six, Po'ipu Bay Golf Course (p525) at number 12 and Princeville's Makai Course (p504) at number 14.

GETTING THERE & AWAY
Air

All commercial flights land at **Lihu'e airport** (LIH; Map p467; ☎ 246-1448; www.hawaii.gov/dot/airports /kauai/lih; ☺ visitor hotline 6:30am-9pm). Three airlines (plus those flying chartered vacation tours) fly directly from the US mainland to Lihu'e Airport:

American Airlines (☎ 800-223-5436; www.aa.com)
United Airlines (☎ 800-241-6522; www.ual.com)
US Airways (☎ 800-428-4322; www.usairways.com)

But most visitors from overseas and from the US mainland arrive first in Honolulu, from which the flight time to Lihu'e is 25 minutes. Kaua'i also has two small airports – Burns Field (p535) in Hanapepe and Princeville Airport (p504) – that serve helicopter tours.

For the interisland flights, there are currently four carriers, which fly from Kahului (Maui), Kona (Big Island) and mainly from Honolulu:

Aloha Airlines (☎ 800-367-5250; www.alohaairlines.com)
go! (☎ 888-435-9462; www.iflygo.com)
Hawaiian Airlines (☎ 800-367-5320; www.hawaiianair.com)
Island Air (☎ US mainland 800-323-3345, Neighbor Islands 800-652-6541; www.islandair.com)

Boat

In 2007 **Hawaii Superferry** (www.hawaiisuperferry.com) launched an interisland ferry service from O'ahu to Kaua'i, Maui and the Big Island. The trip from Honolulu Harbor (O'ahu) to Nawiliwili Harbor (Kaua'i) takes three hours and one-way fares cost $42 to $60, depending on advance purchase and travel days. Transporting your car will cost $55 to $65.

As for island-hopping cruises, the most popular are the **Norwegian Cruise Line** (☎ 800-327-7030; www.ncl.com) cruises between the Hawaiian Islands that start and end within the state, launching either in Honolulu or on Maui. On Kaua'i, ships dock at Nawiliwili Harbor for one night.

GETTING AROUND
To/From the Airport

For car rentals, check in at the appropriate booth outside the baggage-claim area. Vans transport you to nearby car lots. If there's a queue, go directly to the lot, where check-ins are quicker.

Bicycle

Cyclists will encounter the gamut of terrain and weather. Winter months are particularly wet, but showers are common year-round.

Worse problems are the lack of bicycle lanes and the narrow, winding and busy roads.

An 18-mile coastal bicycle path is slated to run from Lihu'e all the way to Anahola by 2008 and the path is partly completed. Selective bike transportation would work well but, among locals, cycling means occasional recreation, not real transportation.

Bus

Let's face it, Kaua'i is no shining model of public transit. It's far too rural, with too many destinations inaccessible by conventional buses.

Kaua'i Bus (☎ 241-6410; www.kauai.gov; 3220 Ho'olako St, Lihu'e; per trip adult/senior & youth 7-18 $1.50/75¢; ⏰ 7:45am-4:30pm Mon-Fri), the county public bus, offers bare-bones islandwide service Monday to Friday, with a more limited service on Saturday. There is no service on Sunday and county holidays. Schedules are available at the **Kaua'i Visitors Bureau** (Map p472; ☎ 245-3971, 800-262-1400; www.kauaidiscovery.com; Suite 101, 4334 Rice St, Lihu'e). Check the website for current information. All buses stop in Lihu'e. On longer routes, eg Lihu'e to Po'ipu, only one bus departs daily from each end.

Car & Motorcycle

Kaua'i has one belt road running three-quarters of the way around the island, from Ke'e Beach in the north to Polihale in the west. The **Ready Mapbook of Kaua'i** ($11) is an invaluable road atlas, sold online at www.geckofarms.com and at island bookstores.

Congestion is rampant, especially between Lihu'e and Kapa'a where rush-hour traffic is a

ROAD DISTANCES & TIMES FROM LIHUE

Destination	Miles	Duration
Anahola	14	25min
Hanalei	31	1hr
Hanapepe	16	30min
Kapa'a	8	15min
Ke'e Beach	40	1¼hr
Kilauea Lighthouse	25	40min
Po'ipu	10	20min
Port Allen	15	25min
Princeville	28	45min
Waimea	23	40min
Waimea Canyon	42	1½hr

given. To combat traffic, a 'contra-flow' lane is created weekdays from 5am to 10:30am on Kuhio Hwy (Hwy 56) in the Wailua area; this turns a northbound lane into a southbound lane by reversing the flow of traffic, so that commuters to Lihu'e have an extra lane open.

Gas prices are especially steep on Kaua'i. Prices vary across the island, so check www .kauaiworld.com/gasprices for the current highs and lows.

Regarding motorcycles, riding anywhere on Kaua'i, particularly in upland areas, requires hardcore rain gear, which some rental shops also supply.

For car rentals, renting from major agencies is most convenient. The following all have a branch at Lihu'e airport.

Alamo (☎ 800-327-9633, Lihu'e 246-0645; www.alamo .com)

Avis (☎ 800-831-2847, Lihu'e 245-7995; www.avis.com)

Budget (☎ 800-527-0700, Lihu'e 245-9031; www .budget.com)

Dollar (☎ 800-800-4000, Lihu'e 742-8351; www .dollarcar.com)

Hertz (☎ 800-654-3011, Lihu'e 245-3356; www.hertz .com)

ON THE ROAD

If you ask Kaua'i locals for driving directions, be prepared for island-style lingo:

- Instead of giving standard north/east/ south/west directions, locals simply refer to *mauka* (toward the mountains; inland) and *makai* (toward the ocean; seaward).

- Highways are known by their Hawaiian common names, not by number. See Highway Nicknames, right.

- Locals invariably refer to landmarks ('turn right at the Shell station' or 'go past Longs Drugs') rather than cross streets or driving mileage, so be eagle-eyed when checking out your surroundings.

- Mainlanders generally talk *much* faster than locals, who take their time getting to the point. If you find yourself growing impatient when trying to extract simple directions, take a deep breath and keep your mouth shut. Relaaaax, you're on vacation.

HIGHWAY NICKNAMES

Locals call highways by nickname rather than by number. Memorize them:

Hwy 50 Kaumuali'i Hwy
Hwy 51 Kapule Hwy
Hwy 56 Kuhio Hwy
Hwy 58 Nawiliwili Rd
Hwy 520 Maluhia Rd (Tree Tunnel) and Po'ipu Rd
Hwy 530 Koloa Rd
Hwy 540 Halewili Rd
Hwy 550 Waimea Canyon Dr
Hwy 560 Kuhio Hwy (continuation of Hwy 56)
Hwy 552 Koke'e Rd
Hwy 570 Ahukini Rd
Hwy 580 Kuamo'o Rd
Hwy 581 Kamalu Rd and Olohena Rd
Hwy 583 Ma'alo Rd

National (☎ 888-868-6207, Lihu'e 245-5636; www .nationalcar.com)

Thrifty (☎ 800-847-4389, Lihu'e 866-450-5101; www .thrifty.com)

Local car-rental agencies are generally reliable and cheaper. The best is **Island Cars** (Map p467; ☎ 246-6000; www.islandcars.net; 2983 Aukele St, Lihu'e), whose daily/weekly rates start at $24/135, taxes included, for just the basics (ie cars five to 15 years old, no air-con). Minimum age is 21; major credit card not required. Pay more for newer cars with air-con.

No helmet laws and the wide, open roads make motorcycle rentals, particularly Harley Davidsons, popular. You must have a motorcycle license or endorsement; you might need previous Harley experience to rent one. Rates hover around $100/170 for 10/24 hours.

Cycle City Kaua'i/Two Wheels (☎ 822-7283, 800-996-9903; www.cyclecitykauai.com; 4555 Pouli Rd, Waipouli)

Kaua'i Harley-Davidson (Map p467; ☎ 241-7020, 877-212-9253; www.kauaih-d.com; 3-1866 Kaumuali'i Hwy, Lihu'e) Located outside Lihu'e in Puhi, this official Harley dealer also sells the gear.

Taxi

Taxicabs (or phones to call one) are available curbside of the baggage-claim area. Taxis charge $3 at flag fall and $3 per subsequent mile, metered in 30¢ increments. Call the following:

Akiko's Taxi (☎ 822-7588, 877-722-7588) Based in Lihu'e and Kapa'a.

BIRD'S-EYE VIEW OF KAUA'I

Loud, noisy and ubiquitous on Kaua'i, helicopters are easy to criticize. Yet almost anyone with a deep appreciation of nature secretly relishes the bird's-eye view.

Helicopters can swoop around Kaua'i's otherwise inaccessible cliffs, valleys and mountains – and only from the air will you witness Mt Wai'ale'ale from inside the mysterious crater, all misty and ringed by waterfalls. Helicopters provide those with mobility problems their only way to see the Na Pali Coast.

Schedule a chopper tour early in your trip in case it's cancelled due to bad weather. Choose a company that uses noise-canceling headphones and helicopters with large windows; passengers in middle seats often feel cheated due to lower visibility.

Most companies fly A-Star helicopters, which fit four passengers in back and two with the pilot in front. Highly recommended are the open-door rides offered only by Inter-Island Helicopter (p535). Most tours leave from Lihu'e (p472). The going rate is around $200 for an hour's flight.

North Shore Cab (☎ 639-7829; www.northshorecab .com) Based in Princeville. Offers tours (per hour $60 for one car, maximum six passengers).
Southshore Cab (☎ 742-1525) Based in Po'ipu.

LIHU'E

pop 5674
The heart of the island's capital, Lihu'e, is hard to pinpoint. With no town square and businesses scattered beyond walking distance, it's a drive-in, drive-out place. Weekday commuters face traffic jams in either direction.

Nevertheless, Lihu'e is worth a stop for economical eating and shopping. Unlike resort towns, it presents itself as a down-to-earth, ordinary place. You'll find longtime family-run businesses tucked away in nondescript buildings – and you're bound to stop at Kukui Grove Shopping Center, an 'anytown' suburban-style cluster of mom-and-pop shops and national chains, including Costco, one of the world's largest warehouse chains.

The ethnic makeup of Lihu'e and its vicinity reflects the island's plantation history: here, the largest ethnic group is the Japanese at just under 30%, followed by Caucasian and mixed-race individuals, each about 20% of the population. The virtually contiguous communities of Puhi (population 1186) and Hanama'ulu (population 3272) both comprise majority Filipino populations.

Lihu'e's resort strip near Kalapaki Beach and Kaua'i Lagoons Golf Club cannot compete with the cachet of Po'ipu or Princeville, but it might become a hotspot yet. Three times a week, Norwegian Cruise Line ships dock at Nawiliwili Harbor, releasing over 2000 passengers for a one-night jaunt.

HISTORY
Lihu'e arose as a plantation town back in the day when sugar was king and the massive Lihu'e Plantation sugar mill (still standing south of town along Kaumuali'i Hwy) was Kaua'i's largest. The plantation relied solely on rainwater during its early years, but then William Harrison Rice, who bought the company in the early 1860s, became the first planter in Hawaii to irrigate sugarcane fields. The plantation closed in 2001, ending more than a century of operation.

Now Lihu'e's economy relies not only on tourism but on retail, which is obvious from all the big-box stores at Kukui Grove Shopping Center. You might not think an island of 62,000 needs a Costco but, in October 2006, it got one.

ORIENTATION
Lihu'e is surrounded on all sides by highways: the Kuhio Hwy (Hwy 56) to the west and the Kapule Hwy (Hwy 51) to the east, while Ahukini Rd (Hwy 570) and Nawiliwili Rd (Hwy 58) roughly represent north and south borders respectively. The town's main drag, Rice St, runs east–west through the heart of town.

INFORMATION
Bookstores
Beach Books (Map p467; Harbor Mall, 3501 Rice St; ☺ 8:30am-7:30pm Mon-Sat) Cheap new and used beach reading.
Borders (Map p467; ☎ 246-0862; Kukui Grove Shopping Center, 4303 Nawiliwili Rd; ☺ 9am-10pm Mon-Thu, to

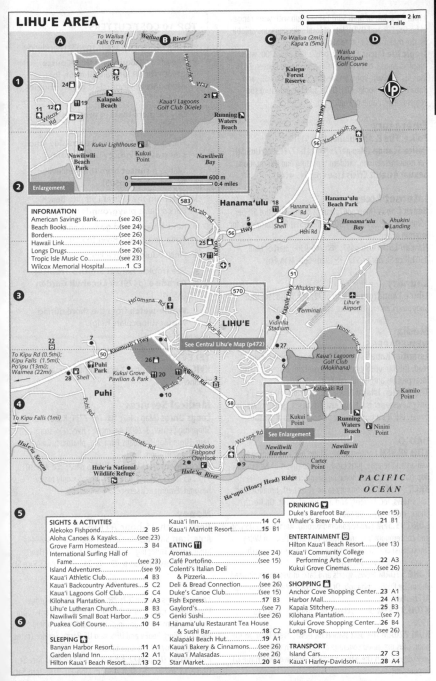

LIHU'E AREA

KAUA'I

11pm Fri & Sat, to 8pm Sun) Large chain with wide range of books, CDs and DVDs; lots of local selections unavailable on the mainland. In-store Starbucks café.

Tropic Isle Music Co (Map p467; ☎ 245-8700; www .tropicislemusic.com; Anchor Cove Shopping Center, 3416 Rice St; ☻ 9am-9pm) Impressive stock of Hawaii- and Kaua'i-specific books, CDs, DVDs and the gamut of souvenirs (all available online).

Emergency

Police, Fire & Ambulance (☎ 911)
Police Station (Map p472; ☎ 241-1771; 3060 Umi St) For nonemergencies, incident reporting and information.
Sexual Assault Crisis Line (☎ 245-4144)

Internet Access

Beach Books (Map p467; Harbor Mall, 3501 Rice St; per 15min $3; ☻ 8:30am-7:30pm Mon-Sat) One computer for internet access.
Hawaii Link (Map p467; ☎ 246-9300; Harbor Mall, 3501 Rice St; per hr $12; ☻ 9am-6pm Mon-Fri)

Laundry

Lihu'e Laundromat (Map p472; ☎ 332-8356; Rice Shopping Center, 4303 Rice St; ☻ 6am-9pm)

Media

NEWSPAPERS

Essential Kaua'i (www.essentialkauai.com) A quick read, this bimonthly publication contains current events, local profiles and handy reviews.
The Garden Island (www.kauaiworld.com) Kaua'i's daily newspaper is a lean, 'just the basics,' small-town paper, but it's a good source of local events and issues.

RADIO

KITH 98.9FM Contemporary island music, including Hawaiian and reggae, plus local-favorite covers of American pop classics. Upbeat choice for island cruising.
KKCR 91.9FM Community radio at its best, broadcasting talk shows, local events and a range of music. On North Shore, frequency is 90.9FM.
KONG 93.5FM (www.kongradio.com) Mainstream US pop and contemporary island music. Excellent DJs Ron Wiley (mornings) and Marc Valentine (afternoons). On North Shore, frequency is 94.5FM.
KONG 570AM News, sports and talk, including syndicated shows by Rush Limbaugh, Dr Dean Edell, Mitch Albom and Al Franken.
KTOH 99.9FM Oldies, classic hits from the 1960s to 1990s.
KUAI 720AM The best station for news, every hour on the hour, plus extended coverage at 7am, noon and 5pm on weekdays. Catch the early-morning show with longtime DJ Reggie DeRoos.

TOP 10 COST CUTTERS

- Hike for free on **trails** (p463) islandwide.
- Tee off at **Kukuiolono Golf Course** (p530) for $8, or wait till noon for discounts at world-class **resort courses** (p463).
- Buy **farmers-market produce** (p475).
- Fill your **gas tank** on the Eastside (and never at the Princeville Chevron!).
- Watch a **sunset** from the Princeville Resort...lawn (p503).
- Entertain the kids at Lydgate Beach Park's giant **playgrounds** (p479).
- Rent a **kayak** and go solo on the manageable Hanalei River (p509).
- Find lodging with a kitchen and eat in.
- See tropical flora at **Smith's Tropical Paradise** (p479) or **Limahuli Garden** (p514).
- **Whale-watch** from the shore during winter (binoculars help).

TELEVISION

KVIC A televised loop of Kaua'i tourist information on channel 3.

Medical Services

Longs Drugs (Map p467; ☎ 245-7771; Kukui Grove Shopping Center, 3-2600 Kaumuali'i Hwy; ☻ store 7am-10pm Mon-Sat, 8am-8pm Sun, pharmacy 8am-9pm Mon-Sat, 9am-6pm Sun)
Wilcox Memorial Hospital (Map p467; ☎ 245-1010, TTY 245-1133; 3420 Kuhio Hwy) Kaua'i's only major hospital. Emergency services 24 hours.

Money

Banks with 24-hour ATMs:
American Savings Bank (Map p467; ☎ 246-8844; Kukui Grove Shopping Center, 3-2600 Kaumuali'i Hwy)
Bank of Hawaii (Map p472; ☎ 245-6761; 4455 Rice St)

Post

Longs Drugs (Map p467; ☎ 245-7771; Kukui Grove Shopping Center, 3-2600 Kaumuali'i Hwy; ☻ 7am-10pm Mon-Sat, 8am-8pm Sun) In-store postal center offers photocopying, FedEx and UPS, and US Postal Service (rates are slightly lower at a post office).
Post office (Map p472; ☎ 800-275-8777; 4441 Rice St, Lihu'e, HI 96766; ☻ 8am-4:30pm Mon-Fri, 9am-1pm Sat)

Main post office holds poste restante (general delivery) mail for a maximum of 30 days.

Tourist Information

Kaua'i Visitors Bureau (Map p472; ☎ 245-3971, 800-262-1400; www.kauaidiscovery.com; Suite 1014, 334 Rice St) offers a monthly calendar of events, bus schedules and list of county-managed Sunshine Markets (farmers markets) for the sale of Kaua'i produce. Order a free 'vacation planning kit' online.

Travel Agencies

Mokihana Travel (Map p472; ☎ 245-5338; Suite 3, 3016 Umi St; ☒ 8am-5pm Mon-Fri, to noon Sat)

SIGHTS
Kaua'i Museum

For a grounding in Kaua'i's history, check out this modest but interesting **museum** (Map p472; ☎ 245-6931; www.kauaimuseum.org; 4428 Rice St; adult/child 6-12/youth 13-17/senior $7/1/3/5, 1st Sat of month free; ☒ 9am-4pm Mon-Fri, 10am-4pm Sat). If you're new to the islands, it's worth taking a **guided tour** (free with admission; ☒ 10:30am Tue, Wed & Thu); call for reservations. Free **Hawaiian quilting demonstrations** (☒ 9am-noon Wed & Thu) and **lauhala-hat weaving demonstrations** (☒ 1pm Mon & Wed) are given year-round.

Straightforward, well-written displays explain the Hawaiian Islands' volcanic genesis and the formation of the island chain from the ocean floor, as well as Kaua'i's unique ecosystems. Collections include early Hawaiian artifacts such as *kapa* (bark cloth), wooden bowls and ceremonial lei. Upstairs the collection covers the sugar and pineapple plantation era. One telling display juxtaposes replicas of a plantation worker's spartan shack and the spacious bedroom of an early missionary's house, furnished with an extravagant koa four-post bed and Hawaiian quilts.

Kalapaki Beach

Hidden behind Kaua'i Marriott Resort (p474), Lihu'e's best beach (Map p467) is often overlooked by tourists. But local surfers and bodyboarders trot toward the swells, while resort guests bask on golden sand lined with coconut trees. Sheltered by points and breakwaters at Nawiliwili Bay, waters are quite hospitable to swimmers. While it might appear to be a private resort beach, it's open to the public (find free parking close to the water at the hotel's north side).

Fronting the beach is the **International Surfing Hall of Fame** (Map p467; ☎ 632-2270; Anchor Cove Shopping Center; adult/child under 12 $10/free; ☒ 9am-9pm). In existence since 1966 but without a bricks-and-mortar home until 2004, this long-overdue museum exhibits boards, memorabilia and original art in cool digs replete with thatched roof and piped-in surfing tunes. The museum screening room shows classic surf movies.

If you've got time to kill, cross the footbridge from Kalapaki Beach, over Nawiliwili Stream, to **Nawiliwili Beach Park** (Map p467). It ain't a showstopper, with a seawall running its length. But from here you can see the light beacon on Kukui Point and, from the far end of the parking lot, you can also see the distant lighthouse on Ninini Point. Gargantuan cruise ships dock at Nawiliwili Harbor and smaller boats, including deep-sea fishing charters and kayak tours, leave from nearby Nawiliwili Small Boat Harbor.

Wailua Falls

Wind your way 4 miles north of Lihu'e to the falls made famous in the opening credits of the *Fantasy Island* TV series. While officially listed as 80ft, the falls have been repeatedly measured at between 125ft to 175ft. Indeed, this gushing double waterfall (Wailua means 'two waters') misting the surrounding tropical foliage is a fantastic photo op, especially when the falls merge into one wide cascade after downpours.

At the lookout spot, a sign reads: 'Slippery rocks at top of falls. People have been killed.' Of course, this tempts folks to scramble down the unmaintained path for the thrill of swimming beneath the falls. The path is steep and people actually do slide off the rocks.

The falls plummet into a deep pool, spurring the truly intrepid to dive from the top, as ancient Hawaiians did to prove their manhood. The display was often fatal then – and it remains so today. In 2000 two 22-year-old men from California leaped, and a local 22-year-old man slipped, from the top, all in the same week. Thereafter the county stated that future jumpers would be billed for rescue costs ($1500).

To get here from Lihu'e, follow Kuhio Hwy north and turn left onto Ma'alo Rd (Hwy 583), which ends at the falls after 4 miles.

Kilohana Plantation

Amid sprawling, manicured lawns, this **plantation estate** (Map p467; www.kilohanakauai.com; Kaumuali'i

Hwy; admission free; ⏰ 9:30am-9:30pm Mon-Sat, to 5pm Sun) is now a tourist magnet featuring Gaylord's restaurant (p475), estate tours and one-stop upscale shopping. Sugar baron Gaylord Parke Wilcox, once the head honcho of Grove Farm Homestead, built the house in 1935. Trivia buffs take note: the Wilcox family was the model for James Michener's famous epic, *Hawaii*.

The 15,000-sq-ft Tudor-style mansion has been painstakingly restored and its legacy as one of Kaua'i's distinguished historic houses is unquestioned. Antique-filled rooms and Oriental carpets laid over hardwood floors lead you past cases of poi pounders, koa bowls and other Hawaiiana to a row of gallery shops.

Clydesdale horses take visitors on **carriage rides** (☎ 246-9529; 20min ride adult/child $12/6; ⏰ 11am-5pm) across the 35-acre grounds, including gardens and livestock barns – rather hokey but fun for kids.

A new attraction, launched in early 2007, is the 2.5-mile recreational **railway** (☎ 245-5608; 30min ride adult/child under 12 $18/10; ⏰ 10am-3:30pm). Its retro-style trains pass staple island crops (sugarcane, pineapple, coffee and taro) and groves of tropical fruits; passengers can sample and buy edibles at a farmers market and gift shop.

Alekoko (Menehune) Fishpond

Although the view is distant, you won't regret a quick stop to look at this tranquil 39-acre pond (Map p467), an ancient *loko wai* (freshwater pond), surrounded by a vast area of forest. According to legend, Kaua'i's *menehune* (little people) formed the fishpond overnight when they built the stone wall running along a bend in Hule'ia River. The stone wall is now covered by a thick green line of mangrove trees.

The pond was in great condition until 1824, when Kaua'i's leader Kaumuali'i died and *ali'i* (chiefs) from O'ahu and Maui ruled the island as absentee landlords. With no *ali'i* to feed and maintain the pond, it sorely declined. Later the surrounding area was planted with taro and rice.

Today the US Fish & Wildlife Service owns the lands surrounding the fishpond (238 acres of river basin and steep forested slopes along the north side of Hule'ia River). In 1973 the area was designated the **Hule'ia National Wildlife Refuge** (http://pacificislands.fws.gov/wnwr/khuleianwr .html) and now provides breeding and feeding grounds for endemic water birds. The refuge is closed to the public, but kayak tours (opposite) along Hule'ia River drift through it.

To get to the overlook, drive up Hulemalu Rd for 0.5 miles.

Ninini Point

You'll enjoy solitude from other tourists here (Map p467), where 360-degree vistas show jets swooping in the sky above and waves crashing against the rocks below. Looking east, soaring cliffs cut off rainbows and, closer in, golfers tee off near a beckoning scoop of beach. These terrific views from Ninini Point are made more so by its 100ft **lighthouse** marking the northern entrance to Nawiliwili Bay. Here, Hawaiians still fish, pick *opihi* (edible limpet) and gather *limu* (edible seaweed).

The road to the lighthouse begins off Kapule Hwy, just over 0.5 miles south of the intersection with Ahukini Rd and marked with two concrete slabs. You'll pass a guard gate (usually empty) and through Hole 12 of the Mokihana Golf Course, for a total of just over 2 miles, most of it rutted dirt road, before you reach the short spur to the lighthouse.

Running Waters Beach (the little slice of sand visible from Ninini Point) is not swimmable but makes a nice picnic spot. To find it, return to Hole 12 and park in the lot just before it, then follow the signs for 'Shore Access.' Turn right at Whaler's Brew Pub and descend to its parking lot, where you'll see another 'Shore Access' sign to your left. It's a steep, quick walk to the beach below.

Grove Farm Homestead

History buffs might enjoy this **plantation museum** (Map p467; ☎ 245-3202; Nawiliwili Rd; 2hr tour adult/child under 12 $5/2; ⏰ tours 10am & 1pm Mon, Wed & Thu), open only for pre-arranged tours, but kids might grow restless. Grove Farm was among the most productive sugar companies on Kaua'i and George Wilcox, the son of missionaries Abner and Lucy Wilcox, built this well-preserved farmhouse in 1864. It feels suspended in time, with rocking chairs sitting dormant on a covered porch and untouched books lining the shelves of the musty library.

Lihu'e Lutheran Church

Atop a curvy country lane just off Kaumuali'i Hwy (Hwy 50) is Hawaii's oldest Lutheran **church** (Map p467; ☎ 245-2145; 4602 Ho'omana Rd; ⏰ services 8am & 10:30am Sun), a quaint clapboard house of worship, with an incongruously slanted floor that resembles a ship's deck and a balcony akin to a captain's bridge. German immigrants built

---

LEAP OF FAITH

The easy way to satisfy your Tarzan fantasy? Go ziplining. No special skill or training needed, but you must pass weight and age restrictions. Inquire first, as restrictions vary by company.

Most ziplining parks are located near Lihu'e. **Just Live** (☎ 482-1295; www.justlive.org; Kuhio Hwy; tour incl snack $115) offers the only canopy-based zipping, meaning you never touch ground after your first zip. The three-hour treetop tour includes six ziplines, 60ft to 70ft off the ground in 200ft Norfolk pines. Too tame? Inquire about the two exciting ropes-challenge courses that test your personal 'fear factor.' Groups are nice and small (a max of eight per two affable and exceptionally professional guides). Profits from commercial tours go to the company's community youth programs.

Kaua'i Backcountry Adventures (Map p467; ☎ 245-2506, 888-270-0555; www.kauaibackcountry.com; Kuhio Hwy; tour incl lunch $120) offers a 3½-hour zipline tour with seven lines, elevated as high as 200ft above the ground and running as far as 900ft (three football fields). Afterward, refuel on a picnic lunch at a swimming pond. Groups max out at 11 here.

On the Kipu Falls Zipline Trek, run by **Outfitters Kaua'i** (Map pp522-3; ☎ 742-9667, 888-742-9887; www.outfitterskauai.com; Po'ipu Plaza, 2827-A Po'ipu Rd; tour incl snack per adult/child 7-14 $115/90), you'll view the scenic Hule'ia National Wildlife Refuge from suspension bridges and other aerial walkways, four ziplines, and a 'zippel' line that simulates rappelling down a mountain. Cap the 4½-hour tour at Kipu Falls for swimming and, if you dare, rope-swinging. Larger groups up to 13.

On the North Shore, Princeville Ranch Adventures (p504) has eight ziplines.

---

this church, styling it after their own late-19th-century boat. The building is actually a faithful 1983 reconstruction of the 1885 original, which was leveled in Hurricane 'Iwa in 1982.

ACTIVITIES
Golf
The two Jack Nicklaus–designed 18-hole par-72 courses at **Kaua'i Lagoons Golf Club** (Map p467; ☎ 241-6000, 800-634-6400; www.kauailagoonsgolf .com; Kaua'i Marriott, 3351 Ho'olaule'a Way; Kiele green fees nonguest/guest morning $170/125, afternoon $115/105, Mokihana nonguest/guest morning $120/75, afternoon $65/59, club rental $35) include the highly regarded and challenging Kiele Course, surrounded by crashing waves, with each hole named for an animal (note the marble statues at each tee), the last being an aptly named golden bear. The adjacent Mokihana Course is less dramatic but gentler and better for higher handicaps.

The lush cliffs of Mt Ha'upu serve as a backdrop to the Robin Nelson–designed **Puakea Golf Course** (Map p467; ☎ 245-8756, 866-773-5554; www.puakeagolf.com; 4315 Kalepa Rd; green fees incl cart before/after 1pm $125/65, club rental $30/20), which first opened in 1997 (with an odd 10 holes) and became an 18-hole course in 2003. Located near Kukui Grove Shopping Center.

Kayaking & Canoeing
Outfitters Kaua'i (Map pp522-3; ☎ 742-9667, 888-742-9887; www.outfitterskauai.com; Po'ipu Plaza, 2827-A Po'ipu Rd, Po'ipu Beach; tour per adult/child 3-14 with lunch $104/80, without lunch $94/75; ⓨ check-in 8am or 9:30am Mon-Sat) offers a pleasant kayaking and hiking tour in the Hule'ia National Wildlife Refuge. The kayak trip is only 2 miles, downwind, and then you return on a motorized canoe.

Island Adventures (☎ 246-6333; www.kauaifun .com; Nawiliwili Small Boat Harbor; adult/child 8-12 $89/69; ⓨ check-in 8am Mon-Sat) offers an 4½-hour tour in the Hule'ia National Wildlife Refuge, where you'll paddle 2.5 miles, walk along a forest trail, ride a van, then hike to two private waterfalls.

Owned and operated by Hawaiians, **Aloha Canoes & Kayaks** (Map p467; ☎ 246-6804, 877-473-5446; www.hawaiikayaks.com; Anchor Cove Shopping Center, 3416 Rice St, Lihu'e; double-hull canoe adult/child 3-11 $82/70; ⓨ check-in 9am Tue, Thu & Sat) offers a 3½-hour tour that allows you to paddle a 12-person canoe in the Hule'ia River, swim and rope-jump. Kayaking tours are offered, too.

Tubing
Too lazy to paddle? Try tubing instead. Folks of all ages can climb onto inner tubes and float down former irrigation ditches with **Kaua'i Backcountry Adventures** (Map p467; ☎ 245-2506, 888-270-0555; www.kauaibackcountry.com; Kuhio Hwy; tour incl lunch per person $99; ⓨ departures 9am, 10:30am, 1pm & 2:30pm Mon-Sat, 9am & 1pm Sun). The three-hour tour ends with lunch at a swimming hole. Great for the whole family (including kids as young as five).

KAUA'I

ATVs

Driving an obnoxious ATV across the private, pristine 3000-acre Kipu Ranch sounds destructive, but accessing a hiking trail in a 4WD is no less questionable. The two tours offered by **Kipu Ranch Adventures** (☎ 246-9288; www.kiputours.com; waterfall tour adult/child/senior $140/90/120) are actually considered ecotours because they introduce visitors to diverse landscapes and their history. The backdrop of the Ha'upu mountain range and Kipu Kai coast are gorgeous and otherwise inaccessible.

Fishing

Kaua'i waters are well stocked with fish, from deep-sea biggies like marlin and tuna to more manageable inshore species like gray snapper. See p462 for more on fishing. Recommended outfitters departing from Nawiliwili Small Boat Harbor (Map p467) include the following:

Kai Bear (☎ 652-4556; 4hr shared charter per person $139-179)

True Blue Charters (☎ 246-6333, 888-245-1707; www.truebluecharters.com; charter 4hr shared per

$139-239, private per 6 anglers $850) Shared charters include standard (maximum 10 anglers) and deluxe (maximum four anglers). Spectators can ride for half price.

Wild Bill's (☎ 822-5963; 4hr shared charter per person $115)

Fitness

Kaua'i Athletic Club (Map p467; ☎ 245-5381; 4370 Kukui Grove St; per day/week/month $12/40/80; 🕑 5:30am-9pm Mon-Fri, 8am-5pm Sat & Sun) offers aerobic and resistance machines, free weights, outdoor swimming pool (48ft long), classes and courts.

TOURS

Most helicopter tours fly from Lihu'e Airport (Map p467). The going rate for a 60-minute flight is about $200; see p466) for more on helicopter tours. The following companies are recommended:

Air Kaua'i (☎ 246-4666, 800-972-4666; www.airkauai .com) Cushy A-Star helicopters with large windows, air-con and excellent narration.

Jack Harter Helicopters (☎ 245-3774, 888-245-2001; www.helicopters-kauai.com)

Safari Helicopters (☎ 246-0136, 800-326-3356; www .safariair.com)

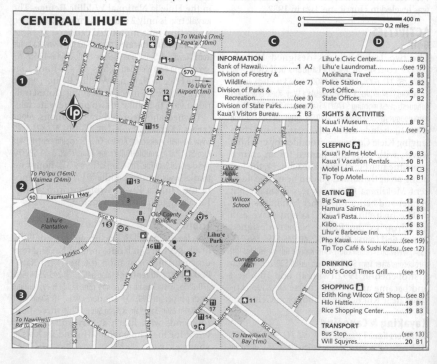

CENTRAL LIHU'E

0   400 m
0   0.2 miles

INFORMATION	
Bank of Hawaii	1 A2
Division of Forestry & Wildlife	(see 7)
Division of Parks & Recreation	(see 3)
Division of State Parks	(see 7)
Kaua'i Visitors Bureau	2 B3
Lihu'e Civic Center	3 B2
Lihu'e Laundromat	(see 19)
Mokihana Travel	4 B3
Police Station	5 B2
Post Office	6 B2
State Offices	7 B2

SIGHTS & ACTIVITIES	
Kaua'i Museum	8 B2
Na Ala Hele	(see 7)

SLEEPING 🛏	
Kaua'i Palms Hotel	9 B3
Kaua'i Vacation Rentals	10 B1
Motel Lani	11 C3
Tip Top Motel	12 B1

EATING 🍴	
Big Save	13 B2
Hamura Saimin	14 B3
Kaua'i Pasta	15 B1
Kiibo	16 B3
Lihu'e Barbecue Inn	17 B3
Pho Kauai	(see 19)
Tip Top Café & Sushi Katsu	(see 12)

DRINKING	
Rob's Good Times Grill	(see 19)

SHOPPING 🛍	
Edith King Wilcox Gift Shop	(see 8)
Hilo Hattie	18 B1
Rice Shopping Center	19 B3

TRANSPORT	
Bus Stop	(see 13)
Will Squyres	20 B1

FESTIVALS & EVENTS

E Pili Kakou I Ho'okahi Lahui (☎ 246-4752; www
.epilikakou.org) Popular annual two-day hula retreat in
late January at the Kaua'i Marriott Resort.

Spring Gourmet Gala (☎ 245-8359; Kaua'i Community College; admission $75; ☉ 6pm) Famous local chefs
headline this food and wine fundraiser in early April for
Kaua'i Community College's culinary arts program.

May Day Lei Contest and Fair (☎ 245-6931; www
.kauaimuseum.org; admission free) Established in the early
1980s, the annual Kaua'i Museum lei contest on May 1
spawns legendary floral art.

Kaua'i Polynesian Festival (☎ 335-6466; www
.kauai-polyfest.com) This four-day event in late May
features Hawaiian and Polynesian dance, food booths and
cultural workshops.

Fourth of July Concert in the Sky (☎ 246-2440)
Enjoy island foods, live entertainment and the grand finale
fireworks show set to music at Lihu'e's Vidinha Stadium
(Map p467).

Kaua'i County Farm Bureau Fair (☎ 828-2120;
admission adult/child $3/2) Old-fashioned family fun at
Vidinha Stadium in late August, with carnival rides and
games, livestock show, petting zoo, hula performances and
lots of local-food booths.

Aloha Festivals Ho'olaule'a & Parade (☎ 245-8508;
www.alohafestivals.com; admission free) This statewide
event in early September starts on Kaua'i with a parade from
Vidinha Stadium to the historic county building lawn. The
ho'olaule'a includes an appearance by Kaua'i's royal court.

Kaua'i Composer's Contest & Concert (☎ 822-
2166; www.mokihana.kauai.net; Kaua'i Community
College; admission $10-15; ☉ 7pm) The signature event
of the Kaua'i Mokihana Festival, this contest in mid- to late
September showcases local composing talent.

'Kaua'i Style' Hawaiian Slack Key Guitar Festival
(☎ 239-4336; www.hawaiianslackkeyguitarfestivals.com,
www.livefromkauai.org; Kaua'i Beach Resort; admission
free; ☉ noon-6pm) Held in mid-November, this opportunity to see master slack-key guitarists like Ledward
Ka'apana for free is not to be missed.

Lights on Rice Parade (☎ 246-1004; admission free;
☉ 6:30pm) See a dazzling array of floats bedecked with
lights along Rice St in early December.

SLEEPING
Budget

Motel Lani (Map p472; ☎ 245-2965; 4240 Rice St; r $45;
☒) If the bottom line is your bottom line,
consider Motel Lani. The salmon-pink, six-
room flat on Lihu'e's modest main street of-

fers tiny, shabby rooms. But they are clean
and come with a small refrigerator (no TV
or phone). During weekdays Neighbor Island
construction workers book up the place.

Tip Top Motel (Map p472; ☎ 245-2333; tiptop@aloha
.net; 3173 Akahi St; r $65; ☒) The depressingly in-
stitutional, 34-room Tip Top has one saving
grace: yummy pancakes at the on-site restaurant. Otherwise, you're stuck with white
cinder-block walls, linoleum floors, iron-
gated windows, fluorescent lighting and an
antiseptic odor. Rooms do include TV and
window-box air-con.

Kaua'i Palms Hotel (Map p472; ☎ 246-0908; www
.kauaipalmshotel.com; 2931 Kalena St; r $65-95; ☉ office
7am-8pm) On a quiet side street, Kaua'i Palms is
definitely the best bargain in Lihu'e. The two-
story, open-air main building houses 15 compact rooms with refrigerator and flat-screen
cable TV. Windows on opposite walls allow
a cooling cross-breeze. The best rooms are
upstairs, with king beds (the smaller downstairs rooms have queen beds). Coin-operated
laundry available.

Midrange & Top End

Kaua'i Inn (Map p467; ☎ 245-9000, 800-808-2330; www
.kauai-inn.com; 2430 Hulemalu Rd; r with kitchenette incl
breakfast $80-110; ☒) Located inland, off the
beaten track, this peaceful property near Ale-
koko Fishpond is Kaua'i's oldest hotel. While
not fancy, the 40 rooms are clean and quite
spacious, with sliding doors leading to back
porches. Rooms in the same category vary in
size, view and decor.

Garden Island Inn (Map p467; ☎ 245-7227, 800-
648-0154; www.gardenislandinn.com; 3445 Wilcox Rd; r with
kitchenette $95-105, ste with kitchenette $125-155; ☒) At
this friendly inn, find colorful door murals,
tropical decor and the best ocean-view deals in
town. Ground-floor units are nicely appointed
with overhead fans, quality double beds, rattan furniture and kitchenettes. Rooms on the
2nd and 3rd floors are more inviting still, with
bigger living space and lanai (veranda). Available downstairs is a well-equipped wheelchair-
accessible room.

Banyan Harbor Resort (Map p467; ☎ 245-7333, 800-
422-6926; www.vacation-kauai.com; 3411 Wilcox Rd; 1-/2-
bedroom units $125/155; ☒) The pros: this 148-unit
condo offers spacious rooms and convenient
amenities such as full kitchen and washer-
dryer. And the cons: quality is extremely
variable and you might end up in a unit that
has clearly housed a cigarette smoker. The

two-bedroom units are either 'townhouses' (two-story, with one full-size and one half bathroom) or 'ramblers' (one-story, with two full bathrooms).

Hilton Kaua'i Beach Resort (Map p467; ☎ 245-1955, 888-805-3843, www.hilton.com; 4331 Kaua'i Beach Dr; r from $189; 🗱 🗶) Located north of Lihu'e, this former Radisson became a 350-room Hilton condo-hotel and underwent major renovation. The rooms are pleasant enough, as are the pool and lobby bar. Yet the place is oddly bland. You won't regret staying here, you just might not remember it.

Kaua'i Marriott Resort (Map p467; ☎ 245-5050, 800-220-2925; www.marriotthotels.com; Kalapaki Beach; r from $259; 🗱 🗶) If sprawling tropical resorts are your thing, you can't go wrong here. This timeshare condo is the best of the Eastside biggies, with a tropical grandeur sure to impress: nene (Hawaiian geese) wander around koi-stocked ponds, the koa canoe *Princess* gleams in the lobby and room decor features island-style orchid bedspreads and botanical prints. And wait till you see the spectacular 26,000-sq-ft, four-part swimming pool…ahh.

EATING
Budget

Hamura Saimin (Map p472; ☎ 245-3271; 2956 Kress St; noodles $3.75-4.50; 🕙 10am-11:30pm Mon-Thu, to late Fri & Sat, to 9:30pm Sun) An island institution, Hamura's is your classic hole-in-the-wall. Expect crowds at lunchtime, slurping noodles elbow-to-elbow at orange U-shaped counters. The famous homemade saimin noodles are peerless. Another specialty is the *liliko'i* (passion fruit) chiffon pie. Stifling interior due to boiling vats and no air-con.

Kalapaki Beach Hut (Map p467; ☎ 246-6330; 3474 Rice St; breakfast & burgers $4-7; 🕙 7am-7pm) Sure, it's touristy. But this archetypal beachside café faces Kalapaki Beach and features big breakfasts, from egg-and-cheese sandwiches to tasty omelettes sautéed with fresh *ono* (white-fleshed wahoo). The fast-food lunch menu features belly-pleasing burgers and sandwiches.

Tip Top Café & Sushi Katsu (Map p472; ☎ 245-2333; 3173 Akahi St; breakfast mains $4.50-7, lunch mains $4.50-8.25; 🕙 Café 6:30am-2pm, Sushi Katsu 11am-2pm & 5:30-9pm Tue-Sun) The white, cinder-block building is lacking in atmosphere, but the main draws are its famous pancakes and oxtail soup. Meat eaters, go local with *loco moco* (two fried eggs, hamburger patty, rice and gravy), saimin (egg noodle and broth soup) and beef stew. Located inside, Sushi Katsu offers value-priced sushi and Japanese dishes.

Fish Express (Map p467; ☎ 245-9918; 3343 Kuhio Hwy; lunch $6-7.50; 🕙 10am-7pm Mon-Sat, to 5pm Sun, lunch served to 3pm daily) Try it once and we guarantee you'll be hooked. The take-out menu includes mouthwatering fish preparations, such as macadamia-crusted '*ahi* (yellowfin tuna) in *liliko'i*-dill sauce, which come with rice and salad. Outside of lunch hours, snag something from the deli case, perhaps a sample of *poke* (cubed, marinated raw fish).

Pho Kauai (Map p472; ☎ 245-9858; Rice Shopping Center, 4303 Rice St; bowls under $8; 🕙 10am-9pm Mon-Sat) Fill up on steaming bowls of well-made *pho* (Vietnamese noodle soup). Choose meat or veg toppings, such as curry chicken, grilled shrimp, snow peas or eggplant. No credit cards.

Kiibo (Map p472; ☎ 245-2650; 2991 Umi St; mains $6-15; 🕙 11am-1:30pm & 5:30-9pm Mon-Sat) If you're craving Japanese food but protecting your pocketbook, Kiibo is your ticket. Here you'll find standbys including tempura udon or soba (noodles in broth), *unagi* (eel) over rice, and grilled mackerel or salmon. Locals love the unpretentious setting and under-$10 meals.

Kaua'i Pasta (Map p472; ☎ 245-2227; 4-939B Kuhio Hwy; mains $9-15; 🕙 11am-2pm, 5-9pm) Locals prefer rice to pasta, but Kaua'i Pasta has proven popular. Colorful salads meld diverse flavors, such as peppery arugula, creamy goat cheese and sweet tomatoes. Hot foccacia sandwiches, classic pasta mains and luscious tiramisu are well made and generous.

Colenti's Italian Deli & Pizzeria (Map p467; ☎ 246-4940; 4303 Nawiliwili Rd; pizzas $12-25; 🕙 11am-9pm) For tasty, consistent, casual Italian fare, go here. Pizzas are New York–style (thin crust that can fold in half); calzones and subs overflow with fillings; staff is friendly – you can't go wrong.

At Kukui Grove Shopping Center, you'll find the usual chain eateries, plus a few gems:

Deli & Bread Connection (Map p467; ☎ 245-7115; Kukui Grove Shopping Center; 3-2600 Kaumuali'i Hwy; sandwiches $4.50-6.50; 🕙 9:30am-7pm Mon-Thu & Sat, to 9pm Fri, 10am-6pm Sun) For good, old-fashioned sandwiches. Classics feature the whole range of deli meats (plus a veg burger), all on freshly baked breads.

Genki Sushi (Map p467; ☎ 632-2450; Kukui Grove Shopping Center, 3-2600 Kaumuali'i Hwy; à la carte nigiri & rolled sushi from $1.60, bento from $8.50; 🕙 11am-8pm Sun-Thu, to 10pm Fri, to 9pm Sat) In a no-frills diner setting, you order from a set menu of individual items topping out at $4.60.

FRESH FROM THE FARM

For farm-fresh fruits and vegetables, find a farmers market. Arrive early because once the whistle blows people rush in, scooping things up quickly. Depending on the location, it can all wrap up within an hour or so. Sellers typically offer $1 or $2 bundles so bring lots of dollar bills.

Monday

- Noon at Knudsen Park, Maluhia Rd, Koloa
- 3pm at Kukui Grove Shopping Center, Kaumuali'i Hwy, Lihu'e (Map p467)

Tuesday

- 2pm in Waipa, inland side of Kuhio Hwy, slightly west of Hanalei
- 3pm at Kalaheo Neighborhood Center, Papalina Rd, Kalaheo
- 3pm at Wailua Homesteads Park, Malu Rd (Map pp480–1)

Wednesday

- 3pm at Kapa'a New Park, Kahau St, Kapa'a (Map p491)

Thursday

- 3:30pm at Hanapepe Town Park, behind the fire station
- 4:30pm at Kilauea Neighborhood Center, Keneke St, Kilauea (Map p500)

Friday

- 3pm at Vidinha Stadium, Ho'olako Rd and Kapule Hwy, Lihu'e (Map p467)

Saturday

- 9am at Kekaha Neighborhood Center, Elepaio Rd, Kekaha
- 9am at Christ Memorial Episcopal Church, Kolo Rd, Kilauea (Map p500)
- 9:30am near Hanalei Community Center, Hanalei, Kuhio Hwy

Kaua'i Bakery and Cinnamons (Map p467; 246-4765; www.kauaibakery.com; Kukui Grove Shopping Center, 3-2600 Kaumuali'i Hwy; pastries 49¢-$1.75, cakes & pies $8-16; 7am-7pm Mon-Thu & Sat, to 9pm Fri, to 6pm Sun) You'll blast to the past with old-fashioned cinnamon rolls, apple turnovers, bread pudding and *malasada* (Portuguese doughnuts without a hole).

Kaua'i Malasadas (Map p467; Kukui Grove Shopping Center, 3-2600 Kaumuali'i Hwy; 3 pieces $1.25; from 8am) Get 'em piping hot from the stand outside Kmart. They do one thing – and they do it well. The stand is open from morning to *pau* (finished).

For groceries, the two major supermarkets are **Big Save** (Map p472; 245-6571; 4444 Rice St; 7am-11pm), near the government buildings in the heart of town (enter on Hardy St), and **Star Market** (Map p467; 245-7777; Kukui Grove Shopping Center; 6am-11pm).

Midrange & Top End

Lihu'e Barbecue Inn (Map p472; 245-2921; 2982 Kress St; lunch $5-12, dinner $19-24; 10:30am-1:30pm & 5-8:30pm Mon-Thu, 10:30am-1:30pm & 4:30-9pm Fri & Sat) Dark and deserted on the outside, the food and friendly service inside are a surprise. The menu is almost a book, with a wide selection

(but inexplicably no real BBQ). Don't expect gourmet dining, but the fish dishes are delicious, especially the seared 'ahi salad.

Hanama'ulu Restaurant Tea House & Sushi Bar (Map p467; 245-2511, 245-3225; 3-4291 Kuhio Hwy; mains $7-10, special platters $17-20; 11:30am-9:30pm Tue-Sun). The name sounds fancier than it is, but this longstanding eatery on the outskirts of Lihu'e serves decent Japanese cuisine. The menu suspiciously includes Chinese dishes, too, but that's common in Hawaii. Specializing in crispy fried dishes, from Chinese ginger chicken to Japanese tempura and *tonkatsu* (breaded cutlets).

Aromas (Map p467; 245-9192; Harbor Mall, Suite 207, 3501 Rice St; breakfast mains $7.25-8.50, lunch mains $10.50-12.50, dinner mains $18-27; 7am-9:30pm Tue-Fri, 8am-9:30pm Sat & Sun) You'll forget the tourist-mall setting inside the casually chic dining room of Aromas, a Pacific-Mediterranean bistro that bridges 'local' and 'gourmet' cuisine. Lunch salads, like the papaya and cashew-chicken salad, make a meal. Start dinner with the 'Poketian,' layered 'ahi poke (cubed raw yellowfin tuna mixed with shoyu, sesame oil, salt and chili pepper), crab, shrimp and rice in a martini glass.

Gaylord's (Map p467; 245-9593; www.kilohanakauai .com/gaylords.htm; Kilohana Plantation, Kaumuali'i Hwy; lunch $8-14, dinner $20-35; 7:45-10am, 11am-2pm & 5:30-9pm

Mon-Sat, 7:45am-2pm & 5:30-9pm Sun) If you're curious about the life of a plantation baron, dine here at the Wilcox estate. The manicured lawn, white tablecloths and clubby tone match the menu, with dishes like filet mignon bathed in *liliko'i* sauce, and shiitake and prime rib salad featuring Maui onions and Kamuela tomatoes. Big breakfast eaters, try the generous daily buffet or Sunday brunch.

Café Portofino (Map p467; ☎ 245-2121; www.caféporto fino.com; Kaua'i Marriott Resort, Kalapaki Beach; appetizers $8-12, mains $16-29; ◔ 5-9pm) If you cringe at white tablecloths, low lighting and live harpists, keep looking. Otherwise, the traditional Italian menu features fine pastas and lots of veal, such as house specialty *osso buco* (veal shank). The atmosphere is rather formal and kids are barely tolerated.

Duke's Canoe Club (Map p467; ☎ 246-9599; Kaua'i Marriott Resort; appetizers $7-9, mains $18-28; ◔ 11am-11pm) Yes, Duke's is an oceanside, open-air dining cliché. But if you want that tropical ambience, this is one of the best Eastside places to find it. The flavorful food won't disappoint. Start with savory appetizers like spicy sugarcane shrimp or crab wontons and don't miss the seven-spiced *'ahi* with papaya-mustard vinaigrette.

DRINKING & ENTERTAINMENT
Bars & Nightclubs
Duke's Barefoot Bar (Map p467; ☎ 246-9599; Kaua'i Marriott Resort, Kalapaki Beach; ◔ 11am-midnight) Leave your shoes at the door at this chill-out place right on Kalapaki Beach. A good mix of Hawaiian, rock and pop music livens things up nightly.

Whaler's Brew Pub (Map p467; ☎ 245-2000; 3132 Ninini Point; ◔ 11:30am-2am Mon-Sat, DJs from 10pm Thu-Sat) You can sample a handful of beers brewed on-site at this pub overlooking Nawiliwili Harbor and the lighthouse on Ninini Point. By day there's a simple bar menu; by night, dancing and DJs.

Rob's Good Times Grill (Map p472; ☎ 246-0311; Rice Shopping Center, 4303 Rice St; ◔ 9pm-2am) The atmosphere might be a little hokey, but a young, energetic crowd comes out to boogie to a live DJ Thursday through Saturday. Sunday through Tuesday is karaoke and Wednesday is…country line dancing (yeehaw!).

Cinemas
Kukui Grove Cinemas (Map p467; ☎ 245-5055; Kukui Grove Shopping Center, 3-2600 Kaumuali'i Hwy; adult/child $6/4, before 5pm $4) Catch a movie at this fourplex.

This is one of the venues for the Hawaii International Film Festival: www.hiff.org.

Concerts
The **Community College Performing Arts Center** is home of the **Kaua'i Concert Association** (☎ 245-7464; www.kauai-concert.org) and offers classical, jazz and dance concerts (tickets $20 to $30) at 7pm. Past performers have included Poncho Sanchez, Kronos Quartet and Ernie Watts.

Shows
Luau are not offered in Lihu'e any more: the well-regarded Kilohana Plantation luau is now independently run and available only to Norwegian Cruise Line passengers. But a fine substitute is 'South Pacific,' an entertaining dinner-theater production of Rodgers and Hammerstein's *South Pacific*, directed by Brenda Turville and produced by Alain Dussaud and the Hawaii Association of Performing Arts, at **Hilton Kaua'i Beach Resort** (Map p467; ☎ 246-0111; 4331 Kaua'i Beach Dr; adult/child incl tax $71/63; ◔ 5:30pm Wed). Line up early; seating is first-come, first-served.

SHOPPING
Malls
Kukui Grove Shopping Center (Map p467; ☎ 245-7784; 3-2600 Kaumuali'i Hwy) Kaua'i's only true 'mall' includes major department and big-box chains including Macy's, Sears, Longs Drugs, Borders, Kmart, Star Market, Radio Shack and banks. It resembles any suburban mall; don't expect designer boutiques or fancy restaurants.

Smaller malls include the following:
Anchor Cove Shopping Center (Map p467; ☎ 246-0634; 3416 Rice St) Near Nawiliwili Harbor.
Harbor Mall (Map p467; ☎ 245-6255; 3501 Rice St) Near Nawiliwili Harbor.
Rice Shopping Center (Map p472; 4303 Rice St) In central Lihu'e.

Stores
Longs Drugs (Map p467; ☎ 245-7771; Kukui Grove Shopping Center, 3-2600 Kaumuali'i Hwy; ◔ 7am-10pm Mon-Sat, 8am-8pm Sun) Longs is the local favorite catchall store. Find a wide range of gifts – from classic macadamia treats to locally published children's books – plus snorkeling gear, bodyboards and cheap *rubbah slippah* (rubber flip-flops).

Hilo Hattie (Map p472; ☎ 245-3404; www.hilohattie .com; 3-3252 Kuhio Hwy; ◔ 8:30am-6:30pm) Ubiquitous statewide, this tourist chain sure draws

---

DETOUR: KIPU FALLS

Admit it. You fantasize about those ol' Mountain Dew commercials, where pretty young things splash in a sun-dappled swimming hole. Now you can experience the island version at Kipu Falls, near Lihu'e. This waterfall pond was a low-key, locals-only favorite until word got out. To minimize tourist impact, come on weekdays (leave weekends for residents) and keep it clean.

Note that Kipu Falls is private property. People have been injured here and too many accidents might prompt the landowner to close it to trespassers. Don't take undue risks and ruin the fun for everyone.

To get here, take Kipu Rd off Kaumuali'i Hwy at the 3-mile marker. A dirt path leading to the falls is just under a mile, starting before the one-lane bridge. Don't leave anything valuable in your car.

---

in the tour-bus crowd. While it's a convenient one-stop shop for generic souvenirs (eg macadamias), beware of overpriced edibles or mediocre knickknacks made in China or the Philippines.

Kapaia Stitchery (Map p467; ☎ 245-2281; 3-3551 Kuhio Hwy; ☑ 9am-5pm Mon-Sat) Nirvana for folks who sew, with a wide selection of tropical fabrics, Hawaiian quilt and pillow kits and needlepoint designs. Custom-made aloha shirts and other handmade items on sale for those who can't thread a needle.

Edith King Wilcox Gift Shop (Map p472; Kaua'i Museum, 4428 Rice St) Located at Kaua'i Museum, this shopping delight features a broad selection of Hawaiiana books, plus koa bowls and other handicrafts. Enter the shop, free of charge, through the museum lobby.

Kilohana Plantation (Map p467; www.kilohanakauai .com/shopping.htm; Kaumuali'i Hwy) While touristy, this classy collection of shops boasts a scenic historic-manor setting and quality goods. Find intricate Ni'ihau shell lei, scrimshaw, dolls, woodcarvings and contemporary paintings by local artists. The aloha shirts at Kilohana Clothing Company are top-notch.

GETTING THERE & AROUND
Bus

The **Kaua'i Bus** (☎ 241-6410; www.kauai.gov; 3220 Ho'olako St; per trip adult/senior & youth 7-18 $1.50/75¢; ☑ 7:45am-4:30pm Mon-Fri) serves Lihu'e with two main routes: routes 100, 100E, 200 and 200E stop at Wal-Mart, Wilcox Memorial Hospital, Big Save, Kukui Grove Shopping Center and Lihu'e Airport. These then continue from Lihu'e to Koloa, Po'ipu and the Westside. Service is limited, with frequency ranging from 40 minutes to two hours, Monday to Saturday.

Within Lihu'e, route 700 offers more stops within town, including Kukui Grove Shopping Center, Garden Island Inn (Kalapaki Beach), Big Save, Wal-Mart and Wilcox Memorial Hospital, running hourly from 8am to 3pm Monday to Friday.

Car & Motorcycle

Kaua'i is a driving town, so most businesses have parking lots and street parking is relatively easy to find. Metered parking in Lihu'e costs 25¢ for 30 minutes. For information about car and motorcycle rentals, see p464.

EASTSIDE

At first glance, the Eastside might assault the senses with too many mundane shopping strips and bumper-to-bumper traffic. But look beyond the highway and find a majestic river, thundering waterfalls, miles of beaches, coconut trees galore and plenty of shopping and dining options.

The Eastside's resort stretch – dubbed the 'Coconut Coast' by the tourist industry (but never by locals) – spans Wailua to Kapa'a. Thus the bulk of Kaua'i's population lives here. Thus the Eastside feels more homey and less touristy than Kaua'i's swankier resort strongholds in Po'ipu and Princeville.

Budget travelers, especially, will find the best selection of lodging here. Live among residents in upland neighborhoods amid backyard orchards and rolling pastures. Seaside condos are unassuming gems, especially in Wailua, with swimmable waters and conveniently coarse-grained sand (it brushes off!).

We divide the Eastside by town: Wailua, Waipouli and Kapa'a. But on the ground, their boundaries are fuzzy. Between the Eastside and the North Shore is Anahola, a rustic

KAUA'I

territory where Native Hawaiians constitute 70% of the population.

WAILUA & AROUND
pop Wailua, incl Wailua Homesteads 6650

Wailua boasts the island's best playground and an absolutely lovely upland residential neighborhood – and a magnificent river runs through it. Of course, from Kuhio Hwy (Hwy 56), you view mainly shopping strips and condos.

The Wailua Homesteads neighborhood (population 4567) sits to the west of Nounou Mountain, the unmistakable (to most) Sleeping Giant. Further west, the Makaleha mountain range rises dramatically; its apt Hawaiian

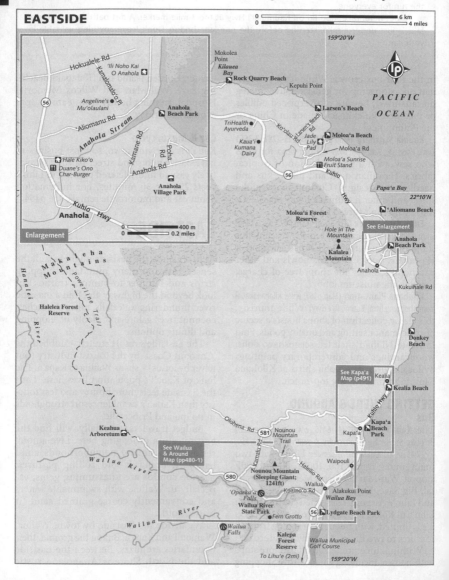

EASTSIDE

name means 'eyes looking about as in wonder and admiration.'

Orientation

The main roads in Wailua are Kuhio Hwy (Hwy 56) and Kuamo'o Rd (Hwy 580), which leads both to residences and to a handful of notable sights. If you are headed to Kapa'a or beyond, take the Kapa'a Bypass Rd, from Coconut Plantation to north Kapa'a.

Sights

LYDGATE BEACH PARK

Local and tourist families flock to this clean, safe, conveniently located **beach park** (www .kamalani.org). Here you'll find calm waters in a large seawater pool, protected by a stone breakwater. It's ideal for shallow swimming and beginning snorkeling. Beware of the open ocean beyond the pool, where currents are strong. Amenities here include changing rooms, rest rooms, showers, drinking water, picnic pavilions, lifeguard and ample parking. The Eastside paved coastal path runs through the park.

In 1994 thousands of local volunteers helped build the enchanting **Kamalani Playground** at the northern end of the park. This massive 16,000-sq-ft wooden castle has swings, slides, mirror mazes, a suspension bridge and other kid-pleasing contraptions. At the southern end of the park, the **Kamalani Kai Play Bridge** is reason alone to stop here. Another community-built, giant wooden labyrinth with spiral slides, confounding ramps and stairs to nowhere, plus kid art strewn throughout, this fanciful bridge fosters serious playtime. When we visited, construction was under way for soccer fields.

To get here, turn *makai* (seaward) on Kuhio Hwy between the 5- and 6-mile markers.

SMITH'S TROPICAL PARADISE

The setting can seem a tad hokey, with a Disney-esque Easter Island figure and trams full of sunburnt, aloha-attired tourists. But don't underestimate the garden's variety of plants, serene pond setting and unpretentious appeal. The loop trail through theme gardens at **Smith's Tropical Paradise** (☎ 821-6895/6; www .smithskauai.com/tropical_garden.html; Wailua River Marina; adult/child under 12 $6/3; ☼ 8:30am-4pm) is a good deal. Forgo the tram ride for a leisurely stroll. If you're catching the luau (p486) here, you'll have ample time to tour the grounds before dinner.

> **KAUA'I FOR NA KEIKI**
>
> ■ Gargantuan jungle gym at **Kamalani Playground & Kamalani Play Bridge** (left)
>
> ■ Flying between towering trees on a **zipline tour** (p471)
>
> ■ Children's Garden at **Na 'Aina Kai Botanical Gardens** (p497)
>
> ■ Indoor fun at **Kaua'i Children's Discovery Museum** (p487)
>
> ■ Video games at **Fun Factory** (p487)
>
> ■ Gentle waters at **Lydgate Beach Park** (left), **Po'ipu Beach Park** (p521), **Baby Beach** (p523) and **Salt Pond Beach Park** (p534)
>
> ■ **Snorkeling cruises** (p533) off the Na Pali Coast
>
> ■ Floating along irrigation ditches in old-fashioned inner **tubes** (p471)
>
> ■ Hiking the first mile or two of the **Kalalau Trail** (p516)
>
> ■ Shopping at **Kokonut Kids** (p512) or, for girly girls, **Marta's Boat** (p489)

KAUA'I'S HINDU MONASTERY

On an island virtually devoid of Hinduism, the splendid Kaua'i Aadheenam, commonly called simply **Kaua'i's Hindu Monastery** (☎ 822-3012; www.himalayanacademy.com/ssc/hawaii; 107 Kaholalele Rd), is both serious monastery and growing tourist attraction. Located on 458 acres of lush rainforest above Wailua River, the traditional South Indian Saivite (Shiva-worshipping) monastery is a sprawling garden oasis, with a meditation hall and Ganesha statues sitting amid wildly tropical landscaping.

Access is limited to **tours** (tours free, donations welcome; ☼ 9am) three or four times a month, which are well worth the time. Check the website for tour dates.

In **Kadavul Temple** (☼ 9am-noon), guests can see the world's largest single-pointed quartz crystal, a 50-million-year-old, six-sided wonder that weighs 700lb and stands over 3ft tall. In the temple, meditating monks have been rotating in three-hour vigils round the clock since the temple was established in 1973.

The highlight of the tour is the Chola-style **Iraivan Temple**, a monumental work-in-progress that is being entirely hand-carved from white

WAILUA & AROUND

SIGHTS & ACTIVITIES
Coco Palms.............................1	G3
Hikina Akala Heiau.................2	G3
Holoholoku Heiau....................3	G2
Kamalani Kai Play Bridge......4	G3
Kamalani Playground.............5	G3
Kamokila Hawaiian Village....6	E3
Kaua'i's Hindu Monastery......7	B2
Kayak Kaua'i.....................(see 33)	
Kukui Heiau.............................8	H2
Mala'e Heiau...........................9	G3
Poli'ahu Heiau......................10	E3
Smith's Motor Boat Service..(see 32)	
Wailua Kayak & Canoe.........11	G3
Water Ski, Surf & Kayak	
Company........................(see 31)	

SLEEPING
Aloha Beach Resort..............12	G3
Best Western Plantation Hale.13	H2
Bunkhouse at Rosewood	
B&B.................................(see 27)	
Fern Grotto Inn....................14	E3
Garden Room........................15	C1
Hale Lani B&B......................16	B1
Inn Paradise.........................17	D1
Kapa'a Sands.......................18	G2
Kaua'i Coast Resort at the	
Beachboy.........................19	H2

Kaua'i Sands Hotel...............20	H2
Lae Nani............................21	H2
Lani Keha.............................22	E1
Lanikai...............................23	H2
Magic Sunrise Hawaii............24	D2
ResortQuest Islander on the	
Beach..............................25	H2
ResortQuest Kaua'i Beach at	
Makaiwa.........................26	H2
Rosewood B&B.....................27	E1

EATING
Caffé Coco............................28	G2
Hukilau Lanai....................(see 19)	
Kintaro...............................29	G2
Korean Bar-B-Q Restaurant..(see 31)	
Mema..................................30	G3
Monico's Taqueria................31	G2

DRINKING
Kuhio Lounge.....................(see 12)	
Tradewinds.......................(see 33)	

ENTERTAINMENT
Aloha Beach Resort..............(see 12)	
Coconut Marketplace	
Cinemas........................(see 33)	
Coconut Marketplace..........(see 33)	
ResortQuest Kaua'i Beach at	
Makaiwa.......................(see 26)	
Smith's Tropical Paradise......32	G3

SHOPPING
Coconut Marketplace...........33	H2
Kaua'i's Hindu Monastery Gift	
Shop..............................(see 7)	
Tin Can Mailman................(see 31)	

granite by a village of artisans founded in Bangalore, India, specifically for this project.

KAMOKILA HAWAIIAN VILLAGE

Established in 1979, this restored **Hawaiian village** (☎ 823-0559; www.kamokila.com; self-guided tour adult/child $5/3; ☉ 9am-5pm), perched on the north bank of Wailua River, remains a relatively off-the-radar attraction. Run by a Hawaiian family, the modest site includes grass huts, an assembly house and a shaman's house, and approximates a traditional indigenous settlement. A small map gives the gist of each building's purpose. As you walk around, you might recognize the village as that used in the movie *Outbreak*.

While the village is not a must-see, the outrigger canoe **tours** (adult/child $30/20; ☉ departures hourly 9:30am-2:30pm) on the Wailua are personalized and unique. They include a paddle, hike and waterfall swim – an interesting variation on the regular Wailua River kayak trip (opposite) – as they leave from the village and a Hawaiian guide is guaranteed. Canoes hold about seven.

Kamokila is on the south side of Kuamo'o Rd, opposite 'Opaeka'a Falls, at the end of a steep, narrow half-mile paved road.

'OPAEKA'A FALLS

While neither the highest nor the prettiest, this 40ft waterfall became a major tourist attraction because tour buses can easily stop here. Just head up on Kuamo'o Rd for 1.5 miles and turn right into the lookout parking lot. You're likely to encounter a herd of camera-toting sightseers all capturing exactly the same shot.

Cross the road for an overhead view of the Wailua River. Note that hiking down to the base of the falls is perilous and not recommended, especially after two tourists plunged to their death in 2006.

KEAHUA ARBORETUM

Amid towering trees, a gurgling stream and cool misty rain, this arboretum, east of town, makes a nice little picnic spot. The Department of Land & Natural Resources planted mini groves of teak, eucalyptus and shower trees in the 1940s to create an outdoor nature classroom, showcasing the benefits of forest management.

Avoid the area at night, when it becomes the scene for rave parties.

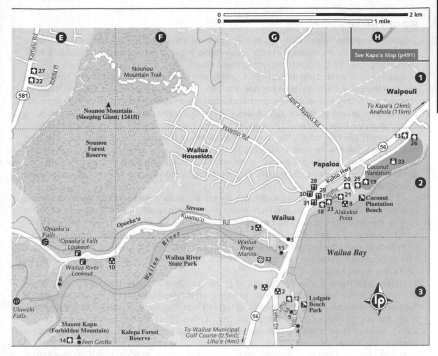

WAILUA RIVER STATE PARK

From a distance, the Wailua River's emerald surface gleams under a jungly canopy and appears gentle and still – nothing like the capricious Pacific Ocean into which it feeds. At 12 miles long, it is the state's only navigable river, formed by the convergence of two large streams, known as its north and south forks, both fed by Wai'ale'ale.

By far the most popular river activity is kayaking, as it is relatively easy and tours are ubiquitous. But kayakers do share the waterway with riverboats, waterskiers and wakeboarders. See p484 for details.

WAILUA BAY

At the mouth of the Wailua River, this sweeping bay of golden sand is rather too visible from the highway. But swimming is possible along the edges. As always, avoid the river's mouth because currents and water depth here is unpredictable. Toward the south, a summer surf break draws locals and also surf students. The long stretch of sand is ideal for walking and, since the bay is so centrally located, it makes a convenient stop for a quick jog or stroll.

Activities
KAYAKING

Among the must-do activities on Kaua'i is kayaking the Wailua River. No surprise: the 5-mile round-trip is doable by most folks. The centrally located launch site is convenient and kayak rentals are available right at the boat ramp.

The route typically doesn't pass the Fern Grotto and instead takes a fork in the river leading to a mile-long side hike through dense forest to Uluwehi Falls (aka Secret Falls), a 130ft waterfall. An alternate tour takes you past the Fern Grotto to a swimming hole. Kayakers must stay on the north side of the river, while the Smith's boats (see p483) cruise in the center.

The county strictly regulates commercial kayak use of the river, due to congestion. Only 15 tour companies are allowed to lead groups of 12 people (typically in six double kayaks) twice per day. Most tours include lunch and leave around 7am or noon; call for exact check-in times. As for individual kayak rentals, the county is even more prohibitive, allowing only four companies to rent them (with a maximum of six in the river at any time). No kayak tours or rentals are allowed on Sundays.

KAUA'I

HIDDEN HEIAU

Spotting a Hawaiian heiau (religious site) takes genuine interest, supreme patience and an eagle eye. Too often they are abandoned ruins, resembling a pile of rocks covered by weeds. If keen on spotting one, the Eastside is rife with ancient sites.

One is located within Lydgate Beach Park (p479), while the other is visible from the park: first, if you look straight out across Wailua Bay from the park, you can see the remains of **Kukui Heiau** on Alakukui Point. Only its foundation stones are discernible. In ancient times torches were lit on the point at night to help guide outrigger canoes. If you walk straight down to the beach while looking toward Alakukui Point, you might find ancient stones with petroglyphs carved into the rock.

At Lydgate's north end sits the ruins of **Hikina Akala Heiau** (Rising of the Sun). In its heyday, the long, narrow temple (c AD 1200) was aligned directly north to south. Boulders still outline the shape, so you get a sense of its original size, though most of the stones are long gone. A bronze plaque reads 'Hauola, City of Refuge,' marking the former refuge for *kapu* (taboo) breakers.

All heiau require a leap of imagination, but the ruins of **Mala'e Heiau** ancient Hawaiian temple, in particular, are lost in the thicket. From Aloha Beach Resort (p485), look 40ft inland past Kuhio Hwy, at the edge of an abandoned cane field. This was once Kaua'i's largest heiau, perhaps 275ft by 325ft, covering 2 acres, but today it's smothered by grasses and Java plum trees.

In ancient times, human sacrifices were made here. In the 1830s Christian missionaries converted Deborah Kapule, the last queen of Kaua'i, and she transformed the interior of Mala'e Heiau into a cattle pen.

Holoholoku Heiau is a *luakini* (temple of human sacrifice) a quarter mile up Kuamo'o Rd on the left. The whole area used to be royal property; on the west side of the grounds, against the flat-backed birthstone, queens gave birth to future kings. This stone is marked by a plaque that reads 'Pohaku Ho'ohanau' (royal birthstone). Only a male child born here could become king of Kaua'i. Another stone a few yards away, marked 'Pohaku Piko,' was where the *piko* (umbilical cords) of the babies were left.

Perched high on a hill overlooking the meandering Wailua River, **Poli'ahu Heiau**, another *luakini*, is named after the snow goddess Poli'ahu, one of Pele's sisters. Poli'ahu Heiau is immediately before the 'Opaeka'a Falls lookout, on the opposite side of the road.

The following companies offer both kayak tours and individual rentals for the Wailua River. While the larger two companies, Kayak Kaua'i and Outfitters Kaua'i, are excellent, especially for their other, more adventurous tours, the smaller two companies' cheaper deals are fine for this paddle.

Kayak Kaua'i (☎ 826-9844, 800-437-3507; www.kayak kauai.com; Coconut Marketplace, Wailua; double kayak per day $75, tour per adult/child $85/60; ☺ check-in 7:45am & 12:15pm), with shop locations in both Wailua and Hanalei, offers river and sea kayaking tours, including the Na Pali trip. Japanese- and Spanish-speaking guides are available.

At **Outfitters Kaua'i** (Map pp522-3; ☎ 742-9667, 888-742-9887; www.outfitterskauai.com; Po'ipu Plaza, 2827-A Poipu Rd, Po'ipu; kayak per person per day $45, tour adult/child 5-14 $94/75; ☺ check-in 7:45am) you can pick up kayaks from Wailua Kayak & Canoe so there's no need to transport them from Po'ipu.

Wailua Kayak Adventures (☎ 822-5795, 639-6332; www.kauaiwailuakayak.com; Kuhio Hwy, Waipouli; single/

double kayaks $25/50, tour per couple $85; ☺ check-in 7am & 1pm) has a choice of three Wailua River tours, often discounted. Call for times, as they vary slightly for each tour. It's located behind Coconuts restaurant in Waipouli.

In business since the mid-1990s, the Hawaiian-owned **Wailua Kayak & Canoe** (☎ 821-1188; wkc@aloha.net; Wailua River State Park; single/double kayak per 5hr $45/75, tour per person $40) is friendly, honest and the only rental outfit right at the boat ramp. Its tour is 'bring your own lunch' (it provides coolers). Check well-worn equipment carefully. Direct bookings only.

HIKING

Eastside trails can be quite steep but allow stupendous views. Be aware that hunting is allowed in this area on weekends, holidays and Monday.

One-way mileage distances are given below. Lonely Planet's *Kaua'i* book describes the trails in more detail.

Kuilau Ridge & Moalepe Trails

While they are indeed independent trails, the Kuilau Ridge Trail (2.1 miles) and Moalepe Trail (2.25 miles) are often mentioned together because they connect and can be hiked in sequence. Both are moderate hikes and, for the effort, they are among the most visually rewarding on Kaua'i. Together they make an easy 9-mile hike or bike, with sweeping views of lush valleys, mist-covered mountains and the sparkling ocean beyond. The trails don't complete a circuit so you either have to retrace your steps or persuade someone to pick you up at one end.

The Kuilau Ridge Trail starts at a marked trailhead on the right just before Kuamo'o Rd crosses the stream at the Keahua Arboretum, 4 miles above the junction of Kuamo'o Rd and Kamalu Rd. The Moalepe Trail trailhead is at the end of Olohena Rd where it bends into Waipouli Rd.

While both are interesting, the Kuilau Ridge Trail is recommended because it takes you immediately into the forest wilderness, while the first mile of the Moalepe Trail crosses the simple, treeless pastureland of the Wailua Game Management Area. Both trails are well maintained and signposted.

Nounou Mountain Trails

There are three trails that trek along Nounou Mountain, the famous Eastside landmark known as Sleeping Giant: Nounou Mountain East Trail (1.75 miles) starts from the east, Nounou Mountain West Trail (1.5 miles) from the west and Kuamo'o-Nounou Trail (2 miles) climbs from south to northeast – and they all meet near the center.

Each trail has its benefits, but mainlanders tend to prefer the **Nounou Mountain East Trail** because it is most exposed and offers ocean views. The well-maintained trail takes 1½ to two hours round-trip and provides a hardy workout.

It begins at a parking lot a mile up Haleilio Rd in the Wailua Houselots neighborhood. The trail is steep, with switchbacks almost to the ridge. This is a wonderful walk to do early in the morning, when it's relatively cool and you can watch the light spread across the valley. The hard-packed dirt trail is exceedingly slippery when wet; look for a walking stick, which hikers sometimes leave near the trailhead. The trail ends at a picnic-table shelter at the summit and joins the west trail near the 1.5-mile post.

The **Nounou Mountain West Trail** is steeper but equally pleasant and ideal if you prefer a cooler, shaded forest trail. There are two ways to access the trailhead: from Kamalu Rd, near telephone pole No 11, or from the end of Lokelani Rd, off Kamalu Rd. Walk through a metal gate marked as a forestry right-of-way.

The **Kuamo'o-Nounou Trail** runs through groves of trees planted in the 1930s by the Civilian Conservation Corps; it connects with the west trail. The trailhead is right on Kuamo'o Rd, near a grassy field between the 2- and 3-mile markers.

TAKE ME TO THE GROTTO

Since 1946 **Smith's Motor Boat Service** (Map pp480-1; ☎ 821-6892; www.smithskauai.com; adult/child 2-12 $20/10; ⊗ departures every 30min 9-11:30am, 12:30-3:30pm) has delighted countless tourists with its leisurely, open-air riverboat rides. During the 1½-hour round-trip to the **Fern Grotto**, jovial guides share historical tidbits, and hula dancers cajole passengers to let loose.

The scenic grotto is an overhanging cliff at the base of Maunu Kapu (Forbidden Mountain), which looms from the river, dripping with yard-long sword ferns and delicate maidenhair. The grotto provides ideal acoustics and musicians serenade with favorites, including 'Ke Kali Nei Au,' better known as the 'Hawaiian Wedding Song' after Elvis Presley sang it in English in *Blue Hawaii*. Actually, it is not a wedding song, but its fate seems set – and couples from around the world come to marry at the Fern Grotto to the Elvis version.

Since the mid-1990s the grotto has struggled to survive. The end of the sugar era caused a localized drought when cane fields above the cliffs went out of production and irrigation stopped, leaving no water to seep through crevices into the natural amphitheater. In 2003 the Hawai'i Tourism Authority provided $245,000, and Kaua'i County added $50,000, to remedy the problem.

By 2005 the drought problem was solved but rain storms in early 2006 caused massive rock slides into the grotto. For many months, the grotto remained closed and riverboat rides were discounted.

KAUA'I

Powerline Trail

The Powerline Trail (13 miles) is actually a former maintenance road for the electric powerlines running along the mountains between Wailua and the North Shore. When the powerlines were established back in the 1930s, county officials used land vehicles to access them. Today helicopters are the mode of choice, so the road has fallen into disuse.

The trek is long, exposed and, especially toward the north, rather monotonous. But it is also peaceful and surrounded by dense foliage. Beware of hidden, steep drop-offs.

The south end of the trail begins across the stream at the Keahua Arboretum, at the end of Kuamo'o Rd.

GOLF

Ranked among the finest municipal golf courses nationally, the **Wailua Municipal Golf Course** (☎ 241-6666; green fees weekday/weekend & holidays $32/44, optional cart rental $16, club rental from $15) is an 18-hole, par-72 course off Kuhio Hwy north of Lihu'e. Plan ahead because morning tee times are reserved perhaps a week in advance at this popular course, designed by former head pro Toyo Shirai. After 2pm, green fees drop by half and no reservations are taken.

WATERSKIING AND WAKEBOARDING

The only non-ocean waterskiing in the state is found here on the Wailua, only from the Wailua Bridge to the first big bend in the river.

Try waterskiing or wakeboarding with a tow by **Water Ski, Surf & Kayak Company** (☎ 822-3574; Kinipopo Shopping Village, 4-356 Kuhio Hwy; per 30/60min $65/120). The company also rents water equipment, including surfboards (per day/week $10/50, $200 deposit), bodyboards (per day/week $5/20, $75 deposit) and snorkel gear (per day/week $5/15, $75 deposit).

Festivals & Events

A Taste of Hawaii (☎ 246-6983; Smith's Tropical Paradise; admission $75-80; ⊗ 11:30am-4pm) The Rotary Club of Kapa'a hosts an 'Ultimate Sunday Brunch' in early June, featuring culinary creations by over 40 of Hawaii's distinguished chefs. Additional booths provide wines, microbrews, ice cream, desserts and live entertainment.

Aloha Festivals Royal Court Investiture (☎ 332-7888; www.alohafestivals.com; admission incl lunch $18) The statewide Aloha Festivals in late August is launched on each island with presentation of a royal court. Held at Kamokila Hawaiian Village, the event includes special ceremonies of traditional chanting and hula.

Sleeping

Wailua, Waipouli and Kapa'a are practically the same town. Consider options in all three towns when planning Eastside lodging.

Book hotels and condos online to avoid exorbitant rack rates. Inquire about AAA and other discounts.

By 2008 visitors should be able to book accommodation at the **Coco Palms Resort** (www.cocopalms.com), first constructed in 1953 and the set of various movies in the '50s and '60s. It was demolished by Hurricane 'Iniki and was under reconstruction at the time of writing.

BUDGET

Bunk House at Rosewood B&B (☎ 822-5216; www.rosewoodkauai.com; 872 Kamalu Rd; r with shared bathroom $45-55) For the price, you can't beat this trio of cheerful, tidy, modern rooms. All sleep two and have private entrances and kitchenettes. Share a bathroom, outdoor shower and gas grill.

Lani Keha (☎ 822-1605; www.lanikeha.com; 848 Kamalu Rd; s/d from $55/65) In a low-key, communal house, Lani Keha is a reliable budget option. Nothing fancy, the three rooms feature *lauhala* (pandanus leaf) mat flooring, king beds and well-worn but clean furnishings. Gather 'round the kitchen and common rooms.

Magic Sunrise Hawaii (☎ 821-9847; www.magicsunrisehawaii.com; 139 Royal Dr; r with shared bathroom $55-70, apt from $99, cottages from $111; 🖳 🖳) At this stylishly New Age, communal inn, the three rooms

---

TOP BUDGET SLEEPS

Budget travelers, good news! Except on the North Shore, you can sleep comfortably for $50 to $80 a night at the following gems:

- **Aloha Hale Orchids** (p492)
- **Boulay Inn** (p520)
- **Garden Room** (opposite)
- **Hale Ikena Nui** (p530)
- **Hale Kiko'o** (p495)
- **Hibiscus Hollow** (p492)
- **Kalaheo Inn** (p530)
- **Kaua'i Palms Hotel** (p473)
- **Prince Kuhio Resort** (p526)
- **Seaview Suite** (p530)
- **Waimea Rock Cabin** (p539)

(with shared bathroom) feature Indonesian-type bamboo beds and hardwood floors. For more space and privacy, book the three-bedroom cottage with kitchen and washer-dryer. French and German spoken here.

Garden Room (☎ 822-5216, 822-3817; 6430 Ahele Dr; r $65) Don't hesitate for a moment. The aptly named Garden Room is the sweetest deal. In a sparkling in-law unit, enjoy a private entrance, fully equipped kitchenette and lush backyard with waterlily and koi pond. The hosts are longtime Kaua'i residents who make guests feel welcome.

MIDRANGE
B&Bs & Inns
Inn Paradise (☎ 822-2542; www.affordable-paradise.com /kauai87_e.html; 6381 Makana Rd; r $75, ste $90-100) Classy units. Spectacular garden view. Charming longtime innkeepers. No surprise, Inn Paradise is consistently ranked No 1 by travelers. Pick from three different-sized units, all with private entrance and kitchen or kitchenette. Reasonable rates, scrumptious breakfast fixings and washer-dryer clinch the deal.

Rosewood B&B (☎ 822-5216; www.rosewoodkauai .com; 872 Kamalu Rd; r $85, cottages $125-145; 🖵) With lodging options for all pocketbooks, Rosewood is a well-managed gem. Choose B&B bedrooms in the main house or picturesque cottages that come with generous welcome baskets. A sweet deal, the spacious 'Victorian Cottage' includes full kitchen, washer-dryer, computer and two bedrooms.

Fern Grotto Inn (☎ 821-9836; www.ferngrottoinn.com; 4561 Kuamo'o Rd; cottages $100-250; 🗵 🖵) Choose from four cozy cottages, amid tropical foliage overlooking the Wailua River near the dock. Operated by a friendly young couple, all are remodeled plantation buildings with hardwood floors, TV/DVD, wi-fi, shared laundry, and kitchen or kitchenette.

Hale Lani B&B (☎ 823-6434, 877-423-6434; www.hale lani.com; 283 Aina Lani Pl; studios $110-120, 2-bedroom ste $150, cottages $165, all incl breakfast; 🖵) If you want a B&B but need more space than a bedroom, try Hale Lani. Located 4.5 miles up Kuamo'o Rd, the cheerful units make efficient use of space and include kitchen or kitchenette, wi-fi and private outdoor hot tub. Home-cooked breakfasts come in a convenient take-out cooler.

Hotels
ResortQuest Islander on the Beach (☎ 822-7417, 877-997-6667; www.resortquesthawaii.com; 440 Aleka Pl;

r $144-228; 🗵 🖵 🖲) The Islander is the best midrange hotel on the island. All 186 rooms were renovated in fall 2005 and, with granite countertops, flat-panel TVs and stainless-steel and teak furnishings, they feel more upscale than their peers. Buildings are named after the Hawaiian Islands – rooms in the Kaua'i and Ni'ihau buildings enjoy the best ocean views.

ResortQuest Kaua'i Beach at Makaiwa (☎ 822-3455, 800-760-8555; www.resortquesthawaii.com; 650 Aleka Loop; r $180-353; 🗵 🖵 🖲) Coconut Beach Resort? Courtyard by Marriott? Don't let the name changes confuse you. Now, as a ResortQuest, the 300-plus-room hotel remains the Eastside's fanciest. Here you'll find an airy lobby full of plush seating, a small fitness center and sedately pleasant pool. Rooms pamper the business traveler with dark woods, black-marble counters and work desk with rolling chair.

Other recommendations:

Kaua'i Sands Hotel (☎ 822-4951, 800-560-5553; www.kauaisandshotel.com; 420 Papaloa Rd; r $88-128; 🗵 🖲) The good news? Cheap and oceanside. The bad news? Cavernous rooms are more motel than hotel. Expect long waits at the front desk and lots of geezer tour groups.

Aloha Beach Resort (☎ 823-6000, 888-823-5111; www.abrkauai.com; 3-5920 Kuhio Hwy; r $115-149, cottages from $215-249) Sitting pretty beside kid-friendly Lydgate Beach Park, this hotel thinks it's grander than it is. The rooms (renovated in 2007) and one-bedroom cottages are pleasant enough – but not worth the rates during busy periods.

Condos
Kapa'a Sands (☎ 822-4901, 800-222-4901; www.kapaa sands.com; 380 Papaloa Rd; studios/2-bedroom units from $110/155; 🖲) Booked solid by returnees, Kapa'a Sands comprises 24 units adjacent to a gentle, swimmable beach. The units are not new or fancy, but all offer an ocean view and they're clean, comfy and have been managed by the same staff for decades. The place is 100% non-smoking (banned even on lanai).

Best Western Plantation Hale (☎ 822-4941, 800-775-4253; www.plantation-hale.com; 4-484 Kuhio Hwy; 1-bedroom units from $119; 🗵 🖲) While located closer to the highway and Coconut Market-place than to the beach, Plantation Hale is a reliable economy condo. Of its 160 units, Best Western manages 111. While not new or plush, units include full kitchen and lanai.

Kaua'i Coast Resort at the Beachboy (☎ 822-3441, 877-977-4355; www.kauaicoastresort.com; 520 Aleka Loop; r from $180, 1-/2-bedroom units from $225/310; 🗵 🖲) An upscale time-share condo that resembles

KAUA'I

a full-service hotel, the Beachboy is well ap-pointed and spotlessly clean, with units so pleasant you'll wish you *lived* here. Ameni-ties include fitness center, spa, tennis courts, swimming pools and Hukilau Lanai restau-rant (right).

TOP END

We list the management company with the majority of units, but search online for better deals on other units. **Rosewood Kaua'i** (☎ 822-5216; www.rosewoodkauai.com) manages exception-ally fine units at Lae Nani and Lanikai.

Lae Nani (☎ 822-4938, 800-688-7444; www.outrigger .com; 410 Papaloa Rd; 1-/2-bedroom units from $215/235; ⚇ 🖳 🏊) For the location, price and quality, Lae Nani is outstanding. The five-building cluster is set beside a pleasant stretch of beach, far enough from the highway for nighttime quiet. Outrigger manages over 60 of the 84 units and provides on-site support. Buildings 3 and 5 include the most oceanfront units; building 1 is furthest from the highway.

Lanikai (☎ 822-7700, 800-367-5004; www.castleresorts .com; 390 Papaloa Rd; 2-bedrooom units from $299; ⚇ 🖳 🏊) With only 14 units, Lanikai feels like an upscale apartment by the sea. The spacious two-bedroom, two-bathroom units include washer-dryer. The only flaw: bedrooms on the highway side can be noisy. Castle manages eight units and provides on-site support.

Eating

Korean Bar-B-Q Restaurant (☎ 823-6744; Kinipopo Shop-ping Village, 4-356 Kuhio Hwy; plates $7-14; ⚇ 10am-9pm Mon-Sat, to 8pm Sun) While more local than Korean, the generous, meaty plates do include kimchi. Non-meat eaters might be wary, but fish and veg options are available. Grungy diner atmos-phere. Health nuts, look elsewhere.

Monico's Taqueria (☎ 822-4300; Kinipopo Shopping Village, 4-356 Kuhio Hwy; mains $8-14; ⚇ 11am-3pm & 5-9pm, closed Tue) Hawaii is no hotbed of Mexican food so the piquantly authentic dishes made by a local girl and her Mexican husband are special indeed. Fish burritos and tacos feature the day's catch, while fresh guacamole and homemade red or green sauces awaken your tastebuds.

Mema (☎ 823-0899; 4-369 Kuhio Hwy; mains $9-18; ⚇ 11am-2pm Mon-Fri, 5-9pm nightly) Not the best, not the worst, Mema serves savory dishes that can be tailored to your meat-philic or meat-phobic preference: you choose either tofu, chicken, pork, beef, fish or shrimp. The stir-fried eggplant with basil and red chili with coconut milk are favorites.

Caffè Coco (☎ 822-7990; 4-369 Kuhio Hwy; salads & sandwiches $5-14.50, meals $16-21; ⚇ 11am-9pm Tue-Fri, 5-9pm Sat & Sun) At this casually romantic hidea-way, Coco chefs have created a winning fusion menu with staples such as the tofu-veggie pea-nut wrap, and Moroccan-spiced 'ahi (yellowfin tuna) with banana chutney and a curried pur-ple-sweet-potato samosa. Sinful desserts and quality coffees are irresistible finales. Beware of voracious mosquitoes (protect your ankles!).

Kintaro (☎ 822-3341; 4-370 Kuhio Hwy; appetizers $3.50-6, meals $14-20; ⚇ 5:30-9:30pm Mon-Sat) Longtime local-fave Kintaro is always packed. No wonder: from thick-cut slices of sashimi to a shrimp-fish-veg tempura combination, mains shine in quality and quantity. The owner is Korean, but the cui-sine is authentic Japanese. A specialty is sizzling, crowd-wowing *teppanyaki*, when chefs show their stuff tableside on steel grills.

Hukilau Lanai (☎ 822-0600; Kaua'i Coast Resort at the Beachboy; dinner $16-27; ⚇ 5-9pm Tue-Sun) Locals rarely frequent touristy resort restaurants, but Hukilau Lanai is an exception. Here, find Ha-waiian Regional Cuisine in a casually elegant setting. Standouts include fish preparations, feta-and-sweet-potato ravioli and 'ahi poke nachos. If you're an early-bird diner, the tast-ing menu pairs six courses with five wines ($40; food only $28) from 5pm to 6pm.

Drinking & Entertainment
BARS & NIGHTCLUBS

Tradewinds (☎ 882-1621; www.tradewinds-kauai.com; Coconut Marketplace; ⚇ 10am-2am) A tropical sports bar featuring a daily happy hour from 2pm to 7pm and a 24oz 'Big Ass Draft' (the ass-shaped glass is yours to keep). No food, but neighboring mall restaurants deliver for free. Lively fun with darts, karaoke, live bands on weekends and nine TVs. During NFL sea-son, it opens at 7am (8am when the mainland switches to daylight saving time).

Kuhio Lounge (☎ 823-6000; Aloha Beach Resort, 3-5920 Kuhio Hwy; admission $5; ⚇ 10pm-2am) This hotel bar is indistinguishable from the pack, but drinks are decent. Live music from 9pm to 1:30am.

LUAU & HULA

Smith's Tropical Paradise (☎ 821-6895; www.smiths kauai.com; Wailua River Marina; luau adult/child 3-6/child 7-13 $65/19/30; ⚇ 5pm Mon, Wed & Fri) Started in 1985, the Smith Family Garden Luau is today a

Kaua'i institution, attracting droves of tourists. It's a lively affair, run with lots of aloha spirit by four generations at the lovely 30-acre garden. The multicultural show features Hawaiian, Tahitian, Samoan, Filipino, Chinese, Japanese and New Zealand dances.

ResortQuest Kaua'i Beach at Makaiwa (☎ 822-3455, 800-760-8555; www.resortquesthawaii.com; 4-484 Kuhio Hwy; luau adult/child 3-12/child 13-18/senior over 60 $65/32/42/59; ⏲ 6pm Tue-Sun) Performed daily except on Monday, this Tahitian-themed Tihati 'Hiva Pasefika' luau is rather Vegasy, with a passable buffet dinner, open bar, *imu* oven unearthing and Polynesian revue – plus a 'pareo fashion show' (wraparound skirt). It lacks the down-home charm of family-run affairs, but performers are quite impressive.

Aloha Beach Resort (☎ 635-7670, 823-6000; www .abrkauai.com; 3-5920 Kuhio Hwy; luau adult $60-65, child 6-12 $30-35, youth 13-20 $40-45; ⏲ 6pm Tue) Presented by the famous Punua hula *halau* (troupe), this luau is both flashy and family-oriented, featuring *keiki* (child) to *tutu* (grandparent) dancers. Wallis and Shana Punua, who direct the show, follow in the footsteps of Kumu Hula Ku'ulei Punua, a senior hula teacher on Kaua'i. The dinner is your typical generous but standard open-bar, all-you-can-eat buffet.

Coconut Marketplace (☎ 822-3641; ⏲ 5pm Wed) While the hula shows (free admission) are light and touristy, they're lively and, hey, you're in Hawaii.

CINEMAS
Coconut Marketplace Cinemas (☎ 821-2324; 4-484 Kuhio Hwy; adult/child/senior $7.25/4.25/5.50, shows before 6pm $4.25) Screens first-run movies in a mall setting.

Shopping
Tin Can Mailman (☎ 822-3009; tincan.mailman@verizon .net; Kinipopo Shopping Village, 4-356 Kuhio Hwy; ⏲ 11am-7pm Mon-Fri, noon-4pm Sat) Bibliophiles and collectors, enter your heaven. This jam-packed shop lives up to its description, 'Fine Books and Curiosities.' Amid shelves of new, used and rare books, find delightful Hawaiiana collectibles: vintage LPs, aloha shirts, maps, photos, postcards and more.

Kaua'i's Hindu Monastery Gift Shop (☎ 822-3012; www.himalayanacademy.com/ssc/hawaii; 107 Kaholalele Rd; ⏲ 9am-noon) While not Hawaiian or local, the souvenirs here are unusual – chanting CDs, alarm clocks with the Great Crystal on the face, granite lingams and tiger-eye Ganesha figurines.

Getting There & Around
A car is necessary to go beyond Kuhio Hwy. Otherwise, the **Kaua'i Bus** (☎ 241-6410) offers limited service between Wailua and Lihu'e, and Wailua and Hanalei, Monday to Friday. Main stops are at Coconut Marketplace going north and Wailua Family Restaurant, near Haleilio Rd, going south.

WAIPOULI
Waipouli is a mile-long strip of shopping malls between Wailua and Kapa'a. Nothing fancy, Waipouli is where you find the necessities, including supermarkets and a business center. In fall 2006 the Outrigger Waipouli Beach Resort, a luxury condo, was built on one of the last two vacant properties in Waipouli.

Information
There are ATMs inside Foodland supermarket in Waipouli Town Center and, just a minute north, inside Safeway in Kaua'i Village. Both are located on the *mauka* side of Kuhio Hwy.

ComputerWeb (☎ 821-0077; www.computerweb .us; Kaua'i Village, 4-831 Kuhio Hwy; per 10min $2; ⏲ 9am-9pm Mon-Sat) One-stop shop for internet access, photocopies, faxes, CDs, video games and computer repairs. Interior is bare-bones basic, but staff is helpful and parking is easy.

Longs Drugs (☎ 822-4915; Kaua'i Village; ⏲ store 7am-10pm Mon-Sat, 8am-8pm Sun, pharmacy 8am-9pm Mon-Sat, 9am-6pm Sun) Pharmacy and over-the-counter drugs, plus excellent prices on household products, beach supplies, grocery items and souvenirs.

Sights
On rainy days, head to the nonprofit **Kaua'i Children's Discovery Museum** (☎ 823-8222; www.kcdm .org; Kaua'i Village; adult/child $5/4; ⏲ 9am-5pm Tue-Sat), an educational indoor playground for the elementary set. Kid-size replicas of Filipino, Japanese and South Indian abodes portray different cultures, while a black-light tunnel and volcano slide make science fun. The museum also offers a day camp (all day $50, per hour $10) for kids in kindergarten to fourth grade, plus a well-stocked gift shop.

Another rainy-day option is **Fun Factory** (Waipouli Town Center; games 50¢-$1; ⏲ 10am-10pm, to midnight Fri & Sat), a very '80s place that resembles a carnival arcade, with sports and shooting games, video games and mini carousel rides.

Activities

Bear in mind that you can rent equipment here, but you do the activities elsewhere.

SURFING

Stop at **Ambrose's Kapuna** (☎ 822-3926; ambrose .curry@verizon.net; 770 Kuhio Hwy; lessons per hr $25), where you can enroll in lessons 'for the obtuse' given by surf guru Ambrose Curry in waters he's ridden since 1968. Post-lesson you can buy a board shaped by Curry or take home a piece of his art.

Also teaching newbies is the **Wailua Bay Surf Company** (☎ 823-1129, 645-1067; 5111 Nounou Rd; 2hr lesson $45).

SNORKELING

The cool thing about **Snorkel Bob's** (☎ 823-9433; www.snorkelbob.com; 4-734 Kuhio Hwy; basic snorkel sets per day/week $2.50/9, good sets $8/32, bodyboards $6.50/26; ☷ 8am-5pm Mon-Sat), if you're island-hopping you can rent gear on Kaua'i and return it on the Big Island, O'ahu or Maui.

BICYCLING

Kaua'i Cycle & Tour (☎ 821-2115; www.bikehawaii .com/kauaicycle; 4-934 Kuhio Hwy, Waipouli; per day/week 18-speed cruiser $15/75, quality mountain-bike with front suspension $20/95, full suspension $35/150; ☷ 9am-6pm Mon-Fri, to 4pm Sat) rents bikes maintained by experienced cyclists. Also sells and services bikes.

CAN YOU SEE HIM?

On clear days you can see the outline of the **Nounou Mountain** (commonly called the Sleeping Giant) atop Nounou Ridge from a marked viewpoint just north of the Waipouli Complex.

According to legend, the amicable giant fell asleep on the hillside after gorging on poi at a luau. When his *menehune* friends needed his help, they tried to rouse him by throwing stones. But the stones bounced from the giant's full belly into his open mouth and lodged in his throat. He died in his sleep and turned into rock.

Now he rests, stretched out on the ridge with his head in Wailua and his feet in Kapa'a. At an elevation of almost 1250ft, the giant's forehead is the highest point on the ridge.

Tours

In air-conditioned 'theaters on wheels,' movie buffs can cruise the island with **Hawaii Movie Tours** (☎ 822-1192, 800-628-8432; www.hawaiimovietour .com; 4-885 Kuhio Hwy; adult/child under 12 from $111/92; ☷ office 7:30am-6pm), stopping at film sites while viewing movie clips on a video monitor. The standard land tour is fine, but it's worth paying extra for the 4WD option (adult/child aged five to 11 $123/113), an adventurous ecotour that takes you off-road to the base of Mt Wai'ale'ale (Jurassic Park territory) and includes lunch at Lydgate Beach Park. Both tours include a look at the private Coco Palms property (p482), where you can pay homage to Elvis.

Sleeping

Accommodations are scarce in Waipouli, but luckily it's sandwiched between Wailua (p484) and Kapa'a (p492), both with plentiful options.

Mokihana of Kaua'i (☎ reservations 360-676-1434, front desk 822-3971; www.hawaii-kailani.com; 796 Kuhio Hwy; studio units $85; ☷) Sure, you can find bigger, better digs for the same price – but not near the beach. That's why Mokihana is booked solid, especially in winter when snowbird owners return for months. Units are open to non-owners from March 1 to December 15 only. Don't book units ending in 12 or 14 because they abut the laundry room.

Outrigger Waipouli Beach Resort & Spa (☎ 822-6000, 800-688-7444; www.outriggerwaipouli.com; 4-820 Kuhio Highway; 1-/2-bedroom units from $199/325; ☷ ☷) Ah, the thrill of newness. The Eastside's newest and poshest condo, built in late 2006, trumps its competition in dazzling luxury. Units feature upscale furnishings, subzero stainless-steel refrigerators, double dishwashers and central air-con – plus an 'extra' bathroom (two per one-bedroom and three per two-bedroom unit). The saltwater 'lazy river' pool, sand-bottom hot tubs and Aveda spa pamper from head to toe.

Eating & Drinking

Coffee Bean & Tea Leaf (☎ 822-4754; www.coffee beanhawaii.com; Waipouli Town Center, 4-771 Kuhio Hwy; drinks from $4; ☷ 6am-9pm, to 9:30pm Fri & Sat) At this clean-cut franchise, indulge in the gamut of coffee·and tea concoctions. Starbucks fans will fit in here.

Papaya's Natural Foods (☎ 823-0190; Kaua'i Village, 4-831 Kuhio Hwy; dishes $5-8, salad per lb $7; ☷ 9am-8pm Mon-Sat, deli to 7pm Mon-Sat) Find your typical un-

ON LOCATION IN KAUA'I

Hollywood has tapped Kaua'i over 75 times when looking for fantasy film and TV locations. Keep your eyes peeled for these famous settings:

- *South Pacific* (1957): the North Shore's Lumaha'i Beach, with Makana mountain in the background, became an icon.
- *Blue Hawaii* (1961): Elvis remains omnipresent at Wailua's Coco Palms Resort.
- *Donovan's Reef* (1963): the Nawiliwili Harbor area, including the original Kaua'i Inn, were backdrops for Lee Marvin and John Wayne.
- *Gilligan's Island* pilot (1963): Moloa'a Bay was the pilot site for the shipwrecked SS *Minnow*.
- *King Kong* (1976): remote Honopu Valley on the Na Pali Coast was the giant gorilla's island home.
- *Fantasy Island* (1978–84): the waterfall shown during this TV series' opening credits is Kaua'i's own Wailua Falls.
- *Raiders of the Lost Ark* (1981): rugged landscapes near Hule'ia Stream outside Lihu'e and Kalalea Mountain north of Anahola stood in for South American jungles.
- *The Thorn Birds* (1983): old Hanapepe town became outback Australia in the Richard Chamberlain TV mini-saga.
- *Honeymoon in Vegas* (1992): Lihu'e sites including the airport, police station and hospital make an appearance along with Nicholas Cage; the manager of Hanalei Inn stars in a bit part as an airline pilot.
- *Jurassic Park* (1993): Hanapepe and Lawa'i Valleys became the valley of the dinosaurs for Steven Spielberg's original and sequels: *The Lost World: Jurassic Park* (1997) and *Jurassic Park III* (2001). All three films in the series were partly filmed on the Garden Isle.
- *Six Days/Seven Nights* (1998): Stunt doubles for Harrison Ford and Anne Heche jump off Makawehi Pt at Shipwreck Beach.
- *Dragonfly* (2002): Upland Wailua's dense forest land stands in for the Venezuelan jungle where Kevin Costner's wife mysteriously disappears.

washed, pierced and dreadlocked clientele here, at Kaua'i's biggest and best health-food store. Stock up on bulk items, vitamins and supplements, organic produce (pricey), bottled water and deli fixings.

King & I (☎ 822-1642; Waipouli Plaza, 4-901 Kuhio Hwy; mains $7-11; ☽ 4:30-9:30pm) Ranked number one by locals, this friendly, family-run restaurant offers a lengthy menu featuring flavors such as curries popping with kaffir lime and lemongrass, fiery or not, as you like. Vegetarians will find loads of options, like flavorful eggplant and tofu in chili oil or a mound of traditional pad thai with tofu.

Kaua'i Pasta (☎ 822-7447; 4-939B Kuhio Hwy; mains $9-15; ☽ 5-9pm Tue-Sun) Real Italian cuisine is rare on Kaua'i so, if you're craving the classics, head to this nondescript joint. The chef, who cut his teeth at Roy's (p528) in Po'ipu, serves savory *panini* (hot sandwiches), classic pasta dishes and a perfectly simple (or simply

perfect) Caprese salad with local basil and tomatoes and fresh mozzarella.

Of the two supermarkets in Waipouli, chain giant **Safeway** (☎ 822-2464; Kaua'i Village, 4-831 Kuhio Hwy; ☽ 24hr) is clearly the tourist choice. Well stocked, with a deli counter, bakery and fish counter, it caters to mainland-haole (Caucasian) tastes. The better option is local chain **Foodland** (Waipouli Town Center; ☽ 6am-11pm), with a good selection of produce and gourmet and health brands, eg Kashi and Scharffen Berger. At both supermarkets, get instant discounts with a store card.

Shopping

Waipouli's two main shopping malls are Waipouli Town Center and Kaua'i Village. One notable shop is the whimsical **Marta's Boat** (☎ 822-3926; 770 Kuhio Hwy; ☽ 10am-6pm Mon-Sat), which will delight 'princesses of all ages' with feminine and sexy threads from Paris, LA and New York. Distinctive lingerie and frocks shine, but jewelry and excruciatingly cute little-girl clothes also enchant. Be prepared for big-city price tags.

KAPA'A

pop 9472

The hub of the Eastside, Kapa'a is a charming town, albeit a tiny one, populated by an eclectic mix of old timers, nouveau hippies and tourists. Historically it was a plantation community, but the last sugar mill closed in the 1940s and the last pineapple plant in the early 1960s. But since the 1970s tourism has mushroomed here.

Today, centrally located Kapa'a is a convenient roadside tourist stop. There's a yuppie/hippie vibe, with espresso cafés, live jazz, Bikram yoga and a noticeable contingent of organic/vegan/raw eateries. Granted, most patrons of such establishments are mainland transplants or tourists (read: haole). Interspersed among the new establishments are longtime diners and shops, still going strong.

On the downside, traffic is a nightmare. During commute hours, cars literally crawl along Kuhio Hwy in both directions. If you're traveling between the north end of Kapa'a and Wailua or beyond, by all means take the Kapa'a Bypass Rd. Except in the heart of Kapa'a, you will definitely need a car.

Information

INTERNET ACCESS

Akamai Computer Technologies (☎ 823-0047; www.akamaicomputers.com; 4-1286-A Kuhio Hwy; per 10min $2; ☽ 9am-4pm Mon-Thu, 9am-noon Fri) Internet access and computer repairs (per hour $65). Park in the Ono Family Restaurant lot.

Business Support Services (☎ 822-5504; fax 822-2148; 4-1191 Kuhio Hwy; per hr $10; ☽ 8am-6pm Mon-Sat, 10am-6pm Sun) No atmosphere but cheap internet access, plus faxing, copies and stamps.

Java Kai (☎ 823-6887; 4-1384 Kuhio Hwy; wi-fi per 15/120min $3/12; ☽ 6am-5pm) Café with limited patio seating.

LAUNDRY

Kapa'a Laundry Center (☎ 822-3113; Kapa'a Shopping Center, 4-1105 Kuhio Hwy; ☽ 7:30am-9:30pm, last wash 8pm) Cramped and lacking wheeled carts, but featuring lively piped-in island tunes.

MEDICAL SERVICES

Samuel Mahelona Memorial Hospital (☎ 822-4961; fax 823-4100; 4800 Kawaihau Rd) Primarily a long-term-care facility, this longstanding hospital expanded services to include basic emergency care in late 2005. Serious cases are transferred to Lihu'e's Wilcox Memorial Hospital.

MONEY

First Hawaiian Bank (☎ 822-4966; 4-1366 Kuhio Hwy) 24-hour ATM.

POST

Post office (☎ 800-275-8777; Kapa'a Shopping Center, 4-1101 Kuhio Hwy; ☽ 8am-4pm Mon-Fri, 9am-2pm Sat)

Sights

KAPA'A BEACH PARK

Low-key and local, this county beach park is a mile-long ribbon of beach beginning at Kapa'a's north end, where there's a ball field, picnic tables and a public pool. At the south end of the beach, near Pono Kai Resort, there's a nice sandy area.

A pretty, shoreline **foot-and-bicycle path** runs the length of the beach park, crossing over a couple of old bridges where families and old-timers drop fishing lines. The path makes an appealing alternative to walking along the highway to and from town.

Activities

There are free **tennis courts** and a **skateboarding park**, along with a field for baseball, football and soccer in Kapa'a New Park, and a public **swimming pool** (☎ 822-3842; admission free; ☽ 10am-4:30pm Thu-Mon) at Kapa'a County Beach Park.

DIVING

No, there's no good diving off Kapa'a's coast, but there are good outfits. From here, you must then head to the North Shore or South Shore.
Ocean Quest Watersports (☎ 742-6991, 800-972-3078; www.fathomfive.com) This satellite location of the superlative Fathom Five (p519) outfit in Koloa is geared for the excellent North Shore dive at Tunnels reef.
Seasport Divers (☎ 823-9222, 800-685-5889; www.seasportdivers.com; 4-976 Kuhio Hwy) Rents gear, leads dives, including to Ni'ihau, and offers certification courses. Snorkel gear is available. Its main location is in Po'ipu (p524).

Use **Dive Kaua'i** (☎ 822-0452, 800-828-3483; www.divekauai.com; 1038 Kuhio Hwy; ☽ 8am-5:30pm Mon-Sat, 9am-3pm Sun) only as Plan B.

FISHING

Join gregarious Captain Terry of **Hawaiian Style Fishing** (☎ 635-7335; half-day charter per person $100) on

KAPA'A

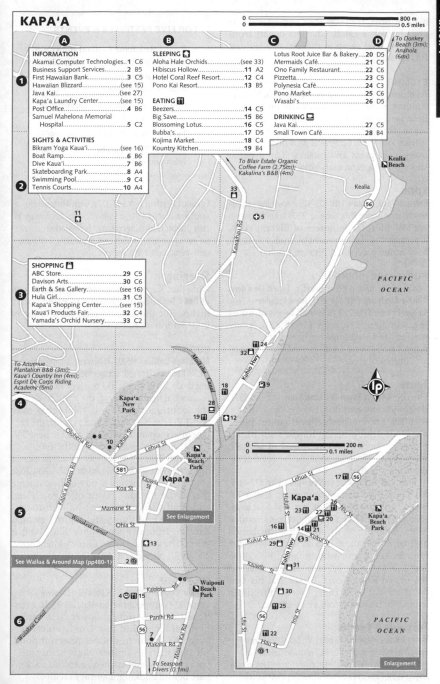

0 _____ 800 m
0 _____ 0.5 miles

INFORMATION
Akamai Computer Technologies..**1** C6
Business Support Services...........**2** B5
First Hawaiian Bank.....................**3** C5
Hawaiian Blizzard.....................(see 15)
Java Kai.................................(see 27)
Kapa'a Laundry Center............(see 15)
Post Office..................................**4** B6
Samuel Mahelona Memorial
    Hospital.................................**5** C2

SIGHTS & ACTIVITIES
Bikram Yoga Kaua'i................(see 16)
Boat Ramp.................................**6** B6
Dive Kaua'i................................**7** B6
Skateboarding Park.....................**8** A4
Swimming Pool...........................**9** C4
Tennis Courts............................**10** A4

SHOPPING 🛍
ABC Store.................................**29** C5
Davison Arts.............................**30** C6
Earth & Sea Gallery.................(see 16)
Hula Girl...................................**31** C5
Kapa'a Shopping Center.........(see 15)
Kaua'i Products Fair..................**32** C4
Yamada's Orchid Nursery.........**33** C2

SLEEPING 🏠
Aloha Hale Orchids................(see 33)
Hibiscus Hollow.......................**11** A2
Hotel Coral Reef Resort............**12** C4
Pono Kai Resort.......................**13** B5

EATING 🍴
Beezers....................................**14** C5
Big Save...................................**15** B6
Blossoming Lotus.....................**16** C5
Bubba's....................................**17** D5
Kojima Market...........................**18** C4
Kountry Kitchen.......................**19** B4

Lotus Root Juice Bar & Bakery....**20** D5
Mermaids Café.........................**21** C5
Ono Family Restaurant.............**22** C6
Pizzetta....................................**23** C5
Polynesia Café.........................**24** C3
Pono Market.............................**25** C6
Wasabi's...................................**26** D5

DRINKING 🍸
Java Kai...................................**27** C5
Small Town Café......................**28** B4

To Donkey
Beach (3mi);
Anahola
(6mi)

Kealia
Beach

To Blair Estate Organic
Coffee Farm (2.75mi);
Kakalina's B&B (4mi)

Kealia

56

PACIFIC
OCEAN

To Anuenue
Plantation B&B (3mi);
Kaua'i Country Inn (4mi);
Esprit De Corps Riding
Academy (5mi)

Kapa'a
New
Park

Kapa'a
Beach
Park

Kapa'a

See Enlargement

See Wailua & Around Map (pp480-1)

Waipouli
Beach
Park

To Seasport
Divers (0.1mi)

0 _____ 200 m
0 _____ 0.1 miles

Kapa'a

Kapa'a
Beach
Park

PACIFIC
OCEAN

Enlargement

his 25ft boat. He takes four anglers at most and shares the catch. Charters depart from the small boat ramp at the end of Kaloloku Rd, off Kuhio Hwy.

CYCLING

A smooth 6-mile coastal pedal starts in Kapa'a, running along Kealia Beach and on to Anahola, before turning into a rough single track for another 9 miles. The jarringly bumpy ride is truly off-road, on gravel and dirt, through overgrown grass and bushes. The pristine shoreline is spectacular, however.

YOGA

Bikram Yoga Kaua'i (☎ 822-5053; www.bikramyogaretreats.com; Dragon Bldg, Suite 10, 4504 Kukui St; drop-in class $15). Ideal for followers of Bikram yoga, especially the classes taught by studio director Judy Louie, a certified Bikram teacher.

HORSEBACK RIDING

More than just a tour outfit, **Esprit De Corps Riding Academy** (☎ 822-4688; www.kauaihorses.com; Kualapa Pl; tours $112-216) offers all levels of training, summer day-camps for all ages, 'pony parties,' and weddings on horseback. Tours ranges from basic to advanced, and groups are limited to five.

Tours

On the **Kapa'a Town Walking Tour** (☎ 245-3373; khs@hawaiilink.net; adult/child $15/5; 🕒 10am & 4pm Tue, Thu & Sat), knowledgeable local guides point out landmarks, describe Kapa'a's sugar and pineapple boom days and, best of all, talk story and answer questions. Advance reservations are required.

Blair Estate Organic Coffee Farm (☎ 822-4495, 800-750-5662; www.blairestatecoffee.com, 6200-B Kawaihau Rd; 1hr tour free; 🕒 9am Mon, Wed & Sat by appointment only) is Kaua'i's only organic coffee farm. Established in 2001, this husband-and-wife operation is a labor of love for founder Les Drent, who initiated his coffee career in the early 1990s, roasting coffee on the famed Kona Coast. Check out his free publication, *Coffee Times* (www.coffeetimes.com). No unannounced visits allowed.

Festivals & Events

Heiva I Kaua'i Iaorana Tahiti (☎ 245-5010) Dance troupes from as far away as Tahiti, Japan and Canada join groups from Hawaii in this Tahitian dance competition in early August at the Kapa'a Beach Park; drumming contests, too.

TOP FIVE FESTIVALS & EVENTS

- **Kaua'i Mokihana Festival Hula Competition** (Po'ipu, September; p526)
- **Eo e Emalani I Alaka'i** (Koke'e State Park, October; p549)
- **Koloa Plantation Days Celebration** (Koloa, July; p520)
- **Taste of Hawaii** (Wailua, June; p484)
- **Waimea Town Celebration** (Waimea, February; p539)

Coconut Festival (☎ 651-3273; www.kbakauai.org; admission adult/child/teen $5/free/2) Two-day homage in early October to all things coconut! Events include coconut-pie-eating contests, coconut cook-off, cooking demonstrations, music, hula, crafts and food.

Sleeping

Note that Kapa'a's longstanding budget icon **KK Bed & Bath** (www.kkbedbath.com) is on temporary hiatus. But the website remains a fount of information on Kapa'a.

BUDGET

Aloha Hale Orchids (☎ 822-4148; www.yamadanursery.com; 5087-A Kawaihau Rd; r $50, cottages $80) Two outstanding deals amid an orchid nursery in a low-key residential neighborhood: the spick-and-span studio includes queen bed, mini refrigerator and TV. For more space and privacy, the cottage offers separate bedroom, full kitchen, TV, lots of windows, washer and clothesline.

Hibiscus Hollow (☎ 823-9004; www.akauaivacationrental.com; 4906 Laipo Rd; d/tr/q incl tax $60/65/70) Close your eyes and picture a one-bedroom suite that a surfer buddy might offer you: clean and comfy, if slightly lived-in, with island-style rattan furnishings and colorful mobiles dangling from an open-beam ceiling. Well, it exists. The suite includes a handy kitchenette, TV-VCR, phone and lanai.

MIDRANGE

Kakalina's B&B (☎ 822-2328, 800-662-4330; www.kakalina.com; 6781 Kawaihau Rd; r incl breakfast $85-90) In a rustic setting on a tropical-flower farm 4 miles north of town, find four comfy units overlooking a serene freshwater reservoir pond. All units share an unpretentious, homey feel – but vary in size and kitchen amenities, so compare before booking. Laundry facility.

Kaua'i Country Inn (☎ 821-0207; www.kauaicountry inn.com; 6440 Olohena Rd; ste $99-159, 3-bedroom cottages from $225; 🖳) We dare you to find an inn classier than this, located about 4 miles out of town. With gleaming hardwood floors and upscale furnishings, the four spacious suites all include cable TV/DVD, Macintosh computers, wi-fi, and kitchen or kitchenette. Kids under 12 are not allowed in suites, but welcome in the three-bedroom cottage. Guests are privileged to view the owner's astounding collection of valuable Beatles memorabilia. Big thumbs up!

Hotel Coral Reef Resort (☎ 822-4481, 800-843-4659; www.hotelcoralreefresort.com; 4-1516 Kuhio Hwy; r $125-249; 🔀) A bit pricey, Coral Reef is Kapa'a's only hotel – and the only in-town, beachside lodging. The tastefully furnished rooms are small but, renovated recently, include upgraded touches like flat-screen TVs. The central location lets you forgo driving in Kapa'a.

Pono Kai Resort (☎ 822-9831, 800-456-0009; www .ponokai.com; 4-1250 Kuhio Hwy; studios from $79, 1-/2-bedroom units from $135/150; 🔀 🔁) While the 240-unit Pono Kai Resort's time-shares are consistent in quality, the 30 to 35 condo vacation rentals are a mixed bag. The key selling point: it's within walking distance of town. One- and two-bedroom units are quite spacious, all with full kitchen.

Eating & Drinking
BUDGET
Hawaiian Blizzard (✹ noon-5pm Mon-Fri) For the island's best shave ice, stop at the white van parked outside Big Save. Owner Aaron Furugen is the low-key guru of shave ice, perfecting the art since the 1980s. Kids flock here after school and neighborhood regulars hang out and talk story.

Java Kai (☎ 823-6887; 4-1384 Kuhio Hwy; coffee drinks $1.50-4.50; ✹ 6am-5pm), A mostly local chain, Java Kai is a nice alternative to Starbucks. Choose from a mind-boggling selection of java drinks, along with coffee beans. Yummy muffins, fruity smoothies and limited sidewalk seating.

Lotus Root Juice Bar & Bakery (☎ 823-6658; www .blossominglotus.com; 4-1384 Kuhio Hwy; cookies & scones $2.50-3; ✹ 7am-6pm) Both hippies and health nuts will appreciate the vegan treats from coconut-lavender cookies to chai-spirulina concoctions.

Small Town Café (☎ 821-1604; 4-1495 Kuhio Hwy; coffee drinks $3-5; ✹ 5:30am-9pm Mon-Sat, to 6pm Sun) With well-worn furniture and a hippie-boho vibe, this neighborhood hangout is the spot for leisurely chats or websurfing (free wi-fi). Enjoy organic, free-trade coffees and teas, plus live music in the evening.

Beezers (☎ 822-4411; 4-1380 Kuhio Hwy; items $4-8.50; ✹ 11am-9:30pm) At this nostalgic ice-cream parlor, splurge on banana splits, root-beer floats and ice-cream sundaes amid quaint 1960s decor. Forget the diet again with diner classics from sloppy joes to double-decker deli sandwiches.

Bubba's (☎ 823-0069; www.bubbaburger.com; 4-1421 Kuhio Hwy; burgers $3-5; ✹ 10:30am-8pm) Locals hardly go here but this local chain has become the haole-tourist mecca. The 100% Kaua'i-beef burgers are fine (and vegetarians can opt for ginger-teriyaki tempeh burgers) but try the locals' fave, Duane's Ono Char Burger (p495) instead.

Kountry Kitchen (☎ 822-3511; 4-1485 Kuhio Hwy; meals $4-8; ✹ 6am-2pm) An excellent down-home diner, Kountry Kitchen lets you tailor your meal. Build your own light and crepelike omelette (from $5.25) from a variety of fillings. Choose either one, two or three pancakes ($3 to $5.75), either banana, strawberry or chocolate-chip. Breakfast served all day, lunch from 11am.

Pono Market (☎ 822-4581; 4-1300 Kuhio Hwy; plate lunch $6; ✹ 7am-7pm Mon-Fri, 7am-6pm Sun) At this hole-in-the-wall corner store, try the ono grinds from the take-out deli counter: generous plate lunches, fresh sushi rolls and Hawaiian food, eg *kalua* (pig cooked in an underground pit) with poi.

Ono Family Restaurant (☎ 822-1710; 4-1292 Kuhio Hwy; breakfast mains $7-8.50, burgers & sandwiches $4.50-8.25; ✹ 7am-1:30pm) Kaua'i's old-time diners take their omelettes and pancakes seriously – and you can taste the results at Ono's, a fixture in Kapa'a. Choose from 18 types of omelette or opt for the incomparable tropical pancakes ($6 to $8) with bananas, macadamia nuts and coconut.

Mermaids Café (☎ 821-2026; 4-1384 Kuhio Hwy; meals $9; ✹ 11am-8:45pm) Plate lunches for the hippie-granola set? You bet. And we guarantee you'll be tempted to try everything on the menu, from the classic seared *'ahi* and nori wrap to overflowing plates of coconut curry topping veggies, tofu or chicken.

For groceries, Waipouli's supermarkets are generally better than Kapa'a's two: **Kojima Market** (☎ 822-5221; 4-1543 Kuhio Hwy; ✹ 8am-7pm Mon-Fri, to 6pm Sat, to 1pm Sun), a smaller grocer that carries local meats, and local chain **Big Save** (☎ 822-4971; Kapa'a Shopping Center; ⊙ 7am-11pm).

MIDRANGE

Wasabi's (☎ 822-2700; 4-1388 Kuhio Hwy; sushi rolls $3.50-13, mains $8-18; ⊙ 11am-9pm) With marine-blue walls, well-worn furniture and funky 'under the sea' decor, Wasabi's has just enough grime for a boho-urban vibe – but not enough to produce the yuck factor. Try the house specialties like Lollypop Roll with paper-thin cucumber hugging succulent *hamachi* (yellowtail), *maguro* (tuna) and salmon ($12).

Blossoming Lotus (☎ 822-7678; www.blossominglotus .com; Dragon Bldg, 4504 Kukui St; mains $7-14; ⊙ 6-9:30pm) You'll either love it or hate it. After initial rave reviews since its opening in 2003, Blossoming Lotus's 'vegan world fusion cuisine' seems hit or miss. The savory appetizers and marinated tofu or tempeh dishes are the most creative.

Olympic Café (☎ 822-5825; 4-1354 Kuhio Hwy; breakfast & lunch mains $8-14, dinner mains $12-24; ⊙ 6am-9pm Sun-Thu, to 10pm Fri & Sat) If you need to satisfy eclectic tastebuds and appetites, the menu here can please all. In a sprawling space overlooking the highway, it's a casual, tropical-setting (if LA-inspired) diner. Fill up with the egg and spinach scramble with sundried tomatoes and artichoke hearts ($9) or the whopping *kalua* pig burrito ($10.50).

Polynesia Café (☎ 822-1945; 4-1639 Kuhio Hwy; mains $10-19; ⊙ 7am-9:30pm) It might resemble a typical touristy joint, but this is a step above. Its signature *ahi* (or tofu) plates are yummy and filling, and the breads and sauces are freshly house-made. The Asian-Hawaiian-Mexican menu might seem a random hodgepodge but, hey, they make it work.

Pizzetta (☎ 823-8882; 4-1387 Kuhio Hwy; pizzas $14-23, pastas $9-17; ⊙ 11am-10pm) Rather a tourist trap but the crust is decent and, on the Eastside, your only other option is Pizza Hut. Try the Milano (fire-roasted veg and feta) or shrimp puttanesca (shrimp, capers, kalamata olives, roma tomatoes and spicy sauce). Daily happy hour is 3pm to 6pm. Taste the house Rooster Brew is made by local microbrewery Keoki Brewing Company.

Shopping

ABC Store (☎ 823-0081; 4-1359 Kuhio Hwy; ⊙ 6am-11pm) This local catchall chain carries everything from snacks and T-shirts to souvenirs and beer. Prices are competitive.

Kaua'i Products Fair (☎ 246-0988; 4-1621 Kuhio Hwy; ⊙ 9am-5pm Thu-Sun) Worth a browse, this outdoor fair on the north side of town sells handmade souvenirs, photography, aloha wear, produce, herbal remedies and more.

Earth & Sea Gallery (☎ 821-2831; Dragon Bldg, 4504 Kukui St; ⊙ 9am-9pm) All pocketbooks can find a gift here, from 'beanbag' geckos (filled with Kaua'i sand) to intricately carved wooden frames ($75 to $125) and coconut-shell lamps ($85).

Yamada's Orchid Nursery (☎ 822-4148; www.yamada nursery.com; 5087-A Kawaihau Rd; ⊙ by appointment) Take home a living, blooming souvenir. You can carry orchids on your flight or have them shipped to your home.

Hula Girl (☎ 822-1950; www.welovehulagirl.com; 4-1340 Kuhio Hwy; ⊙ 9am-6pm Mon-Sat, 10am-5pm Sun) Aloha-shirt aficionados will find a wide selection of quality, name-brand shirts ($40 to $125). Feel the silky soft Tori Richard line in cotton lawn ($70 to $75). Also sells women's dresses, jewelry, island-made ceramics, art prints and other souvenirs.

Davison Arts (☎ 821-8022; www.davisonarts.com; 4-1322 Kuhio Hwy; ⊙ 9:30am-noon Mon, to 5pm Tue-Fri, 10am-2pm Sat) View Hayley Davison's exquisite wood furniture and John Davison's striking paintings inspired by Kaua'i's landscapes. Ready to shell out $2400 for a lustrous koa rocker?

NORTHEAST COAST

Beyond Kapa'a, the landscape suddenly opens into a vast swath of greens and blues. Gone are the hulking resorts, jammed parking lots and bumper-to-bumper traffic. You are entering a part of Kaua'i well known only by locals; see the Eastside map (Map p478) for this area.

Kealia Beach

Mainly a locals' surf and bodyboarding spot, this scenic beach, at the 10-mile marker, is recommended mainly for experts. The powerful waves are mesmerizing but treacherous. A breakwater protects the north end, so swimming and snorkeling are occasionally possible there – but not recommended. After rainstorms, the sand may be heavily littered with tree limbs carried down Kealia Stream, which empties at the beach's south side.

Donkey Beach

An easy 10-minute walk down from the highway takes you to golden Donkey Beach, Kaua'i's best-known nudist beach. But nudity is illegal on Kaua'i and police occasionally bust those in the buff. The site is also popular as a gay beach.

Summer swells are manageable here but from October to May dangerous rip currents and a powerful shorebreak take over. Blustery winds whip ironwood trees away from the shore, which are bent so low they resemble shrubs. *Naupaka* and *'ilima*, native ground-creeping flowers, add dashes of color to the sand. Shade is minimal so bring sun protection.

To get to the beach, stop at the paved parking lot at the ocean side of Kuhio Hwy, about halfway between the 11- and 12-mile markers; look for the small 'Public Shoreline Access' sign.

Anahola

pop 1932

Blink and you'll miss the predominantly Native Hawaiian village of Anahola, where there are subdivisions of Hawaiian Homestead lots at the southern and northern ends. Pineapple and sugar plantations once thrived here but today the area is mainly residential. The few who lodge here will find themselves in rural seclusion among true locals.

Grouped together at the side of Kuhio Hwy, just south of the 14-mile marker, Anahola's modest commercial center includes a **post office** (8am-4pm Mon-Fri, 9:30-11:30am Sat), burger stand and convenience store.

SIGHTS & ACTIVITIES

Anahola Beach Park

A county park on Hawaiian Home Lands, Anahola Beach Park sits at the south side of Anahola Bay. The wide bay fringed with lovely sandy beach was an ancient surfing site and the break is still popular with local surfers. To get here, turn off Kuhio Hwy onto Kukuihale Rd at the 13-mile marker, drive a mile down and then turn onto the dirt beach road. You can also access the north end of the beach from 'Aliomanu Rd (the 'first' 'Aliomanu Rd at the 14-mile marker, not the 'second' one a mile north).

'Aliomanu Beach

Secluded 'Aliomanu Beach is another spot frequented primarily by locals, who pole- and throw-net fish and gather *limu* (seaweed). It's a mile-long stretch of beach; you can get to the prettier north end by turning onto 'Aliomanu Rd (second), just past the 15-mile marker on Kuhio Hwy. Turn left onto Kalalea View

Dr, go 0.5 miles and turn right at the beach access sign.

Massage

Angeline's Mu'olaulani (☎ 822-3235; www.auntyangel ines.com; Kamalomalo'o Pl; signature treatment $130; ☺ 9am-3pm Mon-Fri by appointment only) Experience authentic *lomilomi* (traditional Hawaiian massage) at this longstanding bodywork center. With outdoor shower, open-air deck, massage tables separated by curtains, and simple sarongs to cover up, Angeline's is rustic and a real contrast to ritzy resort spas. The signature treatment includes a steam, vigorous salt scrub and a special four-hands (two-person) *lomilomi*.

TriHealth Ayurveda (☎ 828-2104, 800-455-0770; www.oilbath.com; Kuhio Hwy; treatments $130-275) In a simple bungalow just off the highway, you can sample traditional Ayurvedic therapies, practiced by therapists trained both locally and in Kerala, India. A popular treatment includes a sensual hot-oil massage, synchronized by two therapists, followed by heady relaxation in a rather intimidating horizontal steamer. Located between the 20- and 21-mile markers.

SLEEPING

For information about camping in Anahola Beach Park, see p460.

Hale Kiko'o (☎ 822-3922; www.halekikoo.com; 4-4382-B Kuhio Hwy; s $65-80, d $70-85, plus cleaning fee $50; 🖳) Shh, this charming tropical hideaway is a steal. Choose from two private studios, each with full kitchen: the downstairs unit is chic and spacious (essentially a suite without walls), featuring slate floors, lava-rock pillars, a garden patio and unique outdoor shower. The smaller upstairs unit is plainer but brighter, surrounded by windows and a deck.

'Ili Noho Kai O Anahola (Hawaiian Style Beachfront B&B; ☎ 821-0179, 639-6317; www.kauai.net/anahola; Aliomanu Rd; r with shared bathroom incl breakfast $75) Hang loose at Sondra and Michael Grace's informal guesthouse fronting Anahola Bay. Four compact but tidy rooms (sharing two bathrooms) surround a central lanai, where guests talk story and fill up on home-cooked breakfasts. The hosts are Native Hawaiian activists now running a B&B on Hawaiian Home Lands for which they fought long and hard.

EATING

Duane's Ono Char-Burger (☎ 822-9181; 4-4350 Kuhio Hwy; burgers $5-7; ☺ 10am-6pm Mon-Sat, 11am-6pm Sun) Amid a world of phonies, here's the real deal.

Try the 'old fashioned' (cheddar, onions and sprouts) or the 'local girl' (Swiss cheese, pineapple and teriyaki sauce). Add crispy thin fries and melt-in-your-mouth onion rings. See autographed photos of famous fans, from Chuck Norris to Steve Tyler.

Hole in the Mountain

The *puka* (hole) in Pu'u Konanae is now more like a sliver, since a landslide transformed the once-obvious landmark. Legend says the original hole was created when a giant threw his spear through the mountain, causing the water stored within to gush forth as waterfalls. From slightly north of the 15-mile marker along Hwy 56, look back at the mountain, down to the right of the tallest pinnacle: on sunny days you'll see a smile of light shining through a slit in the rock face.

Ko'olau Road

Ko'olau Rd is a peaceful, scenic loop drive through rich green pastures, dotted with soaring white egrets and bright wild flowers. It makes a nice diversion and is the way to reach untouristed Moloa'a Beach or Larsen's Beach (no facilities at either). Ko'olau Rd connects with Kuhio Hwy 0.5 miles north of the 16-mile marker and again 180yd south of the 20-mile marker.

For a quick bite, the **Moloa'a Sunrise Fruit Stand** (☎ 822-1441; Kuhio Hwy & Ko'olau Rd; juices & smoothies $3-6.25, sandwiches $5.50-7; ☑ 7:30am-6pm Mon-Sat, 10am-5pm Sun) offers healthful sandwiches on multigrain bread, taro burgers and brown-rice vegetarian sushi. Located past the 16-mile marker.

MOLOA'A BEACH

Off the tourist path, this classically curved bay appeared in the pilot for *Gilligan's Island*. To the north, there's a shallow protected swimming area good for families; to the south, the waters are rougher but there's more sand. When the surf's up, stay dry and safe – go beach walking instead. Toward the back of the beach, which is fed by Moloa'a Stream, there's plenty of shade, making for an ideal picnic or daydreaming spot.

To get here, follow Ko'olau Rd and turn onto Moloa'a Rd, which ends 0.75 miles down at a few beach houses and a little parking area.

Cross jaw-jarringly unpaved roads to find **Jade Lily Pad** (☎ 822-5216; www.rosewoodkauai.com;

near Moloa'a Rd; 2-bedroom house $298), a beach house on stilts beside a tranquil stream. With two bedrooms, two bathrooms, full kitchen, lanai with Jacuzzi and airy cathedral ceilings, it's a spacious retreat for adventurous couples or families.

LARSEN'S BEACH

This long, golden-sand beach, named after L David Larsen (former manager of C Brewer's Kilauea Sugar Company), is good for solitary strolls and beachcombing. Although shallow, snorkeling can be good when the waters are very calm, usually only in the summer. Beware of a vicious current that runs westward along the beach and out through a channel in the reef.

When the tide is low, you might share Larsen's with Hawaiian families collecting an edible seaweed called *limu kohu*. The seaweed found here is considered to be some of the finest in all of Hawaii. Otherwise, it will be you, the sand and the waves.

To get here, turn onto Ko'olau Rd from whichever end (ie where it intersects either Kuhio Hwy or Moloa'a Rd), go just over a mile then turn toward the ocean on a dirt road (easy to miss from the south: look for it just before the cemetery) and take the immediate left. It's 1 mile to the parking area and then a five-minute walk downhill to the beach.

THE LAST BIG ONE

When Kaua'i residents talk about the 'big one,' they're talking about Hurricane 'Iniki, which slammed the island on September 11, 1992. 'Iniki stormed in with sustained winds of 145mph and gusts of 165mph; a weather-station meter in mountainous Koke'e broke off at 227mph. The hurricane snapped trees by the thousands, ruined 5000 utility poles and affected an estimated 50% of buildings on Kaua'i, damaging 5000 and totally demolishing over 1300 of them. Thirty-foot waves washed away entire wings of beachfront hotels – Po'ipu and Princeville were particularly hard hit.

Miraculously, only four people died, but the total value of the damage to the island was $1.6 billion. Today locals still notice the changed landscape, but newcomers would never realize the havoc wreaked 15 years ago.

NORTH SHORE

It's futile to describe the North Shore's other-worldly natural beauty without sounding clichéd. But those perfectly curved bays, the fine golden sand, lush valleys, thundering waterfalls and sheer cliffs…truly do exist.

For years the North Shore was tropical hinterland, seen only by surfers, trekkers and escapees from civilization. But today the it's a must-see and cars zoom nonstop to the end of the road. The 1970s development of Princeville, which is among the priciest second-home markets in the USA, was a major impetus for North Shore tourism, for better or worse.

Still, the vibe here is noticeably laid-back and rural. Residents are a motley mix of long-time farming families, '70s hippie settlers, surf bums of all ages, retirees, part-time-resident homeowners and a new youthful generation seeking 'the good life.' Surfing is *the* sport of choice – and catching a few waves every day *pau hana* (after work) is the fantasy lifestyle come true.

KILAUEA
pop 2092

While still a no-stoplight town, Kilauea's modest commercial stretch is worth a stop. The main attractions are the picturesque lighthouse and seabird sanctuary at Kilauea Point, but you'll also find a handful of destination eateries, selling artisan breads, fresh fish and island produce. Vacation rentals are springing up in quiet neighborhoods.

Sights & Activities
KILAUEA POINT

The **Kilauea Point National Wildlife Refuge** (☎ 828-0383; www.fws.gov/pacificislands/wnwr/kkilaueanwr.html; adult/child under 16 $3/free; ⏰ 10am-4pm, closed federal holidays) is the northernmost point of the inhabited Hawaiian Islands. Topped by **Kilauea Lighthouse**, built in 1913, the refuge is picture-postcard material. The paved path to the lighthouse is disabled-accessible.

Even if birds bore you, it's worth driving to the end of Kilauea Rd for the stunning view of the lighthouse (with the biggest clamshell lens in the world) and cliffs beyond. Most of the surrounding refuge is closed to the public, to protect the wildlife habitat.

Four species of bird come to Kilauea to nest: red-footed boobies, wedge-tailed shear-

TOP 5 GARDENS

- **Allerton Garden** (p521): magnificent land-to-sea landscaping in historically prized valley

- **Limahuli Garden** (p514): thriving native, Polynesian and modern plants with the backdrop of Makana Mountain

- **McBryde Garden** (p521): vast grounds of lush tropical jungle, perfect for strolling

- **Na 'Aina Kai Botanical Gardens** (below): meticulously landscaped gardens with surprises from bronze statues to a delightful maze

- **Smith's Tropical Paradise** (p479): relaxing park with still ponds, grassy lawns, shady trees and colorful birdlife

waters, red-tailed and white-tailed tropic birds and Laysan albatrosses. You might also see one of Kaua'i's estimated 100 nene, the endangered Hawaiian goose that was reintroduced here in 1982. Scan for sea turtles and spinner dolphins in spring and summer and for humpback whales in winter.

NA 'AINA KAI BOTANICAL GARDENS

Joyce and Ed Doty moved to Kaua'i from California in 1982 and began landscaping the grounds of their home. Today the Dotys are in their 80s and their retirement project is a 240-acre extravaganza of **botanical gardens** (☎ 828-0525; www.naainakai.com; 4101 Wailapa Rd; tours $25-70), all meticulously groomed.

The expansive grounds include 13 gardens, including the 'Formal Garden' where over 70 life-sized bronze statues romp in Norman Rockwell-inspired poses. A unique attraction is the Poinciana maze, where paths lead you to topiary and statues. Also on the grounds: a beach, a bird-watching marsh and a sprawling forest of around 60,000 South and East Asian hardwood trees.

The gardens are a tad contrived, as they lack the historical context imbued at the National Tropical Botanical Garden (p521). That said, no one will walk away disappointed by the botanical splendor.

Among the tour options is a two-hour riding tour ($35) ideal for people with limited mobility. To reach the gardens, turn right

NORTH SHORE

onto Wailapa Rd, between the 21- and 22-mile markers on Kuhio Hwy.

GUAVA KAI PLANTATION

The token 'visitors center' at this 480-acre guava **plantation** (☎ 828-6121; www.guavakai.com; Kuawa Rd; admission free; ☒ 9am-5pm) is not a must-see. But the neatly planted orchard is pleasant enough. At the visitors center, you can sample juice and buy guava, jams, hot sauces and syrups. You can also stroll a pleasant path through a tropical-flower garden and enter the orchards to pick unlimited guavas.

To get here, turn inland onto Kuawa Rd from Kuhio Hwy, just north of the 23-mile marker.

ROCK QUARRY BEACH

Broad and sandy, with a pretty fringe of iron-wood trees, Rock Quarry Beach (also called Kalihi Beach) is a river mouth for Kilauea Stream, so the water can be murky. Nevertheless, it offers rich fishing and, on occasion, surfing. If the waves are big enough to ride, swimmers should take extreme caution with strong near-shore currents.

Public access is via Wailapa Rd, which begins midway between the 21- and 22-mile markers on Kuhio Hwy. Follow Wailapa Rd north for less than 0.5 miles beyond Kuhio Hwy and then turn left on the unmarked dirt road (4WD recommended) that begins at a bright-yellow water valve.

CHRIST MEMORIAL EPISCOPAL CHURCH

After turning onto Kolo Rd, just past the 23-mile marker on Kuhio Hwy, look immediately for this striking church. Built in 1941 of lava rock, the headstones (also of lava rock) in the churchyard are much older, dating back to when the original Hawaiian Congregational Church stood here.

Sleeping

No hotels or condos in Kilauea, thank goodness, but higher-end vacation rentals are burgeoning. Search the **Vacation Rentals by Owner** (VRBO; www.vrbo.com) website or contact the agencies listed on p505.

Aloha Plantation Kaua'i (☎ 828-6872, 877-658-6977; www.alohaplantation.com; 4481 Malulani Rd; r $69-99) Vintage collectors will be intrigued by this 1920s

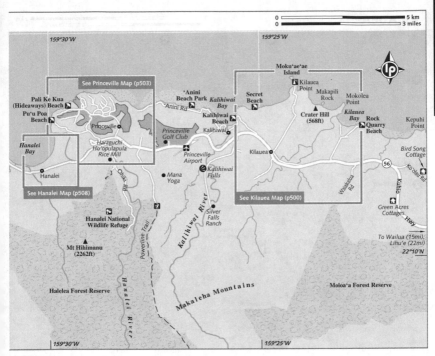

plantation house filled with antiques, from classic barber chairs to bobble-head hula dolls. The in-house rooms resemble an eccentric aunt's house or a mini museum, rather cluttered and furnished with retro rattan and wrought-iron pieces. The best deal is the detached studio ($99) with kitchenette.

Green Acres Cottages (Map pp498–9; ☎ 828-0478, 866-484-6347; www.greenacrescottages.com; 5-0421-C Kuhio Hwy; cottages $75-90) Cozy and country-cute, these top-value studios overlook a neatly planted citrus orchard. Dubbed 'cottages,' the studios are small and situated close together – but each has a private entrance plus kitchenette, phone and wi-fi. The location, right off Kuhio Hwy, requires eagle eyes at night.

Bird Song Cottage (Map pp498–9; ☎ 828-6797, 652-2585; www.kauaibirdsongcottage.com; cottages per night $150) Escape the madding crowd in a lush oasis of greenery. Also known as Manu Mele ('Bird Song' in Hawaiian), this stylish cottage features a sweeping 12ft ceiling, hardwood furniture, luxurious tub made of India-imported granite, full kitchen, canopy bed and washer-dryer. There's a one-time cleaning fee of $100. Privacy is guaranteed here, where

6 acres of grassy valley and tropical foliage is all that's around.

Eating

Kilauea Bakery & Pau Hana Pizza (☎ 828-2020; Kong Lung Center, Kilauea Rd; pastries $2, pizza $10-30; 6:30am-9pm, pizza from 10:30am) Go early for the best selection of gooey mac-nut sticky buns, sourdough loaves, tropical Danish pastries, etc – they can sell out before noon. The pizza is rather bready, but features tasty toppings like smoked *ono*, Kilauea goat cheese and fresh sugarloaf pineapple.

Mango Mama's (☎ 828-1020; cnr Kuhio Hwy & Ho'okui Rd; smoothies $4-5.50, sandwiches $5-6.50; 7am-6pm Mon-Sat) Proudly painted pink, this casual eatery serves healthful fast food: smoothies, sandwiches, burgers (meat or veg), baked goods and coffee drinks. Order at the counter and either take out or find a patio table.

Kilauea Fish Market (☎ 828-6244; 4270 Kilauea Rd; plates & wraps $8-11; 11am-8pm Mon-Sat) At last, yummy plate lunches that won't clog your arteries. One taste and you'll be addicted to the generous plates of seared-'ahi poke salad with organic greens, wraps stuffed with

KAUA'I

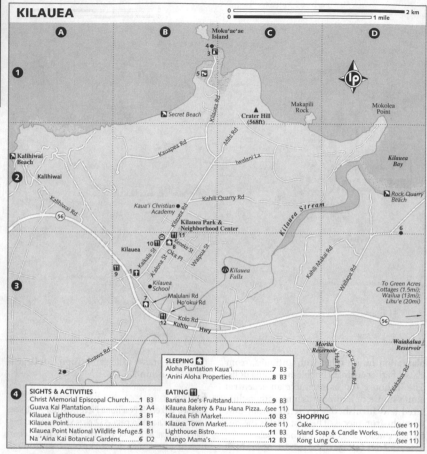

KILAUEA

SLEEPING 🏠
Aloha Plantation Kaua'i...................**7** B3
'Anini Aloha Properties...................**8** B3

SIGHTS & ACTIVITIES
Christ Memorial Episcopal Church.....**1** B3
Guava Kai Plantation.........................**2** A4
Kilauea Lighthouse............................**3** B1
Kilauea Point....................................**4** B1
Kilauea Point National Wildlife Refuge.**5** B1
Na 'Aina Kai Botanical Gardens.........**6** D2

EATING 🍴
Banana Joe's Fruitstand...................**9** B3
Kilauea Bakery & Pau Hana Pizza...(see 11)
Kilauea Fish Market........................**10** B3
Kilauea Town Market......................(see 11)
Lighthouse Bistro...........................**11** B3
Mango Mama's...............................**12** B3

SHOPPING
Cake..(see 11)
Island Soap & Candle Works..........(see 11)
Kong Lung Co.................................(see 11)

sautéed *'ahi*, or tofu with brown rice and lots of veggies.

Lighthouse Bistro (☎ 828-0480; Kong Lung Center, 2484 Keneke St; lunch mains $6-12, dinner mains $18-28; ☜ noon-2pm & 5:30-9pm Mon-Sat, 5:30-9pm Sun) Kilauea's sole sit-down restaurant is especially atmospheric at night, when the open-air dining room glows with mellow lights and rich woods. The menu focuses on local ingredients, such as Kilauea greens and goat cheese. Vegans can enjoy the Napoleon, a towering stack of polenta, grilled vegetables and greens ($18).

For groceries, stop at **Banana Joe's Fruitstand** (☎ 828-1092; www.bananajoekauai.com; 5-2719 Kuhio Hwy; ☜ 9am-6pm Mon-Sat), a banana-yellow (duh!) shack near the 24-mile marker, for fresh produce and local honey, poi, cheeses and

preserves. Try the velvety 'frosty' (frozen fruit run through a juicer), which can almost pass for ice cream. Also worth a browse is **Kilauea Town Market** (☎ 828-1512; Kong Lung Center, Kilauea Rd; deli items $4-7; ☜ 8am-8pm Sun-Thu, to 8:30pm Fri & Sat) for gourmet beer and wine, olives, boutique cheeses, flatbreads and other goodies suited to the yuppie palate.

Shopping

Island Soap & Candle Works (☎ 828-1955; www.island soap.com; Kong Lung Center, 2474 Keneke St; ☜ 9am-9pm) While not exclusive to Kaua'i or Kilauea, each store makes its own soaps and candles, so you know they're fresh and oh-so-fragrant.

Kong Lung Co (☎ 828-1822; Kong Lung Center, 2484 Keneke St; ☜ 11am-6pm) If you appreciate fine furnishings and Asian design, Kong Lung is a must. Browse the high-quality lifestyle wares, including classic Japanese pottery, imaginative chopsticks, designer aloha shirts, glossy collector books and unique children's toys.

Cake (☎ 828-6412; Kong Lung Center, 2484 Keneke St; ☽ 10am-6pm) Fun boutique for the young and hip, with sexy strapless dresses, designer jeans and a rainbow of fitted tees and tanks.

KALIHIWAI

pop 717

The main reason to venture to Kalihiwai ('water's edge' in Hawaiian) is to discover its relatively remote beaches. Kalihiwai Rd was a loop road going down past Kalihiwai Beach, connecting with the highway at two points, until the tidal wave of 1957 washed out the Kalihiwai River bridge. The bridge was never rebuilt and now there are two Kalihiwai Rds, one on each side of the river.

Sights & Activities

KALIHIWAI BEACH

With a wide, deep bay, this sandy stretch of beach (Map p500) is popular for many activities, such as swimming and, when the winter northwest swells roll in, daredevil bodyboarding and surfing along the cliff at the east end of the bay.

If you enjoy kayaking, the Kalihiwai Stream, which empties into the bay, offers perhaps the prettiest scenery of the island's rivers. Launch at the bay and paddle up into Kalihiwai Valley, where you can see or hike to Kalihiwai Falls (Map pp498–9). Note: the falls are on land leased by Princeville Ranch Stables and you might be shooed away). The beach has no facilities. For kayak rentals see p509.

To get here, take the first Kalihiwai Rd, 0.5 miles west of Kilauea.

SECRET BEACH

While no longer a secret, this gorgeous, golden-sand beach (Map p500) backed by sea cliffs and jungly foliage is still frequented mainly by Kaua'i's alternative community – perhaps because it's accessible only by a steep (and slippery) 10- to 15-minute hike. Also known as Kauapea Beach, its waters are swimmable only during summer.

To get to Secret Beach, turn down Kalihiwai Rd 0.5 miles west of Kilauea and then turn right onto the first dirt road, which is just 0.1 miles from Kuhio Hwy. Less than 0.5

miles down, the road ends at a parking area where the well-defined trail begins. Don't go during rainy periods.

PILATES

Up your fitness at **Pilates Kaua'i** (☎ 639-3074; www.pilateskauai.com; 2540 Halaulani Rd; private sessions per hr $65), an airy, well-equipped studio with spectacular valley views. Owner Laurie Cole, a longtime bodyworker and former dancer, is an adept and professional instructor. Ask about mat classes and semi/group sessions.

HORSEBACK RIDING

You can satiate your appetite for North Shore landscapes on a scenic horseback ride at **Silver Falls Ranch** (Map pp498-9 ☎ 828-6718; www.silverfallsranch .com; Kamo'okoa Rd; 90min trail ride $80, 2/3hr ride $100/120), at the end of Kamo'okoa Rd. Daily rides include a leisurely jaunt or a combo ride, swim and picnic lunch.

'ANINI

Countless 'vacation rental' houses line the road fronting idyllic 'Anini Beach. But this secluded area remains a best-kept secret. The beach park is spacious, with calm water perfect for kids, lazy kayaking, easy snorkeling and the best beginner windsurfing on the island.

To get here, cross Kalihiwai Bridge, turn onto the second Kalihiwai Rd and then bear left onto 'Anini Rd.

Sights & Activities

'ANINI BEACH PARK

You can't ask for a gentler stretch of beach than this (Map pp498–9). The water is flat as glass within the lagoon, which is protected by one of the longest and widest fringing reefs in the Hawaiian Islands. At its widest point, the reef extends over 1600ft offshore. The park is unofficially divided into day-use, camping and windsurfing areas. While weekends might draw crowds, weekdays are low key. Facilities include rest rooms, showers, changing rooms, drinking water, picnic pavilions and BBQ grills.

SWIMMING & SNORKELING

With practically no shorebreak and average water depth at 4ft to 5ft, kayaking and lap swimming are practically effortless.

Swimming and snorkeling are good in the day-use area and in front of the camping area;

HEALING RETREATS

In search of healing for your body and mind? Kaua'i is chock-full of massage therapists, yoga teachers and alternative healers. Unfortunately most are only mediocre lightweights geared toward undiscriminating tourists. On the North Shore, experience true rejuvenation at Michaelle Edwards' **Mana Yoga** (Map pp498-9; ☎ 826-9230; www.kauainorthshorevacationrentals.com; 3812 Ahonui Pl; yoga/massage per hr $80).

At her private, rustic home studio southeast of Princeville, Edwards combines yoga, massage and spinal alignment into YogAlign, an effective, no-nonsense therapy for folks of all levels. While trained in traditional yoga methods, Edwards now strives to perpetuate the body's natural alignment rather than to contort it doing strict poses. A warm, perceptive and practical instructor, she analyzes posture and breathing and provides a body 'tune-up.'

Also available are two vacation-rental units on the rural property, surrounded by green hills and fruit orchards (single/double studios $85/95), two-bedroom apartments from $130). Thus you can arrange a personal retreat for yourself or for a group. Longtime Kaua'i resident Edwards is also a professional singer and guitarist (look for her CDs *Tropical Twilight* and *Swinging in Paradise*).

---

conditions are best when the tide is high. The snorkeling is shallow, but the long barrier reef means lots of juvenile fish.

WINDSURFING

'Anini Beach, with its steady gentle breezes and calm bay, is an excellent place to learn windsurfing. Lessons are given by the following outfits; meet at the beach.

'Anini Beach Windsurfing (☎ 826-9463; 1hr lesson $50, board rental per hr/full day $25/50)

Windsurf Kaua'i (☎ 828-6838; windsurfkauai@aol.com; 3hr lesson $75, board rental per hr/half day/full day $25/50/75; ✆ 9am & 1pm Mon-Fri)

Sleeping

To find your dream beach house, search the internet or contact an agency (see p505). 'Anini rentals are pricey, ranging from perhaps $1100 to $10,500 weekly, plus cleaning fees and security deposits.

Try these for starters:

'Anini Beach Hideaway (☎ 828-1051; www.aninibeachhideaway.com; 3635 'Anini Rd; 1-bedroom house per week $875) Sharing an acre of property with a main house, this best-value cottage has lots of fruit trees (guests are invited to pick fruit) but no ocean view.

'Anini Beach Hale (☎ 828-6808, 877-262-6688; www.yourbeach.com; 3649 'Anini Rd; 2-bedroom house per day/week $255/1600) On a large 16,000-sq-ft lot, this two-bedroom, two-bathroom house with large screened lanai is quiet and private. Both bedrooms have king beds; suitable for two couples. Owners are a longtime Kaua'i couple who live in nearby Kilauea.

Noho Kai (☎ 821-1454, 800-769-3285 ext 00; www.nohokai.com; 3617 'Anini Rd; 3-bedroom house per week $2100) Built in 2000, this modern vacation home with

country-white walls is not only spacious at 1750 sq ft but also features sweeping front and back covered lanai (800 sq ft). Very airy, with vaulted ceilings and French doors; two master bedrooms are separated by a large living-room buffer zone. Six people max.

Camping is right on the water, with shaded tent sites. The beach park is relatively spacious, although it crowds up on weekends, when local families arrive. See p460 for county park permit information. No camping is allowed on Tuesdays.

PRINCEVILLE
pop 1698

From the grandiose gateway fountain to the perfectly manicured lawns, you'll either love Princeville or absolutely hate it.

Meet Kaua'i's largest and most exclusive planned community, which emerged after the luxury Princeville Resort was built in 1985. Before then, the promontory between 'Anini Beach and Hanalei Bay was a swath of pristine ranch land.

Today the 11,000-acre community is a resort town that resembles a suburb (albeit suburbia for folks with money). The single thoroughfare is flanked by two celebrated golf greens and well-marked side streets to 1500 condo units and 600 houses (at last count), terminating at the flagship Princeville Resort.

Princeville is, sadly, not pedestrian oriented. A car is imperative here, as shopping and dining options are simply too far away or, considering highway traffic, risky. The vibe is more 'bedroom community' than funky surf town, happening beach strip or lively commercial mecca. (Those would be Hanalei, Po'ipu and Kapa'a, respectively.)

History

Princeville traces its roots to Robert Wyllie, a Scottish doctor who became foreign minister to Kamehameha IV. In the mid-19th century Wyllie established a sugar plantation in Hanalei. When Queen Emma and Kamehameha IV came to visit in 1860, Wyllie named his plantation and the surrounding lands 'Princeville' to honor their two-year-old son, Prince Albert, who died only two years later. The plantation later became a cattle ranch.

Orientation & Information

Kuhio Hwy changes from Hwy 56 to Hwy 560 at the 28-mile marker in front of Princeville. The 10-mile stretch from here to Ke'e Beach is one of the state's most-scenic drives.

In Princeville you'll find the North Shore's only airport, gas station and fire station, plus a shopping center with the basics, such as a supermarket, restaurants and…numerous real-estate agencies. The **post office** (☎ 800-275-8777; Princeville Center; ☺ 10:30am-3:30pm Mon-Fri, to 12:30pm Sat) is located in the shopping center.

Remember, the **Princeville Chevron gas station** (Kuhio Hwy; ☺ 6am-10pm Mon-Sat, to 9pm Sun) is the last stop to buy gas before the end of the road at Ke'e Beach.

Sights

PRINCEVILLE RESORT

Whether or not Princeville suits your fancy, it's worth stopping at Kaua'i's most-glamorous resort to admire its outstanding vantage point. The best time is sunset, when the view of glorious Hanalei Bay and Makana Mountain (commonly called 'Bali Hai' from the movie *South Pacific*) in the distance is unforgettable. Just park in the public lot and join the shutterbugs and couples on the grassy lawn to the right of the lobby.

When it was erected in 1985, locals were livid at losing such a prime lookout spot and nicknamed it 'The Prison.' The original building was indeed dark and unbefitting its spectacular surroundings. Thus it was closed in 1989 and, over the next two years, virtually

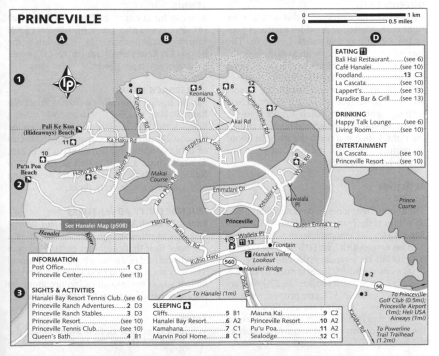

PRINCEVILLE

0 --------- 1 km
0 --------- 0.5 miles

EATING 🍴
Bali Hai Restaurant........(see 6)
Café Hanalei................(see 10)
Foodland.........................**13** C3
La Cascata.....................(see 10)
Lappert's.........................(see 13)
Paradise Bar & Grill......(see 13)

DRINKING
Happy Talk Lounge........(see 6)
Living Room....................(see 10)

ENTERTAINMENT
La Cascata.....................(see 10)
Princeville Resort ....(see 10)

Pali Ke Kua (Hideaways) Beach
Pu'u Poa Beach

See Hanalei Map (p508)
Hanalei River

INFORMATION
Post Office....................................**1** C3
Princeville Center...................(see 13)

SIGHTS & ACTIVITIES
Hanalei Bay Resort Tennis Club..(see 6)
Princeville Ranch Adventures......**2** D3
Princeville Ranch Stables.........**3** D3
Princeville Resort....................(see 10)
Princeville Tennis Club...........(see 10)
Queen's Bath...........................**4** B1

SLEEPING 🛏
Cliffs.............................**5** B1
Hanalei Bay Resort..........**6** A2
Kamahana.....................**7** C1
Marvin Pool Home........**8** C1

Mauna Kai.....................**9** C2
Princeville Resort..........**10** A2
Pu'u Poa.......................**11** A2
Sealodge.....................**12** C1

To Hanalei (1mi)

Hanalei Valley Lookout
Hanalei Bridge

To Princeville Golf Club (0.5mi);
Princeville Airport (1mi); Heli USA Airways (1mi)

To Powerline Trail Trailhead (1.2mi)

Prince Course

KAUA'I

rebuilt. Now another major renovation is afoot and by 2008 the Starwood property will be upgraded to the superior St Regis category.

PALI KE KUA (HIDEAWAYS) & PU'U POA BEACHES
The one complaint about Princeville is the lack of an easily accessible beach. It's true. Pali Ke Kua Beach (also called Hideaways Beach) is a magnificent secluded lozenge of sand, but you must work to reach it. To get here, park in the public lot just after the gatehouse at the Princeville Resort and take the path between the fences. After several minutes, the trail becomes unbelievably steep, with stairs and ropes to aid your descent. The reward? When calm, swimming and especially snorkeling are excellent, and the shady, sandy beach is perfect for sunset year-round.

Nearby is another option, Pu'u Poa Beach, between the Princeville Resort and the mouth of the Hanalei River. To get here, take the path to the left of the gatehouse. While it's less scenic than Pali Ke Kua, you can walk from here all the way to the river mouth.

QUEEN'S BATH
Formed by a lava-rock shelf, this natural pool right at the shoreline provides a natural protected swimming and snorkeling hole. The surf splashes in softly or with a crash, periodically flushing clean the ice-blue pool, which is so salty you float along effortlessly.

To get here, enter the Princeville Resort area and drive just under 1.5 miles before turning right onto Punahele Rd. Park in the area at the end of the road and take the trail to the right. When you reach the shore in about 10 minutes, turn left and walk another five minutes over the rocks.

Activities
GOLF
The Robert Trent Jones Jr–designed championship links at the **Princeville Golf Club** (☎ Prince 826-5000, Makai 826-3580; www.princeville.com; 5-3900 Kuhio Hwy; green fees nonguest/guest Prince $175/150, Makai $125/110, club rental $35) are legendary; the 18-hole par-72 Prince Course, which Jones created in 1990, is Kaua'i's highest-rated course. The 27-hole par-72 Makai Course, c 1971, comprises three aptly named nines – Woods, Lake and Ocean.

Green fees include a cart and a day pass to the spa. Discounts start at noon; save more as the hours pass. Collared shirts are required.

TOP 10 SPLURGES

- **Helicopter ride** (average $100; p466)
- **Brunch** at Princeville Resort (from $53; p503)
- **Ziplining** tour (from $115; p471)
- **Golfing** at a world-renowned course (average $175; p463)
- One-of-a-kind **silk sarong** from the Art of Marbling ($225; p535)
- Taste of **Hawaii culinary extravaganza** (from $75; p484)
- A 17-mile Na Pali Coast **kayaking adventure** (from $175; p510)
- **Spa vacation** at the Outrigger Waipouli Beach Resort and Spa (p488)
- **Scuba diving** off Ni'ihau (average $300; p462)
- Renting your **dream beach house** on the North Shore (sky's the limit; see agency list, opposite)

TENNIS
You can hit at either the **Princeville Tennis Club** (☎ 826-1230; www.princeville.com; Princeville Resort, 5-3900 Kuhio Hwy; court per person per hr $15; ⏰ 9am-5pm) or the **Hanalei Bay Resort Tennis Club** (☎ 826-6522; Hanalei Bay Resort; court per person per hr $6; ⏰ 9am-9pm).

HORSEBACK RIDING
Saddle up for a horseback ride at **Princeville Ranch Stables** (☎ 826-6777; www.princevilleranch.com; Kuhio Hwy; tours $65-170; ⏰ tours Mon-Sat) between the 26- and 27-mile markers, spanning 2500 acres of cattle country, from mountain to ocean. Tours include a jaunt across ranch land to Kalihiwai Falls for picnicking and swimming and a cattle drive for city slickers.

MULTIACTIVITY ADVENTURES
Princeville Ranch Adventures (☎ 826-7669, 888-955-7669; www.adventureskauai.com; tours $79-125) offers a 4½-hour tour that combines eight ziplines, a suspension bridge, a swimming hole and lunch. The minimum age and weight are 12 years and 80lb. If you're not into hikes, inquire about the hiking or kayaking tours to waterfall pools.

Tours
While not the best option available on the island, **Heli USA Airways** (☎ 826-6591, 866-936-1234;

www.heliusahawaii.com; 30/45/60min tours $109/169/199) flies from Princeville Airport, which is handy if you're on the North Shore. This mega outfit, which also runs O'ahu tours, just seems a tad impersonal.

Sleeping

Staying in Princeville probably means staying in a condo. If you know exactly which condo you want, simply do a Google search to find all available units. For more privacy, find a vacation home, which typically start around $250 daily. Expect cleaning fees, minimum stays (typically five to seven nights) and other restrictions.

Check with local agencies:

'Anini Aloha Properties (Map p500; ☎ 828-0067, 800-246-5382; www.aninialoha.com; Suite I-1, 4270 Kilauea Rd, Kilauea 96754) Extensive selection of North Shore rentals, including Princeville condos and dream houses from Anahola to Ha'ena.

Coldwell Banker Bali Hai Realty (Map p508; ☎ 866-400-7368; www.balihai.com; 5-5088 Kuhio Hwy, PO Box 930, Hanalei, HI 96714) Lots of listings for the North Shore, particularly in Hanalei, 'Anini and Kilauea. On-staff Japanese translator available.

Hanalei North Shore Properties (☎ 826-9622, 800-488-3336; www.hanaleinorthshoreproperties.com; PO Box 607, Hanalei, HI 96714) Specializes in unique North Shore vacation rentals, both condos and getaway houses from Anahola to Ha'ena.

Also check listings with **VRBO** (www.vrbo.com). An online agent with plentiful Princeville rentals is **Ahh! Aloha** (☎ 866-922-5642; www.kauai-vacations-ahh.com).

MIDRANGE

If no contact info is listed here, search online or contact agencies. Where the predominant agencies for a condo are mentioned, remember that other agencies or owners might offer better deals. Rates listed are the average: always comparison-shop.

Cliffs (3811 Edward Rd; www.cliffs-princeville.com; 1-bedroom units $100-150; 🖳 🖳) This time-share condo offers spacious suites (1000+ sq ft) with all the comforts of home, such as kitchen, two bathrooms, two lanai, washer-dryer, TV, cable modem. Loft units are a palatial 1500 sq ft. See the management company's website, but use other agencies/owners to avoid exorbitant rates.

Sealodge (☎ 650-573-0636, 800-585-6101, 866-922-5642; Kamehameha Ave; 1-bedroom units $100-150,

2-bedroom units $130-175; 🖳) Who cares if it's slightly weathered, the 86-unit Sealodge boasts a fantastic oceanfront setting – just feel the breeze and hear the surf! The units are comfortable, if basic. Phone numbers of the three main agencies are listed (left), but search online for better deals.

Kamahana (Kamehameha Rd; 1-/2-bedroom units per week $875/1050; 🖳) Most units overlook the sweeping greens of Princeville's Makai Course, so noise is minimal. Because the complex is not oceanfront, units tend to be hotter (without ocean breezes) but also cheaper. Rates vary widely, so shop around.

Mauna Kai (3920 Wyllie Rd; 2-bedroom units per week $900-1200; 🖳) This complex, located near the entrance to Princeville, comprises one- to three-story units with lots of windows and a clean, white look. The distance from the ocean means rates are often reasonable, while the side-street location means peace and quiet. Find a unit by Googling and by contacting Hanalei North Shore Properties (left), which manages three attractive units (ask about the harp-themed No 10).

Marvin Pool Home (☎ 826-9622; www.rentalsonkauai.com; 3583 Keoniana Rd; house per week $1000; 🖳) Ideal for families, with three bedrooms and two bathrooms. While the interior design could use a dose of modern chic, the large private swimming pool more than compensates. Secluded and quiet, except for the hypnotic pounding surf just below the property.

Hanalei Bay Resort (☎ 826-6522, 800-827-4427; www.hanaleibayresort.com; 5380 Hono'iki Rd; r from $205, 1-bedroom units from $370; 🕮 🖳) Named for its panoramic view of Hanalei Bay, this condo-hotel boasts two main advantages: location and variety of unit levels (from basic hotel rooms to two-bedroom suites). While not luxurious, it's pleasantly tropical and offers kitchen amenities in a hotel setting. Quintus Resorts owns and manages 87 of the resort's 137 units; they rarely charge the rack rates quoted here, but check first with other agents/owners. Aloha Condos (☎ 930-1830, 877-782-5642; www.alohacondos.com), located at Hanalei Bay Resort, is your best bet for reasonably priced units: rates can be half those quoted here. Check the website.

TOP END

Pu'u Poa (☎ 826-9394, 800-535-0085; www.marcresorts.com; Ka Haku Rd; 2-bedroom units $275-500; 🖳) While neither modern nor stylish, this condo boasts a prime seaside perch, next door to

KAUA'I

Princeville Resort. Expect so-so conditions (eg thin walls) but mesmerizing views. Pu'u Poa is managed primarily by Marc Resorts, which also manages the adjacent Pali Ke Kua condo (slightly cheaper with one-bedroom units also available) and, across the street, Hale Moi cottages (no pool, no view, noisy and not recommended).

Princeville Resort (☎ 826-9644, 800-325-3589; www .princevillehotelhawaii.com; 5520 Ka Haku Rd; r internet/rack from $365/500, ste internet/rack from $625/875; ✖ ✦) Thanks to its unforgettable view of Hanalei Bay, Princeville Resort is the North Shore's belle of the ball. But until this Starwood property undergoes renovation (and gets promoted from 'The Luxury Collection' to 'St Regis'), expect distinction short of five-star luxury. Positives include the elegant infinity pool, liquid-crystal bathroom windows (which glaze over for privacy), fine restaurants and magnificent views. Negatives are dated room decor, inconsistent service, lack of an easy-access beach, and pricey parking (per day $15, including non-valet). All in all, Princeville Resort will please all except Four Seasons regulars – at least until the renovation.

Eating
BUDGET
Cheap eats are scarce. At Princeville Center, **Paradise Bar & Grill** (☎ 826-1775; Princeville Center; sandwiches $7-8.50; ✖ 11am-11pm) is a casual, touristy hangout serving drinks, burgers and all-American fried stuff. **Lappert's** (☎ 826-7393; 1 scoop $3.10; Princeville Center; ✖ 10am-9pm) features Kaua'i's homegrown premium ice cream.

The biggest supermarket on the North Shore is **Foodland** (☎ 826-9880; Princeville Center; ✖ 6am-11pm), with a better selection than Hanalei's Big Save.

MIDRANGE & TOP END
Café Hanalei (☎ 826-2760; Princeville Resort; breakfast $8.50-14.50, lunch $18-25, dinner $29-40, 3-course prix fixe $58; ✖ 6:30am-2:30pm & 5:30-9:30pm) Enter this breezily elegant restaurant and...wow! A stupendous view of Hanalei Bay. The Asian-inspired island cuisine is good (if short of great). The best value is lunch, from a ⅓lb Kobe beef burger to a bento of teriyaki beef, mango-glazed chicken and fish tempura. Dinners highlight fish, eg pan-seared 'ahi with peanut-miso sauce. Skip the overpriced breakfasts but splurge on the decadent Sunday brunch ($53).

La Cascata (☎ 826-2761; Princeville Resort; dinner mains $29-42, 3-course prix fixe $65; ✖ 6-10pm) In a richly hued, cozy dining room, La Cascata exudes a European feel. The Mediterranean cuisine includes creative starters such as the prawn/scallop/lobster ravioli in arugula pesto. Mains tend toward elaborate preparations, eg rack of lamb with creamy tomato polenta and fig-infused balsamic jus. Awesome sunset views but no patio seating.

Bali Hai Restaurant (☎ 826-6522; Hanalei Bay Resort; breakfast & lunch $8-15, dinner mains $31-38; ✖ 7-11am, 11:30am-2pm & 5-9pm) Another feast for your eyes awaits at this open-air dining room with a panoramic view of Hanalei Bay. For breakfast, go local with poi pancakes and taro hash browns. The dinner menu is heavy on seafood. Cheaper eats are served at Happy Talk Lounge.

Drinking & Entertainment
BARS & NIGHTCLUBS
Happy Talk Lounge (☎ 826-6522; Hanalei Bay Resort; ✖ 11am-9:45pm) Enjoy the same (or better) views here as at the resort's more buttoned-up Bali Hai Restaurant. There's a tasty bar menu ($7 to $15) from 2pm to 9pm, live jazz from 4pm to 7pm Sunday and Hawaiian music most other nights.

Living Room (☎ 826-9644; Princeville Resort; ✖ 3-11pm) A spectacular view of Hanalei Bay makes this a fine place for a sunset drink and sushi rolls. The lovely live music from 7:30pm to 10:30pm swaddles this lounge in ambience.

La Cascata (☎ 826-2761; Princeville Resort; ✖ 6-10pm) Slack-key tunes by Ken Emerson and Poncho Graham on Monday and Tuesday nights at 7:30.

LUAU
Princeville Resort (☎ 826-2788; Princeville Resort; adult/child 6-12/senior 65 & over $69/35/60; ✖ 6pm Mon & Thu) The only luau option on the North Shore. Its spectacular setting raises this otherwise standard dinner-show up a notch.

HANALEI VALLEY
Beyond Princeville lies another world altogether. Colors seem magnified, from emerald cliffs to azure seas to creamy-white blankets of sand. It's the fantasy tropical landscape come alive. The rustic drive itself, on a winding highway with sharp curves and river crossings, only highlights the region's uniqueness.

RULES OF THE ROAD

Drivers: don't play chicken when crossing the one-lane bridges from Hanalei to the end of the road. Follow the local bridge etiquette.

- Stop at the white line. Otherwise you might cause an accident or traffic jam (or receive *da stink eye*).

- If the bridge is empty and you reach it first, go.

- If a car is crossing ahead of you, follow.

- If you see cars approaching from the opposite direction, yield to the entire queue of approaching cars.

- Exception: if you are the sixth or seventh car crossing the bridge, stop and let the opposite side go. It's just common courtesy. And if another person stops and waits to let your side cross, don't forget to give a thank-you wave (or, better yet, the *shaka* (see p582) sign!).

Sights & Activities

HANALEI VALLEY LOOKOUT

Often crowded with cars, this popular lookout (Map p503), located just past Princeville Center, provides a spectacular bird's-eye view of the valley floor with its meandering river and spread of patchwork taro fields. Look to your lower right-hand side to see the North Shore's first one-lane bridge, which opened in 1912. Visible to the south are the twin peaks of Hihimanu ('beautiful' in Hawaiian).

HANALEI BRIDGE

The Hanalei Bridge (Map p503) is the first of seven bridges along the drive from the Hanalei River to the end of the road. They might seem inconvenient but, because big trucks and tour buses are too heavy to cross the bridges, they have successfully prevented further North Shore development.

HANALEI VALLEY SCENIC DRIVE

Birders will enjoy the scenic 2-mile drive through the **Hanalei National Wildlife Refuge** (Map pp498-9; http://pacificislands.fws.gov/wnwr/khanaleinwr .html), which passes taro fields, banana trees, bamboo thickets, *hau* (hibiscus) trees and wild ginger across 917 acres of the valley.

Prior to Western contact, the valley was planted with taro. Then in the mid-1800s rice paddies were planted to feed the Chinese sugar-plantation laborers. After peaking as a major crop in the 1880s, rice eventually waned and today taro again predominates – though at only 5% of its original acreage. Hanalei's wetland taro farms produce two-thirds of Hawaii's commercially grown poi taro and also create a habitat for endangered Hawaiian waterbirds.

The refuge, established in 1972, is closed to the public. But from the roadside birders can spot some of the 49 types of bird using the habitat, including the valley's endangered native species:

ae'o (Hawaiian stilt) slender with black back, white chest and long pink legs
alae ke'oke'o (Hawaiian coot) slate-gray with white forehead
'alae 'ula (Hawaiian moorhen) dark-gray with black head and distinctive red-and-yellow bill
koloa maoli (Hawaiian duck) mottled brown with orange legs and feet

To get here, turn left onto Ohiki Rd immediately after the Hanalei Bridge. You can enter the refuge on the Ho'opulapula Haraguchi Rice Mill Tour (p510).

HANALEI

pop 478

Hanalei is a surf town – and the vibe is palpable. Just count the board-laden trucks heading toward the waves. Here, even the suntanned residents seem permanently in vacation mode, hitting the waves daily after work or school. Many residents are mainland transplants (and former hippies) who came for the waves and the exotic remoteness – and somehow never left.

The entire town of Hanalei sits along the highway, which was just a sleepy road up till the early 1970s. Today the North Shore is a major attraction and traffic through Hanalei is constant. Still, as you cross the Hanalei Bridge and pass the lazy Hanalei River drifting past fields of taro, you know you're crossing a threshold. The town itself combines retro architecture, beach-bum cool and trendy new shops and restaurants.

Unlike many Kaua'i towns, Hanalei does not reflect the island's sugar-plantation history as much as its traditional Hawaiian *kalo* (taro) and fishing roots. The demographics

KAUA'I

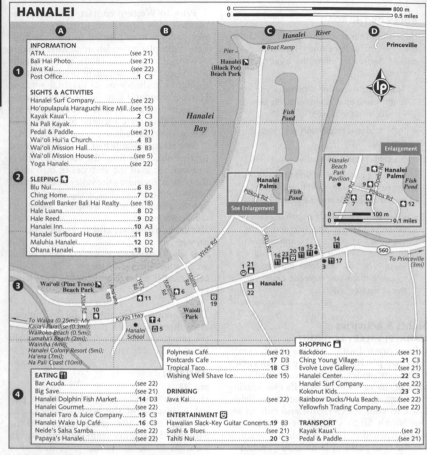

HANALEI

reflect that history, plus the 1970s' flood of mainland haole transplants, with 62% whites, 18% Native Hawaiians and 12% Japanese. Of course, the real demographical factor today is money. Prime Hanalei real estate is affordable mainly to wealthy mainland investors who use the properties for vacation rentals.

Orientation & Information

Nearly anything you might desire can be found in Hanalei Center, on the *mauka* side of Kuhio Hwy, or Ching Young Village, on the *makai* (seaward) side of the highway.

Hanalei has no bank, but there is an ATM in the Ching Young Village's Big Save supermarket.

Bali Hai Photo (☎ 826-9181; Ching Young Village; per hr $9; ☯ 8am-8pm Mon-Fri, 9am-5pm Sat, 10am-5pm Sun) Internet access.

Java Kai (☎ 826-6717; Hanalei Center; ☯ 6:30am-6pm) Lively, open-air hangout spot with wi-fi internet access only.

Post office (☎ 800-275-8777; 5-5226 Kuhio Hwy) In the village center.

Sights
HANALEI BAY
Captured in countless photographs, the perfectly curved Hanalei Bay is always scenic, but not always swimmable. The wave action here is changeable: flat in summer and pounding in winter, when surfers arrive in droves. The best beaches are at Hanalei (Black Pot) Beach Park and Wai'oli (Pine Trees) Beach

Park, which both have rest rooms, showers, drinking water, picnic tables and grills. Another easy-access public beach is found at the **Hanalei Beach Park Pavilion** (also with facilities) on Weke Rd near Aku Rd. Conditions are best for surfing and bodyboarding; swimming is less than ideal due to the shorebreak.

Hanalei (Black Pot) Beach Park

Often dubbed simply 'Hanalei Pier,' due to its unmistakable landmark, this stretch of sand shaded by ironwood trees at Hanalei Beach Park is popular mainly with surfers. The sandy-bottom beach slopes gently, making it very safe for beginners. Lessons are typically taught here, just west of the pier, where you find surf schools lining up big ol' softboards and rashguards daily. In summer, swimming and snorkeling are decent, as are camping and kayaking. As always, take extreme caution during periods of high surf as dangerous shorebreaks and rip currents are common.

At the eastern end of the park the mouth of the Hanalei River opens into the beach and you'll find a small boat ramp where kayakers launch for trips up the river. This spot is called **Black Pot**, after a big black wok owned by Henry Tai Hook, who used to cook community meals here in the late 1800s or early 1900s.

Wai'oli (Pine Trees) Beach Park

Come here in winter to see the North Shore's highest surf – or in spring for surfing contest such as the **Pine Trees Longboard Classic**, held in late April, which showcases local talent from up-and-coming kids to aging legends. Pro surfers Andy and Bruce Irons cut their teeth here and each February they sponsor the Pine Trees Classic, an event for kids to compete, meet their idols and win prizes.

Swimming is hazardous here except during the calmest summer surf. A section, known locally as **Toilet Bowls**, at the end of Ama'ama Rd has rest rooms and showers.

Waikoko Beach

Protected by a reef on the western bend of Hanalei Bay, this sandy-bottomed beach (no facilities) offers shallower and calmer waters than the middle of the bay. Pull off the highway between the 4- and 5-mile markers. Winter surfing is sometimes good off Makahoa Point, the western point of the bay; surfers call this break **Waikokos**.

WAI'OLI HUI'IA CHURCH & MISSION HOUSE

A popular site for quaint church weddings, Wai'oli Hui'ia Church was built by Hanalei's first missionaries, Reverend and Mrs William Alexander, who arrived in 1834 in a double-hulled canoe. Their church, hall and mission house remain in the middle of town, set on a huge manicured lawn with a beautiful mountain backdrop.

The pretty green wooden **church** retains an airy Pacific feel, with large, outward-opening windows and high ceilings. The doors remain open during the day and visitors are welcome. A Bible printed in Hawaiian and dating from 1868 is displayed on top of the old organ. The Wai'oli Church Choir, the island's best, sings hymns in Hawaiian at the 10am Sunday service.

The hall, which originally served as the church, was built of coral lime and plaster with a steeply pitched roof to handle Hanalei's heavy rains.

Adjacent are **Wai'oli Mission Hall**, c 1836, and **Wai'oli Mission House** (☎ 245-3202; admission by donation; ◷ 9am-3pm Tue, Thu & Sat), a New England house that the Alexanders built in 1837 to replace their grass shack.

To get to the inconspicuous parking lot, turn inland immediately east of Hanalei School. Turn left on the dirt driveway opposite the water hydrant.

Activities

KAYAKING

While the Wailua River scenery is more lush, kayaking is more peaceful and solitary along the Hanalei River. The approximately 6-mile round-trip journey through the Hanalei National Wildlife Refuge passes beside grassy banks, occasionally canopied by overhanging trees. Your paddling distance can reach 7.5 miles, depending on the water level in the river.

The Hanalei River is perfect for novice paddlers to practice solo. You can launch your kayak right at the boat ramp and it's impossible to get lost. A self-guided paddle is nice and flexible: you can paddle all day or for just an hour.

For kayak rentals try **Pedal & Paddle** (☎ 826-9069; www.pedalnpaddle.com; Ching Young Village; single kayaks per day/week $15/60, double kayaks $35/140; ◷ 9am-6pm), which offers the gamut of sports and camping equipment.

KAUA'I

Hardcore paddlers, don't miss the 17-mile Na Pali Coast trip. This strenuous, all-day paddle is only possible from May to September, due to rough seas. But, even in summer, the biggest obstacle is seasickness. The put-in is at Ha'ena and the take-out at Polihale, where a van picks you up to return to Hanalei, meaning you circumnavigate Kaua'i in a day.

For the Na Pali Coast trip:

Kayak Kaua'i (☎ 826-9844, 800-437-3507; www .kayakkauai.com; Kuhio Hwy; single kayaks per day/week $28/112, double kayaks $52/208; ☒ 8am-5pm, to 8pm in summer) Tours include a Na Pali Coast thriller ($185) from May to September, Blue Lagoon kayak and snorkel ($60), or open-ocean paddle on the South Shore (winter; $115).

Na Pali Kayak (☎ 826-6900, 866-977-6900; www .napalikayak.com; Kuhio Hwy; tours $175) The Na Pali Coast trip is the only tour these folks lead and their guides have over a decade of experience paddling these waters.

Outfitters Kaua'i (☎ 742-9667, 888-742-9887; www .outfitterskauai.com; Po'ipu Plaza, 2827-A Po'ipu Rd; Na Pali Coast tour $185; ☒ reservations taken 8am-9pm) Located in Po'ipu, but offers tours islandwide.

SNORKELING

While most snorkeling cruises depart from Port Allen on the Westside, those starting from the North Shore allow more time at the lushest parts of Na Pali. These catamarans depart from Hanalei:

Na Pali Catamaran (☎ 826-6853, 866-255-6853; www.napalicatamaran.com) Offers four-hour tours (adult/child $135/110), morning and afternoon, in summer months, generally May to September. On calm days the 34ft cat (16 passengers maximum) enters sea caves. No shade.

Captain Sundown (☎ 826-5585; www.captain sundown.com) Long, six-hour tour (adult/child 10-12 $162/138) is comfortable on a 40ft sailing cat, but the crew cannot go as far toward the coast (or into sea caves) as Na Pali Catamaran does. Summer only.

SURFING

With its sandy bottom, Hanalei Bay is ideal for newbies.

Hanalei Surf Company (☎ 826-9000; www.hanalei surf.com; Hanalei Center, 5-5161 Kuhio Hwy; 2½hr lesson $65-150, surfboards per day/week $15/65, bodyboards per day/week $5/20; ☒ 8am-9pm) Surf instructors here (Russell Lewis and Ian Vernon) have an excellent reputation and are especially suited for advanced surfers.

Hawaiian School of Surfing (☎ 652-1116; 1½hr lesson $65; ☒ lessons 8am, 10am & noon) Stop by (or call in advance) for a lesson by legendary pro big-wave surfer Titus Kinimaka or, more likely, one of his guys, who line up

the boards and red rashguards daily at the pier. No more than three students per instructor.

Hawaiian Surfing Adventures (☎ 482-0749; www .hawaiiansurfingadventures.com; 2hr lesson group/private $55/75, surfboards per day/week $30/100; ☒ 8am-2pm) Longtime Kaua'i surfer Mitchell Alapa and his team give group (up to four but often fewer) or private (single or couple) lessons. Generous lesson includes a half-hour on land, one hour in the water and another hour of solo practice. Look for the yellow rashguards on the beach.

Kayak Kaua'i (☎ 826-9844; www.kayakkauai.com; Kuhio Hwy; 1hr lesson $50, surfboards per day $20, bodyboards per day $6; ☒ lessons 10am & 2pm) If you rent gear for four days, you get three more days free.

YOGA

For Ashtanga yoga, **Yoga Hanalei** (☎ 826-9642; www.yogahanalei.com; Hanalei Center, 2nd fl, 5-5161E Kuhio Hwy, upstairs; per class $15), directed by Bhavani Maki, is your best bet on Kaua'i.

Tours

Ho'opulapula Haraguchi Rice Mill Tour (☎ 651-3399; www.haraguchiricemill.org; Kuhio Hwy; 3hr tour incl lunch per person $65) The Haraguchi family, who also own the Hanalei Taro & Juice Company, offers tours (by appointment only) of their historic rice mill and wetland taro farm. See the otherwise inaccessible Hanalei National Wildlife Refuge (p507) and learn about Hawaii's immigrant history. Tours are limited to 14.

Sleeping

BUDGET

The cheapest way to stay in Hanalei? Camping at Hanalei (Black Pot) Beach Park, permitted on Friday, Saturday and holidays only, with a county permit (see p460).

MIDRANGE & TOP END

Ohana Hanalei (☎ 826-4116; www.hanalei-kauai.com; Pilikoa Rd; r per day/week $95/615) Just half a block from the beach, this large studio is Hanalei's sweetest deal. The downstairs room is clean and comfy (nicely remodeled), with kitchenette, private entrance, phone, cable TV and convenient parking. The hosts are easygoing, longtime residents who give guests lots of privacy.

Hanalei Inn (☎ 826-9333; www.hanaleiinn.com; 5-5468 Kuhio Hwy; r $119) If you're a no-frills type, the four studios with kitchens at Hanalei Inn should suffice. The compact rooms sport hardwood floors, stone-tile bathrooms, small dining table and wi-fi. Stay for a week, pay no taxes. The amiable on-site manager, Bill Gaus, is an excellent local source.

My Kaua'i Paradise (☎ 826-8968, 866-369-8968; www.mykauaiparadise.com; 5-5851 Kuhio Hwy; 1-bedroom units $150-250; 🖳) Find solitude on a riverbed with waterfowl and wetland taro. In a two-story home near Waikoko Beach, the upstairs unit boasts full kitchen and floor-to-ceiling glass with tranquil mountain vista. Minimalist design, with hardwood floors, high ceilings, wi-fi and washer-dryer. Downstairs unit is smaller but thriftier.

Hale Luana (☎ 826-6931; Opelu Rd; ste $150) Utterly charming, this enormous loft suite might be your trip highlight. A private entrance leads to the one-bedroom suite, painted in classic white, with a soaring cathedral ceiling. The romantic, open-air spiral staircase overlooks a spacious kitchen and dining room. In the loft bedroom you can laze in bed, gazing at the ocean through a window. Washer-dryer available. There's a one-time cleaning fee of $85.

Hanalei Surfboard House (☎ 826-9825; www.hanalei surfboardhouse.com; 5459 Weke Rd; r $175-225; 🐾) Host Simon Potts takes the white picket fence to another realm with his…surfboard fence (featuring real, used boards)! A truly distinctive (if slightly pricey) property, its unforgettable attributes are imaginative interior design and charming Potts himself. The three immaculate studios include kitchenette, wi-fi, TV and unique decor, from vintage Hawaiiana to a shower floor handcrafted with Kaua'i sand. The costlier detached unit features air-con and surround-sound stereo.

Ching Home (☎ 826-9622, 800-488-3336; 5119 Weke Rd; studios per week $600, 1-/2-bedroom ste per week $850/$950) Welcome, surfers! This place is ideal for dudes and chicks who don't mind the 'public' location across Hanalei Pavilion. Upstairs is the airy one-bedroom suite.

Hale Reed (☎ 415-459-1858; www.hanalei-vacation .com; 4441 Pilikoa Rd; 2-/3-bedroom apt per week from $1000/$1500; 🖳) If you care about details, rent this impeccable house, with touches including all-matching silverware, luxury linens and wi-fi. The 2nd-floor three-bedroom apartment is the airy main house, with well-stocked kitchen and fantastic 'attic' room, streaming with sunlight and panoramic views. The ground floor, two-bedroom apartment is simpler but comfortable, with full kitchen. Rates rise depending on season and number of guests. You'll be asked for a (partly refundable) $300 to $500 security deposit.

Maluhia Hanalei (☎ 415-382-8918, 415-310 1919; www.hanaleivacationrental.com; Pilikoa Rd; 2-bedroom ste per day/week $150/1050, 3-bedroom ste per day/week $235/1600) At the end of a quiet cul-de-sac, find an island-style house ideal for large groups. The downstairs two-bedroom unit is a bargain, with compact kitchen, classy tile floor and modern tropical furnishings. There's a partly refundable security deposit of $500.

Blu Nui (☎ 826-9622, 800-488-3336; 4435 Mahimahi Rd; 2-bedroom house per week $1500) On a side street near Hanalei Bay, Blu Nui is not the greatest bargain for two bedrooms without a view, but you get a freestanding house with hardwood floor and high ceiling, full kitchen, covered garage and backyard patio.

Eating & Drinking
BUDGET
Wishing Well Shave Ice (Kuhio Hwy; shave ice from $2; ◔ noon-5pm Tue-Sun) Can't miss the colorful van parked near the Hanalei Taro & Juice Company kiosk! While its claim to be the oldest shave-ice vendor on Kaua'i may or may not be true, it does serve a fine product.

Hanalei Taro & Juice Company (☎ 826-1059; 5-5070-B Kuhio Hwy; smoothies $3-4.50, sandwiches $6.50; ◔ 10:30am-5pm Mon-Sat) In a kiosk near the town's east end, this family business specializes in taro edibles. Try fruit-taro smoothies, taro-leaf pita rolls, taro-coconut *mochi* (a Japanese sticky-rice dessert) and freshly made deli sandwiches.

Tropical Taco (☎ 827-8226; 5-5088-A Kuhio Hwy; mains $7-9; ◔ 11am-5pm Mon-Sat) Don't miss the fresh Mexican fare, island-style, at this Hanalei favorite. Wholesome and delicious tacos, tostadas and burritos are made to order with either beef, fish, or veg.

Java Kai (☎ 826-6717; Hanalei Center; ◔ 6:30am-6pm) Take your coffee and tempting pastries on the lanai at casual Java Kai.

Hanalei Wake Up Café (☎ 826-5551; cnr Kuhio Hwy & Aku Rd; breakfast $5-7; ◔ 6-11:30am) The best place for early birds to find a hot breakfast.

On the run, try the following:

Big Save (☎ 826-6652; Ching Young Village; ◔ 7am-9pm) Bland and basic, this is the only supermarket west of Princeville.

Hanalei Dolphin Fish Market (☎ 826-6113; 5-5016 Kuhio Hwy; ◔ 10am-7pm) 'Ahi sushi rolls, 'ahi poke and clam chowder make yummy picnic fixings.

Papaya's Hanalei (☎ 826-0089; Hanalei Center, 5-5161 Kuhio Hwy; ◔ 9am-8pm) Find tasty deli meals and the usual array of healthy cereals, meat substitutes and soy yogurts. Organic produce is dismayingly expensive.

MIDRANGE & TOP END

Polynesia Café (☎ 826-1999; Ching Young Village; mains $11-17; ☻ 8am-9pm) Its slogan proclaims, it's 'gourmet food on paper plates.' And the food does take the plate lunch to another level. Favorites include the mac-nut or pecan-pesto *'ahi* plates. Vegetarians can opt for flavorful tofu plates. In the dessert showcase, massive pieces of cake and brownies are irresistible.

Hanalei Gourmet (☎ 826-2524; www.hanaleigourmet .com; Hanalei Center; sandwiches $7-10, dinner mains $14-26; ☻ 8am-9:30pm, to 10:30pm summer) The best bets at this lively café-bar-deli are huge sandwiches on house-baked bread. The sit-down meals, from a sampler of lox-style local smoked fish to crunchy mac-nut fried chicken, are tasty and unpretentious, if more mainstream American than local.

Neide's Salsa Samba (☎ 826-1851; Hanalei Center; dishes $9-17; ☻ 11am-2:30pm & 5-9pm) Unique flavors and a quiet veranda are the main attractions at this little owner-run restaurant serving Mexican and Brazilian fare – from familiar huevos rancheros and burritos to traditional Brazilian offerings, such as *panqueca* (a veggie or chicken crepe stuffed with pumpkin).

Bar Acuda (☎ 826-7081; Hanalei Center; small plates $5-12; ☻ 11:30am-2:30pm & 6-9:30pm Tue-Sat) Most fans of this urban-chic tapas bar are mainland tourists or transplants, but there's no denying the culinary mastery. Chef-owner Jim Moffat is from San Francisco and his seasonal menu features unimpeachable Mediterranean cuisine. Dishes include house-smoked trout with roasted beets and lobster risotto with local sweet corn.

Postcards Café (☎ 826-1191; www.postcardscafé.com; 5-5075 Kuhio Hwy; mains $18-27; ☻ 6-9pm) Outside, Postcards looks like a plain old wooden building. Inside, the rustic dining room simultaneously feels special and homey. The creative, healthful, pesci-vegetarian cuisine is well worth the price. Signature items include polenta-crusted taro fritters and the seafood rockets (shrimp, fish and coconut, rolled and fried).

Entertainment

Tahiti Nui (☎ 826-6277; Tahiti Nui Bldg, Kuhio Hwy; ☻ 2pm-2am) This longstanding South Seas-style restaurant and bar was once *the* North Shore gathering place – and home of a popular luau. Today the well-worn hangout remains a lively, loud, local favorite. Although dinner is available, go for the bar action at happy hour (4pm to 6pm Monday to Saturday, all day Sunday) and for nightly live music.

Sushi & Blues (☎ 826-9701; www.sushiandblues.com; Ching Young Village; ☻ 6pm-2am) Only in Hanalei will you find the Abercrombie & Fitch set working as sushi chefs and bartenders at a blues club! Staff displays the nonchalance of youth, but the open-air room and tables set with cobalt goblets are quite pleasant. Diverse drink menu includes martinis, beers, wines, sake and tropical favorites. Live music Tuesday to Friday.

Hawaiian Slack-Key Guitar Concerts (☎ 826-1469; www.hawaiianslackkeyguitar.com; Hanalei Community Center; adult/child & senior $10/8; ☻ 4pm Fri & 3pm Sun) Slack-key guitar and ukulele concerts by longtime musicians Doug and Sandy McMaster year-round, in a refreshingly informal atmosphere.

Shopping

Kokonut Kids (☎ 826-0353; 5-5290 Kuhio Hwy; ☻ 10am-6:30pm Mon-Sat, 10:30am-5pm Sun) A smorgasbord of unique, top-quality, locally made children's clothing and toys. The colorful screen-printed tees and handmade sun hats are irresistible. And where else can you find a tropical-print Barbie camping tent and sleeping bag?

Rainbow Ducks/Hula Beach (☎ 826-4741; Hanalei Center; ☻ 10am-8pm) Stylish, Bohemian-chic clothing for the whole family. Funky bags and accessories, with a Southeast Asian touch.

Hanalei Surf Company (☎ 826-9000; www.hanaleisurf .com; Hanalei Center, 5-5161 Kuhio Hwy; ☻ 8am-9pm) The archetypal surf shop, with lots of gear, board shorts, bikinis and nonchalant staffers.

Backdoor (☎ 826-1900; Ching Young Village; 5-5190 Kuhio Hwy; ☻ 9am-9pm) The Hanalei Surf Company's sister is similar in youthful vibe, but carries skateboards and a wider selection of alternative street clothes by brands including Luci Love, Volcom, Paul Frank and Billabong.

Evolve Love Gallery (☎ 826-6441; Ching Young Village; ☻ 10am-6pm) Fine selection of art by local artists.

Yellowfish Trading Company (☎ 826-1227; Hanalei Center; ☻ 10am-8pm Mon-Sat, to 7pm Sun) At this notable Hawaii memorabilia shop, find an irresistible selection of collectibles, eg vintage aloha shirts, handmade jewelry, glossy photo books and antique ceramics.

Getting There & Around

Simply put, you need a car. Buses cannot cross Hanalei Bridge. Your last chance to fill the tank was back in Princeville.

For bicycle rentals, try **Pedal & Paddle** (☎ 826-9069; www.pedalnpaddle.com; Ching Young Village; ⏱ 9am-6pm) for cruisers (per day/week $10/30) and mountain-bikes ($20/80). **Kayak Kaua'i** (☎ 826-9844; www.kayakkauai.com; Kuhio Hwy; ⏱ 8am-5pm) also with cruisers ($15/60).

AROUND HANALEI
Lumaha'i Beach

If Lumaha'i Beach looks familiar, it's where Mitzi Gaynor promised to wash that man right out of her hair in the 1958 musical *South Pacific*. It's just as spectacular in real life. Plan to stroll this mile-long sandy beach, with jungle growth looming on one side and tempestuous open sea on the other.

Forget swimming. There is no reef barrier and waves are almost always too powerful, with perilous shorebreaks.

There are two ways onto Lumaha'i Beach. The first and more scenic is a three-minute walk that begins at the parking area 0.75 miles past the 4-mile marker on the Kuhio Hwy. The trail slopes to the left at the end of the retaining wall. On the beach, the lava-rock ledges are popular for sunbathing and photo ops, but beware: bystanders have been washed away by high surf and rogue waves.

The other way to access Lumaha'i is along the road at sea level at the western end of the beach, just before crossing the Lumaha'i River Bridge. The beach at this end is lined with ironwood trees.

Wainiha

Steeped in ancient history, the narrow, green recesses of Wainiha Valley were the last hideout of the *menehune*, the legendary little people. As late as the 1850s, 65 people in the

---

HOUSES ON STILTS

Why do otherwise-normal houses along the North Shore, especially around coastal Wainiha and Ha'ena, sit waaaay above the ground? To guard against tsunami flooding. After the last tsunami in 1957, the county required all new homes in flood- and tsunami-prone zones to be built on 'pilings' (poles or concrete posts) 10ft to 16ft high. (Note that existing homes may stay on ground level). Do such stilts work? To date, no big wave has put them to the test.

---

valley were officially listed as *menehune* on the government census!

SLEEPING & EATING

Jungle Cabana (☎ 826-5141, 888-886-4969; www.junglecabana.com; Ala'eke Rd; cottages $125) Secluded by a soothing rushing river and foliage gone wild, this aptly named 350-sq-ft studio (with kitchen) is compact, but charming, clean and airy. Woven bamboo furnishings, windows all around and an outdoor tub/shower create a 'thatched-hut' atmosphere. Geared to couples seeking romance in the tropics.

Hale Ho'omaha B&B (☎ 826-7083, 800-851-0291; www.aloha.net/~hoomaha; 7083 Alamihi Rd; r incl breakfast $150-175; 🖳) Ideal for travelers seeking a communal, B&B experience, island-style. Guests enjoy the run of this handsome Hawaiiana-filled house built on stilts, including the sleekly modern kitchen, airy living room and laundry facility. Bedrooms are richly appointed, bathrooms feature dual shower heads and breakfasts are freshly cooked. Save a buck and forgo the costlier Pineapple Room.

Guest House at River Estate (☎ 826-5118, 800-390-8444; www.riverestate.com; house $350; 🐾) Be king of the castle in this secluded house on stilts, surrounded by lush foliage, fruit orchard and the Wainiha River running through the backyard. Renovated in 2007, the spacious house includes two bedrooms, two bathrooms, gourmet kitchen, wraparound lanai, washer-dryer, TV, air-con and all the other comforts of home. Furnishings are upscale; privacy is guaranteed.

Red Hot Mama's (☎ 826-7266; 5-6607 Kuhio Hwy; meals $6-8.50; ⏱ 11am-5pm) The last eatery before the end of the road, this little counter serves up generous burritos, tacos ($3.25 each) and fresh Caesar or tuna salads. Note the collection of hot sauces displayed outside (with the warning not to disturb any!).

SHOPPING

Wainiha General Store (☎ 826-6251; 5-6600 Kuhio Hwy; ⏱ 10:30am-dusk) Just the basics, but it's the last place to grab groceries or beer before the end of the road.

End of the Rainbow (☎ 826-9980; endoftherainbow@hawaii.rr.com; 5-6607 Kuhio Hwy; ⏱ 10:30am-dusk) Handmade jewelry, island-style clothing and sarongs, art prints and photography featuring mainly Kaua'i artists. The collection of genuine *puka*-shell necklaces ($75 to $200) is a far cry from cheapo fakes. The friendly proprietor makes browsers feel welcome.

HA'ENA

A rural community, Ha'ena (Map pp498–9) harks back to the days when the North Shore was still off the radar. Amid the singular houses on stilts, mysterious caves and still-pristine sandy beaches, you'll find plenty of dream beach houses to rent, plus the only resort beyond Princeville.

Two tsunamis struck Ha'ena in the 20th century: the first in 1946 and the second in 1957. Both devastated homes along the beach. Thus any new house built today must be elevated (see Houses on Stilts, p513).

To learn more about Ha'ena's history, see the outstanding website www.pacificworlds .com/haena.

Sights & Activities

LIMAHULI GARDEN

Learn to distinguish Kaua'i's flora among native, Polynesian-introduced and modern-introduced (alien) species at **Limahuli Garden** (☎ 826-1053; www.ntbg.org; self-guided/guided tour $15/20; ☉ 9:30am-4pm Tue-Fri & Sun), part of the National Tropical Botanical Garden (see p521). Perhaps the most natural of all Kaua'i's gardens, the setting is spectacular, with Makana Mountain standing guard over plants flourishing from the copious rainfall.

At your own pace, navigate the scenic 0.75-mile loop trail. Benches here and there allow stops for rest or contemplation. From a handy free booklet, along with succinct signage, you'll learn that the stereotypical tropical fruits and flowers, eg mango, guava and plumeria, were unknown to ancient Hawaiians.

To get here, turn inland just before the stream that marks the boundary of Ha'ena State Park.

TUNNELS BEACH

A hot spot for snorkeling and diving, Tunnels is a wide, horseshoe-shaped fringing reef with fantastic underwater life viewable during calm summer seas. During such conditions, you can start snorkeling near the east point and let the current carry you westward. It's more adventurous (and less crowded) than Ke'e Beach.

In winter, high surf conditions mean a tubular break (hence the name Tunnels) for expert surfers and perilous risk for the rest

of us. Dangerous rip currents prevail from October to May. It was here on October 21, 2003 that competitive surfer Bethany Hamilton, then 13, lost her left arm in a shark attack. Undaunted, Bethany resumed her surfing career, wrote a book, made a media splash and continues to dominate at national competitions. See www.bethanyhamilton.com for her remarkable story.

To get here, drive past the 8-mile marker and park at either of two spots around the halfway mark (between the 8- and 9-mile markers). If you cannot find parking, you might try walking along the beach from the Hanalei Colony Resort (opposite) area.

HA'ENA BEACH PARK

Ha'ena Beach is yet another beautiful curve of white sand, but beware of astoundingly strong rip currents and shorebreaks from October to May. To the right, you can see the horseshoe shape of Tunnels outlined by breaking waves. To the far left is **Cannons**, a particularly good wall dive, with crevices and lava tubes sheltering all sorts of marine life. Lifeguard (and snack truck) on duty here.

MANINIHOLO DRY CAVE

Directly across Ha'ena Beach Park, Maniniholo Dry Cave is deep and broad and high enough to explore. Drippy and creepy, a constant seep of water from the cave walls keeps the interior damp and humid. The cave is named after the head fisherman of the *menehune* who, according to legend, built ponds and other structures at night.

YOGA & MASSAGE

A wide range of massages, face and body treatments, waxing, manicures, Ayurvedic treatments and yoga classes is offered by the **Hanalei Day Spa** (☎ 826-6621; www.hanaleidayspa .com; Hanalei Colony Resort; massage per 60/90min $85/125; ☉ 11am-7pm Mon-Sat).

Sleeping

For backpackers, Ha'ena Beach Park has campsites, rest rooms and showers. If you plan to hike the entire Kalalau Trail, you might want to park and set up a base camp here because your unattended car will probably be safer. See p460 for county camping permit information.

Upscale travelers will find Ha'ena a hotspot for beach-house rentals. A Google search is most effective, but you can also call the agencies listed on p505. The only resort west of Princeville is **Hanalei Colony Resort** (Map pp498-9; ☎ 826-6235, 800-628-3004; www.hcr.com; Hwy 560; 2-bedroom units from $210; ❄ 🖥 ☎), a longstanding condo near Tunnels Beach. The units are comfortable, with full kitchen and lanai, but quality is mixed: you might find bent screen doors, peeling paint or worn furnishings. Despite its flaws, the remote location is peaceful and the staff is friendly, with a reputation for service.

Eating
Mediterranean Gourmet (☎ 826-9875; Hanalei Colony Resort; dinner mains $15-20; ❄ 11am-9pm Mon-Sat) specializes in Middle-Eastern classics, eg falafel, dolmas (stuffed grape leaves), gyros, kebabs, fish specialties and baklava. The husband-and-wife chefs got their start selling hummus, tabouli and other tasty offerings under the Mediterranean Gourmet label at health-food stores and farmers markets.

HA'ENA STATE PARK
At the 'end of the road,' 230-acre Ha'ena State Park is a fitting finale to the idyllic North Shore drive. Ke'e Beach is postcard pretty, with clear, calm waters framed by the distinctive 1280ft cliff commonly known as Bali Hai, its name in the movie *South Pacific*. Hawaiians prefer to use its Hawaiian name, 'Makana,' which aptly means 'gift.'

Wet Caves
Two wet caves are within the boundaries of Ha'ena State Park. The first, **Waikapala'e Wet Cave**, is just a few minutes' walk uphill from the main road along a rutted dirt drive opposite the visitor parking overflow area. The second, **Waikanaloa Wet Cave**, is right on the south side of the main road. Both caves are deep, dark and dripping, with pools of very cold water.

Ke'e Beach
Picturesque Ke'e Beach can't be beat for colorful snorkeling and easy access. A reef protects the right side of the cove and, except on high surf days, waters are calm and pleasantly swimmable. The left side is open and can have a powerful current, particularly in winter.

On the downside, Ke'e Beach is insanely popular due to both the outstanding snorkeling and the adjacent Kalalau trailhead. From the beach, you can behold the Na Pali Coast by walking the first 30 minutes of the Kalalau Trail (p516). Parking can be a problem (go early and avoid summers and weekends) and break-ins are rampant.

Find showers, drinking water, rest rooms and a pay phone in the woods behind the parking lot.

Kaulu Paoa Heiau
The vague remains of Kaulu Paoa Heiau stand just five minutes' walk from Ke'e Beach. Here,

---

INVASION OF THE HIPPIES

No place was remote enough to escape the '60s hippie invasion – not even out-of-the-way Ha'ena. During the late 1960s Howard Taylor (Elizabeth's brother) acquired a large parcel of what is the current Ha'ena State Park. He wanted to build a house there, but the state was condemning the land and wouldn't grant him a permit, yet required tax payment. In retaliation for his treatment, he lent the land to the 'flower-power people,' who had already been squatting on Kaua'i parks since 1968.

Living in shacks, treehouses and tarp shelters, a hippie community, dubbed Taylor Camp, soon formed. The new 'residents' used a communal shower and open-air toilet, established a Church of the Brotherhood of the Paradise Children, sunbathed nude and relied on junker cars to get themselves around. Some survived on welfare, while others grew *pakalolo* (marijuana) or held conventional jobs elsewhere on the island. At one point, the group numbered over 100, to the chagrin of locals suspicious of the oddball, pot-smoking, unwashed haole flocking to the remote North Shore.

In 1977 the state finally condemned the property for park use, spurred by neighbors' complaints about the lack of modern toilets and garbage disposal. Some say the sanitation problem killed off mullet and other fish formerly plentiful in Ha'ena's waters.

Go to www.pacificworlds.com/haena/memories/memory5.cfm for an intriguing account of Taylor Camp.

beneath a cliff face, large stones create a long flat grassy platform where a thatched-roof hula *halau* (school) once stood. In ancient Hawai'i this *halau* was Kaua'i's most sacred; students aspiring to learn hula came from all of the Hawaiian Islands and the legendary Kaua'i chief Lohi'au trained here. Present-day hula *halau* (troupes) still leave lei and other offerings to Laka (goddess of hula) in crevices in the cliff face.

To find the remains of the heiau, take the path on the western side of the beach. Follow the stone wall as it curves uphill and you'll reach the heiau almost immediately. The overgrown section at the foot of the hill is one of the more intact parts of the heiau.

NA PALI COAST STATE PARK

On virtually every visitor's must-see, must-do list is Na Pali, which in Hawaiian means simply 'the cliffs.' Nowhere else in Hawaii will you see such grand, sharply fluted cliffs (though the highest are on Moloka'i).

Na Pali Coast State Park encompasses the rugged, corrugated 22-mile stretch between the end of the road at Ke'e Beach in the north and the road's opposite end at Polihale State Park in the west.

History

Kalalau, Honopu, Awa'awapuhi, Nu'alolo and Miloli'i are the five major valleys on the Na Pali Coast. Since the first waves of Tahitian settlers, these deep river valleys contained sizable settlements. When winter seas prevented canoes from landing on the northern shore, trails down precipitous ridges and rope ladders provided access.

In the mid-19th century missionaries established a school in Kalalau, the largest valley, and registered the valley population at about 200. Influenced by Western ways, people gradually began moving to towns and by century's end the valleys were largely abandoned.

Sights & Activities

For a close-up view of the Na Pali Coast, hiking the 11-mile Kalalau coastal trail into Hanakapi'ai, Hanakoa and Kalalau Valleys is a backpacking adventure rated among the world's most beautiful. From the opposite side, in Koke'e State Park, a couple of strenuous hikes reach clifftops with gorgeous views into Awa'awapuhi and Nu'alolo Valleys for

a different perspective. You can also access the Na Pali Coast by sea on a 17-mile kayak adventure (p510).

KALALAU TRAIL

Kalalau is Hawaii's premier trail, as the Na Pali Coast is a place of singular beauty. It runs along high sea cliffs and winds up and down across lush valleys before it finally ends below the steep fluted *pali* of Kalalau.

The state parks office in Lihu'e can provide a Kalalau Trail brochure with a map. The hike itself can be divided into three parts:

Ke'e Beach–Hanakapi'ai Valley (2 miles)
Hanakapi'ai Valley–Hanakoa Valley (4 miles)
Hanakoa Valley–Kalalau Valley (5 miles)

The first 2 miles of the trail to Hanakapi'ai Valley are insanely popular: 500,000 people hike it annually, and it shows in the eroded trail edges, muddy passages with ankle-deep puddles and, especially in summer, boisterous children. No permit is required for the hike to Hanakapi'ai Valley.

Fit hikers can do the entire 11-mile trail straight through in seven hours. Until the Hanakoa Valley campground reopens, however, it's not possible to (legally) break the trip beyond Hanakapi'ai.

Even if you're not planning to camp, a permit is officially required to continue on the Kalalau Trail beyond Hanakapi'ai. Free day-use hiking permits are available from the **Division of State Parks** (Map p472; ☎ 274-3444; www .hawaii.gov/dlnr/dsp; Department of Land & Natural Resources, Division of State Parks, Room 306, 3060 Eiwa St, Lihue, HI 96766; ✆ 8am-3:30pm Mon-Fri), which also issues the required camping permits for the Hanakapi'ai (one night maximum) and Kalalau (five nights maximum) Valleys. For more information on permits see p459).

Ke'e Beach to Hanakapi'ai Valley

The 2-mile trail running from Ke'e Beach to Hanakapi'ai Valley is a delightfully scenic hike. Morning is the best time to head west on the first leg of the trail, while afternoon is ideal when returning east, as the sun thus strikes your back and provides good light for photography.

The trail weaves through *hala* (screw pine), *kukui* (candlenut) and ohia trees and then back out to clearings with fine coastal views. About a mile in, it starts to dip under soft-needled ironwoods and through stream

KALALAU TRAIL

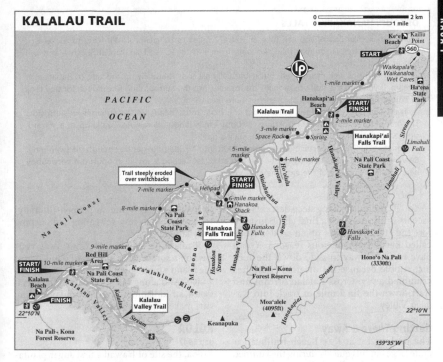

gulches. The smooth rocks on the trail are often coated in mud and thus precariously slippery. At about the 1.5-mile point you'll see a black-and-yellow striped tsunami pole marker, which indicates the lowest point of safety in case of a tsunami.

You will soon reach Hanakapi'ai Valley, where you must ford the stream to continue. Hanakapi'ai Beach is sandy in the summer, but a beach of only boulders during winter, when storms sweep out the sand. With unpredictable rip currents year-round, this beach is the deadliest on the island, causing one drowning per year on average since the 1970s.

The campground closest to the oceanfront cliffs is overused and under-maintained. Another slightly better campground is located a little way up the trail to Hanakapi'ai Falls (see p518).

Hanakapi'ai Valley to Hanakoa Valley

Soon after you leave Hanakapi'ai Valley the trail goes into bush and the next coastal view is not for another mile. Craggy cliffs begin to tower overhead following well-cut, but hot

and exposed, switchbacks that climb 800ft in elevation. The trail keeps climbing past the 3-mile marker and the switchbacks over rocks and mud can be brutally steep. Soon the trail reaches its highest point at **Space Rock**, a prominent boulder overlooking the coast.

Winding from waterfall gulch to ridge and back again, the trail then passes through several mini-valleys within the greater Ho'olulu Valley, finally reaching Waiahuakua Valley. These are 'hanging valleys,' which end abruptly at sea cliffs rather than gradually sloping into a beach.

Hanakoa Valley to Kalalau Valley

By far the narrowest and steepest part of the trail, the last 5 miles are also without question the most beautiful. Make sure you have at least three hours of daylight left.

About a mile out of Hanakoa Valley, ascending past coffee shrubs and *ti* plants, you'll reach the coast again and begin to get fantastic views of Na Pali's jagged edges. The red-dirt switchbacks show extensive erosion due to salty seaspray, sparse rainfall and feral goats that consume the vegetation.

DETOUR: HANAKAPI'AI FALLS

From Hanakapi'ai Beach, you can hike an extra 2 miles to Hanakapi'ai Falls. Due to tricky rock crossings, this trek is tougher than the walk from Ke'e Beach to Hanakapi'ai Beach – and will add at least 2½ hours round-trip.

The trail is not well maintained, but it basically ascends gradually up the side of Hanakapi'ai Stream. If you find the trail occasionally disappears into the surrounding forest, look for tiny tags of colored plastic ribbon tied to branches here and there.

Trails line both sides of the stream, but the main route heads up the stream's western side. The first of three major stream crossings is about a mile (about 25 minutes' walk) up, at a 'hazard' sign. Step gingerly on rocks covered with slick algae.

Hanakapi'ai Falls is spectacular, dropping 100ft into a wide pool gentle enough for swimming. Beware of falling rocks directly under the cascade. The setting is idyllic, though not very sunny near the falls because of the extreme steepness.

You'll continue making steep descents and ascents until you reach a final climb just before the 10-mile marker on an eroded slope called **Red Hill**, for obvious reasons. You'll have to find a way to slide down the red-dirt rubble because the original route has crumbled away. Cross Kalalau Stream and start down the final mile of track into Kalalau Valley.

Getting There & Away

The parking lot at Ke'e Beach trailhead is quite large but fills quickly during the jammed summer months. Break-ins are rampant; some people advise leaving cars empty and unlocked to prevent damage. Campers, consider parking at the campground at Ha'ena Beach Park (Map pp498–9) or storing your belongings elsewhere and catching a cab to the trailhead.

SOUTH SHORE

For the archetypal beach vacation, Kaua'i's crowd-pleaser is the sun-drenched South Shore. Here, the weather is less rainy and the waves less changeable than on the North Shore. And, located off the highway, it feels more exclusive than the Eastside or Lihu'e.

Sunsets blaze at the horizon – and numerous beachfront restaurants capitalize on that million-dollar view. If you're seeking a convivial atmosphere, Po'ipu has enough critical mass for that resort vibe.

Just inland are the former plantation towns Koloa and Kalaheo. Koloa's restored 'old town' is the South Shore's lively, but touristy, commercial center. Kalaheo, gateway to the Westside, is a one-stop town (literally) with refreshingly low-key eating and sleeping alternatives.

It might be tempting to while away your days on resort beaches but, near Po'ipu, two of the island's finest botanical gardens are worth a visit. And along the southeast Maha'ulepu Coast, striking limestone cliffs and pounding surf make a unique beach walk.

KOLOA

pop 1942

Koloa, the site of Hawaii's first sugar plantation, was a thriving commercial center until it largely went bust after WWII. All the old plantation towns tell the same story: the history is sugar, the present is tourism.

Today, Koloa is reborn as a lively tourist town. With its aging wooden buildings and false storefronts, it resembles a clean-cut version of the Old West. The former produce markets, barbershops, bathhouses and beer halls have become boutiques, galleries and restaurants. The adjacent residential towns of Lawa'i (pop 1984) and Omao (pop 1221) are low-key, neighborly and blooming with foliage.

History

Sugarcane first arrived in Hawaii with the original Polynesian settlers, while the earliest Chinese immigrants brought small-scale refinery savvy. When William Hooper, an enterprising 24-year-old Bostonian, arrived on Kaua'i in 1835, however, sugar production went big time.

With financial backing from Honolulu businesspeople, he leased land in Koloa from the king and paid the *ali'i* a stipend to release commoners from their traditional work obligations. He then hired Hawaiians as wage laborers and Koloa became Hawaii's first plantation town.

Orientation & Information

From the west, Koloa Rd (Hwy 530), which runs between Lawa'i and Koloa, is the best way in and out. From Lihu'e, take the scenic Maluhia Rd (Hwy 520), through the enchanting Tree Tunnel.

Services are minimal:

First Hawaiian Bank (☎ 742-1642; 3506 Waikomo Rd) At the east end of town.

Post office (☎ 800-275-8777; 5485 Koloa Rd) Serves both Koloa and Po'ipu.

Sights

TREE TUNNEL

If driving from Lihu'e, take Maluhia Rd (Hwy 520) to navigate under the fairy-tale Tree Tunnel, a mile-long canopy of towering swamp mahogany trees (a type of eucalyptus). Pineapple baron Walter McBryde planted the trees as a community project in 1911, when he had leftover trees after landscaping his estate at Kukuiolono (p529).

KOLOA HISTORIC BUILDINGS

East of town, find **Koloa Jodo Mission** (☎ 742-6735; 2480 Waikomo Rd; ☼ services 6pm Mon-Fri, 9:30am Sun), which follows Pure Land Buddhism, a nonmeditating form, popular in Japan since the 12th century. The Buddhist temple on the left is the original, which dates back to 1910, while the larger temple on the right is currently used for services.

St Raphael's Catholic Church (☎ 742-1955; 3011 Hapa Rd), Kaua'i's oldest Catholic church, is the burial site of some of Hawaii's first Portuguese immigrants. The original church, built in 1854, was made of lava rock and coral mortar with walls 3ft thick – a type of construction visible in the ruins of the adjacent rectory. When the church was enlarged in 1936 it was plastered over, creating a more-typical whitewashed appearance.

Activities

A handful of outfits set up shop in Koloa.

DIVING

The island's best dive outfit, **Fathom Five Divers** (☎ 742-6991, 800-972-3078; www.fathomfive.com; 3450 Po'ipu Rd; shore dives $65-95, boat dives $100-140), is run by a husband-and-wife team, Jeannette and George Thompson. They offer the whole range, from Ni'ihau boat dives to night dives to certification courses. Groups max out at six and they avoid mixing skill levels. Their shore-diving sister company is Ocean Quest Watersports (p490) but all bookings are handled here. Call well in advance.

SNORKELING

For snorkel gear rental and sales, a standby is **Snorkel Bob's** (☎ 742-2206; www.snorkelbob.com; 3236 Po'ipu Rd; rental mask, snorkel & fins per week $9-32; ☼ 8am-5pm), which also rents bodyboards (per day/week $6.50/26).

BROKEN ALARM CLOCK

The first wildlife you'll see – and hear – on Kaua'i will probably be a chicken. They're ubiquitous!

Chickens first arrived in Hawaii with the Polynesians, who brought red junglefowl (*moa*). Later Westerners brought domestic chickens. In the sugarcane plantation days, Kaua'i's wild-chicken population was kept in check by field fires (a regular event before harvest, to allow more-efficient reaping). In the 1980s, as Hawaii's sugar industry declined, chickens inevitably proliferated.

Further, when Hurricane 'Iwa and Hurricane 'Iniki struck in 1982 and 1992 respectively, they obliterated the cages of Kaua'i's fighting cocks, releasing them into the wild. Finally, Kaua'i has no mongoose or snake population to prey on birds, including chickens.

When other islands see their wild-chicken numbers increase, they act quickly to stop it. But Kaua'i's attitude is accommodating. Some consider the chickens a sign of post-hurricane recovery. Today you will find souvenirs, T-shirts and logos featuring chickens.

One downside: if a rooster happens to live outside your bedroom window, you can forget about sleeping in. Known as Kaua'i's 'broken alarm clock,' local roosters crow at random hours, even midnight. The trick? Keep the lights off.

Tours

Kaua'i ATV Tours (☎ 742-2734, 877-707-7088; www .kauaiatv.com; 5330 Koloa Rd; tours $99-145) takes groups from six to 12 over 22,000 acres of pastureland inland of Koloa and Lihu'e, a vast area that's middling in scenery until you reach the lusher upcountry. Don't expect to let loose; guides keep riders under control. Private tours, including transportation to a wedding site by ATV, can be arranged.

Festivals & Events

In late July, **Koloa Plantation Days Celebration** (☎ 822-0734; www.koloaplantationdays.com), the South Shore's biggest annual celebration, spans nine days of family fun with a parade, block party, golf tournaments, guided walks and more.

Sleeping

There are several options near Koloa.

Strawberry Guava B&B (☎ 332-0385, 634-5539; http://homepages.hawaiian.net/lauria; 4896-Z Kua Rd; r incl breakfast $60-85) Run by a friendly couple with three young kids, this B&B set amid jungly foliage exudes down-to-earth warmth. The three rooms are rather spartan, but they're clean and open to a common dining area for home-cooked breakfasts.

Boulay Inn (☎ 742-1120, 635-5539; http://home .hawaii.rr.com/boulayinn; apt per day/week/month $75/ 450/1400) A private one-bedroom apartment with wraparound lanai, full kitchen and free laundry facility for $75? You're not dreaming. This breezy apartment is a comfy home-away-from-home in a low-key neighborhood. The 2nd-floor unit sits atop the owners' garage, so there are no shared walls.

Kaua'i Banyan Inn (☎ 888-786-3855; www.kauai banyan.com; 3528-B Mana Hema Pl; r $90-125; ▢) Stylish, affordable and professionally run, this inn is guaranteed to please discerning guests. First you'll admire the gargantuan banyan tree, standing guard out front. Then you'll appreciate the immaculate units, each with kitchenette, polished hardwood floors, vaulted ceilings, fine furnishings and private lanai. Pay more for better views.

Hale Kua (☎ 332-8570, 800-440-4353; www.halekua .com; 4896-E Kua Rd, Lawa'i; 1-/3-bedroom apt $115/$145, 1-bedroom cottages $125) Escape into a jungle world of misty rain, giant trees and…modern apartments with every creature comfort you could desire. The spacious units resemble upscale townhouses and each includes lanai, washer-dryer and full kitchen.

Marjorie's Kaua'i Inn (☎ 332-8838, 800-717-8838; PO Box 866, Lana'i; www.marjorieskauaiinn.com; r $130-160; ▢) Classy to the nth degree, this three-room inn off Koloa Rd overlooks a magnificent vista of Lawa'i Valley. Each room features an expansive private lanai, glossy hardwood floors, luxury linens and kitchenettes. All guests can use the inviting 50ft lap pool, plus a poolside BBQ grill.

Eating

Lappert's (☎ 742-1272; Koloa Rd; single-scoop ice cream $3.50; ⊙ 6am-10pm) You can find Kaua'i's famous premium ice cream at four locations on the island. This one was where the late founder Walter Lappert often hung out.

Koloa Fish Market (☎ 742-6199; 5482 Koloa Rd; lunch $4-7; ⊙ 10am-6pm Mon-Fri, to 5pm Sat) Your best bet for take-out: bento boxes, sushi, plate lunches and fresh fish. The *poke* comes in mouthwatering varieties and the seared-'*ahi* slices are gourmet quality.

Mi Casita (☎ 742-2323; 5470 Koloa Rd; appetizers $6-9.50, meals $6-19; ⊙ 5-9pm Mon-Sat) The colorful mural and lively piped-in music add just the right atmosphere for the filling Mexican fare served at this cozy family-run restaurant. Standouts include the seafood lover's fajitas, with sautéed *ono* and tiger shrimp, and fresh fish tacos.

Pizzetta (☎ 742-8881; 5408 Koloa Rd; pizzas $14-23, pastas $9-17; ⊙ 11am-9:30pm) The setting is touristy (and most patrons are tourists), but the Italian fare is tasty and reasonable. Pizzas feature gourmet toppings such as fire-roasted veg and feta, with or without grilled chicken. On the run, try pizza by the slice (from 11am to 6pm).

Grocery stores:

Big Save (cnr Waikomo Rd & Koloa Rd; ⊙ 6am-11pm) One of the better Big Save branches, with deli.

Koloa Natural Foods (☎ 742-8910; 5356 Koloa Rd; ⊙ 10am-8pm Tue-Sat, to 4pm Sun & Mon) Limited selection of bulk and packaged items, fresh produce, natural toiletries and supplements – all rather pricey.

Sueoka Store (☎ 742-1611; 5392 Koloa Rd; ⊙ 7am-9pm) Small local market with limited selection but with decent island produce and Japanese take-out meals. Also try their Snack Shop outside for local-style fast food.

Shopping

Progressive Expressions (☎ 742-6041; www.progres siveexpressions.com; 5420 Koloa Rd; ⊙ 9am-9pm) Established in 1972, this was the South Shore's first surf shop. Original owners Marty and Joe Kuala sold the shop to the Hanalei Surf Company in 2005 but Joe still designs and crafts boards sold here.

Pohaku T's (☎ 742-7500; www.pohaku.com; 3430 Po'ipu Rd; ❤ 10am-8pm Mon-Sat, to 6pm Sun) A smorgasbord of quality tees and tanks showcase original Kaua'i-theme designs. Also available are handmade aloha shirts, kids' clothing and other Kaua'i-made items.

Island Soap & Candle Works (☎ 742-1945, 888-528-7627; www.kauaisoap.com; 5428 Koloa Rd; ❤ 9am-10pm) Follow your nose toward the soothing fragrances of plumeria, pineapple and dozens more. Established in 1984 to recreate the art of soap- and candle-making, the company is now a mini-chain.

Jungle Girl (☎ 742-9649; 5424 Koloa Rd; ❤ 9am-9pm) Trendy fashions for females of all ages, from flowing, earthy skirts to bikinis.

Crazy Shirts (☎ 742-7161; 5356 Koloa Rd; ❤ 10am-9pm Mon-Sat, to 6pm Sun) Across the Hawaiian Islands, Crazy Shirts is ubiquitous, selling top-quality, clean-cut, island-inspired T-shirts. Grungy bohos, look elsewhere.

PO'IPU

pop 1075

Tourists absolutely adore Po'ipu (which ironically means 'completely overcast' in Hawaiian) for its dependable sun and easy-access beaches. Numerous condos and time-shares, plus two major hotels, crowd near the shore, engulfing the original cluster of homes scattered here and there. Alas, no Po'ipu 'town' exists – so dining is limited and traveling by foot is challenging except along the beaches.

Orientation & Information

The main entry road is Po'ipu Rd (Hwy 520), which leads you to Lawa'i Rd (toward Spouting Horn Beach Park) if you veer right. If you stay left, you will remain on Po'ipu Rd, where most accommodations are located.

Shopping is limited to **Po'ipu Shopping Village** (☎ 742-2831; 2360 Kiahuna Plantation Dr; ❤ 9am-9pm Mon-Sat, 10am-7pm Sun), a generic mall with shops geared to tourists (selling aloha attire, jewelry, T-shirts and swimwear) and the bulk of Po'ipu's restaurants. Also at the mall is **Bank of Hawaii** (☎ 742-6800; Po'ipu Shopping Village, 2360 Kiahuna Plantation Dr; ❤ 8:30am-4pm Mon-Thu, to 6pm Fri); no cashing of checks or traveler's checks at this branch.

Sights

NATIONAL TROPICAL BOTANICAL GARDEN

If plants aren't your thing, **National Tropical Botanical Garden** (NTBG; ☎ 742-2623; www.ntbg.org; 4425 Lawa'i Rd; tours $20-35; ❤ 8:30am-5pm) might inspire you to develop that green thumb. NTBG, a nonprofit working to propagate tropical and endangered species, manages five gardens (three on Kaua'i, one on Maui and one in Florida).

In Po'ipu's NTBG, don't miss the 80-acre **Allerton Garden**, a stunning landscape masterpiece, showcasing giant Moreton Bay fig trees (seen in *Jurassic Park*), an 'undulating' fountain, golden bamboo groves, pristine lagoon and valley walls blanketed with purple bougainvillea during summer. In 1870 Queen Emma, the wife of Kamehameha IV, lived in Lawa'i Valley – and her summer cottage still stands today. The garden's namesake is Chicago industrialist Robert Allerton, who in 1938 bought, then sumptuously landscaped, the coastal part of the valley.

You can visit Allerton only by guided tour ($35). Guides are knowledgeable guides and pepper the tour with interesting tidbits.

The adjacent **McBryde Garden** is less manicured and fancy than Allerton Garden, showcasing palms, flowering and spice trees, orchids and rare native species, plus a pretty stream and waterfall. You can explore the vast grounds on a self-guided tour ($20).

PO'IPU (SHERATON) BEACH

The Sheraton Kaua'i Resort scored big-time with its location at Po'ipu Beach, which runs east to Po'ipu Beach Park (see below). An off-shore reef tames the waves enough for swimming, snorkeling and moderate windsurfing, bodyboarding and surfing.

Cowshead, the rocky outcropping at the west end of the beach near the Sheraton, offers Po'ipu Beach's best bodyboarding breaks. For experts only, challenging offshore surfing spots include **First Break**, in front of the Sheraton; beginners should always remain inshore. **Waiohai**, at the east end of the beach in front of the sprawling Marriott Waiohai Beach Club time-share, also sees major swells.

To get here, drive to the end of Ho'onani Rd.

PO'IPU BEACH PARK

No monster waves or idyllic solitude here. But if you're seeking a safe, lively, family-

PO'IPU

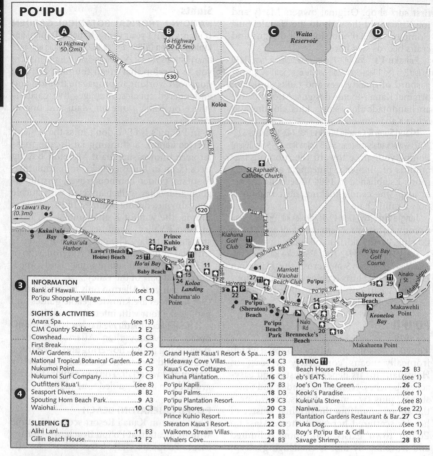

friendly beach, this is it. Located at the end of Ho'owili Rd, it features a lifeguard station and shallow, gentle waters. The narrow beach is crowded, especially during weekends, but it's a convivial scene; kids without siblings can quickly find playmates, and parents end up recognizing familiar faces among their ilk. Older kids can snorkel here, as fish are plentiful enough.

Nukumoi Point extends into the water at the western side of the park. Also known as Tortugas, it is indeed home to many green sea turtles. At low tide, you can walk out on the point and explore tide pools that shelter small fish. The best snorkeling is west of the point, where there are swarms of curious fish. It's also a good, shallow diving spot for beginners.

Beach facilities include rest rooms, showers and picnic tables.

BRENNECKE'S BEACH
No surfboards are allowed near shore here so bodysurfers and bodyboarders can claim this awesome shorebreak for themselves. Note that waves break really close to shore, making it dangerous for novices. Surf is highest in summer, but the winter action is respectable, too. Beware of strong rips during high surf. The beach is only a small pocket of sand and waters can get crowded.

SHIPWRECK BEACH
Expert surfers, bodyboarders and bodysurfers flock to the half-mile-long sandy beach at

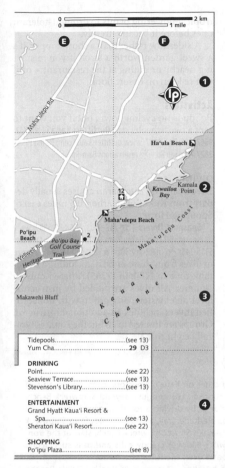

access post that marks the pathway between the road and the beach. Big kids can find deeper water with fewer rocks just a short stroll west.

LAWA'I (BEACH HOUSE) BEACH

Abutting Lawa'i Rd in plain view of passersby, this beach (nicknamed 'Beach House Beach' for the adjacent restaurant) is neither scenic nor sandy. The entry is rocky, with just a roadside strip of sand. Yet it draws a regular contingent of tourist snorkelers. One reason is the location near scads of condos and time-shares. But when waters are calm during winter, it is rich snorkel turf. When the surf's up in summer, come to watch surfers show their stuff. Across from the beach are rest rooms, a shower and public parking.

SPOUTING HORN BEACH PARK

A famous but fickle **geyser**, Spouting Horn somehow became a mandatory stop on the tour-bus circuit. Don't expect Yellowstone's Old Faithful. Spouting Horn is less predictable, less lengthy and less high. Its seawater eruptions are typically under 30ft and last only seconds, when the sea shoots through a hole in the lava reef. But the sea spray creates lovely rainbows – a sweet photo op.

To get here, turn right off Po'ipu Rd onto Lawa'i Rd, just past Po'ipu Plaza and continue for 1.75 miles.

PRINCE KUHIO PARK

In a quiet field of green, a **monument** commemorates Prince Jonah Kuhio Kalaniana'ole, born nearby in 1871. He was the Territory of Hawaii's first delegate to the US Congress and he spearheaded the Hawaiian Homes Commission Act, which set aside 200,000 acres of land for indigenous Hawaiians, many of whom are still waiting for it. You'll also find **Ho'ai Heiau**, the remains of a fishpond and an ancient Hawaiian house platform. The park is about 0.5 miles down Lawa'i Rd, across from Ho'ai Bay.

KOLOA LANDING

Koloa Landing, at the mouth of Waikomo Stream, was once Kaua'i's largest port. In the 1850s farmers used it to ship Kaua'i-grown sugar, oranges and sweet potatoes, and it was the third busiest whaling port among the Hawaiian Islands, surpassed only by Honolulu and Lahaina, Maui. The landing waned after

Keoneloa Bay, which fronts the Grand Hyatt Kaua'i Resort & Spa. The pounding shore-break and high surf are ideal for advanced riders but novices and swimmers should go elsewhere. A couple of near-shore breaks attract local board surfers as well. Toward the left of the bay, daredevils leap off **Makawehi Point**, the gigantic rock cliff.

The name comes from, yes, a shipwrecked wooden boat that washed ashore and remained for years. In 1982 Hurricane 'Iwa swept the boat back to sea.

BABY BEACH

Shallow and safe for little kids, this protected swimming beach is located off Ho'ona Rd, east of Prince Kuhio Park. Look for the beach

the road system was built and it was abandoned in the 1920s. Today only a small boat ramp remains.

Underwater, it's another story: Koloa Landing is popular for **snorkeling** and the best **shore-diving** spot on the South Shore. Its protected waters reach depths of about 30ft and it's generally calm all year. See underwater tunnels, a variety of coral and fish, sea turtles and monk seals. The best sights are located toward the west.

MOIR GARDENS

If cacti are your fancy, **Moir Gardens** (☎ 742-6411; Kiahuna Plantation, 2253 Po'ipu Rd; admission free; ☽ sunrise-sunset) offers a modest oasis on the grounds of the Kiahuna Plantation condo. It's a low-key, approachable collection of mature cacti and succulents, interspersed with winding paths, a lily pond and colorful shocks of orchids.

The gardens, established in the 1930s and now part of the Kiahuna Plantation resort, were originally the estate of Hector Moir, manager of Koloa Sugar Plantation, and Alexandra 'Sandie' Knudsen Moir. The Moirs were once avid gardeners who switched from

tropical flowering plants to drought-tolerant ones before it became trendy.

A sideshow rather than a showstopper, it's a sweet garden worth a stroll if you're staying nearby or dining at the restaurant – or if you're keen on desert flora.

Activities

Po'ipu is no cycling town, but if you want to rent a two-wheeler, try **Outfitters Kaua'i** (☎ 742-9667, 888-742-9887; www.outfitterskauai.com; Po'ipu Plaza, 2827-A Po'ipu Rd; ☽ reservations 8am-9pm).

DIVING

Dive boats and catamaran cruises usually depart from Kukui'ula Harbor, 0.5 miles east of Spouting Horn.

Seasport Divers (☎ 742-9303, 800-685-5889; www.seasportdivers.com; Po'ipu Plaza, 2827 Po'ipu Rd; 2-tank dive $115-145; ☽ check-in 7:30am & 12:45pm) leads a range of dives from shore or boat, including a three-tank dive to Ni'ihau ($265), offered only in summer. All dives are guided by instructor-level divemasters; any group with noncertified divers includes an additional instructor. Groups are limited to 18 but the count is typically eight to 12.

DETOUR: MAHA'ULEPU HERITAGE TRAIL

The windswept Maha'ulepu Coast resembles no other on Kaua'i: limestone cliffs, pounding surf and three pristine beaches still free from mass tourism. Located just beyond Shipwreck Beach, it's not far. But the coast is accessible only by foot or by driving a rough unpaved road.

The best way to get here: hike the Maha'ulepu Heritage Trail, an easy 2 miles from Shipwreck Beach. Park in the Grand Hyatt lot at the end of Ainako St. At Shipwreck Beach, start at the ironwood trees on the east. Along the coast, you will walk over craggy cliffs and pass spectacular lime-sand formations, tide pools in rocky coves and even the ruins of a heiau.

The Maha'ulepu coast comprises a string of beaches – Maha'ulepu Beach (Gillin's Beach), Kawailoa Bay and Ha'ula Beach – from west to east. Waters are choppy and better suited for experienced swimmers than once-a-year tourists but hiking is enticing all year round. Near Maha'ulepu Beach you'll see the sole house on the entire coast, the **Gillin Beach House** (☎ 742-7561; www.gillinbeachhouse.com; per week from $2675), originally built in 1946 by Elbert Gillin, a civil engineer with the Koloa Sugar Plantation.

Kawailoa Bay is surrounded by sand dunes to the west and protected by jutting sea cliffs to the east. Windsurfers and kitesurfers skim across the surf here. Ironwood trees backing the beach make a pleasant spot for picnicking. Continue on until you reach Ha'ula Beach, a stunning curved bay with pounding, white-crested waves. The coastline is exposed so come prepared for sun and wind.

If you prefer to drive, go past the Grand Hyatt, proceed for 1.5 miles on the unpaved road and turn right where it dead-ends at a **gate** (☽ 7:30am-6pm, to 7pm summer). Continue past the gatehouse until you reach the beach parking area. Access hours are strictly enforced.

Two excellent resources are the Maha'ulepu Heritage Trail **website** (www.hikemahaulepu.org) and *Kaua'i's Geologic History: A Simplified Guide* by Chuck Blay and Robert Siemers. Also see **Malama Maha'ulepu** (www.malama-mahauleps.org), a nonprofit working to preserve the coast.

IT'S THEIR TURF

You're almost guaranteed to spot **monk seals** along the Po'ipu coast–half-ton piles of dark blubber. But they're among the most endangered species on Kaua'i – and one of Hawaii's only two endemic mammals, found nowhere else in the world (the other is a species of bat). The once-thriving monk seal population across the Hawaiian Islands is today estimated at about 1300 and declining by 4% annually. Most live on the remote Northwestern Hawaiian Islands but 50 to 100 live in the state of Hawaii and at least half on Kaua'i.

If you see a monk seal, remember that you are intruding in its natural habitat. Keep a distance of 100ft and do not provoke it to move or to 'do something.'

For more information see the website of the **Kaua'i Monk Seal Watch Program** (www.kauai monkseal.com).

Also see Fathom Five Divers in Koloa (p519).

KAYAKING

Outfitters Kaua'i (☎ 742-9667, 888-742-9887; www .outfitterskauai.com; Po'ipu Plaza, 2827-A Po'ipu Rd; ✆ reservations taken 8am-9pm) offers a sea kayaking tour (per adult/child 12 to 14 $135/110); the eight-hour paddle makes a good training prelude to the grueling Na Pali challenge.

SURFING

Po'ipu is a popular spot for lessons because it's got some killer breaks and year-round sun. Beware of large classes, though; four is maximum density.

Aloha Surf Lessons (☎ 639-8614; 2hr lesson group/ private $60/125; ✆ lessons 9am, 11am, 1pm & 3pm) Pro surfer Chava Greenlee and his staff teach groups of six max, with 15 minutes on land, 45 minutes in water with instructor and one hour on your own.

Garden Island Surf School (☎ 652-4841; www .gardenislandsurfschool.com; 2hr lesson $60; ✆ lessons 8am, 10am, noon & 2pm) The lesson includes one hour with instructor and one hour free surfing. Groups can max out at six.

Kaua'i Surf School (☎ 742-8019; www.kauaisurf school.com; 2hr lesson $60). Classes meet at the Nukumoi Surf Company.

Margo Oberg's Surfing School (☎ 332-6100, 888-742-6924; 2hr lesson $48) Offers highly regarded classes designed by this World Cup surfing champion.

Nukumoi Surf Company (☎ 742-8019; www .nukumoi.com; 2100 Ho'one Rd; soft-top boards rental per hour/day/week $5/20/60, hard boards $7.50/30/80, bodyboards per day/week $5/15; ✆ 7:45am-6:30pm Mon-Sat, 10:45am-6pm Sun) This well-stocked surf shop rents equipment.

Progressive Expressions (☎ 742-6041; www.progres siveexpressions.com; 5420 Koloa Rd, Koloa; ✆ 9am-9pm) Koloa surf shop; rents boards for comparable prices.

Seasport Divers (☎ 742-9303, 800-685-5889; www .seasportdivers.com; Po'ipu Plaza, 2827 Po'ipu Rd; surfboard rental per day/week $20/100, bodyboards from $4/15)

HORSEBACK RIDING

If you want a break from hoofin' it yourself, you can hop on a horse at **CJM Country Stables** (☎ 742-6096; www.cjmstables.com; tours from $90; ✆ tours Mon-Sat). The rides are the slow, nose-to-tail, follow-the-leader variety, so they're safe but might bore experienced riders.

GOLF

The economical **Kiahuna Golf Club** (☎ 742-9595; www.kiahunagolf.com; 2545 Kiahuna Plantation Dr; green fees incl cart before/after 2pm $110/75, club rental $40) is a relatively forgiving 18-hole, par-70 Robert Trent Jones Jr course. Established in 1983, this compact, inland course uses smaller targets and awkward stances to pose challenges.

The South Shore's jewel is the **Po'ipu Bay Golf Course** (☎ 742-8711, 800-858-6300; www.kauai.hyatt .com/hyatt/hotels/activities/golf; 2250 Ainako St; green fees incl cart nonguest/guest $185/125, club rental $40). This 18-hole, par-72 course adjacent to the Grand Hyatt covers 210 seaside acres. Rates drop at noon and again at 2:30pm.

BODYWORK & FITNESS

Anara Spa (☎ 742-1234, 800-554-9288; www.anaraspa .com; Grand Hyatt Kaua'i, 1571 Po'ipu Rd; massage per hr $75-250, treatments $65-75) offers all manner of massages, herbal wraps, body scrubs and polishing in a lush, indulgent setting. The spa also includes plush weight and fitness rooms, a 25yd pool and classes.

Tours

Sunset cruises, however clichéd, draw 'em in year-round. **Capt Andy's Sailing Adventures** (☎ 335-6833, 800-535-0830; www.napali.com; Port Allen

Marina Center, Waialo Rd; adult/child 2-12 $69/50) departs from Kukui'ula Harbor between 4pm and 5pm for a scenic two-hour cruise. Also check the myriad cruise options departing from Port Allen Marina Center (p533), further west along the coast.

Festivals & Events

Prince Kuhio Celebration of the Arts (☎ 240-6369; admission free except luau) Day-long celebration, in late March, to honor Prince Johah Kuhio Kalaniana'ole, who was born in 1872 on the site of Prince Kuhio Park (p523). Events include Hawaiiana workshops and an evening luau.

Kaua'i Products Council Craft Fair (☎ 823-8714) When on Kaua'i, buy Kaua'i-made. At this all-day fair in mid-August, you'll find quality products made primarily on Kaua'i, secondarily within Hawaii. Usually located opposite Po'ipu Beach Park.

Kaua'i Mokihana Festival Hula Competition (☎ 822-2166; www.mokihana.kauai.net; Grand Hyatt Po'ipu Resort & Spa; admission $5-10) Three days of serious hula performances in late September, both *kahiko* (ancient) and *'auana* (modern).

Hawaiiana Festival (☎ 742-1234; www.alohafestivals .com; Grand Hyatt Kaua'i Resort & Spa; admission free except luau; ⊙ 8am-noon) Part of the Aloha Festival, this mid-October three-day event features Hawaiian crafts, demonstrations, hula and a luau.

New Year's Eve Fireworks (☎ 742-7444; www .poipubeach.org) Free fireworks on the beach at Po'ipu Beach Park on December 31.

Sleeping

Start by browsing the website listings of **Po'ipu Beach Resort Association** (☎ 742-7444; www.poipu beach.org; PO Box 730, Po'ipu, HI 96756) and **Vacation Rentals By Owner** (www.vrbo.com).

The following vacation rental companies are good starting points:

Grantham Resorts (☎ 742-2000, 800-325-5701; www.grantham-resorts.com; 3176 Po'ipu Rd, Ste 1, Koloa, HI 96756) Well established; main agency for Waikomo Stream Villas and Nihi Kai Villas.

Kaua'i Vacation Rentals (Map p472; ☎ 245-8841, 800-367-5025; www.kauaivacationrentals.com; 3-3311 Kuhio Hwy, Lihu'e, HI 96766) Longtime all-island agency.

Po'ipu Beach Vacation Rentals (☎ 742-2850, 800-684-5133; www.pbvacationrentals.com; PO Box 1258, Koloa, HI 96756) Excellent selection in all price ranges; easy-to-navigate website.

Po'ipu Connection Realty (☎ 800-742-2260; www .poipuconnection.com; PO Box 1022, Koloa, HI 96756) Personalized service; limited selection but includes gems in small, oceanfront complexes.

BUDGET

Prince Kuhio Resort (5061 Lawa'i Rd; studios/1-bedroom units from about $75/135; ⊠ ⊠) While neither new nor spotless, you cannot beat the 90-unit Prince Kuhio for value. Located across the road from Lawa'i (Beach House) Beach, the grounds are pleasantly landscaped with tall trees and a decent-size pool. Units vary markedly in quality. Search online for owners or contact agencies. Po'ipu Connection Realty manages 16 units, including a gem, Unit 331 (per night $75 to $100).

MIDRANGE

Waikomo Stream Villas (☎ 742-7220, 800-325-5701; www.grantham-resorts.com; 2721 Po'ipu Rd; 1-/2-bedroom units from $119/149; ⊠ ⊠) Amid gardens along the serene Waikomo Stream, this 60-unit condo will please the discerning yet thrifty traveler. It feels upscale despite low rates. The 60 units are modern, clean and spacious (averaging 1100 to 1500 sq ft), with lanai, a well-equipped kitchen and washer-dryer. Upgrade to a split-level two-bedroom for vaulted ceilings with lots of light. Po'ipu Beach Vacation Rentals' rates are lower.

Kaua'i Cove Cottages (☎ 651-0279, 800-631-9313; www.kauaicove.com; 2672 Pu'uholo Rd; studio units $125-145) From the outside, the units look boxy and plain. But inside – wow! Bamboo canopy beds, open-beam ceilings, reams of sheer mosquito netting and lots of windows create a romantic tropical retreat. The patios are small, but the kitchens are fully loaded and the cool hardwood floors refresh beached-out feet. Parking stalls are conveniently located at your doorstep.

Po'ipu Plantation Resort (☎ 742-6757, 800-634-0263; www.poipubeach.com; 1792 Pe'e Rd; r incl breakfast $125-210, 1-/2-bedroom units from $135/175; ⊠ ⊠) For a personal touch, choose this nine-unit condo – fantastic value because it's not oceanfront, but the beach is a quick walk away and the units feature spacious rooms, high ceilings, hardwood floors, bedding for four, fully equipped kitchens and lanai.

Hideaway Cove Villas (☎ 635-8785, 866-849-2426; www.hideawaycove.com; 2307 & 2315 Nalo Rd; studios $155-170, 1-/2-bedroom units from $190/255; ⊠ ⊠) Impeccable, modern and professionally managed, Hideaway Cove offers a variety of units in two outstanding villas. All units feature private lanai, hardwood floors, four-post beds, air-con, wi-fi and new appliances that spell upscale. No detail is forgotten: even the full

---

TOP 5 SUNSET SPOTS

- **Hanalei Bay** (p508), especially from the pier
- **Princeville Resort lawn** (p503)
- **Polihale State Park** (p542) or **Kekaha Beach Park** (p541), to spare your car
- **Beach House Restaurant** (p528)
- **Aboard a catamaran** sailing the South Shore (p533)

---

complement of kitchen utensils match! Larger units available.

Po'ipu Palms (☎ 800-742-2260; www.poipuconnection .com; 1697 Pe'e Rd; 2-bedroom units $165-225; ☒) Location, location, location. Po'ipu Palms might resemble a modest one-story complex, but its primo perch overlooking the ocean catapults it to Class A status. The 12 two-bedroom, two-bathroom oceanfront units are 900 sq ft and all decently appointed, but they definitely vary in chic appeal. All include washer-dryer and the soothing soundtrack of endless waves.

Kiahuna Plantation (☎ 742-6411, 800-688-7444; www.outrigger.com; 2253 Po'ipu Rd; 1-/2-bedroom units from $165/289; ☒) Amid luxuriant trees and giant monstera leaves, these airy units are spread between Po'ipu Rd and a swimmable bit of Po'ipu Beach. Each has a fully equipped kitchen, living room and large lanai. The only thing missing is an in-unit washer-dryer. Rates vary widely depending on seasonal availability.

Po'ipu Shores (☎ 742-7700; www.castleresorts.com; 1775 Pe'e Rd; 1-/2-bedroom units from $199/299; ☐ ☒) Believe it or not, the sound of crashing waves is too loud for some. All 39 units are oceanfront, overlooking lava rock and pounding surf. While not extraordinary in style, they're perfectly decent in amenities, with private lanai, full kitchen, washer-dryer, wi-fi and cable TV.

TOP END

In September 2006 the iconic Gloria's Spouting Horn B&B closed when longtime host Gloria Merkle retired.

Alihi Lani (☎ 800-742-2260; www.poipuconnection .com; 2564 Ho'onani Rd; per week $1600; ☒ ☒) For a contemporary boutique condo (with only six units) overlooking the ocean, Alihi Lani's two-bedroom, two-bathroom units should more

than satisfy. At 1150 sq ft, they're spacious, with huge full kitchens, washer-dryer and wide doors begging to be flung open toward the lanai and glorious ocean beyond.

Po'ipu Kapili (☎ 742-6449, 800-443-7714; www .poipukapili.com; 2221 Kapili Rd; 1-/2-bedroom units from $230/320; ☒) Epitomizing functional luxury, this condo shines. While not beachfront, it's close to Po'ipu Beach, with 60 spacious units featuring lots of hardwood, big plush beds, two bathrooms, digital cable and internet access. Only two-bedroom units include washer-dryer.

Sheraton Kaua'i Resort (☎ 742-1661, 800-782-9488; www.sheraton-kauai.com; 2440 Ho'onani Rd; r from $240; ☒ ☒) An open-air design takes advantage of the Sheraton's awesome location on Po'ipu's finest family beach. But the hotel sprawls like an amoeba. Until you reach the pricey Deluxe Garden category (from $375), you'll be in the so-so wing across the road. Ideal for families, this is a decent business-class hotel, not a luxury property.

Grand Hyatt Kaua'i Resort & Spa (☎ 742-1234, 800-554-9288; www.kauai.hyatt.com; 1571 Po'ipu Rd; r internet $340-520, rack $455-685; ☒ ☒) At Po'ipu's top hotel, the island-style architecture manages to complement the natural magnificence outside. Inside, the room decor is typically tropical, but obviously a class above. Highlights include Anara Spa (p525), Po'ipu Bay Golf Course (p525) and a swimming-pool extravaganza featuring a 150ft waterslide. The only downside is its distance from swimmable waters (eg 1 mile to Brennecke's Beach).

Whalers Cove (☎ 742-7571, 800-225-2683; www .whalers-cove.com; 2640 Pu'uholo Rd; 1-/2-bedroom units from $349/479; ☒ ☒ ☐) Whalers Cove, the most luxurious condo in Po'ipu, is perfect for discriminating travelers who want luxury without a smidgen of tourist fuss. Units are spacious, elegant and utterly immaculate, with markedly upmarket furniture, gleaming marble-tile floors and carpeting that pampers your toes. Daily maid service and gracious staff. Call for best offers.

Eating

Take your pick from expensive resort restaurants or mall venues at Po'ipu Shopping Village.

BUDGET

eb's EATS (☎ 742-1979; Po'ipu Shopping Village; breakfast $6, lunch $6-10, dinner $10-12; ☺ 9am-9pm Mon-Fri,

10am-5pm Sat & Sun) For 'healthy gourmet' eats, both vegetarians and omnivores will find satisfaction at this casual counter with patio tables. Sandwiches are especially creative, eg oven-roasted turkey with pesto mayo and wild-mushroom meatloaf. Save room for scrumptious baked goodies.

Joe's on the Green (☎ 742-9696; Kiahuna Plantation Dr; breakfast $5-8, lunch $7-10; ⏱ 7am-5:30pm) Join the locals at this open-air eatery at Kiahuna Golf Club for the early-bird special ($5, served until 9am, Monday to Saturday). For a casual clubhouse setting, the food is quite gourmet, from shrimp cakes with chipotle aioli to 'ahi tempura rolls, to smoked pork ribs falling off the bone.

Puka Dog (☎ 742-6044; www.pukadog.com; Po'ipu Shopping Village; hot dogs $6; ⏱ 11am-6pm Mon-Sat) Homemade hot dogs go gourmet, with toasty buns, a choice of Polish sausage or veggie dog, mild to hot sauce and tropical fruit relish (from mango to pineapple). Wash it down with freshly squeezed lemonade.

Savage Shrimp (☎ 635-0267; cnr Po'ipu & Ho'onani Rds; meals $10; ⏱ 11am-2pm) If you're a fan of garlic and shrimp, find the white van parked on a grassy roadside patch near Koloa Landing for heaped plates of Brazilian-style shrimp cooked with garlic, coconut milk, cilantro and tomatoes. Be prepared for blazing sun and greasy fingers (the shrimp is unpeeled).

Kukui'ula Store (☎ 742-1601; Po'ipu Plaza, 2827 Po'ipu Rd; ⏱ 8am-6:30pm) If you need groceries, head to this small but well-stocked supermarket.

MIDRANGE & TOP END

Yum Cha (☎ 742-1515; Po'ipu Bay Golf Clubhouse; plates $6-20; ⏱ 5-9pm Tue-Sat) Here, Asian-fusion cuisine is presented tapas style. Flavors cover the gamut, from Chinese (dim sum–style dumplings, crispy Mandarin chicken) to Thai (green-papaya salad, lemongrass-and-prawn soup) to Vietnamese (lettuce wraps).

Keoki's Paradise (☎ 742-7535; Po'ipu Shopping Village; café menu $5-11, dinner $17-25; ⏱ 11am-10pm, bar to 11pm) If you're a fan of tiki restaurants, you'll love the tropical onslaught here. Although the whole experience shouts 'touristy,' the food is colorful and tasty. Stick with the fresh fish and the simplest 'naturally grilled' preparation. Save room for Hula Pie, a decadent hunk of macnut ice cream over chocolate-cookie crust.

Roy's Po'ipu Bar & Grill (☎ 742-5000; www.roys restaurant.com; Po'ipu Shopping Village; appetizers $7-12, mains $19-25; ⏱ 5:30-9:30pm) Roy's, poster child of Hawaii Regional Cuisine, is suited to risk-averse foodies. Signature dishes such as pesto-steamed whitefish with cilantro-ginger-peanut oil and grilled shrimp with smoked tomato *beurre blanc* (classic French butter sauce) nicely blend local ingredients with gourmet preparations. Brace for long waits and loud crowds.

Plantation Gardens Restaurant & Bar (☎ 742-2121; www.pgrestaurant.com; Kiahuna Plantation, 2253 Po'ipu Rd; appetizers $8-15, mains $19-26; ⏱ pupu 4pm, dinner 5:30-9pm) If you are sick of the beach-sunset hype, enjoy dinner in a lovely garden setting instead. The menu is mercifully concise and features locally grown ingredients, kiawe (mesquite) grilling (for a rich, smoky flavor) and lots of seafood, eg island-style bouillabaisse (seafood stew) in curry-coconut broth.

Tidepools (☎ 742-6260; Grand Hyatt Kaua'i Resort & Spa, 1571 Po'ipu Rd; mains $23-30; ⏱ 6-10pm) If you're a sucker for the classic 'romantic dinner for two,' you'll enjoy Tidepools, which matches the Grand Hyatt setting in island-style extravagance. The menu favors seafood, from silky sashimi to crab-lobster cakes to the wok-seared 'ahi. Vegetarians are not forgotten, with savory grilled tofu or Shiitake mushroom mains as creative as the rest.

Beach House Restaurant (☎ 742-1424; www.the -beach-house.com; 5022 Lawa'i Rd; dinner mains $20-32; ⏱ 6-10pm) A South Shore icon, the Beach House boasts an outstanding oceanfront setting and good Hawaii Regional Cuisine. The focus is fresh fish; the signature 'ahi taster includes 'ahi poke sushi, 'ahi tostadas and 'ahi hash spring roll. The kids menu will delight.

Naniwa (☎ 742-1661; Sheraton Kaua'i Resort, 2440 Ho'onani Rd; dinner mains $25-45; ⏱ 6-9:30pm Tue-Sat) If you're stuck in Po'ipu with sushi cravings, your only option is Naniwa, which serves flawlessly fresh, impeccably presented, expensive Japanese cuisine. Two-piece nigiri average $11 and maki rolls are $12 to $16, but the combinations are creative.

Drinking & Entertainment

For nighttime entertainment in Po'ipu, the Grand Hyatt's gloss is hard to top.

BARS

Stevenson's Library (☎ 742-1234, 800-554-9288; Grand Hyatt Kaua'i Resort & Spa; 1571 Po'ipu Rd; ⏱ 6-11:45pm) An exclusive gentleman's-club library…on the beach. Might seem incongruous but, hey, why not? From the gleaming 27ft koa-wood bar, enjoy an impressive selection of liquors, fine cigars, live jazz, pool and chess.

Seaview Terrace (☎ 742-1234, 800-554-9288; Grand Hyatt Kaua'i Resort & Spa; 1571 Po'ipu Rd; 🕑 4-11pm) Catch the sunset from indoors here, as the aptly named bar boasts a perfect view. Entertainment includes a nightly torch-lighting ceremony at sunset and either Hawaiian music or *keiki* hula shows (times vary depending on season).

Point (☎ 742-1661; Sheraton Kaua'i Resort; 🕑 11am-midnight) Primo spot for sunset viewing and people-watching. Bar fare is offered but the tropical-umbrella drinks and beer on tap are the main draws – besides the setting.

LUAU & HULA

Grand Hyatt Kaua'i Resort & Spa (☎ 240-6456; 1571 Po'ipu Rd; adult/junior 13-20/child 6-12 $78/68/40; 🕑 5:15pm Sun & Thu) The Drums of Paradise Luau is a well-oiled production befitting the Grand Hyatt setting. For an all-you-can-eat buffet, the food is decent. The indoor show is more glossy than homey and of course includes the Samoan fire dance.

Sheraton Kaua'i Resort (☎ 742-8200; www .sheraton-kauai.com; 2440 Ho'onani Rd; adult/child 6 to 12 $75/37; 🕑 6pm Mon & Fri) Advertised as Kaua'i's only 'oceanfront' luau, the Sheraton's 'Surf to Sunset Luau' is the standard all-you-can-eat buffet and bar, followed by a Polynesian revue.

KALAHEO

pop 3913

Kalaheo is definitely off the tourist track, but, tucked away, you'll find peaceful accommodations that let you become part of the neighborhood. If you plan to hike at Waimea Canyon and Koke'e State Parks but also want easy access to Po'ipu beaches, Kalaheo's central location is ideal.

The town's post office and handful of restaurants are clustered around the intersection of Kaumuali'i Hwy and Papalina Rd.

Sights

KUKUIOLONO PARK

Whether or not you golf, this **park** (🕑 6:30am-6:30pm) is nice for jogging or strolling. You'll see only locals here – along with a panoramic vista of the South Shore, including verdant Lawa'i Valley, the resorts in Po'ipu and the endless Pacific beyond.

Kukuiolono means 'light of Lono,' referring to the torches that Hawaiians once placed on this hill to help guide canoes safely to the shore. In 1860 King Kamehameha III leased the land to Duncan McBryde, whose son, Walter, the pineapple baron, eventually purchased the 178-acre estate. He built the public golf course here in 1929 and later he deeded the entire site to an irrevocable trust, for use as a public park upon his death. Walter McBryde is now buried near the 8th hole of the golf course, which features a modest Japanese garden.

To get here, turn left onto Papalina Rd from Kaumuali'i Hwy (heading west).

HANAPEPE VALLEY LOOKOUT

The scenic lookout that pops up shortly after the 14-mile marker offers a view deep into Hanapepe Valley. The red-clay walls of the cliffs are topped by a layer of green cane, like frosting on a cake. This sight is but a teaser of the dramatic vistas awaiting at Waimea Canyon.

While old king sugar might still dominate Hanapepe Valley, look across the highway toward the ocean to see Kaua'i's current major commercial crop, coffee.

DETOUR: PU'U ROAD SCENIC DRIVE

Pu'u Rd is a scenic side-loop passing small ranches, grand mango trees and fine coastal views. It's a winding country road, only one lane with some blind curves, but nothing tricky if you go slow and honk on the hairpins. And it's so quiet, you might not even encounter another car.

After leaving Kukuiolono Park, turn right onto Pu'u Rd to start the drive. It's just over 3 miles back to Kaumuali'i Hwy this way. About halfway along, you'll look down on Port Allen's oil tanks and the town of Numila, with its old sugar mill.

Down the slope on the west side of the road are coffee trees, part of a total of 4000 acres that have been planted between Koloa and 'Ele'ele – an attempt to diversify the former sugarcane land.

Activities

Kukuiolono Golf Course (☎ 332-9151; Kukuiolono Park; green fees adult/child $8/3, pull carts $6; ⏰ 6:30am-6:30pm) is an unassuming, nine-hole, par-36 golf course with scenic ocean and valley views and earthy appeal (see bags of chicken feed for the fowl on the fairway). Grab a bucket of balls for $2 and hit the driving range, first-come, first-served.

Others might prefer **Poise Pilates** (☎ 651-5287; 4432 Papalina Rd; private session per hr $65), where owner and instructor Theresa Ouano is a model of energy and fitness.

Sleeping

Seaview Suite (☎ 332-9744; www.seakauai.com; 3913 Uluali'i St; studios/ste $75/85) In a quiet neighborhood, find two comfy ground-floor units with lovely sunset and ocean views. The one-bedroom suite includes full kitchen, separate living and dining areas and bedding for four. Budget travelers can bunk in the Ti Room, a cozy studio with kitchenette (including full-size refrigerator).

Hale Ikena Nui (☎ 332-9005, 800-550-0778; www .kauaivacationhome.com; 3957 Uluali'i St; r incl breakfast $75, 1-bedroom units $95; 🖳) Home sweet home: the large B&B room in a clean, airy, island house includes private bathroom and use of owner's kitchen, living room and wraparound deck. The spacious one-bedroom unit (1000 sq ft) includes a sofabed, full kitchen and washer-dryer. Wi-fi and irresistible pet dog on site.

Kalaheo Inn (☎ 332-6023, 888-332-6023; www.kala heoinn.com; 4444 Papalina Rd; studios/1-/2-bedroom units from $80/90/120) Like the surrounding town, Kalaheo Inn is unpretentious, dependable and quietly pleasant. The 14 tidy units come in a range of sizes, configurations and bed types. All feature modern furnishings, kitchen or kitchenette and TV-VCR. Studio 13, which includes a full-sized fridge, is the best value. Wi-fi in the office only, but you might be able to catch it (especially if you're nearby in one-bedroom units 1, 2 or 3).

Bamboo Jungle House (☎ 332-5515, 888-332-5115; www.bamboojunglehouse.com; 3829 Waha Rd; r incl breakfast $130-160; 🖳🖳) Behold a tropical oasis at this upscale B&B, complete with garden lap pool amid jungly foliage, lava-rock waterfall and gazebo (where massages can be arranged). The three units are immaculate, with snow-white walls, fluffy canopy beds, sparkling French doors and wi-fi. A distinctive property, it's geared toward couples and no kids are allowed.

Eating

Mark's Place (☎ 332-0050; 2-3687 Kaumuali'i Hwy; plates $6-7; ⏰ 10am-8pm Mon-Fri) East of Kalaheo, this local fave has opened a second location. The classic, generous plate lunches feature meaty mains from teriyaki beef to Korean chicken – plus brown/white rice and green/macaroni salad. Daily specials go gourmet, with mains such as salmon atop greens with soy-wasabi vinaigrette.

Kalaheo Café & Coffee Co (☎ 332-5858; www.kala heo.com; 2-2560 Kaumuali'i Hwy; breakfast & lunch $6-10, dinner $16-26; ⏰ 6am-2:30pm daily, 5:30-8:30pm Wed-Sat) First known for its breakfasts and melt-in-your-mouth 'cinnamon knuckle' pastry, this neighborhood café now serves gourmet, if eclectic, dinners. Hunan-style pork tenderloin is paired with pineapple marmalade and mashed potato, while the fresh-catch enchilada features herb polenta. Economize by ordering grilled sandwiches from the lunch menu till closing.

Brick Oven Pizza (☎ 332-8561; Kaumuali'i Hwy; 10-/12-/15-inch pizza from $10/14/20; ⏰ 11am-10pm Tue-Sun) Always jammed with tourists, Brick Oven has developed a cult following. The brick-oven pies are tasty, but mainland aficionados might be underwhelmed. Ideal for vegetarians: a truly meatless combo piled with premium veggies and stock-free sauce.

Camp House Grill (☎ 332-9755; Kaumuali'i Hwy; breakfast & burgers $4-6, dinner $10-12; ⏰ 6:30am-9:30pm) Set in a weathered ol' plantation building, this diner is known for its burgers and, especially, its pies (per slice $3.50, whole $10 to $15), from pineapple cream cheese to chocolate-chip macadamia. Mains are generous standards: catch of the day, *huli huli* (rotisserie) chicken, barbecued ribs. Expect neither fancy nor spotless.

Pomodoro (☎ 332-5945; Rainbow Plaza, Kaumuali'i Hwy; dinner mains $10-20; ⏰ 6-9pm) The casual, neighborly Pomodoro, run by a longtime Kaua'i couple, features traditional Italian food, a rarity on Kaua'i. Try the hearty minestrone soup with fresh veggies and homemade pastas. Service is prompt and friendly.

Kalaheo Steak House (☎ 332-9780; 4444 Papalina Rd; dinner $20-33; ⏰ 6-10pm) An island fixture, Kalaheo Steak House is masculinely cozy and dimly lit, with faux-leather-upholstered booths, an empty adjoining bar and a working-class clubby feel. Dig into 'real food,' like steak, from a 12oz sirloin to an insanely huge 24oz prime rib.

WESTSIDE

The Westside is Kaua'i's rugged last frontier. The striking red-dirt landscape might seem stark compared with the sublime, fertile beauty of the North Shore. In this big-sky country, the palette is earthy, with dusty maroon hills alongside fields of cane and coffee. Straight swaths of sandy beach seem endless, as does the sweeping Pacific horizon.

With no major resorts and only a handful of restaurants, the Westside remains rural, rough around the edges and very local in flavor. Quiet villages are throwbacks to the plantation era. 'God's Country' they call the Westside, for its multitude of Christian churches, simple wooden structures that match the surroundings.

Of its three major towns (all with populations less than 3500), Hanapepe is the quaintest, with an artists colony amid Old West architecture. Waimea boasts the most commercial development, with inns and cottages, plus the island's largest brewpub. Kekaha, while still a sleepy beach community, is an oft-missed fount of accommodations, with dozens of vacation-rental homes for all pocketbooks.

Of course, nature is the real draw – and the star attraction is Waimea Canyon, a massive chasm revealing layers of ancient lava flows. Steep hikes in and around the canyon illustrate Kaua'i's unique geology and ecology – and challenge even the most surefooted trekkers.

'ELE'ELE & NUMILA
pop 2040

It's just a tiny residential cluster, but **'Ele'ele** draws folks from surrounding towns for its mini strip mall at the 16-mile marker. Nothing special: supermarket, bank, launderette and **post office** (8am-4pm Mon-Fri, 9-11am Sat).

You'll also find two decent eateries: in a nondescript setting, **Toi's Thai Kitchen** (335-3111; 'Ele'ele Shopping Center, 4469 Waialo Rd; mains $12-18; take-out 11am-2pm Tue-Sat, restaurant 5:30-9pm Tue-Sat) offers plenty of tasty family-style dishes. At **Grinds Café** (335-6027; www.grindscafé.net; 'Ele'ele Shopping Center, 4469 Waialo Rd; breakfast $4-7, lunch $4.50-9; 5:30am-6pm) you'll find hearty diner food like omelettes, deli sandwiches, salads and local-style meaty plates. Dressings, breads and hamburger patties are homemade.

Nearby **Numila** is a former cane town with tin-roof wooden houses surrounding a defunct sugar mill. At the southwest edge of town is **Kaua'i Coffee Company** (335-0813, 800-545-8605; www.kauaicoffee.com; Halewili Rd; 9am-5pm), the state's largest coffee operation. The little **museum** (admission free) is mainly an inducement to buy coffee, which you can sample for free at the on-site café. To get here, take Halewili Rd (Hwy 540), which passes acres of coffee fields and intersects Kaumuali'i Hwy near Kalaheo and 'Ele'ele.

PORT ALLEN

In the late 1800s Port Allen, located immediately south of 'Ele'ele on Hanapepe Bay, was a major port called 'Ele'ele Landing. Today the port is Kaua'i's busiest recreational boat harbor.

Don't expect a picturesque dock: Port Allen is the unloading point for fuel serving the adjacent electric plant and it provides a dock for vessels working with the Pacific Missile Range

---

THAR SHE BLOWS!

On Kaua'i, the first sign of winter is not snow or ice, it's the arrival of 2000 to 5000 whales. Shallow, warm Hawaiian waters are a key habitat for the endangered humpback whale. Nearly two-thirds of the entire North Pacific population migrates here from the Gulf of Alaska between November and May.

In Hawaiian waters they breed, calve and nurse their young. Males compete for female attention, slamming each other with their powerful tail flukes and emitting mysterious sounds. The females and the young are showy too, slapping the surface of the water with their distinctively long pectoral fins and by breaching (launching into the air).

To learn more, check the website of the **Hawaiian Islands Humpback Whale National Marine Sanctuary** (246-2860; www.hawaiihumpbackwhale.noaa.gov; Suite 206, 4370 Kukui Grove Street, Lihu'e, HI 96766).

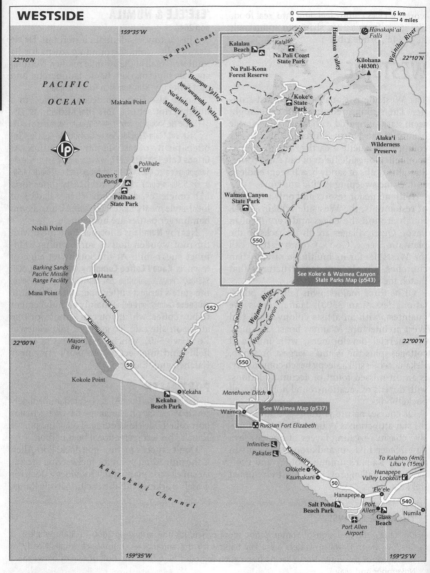

WESTSIDE

Facility (p541). There are no accommodations or eateries in Port Allen: your nearest best bets are Hanapepe, less than a mile away, for eats, and Kaleheo, 5 miles away, for sleeps.

Information

The Port Allen Marina Center just up from the harbor has most of the tour offices.

West Side Copy Center (☎ 335-9990; Port Allen Marina Center, 4353 Waialo Rd; per hr $6; ☷ 8am-6pm Mon-Fri, 8am-noon Sat) has internet access.

Sights

Colorful bits of sea glass decorate the sand along **Glass Beach**, just to the east of Port Allen. The smooth glass 'pebbles' originated from a long-abandoned dumpsite nearby, worn and weathered after decades of wave action. Sometimes the glass is plentiful, other times most is washed out to sea.

To get to the little cove, take Aka'ula St, the last left before entering the Port Allen commercial harbor, go past the fuel storage tanks and then curve to the right down a rutted dirt road that leads 100yd to the beach.

Activities

DIVING

Mana Divers (☎ 335-0881; www.manadivers.com; Bay 3, Port Allen Boat Harbor, 4310 Waialo Rd) offers boat dives, night dives and certification courses, but Fathom Five Divers (p519) in Koloa is superior.

SNORKELING & WHALE-WATCHING

Port Allen is the launching point for the majority of Kaua'i's catamaran and raft tours, but also consider the tours departing from Hanalei Bay (p510), during summer months only, and Kikialoha Small Boat Harbor (p538) in Kekaha, both of which start closer to the North Shore.

Most snorkeling tours head to the Na Pali Coast and the main decision is whether to go by catamaran (motorized or sailing) or by raft. Certainly rafts are the most exhilarating, bouncing along the water and entering caves (in mellower weather), but most lack rest rooms and shade. Catamarans are cushier, with smooth rides, rest rooms, ample shade and amenities such as water slides and trampolines for sunning.

Catamarans

A major player in the cruise business, **Holoholo Charters** (☎ 335-0815, 800-848-6130; www.holoholo charters.com; Port Allen Marina Center, Waialo Rd; ☽ 6am-8pm) sails two catamarans, a 50ft sailing 'cat' and a 65ft power vessel. Snorkel tours include a seven-hour Ni'ihau and Na Pali snorkel tour (adult/child aged six to 12 $175/125) and a five-hour morning tour (adult/child aged five to 12 $135/95). The big boat, especially, is fast and cushy.

The longtime Hawaiian-owned **Catamaran Kahanu** (☎ 645-6176, 888-213-7711; www.catamaran kahanu.com; Port Allen Marina Center, Waialo Rd) offers five-hour snorkeling tours (adult/child aged four to 11 $135/85). This outfit feels local and less commercial, and on tour you can watch a demonstration on weaving *ti* leaves and *hau* (pandanas) and coconut fibers into fishing lines, nets, etc.

WISE WORDS

A T-shirt is a T-shirt is a T-shirt is a T-shirt? Minds might differ, but on Kaua'i it's *caveat emptor* regarding the iconic Kimo's Hawaiian Rules T-shirts and paraphernalia. The authentic producer of those words is **Nite Owl T-Shirts** (☎ 335-6110, 888-430-9907; www.niteowlt-shirts.com; Waialo Rd; ☽ 9am-5pm Fri-Tue, 7am-4pm Wed & Thu), a screenprinting company established in 1985. Don't be fooled by copycats who have swiped their famous words. You can find reasonably priced shirts in assorted styles, including femme tanks and extra-extra-extra-large sizes, at the Port Allen headquarters.

Kimo's Hawaiian Rules

▪ Never judge a day by the weather.

▪ The best things in life aren't things.

▪ Tell the truth – there's less to remember.

▪ Speak softly and wear a loud shirt.

▪ Goals are deceptive – the unaimed arrow never misses.

▪ He who dies with the most toys – still dies.

▪ Age is relative – when you're over the hill you pick up speed.

▪ There are two ways to be rich – make more or desire less.

▪ Beauty is internal – looks mean nothing.

▪ No rain – no rainbows®.

The power catamaran tours run by **Capt Andy's Sailing Adventures** (☎ 335-6833, 800-535-0830; www.napali.com; Port Allen Marina Center, Waialo Rd) go to Na Pali for five hours of snorkeling (adult/child aged two to 12 $139/99). Prices often drop by $10 online. Groups tend to be large.

Blue Dolphin Charters (☎ 335-5553, 877-511-1311; www.kauaiboats.com; Port Allen Marina Center, Waialo Rd) offers snorkeling and diving tours, including a seven-hour Ni'ihau jaunt (internet/regular price $175/196) and the standard five-hour Na Pali deal (internet/regular $126/147). Prices include tax.

Kaua'i Sea Tours (☎ 826-7254, 800-733-7997; www.kauaiseatours.com; Aka'ula St, Port Allen) offers Na Pali tours by catamaran (adult/child from $139/99) or by rigid hull raft (adult/child from $129/89).

Most companies also offer sunset tours (no snorkeling) that include drinks and dinner or *pupu* (appetizers). Some try to up the 'romance' factor with no-children cruises.

Rafts

For zippier excitement, tour Na Pali in Zodiac rafts instead. Capt Andy's sister outfit, **Captain Zodiac Raft Adventures** (☎ 335-6833, 800-535-0830; www.napali.com; Port Allen Marina Center, Waialo Rd), offers a 5½-hour tour (adult/child $129/89) year-round. Remember, no shade and no rest rooms.

Shopping

Kauai Chocolate Company (☎ 335-0448; www.kauaichocolate.com; 4341 Waialo Rd; ☺ 11am-5pm Mon-Sat, noon-5pm Sun) Chocoholics, this is *the* place to get your fix. Signature treats include the Krabs (with caramel, pretzels and macs), luscious fudge, Piko Bars (edible body goo) and lots of sugar-free options. For massive decadence, buy Da Brick ($18.50), a 16oz hunk of macadamia toffee, caramel, chocolate and more.

HANAPEPE

pop 2153

At first glance, Hanapepe resembles the Wild West, with retro wooden buildings and dusty roads baking under the sun. But behind the quaint facades are over a dozen art galleries, plus a handful of unique shops and restaurants. It's worth a stop, especially on Friday night (see opposite).

Locals are proud of Hanapepe's vintage architecture, which includes over 40 sites

that meet State or Federal National Historic Register criteria. Unfortunately Hurricane 'Iniki obliterated about half of Hanapepe's irreplaceable buildings in 1992, but the town's traditional essence remains.

Indeed Hanapepe substituted for the Australian outback in the TV miniseries *The Thorn Birds*, for the Filipino Olongapo City in the movie *Flight of the Intruder* and for any Hawaiian town in Disney's animated movie *Lilo and Stitch*.

History

In the early 1800s Hanapepe was a thriving, taro-farming, Native Hawaiian community. But Hanapepe's native population declined from introduced diseases and by 1870 only a small village remained. Chinese rice growers arrived in the 1860s, while Japanese plantation workers came in the early 1900s. Hanapepe became a haven for the sugar-plantation malcontents, including labor-union organizers and restless, entrepreneurial laborers who started small businesses or farms.

In the early 1900s, Hanapepe was a bustling commercial center, popular for military R&R, but in the late 1930s, Lihue became the island's shipping, business and political seat. Hanapepe ebbed further when the main highway bypassed the town center, but today the town is transforming itself into an artists colony and tourist stop.

Orientation & Information

Veer *mauka* onto Hanapepe Rd at the 'Kaua'i's Biggest Little Town' sign.

American Savings Bank (☎ 335-3118; 4548 Kona Rd)

Bank of Hawaii (☎ 335-5021; 3764 Hanapepe Rd) On the western end of Hanapepe Rd.

Post office (☎ 335-5433, 800-275-8777; 3817 Kona Rd; ☺ 8:30am-12:30pm & 1-4pm Mon-Fri, 9:30-11:30am Sat)

Sights & Activities

Find a copy of Hanapepe's 'Walking Tour Map' ($2), which describes the town's historic buildings. On your stroll, don't miss the **Swinging Bridge**, which crosses the Hanapepe River. Its funky old predecessor fell victim to 'Iniki, but in a community-wide effort this new bridge was erected in 1996.

SALT POND BEACH PARK

Salt Pond Beach Park is one of Kaua'i's best family beaches – and even better because it

---

MEET THE ARTISTS

A sleepy village by day, Hanapepe boasts one of the best weekly nighttime events on the island: **Hanapepe Art Night** (6-9pm Fri). Along the main street, Hanapepe Rd, shops and galleries stay open late, offering refreshments and a chance to meet the artists. Most of the 15 or so galleries are owner-run, making Hanapepe a true artists colony.

Notables include the following:

Arius Hopman Gallery (☎ 335-0227; www.hopmanart.com; 3840-C Hanapepe Rd; 10:30am-3:30pm Mon-Thu, to 9pm Fri) A Kaua'i resident since the early 1990s, the well-traveled Hopman is an engineer-turned- watercolorist; his representational renderings of Kaua'i are easy on the eye.

Art of Marbling (☎ 482-1472; 3890 Hanapepe Rd; 10am-5pm Sat-Thu, to 9pm Fri) Becky J Wold creates exquisite marbled silks, which make unique scarves, sarongs, wraps or wall art. Also on display are Robert Bader's gorgeous wood sculpture, including translucent Norfolk pine bowls.

Banana Patch (☎ 335-5944; 800-914-5944; www.bananapatchstudio.com; 3865 Hanapepe Rd; square tiles 4/6in $17/28; 10am-4:30pm Sat-Thu, to 9pm Fri) Home of the colorfully painted 'Mahalo for removing your shoes' hanging tiles, originated by Joanna Carolan. Also find handpainted platters and bowls, fine jewelry and other gifts.

Kauai Fine Arts (☎ 335-3778; www.brunias.com; 3751 Hanapepe Rd; 9:30am-4:30pm Mon-Thu & Sat, to 9pm Fri) A wide-ranging collection of antique maps and prints, plus Ni'ihau shell jewelry and other exquisite handiwork.

Talk Story: The Bookstore (☎ 335-6469; www.talkstorybookstore.com; 3785 Hanapepe Rd; 10:30am-5:30pm Mon-Thu, 10:30am-10pm Fri) A used bookstore that's also the town's gathering place: live music (7pm to 10pm Friday), cribbage (1pm Tuesday), chess (4pm Thursday), wi-fi (per 15 minutes $2.50) and book signings. Owners Ed and Cynthia exude aloha spirit.

Vintage Aloha (☎ 335-5797; www.vintagealohagallery.com; 3900 Hanapepe Rd; 11-5pm Mon, Wed, Thu, & Sat, 1-9pm Fri) Gallery owner Melinda Morey has created an attractive space to showcase fine vintage Hawaiiana, jewelry, artsy books, home furnishings and her own vivid paintings.

---

has remained untouristy. Beyond the long stretch of sand, the water in the cove reaches up to a depth of 10ft and works well for swimming laps (four times across is equivalent to 0.5 miles) and also for windsurfing. Both ends of the cove are shallow and good for kids. Along with a lifeguard, amenities include picnic tables, BBQ grills, showers and campsites.

The park is named for its famous salt ponds toward the eastern edge, where Hawaiians have traditionally made rock salt from seawater. Often, this *alae* salt is tinted red from adding a bit of Kaua'i's ubiquitous iron-rich earth.

To get here, turn left just just after passing the 17-mile marker, onto Lele Rd, then right onto Lokokai Rd.

FLYING
For a real adrenaline high, take an ultralight lesson with **Birds in Paradise** (☎ 822-5309; www.birdsinparadise.com; Burns Field, Puolo Rd; 30-min/1hr lesson $96/165). You can also do a round-the-island lesson on one of these powered hang gliders for $300. Take the road for Salt Pond Beach Park to reach the airport.

Tours
For anyone with fantasies of riding M*A*S*H copters with Hawkeye, **Inter-Island Helicopter** (☎ 335-5009, 800-656-5009; www.interislandhelicopters.com; 1-3410 Kaumuali'i Hwy; flights regular/waterfall $185/250) is the only way to go. Their copters fly without doors, meaning you feel the wind on your face (and perhaps a spray of mist) and enjoy panoramic views. Tours depart from Burns Field on Lokokai Rd, en route to Salt Pond Beach Park.

For a truly off-the-beaten-track trip, fly to Ni'ihau with Ni'ihau Helicopters (p457).

Sleeping & Eating
Hanapepe is more a daytripper spot than a home base, but Salt Pond Beach Park offers convenient camping (see p460 for permit information). Rentals are scarce here, but one sweet deal within walking distance of town is **Hanapepe Riverside** (☎ 261-1693; www.affordable-paradise.com; 4466 Puolo Rd; 1-bedroom units $85), a sizeable, upstairs unit with full kitchen, use of washer-dryer and expansive deck overlooking Hanapepe River.

Kaua'i Pupu Factory (☎ 335-0084; 1-3566 Kaumuali'i Hwy; plate lunch $6.25, 'ahi poke per lb $9; 9am-5:30pm

Mon-Fri, to 3pm Sat) Stop for local grinds, including dried, smoked fish, deep-fried *ika* (squid) and purple-sweet-potato tempura. If you're curious to try Hawaiian food, don't miss the mouthwatering plate lunch with *laulau* or *kalua* pork with rice, *lomilomi* salmon and *poke* (see p56 if you're baffled by these dishes).

Omoide Bakery & Wong's Chinese Restaurant (☎ 335-5066, 335-5291; 1-3543 Kaumuali'i Hwy; mains $7.50-9.75; ☒ 9:30am-9pm Tue-Sat) Established in 1956, this slightly divey Chinese diner also specializes in pies – *liliko'i* chiffon pie, a Kaua'i obsession. The Hong Kong and Cantonese menu features the usual laundry list of chicken, beef, pork and seafood dishes. It is on the seaward side of the highway.

Hanapepe Café (☎ 335-5011; 3830 Hanapepe Rd; lunch $6-10, dinner $18-25; ☒ 11am-3pm Mon-Thu, 11am-2pm & 6-9pm Fri) Hanapepe's only upscale restaurant happens to be a gourmet destination. The food is elegant, from the smoked-mozzarella frittata to Swiss-chard-filled ravioli. The Friday dinner menu changes fortnightly but might include seared *ono* in saffron sauce or Mediterranean veg over garlic-smashed potatoes. Live music by notable slack-key artist Cindy Combs.

Assuage a snack attack with shave ice and crack seed at **Hawaiian Hut Delights** (☎ 335-3781; Hanapepe Rd; shave ice from $2; ☒ noon-5pm Mon-Fri) or irresistible taro chips from **Taro Ko Chips Factory** (☎ 335-5586; 3940 Hanapepe Rd; per small bag $2.50; ☒ 8am-5pm), a dilapidated kitchen 'factory' where elderly Mrs Nagamine still fries the sliced taro (and potato and purple sweet potato) in massive black woks at dawn. In Hanapepe you'll find the Kaua'i headquarters and factory of **Lappert's** (☎ 335-6121; www.lapperts.com; 1-3555 Kaumuali'i Hwy; ☒ 10am-6pm), which sells Hawaii's most famous premium ice cream.

OLOKELE & KAUMAKANI

Olokele exists only for the Olokele Sugar Company, the last remaining sugar producer on Kaua'i, and Kaumakani exists only as the headquarters of **Gay & Robinson** (☎ 335-2824; www.robinsonadventures.com; 2 Kaumakani Ave), owners of this plantation and the island of Ni'ihau (see p456).

Sugar once ruled Kaua'i's economy but, when Lihue Plantation closed in 2000 due to unprofitability, Gay & Robinson became the sole diehard. In the entire state, only one other

sugar company remains: Hawaii Commercial & Sugar on Maui.

The road to Gay & Robinson headquarters and the sugar mill, which comes up immediately after the 19-mile marker on Kaumuali'i Hwy, is shaded by lovely tall trees and lined with classic century-old lampposts. Taking this short drive offers a glimpse into plantation life. Everything is covered with a layer of red dust from the surrounding fields. Quite a few indigenous Ni'ihauans live in this area, many of them working for the Robinsons.

At the end of the road is a simple **visitors center** (admission free; ☒ 8am-4pm Mon-Fri, 11am-3pm Sat), which is more gift shop than anything. More interesting are the two-hour **mill tours** (☒ 8:45am & 12:45pm Mon-Fri), especially when the mill is actually munching the cane and cranking out the sugar, which isn't always the case. To further explore the vast ranchland, Gay & Robinson also offers ATV tours ($99 to $145; reservations required). Unlike other ATV tours, this one focuses on the landscape and history, not thrill-riding, and reaches an elevation of 1500ft.

WAIMEA
pop 1787

Although Waimea (literally 'reddish water') is no longer a major destination, it boasts a storied history. Captain Cook of the British navy first came ashore the Hawaiian Islands here in 1778. King Kaumuali'i welcomed the first missionaries here in 1820. In 1884 Waimea Sugar moved in and the settlement bloomed into a plantation town. In fact, Waimea was the capital of Kaua'i until the mid-1800s.

Today it remains the Westside's major town, but it's tiny. Don't expect more than basic shopping and a handful of eateries. While nightlife is nonexistent, Waimea boasts the only movie theater on the Westside and South Shore. It makes a convenient base for exploring Waimea Canyon and Koke'e State Parks.

Note that Waimea also refers to a district, a river, a valley and a town on Kaua'i – and there is a Waimea valley on O'ahu and another Waimea town on the Big Island.

Information

Check the website of **West Kaua'i Business and Professional Association** (www.wkbpa.org) to learn more about Waimea.

First Hawaiian Bank (☎ 338-1611; 4525 Panako Rd) On Waimea's central square.

Na Pali Explorer (☎ 338-9999, 877-335-9909; www
.napali-explorer.com; Kaumuali'i Hwy; internet per 30
min $3; ☺ 7am-5pm) A one-stop shop for internet
access, simple souvenirs, light snacks and snorkel-cruise
bookings.

Post office (☎ 800-275-8777; 9911 Waimea Rd)

West Kaua'i Medical Center (☎ 338-9431; Waimea
Canyon Dr) Emergency-room services 24 hours.

Sights
HISTORIC TOWN CENTER
Downtown Waimea's classic style comes from
wooden buildings with historic facades, such
as the neoclassical **First Hawaiian Bank** (1929)
and the Art Deco **Waimea Theatre** (1938).

The **statue** of Captain Cook in the center of
town is a replica of the original statue by Sir
John Tweed that stands in Whitby, England.
The great navigator, clutching his charts and
decked out in his finest captaining threads,
now watches over traffic on Kaumuali'i
Hwy.

Waimea Foreign Mission Church (cnr Huakai & Makeke
Rds) was originally a thatched structure built
in 1826 by the Reverend Samuel Whitney,
the first missionary to Waimea. The present
church was built of sandstone blocks and coral
mortar in 1858 by another missionary, the
Reverend George Rowell.

In 1865 Reverend Rowell had a spat with
some folks in the congregation and went off to
build the **Waimea Hawaiian Church** (Kaumuali'i Hwy;
☺ service 8:30am Sun), a wooden-frame church
that was downed in the 1992 hurricane but has

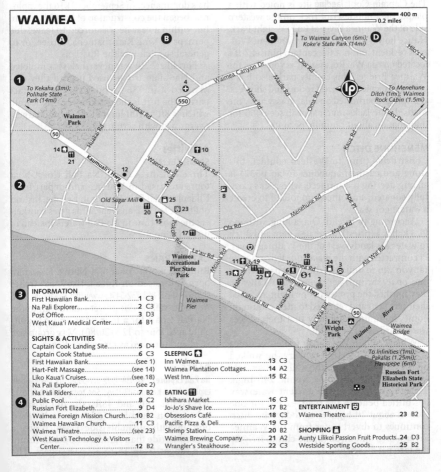

WAIMEA

0 ——————— 400 m
0 ——————— 0.2 miles

KAUA'I

been rebuilt. Sunday services include hymns sung in Hawaiian.

WEST KAUA'I TECHNOLOGY & VISITORS CENTER

While not a must-see, this state-funded center (☎ 338-1332; 9565 Kaumuali'i Hwy; admission free; ☽ 9:30am-5pm Mon-Fri) offers interesting photo and artifact displays on local history from a technology perspective, plus a great assortment of books for sale. Volunteers from the center lead 90-minute walking tours (donations accepted; ☽ 9:30am Mon) of historic Waimea and free lei-making workshops (donations accepted; ☽ 9:30am Fri); reservations preferred.

LUCY WRIGHT PARK

The Captain Cook landing site is noted with a plaque on a nondescript rock on the western side of the Waimea River at Lucy Wright Park. Notice how it's named after a prominent Waimea resident and not the captain himself? It's located on Ala Wai Rd, as soon as you cross the Waimea Bridge. This county park also has a ball field, picnic tables, rest rooms and showers. Camping is permitted on a flat grassy area, the roadside site lacks much appeal; see p460 for information about camping permits.

MENEHUNE DITCH

Constructed prior to Western contact, this stone and earthen aqueduct (Map p532) is an engineering masterpiece, with rocks carefully squared, smoothed and joined to create a watertight seal.

According to legend, Ola, a king, ordered Pi, a kahuna (priest), to create a dam and ditch to water his lands west of the Waimea River. Pi contracted with the *menehune* living on the canyon rim to build the ditch for payment of one '*opae* (shrimp) per *menehune*. As always, they finished the project in one night, received their payment and returned to their mountain home, humming so loudly that their voices were heard as far as O'ahu.

When Captain Vancouver visited Waimea at the close of the 18th century, he walked up the river valley atop the wall of this ditch, estimating the walls to be around 24ft high. These days most of the ancient waterway lies buried beneath the road, except for one section about 2ft high. Even today, the ditch continues to divert water from the Waimea River along, and through, the cliff to irrigate the taro patches below.

To get here, turn at the police station onto Menehune Rd and go almost 1.5 miles up the Waimea River. The ditch is along the left side of the road after a tiny parking area.

RUSSIAN FORT ELIZABETH

The remains of this fort (1816–64) stand above the east bank of the Waimea River. It looks like a boring abandoned stone wall but the historical backstory might surprise you.

In a nutshell, the Russians were interested in Hawaii as a supply spot between Russia and the Pacific Northwest, where they monopolized the seal and otter fur trade. A Russian diplomat ingratiated himself with Kaua'i's King Kaumuali'i, who figured the Russians might help him overcome King Kamehameha's dominance. In September 1816 the diplomat began the construction of Fort Elizabeth, but within a year he was forced to leave, due perhaps to King Kamehameha's orders or to general suspicion of the Russians.

Fort Elizabeth was nevertheless completed and Hawaiian troops used it until they dismantled it in 1864. Today the most intact part of the fort is the exterior lava-rock wall, which is 8ft to 10ft high in places and largely overgrown with scrub.

Activities

SNORKELING

Three outfitters doing Na Pali Coast boat tours are based in Waimea and depart from Kikiaola Small Boat Harbor in Kekaha, instead of Port Allen in Hanapepe. This gives snorkelers the most time in Na Pali waters instead of just cruising there.

CATAMARANS

Run by Liko Ho'okano, a Native Hawaiian born and raised on Kaua'i, Liko Kaua'i Cruises (☎ 338-0333, 888-732-5456; www.liko-kauai.com; 9875 Waimea Rd) sails a 49ft power catamaran to the Na Pali Coast for a four-hour cruise (adult/child aged four to 12 $120/80). Max group size is 34 and tours go as far as Ke'e Beach.

RAFTS

Na Pali Explorer (☎ 338-9999, 877-335-9909; www.napali-explorer.com; Kaumuali'i Hwy; 5hr tour adult/child 5-12 $125/85) has 26ft and 48ft rafts doing snorkel trips on rigid-hull inflatable rafts (hard bottom with inflatable sides), which give a smoother ride than standard Zodiacs. Group size ranges from 16 to 35 passengers. The larger raft includes a rest room and canopy for shade.

If you want a wild raft adventure, **Na Pali Riders** (☎ 742-6331; www.napaliriders.com; Kaumuali'i Hwy; 4hr tour adult/child 5-12 $99/89) fits the bill – but the rigid-hull inflatables are markedly more comfortable. The four-hour tour explores the entire Na Pali Coast, enters sea caves, encounters dolphins and other marine life and bounces you up and down with each wave. If waters are choppy, you'll feel it.

SURFING

Just before the entrance to Russian Fort Elizabeth, immediately after the 21-mile marker, you'll notice cars parked on the side of the highway. This is the access point to a popular surf break called **Pakalas**. Park here and take the short dirt path to the beach. East of the stone jetty, you'll find good-sized swells and a stretch of gorgeous golden beach backed by swaying palms. Another break nearby is called **Infinities** for its lengthy ride. Both are suitable for experienced surfers only.

MASSAGE & YOGA

Hart-Felt Massage (☎ 338-2240; www.hartfeltmassage.com; Waimea Plantation Cottages, Unit 40, 9400 Kaumuali'i Hwy; massage $46-155; spa & skin treatments $55-130; ☺ 9am-6pm Mon-Sat, by appointment Sun) offers an array of massages, spa and skin treatments. Also offered is an oceanfront **yoga class** (☎ 338-2240; $13; ☺ 5pm Tue, 8:30am Sat & Sun), which might provide an adequate intro for newbies. Serious yoga students: don't bother.

SWIMMING

For lap swimming, there's a **public pool** (☎ 338-1271; 9707 Tsuchiya Rd) at Waimea High School; call for schedule.

Festivals & Events

Waimea Town Celebration (☎ 338-1332; www.wkbpa.org; admission free) Free fun in mid-February includes rodeo, canoe race, food, crafts, and lei and hula competitions.

Waimea Lighted Christmas Parade (☎ 338-9957) Watch lighted floats through Waimea town. Parade starts at dusk, a week before Christmas.

Sleeping

For a rural town, Waimea lodging is steep. Also check nearby Kekaha's listings (p541).

Waimea Rock Cabin (☎ 822-7944, 338-9015; www.a1vacations.com/kauaiwaimearockcabin/1; Menehune Rd;

cabin per day/week $50/300) No touristy hubbub in this simple studio cabin amid stark, red-dirt vistas, about 1.5 miles northeast of town. It's clean and quiet, surrounded by citrus trees and local neighbors. The king bed, kitchenette, satellite TV and phone make for a cozy stay. Ideal for no-frills travelers planning multiple trips up to the canyon.

Inn Waimea (☎ 338-0031; www.innwaimea.com; 4469 Halepule Rd; r from $135, cottages $150; ☐) Close to the heart of Waimea, this lovely old missionary home with four guest rooms combines historic character with modern comforts. Rooms include the expected amenities plus high-speed internet connections and shared living room. The two-bedroom cottages give you more for your money.

West Inn (☎ 338-1107, 866-937-8466; www.thewestinn.com; 9686 Kaumuali'i Hwy; r $139; ☒ ☐) You can't miss this little motel-style inn, located right on the main drag, across from Waimea Theatre. Rooms are Best Western motel quality: clean and comfy, with either king or double beds, phone, cable TV, wi-fi, lanai and kitchenette. Rather steep, but competition is scarce around here.

Waimea Plantation Cottages (☎ 338-1625, 800-992-7866; www.waimea-plantation.com; 9400 Kaumuali'i Hwy; 1-/2-/3-bedroom cottages from $220/275/325; ☒) No doubt you've read about these perennially popular cottages. They're media darlings. But whether they are worth the expense is debatable. All include the basics (eg cable TV, stereo and full kitchen) but they widely vary in quality and can be noisy due to wild chickens and the Waimea Brewing Company on site. The rustic setting is a refreshing change from touristy resorts, but for the price, you could do better.

Eating & Drinking

BUDGET

Jo-Jo's Shave Ice (9740 Kaumuali'i Hwy; shave ice $2-4; ☺ 10am-6pm) While still a worthwhile stop with dozens and dozens of syrup flavors, the quality is inconsistent (eg skimpy syrup or gritty ice). Still, the colorful sign above the rickety screen door is a beacon and, heck, a small cup is just two bucks. Try unusual flavors like lychee, tamarind and rum.

Shrimp Station (☎ 338-1242; 9652 Kaumuali'i Hwy; dishes $4.75-12; ☺ 11am-5pm) Follow your nose to this little roadside lunch window serving fresh, aromatic shrimp plates. Varieties include coconut and sweet chili. Each comes

KAUA'I

BUY LOCAL

Why buy generic national brands when you can buy local? Look for locally made products at gift shops, art galleries, craft fairs and farmers markets.

Look for the 'Kaua'i Made' label attached to products either made on Kaua'i or made with Kaua'i materials. Find a list of local manufacturers at www.kauaimade.net. Of course, the list is not exhaustive.

Don't miss the following, sold at island shops, farmers markets, craft fairs and/or online.

Aunty Lilikoi Passion Fruit Products Passion-fruit preserves, mustards, dressings and beauty products. See below.

Barkaroo Bakery (www.barkaroobakery.com) Wholesome pet treats shaped into palm trees, hula girls, sushi and more.

Caitlin Ross Odom (www.caitlinrossodom.com) Exquisite sterling-silver jewelry featuring sea glass from Glass Beach.

Denise Tjarks (www.denisetjarks.com) Unique bags handmade from vintage and collectible fabrics.

Kauai Kunana Dairy (www.kauaikunanadairy.com) Gourmet goat cheeses and beauty products.

Keiki Kovers (☎ 335-0482; (www.keikilovers.com) 4545 Kona Rd, Hanapepe, HI 96716; ☺ 9am-2:30pm) Handmade tropical-print clothing and hats for babies and children.

with ½lb of the critters and, of course, two scoops of rice.

Obsessions Café (☎ 338-1110; 9875 Waimea Rd; breakfast & lunch $6-7; ☺ 8am-2pm) If you miss Mom's home cooking, find comfort here. The food is hearty and all homemade, from cheese-filled omelettes to freshly baked pastries. Sandwiches and wraps are particularly satisfying.

Ishihara Market (☎ 338-1751; 9894 Kaumuali'i Hwy; ☺ 6am-8:30pm Mon-Fri, 7am-8:30pm Sat & Sun) The town's best grocer is an indie with an extensive deli selling take-out sushi, green salads and a mouthwatering selection of 'ahi poke.

MIDRANGE & TOP END

Pacific Pizza & Deli (☎ 338-1020; 9850 Kaumuali'i Hwy; pizza $9-22; ☺ 11am-9pm Mon-Sat) Traditional or wacky, it's all here, from Mexican (ground beef and refried beans) to Filipino (Langanisa sausage and grilled eggplant) to *lomilomi* salmon. The calzones, offered in each pizza-combo flavor, are ideal for single diners.

Waimea Brewing Company (☎ 338-9733; www .waimea-plantation.com/brew; Waimea Plantation Cottages, 9400 Kaumuali'i Hwy; appetizers $7-13, dishes $9-30; ☺ 11am-10pm Sun-Thu, to 2am Fri & Sat) It resembles a suburban mall joint but the open-air plantation building and swaying coconut trees are pleasant and the island-inspired pub food is tasty. Two creative uses of *'ahi poke*: a seared *poke* wrap and a sushi roll filled with *poke* and flash-fried. As for the US's westernmost microbrewery's beers, aficionados find them only passable.

Wrangler's Steakhouse (☎ 338-1218; dinner mains $17-25; 9852 Kaumuali'i Hwy; ☺ 11am-9pm Mon-Fri, 4-9pm Sat) Those with hearty appetites will enjoy this cozy, ranch-style restaurant. Meat eaters should sample the signature 'sizzling' New York–cut steak, juicy and prepared to your liking, while those more indecisive types can choose a main of Japanese tempura, teriyaki beef and sashimi. Vegetarians, keep looking.

Entertainment

Waimea Theatre (☎ 338-0282; 9691 Kaumuali'i Hwy; ☺ 7:30pm Wed-Sun) A variety of movies, including new releases, indies and classics, are shown here. This is also a venue for the Hawaii International Film Festival (see its website at www.hiff.org).

Shopping

Aunty Lilikoi Passion Fruit Products (☎ 866-545-4564; www.auntylilikoi.com; 9875 Kaumuali'i Hwy; condiments per 10oz $5; ☺ 10am-5pm) This mom-and-pop shop operated by Tony and Lori Cardenas concocts the gamut of delectable passion-fruit jellies and other condiments. The *liliko'i*-wasabi mustard beat more than 300 rivals to win the 2005 Grand Champion Medal in the Napa Valley Mustard Competition. The *liliko'i* is the same variety that you see growing wild on Kaua'i (with yellow skin and seedy orange pulp), but a pure fruit puree that is imported from Ecuador is used because the locally grown fruit isn't available in such quantity or quality yet.

Westside Sporting Goods (☎ 338-1411; 9681 Kaumuali'i Hwy; ◔ 9:30am-5:30pm Mon-Fri, to 4:30pm Sat) Head here for outdoor gear, including camping and hiking supplies such as fleece sleeping bags ($15), camp-stove fuel, *tabi* (reef-walking sandals) and first-aid kits.

KEKAHA

pop 3175

Kekaha is strictly a residential town but, due to its beachside location, there are dozens of vacation-rentals available here. Heavy-duty hikers planning for multiple forays up around the canyon will find Kekaha a convenient home base, as would anyone seeking solitude. For others, it might be too out of the way.

Driving here, the coastal highway seems to stretch forever, along a glorious carpet of golden sand as far as the eye can see. Kekaha Beach Park is perfect for vigorous beach walking or sunset strolling – or you can drive all the way to Polihale State Park (with a 4WD and a dose of patience).

Rural by choice, Kekaha is rarely visited, even by locals. But in the 2000s real-estate values have jumped, ironically because Kekaha is the last affordable area on Kaua'i.

Check out **The Unofficial Guide to Kekaha Town** (http://home.hawaii.rr.com/webguides/kekaha.html) for a hilarious introduction to the westernmost town in the state.

Orientation

Kaumuali'i Hwy borders the coastline while Kekaha Rd (Hwy 50), the main drag, lies parallel and a few blocks inland. All you'll find in town are a post office and a couple of stores. On its eastern end, Kekaha Rd and Kaumuali'i Hwy meet near the Kikiaola Small Boat Harbor, a state harbor with a launch ramp.

Sights & Activities

KEKAHA BEACH PARK

Just west of Kekaha town, this vast beach is ideal for solitary walking. Without any shade, however, the sun is brutal. Before you jump in, watch the tide carefully. This is unprotected open ocean and when the surf is high currents are extremely dangerous; under the right conditions it can be good for **surfing** and **bodyboarding**.

Ni'ihau and its offshore islet, Lehua, are visible from the beach. An inconspicuous shower can be found just inland from the highway between Alae and Amakihi Rds; rest rooms and picnic tables are nearby.

Sleeping & Eating

For lodging listings, see **Kekaha Oceanside** (www.kekahaoceansidekauai.com).

Mindy's (☎ 337-9275; mindys@hgea.org; 8842 Kekaha Rd; s/d $75/85) This sunny 2nd-story apartment is a charmer, with private deck and peaceful mountain views combined with full kitchen, TV, sofa bed for additional guests (per person $5), and ceiling fans throughout. Complimentary fruit and coffee are provided.

Boathouse (☎ 332-9744; www.seakauai.com; 4518-A Nene St; r $85) Within walking distance of an uncrowded sandy beach, the Boathouse is a clean, spacious, ground-floor studio with wraparound covered lanai. It's perfect for either one or two, with kitchenette, king bed and TV. Free use of washer-dryer. The friendly owners also rent the Seaview Suite in Kalaheo.

Eating options are scarce. For snacks, try **Menehune Food Mart** (☎ 337-1335; Waimea Canyon Plaza, 8171 Kekaha Rd; ◔ 5:30am-8pm Wed-Sat, to 6pm Sun-Tue).

BARKING SANDS

Between Kekaha Beach Park and Polihale State Park, the beach stretches for approximately 15 miles. However, there is only limited public access near the US navy base at **Barking Sands Pacific Missile Range Facility** (PMRF; ☎ general information 335-4229, beach access 335-4111). Following the September 11 terrorist attacks, the navy barred access except to Kaua'i residents without felony convictions or to people with military connections. The navy is Kaua'i's largest employer and it controversially occupies and prohibits access to indigenous Hawaiian territory. Any move by the military to occupy more land generates fervent protest.

Barking Sands earned its nickname because on days both sunny and windy (with the planets lined up just right) the moving sands make sounds akin to those of barking dogs. (Please send us a recording if you hear them.) The missile-range facility at Barking Sands provides the aboveground link to a sophisticated sonar network that tracks more than 1000 sq miles of the Pacific. Established during WWII, it's been developed into the world's largest underwater listening device.

KAUA'I

DETOUR: POLIHALE STATE PARK

Escape civilization in miles of solitary white-sand **beach** at Polihale, where nothing mars the endless horizon. The magnitude of sand, sea and sky is almost overwhelming. Expert surfers shred at Polihale but strong rip currents mean the waters are too treacherous for swimming. Instead, come here to meditate on wave after wave pounding the shore, or to admire the fiery show at sunset. Not a single tree shades the beach so bring sun protection.

Getting here is tricky, however. Locals cruise here in monster trucks but tourists' standard rental cars might be challenged. Drop your tire pressure to 20lb for the best traction in the sand or, better yet, rent a 4WD. If it's rainy, go elsewhere.

Polihale State Park requires a 3.5-mile drive over unpaved road. To get here, pass the 32-mile marker and then turn left at the park sign, 0.75 miles north of the PMRF entrance.

After almost 3.5 miles, turn left at a large monkeypod tree in the middle of the road to reach the only safe swimming spot here. Follow the road north, up the hill toward the sand dunes. Walk north along the beach to **Queen's Pond**, where a large semicircular reef almost reaches the shore, creating a protected pool – but only during calm surf.

For **camping**, start from the monkeypod tree, turn right and continue another mile. A left turnoff leads to a camping area with rest rooms, outdoor showers, drinking water and a picnic pavilion. See p459 for permit information.

WAIMEA CANYON STATE PARK

Of all Kaua'i's unique wonders, none can touch Waimea Canyon for utter grandeur. While one expects to find tropical beaches and gardens here, few expect a gargantuan chasm of ancient lava rock, 13 miles long and 2500ft deep to the riverbed (or 3700ft above sea level). Flowing through the canyon is the Waimea River, Kaua'i's longest, which is fed by three eastern tributaries that bring reddish-brown waters from the mountaintop bog, Alaka'i Swamp.

From afar, the view of the canyon tends to be hazy. The optimum viewing conditions are sunny days following heavy rain, when the lava layers turn deeper red and waterfalls cascade throughout the canyon.

Waimea Canyon was formed when Kaua'i's original shield volcano, Wai'ale'ale, slumped along an ancient fault line, creating a sharp east-facing line of cliffs. Then another shield volcano, Lihu'e, developed the island's east side, producing new lava flows that ponded against the cliffs. Thus the western canyon walls are taller, thinner and more eroded – a contrast most theatrically apparent while hiking along the canyon floor. The black and red horizontal striations along the canyon walls represent successive volcanic eruptions; the red color indicates that water seeped through the rocks, creating rust from the iron inside.

Orientation

The southern boundary of Waimea Canyon State Park is about 6 miles up the road from Waimea. You can reach the park by two roads: Waimea Canyon Dr (Hwy 550) starts in Waimea just beyond the 23-mile marker, while Koke'e Rd (Hwy 552) starts in Kekaha off Mana Rd. They merge between the 6-mile and 7-mile markers.

State officials generally prefer visitors to use Waimea Canyon Dr, which is 19 miles long and passes the canyon lookouts with terrific views into Kalalau Valley on the Na Pali Coast. Koke'e Rd is shorter by 3 miles and also offers scenic views, but not of the canyon.

Dangers & Annoyances

Rain creates hazardous conditions in the canyon. The red-dirt trails quickly become slick and river fords rise to impassable levels. Try hiking poles or a sturdy walking stick to ease the steep descent into the canyon.

Note the time of sunset and plan to return well before it's dark. Note that daylight will fade inside the canyon long before sunset.

While packing light is recommended, take enough water for your entire trip, especially the uphill return journey. Do not drink fresh water along the trails without treating it.

Cell phones do not work here. If possible, hike with a companion or at least tell someone your expected return time.

Sights

Along Waimea Canyon Dr, you can see naturally growing examples of native trees, including kiawe and wiliwili. The valuable hardwood

KAUA'I

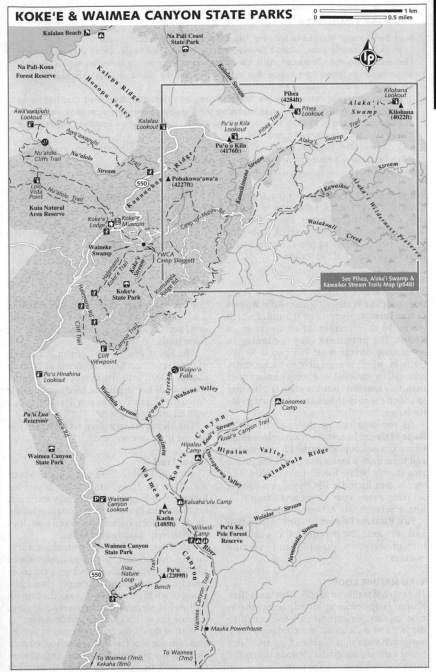

KOKE'E & WAIMEA CANYON STATE PARKS

0 ——————— 1 km
0 ——————— 0.5 miles

Kalalau Beach

Na Pali Coast State Park

Na Pali-Kona Forest Reserve

Kalepa Ridge

Honopu Valley

Awa'awapuhi Lookout

Nu'alolo Cliffs Trail

Awa'awapuhi Trail

Nu'alolo

Nu'alolo Stream

Lolo Vista Point

Nu'alolo Trail

Kuia Natural Area Reserve

Kalalau Lookout

Kalalau Stream

Kaunuohua Ridge

550

Pohakuwa'awa'a (4227ft)

Koke'e Lodge

Koke'e Museum

Waineke Swamp

Haleманu Koke'e Trail

Koke'e State Park

Koke'e Stream

YWCA Camp Sloggett

Kumuwela Ridge Rd

Haleманu Rd

Cliff Trail

Cliff Viewpoint

Pu'u Hinahina Lookout

Waialuula Stream

Canyon Trail

Waipo'o Falls

Po'omau Stream

Wahane Valley

Pu'u Lua Reservoir

Koke'e Rd

Waimea Canyon State Park

Waimea

Waimea Canyon

Koai'e Canyon Trail

Hipalau Camp

Koai'e Stream

Onepaewaa Valley

Hipalau Valley

Kaluaha'ula Ridge

Lonomea Camp

Waimea Canyon Lookout

Po'o Kaeha (1485ft)

Kaluaha'ulu Camp

Wiliwili Camp

Waialae Stream

Pu'u Ka Pele Forest Reserve

Nawaimaka Stream

Koai'e Canyon Trail

Waimea Canyon State Park

Iliau Nature Loop

Kukui Trail

Pu'u (2209ft)

Bench

Waimea River

Waimea Canyon

Waimea Canyon Trail

Mauka Powerhouse

To Waimea (7mi); Kekaha (8mi)

To Waimea (7mi)

Pihea (4284ft)

Pihea Lookout

Pihea Trail

Kilohana Lookout

Alaka'i Swamp

Kilohana (4022ft)

Pu'u o Kila Lookout

Pu'u o Kila (4176ft)

Alaka'i Swamp Trail

Kauaikinana Stream

Alaka'i Swamp

Camp 10-Mohihi Rd

Kawaikoi

Alaka'i Wilderness Preserve

Stream

Waiakoali Creek

See Pihea, Alaka'i Swamp & Kawaikoi Stream Trails Map (p548)

THE MARK TWAIN MYTH

Mark Twain called Waimea Canyon the 'Grand Canyon of the Pacific'... Not!

In their excellent book, *Kaua'i's Geologic History: A Simplified Guide*, Chuck Blay and Robert Siemers debunk this oft-quoted myth. Twain did spend time on the Hawaiian Islands in 1866, when he wrote *Letters from Hawaii*. But he never visited the island of Kaua'i nor saw Waimea Canyon. His writings mention neither.

Further, extensive research by the Bishop Museum in Honolulu discovered that renowned geologist John Wesley Powell began exploring the Colorado River canyon in 1867, ultimately publishing his findings in 1875. Only in 1908 did US President Theodore Roosevelt establish the 'Grand Canyon' as a national monument.

So, unless Mark Twain also coined the Grand Canyon's name, too (before it was even on the map), he could not have compared the two. Twain died in 1910.

koa proliferates at the hunter's check station along the way. Look for the trees with narrow, crescent-shaped leaves. (Note: the area is popular for deer hunting, which is obvious by the photo collage of proud hunters with their fallen quarry at the station.)

SCENIC LOOKOUTS

The most scenic of the lookout points along this stretch of Waimea Canyon Rd is **Waimea Canyon Lookout**, signposted 0.3 miles north of the 10-mile marker, at an elevation of 3400ft. The prominent canyon running in an easterly direction off Waimea is Koai'e Canyon, which is accessible to backcountry hikers. Conventional tour buses go no further than this lookout (but the state is planning to widen the road to Kalalau Lookout (p546) for buses).

As you continue up the road, the 800ft **Waipo'o Falls** can be seen from a couple of small unmarked lookouts before the 12-mile marker and then from a lookout opposite the picnic area shortly before the 13-mile marker. The picnic area includes BBQ pits, rest rooms, drinking water, a pay phone and Camp Hale Koa, a Seventh Day Adventist camp.

Pu'u Hinahina Lookout (3640ft) offers two lookouts near the parking lot at a marked turnoff between the 13- and 14-mile markers.

ILIAU NATURE LOOP

The marked trailhead for the 10-minute Iliau Nature Loop comes up shortly before the 9-mile marker. Be sure to pass the bench to the left and walk about three minutes for a top-notch vista into Waimea Canyon. After heavy rainfall, waterfalls explode down the sheer rock walls across the gorge.

The trail is named for the *iliau,* a plant endemic to Kaua'i's Westside, which grows along the trail and produces stalks up to 10ft high. Like the silversword, *iliau* grows to a ripe old age. Then for a grand finale it bursts into blossom and dies.

Activities

HIKING

For serious hikers, there are trails that lead deep into Waimea Canyon. During weekends and holidays, pig and deer hunters use these trails.

The Kukui and Koai'e Canyon Trails, two of the steepest on Kaua'i, connect at Wiliwili Camp, 2000ft into the canyon. If the entire trek sounds too strenuous, hike just one mile down the Kukui Trail, as you'll reach a bench with an astounding view.

The hiking mileage given for each trail following is for one way only.

Kukui Trail

The Kukui Trail (2.5 miles) trailhead, which also starts the Iliau Nature Loop, is just before the 9-mile marker. It officially starts just beyond it at a hunter checking station on the right. The trail is quite exposed and thus dries out relatively quickly after rains.

You'll encounter many switchback turns during the descent. When in doubt about where the trail actually is, stick with the more level forks and ignore the steeply rutted bits going down the deepest gashes in the canyon wall. Avoid perching on canyon outcroppings because the soil is crumbly and unstable.

Further down, the trail continues to switchback. Do not veer toward the tree-topped *pu'u* (hill) with a big gash in its side. Instead look for a small sign directing hikers to turn left and hike steeply down with the hill behind you.

Eventually the trail enters thick forest and tree roots form natural steps going downhill. The first of the forested switchbacks are the steepest, gradually easing as the path travels downhill. As the sounds of rushing river water become clearly audible, the picnic shelter and toilet of Wiliwili Camp come into view.

Overnight camping is allowed at Wiliwili Camp, but mostly hunters use it. Facilities include only an open-air picnic shelter and pit toilet.

Koai'e Canyon Trail

Near Wiliwili Camp, the Kukui Trail leads to the Koai'e Canyon Trail (3 miles), a wide dirt road running north across a small streambed then uphill on switchbacks. Ignore false spur trails that misguide you back down to the river. Tricky spots include a plank across a stream and a stretch where the trail narrows to only a foot's width along a slippery, mossy rock face above the river. Later, when the trail rejoins the old dirt road, it quickly descends back to the river, then crosses over it.

Along the way you'll find three backcountry camps. After passing the first, Kaluaha'ulu Camp, stay on the eastern bank of the river and do not cross it. Finally you will reach a Na Ala Hele trailhead for the Koai'e Canyon Trail. The trail is overgrown at this point, requiring minor bushwhacking, and spongy, loose soil can conceal steep drop-offs alongside the path.

Next you'll reach Hipalau Camp, after which the trail becomes indistinct. Keep heading north. Do not veer toward the river, but continue ascending at approximately the same point midway between the canyon walls and the river.

Growing steeper, the trail then enters Koai'e Canyon, recognisable by the red-rock walls rising to the left. The last camp is Lonomea Camp. Find the best views at the emergency helipad, a grassy area perfect for picnicking. When ready, retrace your steps.

Waimea Canyon Trail

A third trail in this area is the 8-mile Waimea Canyon Trail, which runs south from Wiliwili Camp to the town of Waimea, ending on Menehune Rd, but it's not recommended. Much of the trail is along a 4WD road that leads to a hydroelectric power station and it's not particularly scenic. Further, there are numerous river crossings that are frequently impassable.

CYCLING

Coast downhill for 13 miles, from the rim of Waimea Canyon (elevation 3500ft) to sea level with **Outfitters Kaua'i** (☎ 742-9667, 888-742-9887; www.outfitterskauai.com; Po'ipu Plaza, 2827-A Po'ipu Rd, Po'ipu; tour adult/child 12-14 $94/75; ⏱ check-in 6am & 2:30pm), who will supply all the necessary cruisers, helmets and snacks. Remember, you'll be a target for the setting sun during the afternoon ride.

Mountain bikers can also find miles of bumpy, 4WD hunting-area roads off Waimea Canyon Dr. Even when the yellow gates are closed on nonhunting days, cyclists are still allowed to go around and use them – except for Papa'alai Rd, which is managed by the Department of Hawaiian Home Lands and open for hunting, but not recreational use.

Sleeping

All four camps on the canyon trails are part of the forest reserve system. They have open-air picnic shelters and pit toilets, but no other facilities; all freshwater must be treated before drinking. See p459 for camping permit information.

KOKE'E STATE PARK

Sprawling Koke'e State Park is the starting point for almost 50 miles of outstanding hiking trails. Here, you'll see terrain unlike that found anywhere else on the island, including the largest concentration of extant native bird species in Hawaii. Remote Alaka'i Swamp in particular is a unique view of Kaua'i's native ecosystem; not only is the swamp inhospitable to exotic species but, due to its high elevation, it is one of the few places across Hawaii where mosquitoes, which transmit avian diseases, do not flourish.

Ancient Hawaiians never established a permanent village in these chilly highlands and came mainly to collect feathers from forest birds and to cut koa trees for canoes. But an extraordinarily steep ancient Hawaiian trail once ran down the cliffs from Koke'e (ko-*keh*-eh) to Kalalau Valley on the Na Pali Coast. Today the park's only paved road will take you to the Kalalau Lookout, a coastal overlook among the most breathtaking across the Hawaiian islands.

Orientation & Information

This park's boundary starts beyond the Pu'u Hinahina Lookout. After the 15-mile marker, you'll pass a brief stretch of park cabins, restaurant, museum and campground.

The helpful people at the Koke'e Museum sell inexpensive trail maps and provide basic information on trail conditions; you can also call them for real-time **mountain weather reports** (☎ 335-9975).

Remember, the nearest place for provisions and gas is Waimea, 15 miles away.

Dangers & Annoyances

All of the suggestions listed for Waimea Canyon State Park (p542) apply. Further, the higher elevation produces a cooler and wetter climate, so take appropriate attire.

Sights

KOKE'E NATURAL HISTORY MUSEUM

Learn about local flora, fauna, climate and geology at this small **museum** (☎ 335-9975; www .kokee.org; donation $1; ☯ 10am-4pm). Also find detailed topographical maps and a display of poi pounders, stone adze heads and other artifacts.

Obtain a brochure ($1.50 or borrow for free) for the short **nature trail** out back. It offers interpretive information corresponding to the trail's numbered plants and trees, including many native species.

The chickens that congregate in the museum's parking lot are not the common garden variety but *moa* (red junglefowl), brought to Hawaii by early Polynesian settlers. Among the major Hawaiian Islands today, *moa* exists solely on Kaua'i.

KALALAU LOOKOUTS

At the 18-mile marker, the 4000ft **Kalalau Lookout** faces the emerald depths of the valley and straight out to sea. On clear days, late-afternoon rainbows sweep so deeply into Kalalau Valley that the bottom part of the bows curve back inward. Bright-red 'apapane birds feed from the ohia-lehua flowers near the lookout railings.

Kalalau Valley was once the site of a large settlement and was joined to Koke'e by a very steep trail that ran down the cliffs. Today the only way into the valley is along the coastal Kalalau Trail (p516) from Ha'ena on the North Shore or by kayak (p509).

The paved road continues another mile to **Pu'u o Kila Lookout**, where it dead-ends at a parking lot. At the time of research, this last stretch of road was closed to vehicular traffic; thus you must walk a mile to the lookout. From this lookout, you'll find another grand view into Kalalau Valley and a glance inland toward the Alaka'i Wilderness Preserve.

Activities

HIKING

Almost 50 miles of hiking trails offer varied terrain for all fitness levels. Generally the toughest trails are those with the steepest changes in elevation. Be aware that pig, deer and goat hunters use some of these trails, so you might want to bust out that garish orange jacket.

The starting point for several scenic hikes, Halemanu Rd is just north of the 14-mile marker on Waimea Canyon Dr. Whether or not the road is passable in a non-4WD vehicle depends on recent rainfall. The wet clay roads here make for a skid fest. Even if you can drive in, an unexpected shower might mean you cannot get out. Thus, if you're without 4WD, park on the west shoulder of Waimea Canyon Dr, opposite Halemanu Rd, and walk the 0.8 miles down.

During summer weekends, trained volunteers lead **Wonder Walks** (June to September, nominal donation), guided hikes on various trails at Waimea Canyon and Koke'e State Parks. Contact the **museum** (☎ 335-9975; www .kokee.org) for schedules and reservations.

Bear in mind, the trails described below are only a sampling. If you hate backtracking, you can probably find other trails that intersect them.

Cliff & Canyon Trails

The first of the hikes off Halemanu Rd is the **Cliff Trail** (0.1 miles), a short, simple walk that ends at an overlook peering into Waimea Canyon. From there, you can continue on the **Canyon Trail** (1.8 miles), a steep, but not terribly strenuous hike that follows the canyon rim, passes Waipo'o Falls and ends at **Kumuwela Lookout**.

Starting from the highway, walk down Halemanu Rd for just over 0.5 miles to a well-signed junction. Veer to the right and continue to the next fork in the road, keeping Halemanu Stream on the left and ignoring a hunting trail-of-use on the right. Then turn right onto the footpath leading to both the Cliff and Canyon Trails.

At the next junction, the Cliff Trail veers right and wanders for less than 0.25 miles uphill to the **Cliff Viewpoint**.

For the Canyon Trail, backtrack to the previous junction. This trail descends though koa, blackberry and *'iliahi* (Hawaiian sandalwood) to the edge of Waimea Canyon. Beware of eroded areas and strong winds. Views are tremendous but don't venture too close to the edges, as the soil is unstable.

In less than an hour, the Canyon Trail veers away from the rim into another gulch en route to the 800ft **Waipo'o Falls**. A sign might still be standing, identifying 'Falls No 1.' Further along is 'Falls No 2,' which might be tricky to cross. If the water levels and speed look menacing, turn around here.

Otherwise, after hopping boulders across the stream, follow the trail to Kumuwela Ridge at the canyon rim. The trail ends at **Kumuwela Lookout**, where you can rest at a picnic table before backtracking to Halemanu Rd.

Halemanu-Koke'e Trail

Another trail off Halemanu Rd, which starts further down the road than the Cliff and Canyon Trails is **Halemanu-Koke'e Trail** (1.25 miles). An easy recreational nature trail, it passes through a native forest of koa and ohia trees that provide a habitat for native birds. One of the common plants found on this trail is banana *poka*, a member of the passion-fruit family and a serious invasive pest. It has pretty pink flowers, but it drapes the forest with its vines and chokes out less-aggressive native plants. The trail ends near YWCA Camp Sloggett, about 0.5 miles from Koke'e Lodge.

Awa'awapuhi & Nu'alolo Trails

The Awa'awapuhi Trail (3.25 miles) and the Nu'alolo Trail (3.75 miles) each traverses the edges of sheer 2000ft cliffs, allowing you a bird's-eye view into valleys otherwise accessible only by boat. These trails connect via the **Nu'alolo Cliffs Trail** (2 miles), which contains nerve-wrackingly narrow and washed-out stretches, right along precipices thousands of feet below. Not recommended for acrophobics! The Nu'alolo Cliffs Trail connects to the Nu'alolo Trail near the 3.25-mile mark and to the Awa'awapuhi Trail just short of the 3-mile mark.

If you're undecided as to which trail to take, Awa'awapuhi Trail is recommended because the Nu'alolo Trail is steeper and, especially when muddy, ascending it can be rather treacherous. Also, if you are a solo hiker, you'll encounter more traffic, which is preferable for safety. The views of Nu'alolo Valley clear to the Pacific Ocean are outstanding on both trails.

If you're up for a hardcore day hike of all three trails, do the Nu'alolo Trail first to avoid its merciless ascent, especially near the top. Also, if you start on the Nu'alolo Trail, your car will be parked 2 miles downhill (rather than uphill) at the Nu'alolo Trail trailhead.

The trailhead for the **Awa'awapuhi Trail** is just after the 17-mile marker. The trail starts atop Kaunuohua Ridge, descending in an ohia and koa forest. You'll soon see lush valleys over Honopu Ridge toward the ocean, with the sharply eroded *pali* (cliff) dropping away below the trail.

Shortly after the 2.5-mile marker you'll find a jaw-dropping **viewpoint** right at the level of the clouds, where on clear days the blues of sky and of ocean merge seamlessly.

The trail later traverses overgrown forested land, so be careful of steep drop-offs. At the next trail junction, before the 3-mile mark, the **Nu'alolo Cliffs Trail** appears on the left. But first, segue to the right to reach **Awa'awapuhi Lookout**, 0.25 miles further. The views into Awa'awapuhi Valley straight ahead, and Nu'alolo Valley off to the left, are indescribable. Don't venture past the guard rails as the high winds and unstable soil are extremely perilous. If you slip, the drop is 2000ft.

To complete the entire three-trail trek, start on the **Nu'alolo Trail** near Koke'e Lodge, off Waimea Canyon Dr. It begins in cool upland forest and descends 1500ft, ending after a badly eroded stretch at **Lolo Vista Point**, a lookout on the valley rim. After turning onto the Nu'alolo Cliffs Trail, hikers contour above the valley for less than 2 miles, passing a waterfall, to the crossroads with the Awa'awapuhi Trail.

Pihea Trail to Alaka'i Swamp Trail

The Alaka'i Swamp Trail (3.5 miles) and the Pihea Trail (3.75 miles) are often hiked in conjunction because they cross paths, allowing you to traverse parts of both. Most hikers start on the Pihea Trail because the trailhead is accessible by the paved road to **Pu'u o Kila Lookout** (opposite); at the time of research, the road was closed to vehicular traffic after the

Kalalau Lookout, so hikers must walk an extra mile to the trailhead. For the alternate Alaka'i Swamp Trail starting point, see right. The trails are well maintained, with mile markers and signs.

The Pihea Trail trailhead is just beyond the lookout. The first mile of the trail runs along the ridge, offering fine views into Kalalau Valley, before coming to the small fork for **Pihea Vista**, a viewpoint that requires a steep scramble to reach. It then turns inland through wetland forest and, at about 1.75 miles, arrives at aptly named **Alaka'i Crossing**. At this fairy-tale crossroads deep in the misty forest, four boardwalks intersect and lead in opposite directions.

Taking a hard left, the trail continues for 2 miles through rain forest and exposed bogs filled with ferns, perfectly blossoming ohia and old telephone poles before reaching **Kilohana Lookout**, which is the turn-around point for this hike.

While most of the swamp trail has been spanned with boardwalks, it can still be extremely wet and slippery. The stretch between Alaka'i Crossing and Kilohana Lookout includes hundreds of steps, which can be hell on your knees.

Alaka'i Swamp Trail to Pihea Trail

If your vehicle has 4WD, you can start at the Alaka'i Swamp trailhead, located on Camp 10-Mohihi Rd, which is up past the Koke'e Museum on the right. If you drive an ordinary car on this rutted dirt road, you're asking for trouble, especially in wet weather.

Starting on the Alaka'i Swamp Trail means you can avoid the most strenuous, muddy parts of the Pihea Trail, substituting a gentle stroll on a grassy ridge and then over boardwalks through the swamp to Alaka'i Crossing.

From here continue straight (heading east) to Kilohana Lookout. On the return from the lookout, you can either retrace your steps or detour at Alaka'i Crossing onto the Pihea Trail by turning left and hiking to Kawaikoi Camp. From here you must walk back up Mohihi Rd to retrieve your vehicle at the Alaka'i Swamp trailhead. This combination of trails lets you experience the swamp and the unusual boardwalk trail and then hike on a dirt path that borders and crosses Kawaikoi Stream.

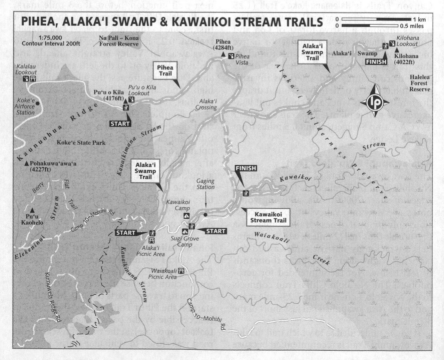

Kawaikoi Stream Trail

A scenic mountain stream trail, the Kawaikoi Stream Trail (1.7 miles) begins between the Sugi Grove and Kawaikoi campgrounds, off Camp 10-Mohihi Rd. It initially follows the southern bank of Kawaikoi Stream and then heads away from the stream and makes a loop, coming down the northern side of the stream before reconnecting with the southern side. If the stream is running high, don't try to cross it.

Festivals & Events

Hula *halau* (troops) from all over Hawaii participate in the one-day **Eo e Emalani I Alaka'i** (☎ 335-9975; www.kokee.org/details.html; admission free; ❧ 10am), an outdoor dance festival at Koke'e Natural History Museum in early October, which re-enacts the historic 1871 journey of Queen Emma to Alaka'i Swamp. The festival includes a royal procession, hula, music and crafts.

Sleeping

Koke'e State Park Cabins (Koke'e Lodge; ☎ 335-6061; PO Box 819, Waimea, HI 96796; cabin $35-45) Minimally maintained, the 12 cabins are suited only to folks seeking a remote, rustic, rather grimy experience. Both the cheaper studio cabins and the newer two-bedroom ones include a double and four twin beds, kitchen, shower, wood stove (your only heating source), linens and blankets – all of dubious cleanliness. While some have complained of roaches, lead paint, loud roosters and gross showers, others find roughin' it to be extraordinarily memorable. Come prepared with extra firewood, cleaning supplies and groceries.

YWCA Camp Sloggett (☎ 245-5959; www.camping kauai.com; campsites per person $10, dm $20, 1-bedroom cabin $65) Choose your comfort level from a one-bedroom cottage, a bunkhouse with beds and tent camping on the grass. Guests must provide their own linens for the bunkhouse. No reservations needed except for the cabin. Groups of five to 11, inquire about the two-bedroom lodge. Camp Sloggett is about 0.5 miles east of the park museum down a rutted dirt road passable by standard cars, except when muddy.

For **camping**, you have three options. The most accessible camping area is the Koke'e State Park Campground, near Koke'e Lodge. The campsites come with picnic tables, drinking water, rest rooms and showers.

Off the beaten track, Kawaikoi and Sugi Grove campgrounds are about 4 miles east of Koke'e Lodge, off the 4WD Camp 10-Mohihi Rd in the forest reserve adjacent to the state park. Each campground has pit toilets, picnic shelters and fire pits. But there's no potable water source (stream water must be treated). See p459 for details on obtaining permits.

Eating

Koke'e Lodge (☎ 335-6061; snacks $3-7; ❧ 9am-3:30pm) Step right up, folks. This is the only eatery within 20 miles. Luckily the food is surprisingly good. Find smoked-salmon quiche, granola and other breakfast fare all day long, plus hearty soups, sandwiches and interesting salads, like the Moroccan sampler with couscous, hummus and Mediterranean veggies.

PAPAHANAUMOKUAKEA MARINE NATIONAL MONUMENT

On June 15 2006, President Bush declared the Northwestern Hawaiian Islands the USA's first Marine National Monument. Encompassing around 140,000 sq miles and containing 33 islands and atolls, it is now the largest protected marine area in the world, seven times larger than all US marine sanctuaries combined.

This breathtaking act of stewardship caught most observers by surprise, since President Bush is not known for his environmentalism. He was apparently moved by a personal appeal from Governor Linda Lingle, and by seeing the 2006 PBS film *Voyage to Kure* by Jean-Michel Cousteau. A few fishers have commercial interests in the islands, but their licenses will expire in 2011.

The Northwestern Hawaiian Islands begin about 130 miles northwest of Kaua'i and stretch for 1400 miles. They contain the largest and healthiest coral-reef system in the US, which is home to 7000 marine species, a quarter of which are endemic to Hawaii. The islands also support around 14 million seabirds, including 19 species of native seabirds. In addition, island beaches are the primary breeding ground for the endangered Hawaiian monk seal (p67) and green sea turtles (p66).

However, the islands are not absolutely 'pristine.' Pacific Ocean currents bring an estimated 45 to 60 tons of debris to the islands annually, and a major cleanup from 1998 to 2005 removed 544 tons of entangled fishing nets, plastic bottles and trash.

The Northwestern Hawaiian Islands are grouped into 10 island clusters, which contain atolls (low sandy islands formed on top of coral reefs) and some single-rock islands. From east to west, the clusters are: Nihoa Island, Mokumanamana (Necker Island), French Frigate Shoals, Gardner Pinnacles, Maro Reef, Laysan Island, Lisianski Island, Pearl and Hermes Atoll, Midway Atoll and Kure Atoll. The total land area of the Northwestern Hawaiian Islands is just under 5 sq miles.

Human history on the islands extends back to the first Polynesian voyagers to arrive in Hawaii. In modern times, the most famous island has been, of course, Midway Atoll, which is the only island open to visitors.

NIHOA & MOKUMANAMANA

Nihoa and Mokumanamana (Necker Island), the two islands closest to Kaua'i, were home to Native Hawaiians from around AD 1000 to AD 1700. An abundance of archaeological remains have been found, including stone temple platforms, house sites, terraces, burial caves and carved stone images. Speculation is that about 175 people may have lived on Nihoa and traveled to the much smaller Mokumanamana for religious ceremonies.

That anyone could live at all on these dots is remarkable. Nihoa is only 1 sq km, and Mokumanamana is one-sixth that size. Nihoa juts from the sea steeply, like a broken tooth, and is the tallest of the Northwestern Hawaiian Islands, with one peak reaching 910ft.

Two endemic land birds live on Nihoa. The Nihoa finch, which like the Laysan finch is a raider of other birds' eggs, has a population of a few thousand. The gray Nihoa millerbird, related to the Old World warbler family, numbers between 300 and 700.

FRENCH FRIGATE SHOALS

With 67 acres of land surrounded by 938 acres of coral reef, the French Frigate Shoals contains the Monument's greatest variety of coral (41 species). It is also where most of Hawaii's green sea turtles and Hawaiian monk seals come to nest. The reef forms a classic comma-shaped atoll on top of an eroded volcano, in the center of which 135ft La Perouse Pinnacle rises like a ship; this rock was named after the French explorer who almost wrecked here in 1786. A small sand island, Tern Island is dominated by an airfield, which was built as a refueling stop during WWII. Today, Tern Island is a US Fish & Wildlife Service field station housing two full-time refuge managers and a few volunteers.

LAYSAN ISLAND

Not quite 1.5 sq miles, Laysan is the second biggest of the Northwestern Hawaiian Islands. The grassy island has the most bird species in the Monument, and to see the huge flocks of

Laysan albatross, shearwaters and curlews – plus the endemic Laysan duck chasing brine flies around the super salty inland lake – you'd never know how close this island came to becoming a barren wasteland.

Beginning in the late 19th century, humans began frequenting Laysan to mine phosphate-rich guano – or bird droppings – to use as fertilizer; they also killed hundreds of thousands of albatross for their feathers (to adorn hats) and took eggs for albumen, a substance used in photo processing. Albatross lay just one egg a year, so an 'egging' sweep could destroy an entire year's hatch. Traders built structures and brought pack mules and, oddly enough, pet rabbits.

The rabbits ran loose and multiplied (as only they can), and within 20 years their nibbling destroyed 21 of the island's 25 plant species. Without plants, three endemic Laysan land birds – the Laysan flightless rail, Laysan honeycreeper and Laysan millerbird – perished. About 100 Laysan finch and the last 11 Laysan duck seemed doomed to follow. Then, in 1909, public outcry led President Theodore Roosevelt to create the Hawaiian Islands Bird Reservation, and the Northwestern Hawaiian Islands have been under some kind of protection ever since.

By 1923 every last rabbit was removed, and the rehabilitation of Laysan began. Incredibly, with weed-abatement assistance, native plant life recovered, and so did the birds. The Laysan finch is again common, and the Laysan duck numbers about 300 (another small population has recently been established on Midway). About 160,000 pairs of Laysan albatross now live on the island, making it again one of the world's largest colonies. Nearly the same sequence of events unfolded on nearby Lisianski Island and, together, these islands are a success story that Fish & Wildlife officials consider one of their finest moments.

MIDWAY ISLANDS

The Midway Islands were an important naval air station during WWII, but they are best known as the site of a pivotal battle in June 1942, when American forces surprised an attacking Japanese fleet and defeated it. This victory is credited with turning the tide in the Pacific theater. Postwar, Midway became a staging point for Cold War air patrols.

By 1996 the military no longer needed Midway, and they transferred jurisdiction to the US Fish & Wildlife Service (FWS). Before leaving, it conducted an extensive cleanup program to remove debris, contaminants, rats and nonnative plants. Midway was then developed for tourism: barracks became hotel rooms, the mess hall a cafeteria. A museum and restaurant were added. A gym, theater (for movies), bowling alley and library were part of the original military facility. On Sand Island, various military structures (like gun emplacements) were designated a National Historical Landmark. Until 2002, up to 100 visitors a day were allowed, then the concessionaire pulled out (due to financial losses) and visitation ended. However, in 2007, FWS plans to resume visitation, running the services themselves.

Today, the prime highlight at Midway are the more than two million seabirds who nest here, including the world's largest colony of Laysan albatross, which are so thick between November and July that they virtually blanket the ground. Also, Midway's coral reefs are unusually rich and are frequented by dolphins, sea turtles and Hawaiian monk seals.

VISITING THE MONUMENT

The **Papahanaumokuakea Marine National Monument** (www.hawaiireef.noaa.gov) can be visited virtually online or in Hilo, Hawai'i, at the **Mokupapapa Discovery Center** (p272). In 2007, visitation to Midway will resume, and it will be managed by the **US Fish & Wildlife Service** (www.fws.gov /midway). Until 2011, current plans are to allow visitation only from November through July (to coincide with albatross season) for up to 50 overnight visitors per day; costs will run at around $230 a day (including meals, room and fees), plus $2000 for the airfare. FWS will be reconstructing facilities over the next few years, so expect changes – and expect slots to fill up fast.

Good places to learn more about the monument include **Northwestern Hawaiian Islands Multi-Agency Education Project** (www.hawaiianatolls.org) and **Kahea** (www.kahea.org/nwhi).

Directory

CONTENTS

ACCOMMODATIONS

With prices to suit all budgets, Hawaii accommodations are as varied as they come – choose from campgrounds, rustic cabins, hostels, rural and upscale B&Bs, a wide range of hotels, all-inclusive resorts, condominiums and 'vacation rental' homes.

During high season – mid-December through March and June through August – lodgings will be the most expensive and in demand. In off or shoulder seasons expect discounts and easier booking, though family-friendly resorts rarely lower their rates. Certain big holidays (p559) and major events (p559) command premium prices, and for

---

BOOK ACCOMMODATIONS ONLINE

For more accommodations reviews and recommendations by Lonely Planet authors, check out the online booking service at www.lonelyplanet.com. You'll find the true, insider lowdown on the best places to stay. Reviews are thorough and independent. Best of all, you can book online.

---

these, lodgings can book up a year ahead. Reviews throughout this book note when there are large fluctuations between high- and low-season rates, and when it's common to get internet specials well below advertised 'rack rates.'

All that said, jockeying for the 'best rate' in Hawaii is a constant game that some elevate to an avocation. Be bold and inquisitive, and work every angle you can think of. You might also check out **Trip Advisor** (www.tripadvisor.com) for accommodations reviews and traveler advice.

For last-minute deals, check out:

- www.expedia.com
- www.orbitz.com
- www.priceline.com
- www.travelocity.com

In this guide, our reviews indicate rates for single occupancy (s), double (d) or simply the room (r), when there's no difference in the rate for one or two people. A double room in our budget category usually costs $80 or less; midrange doubles cost $80 to $210; and top-end rooms start at $210. The only exception to this is Waikiki, where the midrange category is $100 to $300.

Unless noted, breakfast is *not* included, bathrooms are private and all lodging is open year-round; rates generally don't include taxes of a whopping 11.41%.

For an explanation of the icons used in this book see the Quick Reference on the inside front cover.

A reservation guarantees your room, but most reservations require a deposit, after which, if you change your mind, the establishment will only refund your money if it's able to rebook your room within a certain period. Note the cancellation policies and other restrictions before making a deposit.

B&Bs & Vacation Rentals

In Hawaii 'B&B' is a wide-ranging category: these accommodations can run from spare bedrooms in family households to historic homes to plush, pull-out-the-stops romantic hideaways. Most times, these are family-run operations; they provide a much more personal experience than hotels, but offer fewer services. B&Bs discourage unannounced drop-ins, and for that reason, they may not appear on maps in this book. Because hosts are often out during the day, same-day reservations are hard to get, so try to book B&Bs in advance. Most B&Bs book full weeks in advance, especially in winter. B&Bs frequently have two- and three-night minimum stay requirements, though some will waive this if you pay a slightly higher one-night rate (it's more work to turn over rooms nightly). Simple, rural B&Bs begin around $65; most B&B rates average closer to $100, and historic or exclusive properties typically run $150 to $250. Most B&Bs offer continental breakfast or provide food for guests to cook their own.

Sometimes, the distinction between a B&B and a 'vacation rental' is very slim. Typically, a vacation rental means renting an entire house (with no on-site manager and no breakfast provided), but many B&Bs also rent stand-alone cottages, and often all these kinds of properties are handled by the same rental agencies. In some communities (such as Kailua on O'ahu, p160), there is a growing tension over the proliferation of 'unlicensed' vacation rentals/B&Bs in residential neighborhoods.

This book includes B&Bs that can be booked directly, but there are others that can be booked only through B&B reservation services. Some islands have B&B associations, such as the **Hawaii Island B&B Association** (www .stayhawaii.com) on the Big Island. Island-wide B&B agencies include:

Affordable Paradise Bed & Breakfast (☎ 261-1693; www.affordable-paradise.com) Books reasonably priced B&Bs and cottages.

All Islands Bed & Breakfast (☎ 263-2342, 800-542-0344; www.all-islands.com) Books scores of host homes.

Bed & Breakfast Hawaii (☎ 822-7771, 800-733-1632; www.bandb-hawaii.com) A larger statewide service.

Vacation Rental by Owner (www.vrbo.com) Facilitates renting vacation homes directly from the owners.

Note that some B&Bs, to preserve a romantic atmosphere have minimum ages for, or don't allow, children. Be sure to ask about these kinds of policies before making reservations.

Camping & Cabins

While Hawaii has, no surprise, some stellar public campgrounds, it has no full-service private campgrounds, and the overall quality of facilities ranges from great to terrible. The best facilities are in national parks, next best are state parks and typically the least well-cared-for are county parks. Sites are less busy during the week than on weekends.

For safety reasons, a few county and state parks are expressly not recommended because they are either very isolated or they are regular late-night carousing spots. Theft and violence aimed at campers has decreased in recent years, but you should still choose your campgrounds carefully. See the recommendations in this guide, and also get advice from local county and state parks departments; they are usually very upfront about campground conditions and safety.

Hawaii's two national parks – Maui's Haleakala National Park (p403) and the Big

---

PRACTICALITIES

- Voltage is 110/120V, 60 cycles, as elsewhere in the USA.

- Most accommodations have inexpensive coin-operated washers and dryers; other convenient laundry locations are listed in individual island chapters.

- Hawaii's daily newspaper, the *Honolulu Advertiser*, is available throughout the islands.

- Hawaii has about 50 radio stations; all the major US TV networks are represented, as well as cable channels offering tourist information and Japanese-language programs.

- Video systems use the NTSC standard, which is not compatible with the PAL system.

- As on the mainland, distances are measured in feet, yards and miles; weights in ounces, pounds and tons.

Island's Hawai'i Volcanoes National Park (p288) – have excellent camping. Both have free drive-up campgrounds, cabins for rent and backcountry campsites; campgrounds are rarely full.

The five largest islands offer camping at state parks. The parks usually have picnic tables, BBQ grills, drinking water, toilets and showers. You may obtain permits ($5 per night per site) from any Division of State Parks office. The main office, Division of State Parks, **Department of Land and Natural Resources** (Map pp106-7; ☎ 587-0300; www.hawaii.gov/dlnr/dsp; Room 131, 1151 Punchbowl St, PO Box 621, Honolulu, HI 96809; ⊗ 8am-3:30pm Mon-Fri), handles reservations for all islands.

Some county parks are in fact quite wonderful, with white-sand beaches and good facilities. The key thing to keep in mind is that just because you *can* camp somewhere, it doesn't necessarily mean you'll *want* to. Check out the campground before committing yourself.

The state and counties also oversee some basic housekeeping cabins. For more specifics, see the O'ahu (p92), Big Island (p191), Maui (p309), Moloka'i (p429) and Kaua'i (p459) chapters.

Condominiums

More spacious than hotel rooms, condominiums are individually owned apartments furnished with everything a visitor needs – from a kitchen to washers and dryers (usually) to lanais. They're almost always cheaper than all but the budget hotel rooms, especially if you're traveling with a group. Most units have a three- to seven-day minimum stay. The weekly rate is often six times the daily rate and the monthly is three times the weekly.

Most condos are rented through agencies, which are listed in individual island chapters. To save money, try booking directly first, then go through the agencies. You can also do your own web searches for online classifieds. Don't forget to ask about cleaning fees, which will be tacked onto your bill and vary depending on how long you stay.

Hostels

Hawaii has only three hostels associated with **Hostelling International** (HI; www.hiusa.org). Two are in Honolulu (p123) and another is near Hawai'i Volcanoes National Park (p288) on the Big Island. All cities and most midsize towns have a small selection of private hostels. A few are appealing, friendly and well kept, but the majority are aimed at backpackers and traveling school groups, and are essentially worn-out crash pads. Most are spartan, offer a common kitchen and internet access, and have bulletin boards thick with useful postings. Dorm beds generally cost $16 to $20. Some are listed at **The Hostel Handbook** (www.hostelhandbook.com).

Hotels

It's very common for Hawaii hotels, particularly larger beach hotels, to discount their published rack rates, most often when you book ahead via the internet. Others discount by the season, week or day depending on demand; others throw in a free rental car. Ask about specials before booking. Within a particular hotel, the main thing that impacts room rates is the view and floor. An ocean view can cost 50% to 100% more than a parking-lot view (euphemistically called a 'garden view'). The higher the rate, usually the quieter the room.

Resorts

Hawaii resorts don't mess around: they are designed to be pleasure palaces that anticipate your every need and provide 'the best' of everything (to keep you on the property every minute of the day). They provide a myriad of dining options, multiple swimming pools, children's programs, nightly entertainment and fitness centers. At the priciest ones, beach sands are without blemishes, coconut trees are trimmed of drooping fronds and every aspect of your experience is managed (in an oh-so-seamless way). They are intentionally contrived visions of paradise – and once you accept that, they're really quite nice.

ACTIVITIES

Hawaii is famous for the range and excellence of its outdoor activities. Whether on land or in the sea, Hawaii provides some of the top experiences you'll find anywhere in the world, and there are very few things you can't do at all. Rock climbing? No, there's really no rock climbing. White-water rafting? No, not that either. Skiing? Actually, yes. It won't ever make top 10 lists, but it can be done on Mauna Kea (p257). After that? Yep, pretty much everything else.

See the Hawaii Outdoors chapter for a real introduction to what you can do in Hawaii. To whet your whistle, here's a list of possibilities:

- Paddle an outrigger canoe
- Sea kayak in the shadow of 2000ft cliffs
- River kayak to waterfalls
- Hike in rain forests and across active volcanoes
- Sunbathe on green-, black- or white-sand beaches
- Surf waves big and small
- Bodyboard and bodysurf
- Ride horses into sacred valleys
- Snorkel lava-rock tide pools
- Scuba dive coral reefs and sunken ships
- Spelunk in lava tubes
- Race marathons and triathlons
- Windsurf and kitesurf
- Hangglide and skydive
- Golf the world's best courses
- Play tennis beneath palm trees
- Practice yoga in forest retreats
- Go charter fishing for blue marlin
- Whale watch on land and on sea
- Bird-watch till your eyes bleed
- Take a catamaran cruise
- Take a helicopter tour over hot lava
- Mountain bike dirt roads to secluded beaches
- Cycle from crater to coastline

Oh, and we almost forgot. No dog-sledding.

BUSINESS HOURS

Unless there are variations of more than a half-hour in either direction, the following are the opening hours for entries listed in this book:

Banks 8:30am to 4pm Monday to Friday; some banks open to 6pm Friday and 9am to noon or 1pm Saturday.

Businesses 8:30am to 4:30pm Monday to Friday; some post offices open 9am to noon Saturday.

Restaurants breakfast 6am to 10am, lunch 11:30am to 2pm, dinner 5pm to 9:30pm.

Shops 9am to 5pm Monday to Saturday, some also open noon to 5pm Sunday; major shopping areas and malls keep extended hours.

CHILDREN (NA KEIKI)

A parent would like to hope that Hawaii, of all places, would be enough to satisfy any child. It offers tons of beaches and outdoor activities for all ages and abilities – plus hotels have pools, malls have arcades and movies, and the trees have coconuts and ripe fruit.

It's easy to meet local kids and their families at parks and beaches, and teens have many avenues – through music, arts and other programs – to encounter Hawaii's fascinating multiethnic society.

Nevertheless, even Hawaii is no cure-all for the boredom of a child. Don't leave home without your usual assortment of books, treats and amusements, and make sure you know where the nearest shave ice is sold.

That warning aside, traveling with kids in Hawaii is as easy (and hard) as anywhere in the US. Traveling families are common, most hotels and restaurants are ready to accommodate them and locals welcome and enjoy them. So long as you keep your kids covered in sunblock and don't try to do or see too much in any one day, you don't need to worry about having a successful Hawaii trip with your family.

Some activities (like horseback riding, surf lessons and helicopter tours) require that children be of a certain age, height or weight to participate. Always ask if restrictions apply. Each island chapter includes specific advice for the best kid-friendly activities; see O'ahu (p142), the Big Island (p205), Maui (p356), Lana'i (p423), Moloka'i (p439) and Kaua'i (p479).

If you forget some critical piece of equipment, **Baby's Away** (☎ on the Big Island 800-996-9030, on O'ahu 800-496-6386, on Maui 800-942-9030; www .babysaway.com) rents cribs, strollers, playpens, high chairs and more. The easiest and most reliable way to find babysitters is to ask the hotel concierge.

For general advice about traveling with children, subscribe to the newsletter **Have Children Will Travel** (☎ 885-0333; www.havechildrenwilltravel .com); it's published in Hawaii but covers the world, and is packed with road-tested advice. Also, Lonely Planet's *Travel with Children* has lots of valuable tips and amusing tales.

Na keiki are welcome most everywhere in Hawaii (except at some B&Bs). Children under 17 or 18 often stay free when sharing a room with their parents and using existing bedding. But always ask. Cots and roll-away beds are usually available (for an additional fee) at hotels and resorts.

Because children are seen as well as heard in Hawaii, many restaurants have children's menus and high chairs are usually available – but if a high chair is a necessity at every meal, bring a collapsible seat.

DIRECTORY

Car-rental companies (p571) are required to provide child-safety seats, but the truth is they don't always have them on hand; reserve in advance or bring your own.

CLIMATE CHARTS

Native Hawaiians have about as many words for rain and wind as Native Alaskans have for snow. However, if each day's weather is impossible to predict, the overall climate is remarkably even tempered.

Average temperatures in Hawaii differ only about 7°F from winter to summer. Near the coast, average highs are about 83°F and lows around 68°F. Hawaii's mountains trap trade winds blowing from the northeast, blocking clouds and bringing abundant rainfall to each island's windward side. Conversely, those same mountains block wind and rain from the southwesterly, or leeward, side where it's the driest and sunniest.

During *kona* (leeward) weather, winds blow from the south, turning snorkeling spots into surfing spots and vice versa. *Kona* storms usually occur in winter and are very unpredictable.

The Honolulu office of the **National Weather Service** (www.prh.noaa.gov/hnl/) offers a comprehensive online weather forecast, but for the coolest infrared and satellite images, visit the **University of Hawaii Meteorology Department** (www.weather.hawaii.edu) website.

COURSES

Some resorts and shopping centers, for example Whalers Village on Maui (p335), offer free or low-cost classes and workshops in hula, traditional Hawaiian arts and the like. Since many schedules are unpredictable, keep your eyes and ears open. The hotel concierge is always a good source of information. Also, check out the East Hawaii Cultural Center

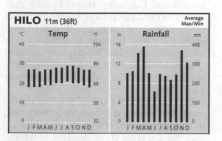

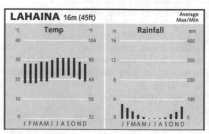

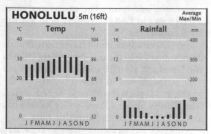

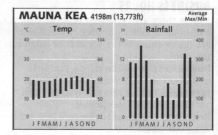

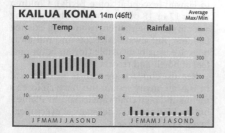

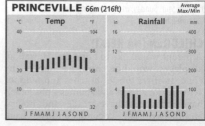

SMOKE-FREE HAWAII

On November 16, 2006 Hawaii became the 14th state in the US to pass comprehensive antismoking legislation. It is now illegal to light up a cigarette in any public building, or within 20ft of a building's entrance. This includes restaurants, bars, offices, hotel lobbies and many other places – though you can still smoke in your car and outside in the park. Because smoking is now largely banned, this guide does not use a nonsmoking icon (☒). Note that if you break the law, you can be fined $50, plus a $25 court fee. (For complete information on Hawaii's nonsmoking regulations, visit www.hawaiismokefree.com.)

Surveys show that 85% of Hawaiians favor the law. But there is still that disgruntled 15%. On the Big Island, some consider the law absurd, seeing as how they live with a 'smoking' volcano – Kilauea – that puffs out some 2000 tons of sulfur dioxide daily. That, indeed, is some killer second-hand smoke.

(p272) and the Volcano Art Center (p292) on the Big Island, and the Hui No'eau Visual Arts Center (p395) on Maui.

For an overview of mediation, yoga and so-called 'alternative healing' classes and retreats on the islands, see p87.

The main venue for courses is the **University of Hawai'i** (UH; www.hawaii.edu), which has its main campus at Manoa on O'ahu and a smaller campus in Hilo on the Big Island. UH offers full-time university attendance and summer-school courses. The summer session consists primarily of two six-week terms. For a catalog, contact the **Outreach College office** (☎ 956-5666, 800-862-6628; www.outreach .hawaii.edu/summer; Room 101, Krauss Hall, 2500 Dole St, Honolulu, HI 96822).

CUSTOMS

Each visitor is allowed to bring 1L of liquor and 200 cigarettes duty-free into the USA, but you must be at least 21 years old to possess the former and 18 years old to possess the latter. In addition, each traveler is permitted to bring up to $100 worth of gift merchandise into the USA without incurring any duty.

Most fresh fruits and plants are restricted from entry into Hawaii, and customs officials are militant. In order to help prevent the pestilent spread of invasive alien species (see Environmental Issues, p70), it's also important to clean shoes and outdoor gear before bringing it to the islands. Because Hawaii is a rabies-free state, the pet quarantine laws are draconian, but you may be able to slice the time and expense to 30 days ($655) or five days ($225). For complete details, contact the **Hawaiian Department of Agriculture** (☎ 808-973-9560; www.hawaiiag.org).

DANGERS & ANNOYANCES

In general, Hawaii is a very safe place to visit. For travelers, the two main concerns are car break-ins (common) and natural disasters (rare but serious). Since tourism is so important to Hawaii, state officials have established the **Visitor Aloha Society of Hawaii** (VASH; ☎ 808-926-8274; www.visitoralohasocietyofhawaii.org), which provides aid to visitors who become the victims of accidents or crimes while vacationing in Hawaii.

For health concerns, see the Health chapter.

Drugs

Pakalolo (marijuana) remains a billion-dollar underground industry, and the use of 'ice' (crystal methamphetamine) has been an ongoing social and law-enforcement issue since the 1990s, especially in rural communities. The 'ice epidemic' has abated somewhat recently (as a result of enforcement efforts), but ice-related crimes continue and social-service agencies still struggle to provide treatment for addicts.

Scams

The main scams directed toward visitors in Hawaii involve fake activity-operator booths and timeshare booths. Salespeople at the latter will offer you all sorts of deals, from free luaus to sunset cruises, if you'll just come to hear their 'no obligation' pitch. *Caveat emptor.*

Theft & Violence

The islands are notorious for rip-offs from parked rental cars. It can happen within seconds, whether from a secluded parking area at a trailhead or from a crowded hotel parking lot. As much as possible, do not to leave anything valuable in your car, ever. If you must, pack things well out of sight *before* you arrive at your destination; thieves wait and watch to see what you put in the trunk. Many locals leave their car doors unlocked to avoid paying for broken windows.

Otherwise, the most common problem is being hassled by drunks on beaches and in campgrounds, mainly at night. Wherever you are, stay tuned to the general vibe (see also Women Travelers, p565). Don't leave valuables in your tent, and watch your belongings in hostels.

Overall, violent crime is lower in Hawaii than in most of mainland USA, but Honolulu is a major city of nearly a million people and it suffers from the gamut of typical big-city problems, including a growing homeless population (p185). Don't forget your street smarts just because you're in Hawaii.

Natural Disasters

Hurricanes, tsunami and earthquakes all occur in Hawaii, sometimes to devastating effect. In 2006 the Big Island was shaken by a 6.7 earthquake that caused $200 million in damage, but no deaths (see the boxed text, p198). In 1992 Hurricane 'Iniki wrecked large swathes of Kaua'i (see the boxed text, p496), and in 1946 the largest tsunami in Hawaii's history killed 159 people and caused enormous damage (see p265).

On average, tsunami (incorrectly called tidal waves – the Japanese term *tsunami* means 'harbor wave') have occurred once a decade over the last century and killed more people statewide than all other natural disasters combined. In 1948 Hawaii installed a tsunami warning system, aired through yellow speakers mounted on telephone poles around the islands. They're tested on the first working day of each month at 11:45am for about one minute.

Of course, it's highly unlikely that a natural disaster will occur while you're here. Usually, there is ample warning prior to hurricanes. If you hear tsunami warning sirens, head for higher ground immediately. The front sections of telephone books have maps of tsunami safety evacuation zones. Earthquakes usually provide no warning; if one occurs, get clear of buildings or brace yourself in doorways.

For more information, visit the websites of the **International Tsunami Information Center** (www.tsunamiwave.info); the **National Hurricane Center** (www.nhc.noaa.gov); and the **Pacific Disaster Center** (www.pdc.org).

DISCOUNTS

Glossy, free tourist magazines are distributed widely; all contain discount coupons for activities and restaurants. However, for hotels and activities, usually the best deals are offered when you book in advance through their websites.

Children, students, seniors and military personnel usually receive discounts into museums and other sights. All but children need valid identification confirming their status. Since Hawaii is a popular destination for retirees, senior discounts are available more widely than others; for instance, Hawaii's biggest hotel chain, Outrigger, offers across-the-board discounts to seniors. If you have reached 'that age,' consider joining the nonprofit **American Association of Retired Persons** (AARP; ☎ 888-687-2277; www.aarp.org; 601 E St NW, Washington, DC 20049), which is a good source for travel bargains.

EMBASSIES & CONSULATES

The **US Department of State** (http://usembassy.state.gov) website has links for all US embassies abroad:

Australia (☎ 02-6214 5600; Moonah Pl, Yarralumla, Canberra, ACT 2600)
Canada (☎ 613-238 5335; 490 Sussex Dr, Ottawa, Ontario K1N 1G8)
France (☎ 33 1 43 12 22 22; 2 Av Gabriel, 75382 Paris Cedex 08)
Germany (☎ 030-238 5174; Neustádtische Kirchstrasse 4-5, 10117 Berlin)
Ireland (☎ 353-1-668 8777; 42 Elgin Rd, Ballsbridge, Dublin 4)
Italy (☎ 39-06-4674-1; Via Vittorio Veneto 119/A, 00187 Rome)
Japan (☎ 03-3224-5000; 1-10-5 Akasaka, Minato-ku, Tokyo 107-8420)
Netherlands (☎ 31-70-310 9209; Lange Voorhout 102, 2514 EJ, The Hague)
New Zealand (☎ 04-462 6000; 29 Fitzherbert Terrace, Thorndon, Wellington)
UK (☎ 020-7499 9000; 24 Grosvenor Sq, London W1A 1AE)

Consulates in Honolulu:
Australia (Map pp106-7; ☎ 524-5050; 1000 Bishop St)
Germany (Map pp136-7; ☎ 946-3819; 252 Paoa Pl)
Italy (Map pp106-7; ☎ 531-2277; Suite 201, 735 Bishop St)
Japan (☎ 543-3111; 1742 Nu'uanu Ave)
Netherlands (Map pp106-7; ☎ 531-6897; Suite 702, 745 Fort St Mall)
New Zealand (Map pp106-7; ☎ 547-5117; Suite 414, 900 Richards St)
Philippines (☎ 595-6316; 2433 Pali Hwy)

FESTIVALS & EVENTS

Hawaii is an almost year-round festival. There are far too many to list, but here are some of the major festivals and events. See also p23 for our list of recommended festivals. The **Hawaii Visitors & Convention Bureau** (www.gohawaii .com) posts a complete events calendar on its website. For holidays, see right.

January to March
NFL Pro Bowl (O'ahu) Early January
Hula Bowl (O'ahu) January
Chinese New Year (statewide) Mid-January to mid-February
Cherry Blossom Festival (mostly on O'ahu) February to early March
St Patrick's Day Parade (Waikiki, O'ahu) March 17
Merrie Monarch Festival (Hilo, the Big Island, p276) Starts Easter Sunday

April to May
May Day (all islands) May 1
Moloka'i Ka Hula Piko (Moloka'i; p436) May

June to July
Pan-Pacific Festival (Honolulu, O'ahu) First weekend of June
Prince Lot Hula Festival (Honolulu, O'ahu, p122) July
Transpacific Yacht Race (Honolulu, O'ahu) Early to mid-July
July 4 Rodeos (Waimea, the Big Island, p249; and Makawao, Maui, p396) July 4

August to October
Aloha Festivals (all islands, p122) Late August through early October
Princess Ka'iulani Commemoration Week (Waikiki, O'ahu) Third week in October
Hawaii International Film Festival (all islands, p122) Late October

November to December
Kona Coffee Cultural Festival (Kailua-Kona, the Big Island; p207) Early November
Triple Crown of Surfing (North Shore of O'ahu, p79) November through December
Pearl Harbor Day (Honolulu, O'ahu) December 7
Bodhi Day (statewide) December 8

FOOD

Reviews in the Eating section for each destination are broken down into three price categories: budget (for meals costing $12 or less), midrange (where most main dishes cost $12 to $30) and top end (where most dinner mains cost more than $30). These price estimates do not include taxes, tips or beverages.

For details about Hawaiian cuisine and local grinds, see the Food & Drink chapter.

GAY & LESBIAN TRAVELERS

Hawaii has a heritage of Polynesian tolerance that extends to gays and lesbians – despite the sometimes homophobic statements of a few contemporary Hawaiian elders. However, locals also tend to be very private about their personal lives in general, so you will not see much public hand-holding and open displays of affection of any kind, much less between gays. Even in Waikiki, which is without question the home of Hawaii's main gay scene, that 'scene' is muted by mainland standards (say, compared to San Francisco or Los Angeles). Everyday queer life is low-key – it's more about picnics and potlucks, not nightclubs.

That said, Hawaii remains a very popular destination for gay and lesbian travelers, who are served by a network of B&Bs, resorts and tours. A good source of information on local issues is the **Gay & Lesbian Community Center** (Map pp106-7; ☎ 545-2848; www.thecenterhawaii.org; Suite 105, 614 South St, Honolulu, HI 96813), which has support groups, movie nights, a community newspaper and a library. The monthly **Odyssey** (www .odysseyhawaii.com), free at gay-friendly businesses throughout Hawaii, covers the island-wide gay scene.

For more information on gay Hawaii, and recommendations about places to stay, gay beaches, travel arrangements and so on, visit the following sites:
Gay Hawaii (www.gayhawaii.com)
Out in Hawaii (www.outinhawaii.com)
Pacific Ocean Holidays (☎ 944-4700, 800-735-6599; PO Box 88245, Honolulu, HI 96830; www.gayhawaii vacations.com) Arranges packages.
Rainbow Handbook Hawai'i (www.rainbowhand book.com)

HOLIDAYS

Also see Festivals & Events (left).
New Year's Day January 1
Martin Luther King Jr Day Third Monday of January
Presidents Day Third Monday of February
Easter March or April
Memorial Day Last Monday of May
King Kamehameha Day June 11
Independence Day July 4

DIRECTORY

Admission Day Third Friday of August
Labor Day first Monday of September
Columbus Day Second Monday of October
Election Day Second Tuesday of November
Veterans Day November 11
Thanksgiving Fourth Thursday of November
Christmas Day December 25

THE LEGAL AGE FOR...

- Drinking: 21
- Driving: 16
- Sex: 16
- Voting: 18

INSURANCE

It's expensive to get sick, crash a car or have things stolen from you in the USA. For car-rental insurance, see p571, and for health insurance, see p573. Consult your home-owner's (or renter's) insurance policy before leaving home to see if and to what extent you are covered should items be stolen from your rental car.

INTERNET ACCESS

If you usually access your email through your office or school, you'll find it easier to open a free account with **Yahoo!** (www.yahoo.com) or **Hotmail** (www.hotmail.com).

If you bring a laptop from outside the USA, invest in a universal AC and plug adapter. Also, your PC card modem may not work once you leave your home country – but you won't know until you try. The safest option? Buy a reputable 'global' modem before leaving home. Ensure that you have at least a US RJ-11 telephone adapter that works with your modem. For more technical help, visit **TeleAdapt** (www.teleadapt.com).

On the main islands, cybercafés and business centers offer inexpensive online computer access (see the 'Information' sections in this book). Public libraries provide free internet access, but you need to purchase a temporary three-month nonresident library card ($10); for details, visit **Hawaii State Public Library System** (www.librarieshawaii.org).

When accommodations provide an internet terminal for their guests, this is noted with the icon 🖳. An increasing number of hotels, B&Bs and cafés offer wi-fi; this is often but not always noted in text. Call the hotel to confirm. Also, visit **Wi-Fi Alliance** (www.wi-fi.org) or **Wi-Fi Free Spot** (www.wififreespot.com) for a list of wi-fi hotspots in Hawaii (plus tech and access info).

LEGAL MATTERS

You have the right to an attorney from the very first moment you are arrested. If you can't afford one, the state must provide one for free. The **Hawaii State Bar Association** (☎ 537-9140, 800-808-4722) makes attorney referrals, but foreign visitors may want to call their consulate for advice.

In Hawaii, anyone driving with a blood alcohol level of 0.08% or higher is guilty of driving 'under the influence,' which carries severe penalties. As with most places, the possession of marijuana and narcotics is illegal in Hawaii.

Hawaii's **Department of Commerce & Consumer Affairs** (www.hawaii.gov/dcca) has a Consumer Resource Center with contact numbers for each island if you want to lodge a complaint against a company or get more information on your rights.

According to the letter of the law, hitchhiking is illegal statewide.

MAPS

First things first: the maps in this book are sufficient for quite a bit of exploring! And staying within the family for another minute, Lonely Planet's *Honolulu & O'ahu City Map* is invaluable.

By far, the most detailed street maps are the *Ready Mapbook* series. These atlas-style books (about $10 each) cover virtually every road on each of the main islands. (Lana'i and Moloka'i are included in the book for Maui.) Bookstores and convenience stores in Honolulu and Waikiki also stock street maps of the city area.

Serious hikers should get topographical island and sectional maps published by the **US Geological Survey** (USGS; ☎ 888-275-8747; www.usgs.gov); however, note the dates on the maps, as some were drawn decades ago. USGS maps can be purchased at the national parks on Maui and the Big Island and at good bookstores; see 'Information' sections in island chapters.

Divers and snorkelers should try **Franko's Maps** (www.frankosmaps.com), a series of laminated, waterproof maps (about $7) of each island showing snorkeling and diving spots.

MONEY

The US dollar is the only currency used in Hawaii. The dollar (commonly called a buck) is divided into 100 cents. Coins come in denominations of one cent (penny), five cents (nickel), 10 cents (dime), 25 cents (quarter) and the rare 50-cent piece (half dollar). Notes come in one-, five-, 10-, 20-, 50- and 100-dollar denominations.

See the Quick Reference inside the front cover for exchange rates, and Getting Started (p22) for information on costs.

ATMs, Cash & Checks

ATMs are everywhere, and their ease and availability have largely negated the need for traveler's checks. However, most ATM withdrawals using out-of-state cards incur surcharges of $1.50 to $2.

The **Bank of Hawaii** (www.boh.com) and **First Hawaiian Bank** (www.fhb.com) both have extensive ATM networks that will give cash advances on major credit cards and allow cash withdrawals with affiliated ATM cards. Most ATMs in Hawaii accept bank cards from both the Plus and Cirrus systems. Look for ATMs outside banks, and in large grocery stores, shopping centers, convenience stores and gas stations.

If you're carrying foreign currency, it can be exchanged for US dollars at the Honolulu International Airport and larger banks around Hawaii.

Personal checks not drawn on a Hawaiian bank are generally not accepted.

Credit Cards

Major credit cards are widely accepted in Hawaii, including at car-rental agencies and most hotels, restaurants, gas stations, grocery stores and tour operators. Many B&Bs and some condominiums – particularly those handled through rental agencies – do not accept credit cards, however.

Tipping

In restaurants, good waiters are tipped at least 15%, while dissatisfied customers make their ire known by leaving 10%. There has to be real cause for not tipping at all. Taxi drivers and hairstylists are typically tipped about 10% and hotel bellhops about $1 per bag.

Traveler's Checks

Traveler's checks provide protection from theft and loss. Keeping a record of the check numbers and those you have used is vital for replacing lost checks, so keep this information separate from the checks themselves. For refunds on lost or stolen travelers checks, call **American Express** (☎ 800-992-3404) or **Thomas Cook** (☎ 800-287-7362).

Foreign visitors carrying traveler's checks will find things infinitely easier if the checks are in US dollars. These are accepted like cash at most midrange and top-end restaurants, hotels and shops, but rarely if ever by budget lodgings and cheap diners.

PHOTOGRAPHY

For a course on photographic sins and excellence, consult Lonely Planet's *Travel Photography*.

Both print and slide film are readily available in Hawaii. Disposable underwater cameras (about $15) deliver surprisingly good snaps.

While in Hawaii, try to develop each roll as you finish it, as the high temperature and humidity greatly accelerate the deterioration of exposed film. Longs Drugs is one of the cheapest places for developing film. All the main tourist enclaves have one-hour print shops.

Don't even think about taking snaps of military installations.

With the implementation of high-powered X-ray at airports, don't pack film into checked luggage or carry-on bags. Instead carry your film in a baggie to show separately to airport security officials (known as a hand check). Remember to finish off the roll in your camera and take it out, too, or those photos may end up foggy.

For video information, see p553.

POST

Mail delivery to and from Hawaii usually takes a little longer than similar services on the US mainland via the **US postal service** (USPS; ☎ 800-275-8777; www.usps.gov).

First-class mail between Hawaii and the mainland goes by air and usually takes three to four days. For 1st-class mail sent and delivered within the USA, postage rates are 37¢ for letters up to 1oz (23¢ for each additional ounce) and 23¢ for standard-size postcards.

International airmail rates for letters up to 1oz are 60¢ to Canada or Mexico, 80¢ to other countries. Postcards cost 50¢ to Canada or Mexico, 70¢ to other countries.

You can have mail sent to you c/o General Delivery at most big post offices in Hawaii. On O'ahu, all general-delivery mail addressed to Honolulu or Waikiki is delivered to the main post office adjacent to Honolulu International Airport. General delivery mail is usually held for up to 30 days. Most hotels will also hold mail for incoming guests.

SHOPPING

Looking for a souvenir? Hmmm, Hawaii might have *something*...

In a nation known for its kitsch, Hawaii may be the (plastic) jewel in the crown. It is also one of the USA's top places for quality handmade crafts. The only question is: are you a hula girl bobble-figure type person or a hand-carved koa bowl type person?

If you're the latter, prepare for high prices; the real stuff isn't cheap. If you do find 'an amazing deal,' it's likely not to be authentic. Farmers markets are great places for well-priced crafts and local art – often sold by the artist – but it may be hard to distinguish fake from genuine articles.

The best way to ensure that what you buy is authentic Hawaiiana is to shop at well-respected art galleries and artist's cooperatives. These are noted in island chapters, but a sampling of the best includes: the granddaddy of them all, the Bishop Museum on O'ahu (p115); the Volcano Art Center on the Big Island (p292); and the Hui No'eau Visual Arts Center (p395) and Maui Crafts Guild (p373), both on Maui. On Kaua'i, the little town of Hanapepe (p534) has a number of fine galleries; also visit the website www.kauaimade.org for other bona fide sellers.

See p50 for more information on Hawaiian arts and crafts.

In addition to Hawaiian music, aloha shirts, flower-print dresses and more T-shirts than there are fish in the sea, Hawaii has a number of food items that make great gifts. Nothing says Hawaii like macadamia nuts and Kona coffee, but also look for high-quality *liliko'i* (passion fruit) preserves, mango chutneys, crack seed (p55) and specialty chocolates. Make sure that any unsealed food item has been verified as approved for travel (or you'll be forced to surrender your papayas and mangoes at the airport).

Flowers such as orchids, anthuriums and proteas make good gifts if you're flying straight home. Proteas stay fresh for about 10 days and then can be dried. Foreign visitors should check with their airline, however, as there are often restrictions on taking agricultural products across international borders (see p557).

SOLO TRAVELERS

Travel, including solo travel, is generally safe and easy. In general, women need to exercise more vigilance in large cities than in rural areas. Everyone, though, should avoid hiking, cycling long distances or camping alone, especially in unfamiliar places. For more safety advice, see Women Travelers (p565) and Dangers & Annoyances (p557).

TELEPHONE

Always dial '1' before toll-free (☎ 800, 888 etc) and domestic long-distance numbers. Some toll-free numbers may only work within the state or from the US mainland, for instance, while others may work from Canada, too. But you'll only know if it works by making the call.

Pay phones are readily found in shopping centers, beach parks and other public places. Calls from one point on an island to another point on that island are considered local and cost 25¢ or 50¢. Calls from one island to another are always long distance and more expensive. Hotels often add a hefty service charge ($1 and more) for calls from a room phone.

Private prepaid phone cards are available from convenience stores, supermarkets and pharmacies. Cards sold by major telecommunications companies, such as AT&T, may offer better deals than upstart companies.

Cell (Mobile) Phones

The USA uses a variety of mobile-phone systems, 99% of which are incompatible with the GSM 900/1800 standard used throughout Europe and Asia. Check with your cellular service provider before departure about using your phone in Hawaii. Verizon has the most extensive cellular network on the islands, but AT&T, Cingular and Sprint also have decent coverage. Cellular coverage is quite good on O'ahu, but more spotty on the Neighbor Islands. Coverage is nonexistent in many remote regions and on hiking trails.

Long-Distance & International Calls

To make international calls direct from Hawaii, dial ☎ 011 + country code + area code + number. (An exception is to Canada, where you dial ☎ 1 + area code + number, but international rates still apply.)

For international operator assistance, dial ☎ 0. The operator can provide specific rate information and tell you which time periods are the cheapest for calling.

If you're calling Hawaii from abroad, the international country code for the USA is ☎ 1. All calls to Hawaii are then followed by the area code ☎ 808 and the seven-digit local number. Also dial the area code when making a call from one island to another (eg O'ahu to Maui).

TIME

Hawaii does not observe daylight saving time. It does, though, have about 11 hours of daylight in midwinter (December) and almost 13½ hours in midsummer (June). In midwinter the sun rises at about 7am and sets at about 6pm. In midsummer it rises before 6am and sets after 7pm.

And then there's 'Hawaiian' or 'island time,' which is either a relaxed pace or a euphemism for being late.

When it's noon in Hawaii, it's 2pm in Los Angeles, 5pm in New York, 10pm in London, 7am the next day in Tokyo, 8am the next day in Melbourne and 10am the next day in Auckland.

TOURIST INFORMATION

In addition to the tourist bureaus listed here, you can get a good deal of useful tourist information from two very similar free publications, which are piled up everywhere on all four main islands: **101 Things to Do** (www.101thingstodo .com) and **This Week** (www.thisweek.com).

Big Island Visitors Bureau Hilo (Map p268; ☎ 961-5797, 800-648-2441; www.bigisland.org; 250 Keawe St, Hilo 96720); Waikoloa (☎ 886-1655; Suite B14, King's Shops, 250 Waikoloa Beach Dr, Waikoloa 96738)

Destination Lana'i (☎ 565-7600, 800-947-4774; www.visitlanai.net)

Hawaii Visitors & Convention Bureau (Map pp106-7; ☎ 800-464-2924; www.gohawaii.com; Suite 801, 2270 Kalakaua Ave, Honolulu, HI 96815) Will mail a free Visitor Guide.

Kauai Visitors Bureau (Map p467; ☎ 245-3971, 800-262-1400; www.kauaivisitorsbureau.org; Suite 101, 4334 Rice St, Lihu'e)

Maui Visitors Bureau (Map p351; ☎ 244-3530, 800-525-6284; www.visitmaui.com; 1727 Wili Pa Loop, Wailuku) Also represents Lana'i and Moloka'i.

Moloka'i Visitors Association (Map p435; ☎ 553-3876; www.molokai-hawaii.com; Suite 200, 2 Kamoi St, Kaunakakai 96748)

O'ahu Visitors Bureau (☎ 877-525-6248; www .visit-oahu.com)

TOURS

See p567 for package tours and p568 for cruises to the Hawaiian Islands.

A number of companies operate half- and full-day sightseeing bus tours on each island. Specialized adventure tours, like whale-watching cruises, bicycle tours down Haleakala, snorkeling trips to Lana'i and boat cruises along the Kona Coast, are also available. All of these tours can be booked after arrival in Hawaii. For details, consult the Activities sections near the front of island chapters.

Helicopter tours get you to some amazing places, with flights over active volcanoes, along towering coastal cliffs and above inaccessible waterfalls. Prices vary depending on the destination and the length of the flight, with a 45-minute tour averaging $175 per passenger. For details, see the Tours section near the front of each island chapter.

If you want to visit another island while you're in Hawaii but only have a day or two to spare, consider an island-hopping tour to the Neighbor Islands. The largest company specializing in 'overnighters' is **Roberts Hawaii** (☎ on O'ahu 523-9323, from the Neighbor Islands & US mainland 800-899-9323; www.robertsovernighters.com).

Elderhostel (☎ 800-454-5768; www.elderhostel.org) offers educational programs for those aged 55 or older. Many of these focus on Hawaii's people and culture, while others explore the natural environment. Fees cost $800 to $3500 for one- to two-week programs, including accommodations, meals and classes, but excluding airfare.

TRAVELERS WITH DISABILITIES

Many of the major resort hotels and tourist areas have elevators, TTD-capable phones, wheelchair-accessible rooms and other features to smooth the day. Beyond that, few generalizations can be made islandwide. For specifics, contact the **Disability and Communication Access Board** (DCAB; ☎ 586-8121; www.hawaii .gov/health/dcab; Room 101, 919 Ala Moana Blvd, Honolulu, HI 96814). From its website, you can download Travel Tips brochures with information on airlines, transportation, medical and other support services on each island.

Seeing-eye and guide dogs are not subject to the same quarantine as other pets, provided they meet the Department of Agriculture's minimum requirements (see p557).

Wheelchair Getaways of Hawaii (☎ 800-638-1912; www.wheelchairgetaways.com) rents wheelchair-accessible vans on all the islands.

For a list of services available to disabled passengers by airline, go to **The Allgohere Airline Directory** (www.everybody.co.uk/airindex.htm).

On mainland USA, the **Society for the Advancement of Travel for the Handicapped** (SATH; ☎ 212-447-7284; www.sath.org; Suite 610, 347 Fifth Ave, New York, NY 10016) publishes a quarterly magazine and has various information sheets on travel for the disabled.

VISAS

The US continues to fine-tune its entry requirements and security guidelines post-September 11, so it's imperative that all foreign visitors double-check visa guidelines. The introductory portal for US visa information is **Destination USA** (www.unitedstatesvisas.gov). The **US State Department** (www.travel.state.gov) maintains the most comprehensive visa information and has application forms that can be downloaded.

US Citizenship & Immigration Services (www.uscis .gov) mainly focuses on immigrants, not temporary visitors.

With the exception of Canadians and visitors who qualify for the Visa Waiver Program (right), foreign visitors to the USA need a visa. To apply, you need a passport that's valid for at least six months longer than your intended stay and a recent photo (50.8mm x 50.8mm). All students and males aged 16 to 45 must fill out supplemental documents detailing their travel plans (though this can be required of anyone). Documents of financial stability and/or guarantees from a US resident are sometimes required, particularly for those from developing countries. Visa applicants may be required to 'demonstrate binding obligations' that will ensure their return home. Because of this requirement, those planning to travel through other countries before arriving in the USA are better off applying for their US visa in their home country rather than while they are on the road.

The validity period for a US visitor visa depends on your home country. The actual length of time you'll be allowed to stay in the USA is determined by US officials at the port of entry. If you want to stay in the USA longer than the date stamped on your passport, go to the Honolulu office of the **Citizenship & Immigration Service** (☎ 532-3721; 595 Ala Moana Blvd, Honolulu) before the stamped date to apply for an extension.

The Visa Waiver Program allows citizens of certain countries to enter the USA for stays of 90 days or less without first obtaining a US visa. There are 27 countries currently participating; they are Andorra, Australia, Austria, Belgium, Brunei, Denmark, Finland, France, Germany, Iceland, Ireland, Italy, Japan, Liechtenstein, Luxembourg, Monaco, the Netherlands, New Zealand, Norway, Portugal, San Marino, Singapore, Slovenia, Spain, Sweden, Switzerland and the UK. Under this program you must have a return ticket (or onward ticket to any foreign destination) that is nonrefundable in the USA. You also need a machine-readable passport (or if your passport was issued/renewed after October 26, 2006 an 'e-passport' with digital chip). Note that you will not be allowed to extend your stay beyond 90 days.

Upon arriving in the US, all foreign visitors must register in the US-Visit program. This entails having their two index fingers scanned and a digital photo taken. For more information, see the website of the **Department of Homeland Security** (www.dhs.gov).

VOLUNTEERING

Volunteer opportunities abound in Hawaii, and they provide a memorable experience of Hawaii's people and land you'll never get by just passing through. Some require time commitments, typically a week or so, but lots ask for just a day. Longer programs may provide meals and lodging (and charge a fee to offset costs), but none provide transportation to Hawaii.

The best central place to find out about volunteer opportunities is **Malama Hawaii** (www .malamahawaii.org), a partnership network of community and nonprofit organizations. It posts a wide-ranging calendar that also includes fundraising concerts, educational events and cultural workshops. Volunteer by pulling invasive weeds, doing trail maintenance, restoring taro patches, cleaning streams and much more.

The **Sierra Club** (www.hi.sierraclub.org) and the **Hawaii Audubon Society** (www.hawaiiaudubon.com) are great organizations that conduct programs on all the islands. The **Division of Forestry & Wildlife** (DOFAW; www.dofaw.net) coordinates volunteers at state reserves and parks.

The **National Park Service** (www.nps.gov/volunteer) coordinates volunteers at Hawai'i Volcanoes National Park (p288) on the Big Island and Haleakala National Park (p403) on Maui.

Volunteer Zone (www.volunteerzone.org) is aimed at residents (mostly on O'ahu) but is open to visitors; it also lists places to contribute donations. Volunteer with O'ahu's **Hawaii Nature Center** (www.hawaiinaturecenter.org) and you can nurture both children and the outdoors.

One of the most memorable volunteer opportunities is the five-day trip to the uninhabited island of Kaho'olawe (p412) run by **Protect Kaho'olawe 'Ohana** (www.kahoolawe.org).

On Kaua'i, the **Koke'e Resource Conservation Program** (www.krcp.org) conducts weed-control projects in Koke'e, Waimea Canyon and Na Pali Coast State Parks.

The **Hawaiian Islands Humpback Whale National Marine Sanctuary** (www.hawaiihumpbackwhale.noaa.gov) needs volunteers (mostly on Maui); if you're here during the first three months of the year, consider joining the annual Sanctuary Ocean Count.

Those with more time and an interest in dolphins should contact **Wild Dolphin Foundation** (www.wilddolphin.org/volunteer.html) about assisting its ongoing research.

You can also assist scientists with field research through **Earthwatch International** (www.earthwatch.org), which has occasional Hawaii projects.

WOMEN TRAVELERS

Hawaii presents few unique problems for women travelers and may be more relaxed and comfortable than many mainland destinations. The one place where women – especially solo travelers – might feel uneasy is in local bars, but no more nor less than anywhere else in the world.

If you're camping, opt for secure, well-used camping areas over isolated locales where you might be the only camper; this advice pertains to anyone. Some county parks and their campgrounds (see p553) are notorious as late-night party spots. This can be true of beaches after dark as well, and women should be careful walking alone on beaches at night.

WORK

US citizens can pursue work in Hawaii as they would in any other state – the problem is finding a decent job. Foreign visitors in the USA on tourist visas are not legally allowed to take up employment.

Finding serious 'professional' employment is difficult since Hawaii has a tight labor market. The biggest exceptions are for teachers and nurses. Waiting on tables at restaurants or cafés is probably what you can expect. Folks with language, scuba, fishing or guiding skills might investigate employment with resorts. But most housekeeping or groundskeeping jobs at megaresorts go to locals.

Check notice boards in larger cities, at hostels (which often offer room and board in exchange for work), at coffee shops and cafés, and at natural food stores. Also check the classified job ads in the *Honolulu Advertiser* (www.honoluluadvertiser.com). Continue surfing at **JobsHawaii.com** (www.jobshawaii.com) and at **Hire Net Hawaii** (www.hirenethawaii.com), which is run by the **State Department of Labor & Industrial Relations** (☎ 586-8700; www.hawaii.gov/labor; 830 Punchbowl St, Honolulu, HI 96813).

Transportation

CONTENTS

GETTING THERE & AWAY

Roughly 99% of visitors to Hawaii arrive by air, and the majority of flights – international and domestic – arrive at Honolulu International Airport (below), though recently direct flights to Neighbor Islands have increased.

Flights and tours can be booked online at www.lonelyplanet.com/travel_services.

ENTERING THE COUNTRY

A passport is required for all foreign citizens, who must register with the US-Visit program. Unless eligible under the Visa Waiver Program, foreign travelers must also have a tourist visa. Always reconfirm US entrance requirements prior to boarding your plane. See p564 for details.

AIR

Hawaii is a very competitive market for US domestic and international airfares, which vary tremendously by season, demand, number of stopovers and ticket details. At any given time, any airline may have the cheapest fare.

Airports & Airlines

Because of the sheer distance, travelers arriving from Europe will often have to change planes on the US mainland. Major gateway airports include the following:

Atlanta International Airport (ATL; ☎ 800-897-1910; www.atlanta-airport.com)
Chicago O'Hare International Airport (ORD; ☎ 773-686-2200; www.ohare.com)
Denver International Airport (DEN; ☎ 303-342-2000; www.flydenver.com)
Los Angeles International Airport (LAX; ☎ 310-646-5252; www.los-angeles-lax.com)
New York JFK International Airport (JFK; ☎ 718-244-4444; www.panynj.gov)
San Francisco International Airport (SFO; ☎ 650-821-8211; www.flysfo.com)

The majority of incoming flights from overseas and the US mainland arrive on O'ahu at **Honolulu International Airport** (HNL; ☎ 836-6413; www.honoluluairport.com). Airlines flying into Honolulu:

Air Canada (AC; ☎ 888-247-2262; www.aircanada.com)
Air New Zealand (NZ; ☎ 800-262-1234; www.airnewzealand.com)
Air Pacific (Fj; ☎ 800-227-4446; www.airpacific.com)
Alaska Airlines (AS; ☎ 800-252-7522; www.alaskaair.com)
Aloha Airlines (AQ; ☎ 800-367-5250; www.alohaairlines.com)
American Airlines (AA; ☎ 800-433-7300; www.aa.com)
China Airlines (CI; ☎ 800-227-5118; www.china-airlines.com)
Continental (CO; ☎ 800-523-3273; www.continental.com)
Delta (DL; ☎ 800-221-1212; www.delta.com)
Hawaiian Airlines (HA; ☎ 800-367-5320; www.hawaiianair.com)
Japan Airlines (JL; ☎ 800-525-3663; www.japanair.com)
Korean Airlines (KE; ☎ 800-438-5000; www.koreanair.com)
Northwest (NW; ☎ 800-225-2525; www.nwa.com)
Philippine Airlines (PR; ☎ 800-435-9725; www.philippineair.com)
Qantas Airways (QF; ☎ 800-227-4500; www.qantas.com.au)
United Airlines (UA; ☎ 800-241-6522; www.ual.com)
US Airways (US; ☎ 800-428-4322; www.usairways.com/awa)

For information on most airlines, visit **Seat Guru** (www.seatguru.com). For more information on flights to individual islands, see the Getting There & Away sections near the front of each island chapter. To reach Lana'i or Moloka'i, you'll have to fly via Honolulu or Maui.

For information on Neighbor Island airports, visit www.hawaii.gov/dot/airports. Following are the main ones:

Hilo International Airport (ITO; ☎ 934-5840; Hawai'i)
Kahului airport (OGG; ☎ 872-3893; Maui)
Kona International Airport at Keahole (KOA; ☎ 329-3423; Hawai'i)
Lana'i airport (LNY; ☎ 565-6757; Lana'i)
Lihu'e airport (LIH; ☎ 246-1448; Kaua'i)
Moloka'i airport (MKK; ☎ 567-6361; Moloka'i)

Tickets

The best deals are often found on the internet. Start searching at **Travelocity** (www.travelocity.com), **Expedia** (www.expedia.com), **Orbitz** (www.orbitz.com) or **Kayak** (www.kayak.com). You could also try **Priceline** (www.priceline.com), but first get advice at **BiddingForTravel.com** (www.biddingfortravel.com).

In Hawaii, larger travel agencies specializing in discount tickets and packages include **King's Travel** (Map p112; ☎ 593-4481, 800-801-4481; www.kingstravel.com; 725 Kapi'olani Blvd, Honolulu) and **Panda Travel** (Map pp136-7; ☎ 738-3898, 800-303-6702; www.pandaonline.com; 1017 Kapahulu Ave, Honolulu).

Round-the-world (RTW) tickets allow you to fly around the world using an alliance of airlines; Circle Pacific tickets are similar, but itineraries focus on the Pacific region. Only consider them if you want to visit other parts of the world in addition to Hawaii. The two main alliances are **One World** (www.oneworld.com) and the **Star Alliance** (www.staralliance.com).

US Mainland

Competition is high among airlines flying to Honolulu from major mainland cities, and the 'lowest fare' fluctuates constantly. In general, return fares from the US mainland to Hawaii cost $350 (during off-season deals from the West Coast) to $800+ (during high season from the East Coast). Package-tour companies can sometimes offer the best airfare deals, but you'll need to consider the whole 'package.'

Most mainland flights fly into Honolulu, but direct flights to Maui, Kaua'i and the Big Island are possible from San Francisco, Los Angeles, Seattle and Las Vegas. The greatest number of carriers, flights and nonstop options originate from West Coast cities. A few nonstops originate further east, but most often you will have to add one or even two stops from East Coast cities (certainly if you want the cheapest fare).

> **THINGS CHANGE...**
>
> The information in this chapter is particularly vulnerable to change. Check directly with the airline or a travel agent to make sure you understand how a fare (and ticket you may buy) works and be aware of the security requirements for international travel. Shop carefully. The details given in this chapter should be regarded as pointers and are not a substitute for your own careful, up-to-date research.

For those with limited time, package tours can sometimes be the cheapest option. Basic ones cover airfare and accommodations, while deluxe packages include car rental, island hopping and activities. **Pleasant Holidays** (☎ 800-742-9244; www1.pleasantholidays.com) has departures from various US mainland points.

And then there's the Air Tech Space-Available FlightPass, which is often the cheapest way to fly between the West Coast and Hawaii. **Air Tech** (☎ 212-219-7000; www.airtech.com) offers super deals (from $130 to $170 one way), but you must be flexible with your travel time; it offers unsold seats at the last minute and doesn't guarantee a specific flight. Currently, flights to Honolulu, Kaua'i, and Maui depart from San Francisco and Los Angeles.

The nonstop flight time to Hawaii is about 5½ hours from the West Coast. East Coast flights range from 11 to 15 hours, depending on stops.

Australia

Hawaiian Airlines flies nonstop between Sydney and Honolulu. Qantas flies to Honolulu from Sydney and Melbourne. Agents serving Australia include **Flight Centre** (☎ 1300-133-133; www.flightcentre.com.au) and **STA Travel** (☎ 1300-733-035; www.statravel.com.au).

Canada

Air Canada offers flights to Honolulu from Vancouver, Calgary, Edmonton and Toronto. Agents serving Canada include **Travel Cuts** (☎ 866-246-9762; www.travelcuts.com) and **Travelocity** (☎ 877-282-2925; www.travelocity.ca).

Japan

Japan Airlines flies to Honolulu from Tokyo, Osaka, Nagoya and Fukuoka. Continental and Northwest have several flights to Honolulu from Tokyo and Osaka. Agents serving Japan include **STA Travel** (☎ 03-5391-2922; www.statravel .co.jp).

Micronesia & New Zealand

Continental has nonstop flights from Guam to Honolulu, and Air New Zealand flies from Auckland. Agents serving New Zealand include **Flight Centre** (☎ 0800-24-35-44; www.flight centre.co.nz) and **STA Travel** (☎ 0800-474-400; www .statravel.co.nz).

South Pacific Islands

Hawaiian Airlines flies to Honolulu from Tahiti and American Samoa. Air New Zealand offers return flights from Fiji to Honolulu via Auckland; it also flies to Honolulu from Tonga, the Cook Islands and Western Samoa.

Southeast Asia

Northwest flies to Honolulu from Hong Kong, Bangkok, Manila, Seoul and Singapore. Korean Air, China Airlines, Philippine Airlines and others also offer numerous flights between Southeast Asian cities and Honolulu.

Bucket shops in Bangkok, Singapore and Hong Kong should be able to beat standard fares, perhaps by half price. Agents serving Southeast Asia include **STA Travel** (☎ 2148-9800; www.statravel.com.my), **Concorde Travel** (☎ 2526-3391; www.concorde-travel.com) and **Traveller Services** (☎ 2375-2222; www.taketraveller.com).

UK & Continental Europe

In addition to other national carriers, American, United, Delta and Continental offer flights to Honolulu from various European cities. The most common route to Hawaii from Europe is west via New York, Chicago or Los Angeles. If you're interested in heading east with stops in Asia, consider getting a RTW ticket.

London is arguably the world's headquarters for bucket shops specializing in discount tickets. Two good, reliable agents for cheap tickets in London are **STA Travel** (☎ 0870-162-7551; www.statravel.co.uk) and **Trailfinders** (☎ 0845-058-5858; www.trailfinders.com).

SEA

In recent years a handful of cruise ships has begun offering tours that include Hawaii. Most cruises last 10 to 12 days, and airfare to and from the departure point costs extra.

Most Hawaiian cruises include stopovers in Honolulu, Maui, Kaua'i and the Big Island. Cruise lines include the following:
Holland America Cruise Line (☎ 877-724-5425; www.hollandamerica.com) Typically departs from San Diego, Seattle or Vancouver.
Princess Cruises (☎ 800-568-3262; www.princess .com) Offers the most cruises; most depart from Los Angeles and Vancouver.

GETTING AROUND

Most interisland travel is by plane, but the recent launching of the Superferry (p570) now connects O'ahu, Kaua'i and Maui by sea.

AIR

The major airports handling most interisland traffic are Honolulu (on O'ahu), Kahului (on Maui), Kona and Hilo (both on the Big Island), and Lihu'e (on Kaua'i). See p566 for details.

Moloka'i and Lana'i are usually approached by ferry service from Maui.

Airlines in Hawaii

In 2006 Hawaiian Airlines and Aloha Airlines – longtime major interisland carriers – were joined by upstart go! (an affiliate of Mesa Air). All three offer frequent flights in full-bodied planes between the four main islands (opposite). Their advantage over the smaller carriers is frequency and dependability of service. Island Air (opposite), an affiliate of Aloha Airlines, provides service to the main islands as well as less-frequent connections to Moloka'i and Lana'i; it's the largest commuter airline and offers an extensive schedule, but it's infamous for late and cancelled flights.

Smaller airports – such as Hana on Maui and Waimea-Kohala on the Big Island – are served by Island Air as well as by Pacific Wings and Moloka'i Air Shuttle, which use prop planes. These carriers often have competitive fares, and they fly so low to the ground they almost double as sightseeing planes.

The advance reservations versus walk-up policies vary by commuter company. Also, airline regulations concerning surfboards and oversize equipment vary and can be very restrictive; make sure to check before booking.

CLIMATE CHANGE & TRAVEL

Climate change is a serious threat to the ecosystems that humans rely upon, and air travel is the fastest-growing contributor to the problem. Lonely Planet regards travel, overall, as a global benefit, but believes we all have a responsibility to limit our personal impact on global warming.

Flying & climate change

Pretty much every form of motorized travel generates CO_2 (the main cause of human-induced climate change) but planes are far and away the worst offenders, not just because of the sheer distances they allow us to travel, but because they release greenhouse gases high into the atmosphere. The statistics are frightening: two people taking a return flight between Europe and the US will contribute as much to climate change as an average household's gas and electricity consumption over a whole year.

Carbon offset schemes

Climatecare.org and other websites use 'carbon calculators' that allow travelers to offset the level of greenhouse gases they are responsible for with financial contributions to sustainable travel schemes that reduce global warming – including projects in India, Honduras, Kazakhstan and Uganda.

Lonely Planet, together with Rough Guides and other concerned partners in the travel industry, support the carbon offset scheme run by climatecare.org. Lonely Planet offsets all of its staff and author travel.

For more information check out our website: www.lonelyplanet.com.

Air Passes

At the time of writing the four largest carriers – Hawaiian Airlines, Aloha Airlines, go! and Island Air – were engaged in fierce fare wars that had cut one-way interisland airfares to $30 or $40. Competition from the Superferry may keep airfares low; stay tuned (in the past, one-way fares cost $70 to $100).

Interisland carriers offer a range of deals and schemes – from frequent-flyer programs to discounts for advance internet booking – but fares are currently about as low as they can go. In general, the further you fly, the more it will cost.

Aloha Airlines (☎ 800-367-5250, on O'ahu 484-1111; www.alohaairlines.com) Flies over 100 daily routes on 737s between Honolulu, Kaua'i, Maui and the Big Island.

George's Aviation (☎ 834-2120, 866-834-2120; www .georgesaviation.com) Flies charter prop planes between Honolulu, Maui and Moloka'i.

go! (☎ 888-435-9462; www.iflygo.com) Flies frequently from Honolulu to Kaua'i, Maui and the Big Island.

Hawaiian Airlines (☎ 800-367-5320, on O'ahu 838-1555; www.hawaiianair.com) Flies over 100 daily routes on 717s between Honolulu, Kaua'i, Maui and the Big Island.

Island Air (☎ 800-652-6541, on O'ahu 484-2222; www.islandair.com) Flies small 37-passenger planes between Honolulu, Moloka'i, Lana'i, Maui, Kaua'i and the Big Island.

Moloka'i Air Shuttle (☎ 567-6847, on O'ahu 545-4988) Flies prop planes between Honolulu and Moloka'i.

Pacific Wings (☎ 888-575-4546; www.pacificwings .com) Flies charter prop planes between all six main islands.

Paragon Air (☎ 800-428-1231, on Maui 244-3356; www.paragon-air.com) Flies charter prop planes from Maui; it specializes in trips to Moloka'i, but flies to all islands.

BICYCLE

We would never discourage dedicated cyclists, but realistically, getting around the islands solely by bicycle is challenging. It can entail blistering heat, strong headwinds, narrow roads and dangerous traffic. Long-distance cycling is best done with the support of a tour group, but if you're adventurous and in good shape, it can be done on your own. For island-specific details and advice, see the opening Activities section of island chapters.

The Superferry (p570) may make cycle touring much easier. It costs an extra $20 to $25 to wheel a bike onto the ferry, which allows cyclists to see O'ahu, Kaua'i and Maui without cumbersome interisland flights. Tour as much as you feel like, then ferry over to the next island!

Bringing your own bike to Hawaii costs upwards of $100 on flights from the mainland;

interisland flights charge an additional $25 or more. The bicycle can be checked at the airline counter, the same as any baggage, but you'll need to prepare the bike by wrapping the handlebars and pedals in foam or by fixing the handlebars to the side and removing the pedals.

In general, bicycles are required to follow the same state laws and rules of the road as cars. For island-specific cycling information, see the Activities and Getting Around sections of the island chapters. See also p86.

BOAT

The new **Hawaii Superferry** (www.hawaiisuperferry .com) is a four-story, state-of-the-art catamaran that carries both passengers and cars and makes two round-trips daily: one between Honolulu and Kaua'i and one between Honolulu and Maui. Service had not begun at the time of research, but both trips take three hours. Passenger fares are $50/60 off-peak/peak; standard cars are an additional $55/65. Peak days are Friday to Monday; off-peak Tuesday to Thursday. Canoes and surfboards are free on vehicles ($20 to $30 as carry-ons); bikes are $20 to $25. At the time of writing, it's hard to say how far in advance reservations will be necessary.

The Superferry promises to be a very comfortable ride; it includes dining areas and bars, games and wi-fi, TV and gift shops. For an extra $20, you can access a special lounge. Its capacity is 866 passengers and 282 cars. In 2009 a second ship will enter service and sail between Honolulu and the Big Island.

Separate from the Superferry, passenger-only ferries also operate between Lahaina, Maui, and Lana'i (p416), and between Lahaina and Moloka'i (p433).

Norwegian Cruise Line (☎ 800-327-7030; www .ncl.com) is the only company that operates a cruise between the Hawaiian Islands that starts and ends in Hawaii. The seven-day interisland cruises make round-trips from Maui and Honolulu and visit the four main islands. Longer 10- and 11-day itineraries are possible.

BUS

O'ahu's excellent islandwide public system, called TheBus (p100), makes O'ahu the easiest island to navigate without a car. Schedules are frequent, service is reliable and fares are $2 per ride regardless of your destination.

Public bus systems on the Neighbor Islands are geared solely to resident commuters; service is infrequent and limited to main towns, sometimes bypassing tourist destinations entirely. After O'ahu, the next best system is probably the Maui Bus (p315), but as above, it's only good for getting between main towns.

Bus service on the Big Island will get you around the island (and includes Hawai'i Volcanoes National Park), but service is extremely limited; it's not good for sightseeing. Nonetheless, it's free and called the Hele-On Bus (p199).

The limited Kauai Bus (p464) can take visitors between the major island towns and as far north as Hanalei, but it won't get you to main tourist destinations like Waimea Canyon.

CAR

The majority of visitors to Hawaii rent their own vehicles, particularly US visitors to Neighbor Islands. So to most of you, we say: read on.

The minimum age for driving in Hawaii is 18 years, though car-rental companies usually have higher age restrictions. If you're under 25 years, you should call the car-rental agencies in advance to check their policies regarding restrictions and surcharges.

Automobile Associations

The **American Automobile Association** (AAA; Map p102; ☎ 593-2221, from Neighbor Islands 800-736-2886; www .aaa-hawaii.com; 1130 N Nimitz Hwy, Honolulu) has its only Hawaii office in Honolulu. It provides members with maps and other information. Members also get discounts on car rental, air tickets, some hotels, some sightseeing attractions, as well as emergency road service and towing (☎ 800-222-4357). AAA has reciprocal agreements with automobile associations in other countries, but be sure to bring your membership card from your country of origin.

Driver's License

An International Driving Permit, obtained before you leave home, is only necessary if your country of origin is a non-English-speaking one.

Fuel & Towing

Fuel is readily available everywhere except along a few particular roads, which are noted in the text (like Saddle Rd on the Big Island

and the Road to Hana on Maui). Expect to pay at least 50¢ more per US gallon than on the mainland. Currently the average gas price statewide is about $2.85 per US gallon, but it varies island to island, from about $2.75 in Honolulu to $3.10 on Maui.

If you get into trouble with your car, towing is mighty expensive in Hawaii and therefore it is to be avoided at all costs. Figure the fees at about $65 to start, plus $6.50 for every mile you need to be towed. How to avoid it? Don't drive your standard car on 4WD roads (such as to Mauna Kea's summit), which is, in any case, usually prohibited by rental companies. Always ask when booking if the company has any road restrictions for its vehicles.

Rental

Cars for <u>rent</u> are readily available except on Lana'i and Moloka'i, where you should reserve as early as possible. With advance reservations (highly recommended anywhere), the daily rate for a small car ranges from $25 to $50, while typical weekly rates are $175 to $250. (Rates for midsize cars or even 4WD vehicles are sometimes only a tad higher.) When getting quotes, always ask for the full rate, *including taxes,* which can add more than $5 a day and over $100 to a multiweek rental.

Getting the best deal on a car rental is 10% timing, 10% science and 90% persistence (that's right, it takes 110%). Auto clubs and frequent-flier programs sometimes offer discounts, so ask them first. Shop around between rental companies, and check their offers against online agencies (use the same ones as for airline tickets, p567). Like the ancient *menehune* (the legendary 'little people' who built many of Hawaii's heiau and other stonework), the $15 per day car rental may seem a myth, but people will swear they've gotten them.

Rental rates usually include unlimited mileage. Sometimes, as in Honolulu, you might get a better deal if you pick up and drop off from a city (rather than an airport) location, but be careful of dropping off and picking up at different locations, which usually requires a hefty additional fee.

Having a major credit card greatly simplifies the rental process. Without one, some agents simply will not rent vehicles, while others require prepayment, a deposit of $200

per week, pay stubs, proof of return airfare and more.

Toll-free numbers for the following companies operating in Hawaii work from the US mainland:

Alamo (☎ 800-462-5266; www.alamo.com)
Avis (☎ 800-331-1212; www.avis.com)
Budget (☎ 800-527-0700; www.budget.com)
Dollar (☎ 800-800-4000; www.dollarcar.com)
Hertz (☎ 800-654-3131; www.hertz.com)
National (☎ 800-227-7368; www.nationalcar.com)

There is a handful of local agencies (see the Getting Around section of each island chapter), but for the most part, big companies offer newer, more reliable cars and fewer hassles.

Insurance

Liability insurance covers people and property that you might hit. For damage to the actual rental vehicle, a collision damage waiver (CDW) is available for about $15 a day. If you have collision coverage on your vehicle at home, it might cover damages to car rentals; inquire before departing. Additionally, some credit cards offer reimbursement coverage for collision damages if you rent the car with that credit card; again, check before departing. Most credit-card coverage isn't valid for rentals of more than 15 days or for exotic models, jeeps, vans and 4WD vehicles.

Road Conditions & Hazards

Drunk drivers can be a hazard, and in some rural areas, so can livestock on the road. However, the main hazards are usually narrow, winding or steep roads that sometimes wash out after heavy rains. Every island has several, and they are noted in the text.

For one-lane-bridge crossings, one direction of traffic usually has the right of way while the other must obey the posted yield sign. Downhill traffic must yield to uphill traffic where there is no sign.

Street addresses on some Hawaiian highways may seem quirky, but there's a pattern. For hyphenated numbers, such as 4-734 Kuhio Hwy, the first part of the number identifies the post office district and the second part identifies the street address. Thus, it's possible for 4-736 to be followed by 5-002; you've just entered a new district, that's all.

TRANSPORTATION

Road Rules

As with mainland USA, driving is (mostly) on the right-hand side of the road. On unpaved or potholed roads, locals tend to hog the middle stripe until an oncoming car approaches.

'Right on red' is allowed (unless a sign prohibits it), but island drivers usually wait for the green light. Indeed, in Hawaii, slow, courteous driving is the rule, not the exception. Locals don't honk (unless they're about to crash or cattle block the road), they don't follow close and they let people pass. Do the same, and you may get an appreciative *shaka* (Hawaiian hand greeting) from other drivers.

Hawaii requires the use of seat belts (tickets are expensive), and children aged four and under must use a child-safety seat. Car-rental companies (p571) are required to provide them on request, but only if you reserve in advance.

Speed limits are posted *and* enforced. If you're stopped for speeding, expect a ticket, as Hawaii police rarely just give warnings.

HITCHING

Hitchhiking, though technically illegal statewide, is not unusual. In certain areas, it's an accepted way to get around easily (sometimes as noted in the text). However, hitchhiking anywhere is not without risks, and Lonely Planet does not recommend it. Get local advice, never hitchhike alone and size up each situation carefully before getting in a car. Travelers should understand that, by hitchhiking, they are always taking a small but serious risk.

MOPED & MOTORCYCLE

Motorcycle hire is not common in Hawaii, but mopeds are a transportation option in some resort areas. You can legally drive either vehicle in Hawaii as long as you have a valid driver's license issued by your home country. The minimum age for renting a moped is 16; for a motorcycle it's 21.

There are no helmet laws in the state of Hawaii, but rental agencies often provide free helmets, and cautious riders will use them. Also remember that the windward sides of the islands generally require hardcore foul-weather gear, since it rains often.

State law requires mopeds to be ridden by one person only and prohibits their use on sidewalks and freeways. Mopeds must always be driven in single file and may not be driven at speeds in excess of 30mph. Bizarrely, mopeds can be more expensive to rent than cars.

TAXI

All the main islands have taxis, with fares based on mileage regardless of the number of passengers. Since taxis are often station wagons or minivans, they're good value for groups (a particularly smart idea if the designated driver decides to join the partying). Rates vary, as they're set by each county, but average around $2.50 at flag-down, then about $2 per additional mile. Outside of Honolulu and Waikiki, and at most hotels and resorts, travelers will have to call ahead to book a taxi. Pick-ups from remote locations (such as after a long one-way hike) can sometimes be arranged in advance.

Health

CONTENTS

Hawaii encompasses an extraordinary range of climates and terrains, from the freezing heights of volcanic summits to tropical rain forests. Because of the high level of hygiene, infectious diseases will not be a significant concern for most travelers, who will experience nothing worse than mild sunburn.

BEFORE YOU GO

INSURANCE

The USA offers possibly the finest health care in the world. The problem is that, unless you have good insurance, it can be prohibitively expensive. It's essential to purchase travel-health insurance if your regular policy doesn't cover you when you are overseas. For more information, check the **Lonely Planet website** (www.lonelyplanet.com/travel_services/insurance/travel_insurance.cfm). Make sure you find out in advance if your insurance will make payments directly to providers or reimburse you later for overseas health expenditures.

Bring any medications you may need in their original containers, clearly labeled. A signed, dated letter from your physician describing all medical conditions and medications, including generic names, is also handy.

MEDICAL CHECKLIST

- acetaminophen (eg Tylenol) or aspirin
- anti-inflammatory drugs (eg ibuprofen)
- antihistamines (for hay fever and allergic reactions)
- antibacterial ointment (eg Neosporin) for cuts and abrasions

- steroid cream or cortisone (for poison ivy and other allergic rashes)
- bandages, gauze, gauze rolls
- adhesive or paper tape
- scissors, safety pins, tweezers
- thermometer
- pocket knife
- DEET-containing insect repellent for the skin
- permethrin-containing insect spray for clothing, tents and bed nets
- sunblock

INTERNET RESOURCES

There is a wealth of travel-health advice on the internet. The World Health Organization publishes a superb book, called *International Travel and Health,* which is revised annually and is available online at no cost at www.who.int/ith. Another website of general interest is MD Travel Health at www.mdtravelhealth.com, which provides complete travel-health recommendations for every country, updated daily, also at no cost.

It's usually a good idea to consult your government's travel-health website before departure, if one is available:
Australia (www.smartraveller.gov.au)
Canada (www.hc-sc.gc.ca/index_e.html)
UK (www.dh.gov.uk/PolicyAndGuidance/HealthAdviceForTravellers/fs/en)
USA (www.cdc.gov/travel)

IN HAWAII

AVAILABILITY & COST OF HEALTH CARE

For immediate medical assistance anywhere in Hawaii, call ☎ 911. In general, if you have a medical emergency, the best bet is to find the nearest hospital and go to its emergency room. If the problem isn't urgent, you can call a nearby hospital and ask for a referral to a local physician, which is usually cheaper than a trip to the emergency room. In Hawaii the nearest hospital could be a fair distance away, so the best choice may be an expensive stand-alone, for-profit, urgent-care center. Also keep in mind that medical helicopter evacuation may not always be possible from remote areas. See the Information sections of island chapters for local hospitals.

Pharmacies are abundantly supplied, but you may find that some medications that are available over the counter in your home country require a prescription in the USA, and, as always, if you don't have insurance to cover the cost of prescriptions, they can be shockingly expensive.

Covering all the islands, the **Hawaii Health Guide** (www.hawaiihealthguide.com) is the most comprehensive central resource for finding local hospitals, health services, practitioners and wellness programs.

INFECTIOUS DISEASES

In addition to more common ailments, there are several infectious diseases are present in Hawaii. Most of these diseases are acquired by mosquito or tick bites, or through environmental exposure. Currently Hawaii is rabies-free.

Dengue Fever

Dengue is transmitted by aedes mosquitoes, which bite preferentially during the daytime and are usually found close to human habitations, often indoors. They breed primarily in artificial water containers such as jars, barrels, cisterns, metal drums, plastic containers and discarded tires. As a result, dengue is especially common in densely populated, urban environments. In Hawaii the last outbreak of this mosquito-borne disease was in 2002. For updates, consult the **Hawaii State Department of Health website** (www.state.hi.us/doh).

Dengue usually causes flulike symptoms, including fever, muscle aches, joint pains, headaches, nausea and vomiting, often followed by a rash. There is no treatment for dengue fever except to take analgesics such as acetaminophen/paracetamol (eg Tylenol) – do not take aspirin as it increases the likelihood of hemorrhaging – and drink plenty of fluids. See a doctor to be diagnosed and monitored. Severe cases may require hospitalization for intravenous fluids and supportive care. There is no vaccine. The cornerstone of prevention is insect protection measures.

Giardiasis

This parasitic infection of the small intestine occurs throughout the world. Symptoms may include nausea, bloating, cramps and diarrhea, and may last for weeks. To protect yourself, you should avoid drinking directly from waterfalls, ponds, streams and rivers, which may be contaminated by animal or human feces. The infection can also be transmitted from person to person if proper hand washing is not done. Giardiasis is easily diagnosed by a stool test and readily treated with antibiotics.

Leptospirosis

Leptospirosis is acquired by exposure to water contaminated by the urine of infected animals such as rats and feral pigs. Outbreaks often occur at times of flooding, when sudden overflow may contaminate water sources downstream from animal habitats. Even an idyllic waterfall may, in fact, be infected with leptospirosis. The initial symptoms, which resemble a mild flu, usually subside uneventfully in a few days, but a minority of cases are complicated by jaundice or meningitis. It can also cause hepatitis and renal failure, which might be fatal. Diagnosis is through

---

RECOMMENDED VACCINATIONS

No special vaccines are required or recommended for travel to the USA. All travelers should be up to date on routine immunizations, listed below.

Vaccine	Recommended for	Dosage	Side effects
tetanus-diphtheria	all travelers who haven't had booster within 10 years	one dose lasts 10 years	soreness at injection site
measles	travelers born after 1956 who've had only one measles vaccination	one dose	fever; rash; joint pains; allergic reactions
chicken pox	travelers who've never had chicken pox	two doses a month apart	fever; mild case of chicken pox
influenza	all travelers during flu season (Nov–Mar)	one dose	soreness at the injection site; fever

blood tests and the disease is easily treated with doxycycline. There is no vaccine. You can minimize your risk by staying out of bodies of freshwater (eg pools, streams) that may be contaminated, especially if you have any open cuts or sores. Because hikers account for many of the cases of leptospirosis in Hawaii, the state posts warning signs at trailheads. If you're camping, water purification is essential.

West Nile Virus

These infections were unknown in the USA until a few years ago, but have now been reported in almost every state. Humans in Hawaii have not been affected so far, but the rising number of reported cases in California – as well as documented cases of West Nile virus in Maui birds – is cause for concern. The virus is transmitted by culex mosquitoes, which are active in late summer and early fall and generally bite after dusk (see also Mosquito Bites, p596). Most infections are mild or asymptomatic, but the virus may infect the central nervous system, leading to fever, headache, confusion, lethargy, coma and sometimes death. There is no treatment for West Nile virus.

For the latest update on the areas affected by West Nile, go to the **US Geological Survey website** (http://diseasemaps.usgs.gov).

ENVIRONMENTAL HAZARDS

Vog, a visible haze or volcanic smog from active volcanoes, is usually dispersed by trade winds and is not generally hazardous. When it occasionally hangs over the islands, though, it can create breathing problems for some.

See p78 for advice on ocean safety.

Altitude Sickness

Acute Mountain Sickness (AMS), aka 'altitude sickness,' may develop in those who ascend rapidly to altitudes greater than 7500ft, as on Mauna Kea (see p251) and Mauna Loa (see p258) on the Big Island. Being physically fit offers no protection. Those who have experienced AMS in the past are prone to future episodes. The risk increases with faster ascents, higher altitudes and greater exertion. Symptoms may include headaches, nausea, vomiting, dizziness, malaise, insomnia and loss of appetite. Severe cases may be complicated by fluid in the lungs (high-altitude pulmonary edema) or swelling of the brain (high-altitude cerebral edema).

The best treatment for AMS is descent. If you are exhibiting symptoms, do not ascend. If symptoms are severe or persistent, descend immediately. When traveling to high altitudes, it's also important to avoid overexertion, eat light meals and abstain from alcohol. If your symptoms are more than mild or don't resolve promptly, see a doctor. Altitude sickness should be taken seriously; it can be life-threatening when severe.

Bites & Stings

Hawaii has no established snake population in the wild, although snakes have been sighted recently in the wild, especially in sugarcane fields.

Leeches are found in humid rain-forest areas. They do not transmit any disease but their bites are often intensely itchy for weeks afterwards and can easily become infected. Apply an iodine-based antiseptic to any leech bite to help prevent infection.

Bee and wasp stings mainly cause problems for people who are allergic to them. Anyone with a serious bee or wasp allergy should carry an injection of adrenaline for emergency treatment. For others pain is the main problem – apply ice to the sting and take painkillers.

Commonsense approaches to these concerns are the most effective: wear long sleeves and pants, hats and shoes (rather than sandals) to protect yourself.

MAMMAL BITES

Do not attempt to pet, handle or feed any animal, with the exception of domestic animals known to be free of any infectious disease. Most animal injuries are directly related to a person's attempt to touch or feed the animal.

Any bite or scratch by a mammal, including bats or feral pigs, goats etc, should be promptly and thoroughly cleansed with large amounts of soap and water, followed by application of an antiseptic such as iodine or alcohol. It may also be advisable to start an antibiotic, since wounds caused by animal bites and scratches frequently become infected.

MARINE ANIMALS

Marine spikes, such as those found on sea urchins, scorpion fish and Hawaiian lionfish, can cause severe local pain. If this occurs, immediately immerse the affected area in hot water (as high a temperature as can be

HEALTH

tolerated). Keep topping up with hot water until the pain subsides and medical care can be reached. The same advice applies if you are stung by a cone shell.

Marine stings from jellyfish and Portuguese man-of-war (aka 'bluebottles,' which have translucent, bluish, bladder-like floats) also occur in Hawaii's tropical waters. Even touching a bluebottle a few hours after it's washed up onshore can result in burning stings. Jellyfish are often seen eight to 10 days after a full moon when they float into shallow nearshore waters such as at Waikiki; the influx usually lasts for three days. If you are stung, first aid consists of washing the skin with vinegar to prevent further discharge of remaining stinging cells, followed by rapid transfer to a hospital; antivenoms are widely available.

Despite extensive media coverage, the risk of shark attack in Hawaiian waters is no greater than in other countries with extensive coastlines. Avoid swimming in waters with runoff after heavy rainfall (eg around river mouths) and those areas frequented by commercial fishing operators. Do not swim if you are actively bleeding, as this attracts sharks. Check with lifeguards about local risks. Keep in mind that your chances of being hit by a falling coconut on the beach are greater than of shark attack, though!

MOSQUITO BITES

When traveling in areas where West Nile or other mosquito-borne illnesses have been reported, keep yourself covered and apply a good insect repellent, preferably one containing DEET, to exposed skin and clothing. In general, adults and children over 12 should use preparations containing 25% to 35% DEET, which usually lasts about six hours. Children between two and 12 years of age should use preparations containing no more than 10% DEET, applied sparingly, which will usually last about three hours. Neurologic toxicity has been reported from DEET, especially in children, but appears to be extremely uncommon and generally related to overuse. DEET-containing compounds should not be used on children under age two.

Insect repellents containing certain botanical products, including oil of eucalyptus and soybean oil, are effective but last only 1½ to two hours. Products based on citronella are not effective.

Visit the **Center for Disease Control's website** (CDC; www.cdc.gov/ncidod/dvbid/westnile/qa/prevention.htm) for prevention information.

SPIDER BITES

Although there are many species of spiders in the USA, the only ones that cause significant human illness are the black widow, brown recluse and hobo spiders. It is a matter of debate which of these species are conclusively found in Hawaii. The black widow is black or brown in color, measuring about 15mm in body length, with a shiny top, fat body and distinctive red or orange hourglass figure on its underside. It's found usually in woodpiles, sheds and bowls of outdoor toilets. The brown recluse spider is brown in color, usually 10mm in body length, with a dark violin-shaped mark on the top of the upper section of the body. It's active mostly at night, lives in dark sheltered areas such as under porches and in woodpiles, and typically bites when trapped. The symptoms of a hobo-spider bite are similar to those of a brown recluse, but milder.

If bitten by a black widow, you should apply ice and go immediately to emergency. Complications of a black widow bite may include muscle spasms, breathing difficulties and high blood pressure. The bite of a brown recluse or hobo spider typically causes a large, inflamed wound, sometimes associated with fever and chills. If bitten, apply ice and see a physician.

Cold

Cold exposure may be a problem in certain areas. To prevent hypothermia, keep all body surfaces covered, including the head and neck. Synthetic materials such as Gore-Tex and Thinsulate provide excellent insulation. Because the body loses heat faster when wet, stay dry at all times. Change inner garments promptly when they become moist. Keep active, but get enough rest. Consume plenty of food and water. Be especially sure not to have any alcohol. Caffeine and tobacco should also be avoided.

Watch out for the 'Umbles' – stumbles, mumbles, fumbles and grumbles – which are important signs of impending hypothermia. If someone appears to be developing hypothermia, you should insulate them from the ground, protect them from the wind, remove wet clothing or cover with a vapor barrier such as a plastic bag, and transport immediately to a warm environment and a medical facility. Warm fluids (but not coffee or tea) may be given if the person is alert enough to swallow.

Diving & Snorkeling Hazards

Divers, snorkelers and surfers should seek specialized advice before they travel to ensure their medical kit contains treatment for coral cuts and tropical ear infections, as well as the standard problems. Divers should check their insurance covers them for decompression illness – get specialized dive insurance through an organization such as **Divers Alert Network** (DAN; www.diversalertnetwork.org). Have a dive medical before you leave your home country – there are certain medical conditions that are incompatible with diving that your dive operator may not always ask you about.

Heat

Travelers should drink plenty of fluids and avoid strenuous exercise when the temperature is high.

Dehydration is the main contributor to heat exhaustion. Symptoms include feeling weak, headache, irritability, nausea or vomiting, sweaty skin, a fast, weak pulse and a normal or slightly elevated body temperature. Treatment involves getting out of the heat and/or sun, fanning the victim and applying cool, wet cloths to the skin, laying the victim flat with their legs raised and rehydrating with water containing one-quarter of a teaspoon of salt per liter. Recovery is usually rapid and it is common to feel weak for some days afterwards.

Heatstroke is a serious medical emergency. Symptoms come on suddenly and include weakness, nausea, a hot, dry body with a body temperature of over 106°F, dizziness, confusion, loss of coordination, fits and eventually collapse and loss of consciousness. Seek medical help and commence cooling by getting the person out of the heat, removing their clothes, fanning and applying cool, wet cloths or ice to their body, especially to the groin and armpits.

HEALTH

Language

Hawaii has two official state languages: English and Hawaiian. Although English has long replaced Hawaiian as the dominant language, many Hawaiian words and phrases are commonly used in speech and in print.

Prior to the arrival of Christian missionaries in 1820, the Hawaiians had no written language. Knowledge was passed on through complex oral genealogies, stories, chants, songs and descriptive place names. The missionaries rendered the spoken language into the Roman alphabet and established the first presses in the islands, which were used to print the Bible and other religious instructional materials in Hawaiian.

Throughout the 19th century, as more and more foreigners (particularly the Americans and the British) settled in the islands, the everyday use of Hawaiian declined. In the 1890s English was made the official language of government and education.

The push for statehood, from 1900 to 1959, added to the decline of the Hawaiian language. Speaking Hawaiian was seen as a deterrent to American assimilation, thus adult native speakers were strongly discouraged from teaching their children Hawaiian as the primary language in the home.

This attitude remained until the early 1970s when the Hawaiian community began to experience a cultural renaissance. A handful of young Hawaiians lobbied to establish Hawaiian language classes at the University of Hawai'i, and Hawaiian language immersion preschools followed in the 1980s. These preschools are modeled after Maori *kohanga reo* (language nests), where the primary method of language perpetuation is through speaking and hearing the language on a daily basis. In Hawai'i's 'Aha Punana Leo preschools, all learning and communication takes place in the mother tongue – *ka 'olelo makuahine.*

Hawaiian has now been revived from the point of extinction and is growing throughout the community. Record numbers of students enroll in Hawaiian language classes in high schools and colleges, and immersion-school graduates are raising a new generation of native speakers.

If you'd like to discover more about the Hawaiian language, get a copy of Lonely Planet's *South Pacific Phrasebook.*

PRONUNCIATION

Written Hawaiian uses just 13 letters: five vowels (**a**, **e**, **i**, **o**, **u**), seven consonants (**h**, **k**, **l**, **m**, **n**, **p**, **w**) and the glottal stop (**'**). The letters **h**, **l**, **m** and **n** are pronounced much the same as in English. Usually every letter in Hawaiian words is pronounced, and each vowel has a different pronunciation depending on whether it is stressed or unstressed.

Consonants

p/k	similar to English, but with less aspiration; **k** may be replaced with **t**
w	after **i** and **e**, usually a soft English 'v;' thus the town of Hale'iwa is pronounced 'Haleiva.' After **u** or **o** it's often like English 'w,' thus Olowalu is pronounced as written. After **a** or at the beginning of a word it can be as English 'w' or 'v,' thus you'll hear both Hawai'i and Havai'i (The Big Island).

Unstressed vowels (without macron)

a	as in 'ago'
e	as in 'bet'
i	as the 'y' in 'city'
o	as in 'sole'
u	as in 'rude'

Glottal Stops & Macrons

Written Hawaiian uses both glottal stops ('), called *'okina*, and macrons (a straight bar above a vowel, eg **ā**), called *kahakō*. In modern print both the glottal stop and the macron are often omitted. In this guidebook, the macrons have been omitted, but glottal stops have been included, as they can be helpful in striving to pronounce common place names and words correctly.

The glottal stop indicates a break between two vowels, producing an effect similar to saying 'oh-oh' in English. For example, *'a'a*, a type of lava, is pronounced 'ah-ah,' and Ho'okena, a place name, is pronounced 'Ho-oh-kena.' A macron inidicates that the vowel is stressed and has a long pronunciation.

Glottal stops and macrons not only affect pronunciation, but can give a word a completely different meaning. For example, *ai* (with no glottal) means 'sexual intercourse,' but *'ai* (with the glottal) means 'food.' Similarly, the word *ka'a* (with no macron over the second **a**) means 'to roll, turn or twist,' but *ka'ā* (with a macron over the second **a**) is a thread or line used in fishing.

Compound Words

In the written form, many Hawaiian words are compound words made up of several different words. For example, the word *humuhumunukunukuapua'a* can be broken down as follows: *humuhumu-nukunuku-a-pua'a* (literally, 'trigger fish snout of pig'), meaning 'the fish with a snout like a pig.' The place name Waikiki is also a compound word: *wai-kiki* (literally, 'freshwater sprouting'), referring to the freshwater swamps once found in the area. Some words are doubled to emphasize their meaning, much like in English. For example, *wiki* means 'quick,' while *wikiwiki* means 'very quick.'

Common Hawaiian Words

For more Hawaiian words, see the Glossary (p580).

aloha – love, hello, welcome, goodbye
hale – house
heiau – religious temple
kane – man
kapu – taboo, restricted
lu'au – traditional Hawaiian feast
mahalo – thank you
mahimahi – dolphinfish, popular in restaurants
mauka – a direction, toward the mountains
makai – a direction, toward the sea
'ono – delicious, tasty
pau – finished, completed
poi – staple food made from taro
ukulele – four-stringed musical instrument, used in modern Hawaiian music (literally, 'leaping flea,' because of the action of the fingers when playing)
wahine – woman

PIDGIN

Hawaii pidgin is a distinct language, spoken by over 500,000 people. It developed on sugar plantations where the *luna* (foreman) had to communicate with field laborers from many foreign countries. Early plantation pidgin used a very minimal and condensed

form of English as the root language, to which elements from Cantonese, Hawaiian and Portuguese were added. It became the second language of first-generation immigrants and many Hawaiians.

As this English-based pidgin evolved, it took on its own grammatical structure and syntax. Many words were pronounced differently and combined in ways not found in English. Rather than a careless or broken form of English, it evolved into a separate language, called Hawaii Creole by linguists.

Today, there is ongoing controversy about the validity of pidgin, with opponents saying that it erodes standard English and becomes a barrier to social and educational advancement. Proponents argue that pidgin is a rich and vibrant language that should not be looked down upon or banned from schools, and that pidgin speakers are often unjustly seen as less intelligent.

In recent years numerous award-winning plays, books and poetry have been written in pidgin by local authors who are passionate in their determination to keep pidgin alive in the community.

Common Pidgin Words & Phrases

brah – shortened form of *braddah* (brother); also used as 'hey you'
broke da mout – delicious; as in 'My auntie make broke da mout kine fish!'
buggahs – guys; as in 'Da buggahs went to without me!'
bumbye – later on; as in 'We go movies bumbye den (then).'
bummahs – bummer; an expression of disappointment or regret
chicken skin – goose bumps
cockaroach – to steal; as in 'Who went cockaroach my slippahs?'
da kine – whatchamacallit; used whenever you can't think of the word you want
Fo' real? – Really? Are you kidding me?
funny kine – strange or different; as in 'He stay acking (acting) all funny kine.'
geev 'um – Go for it! Give it all you got!
How you stay? – How are you doing these days?
Howzit? – Hi, how's it going? As in 'Eh, howzit brah?'
kay den – 'OK then'; as in 'Kay den, we go beach.'
laydahs – Later on. I'll see you later, as in, 'Kay den, laydahs.'
no ack – (literally, 'no act') Stop showing off, cool it.
rubbah slippahs – (rubber) thongs, flip-flops
talk story – any kind of casual conversation
to da max – a suffix that adds emphasis to something; as in 'Da waves was big to da max!'

Glossary

For more food terms, see p62. Also see the Language chapter.

'a'a – type of lava that is rough and jagged

'ahi – yellowfin tuna

'ahinahina – silversword plant with pointed silver leaves

ahu – stone cairns used to mark a trail; an altar or shrine

ahupua'a – traditional land division, usually in a wedge shape that extends from the mountains to the sea

aikane – friend

'aina – land

'akala – Hawaiian raspberry; also called a thimbleberry

akamai – clever

'akepa – endangered crested honeycreeper

aku – bonito (skipjack tuna)

akua – god, spirit, idol

'alae ke'oke'o – endangered Hawaiian coot

'alala – Hawaiian crow

ali'i – chief, royalty

aloha – the traditional greeting meaning love, welcome, good-bye

aloha 'aina – love of the land

'ama'ama – mullet

'amakihi – small, yellow-green bird; one of the more common native birds

anchialine pool – contains a mixture of seawater and freshwater

'a'o – Newell's shearwater (a seabird)

'apapane – bright red native Hawaiian honeycreeper

'aumakua – protective deity, deified ancestor or trustworthy person

awa – milkfish

'awa – see *kava*

'awapuhi – wild ginger

azuki bean – often used as a topping for shave ice (in paste or as whole beans)

banh hoi – Vietnamese version of fajitas

bento – Japanese-style box lunch

broke da mout – delicious; literally, 'broke the mouth'

chicken skin – goosebumps

crack seed – Chinese preserved fruit; a salty, sweet and/or sour snack

'elepaio – a brownish native bird with a white rump, common to O'ahu forests

fuku-bonsai – Hawaiian-style potted dwarf trees

goza – rolled-up straw mats used at the beach

grinds – food

hala – pandanus tree; the leaves are used in weaving mats and baskets

hale – house

hana – work; a bay, when used as a compound in place names

haole – Caucasian; literally, 'without breath'

hapa – portion or fragment; person of mixed blood

hau – indigenous lowland hibiscus tree whose wood is often used for making canoe outriggers (stabilizing arms that jut out from the hull)

Hawai'i nei – all the Hawaiian Islands taken as a group

heiau – ancient stone temple; a place of worship in Hawaii

hele on – to get moving

Hina – Polynesian goddess (wife of Ku, one of the four main gods)

holoholo – to walk, drive or ramble around for pleasure

holua – sled or sled course

honu – turtle

ho'olaule'a – celebration, party

ho'onanea – to pass the time in ease, peace and pleasure

huhu – angry

hui – group, organization

hukilau – fishing with a *seine* (a large net), involving a group of people who pull in the net

hula – Hawaiian dance form, either traditional or modern

hula 'auana – modern hula, developed after the introduction of Western music

hula halau – hula school or troupe

hula kahiko – traditional hula

hula ohelo – a hula dance style in which the some of the dancer's motions imitate sexual intercourse

humuhumunukunukuapua'a – rectangular triggerfish; Hawaii's unofficial state fish

'i'iwi – a bright red Hawaiian honeycreeper with a curved, salmon-colored beak

'iliahi – Hawaiian sandalwood

'ili'ili – small stones

'ilima – native plant, a ground cover with delicate yellow-orange flowers

'io – Hawaiian hawk

issei – first-generation Japanese immigrants

kahili – a feathered standard, used as a symbol of royalty

kahuna – knowledgable person in any field; commonly a priest, healer or sorcerer

kahuna nui – high priest
kama'aina – person born and raised or a longtime resident in Hawaii; literally, 'child of the land'
kanaka – man, human being, person; also Native Hawaiian
Kanaloa – god of the underworld
kane/Kane – man; also the name of one of four main Hawaiian gods
kapa – see *tapa*
kapu – taboo, part of strict ancient Hawaiian social and religious system
kaukau wagon – lunch wagon
kaunaoa – a groundcover vine with yellow tendrils used to make lei
kava – a mildly narcotic drink ('awa in Hawaiian) made from the roots of *Piper methysticum*, a pepper shrub
keiki – child
ki – see *ti*
kiawe – a relative of the mesquite tree introduced to Hawaii in the 1820s, now very common; its branches are covered with sharp thorns
ki'i – image, statue (often of a deity)
kilau – a stiff, weedy fern
kipuka – an area of land spared when lava flows around it; an oasis
ko – sugarcane
ko'a – fishing shrine
koa – native hardwood tree often used in making native crafts and canoes
kohola – whale
koki'o ke'oke'o – native Hawaiian white hibiscus tree
kokua – help, cooperation
kona – leeward side; a leeward wind
konane – a strategy game similar to checkers
ko'olau – windward side
Ku – Polynesian god of many manifestations, including god of war, farming and fishing (husband of Hina)
kukui – candlenut tree and the official state tree; its oily nuts were once burned in lamps
kumulipo – Native Hawaiian creation story or chant
kupuna – grandparent, elder
ku'ula – a stone idol placed at fishing sites, believed to attract fish

Laka – goddess of the hula
lama – native plant in the persimmon family
lanai – veranda
lau – leaf
lauhala – leaves of the hala plant used in weaving
lei – garland, usually of flowers, but also of leaves or shells
limu – seaweed
lio – horse
loko i'a – fishpond
lolo – stupid, feeble-minded, crazy

lomi – to rub or soften
lomilomi – traditional Hawaiian massage
Lono – Polynesian god of harvest, agriculture, fertility and peace
loulu – native fan palms
luakini – a type of *heiau* dedicated to the war god Ku and used for human sacrifices
luau – traditional Hawaiian feast

mahalo – thank you
mahele – to divide; usually refers to the missionary-initiated land divisions of 1848
mahimahi – dolphinfish or dorado; not related to the mammal dolphin
mai ho'oka'awale – leprosy; literally, 'the separating sickness'
mai'a – banana
maile – native plant with twining habit and fragrant leaves; often used for lei
maka'ainana – commoners; literally, 'people who tend the land'
makaha – a sluice gate, used to regulate the level of water in a fishpond
makahiki – traditional annual wet-season winter festival dedicated to the agricultural god Lono
makai – toward the sea
makaku – creative, artistic imagination
malihini – newcomer, visitor
malo – loincloth
mamane – a native tree with bright yellow flowers; used to make lei
mana – spiritual power
manini – convict tang (a reef fish); also used to refer to something small or insignificant
mauka – toward the mountains; inland
mele – song, chant
menehune – 'little people' who, according to legend, built many of Hawaii's fishponds, heiau and other stonework
milo – a native shade tree with beautiful hardwood
moa pahe'e – a game, similar to 'ulu maika, using wooden darts and spears
mokihana – an endemic tree or shrub, with scented green berries; used to make lei
mo'i – king
mo'o – water spirit, water lizard or dragon
mu – a 'body catcher' who secured sacrificial victims for the heiau altar
muumuu – a long, loose-fitting dress introduced by the missionaries

naupaka – a native shrub with delicate white flowers
Neighbor Islands – the term used to refer to the main Hawaiian Islands outside of O'ahu
nene – a native goose; Hawaii's state bird
nisei – second-generation Japanese immigrants

niu – coconut palm

noni – Indian mulberry; a small tree with yellow, smelly fruit that is used medicinally

nuku pu'u – a native honeycreeper with a yellow-green underbelly

ogo – seaweed

'ohana – family, extended family

'ohi'a lehua – native Hawaiian tree with tufted, feathery, pom-pom–like flowers

'okole – buttocks

olo – traditional long, wooden surfboard

one hanau – birthplace, homeland

'ono – delicious

'o'o ihe – spear-throwing

pahoehoe – type of lava that is quick and smooth-flowing

pakalolo – marijuana; literally, 'crazy smoke'

palaka – Hawaiian-style plaid shirt made from sturdy cotton

pali – cliff

palila – endemic honeycreeper

paniolo – cowboy

panquela – Brazilian crepe stuffed with pumpkin

pau – finished, no more

Pele – goddess of fire and volcanoes; her home is in Kilauea Caldera

pigdin – distinct Hawaiian language or dialect (see p578)

piko – navel, umbilical cord

pili – a bunchgrass, commonly used for thatching houses

pilo – native shrub of the coffee family

pohaku – rock

pohuehue – morning glory

poi – staple Hawaiian starch made of steamed, mashed taro

Poliahu – goddess of snow

po'ouli – endangered endemic creeper

pua aloalo – a hibiscus flower

pueo – Hawaiian owl

puhi – eel

pu'ili – bamboo sticks used in hula performances

puka – any kind of hole or opening; small shells that are made into necklaces

pukiawe – native plant with red and white berries and evergreen leaves

pulu – the silken clusters encasing the stems of hapu'u ferns

pupu – snack or appetizer; also a type of cowry shell

pu'u – hill, cinder cone

pu'uhonua – place of refuge

raku – a style of Japanese pottery characterized by a rough, handmade appearance

rakusen kaiseki – multicourse chef's tasting menu

ryokan – traditional Japanese inn

rubbah slippah – rubber thongs

sansei – third-generation Japanese immigrants

shaka – hand gesture used in Hawaii as a greeting or sign of local pride

stink-eye – dirty look

tabi – Japanese reef-walking shoes

talk story – to strike up a conversation, make small talk

tapa – cloth made by pounding the bark of paper mulberry, used for early Hawaiian clothing (*kapa* in Hawaiian)

ti – common native plant; its long shiny leaves are used for wrapping food and making hula skirts (*ki* in Hawaiian)

tiki – see *ki'i*

tutu – grandmother or grandfather; also term of respect for any member of that generation

'ua'u – dark-rumped petrel

ukulele – a stringed musical instrument derived from the braguinha, which was introduced to Hawaii in the 1800s by Portuguese immigrants

'uli'uli – gourd rattle containing seeds and decorated with feathers

'ulu maika – ancient Hawaiian bowling game

unagi – eel

wahine – woman

wikiwiki – hurry, quick

wiliwili – the lightest of the native woods

zazen – Zen meditation

zendo – communal Zen meditation hall

The Authors

JEFF CAMPBELL
Coordinating Author; Environment; Outdoors; Windward Hawai'i (The Big Island); Northwestern Hawaiian Islands; Kaho'olawe

Jeff fell in love on the Big Island, and yes, cliché though it is, spent his honeymoon on Kaua'i – does it help that he and his bride were camping and hiking? No matter, his fondness for the archipelago runs deep. For Lonely Planet, Jeff has been the coordinating author of *USA* (which won the 2004 Society of American Travel Writers Silver Award for best guidebook), *Southwest USA* and *Zion & Bryce Canyon National Parks*, among others. He now lives, ahem, in New Jersey.

CHINA WILLIAMS
O'ahu

In all honesty, China thought Hawaii was a little too 'soft' for her usual traveling itinerary in Southeast Asia. But she was pleasantly surprised at Asian-influenced Honolulu and the rainbow hills of interior O'ahu. China grew up in South Carolina and has migrated back and forth across the mainland with almost military itinerancy. Nearly twice a year she hops across the Pacific to update books for Lonely Planet to Thailand and its neighbors. Home is currently in Montana with her husband, Matt, and baby son, Felix.

LUCI YAMAMOTO
The Culture; Food & Drink; Kaua'i; Ni'ihau

Luci Yamamoto is a fourth-generation native of Hawaii. She grew up in Hilo before leaving for college in Los Angeles and law school in Berkeley. Following a short stint practicing law in California, she inevitably switched careers to pursue writing. Her past Lonely Planet titles include *Kaua'i*, *Hawai'i: the Big Island* and *Hawaii*. Currently living in Vancouver, she feels privileged when she returns to Hawaii and local folks still consider her a 'local girl.'

MOLLY GREEN   Leeward Hawai'i (The Big Island); Moloka'i

Thanks to a half-Hawaiian best friend, Molly was exposed to pidgin-speaking aunties and steaming saimin (noodle soup) at a young age. She hula danced (the real kind) her way through several grade-school talent shows and made her first trip to Hawaii at age seven. After working in the Cartography department in Lonely Planet's Oakland office, she has contributed to several titles, including *Brazil*. She hails from Santa Cruz, California.

NED FRIARY & GLENDA BENDURE   Maui; Lana'i

Ned and Glenda first discovered Maui as the glorious last stop on a round-the-world trip. They've since returned to Hawaii a dozen times to hit the surf and trek the trails while researching the islands from top to bottom for Lonely Planet. One thing they love about Maui is the constant evolution, with hot new things popping up all the time. They're also the authors of LP's *O'ahu* guide.

CONTRIBUTING AUTHORS

Lisa Dunford wrote the Hawaiian Quilting boxed text in The Culture chapter. Long a Hawaiiophile, Lisa found a new dimension to her passion when she started quilting eight years ago. Her first effort at appliquéing a Hawaiian-style quilt was not such a success, but she kept at it. Lisa gets back to the islands as often as possible for inspiration.

Dr David Goldberg wrote the material from which the Health chapter was adapted. He completed his training at Columbia-Presbyterian Medical Center in New York City and is an infectious diseases specialist and the editor-in-chief of www.mdtravelhealth.com.

Jake Howard contributed the Surfing boxed texts in the Outdoors special section and in the O'ahu, Big Island, Maui, Lana'i, Moloka'i and Kaua'i chapters. Jake grew up surfing the rugged Northern California coast. He is now working as the Senior Editor at *Surfer* magazine and lives in San Clemente, California. He has traveled extensively through the Pacific Islands and Indonesia, as well as Central and South America.

Nanette Naioma Napoleon wrote the History chapter. Nanette is a freelance researcher and writer from Kailua, O'ahu, who specializes in the history and cultures of Hawaii. She previously wrote a daily history column for the *Honolulu Star-Bulletin* newspaper, and currently writes history features for the *'Oiwi Files News Journal,* a Native Hawaiian newspaper.

Behind the Scenes

THIS BOOK

This guidebook was commissioned in Lonely Planet's Oakland office and was produced by the following:

Commissioning Editor Emily K Wolman
Coordinating Editors Yvonne Byron, Liani Solari, Louise Clarke
Coordinating Cartographer Jolyon Philcox
Coordinating Layout Designer Carol Jackson
Managing Editors Bruce Evans, Melanie Dankel
Managing Cartographer Alison Lyall
Assisting Editors Elisa Arduca, Sarah Bailey, Janice Bird, Gennifer Ciavarra, Craig Kilburn, Kristin Odijk, Phillip Tang
Assisting Cartographers Tony Fankhauser, Sophie Richards
Cover Designer Pepi Bluck

Color Designer Evelyn Yee
Project Manager Kate McLeod
Language Content Coordinator Quentin Frayne
Thanks to Sin Choo, Erin Corrigan, Sally Darmody, James Hardy, Rebecca Lalor, Stephanie Pearson, Raphael Richards, Averil Robertson, Wibowo Rusli, Celia Wood

THANKS
JEFF CAMPBELL

First, thanks to our crackerjack team of writers, and to LP commisioning editor Emily Wolman – you've made this a dream project. Many folks helped me get inside island life – none more than Bobby Camara. *Mahalo nui loa!* Others who graciously 'talked story' with me include Mauna Kea's Kimo Pihana and David Byrne, HAVO rangers

---

LONELY PLANET: TRAVEL WIDELY, TREAD LIGHTLY, GIVE SUSTAINABLY

The Lonely Planet Story

The story begins with a classic travel adventure: Tony and Maureen Wheeler's 1972 journey across Europe and Asia to Australia. There was no useful information about the overland trail then, so Tony and Maureen published the first Lonely Planet guidebook to meet a growing need.

From a kitchen table, Lonely Planet has grown to become the largest independent travel publisher in the world, with offices in Melbourne (Australia), Oakland (USA) and London (UK). Today Lonely Planet guidebooks cover the globe. There is an ever-growing list of books and information in a variety of media. Some things haven't changed. The main aim is still to make it possible for adventurous individuals to get out there – to explore and better understand the world.

At Lonely Planet we believe travelers can make a positive contribution to the countries they visit – if they respect their host communities and spend their money wisely. Every year 5% of company profit is donated to charities around the world.

The Lonely Planet Foundation

The Lonely Planet Foundation proudly supports nimble nonprofit institutions working for change in the world. Each year the foundation donates 5% of Lonely Planet company profits to projects selected by staff and authors. Our partners range from Kabissa, which provides small nonprofits across Africa with access to technology, to the Foundation for Developing Cambodian Orphans, which supports girls at risk of falling victim to sex traffickers.

Our nonprofit partners are linked by a grass-roots approach to the areas of health, education or sustainable tourism. Many projects we support – such as one with BaAka (Pygmy) children in the forested areas of Central African Republic – choose to focus on women and children as one of the most effective ways to support the whole community.

Sometimes foundation assistance is as simple as restoring a local ruin like the Minaret of Jam in Afghanistan; this incredible monument now draws intrepid tourists to the area and its restoration has greatly improved options for local people.

Just as travel is often about learning to see with new eyes, so many of the groups we work with aim to change the way people see themselves and the future for their children and communities.

BEHIND THE SCENES

Mardie Lane and BG Horvat, Wayne Subica, the eminent Dr Samuel Gon, Estelle Young, Phil Terry, Lani Stackel, Lisa Gold, Greg Ambrose, Mark Fragale, Grant Matsushige, Bob Tedeschi, Monica Nucciarone and Matt Warshaw. I dedicate my efforts to my island girl.

CHINA WILLIAMS
People on O'ahu are awesome. The update was easy and easy-going and I made a few friends along the way. Thanks to Leela for the lunch and chat, to Lesa Griffith for the restaurant run-down, *Honolulu Weekly* for the entertainment insights. Great thanks to Tonic Bille for saving me from the earthquake and from crashing into her hedges. Noreen and Rocky showed me a fabulous time on the Wai'anae Coast. And thanks to Dave and Debbie for the Hawaiian style muddin' trip. Big heaps to Cherie Isabella, as well as Emily Wolman, Jeff Campbell and the LP production team.

LUCI YAMAMOTO
Mahalo to my Kaua'i insiders: Todd Vines of Essential Kaua'i (who gave countless answers to my countless questions); Jon Letman, NTBG source and fellow writer; Richard Sugiyama, expert on the Eastside and all things local (especially shave ice); and Michaelle Edwards, the best yoga teacher on Kaua'i. I must also recognize the generosity of Rosemary Smith, Bruna Stude, and Craig Koga. Special thanks to Lonely Planet's Emily Wolman for another opportunity to write about my beautiful home state. Aloha to my family in Hilo, in Santa Cruz and in Vancouver. You know who you are.

MOLLY GREEN
A warm *mahalo* to: supportive Mama Frieda, loving Funi de Pheida, snorkel gear–lending Greg and Rebecca; (for local hook-ups) Jared, Eric and Yoav; (Big Island) Saifon and Kris for megaaloha, and Melanie, Colher, Spruce, Kaya, Kawa Hou, Diver Dan, Luana Inn for tips; (Moloka'i) Abbey, Rose and Juno for taking us in; (O'ahu) Mikki Mangosing for local aloha, BYU library for saving my ass, Cuica for stinking and running, and Bubba, Lisa, Boogie, Megan, Jade and Torri for distraction. Endless thanks to my love Daniel, who inspired, helped and supported me through this difficult project. [Text inspired by Nacho Libre.]

NED FRIARY & GLENDA BENDURE
Of the many people who helped us along the way, a special thanks to Allen Tom, Ed Lyman and David Mattila of the Hawaiian Islands Humpback Whale National Marine Sanctuary for a most fascinating day. Thanks also to Pat Savino of the Kealia Pond National Wildlife Refuge and Nan Cabatbat of the Hawai'i Natural History Association for sharing their insights into Maui's natural wonders. A hearty *mahalo* to Emily Wolman at the LP base camp for her inspiration and guidance, and to Jeff Campbell for his always-super coordinating efforts.

OUR READERS
Many thanks to the travelers who used the last edition and wrote to us with helpful hints, useful advice and interesting anecdotes:
Sebastien Ananian-Cooper, Chris Bennack, Walter Bono, Francesca Brice, Gen Cain, Claudia Crenshaw, Bianca Falace, Maurice Friedman, Evan Garner, Tony Gordon, Kirby Guyer, Aline Huntly, Jan-Peter Idel, Nina Innocenti, Deb Kim, Patty Lisieski, Michael Marquardt, Robert Masters, Marci Mowery, Barbara Murphy, Elke Obermeier, Marlene Pakrastins, Chris Ploegaert, Emma Rayson, Gill, Steve, Hayley & Shelley Reynolds, Emilio Salamí, Catherine Ulrich, Joy Vanbuhler, KI Waugh, William Wilson

ACKNOWLEDGMENTS
Many thanks to the following for the use of their content:
Wise Words boxed text on p553 ®Nite Owl T-Shirts LLC

SEND US YOUR FEEDBACK

We love to hear from travelers – your comments keep us on our toes and help make our books better. Our well-traveled team reads every word on what you loved or loathed about this book. Although we cannot reply individually to postal submissions, we always guarantee that your feedback goes straight to the appropriate authors, in time for the next edition. Each person who sends us information is thanked in the next edition – and the most useful submissions are rewarded with a free book.

To send us your updates – and find out about Lonely Planet events, newsletters and travel news – visit our award-winning website: **www.lonelyplanet.com/contact**.

Note: we may edit, reproduce and incorporate your comments in Lonely Planet products such as guidebooks, websites and digital products, so let us know if you don't want your comments reproduced or your name acknowledged. For a copy of our privacy policy visit www.lonelyplanet.com/privacy.

Globe on title page © Mountain High Maps 1993 Digital Wisdom, Inc.

Internal photographs: p390 Jeff Campbell; p388 Ned Friary & Glenda Bendure; p389 Molly Green; p386 China Williams; p392 Lucy Yamamoto. All other photographs by Lonely Planet Images, and by p13 (#2) John Borthwick; p6 (#4), p8 (#5), p9 (#2), p10 (#6), p11 (#1, #2), p12 (#5), p13 (#3), p14 (#4) Ann Cecil; p5 Linda Ching; p9 (#1) Scott Darsney; p6 (#6), p7 (#1) John Elk III; p12 (#1), p14 (#3) Peter Hendrie; p10 (#3), p15 (#1, #2) Karl Lehmann; p7 (#2) Holger Leue; p8 (#6) Woodward Payne & Beverly Anderson; p16 Woods Wheatcroft; p83 Laurence Worcester.

All images are the copyright of the photographers unless otherwise indicated. Many of the images in this guide are available for licensing from Lonely Planet Images: www.lonelyplanetimages.com.

Index

INDEX

INDEX

INDEX

000 Map pages
000 Photograph pages

INDEX

000 Map pages
000 Photograph pages

INDEX

INDEX

000 Map pages
000 Photograph pages